Deciding Communication Law

Key Cases in Context

LEA's Communication Series
Jennings Bryant/Dolf Zillmann, General Editors

Selected titles in Mass Communication (Alan Rubin, Advisory Editor), include:

Alexander/Owers/Carveth/Hollifield/Greco • Media Economics: Theory and Research, Second Edition

Bunker • Critiquing Free Speech: First Amendment Theory and the Challenge of Interdisciplinarity

Gunter • Media Sex: What Are the Issues?

Harris • A Cognitive Psychology of Mass Communication, Third Edition

Moore • Mass Communication Law and Ethics, Second Edition

Perse • Media Effects and Society

Wicks • Understanding Audiences: Learning to Use the Media Constructively

Van Evra • Television and Child Development, Third Edition

For a complete listing of titles in LEA's Communication Series,
contact Lawrence Erlbaum Associates, Inc. at www.erlbaum.com.

Deciding Communication Law

Key Cases in Context

❧

Susan Dente Ross

Edward R. Murrow School of Communication
Washington State University

LEA

LAWRENCE ERLBAUM ASSOCIATES, PUBLISHERS

2004   Mahwah, New Jersey   London

Lawrence Erlbaum Associates, Inc., Publishers
10 Industrial Avenue
Mahwah, NJ 07430

Cover design by Kathryn Houghtaling Lacey

Library of Congress Cataloging-in-Publication Data

Deciding Communication Law: Key Cases in Context, by Susan Dente Ross
p. cm.
Includes bibliographical references and index.
ISBN 0-8058-4698-0 (cloth : alk. paper)

Copyright information for this volume can be obtained by contacting the Library of Congress

Books published by Lawrence Erlbaum Associates are printed on acid-free paper,
and their bindings are chosen for strength and durability.

Printed in the United States of America

10 9 8 7 6 5 4 3 2 1

For Matthew, Jonathan, and Steven.

And for my whole family,

whose talents and travails encourage and guide me

Contents

Foreword

The U.S. Constitution is based on the Enlightenment principle that the people are sovereign, the ultimate source of authority. That document, the world's oldest written national constitution, created a government of limited powers and recognized certain rights. The text still says Congress makes all federal laws and shall make "no law" abridging freedom of the press. Beyond that, what is protected and what is not by the press guarantee has been subject to debate.

Final decisions about the freedom to exchange ideas and information had to be left either to the officeholders the founders so profoundly distrusted or to anyone who had a means of communication. Some researchers have argued that the term "freedom of the press" had a very narrow meaning in the eighteenth century and that officials were left with the power to determine what is acceptable. Others have concluded that the expression of a sovereign people cannot be restricted by their servants in government and have contended that suppression is unconstitutional.

Scholars may disagree about the original boundaries of the press clause, but it remains possible to believe that "no law" means "no law" or, at least, that the Constitution forbids governmental control of privately produced media content. Individuals may sue communicators for violations of their rights, but if the First Amendment means what it plainly says, then the three official branches of government were given no authority over the choices made by the unofficial fourth branch, an independent press. Freedom may involve inconvenience and risk, but unfettered thought and expression are so essential to democracy that they must be protected to the fullest extent possible. Tolerance of the unconventional and the annoying is necessary not only because of the respect due to individual rights, but also because today's radical can be tomorrow's visionary. The founders themselves challenged the status quo and wanted to preserve for posterity the rights they exercised.

In practice, of course, the temptations can be great to find exceptions to any liberty. The press protection that eighteenth-century Americans demanded and ratified has been under siege ever since. As James Madison said, the mere "parchment barriers" of the Constitution are subject to the pressures of the moment. If the founders preferred to let the press make its own decisions, they surely would be displeased by the escalation of First Amendment conflicts that began in the early twentieth century as government and corporate power grew.

Since the eighteenth century, the nation's mass communication infrastructure has expanded enormously. No longer limited to lumbering, hand-operated printing presses, people can send messages across the planet with the tap of a finger. A substantial portion of the American economy depends on media technology and intellectual property. The stakes are high when regulations are tightened or relaxed.

Maintaining a thriving media environment for democratic debate is always a challenge. Communication workers, media activists, educators and citizens in general should be prepared for the increasingly complex issues ahead. Rights such as freedom of expression wither without a continuing commitment to fundamental principles and everyday practices that keep a liberty alive.

The founders feared the United States, like ancient republics, would lose its liberties over time. Expediency can seem compelling. Courts and commentators often have relied on prudential and doctrinal arguments rather than the founders' words, democratic theory or thorough historical analysis. If the Constitution is to be more than a mere façade for makeshift reasoning and shaky solutions, then critical analysis must be applied to limitations of basic freedoms. When a liberty is threatened, every person should be prepared to question the restriction and to articulate the reasons for the right.

The justices of the Supreme Court of the United States have the paramount position for defining freedoms and should be defending them against repression. Their decisions, unfortunately, can be flawed and even foolish. They often disagree among themselves and can mangle the press clause in their written mêlées. Distinguishing between sound and unsound jurisprudence is the task of every student of communication law.

Writings on law should be considered with caution. The impressive trappings of the legal system can conceal much that is worth knowing. Many disputes never reach the courtroom. When they do, fallible human beings apply the law and may issue a written opinion. Centuries of thought on an issue can be compressed into a small number of pages with little historical context. Ideology and emotion can affect judgment. Attempts to refine an area of law can produce incoherence.

At first, court decisions may seem composed of indecipherable terminology and intricate logic, but each one fits within developments over time. The study of case law rests on careful attention to both the details and the larger picture. The discerning reader ponders, unravels, compares and assesses.

A court's ruling is not necessarily the final word. Decisions can be modified or overturned later and can be more or less disregarded by law enforcement officials and the public at large. People can be ignorant of the law, can prefer civil disobedience or can simply not fear the possible consequences. The various forces at work make the American legal system both dynamic and disconcerting.

The study of cases shows how liberties can be lost or maintained. Each legal contest pits competing interests in often intriguing ways. Attempts to control expression are frequently futile, but damaging precedents can be set. When the press protections of the federal or state constitutions are placed at risk, courts should keep in mind the values long associated with freedom of expression: self-fulfillment, self-government, the advancement of knowledge, the exposure of wrongdoing and the resolution of conflict.

This book, written by one of the country's leading scholars of media law, provides a clear, insightful introduction to the "hows" and "whys" of reading communication cases. The focus on analyzing the text of key decisions gives readers an effective way of understanding the most significant concepts and approaches. Readers will be prepared for their own further inquiry in an area of law that affects every media consumer every day.

Jeffery A. Smith
University of Wisconsin–Milwaukee

Preface

"I thought I'd hate this class, but now I really like the law, and I even agree with Justice Scalia some of the time." That's what students have told me again and again during the class in media law that spawned this book. It seems it's almost always a surprise to these students – graduates and undergraduates alike – that they not only understand the cases but also enjoy reading the decisions that form American common law. Once they overcome their initial timidity and learn a bit of legal jargon, they are fascinated by the drama of the law and by the profound disagreements and biting rhetoric exchanged by the judges who hand down these rulings. This is the stuff of real life, real disputes, real rulings: the real thing. It's no at all like reading books that talk about cases.

This book is a response to the feelings, suggestions and desires of many of the media law students I have had the good fortune to teach over the past decade or so. It is the distillation of lessons learned from those students, in the classroom and out, about what will assist their own reading of the law and what will stimulate their critical thinking and enthusiastic self-directed learning.

My contribution to this text, beyond selecting and editing the key cases herein, is to act as the reader's guide. I provide a foundation in each area of the law but stop far short of detailing all the relevant nuances or developing a comprehensive summary of the topic. This book does not offer an encyclopedic treatment of the topics herein. Rather it seeks to survey the terrain, highlight the landmarks and suggest useful signposts to guide individual navigation of the law. A vast array of in-depth and summary treatments of these topics exists for readers who want a more constant or more assertive companion on their voyage through the law. But I would encourage even the most timorous reader to dive in to the cases themselves.

This book offers a solid grounding in a number of key communication law issues. After introducing readers to the basic system of law, it provides an overview of the often complex legal doctrines that guide judicial decision making. After that, the third section of the book is devoted to distinctions among different classes of speech, a thicket the Supreme Court chose not to enter when in 2003 it reversed its decision to review *Nike v. Kasky*.

The fourth section of the book explores distinctions among various types of speakers, including differential treatment of various types of media and the issue of student speech. The fifth section examines cases in which important concerns, such as those of reputation, privacy and intellectual property, compete with free speech interests. The final section of the book explores a number of important reporting issues, including open government laws and other legal issues of particular concern to journalists.

This book may serve as the cornerstone of many undergraduate and graduate courses in media law and related fields. But whether the book serves as a primary text, a supplementary reading, a reference work or an introduction to an area of personal interest, it serves best as a stimulant to further reading, discussion and research. Suggested readings in each chapter point the interested reader toward related cases that offer different, and sometimes contradictory, insights into the topic. These too are but a sampling of the wealth of case law that surrounds each field. My hope is that this text and its suggestions will assist many readers in developing a lifelong habit of finding and reading the law.

Of all those who contributed to this work, I most want to thank my former students for their challenging perspectives and engagement. Numerous others who have shaped my understanding of the law and my approach to teaching know who they are and will remain unnamed so they will not suffer from any errors of omission or commission by me in this text. However, my special thanks go to Bill Chamberlin, who guided me through my doctoral work and whose example as a dedicated teacher continues to inspire me today. Thanks also to Linda Bathgate, my editor, and to Lawrence Erlbaum Associates, who dared to support a textbook intended primarily for graduate students of media law. Thanks also to Alex Tan and Washington State University for supporting the sabbatical during which I found time to write this book.

Susan Dente Ross
Washington State University
Summer 2003

Reading This Book

I was pleased to hear that Susan Ross was planning to write the book you hold in your hand. I know Professor Ross to be a serious and deeply knowledgeable communication law scholar, so I was sure this book would be thoughtfully prepared. Not only that, this volume fills an important need in our field.

When it comes to communication law – or almost any field of law, for that matter – there is simply no substitute for reading the cases. Cases tell the story in a way that hornbooks, treatises and other narrative secondary sources simply can't replicate. As helpful as serious communication law treatises often are to students and teachers alike, to know the law only through these sources is to know the lyrics but not the music.

With the cases, you get the law in all its untidy glory. You see the institutional compromises, the factual elisions and the numerous doctrinal roads almost but not quite taken. Over time, you also develop that sixth sense – dubbed "thinking like a lawyer" – about where the rules will likely run out or conflict with other important principles.

For the reader just starting out in the study of communication law, this book is a great beginning. I urge you not to stop here, however. Read lower court cases, where the principles created by the High Court are refined and sometimes (*sub silentio*) altered. The U. S. Supreme Court visits some areas of communication law infrequently enough that the lower courts are given years, and sometimes decades, to put their own spin on the development of the law. Read the major legal theorists as well – Emerson, Dworkin, Posner, Sunstein, Blasi and the rest. The thought of influential theorists, while not always directly influencing legal doctrine, nonetheless often impinges on the development of the law. By reading the theorists, you'll see the cases through a variety of philosophical lenses that will deepen your understanding of what the judges are up to.

As you read the cases, notice the different types of legal arguments the courts deploy. One judge bases a decision on the text of the Constitution, while another seemingly ignores the text altogether and focuses on past precedents. A third draws from the overall structure of the Constitution, while yet another makes much of the intention of the framers. (As if it were easy to determine what eighteenth-century folks might think about twenty-first century developments!) These different types of legal argument (or modalities, in legal theorist Philip Bobbitt's influential terminology[1]) don't always, or perhaps even often, suggest the same result in a given case. As you read, try to ascertain why different arguments deployed.

---

[1] Philip Bobbitt, Constitutional Interpretation (Blackwell 1991).

At the same time, be somewhat skeptical of the explanations offered in the opinions. Ask yourself whether the legal doctrine is sufficiently determinate to produce the result the court wants to reach. Is the doctrine doing any real work in the case, or does it appear to be simply rhetorical window dressing? Try to determine what extra-judicial forces may have influenced or led to the decision. In doing so, you'll be following an intellectual trend in legal studies that began with Oliver Wendell Holmes, Jr., and the "legal realists" and continues to this day in various forms.

Despite the skeptical eye, I think it's better to avoid total cynicism. Like any human institution, the law is flawed in many ways, but the reductive perspective that legal doctrine is based simply on what the judge had for breakfast is, in my view, untenable. Judges unquestionably have discretion, and at times their political views clearly affect their rulings. Nonetheless, despite some uncertainty, legal rules by and large can yield reasonably consistent adjudication. Many legally trained observers felt somewhat dispirited, if not outraged, after what many viewed as the nakedly partisan (and constitutionally suspect) U. S. Supreme Court decision in the *Bush v. Gore* case that decided the 2000 presidential election. Still, that sort of decision seems to be the exception rather than the rule. Assuming, in the main, good faith on the part of constitutional interpreters, there are ways, as legal theorist Ronald Dworkin has argued, to decide cases so as to put the Constitution in its best light. The more cases you read and the more you understand the art of judging, I think you may agree that most judges, most of the time, are trying to play it straight and reach the soundest decision possible given the legal materials.

Reading and understanding the cases is important not just for lawyers, but for informed citizens. When the law becomes a game for insiders only, something has gone dreadfully wrong. The judiciary, which Hamilton perhaps naively characterized as "the least dangerous branch," now exercises tremendous power in shaping the meaning of the Constitution and, by extension, the ambit of our rights. Citizens in a democracy need to keep close tabs on all government officials, including those life-tenured ones in black robes.

Matthew D. Bunker
University of Alabama

The System of Law

The sources and hierarchy of the law and the judicial system

The United States is a nation governed by the rule of law. The rule of law is the framework of this society in which pre-established norms and procedures provide for decisions to be made consistently and without favoritism. The law, after all, is simply a compact among the citizens to establish a system of rules to govern society. The law dictates acceptable behavior for citizens and government, and it settles disputes among members of society, and between citizens and their government. The law is not merely a friendly agreement, though; government enforces the law through sanctions against violators, and those penalties include the elimination of basic individual rights and liberties.

To function effectively, laws must be sufficiently specific to inform citizens of the line between proper and improper behavior. A vague or unclear law fails to provide adequate notice to people who would willingly obey laws they understood. Good laws are tailored carefully to achieve their goals; they regulate only those people or activities necessary to advance an identified government interest or to prevent a certain kind of harm. Finally, laws should be fairly stable. If laws change too rapidly, members of society have difficulty staying informed and adhering to the law.

Yet laws are subject to interpretation and to change. Laws take on new meaning, proliferate and evolve in response to changes in society. The body of law in this nation has expanded as American society has become more diverse and more complex, and laws have taken on new meaning through application to new and unique situations. Many laws that govern communications in the 21st Century did not exist in the 1700s; neither did the communications technologies themselves. Technology has not been the sole force driving legal change, however. Advertising is one area in which laws have emerged, exploded and evolved as society has developed different perceptions of the rights and responsibilities of corporations in society. Similarly, the law of defamation, a long-standing legal concept, has shifted to reflect altered societal priorities, new understanding of the power of mass media to affect the lives of individuals and a commitment to the role of mass communication in a democratic state.

SOURCES OF LAW

In the United States, communication law develops from five primary sources: constitutional law, statutory law, executive orders, administrative law and common law. Another source of law, equity, less frequently determines the outcome of communication law issues. Briefly, equity law empowers judges to ensure fairness by issuing decrees to remedy or prevent harms. Restraining orders and injunctions fall within the equity power of judges.

Constitutional Law

Constitutions at the city, state and federal levels establish the form and functions of government and guarantee fundamental rights to the people. Constitutions tend to provide broad outlines rather than detailed descriptions. In relatively few words, the U.S. Constitution, ratified in 1779, established the three branches of federal government, delegated powers among the executive, the judicial and the legislative branches, and established the relationship among citizens, the states and the federal government.

As the supreme law of the land, the U.S. Constitution is quite difficult to amend. Constitutional amendments must be proposed in either of two ways: by a two-thirds vote of both houses of Congress or by a special constitutional convention called by votes of two-thirds of the state legislatures. Amendments are ratified only after three-fourths of the states approve them. In more than two hundred years, Congress has approved only thirty-three of the thousands of proposed constitutional amendments, and only twenty-six amendments have been ratified. In fewer than five hundred words, the first ten amendments to the Constitution – generally known as the Bill of Rights – guarantee the fundamental rights and freedoms of Americans and limit the power of government. In particular, the First Amendment protects the people's freedom of speech, assembly, petition and exercise of religion, and prevents government from abridging the freedom of the press.

Although the text of the Constitution is very stable, its meaning is not static. Constitutional law can evolve and change based on the decisions of the courts. Many view the Constitution as a living document because the courts continually give it new life and meaning by re-examining and re-interpreting the Constitution's language. Through its self-appointed power of judicial review, the U.S. Supreme Court determines the meaning of the language of the First Amendment and all the provisions of the Constitution. State supreme courts also interpret their state constitutions, but no law – state or federal – may conflict with the U.S. Constitution. The Supreme Court reshapes the meaning of constitutional law by applying the Constitution to novel situations and by voiding any regulations or statutes "repugnant to the Constitution."[1]

Statutory Law

Under the terms of the U.S. Constitution, the popularly elected legislative branch of government – the U.S. Congress and state, county and city legislatures – makes an ever-increasing body of law by enacting statutes. Statutes, like the Constitution, are a form of black letter law; they are formally adopted and relatively stable because they are written down. In addition, like the Constitution, statutory law can be ambiguous and is subject to judicial interpretation and application. Court review of statutes is known as statutory construction. In general, courts prefer to limit the meaning and application of statutes to the clear letter and intent of the law and refuse to expand statutes by implication or inference.[2] Statutory laws form a hierarchy; some federal laws pre-empt state laws, which in turn may pre-empt city statutes. Courts may invalidate state statutes that conflict with federal laws or city statutes that conflict with either state or federal law.

Unlike the Constitution, statutory law frequently responds to specific problems. Thus statutory law often is extremely detailed and fact specific. Statutes often define the limits of acceptable behavior. For example, all criminal laws are statutes. Statutes also establish the rules of electronic

---

[1] Marbury v. Madison, 1 Cranch (5 U.S.) 137, 180 (1803).
[2] *See, e.g.*, Singer, N.J. Statutes and Statutory Construction (1999).

copyright, broadcasting, advertising and access to government meetings and information. Statutes can also anticipate and prevent problems, such as when Congress prohibited all citizens from distributing child pornography over the Internet.

Executive Orders

Constitutions vest the executive branch of government with power to execute laws. Under this authority, local, county, state and federal executives may implement laws enacted by the legislature and may issue orders that have the power of law. These executives – the president, governors and mayors – also may delegate authority to administrative authorities to interpret and implement statutes (see Administrative Law below).

Recent executive orders from the U.S. president have limited media access to military zones, excluded media from meetings of groups advising the president on energy policy and redefined access to presidential records. Similarly, mayors and governors have issued orders – particularly under perceived emergency conditions – that severely limited public freedom of movement. In 1999, for example, the mayor of Seattle imposed a curfew on the city and excluded many citizens from a large section of downtown after individuals protesting the meeting of the World Trade Organization there became unruly and vandalized a number of downtown businesses. Although some executive orders may have dramatic effects on communications, they generally are not a major force in communication law.

Administrative Law

A vast array of state and federal administrative agencies established by statute in the executive branch of government oversees activities in specific areas of expertise. These agencies incorporate both legislative and judicial functions. Administrative agencies, like the Federal Communications Commission that oversees interstate electronic communication, propose and adopt orders, rules and regulations to carry out their delegated duties. Administrative agencies also enforce administrative law; they conduct hearings in which they grant relief, resolve disputes, and levy fines or penalties. This body of rules has the force of law. Administrative law may constitute the largest proportion of contemporary law in this country.

Administrative laws and agency dispute resolutions generally are subject to review by courts after administrative remedies have been exhausted. While courts may overturn unconstitutional agency actions and void agency decisions that violate agency rules or exceed agency authority, courts recognize that agencies have specialized knowledge and are vested by law with discretionary power to exercise authority over specified subjects. Therefore, courts frequently defer to the judgment of administrative agencies. Administrative agencies' scope of authority and even their existence also are subject to reconsideration by the legislative bodies that granted them power. Legislatures may adopt new statutes or amend pre-existing laws to revise the purview of administrative agencies. Thus, Congress adopted the Telecommunications Act of 1996, which substantially clarified and revised the responsibilities of the Federal Communications Commission, originally established by the Communications Act of 1934.

Common Law

The common law consists of rules and principles developed through time from custom and the judgments of the courts. The common law is a vast and unwritten body of legal principles and precedents established through thousands of court rulings reaching back hundreds of years and across the Atlantic to England. For centuries before the settlement of the American colonies, English judges made the law. They resolved disputes based on custom and the legal precedents established by judges in previous court rulings. These judicial decisions, and the reasoning for them, formed the English common law, which became the foundation of American common law.

Common law rests on history, tradition and the presumption that precedent should guide future decisions. The Latin phrase for this fundamental premise of common law is *stare decisis*, which means stand by or adhere to the decision. The concept is that once a court has laid down a principle relevant to a certain set of facts, future courts will adhere to that principle when the facts of a new question are reasonably similar. In this way, courts exercise authority because their precedents direct the subsequent decisions of lower courts within their jurisdiction. This principle assures predictability and stability among different courts treating similar questions. Common law principles pervade the law, and common law strongly influences the contemporary law of privacy.

However, courts do not always adhere to precedent. The common law is adaptable because it is not written down and is subject to interpretation, and courts may depart from precedent with good reason. Courts examining a new but similar question may find it necessary to modify precedent to reflect new understanding. Courts also may distinguish the new set of facts from those in the precedent case and so free themselves from the strictures of *stare decisis*. Finally, courts may overturn a precedent outright to remedy past injustices, but courts rarely and very reluctantly overturn precedent because of the strength of the *stare decisis* doctrine.

THE COURT SYSTEM

It is important to understand the structure of the courts that are so central to communication law in America. The courts create the common law, and apply and interpret constitutions, statutes and orders. Through their judgments, courts can reshape the law or even throw out laws as unconstitutional.

Every state, the District of Columbia and the federal government each has its own court system. Each system of courts operates independently under the authority of the relevant constitution. For example, the U.S. Constitution requires the establishment of the Supreme Court of the United States and authorizes Congress to establish other courts it deems necessary to the proper functioning of the federal judiciary. Every court has its own jurisdiction; each has either a geographic or a topical area of responsibility and authority. Within their geographic regions, federal courts exercise authority over cases that involve the federal government, interstate or international controversies, and cases that interpret and apply federal laws, treaties and the U.S. Constitution.

The fifty-two separate court systems in this country are organized similarly; most court systems have three tiers. At the lowest level of the court systems are trial courts. Trial courts examine facts and apply existing law. They are the only courts to use juries, and they have original jurisdiction over a case. Trial courts base their decisions on the unique facts of the case before them and do not establish precedent. Each state houses at least one of the nation's ninety-four trial-level federal courts; these courts are called federal district courts.

In contrast to the fact-based decisions of trial courts, courts of appeals generally do *not* review the facts. It is the responsibility of appellate courts to examine the procedure of the lower courts to determine whether the proper law was applied and whether the judicial process was fair and appropriate. Appellate courts review the law based on legal briefs and short oral arguments from attorneys representing the two sides of the question. Rather than consider facts *de novo*, courts of appeal generally remand cases to the trial courts when they determine the facts require review or a more complete record should be developed through additional fact finding. Courts of appeal establish precedent for lower courts within their jurisdiction; the precedent is binding on courts within the same court system and may be persuasive to courts in other court systems or jurisdictions.

There generally are two levels of appellate courts: the intermediate courts of appeal and the supreme courts. In the federal court system, there are thirteen intermediate-level appellate courts called circuit courts. A panel of three judges hears all except the most important cases in the federal circuit courts of appeal. In rare cases, all the judges of the circuit court will sit *en banc* to hear an appeal. Twelve of the federal circuits represent geographic regions. For example, the U.S. Court of Appeals for the Ninth Circuit bears responsibility for the entire West Coast and Hawaii and Alaska, while the U.S. Court of Appeals for the D.C. Circuit covers the District of Columbia. The thirteenth circuit, the U.S. Court of Appeals for the Federal Circuit, handles specialized appeals.

The U.S. Supreme Court

The Supreme Court of the United States is the nation's highest court and sits atop both the state and federal court systems. The president appoints and the Senate confirms the nine justices of the U.S. Supreme Court who hand down legal precedents that bind all lower courts in the country. The appointment of Supreme Court justices, who sit for life, gives the president influence over the Court's political ideology.

Most cases reach the Supreme Court on petitions for review, which are called *writs of certiorari*. The Supreme Court receives thousands of petitions to hear appeals each year and accepts only a small fraction (usually less than five percent) of the petitioned cases. In the remaining cases, when the Court denies *cert.*, the lower court ruling remains in place. By denying *cert.*, the Supreme Court neither affirms nor rejects the lower court opinion, and the denial should not be interpreted to signal any orientation of the Court toward the issue under review. The Court also has original jurisdiction over a few kinds of legal problems (such as disputes between two states) and is required to accept a few cases in which the losing party has an automatic right of appeal. In recent years, the Supreme Court generally has issued fewer than a hundred signed opinions each year.

In deciding which *writs of certiorari* to accept and which to refuse, the Court may favor cases that raise unique or significant legal questions or cases in which lower courts are in conflict. The Court may also consider whether an issue is *ripe* for consideration, meaning that the case presents a real and present controversy rather than a hypothetical concern. In addition, the Court may reject some petitions as moot because the controversy is no longer "live" and their decision would have no real effect on the outcome of the dispute. Mootness may be an issue, for example, when a student who has challenged school policy graduates before the case ultimately has been resolved. Courts generally will not reject a case as moot if the issue involved is "capable of repetition, yet evading review."[3] In what is known as the rule of four, four justices must vote to grant a *writ of cert.* before the Supreme Court will hear a case.

As the nation's highest appellate court, the Supreme Court of the United States establishes legal precedent for the nation when it issues a majority opinion. However, if a majority of five justices does not agree on a point of law or even the outcome of the case, the Court may issue a plurality opinion. A plurality opinion decides the issue but does not establish binding precedent. Historically, however, a majority of the Supreme Court often has later endorsed plurality opinions (and even a number of concurring or dissenting opinions as well). The Supreme Court may also issue a *per curiam* opinion, which is an unsigned opinion "by the court."

THE JUDICIAL PROCESS

Although each court and each case pursues a slightly idiosyncratic path, the judicial process follows some general patterns. In criminal cases, the government initiates an investigation into a possible crime. Based on evidence gathered, the police arrest an individual they suspect of committing a crime such as robbery, rape or murder. A preliminary, pretrial hearing may be held to determine whether there is probable cause to proceed to trial. If probable cause exists, the judge may set bail. At this point, either the prosecutor charges the suspect or a grand jury convenes to issue an indictment. Next an arraignment in court involves the formal, public reading of the charges against the defendant, and the defendant enters a plea of guilty or not guilty. Proof beyond

---

[3] Southern Pacific Terminal Co. v. Interstate Commerce Commission, 219 U.S. 498, 515 (1911).

a reasonable doubt is required to establish guilt in a criminal trial. Upon a verdict of guilty, the judge announces the sentence.

Civil cases generally involve two private individuals who cannot resolve a dispute. In a civil suit, one person claims he has been harmed by an intrusion on his privacy or the inaccuracy of a news report, for example. The civil harm involved in such cases is called a tort. Most communication lawsuits are civil suits in which the plaintiff must prove his case by the preponderance of evidence. This standard of proof is lower than in criminal cases.

Civil suits begin when the plaintiff files a legal complaint with the clerk of courts against the other person, the defendant. The court then serves a summons on the defendant, notifying her of the complaint and requiring her to appear in court. The defendant may answer the complaint by filing a counter-suit, by denying the charge or by filing a motion for summary judgment. A case ends in summary judgment when the judge decides the two sides agree on the facts in the case and the facts legally support one party. Sometimes the disputing parties will agree to an out-of-court settlement at this point. When this occurs, there is no public record of the outcome of the case, and terms of the settlement may prohibit the parties from discussing the particulars of the settlement.

More often, however, the two sides do not agree on the facts and begin to gather evidence through a process called discovery. In trying to build a case, each side may issue subpoenas that require someone, sometimes a journalist, to testify in court. With few exceptions, citizens generally have a legal obligation to participate in the judicial process and to comply with subpoenas. The judge may issue a contempt of court ruling against individuals who refuse to comply with subpoenas. Contempt citations sometimes land journalists in jail. The discovery process can last for months, during which either side may file new motions or amend earlier statements or complaints. Throughout this pre-trial period, the litigants may attempt to "spin" their case in the media. Judges are sensitive to the potential harmful effects of such pre-trial publicity on the fairness of trials.

The dispute then is heard in court. Roughly half of all civil suits are heard in a jury trial. In fact, a jury trial is required if either party requests it. The court then selects jurors to form an impartial panel to hear the evidence. The hearing may begin with the defendant filing a motion to dismiss the case, a demurrer. In a demurrer, the defendant agrees to the claims of the plaintiff but denies that the actions caused any harm to the plaintiff. Plaintiffs in civil suits often seek damages, payment to compensate for their losses from the alleged harmful act or to punish the defendant. To receive a damage award, a plaintiff generally has to show that the harm occurred, the defendant was in the wrong, and the defendant acted either negligently or with malicious intent.

After the evidence is presented at trial, the judge instructs the jury on how the law should be applied to the facts of the case. If the jury cannot reach a verdict, a new trial may begin. More typically, a jury verdict is entered in the case. However, the judge has the authority to overturn the verdict if she believes the jury has reached a verdict contrary to law. After the judgment of the court is entered, either the plaintiff or the defendant may appeal. The person who appeals, the petitioner, challenges the decision of the court. The respondent to the appeal wants the verdict to be affirmed. It can take years and cost hundreds of thousands of dollars to appeal a case up to the Supreme Court, and there is no guarantee the Court will agree to hear your case.

Reading the Law

Understanding and locating legal texts

This casebook is a first step toward advanced study and independent research in the law. A basic premise of this text is that you learn the law best by reading the law *not* by reading about the law. Therefore, this text is designed to assist your critical, analytical reading of the key court decisions that form the foundation of communication law. This text also will introduce some of the basic skills and strategies you will need to study the law further and independently.

There is no substitute for reading the law in full and verbatim. Only by reading legal texts does the law come alive. Reading the opinions of various judges and justices, the arguments of legislators and lobbyists, the rules and orders of administrative agencies demonstrates the discretion of those who make and apply the laws. The eloquent and sometimes heated disagreement among the justices of the U.S. Supreme Court about the proper resolution of groundbreaking cases demonstrates the flexibility and subjectivity of the law. Reading the law provides direct experience with the maze of tests, standards and doctrines that guides courts toward their frequently complex, inconsistent and sometimes contradictory rulings. Reading legal texts also makes it possible to engage directly with the law itself and develop a facility for unearthing key concepts and deciphering unclear language.

WHAT TO STUDY

To students of the law, it seems obvious they must decode legal texts before they can fully understand them. Like a foreign language, legal language is both unfamiliar and opaque. Yet, legal scholars have not always recognized this fact.[1] Traditional formalist legal scholarship has maintained that understanding the law requires the researcher only to find the relevant legal rules and precedents, read them, and then apply them to the issue or question at hand.[2] In this view, both the process and the outcome of legal research are clear. Read the law; apply the law. Legal scholars need not go beyond the conventional legal sources of briefs, digests, codes, legislative records and case reporters to answer legal questions. No unique methods are needed; the conclusions of legal research are as clear and certain as the answer to a mathematical formula. For

---

[1] *See, e.g.,* Mark Tushnet, *Critical Legal Studies*, 36 J. LEGAL EDUC. 505 (1986) (critiquing this assumption).

[2] *See, e.g.,* Thomas C. Grey, *Langdell's Orthodoxy*, 45 U. PITT. L. REV. 1 (1983).

formal positivist scholars, the greatest research hurdle is locating the legal texts that are the appropriate and sufficient realm of the specific study.

Other scholars adopt a more holistic, humanistic approach to the study of law and suggest that legal texts – constitutions, statutes, regulations, legislative records and the like – should not be the solitary or even the primary focus of legal study. Legal realists, for example, view the law as a product of human endeavor that is shaped by numerous factors beyond the law itself. [3] Legal realists see the law as fluid, responsive to social pressures and change. From this perspective, judges do not discover but make the law. Legal rules are not immutable; regardless of their detail and specificity, laws do not predict future legal decisions. Instead, the ambiguity of legal language empowers government officials to use their discretion to determine the law. For legal realists, then, conceptually sound study of the law requires examination of the individuals who make legal judgments and the context in which legal decisions are made as well as the published law. For these scholars, the research strategies and the materials scrutinized are as vast and varied as the issues touched by the law.

These differences in defining the proper materials to be examined by legal scholars are echoed in broad divergence in legal research methods. Legal scholarship includes both its own unique approach to knowledge and many of the leading contemporary research theories and methods. Much legal scholarship is doctrinal, interpretive or normative; it seeks to persuade as well as inform. [4] Such research may explain disparate lines of precedent, fit new laws into a coherent whole, provide original insights into landmark decisions, or analyze the internal logic of one or more legal materials.

Other legal scholars employ quantitative social-science methods – such as content analyses or surveys – to produce statistically reliable, verifiable, replicable data that can be generalized to explain past legal outcomes and predict future events. A separate array of legal scholars adopts qualitative, rhetorical, historical, critical and feminist methodologies – to name but a few – to richly inform their understanding of the law. Still other legal researchers apply multiple methods to address their questions more thoroughly. Indeed, a separate group of legal scholars is conducting studies to assess which research methods most effectively answer specific legal topics. [5]

UNDERSTANDING THE LAW

Clearly there is no one correct way to study the law. What follows, however, is an outline of how to read cases and where to find the primary legal sources generally relied upon as the core of both positivist and realist scholarship, both quantitative and qualitative legal research.

Reading and Briefing Cases

Reading case law poses unique problems because the material is dense and the legal terminology often is unfamiliar. Briefing cases is an efficient strategy used by practicing lawyers, scholars and students of the law to identify and summarize the important elements of a case. The goal of a case brief is to summarize clearly the key aspects of a court decision with reference to the central precedents, rules or tests used by the court. Briefing cases requires careful reading to determine what the court decided and why.

When done well, briefing a case clarifies opinions, increases retention of the material and produces ready one- to two-page reference summaries on important judicial decisions. Briefing forces readers of case law to sort out the essential facts, issues, reasoning, tests, holding and rule of

---

[3] *See, e.g.,* KARL LLEWELLYN, THE BRAMBLE BUSH (1960).

[4] Goldsmith, J. & Vermeule, A. Empirical methodology and legal scholarship, 69:1 THE UNIV. OF CHICAGO L. REV. 153 (Winter 2002).

[5] *See, e.g.,* LaFond, C., Toomey, T. L., Rothstein, C., Manning, W. & Wagenaar, A. C., *Policy evaluation research: Measuring the independent variables,"* 24:1 EVALUATION REV. 92 (Feb. 2000).

law in each case. Briefing also attunes readers to the eloquence of the law – the particularly apt turn of phrase or pithy quote – and focuses attention on the legal foundations upon which the court based its opinion.

It may be useful to read a case twice when you first begin reading and briefing case law. A quick read through the case familiarizes the reader with the basics; the second reading attends to details and allows for note taking. While there are many different styles of briefs, most briefs contain the same basic elements in a fixed format. Those elements are:

Citation. Every case has a proper name and an official citation. While many cases appear in more than one reporter, there is only one official reporter, e.g., U.S. for U.S. Supreme Court decisions. A proper legal citation contains, in this order: the names of the parties, the volume number of the reporter in which the case is published, the abbreviation for the legal reporter, the number of the first page on which the case appears and the year in which the case was decided. Thus, *Near v. Minnesota*, 282 U.S. 697 (1931) is the correct, official citation for this case about prior restraint. This citation means that the U.S. Supreme Court decision in the challenge brought by Near against a Minnesota statute was handed down in 1931 and may be found in volume 282 of the *United States Reports* beginning on page 697.

Facts. This section summarizes briefly the key events or actions that led to the initial legal dispute. It also outlines the process the case followed through the judicial system, highlighting the outcome at each stage in the judicial process and noting key aspects of each lower court's reasoning.

Issue(s) or Legal Question(s). This section poses the central legal question(s) considered by the court. There may be more than one. In general, briefs present each issue as a separate question that can be answered yes or no. Sometimes courts identify the issue with a phrase that begins, "The issue before the court is whether ..." The legal questions generally relate to the facts of the case but also point toward a more general legal concern.

Outcome. This answers each of the questions presented in the preceding section either yes or no based on the court's majority opinion. This section also tells whether the lower court decision is affirmed, reversed or remanded, names the justice (or judge) who wrote the majority opinion and reports the vote (in parentheses).

Analysis or Reasoning. Here, the brief explains the foundation for the court's majority opinion. What statutes, precedents, tests, doctrines or rationales did the court use to justify its decision? What facts or factors of the case did the court consider most significant? What factors did the court ignore or dismiss as irrelevant? This section often includes direct quotations from the opinion, but it should exclude *dicta*, comments by the court that are not directly germane to the court's decision.

Concurrence(s) or Dissent(s). If such opinions exist, this section reports each one separately by identifying the author and, in parentheses, the number of judges joining the opinion. Then it briefly states the primary reason(s) for each concurrence or dissent, focusing on where and why this opinion's author differs from the majority. Sometimes a direct quotation aptly summarizes the unique position of the opinion writer.

Rule of Law. The legal principle or test established, confirmed or modified by this case should be stated in one sentence. The rule of law is the essence of case precedent. It is not limited to the facts of this case but rather establishes a more general principle or process to govern future analogous cases.

Standard briefs are limited to two typed pages in length, with the content of each of the elements single-spaced and a double space between elements. Standardized briefs include the names of each of the elements (except Citation) and present them in the following way.

Name of Case
Official Citation
(Date of Decision)

FACTS:

ISSUE:

OUTCOME: Answer. Judge. (Vote).

ANALYSIS:

CONCURRENCE(S) OR DISSENT(S) [If any]: Judge. (Number joining the opinion). Reasoning.

RULE OF LAW:

Finding the Law

Students of communication law will begin exploring that body of the law through the materials in this book. However, successful legal scholars, researchers and practitioners perform an extensive amount of research using legal encyclopedias, case law, articles from legal and scholarly journals, historical records and the text of the law itself. The diversity of specialized documents that comprise the law appears in a variety of forms, but the law is organized into a highly structured and extremely useful cross-referencing scheme.

As in all fields of research, legal research incorporates both primary and secondary sources. Primary sources are original or first-hand, direct records of the law itself. Secondary sources encompass summaries, analyses, commentaries and compilations of various aspects of the law. While secondary sources generally are considered inferior to primary sources because they are a step removed from the actual law, both types of documents are valuable in legal research.

RESEARCH STRATEGY

It is not helpful to tell a beginning legal researcher that legal research begins at its logical starting point. Unfortunately, however, that is true. Effective legal research sometimes begins with secondary sources, sometimes with cases, sometimes with statutes. The choice of where to start essentially involves determining what will be the most effective strategy for answering the specific legal question at hand.[6]

Sometimes the choice of where to begin is as simple as using the materials already in the researcher's possession. Thus, each case in this text could be the logical starting point for research; the legal materials cited in every case provide a preliminary research map to the historical legal foundations of that case. Then each of these sources directs the reader back to another set of sources, and so on, in an expanding tree of precedent materials. To update the law from the original case, a unique legal tool, Shepardizing, directs the researcher to subsequent decisions that cite that case. If a researcher knows a statute rather than a case, however, annotated statutes direct readers to cases that have interpreted and applied the law and to relevant law journal articles. Annotated statutes also provide guidance to the history of the law through a summary legislative history at the end of the statutory text.

---

[6] For more detail on the legal research process, see, e.g., MERSKY, R. M., DUNN, D. J. & JACOBSTEIN, J. M. FUNDAMENTALS OF LEGAL RESEARCH: LEGAL RESEARCH ILLUSTRATED (2002); KUNZ, C. L. , SCHMEDEMANN, D. A., DOWNS, M. P. & BATESON, A. L. THE PROCESS OF LEGAL RESEARCH (2000); WREN, C. G. & WREN, J. R. THE LEGAL RESEARCH MANUAL (1992); AND ELIAS, S. & LEVINKIND, S. LEGAL RESEARCH: HOW TO FIND AND UNDERSTAND THE LAW (2002).

In many cases, however, the researcher will have neither case nor statute from which to begin. Then secondary sources are most useful. Secondary sources are enormously effective tools for summarizing the law and providing citations to key cases and analyses on point, but they represent only the opinion of the commentator. They are not authoritative statements of the law.

Perhaps the most useful secondary sources for beginning researchers in communication law are *American Law Reports, American Jurisprudence, Corpus Juris Secundum* and *Media Law Reporter*. The first three provide topical encyclopedia-style summaries on key legal subjects. *Media Law Reporter* provides both topical summaries and excerpts of key media law cases organized by subject. These secondary sources provide an excellent starting point and overview of unfamiliar topics of law, but they require some rather complicated research in supplements (called pocket parts) and through indexing to assure their information is comprehensive and up-to-date.

Legal and scholarly periodicals provide invaluable resources. A contemporary article in a credible law or communication journal related to the research subject is an excellent source for timely commentary, summary and citations. In addition to numerous general law reviews that treat communication law topics, journals of special interest include *Cardozo Arts & Entertainment Law Journal, Communication Law & Policy, Communications & the Law, Federal Communication Law Journal, Free Speech Yearbook, Hastings Communications & Entertainment Law Journal, Journal of Broadcasting and Electronic Media, Journalism & Mass Communication Quarterly* and *News Media & the Law*.

Finding Tools and Indexes

Many legal resources are available through databases such as *LEXIS-NEXIS* or *Westlaw*, online through the Internet and in print in research and law libraries. A number of indexes and finding tools help researchers locate legal materials in each of these formats.

- **Current Law Index** indexes a broad variety of post-1980 law journal articles by subject, author and key cases. The case index provides an alphabetical list of the cases that have been the focus of journal articles, an invaluable tool for finding secondary commentary on cases related to your area of interest.

- **Index to Legal Periodicals** provides a subject, author and key-case index to fewer journals than Current Law Index, but it indexes articles back to 1908.

- **Online search engines** particularly useful to legal scholars include Findlaw (http://www.findlaw.com/), LawCrawler (http://www.lawcrawler.com/) and Meta-Index for Legal Research (http://www.gxu.edu/lawadm/lawform.html/). These search tools access both primary and secondary legal resources.

- **LegalTrac** is an online index of law articles in nearly two thousand legal and non-legal periodicals since 1981. Searchable by keyword or subject, LegalTrac provides some citations, some short abstracts and even some full-text articles.

- **LEXIS-NEXIS**, available at many universities through the online Academic Universe option, is a full-text database of primary and secondary legal sources, business and financial information, and news. It has multiple search options, including keyword, case names and detailed Boolean searches.

- **West Digests**, created by the publishers of a leading series of court reporters, index court decisions at all levels by subject matter. The digests also assign "key numbers" to each sub-area within a major topic of the law. These key numbers allow researchers to find any case in any West reporter related to a given sub-area.

Primary Legal Resources

Primary legal resources can be accessed in a variety of ways and in a range of formats. This section introduces these resources and some of the mechanisms for obtaining them.

Court Decisions. The legal databases, *Westlaw* and *Lexis-Nexis*, likely are the fastest and most inclusive sources for court decisions, but many of the decisions also are available in bound volumes called reporters. [Note: Few decisions at the trial court level are reported in print or online.] Several reporters publish U.S. Supreme Court cases. The official reporter, *United States Reports* (abbreviated as U.S.), establishes the official citation for U.S. Supreme Court cases but is extremely slow to appear in print. Thus, both Lawyers Cooperative (*Lawyer's Edition* abbreviated as L. Ed.) and West Publishing (*Supreme Court Reporter* abbreviated as S. Ct.) issue a more timely record of Supreme Court decisions through their own reporters. The fastest print source of U.S. Supreme Court decisions is *United States Law Week* (abbreviated U.S.L.W.), which publishes Supreme Court rulings and important federal agency and lower federal and state court decisions weekly in loose leaf.

West also publishes a series of reporters for decisions of the U.S. Circuit Courts of Appeals (*Federal Reporters* abbreviated as F., F.2d, F.3d) and the U.S. District Courts (*Federal Supplements* abbreviated as F.Supp., F.Supp.2d). The courts of each state have an official reporter for their highest court decisions and may have reporters for their lower courts. West also publishes seven regional reporters (e.g., *Pacific Reporter* abbreviated as P., P.2d) that print state appellate court decisions within a specific geographic region. Many court decisions also are available online through a number of sites including the Legal Information Institute at Cornell University (http://www.law.cornell.edu) and the U.S.C. Law School site (http://www.use.edu/dept/law-lib/legal/topiclst.html).

Statutes, Rules and Regulations. Similar to case law, statutes, rules and regulations are available in a number of volumes. For example, federal statutes are published chronologically (not an efficient organization for topical searches) in *United States Statutes at Large*. The same statutes also can be found arranged into fifty titles, or topic areas, in the *United States Code* (abbreviated U.S.C.). West's *United States Code Annotated* (U.S.C.A.) and Lawyers Cooperative's *United States Code Service* (U.S.C.S.). provide notes and references on changes and applications of the law in their annotated editions. The two volumes also offer a popular name index that allows researchers to locate statutes by their common names. Federal statutes may be found online at http://uscode.house.gov/usc.htm, and state laws generally are available through state government sites.

Rules and regulations proposed and promulgated by federal administrative agencies appear in the *Federal Register* (Fed. Reg.). The *Code of Federal Regulations* (C.F.R.) organizes this enormous body of law into fifty titles arranged by subject, and a variety of official reports from each administrative agency publishes narrower categories of decisions. The Federal Communications Commission, for example, issues a record (F.C.C.R.). Like most federal agencies, the FCC maintains its own web site at www.fcc.gov. Select FCC materials also are available online through http://www.gpo.gov/su_docs/aces/aces140, http://www.gpo.gov/nara/cfr/index.html, and some also can be found at http://hraunfoss.fcc.gov/edocs_public/Silve. But perhaps the most effective way to navigate the morass of FCC rulings is to use the regularly updated and indexed service of *Pike and Fischer's Radio Regulations* (P&F Rad. Reg.) available in print and online via a subscription service.

Legislative Records. The *Congressional Record* (Cong. Rec.) is the official report of what transpires in Congress. Federal depository libraries also hold copies of most documents printed by the federal printing office, including House and Senate bills, hearing transcripts, committee reports and studies. Congressional and other federal documents generally are available online through http://thomas.loc.gov. Congressional session laws and bills also may be accessed through http://www.access.gpo.gov/nara/nara005.html and http://www.access.gpo.gov/su_doc/aces/.

Chapter

3

First Amendment Theory and Prior Restraint

The history, meanings and boundaries of freedom of speech and of the press

Focal cases:
Near v. Minnesota, 283 U.S. 697 (1931)
New York Times Co. v. United States, 403 U.S. 713 (1971)

> Congress shall make no law respecting an establishment of religion, or prohibiting the exercise thereof; or abridging the freedom of speech, or of the press; or the right of the people peaceably to assemble, and to petition the Government for a redress of grievances.

Those forty-five words are the complete text of the First Amendment to the U.S. Constitution. Since their adoption in 1791, the fourteen words that limit government authority over "freedom of speech, or of the press" have shaped the American concept of free expression, formed the foundation of much media law and come to embody many of the nation's values and aspirations.

If interpreted literally, the First Amendment's free speech and press clauses would limit only the U.S. Congress from "abridging the freedom" of the people and the press. However, the First Amendment is not read literally. Instead, it has been applied to overturn Congressional statutes, federal judicial and executive decisions[1] and state actions.[2] In 1925, the U.S. Supreme Court stated unequivocally that the freedoms of speech and the press are "fundamental personal rights and liberties protected [against state actions] by the due process clause of the Fourteenth Amendment."[3] Today, the First Amendment's protection against government action extends equally to all levels of government.

---

[1] *See, e.g.,* New York Times Co. v. United States, 403 U.S. 713 (1971).

[2] Near v. Minnesota, 283 U.S. 697 (1931).

[3] Gitlow v. New York, 268 U.S. 652 (1925).

But what does that protection mean? What are the "speech" and "the press" freedoms that government may not abridge? The answers to those questions are not clear. In fact, in some ways they are the focus of much of the content of this book. Experts disagree both on the answers and on how to properly determine the correct answers to these questions. Some justices and scholars suggest that the meaning is clear from the text itself, but even the most conservative textualists do not ascribe to the amendment's absolute ban on government action.[4] Among other uncertainties, parsing the First Amendment necessitates judgments about whether a given government action actually "abridges" the protected freedoms. An array of scholars argues that some laws – including laws that assure citizen access to the media[5] or advance the equal participation of minorities in contemporary society or punish discriminatory and hateful speech[6] – are permissible under the First Amendment because they enhance rather than abridge protected freedoms.

Some who reject a close textual reading of the First Amendment as sufficient to guide a coherent philosophy of law, or jurisprudence, believe the original intent of those who wrote the amendment establishes the correct interpretation and application of the clause. Unfortunately, intent is a slippery thing, and the framers of the Bill of Rights left behind only a scant record of their discussions and their intent. Moreover, social values and conditions have changed in the two hundred years since the adoption of the Bill of Rights, and many argue that a static interpretation of its language undermines the contemporary relevance of the First Amendment.

Although scholars long have sought a consistent, unified theory to direct First Amendment decision-making, courts have tended to favor *ad hoc*, or issue specific, reasoning. Often called balancing, *ad hoc* reasoning requires the court to weigh the individual's constitutional rights against the competing rights of others. There is no clear formula to dictate the outcome of this process; the determination of which rights should dominate requires careful examination of the unique issues and conflicts involved.

Despite the ambiguity of First Amendment jurisprudence, constitutional scholars tend to agree on several things. First, scholars generally agree the First Amendment was never an absolute ban on all government actions involving freedom of speech or press. Second, scholars agree that, at a minimum, the First Amendment was intended to prevent the U.S. government from enacting the suppressive laws that flourished in England during the three hundred years following the introduction of the printing press in 1476. Finally, most scholars acknowledge that the First Amendment guarantee of freedom of speech and press did not eliminate the common law of sedition libel, which made it a crime to criticize government officials.[7]

ANTECEDENTS TO THE FIRST AMENDMENT

The First Amendment was, and is, a product of its history and its context. At the time of the adoption of the First Amendment, licensing of presses by the British crown had prevailed in England since the early 1500s. King Henry VIII and the Roman Catholic Church feared that the wholesale distribution of printed materials made possible by the printing press would undermine their control of information and, so, their control of the people. To maintain their power, the church and the crown sought to suppress alternative ideas by licensing the press and by outlawing

---

[4] Even Justice Hugo Black, generally viewed as a rare, nearly absolutist Supreme Court justice, acknowledged that certain restraints on speech had been accepted by those who wrote the text of the First Amendment.

[5] *See, e.g.,* Jerome Barron, *Access to the Press – A New First Amendment Right*, 80 HARV. L. REV. 1641 (1967).

[6] *See, e.g.,* Richard Delgado & Jean Stefancic, *Images of the Outsider in American Law and Culture: Can Free Expression Remedy Systemic Social Ills?*, 77 CORNELL L. REV. 1258 (1992); RICHARD DELGADO & JEAN STEFANCIC (EDS.), CRITICAL RACE THEORY: THE CUTTING EDGE (2D ED., 2000).

[7] *See, e.g.,* LEONARD LEVY, LEGACY OF SUPPRESSION (1960); LEONARD LEVY, EMERGENCE OF A FREE PRESS (1985).

critical views as heresy or sedition. They joined forces, imposed a strict system of prior review of all texts, licensing and bond fees on printers, through which they attempted to control all publishing. King's officers banned books and censored disfavored ideas.

The crown also provided lucrative monopoly printing contracts for certain works, including the Bible, to favored printers who were then enlisted to help enforce the government's prior restraint policies. These printers searched and destroyed competitors' businesses with impunity. Although unlicensed texts continued to appear in England, such publishing was extremely dangerous. Printers suspected of publishing or distributing unauthorized or outlawed texts faced fines, prison, torture or even execution.

THE FOUNDATIONS OF FIRST AMENDMENT THEORY

Although the power of prior review shifted from the king's officers to the British Parliament in 1643, all publications remained subject to prior review by government censors. Writers of the day protested these government-imposed limits and developed theories to justify freedom of the press. In 1644, for example, John Milton's unlicensed *Areopagitica* argued that an open marketplace of ideas advanced the interests of mankind and society. The free exchange of ideas was vital to the discovery of truth, Milton said.

Though all the winds of doctrine were let loose to play upon the earth, so Truth be in the field, we do injuriously by licensing and prohibiting to misdoubt her strength. Let her and Falsehood grapple; who ever knew Truth put to the worse in a free and open encounter?[8]

By the late 1600s, John Locke would argue that government censorship was an improper exercise of power.[9] Locke asserted that all people have fundamental natural rights – including the rights of liberty and self-fulfillment – that may not legitimately be limited by government. Freedom of expression is central to these natural rights. Locke also argued for a revolutionary new vision of government. Government, he said, existed not on its own authority but through a grant of power from the people. Under this social contract, Locke said, the people grant government limited power in exchange for assurance that government will protect the people's rights. Thus, a legitimate government must advance, not restrict, the rights of the people. In Locke's view, government censorship violates this fundamental contract and can never be justified.

In 1694, the Parliament of England failed to renew the Licensing Act, but for the next one hundred years, the government continued to enact and enforce laws that punished immoral, illegal or dangerous speech *after* the fact. The intelligentsia of the day believed legal action after the fact raised few of the problems inherent in prior restraint. *Post hoc* punishment, in this view, was not censorship. Punishment after the fact allowed citizens to receive information and individuals to express themselves freely, but it held speakers responsible for their unacceptable or dangerous ideas. Indeed, the prevalent understanding of freedom of the press in England at the time of the colonization of America accepted after-the-fact punishment for abuse of the rights of free speech and press. In 1769, Sir William Blackstone, leading chronicler of English law, described the state of the law:

The liberty of the press is indeed essential to the nature of a free state, but this consists in laying no *previous* restraints upon publications, and not in freedom from censure for criminal matter when published. Every freeman has an undoubted right to lay what sentiments he pleases before the public: to forbid this is to destroy the freedom of the

---

[8] JOHN MILTON, AEROPAGITICA (1st Ed. n.p. 1644) in GREAT BOOKS OF THE WESTERN WORLD (1952) 409.
[9] JOHN LOCKE, THE SECOND TREATISE OF CIVIL GOVERNMENT (1690). *See also*, JEAN-JACQUES ROUSSEAU, OF THE SOCIAL CONTRACT (1762).

press: but if he publishes what is improper, mischievous, or illegal, he must take the consequences of his own temerity.[10]

England attempted to impose this view of freedom of the press upon the developing American colonies through British licensing, taxation and sedition laws. These efforts were undermined by the growing independence of colonial administrators and juries that refused to convict under the law (a practice called jury nullification). Colonial convictions for sedition effectively ended in 1734 with the jury acquittal of John Peter Zenger, a German printer who clearly had broken the sedition law by publishing criticism of the New York colonial governor, William Cosby. When colonial juries refused to punish for publication of truthful seditious libel, colonial legislatures stepped in, employing their power of contempt to question, convict, jail and fine publishers with whom they were displeased.

Thus, the popular meaning of freedom of speech and press in the late 1700s in America is unclear, and the framers of the First Amendment left no clear record indicating whether they meant the clause narrowly – as only a ban on prior restraints – or more broadly. Vague indications of original intent do not establish whether the First Amendment was meant to prevent the newly formed government from punishing people both before and after the fact for speech that was criminal in England, such as seditious libel.[11]

The passage of the Alien and Sedition Acts within seven years of the adoption of the First Amendment further clouds the issue. These laws enacted in 1798 severely restricted the fundamental rights of aliens in the United States and imposed heavy fines and jail time on individuals convicted of stirring up emotions or expressing malicious or scandalous views against the federal government. As the 18th Century ended, more than a dozen prosecutions and convictions under these laws targeted outspoken publishers, editors and political opponents of John Adams' government.[12] The U.S. Supreme Court never reviewed the constitutionality of the federal Sedition Act, which expired in 1801.

FIRST AMENDMENT VALUES

Given the inability of historical records to provide a definitive interpretation of the First Amendment, jurists and legal scholars have looked to theory to define the expanse of its protection for freedom of expression. Theories have not succeeded in this role, as the following quick review of some leading First Amendment theories suggests.

At the most basic level, theorists tend to view the First Amendment either as a tool to achieve other goals or as an expression of a fundamental, intrinsic value. In the first view, freedom of speech and press are protected under the First Amendment because they embody the means to advance societal interests. For example, several utilitarian scholars argue that the primary value of the First Amendment is to assure the proper functioning of democracy.[13] These theorists assert that the First Amendment should protect only those forms of expression that improve the ability of citizens to engage in democratic deliberation or to oversee their government representatives. Other functionalist scholars believe the First Amendment should be interpreted to support a broad marketplace of ideas that advances society's search for truth,[14] or to improve the ability of

---

[10] WILLIAM BLACKSTONE, COMMENTARIES ON THE LAWS OF ENGLAND, vol. 4 (London: 1769) 151-52.

[11] *But see* ZECHARIAH CHAFEE, FREE SPEECH IN THE UNITED STATES 2 (1941) (arguing that the First Amendment was designed to eliminate the law of sedition forever).

[12] *See* JAMES MORTON SMITH, FREEDOM'S FETTERS (1956).

[13] *See, e.g.,* ALEXANDER MEIKLEJOHN, FREE SPEECH AND ITS RELATION TO SELF-GOVERNMENT (1948); CASS SUNSTEIN, DEMOCRACY AND THE PROBLEM OF FREE SPEECH; Vincent Blasi, *The Checking Value in First Amendment Theory,* 1977 AM. B. FOUND. RES. J. 521 (1977).

[14] *See, e.g.,* JOHN MILTON, ON LIBERTY (1859); THOMAS I. EMERSON, THE SYSTEM OF FREE EXPRESSION (1970).

minority groups in society to be heard effectively,[15] or to encourage the development of a tolerant society.[16]

The various functionalist approaches to understanding the First Amendment have been criticized for requiring jurists to draw untenable distinctions. There are no bright lines to define what expression does, and does not, contribute to informed democratic deliberation, for example. Critics also argue that utilitarian theories allow certain types of speech to be favored by government, while other types of speech legitimately may be disfavored or regulated without harm to the freedom of speech embraced by the First Amendment. Some observers have noted that government is most likely to judge speech critical of its own actions to be criminal or dangerous, and this speech is most needy of protection in a democracy.

In contrast, some scholars argue that the core purpose of the First Amendment is to provide the opportunity for the expression of dissent.[17] While this might be considered an instrumentalist theory – to value dissent because it increases the diversity of expressed ideas and so enriches the marketplace of ideas – it more often represents a vision of freedom of expression as an end in itself. Dissent is good not because it enhances discussion; dissent is good because it embodies an element of individual natural liberty and enables each human to express, fulfill and constitute him or herself.[18] These theorists echo Locke and argue that the freedom to speak and print ideas is a fundamental good inherent in every individual that is never the legitimate domain of government action.

Critics argue that this natural liberty approach has no logical end. Individuals do not express themselves simply through words. They express themselves through dress, occupation, gesture and action. If the First Amendment is interpreted to broadly protect individual self-expression and self-fulfillment, virtually everything falls under the First Amendment umbrella. If everything is speech, nothing benefits from special constitutional protection. Moreover, this approach seems to privilege individual autonomy to the detriment of communal social values. Some say the First Amendment should not enshrine individuality as supreme; free expression offers the promise of rich social interaction.

CONTEMPORARY PRIOR RESTRAINT

No single First Amendment theory has dominated the jurisprudence of free expression. Instead, the legal interpretation and application of the free speech and press clause have developed in response to historical pressures and the specific legal challenges brought before the U.S. Supreme Court. Nevertheless, there is one bedrock principle that harkens back to the 1700s: freedom of the press cannot co-exist with prior restraint. Prior restraints generally are presumed to be unconstitutional because they pose an unacceptable risk of enforcing a government-prescribed orthodoxy by eliminating potentially valuable but disfavored concepts from the marketplace of ideas. It is generally agreed that a prior restraint on expression – particularly any outright ban on certain ideas or forms of expression – is the least acceptable form of government regulation of speech.

---

[15] See, e.g., CATHERINE MACKINNON, FEMINISM UNMODIFIED, DISCOURSES ON LIFE AND LAW (1987); MARI J. MATSUDA, CHARLES R. LAWRENCE, RICHARD DELGADO & KIMBERLE WILLIAMS CRENSHAW, (eds.), WORDS THAT WOUND: CRITICAL RACE THEORY, ASSAULTIVE SPEECH, AND THE FIRST AMENDMENT (1993).
[16] See, e.g., LEE BOLLINGER, THE TOLERANT SOCIETY: FREEDOM OF SPEECH AND EXTREMIST SPEECH IN AMERICA (1986).
[17] See, e.g., STEVEN SHIFFRIN, DISSENT, INJUSTICE AND THE MEANINGS OF AMERICA (1999); Vincent Blasi, *The Pathological Perspective and the First Amendment*, 85 COLUM. L. REV. 449 (1985).
[18] See, e.g., C. Edwin Baker, *Scope of the First Amendment Freedom of Speech*, 25 U.C.L.A. L. REV. 964 (1978).

For the past seventy years, the Supreme Court has attempted to clarify what constitutes an impermissible prior restraint of speech. In its classic sense, a prior restraint has three components. First, a prior restraint is broad; it subjects all speech or publication to government oversight. Second, a prior restraint employs government reviewers or censors who, based on their subjective evaluations, determine what content is acceptable. Third, the government censors impose their judgment on publications before they are published.

In developing its contemporary doctrine against prior restraint, the Supreme Court has said the First Amendment is a *nearly* absolute prohibition on the imposition of government control before speech or publication occurs. The Supreme Court first established the doctrine against prior restraint in the 1931 case of *Near v. Minnesota*.[19] In *Near*, the Court struck down a perpetual injunction on "nuisance" publications. The Court said the Constitution prohibited a Minnesota state criminal law that allowed government to permanently stop, or enjoin, a publication that previously had been found to contain libel – including criticism of government.

Forty years later, in *New York Times Co. v. United States*,[20] the Court said the federal government's effort to stop newspaper publication of classified military information was an unconstitutional prior restraint. In *New York Times Co.*, the Court considered whether publication of classified documents related to the War in Vietnam posed an unacceptable risk to national security, fighting soldiers, international alliances and U.S. prisoners of war. The Court struck down the injunction because the government failed to show that publication of "the Pentagon Papers" would seriously harm national security. This decision left open the possibility that prior restraints might be constitutional if they were shown to be necessary to prevent serious harms to fundamental government interests.

More recently, a 1994 *per curiam* decision by Justice Blackmun struck down a state court injunction preventing the scheduled broadcast of an investigative news report. *CBS v. Davis*[21] involved footage taken inside a South Dakota meatpacking plant by a plant employee wearing a hidden camera during his shift. As a basic tenet, Blackmun said indefinite delay of news broadcasts is unacceptable under the First Amendment because such delay likely will cause irreparable harm to the news media and to the public. Writing for the Court, Blackmun said that although the footage obtained through "calculated misdeeds" by CBS might result in significant harm to the meatpacking company, the injunction was unwarranted because the company had failed to meet its burden to show that the exceptional remedy of a prior restraint was necessary. Blackmun said a prior restraint on the media would be justified only if the party seeking the restraint : (1) could demonstrate that the harm to be caused by the publication was great and certain and could not be addressed by less intrusive measures or (2) that the news media likely had engaged in criminal activity to obtain the material in question.

Not all government actions that seem to prevent or limit citizens' ability to express themselves are considered prior restraints. In 1993, for example, the U.S. Supreme Court upheld the right of government to seize all the materials in an adult entertainment business as punishment for illegal speech. The business owner seeking redress in *Alexander v. United States*[22] had been convicted of selling three obscene tapes and four obscene magazines. The Supreme Court reasoned that although most of the confiscated sexual magazines and videos were protected by the First Amendment, their destruction was a constitutional punishment for the owner's illegal distribution

---

[19] 283 U.S. 697 (1931).
[20] 403 U.S. 713 (1971).
[21] 510 U.S. 1315 (1994).
[22] 509 U.S. 544 (1993).

of obscenity. The seizure did not constitute a prior restraint because the owner remained free to open a new store and buy and sell the same materials again, the Court said.

Some prior restraints do exist today. Police may legally step in to prevent you from verbally conspiring to commit a crime or inciting others to violence, and government may impose prior restraints to prevent speech that threatens national security. Cities can require permits prior to parades in the streets or to coordinate use of public parks and meeting areas. The U.S. Supreme Court also has upheld the constitutionality of laws banning protests within a certain distance of abortion facilities and stopping distribution of election materials within a certain distance of the polls. Judges' orders prohibiting trial participants from discussing the trial generally are acceptable. Laws that limit use of copyrighted material are mandated by the Constitution, and laws that criminalize the production and distribution of obscenity are accepted.

READING THE PRIOR RESTRAINT CASES

Guidance on what is, and is not, an unconstitutional prior restraint is best gleaned from the Supreme Court's own words. To enrich your understanding, the full text of one foundational prior restraint case, *Near v. Minnesota*, and excerpts from the Supreme Court's ruling in *New York Times Co. v. United States* follow. (Note that throughout this text, the Supreme Court's pagination is indicated in the body of the cases by numbers in brackets, e.g. [155].)

A number of other cases also should inform a full understanding of prior restraint law in America. Other key cases of interest that you may wish to read include:

- *Snepp v. United States*, 444 U.S. 507 (1980) (upholding CIA prior review of present or past employee's dissemination of CIA-related information).
- *Pittsburgh Press Co. v. Pittsburgh Commission on Human Relations*, 413 U.S. 376 (1973) (enjoining publication of sex-designated help wanted ads).
- *Organization for a Better Austin v. Keefe*, 402 U.S. 415 (1971) (dissolving an injunction stopping distribution of pamphlets criticizing a real estate developer).
- *Times Film Corp. v. Chicago*, 365 U.S. 43 (1961) (upholding statute requiring city review of films prior to public exhibition).
- *Kingsley Books v. Brown*, 354 U.S. 436 (1957) (enjoining distribution of obscene pamphlets).
- *Lorain Journal Co. v. United States*, 342 U.S. 143 (1951) (affirming injunction on newspaper attempt to monopolize commerce by refusing to carry ads from businesses advertising in other local media).

The following questions are designed to help you read and understand the important elements of the following cases.

- What law or government action is being challenged in each of these cases?
- What government interest is the statute or government action designed to serve?
- Does the majority accept the notion that the statute or government action serves a real interest or addresses a real harm?
- Does the majority believe the statute or government action discriminates against certain types of content or certain ideas? How does this affect the ruling?
- How does the Supreme Court define "prior restraint"? In other words, what elements does the Supreme Court examine to determine whether the government action constitutes prior restraint?
- What evidence or proof would the Supreme Court require to justify a prior restraint?
- Who bears the burden of proof and under what conditions might a prior restraint be permitted?

- Does the Supreme Court decide the case based on a clear rule or test, or does it engage in some form of *ad hoc* reasoning? Explain.
- What precedents does the Court rely on to reach its decision?
- Does the Court review the intent, the text or the effect of the statute or government action?
- What is the core reason for the separate opinions? Do the opinions disagree on outcome, reasoning, or both?

Near v. Minnesota
283 U.S. 697
(1931)

PRIOR HISTORY: Appeal from the Supreme Court of Minnesota.

JUDGES: Hughes, Holmes, Van Devanter, McReynolds, Brandeis, Suther-land, Butler, Stone, Roberts

OPINION: [701] MR. CHIEF JUSTICE HUGHES delivered the opinion of the Court.

Chapter 285 of the Session Laws of Minnesota for the year 1925[1] provides for the abatement, as a public nuisance, of a "malicious, scandalous and defamatory newspaper, [702] magazine or other periodical." Section one of the Act is as follows:

"Section 1. Any person who, as an individual, or as a member or employee of a firm, or association or organization, or as an officer, director, member or employee of a corporation, shall be engaged in the business of regularly or customarily producing, publishing or circulating, having in possession, selling or giving away.

(a) an obscene, lewd and lascivious newspaper, magazine, or other periodical,

or (b) a malicious, scandalous and defamatory newspaper, magazine or other periodical, is guilty of a nuisance, and all persons guilty of such nuisance may be enjoined, as hereinafter provided.

"Participation in such business shall constitute a commission of such nuisance and render the participant liable and subject to the proceedings, orders and judgments provided for in this Act. Ownership, in whole or in part, directly or indirectly, of any such periodical, or of any stock or interest in any corporation or organization which owns the same in whole or in part, or which publishes the same, shall constitute such participation.

"In actions brought under (b) above, there shall be available the defense that the truth was published with good motives and for justifiable ends and in such actions the plaintiff shall not have the right to

report (sic) to issues or editions of periodicals taking place more than three months before the commencement of the action."

Section two provides that whenever any such nuisance is committed or exists, the County Attorney of any county where any such periodical is published or circulated, or, in case of his failure or refusal to proceed upon written request in good faith of a reputable citizen, the Attorney General, or upon like failure or refusal of the latter, any citizen of the county, may maintain an action in the district court of the county in the name of the State to enjoin [703] perpetually the persons committing or maintaining any such nuisance from further committing or maintaining it. Upon such evidence as the court shall deem sufficient, a temporary injunction may be granted. The defendants have the right to plead by demurrer or answer, and the plaintiff may demur or reply as in other cases.

The action, by section three, is to be "governed by the practice and procedure applicable to civil actions for injunctions," and after trial the court may enter judgment permanently enjoining the defendants found guilty of violating the Act from continuing the violation and, "in and by such judgment, such nuisance may be wholly abated." The court is empowered, as in other cases of contempt, to punish disobedience to a temporary or permanent injunction by fine of not more than $ 1,000 or by imprisonment in the county jail for not more than twelve months.

Under this statute, clause (b), the County Attorney of Hennepin County brought this action to enjoin the publication of what was described as a "malicious, scandalous and defamatory newspaper, magazine and periodical," known as "The Saturday Press," published by the defendants in the city of Minneapolis. The complaint alleged that the defendants, on September 24, 1927, and on eight subsequent dates in October and November, 1927, published and circulated editions of that periodical which were "largely devoted to malicious, scandalous and defamatory articles" concerning

---

[1] Mason's Minnesota Statutes, 1927, 10123-1 to 10123-3.

Charles G. Davis, Frank W. Brunskill, the Minneapolis Tribune, the Minneapolis Journal, Melvin C. Passolt, George E. Leach, the Jewish Race, the members of the Grand Jury of Hennepin County impaneled in November, 1927, and then holding office, and other persons, as more fully appeared in exhibits annexed to the complaint, consisting of copies of the articles described and constituting 327 pages of the record. While the complaint did not so allege, it [704] appears from the briefs of both parties that Charles G. Davis was a special law enforcement officer employed by a civic organization, that George E. Leach was Mayor of Minneapolis, that Frank W. Brunskill was its Chief of Police, and that Floyd B. Olson (the relator in this action) was County Attorney.

Without attempting to summarize the contents of the voluminous exhibits attached to the complaint, we deem it sufficient to say that the articles charged in substance that a Jewish gangster was in control of gambling, bootlegging and racketeering in Minneapolis, and that law enforcing officers and agencies were not energetically performing their duties. Most of the charges were directed against the Chief of Police; he was charged with gross neglect of duty, illicit relations with gangsters, and with participation in graft. The County Attorney was charged with knowing the existing conditions and with failure to take adequate measures to remedy them. The Mayor was accused of inefficiency and dereliction. One member of the grand jury was stated to be in sympathy with the gangsters. A special grand jury and a special prosecutor were demanded to deal with the situation in general, and, in particular, to investigate an attempt to assassinate one Guilford, one of the original defendants, who, it appears from the articles, was shot by gangsters after the first issue of the periodical had been published. There is no question but that the articles made serious accusations against the public officers named and others in connection with the prevalence of crimes and the failure to expose and punish them.

At the beginning of the action, on November 22, 1927, and upon the verified complaint, an order was made directing the defendants to show cause why a temporary injunction should not issue and meanwhile forbidding the defendants to publish, circulate or have in their possession any editions of the periodical from September [705] 24, 1927, to November 19, 1927, inclusive, and from publishing, circulating, or having in their possession, "any future editions of said The Saturday Press" and "any publication, known by any other name whatsoever containing malicious, scandalous and defamatory matter of the kind alleged in plaintiff's complaint herein or otherwise."

The defendants demurred to the complaint upon the ground that it did not state facts sufficient to constitute a cause of action, and on this demurrer challenged the constitutionality of the statute. The District Court overruled the demurrer and certified the question of constitutionality to the Supreme Court of the State. The Supreme Court sustained the statute (174 Minn. 457; 219 N. W. 770), and it is conceded by the appellee that the Act was thus held to be valid over the objection that it violated not only the state constitution but also the Fourteenth Amendment of the Constitution of the United States.

Thereupon, the defendant Near, the present appellant, answered the complaint. He averred that he was the sole owner and proprietor of the publication in question. He admitted the publication of the articles in the issues described in the complaint but denied that they were malicious, scandalous or defamatory as alleged. He expressly invoked the protection of the due process clause of the Fourteenth Amend-ment. The case then came on for trial. The plaintiff offered in evidence the verified complaint, together with the issues of the publication in question, which were attached to the complaint as exhibits. The defendant objected to the introduction of the evidence, invoking the constitutional provisions to which his answer referred. The objection was overruled, no further evidence was presented, and the plaintiff rested. The defendant then rested, without offering evidence. The plaintiff moved that the court direct the issue of a permanent injunction, and this was done.

[706] The District Court made findings of fact, which followed the allegations of the complaint and found in general terms that the editions in question were "chiefly devoted to malicious, scandalous and defamatory articles," concerning the individuals named. The court further found that the defendants through these publications "did engage in the business of regularly and customarily producing, publishing and circulating a malicious, scandalous and defamatory newspaper," and that "the said publication" "under said name of The Saturday Press, or any other name, constitutes a public nuisance under the laws of the State." Judgment was thereupon entered adjudging that "the newspaper, magazine and periodical known as The Saturday Press," as a public nuisance, "be and is hereby abated." The judgment perpetually enjoined the defendants "from producing, editing, publishing, circulating, having in their possession, selling or giving away any publication whatsoever which is a malicious, scandalous or defamatory newspaper, as defined by law," and also "from further conducting said nuisance under the name and title of said The Saturday Press or any other name or title."

The defendant Near appealed from this judgment to the Supreme Court of the State, again asserting his right under the Federal Constitution, and the judgment was affirmed upon the authority of the former decision. 179 Minn. 40; 228 N. W. 326. With respect to the contention that the judgment went too far, and prevented the defendants from publishing any kind of a newspaper, the court observed that the assignments of error did not go to the form of the judgment and that the lower court had not been asked to modify it. The court added that it saw no reason "for defendants to construe the judgment as restraining them from operating a newspaper in harmony with the public welfare, to which all must yield," that the allegations of the complaint had been [707] found to be true, and, though this was an equitable action, defendants had not indicated a desire "to conduct their business in the usual and legitimate manner."

From the judgment as thus affirmed, the defendant Near appeals to this Court.

This statute, for the suppression as a public nuisance of a newspaper or periodical, is unusual, if not unique, and raises questions of grave importance transcending the local interests involved in the particular action. It is no longer open to doubt that the liberty of the press, and of speech, is within the liberty safeguarded by the due process clause of the Fourteenth Amendment from invasion by state action. It was found impossible to conclude that this essential personal liberty of the citizen was left unprotected by the general guaranty of fundamental rights of person and property. Gitlow v. New York, 268 U.S. 652, 666; Whitney v. California, 274 U.S. 357, 362, 373; Fiske v. Kansas, 274 U.S. 380, 382; Stromberg v. California, ante, p. 359. In maintaining this guaranty, the authority of the State to enact laws to promote the health, safety, morals and general welfare of its people is necessarily admitted. The limits of this sovereign power must always be determined with appropriate regard to the particular subject of its exercise.

Thus, while recognizing the broad discretion of the legislature in fixing rates to be charged by those undertaking a public service, this Court has decided that the owner cannot constitutionally be deprived of his right to a fair return, because that is deemed to be of the essence of ownership. Railroad Commission Cases, 116 U.S. 307, 331; Northern Pacific Ry. Co. v. North Dakota, 236 U.S. 585, 596. So, while liberty of contract is not an absolute right, and the wide field of activity in the making of contracts is subject to legislative supervision (Frisbie v. United States, 157 U.S. 161, 165), this Court has held that the power of the State stops short of interference with what are deemed [708] to be certain indispensable requirements of the liberty assured, notably with respect to the fixing of prices and wages. Tyson Bros. v. Banton, 273 U.S. 418; Ribnik v. McBride, 277 U.S. 350; Adkins v. Children's Hospital, 261 U.S. 525, 560, 561. Liberty of speech, and of the press, is also not an absolute right, and the State may punish its abuse. Whitney v. California, supra; Stromberg v. California, supra. Liberty, in each of its phases, has its history and connotation and, in the present instance, the inquiry is as to the historic conception of the liberty of the press and whether the statute under review violates the essential attributes of that liberty.

The appellee insists that the questions of the application of the statute to appellant's periodical, and of the construction of the judgment of the trial court, are not presented for review; that appellant's sole attack was upon the constitutionality of the statute, however it might be applied. The appellee contends that no question either of motive in the publication, or whether the decree goes beyond the direction of the statute, is before us. The appellant replies that, in his view, the plain terms of the statute were not departed from in this case and that, even if they were, the statute is nevertheless unconstitutional under any reasonable construction of its terms. The appellant states that he has not argued that the temporary and permanent injunctions were broader than were warranted by the statute; he insists that what was done was properly done if the statute is valid, and that the action taken under the statute is a fair indication of its scope.

With respect to these contentions it is enough to say that in passing upon constitutional questions the court has regard to substance and not to mere matters of form, and that, in accordance with familiar principles, the statute must be tested by its operation and effect. Henderson v. Mayor, 92 U.S. 259, 268; Bailey v. Alabama, 219 U.S. 219, 244; [709] United States v. Reynolds, 235 U.S. 133, 148, 149; St. Louis Southwestern Ry. Co. v. Arkansas, 235 U.S. 350, 362; Mountain Timber Co. v. Washington, 243 U.S. 219, 237. That operation and effect we think is clearly shown by the record in this case. We are not concerned with mere errors of the trial court, if there be such, in going beyond the direction of the statute as construed by the Supreme Court of the State. It is thus important to note precisely the purpose and effect of the statute as the state court has construed it.

First. The statute is not aimed at the redress of individual or private wrongs. Remedies for libel remain available and unaffected. The statute, said the state court, "is not directed at threatened libel but at an existing business which, generally speaking, involves more than libel." It is aimed at the distribution of scandalous matter as "detrimental to public morals and to the general welfare," tending "to disturb the peace of the community" and "to provoke assaults and the commission of crime." In order to obtain an injunction to suppress the future publication of the newspaper or periodical, it is not necessary to prove the falsity of the charges that have been made in the publication condemned. In the present action there was no allegation that the matter published was not true. It is alleged, and the statute requires the allegation, that the publication was "malicious." But, as in prosecutions for libel, there is no requirement of proof by the State of malice in fact as distinguished from malice inferred from the mere publication of the defamatory matter.[2] The judgment in this case proceeded upon the mere proof of publication. The statute permits the defense, not of the truth alone, but only that the truth was published with good motives and [710] for justifiable ends. It is apparent that under the statute the publication is to be regarded as defamatory if it injures reputation, and that it is scandalous if it circulates charges of reprehensible conduct, whether criminal or otherwise, and the publication is thus deemed to invite public reprobation and to constitute a public scandal. The court sharply defined the purpose of the statute, bringing out the precise point, in these words: "There is no constitutional right to publish a fact merely because it is true. It is a matter of common knowledge that prosecutions under the criminal libel statutes do not result in efficient repression or suppression of the evils of scandal. Men who are the victims of such assaults seldom resort to the courts. This is especially true if their sins are exposed and the only question relates to whether it was done with good motives and for justifiable ends. This law is not for the protection of the person attacked nor to punish the wrongdoer. It is for the protection of the public welfare."

Second. The statute is directed not simply at the circulation of scandalous and defamatory statements with regard to private citizens, but at the continued publication by newspapers and periodicals of charges against public officers of corruption, malfeasance in office, or serious neglect of duty. Such charges by their very nature create a public scandal. They are scandalous and defamatory within the meaning of the statute, which has its normal operation in relation to publications dealing prominently and chiefly with the alleged derelictions of public officers.[3]

---

[2] Mason's Minn. Stats. 10112, 10113; State v. Shipman, 83 Minn. 441, 445; 86 N. W. 431; State v. Minor, 163 Minn. 109, 110; 203 N. W. 596.

[3] It may also be observed that in a prosecution for libel the applicable Minnesota statute (Mason's Minn. Stats., 1927, §§ 10112, 10113), provides that the publication is justified "whenever the matter charged as libelous is true and was published with good motives and for justifiable ends," and also "is excused when honestly made, in belief of its truth, and upon reasonable grounds for such belief, and consists of fair comments upon the conduct of a person in respect to

[711] Third. The object of the statute is not punishment, in the ordinary sense, but suppression of the offending newspaper or periodical. The reason for the enactment, as the state court has said, is that prosecutions to enforce penal statutes for libel do not result in "efficient repression or suppression of the evils of scandal." Describing the business of publication as a public nuisance, does not obscure the substance of the proceeding which the statute authorizes. It is the continued publication of scandalous and defamatory matter that constitutes the business and the declared nuisance. In the case of public officers, it is the reiteration of charges of official misconduct, and the fact that the newspaper or periodical is principally devoted to that purpose, that exposes it to suppression. In the present instance, the proof was that nine editions of the newspaper or periodical in question were published on successive dates, and that they were chiefly devoted to charges against public officers and in relation to the prevalence and protection of crime. In such a case, these officers are not left to their ordinary remedy in a suit for libel, or the authorities to a prosecution for criminal libel. Under this statute, a publisher of a newspaper or periodical, undertaking to conduct a campaign to expose and to censure official derelictions, and devoting his publication principally to that purpose, must face not simply the possibility of a verdict against him in a suit or prosecution for libel, but a determination that his newspaper or periodical is a public nuisance to be abated, and that this abatement and suppression will follow unless he is prepared with legal evidence to prove the truth of the charges and also to satisfy the court that, in [712] addition to being true, the matter was published with good motives and for justifiable ends.

This suppression is accomplished by enjoining publication and that restraint is the object and effect of the statute.

Fourth. The statute not only operates to suppress the offending newspaper or periodical but to put the publisher under an effective censorship. When a newspaper or periodical is found to be "malicious, scandalous and defamatory," and is suppressed as such, resumption of publication is punishable as a contempt of court by fine or imprisonment. Thus, where a newspaper or periodical has been suppressed because of the circulation of charges against public officers of official misconduct, it would seem to be clear that the renewal of the publication of such charges would constitute a contempt and that the judgment would lay a permanent restraint upon the publisher, to escape which he must satisfy the court as to the character of a new publication. Whether he

---

public affairs." The clause last mentioned is not found in the statute in question.

would be permitted again to publish matter deemed to be derogatory to the same or other public officers would depend upon the court's ruling. In the present instance the judgment restrained the defendants from "publishing, circulating, having in their possession, selling or giving away any publication whatsoever which is a malicious, scandalous or defamatory newspaper, as defined by law." The law gives no definition except that covered by the words "scandalous and defamatory," and publications charging official misconduct are of that class. While the court, answering the objection that the judgment was too broad, saw no reason for construing it as restraining the defendants "from operating a newspaper in harmony with the public welfare to which all must yield," and said that the defendants had not indicated "any desire to conduct their business in the usual and legitimate manner," the manifest inference is that, at least with respect to a [713] new publication directed against official misconduct, the defendant would be held, under penalty of punishment for contempt as provided in the statute, to a manner of publication which the court considered to be "usual and legitimate" and consistent with the public welfare.

If we cut through mere details of procedure, the operation and effect of the statute in substance is that public authorities may bring the owner or publisher of a newspaper or periodical before a judge upon a charge of conducting a business of publishing scandalous and defamatory matter – in particular that the matter consists of charges against public officers of official dereliction – and unless the owner or publisher is able and disposed to bring competent evidence to satisfy the judge that the charges are true and are published with good motives and for justifiable ends, his newspaper or periodical is suppressed and further publication is made punishable as a contempt. This is of the essence of censorship.

The question is whether a statute authorizing such proceedings in restraint of publication is consistent with the conception of the liberty of the press as historically conceived and guaranteed. In determining the extent of the constitutional protection, it has been generally, if not universally, considered that it is the chief purpose of the guaranty to prevent previous restraints upon publication. The struggle in England, directed against the legislative power of the licenser, resulted in renunciation of the censorship of the press.[4] The liberty deemed to be established was thus described by Blackstone: "The liberty of the press is indeed essential to the nature of

a free state; but this consists in laying no previous restraints upon publications, and not in freedom from censure for criminal matter when published. Every freeman has an [714] undoubted right to lay what sentiments he pleases before the public; to forbid this, is to destroy the freedom of the press; but if he publishes what is improper, mischievous or illegal, he must take the consequence of his own temerity." 4 Bl. Com. 151, 152; see Story on the Constitution, §§ 1884, 1889. The distinction was early pointed out between the extent of the freedom with respect to censorship under our constitutional system and that enjoyed in England. Here, as Madison said, "the great and essential rights of the people are secured against legislative as well as against executive ambition. They are secured, not by laws paramount to prerogative, but by constitutions paramount to laws. This security of the freedom of the press requires that it should be exempt not only from previous restraint by the Executive, as in Great Britain, but from legislative restraint also." Report on the Virginia Resolutions, Madison's Works, vol. IV, p. 543. This Court said, in Patterson v. Colorado, 205 U.S. 454, 462: "In the first place, the main purpose of such constitutional provisions is 'to prevent all such previous restraints upon publications as had been practiced by other governments,' and they do not prevent the subsequent punishment of such as may be deemed contrary to the public welfare. Commonwealth v. Blanding, 3 Pick. 304, 313, 314; Respublica v. Oswald, 1 Dallas, 319, 325. The preliminary freedom extends as well to the false as to the true; the subsequent punishment may extend as well to the true as to the false. This was the law of criminal libel apart from statute in most cases, if not in all. Commonwealth v. Blanding, ubi sup.; 4 Bl. Com. 150."

The criticism upon Blackstone's statement has not been because immunity from previous restraint upon publication has not been regarded as deserving of special emphasis, but chiefly because that immunity cannot be deemed to exhaust the conception of the liberty guaranteed by [715] state and federal constitutions. The point of criticism has been "that the mere exemption from previous restraints cannot be all that is secured by the constitutional provisions"; and that "the liberty of the press might be rendered a mockery and a delusion, and the phrase itself a by-word, if, while every man was at liberty to publish what he pleased, the public authorities might nevertheless punish him for harmless publications." 2 Cooley, Const. Lim., 8th ed., p. 885. But it is recognized that punishment for the abuse of the liberty accorded to the press is essential to the protection of the public, and that the common law rules that subject the libeler to responsibility for the public offense, as well as for the private injury, are

---

[4] May, Constitutional History of England, vol. 2, chap. IX, p. 4; DeLolme, Commentaries on the Constitution of England, chap. IX, pp. 318, 319.

not abolished by the protection extended in our constitutions. id. pp. 883, 884. The law of criminal libel rests upon that secure foundation. There is also the conceded authority of courts to punish for contempt when publications directly tend to prevent the proper discharge of judicial functions. Patterson v. Colorado, supra; Toledo Newspaper Co. v. United States, 247 U.S. 402, 419.[5] In the present case, we have no occasion to inquire as to the permissible scope of subsequent punishment. For whatever wrong the appellant has committed or may commit, by his publications, the State appropriately affords both public and private redress by its libel laws. As has been noted, the statute in question does not deal with punishments; it provides for no punishment, except in case of contempt for violation of the court's order, but for suppression and injunction, that is, for restraint upon publication.

The objection has also been made that the principle as to immunity from previous restraint is stated too [716] broadly, if every such restraint is deemed to be prohibited. That is undoubtedly true; the protection even as to previous restraint is not absolutely unlimited. But the limitation has been recognized only in exceptional cases: "When a nation is at war many things that might be said in time of peace are such a hindrance to its effort that their utterance will not be endured so long as men fight and that no Court could regard them as protected by any constitutional right." Schenck v. United States, 249 U.S. 47, 52. No one would question but that a government might prevent actual obstruction to its recruiting service or the publication of the sailing dates of transports or the number and location of troops.[6] On similar grounds, the primary requirements of decency may be enforced against obscene publications. The security of the community life may be protected against incitements to acts of violence and the overthrow by force of orderly government. The constitutional guaranty of free speech does not "protect a man from an injunction against uttering words that may have all the effect of force. Gompers v. Buck Stove & Range Co., 221 U.S. 418, 439." Schenck v. United States, supra. These limitations are not applicable here. Nor are we now concerned with questions as to the extent of authority to prevent publications in order to protect private rights according to the principles governing the exercise of the jurisdiction of courts of equity.[7]

The exceptional nature of its limitations places in a strong light the general conception that liberty of the press, historically considered and taken up by the Federal Constitution, has meant, principally although not exclusively, immunity from previous restraints or censorship. The conception of the liberty of the press in this country had broadened with the exigencies of the colonial [717] period and with the efforts to secure freedom from oppressive administration.[8] That liberty was especially cherished for the immunity it afforded from previous restraint of the publication of censure of public officers and charges of official misconduct. As was said by Chief Justice Parker, in Commonwealth v. Blanding, 3 Pick. 304, 313, with respect to the constitution of Massachusetts: "Besides, it is well understood, and received as a commentary on this provision for the liberty of the press, that it was intended to prevent all such previous restraints upon publications as had been practiced by other governments, and in early times here, to stifle the efforts of patriots towards enlightening their fellow subjects upon their rights and the duties of rulers. The liberty of the press was to be unrestrained, but he who used it was to be responsible in case of its abuse." In the letter sent by the Continental Congress (October 26, 1774) to the Inhabitants of Quebec, referring to the "five great rights" it was said:[9] "The last right we shall mention, regards the freedom of the press. The importance of this consists, besides the advancement of truth, science, morality, and arts in general, in its diffusion of liberal sentiments on the administration of Government, its ready communication of thoughts between subjects, and its consequential promotion of union among them, whereby oppressive officers are shamed or intimidated, into more honourable and just modes of conducting affairs." Madison, who was the leading spirit in the preparation of the First Amendment of the Federal Constitution, thus described the practice and sentiment which led to the guaranties of liberty of the press in state constitutions:[10]

[718] "In every State, probably, in the Union, the press has exerted a freedom in canvassing the merits and measures of public men of every description which has not been confined to the strict limits of the common law. On this footing the freedom of the press has stood; on this footing it yet stands. . . . Some degree of abuse is inseparable from the proper use of everything, and in no instance is this more true

---

[5] See Huggonson's Case, 2 Atk. 469; Respublica v. Oswald, 1 Dallas 319; Cooper v. People, 13 Colo. 337, 373; 22 Pac. 790; Nebraska v. Rosewater, 60 Nebr. 438; 83 N. W. 353; State v. Tugwell, 19 Wash. 238; 52 Pac. 1056; People v. Wilson, 64 Ill. 195; Storey v. People, 79 Ill. 45; State v. Circuit Court, 97 Wis. 1; 72 N. W. 193.

[6] Chafee, Freedom of Speech, p. 10.

[7] See 29 Harvard Law Review, 640.

[8] See Duniway, "The Development of Freedom of the Press in Massachusetts," p. 123; Bancroft's History of the United States, vol. 2, 261.

[9] Journal of the Continental Congress, 1904 ed., vol. I, pp. 104, 108.

[10] Report on the Virginia Resolutions, Madison's Works, vol. iv, 544.

than in that of the press. It has accordingly been decided by the practice of the States, that it is better to leave a few of its noxious branches to their luxuriant growth, than, by pruning them away, to injure the vigour of those yielding the proper fruits. And can the wisdom of this policy be doubted by any who reflect that to the press alone, chequered as it is with abuses, the world is indebted for all the triumphs which have been gained by reason and humanity over error and oppression; who reflect that to the same beneficent source the United States owe much of the lights which conducted them to the ranks of a free and independent nation, and which have improved their political system into a shape so auspicious to their happiness? Had 'Sedition Acts,' forbidding every publication that might bring the constituted agents into contempt or disrepute, or that might excite the hatred of the people against the authors of unjust or pernicious measures, been uniformly enforced against the press, might not the United States have been languishing at this day under the infirmities of a sickly Confederation? Might they not, possibly, be miserable colonies, groaning under a foreign yoke?"

The fact that for approximately one hundred and fifty years there has been almost an entire absence of attempts to impose previous restraints upon publications relating to the malfeasance of public officers is significant of the deep-seated conviction that such restraints would violate constitutional right. Public officers, whose character and [719] conduct remain open to debate and free discussion in the press, find their remedies for false accusations in actions under libel laws providing for redress and punishment, and not in proceedings to restrain the publication of newspapers and periodicals. The general principle that the consti-tutional guaranty of the liberty of the press gives immunity from previous restraints has been approved in many decisions under the provisions of state constitutions.[11]

---

[11] Dailey v. Superior Court, 112 Cal. 94, 98; 44 Pac. 458; Jones, Varnum & Co. v. Townsend's Admx., 21 Fla. 431, 450; State ex rel. Liversey v. Judge, 34 La. 741, 743; Commonwealth v. Blanding, 3 Pick, 304, 313; Lindsay v. Montana Federation of Labor, 37 Mont. 264, 275, 277; 96 Pac. 127; Howell v. Bee Publishing Co., 100 Neb. 39, 42; 158 N. W. 358; New Yorker Staats-Zeitung v. Nolan, 89 N. J. Eq. 387; 105 Atl. 72; Brandreth v. Lane, 8 Paige 24; New York Juvenile Guardian Society v. Roosevelt, 7 Daly 188; Ulster Square Dealer v. Fowler, 111 N. Y. Supp. 16; Star Co. v. Brush, 170 id. 987; 172 id. 320; 172 id. 851; Dopp v. Doll, 9 Ohio Dec. Rep. 428; Respublica v. Oswald, 1 Dall. 319, 325; Respublica v. Dennie, 4 Yeates 267, 269; Ex parte Neill, 32 Tex. Cr. 275; 22 S. W. 923; Mitchell v. Grand Lodge, 56 Tex. Civ. App. 306, 309; 121 S. W. 178; Sweeney v. Baker, 13 W. Va. 158, 182; Citizens Light, Heat & Power Co. v. Montgomery Light & Water Co., 171 Fed. 553, 556; Willis v.

The importance of this immunity has not lessened. While reckless assaults upon public men, and efforts to bring obloquy upon those who are endeavoring faithfully to discharge official duties, exert a baleful influence and deserve the severest condemnation in public opinion, it cannot be said that this abuse is greater, and it is believed to be less, than that which characterized the period in which our institutions took shape. Meanwhile, the administration of government has become more complex, the opportunities for malfeasance and corruption have multiplied, crime has grown to most serious proportions, and the danger of its protection by unfaithful officials and of the impairment of the fundamental security of life and [720] property by criminal alliances and official neglect, emphasizes the primary need of a vigilant and courageous press, especially in great cities. The fact that the liberty of the press may be abused by miscreant purveyors of scandal does not make any the less necessary the immunity of the press from previous restraint in dealing with official miscon-duct. Subsequent punishment for such abuses as may exist is the appropriate remedy, consistent with constitutional privilege.

In attempted justification of the statute, it is said that it deals not with publication per se, but with the "business" of publishing defamation. If, however, the publisher has a constitutional right to publish, without previous restraint, an edition of his newspaper charging official derelictions, it cannot be denied that he may publish subsequent editions for the same purpose. He does not lose his right by exercising it. If his right exists, it may be exercised in publishing nine editions, as in this case, as well as in one edition. If previous restraint is permissible, it may be imposed at once; indeed, the wrong may be as serious in one publication as in several. Characterizing the publication as a business, and the business as a nuisance, does not permit an invasion of the constitutional immunity against restraint. Similarly, it does not matter that the newspaper or periodical is found to be "largely" or "chiefly" devoted to the publication of such derelictions. If the publisher has a right, without previous restraint, to publish them, his right cannot be deemed to be dependent upon his publishing something else, more or less, with the matter to which objection is made.

Nor can it be said that the constitutional freedom from previous restraint is lost because charges are made of derelictions which constitute crimes. With the multiplying provisions of penal codes, and of municipal charters and ordinances carrying penal sanctions, the conduct of [721] public officers is

---

O'Connell, 231 Fed. 1004, 1010; Dearborn Publishing Co. v. Fitzgerald, 271 Fed. 479, 485.

very largely within the purview of criminal statutes. The freedom of the press from previous restraint has never been regarded as limited to such animadversions as lay outside the range of penal enactments. Historically, there is no such limitation; it is inconsistent with the reason which underlies the privilege, as the privilege so limited would be of slight value for the purposes for which it came to be established.

The statute in question cannot be justified by reason of the fact that the publisher is permitted to show, before injunction issues, that the matter published is true and is published with good motives and for justifiable ends. If such a statute, authorizing suppression and injunction on such a basis, is constitutionally valid, it would be equally permissible for the legislature to provide that at any time the publisher of any newspaper could be brought before a court, or even an administrative officer (as the constitutional protection may not be regarded as resting on mere procedural details) and required to produce proof of the truth of his publication, or of what he intended to publish, and of his motives, or stand enjoined. If this can be done, the legislature may provide machinery for determining in the complete exercise of its discretion what are justifiable ends and restrain publication accordingly. And it would be but a step to a complete system of censorship. The recognition of authority to impose previous restraint upon publication in order to protect the community against the circulation of charges of misconduct, and especially of official misconduct, necessarily would carry with it the admission of the authority of the censor against which the constitutional barrier was erected. The preliminary freedom, by virtue of the very reason for its existence, does not depend, as this Court has said, on proof of truth. Patterson v. Colorado, supra.

Equally unavailing is the insistence that the statute is designed to prevent the circulation of scandal which tends [722] to disturb the public peace and to provoke assaults and the commission of crime. Charges of reprehensible conduct, and in particular of official malfeasance, unquestionably create a public scandal, but the theory of the constitutional guaranty is that even a more serious public evil would be caused by authority to prevent publication. "To prohibit the intent to excite those unfavorable sentiments against those who administer the Government, is equivalent to a prohibition of the actual excitement of them; and to prohibit the actual excitement of them is equivalent to a prohibition of discussions having that tendency and effect; which, again, is equivalent to a protection of those who administer the Government, if they should at any time deserve the contempt or hatred of the people, against being exposed to it by free animadversions

on their characters and conduct." There is nothing new in the fact that charges of reprehensible conduct may create resentment and the disposition to resort to violent means of redress, but this well-understood tendency did not alter the determination to protect the press against censorship and restraint upon publication. As was said in New Yorker Staats-Zeitung v. Nolan, 89 N. J. Eq. 387, 388; 105 Atl. 72: "If the township may prevent the circulation of a newspaper for no reason other than that some of its inhabitants may violently disagree with it, and resent its circulation by resorting to physical violence, there is no limit to what may be prohibited." The danger of violent reactions becomes greater with effective organization of defiant groups resenting exposure, and if this consideration warranted legislative interference with the initial freedom of publication, the constitutional protection would be reduced to a mere form of words.

For these reasons we hold the statute, so far as it authorized the proceedings in this action under clause (b) [723] of section one, to be an infringement of the liberty of the press guaranteed by the Fourteenth Amendment. We should add that this decision rests upon the operation and effect of the statute, without regard to the question of the truth of the charges contained in the particular periodical. The fact that the public officers named in this case, and those associated with the charges of official dereliction, may be deemed to be impeccable, cannot affect the conclusion that the statute imposes an unconstitutional restraint upon publication.

Judgment reversed.

DISSENT: MR. JUSTICE BUTLER, dissenting.

MR. JUSTICE VAN DEVANTER, MR. JUSTICE McREYNOLDS, and MR. JUSTICE SUTHERLAND concur in this opinion.

The decision of the Court in this case declares Minnesota and every other State powerless to restrain by injunction the business of publishing and circulating among the people malicious, scandalous and defamatory periodicals that in due course of judicial procedure has been adjudged to be a public nuisance. It gives to freedom of the press a meaning and a scope not heretofore recognized and construes "liberty" in the due process clause of the Fourteenth Amendment to put upon the States a federal restriction that is without precedent.

Confessedly, the Federal Constitution prior to 1868, when the Fourteenth Amendment was adopted, did not protect the right of free speech or press against state action. Barron v. Baltimore, 7 Pet. 243, 250. Fox v. Ohio, 5 How. 410, 434. Smith v. Maryland, 18 How. 71, 76. Withers v. Buckley, 20 How. 84, 89-91. Up to that time the right was safeguarded solely by the constitutions and laws of the States and, it may be added, they operated adequately to protect it. This Court was not called on until 1925 to decide whether the "liberty" protected by the Fourteenth Amendment includes the right of free speech and press. That question has been finally answered [724] in the affirmative. Cf. Patterson v. Colorado, 205 U.S. 454, 462. Prudential Ins. Co. v. Cheek, 259 U.S. 530, 538, 543. See Gitlow v. New York, 268 U.S. 652. Fiske v. Kansas, 274 U.S. 380. Stromberg v. California, ante, p. 359.

[725]The record shows, and it is conceded, that defendants' regular business was the publication of malicious, scandalous and defamatory articles concerning the principal public officers, leading newspapers of the city, many private persons and the Jewish race. It also shows that it was their purpose at all hazards to continue to carry on the business. In every edition slanderous and defamatory matter predominates to the practical exclusion of all else. Many of the statements are so highly improbable as to compel a finding that they are false. The articles themselves show malice.[12]

---

[1] The following articles appear in the last edition published, dated November 19, 1927:

"FACTS NOT THEORIES.

"'I am a bosom friend of Mr. Olson,' snorted a gentleman of Yiddish blood, 'and I want to protest against your article,' and blah, blah, blah, ad infinitum, ad nauseam.

"I am not taking orders from men of Barnett faith, at least right now. There have been too many men in this city and especially those in official life, who HAVE been taking orders and suggestions from JEW GANGSTERS, therefore we HAVE Jew Gangsters, practically ruling Minneapolis.

"It was buzzards of the Barnett stripe who shot down my buddy. It was Barnett gunmen who staged the assault on Samuel Shapiro. It is Jew thugs who have 'pulled' practically every robbery in this city. It was a member of the Barnett gang who shot down George Rubenstein (Ruby) while he stood in the shelter of Mose Barnett's ham-cavern on Hennepin avenue. It was Mose Barnett himself who shot down Roy Rogers on Hennepin avenue. It was at Mose Barnett's place of 'business' that the '13 dollar Jew' found a refuge while the police of New York were combing the country for him. It was a gang of Jew gunmen who boasted that for five hundred dollars they would kill any man in the city. It was Mose Barnett, a Jew, who boasted that he held the chief of police of Minneapolis in his hand – had bought and paid for him.

"It is Jewish men and women – pliant tools of the Jew gangster, Mose Barnett, who stand charged with having falsified the election records and returns in the Third ward. And it is Mose Barnett himself, who, indicted for his part in the Shapiro assault, is a fugitive from justice today.

"Practically every vendor of vile hooch, every owner of a moonshine still, every snake-faced gangster and embryonic yegg in the Twin Cities is a JEW.

"Having these examples before me, I feel that I am justified in my refusal to take orders from a Jew who boasts that he is a 'bosom friend' of Mr. Olson.

"I find in the mail at least twice per week, letters from gentlemen of Jewish faith who advise me against 'launching an attack on the Jewish people.' These gentlemen have the cart before the horse. I am launching, nor is Mr. Guilford, no attack against any race, BUT:

"When I find men of a certain race banding themselves together for the purpose of preying upon Gentile or Jew; gunmen, KILLERS, roaming our streets shooting down men against whom they have no personal grudge (or happen to have); defying OUR laws; corrupting OUR officials; assaulting business men; beating up unarmed citizens; spreading a reign of terror through every walk of life, then I say to you in all sincerity, that I refuse to back up a single step from that 'issue' – if they choose to make it so.

"If the people of Jewish faith in Minneapolis wish to avoid criticism of these vermin whom I rightfully call 'Jews' they can easily do so BY THEMSELVES CLEANING HOUSE.

"I'm not out to cleanse Israel of the filth that clings to Israel's skirts. I'm out to 'hew to the line, let the chips fly where they may.'

"I simply state a fact when I say that ninety per cent. of the crimes committed against society in this city are committed by Jew gangsters.

"It was a Jew who employed JEWS to shoot down Mr. Guilford. It was a Jew who employed a Jew to intimidate Mr. Shapiro and a Jew who employed JEWS to assault that gentleman when he refused to yield to their threats. It was a JEW who wheedled or employed Jews to manipulate the election records and returns in the Third ward in flagrant violation of law. It was a Jew who left two hundred dollars with another Jew to pay to our chief of police just before the last municipal election, and:

"It is Jew, Jew, Jew, as long as one cares to comb over the records.

"I am launching no attack against the Jewish people AS A RACE. I am merely calling attention to a FACT. And if the people of that race and faith wish to rid themselves of the odium and stigma THE RODENTS OF THEIR OWN RACE HAVE BROUGHT UPON THEM, they need only to step to the front and help the decent citizens of Minneapolis rid the city of these criminal Jews.

"Either Mr. Guilford or myself stand ready to do battle for a MAN, regardless of his race, color or creed, but neither of us will step one inch out of our chosen path to avoid a fight IF the Jews want to battle.

"Both of us have some mighty loyal friends among the Jewish people but not one of them comes whining to ask that we 'lay off' criticism of Jewish gangsters and none of them who comes carping to us of their 'bosom friendship' for any public official now under our journalistic guns."

"GIL'S [Guilford's] CHATTERBOX.

"I headed into the city on September 26th, ran across three Jews in a Chevrolet; stopped a lot of lead and won a bed for myself in St. Barnabas Hospital for six weeks. . . .

"Whereupon I have withdrawn all allegiance to anything with a hook nose that eats herring. I have adopted the sparrow as my national bird until Davis' law enforcement league or the K. K. K. hammers the eagle's beak out straight. So if I seem to act crazy as I ankle down the street, bear in mind that I am merely saluting MY national emblem.

"All of which has nothing to do with the present whereabouts of Big Mose Barnett. Methinks he headed the local delegation to the new Palestine-for-Jews-only. He went ahead of the boys so he could do a little fixing with the Yiddish chief of

The defendant here has no standing to assert that the statute is invalid because it might be construed so as to violate the Constitution. His right is limited solely to [726] the inquiry whether, having regard to the points properly raised in his case, the effect of applying the statute is to deprive him of his liberty without due process of law. [727] This Court should not reverse the judgment below upon the ground that in some other case the statute may be applied in a way that is repugnant to the freedom of the press protected by the Fourteenth Amendment. Castillo v. McConnico, 168 U.S. 674, 680. Williams v. Mississippi, 170 U.S. 213, 225. Yazoo & Miss. R. Co. v. Jackson Vinegar Co., 226 U.S. 217, 219-220. Plymouth Coal Co. v. Pennsylvania, 232 U.S. 531, 544-546.

This record requires the Court to consider the statute as applied to the business of publishing articles that are in fact malicious, scandalous and defamatory. The statute provides that any person who "shall be engaged in the business of regularly or customarily producing, publishing or circulating" a newspaper, magazine or other periodical that is (a) "obscene, lewd and lascivious" or (b) "malicious, scandalous and defamatory" [728] is guilty of a nuisance and may be enjoined as provided in the Act. It will be observed that the qualifying words are used conjunctively. In actions brought under (b) "there shall be available the defense that the truth was published with good motives and for justifiable ends."

The complaint charges that defendants were engaged in the business of regularly and customarily publishing "malicious, scandalous and defamatory newspapers" known as the Saturday Press, and nine editions dated respectively on each Saturday commencing September 25 and ending November

19, 1927, were made a part of the complaint. These are all that were published.

On appeal from the order of the district court overruling defendants' demurrer to the complaint the state supreme court said (174 Minn. 457, 461; 219 N. W. 770): "The constituent elements of the declared nuisance are the customary and regular dissemination by means of a newspaper which finds its way into families, reaching the young as well as the mature, of a selection of scandalous and defamatory articles treated in such a way as to excite attention and interest so as to command circulation. . . . The statute is not directed at threatened libel but at an existing business which, generally speaking, involves more than libel. The distribution of scandalous matter is detrimental to public morals and to the general welfare. It tends to disturb the peace of the community. Being defamatory and malicious, it tends to provoke assaults and the commission of crime. It has no concern with the publication of the truth, with good motives and for justifiable ends. . . . In Minnesota no agency can hush the sincere and honest voice of the press; but our constitution was never intended to protect malice, scandal and defamation when untrue or published with bad motives or without justifiable ends. . . . It was never the intention of the constitution to afford protection [729] to a publication devoted to scandal and defamation. . . . Defendants stand before us upon the record as being regularly and customarily engaged in a business of conducting a newspaper sending to the public malicious, scandalous and defamatory printed matter."

The case was remanded to the district court. Near's answer made no allegations to excuse or justify the business or the articles complained of. It formally denied that the publications were malicious, scandalous or defamatory, admitted that they were made as alleged, and attacked the statute as unconstitutional. At the trial the plaintiff introduced evidence unquestionably sufficient to support the complaint. The defendant offered none. The court found the facts as alleged in the complaint and specifically that each edition "was chiefly devoted to malicious, scandalous and defamatory articles" and that the last edition was chiefly devoted to malicious, scandalous and defamatory articles concerning Leach (mayor of Minneapolis), Davis (representative of the law enforcement league of citizens), Brunskill (chief of police), Olson (county attorney), the Jewish race and members of the grand jury then serving in that court; that defendants in and through the several publications "did thereby engage in the business of regularly and customarily producing, publishing and circulating a malicious, scandalous and defamatory newspaper."

---

police and get his twenty-five per cent. of the gambling rake-off. Boys will be boys and 'ganefs' will be ganefs."
"GRAND JURIES AND DITTO.
"There are grand juries, and there are grand juries. The last one was a real grand jury. It acted. The present one is like the scion who is labelled 'Junior.' That means not so good. There are a few mighty good folks on it – there are some who smell bad. One petty peanut politician whose graft was almost pitiful in its size when he was a public official, has already shot his mouth off in several places. He is establishing his alibi in advance for what he intends to keep from taking place. "But George, we won't bother you. [Meaning a grand juror.] We are aware that the gambling syndicate was waiting for your body to convene before the big crap game opened again. The Yids had your dimensions, apparently, and we always go by the judgment of a dog in appraising people. "We will call for a special grand jury and a special prosecutor within a short time, as soon as half of the staff can navigate to advantage, and then we'll show you what a real grand jury can do. Up to the present we have been merely tapping on the window. Very soon we shall start smashing glass."

Defendant Near again appealed to the supreme court. In its opinion (179 Minn. 40; 228 N. W. 326) the court said: "No claim is advanced that the method and character of the operation of the newspaper in question was not a nuisance if the statute is constitutional. It was regularly and customarily devoted largely to malicious, scandalous and defamatory matter. . . . The record presents the same questions, upon which we have already passed."

[730] Defendant concedes that the editions of the newspaper complained of are "defamatory per se." And he says: "It has been asserted that the constitution was never intended to be a shield for malice, scandal, and defamation when untrue, or published with bad motives, or for unjustifiable ends. . . . The contrary is true; every person does have a constitutional right to publish malicious, scandalous, and defamatory matter though untrue, and with bad motives, and for unjustifiable ends, in the first instance, though he is subject to responsibility therefor afterwards." The record, when the substance of the articles is regarded, requires that concession here. And this Court is required to pass on the validity of the state law on that basis.

No question was raised below and there is none here concerning the relevancy or weight of evidence, burden of proof, justification or other matters of defense, the scope of the judgment or proceedings to enforce it or the character of the publications that may be made notwithstanding the injunction.

There is no basis for the suggestion that defendants may not interpose any defense or introduce any evidence that would be open to them in a libel case, or that malice may not be negatived by showing that the publication was made in good faith in belief of its truth, or that at the time and under the circumstances it was justified as a fair comment on public affairs or upon the conduct of public officers in respect of their duties as such. See Mason's Minnesota Statutes, §§ 10112, 10113.

The scope of the judgment is not reviewable here. The opinion of the state supreme court shows that it was not reviewable there, because defendants' assignments of error in that court did not go to the form of the judgment, and because the lower court had not been asked to modify the judgment.

[731] The Act was passed in the exertion of the State's power of police, and this court is by well established rule required to assume, until the contrary is clearly made to appear, that there exists in Minnesota a state of affairs that justifies this measure for the preservation of the peace and good order of the State. Lindsley v. Natural Carbonic Gas Co., 220 U.S. 61, 79. Gitlow v. New York, supra, 668-669. Corporation Commission v. Lowe, 281 U.S. 431, 438. O'Gorman & Young v. Hartford Ins. Co., 282 U.S. 251, 257-258.

The publications themselves disclose the need and propriety of the legislation. They show: In 1913 one Guilford, originally a defendant in this suit, commenced the publication of a scandal sheet called the Twin City Reporter; in 1916 Near joined him in the enterprise, later bought him out and engaged the services of one Bevans. In 1919 Bevans acquired Near's interest, and has since, alone or with others, continued the publication. Defendants admit that they published some reprehensible articles in the Twin City Reporter, deny that they personally used it for blackmailing purposes, admit that by reason of their connection with the paper their reputation did become tainted and state that Bevans, while so associated with Near, did use the paper for blackmailing purposes. And Near says it was for that reason he sold his interest to Bevans.

In a number of the editions defendants charge that, ever since Near sold his interest to Bevans in 1919, the Twin City Reporter has been used for blackmail, to dominate public gambling and other criminal activities and as well to exert a kind of control over public officers and the government of the city.

The articles in question also state that, when defendants announced their intention to publish the Saturday Press, they were threatened, and that soon after the first publication [732] Guilford was waylaid and shot down before he could use the firearm which he had at hand for the purpose of defending himself against anticipated assaults. It also appears that Near apprehended violence and was not unprepared to repel it. There is much more of like significance.

The long criminal career of the Twin City Reporter – if it is in fact as described by defendants – and the arming and shooting arising out of the publication of the Saturday Press, serve to illustrate the kind of conditions, in respect of the business of publishing malicious, scandalous and defamatory periodicals, by which the state legislature presumably was moved to enact the law in question. It must be deemed appropriate to deal with conditions existing in Minnesota.

It is of the greatest importance that the States shall be untrammeled and free to employ all just and appropriate measures to prevent abuses of the liberty of the press.

In his work on the Constitution (5th ed.) Justice Story, expounding the First Amendment which declares: "Congress shall make no law abridging the freedom of speech or of the press," said (§ 1880): "That this amendment was intended to secure to every citizen an absolute right to speak, or write, or print whatever he might please, without any responsibility, public or private, therefore, is a supposition too wild to be indulged by any rational man. This would be to allow to every citizen a right to destroy at his pleasure the reputation, the peace, the property, and even the personal safety of every other citizen. A man might, out of mere malice and revenge, accuse another of the most infamous crimes; might excite against him the indignation of all his fellow-citizens by the most atrocious calumnies; might disturb, nay, overturn, all his domestic peace, and embitter his parental affections; might inflict the most distressing punishments upon the weak, the timid, and the innocent; [733] might prejudice all a man's civil, and political, and private rights; and might stir up sedition, rebellion, and treason even against the government itself, in the wantonness of his passions or the corruption of his heart. Civil society could not go on under such circumstances. Men would then be obliged to resort to private vengeance to make up for the deficiencies of the law; and assassination and savage cruelties would be perpetrated with all the frequency belonging to barbarous and brutal communities. It is plain, then, that the language of this amendment imports no more than that every man shall have a right to speak, write, and print his opinions upon any subject whatsoever, without any prior restraint, so always that he does not injure any other person in his rights, person, property, or reputation; and so always that he does not thereby disturb the public peace, or attempt to subvert the government. It is neither more nor less than an expansion of the great doctrine recently brought into operation in the law of libel, that every man shall be at liberty to publish what is true, with good motives and for justifiable ends. And with this reasonable limitation it is not only right in itself, but it is an inestimable privilege in a free government. Without such a limitation, it might become the scourge of the republic, first denouncing the principles of liberty, and then, by rendering the most virtuous patriots odious through the terrors of the press, introducing despotism in its worst form."

The Court quotes Blackstone in support of its condemnation of the statute as imposing a previous restraint upon publication. But the previous restraints referred to by him subjected the press to the arbitrary will of an administrative officer. He describes the practice (Book IV, p. 152): "To subject the press to the restrictive power of a licenser, as was formerly done, both before and since the revolution [of 1688], is to subject all freedom [734] of sentiment to the prejudices of one man, and make him the arbitrary and infallible judge of all controverted points in learning, religion, and government."[13]

Story gives the history alluded to by Blackstone (§ 1882):

"The art of printing soon after its introduction, we are told, was looked upon, as well in England as in other countries, as merely a matter of state, and subject to the coercion of the crown. It was, therefore, regulated in England by the king's proclamations, prohibitions, charters of privilege, and licenses, and finally by the decrees of the Court of Star-Chamber, which limited the number of printers and of presses which each should employ, and prohibited new publications, unless previously approved by proper licensers. On the demolition of this odious jurisdiction, in 1641, the Long Parliament of Charles the First, after their rupture with that prince, assumed the same powers which the Star-Chamber exercised with respect to licensing books; and during the Commonwealth (such is human frailty and the love of power even in republics!) they issued their ordinances for that purpose, founded principally upon a Star-Chamber decree of 1637. After the restoration of Charles the Second, a statute on the same subject was passed, copied, with some few alterations, from the parliamentary ordinances. The act expired in 1679, and was revived and continued for a few years after the revolution of 1688. Many attempts were made by the government to keep it in force; but it was [735] so strongly resisted by Parliament that it expired in 1694, and has never since been revived."

It is plain that Blackstone taught that under the common law liberty of the press means simply the absence of restraint upon publication in advance as distinguished from liability, civil or criminal, for libelous or improper matter so published. And, as above shown, Story defined freedom of the press guaranteed by the First Amendment to mean that "every man shall be at liberty to publish what is true, with good motives and for justifiable ends." His statement concerned the definite declaration of the First Amendment. It is not suggested that the freedom of press included in the liberty protected by the Fourteenth Amendment, which was adopted after Story's definition, is greater than that protected against congressional action. And see 2 Cooley's Constitutional Limitations, 8th ed., p. 886. 2 Kent's Commentaries (14th ed.) Lect. XXIV, p. 17.

The Minnesota statute does not operate as a previous restraint on publication within the proper meaning of that phrase. It does not authorize administrative control in advance such as was formerly exercised by the licensers and censors but prescribes a remedy to be enforced by a suit in equity. In this case there was previous publication

[2] May, Constitutional History of England, c. IX. Duniway, Freedom of the Press in Massachusetts, cc. I and II. Cooley, Constitutional Limitations (8th ed.) Vol. II, pp. 880-881. Pound, Equitable Relief against Defamation, 29 Harv. L. Rev. 640, 650 et seq. Madison, Letters and Other Writings (1865

ed.) Vol. IV, pp. 542, 543. Respublica v. Oswald, 1 Dall. 319, 325. Rawle, A View of the Constitution (2d ed. 1829) p. 124. Paterson, Liberty of the Press, c. III.

made in the course of the business of regularly producing malicious, scandalous and defamatory periodicals. The business and publications unquestionably constitute an abuse of the right of free press. The statute denounces the things done as a nuisance on the ground, as stated by the state supreme court, that they threaten morals, peace and good order. There is no question of the power of the State to denounce such transgressions. The restraint authorized is only in respect of continuing to do what has been duly adjudged to constitute a nuisance. The controlling words are "All persons guilty of such nuisance may be enjoined, as hereinafter [736] provided. . . . Whenever any such nuisance is committed . . . an action in the name of the State" may be brought "to perpetually enjoin the person or persons committing, conducting or maintaining any such nuisance, from further committing, conducting or maintaining any such nuisance. . . . The court may make its order and judgment permanently enjoining . . . defendants found guilty . . . from committing or continuing the acts prohibited hereby, and in and by such judgment, such nuisance may be wholly abated. . . ." There is nothing in the statute[3] purporting to prohibit publications that have not been adjudged to constitute a nuisance. It is fanciful to suggest similarity between the granting or enforcement of the decree authorized by this statute to prevent further publication of malicious, scandalous and defamatory articles and the previous restraint upon the press by licensers as referred to by Blackstone and described in the history of the times to which he alludes.

[737] The opinion seems to concede that under clause (a) of the Minnesota law the business of regularly publishing and circulating an obscene periodical may be enjoined as a nuisance. It is difficult to perceive any distinction, having any relation to constitutionality, between clause (a) and clause (b) under which this action was brought. Both nuisances are offensive to morals, order and good government. As that resulting from lewd publications constitutionally may be enjoined it is hard to understand why the one resulting from a regular business of malicious defamation may not.

It is well known, as found by the state supreme court, that existing libel laws are inadequate effectively to suppress evils resulting from the kind of business and publications that are shown in this case. The doctrine that measures such as the one before us are invalid because they operate as previous restraints to infringe freedom of press exposes the peace and good order of every community and the business and private affairs of every individual to the constant and protracted false and malicious [738] assaults of any insolvent publisher who may have purpose and sufficient capacity to contrive and put into effect a scheme or program for oppression, blackmail or extortion.

The judgment should be affirmed.

---

[3] § 1. Any person who, as an individual, or as a member or employee of a firm, or association or organization, or as an officer, director, member or employee of a corporation, shall be engaged in the business of regularly or customarily producing, publishing or circulating, having in possession, selling or giving away.
(a) an obscene, lewd and lascivious newspaper, magazine, or other periodical, or
(b) a malicious, scandalous and defamatory newspaper, magazine, or other periodical, is guilty of a nuisance, and all persons guilty of such nuisance may be enjoined, as hereinafter provided.
* * * * *
In actions brought under (b) above, there shall be available the defense that the truth was published with good motives and for justifiable ends and in such actions the plaintiff shall not have the right to report [resort] to issues or editions of periodicals taking place more than three months before the commencement of the action.
§ 2. Whenever any such nuisance is committed or is kept, maintained, or exists, as above provided for, the County Attorney of any county where any such periodical is published or circulated . . . may commence and maintain in the District Court of said county, an action in the name of the State of Minnesota . . . to perpetually enjoin the person or persons committing, conducting or maintaining any such nuisance, from further committing, conducting, or maintaining any such nuisance. . . .
§ 3. The action may be brought to trial and tried as in the case of other actions in such District Court, and shall be governed by the practice and procedure applicable to civil actions for injunctions.
After trial the court may make its order and judgment permanently enjoining any and all defendants found guilty of violating this Act from further committing or continuing the acts prohibited hereby, and in and by such judgment, such nuisance may be wholly abated.
The court may, as in other cases of contempt, at any time punish, by fine of not more than $1,000, or by imprisonment in the county jail for not more than twelve months, any person or persons violating any injunction, temporary or permanent, made or issued pursuant to this Act.

New York Times Co. v. United States
403 U.S. 713
(1971)
(Excerpts only. Footnotes omitted.)

Author's Note: The federal government had been granted an injunction to stop *The New York Times* and the *Washington Post* from publishing reports based on classified documents the government said would jeopardize American troops and disclose strategic objectives and planned troop movements in Vietnam. The newspapers claimed the documents revealed a concerted government campaign to manipulate public opinion and misrepresent troop losses in Vietnam.

PER CURIAM

OPINION: [714] We granted certiorari in these cases in which the United States seeks to enjoin the New York Times and the Washington Post from publishing the contents of a classified study entitled "History of U.S. Decision-Making Process on Viet Nam Policy." Post, pp. 942, 943.

"Any system of prior restraints of expression comes to this Court bearing a heavy presumption against its constitutional validity." Bantam Books, Inc. v. Sullivan, 372 U.S. 58, 70 (1963); see also Near v. Minnesota, 283 U.S. 697 (1931). The Government "thus carries a heavy burden of showing justification for the imposition of such a restraint." Organization for a Better Austin v. Keefe, 402 U.S. 415, 419 (1971). The District Court for the Southern District of New York in the New York Times case and the District Court for the District of Columbia and the Court of Appeals for the District of Columbia Circuit in the Washington Post case held that the Government had not met that burden. We agree.

The judgment of the Court of Appeals for the District of Columbia Circuit is therefore affirmed. The order of the Court of Appeals or the Second Circuit is reversed and the case is remanded with directions to enter a judgment affirming the judgment of the District Court for the Southern District of New York. The stays entered June 25, 1971, by the Court are vacated. The judgments shall issue forthwith.

So ordered.

CONCUR: MR. JUSTICE BLACK, with whom MR. JUSTICE DOUGLAS joins, concurring.

I adhere to the view that the Government's case against the Washington Post should have been dismissed and that the injunction against the New York Times should have been vacated without oral argument when the cases were first presented to this Court. I believe [715] that every moment's continuance of the injunctions against these newspapers amounts to a flagrant, indefensible, and continuing violation of the First Amendment.

... [717] In the First Amendment the Founding Fathers gave the free press the protection it must have to fulfill its essential role in our democracy. The press was to serve the governed, not the governors. The Government's power to censor the press was abolished so that the press would remain forever free to censure the Government. The press was protected so that it could bare the secrets of government and inform the people. Only a free and unrestrained press can effectively expose deception in government. And paramount among the responsibilities of a free press is the duty to prevent any part of the government from deceiving the people and sending them off to distant lands to die of foreign fevers and foreign shot and shell. In my view, far from deserving condemnation for their courageous reporting, the New York Times, the Washington Post, and other newspapers should be commended for serving the purpose that the Founding Fathers saw so clearly. In revealing the workings of government that led to the Vietnam war, the newspapers nobly did precisely that which the Founders hoped and trusted they would do.

... [719] The word "security" is a broad, vague generality whose contours should not be invoked to abrogate the fundamental law embodied in the First Amendment. The guarding of military and diplomatic secrets at the expense of informed representative government provides no real security for our Republic. The Framers of the First Amendment, fully aware of both the need to defend a new nation and the abuses of the English and Colonial governments, sought to give this new society strength and security by providing that freedom of speech, press, religion, and assembly should not be abridged.

CONCUR: ... [720] MR. JUSTICE DOUGLAS, with whom MR. JUSTICE BLACK joins, concurring.

While I join the opinion of the Court I believe it necessary to express my views more fully.

It should be noted at the outset that the First Amendment provides that "Congress shall make no law . . . abridging the freedom of speech, or of the press." That leaves, in my view, no room for governmental restraint on the press.

... [723] The dominant purpose of the First Amendment was to prohibit the widespread practice of governmental suppression [724] of embarrassing information. It is common knowledge that the First Amendment was adopted against the widespread use of the common law of seditious libel to punish the dissemination of material that is embarrassing to the powers-that-be. See T. Emerson, The System of Freedom of Expression, c. V (1970); Z. Chafee, Free Speech in the United States, c. XIII (1941). The present cases will, I think, go down in history as the most dramatic illustration of that principle. A debate of large proportions goes on in the Nation over our posture in Vietnam. That debate antedated the disclosure of the contents of the present documents. The latter are highly relevant to the debate in progress.

Secrecy in government is fundamentally anti-democratic, perpetuating bureaucratic errors. Open debate and discussion of public issues are vital to our national health. On public questions there should be "uninhibited, robust, and wide-open" debate. New York Times Co. v. Sullivan, 376 U.S. 254, 269-270.

CONCUR: ... MR. JUSTICE BRENNAN.

... [725] The error that has pervaded these cases from the outset was the granting of any injunctive relief whatsoever, interim or otherwise. The entire thrust of the Government's claim throughout these cases has been that publication of the material sought to be enjoined "could," or "might," or "may" prejudice the national interest in various ways. But the First Amendment tolerates absolutely no prior judicial restraints of the press predicated upon surmise or conjecture that untoward consequences [726] may result. Our cases, it is true, have indicated that there is a single, extremely narrow class of cases in which the First Amendment's ban on prior judicial restraint may be overridden. Our cases have thus far indicated that such cases may arise only when the Nation "is at war," Schenck v. United States, 249 U.S. 47, 52 (1919), during which times "no one would question but that a government might prevent actual obstruction to its recruiting service or the publication of the sailing dates of transports or the number and location of troops." Near v. Minnesota, 283 U.S. 697, 716 (1931). Even if the present world situation were assumed to be tantamount to a time of war, or if the power of presently available armaments would justify even in peacetime the suppression of information that would set in motion a nuclear holocaust, in neither of these actions has the Government presented or even alleged that publication of items from or based upon the material at issue would cause the happening of an event of that nature. "The chief purpose of [the First Amendment's] guaranty [is] to prevent previous restraints upon publication." Near v. Minnesota, supra, at 713. Thus, only governmental allegation and proof that publication must inevitably, directly, [727] and immediately cause the occurrence of an event kindred to imperiling the safety of a transport already at sea can support even the issuance of an interim restraining order. In no event may mere conclusions be sufficient: for if the Executive Branch seeks judicial aid in preventing publication, it must inevitably submit the basis upon which that aid is sought to scrutiny by the judiciary. And therefore, every restraint issued in this case, whatever its form, has violated the First Amendment – and not less so because that restraint was justified as necessary to afford the courts an opportunity to examine the claim more thoroughly. Unless and until the Government has clearly made out its case, the First Amendment commands that no injunction may issue.

CONCUR: ... MR. JUSTICE STEWART, with whom MR. JUSTICE WHITE joins, concurring.

... [728] If the Constitution gives the Executive [729] a large degree of unshared power in the conduct of foreign affairs and the maintenance of our national defense, then under the Constitution the Executive must have the largely unshared duty to determine and preserve the degree of internal security necessary to exercise that power successfully. It is an awesome responsibility, requiring judgment and wisdom of a high order. I should suppose that moral, political, and practical considerations would dictate that a very first principle of that wisdom would be an insistence upon avoiding secrecy for its own sake. For when everything is classified, then nothing is classified, and the system becomes one to be disregarded by the cynical or the careless, and to be manipulated by those intent on self-protection or self-promotion. I should suppose, in short, that the hallmark of a truly effective internal security system would be the maximum possible disclosure, recognizing that secrecy can best be preserved only when credibility is truly maintained. But be that as it may, it is clear to me that it is the constitutional duty of the Executive – as a matter of sovereign prerogative and not as a matter of law as the courts know law – through the promulgation and enforcement of executive regulations, to protect [730] the confidentiality necessary to carry out its responsibilities in the fields of international relations and national defense.

CONCUR: ... MR. JUSTICE WHITE, with whom MR. JUSTICE STEWART joins, concurring.

I concur in today's judgments, but only because of the concededly extraordinary protection against prior restraints [731] enjoyed by the press under our constitutional system. I do not say that in no circumstances would the First Amendment permit an injunction against publishing information about government plans or operations. Nor, after examining the materials the Government characterizes as the most sensitive and destructive, can I deny that revelation of these documents will do substantial damage to public interests. Indeed, I am confident that their disclosure will have that result. But I nevertheless agree that the United States has not satisfied the very heavy burden that it must meet to warrant an injunction against publication in these cases, at least in the absence of express and appropriately limited congressional authorization for prior restraints in circumstances such as these.

DISSENT: ... [748] MR. CHIEF JUSTICE BURGER, dissenting.

... [751] As I see it, we have been forced to deal with litigation concerning rights of great magnitude without an adequate record, and surely without time for adequate treatment either in the prior proceedings or in this Court. It is interesting to note that counsel on both sides, in oral argument before this Court, were frequently unable to respond to questions on factual points. Not surprisingly they pointed out that they had been working literally "around the clock" and simply were unable to review the documents that give rise to these cases and [752] were not familiar with them. This Court is in no better posture. I agree generally with MR. JUSTICE HARLAN and MR. JUSTICE BLACKMUN but I am not prepared to reach the merits.

DISSENT: ... MR. JUSTICE HARLAN, with whom THE CHIEF JUSTICE and MR. JUSTICE BLACKMUN join, dissenting.

...[757] The power to evaluate the "pernicious influence" of premature disclosure is not, however, lodged in the Executive alone. I agree that, in performance of its duty to protect the values of the First Amendment against political pressures, the judiciary must review the initial Executive determination to the point of satisfying itself that the subject matter of the dispute does lie within the proper compass of the President's foreign relations power.

Constitutional considerations forbid "a complete abandonment of judicial control." Cf. United States v. Reynolds, 345 U.S. 1, 8 (1953). Moreover, the judiciary may properly insist that the determination that disclosure of the subject matter would irreparably impair the national security be made by the head of the Executive Department concerned – here the Secretary of State or the Secretary of Defense – after actual personal consideration by that officer. This safeguard is required in the analogous area of executive claims of privilege for secrets of state. See id., at 8 and n. 20; Duncan v. Cammell, Laird & Co., [1942] A. C. 624, 638 (House of Lords).

But in my judgment the judiciary may not properly go beyond these two inquiries and redetermine for itself the probable impact of disclosure on the national security.

DISSENT: ...[760] MR. JUSTICE BLACKMUN.

...[761] The First Amendment, after all, is only one part of an entire Constitution. Article II of the great document vests in the Executive Branch primary power over the conduct of foreign affairs and places in that branch the responsibility for the Nation's safety. Each provision of the Constitution is important, and I cannot subscribe to a doctrine of unlimited absolutism for the First Amendment at the cost of downgrading other provisions. First Amendment absolutism has never commanded a majority of this Court. See, for example, Near v. Minnesota, 283 U.S. 697, 708 (1931), and Schenck v. United States, 249 U.S. 47, 52 (1919). What is needed here is a weighing, upon properly developed standards, of the broad right of the press to print and of the very narrow right of the Government to prevent. Such standards are not yet developed.

Chapter

4

The First Amendment, Content-Based and Content-Neutral Laws

An approach to First Amendment balancing

Focal Cases:
United States v. O'Brien, 391 U.S. 367 (1968)
Ward v. Rock Against Racism, 491 U.S. 781 (1989)
Texas v. Johnson, 491 U.S. 397 (1989)
Simon & Schuster, Inc. v. New York Crime Victims Board, 502 U.S. 105 (1991)

In the two centuries since the adoption of the Bill of Rights, the U.S. Supreme Court has developed a number of strategies to guide its First Amendment jurisprudence. The U.S. Supreme Court has said that all laws that affect First Amendment interests are not equal. As seen in the previous chapter, the Supreme Court in 1931 established that prior restraint, especially any prior restraint that involves an outright ban on expression, is the least tolerable form of government intervention in the speech marketplace.[1] The Supreme Court also has developed a number of other doctrines to guide its First Amendment decisions. In various First Amendment cases, the Court has evaluated the competing rights and interests involved (See Chaps. 14-16.), the nature of the speaker (See Chaps. 12 & 13.), the costs and benefits of the speech (See Chaps. 6-11.), the location of the speech (See Chap. 5.), and the type of government action being challenged.

This chapter focuses on the Court's evaluation of government regulations based on distinctions between laws that target the content of expression and laws directed at speech externalities.[2] The Court calls the first type of law content-based and the second, content-neutral. Content-based laws regulate what is being said; they single out certain messages, ideas or subject matter for punishment. Laws prohibiting the use of racial, religious or other slurs are content-based. Content-neutral laws regulate where, when and how expression occurs; they often advance

---

[1] Near v. Minnesota, 283 U.S. 697 (1931).

[2] The concept of externalities is employed in economics to identify the often unintended and peripheral costs and benefits of individual choices. An example of a positive externality is the pleasure neighbors and passersby receive from a beautiful garden in someone's front yard. A negative externality is the displeasure these same individuals experience if the yard is filled instead with junked cars and refuse.

public interests unrelated to speech. Noise or assembly restrictions in school and residential zones, for example, limit the volume of permissible speech but create environments conducive to activities in those institutions.[3]

The Supreme Court generally views content-based laws as presumptively invalid because they pose a direct and serious threat of government censorship of disfavored ideas. Therefore, the Supreme Court reviews content-based laws in the most rigorous fashion, imposing what is called strict scrutiny. The Court reviews content-neutral laws less stringently because it believes content-neutral laws impose a reduced danger of censorship. The Court employs some form of balancing, or intermediate scrutiny, to determine when content-neutral laws are constitutional. The Court applies a third level of judicial scrutiny – called rational review or minimum scrutiny – to regulations that raise no constitutional concerns.

Content-Based Laws

Through content-based laws, the state attempts to control dangerous, undesirable or offensive speech. Such laws generally are unconstitutional. In 1989, the Supreme Court said, "If there is a bedrock principle underlying the First Amendment, it is that the government may not prohibit the expression of an idea simply because society finds the idea itself offensive or disagreeable."[4] In *Texas v. Johnson,* a deeply divided Supreme Court invalidated a Texas statute that outlawed desecration of the American flag. In this case involving symbolic speech,[5] the Supreme Court said the Texas law was content-based because the state regulated flag desecration precisely because government disfavored the viewpoint expressed by flag burning. In other cases, the Court has said laws may be unconstitutionally content-based even if they do not reflect illicit or discriminatory government motives but differentially treat certain messages or speakers. Thus, in *Simon & Schuster, Inc. v. New York Crime Victims Board,*[6] the U.S. Supreme Court struck down as content-based a New York state law that required authors of descriptions of crimes to turn resulting income over to the state to compensate crime victims.

The Court applied strict scrutiny to review the statutes in both of these cases. Rather than presume the constitutionality of content-based regulations, strict scrutiny imposes a heavy burden on government to demonstrate the constitutionality of its law. The Court requires the government to justify its regulation by showing that the law is essential to achieve a government interest of the highest order. The Court examines both the law's purpose or intent and its effect. To be found constitutional, a law evaluated under strict scrutiny must 1) employ the least intrusive means to 2) achieve a compelling government interest.

A law employs the least-intrusive means if it limits no more speech than necessary to attain its goal. To determine whether a law meets this standard, the Court often examines alternative methods available to the government. A law is least intrusive if none of the available alternatives would be less harmful to free expression rights. In 1992 in *Simon & Schuster,* New York State argued that its statute, known as the "Son of Sam" law, effectively prohibited criminals from benefiting from the fruits of their crimes. The Supreme Court, however, found the law unconstitutionally overbroad, or overinclusive, because it imposed a state penalty on too wide an range of protected speech and did not use the least intrusive means to achieve the state's goal. The

---

[3] *But see* Police Dept. of Chicago v. Mosley, 408 U.S. 92 (1972) (striking down as content-based a law exempting labor picketing from a ban on picketing outside schools); Carey v. Brown, 447 U.S. 455 (1980) (striking down as overbroad a law banning all picketing, except picketing related to labor disputes, in residential areas).

[4] Texas v. Johnson, 491 U.S. 397, 414 (1989) (striking down a conviction for flag burning).

[5] The Supreme Court has said symbolic speech exists and warrants First Amendment protection when: 1) speech and action combine, 2) there is an intent to convey a message, and 3) witnesses are likely to understand that message.

[6] 502 U.S. 105 (1992).

Court said the statute effectively taxed not only the fruits of crime but criminals writing on any subject and authors who had not been charged or convicted of a crime who might express even passing comments about actual crimes.

In contrast, the Supreme Court found the state's interests – to compensate crime victims and limit the profitability of crime – in the Son in Sam law compelling. Under strict scrutiny, a government interest is compelling when it is paramount rather than merely important or routine. A compelling interest does more than simply improve efficiency of government; a compelling interest relates directly to core constitutional interests and to the most significant functions of government. The Supreme Court is more likely to find a government interest compelling if it pertains closely to public health or safety. A frequently cited compelling government interest is national security.

Some observers assert that when the Court imposes strict scrutiny, it is outcome determinative. In other words, the Supreme Court automatically finds state actions reviewed under strict scrutiny to be unconstitutional. This is not entirely true. While strict scrutiny is an extremely rigorous standard, some content-based regulations have passed constitutional muster under this standard. The Supreme Court has upheld content-based laws that target low value speech (such as fighting words)[7] or that protect fundamental constitutional rights (such as voting).[8] In addition, the Court has affirmed the authority of government to limit or punish speech that threatens to harm the government, individuals or society's morals.[9]

CONTENT-NEUTRAL LAWS

While the Supreme Court strongly disfavors state actions that target speech because of the content of its message, the Court has been more lenient with content-neutral laws. The Court has decided that content-neutral laws are more acceptable under the First Amendment because they apply equally to all communications regardless of the message they contain and generally regulate non-speech elements, such as the time, the place or the manner (volume) in which the speech occurs. Many content-neutral laws thus are called time/place/manner or TPM restrictions. Content-neutral laws do not censor specific ideas, but they can reduce the overall quantity and diversity of speech available in the marketplace of ideas and inhibit the freedom of individuals to express themselves.

The Court has developed an intermediate level of scrutiny, sometimes called a balancing test, to determine the constitutionality of content-neutral laws. One form of intermediate scrutiny was established in *United States v. O'Brien*.[10] David O'Brien was arrested for publicly burning his draft card to protest the war in Vietnam in violation of a federal statute requiring all American males over 18 to carry a military draft card at all times. In reviewing the federal law, the Supreme Court ruled that the First Amendment's protection of O'Brien's symbolic speech did not outweigh the government's important interest in recruiting and maintaining enlistment in the military.

In *O'Brien*, the Court established that a content-neutral law will be found constitutional if: 1) it advances an important government interest, 2) the government interest is not related to suppressing free expression, and 3) the law's restriction on free expression is incidental and no greater than needed to achieve the government interest. The Supreme Court has said a government interest is important when it is more than convenient or reasonable; an important government interest is substantial, weighty or significant. The Court has been less than consistent in determining when an interest is unrelated to suppression of speech. Generally, a law will survive

---

[7] Chaplinsky v. New Hampshire, 315 U.S. 568 (1942).
[8] Burson v. Freeman, 504 U.S. 191 (1992).
[9] *See generally* Chap. 6 on antiterrorism laws, Chap. 9 on obscenity and Chap. 14 on libel.
[10] 391 U.S. 367 (1968).

the second prong of the *O'Brien* test if it targets non-speech and serves a government function unrelated to content. However, the Court has ruled that some laws designed to increase the diversity of ideas available to the public are content-neutral while some are not.[11] The key to this apparent discrepancy is that the Court's judgment turns on the identity of the speaker or the value of the speech (This will be discussed in greater depth in Ch. 6-13.).[12]

The third prong of the *O'Brien* test, sometimes called the narrow-tailoring standard, usually requires that alternative means of expression exist for the regulated speech. As a result, most complete bans are not constitutional because their harm to speech is more than merely incidental or peripheral. However, narrow tailoring is not the same as the least-restrictive-means standard applied to content-based laws. Rather, a law is narrowly tailored when it "fits" its purpose, advances the government interest directly, and does not impose a burden on substantially more speech than needed to achieve the government's goal.[13] The calculation is not exact, and the Supreme Court often defers to the expertise of administrative agencies and legislatures to determine the appropriate legal mechanism for achieving government objectives. Most laws reviewed under intermediate scrutiny are upheld.

The Court at times has acknowledged that facially content-neutral laws of general application may hide illicit government motives that trigger strict scrutiny review. An illicit legislative motive could exist, for example, if a law setting size and placement requirements for billboards was adopted not to improve traffic safety but to prevent the Aryan Nations from posting messages of hate on billboards throughout the community.

The Supreme Court also has expressed concern that laws that appear content neutral may be applied in a way that discriminates against disfavored ideas. The Court employs the narrow-tailoring requirement of *O'Brien* to assure that laws do not provide the opportunity for abuse by granting unlimited discretion to officials. For example, the Court has said regulations that give officials unfettered authority to determine the fee to be charged for a parade permit invite discrimination and are unconstitutional.[14] To assure that facially neutral laws will not be discriminatorily applied, the Court often examines both the specific legal limits placed on officials' discretion and the history of how the rule has been applied. Laws must be clear and specific and may not vest officials with vague or unlimited power.

THE JURISPRUDENCE OF CONTENT NEUTRALITY

The Supreme Court's distinction between content-based and content-neutral laws has been controversial. While content-based laws may eliminate certain topics from public discourse (e.g., obscenity), it is not obvious that content-neutral laws are always less pernicious to speech. Some scholars argue that the Supreme Court has failed to justify adequately why lesser scrutiny applies to content-neutral laws that may have far-reaching effects, such as banning billboards from public rights-of-way or setting parade routes outside the downtown business area.[15] In reading the following cases and case excerpts, decide whether you believe the content-based/content-neutral distinction advances the goals of the First Amendment. Also, ask yourself whether the Supreme Court has established a bright line between the two categories that permits the development of coherent free-speech jurisprudence.

---

[11] *See, e.g.,* Turner Broadcasting System, Inc., v. FCC, 512 U.S. 622 (1994); Red Lion Broadcasting Co. v. FCC, 395 U.S. 367 (1969). But see Miami Herald Pub. Co. v. Tornillo, 418 U.S. 241 (1974).

[12] *See, e.g.,* Susan D. Ross, *Reconstructing First Amendment Doctrine: The 1990s [R]Evolution of the Central Hudson and O'Brien Tests,* 23 COMM/ENT 723 (2001).

[13] Ward v. Rock Against Racism, 491 U.S. 781 (1989). See also Matthew D. Bunker & Emily Erickson, *The Jurisprudence of Precision: Contrast Space and Narrow Tailoring in First Amendment Doctrine,* 6 COMM. L. & POL'Y 259 (2001).

[14] Forsyth County, Ga. v. The Nationalist Movement, 505 U.S. 123 (1992).

[15] *See, e.g.,* Geoffrey Stone, *Content-Neutral Restrictions,* 54 U. CHI. L. REV. 46 (1987).

The following cases appear in chronological order, beginning with the full text of the foundational content-neutrality case, *United States v. O'Brien*. Then you move on to excerpts from the Supreme Court's ruling in *Ward v. Rock Against Racism*, in which the Court considered whether a New York City regulation requiring city employees to control the volume and sound mix for performers in Central Park was a permissible content-neutral law. The case law on content-based regulations is vast and varied. Below you will read excerpts from the flag-burning case, *Texas v. Johnson*, and the complete decision in *Simon & Schuster, Inc. v. New York State Crime Victims Board*.

The cases cited here will enrich your understanding of content distinctions and provide a starting point for related legal research projects. These are but a sampling of the numerous cases exploring this area of First Amendment law.

- *Legal Services Corp. v. Velazquez*, 531 U.S. 533 (2001) (federal ban on client representation in specific types of cases violates the First Amendment requirement of content neutrality).
- *Schenck v. Pro-Choice Network of Western New York*, 519 U.S. 357 (1997) (finding a fixed, no-protest buffer zone around abortion clinics constitutional but a floating zone unconstitutional).
- *Turner Broadcasting System, Inc. v. Federal Communications Commission*, 512 U.S. 622 (1994) (intermediate-level scrutiny is the proper standard to evaluate constitutionality of content-neutral cable "must-carry" provisions).
- *City of Ladue v. Gilleo*, (1994) (striking down a law prohibiting residential signs that included numerous content exceptions).
- *United States v. Eichman*, 496 U.S. 310 (1990) (invalidating anti-flag desecration law).
- *City of Lakewood v. Plain Dealer Publishing Co.*, 486 U.S. 750 (1988) (discretionary law allowing city to determine placement and design of news racks violates the First Amendment).
- *Boos v. Barry*, 485 U.S. 312 (1988) (invalidating city ordinance that prohibited critical picket signs in front of foreign embassies).
- *Clark v. Community for Creative Non-Violence*, 468 U.S. 288 (1984) (camping ban on the Mall in Washington, D.C., does not violate the First Amendment).
- *Hefron v. International Society for Krishna Consciousness*, 452 U.S. 640 (1981) (rule requiring all distributions of literature and fund solicitations on fair grounds be made from a booth does not violate the First Amendment).
- *Carey v. Brown*, (1980) (a law exempting labor picketing from a picketing ban outside schools is unconstitutional).
- *Smith v. Goguen*, 415 U.S. 566 (1974) (finding criminal law that prohibits contemptuous treatment of the flag unconstitutional).
- *Police Dept. of Chicago v. Mosley*, 408 U.S. 92 (1972) (a law exempting labor picketing from a picketing ban in residential areas violates the First Amendment).
- *Thornhill v. Alabama*, 310 U.S. 88 (1940) (finding state ban on business picketing violates the First Amendment).
- *Schneider v. New Jersey*, 308 U.S. 147 (1939) (finding unconstitutional a law banning distribution of handbills).
- *Lovell v. Griffin*, 303 U.S. 444 (1938) (discretionary law allowing city manager to decide who could distribute literature violates the First Amendment).

Reading the Content Jurisprudence Cases

The following questions will direct your attention to important elements of the following cases.

- How does the Court define symbolic speech?
- How does the Court determine whether the state action is content based or content neutral?
- What test does the Court apply, and how does it define the tests' prongs, particularly the prong related to the "fit" of the regulation with its objective?
- What is the asserted government interest to be served by the state action, and how does the Court determine whether that interest is compelling, important or merely efficient?
- Does the Court examine the intent, the text or the effect of the state action? Does the law hide any illicit content-based motivation?
- What type of expression does the law affect, and how does this influence the Court's decision? Does the law target "pure" speech? Political speech? Symbolic speech?
- How does the Court determine whether the infringement on expression is direct or incidental?
- Does the Supreme Court balance the competing interests involved or expressly examine alternate regulatory options?
- What are the primary concerns expressed by the separate opinions? Do they address facts in these cases or reach to broader issues of legal rules and doctrines?

United States v. O'Brien
391 U.S. 367
(1968)

PRIOR HISTORY: Certiorari to the United States Court of Appeals for the First Circuit.

JUDGES: Warren, Black, Douglas, Harlan, Brennan, Stewart, White, Fortas; Marshall took no part in the consideration or decision of these cases

OPINION: [369] MR. CHIEF JUSTICE WARREN delivered the opinion of the Court.

On the morning of March 31, 1966, David Paul O'Brien and three companions burned their Selective Service registration certificates on the steps of the South Boston Courthouse. A sizable crowd, including several agents of the Federal Bureau of Investigation, witnessed the event.[1] Immediately after the burning, members of the crowd began attacking O'Brien and his companions. An FBI agent ushered O'Brien to safety inside the courthouse. After he was advised of his right to counsel and to silence, O'Brien stated to FBI agents that he had burned his registration certificate because of his beliefs, knowing that he was violating federal law. He produced the charred remains of the certificate, which, with his consent, were photographed.

For this act, O'Brien was indicted, tried, convicted, and sentenced in the United States District Court for the District of Massachusetts.[2] He did not contest the fact [370] that he had burned the certificate. He stated in argument to the jury that he burned the certificate publicly to influence others to adopt his antiwar beliefs, as he put it, "so that other people would reevaluate their positions with Selective Service, with the armed forces, and reevaluate their place in the culture of today, to hopefully consider my position."

The indictment upon which he was tried charged that he "willfully and knowingly did mutilate, destroy, and change by burning [his] Registration Certificate (Selective Service System Form No. 2); in violation of Title 50, App., United States Code, Section 462 (b)." Section 462 (b) is part of the Universal Military Training and Service Act of 1948. Section 462 (b)(3), one of six numbered subdivisions of § 462 (b), was amended by Congress in 1965, 79 Stat. 586 (adding the words italicized below), so that at the time O'Brien burned his certificate an offense was committed by any person, "who forges, alters, knowingly destroys, knowingly mutilates, or in any manner changes any such certificate . . . ."

---

[1] At the time of the burning, the agents knew only that O'Brien and his three companions had burned small white cards. They later discovered that the card O'Brien burned was his registration certificate, and the undisputed assumption is that the same is true of his companions.

[2] He was sentenced under the Youth Corrections Act, 18 U. S. C. § 5010 (b), to the custody of the Attorney General for a maximum period of six years for supervision and treatment.

In the District Court, O'Brien argued that the 1965 Amendment prohibiting the knowing destruction or mutilation of certificates was unconstitutional because it was enacted to abridge free speech, and because it served no legitimate legislative purpose.[3] The District Court rejected these arguments, holding that the statute on its face did not abridge First Amendment rights, that the court was not competent to inquire into the motives of Congress in enacting the 1965 Amendment, and that the [371] Amendment was a reasonable exercise of the power of Congress to raise armies.

On appeal, the Court of Appeals for the First Circuit held the 1965 Amendment unconstitutional as a law abridging freedom of speech.[4] At the time the Amendment was enacted, a regulation of the Selective Service System required registrants to keep their registration certificates in their "personal possession at all times." 32 CFR § 1617.1 (1962).[5] Willful violations of regulations promulgated pursuant to the Universal Military Training and Service Act were made criminal by statute. 50 U. S. C. App. § 462 (b)(6). The Court of Appeals, therefore, was of the opinion that conduct punishable under the 1965 Amendment was already punishable under the non-possession regulation, and consequently that the Amendment served no valid purpose; further, that in light of the prior regulation, the Amendment must have been "directed at public as distinguished from private destruction." On this basis, the court concluded that the 1965 Amendment ran afoul of the First Amendment by singling out persons engaged in protests for special treatment. The court ruled, however, that O'Brien's conviction should be affirmed under the statutory provision, 50 U. S. C. App. § 462 (b)(6), which in its view made violation of the non-possession regulation a crime, because it regarded such violation to be a lesser included offense of the crime defined by the 1965 Amendment.[6]

[372] The Government petitioned for certiorari in No. 232, arguing that the Court of Appeals erred in holding the statute unconstitutional, and that its decision conflicted with decisions by the Courts of Appeals for the Second[7] and Eighth Circuits[8] upholding the 1965 Amendment against identical constitutional challenges. O'Brien cross-petitioned for certiorari in No. 233, arguing that the Court of Appeals erred in sustaining his conviction on the basis of a crime of which he was neither charged nor tried. We granted the Government's petition to resolve the conflict in the circuits, and we also granted O'Brien's cross-petition. We hold that the 1965 Amendment is constitutional both as enacted and as applied. We therefore vacate the judgment of the Court of Appeals and reinstate the judgment and sentence of the District Court without reaching the issue raised by O'Brien in No. 233.

When a male reaches the age of 18, he is required by the Universal Military Training and Service Act to register with a local draft board.[9] He is assigned a Selective Service number,[10] and within five days he is issued a [373] registration certificate (SSS Form No. 2).[11] Subsequently, and based on a questionnaire completed by the registrant,[12] he is assigned a classification denoting his eligibility for induction,[13] and "as soon as practicable" thereafter he is issued a Notice of Classification (SSS Form No. 110).[14] This initial classification is not necessarily permanent,[15] and if in the interim before induction the registrant's status changes in some relevant way, he may be reclassified.[16] After such a reclassification, the local board "as soon as practicable" issues to the registrant a new Notice of Classification.[17]

---

[3] The issue of the constitutionality of the 1965 Amendment was raised by counsel representing O'Brien in a pretrial motion to dismiss the indictment. At trial and upon sentencing, O'Brien chose to represent himself. He was represented by counsel on his appeal to the Court of Appeals.

[4] O'Brien v. United States, 376 F.2d 538 (C. A. 1st Cir. 1967).

[5] The portion of 32 CFR relevant to the instant case was revised as of January 1, 1967. Citations in this opinion are to the 1962 edition which was in effect when O'Brien committed the crime, and when Congress enacted the 1965 Amendment.

[6] The Court of Appeals nevertheless remanded the case to the District Court to vacate the sentence and re-sentence O'Brien. In the court's view, the district judge might have considered the violation of the 1965 Amendment as an aggravating circumstance in imposing sentence. The Court

---

of Appeals subsequently denied O'Brien's petition for a rehearing, in which he argued that he had not been charged, tried, or convicted for non-possession, and that non-possession was not a lesser included offense of mutilation or destruction. O'Brien v. United States, 376 F.2d 538, 542 (C. A. 1st Cir. 1967).

[7] United States v. Miller, 367 F.2d 72 (C. A. 2d Cir. 1966), cert. denied, 386 U.S. 911 (1967).

[8] Smith v. United States, 368 F.2d 529 (C. A. 8th Cir. 1966).

[9] See 62 Stat. 605, as amended, 65 Stat. 76, 50 U. S. C. App. § 453; 32 CFR § 1613.1 (1962).

[10] 32 CFR § 1621.2 (1962).

[11] 32 CFR § 1613.43a (1962).

[12] 32 CFR §§ 1621.9, 1623.1 (1962).

[13] 32 CFR §§ 1623.1, 1623.2 (1962).

[14] 32 CFR § 1623.4 (1962).

[15] 32 CFR § 1625.1 (1962).

[16] 32 CFR §§ 1625.1, 1625.2, 1625.3, 1625.4, and 1625.11 (1962).

[17] 32 CFR § 1625.12 (1962).

Both the registration and classification certificates are small white cards, approximately 2 by 3 inches. The registration certificate specifies the name of the registrant, the date of registration, and the number and address of the local board with which he is registered. Also inscribed upon it are the date and place of the registrant's birth, his residence at registration, his physical description, his signature, and his Selective Service number. The Selective Service number itself indicates his State of registration, his local board, his year of birth, and his chronological position in the local board's classification record.[18]

The classification certificate shows the registrant's name, Selective Service number, signature, and eligibility classification. It specifies whether he was so classified by his local board, an appeal board, or the President. It [374] contains the address of his local board and the date the certificate was mailed. Both the registration and classification certificates bear notices that the registrant must notify his local board in writing of every change in address, physical condition, and occupational, marital, family, dependency, and military status, and of any other fact which might change his classification. Both also contain a notice that the registrant's Selective Service number should appear on all communications to his local board.

Congress demonstrated its concern that certificates issued by the Selective Service System might be abused well before the 1965 Amendment here challenged. The 1948 Act, 62 Stat. 604, itself prohibited many different abuses involving "any registration certificate, . . . or any other certificate issued pursuant to or prescribed by the provisions of this title, or rules or regulations promulgated hereunder . . . ." 62 Stat. 622. Under §§ 12 (b)(1)-(5) of the 1948 Act, it was unlawful (1) to transfer a certificate to aid a person in making false identification; (2) to possess a certificate not duly issued with the intent of using it for false identification; (3) to forge, alter, "or in any manner" change a certificate or any notation validly inscribed thereon; (4) to photograph or make an imitation of a certificate for the purpose of false identification; and (5) to possess a counterfeited or altered certificate. 62 Stat. 622. In addition, as previously mentioned, regulations of the Selective Service System required registrants to keep both their registration and classification certificates in their personal possession at all times. 32 CFR § 1617.1 (1962) (Registration Certificates);[19] 32 CFR §

1623.5 [375] (1962) (Classification Certificates).[20] And § 12 (b)(6) of the Act, 62 Stat. 622, made knowing violation of any provision of the Act or rules and regulations promulgated pursuant thereto a felony.

By the 1965 Amendment, Congress added to § 12 (b)(3) of the 1948 Act the provision here at issue, subjecting to criminal liability not only one who "forges, alters, or in any manner changes" but also one who "knowingly destroys, [or] knowingly mutilates" a certificate. We note at the outset that the 1965 Amendment plainly does not abridge free speech on its face, and we do not understand O'Brien to argue otherwise. Amended § 12 (b)(3) on its face deals with conduct having no connection with speech. It prohibits the knowing destruction of certificates issued by the Selective Service System, and there is nothing necessarily expressive about such conduct. The Amendment does not distinguish between public and private destruction, and it does not punish only destruction engaged in for the purpose of expressing views. Compare Stromberg v. California, 283 U.S. 359 (1931).[21] A law prohibiting destruction of Selective Service certificates no more abridges free speech on its face than a motor vehicle law prohibiting the destruction of drivers' licenses, or a tax law prohibiting the destruction of books and records.

[376] O'Brien nonetheless argues that the 1965 Amendment is unconstitutional in its application to him, and is unconstitutional as enacted because what he calls the "purpose" of Congress was "to suppress freedom of speech." We consider these arguments separately.

O'Brien first argues that the 1965 Amendment is unconstitutional as applied to him because his act of burning his registration certificate was protected "symbolic speech" within the First Amendment. His argument is that the freedom of expression which the First Amendment guarantees includes all modes of "communication of ideas by conduct," and that his conduct is within this definition because he did it in "demonstration against the war and against the draft."

We cannot accept the view that an apparently limitless variety of conduct can be labeled "speech"

---

[18] 32 CFR § 1621.2 (1962).

[19] 32 CFR § 1617.1 (1962), provides, in relevant part:
"Every person required to present himself for and submit to registration must, after he is registered, have in his personal possession at all times his Registration Certificate (SSS Form No. 2) prepared by his local board which has not been

altered and on which no notation duly and validly inscribed thereon has been changed in any manner after its preparation by the local board. The failure of any person to have his Registration Certificate (SSS Form No. 2) in his personal possession shall be prima facie evidence of his failure to register."

[20] 32 CFR § 1623.5 (1962), provides, in relevant part:
"Every person who has been classified by a local board must have in his personal possession at all times, in addition to his Registration Certificate (SSS Form No. 2), a valid Notice of Classification (SSS Form No. 110) issued to him showing his current classification."

[21] See text, infra, at 382.

whenever the person engaging in the conduct intends thereby to express an idea. However, even on the assumption that the alleged communicative element in O'Brien's conduct is sufficient to bring into play the First Amendment, it does not necessarily follow that the destruction of a registration certificate is constitutionally protected activity. This Court has held that when "speech" and "non-speech" elements are combined in the same course of conduct, a sufficiently important governmental interest in regulating the non-speech element can justify incidental limitations on First Amendment freedoms. To characterize the quality of the governmental interest which must appear, the Court has employed a variety of descriptive terms: compelling;[22] substantial;[23] subordinating;[24] [377] paramount;[25] cogent;[26] strong.[27] Whatever imprecision inheres in these terms, we think it clear that a government regulation is sufficiently justified if it is within the constitutional power of the Government; if it furthers an important or substantial governmental interest; if the governmental interest is unrelated to the suppression of free expression; and if the incidental restriction on alleged First Amendment freedoms is no greater than is essential to the furtherance of that interest. We find that the 1965 Amendment to § 12 (b)(3) of the Universal Military Training and Service Act meets all of these requirements, and consequently that O'Brien can be constitutionally convicted for violating it.

The constitutional power of Congress to raise and support armies and to make all laws necessary and proper to that end is broad and sweeping. Lichter v. United States, 334 U.S. 742, 755-758 (1948); Selective Draft Law Cases, 245 U.S. 366 1918); see also Ex parte Quirin, 317 U.S. 1, 25-26 (1942). The power of Congress to classify and conscript manpower for military service is "beyond question." Lichter v. United States, supra, at 756; Selective Draft Law Cases, supra. Pursuant to this power, Congress may establish a system of registration for individuals liable for training and service, and may require such individuals within reason to cooperate in the registration system. The issuance of certificates indicating the registration and eligibility classification of individuals is a legitimate and substantial administrative aid in the

functioning of this system. And legislation [378] to insure the continuing availability of issued certificates serves a legitimate and substantial purpose in the system's administration.

O'Brien's argument to the contrary is necessarily premised upon his unrealistic characterization of Selective Service certificates. He essentially adopts the position that such certificates are so many pieces of paper designed to notify registrants of their registration or classification, to be retained or tossed in the wastebasket according to the convenience or taste of the registrant. Once the registrant has received notification, according to this view, there is no reason for him to retain the certificates. O'Brien notes that most of the information on a registration certificate serves no notification purpose at all; the registrant hardly needs to be told his address and physical characteristics. We agree that the registration certificate contains much information of which the registrant needs no notification. This circumstance, however, does not lead to the conclusion that the certificate serves no purpose, but that, like the classification certificate, it serves purposes in addition to initial notification. Many of these purposes would be defeated by the certificates' destruction or mutilation. Among these are:

The registration certificate serves as proof that the individual described thereon has registered for the draft. The classification certificate shows the eligibility classification of a named but undescribed individual. Voluntarily displaying the two certificates is an easy and painless way for a young man to dispel a question as to whether he might be delinquent in his Selective Service obligations. Correspondingly, the avail-ability of the certificates for such display relieves the Selective Service System of the administrative burden it would otherwise have in verifying the Registration and classification of all suspected delinquents Further, since both certificates are in the nature of "receipts" attesting that the registrant [379] has done what the law requires, it is in the interest of the just and efficient administration of the system that they be continually available, in the event, for example, of a mix-up in the registrant's file. Additionally, in a time of national crisis, reasonable availability to each registrant of the two small cards assures a rapid and uncomplicated means for determining his fitness for immediate induction, no matter how distant in our mobile society he may be from his local board.

The information supplied on the certificates facilitates communication between registrants and local boards, simplifying the system and benefiting all concerned. To begin with, each certificate bears the address of the registrant's local board, an item unlikely to be committed to memory. Further, each card bears the registrant's Selective Service number,

---

[22] NAACP v. Button, 371 U.S. 415, 438 (1963); see also Sherbert v. Verner, 374 U.S. 398, 403 (1963).

[23] NAACP v. Button, 371 U.S. 415, 444 (1963); NAACP v. Alabama ex rel. Patterson, 357 U.S. 449, 464 (1958).

[24] Bates v. Little Rock, 361 U.S. 516, 524 (1960).

[25] Thomas v. Collins, 323 U.S. 516, 530 (1945); see also Sherbert v. Verner, 374 U.S. 398, 406 (1963).

[26] Bates v. Little Rock, 361 U.S. 516, 524 (1960).

[27] Sherbert v. Verner, 374 U.S. 398, 408 (1963).

and a registrant who has his number readily available so that he can communicate it to his local board when he supplies or requests information can make simpler the board's task in locating his file. Finally, a registrant's inquiry, particularly through a local board other than his own, concerning his eligibility status is frequently answerable simply on the basis of his classification certificate; whereas, if the certificate were not reasonably available and the registrant were uncertain of his classification, the task of answering his questions would be considerably complicated.

Both certificates carry continual reminders that the registrant must notify his local board of any change of address, and other specified changes in his status. The smooth functioning of the system requires that local boards be continually aware of the status and whereabouts of registrants, and the destruction of certificates deprives the system of a potentially useful notice device.

The regulatory scheme involving Selective Service certificates includes clearly valid prohibitions against the alteration, forgery, or similar deceptive misuse of certificates. [380] The destruction or mutilation of certificates obviously increases the difficulty of detecting and tracing abuses such as these. Further, a mutilated certificate might itself be used for deceptive purposes.

The many functions performed by Selective Service certificates establish beyond doubt that Congress has a legitimate and substantial interest in preventing their wanton and unrestrained destruction and assuring their continuing availability by punishing people who knowingly and willfully destroy or mutilate them. And we are un-persuaded that the pre-existence of the non-possession regulations in any way negates this interest.

In the absence of a question as to multiple punishment, it has never been suggested that there is anything improper in Congress' providing alternative statutory avenues of prosecution to assure the effective protection of one and the same interest. Compare the majority and dissenting opinions in Gore v. United States, 357 U.S. 386 (1958).[28] Here, the pre-existing avenue of prosecution was not even statutory. Regulations may be modified or revoked from time to time by administrative discretion. Certainly, the Congress may change or supplement a regulation.

Equally important, a comparison of the regulations with the 1965 Amendment indicates that they protect overlapping but not identical governmental interests, and that they reach somewhat different classes of wrongdoers.[29] The gravamen of the offense defined by the statute is the deliberate rendering of certificates un-available for the various purposes which they may serve. Whether registrants keep their certificates in their personal [381] possession at all times, as required by the regulations, is of no particular concern under the 1965 Amendment, as long as they do not mutilate or destroy the certificates so as to render them unavailable. Although as we note below we are not concerned here with the non-possession regulations, it is not inappropriate to observe that the essential elements of non-possession are not identical with those of mutilation or destruction. Finally, the 1965 Amendment, like § 12 (b) which it amended, is concerned with abuses involving any issued Selective Service certificates, not only with the registrant's own certificates. The knowing destruction or mutilation of someone else's certificates would therefore violate the statute but not the non-possession regulations.

We think it apparent that the continuing availability to each registrant of his Selective Service certificates substantially furthers the smooth and proper functioning of the system that Congress has established to raise armies. We think it also apparent that the Nation has a vital interest in having a system for raising armies that functions with maximum efficiency and is capable of easily and quickly responding to continually changing circumstances. For these reasons, the Government has a substantial interest in assuring the continuing availability of issued Selective Service certificates.

[11] It is equally clear that the 1965 Amendment specifically protects this substantial governmental interest. We perceive no alternative means that would more precisely and narrowly assure the continuing availability of issued Selective Service certificates than a law which prohibits their willful mutilation or destruction. Compare Sherbert v. Verner, 374 U.S. 398, 407-408 (1963), and the cases cited therein. The 1965 Amendment prohibits such conduct and does nothing more. In other words, both the governmental interest and the operation of the 1965 Amendment are limited to the non-communicative [382] aspect of O'Brien's conduct. The governmental interest and the scope of the 1965 Amendment are limited to preventing harm to the smooth and efficient functioning of the Selective Service System. When O'Brien deliberately rendered unavailable his Registration certificate, he willfully frustrated this governmental interest. For this non-communicative impact of his conduct, and for nothing else, he was convicted.

---

[28] Cf. Milanovich v. United States, 365 U.S. 551 (1961); Heflin v. United States, 358 U.S. 415 (1959); Prince v. United States, 352 U.S. 322 (1957).

[29] Cf. Milanovich v. United States, 365 U.S. 551 (1961); Heflin v. United States, 358 U.S. 415 (1959); Prince v. United States, 352 U.S. 322 (1957).

The case at bar is therefore unlike one where the alleged governmental interest in regulating conduct arises in some measure because the communication allegedly integral to the conduct is itself thought to be harmful. In Stromberg v. California, 283 U.S. 359 (1931), for example, this Court struck down a statutory phrase which punished people who expressed their "opposition to organized government" by displaying "any flag, badge, banner, or device." Since the statute there was aimed at suppressing communication it could not be sustained as a regulation of non-communicative conduct. See also, NLRB v. Fruit & Vegetable Packers Union, 377 U.S. 58, 79 (1964) (concurring opinion).

In conclusion, we find that because of the Government's substantial interest in assuring the continuing availability of issued Selective Service certificates, because amended § 462 (b) is an appropriately narrow means of protecting this interest and condemns only the independent non-communicative impact of conduct within its reach, and because the non-communicative impact of O'Brien's act of burning his registration certificate frustrated the Government's interest, a sufficient governmental interest has been shown to justify O'Brien's conviction.

[12] O'Brien finally argues that the 1965 Amendment is unconstitutional as enacted because what he calls the "purpose" of Congress was "to suppress freedom of [383] speech." We reject this argument because under settled principles the purpose of Congress, as O'Brien uses that term, is not a basis for declaring this legislation unconstitutional.

[13] It is a familiar principle of constitutional law that this Court will not strike down an otherwise constitutional statute on the basis of an alleged illicit legislative motive. As the Court long ago stated:

"The decisions of this court from the beginning lend no support whatever to the assumption that the judiciary may restrain the exercise of lawful power on the assumption that a wrongful purpose or motive has caused the power to be exerted." McCray v. United States, 195 U.S. 27, 56 (1904).

This fundamental principle of consti-tutional adjudication was reaffirmed and the many cases were collected by Mr. Justice Brandeis for the Court in Arizona v. California, 283 U.S. 423, 455 (1931).

[14][15][16][17] Inquiries into congressional motives or purposes are a hazardous matter. When the issue is simply the interpretation of legislation, the Court will look to statements by legislators for guidance as to the purpose of the legislature,[30] because the benefit to sound decision-making in [384] this circumstance is thought sufficient to risk the possibility of misreading Congress' purpose. It is entirely a different matter when we are asked to void a statute that is, under well-settled criteria, constitutional on its face, on the basis of what fewer than a handful of Congressmen said about it. What motivates one legislator to make a speech about a statute is not necessarily what motivates scores of others to enact it, and the stakes are sufficiently high for us to eschew guesswork. We decline to void essentially on the ground that it is unwise legislation which Congress had the undoubted power to enact and which could be reenacted in its exact form if the same or another legislator made a "wiser" speech about it.

[18] O'Brien's position, and to some extent that of the court below, rest upon a misunderstanding of Grosjean v. American Press Co., 297 U.S. 233 (1936), and Gomillion v. Lightfoot, 364 U.S. 339 (1960). These cases stand, not for the proposition that legislative motive is a proper basis for declaring a statute unconstitutional, but that the inevitable effect of a statute on its face may render it unconstitutional. Thus, in Grosjean the Court, having concluded that the right of publications to be free from certain kinds of taxes was a freedom of the press protected by the First Amendment, struck down a statute which on its face did nothing other than impose [385] just such a tax. Similarly, in Gomillion, the Court sustained a complaint which, if true, established that the "inevitable effect," 364

---

[30] The Court may make the same assumption in a very limited and well-defined class of cases where the very nature of the constitutional question requires an inquiry into legislative purpose. The principal class of cases is readily apparent – those in which statutes have been challenged as bills of attainder. This Court's decisions have defined a bill of attainder as a legislative Act which inflicts punishment on named individuals or members of an easily ascertainable group without a judicial trial. In determining whether a particular statute is a bill of attainder, the analysis necessarily requires an inquiry into whether the three definitional elements – specificity in identification, punishment, and lack of a judicial trial – are contained in the statute. The inquiry into whether the challenged statute contains the necessary element of punishment has on occasion led the Court to examine the legislative motive in enacting the statute. See, e.g., United States v. Lovett, 328 U.S. 303 (1946). Two other decisions not involving a bill of attainder analysis contain an inquiry into legislative purpose or motive of the type that O'Brien suggests we engage in this case. Kennedy v. Mendoza-Martinez, 372 U.S. 144, 169-184 (1963); Trop v. Dulles, 356 U.S. 86, 95-97 (1958). The inquiry into legislative purpose or motive in Kennedy and Trop, however, was for the same limited purpose as in the bill of attainder decisions – i.e., to determine whether the statutes under review were punitive in nature. We face no such inquiry in this case. The 1965 Amendment to § 462 (b) was clearly penal in nature, designed to impose criminal punishment for designated acts.

U.S., at 341, of the redrawing of municipal boundaries was to deprive the petitioners of their right to vote for no reason other than that they were Negro. In these cases, the purpose of the legislation was irrelevant, because the inevitable effect – the "necessary scope and operation," McCray v. United States, 195 U.S. 27, 59 (1904) – abridged constitutional rights. The statute attacked in the instant case has no such inevitable unconstitutional effect, since the destruction of Selective Service certificates is in no respect inevitably or necessarily expressive. Accordingly, the statute itself is constitutional.

We think it not amiss, in passing, to comment upon O'Brien's legislative-purpose argument. There was little floor debate on this legislation in either House. Only Senator Thurmond commented on its substantive features in the Senate. 111 Cong. Rec. 19746, 20433. After his brief statement, and without any additional substantive comments, the bill, H. R. 10306, passed the Senate. 111 Cong. Rec. 20434. In the House debate only two Congressmen addressed themselves to the Amendment – Congressmen Rivers and Bray. 111 Cong. Rec. 19871, 19872. The bill was passed after their statements without any further debate by a vote of 393 to 1. It is principally on the basis of the statements by these three Congress-men that O'Brien makes his congressional-"purpose" argument. We note that if we were to examine legislative purpose in the instant case, we would be obliged to consider not only these statements but also the more authoritative reports of the Senate and House Armed Services Committees. The portions of those reports explaining the purpose of the Amendment are reproduced in the Appendix in their entirety. While both reports make clear a concern with the "defiant" [386] destruction of so-called "draft cards" and with "open" encouragement to others to destroy their cards, both reports also indicate that this concern stemmed from an apprehension that unrestrained destruction of cards would disrupt the smooth functioning of the Selective Service System.

[19] Since the 1965 Amendment to § 12 (b)(3) of the Universal Military Training and Service Act is constitutional as enacted and as applied, the Court of Appeals should have affirmed the judgment of conviction entered by the District Court. Accordingly, we vacate the judgment of the Court of Appeals, and reinstate the judgment and sentence of the District Court. This disposition makes unnecessary consideration of O'Brien's claim that the Court of Appeals erred in affirming his

conviction on the basis of the non-possession regulation.[31]

It is so ordered.

MR. JUSTICE MARSHALL took no part in the consideration or decision of these cases.

APPENDIX TO OPINION OF THE COURT.

PORTIONS OF THE REPORTS OF THE COMMITTEES ON ARMED SERVICES OF THE SENATE AND HOUSE EXPLAINING THE 1965 AMENDMENT.

The "Explanation of the Bill" in the Senate Report is as follows:

"Section 12 (b)(3) of the Universal Military Training and Service Act of 1951, as amended, provides, among other things, that a person who forges, alters, or changes [387] a draft registration certificate is subject to a fine of not more than $ 10,000 or imprisonment of not more than 5 years, or both. There is no explicit prohibition in this section against the knowing destruction or mutilation of such cards.

"The committee has taken notice of the defiant destruction and mutilation of draft cards by dissident persons who disapprove of national policy. If allowed to continue unchecked this contumacious conduct represents a potential threat to the exercise of the power to raise and support armies.

"For a person to be subject to fine or imprisonment the destruction or mutilation of the draft card must be 'knowingly' done. This qualification is intended to protect persons who lose or mutilate draft cards accidentally." S. Rep. No. 589, 89th Cong., 1st Sess. (1965). And the House Report explained:

"Section 12 (b)(3) of the Universal Military Training and Service Act of 1951, as amended, provides that a person who forges, alters, or in any manner changes his draft registration card, or any notation duly and validly inscribed thereon, will be subject to a fine of $10,000 or imprisonment of not more than 5 years. H. R. 10306 would amend this provision to make it apply also to those persons who knowingly destroy or knowingly mutilate a draft registration card.

"The House Committee on Armed Services is fully aware of, and shares in, the deep concern expressed through-out the Nation over the increasing incidences in which individuals and large groups of individuals openly defy and encourage others to defy the authority of their Government by destroying or mutilating their draft cards.

"While the present provisions of the Criminal Code with respect to the destruction of Government

---

[31] The other issues briefed by O'Brien were not raised in the petition for certiorari in No. 232 or in the cross-petition in No. 233. Accordingly, those issues are not before the Court.

property [388] may appear broad enough to cover all acts having to do with the mistreatment of draft cards in the possession of individuals, the committee feels that in the present critical situation of the country, the acts of destroying or mutilating these cards are offenses which pose such a grave threat to the security of the Nation that no question whatsoever should be left as to the intention of the Congress that such wanton and irresponsible acts should be punished.

"To this end, H. R. 10306 makes specific that knowingly mutilating or knowingly destroying a draft card constitutes a violation of the Universal Military Training and Service Act and is punishable thereunder; and that a person who does so destroy or mutilate a draft card will be subject to a fine of not more than $10,000 or imprisonment of not more than 5 years." H. R. Rep. No. 747, 89th Cong., 1st Sess. (1965).

CONCUR: MR. JUSTICE HARLAN, concurring.

The crux of the Court's opinion, which I join, is of course its general statement, ante, at 377, that:
I wish to make explicit my understanding that this passage does not foreclose consideration of First Amendment claims in those rare instances when an "incidental" restriction upon expression, imposed by a regulation which furthers an "important or substantial" governmental interest and satisfies the Court's other criteria, in practice has the effect of entirely I wish to make explicit my understanding that this passage does not foreclose consideration of First Amendment claims in those rare instances when an "incidental" restriction upon expression, imposed by a regulation which furthers an "important or substantial" governmental interest and satisfies the Court's other criteria, in practice has the effect of entirely preventing a "speaker" [389] from reaching a significant audience with whom he could not otherwise lawfully communicate. This is not such a case, since O'Brien manifestly could have conveyed his message in many ways other than by burning his draft card.

DISSENT: MR. JUSTICE DOUGLAS.

The Court states that the constitutional power of Congress to raise and support armies is "broad and sweeping" and that Congress' power "to classify and conscript manpower for military service is 'beyond question.'" This is undoubtedly true in times when, by declaration of Congress, the Nation is in a state of war. The underlying and basic problem in this case, however, is whether conscription is permissible in the absence of a declaration of war.[1]

---

[1] Neither of the decisions cited by the majority for the proposition that Congress' power to conscript men into the armed services is "'beyond question'" concerns peacetime

That question has not been briefed nor was it presented in oral argument; but it is, I submit, a question upon which the litigants and the country are entitled to a ruling. I have discussed in Holmes v. United States, post, p. 936, the nature of the legal issue and it will be seen from my dissenting opinion in that case that this Court has never ruled on [390] the question. It is time that we made a ruling. This case should be put down for re-argument and heard with Holmes v. United States and with Hart v. United States, post, p. 956, in which the Court today denies certiorari.[2]

The rule that this Court will not consider issues not raised by the parties is not inflexible and yields in "exceptional cases" (Duignan v. United States, 274 U.S. 195, 200) to the need correctly to decide the case before the court. E.g., Erie R. Co. v. Tompkins, 304 U.S. 64; Terminiello v. Chicago, 337 U.S. 1. In such a case it is not unusual to ask for re-argument (Sherman v. United States, 356 U.S. 369, 379, n. 2, Frankfurter, J., concurring) even on a constitutional question not raised by the parties. In Abel v. United States, 362 U.S. 217, the petitioner had conceded that an administrative deportation arrest warrant would be valid for its limited purpose even though not supported by a sworn affidavit stating probable cause; but the Court ordered re-argument on the question whether the warrant had been validly issued in petitioner's case. 362 U.S., at 219, n., par. 1; 359 U.S. 940.

In Lustig v. United States, 338 U.S. 74, the petitioner argued that an exclusionary rule should apply to the fruit of an unreasonable search by state officials solely because they acted in concert with federal officers (see Weeks v. United States, 232 U.S. 383; Byars v. United States, 273 U.S. 28). The Court ordered re-argument on the question raised in a then pending case, Wolf v. Colorado, 338 U.S. 25: applicability of the Fourth Amendment to the

---

conscription. As I have shown in my dissenting opinion in Holmes v. United States, post, p. 936, the Selective Draft Law Cases, 245 U.S. 366, decided in 1918, upheld the constitutionality of a conscription act passed by Congress more than a month after war had been declared on the German Empire and which was then being enforced in time of war. Lichter v. United States, 334 U.S. 742, concerned the constitutionality of the Renegotiation Act, another wartime measure, enacted by Congress over the period of 1942-1945 (id., at 745, n. 1) and applied in that case to excessive war profits made in 1942-1943 (id., at 753). War had been declared, of course, in 1941 (55 Stat. 795). The Court referred to Congress' power to raise armies in discussing the "background" (334 U.S., at 753) of the Renegotiation Act, which it upheld as a valid exercise of the War Power.

[2] Today the Court also denies stays in Shiffman v. Selective Service Board No. 5, and Zigmond v. Selective Service Board No. 16, post, p. 930, where punitive delinquency regulations are invoked against registrants, decisions that present a related question.

States. U.S. Sup. Ct. Journal, October Term, 1947, p. 298. In Donaldson v. Read Magazine, 333 U.S. 178, the only issue presented, [391] according to both parties, was whether the record contained sufficient evidence of fraud to uphold an order of the Postmaster General. Re-argument was ordered on the constitutional issue of abridgment of First Amendment freedoms. 333 U.S., at 181-182; Journal, October Term, 1947, p. 70. Finally, in Musser v. Utah, 333 U.S. 95, 96, re-argument was ordered on the question of unconstitutional vagueness of a criminal statute, an issue not raised by the parties but suggested at oral argument by Justice Jackson. Journal, October Term, 1947, p. 87.

These precedents demonstrate the appropriateness of restoring the instant case to the calendar for re-argument on the question of the constitutionality of a peacetime draft and having it heard with Holmes v. United States and Hart v. United States.

Ward v. Rock Against Racism
491 U.S. 781
(1989)
(Excerpts only. Footnotes omitted.)

Author's Note: After Rock Against Racism's concerts in New York City's Central Park prompted several noise complaints, the city adopted a policy to require that the city provide sound-amplification equipment and a sound technician to control the volume of concerts in the Central Park band shell. The Court voted 6-3 to reverse the lower court and find that the policy was a reasonable regulation of the place and manner of speech under the First Amendment.

JUDGES: Kennedy, J., delivered the opinion of the Court, in which Rehnquist, C. J., and White, O'Connor, and Scalia, JJ., joined. Blackmun, J., concurred in the result. Marshall, J., filed a dissenting opinion, in which Brennan and Stevens, JJ., joined.

OPINION: [789] We granted certiorari, 488 U.S. 816 (1988), to clarify the legal standard applicable to governmental regulation of the time, place, or manner of protected speech. Because the Court of Appeals erred in requiring the city to prove that its regulation was the least intrusive means of furthering its legitimate [790] governmental interests, and because the ordinance is valid on its face, we now reverse. ...We decide [791] the case as one in which the band shell is a public forum for performances in which the government's right to regulate expression is subject to the protections of the First Amendment.

Our cases make clear, however, that even in a public forum the government may impose reasonable restrictions on the time, place, or manner of protected speech, provided the restrictions "are justified without reference to the content of the regulated speech, that they are narrowly tailored to serve a significant governmental interest, and that they leave open ample alternative channels for communication of the information." Clark v. Community for Creative Non-Violence, 468 U.S. 288, 293 (1984). ...The principal inquiry in determining content neutrality, in speech cases generally and in time, place, or manner cases in particular, is whether the government has adopted a regulation of speech because of disagreement with the message it conveys. The government's purpose is the controlling consideration. A regulation that serves purposes unrelated to the content of expression is deemed neutral, even if it has an incidental effect on some speakers or messages but not others.

...[792] On this record, the city's concern with sound quality extends only to the clearly content-neutral goals of ensuring adequate [793] sound amplification and avoiding the volume problems associated with inadequate sound mix. n4 Any governmental attempt to serve purely esthetic goals by imposing subjective standards of acceptable sound mix on performers would raise serious First Amendment concerns, but this case provides us with no opportunity to address those questions.

... [795] The dissent's suggestion that the guideline constitutes a prior restraint is not consistent with our cases. As we said in Southeastern Promotions, Ltd. v. Conrad, 420 U.S. 546 (1975), the regulations we have found invalid as prior restraints have "had this in common: they gave public officials the power to deny use of a forum in advance of actual expression." Id., at 553. ... The relevant question is whether the challenged regulation authorizes suppression of speech in advance of its expression, and the sound-amplification guideline does not. ... [796] The city's regulation is also "narrowly tailored to serve a significant governmental interest." ... [797] The city enjoys a substantial interest in ensuring the ability of its citizens to enjoy whatever benefits the city parks have to offer, from amplified music to silent meditation. The Court of Appeals recognized the city's substantial interest in limiting the sound emanating from the band shell. See 848 F. 2d, at 370. The court concluded, however, that the city's sound-amplification guideline was not narrowly tailored to further this interest, because "it has not [been] shown . . . that the requirement of the use of the city's sound system and technician was the least intrusive means of regulating the volume." Id., at 371. In the court's judgment, there were several alternative methods of achieving the desired end that would have been less restrictive of respondent's First Amendment rights.

The Court of Appeals erred in sifting through all the available or imagined alternative means of regulating sound volume in order to determine whether the city's solution was "the least intrusive means" of achieving the desired end. This "less-restrictive-alternative analysis . . . has never been a part of the inquiry into the validity of a time, place, and manner regulation." Instead, our cases quite clearly hold that restrictions on the time, place, or manner of protected speech are not invalid "simply because there is some imaginable alternative that might be less burdensome on speech." ... [798] Lest any confusion on the point remain, we reaffirm today that a regulation of the time, place, or manner of protected speech must be narrowly tailored to serve the government's legitimate, content-neutral interests but that it need not be the least restrictive or least intrusive means of doing so. [799] Rather, the requirement of narrow tailoring is satisfied "so long as the . . . regulation promotes a substantial government interest that would be achieved less effectively absent the regulation." To be sure, this standard does not mean that a time, place, or manner regulation may burden substantially more speech than is necessary to further the government's legitimate interests. Government may not regulate expression in such a manner that a substantial portion of the burden on speech does not serve to advance its goals. So long as the means chosen are not substantially broader than necessary to achieve the government's interest, how-ever, the regulation will not be invalid simply because a court concludes that the government's interest could be adequately served by some less-speech-restrictive alternative.

... [800] The dissent's attempt to analogize the sound-amplification guideline to a total ban on distribution of handbills is imaginative but misguided. The guideline does not ban all concerts, or even all rock concerts, but instead focuses on the source of the evils the city seeks to eliminate – excessive and inadequate sound amplification – and eliminates them without at the same time banning or significantly restricting a substantial quantity of speech that does not create the same evils. This is the essence of narrow tailoring.

... It is undeniable that the city's substantial interest in limiting sound volume is served in a direct and effective way by the requirement that the city's sound technician control the mixing board during performances. Absent this requirement, the city's interest would have been served less well, as is evidenced by the complaints about excessive volume generated by respondent's past concerts. The alternative regulatory methods hypothesized by the Court of Appeals reflect nothing more than a disagreement with the city over how much control of volume is appropriate or how that level of control is to be achieved. The Court of Appeals erred in failing to defer to the city's reasonable determination that its interest in controlling volume would be best served by requiring band shell performers to utilize the city's sound technician. ... [801] It is apparent that the guideline directly furthers the city's legitimate governmental interests and that those interests would have been less well served in the absence of the sound-amplification guideline. ... [802] Since the guideline allows the city to control volume without interfering with the performer's desired sound mix, it is not "substantially broader than necessary" to achieve the city's legitimate ends. The final requirement, that the guideline leave open ample alternative channels of communication, is easily met.

... [803] The city's sound-amplification guideline is narrowly tailored to serve the substantial and content-neutral governmental interests of avoiding excessive sound volume and providing sufficient amplification within the band shell concert ground, and the guide-line leaves open ample channels of communication. Accordingly, it is valid under the First Amendment as a reasonable regulation of the place and manner of expression. The judgment of the Court of Appeals is

Reversed.

DISSENT: ... [803] JUSTICE MARSHALL, with whom JUSTICE BRENNAN and JUSTICE STEVENS join, dissenting.

No one can doubt that government has a substantial interest in regulating the barrage of excessive sound that can plague urban life. Unfortunately, the majority plays to our shared impatience with loud noise to obscure the damage that it does to our First Amendment rights. Until today, a key safeguard of free speech has been government's obligation to adopt the least intrusive restriction necessary to achieve its goals. By abandoning the requirement that time, place, and manner regulations must be narrowly tailored, the majority replaces constitutional scrutiny with mandatory deference. The majority's willingness to give government officials a free hand in achieving their policy ends extends so far as to permit, in this case, government control of speech in advance of its dissemination. Because New York City's Use Guidelines are not narrowly tailored to serve its interest in regulating loud noise, and because they constitute an impermissible prior restraint, I dissent.

[804] ... My complaint is with the majority's serious distortion of the narrow tailoring requirement. ... [805] In practice, the Court has interpreted the narrow tailoring requirement to mandate an examination of alternative methods of serving the asserted governmental interest and a determination whether the greater efficacy of the challenged regulation outweighs the increased burden it places on protected speech. ... The Court's past concern for the extent to which a regulation burdens speech more than would a satisfactory alternative is noticeably absent from today's decision. The majority requires only that government show that its interest cannot be served as effectively without the challenged restriction. It will be enough, therefore, that the challenged regulation advances the government's interest only in the slightest, for any differential burden on speech that results does not enter the calculus. Despite its protestations to the contrary, the majority thus has abandoned the requirement that restrictions on speech be narrowly tailored in any ordinary use of the phrase.

...[807] The majority thus instructs courts to refrain from examining how much speech may be restricted to serve an asserted interest and how that level of restriction is to be achieved. If a court cannot engage in such inquiries, I am at a loss to understand how a court can ascertain whether the government has adopted a regulation that burdens substantially more speech than is necessary. ... By holding that the Guidelines are valid time, place, and manner restrictions, notwithstanding the availability of less intrusive but effective means of controlling volume, the majority deprives the narrow tailoring requirement of all meaning.

... [808] The majority's conclusion that the city's exclusive control of sound equipment is constitutional is deeply troubling for another reason. It places the Court's imprimatur on a quintessential prior restraint, incompatible with fundamental First Amendment values. ... Whether the city denies a performer a band shell permit or grants the permit and then silences or [809] distorts the performer's music, the result is the same – the city censors speech. ... As a system of prior restraint, the Guidelines are presumptively invalid. ... [811] With neither prompt judicial review nor detailed and neutral standards fettering the city's discretion to restrict protected [812] speech, the Guidelines constitute a quintessential, and unconstitutional, prior restraint.

Today's decision has significance far beyond the world of rock music. Government no longer need balance the effectiveness of regulation with the burdens on free speech. After today, government need only assert that it is most effective to control speech in advance of its expression. Because such a result eviscerates the First Amendment, I dissent.

Texas v. Johnson
491 U.S. 397
(1989)

(Excerpts only. Footnotes omitted.)

Author's Note: After a protester burned an American flag During a political protest in Dallas at the time of the 1984 Republican National Convention, he was convicted of violating a Texas statute that prohibited flag desecration. The law sought to insure the public peace and protect the symbolic value of the flag. In a 5-4 decision, the Supreme Court affirmed the state high court's judgment that the law violated the constitutionally protected symbolic speech of the protester.

JUDGES: Brennan, J., delivered the opinion of the Court, in which Marshall, Blackmun, Scalia, and Kennedy, JJ., joined. Kennedy, J., filed a concurring opinion. Rehnquist, C. J., filed a dissenting opinion, in which White and O'Connor, JJ., joined. Stevens, J., filed a dissenting opinion.

OPINION: [404] ... The First Amendment literally forbids the abridgment only of "speech," but we have long ... acknowledged that conduct may be "sufficiently imbued with elements of communication to fall within the scope of the First and Fourteenth Amendments" ... [when] "[a]n intent to convey a particularized message was present, and the likelihood was great that the message would be understood by those who viewed it."

... [406] Johnson burned an American flag as part – indeed, as the culmination – of a political demonstration ... The expressive, overtly political nature of this conduct was both intentional and overwhelmingly apparent. ... The government generally has a freer hand in restricting expressive conduct than it has in restricting the written or spoken word. ... [407] [However,] the governmental interest in question [must] be unconnected to expression in order to come under O'Brien's less demanding rule.

... [410] The State, apparently, is concerned that [flag desecration] will lead people to believe either that the flag does not stand for nationhood and national unity, but instead reflects other, less positive concepts, or that the concepts reflected in the flag do not in fact exist, that is, that we do not enjoy unity as a Nation. These concerns blossom only when a person's treatment of the flag communicates some message, and thus are related "to the suppression of free expression." ... [411] Johnson was not, we add, prosecuted for the expression of just any idea; he was prosecuted for his expression of dissatisfaction with the policies of this country, expression situated at the core of our First Amendment values. Moreover, Johnson was prosecuted because he knew that his politically charged expression would cause "serious offense." ... The Texas law is thus not aimed at protecting the physical integrity of the flag in all circumstances, but is designed instead to protect it only against impairments that would cause serious offense to others. ... [412] Johnson's political expression was restricted because of the content of the message he conveyed. We must therefore subject the State's asserted interest in preserving the special symbolic character of the flag to "the most exacting scrutiny."

... [414] If there is a bedrock principle underlying the First Amendment, it is that the government may not prohibit the expression of an idea simply because society finds the idea itself offensive or disagreeable. We have not recognized an exception to this principle even where our flag has been involved. ... [415] Nothing in our precedents suggests that a State may foster its own view of the flag by prohibiting expressive conduct relating to it. ...[416] Their enduring lesson, that the government may not prohibit expression simply because it disagrees with its message, is not dependent on the particular mode in which one chooses to express an idea. n11 If we were to hold that a State may forbid flag burning wherever it is likely to endanger the flag's symbolic role, but allow it wherever burning a flag promotes that role ... [417] we would be permitting a State to "prescribe what shall be orthodox" by saying that one may burn the flag to convey one's attitude toward it and its referents only if one does not endanger the flag's representation of nationhood and national unity.

... There is, moreover, no indication – either in the text of the Constitution or in our cases interpreting it – that a separate juridical category exists for the American flag alone. Indeed, we would not be surprised to learn that the persons [418] who framed our Constitution and wrote the Amendment that we now construe were not known for their reverence for the Union Jack. The First Amendment does not guarantee that other concepts virtually sacred to our Nation as a whole – such as the principle that discrimination on the basis of race is odious and destructive – will go unquestioned in the market-place of ideas. We decline, therefore, to create for the flag an exception to the joust of principles protected by the First Amendment.

... [419] We are tempted to say, in fact, that the flag's deservedly cherished place in our community will be strengthened, not weakened, by our holding today. Our decision is a reaffirmation of the principles of freedom and inclusiveness that the flag best reflects, and of the conviction that our toleration of criticism such as Johnson's is a sign and source of our strength. ... It is the Nation's resilience, not its rigidity, that Texas sees reflected in the flag – and it is that resilience that we reassert today. The way to preserve the flag's special role is not to punish those who feel differently about these matters. It is to persuade them that they are wrong. ... We do not consecrate the flag by punishing its desecration, for in doing so we dilute the freedom that this cherished emblem represents.

CONCUR: [420] JUSTICE KENNEDY.

... The hard fact is that sometimes we must make decisions we do not like. We make them because they are right, right [421] in the sense that the law and the Constitution, as we see them, compel the result. And so great is our commitment to the process that, except in the rare case, we do not pause to express distaste for the result, perhaps for fear of undermining a valued principle that dictates the decision. This is one of those rare cases.

... It is poignant but fundamental that the flag protects those who hold it in contempt.

DISSENT: [421] CHIEF JUSTICE REHNQUIST, with whom JUSTICE WHITE and JUSTICE O'CONNOR join, dissenting.

... [429] The American flag, then, throughout more than 200 years of our history, has come to be the visible symbol embodying our Nation. It does not represent the views of any particular political party, and it does not represent any particular political philosophy. The flag is not simply another "idea" or "point of view" competing for recognition in the marketplace of ideas. Millions and millions of Americans regard it with an almost mystical reverence regardless of what sort of social, political, or philosophical beliefs they may have. I cannot agree that the First Amendment invalidates the Act of Congress, and the laws of 48 of the 50 States, which make criminal the public burning of the flag.

... [431] As with "fighting words," so with flag burning, for purposes of the First Amendment: It is "no essential part of any exposition of ideas, and [is] of such slight social value as a step to truth that any benefit that may be derived from [it] is clearly outweighed" by the public interest in avoiding a probable breach of the peace.

... [432] The Texas statute deprived Johnson of only one rather inarticulate symbolic form of protest – a form of protest that was profoundly offensive to many – and left him with a full panoply of other symbols and every conceivable form of verbal expression to express his deep disapproval of national policy. Thus, in no way can it be said that Texas is punishing him because his hearers – or any other group of people – were profoundly opposed to the message that he sought to convey. Such opposition is no proper basis for restricting speech or expression under the First Amendment. It was Johnson's use of this particular symbol, and not the idea that he sought to convey by it or by his many other expressions, for which he was punished.

... [435] Surely one of the high purposes of a democratic society is to legislate against conduct that is regarded as evil and profoundly offensive to the majority of people – whether it be murder, embezzlement, pollution, or flag burning....

I would uphold the Texas statute as applied in this case.

DISSENT: [436] JUSTICE STEVENS.

... [437] The value of the flag as a symbol cannot be measured. Even so, I have no doubt that the interest in preserving that value for the future is both significant and legitimate. ... Sanctioning the public desecration of the flag will tarnish its value– both for those who cherish the ideas for which it waves and for those who desire to don the robes of martyrdom by burning it. That tarnish is not justified by the trivial burden on free expression occasioned by requiring that an available, alternative mode of expression – including uttering words critical of the flag – be employed.

[438] ... The Court is ... quite wrong in blandly asserting that respondent "was prosecuted for his expression of dissatisfaction with the policies of this country, expression situated at the core of our First Amendment values." Respondent was prosecuted because of the method he chose to express his dissatisfaction with those policies. Had he chosen to spray-paint – or perhaps convey with a motion picture projector – his message of dissatisfaction on the facade of the Lincoln Memorial, there would be no question about the power of the Government to prohibit his means of expression. The prohibition would be supported by the legitimate interest in preserving the quality of an important [439] national asset. Though the asset at stake in this case is intangible, given its unique value, the same interest supports a prohibition on the desecration of the American flag. ... I respectfully dissent.

Simon & Schuster, Inc. v. New York State Crime Victims Board
502 U.S. 105
(1991)

JUDGES: O'CONNOR, J., delivered the opinion of the Court, in which REHNQUIST, C. J., and WHITE, STEVENS, SCALIA, and SOUTER, JJ., joined. BLACKMUN, J., and KEN-NEDY, J., filed opinions concurring in the judgment. THOMAS, J., took no part in the consideration or decision of the case.

OPINION: [108] JUSTICE O'CONNOR delivered the opinion of the Court.

[1A] New York's "Son of Sam" law requires that an accused or convicted criminal's income from works describing his crime be deposited in an escrow account. These funds are then made available to the victims of the crime and the criminal's other creditors. We consider whether this statute is consistent with the First Amendment.

I A.   In the summer of 1977, New York was terrorized by a serial killer popularly known as the Son of Sam. The hunt for the Son of Sam received considerable publicity, and by the time David

Berkowitz was identified as the killer and apprehended, the rights to his story were worth a substantial amount. Berkowitz's chance to profit from his notoriety while his victims and their families remained uncompensated did not escape the notice of New York's Legislature. The State quickly enacted the statute at issue, N.Y. Exec. Law § 632-a (McKinney 1982 and Supp. 1991).

The statute was intended to "ensure that monies received by the criminal under such circumstances shall first be made available to recompense the victims of that crime for their loss and suffering." Assembly Bill Memorandum Re: A 9019, July 22, 1977, reprinted in Legislative Bill Jacket, 1977 N.Y. Laws, ch. 823. As the author of the statute explained: "It is abhorrent to one's sense of justice and decency that an individual . . . can expect to receive large sums of money for his story once he is captured – while five people are dead, [and] other people were injured as a result of his conduct." [109] Memorandum of Sen. Emanuel R. Gold, reprinted in New York State Legislative Annual, 1977, p. 267.

The Son of Sam law, as later amended, requires any entity contracting with an accused or convicted person for a depiction of the crime to submit a copy of the contract to respondent New York State Crime Victims Board (Board), and to turn over any income under that contract to the Board. This requirement applies to all such contracts in any medium of communication: "Every person, firm, corporation, partnership, association or other legal entity contracting with any person or the representative or assignee of any person, accused or convicted of a crime in this state, with respect to the reenactment of such crime, by way of a movie, book, magazine article, tape recording, phonograph record, radio or television presentation, live entertainment of any kind, or from the expression of such accused or convicted person's thoughts, feelings, opinions or emotions regarding such crime, shall submit a copy of such contract to the board and pay over to the board any moneys which would otherwise, by terms of such contract, be owing to the person so accused or convicted or his representatives." N.Y. Exec. Law § 632-a(1) (McKinney 1982).

The Board is then required to deposit the payment in an escrow account "for the benefit of and payable to any victim . . . provided that such victim, within five years of the date of the establishment of such escrow account, brings a civil action in a court of competent jurisdiction and recovers a money judgment for damages against such [accused or convicted] person or his representatives." Ibid. After five years, if no actions are pending, "the board shall immediately pay over any moneys in the escrow account to such person or his legal representatives." § 632-a(4). This 5-year period in which to bring a civil action against the convicted [110] person begins to run when the escrow account is established, and supersedes any limitations period that expires earlier. § 632-a(7).

Subsection (8) grants priority to two classes of claims against the escrow account. First, upon a court order, the Board must release assets "for the exclusive purpose of retaining legal representation." § 632-a(8). In addition, the Board has the discretion, after giving notice to the victims of the crime, to "make payments from the escrow account to a representative of any person accused or convicted of a crime for the necessary expenses of the production of the moneys paid into the escrow account." Ibid. This provision permits payments to literary agents and other such representatives. Payments under subsection (8) may not exceed one-fifth of the amount collected in the account. Ibid.

Claims against the account are given the following priorities: (a) payments ordered by the Board under subsection (8); (b) subrogation claims of the State for payments made to victims of the crime; (c) civil judgments obtained by victims of the crime; and (d) claims of other creditors of the accused or convicted person, including state and local tax authorities. N.Y. Exec. Law § 632-a(11) (McKinney Supp. 1991).

Subsection (10) broadly defines "person convicted of a crime" to include "any person convicted of a crime in this state either by entry of a plea of guilty or by conviction after trial *and any person who has voluntarily and intelligently admitted the commission of a crime for which such person is not prosecuted.*" § 632-a(10)(b) (emphasis added). Thus a person who has never been accused or convicted of a crime in the ordinary sense, but who admits in a book or other work to having committed a crime, is within the statute's coverage.

As recently construed by the New York Court of Appeals, however, the statute does not apply to victimless crimes. *Children of Bedford, Inc. v. Petromelis*, 77 N.Y.2d 713, 726, 573 N.E.2d 541, 548, 570 N.Y.S.2d 453 (1991).

[111] The Son of Sam law supplements pre-existing statutory schemes authorizing the Board to compensate crime victims for their losses, see N.Y. Exec. Law § 631 (McKinney 1982 and Supp. 1991), permitting courts to order the proceeds of crime forfeited to the State, see N.Y. Civ. Prac. Law §§ 1310-1352 (McKinney Supp. 1991), providing for orders of restitution at sentencing, N.Y. Penal Law § 60.27 (McKinney 1987), and affording prejudgment attachment procedures to ensure that wrongdoers do not dissipate their assets, N.Y. Civ. Prac. Law §§ 6201-6226 (McKinney 1980 and Supp. 1991). The escrow arrangement established by the Son of Sam law enhances these provisions only insofar as the accused or convicted person earns income within the scope of § 632-a(1).

Since its enactment in 1977, the Son of Sam law has been invoked only a handful of times. As might be expected, the individuals whose profits the Board has sought to escrow have all become well known for having committed highly publicized crimes. These include Jean Harris, the convicted killer of "Scarsdale Diet" Doctor Herman Tarnower; Mark David Chapman, the man convicted of assassinating John Lennon; and R. Foster Winans, the former Wall Street Journal columnist convicted of insider trading. Ironically, the statute was never applied to the Son of Sam himself; David Berkowitz was found incompetent to stand trial, and the statute at that time applied only to criminals who had actually been convicted. N.Y. Times, Feb. 20, 1991, p. B8, col. 4. According to the Board, Berkowitz voluntarily paid his share of the royalties from the book Son of Sam, published in 1981, to his victims or their estates. Brief for Respondents 8, n. 13.

This case began in 1986, when the Board first became aware of the contract between petitioner Simon & Schuster and admitted organized crime figure Henry Hill.

[112] B.　　Looking back from the safety of the Federal Witness Protection Program, Henry Hill recalled: "At the age of twelve my ambition was to be a gangster. To be a wiseguy. To me being a wiseguy was better than being president of the United States." N. Pileggi, Wiseguy: Life in a Mafia Family 19 (1985) (hereinafter Wiseguy). Whatever one might think of Hill, at the very least it can be said that he realized his dreams. After a career spanning 25 years, Hill admitted engineering some of the most daring crimes of his day, including the 1978-1979 Boston College basketball point shaving scandal, and the theft of $ 6 million from Lufthansa Airlines in 1978, the largest successful cash robbery in American history. Wiseguy 9. Most of Hill's crimes were more banausic: He committed extortion, he imported and distributed narcotics, and he organized numerous robberies.

Hill was arrested in 1980. In exchange for immunity from prosecution, he testified against many of his former colleagues. Since his arrest, he has lived under an assumed name in an unknown part of the country.

In August 1981, Hill entered into a contract with author Nicholas Pileggi for the production of a book about Hill's life. The following month, Hill and Pileggi signed a publishing agreement with Simon & Schuster, Inc. Under the agreement, Simon & Schuster agreed to make payments to both Hill and Pileggi. Over the next few years, according to Pileggi, he and Hill "talked at length virtually every single day, with not more than an occasional Sunday or holiday skipped. We spent more than three hundred hours together; my notes of conversations with Henry occupy more than six linear file feet." App. 27. Because producing the book required such a substantial investment of time and effort, Hill sought compensation. *Ibid.*

The result of Hill and Pileggi's collaboration was Wiseguy, which was published in January 1986. The book depicts, in colorful detail, the day-to-day existence of organized crime, [113] primarily in Hill's first-person narrative. Throughout Wiseguy, Hill frankly admits to having participated in an astonishing variety of crimes. He discusses, among other things, his conviction of extortion and the prison sentence he served. In one portion of the book, Hill recounts how members of the Mafia received preferential treatment in prison:

"The dorm was a separate three-story building outside the wall, which looked more like a Holiday Inn than a prison. There were four guys to a room, and we had comfortable beds and private baths. There were two dozen rooms on each floor, and each of them had mob guys living in them. It was

like a wiseguy convention – the whole Gotti crew, Jimmy Doyle and his guys, 'Ernie Boy' Abbamonte and 'Joe Crow' Delvecchio, Vinnie Aloi, Frank Cotroni.

"It was wild. There was wine and booze, and it was kept in bath-oil or after-shave jars. The hacks in the honor dorm were almost all on the take, and even though it was against the rules, we used to cook in our rooms. Looking back, I don't think Paulie went to the general mess five times in the two and a half years he was there. We had a stove and pots and pans and silverware stacked in the bathroom. We had glasses and an ice-water cooler where we kept the fresh meats and cheeses. When there was an inspection, we stored the stuff in the false ceiling, and once in a while, if it was confiscated, we'd just go to the kitchen and get new stuff.

"We had the best food smuggled into our dorm from the kitchen. Steaks, veal cutlets, shrimp, red snapper. Whatever the hacks could buy, we ate. It cost me two, three hundred a week. Guys like Paulie spent five hundred to a thousand bucks a week. Scotch cost thirty dollars a pint. The hacks used to bring it inside the walls in their lunch pails. We never ran out of booze, because we had six hacks bringing it in six days a week. Depending on what you wanted and how much you were [114] willing to spend, life could be almost bearable." Wiseguy 150-151.

Wiseguy was reviewed favorably: The Washington Post called it an "'amply detailed and entirely fascinating book that amounts to a piece of revisionist history,'" while New York Daily News columnist Jimmy Breslin named it "'the best book on crime in America ever written.'" App. 5. The book was also a commercial success: Within 19 months of its publication, more than a million copies were in print. A few years later, the book was converted into a film called Goodfellas, which won a host of awards as the best film of 1990.

From Henry Hill's perspective, however, the publicity generated by the book's success proved less desirable. The Crime Victims Board learned of Wiseguy in January 1986, soon after it was published.

C.　On January 31, the Board notified Simon & Schuster: "It has come to our attention that you may have contracted with a person accused or convicted of a crime for the payment of monies to such person." App. 86. The Board ordered Simon & Schuster to furnish copies of any contracts it had entered into with Hill, to provide the dollar amounts and dates of all payments it had made to Hill, and to suspend all payments to Hill in the future. Simon & Schuster complied with this order. By that time, Simon & Schuster had paid Hill's literary agent $ 96,250 in advances and royalties on Hill's behalf, and was holding $27,958 for eventual payment to Hill.

The Board reviewed the book and the contract, and on May 21, 1987, issued a proposed determination and order. The Board determined that Wiseguy was covered by § 632-a of the Executive Law, that Simon & Schuster had violated the law by failing to turn over its contract with Hill to the Board and by making payments to Hill, and that all money owed to [115] Hill under the contract had to be turned over to the Board to be held in escrow for the victims of Hill's crimes. The Board ordered Hill to turn over the payments he had already received, and ordered Simon & Schuster to turn over all money payable to Hill at the time or in the future.

Simon & Schuster brought suit in August 1987, under 42 U. S. C. § 1983, seeking a declaration that the Son of Sam law violates the First Amendment and an injunction barring the statute's enforcement. After the parties filed cross-motions for summary judgment, the District Court found the statute to be consistent with the First Amendment. 724 F. Supp. 170 (SDNY 1989). A divided Court of Appeals affirmed. *Simon & Schuster, Inc. v. Fischetti*, 916 F.2d 777 (CA2 1990).

Because the Federal Government and most of the States have enacted statutes with similar objectives, see 18 U. S. C. § 3681; Note, *Simon & Schuster, Inc. v. Fischetti:* Can New York's Son of Sam Law Survive First Amendment Challenge?, 66 Notre Dame L. Rev. 1075, n. 6 (1991) (listing state statutes), the issue is significant and likely to recur. We accordingly granted certiorari, 498 U.S. 1081 (1991), and we now reverse.

II A.   [2A] [3] A statute is presumptively inconsistent with the First Amendment if it imposes a financial burden on speakers because of the content of their speech. *Leathers v. Medlock*, 499 U.S. 439, 447, 113 L. Ed. 2d 494, 111 S. Ct. 1438 (1991). As we emphasized in invalidating a content-based magazine tax: "Official scrutiny of the content of publications as the basis for imposing a tax is entirely incompatible with the First Amendment's guarantee of freedom of the press." *Arkansas Writers' Project, Inc. v. Ragland*, 481 U.S. 221, 230, 95 L. Ed. 2d 209, 107 S. Ct. 1722 (1987). [2B][4] This is a notion so engrained in our First Amendment jurisprudence that last Term we found it so "obvious" as to [116] not require explanation. *Leathers, supra*, at 447. It is but one manifestation of a far broader principle: "Regulations which permit the Government to discriminate on the basis of the content of the message cannot be tolerated under the First Amendment." *Regan v. Time, Inc.*, 468 U.S. 641, 648-649, 82 L. Ed. 2d 487, 104 S. Ct. 3262 (1984). See also *Police Dept. of Chicago v. Mosley*, 408 U.S. 92, 95, 33 L. Ed. 2d 212, 92 S. Ct.

2286 (1972). In the context of financial regulation, it bears repeating, as we did in *Leathers*, that the government's ability to impose content-based burdens on speech raises the specter that the government may effectively drive certain ideas or viewpoints from the marketplace. 499 U.S. at 448-449. The First Amendment presumptively places this sort of discrimination beyond the power of the government. As we reiterated in *Leathers*: "'The constitutional right of free expression is . . . intended to remove governmental restraints from the arena of public discussion, putting the decision as to what views shall be voiced largely into the hands of each of us . . . in the belief that no other approach would comport with the premise of individual dignity and choice upon which our political system rests.'" *Id.*, at 448-449 (quoting *Cohen v. California*, 403 U.S. 15, 24, 29 L. Ed. 2d 284, 91 S. Ct. 1780 (1971)).

[1B] The Son of Sam law is such a content-based statute. It singles out income derived from expressive activity for a burden the State places on no other income, and it is directed only at works with a specified content. Whether the First Amendment "speaker" is considered to be Henry Hill, whose income the statute places in escrow because of the story he has told, or Simon & Schuster, which can publish books about crime with the assistance of only those criminals willing to forgo remuneration for at least five years, the statute plainly imposes a financial disincentive only on speech of a particular content.

The Board tries unsuccessfully to distinguish the Son of Sam law from the discriminatory tax at issue in *Arkansas Writers' Project*. While the Son of Sam law escrows all of the speaker's speech-derived income for at least five years, [117] rather than taxing a percentage of it outright, this difference can hardly serve as the basis for disparate treatment under the First Amendment. Both forms of financial burden operate as disincentives to speak; indeed, in many cases it will be impossible to discern in advance which type of regulation will be more costly to the speaker.

[5]   The Board next argues that discriminatory financial treatment is suspect under the First Amendment only when the legislature intends to suppress certain ideas. This assertion is incorrect; our cases have consistently held that "illicit legislative intent is not the *sine qua non* of a violation of the First Amendment." *Minneapolis Star & Tribune Co. v. Minnesota Comm'r of Revenue*, 460 U.S. 575, 592, 103 S. Ct. 1365, 75 L. Ed. 2d 295 (1983). Simon & Schuster need adduce "no evidence of an improper censorial motive." *Arkansas Writers' Project, supra*, at 228. As we concluded in *Minneapolis Star:* "We have long recognized that even regulations aimed at proper

governmental concerns can restrict unduly the exercise of rights protected by the First Amendment." 460 U.S. at 592.

[6]   Finally, the Board claims that even if the First Amendment prohibits content-based financial regulation specifically of the *media*, the Son of Sam law is different, because it imposes a general burden on any "entity" contracting with a convicted person to transmit that person's speech. Cf. *Cohen v. Cowles Media Co.*, 501 U.S. 663, 670, 115 L. Ed. 2d 586, 111 S. Ct. 2513 (1991) ("Enforcement of . . . general laws against the press is not subject to stricter scrutiny than would be applied to enforcement against other persons or organizations"). This argument falters on both semantic and constitutional grounds. Any "entity" that enters into such a contract becomes by definition a medium of communication, if it was not one already. In any event, the characterization of an entity as a member of the "media" is irrelevant for these purposes. The government's power to impose content-based financial disincentives on speech surely does not vary with the identity of the speaker.

[118] [7]   The Son of Sam law establishes a financial disincentive to create or publish works with a particular content. In order to justify such differential treatment, "the State must show that its regulation is necessary to serve a compelling state interest and is narrowly drawn to achieve that end." *Arkansas Writers' Project*, 481 U.S. at 231.

B.   [8] The Board disclaims, as it must, any state interest in suppressing descriptions of crime out of solicitude for the sensibilities of readers. See Brief for Respondents 38, n. 38. As we have often had occasion to repeat: "'The fact that society may find speech offensive is not a sufficient reason for suppressing it. Indeed, if it is the speaker's opinion that gives offense, that consequence is a reason for according it constitutional protection.'" *Hustler Magazine, Inc. v. Falwell*, 485 U.S. 46, 55, 99 L. Ed. 2d 41, 108 S. Ct. 876 (1988) (quoting *FCC v. Pacifica Foundation*, 438 U.S. 726, 745, 57 L. Ed. 2d 1073, 98 S. Ct. 3026 (1978)). "'If there is a bedrock principle underlying the First Amendment, it is that the Government may not prohibit the expression of an idea simply because society finds the idea itself offensive or disagreeable.'" *United States v. Eichman*, 496 U.S. 310, 319, 110 L. Ed. 2d 287, 110 S. Ct. 2404 (1990) (quoting *Texas v. Johnson*, 491 U.S. 397, 414, 105 L. Ed. 2d 342, 109 S. Ct. 2533 (1989)). The Board thus does not assert any interest in limiting whatever anguish Henry Hill's victims may suffer from reliving their victimization.

[1C]   There can be little doubt, on the other hand, that the State has a compelling interest in ensuring that victims of crime are compensated by those who harm them. Every State has a body of tort law serving exactly this interest. The State's interest

in preventing wrongdoers from dissipating their assets before victims can recover explains the existence of the State's statutory provisions for prejudgment remedies and orders of restitution. See N.Y. Civ. Prac. Law §§ 6201-6226 (McKinney 1980 and Supp. 1991); N.Y. Penal Law [119] § 60.27 (McKinney 1987). We have recognized the importance of this interest before, in the Sixth Amendment context. See *Caplin & Drysdale, Chartered v. United States*, 491 U.S. 617, 629, 105 L. Ed. 2d 528, 109 S. Ct. 2646, 109 S. Ct. 2667 (1989).

The State likewise has an undisputed compelling interest in ensuring that criminals do not profit from their crimes. Like most if not all States, New York has long recognized the "fundamental equitable principle," *Children of Bedford v. Petromelis*, 77 N.Y.2d at 727, 573 N.E.2d at 548, that "no one shall be permitted to profit by his own fraud, or to take advantage of his own wrong, or to found any claim upon his own iniquity, or to acquire property by his own crime." *Riggs v. Palmer*, 115 N.Y. 506, 511-512, 22 N.E. 188, 190 (1889). The force of this interest is evidenced by the State's statutory provisions for the forfeiture of the proceeds and instrumentalities of crime. See N.Y. Civ. Prac. Law §§ 1310-1352 (McKinney Supp. 1991).

The parties debate whether book royalties can properly be termed the profits of crime, but that is a question we need not address here. For the purposes of this case, we can assume without deciding that the income escrowed by the Son of Sam law represents the fruits of crime. We need only conclude that the State has a compelling interest in depriving criminals of the profits of their crimes, and in using these funds to compensate victims.

The Board attempts to define the State's interest more narrowly, as "ensuring that criminals do not profit from storytelling about their crimes before their victims have a meaningful opportunity to be compensated for their injuries." Brief for Respondents 46. Here the Board is on far shakier ground. The Board cannot explain why the State should have any greater interest in compensating victims from the proceeds of such "storytelling" than from any of the criminal's other assets. Nor can the Board offer any justification for a distinction between this expressive activity and [120] any other activity in connection with its interest in transferring the fruits of crime from criminals to their victims. Thus even if the State can be said to have an interest in classifying a criminal's assets in this manner, that interest is hardly compelling.

We have rejected similar assertions of a compelling interest in the past. In *Arkansas Writers' Project* and *Minneapolis Star*, we observed that while the State certainly has an important interest in raising revenue through taxation, that interest hardly justified selective taxation of the press, as it was completely unrelated to a press/non-press distinction. *Arkansas Writers' Project, supra*, at 231; *Minneapolis Star*, 460 U.S. at 586. Likewise, in *Carey v. Brown*, 447 U.S. 455, 467-469, 65 L. Ed. 2d 263, 100 S. Ct. 2286 (1980), we recognized the State's interest in preserving privacy by prohibiting residential picketing, but refused to permit the State to ban only non-labor picketing. This was because "nothing in the content-based labor/non-labor distinction has any bearing whatsoever on privacy." *Id.*, at 465. Much the same is true here. The distinction drawn by the Son of Sam law has nothing to do with the State's interest in transferring the proceeds of crime from criminals to their victims.

Like the government entities in the above cases, the Board has taken the *effect* of the statute and posited that effect as the State's interest. If accepted, this sort of circular defense can sidestep judicial review of almost any statute, because it makes all statutes look narrowly tailored. As Judge Newman pointed out in his dissent from the opinion of the Court of Appeals, such an argument "eliminates the entire inquiry concerning the validity of content-based discriminations. Every content-based discrimination could be upheld by simply observing that the state is anxious to regulate the designated category of speech." 916 F.2d at 785.

In short, the State has a compelling interest in compensating victims from the fruits of the crime, but little if any interest in limiting such compensation to the proceeds of the [121] wrongdoer's speech about the crime. We must therefore determine whether the Son of Sam law is narrowly tailored to advance the former, not the latter, objective.

C. [1D] As a means of ensuring that victims are compensated from the proceeds of crime, [1F] [9B] the Son of Sam law is significantly overinclusive. As counsel for the Board conceded at oral argument, the statute applies to works on *any* subject, provided that they express the author's thoughts or recollections about his crime, however tangentially or incidentally. See Tr. of Oral Arg. 30, 38; see also App. 109. In addition, the statute's broad definition of "person convicted of a crime" enables the Board to escrow the income of any author who admits in his work to having committed a crime, whether or not the author was ever actually accused or convicted. § 632-a(10)(b).

[1E] [9A] These two provisions combine to encompass a potentially very large number of works. Had the Son of Sam law been in effect at the time and place of publication, it would have escrowed payment for such works as The Autobiography of Malcolm X, which describes crimes committed by the civil rights leader before he became a public figure; Civil Disobedience, in

which Thoreau acknowledges his refusal to pay taxes and recalls his experience in jail; and even the Confessions of Saint Augustine, in which the author laments "my past foulness and the carnal corruptions of my soul," one instance of which involved the theft of pears from a neighboring vineyard. See A. Haley & Malcolm X, The Autobiography of Malcolm X 108-125 (1964); H. Thoreau, Civil Disobedience 18-22 (1849, reprinted 1969); The Confessions of Saint Augustine 31, 36-37 (Franklin Library ed. 1980). *Amicus* Association of American Publishers, Inc., has submitted a sobering bibliography listing hundreds of works by American prisoners and ex-prisoners, many of which contain descriptions of the crimes for which the authors were incarcerated, [122] including works by such authors as Emma Goldman and Martin Luther King, Jr. A list of prominent figures whose autobiographies would be subject to the statute if written is not difficult to construct: The list could include Sir Walter Raleigh, who was convicted of treason after a dubiously conducted 1603 trial; Jesse Jackson, who was arrested in 1963 for trespass and resisting arrest after attempting to be served at a lunch counter in North Carolina; and Bertrand Russell, who was jailed for seven days at the age of 89 for participating in a sit-down protest against nuclear weapons. The argument that a statute like the Son of Sam law would prevent publication of *all* of these works is hyperbole – some would have been written without compensation – but the Son of Sam law clearly reaches a wide range of literature that does not enable a criminal to profit from his crime while a victim remains uncompensated.*

---

* Because the Son of Sam law is so overinclusive, we need not address the Board's contention that the statute is content neutral under our decisions in *Ward* v. *Rock Against Racism*, 491 U.S. 781, 105 L. Ed. 2d 661, 109 S. Ct. 2746 (1989), and *Renton* v. *Playtime Theatres, Inc.*, 475 U.S. 41, 89 L. Ed. 2d 29, 106 S. Ct. 925 (1986). In these cases, we determined that statutes were content neutral where they were intended to serve purposes unrelated to the content of the regulated speech, despite their incidental effects on some speakers but not others. Even under *Ward* and *Renton*, however, regulations must be "narrowly tailored" to advance the interest asserted by the State. *Ward, supra*, at 798; *Renton, supra*, at 52. A regulation is not "narrowly tailored" – even under the more lenient tailoring standards applied in *Ward* and *Renton* – where, as here, "a substantial portion of the burden on speech does not serve to advance [the State's content-neutral] goals." *Ward, supra*, at 799. Thus whether the Son of Sam law is analyzed as content neutral under *Ward* or content based under *Leathers*, it is too overinclusive to satisfy the requirements of the First Amendment. And, in light of our conclusion in this case, we need not decide whether, as JUSTICE BLACKMUN suggests, the Son of Sam law is underinclusive as well as overinclusive. Nor does this case present a need to address

[123] Should a prominent figure write his autobiography at the end of his career, and include in an early chapter a brief recollection of having stolen (in New York) a nearly worthless item as a youthful prank, the Board would control his entire income from the book for five years, and would make that income available to all of the author's creditors, despite the fact that the statute of limitations for this minor incident had long since run. That the Son of Sam law can produce such an outcome indicates that the statute is, to say the least, not narrowly tailored to achieve the State's objective of compensating crime victims from the profits of crime.

III. [1G] The Federal Government and many of the States have enacted statutes designed to serve purposes similar to that served by the Son of Sam law. Some of these statutes may be quite different from New York's, and we have no occasion to determine the constitu-tionality of these other laws. We conclude simply that in the Son of Sam law, New York has singled out speech on a particular subject for a financial burden that it places on no other speech and no other income. The State's interest in compensating victims from the fruits of crime is a compelling one, but the Son of Sam law is not narrowly tailored to advance that objective. As a result, the statute is inconsistent with the First Amendment.

The judgment of the Court of Appeals is accordingly Reversed.

JUSTICE THOMAS took no part in the consideration or decision of this case.

CONCUR: JUSTICE BLACKMUN, concurring in the judgment.

I am in general agreement with what the Court says in its opinion. I think, however, that the New York statute is underinclusive as well as overinclusive and that we should [124] say so. Most other States have similar legislation and deserve from this Court all the guidance it can render in this very sensitive area.

CONCUR: JUSTICE KENNEDY, concurring in the judgment.

The New York statute we now consider imposes severe restrictions on authors and publishers, using as its sole criterion the content of what is written. The regulated content has the full protection of the First Amendment and this, I submit, is itself a full and sufficient reason for holding the statute unconstitutional. In my view it is both unnecessary

---

JUSTICE KENNEDY's discussion of what is a longstanding debate, see G. Gunther, Constitutional Law 1069-1070 (12th ed. 1991), on an issue which the parties before us have neither briefed nor argued.

and incorrect to ask whether the State can show that the statute "'is necessary to serve a compelling state interest and is narrowly drawn to achieve that end.'" *Ante*, at 118 (quoting *Arkansas Writers' Project, Inc. v. Ragland*, 481 U.S. 221, 231, 95 L. Ed. 2d 209, 107 S. Ct. 1722 (1987)). That test or formulation derives from our equal protection jurisprudence, see, *e.g.*, *Wygant v. Jackson Board of Ed.*, 476 U.S. 267, 273-274, 90 L. Ed. 2d 260, 106 S. Ct. 1842 (1986) (opinion of Powell, J.); *Hirabayashi v. United States*, 320 U.S. 81, 100, 87 L. Ed. 1774, 63 S. Ct. 1375 (1943), and has no real or legitimate place when the Court considers the straightforward question whether the State may enact a burdensome restriction of speech based on content only, apart from any considerations of time, place, and manner or the use of public forums.

Here, a law is directed to speech alone where the speech in question is not obscene, not defamatory, not words tantamount to an act otherwise criminal, not an impairment of some other constitutional right, not an incitement to lawless action, and not calculated or likely to bring about imminent harm the State has the substantive power to prevent. No further inquiry is necessary to reject the State's argument that the statute should be upheld.

Borrowing the compelling interest and narrow tailoring analysis is ill advised when all that is at issue is a content-based restriction, for resort to the test might be read as a [125] concession that States may censor speech whenever they believe there is a compelling justification for doing so. Our precedents and traditions allow no such inference.

This said, it must be acknowledged that the compelling interest inquiry has found its way into our First Amendment jurisprudence of late, even where the sole question is, or ought to be, whether the restriction is in fact content based. Although the notion that protected speech may be restricted on the basis of content if the restriction survives what has sometimes been termed "'the most exacting scrutiny,'" *Texas v. Johnson*, 491 U.S. 397, 412, 105 L. Ed. 2d 342, 109 S. Ct. 2533 (1989), may seem familiar, the Court appears to have adopted this formulation in First Amendment cases by accident rather than as the result of a considered judgment. In *Johnson*, for example, we cited *Boos v. Barry*, 485 U.S. 312, 321, 99 L. Ed. 2d 333, 108 S. Ct. 1157 (1988), as support for the approach. *Boos v. Barry* in turn cited *Perry Ed. Assn. v. Perry Local Educators' Assn.*, 460 U.S. 37, 45, 74 L. Ed. 2d 794, 103 S. Ct. 948 (1983), for the proposition that to justify a content-based restriction on political speech in a public forum, the State must show that "the 'regulation is necessary to serve a compelling state interest and that it is narrowly drawn to achieve that end.'" *Boos v. Barry, supra*, at 321. Turning to the appropriate page in *Perry*, we discover that the statement was supported with a citation of *Carey v. Brown*, 447 U.S. 455, 461, 65 L. Ed. 2d 263, 100 S. Ct. 2286 (1980). Looking at last to *Carey*, it turns out the Court was making a statement about equal protection: "When government regulation discriminates among speech-related activities in a public forum, the Equal Protection Clause mandates that the legislation be finely tailored to serve substantial state interests, and the justifications offered for any distinctions it draws must be carefully scrutinized." *Id.*, at 461-462. Thus was a principle of equal protection transformed into one about the government's power to regulate the content of speech in a public forum, and from this to a more general First Amendment statement about the government's power to regulate the content of speech.

[126] The employment of the compelling interest test in the present context is in no way justified by my colleagues' citation of *Arkansas Writers' Project v. Ragland. Ante,* at 118. True, both *Ragland* and the case on which it relied, *Minneapolis Star & Tribune Co. v. Minnesota Comm'r of Revenue*, 460 U.S. 575, 103 S. Ct. 1365, 75 L. Ed. 2d 295 (1983), recite either the compelling interest test or a close variant, see *Ragland, supra,* at 231; *Minneapolis Star, supra,* at 585, but neither is a case in which the State regulates speech for its content.

There are, of course, other cases, some even predating the slow metamorphosis of *Carey v. Brown's* equal protection analysis into First Amendment law, which apply the compelling interest test, but these authorities also address issues other than content censorship. See *Buckley v. Valeo*, 424 U.S. 1, 25, 46 L. Ed. 2d 659, 96 S. Ct. 612 (1976) (upholding content-neutral limitations on financial contributions to campaigns for federal office and striking down content-neutral limitations on financial expenditures for such campaigns); *Cousins v. Wigoda*, 419 U.S. 477, 489, 42 L. Ed. 2d 595, 95 S. Ct. 541 (1975) (content-neutral restriction on freedom of association); *NAACP v. Button*, 371 U.S. 415, 438, 9 L. Ed. 2d 405, 83 S. Ct. 328 (1963) (content-neutral prohibition on solicitation by lawyers); *Shelton v. Tucker*, 364 U.S. 479, 488, 5 L. Ed. 2d 231, 81 S. Ct. 247 (1960) (content-neutral statute compelling teachers in state-supported schools or colleges to disclose all organizations to which they belonged or contributed).

The inapplicability of the compelling interest test to content-based restrictions on speech is demonstrated by our repeated statement that "above all else, the First Amendment means that government has no power to restrict expression because of its message, its ideas, its subject matter, or its content." *Police Dept. of Chicago v. Mosley*, 408 U.S. 92, 95, 33 L. Ed. 2d 212, 92 S. Ct. 2286

(1972). See also *Ragland*, 481 U.S. at 229-230 (citing *Mosley); Regan v. Time, Inc.*, 468 U.S. 641, 648-649, 82 L. Ed. 2d 487, 104 S. Ct. 3262 (1984) ("Regulations which permit the Government to discriminate on the basis of the content of the message cannot be tolerated under the First Amendment"). These [127] general statements about the government's lack of power to engage in content discrimination reflect a surer basis for protecting speech than does the test used by the Court today.

There are a few legal categories in which content-based regulation has been permitted or at least contemplated. These include obscenity, see, *e.g., Miller v. California*, 413 U.S. 15, 37 L. Ed. 2d 419, 93 S. Ct. 2607 (1973), defamation, see, *e.g., Dun & Bradstreet, Inc. v. Greenmoss Builders, Inc.,* 472 U.S. 749, 86 L. Ed. 2d 593, 105 S. Ct. 2939 (1985), incitement, see, *e.g., Brandenburg v. Ohio*, 395 U.S. 444, 23 L. Ed. 2d 430, 89 S. Ct. 1827 (1969), or situations presenting some grave and imminent danger the government has the power to prevent, see, *e.g., Near v. Minnesota ex rel. Olson*, 283 U.S. 697, 716, 75 L. Ed. 1357, 51 S. Ct. 625 (1931). These are, however, historic and traditional categories long familiar to the bar, although with respect to the last category it is most difficult for the government to prevail. See *New York Times Co. v. United States*, 403 U.S. 713, 29 L. Ed. 2d 822, 91 S. Ct. 2140 (1971). While it cannot be said with certainty that the foregoing types of expression are or will remain the only ones that are without First Amendment protection, as evidenced by the proscription of some visual depictions of sexual conduct by children, see *New York v. Ferber*, 458 U.S. 747, 73 L. Ed. 2d 1113, 102 S. Ct. 3348 (1982), the use of these traditional legal categories is preferable to the sort of ad hoc balancing that the Court henceforth must perform in every case if the analysis here used becomes our standard test.

As a practical matter, perhaps we will interpret the compelling interest test in cases involving content regulation so that the results become parallel to the historic categories I have discussed, although an enterprise such as today's tends not to remain *pro forma* but to take on a life of its own. When we leave open the possibility that various sorts of content regulations are appropriate, we discount the value of our precedents and invite experiments that in fact present clear violations of the First Amendment, as is true in the case before us.

To forgo the compelling interest test in cases involving direct content-based burdens on speech would not, of course, [128] eliminate the need for difficult judgments respecting First Amendment issues. Among the questions we cannot avoid the necessity of deciding are: Whether the restricted expression falls within one of the unprotected categories discussed above, *supra,* at 127; whether some other constitutional right is impaired, see *Nebraska Press Assn. v. Stuart*, 427 U.S. 539, 49 L. Ed. 2d 683, 96 S. Ct. 2791 (1976); whether, in the case of a regulation of activity which combines expressive with non-expressive elements, the regulation aims at the activity or the expression, compare *United States v. O'Brien*, 391 U.S. 367, 20 L. Ed. 2d 672, 88 S. Ct. 1673 (1968), with *Texas v. Johnson*, 491 U.S. at 406-410; whether the regulation restricts speech itself or only the time, place, or manner of speech, see *Ward v. Rock Against Racism*, 491 U.S. 781, 105 L. Ed. 2d 661, 109 S. Ct. 2746 (1989); and whether the regulation is in fact content based or content neutral. See *Boos v. Barry*, 485 U.S. at 319-321. However difficult the lines may be to draw in some cases, here the answer to each of these questions is clear.

The case before us presents the opportunity to adhere to a surer test for content-based cases and to avoid using an unnecessary formulation, one with the capacity to weaken central protections of the First Amendment. I would recognize this opportunity to confirm our past holdings and to rule that the New York statute amounts to raw censorship based on content, censorship forbidden by the text of the First Amendment and well-settled principles protecting speech and the press. That ought to end the matter.

With these observations, I concur in the judgment of the Court holding the statute invalid.

Public Forum Doctrine

The First Amendment and government property

Focal Cases:
Cox v. New Hampshire, 312 U.S. 569 (1941)
Hill v. Colorado, 530 U.S. 703 (2000)

I f the U.S. government is said to be a government of, by and for the people, then it should follow that government property is also of, by and for the people. This reasoning is the foundation of the Supreme Court's establishment of public forum doctrine in 1939.[1] In *Hague v. CIO,* the Court wrote:

Wherever the title of streets and parks may rest, they have immemorially been held in trust for the use of the public and, time out of mind, have been used for purposes of assembly, communicating thoughts between citizens, and discussing public questions. Such use of the streets and public places has, from ancient times, been a part of the privileges, immunities, rights, and liberties of citizens.[2]

Public forum doctrine presumes the public has a right to assemble and speak on government property because government is merely the trustee of this property for the public. While public forum doctrine extends First Amendment protection to individuals who wish to use government property for purposes of free speech and association, this protection is neither absolute nor uniform.

TYPES OF FORUMS

The nature of public access provided under the public forum doctrine depends upon the nature of the property involved. In 1972, the Court said: "The nature of a place, the pattern of its normal activities, dictate the kinds of regulations ... that are reasonable. [The] crucial question is whether the manner of expression is basically incompatible with the normal activity of a particular

---

[1] Hague v. Committee for Industrial Organization, 307 U.S. 496 (1939).
[2] 307 U.S. at 515.

place at a particular time."[3] Consequently, public forum doctrine establishes three categories of property that provide a continuum of First Amendment public access rights.[4]

First, quintessentially public lands – such as parks, streets and sidewalks adjacent to public buildings – are considered traditional public forums.[5] Either government fiat or historical usage has established these traditional public forums as places of public assembly, discussion and association. Both tradition and common law support a basic right of public access to these spaces, and the public has a presumptive right to use these places for expression. Consequently, government may not close traditional public forums to the public or ban communication activities there without demonstrating a compelling need and meeting the other requirements imposed under strict scrutiny review. Government may, however, impose content neutral rules to facilitate the efficient and non-disruptive use of traditional public forums.

Second, some government locales that have not historically and do not presently serve primarily as spaces for public speech may become limited or designated public forums when government intentionally designates them as venues for compatible public speech and assembly.[6] Government often constrains the time, place and manner of public use of these places to permit the facilities to serve their primary function unhindered by the noise and confusion that might attend public assemblies. Limited public forums include public schools and university meeting rooms, public libraries, high school newspapers, state fair grounds and statehouses. Once a government facility has been opened for public use, the common law tradition of free speech prevents government from banning expressive access without a compelling reason or from making content-based discriminations among users. The Court generally reviews regulations imposed on limited public forums under intermediate scrutiny, balancing the citizen right of free expression against the primary role of the facility. In general, government may impose well tailored, reasonable, content-neutral licensing and usage regulations to facilitate both governmental and citizen use of limited public forum space. Speech and access compatible with the location's primary function usually must be permitted.

Finally, government may designate its property as non-public forums when public access, assembly and speech would undermine the proper functioning of a government facility and where government has demonstrated no intent or history of open access. In non-public forums, government drops its role as trustee, behaves more like a private property owner and controls the space to achieve government objectives.[7] The Supreme Court has ruled that military bases, prisons, post office walkways, utility poles, airport terminals and mailboxes are among the government spaces that may be closed to the public for speech and assembly purposes.[8] Government may exclude the entire public or certain speakers or messages from non-public forums based on a reasonable or rational, viewpoint-neutral interest.

These three public forum categories are far from absolute. For example, the Supreme Court has permitted government to ban public access and expression from traditional public forums such as sidewalks and streets if the expression endangers core privacy or health interests. Thus, the Court has prohibited targeted picketing outside a doctor's residence and has created non-expressive buffer zones around abortion facilities.[9] In contrast, although the First Amendment generally does not dictate the behavior of private citizens, the Supreme Court occasionally has applied public forum doctrine to require private property owners to open their property to public expression. The Court has said that when private property fulfills a quasi-public purpose or serves the functional equivalent of a public space – such as may occur in the open area of a shopping

---

[3] Grayned v. Rockford, 408 U.S. 104, 116 (1972).

[4] *See, e.g.,* Perry Education Association v. Perry Local Educators' Association, 460 U.S. 37 (1983).

[5] *See, e.g.,* Hague v. Committee for Industrial Organization, 307 U.S. 496 (1939).

[6] *See, e.g.,* Greer v. Spock, 424 U.S. 828 (1976).

mall or a parking lot that is used widely for public assembly and expression – that owner must allow the free expression protected in a traditional public forum.[10]

GOVERNMENT SUBSIDIES

Not all public forums exist in physical space; public forum analysis also has guided some Supreme Court decisions involving taxation and government funding of expression.[11] Because the distribution of or exclusion from government financial benefits can implicate speech, the Court has ruled that state funding or taxation policies that discriminate based on viewpoint violate the Constitution. Although government is not obligated to subsidize private expressive activities, government funding of private expression may create a virtual public forum in which government must respect equal protection interests and eschew viewpoint-based discriminations.[12] Thus, for example, a university may not discriminate against student religious publications when it distributes student funds to support student activities.[13] The same holds true when government imposes taxes or provides tax-exemptions on expression; these obligations or benefits must be non-discriminatory and may not, for example, disfavor large newspapers, general interest magazines or commercial publications.[14]

The Supreme Court has not been entirely clear, however, on when government funding creates a public forum. For instance, the Court has ruled that government funding of the arts through the National Endowment for the Arts does not establish a public forum and may, therefore, incorporate standards to advance the objectives of the NEA that may disfavor indecent or offensive artwork.[15] A plurality of the Court relied upon similar reasoning to rule that although public school librarians may make curriculum and age-based value judgments about content to guide book acquisitions, they may not remove books from school libraries simply because the book's viewpoint is offensive.[16]

GOVERNMENT AS EMPLOYER

As the foregoing suggests, government rarely has power to discriminate among speakers in public forums. Yet, government may impose reasonable speech-related restrictions that differentially affect certain categories of speakers in non-public forums, and it may control some speech of its own workers. Few bright lines exist in the jurisprudence of government employee speech, in part because of the many, weighty interests at stake. Clearly, however, citizens do not

---

[7] *See, e.g.*, Adderley v. Florida, 385 U.S. 39 (1966).

[8] *See, e.g.*, United States v. Albertini, 472 U.S. 675 (1985); Los Angeles City Council v. Taxpayers for Vincent, 466 U.S. 789 (1984); United States v. Kokinda, 497 U.S. 720 (1990).

[9] *See, e.g.*, Frisby v. Schultz, 487 U.S. 474 (1988); Madsen v. Women's Health Center, Inc., 512 U.S. 753 (1994). *But see* Scheidler v. National Organization for Women, 537 U.S. 393 (2003) (removing civil injunction on anti-abortion protesters and rejecting claim that their protests constituted illegal extortion and racketeering).

[10] *See, e.g.*, Amalgamated Food Employees Union v. Logan Valley Plaza, Inc., 391 U.S. 308 (1968); Hudgens v. National Labor Relations Board, 424 U.S. 507 (1976); Pruneyard Shopping Center v. Robins, 447 U.S. 74 (1980). *But see* Lloyd Corp., Ltd. v. Tanner, 407 U.S. 551 (1972).

[11] *See, generally*, Frederick Schauer, *Principles, Institutions and the First Amendment*, 112 HARV. L. REV. 84 (1998).

[12] *See, e.g.*, Board of Regents of the University of Wisconsin System v. Southworth, 529 U.S. 217 (2000); Rosenberger v. Rector and Visitors of the University of Virginia, 515 U.S. 819 (1995).

[13] Rosenberger v. Rector and Visitors of the University of Virginia, 515 U.S. 819 (1995).

[14] *See, e.g.*, Grosjean v. American Press Co., 297 U.S. 233 (1936); Minneapolis Star & Tribune Co. v. Minnesota Commissioner of Revenue, 460 U.S. 575 (1983); Arkansas Writers' Project v. Ragland, 481 U.S. 221 (1987). *But see* Leathers v. Medlock, 499 U.S. 439 (1991).

[15] National Endowment for the Arts v. Finley, 524 U.S. 569 (1998).

[16] Island Trees Union Free School District Board of Education v. Pico, 457 U.S. 853 (1982).

abandon their First Amendment rights when they accept government employ.[17] Nor does the public lose its First Amendment-related interest in access to critical government information when that information is held exclusively by state employees. Nevertheless, it is equally clear that government classification of highly sensitive material would be ineffective if government had no power to control the speech of its workers.[18]

The crux of the issue is to distinguish the right of government to dictate appropriate behavior of its employees from the limit on government power to regulate freedom of expression.[19] In general, government enjoys the discretion of an employer to advance compelling government interests or to control workers' speech that is not of significant public interest. However, if the employee's speech relates to a matter of public concern – particularly if the speech involves issues of self-governance[20] – the Supreme Court employs a form of intermediate scrutiny to review the government's action. Under this standard, the Court has affirmed laws prohibiting political campaigning by federal employees[21] and has protected the right of government employees to communicate privately with their supervisors.[22]

CONTENT-NEUTRAL LAWS IN THE PUBLIC FORUM

Some observers believe public forum doctrine has been vital to dissent in America.[23] In recent times, the doctrine has extended constitutional protection to Nazi marches, anti-Vietnam War protests and Civil Rights sit-ins, assemblies, boycotts and marches.[24] The Court has applied public forum analysis to strike down laws prohibiting leafleting.[25] Yet, somewhat illogically, the doctrine has not rendered unconstitutional various laws banning demonstrations outside abortion clinics.[26]

Most outright bans on speech activity in public forums do not survive constitutional scrutiny. In 2003, however, the Supreme Court said a city provision that banned all access to the city's housing projects for non-residents with no "legitimate business ... or social" purpose was not facially overbroad.[27] The Court said the no-trespass policy and the city's unwritten rule that required permission from the housing manager to distribute leaflets or to demonstrate might be

---

[17] See, e.g., Perry v. Sindermann, 408 U.S. 593 (1972). For discussion of parallel treatment of public school students, see Chap. 13 and Tinker v. Des Moines Independent Community School Dist., 393 U.S. 503 (1969).

[18] See Snepp v. United States, 444 U.S. 507 (1980); SISSELA BOK, SECRETS (1993). But see RICHARD O. CURRY (ed.), FREEDOM AT RISK: SECRECY, CENSORSHIP, AND REPRESSION IN THE 1980S (1998); Benjamin S. DuVal Jr., The Occasions of Secrecy, 47 U. PITT. L. REV. 579 (Spring 1986); DANIEL N. HOFFMAN, GOVERNMENTAL SECRECY AND THE FOUNDING FATHERS: A STUDY IN CONSTITUTIONAL CONTROLS (1981); Seth F. Kreimer, Sunlight Secrets and Scarlet Letters: The Tension Between Privacy and Disclosure in Constitutional Law, 140 U. PA. L. REV. 1 (1991); Kermit L. Hall, The Virulence of the National Appetite for Bogus Revelation, 56 MD. L. REV. 1 (1997).

[19] See, e.g., Pickering v. Board of Education, 391 U.S. 563 (1968); Toni M. Massaro, Significant Silences: Freedom of Speech in the Public Sector Workplace, 61 S.CAL. L. REV. 1 (1987).

[20] See, e.g., Rankin v. McPherson, 483 U.S. 378 (1987).

[21] See, e.g., United Public Workers of America v. Mitchell, 330 U.S. 75 (1947); United States Civil Service Commission v. National Association of Letter Carriers, 413 U.S. 548 (1973).

[22] See, e.g., Givhan v. Western Line Consolidated School District, 439 U.S. 410 (1979).

[23] See, e.g., Susan Dente Ross, An Apologia to Radical Dissent and a Supreme Court Test to Protect It, 7 COMM. L. & POLICY 401 (Autumn, 2002); Ronald J. Krotoszynski, Jr., Essay: Celebrating Selma: The Importance of Context in Public Forum Analysis, 104 YALE L.J. 1411 (April 1995).

[24] See, e.g., Village of Skokie v. National Socialist Party of America, 439 U.S. 916 (1978); Hess v Indiana, 414 U.S. 105 (1973); Brown v. Louisiana, 383 U.S. 131 (1966). Edwards v. South Carolina, 371 U.S. 229 (1963); NAACP v. Claiborne Hardware Co., 458 U.S. 886 (1982); Gregory v. City of Chicago, 394 U.S. 111 (1969); Grayned v. Rockford, 408 U.S. 104 (1972).

[25] See, e.g., Schneider v. New Jersey, 308 U.S. 147 (1939); United States v. Grace, 461 U.S. 171 (1983).

[26] See, e.g., Madsen v. Women's Health Center, 512 U.S. 753 (1994); Schenck v. Pro-Choice Network of Western New York, 519 U.S. 357 (1997); Hill v. Colorado, 530 U.S. 703 (2000).

[27] Virginia v. Hicks, 123 S.Ct. 2191 (2003).

unconstitutional *as applied* if they were employed to prohibit "a substantial amount" of protected speech.[28]

The Court consistently has held that government may impose well-crafted, content-neutral licensing, permit and fee provisions to provide for effective use of public forums and to minimize the risk of violence or disorder as long as the provisions do not give administrators unfettered discretion.[29] While licensing and registration requirements for use of public forums may violate the constitution if they unduly infringe protected free speech,[30] laws dictating the placement of news racks on public sidewalks and establishing standardized application processes and non-discriminatory fees for assembly and parade permits generally are constitutional.

READING THE PUBLIC FORUM CASES

Below you will read excerpts from one of the early public forum cases, *Cox v. New Hampshire*, in which the Supreme Court establishes the authority of government to employ licensing provisions to assure the orderly use of public streets and walkways. Then you will read one of the Court's more recent public forum decisions, *Hill v. Colorado*, in its entirety. *Hill* is the latest in a series of Supreme Court rulings limiting the speech protection of public forum doctrine when free expression in public areas is balanced against individual interests in health and privacy.

To better understand the breadth and the limits of public forum doctrine, you may wish to read some of the following cases. This is not an exhaustive list of public forum decisions. Rather, these cases highlight some of the important areas in which the Supreme Court has applied the doctrine. Other important cases involving public forum doctrine will appear in subsequent chapters of this text.

- *Chicago v. Morales*, 527 U.S. 41 (1999) (striking ban on public loitering by suspected gang members as unconstitutionally vague).
- *National Endowment for the Arts v. Finley*, 524 U.S. 569 (1998) (affirming government authority to consider decency criteria in funding decisions).
- *Rosenberger v. Rector and Visitors of the University of Virginia*, 515 U.S. 819 (1995) (finding disbursement of student fees constitutes a public forum).
- *Madsen v. Women's Health Center, Inc.*, 512 U.S. 753 (1994) (affirming constitutionality of non-protest zone that encompasses public sidewalk).
- *United States v. Kokinda*, 497 U.S. 720 (1990) (holding that post office walkway is not a public forum).
- *Boos v. Barry*, 485 U.S. 313 (1988) (finding ban on demonstrations outside foreign consulates unconstitutional).
- *Pruneyard Shopping Center v. Robins*, 447 U.S. 74 (1980) (applying public forum analysis to private shopping center).
- *Village of Skokie v. National Socialist Party of America*, 439 U.S. 916 (1978) (striking down law prohibiting Nazi march and racist displays).
- *Hague v. Committee for Industrial Organization*, 307 U.S. 496 (1939) (establishing public forum concepts).

Use these questions to help you read critically and focus on the important aspects of the following cases.

---

[28] Hicks at 2199.

[29] *See, e.g.*, Cox v. New Hampshire, 312 U.S. 569 (1941); Cincinnati v. Discovery Network, Inc., 507 U.S. 410 (1993); Thomas v. Chicago Park Dist., 534 U.S. 316 (2002). But see, e.g., City of Lakewood v. Plain Dealer Publishing Co., 486 U.S. 750 (1988); Forsythe County, Ga. v. Nationalist Movement, 505 U.S. 123 (1992).

[30] Watchtower Bible & Tract Society of NY v. Stratton, 536 U.S. 150 (2002).

- What type of public forum is involved in each case?
- What is the burden of proof, and where is it placed?
- Does the Supreme Court require government to justify the precise requirements of its regulatory strategy? Is tailoring an issue?
- What special nature of the place, the speakers or the government regulation is most significant to the Court's ruling?
- How does the Court resolve the conflict between the rights of the group to assemble and speak and the rights of individuals who might wish to use the public streets and walkways for other reasons?
- How does the Court address concerns of equal access and non-discriminatory treatment? Is this concern central to the ruling? Why?
- Does the Court's reliance on public forum doctrine in these cases advance or impede First Amendment interests? Would the case outcome change if evaluated under the rules that apply to content-based and content-neutral regulations?
- What do these cases indicate about the limits of public forum doctrine?
- What are the specific concerns raised by the dissenting justices?

Cox v. New Hampshire
312 U.S. 569
(1941)
(Excerpts only. Footnotes omitted.)

Author's Note: Sixty-eight Jehovah's Witnesses were convicted in the municipal court of Manchester, New Hampshire, for violating a state law requiring a license before conducting a parade or procession on a public street. They had marched peacefully, single-file in four or five groups along the public sidewalks, carrying signs and distributing leaflets. Five members of the group challenged the law as an unconstitutional abridgement of their freedom of worship, speech, press, and assembly. They also argued that the law was unconstitutionally vague and vested undue discretion in the licensing authority. Both lower courts upheld the conviction, and the Supreme Court affirmed.

JUDGES: Hughes, McReynolds, Stone, Roberts, Black, Reed, Frankfurter, Douglas, Murphy

OPINION: [574] The authority of a municipality to impose regulations in order to assure the safety and convenience of the people in the use of public highways has never been regarded as inconsistent with civil liberties but rather as one of the means of safeguarding the good order upon which they ultimately depend. ... As regulation of the use of the streets for parades and processions is a traditional exercise of control by local government, the question in a particular case is whether that control is exerted so as not to deny or unwarrantedly abridge the right of assembly and the opportunities for the communication of thought and the discussion of public questions immemorially associated with resort to public places.

[575]...[It is] significant that the statute prescribed no measures for controlling or suppressing the publication on the highways of facts and opinions, either by speech or by writing; that communication by the distribution of literature or by the display of placards and signs was in no respect regulated by the statute; that the regulation with respect to parades and processions was applicable only to organized formations of persons using the highways; and that the defendants, separately, or collectively in groups not constituting a parade or procession, were under no contemplation of the Act. ... [The] interference with liberty of speech and writing seemed slight.

...[Reviewing the statute] with regard only to considerations of time, place and manner so as to [576] conserve the public convenience ... the court further observed that, in fixing time and place, the license served to prevent confusion by overlapping parades or processions, to secure convenient use of the streets by other travelers, and to minimize the risk of disorder. But the court held that the licensing board was not vested with arbitrary power or an unfettered discretion; that its discretion must be exercised with uniformity of method of treatment upon the facts of each application, free from improper or inappropriate considerations and from unfair discrimination; that a systematic, consistent and just order of treatment, with reference to the convenience of public use of the highways, is the statutory mandate.

If a municipality has authority to control the use of its public streets for parades or processions, as it undoubtedly has, it cannot be denied authority to give consideration, without unfair discrimination, to time, place and manner in relation to the other proper uses of the streets. We find it impossible to say that the limited authority conferred by the licensing provisions of the statute in question as thus construed by the state court contravened any constitutional right.

... There remains the question of license fee[] which, as the court said, ... [577] was held to be not a revenue tax, but one to meet the expense incident to the administration of the Act and to the maintenance of public order in the matter licensed. There is nothing contrary to the Constitution in the charge of a fee limited to the purpose stated. The suggestion that a flat fee should have been charged fails to take account of the difficulty of framing a fair schedule to meet all circumstances, and we perceive no constitutional ground for denying to local governments that flexibility of adjustment of fees which in the light of varying conditions would tend to conserve rather than impair the liberty sought.

HILL v. COLORADO
530 U.S. 703
(2000)

JUDGES: STEVENS, J., delivered the opinion of the Court, in which REHN-QUIST, C. J., and O'CONNOR, SOUTER, GINSBURG, and BREYER, JJ., joined. SOUTER, J., filed a concurring opinion, in which O'CONNOR, GINSBURG, and BREYER, JJ., joined. SCALIA, J., filed a dissenting opinion, in which THOMAS, J., joined. KENNEDY, J., filed a dissenting opinion.

OPINION: [707] JUSTICE STEVENS delivered the opinion of the Court.

[1A] At issue is the constitutionality of a 1993 Colorado statute that regulates speech-related conduct within 100 feet of the entrance to any health care facility. The specific section of the statute that is challenged, Colo. Rev. Stat. § 18-9-122(3) (1999), makes it unlawful within the regulated areas for any person to "knowingly approach" within eight feet of another person, without that person's consent, "for the purpose of passing a leaflet or handbill to, displaying a sign to, or engaging in oral protest, education, or counseling with such other person . . . ."[1] Although the statute prohibits speakers

from [708] approaching unwilling listeners, it does not require a standing speaker to move away from anyone passing by. Nor does it place any restriction on the content of any message that anyone may wish to communicate to anyone else, either inside or outside the regulated areas. It does, however, make it more difficult to give unwanted advice, particularly in the form of a handbill or leaflet, to persons entering or leaving medical facilities.

The question is whether the First Amendment rights of the speaker are abridged by the protection the statute provides for the unwilling listener.

I. Five months after the statute was enacted, petitioners filed a complaint in the District Court for Jefferson County, Colorado, praying for a declaration

---

[1] The entire § 18-9-122 reads as follows:
"(1) The general assembly recognizes that access to health care facilities for the purpose of obtaining medical counseling and treatment is imperative for the citizens of this state; that the exercise of a person's right to protest or counsel against certain medical procedures must be balanced against another person's right to obtain medical counseling and treatment in an unobstructed manner; and that preventing the willful obstruction of a person's access to medical counseling and treatment at a health care facility is a matter of statewide concern. The general assembly therefore declares that it is appropriate to enact legislation that prohibits a person from knowingly obstructing another person's entry to or exit from a health care facility.

"(2) A person commits a class 3 misdemeanor if such person knowingly obstructs, detains, hinders, impedes, or blocks another person's entry to or exit from a health care facility. "(3) No person shall knowingly approach another person within eight feet of such person, unless such other person consents, for the purpose of passing a leaflet or handbill to, displaying a sign to, or engaging in oral protest, education, or counseling with such other person in the public way or sidewalk area within a radius of one hundred feet from any entrance door to a health care facility. Any person who violates this subsection (3) commits a class 3 misdemeanor. "(4) For the purposes of this section, 'health care facility' means any entity that is licensed, certified, or otherwise authorized or permitted by law to administer medical treatment in this state. "(5) Nothing in this section shall be construed to prohibit a statutory or home rule city or county or city and county from adopting a law for the control of access to health care facilities that is no less restrictive than the provisions of this section. "(6) In addition to, and not in lieu of, the penalties set forth in this section, a person who violates the provisions of this section shall be subject to civil liability, as provided in section 13-21-106.7, C. R. S."

that § 18-9- 122(3) was facially invalid and seeking an injunction against its enforcement. They stated that prior to the enactment of the statute, they had engaged in "sidewalk counseling" on the public ways and sidewalks within 100 feet of the entrances to facilities where human abortion is practiced or where medical personnel refer women to other facilities for abortions. "Sidewalk counseling" consists of efforts "to educate, counsel, persuade, or inform passersby about abortion and abortion alternatives by means of verbal or written speech, including conversation and/or display of signs and/or distribution of literature."[2] They further alleged that such activities frequently entail being within eight feet of other persons and that their fear of prosecution under the new statute [709] caused them "to be chilled in the exercise of fundamental constitutional rights."[3]

Count 5 of the complaint claimed violations of the right to free speech protected by the First Amendment to the Federal Constitution, and Count 6 alleged that the impairment of the right to distribute written materials was a violation of the right to a free press.[4] The complaint also argued that the statutory consent requirement was invalid as a prior restraint tantamount to a licensing requirement, that the statute was vague and overbroad, and that it was a content-based restriction that was not justified by a compelling state interest. Finally, petitioners contended that § 18-9-122(3) was content based for two reasons: The content of the speech must be examined to determine whether it "constitutes oral protest, counseling and education"; and that it is "viewpoint-based" because the statute "makes it likely that prosecution will occur based on displeasure with the position taken by the speaker."[5]

In their answers to the complaint, respondents admitted virtually all of the factual allegations. They filed a motion for summary judgment supported by affidavits, which included a transcript of the hearings that preceded the enactment of the statute. It is apparent from the testimony of both supporters and opponents of the statute that demonstrations in front of abortion clinics impeded access to those clinics and were often confrontational.[6] Indeed, it was a common practice to provide escorts for persons entering and leaving the clinics both to ensure their access and to provide [710] protection from aggressive counselors who sometimes used strong and abusive language in face-to-face encounters.[7] There was also evidence that emotional confrontations may adversely affect a patient's medical care.[8] There was no evidence, however, that the "sidewalk counseling" conducted by petitioners in this case was ever abusive or confrontational.

The District Judge granted respondents' motion and dismissed the complaint. Because the statute had not actually been enforced against petitioners, he found that they only raised a facial challenge.[9] He agreed with petitioners that their sidewalk counseling was conducted in a "quintessential" public forum, but held that the statute permissibly imposed content-neutral "time, place, and manner restrictions" that were narrowly tailored to serve a significant government interest, and left open ample alternative channels of communication.[10] Relying on Ward v. Rock Against Racism, [711] 491 U.S. 781, 785, 105 L. Ed. 2d 661, 109 S. Ct. 2746 (1989), he noted that "'the principal inquiry in determining content neutrality . . . is whether the government has adopted a regulation of speech because of disagreement with the message it conveys.'" He found that the text of the statute "applies to all viewpoints, rather than certain viewpoints," and that the legislative history made it clear that the State had not favored one viewpoint over another.[11] He concluded that the "free zone" created by the statute was narrowly tailored under the test announced in Ward, and that it left open ample alternative means of communication because signs and leaflets may be seen, and speech

---

[2] App. 17.

[3] Id. at 18-19.

[4] Counts 1 through 4 alleged violations of the Colorado Constitution, Count 7 alleged a violation of the right to peaceable assembly, and Counts 8 and 9 alleged violations of the Due Process and Equal Protection Clauses of the Fourteenth Amendment.

[5] Id. at 25-26.

[6] The legislature also heard testimony that other types of protests at medical facilities, such as those involving animal rights, create difficulties for persons attempting to enter the facility. App. to Pet. for Cert. 40a.

[7] A nurse practitioner testified that some antiabortion protesters "'yell, thrust signs in faces, and generally try to upset the patient as much as possible, which makes it much more difficult for us to provide care in a scary situation anyway.'" Hill v. Thomas, 973 P.2d 1246, 1250 (Colo. 1999). A volunteer who escorts patients into and out of clinics testified that the protestors "'are flashing their bloody fetus signs. They are yelling, "you are killing your baby." They are talking about fetuses and babies being dismembered, arms and legs torn off . . . a mother and her daughter . . . were immediately surrounded and yelled at and screamed at . . . .'" Id. at 1250-1251.

[8] A witness representing the Colorado Coalition of Persons with Disabilities, who had had 35 separate surgeries in the preceding eight years testified: "Each and every one is tough. And the night before and the morning of any medical procedure that's invasive is the toughest part of all. You don't need additional stressors placed on you while you're trying to do it . . . . We all know about our own personal faith. You don't need somebody standing in your face screaming at you when you are going in for what may be one of the most traumatic experiences of your life anyway. Why make it more traumatic?" App. 108.

[9] App. to Pet. for Cert. 31a.

[10] Id. at 32a.

[11] Id. at 32a-33a.

may be heard, at a distance of eight feet. Noting that the petitioners had stated in their affidavits that they intended to "continue with their protected First Amendment activities," he rejected their overbreadth challenge because he believed "the statute will do little to deter protected speech."[12] Finally, he concluded that the statute was not vague and that the prior restraint doctrine was inapplicable because the "statute requires no license or permit scheme prior to speaking."[13]

The Colorado Court of Appeals affirmed for reasons similar to those given by the District Judge. It noted that even though only seven percent of the patients receiving services at one of the clinics were there to obtain abortion services, all 60,000 of that clinic's patients "were subjected to the same treatment by protesters."[14] It also reviewed our then-recent decision in Madsen v. Women's Health Center, Inc., 512 U.S. 753, 129 L. Ed. 2d 593, 114 S. Ct. 2516 (1994), and concluded that Madsen's reasoning supported the conclusion that the statute was content neutral.[15]

[712] In 1996, the Supreme Court of Colorado denied review,[16] and petitioners sought a writ of certiorari from our Court. While their petition was pending, we decided Schenck v. Pro-Choice Network of Western N.Y., 519 U.S. 357, 137 L. Ed. 2d 1, 117 S. Ct. 855 (1997). Because we held in that case that an injunctive provision creating a speech-free "floating buffer zone" with a 15-foot radius violates the First Amendment, we granted certiorari, vacated the judgment of the Colorado Court of Appeals, and remanded the case to that court for further consideration in light of Schenck. 519 U.S. 1145 (1997).

On remand the Court of Appeals reinstated its judgment upholding the statute. It noted that in Schenck we had "expressly declined to hold that a valid governmental interest in ensuring ingress and egress to a medical clinic may never be sufficient to justify a zone of separation between individuals entering and leaving the premises and protesters" and that our opinion in Ward provided the standard for assessing the validity of a content-neutral, generally applicable statute. Under that standard, even though a 15-foot floating buffer might preclude protesters from expressing their views from a normal conversational distance, a lesser distance of eight feet was sufficient to protect such speech on a public sidewalk.[17]

The Colorado Supreme Court granted certiorari and affirmed the judgment of the Court of Appeals. In a thorough opinion, the court began by commenting on certain matters that were not in dispute. It reviewed the history of the statute in detail and concluded that it was intended to protect both the "citizen's 'right to protest' or counsel against certain medical procedures" and also to ensure "that government protects 'a person's right to obtain medical counseling and treatment.'"[18] It noted that both the trial court and the Court of Appeals had concluded that the statute was content [713] neutral, that petitioners no longer contended otherwise, and that they agreed that the question for decision was whether the statute was a valid time, place, and manner restriction under the test announced in Ward.[19]

The court identified two important distinctions between this case and Schenck. First, Schenck involved a judicial decree and therefore, as explained in Madsen, posed "greater risks of censorship and discriminatory application than do general ordinances."[20] Second, unlike the floating buffer zone in Schenck, which would require a protester either to stop talking or to get off the sidewalk whenever a patient came within 15 feet, the "knowingly approaches" requirement in the Colorado statute allows a protester to stand still while a person moving towards or away from a health care facility walks past her.[21] Applying the test in Ward, the court concluded that the statute was narrowly drawn to further a significant government interest. It rejected petitioners' contention that it was not narrow enough because it applied to all health care facilities in the State. In the court's view, the comprehensive coverage of the statute was a factor that supported its content neutrality. Moreover, the fact that the statute

---

[12] Id. at 35a.

[13] Id. at 36a.

[14] Hill v. Lakewood, 911 P.2d 670, 672 (1995).

[15] Id. at 673-674.

[16] App. to Pet. for Cert. 46a.

[17] Hill v. Lakewood, 949 P.2d 107, 109 (1997).

[18] 973 P.2d at 1249 (quoting § 18-9-122(1)).

[19] "Petitioners concede that the test for a time, place, and manner restriction is the appropriate measure of this statute's constitutionality. See Tape Recording of Oral Argument, Oct. 19, 1998, statement of James M. Henderson, Esq. Petitioners argue that pursuant to the test announced in Ward, the 'floating buffer zone' created by section 18-9- 122(3) is not narrowly tailored to serve a significant government interest and that section 18-9-122(3) does not provide for ample alternative channels of communication. We disagree." Id. at 1251.
"We note that both the trial court and the court of appeals found that section 18-9-122(3) is content-neutral, and that petitioners do not contend otherwise in this appeal." Id. at 1256.

[20] Madsen v. Women's Health Center, Inc., 512 U.S. 753, 764, 129 L. Ed. 2d 593, 114 S. Ct. 2516 (1994).

[21] 973 P.2d at 1257-1258 ("What renders this statute less restrictive than . . . the injunction in Schenck . . . is that under section 18-9-122(3), there is no duty to withdraw placed upon petitioners even within the eight-foot limited floating buffer zone").

was enacted, in part, because the General [714] Assembly "was concerned with the safety of individuals seeking wide-ranging health care services, not merely abortion counseling and procedures," added to the substantiality of the government interest that it served.[22] Finally, it concluded that ample alternative channels remain open because petitioners, and "indeed, everyone, are still able to protest, counsel, shout, implore, dissuade, persuade, educate, inform, and distribute literature regarding abortion. They just cannot knowingly approach within eight feet of an individual who is within 100 feet of a health care facility entrance without that individual's consent. As articulated so well . . . in Ward, ['the fact that § 18-9-122(3)] may reduce to some degree the potential audience for [petitioners'] speech is of no consequence, for there has been no showing that the remaining avenues of communication are inadequate.'"[23]

Because of the importance of the case, we granted certiorari. 527 U.S. 1068 (1999). We now affirm.

II. Before confronting the question whether the Colorado statute reflects an acceptable balance between the constitutionally protected rights of law-abiding speakers and the interests of unwilling listeners, it is appropriate to examine the competing interests at stake. A brief review of both sides of the dispute reveals that each has legitimate and important concerns.

[2] The First Amendment interests of petitioners are clear and undisputed. As a preface to their legal challenge, petitioners emphasize three propositions. First, they accurately explain that the areas protected by the statute encompass all the public ways within 100 feet [715] of every entrance to every health care facility everywhere in the State of Colorado. There is no disagreement on this point, even though the legislative history makes it clear that its enactment was primarily motivated by activities in the vicinity of abortion clinics. Second, they correctly state that their leafleting, sign displays, and oral communications are protected by the First Amendment. The fact that the messages conveyed by those communications may be offensive to their recipients does not deprive them of constitutional protection. Third, the public sidewalks, streets, and ways affected by the statute are "quintessential" public forums for free speech. Finally, although there is debate about the magnitude of the statutory impediment to their ability to communicate effectively with persons in the regulated zones, that ability, particularly the ability to distribute leaflets, is unquestionably lessened by this statute.

[1B] On the other hand, petitioners do not challenge the legitimacy of the state interests that the statute is intended to serve. It is a traditional exercise of the States' "police powers to protect the health and safety of their citizens." Medtronic, Inc. v. Lohr, 518 U.S. 470, 475, 135 L. Ed. 2d 700, 116 S. Ct. 2240 (1996). That interest may justify a special focus on unimpeded access to health care facilities and the avoidance of potential trauma to patients associated with confrontational protests. See Madsen v. Women's Health Center, Inc., 512 U.S. 753, 129 L. Ed. 2d 593, 114 S. Ct. 2516 (1994); NLRB v. Baptist Hospital, Inc., 442 U.S. 773, 61 L. Ed. 2d 251, 99 S. Ct. 2598 (1979). Moreover, as with every exercise of a State's police powers, rules that provide specific guidance to enforcement authorities serve the interest in even-handed application of the law. Whether or not those interests justify the particular regulation at issue, they are unquestionably legitimate.

It is also important when conducting this interest analysis to recognize the significant difference between state restrictions [716] on a speaker's right to address a willing audience and those that protect listeners from unwanted communication. This statute deals only with the latter.

[3A] The right to free speech, of course, includes the right to attempt to persuade others to change their views, and may not be curtailed simply because the speaker's message may be offensive to his audience. But the protection afforded to offensive messages does not always embrace offensive speech that is so intrusive that the unwilling audience cannot avoid it. Frisby v. Schultz, 487 U.S. 474, 487, 101 L. Ed. 2d 420, 108 S. Ct. 2495 (1988). Indeed, "it may not be the content of the speech, as much as the deliberate 'verbal or visual assault,' that justifies proscription." Erznoznik v. Jacksonville, 422 U.S. 205, 210-211, n. 6, 45 L. Ed. 2d 125, 95 S. Ct. 2268 (1975) (citation and brackets omitted). Even in a public forum, one of the reasons we tolerate a protester's right to wear a jacket expressing his opposition to government policy in vulgar language is because offended viewers can "effectively avoid further bombardment of their sensibilities simply by averting their eyes." Cohen v. California, 403 U.S. 15, 21, 29 L. Ed. 2d 284, 91 S. Ct. 1780 (1971).

The recognizable privacy interest in avoiding unwanted communication varies widely in different settings. It is far less important when "strolling through Central Park" than when "in the confines of one's own home," or when persons are "powerless to avoid" it. Id. at 21-22. But even the interest in preserving tranquility in "the Sheep Meadow" portion of Central Park may at times justify official restraints on offensive musical expression. Ward, 491 U.S. at 784, 792. More specific to the facts of this case, we have recognized that "the First Amendment does not demand that

---

[22] Id. at 1258.

[23] Ibid. (quoting Ward v. Rock Against Racism, 491 U.S. 781, 802, 105 L. Ed. 2d 661, 109 S. Ct. 2746 (1989)).

patients at a medical facility undertake Herculean efforts to escape the cacophony of political protests." Madsen, 512 U.S. at 772-773.

[1C] [3B] The unwilling listener's interest in avoiding unwanted communication has been repeatedly identified in our cases. It is an aspect of the broader "right to be let alone" that one of our wisest Justices characterized as "the most comprehensive of rights and the right most valued by civilized men." Olmstead v. United States, 277 U.S. 438, 478, 72 L. Ed. [717] 944, 48 S. Ct. 564 (1928) (Brandeis, J., dissenting).[24] The right to avoid unwelcome speech has special force in the privacy of the home, Rowan v. Post Office Dept., 397 U.S. 728, 738, 25 L. Ed. 2d 736, 90 S. Ct. 1484 (1970), and its immediate surroundings, Frisby v. Schultz, 487 U.S. at 485, but can also be protected in confrontational settings. Thus, this comment on the right to free passage in going to and from work applies equally – or perhaps with greater force – to access to a medical facility:

"How far may men go in persuasion and communication, and still not violate the right of those whom they would influence? In going to and from work, men have a right to as free a passage without obstruction as the streets afford, consistent with the right of others to enjoy the same privilege. We are a social people, and the accosting by one of another in an inoffensive way and an offer by one to communicate and discuss information with a view to influencing the other's action, are not regarded as aggression or a violation of that other's rights. If, however, the offer is declined, as it may rightfully be, then persistence, importunity, following and dogging, become unjustifiable annoyance and obstruction which is likely soon to savor of intimidation. From all of this the person sought to be influenced has a right to be free, and his employer has a right to have him free." American Steel Foundries v. Tri-City Central Trades Council, 257 U.S. 184, 204, 66 L. Ed. 189, 42 S. Ct. 72 (1921).

We have since recognized that the "right to persuade" discussed in that case is protected by the First Amendment, Thornhill v. Alabama, 310 U.S. 88, 84 L. Ed. 1093, 60 S. Ct. 736 (1940), as well as by federal [718] statutes. Yet we have continued to maintain that "no one has a right to press even 'good' ideas on an unwilling recipient." Rowan, 397 U.S. at 738. None of our decisions has minimized the enduring importance of "the right to be free" from persistent "importunity, follow-ing and dogging" after an offer to communicate has been declined. While the freedom to communicate

is substantial, "the right of every person 'to be let alone' must be placed in the scales with the right of others to communicate." Id. at 736. It is that right, as well as the right of "passage without obstruction," that the Colorado statute legitimately seeks to protect. The restrictions imposed by the Colorado statute only apply to communications that interfere with these rights rather than those that involve willing listeners.

The dissenters argue that we depart from precedent by recognizing a "right to avoid unpopular speech in a public forum," post, at 7 (opinion of KENNEDY, J.); see also post, at 10-14 (opinion of SCALIA, J.). We, of course, are not addressing whether there is such a "right." Rather, we are merely noting that our cases have repeatedly recognized the interests of unwilling listeners in situations where "the degree of captivity makes it impractical for the unwilling viewer or auditor to avoid exposure. See Lehman v. [Shaker Heights, 418 U.S. 298, 41 L. Ed. 2d 770, 94 S. Ct. 2714 (1974)]." Erznoznik, 422 U.S. at 209. We explained in Erznoznik that "this Court has considered analogous issues – pitting the First Amendment rights of speakers against the privacy rights of those who may be unwilling viewers or auditors – in a variety of contexts. Such cases demand delicate balancing." Id. at 208 (citations omitted). The dissenters, however, appear to consider recognizing any of the interests of unwilling listeners – let alone balancing those interests against the rights of speakers – to be unconstitutional. Our cases do not support this view.[25]

III. [719] [1D] [4] [5A] All four of the state court opinions upholding the validity of this statute concluded that it is a content-neutral time, place, and manner regulation. Moreover, they all found support for their analysis in Ward v. Rock Against Racism, 491 U.S. 781, 105 L. Ed. 2d 661, 109 S. Ct. 2746 (1989).[26] It is therefore appropriate to comment on the "content neutrality" of the statute. As we explained in Ward:

---

[24] This common-law "right" is more accurately characterized as an "interest" that States can choose to protect in certain situations. See Katz v. United States, 389 U.S. 347, 350-351, 19 L. Ed. 2d 576, 88 S. Ct. 507 (1967).

[25] Furthermore, whether there is a "right" to avoid unwelcome expression is not before us in this case. The purpose of the Colorado statute is not to protect a potential listener from hearing a particular message. It is to protect those who seek medical treatment from the potential physical and emotional harm suffered when an unwelcome individual delivers a message (whatever its content) by physically approaching an individual at close range, i.e., within eight feet. In offering protection from that harm, while maintaining free access to heath clinics, the State pursues interests constitutionally distinct from the freedom from unpopular speech to which JUSTICE KENNEDY refers.
[26] See App. to Pet. for Cert. 32a (Colo. Dist. Ct.); 911 P.2d at 673-674 (Colo. Ct. App.); 949 P.2d at 109 (Colo. Ct. App.), 973 P.2d at 1256 (Colo. Sup. Ct.).

"The principal inquiry in determining content neutrality, in speech cases generally and in time, place, or manner cases in particular, is whether the government has adopted a regulation of speech because of disagreement with the message it conveys." Id. at 791.

The Colorado statute passes that test for three independent reasons. First, it is not a "regulation of speech." Rather, it is a regulation of the places where some speech may occur. Second, it was not adopted "because of disagreement with the message it conveys." This conclusion is supported not just by the Colorado courts' interpretation of legislative history, but more importantly by the State Supreme Court's unequivocal holding that the statute's "restrictions apply equally to all demonstrators, regardless of view-point, and the statutory language makes no reference to the content of the speech."[27] Third, the State's interests in protecting [720] access and privacy, and providing the police with clear guidelines, are unrelated to the content of the demonstrators' speech. As we have repeatedly explained, government regulation of expressive activity is "content neutral" if it is justified without reference to the content of regulated speech. See ibid. and cases cited.

Petitioners nevertheless argue that the statute is not content neutral insofar as it applies to some oral communication. The statute applies to all persons who "knowingly approach" within eight feet of another for the purpose of leafleting or displaying signs; for such persons, the content of their oral statements is irrelevant. With respect to persons who are neither leafletters nor sign carriers, however, the statute does not apply unless their approach is "for the purpose of . . . engaging in oral protest, education, or counseling." Petitioners contend that an individual near a health care facility who knowingly approaches a pedestrian to say "good morning" or to randomly recite lines from a novel would not be subject to the statute's restrictions.[28] Because the content of the oral statements made by an approaching speaker must sometimes be examined to determine whether the knowing approach is covered by the statute, petitioners argue that the law is "content-based" under our reasoning in Carey v. Brown, 447 U.S. 455, 462, 65 L. Ed. 2d 263, 100 S. Ct. 2286 (1980).

Although this theory was identified in the complaint, it is not mentioned in any of the four Colorado opinions, all of which concluded that the statute was content neutral. For that reason, it is likely that the argument has been waived. Additionally, the Colorado Attorney General argues that we should assume that the state courts tacitly construed the terms "protest, education, or counseling" to encompass "all [721] communication."[29] Instead of relying on those arguments, however, we shall explain why petitioners' contention is without merit and why their reliance on Carey v. Brown is misplaced.

[5B] It is common in the law to examine the content of a communication to determine the speaker's purpose. Whether a particular statement constitutes a threat, blackmail, an agreement to fix prices, a copyright violation, a public offering of securities, or an offer to sell goods often depends on the precise content of the statement. We have never held, or suggested, that it is improper to look at the content of an oral or written statement in order to determine whether a rule of law applies to a course of conduct. With respect to the conduct that is the focus of the Colorado statute, it is unlikely that there would often be any need to know exactly what words were spoken in order to determine whether "sidewalk counselors" are engaging in "oral protest, education, or counseling" rather than pure social or random conversation.

Theoretically, of course, cases may arise in which it is necessary to review the content of the statements made by a person approaching within eight feet of an unwilling listener to determine whether the approach is covered by the statute. But that review need be no more extensive than a determination of whether a general prohibition of "picketing" or "demonstrating" applies to innocuous speech. The regulation of such expressive activities, by definition, does not cover social, random, or other everyday communications. See Webster's Third New International Dictionary 600, 1710 (1993) (defining "demonstrate" as "to make a public display of sentiment for or against a person or cause" and "picket" as an [722] effort "to persuade or otherwise influence"). Nevertheless, we have never suggested that the kind of cursory examination that might be required to exclude casual conversation from the coverage of a regulation of picketing would be problematic.[30]

---

[27] Ibid. This observation in Madsen is equally applicable here: "There is no suggestion in this record that Florida law would not equally restrain similar conduct directed at a target having nothing to do with abortion; none of the restrictions imposed by the court were directed at the contents of petitioner's message." 512 U.S. at 762-763.

[28] See Brief for Petitioners 32, n. 23.

[29] "The Colorado Supreme Court's ruling confirms that the statutory language should be interpreted to refer to approaches for all communication, as Colorado has argued since the beginning of this case." Brief for Respondents 21.

[30] In United States v. Grace, 461 U.S. 171, 75 L. Ed. 2d 736, 103 S. Ct. 1702 (1983), after examining a federal statute that was "interpreted and applied" as "prohibiting picketing and leafletting, but not other expressive conduct" within the Supreme Court building and grounds, we concluded that "it is clear that the prohibition is facially content-neutral." Id. at 181, n. 10. Similarly, we have recognized that statutes can equally restrict all "picketing." See, e.g., Police Dept. of Chicago v. Mosley, 408 U.S. 92, 98, 33 L. Ed. 2d 212, 92 S.

In Carey v. Brown we examined a general prohibition of peaceful picketing that contained an exemption for picketing of a place of employment involved in a labor dispute. We concluded that this statute violated the Equal Protection Clause of the Fourteenth Amendment, because it discriminated between lawful and unlawful conduct based on the content of the picketers' messages. That discrimination was impermissible because it accorded preferential treatment to expression concerning one particular subject matter – labor disputes – while prohibiting discussion of all other issues. Although our opinion stressed that "it is the content of the speech that determines whether it is within or without the statute's blunt prohibition," we appended a footnote to that sentence explaining that it was the fact that the statute placed a prohibition on discussion of particular topics, while others were allowed, that was constitutionally [723] repugnant.[31] Regulation of the subject matter of messages, though not as obnoxious as viewpoint-based regulation, is also an objectionable form of content-based regulation. Consolidated Edison Co. of N.Y. v. Public Serv. Comm'n of N.Y., 447 U.S. 530, 538, 65 L. Ed. 2d 319, 100 S. Ct. 2326 (1980).

The Colorado statute's regulation of the location of protests, education, and counseling is easily distinguishable from Carey. It places no restrictions on – and clearly does not prohibit – either a particular viewpoint or any subject matter that may be discussed by a speaker. Rather, it simply establishes a minor place restriction on an extremely broad category of communications with unwilling listeners. Instead of drawing distinctions based on the subject that the approaching speaker may wish to address, the statute applies equally to used car salesmen, animal rights activists, fundraisers, environmentalists, and missionaries. Each can attempt to educate unwilling listeners on any subject, but

without consent may not approach within eight feet to do so.

The dissenters, nonetheless, contend that the statute is not "content neutral." As JUSTICE SCALIA points out, the vice of content-based legislation in this context is that "it lends itself" to being "used for invidious thought-control purposes." Post, at 3. But a statute that restricts certain categories of speech only lends itself to invidious use if there is a significant number of communications, raising the same problem that the statute was enacted to solve, that fall outside the statute's scope, while others fall inside. E.g., Police Dept. of Chicago v. Mosley, 408 U.S. 92, 33 L. Ed. 2d 212, 92 S. Ct. 2286 (1972). Here, [724] the statute's restriction seeks to protect those who enter a health care facility from the harassment, the nuisance, the persistent importuning, the following, the dogging, and the implied threat of physical touching that can accompany an unwelcome approach within eight feet of a patient by a person wishing to argue vociferously face-to-face and perhaps thrust an undesired handbill upon her. The statutory phrases, "oral protest, education, or counseling," distinguish speech activities likely to have those consequences from speech activities (such as JUSTICE SCALIA's "happy speech," post, at 3) that are most unlikely to have those consequences. The statute does not distinguish among speech instances that are similarly likely to raise the legitimate concerns to which it responds. Hence, the statute cannot be struck down for failure to maintain "content neutrality," or for "under-breadth."

Also flawed is JUSTICE KENNEDY's theory that a statute restricting speech becomes unconstitutionally content based because of its application "to the specific locations where that discourse occurs," post, at 3. A statute prohibiting solicitation in airports that was motivated by the aggressive approaches of Hari-Krishnas does not become content based solely because its application is confined to airports – "the specific location where that discourse occurs." A statute making it a misdemeanor to sit at a lunch counter for an hour without ordering any food would also not be "content based" even if it were enacted by a racist legislature that hated civil rights protesters (although it might raise separate questions about the State's legitimate interest at issue). See post, at 3-4.

[6] Similarly, the contention that a statute is "viewpoint based" simply because its enactment was motivated by the conduct of the partisans on one side of a debate is without support. Post, at 4-5 (KENNEDY, J., dissenting). The anti-picketing ordinance upheld in Frisby v. Schultz, 487 U.S. 474, 101 L. Ed. 2d 420, 108 S. Ct. 2495 (1988), a decision in which both of today's dissenters [725] joined, was obviously enacted in response to the activities of

---

Ct. 2286 (1972) ("This is not to say that all picketing must always be allowed. We have continually recognized that reasonable 'time, place, and manner' regulations of picketing may be necessary to further significant governmental interests"), and cases cited. See also Frisby v. Schultz, 487 U.S. 474, 101 L. Ed. 2d 420, 108 S. Ct. 2495 (1988) (upholding a general ban on residential picketing). And our decisions in Schenck and Madsen both upheld injunctions that also prohibited "demonstrating." Schenck v. Pro-Choice Network of Western N.Y., 519 U.S. 357, 366, n. 3, 137 L. Ed. 2d 1, 117 S. Ct. 855 (1997); Madsen, 512 U.S. at 759.

[31] "It is, of course, no answer to assert that the Illinois statute does not discriminate on the basis of the speaker's viewpoint, but only on the basis of the subject matter of his message. 'The First Amendment's hostility to content-based regulation extends not only to restrictions on particular viewpoints, but also to prohibition of public discussion of an entire topic.'" Carey, 447 U.S. at 462, n. 6 (quoting Consolidated Edison Co. of N.Y. v. Public Serv. Comm'n of N.Y., 447 U.S. 530, 537, 65 L. Ed. 2d 319, 100 S. Ct. 2326 (1980)).

antiabortion protesters who wanted to protest at the home of a particular doctor to persuade him and others that they viewed his practice of performing abortions to be murder. We nonetheless summarily concluded that the statute was content neutral. Id. at 482.

[5C] JUSTICE KENNEDY further suggests that a speaker who approaches a patient and "chants in praise of the Supreme Court and its abortion decisions, or hands out a simple leaflet saying, 'We are for abortion rights,'" would not be subject to the statute. Post, at 5. But what reason is there to believe the statute would not apply to that individual? She would be engaged in "oral protest" and "education," just as the abortion opponent who expresses her view that the Supreme Court decisions were incorrect would be "protesting" the decisions and "educating" the patient on the issue. The close approach of the latter, more hostile, demonstrator may be more likely to risk being perceived as a form of physical harassment; but the relevant First Amendment point is that the statute would prevent both speakers, unless welcome, from entering the 8-foot zone. The statute is not limited to those who oppose abortion. It applies to the demonstrator in JUSTICE KENNEDY's example. It applies to all "protest," to all "counseling," and to all demonstrators whether or not the demonstration concerns abortion, and whether they oppose or support the woman who has made an abortion decision. That is the level of neutrality that the Constitution demands. The Colorado courts correctly concluded that § 18-9- 122(3) is content neutral.

IV. [1E] [7] We also agree with the state courts' conclusion that § 18-9-122(3) is a valid time, place, and manner regulation under the test applied in Ward because it is "narrowly tailored." We already have noted that the statute serves governmental interests that are significant and legitimate and that the restrictions [726] are content neutral. We are likewise persuaded that the statute is "narrowly tailored" to serve those interests and that it leaves open ample alternative channels for communication. As we have emphasized on more than one occasion, when a content-neutral regulation does not entirely foreclose any means of communication, it may satisfy the tailoring requirement even though it is not the least restrictive or least intrusive means of serving the statutory goal.[32]

The three types of communication regulated by § 18-9-122(3) are the display of signs, leafleting, and oral speech. The 8-foot separation between the speaker and the audience should not have any adverse impact on the readers' ability to read signs displayed by demonstrators. In fact, the separation might actually aid the pedestrians' ability to see the signs by preventing others from surrounding them and impeding their view. Furthermore, the statute places no limitations on the number, size, text, or images of the placards. And, as with all of the restrictions, the 8-foot zone does not affect demonstrators with signs who remain in place.

With respect to oral statements, the distance certainly can make it more difficult for a speaker to be heard, particularly if the level of background noise is high and other speakers are competing for the pedestrian's attention. Notably, the statute places no limitation on the number of speakers or the noise level, including the use of amplification equipment, although we have upheld such restrictions in past cases. See, e.g., Madsen, 512 U.S. at 772-773. More significantly, this statute does not suffer from the failings that compelled us to reject the "floating buffer zone" in Schenck, 519 U.S. at 377. Unlike the 15-foot zone in Schenck, this 8-foot zone allows the speaker to communicate at a "normal conversational [727] distance." Ibid. Additionally, the statute allows the speaker to remain in one place, and other individuals can pass within eight feet of the protester without causing the protester to violate the statute. Finally, here there is a "knowing" requirement that protects speakers "who thought they were keeping pace with the targeted individual" at the proscribed distance from inadvertently violating the statute. Id. at 378, n. 9.

[1F] It is also not clear that the statute's restrictions will necessarily impede, rather than assist, the speakers' efforts to communicate their messages. The statute might encourage the most aggressive and vociferous protesters to moderate their confrontational and harassing conduct, and thereby make it easier for thoughtful and law-abiding sidewalk counselors like petitioners to make themselves heard. But whether or not the 8-foot interval is the best possible accommodation of the competing interests at stake, we must accord a measure of deference to the judgment of the Colorado Legislature. See Madsen, 512 U.S. at 769-770. Once again, it is worth reiterating that only attempts to address unwilling listeners are affected.

The burden on the ability to distribute handbills is more serious because it seems possible that an 8-foot interval could hinder the ability of a leafletter to deliver handbills to some unwilling recipients. The statute does not, however, prevent a leafletter from simply standing near the path of oncoming pedestrians and proffering his or her material, which the pedestrians can easily accept.[33] And, as in all

---

[32] "Lest any confusion on the point remain, we reaffirm today that a regulation of the time, place, or manner of protected speech must be narrowly tailored to serve the government's legitimate, content-neutral interests but that it need not be the least restrictive or least intrusive means of doing so." Ward v. Rock Against Racism, 491 U.S. at 798.

[33] JUSTICE KENNEDY states that the statute "forecloses peaceful leafletting," post, at 15. This is not correct. All of the

leafleting situations, pedestrians continue to be free to decline the tender. In Heffron v. International Soc. for [728] Krishna Consciousness, Inc., 452 U.S. 640, 69 L. Ed. 2d 298, 101 S. Ct. 2559 (1981), we upheld a state fair regulation that required a religious organization desiring to distribute literature to conduct that activity only at an assigned location – in that case booths. As in this case, the regulation primarily burdened the distributors' ability to communicate with unwilling readers. We concluded our opinion by emphasizing that the First Amendment protects the right of every citizen to "'reach the minds of willing listeners and to do so there must be opportunity to win their attention.' Kovacs v. Cooper, 336 U.S. 77, 87, 93 L. Ed. 513, 69 S. Ct. 448 (1949)." Id. at 655. The Colorado statute adequately protects those rights.

Finally, in determining whether a statute is narrowly tailored, we have noted that "we must, of course, take account of the place to which the regulations apply in determining whether these restrictions burden more speech than necessary." Madsen, 512 U.S. at 772. States and municipalities plainly have a substantial interest in controlling the activity around certain public and private places. For example, we have recognized the special governmental interests surrounding schools,[34] court houses,[35] polling places,[36] and private homes.[37] Additionally, we previously have noted the unique concerns that surround health care facilities:

"'Hospitals, after all, are not factories or mines or assembly plants. They are hospitals, where human ailments are treated, where patients and relatives alike often are under emotional strain and worry, where pleasing and comforting patients are principal facets of the day's activity, and where the patient and [her] family . . . need a restful, uncluttered, relaxing, and [729] helpful atmosphere.'" Ibid. (quoting NLRB v. Baptist Hospital, Inc., 442 U.S. at 783-784, n. 12).

Persons who are attempting to enter health care facilities – for any purpose – are often in particularly vulnerable physical and emotional conditions. The State of Colorado has responded to its substantial and legitimate interest in protecting these persons

from unwanted encounters, confrontations, and even assaults by enacting an exceedingly modest restriction on the speakers' ability to approach.

JUSTICE KENNEDY, however, argues that the statute leaves petitioners without adequate means of communication. Post, at 14-15. This is a considerable over-statement. The statute seeks to protect those who wish to enter health care facilities, many of whom may be under special physical or emotional stress, from close physical approaches by demon-strators. In doing so, the statute takes a prophylactic approach; it forbids all unwelcome demonstrators to come closer than eight feet. We recognize that by doing so, it will sometimes inhibit a demonstrator whose approach in fact would have proved harmless. But the statute's prophylactic aspect is justified by the great difficulty of protecting, say, a pregnant woman from physical harassment with legal rules that focus exclusively on the individual impact of each instance of behavior, demanding in each case an accurate characterization (as harassing or not harassing) of each individual movement within the 8-foot boundary. Such individualized characterization of each individual movement is often difficult to make accurately. A bright-line prophylactic rule may be the best way to provide protection, and, at the same time, by offering clear guidance and avoiding subjectivity, to protect speech itself.

As we explained above, the 8-foot restriction on an unwanted physical approach leaves ample room to communicate a message through speech. Signs, pictures, and voice itself can cross an 8-foot gap with ease. If the clinics in Colorado resemble those in Schenck, demonstrators with leaflets [730] might easily stand on the sidewalk at entrances (without blocking the entrance) and, without physically approaching those who are entering the clinic, peacefully hand them leaflets as they pass by.

Finally, the 8-foot restriction occurs only within 100 feet of a health care facility – the place where the restriction is most needed. The restriction interferes far less with a speaker's ability to communicate than did the total ban on picketing on the sidewalk outside a residence (upheld in Frisby v. Schultz, 487 U.S. 474, 101 L. Ed. 2d 420, 108 S. Ct. 2495 (1988)), the restriction of leafleting at a fairground to a booth (upheld in Heffron v. International Society for Krishna Consciousness, Inc., 452 U.S. 640, 69 L. Ed. 2d 298, 101 S. Ct. 2559 (1981)), or the "silence" often required outside a hospital. Special problems that may arise where clinics have particularly wide entrances or are situated within multipurpose office buildings may be worked out as the statute is applied. This restriction is thus reasonable and narrowly tailored.

V.   [8A] Petitioners argue that § 18-9-122(3) is invalid because it is "overbroad." There are two parts to petitioners' "overbreadth" argument. On the one

---

cases he cites in support of his argument involve a total ban on a medium of expression to both willing and unwilling recipients, see post, at 16-22. Nothing in this statute, however, prevents persons from proffering their literature, they simply cannot approach within eight feet of an unwilling recipient.

[34] See Grayned v. City of Rockford, 408 U.S. 104, 119, 33 L. Ed. 2d 222, 92 S. Ct. 2294 (1972).

[35] See Cox v. Louisiana, 379 U.S. 559, 562, 13 L. Ed. 2d 487, 85 S. Ct. 476 (1965).

[36] See Burson v. Freeman, 504 U.S. 191, 206-208, 119 L. Ed. 2d 5, 112 S. Ct. 1846 (1992) (plurality opinion); Id. at 214-216 (SCALIA, J., concurring in judgment).

[37] See Frisby v. Schultz, 487 U.S. at 484-485

hand, they argue that the statute is too broad because it protects too many people in too many places, rather than just the patients at the facilities where confrontational speech had occurred. Similarly, it burdens all speakers, rather than just persons with a history of bad conduct.[38] On the other hand, petitioners also contend that the statute is overbroad because it "bans virtually the universe of protected expression, including displays of signs, distribution of literature, and mere verbal statements."[39]

The first part of the argument does not identify a constitutional defect. The fact that the coverage of a statute is [731] broader than the specific concern that led to its enactment is of no constitutional significance. What is important is that all persons entering or leaving health care facilities share the interests served by the statute. It is precisely because the Colorado Legislature made a general policy choice that the statute is assessed under the constitutional standard set forth in Ward, 491 U.S. at 791, rather than a more strict standard. See Madsen, 412 U.S. at 764. The cases cited by petitioners are distinguishable from this statute. In those cases, the government attempted to regulate nonprotected activity, yet because the statute was overbroad, protected speech was also implicated. See Houston v. Hill, 482 U.S. 451, 96 L. Ed. 2d 398, 107 S. Ct. 2502 (1987); Secretary of State of Md. v. Joseph H. Munson Co., 467 U.S. 947, 81 L. Ed. 2d 786, 104 S. Ct. 2839 (1984). In this case, it is not disputed that the regulation affects protected speech activity, the question is thus whether it is a "reasonable restriction on the time, place, or manner of protected speech." Ward, 491 U.S. at 791. Here, the comprehensiveness of the statute is a virtue, not a vice, because it is evidence against there being a discriminatory governmental motive. As we have observed, "there is no more effective practical guaranty against arbitrary and unreasonable government than to require that the principles of law which officials would impose upon a minority must be imposed generally." Railway Express Agency, Inc. v. New York, 336 U.S. 106, 112, 93 L. Ed. 533, 69 S. Ct. 463 (1949) (Jackson, J., concurring).

[1G] [8B] [9] [10] The second part of the argument is based on a misreading of the statute and an incorrect understanding of the overbreadth doctrine. As we have already noted, § 18-9-122(3) simply does not "ban" any messages, and likewise it does not "ban" any signs, literature, or oral statements. It merely regulates the places where communications may occur. As we explained in Broadrick v. Oklahoma, 413 U.S. 601, 612, 37 L. Ed. 2d 830, 93 S. Ct. 2908 (1973), the overbreadth doctrine enables litigants "to challenge a statute, not

because their own rights of free expression are violated, but because of a judicial prediction [732] or assumption that the statute's very existence may cause others not before the court to refrain from constitutionally protected speech or expression." Moreover, "particularly where conduct and not merely speech is involved, we believe that the overbreadth of a statute must not only be real, but substantial as well, judged in relation to the statute's plainly legitimate sweep." Id. at 615. Petitioners have not persuaded us that the impact of the statute on the conduct of other speakers will differ from its impact on their own sidewalk counseling. Cf. Members of City Council of Los Angeles v. Taxpayers for Vincent, 466 U.S. 789, 801, 80 L. Ed. 2d 772, 104 S. Ct. 2118 (1984). Like petitioners' own activities, the conduct of other protesters and counselors at all health care facilities are encompassed within the statute's "legitimate sweep." Therefore, the statute is not overly broad.

VI. [11A] Petitioners also claim that § 18-9-122(3) is unconstitutionally vague. They find a lack of clarity in three parts of the section: the meaning of "protest, education, or counseling"; the "consent" requirement; and the determination of whether one is "approaching" within eight feet of another.

[12] A statute can be impermissibly vague for either of two independent reasons. First, if it fails to provide people of ordinary intelligence a reasonable opportunity to understand what conduct it prohibits. Second, if it authorizes or even encourages arbitrary and discriminatory enforcement. Chicago v. Morales, 527 U.S. 41, 56-57, 144 L. Ed. 2d 67, 119 S. Ct. 1849 (1999). [11B]

In this case, the first concern is ameliorated by the fact that § 18-9-122(3) contains a scienter requirement. The statute only applies to a person who "knowingly" approaches within eight feet of another, without that person's consent, for the purpose of engaging in oral protest, education, or counseling. The likelihood that anyone would not understand any of those common words seems quite remote.

Petitioners proffer [733] hypertechnical theories as to what the statute covers, such as whether an outstretched arm constitutes "approaching."[40] And while "there is little doubt that imagination can conjure up hypothetical cases in which the meaning of these terms will be in nice question," American Communications Assn. v. Douds, 339 U.S. 382, 412, 94 L. Ed. 925, 70 S. Ct. 674 (1950), because we are "condemned to the use of words, we can never expect mathematical certainty from our language," Grayned v. City of Rockford, 408 U.S. 104, 110, 33 L. Ed. 2d 222, 92 S. Ct. 2294 (1972). For these reasons, we rejected similar vagueness challenges to the injunctions at issue in Schenck, 519 U.S. at

---

[38] Brief for Petitioners 22-23.

[39] Id. at 25.

[40] Brief for Petitioners 48.

383, and Madsen, 512 U.S. at 775-776. We thus conclude that "it is clear what the ordinance as a whole prohibits." Grayned, 408 U.S. at 110. More importantly, speculation about possible vagueness in hypothetical situations not before the Court will not support a facial attack on a statute when it is surely valid "in the vast majority of its intended applications," United States v. Raines, 362 U.S. 17, 23, 4 L. Ed. 2d 524, 80 S. Ct. 519 (1960).

For the same reason, we are similarly unpersuaded by the suggestion that § 18-9-122(3) fails to give adequate guidance to law enforcement authorities. Indeed, it seems to us that one of the section's virtues is the specificity of the definitions of the zones described in the statute. "As always, enforcement requires the exercise of some degree of police judgment," Grayned, 408 U.S. at 114, and the degree of judgment involved here is acceptable.

VII. [1H][13] Finally, petitioners argue that § 18-9-122(3)'s consent requirement is invalid because it imposes an unconstitutional "prior restraint" on speech. We rejected this argument previously in Schenck, 519 U.S. at 374, n. 6, and Madsen, 512 U.S. at 764, n. 2. Moreover, the restrictions in this case raise an even lesser prior restraint concern than those at issue in Schenck and Madsen where particular speakers were at times completely banned within certain zones. Under this statute, absolutely no channel of communication is foreclosed. No speaker is silenced. And no message is prohibited. Petitioners are simply wrong when they assert that "the statute compels speakers to obtain [734] consent to speak and it authorizes private citizens to deny petitioners' requests to engage in expressive activities."[41] To the contrary, this statute does not provide for a "heckler's veto" but rather allows every speaker to engage freely in any expressive activity communicating all messages and viewpoints subject only to the narrow place requirement imbedded within the "approach" restriction.

Furthermore, our concerns about "prior restraints" relate to restrictions imposed by official censorship.[42] The regulations in this case, however, only apply if the pedestrian does not consent to the approach.[43]

---

[41] Id. at 29.

[42] See Ward, 491 U.S. at 795, n. 5 ("The regulations we have found invalid as prior restraints have 'had this in common: they gave public officials the power to deny use of a forum in advance of actual expression'" (quoting Southeastern Promotions, Ltd. v. Conrad, 420 U.S. 546, 553, 43 L. Ed. 2d 448, 95 S. Ct. 1239 (1975) (emphasis added)).

[43] While we have in prior cases found governmental grants of power to private actors constitutionally problematic, those cases are distinguishable. In those cases, the regulations allowed a single, private actor to unilaterally silence a speaker even as to willing listeners. See, e.g., Reno v. American Civil

Private citizens have always retained the power to decide for themselves what they wish to read, and within limits, what oral messages they want to consider. This statute simply empowers private citizens entering a health care facility with the ability to prevent a speaker, who is within eight feet and advancing, from communicating a message they do not wish to hear. Further, [735] the statute does not authorize the pedestrian to affect any other activity at any other location or relating to any other person. These restrictions thus do not constitute an unlawful prior restraint.

* * *

The judgment of the Colorado Supreme Court is affirmed. It is so ordered.

CONCUR: JUSTICE SOUTER, with whom JUSTICE O'CONNOR, JUSTICE GINSBURG, and JUSTICE BREYER join, concurring.

I join the opinion of the Court and add this further word. The key to determining whether Colo. Rev. Stat. § 18-9-122(3) (1999), makes a content-based distinction between varieties of speech lies in understanding that content-based discriminations are subject to strict scrutiny because they place the weight of government behind the disparagement or suppression of some messages, whether or not with the effect of approving or promoting others. United States v. Playboy Entertainment Group, Inc., 529 U.S. __, (2000) (slip op., at 7); R. A. V. v. St. Paul, 505 U.S. 377, 382, 120 L. Ed. 2d 305, 112 S. Ct. 2538 (1992); cf. Police Dept. of Chicago v. Mosley, 408 U.S. 92, 95-96, 33 L. Ed. 2d 212, 92 S. Ct. 2286 (1972). Thus the government is held to a very exacting and rarely satisfied standard when it disfavors the discussion of particular subjects, Simon & Schuster, Inc. v. Members of N.Y. State Crime Victims Bd., 502 U.S. 105, 116, 116 L. Ed. 2d 476, 112 S. Ct. 501 (1991), or particular viewpoints within a given subject matter, Carey v. Brown, 447 U.S. 455, 461-463, 65 L. Ed. 2d 263, 100 S. Ct. 2286 (1980) (citing Chicago, supra, at 95-96); cf. National Endowment for Arts v. Finley, 524 U.S. 569, 601-602, 141 L. Ed. 2d 500, 118 S. Ct. 2168 (1998) (SOUTER, J., dissenting).

Concern about employing the power of the State to suppress discussion of a subject or a point of view is not, however, raised in the same way when a law addresses not the content of speech but the circumstances of its delivery. The right to express

---

Liberties Union, 521 U.S. 844, 880, 117 S. Ct. 2329, 138 L. Ed. 2d 874 (1997) ("It would confer broad powers of censorship, in the form of a 'heckler's veto,' upon any opponent of indecent speech . . . "). The Colorado statute at issue here confers no such censorial power on the pedestrian.

unpopular views does not necessarily immunize a speaker from liability for resorting to otherwise impermissible [736] behavior meant to shock members of the speaker's audience, see United States v. O'Brien, 391 U.S. 367, 376, 20 L. Ed. 2d 672, 88 S. Ct. 1673 (1968) (burning draft card), or to guarantee their attention, see Kovacs v. Cooper, 336 U.S. 77, 86-88, 93 L. Ed. 513, 69 S. Ct. 448 (1949) (sound trucks); Frisby v. Schultz, 487 U.S. 474, 484-485, 101 L. Ed. 2d 420, 108 S. Ct. 2495 (1988) (residential picketing); Heffron v. International Soc. for Krishna Consciousness, Inc., 452 U.S. 640, 647-648, 69 L. Ed. 2d 298, 101 S. Ct. 2559 (1981) (soliciting). Unless regulation limited to the details of a speaker's delivery results in removing a subject or viewpoint from effective discourse (or otherwise fails to advance a significant public interest in a way narrowly fitted to that objective), a reasonable restriction intended to affect only the time, place, or manner of speaking is perfectly valid. See Ward v. Rock Against Racism, 491 U.S. 781, 791, 105 L. Ed. 2d 661, 109 S. Ct. 2746 (1989) ("Our cases make clear . . . that even in a public forum the government may impose reasonable restrictions on the time, place, or manner of protected speech, provided the restrictions 'are justified without reference to the content of the regulated speech, that they are narrowly tailored to serve a significant governmental interest, and that they leave open ample alternative channels for communication of the information'" (quoting Clark v. Community for Creative Non-Violence, 468 U.S. 288, 293, 82 L. Ed. 2d 221, 104 S. Ct. 3065 (1984)); 491 U.S. at 797 ("Our cases quite clearly hold that restrictions on the time, place, or manner of protected speech are not invalid 'simply because there is some imaginable alternative that might be less burdensome on speech'" (quoting United States v. Albertini, 472 U.S. 675, 689, 86 L. Ed. 2d 536, 105 S. Ct. 2897 (1985)).

It is important to recognize that the validity of punishing some expressive conduct, and the permissibility of a time, place, or manner restriction, does not depend on showing that the particular behavior or mode of delivery has no association with a particular subject or opinion. Draft card burners disapprove of the draft, see United States v. O'Brien, supra, at 370, and abortion protesters believe abortion is morally wrong, Madsen v. Women's Health Center, [737] Inc., 512 U.S. 753, 758, 129 L. Ed. 2d 593, 114 S. Ct. 2516 (1994). There is always a correlation with subject and viewpoint when the law regulates conduct that has become the signature of one side of a controversy. But that does not mean that every regulation of such distinctive behavior is content based as First Amendment doctrine employs that term. The correct rule, rather, is captured in the formulation that a restriction is content based only if it is imposed

because of the content of the speech, see Ward, supra, at 791 ("The principal inquiry in determining content neutrality, in speech cases generally and in time, place, or manner cases in particular, is whether the government has adopted a regulation of speech because of disagreement with the message it conveys"), and not because of offensive behavior identified with its delivery.

Since this point is as elementary as anything in traditional speech doctrine, it would only be natural to suppose that today's disagreement between the Court and the dissenting Justices must turn on unusual difficulty in evaluating the facts of this case. But it does not. The facts overwhelmingly demonstrate the validity of subsection (3) as a content-neutral regulation imposed solely to regulate the manner in which speakers may conduct themselves within 100 feet of the entrance of a health care facility.

No one disputes the substantiality of the government's interest in protecting people already tense or distressed in anticipation of medical attention (whether an abortion or some other procedure) from the unwanted intrusion of close personal importunity by strangers. The issues dividing the Court, then, go to the content neutrality of the regulation, its fit with the interest to be served by it, and the availability of other means of expressing the desired message (however offensive it may be even without physically close communication).

Each of these issues is addressed principally by the fact that subsection (3) simply does not forbid the statement of any position on any subject. It does not declare any view [738] as unfit for expression within the 100-foot zone or beyond it. What it forbids, and all it forbids, is approaching another person closer than eight feet (absent permission) to deliver the message. Anyone (let him be called protester, counselor, or educator) may take a stationary position within the regulated area and address any message to any person within sight or hearing. The stationary protester may be quiet and ingratiating, or loud and offensive; the law does not touch him, even though in some ways it could. See Madsen, supra, at 768-771 (1994) (injunction may bar protesters from 36 foot zone around entrances to clinic and parking lot).

This is not to say that enforcement of the approach restriction will have no effect on speech; of course it will make some difference. The effect of speech is a product of ideas and circumstances, and time, place, and manner are circumstances. The question is simply whether the ostensible reason for regulating the circumstances is really something about the ideas. Here, the evidence indicates that the ostensible reason is the true reason. The fact that speech by a stationary speaker is untouched by this statute shows that the reason for its restriction on approaches goes to the approaches, not to the content of the speech of those approaching. What is prohibited is a close encounter when the person addressed does not want to get close. So, the intended recipient can stay far enough away to prevent the whispered argument, mitigate some of the physical shock of the shouted denunciation, and avoid the unwanted handbill. But the content of the message will survive on any sign readable at eight feet and in any statement audible from that slight distance. Hence the implausibility of any claim that an anti-abortion message, not the behavior of protesters, is what is being singled out.

The matter of proper tailoring to limit no more speech than necessary to vindicate the public interest deserves a few specific comments, some on matters raised by JUSTICE KENNEDY's dissent. Subsection (3) could possibly be applied [739] to speakers unlike the present petitioners, who might not know that the entrance to the facility was within 100 feet, or who might try to engage people within 100 feet of a health facility other than a physician's office or hospital, or people having no business with the facility. These objections do not, however, weigh very heavily on a facial challenge like this. The specter of liability on the part of those who importune while oblivious of the facility is laid to rest by the requirement that a defendant act "knowingly." See Colo. Rev. Stat. § 18-1-503(4) (1999) (culpable mental state requirement deemed to apply to each element of offense, absent clear contrary intent). While it is true that subsection (3) was not enacted to protect dental patients, I cannot say it goes beyond the State's interest to do so; someone facing an hour with a drill in his tooth may reasonably be protected from the intrusive behavior of strangers who are otherwise free to speak. While some mere passersby may be protected needlessly, I am skeptical about the number of health care facilities with substantial pedestrian traffic within 100 feet of their doors but unrelated to the business conducted inside. Hence, I fail to see danger of the substantial overbreadth required to be shown before a statute is struck down out of concern for the speech rights of those not before the Court. Cf. Secretary of State of Md. v. Joseph H. Munson Co., 467 U.S. 947, 964-965, 81 L. Ed. 2d 786, 104 S. Ct. 2839 (1984); Houston v. Hill, 482 U.S. 451, 458, 96 L. Ed. 2d 398, 107 S. Ct. 2502 (1987).

As for the claim of vagueness, at first blush there is something objectionable. Those who do not choose to remain stationary may not approach within eight feet with a purpose, among others, of "engaging in oral protest, education, or counseling." Colo. Rev. Stat. § 18-9-122(3) (1999). While that formula excludes liability for enquiring about the time or the bus schedule within eight feet, "education" does not convey much else by way of

limitation. But that is not fatal here. What is significant is not that the word fails to limit clearly, but that it pretty clearly fails to limit very much at [740] all. It succeeds in naturally covering any likely address by one person approaching another on a street or parking lot outside a building entrance (aside from common social greetings, protests, or requests for assistance). Someone planning to spread a message by accosting strangers is likely to understand the statute's application to "education." And just because the coverage is so obviously broad, the discretion given to the police in deciding whether to charge an offense seems no greater than the prosecutorial discretion inherent in any generally applicable criminal statute. Cf. Grayned v. City of Rockford, 408 U.S. 104, 108, 33 L. Ed. 2d 222, 92 S. Ct. 2294 (1972) (noting that "vague laws may trap the innocent by not providing fair warning" and that "if arbitrary and discriminatory enforcement is to be prevented, laws must provide explicit standards for those who apply them"); Coates v. Cincinnati, 402 U.S. 611, 614, 29 L. Ed. 2d 214, 91 S. Ct. 1686 (1971). "Perfect clarity and precise guidance have never been required even of regulations that restrict expressive activity." Ward, 491 U.S. at 794.

Although petitioners have not argued that the "floating bubble" feature of the 8-foot zone around a pedestrian is itself a failure of narrow tailoring, I would note the contrast between the operation of subsection (3) and that of the comparable portion of the injunction struck down in Schenck v. Pro-Choice Network of Western N.Y., 519 U.S. 357, 377-379, 137 L. Ed. 2d 1, 117 S. Ct. 855 (1997), where we observed that the difficulty of administering a floating bubble zone threatened to burden more speech than necessary. In Schenck, the floating bubble was larger (15 feet) and was associated with near-absolute prohibitions on speech. Ibid. Since subsection (3) prohibits only 8-foot approaches, however, with the stationary speaker free to speak, the risk is less. Whether floating bubble zones are so inherently difficult to administer that only fixed, no-speech zones (or prohibitions on ambulatory counseling within a fixed zone) should pass muster is an issue neither before us nor well suited to consideration on a facial challenge, cf. Ward, 491 U.S. at 794 ("Since respondent does not claim [741] that city officials enjoy unguided discretion to deny the right to speak altogether, it is open to question whether respondent's claim falls within the narrow class of permissible facial challenges to allegedly unconstrained grants of regulatory authority").

DISSENT: JUSTICE SCALIA, with whom JUSTICE THOMAS joins, dissenting.

The Court today concludes that a regulation requiring speakers on the public thoroughfares bordering medical facilities to speak from a distance of eight feet is "not a 'regulation of speech,'" but "a regulation of the places where some speech may occur," ante, at 14; and that a regulation directed to only certain categories of speech (protest, education, and counseling) is not "content-based." For these reasons, it says, the regulation is immune from the exacting scrutiny we apply to content-based suppression of speech in the public forum. The Court then determines that the regulation survives the less rigorous scrutiny afforded content-neutral time, place, and manner restrictions because it is narrowly tailored to serve a government interest — protection of citizens' "right to be let alone" — that has explicitly been disclaimed by the State, probably for the reason that, as a basis for suppressing peaceful private expression, it is patently incompatible with the guarantees of the First Amendment.

None of these remarkable conclusions should come as a surprise. What is before us, after all, is a speech regulation directed against the opponents of abortion, and it therefore enjoys the benefit of the "ad hoc nullification machine" that the Court has set in motion to push aside whatever doctrines of constitutional law stand in the way of that highly favored practice. Madsen v. Women's Health Center, Inc., 512 U.S. 753, 785, 129 L. Ed. 2d 593, 114 S. Ct. 2516 (1994) (SCALIA, J., concurring in judgment in part and dissenting in part). Having deprived abortion opponents of the political right to persuade the electorate that abortion should be restricted by law, the Court today continues [742] and expands its assault upon their individual right to persuade women contemplating abortion that what they are doing is wrong. Because, like the rest of our abortion jurisprudence, today's decision is in stark contradiction of the constitutional principles we apply in all other contexts, I dissent.

I. Colorado's statute makes it a criminal act knowingly to approach within 8 feet of another person on the public way or sidewalk area within 100 feet of the entrance door of a health care facility for the purpose of passing a leaflet to, displaying a sign to, or engaging in oral protest, education, or counseling with such person. Whatever may be said about the restrictions on the other types of expressive activity, the regulation as it applies to oral communications is obviously and undeniably content-based. A speaker wishing to approach another for the purpose of communicating any message except one of protest, education, or counseling may do so without first securing the other's consent. Whether a speaker must obtain permission before approaching within eight feet — and whether he will be sent to prison for failing to do so — depends entirely on what he intends to say when he gets there. I have no doubt that this regulation would be deemed content-based in an instant if the case before us involved antiwar protesters, or union members seeking to "educate" the public about the reasons for their strike. "It is," we would say, "the content of the speech that determines whether it is within or without the statute's blunt prohibition," Carey v. Brown, 447 U.S. 455, 462, 65 L. Ed. 2d 263, 100 S. Ct. 2286 (1980). But the jurisprudence of this Court has a way of changing when abortion is involved.

The Court asserts that this statute is not content-based for purposes of our First Amendment analysis because it neither (1) discriminates among viewpoints nor (2) places restrictions on "any subject matter that may be discussed by a speaker." Ante, at 18. But we have never held that the [743] universe of content-based regulations is limited to those two categories, and such a holding would be absurd. Imagine, for instance, special place-and-manner restrictions on all speech except that which "conveys a sense of contentment or happiness." This "happy speech" limitation would not be "viewpoint-based" — citizens would be able to express their joy in equal measure at either the rise or fall of the NASDAQ, at either the success or the failure of the Republican Party — and would not discriminate on the basis of subject matter, since gratification could be expressed about anything at all. Or consider a law restricting the writing or recitation of poetry — neither viewpoint-based nor limited to any particular subject matter. Surely this Court would consider such regulations to be "content-based" and deserving of the most exacting scrutiny.[1]

"The vice of content-based legislation — what renders it deserving of the high standard of strict scrutiny — is not that it is always used for invidious, thought-control purposes, but that it lends itself to use for those purposes." Madsen, [744] supra, at 794 (opinion of SCALIA, J.) (emphasis omitted). A

---

[1] The Court responds that statutes which restrict categories of speech – as opposed to subject matter or viewpoint – are constitutionally worrisome only if a "significant number of communications, raising the same problem that the statute was enacted to solve, . . . fall outside the statute's scope, while others fall inside." Ante, at 18-19. I am not sure that is correct, but let us assume, for the sake of argument, that it is. The Court then proceeds to assert that "the statutory phrases, 'oral protest, education, or counseling,' distinguish speech activities likely to" present the problem of "harassment, . . . nuisance, . . . persistent importuning, . . . following, . . . dogging, and . . . implied threat of physical touching," from "speech activities [such as my example of 'happy speech'] that are most unlikely to have those consequences," ibid. Well. That may work for "oral protest"; but it is beyond imagining why "education" and "counseling" are especially likely, rather than especially unlikely, to involve such conduct. (Socrates was something of a noodge, but even he did not go that far.) Unless, of course, "education" and "counseling" are code words for efforts to dissuade women from abortion – in which event the statute would not be viewpoint neutral, which the Court concedes makes it invalid.

restriction that operates only on speech that communicates a message of protest, education, or counseling presents exactly this risk. When applied, as it is here, at the entrance to medical facilities, it is a means of impeding speech against abortion. The Court's confident assurance that the statute poses no special threat to First Amendment freedoms because it applies alike to "used car salesmen, animal rights activists, fundraisers, environmentalists, and missionaries," ante, at 18, is a wonderful replication (except for its lack of sarcasm) of Anatole France's observation that "the law, in its majestic equality, forbids the rich as well as the poor to sleep under bridges . . .." see J. Bartlett, Familiar Quotations 550 (16th ed. 1992). This Colorado law is no more targeted at used car salesmen, animal rights activists, fundraisers, environmentalists, and missionaries than French vagrancy law was targeted at the rich. We know what the Colorado legislators, by their careful selection of content ("protest, education, and counseling"), were taking aim at, for they set it forth in the statute itself: the "right to protest or counsel against certain medical procedures" on the sidewalks and streets surrounding health care facilities. Col. Rev. Stat. § 18-9-122(1) (1999) (emphasis added).

The Court is unpersuasive in its attempt to equate the present restriction with content-neutral regulation of demonstrations and picketing – as one may immediately suspect from the opinion's wildly expansive definitions of demonstrations as "'public displays of sentiment for or against a person or cause,'" and of picketing as an effort "'to persuade or otherwise influence.'" Ante, at 16-17, quoting Webster's Third New International Dictionary 600, 1710 (1993). (On these terms, Nathan Hale was a demonstrator and Patrick Henry a picket.) When the government regulates "picketing," or "demonstrating," it restricts a particular manner of expression that is, as the author of today's opinion has several times explained, "'a mixture of conduct and communication.'" [745] Frisby v. Schultz, 487 U.S. 474, 497, 101 L. Ed. 2d 420, 108 S. Ct. 2495 (1988) (STEVENS, J., dissenting), quoting NLRB v. Retail Store Employees, 447 U.S. 607, 618-619, 65 L. Ed. 2d 377, 100 S. Ct. 2372 (1980) (STEVENS, J., concurring in part and concurring in result). The latter opinion quoted approvingly Justice Douglas's statement:

"Picketing by an organized group is more than free speech, since it involves patrol of a particular locality and since the very presence of a picket line may induce action of one kind or another, quite irrespective of the nature of the ideas which are being disseminated. Hence those aspects of picketing make it the subject of restrictive regulation." Bakery Drivers v. Wohl, 315 U.S. 769, 776-777, 86 L. Ed. 1178, 62 S. Ct. 816 (1942) (concurring opinion).

As JUSTICE STEVENS went on to explain, "no doubt the principal reason why handbills containing the same message are so much less effective than labor picketing is that the former depend entirely on the persuasive force of the idea." Retail Store Employees, supra, at 619. Today, of course, JUSTICE STEVENS gives us an opinion restricting not only handbilling but even one-on-one conversation of a particular content. There comes a point – and the Court's opinion today passes it – at which the regulation of action intimately and unavoidably connected with traditional speech is a regulation of speech itself. The strictures of the First Amendment cannot be avoided by regulating the act of moving one's lips; and they cannot be avoided by regulating the act of extending one's arm to deliver a handbill, or peacefully approaching in order to speak. All of these acts can be regulated, to be sure; but not, on the basis of content, without satisfying the requirements of our strict-scrutiny First Amendment jurisprudence.

Even with regard to picketing, of course, we have applied strict scrutiny to content-based restrictions. See Carey, 447 U.S. at 461 (applying strict scrutiny to, and invalidating, an Illinois statute that made "permissibility of residential [746] picketing . . . dependent solely on the nature of the message being conveyed"). As discussed above, the prohibition here is content-based: those who wish to speak for purposes other than protest, counsel, or education may do so at close range without the listener's consent, while those who wish to speak for other purposes may not. This bears no resemblance to a blanket prohibition of picketing – unless, of course, one uses the fanciful definition of picketing ("an effort to persuade or otherwise influence") newly discovered by today's opinion. As for the Court's appeal to the fact that we often "examine the content of a communication" to determine whether it "constitutes a threat, blackmail, an agreement to fix prices, a copyright violation, a public offering of securities, or an offer to sell goods," ante, at 16, the distinction is almost too obvious to bear mention: Speech of a certain content is constitutionally proscribable. The Court has not yet taken the step of consigning "protest, education, and counseling" to that category.

Finally, the Court is not correct in its assertion that the restriction here is content-neutral because it is "justified without reference to the content of regulated speech," in the sense that "the State's interests in protecting access and privacy, and providing the police with clear guidelines, are unrelated to the content of the demonstrators' speech." Ante, at 14-15 (emphasis added). That is not an accurate statement of our law. The Court makes too much of the statement in Ward v. Rock Against Racism, 491 U.S. 781, 105 L. Ed. 2d 661,

109 S. Ct. 2746 (1989), that "the principal inquiry in determining content neutrality . . . is whether the government has adopted a regulation of speech because of disagreement with the message it conveys." Id. at 791, quoted ante, at 14. That is indeed "the principal inquiry" – suppression of uncongenial ideas is the worst offense against the First Amendment – but it is not the only inquiry. Even a law that has as its purpose something unrelated to the suppression of particular content cannot irrationally single out that content for its prohibition. [747] An ordinance directed at the suppression of noise (and therefore "justified without reference to the content of regulated speech") cannot be applied only to sound trucks delivering messages of "protest." Our very first use of the "justified by reference to content" language made clear that it is a prohibition in addition to, rather than in place of, the prohibition of facially content-based restrictions. "Selective exclusions from a public forum" we said, "may not be based on content alone, and may not be justified by reference to content alone." Police Dept. of Chicago v. Mosley, 408 U.S. 92, 96, 33 L. Ed. 2d 212, 92 S. Ct. 2286 (1972) (emphasis added).

But in any event, if one accepts the Court's description of the interest served by this regulation, it is clear that the regulation is both based on content and justified by reference to content. Constitutionally proscribable "secondary effects" of speech are directly addressed in subsection (2) of the statute, which makes it unlawful to obstruct, hinder, impede, or block access to a health care facility – a prohibition broad enough to include all physical threats and all physically threatening approaches. The purpose of subsection (3), however (according to the Court), is to protect "the unwilling listener's interest in avoiding unwanted communication," ante, at 11. On this analysis, Colorado has restricted certain categories of speech – protest, counseling, and education – out of an apparent belief that only speech with this content is sufficiently likely to be annoying or upsetting as to require consent before it may be engaged in at close range. It is reasonable enough to conclude that even the most gentle and peaceful close approach by a so-called "sidewalk counselor" – who wishes to "educate" the woman entering an abortion clinic about the nature of the procedure, to "counsel" against it and in favor of other alternatives, and perhaps even (though less likely if the approach is to be successful) to "protest" her taking of a human life – will often, indeed usually, have what might be termed the "secondary effect" of annoying or deeply upsetting the woman who is planning [748] the abortion. But that is not an effect which occurs "without reference to the content" of the speech. This singling out of presumptively "unwelcome" communications fits precisely the description of prohibited regulation set forth in Boos v. Barry, 485 U.S. 312, 321, 99 L. Ed. 2d 333, 108 S. Ct. 1157 (1988): It "targets the direct impact of a particular category of speech, not a secondary feature that happens to be associated with that type of speech." Ibid. (emphasis added).[2]

In sum, it blinks reality to regard this statute, in its application to oral communications, as anything other than a content-based restriction upon speech in the public forum. As such, it must survive that stringent mode of constitutional analysis our cases refer to as "strict scrutiny," which requires that the restriction be narrowly tailored to serve a compelling state interest. See United States v. Playboy Entertainment Group, Inc., 529 U.S. __, (2000) (slip op., at 8); Perry Ed. Assn. v. Perry Local Educators' Assn., 460 U.S. 37, 45, 74 L. Ed. 2d 794, 103 S. Ct. 948 (1983). Since the Court does not even attempt to support the regulation under this standard, I shall discuss it only briefly. Suffice it to say that if protecting people from unwelcome [749] communications (the governmental interest the Court posits) is a compelling state interest, the First Amendment is a dead letter. And if (as I shall discuss at greater length below) forbidding peaceful, nonthreatening, but uninvited speech from a distance closer than eight feet is a "narrowly tailored" means of preventing the obstruction of entrance to medical facilities (the governmental interest the State asserts) narrow tailoring must refer not to the standards of Versace, but to those of Omar the tentmaker. In the last analysis all of this does not matter, however, since as I proceed to discuss neither the restrictions upon oral communications nor those upon handbilling can withstand a proper application of even the less demanding scrutiny we apply to

---

[2] The Court's contention that the statute is content-neutral because it is not a "'regulation of speech'" but a "regulation of the places where some speech may occur," ante, at 14 (quoting Ward v. Rock Against Racism, 491 U.S. 781, 791, 105 L. Ed. 2d 661, 109 S. Ct. 2746 (1989)), is simply baffling. First, because the proposition that a restriction upon the places where speech may occur is not a restriction upon speech is both absurd and contradicted by innumerable cases. See, e.g., Madsen v. Women's Health Center, Inc., 512 U.S. 753, 129 L. Ed. 2d 593, 114 S. Ct. 2516 (1994); Burson v. Freeman, 504 U.S. 191, 119 L. Ed. 2d 5, 112 S. Ct. 1846 (1992); Frisby v. Schultz, 487 U.S. 474, 101 L. Ed. 2d 420, 108 S. Ct. 2495 (1988); Boos v. Barry, 485 U.S. 312, 99 L. Ed. 2d 333, 108 S. Ct. 1157 (1988); Heffron v. International Soc. for Krishna Consciousness, Inc., 452 U.S. 640, 69 L. Ed. 2d 298, 101 S. Ct. 2559 (1981); Carey v. Brown, 447 U.S. 455, 65 L. Ed. 2d 263, 100 S. Ct. 2286 (1980); Grayned v. City of Rockford, 408 U.S. 104, 33 L. Ed. 2d 222, 92 S. Ct. 2294 (1972); Police Dept. of Chicago v. Mosley, 408 U.S. 92, 33 L. Ed. 2d 212, 92 S. Ct. 2286 (1972). And second, because the fact that a restriction is framed as a "regulation of the places where some speech may occur" has nothing whatever to do with whether the restriction is content-neutral – which is why Boos held to be content-based the ban on displaying, within 500 feet of foreign embassies, banners designed to "'bring into public odium any foreign government.'" 485 U.S. at 316.

truly content-neutral regulations of speech in a traditional public forum.

II. As the Court explains, under our precedents even a content-neutral, time, place, and manner restriction must be narrowly tailored to advance a significant state interest, and must leave open ample alternative means of communication. Ward, 491 U.S. at 802. It cannot be sustained if it "burdens substantially more speech than is necessary to further the government's legitimate interests." Id. at 799.

This requires us to determine, first, what is the significant interest the State seeks to advance. Here there appears to be a bit of a disagreement between the State of Colorado (which should know) and the Court (which is eager to speculate). Colorado has identified in the text of the statute itself the interest it sought to advance: to ensure that the State's citizens may "obtain medical counseling and treatment in an unobstructed manner" by "preventing the willful obstruction of a person's access to medical counseling and treatment at a health care facility." Colo. Rev. Stat. § 18-9-122(1) (1999). In its brief here, the State repeatedly confirms the interest squarely identified in the statute under review. See, e.g., Brief for Respondents 15 ("Each provision of the statute was [750] chosen to precisely address crowding and physical intimidation: conduct shown to impede access, endanger safety and health, and strangle effective law enforcement"); id. at 14 ("This provision narrowly addresses the conduct shown to interfere with access through crowding and physical threats"). The Court nevertheless concludes that the Colorado provision is narrowly tailored to serve . . . the State's interest in protecting its citizens' rights to be let alone from unwanted speech.

Indeed, the situation is even more bizarre than that. The interest that the Court makes the linchpin of its analysis was not only unasserted by the State; it is not only completely different from the interest that the statute specifically sets forth; it was explicitly disclaimed by the State in its brief before this Court, and characterized as a "straw interest" petitioners served up in the hope of discrediting the State's case. Id. at 25, n. 19. We may thus add to the lengthening list of "firsts" generated by this Court's relentlessly pro-abortion jurisprudence, the first case in which, in order to sustain a statute, the Court has relied upon a governmental interest not only unasserted by the State, but positively repudiated.

I shall discuss below the obvious invalidity of this statute assuming, first (in Part A), the fictitious state interest that the Court has invented, and then (in Part B), the interest actually recited in the statute and asserted by counsel for Colorado.

A. It is not without reason that Colorado claimed that, in attributing to this statute the false purpose of protecting citizens' right to be let alone, petitioners were seeking to discredit it. Just three Terms ago,

in upholding an injunction against antiabortion activities, the Court refused to rely on any supposed "'right of the people approaching and entering the facilities to be left alone.'" Schenck v. Pro-Choice Network of Western N.Y., 519 U.S. 357, 383, 137 L. Ed. 2d 1, 117 S. Ct. 855 (1997). It expressed "doubt" that this "right . . . accurately reflects our [751] First Amendment jurisprudence." Ibid. Finding itself in something of a jam (the State here has passed a regulation that is obviously not narrowly tailored to advance any other interest) the Court today neatly repackages the repudiated "right" as an "interest" the State may decide to protect, ante, at 11, n. 24, and then places it onto the scales opposite the right to free speech in a traditional public forum.

To support the legitimacy of its self-invented state interest, the Court relies upon a bon mot in a 1928 dissent (which we evidently overlooked in Schenck). It characterizes the "unwilling listener's interest in avoiding unwanted communication" as an "aspect of the broader 'right to be let alone'" Justice Brandeis coined in his dissent in Olmstead v. United States, 277 U.S. 438, 478, 72 L. Ed. 944, 48 S. Ct. 564. The amusing feature is that even this slim reed contradicts rather than supports the Court's position. The right to be let alone that Justice Brandeis identified was a right the Constitution "conferred, as against the government"; it was that right, not some generalized "common-law right" or "interest" to be free from hearing the unwanted opinions of one's fellow citizens, which he called the "most comprehensive" and "most valued by civilized men." Ibid. (emphasis added). To the extent that there can be gleaned from our cases a "right to be let alone" in the sense that Justice Brandeis intended, it is the right of the speaker in the public forum to be free from government interference of the sort Colorado has imposed here.

In any event, the Court's attempt to disguise the "right to be let alone" as a "governmental interest in protecting the right to be let alone" is unavailing for the simple reason that this is not an interest that may be legitimately weighed against the speakers' First Amendment rights (which the Court demotes to the status of First Amendment "interests," ante, at 9.) We have consistently held that "the Constitution does not permit the government to decide which types of otherwise protected speech are sufficiently offensive to require protection for the unwilling listener or viewer." Erznoznik [752] v. Jacksonville, 422 U.S. 205, 210, 45 L. Ed. 2d 125, 95 S. Ct. 2268 (1975) (emphasis added). And as recently as in Schenck, the Court reiterated that "as a general matter, we have indicated that in public debate our own citizens must tolerate insulting, and even outrageous, speech in order to provide adequate breathing space to the freedoms protected by the First Amendment." 519 U.S. at 383 (internal quotation marks omitted).

The Court nonetheless purports to derive from our cases a principle limiting the protection the Constitution affords the speaker's right to direct "offensive messages" at "unwilling" audiences in the public forum. Ante, at 10. There is no such principle. We have upheld limitations on a speaker's exercise of his right to speak on the public streets when that speech intrudes into the privacy of the home. Frisby, 487 U.S. at 483, upheld a content-neutral municipal ordinance prohibiting picketing outside a residence or dwelling. The ordinance, we concluded, was justified by, and narrowly tailored to advance, the government's interest in the "protection of residential privacy." Id. at 484. Our opinion rested upon the "unique nature of the home"; "the home," we said, "is different." Ibid. The reasoning of the case plainly assumed the nonexistence of the right – common law or otherwise – that the Court relies on today, the right to be free from unwanted speech when on the public streets and sidewalks. The home, we noted, was "'the one retreat to which men and women can repair to escape from the tribulations of their daily pursuits.'" Ibid. (quoting Carey, 447 U.S. at 471). The limitation on a speaker's right to bombard the home with unwanted messages which we approved in Frisby – and in Rowan v. Post Office Dept., 397 U.S. 728, 25 L. Ed. 2d 736, 90 S. Ct. 1484 (1970), upon which the Court also relies – was predicated on the fact that "'we are often 'captives' outside the sanctuary of the home and subject to objectionable speech.'" Frisby, supra, at 484 (quoting Rowan, supra, at 738) (emphasis added). As the universally understood state of First Amendment law is described in a leading treatise: "Outside [753] the home, the burden is generally on the observer or listener to avert his eyes or plug his ears against the verbal assaults, lurid advertisements, tawdry books and magazines, and other 'offensive' intrusions which increasingly attend urban life." L. Tribe, American Constitutional Law § 12-19, p. 948 (2d ed. 1988). The Court today elevates the abortion clinic to the status of the home.[3]

There is apparently no end to the distortion of our First Amendment law that the Court is willing to

---

[3] I do not disagree with the Court that "our cases have repeatedly recognized the interests of unwilling listeners" in locations, such as public conveyances, where "'the degree of captivity makes it impractical for the unwilling viewer or auditor to avoid exposure,'" ante, at 13 (quoting Erznoznik v. City of Jacksonville, 422 U.S. 205, 95 S. Ct. 2268, 45 L. Ed. 2d 125 (1975)). But we have never made the absurd suggestion that a pedestrian is a "captive" of the speaker who seeks to address him on the public sidewalks, where he may simply walk quickly by. Erzoznick itself, of course, invalidated a prohibition on the showing of films containing nudity on screens visible from the street, noting that "the burden normally falls upon the viewer to 'avoid further bombardment of [his] sensibilities simply by averting [his] eyes.'" Id. at 210-211 (quoting Cohen v. California, 403 U.S. 15, 21, 29 L. Ed. 2d 284, 91 S. Ct. 1780 (1971).

endure in order to sustain this restriction upon the free speech of abortion opponents. The labor movement, in particular, has good cause for alarm in the Court's extensive reliance upon American Steel Foundries v. Tri-City Central Trades Council, 257 U.S. 184, 66 L. Ed. 189, 42 S. Ct. 72 (1921), an opinion in which the Court held that the Clayton Act's prohibition of injunctions against lawful and peaceful labor picketing did not forbid the injunction in that particular case. The First Amendment was not at issue, and was not so much as mentioned in the opinion, so the case is scant authority for the point the Court wishes to make. The case is also irrelevant because it was "clear from the evidence that from the outset, violent methods were pursued from time to time in such a way as to characterize the attitude of the picketers as continuously threatening." Id. at 200. No such finding was made, or could be made, here. More importantly, however, as far as our future labor cases [754] are concerned: If a "right to be free" from "persistence, importunity, following and dogging," id., at 204, short of actual intimidation was part of our infant First Amendment law in 1921, I am shocked to think that it is there today. The Court's assertion that "none of our decisions has minimized the enduring importance of 'the right to be free' from persistent 'importunity, following and dogging' after an offer to communicate has been declined," ante, at 12, is belied by the fact that this passage from American Steel Foundries has never – not once – found its way into any of the many First Amendment cases this Court has decided since 1921. We will have cause to regret today's injection of this irrelevant anachronism into the mainstream of our First Amendment jurisprudence.

Of course even if one accepted the American Steel Foundries dictum as an accurate expression of First Amendment law, the statute here is plainly not narrowly tailored to protect the interest that dictum describes. Preserving the "right to be free" from "persistent importunity, following and dogging" does not remotely require imposing upon all speakers who wish to protest, educate, or counsel a duty to request permission to approach closer than eight feet. The only way the narrow-tailoring objection can be eliminated is to posit a state-created, First-Amendment-trumping "right to be let alone" as broad and undefined as Brandeis's Olmstead dictum, which may well (why not, if the Court wishes it?) embrace a right not to be spoken to without permission from a distance closer than eight feet. Nothing stands in the way of that solution to the narrow-tailoring problem – except, of course, its utter absurdity, which is no obstacle in abortion cases.

B. I turn now to the real state interest at issue here – the one set forth in the statute and asserted in Colorado's brief: the preservation of unimpeded access to health care facilities. We need look no further than subsection (2) of the statute to [755] see what a provision would look like that is narrowly tailored to serve that interest. Under the terms of that subsection, any person who "knowingly obstructs, detains, hinders, impedes, or blocks another person's entry to or exit from a health care facility" is subject to criminal and civil liability. It is possible, I suppose, that subsection (2) of the Colorado statute will leave unrestricted some expressive activity that, if engaged in from within eight feet, may be sufficiently harassing as to have the effect of impeding access to health care facilities. In subsection (3), however, the State of Colorado has prohibited a vast amount of speech that cannot possibly be thought to correspond to that evil.

To begin with, the 8-foot buffer zone attaches to every person on the public way or sidewalk within 100 feet of the entrance of a medical facility, regardless of whether that person is seeking to enter or exit the facility. In fact, the State acknowledged at oral argument that the buffer zone would attach to any person within 100 feet of the entrance door of a skyscraper in which a single doctor occupied an office on the 18th floor. Tr. of Oral Arg. 41. And even with respect to those who are seeking to enter or exit the facilities, the statute does not protect them only from speech that is so intimidating or threatening as to impede access. Rather, it covers all unconsented-to approaches for the purpose of oral protest, education, or counseling (including those made for the purpose of the most peaceful appeals) and, perhaps even more significantly, every approach made for the purposes of leafleting or handbilling, which we have never considered, standing alone, obstructive or unduly intrusive. The sweep of this prohibition is breathtaking.

The Court makes no attempt to justify on the facts this blatant violation of the narrow-tailoring principle. Instead, it flirts with the creation of yet a new constitutional "first" designed for abortion cases: "When," it says, "a content-neutral regulation does not entirely foreclose any means of communication, it may satisfy the tailoring requirement even [756] though it is not the least restrictive or least intrusive means of serving the statutory goal." Ante, at 21. The implication is that the availability of alternative means of communication permits the imposition of the speech restriction upon more individuals, or more types of communication, than narrow tailoring would otherwise demand. The Court assures us that "we have emphasized" this proposition "on more than one occasion," ibid. The only citation the Court provides, however, says no such thing. Ward v. Rock Against Racism, 491 U.S. at 798, quoted ante, at 21, n. 32, says only that narrow tailoring is not synonymous with "least restrictive alternative." It does not at all suggest – and to my knowledge no other case does either – that

narrow tailoring can be relaxed when there are other speech alternatives.

The burdens this law imposes upon the right to speak are substantial, despite an attempt to minimize them that is not even embarrassed to make the suggestion that they might actually "assist . . . the speakers' efforts to communicate their messages," ante, at 22. (Compare this with the Court's statement in a non-abortion case, joined by the author of today's opinion: "The First Amendment mandates that we presume that speakers, not the government, know best both what they want to say and how to say it." Riley v. National Federation of Blind of N. C., Inc., 487 U.S. 781, 790-791, 101 L. Ed. 2d 669, 108 S. Ct. 2667 (1988).) The Court displays a willful ignorance of the type and nature of communication affected by the statute's restrictions. It seriously asserts, for example, that the 8-foot zone allows a speaker to communicate at a "normal conversational distance," ante, at 22. I have certainly held conversations at a distance of eight feet seated in the quiet of my chambers, but I have never walked along the public sidewalk – and have not seen others do so – "conversing" at an 8-foot remove. The suggestion is absurd. So is the suggestion that the opponents of abortion can take comfort in the fact that the statute "places no limitation on the number of speakers or the noise level, including the use of amplification [757] equipment," ante, at 21. That is good enough, I suppose, for "protesting"; but the Court must know that most of the "counseling" and "educating" likely to take place outside a health care facility cannot be done at a distance and at a high-decibel level. The availability of a powerful amplification system will be of little help to the woman who hopes to forge, in the last moments before another of her sex is to have an abortion, a bond of concern and intimacy that might enable her to persuade the woman to change her mind and heart. The counselor may wish to walk alongside and to say, sympathetically and as softly as the circumstances allow, something like: "My dear, I know what you are going through. I've been through it myself. You're not alone and you do not have to do this. There are other alternatives. Will you let me help you? May I show you a picture of what your child looks like at this stage of her human development?" The Court would have us believe that this can be done effectively – yea, perhaps even more effectively – by shouting through a bullhorn at a distance of eight feet.

The Court seems prepared, if only for a moment, see ante, at 22-23, to take seriously the magnitude of the burden the statute imposes on simple handbilling and leafleting. That concern is fleeting, however, since it is promptly assuaged by the realization that a leafletter may, without violating the statute, stand "near the path" of oncoming pedestrians and make his "proffer . . .,which the pedestrians can easily accept," ante, at 22-23. It does not take a veteran labor organizer to recognize – although surely any would, see Brief for American Federation of Labor and Congress of Industrial Organization as Amicus Curiae 7-8 – that leafleting will be rendered utterly ineffectual by a requirement that the leafletter obtain from each subject permission to approach, or else man a stationary post (one that does not obstruct access to the facility, lest he violate subsection (2) of statute) and wait for passersby voluntarily to approach an outstretched hand. That simply is not how it is done, and the [758] Court knows it – or should. A leafletter, whether he is working on behalf of Operation Rescue, Local 109, or Bubba's Bar-B-Que, stakes out the best piece of real estate he can, and then walks a few steps toward individuals passing in his vicinity, extending his arm and making it as easy as possible for the passerby, whose natural inclination is generally not to seek out such distributions, to simply accept the offering. Few pedestrians are likely to give their "consent" to the approach of a handbiller (indeed, by the time he requested it they would likely have passed by), and even fewer are likely to walk over in order to pick up a leaflet. In the abortion context, therefore, ordinary handbilling, which we have in other contexts recognized to be a "classic form of speech that lies at the heart of the First Amendment," Schenck, 519 U.S. at 377, will in its most effective locations be rendered futile, the Court's implausible assertions to the contrary notwithstanding.

The Colorado provision differs in one fundamental respect from the "content-neutral" time, place, and manner restrictions the Court has previously upheld. Each of them rested upon a necessary connection between the regulated expression and the evil the challenged regulation sought to eliminate. So, for instance, in Ward v. Rock Against Racism, the Court approved the city's control over sound amplification because every occasion of amplified sound presented the evil of excessive noise and distortion disturbing the areas surrounding the public forum. The regulation we upheld in Ward, rather than "banning all concerts, or even all rock concerts, . . . instead focused on the source of the evils the city seeks to eliminate . . . and eliminates them without at the same time banning or significantly restricting a substantial quantity of speech that does not create the same evils." 491 U.S. at 799, n. 7. In Members of City Council of Los Angeles v. Taxpayers for Vincent, 466 U.S. 789, 808, 80 L. Ed. 2d 772, 104 S. Ct. 2118 (1984), the Court approved a prohibition on signs attached to utility poles which "did no more than eliminate the exact source of [759] the evil it sought to remedy." In Heffron v. International Soc. for Krishna Consciousness, Inc., 452 U.S. 640, 652, 69 L. Ed. 2d 298, 101 S. Ct. 2559 (1981), the Court upheld a regulation prohibiting the sale or distribution on the

state fairgrounds of any merchandise, including printed or written material, except from a fixed location, because that precisely served the State's interest in "avoiding congestion and maintaining the orderly movement of fair patrons on the fairgrounds."

In contrast to the laws approved in those cases, the law before us here enacts a broad prophylactic restriction which does not "respond precisely to the substantive problem which legitimately concerned" the State, Vincent, supra, at 810 – namely (the only problem asserted by Colorado), the obstruction of access to health facilities. Such prophylactic restrictions in the First Amendment context – even when they are content-neutral – are not permissible. "Broad prophylactic rules in the area of free expression are suspect. . . . Precision of regulation must be the touchstone in an area so closely touching our most precious freedoms." NAACP v. Button, 371 U.S. 415, 438, 9 L. Ed. 2d 405, 83 S. Ct. 328 (1963). In United States v. Grace, 461 U.S. 171, 75 L. Ed. 2d 736, 103 S. Ct. 1702 (1983), we declined to uphold a ban on certain expressive activity on the sidewalks surrounding the Supreme Court. The purpose of the restriction was the perfectly valid interest in security, just as the purpose of the restriction here is the perfectly valid interest in unobstructed access; and there, as here, the restriction furthered that interest – but it furthered it with insufficient precision and hence at excessive cost to the freedom of speech. There was, we said, "an insufficient nexus" between security and all the expressive activity that was banned, id. at 181 – just as here there is an insufficient nexus between the assurance of access and forbidding unconsented communications within eight feet.[4]

Compare with these venerable and consistent descriptions of our First Amendment law the defenses that the Court makes to the contention that the present statute is overbroad. (To be sure, the Court is assuming its own invented state interest –

---

[4] The Court's suggestion, ante, at 25, that the restrictions imposed by the Colorado ban are unobjectionable because they "interfere far less with a speaker's ability to communicate," than did the regulations involved in Frisby and Heffron, and in cases requiring "silence" outside of a hospital (by which I presume the Court means Madsen v. Women's Health Center, Inc., 512 U.S. 753, 129 L. Ed. 2d 593, 114 S. Ct. 2516 (1994)), misses the point of narrow-tailoring analysis. We do not compare restrictions on speech to some Platonic ideal of speech restrictiveness, or to each other. Rather, our First Amendment doctrine requires us to consider whether the regulation in question burdens substantially more speech than necessary to achieve the particular interest the government has identified and asserted. Ward, 491 U.S. at 799. In each of the instances the Court cites, we concluded that the challenged regulation contained the precision that our cases require and that Colorado's statute (which the Court itself calls "prophylactic," ante, at 24-25) manifestly lacks.

protection of the "right to be let alone" – rather than the interest that the statute describes, but even so the statements are extraordinary.) "The fact," the Court says, "that the coverage of a statute is broader than the specific concern that led to its enactment is of no constitutional significance." Ante, at 26. That is true enough ordinarily, but it is not true with respect to restraints upon speech, which is what the doctrine of overbreadth is all about. (Of course it is also not true, thanks to one of the other pro-abortion "firsts" announced by the current Court, with respect to restrictions upon abortion, which – as our decision in Stenberg v. Carhart, post, p. ___, exemplifies – has been raised to First Amendment status, even as speech opposing abortion has been demoted from First Amendment status.) Again, the Court says that the overbreadth doctrine is not applicable because this law simply "does not 'ban' any signs, literature, or oral statements," but "merely regulates the places where communications may occur." Ante, at 27. I know of no precedent for the proposition that time, place, and manner restrictions are not subject to the doctrine of overbreadth. Our decision in Grace, supra, demonstrates the contrary: Restriction of speech on the sidewalks around [761] the Supreme Court was invalidated because it went further than the needs of security justified. Surely New York City cannot require a parade permit and a security bond for any individual who carries a sign on the sidewalks of Fifth Avenue.

The Court can derive no support for its approval of Colorado's overbroad prophylactic measure from our decision in Schenck. To be sure, there we rejected the argument that the court injunction on demonstrating within a fixed buffer zone around clinic entrances was unconstitutional because it banned even "'peaceful nonobstructive demonstrations.'" 519 U.S. at 381. The Court upheld the injunction, however, only because the "District Court was entitled to conclude," "based on defendants' past conduct" and "the record in [that] case," that the specific defendants involved would, if permitted within the buffer zone, "continue to do what they had done before: aggressively follow and crowd individuals right up to the clinic door and then refuse to move, or purposefully mill around parking lot entrances in an effort to impede or block the progress of cars." Id. at 382. It is one thing to assume, as in Schenck, that a prophylactic injunction is necessary when the specific targets of that measure have demonstrated an inability or unwillingness to engage in protected speech activity without also engaging in conduct that the Constitution clearly does not protect. It is something else to assume that all those who wish to speak outside health care facilities across the State will similarly abuse their rights if permitted to exercise them. The First Amendment stands as a bar to exactly this type of prophylactic

legislation. I cannot improve upon the Court's conclusion in Madsen that "it is difficult, indeed, to justify a prohibition on all uninvited approaches of persons seeking the services of the clinic, regardless of how peaceful the contact may be, without burdening more speech than necessary to prevent intimidation and to ensure access to the clinic. Absent evidence that the protestors' speech is independently [762] proscribable (i.e., 'fighting words' or threats), or is so infused with violence as to be indistinguishable from a threat of physical harm, this provision cannot stand." 512 U.S. at 774 (citation omitted).

The foregoing discussion of overbreadth was written before the Court, in responding to JUSTICE KENNEDY, abandoned any pretense at compliance with that doctrine, and acknowledged – indeed, boasted – that the statute it approves "takes a prophylactic approach," ante, at 24, and adopts "[a] bright-line prophylactic rule," ante, at 25.[5] I scarcely know how to respond to such an unabashed repudiation of our First Amendment doctrine. Prophylaxis is the antithesis of narrow tailoring, as the previously quoted passage from Button makes clear ("Broad prophylactic rules in the area of free expression are suspect. . . . Precision of regulation must be the touchstone in an area so closely touching our most precious freedoms." 371 U.S. at 438.) If the Court were going to make this concession, it could simply have dispensed with its earlier (unpersuasive) attempt to show that the statute was narrowly tailored. So one can add to the casualties of our whatever-it-takes pro-abortion jurisprudence the First Amendment doctrine of narrow tailoring and overbreadth. R. I. P.

    * * *

Before it effectively threw in the towel on the narrow-tailoring point, the Court asserted the importance of taking [763] into account "'the place to which the regulations apply in determining whether these restrictions burden more speech than necessary.'" Ante, at 23 (quoting Madsen, supra, at 772). A proper regard for the "place" involved in this case should result in, if anything, a commitment by this Court to adhere to and rigorously enforce our speech-protective standards. The public forum

---

[5] Of course the Court greatly understates the scope of the prophylaxis, saying that "the statute's prophylactic aspect is justified by the great difficulty of protecting, say, a pregnant woman from physical harassment with legal rules that focus exclusively on the individual impact of each instance of behavior," ante, at 24-25. But the statute prevents the "physically harassing" act of (shudder!) approaching within closer than eight feet not only when it is directed against pregnant women, but also (just to be safe) when it is directed against 300-pound, male, and unpregnant truck drivers – surely a distinction that is not "difficult to make accurately," ante, at 25.

involved here – the public spaces outside of health care facilities – has become, by necessity and by virtue of this Court's decisions, a forum of last resort for those who oppose abortion. The possibility of limiting abortion by legislative means – even abortion of a live-and-kicking child that is almost entirely out of the womb – has been rendered impossible by our decisions from Roe v. Wade, 410 U.S. 113, 35 L. Ed. 2d 147, 93 S. Ct. 705 (1973), to Stenberg v. Carhart, post, p. ___. For those who share an abiding moral or religious conviction (or, for that matter, simply a biological appreciation) that abortion is the taking of a human life, there is no option but to persuade women, one by one, not to make that choice. And as a general matter, the most effective place, if not the only place, where that persuasion can occur, is outside the entrances to abortion facilities. By upholding these restrictions on speech in this place the Court ratifies the State's attempt to make even that task an impossible one.

Those whose concern is for the physical safety and security of clinic patients, workers, and doctors should take no comfort from today's decision. Individuals or groups intent on bullying or frightening women out of an abortion, or doctors out of performing that procedure, will not be deterred by Colorado's statute; bullhorns and screaming from eight feet away will serve their purposes well. But those who would accomplish their moral and religious objectives by peaceful and civil means, by trying to persuade individual women of the rightness of their cause, will be deterred; and that is not a good thing in a democracy. This Court once recognized, as the Framers surely did, that the freedom to speak and persuade is inseparable from, and antecedent to, the survival [764] of self-government. The Court today rotates that essential safety valve on our democracy one-half turn to the right, and no one who seeks safe access to health care facilities in Colorado or elsewhere should feel that her security has by this decision been enhanced.

It is interesting to compare the present decision, which upholds an utterly bizarre pro-abortion "request to approach" provision of Colorado law, with Stenberg, post, p. ___, also announced today, which strikes down a live-birth abortion prohibition adopted by 30 States and twice passed by both Houses of Congress (though vetoed both times by the President). The present case disregards the State's own assertion of the purpose of its pro-abortion law, and posits instead a purpose that the Court believes will be more likely to render the law constitutional. Stenberg rejects the State's assertion of the very meaning of its antiabortion law, and declares instead a meaning that will render the law unconstitutional. The present case rejects overbreadth challenges to a pro-abortion law that regulates speech, on grounds that have no support in our prior jurisprudence and that instead amount to a total repudiation of the

doctrine of overbreadth. Stenberg applies overbreadth analysis to an antiabortion law that has nothing to do with speech, even though until eight years ago overbreadth was unquestionably the exclusive preserve of the First Amendment. See Stenberg, post, at ___ (THOMAS, J., dissenting); Janklow v. Planned Parenthood, Sioux Falls Clinic, 517 U.S. 1174, 1177-1181, 134 L. Ed. 2d 679, 116 S. Ct. 1582 (1996) (SCALIA, J., dissenting from denial of cert.); Ada v. Guam Soc. of Obstetricians & Gynecologists, 506 U.S. 1011, 1013, 121 L. Ed. 2d 564, 113 S. Ct. 633 (1992) (SCALIA, J., dissenting from denial of cert.).

Does the deck seem stacked? You bet. As I have suggested throughout this opinion, today's decision is not an isolated distortion of our traditional constitutional principles, but is one of many aggressively pro-abortion novelties announced by the Court in recent years. See, e.g., Madsen v. Women's Health Center, Inc., 512 U.S. 753, 129 L. Ed. 2d 593, 114 S. Ct. 2516 (1994); Schenck [765] v. Pro-Choice Network of Western N.Y., 519 U.S. 357, 137 L. Ed. 2d 1, 117 S. Ct. 855 (1997); Thornburgh v. American College of Obstetricians and Gynecologists, 476 U.S. 747, 90 L. Ed. 2d 779, 106 S. Ct. 2169 (1986). Today's distortions, however, are particularly blatant. Restrictive views of the First Amendment that have been in dissent since the 1930's suddenly find themselves in the majority. "Uninhibited, robust, and wide open" debate is replaced by the power of the state to protect an unheard-of "right to be let alone" on the public streets. I dissent.

DISSENT: JUSTICE KENNEDY.

The Court's holding contradicts more than a half century of well-established First Amendment principles. For the first time, the Court approves a law which bars a private citizen from passing a message, in a peaceful manner and on a profound moral issue, to a fellow citizen on a public sidewalk. If from this time forward the Court repeats its grave errors of analysis, we shall have no longer the proud tradition of free and open discourse in a public forum. In my view, JUSTICE SCALIA's First Amendment analysis is correct and mandates outright reversal. In addition to undermining established First Amendment principles, the Court's decision conflicts with the essence of the joint opinion in Planned Parenthood of Southeastern Pa. v. Casey, 505 U.S. 833, 120 L. Ed. 2d 674, 112 S. Ct. 2791 (1992). It seems appropriate in these circumstances to reinforce JUSTICE SCALIA's correct First Amendment conclusions and to set forth my own views.

I. The Court uses the framework of Ward v. Rock Against Racism, 491 U.S. 781, 105 L. Ed. 2d 661, 109 S. Ct. 2746 (1989), for resolution of the case. The Court wields the categories of Ward so that what once were rules to protect speech now become rules to restrict it. This is twice unfortunate. The rules of Ward are diminished in value for later cases; and the Ward analysis ought not have been undertaken at all. To employ Ward's complete [766] framework is a mistake at the outset, for Ward applies only if a statute is content neutral. Colorado's statute is a textbook example of a law which is content based.

A. The statute makes it a criminal offense to "knowingly approach another person within eight feet of such person, unless such other person consents, for the purpose of passing a leaflet or handbill to, displaying a sign to, or engaging in oral protest, education, or counseling with such other person in the public way or sidewalk area within a radius of one hundred feet from any entrance door to a health care facility." Colo. Rev. Stat. § 18-9-122(3) (1999). The law imposes content-based restrictions on speech by reason of the terms it uses, the categories it employs, and the conditions for its enforcement. It is content based, too, by its predictable and intended operation. Whether particular messages violate the statute is determined by their substance. The law is a prime example of a statute inviting screening and censoring of individual speech; and it is serious error to hold otherwise.

The Court errs in asserting the Colorado statute is no different from laws sustained as content neutral in earlier cases. The prohibitions against "picketing" and/or "leafleting" upheld in Frisby v. Schultz, 487 U.S. 474, 101 L. Ed. 2d 420, 108 S. Ct. 2495 (1988), United States v. Grace, 461 U.S. 171, 75 L. Ed. 2d 736, 103 S. Ct. 1702 (1983), and Police Dept. of Chicago v. Mosley, 408 U.S. 92, 33 L. Ed. 2d 212, 92 S. Ct. 2286 (1972), the Court says, see ante, at 17, and n. 30, are no different from the restrictions on "protest, education, or counseling" imposed by the Colorado statute. The parallel the Court sees does not exist. No examination of the content of a speaker's message is required to determine whether an individual is picketing, or distributing a leaflet, or impeding free access to a building. Under the Colorado enactment, however, the State must review content to determine whether a person has engaged in criminal "protest, education, or counseling." When a citizen [767] approaches another on the sidewalk in a disfavored-speech zone, an officer of the State must listen to what the speaker says. If, in the officer's judgment, the speaker's words stray too far toward "protest, education, or counseling" – the boundaries of which are far from clear – the officer may decide the speech has moved from the permissible to the criminal. The First Amendment does not give the government such power.

The statute is content based for an additional reason: It restricts speech on particular topics. Of course, the enactment restricts "oral protest, education, or counseling" on any subject; but a statute of broad application is not content neutral if its terms control the substance of a speaker's message. If oral protest, education, or counseling on every subject within an 8-foot zone present a danger to the public, the statute should apply to every building entrance in the State. It does not. It applies only to a special class of locations: entrances to buildings with health care facilities. We would close our eyes to reality were we to deny that "oral protest, education, or counseling" outside the entrances to medical facilities concern a narrow range of topics – indeed, one topic in particular. By confining the law's application to the specific locations where the prohibited discourse occurs, the State has made a content-based determination. The Court ought to so acknowledge. Clever content-based restrictions are no less offensive than censoring on the basis of content. See, e.g., United States v. Eichman, 496 U.S. 310, 110 L. Ed. 2d 287, 110 S. Ct. 2404 (1990). If, just a few decades ago, a State with a history of enforcing racial discrimination had enacted a statute like this one, regulating "oral protest, education, or counseling" within 100 feet of the entrance to any lunch counter, our predecessors would not have hesitated to hold it was content based or viewpoint based. It should be a profound disappointment to defenders of the First Amendment that the Court today refuses to apply the same structural analysis when the speech involved is less palatable to it.

[768] The Court, in error and irony, validates the Colorado statute because it purports to restrict all of the proscribed expressive activity regardless of the subject. The evenhandedness the Court finds so satisfying, however, is but a disguise for a glaring First Amendment violation. The Court, by citing the breadth of the statute, cannot escape the conclusion that its categories are nonetheless content based. The liberty of a society is measured in part by what its citizens are free to discuss among themselves. Colorado's scheme of disfavored-speech zones on public streets and sidewalks, and the Court's opinion validating them, are antithetical to our entire First Amendment tradition. To say that one citizen can approach another to ask the time or the weather forecast or the directions to Main Street but not to initiate discussion on one of the most basic moral and political issues in all of contemporary discourse, a question touching profound ideas in philosophy and theology, is an astonishing view of the First Amendment. For the majority to examine the statute under rules applicable to content-neutral regulations is an affront to First Amendment teachings.

After the Court errs in finding the statute content neutral, it compounds the mistake by finding the law viewpoint neutral. Viewpoint-based rules are invidious speech restrictions, yet the Court approves this one. The purpose and design of the statute – as everyone ought to know and as its own defenders urge in attempted justification – are to restrict speakers on one side of the debate: those who protest abortions. The statute applies only to medical facilities, a convenient yet obvious mask for the legislature's true purpose and for the prohibition's true effect. One need read no further than the statute's preamble to remove any doubt about the question. The Colorado Legislature sought to restrict "a person's right to protest or counsel against certain medical procedures." Colo. Rev. Stat. § 18-9-122(1) (1999). The word "against" reveals the legislature's desire to restrict [769] discourse on one side of the issue regarding "certain medical procedures." The testimony to the Colorado Legislature consisted, almost in its entirety, of debates and controversies with respect to abortion, a point the majority acknowledges. Ante, at 9. The legislature's purpose to restrict unpopular speech should be beyond dispute.

The statute's operation reflects its objective. Under the most reasonable interpretation of Colorado's law, if a speaker approaches a fellow citizen within any one of Colorado's thousands of disfavored-speech zones and chants in praise of the Supreme Court and its abortion decisions, I should think there is neither protest, nor education, nor counseling. If the opposite message is communicated, however, a prosecution to punish protest is warranted. The anti-speech distinction also pertains if a citizen approaches a public official visiting a health care facility to make a point in favor of abortion rights. If she says, "Good job, Governor," there is no violation; if she says, "Shame on you, Governor," there is. Furthermore, if the speaker addresses a woman who is considering an abortion and says, "Please take just a moment to read these brochures and call our support line to talk with women who have been in your situation," the speaker would face criminal penalties for counseling. Yet if the speaker simply says, "We are for abortion rights," I should think this is neither education or counseling. Thus does the Court today ensure its own decisions can be praised but not condemned. Thus does it restrict speech designed to teach that the exercise of a constitutional right is not necessarily concomitant with making a sound moral choice. Nothing in our law or our enviable free speech tradition sustains this self-serving rule. Colorado is now allowed to punish speech because of its content and viewpoint.

The Court time and again has held content-based or viewpoint-based regulations to be presumptively invalid. See McIntyre v. Ohio Elections Comm'n, 514 U.S. 334, 345-346, 131 L. Ed. 2d 426, 115 S. Ct. 1511 (1995); R. A. V. v. St. Paul, 505 U.S. 377, 382, 120 L. Ed. 2d 305, 112 S. Ct. 2538 (1992); [770] Simon & Schuster, Inc. v. Members of N.Y. State Crime Victims Bd., 502 U.S. 105, 116, 116 L. Ed. 2d

476, 112 S. Ct. 501 (1991) ("'Regulations which permit the Government to discriminate on the basis of the content of the message cannot be tolerated under the First Amendment'" (quoting Regan v. Time, Inc., 468 U.S. 641, 648-649, 82 L. Ed. 2d 487, 104 S. Ct. 3262 (1984)). Here the statute "suppresses expression out of concern for its likely communicative impact." Eichman, 496 U.S. at 317. Like the picketing statute struck down in Boos v. Barry, 485 U.S. 312, 99 L. Ed. 2d 333, 108 S. Ct. 1157 (1998), this prohibition seeks to eliminate public discourse on an entire subject and topic. The Court can cite not a single case where we sustained a law aimed at a broad class of topics on grounds that it is both content and viewpoint neutral. Cf. McIntyre v. Ohio Elections Comm'n, supra, at 345 ("Even though this provision applies evenhandedly to advocates of differing viewpoints, it is a direct regulation of the content of speech"); Boos, supra, at 319 ("[A] regulation that 'does not favor either side of a political controversy' is nonetheless impermissible because the 'First Amendment's hostility to content-based regulations extends . . . to prohibition of public discussion of an entire topic'" (quoting Consolidated Edison Co. of N.Y. v. Public Serv. Comm'n of N.Y., 447 U.S. 530, 537, 65 L. Ed. 2d 319, 100 S. Ct. 2326 (1980)); see also First Nat. Bank of Boston v. Bellotti, 435 U.S. 765, 784-785, 55 L. Ed. 2d 707, 98 S. Ct. 1407 (1978) (invalidating statute which permitted corporations to speak on political issues decided by referenda, but not on other subjects). Statutes which impose content-based or viewpoint-based restrictions are subjected to exacting scrutiny. The State has failed to sustain its burden of proving that its statute is content and viewpoint neutral. See United States v. Playboy Entertainment Group, Inc., 529 U.S. ___, (2000) (slip op., at 12) ("When the Government restricts speech, the Government bears the burden of proving the constitutionality of its actions"). The Ward time, place, and manner analysis is simply inapplicable to this law. I would hold the statute invalid from the very start.

B. [771] In a further glaring departure from precedent we learn today that citizens have a right to avoid unpopular speech in a public forum. Ante, at 11-12. For reasons JUSTICE SCALIA explains in convincing fashion, neither Justice Brandeis' dissenting opinion in Olmstead v. United States, 277 U.S. 438, 478, 72 L. Ed. 944, 48 S. Ct. 564 (1928), nor the Court's opinion in American Steel Foundries v. Tri-City Central Trades Council, 257 U.S. 184, 66 L. Ed. 189, 42 S. Ct. 72 (1921), establishes a right to be free from unwelcome expression aired by a fellow citizen in a traditional public forum: "The Fourteenth Amendment does not permit a State to make criminal the peaceful expression of unpopular views." Edwards v. South Carolina, 372 U.S. 229, 237, 9 L. Ed. 2d 697, 83 S. Ct. 680 (1963).

The Court's reliance on Rowan v. Post Office Dept., 397 U.S. 728, 25 L. Ed. 2d 736, 90 S. Ct. 1484 (1970), and Erznoznik v. Jacksonville, 422 U.S. 205, 45 L. Ed. 2d 125, 95 S. Ct. 2268 (1975), is inapt. Rowan involved a federal statute allowing individuals to remove their names from commercial mailing lists. Businesses contended the statute infringed upon their First Amendment right to communicate with private citizens. The Court rejected the challenge, reasoning that the First Amendment affords individuals some control over what, and how often, unwelcome commercial messages enter their private residences. Id. at 736, 738. Rowan did not hold, contrary to statements in today's opinion, see ante, at 12-13, that the First Amendment permits the government to restrict private speech in a public forum. Indeed, the Court in Rowan recognized what everyone, before today, understood to be true: "We are often 'captives' outside the sanctuary of the home and subject to objectionable speech and other sound . . . ." 397 U.S. at 738.

In Erznoznik, the Court struck down a municipal ordinance prohibiting drive-in movie theaters visible from either a public street or a public place from showing films containing nudity. The ordinance, the Court concluded, imposed a content-based restriction upon speech and was both too broad [772] and too narrow to serve the interests asserted by the municipality. 422 U.S. at 211-215. The law, moreover, was not analogous to the rare, "selective restrictions" on speech previously upheld to protect individual privacy. Id. at 208-209 (citing and discussing Rowan, supra, and Lehman v. Shaker Heights, 418 U.S. 298, 41 L. Ed. 2d 770, 94 S. Ct. 2714 (1974)). The Court did not, contrary to the majority's assertions, suggest that government is free to enact categorical measures restricting traditional, peaceful communications among citizens in a public forum. Instead, the Court admonished that citizens usually bear the burden of disregarding unwelcome messages. 422 U.S. at 211 (citing Cohen v. California, 403 U.S. 15, 21, 29 L. Ed. 2d 284, 91 S. Ct. 1780 (1971)).

Today's decision is an unprecedented departure from this Court's teachings respecting unpopular speech in public fora.

II. The Colorado statute offends settled First Amendment principles in another fundamental respect. It violates the constitutional prohibitions against vague or overly broad criminal statutes regulating speech. The enactment's fatal ambiguities are multiple and interact to create further imprecisions. The result is a law more vague and overly broad than any criminal statute the Court has sustained as a permissible regulation of speech. The statute's imprecisions are so evident that this, too,

ought to have ended the case without further discussion.

The law makes it a criminal offense to "knowingly approach another person within eight feet of such person, unless such other person consents, for the purpose of passing a leaflet or handbill to, displaying a sign to, or engaging in oral protest, education, or counseling with such other person in the public way or sidewalk area within a radius of one hundred feet from any entrance door to a health care facility." Colo. Rev. Stat. § 18-9-122(3) (1999). The operative terms and phrases of the statute are not defined. The case comes [773] to us from the state court system; and as the Colorado courts did not give the statute a sufficient narrowing construction, questions of vagueness and overbreadth should be addressed by this Court in the first instance. See Coates v. Cincinnati, 402 U.S. 611, 613-614, 29 L. Ed. 2d 214, 91 S. Ct. 1686 (1971).

In the context of a law imposing criminal penalties for pure speech, "protest" is an imprecise word; "counseling" is an imprecise word; "education" is an imprecise word. No custom, tradition, or legal authority gives these terms the specificity required to sustain a criminal prohibition on speech. I simply disagree with the majority's estimation that it is "quite remote" that "anyone would not understand any of those common words." Ante, at 28. The criminal statute is subject to manipulation by police, prosecutors, and juries. Its substantial imprecisions will chill speech, so the statute violates the First Amendment. Cf. Kolender v. Lawson, 461 U.S. 352, 358, 360, 75 L. Ed. 2d 903, 103 S. Ct. 1855 (1983); Herndon v. Lowry, 301 U.S. 242, 263-264, 81 L. Ed. 1066, 57 S. Ct. 732 (1937).

In operation the statute's inevitable arbitrary effects create vagueness problems of their own. The 8-foot no-approach zone is so unworkable it will chill speech. Assume persons are about to enter a building from different points and a protestor is walking back and forth with a sign or attempting to hand out leaflets. If she stops to create the 8-foot zone for one pedestrian, she cannot reach other persons with her message; yet if she moves to maintain the 8-foot zone while trying to talk to one patron she may move knowingly closer to a patron attempting to enter the facility from a different direction. In addition, the statute requires a citizen to give affirmative consent before the exhibitor of a sign or the bearer of a leaflet can approach. When dealing with strangers walking fast toward a building's entrance, there is a middle ground of ambiguous answers and mixed signals in which misinterpretation can subject a good-faith speaker to criminal liability. The mere failure to give a reaction, for instance, is a failure to give consent. These elements [774] of ambiguity compound the others.

Finally, as we all know, the identity or enterprise of the occupants of a building which fronts on a public street are not always known to the public. Health care providers may occupy but a single office in a large building. The Colorado citizen may walk from a disfavored-speech zone to a free zone with little or no ability to discern when one ends and the other begins. The statute's vagueness thus becomes as well one source of its overbreadth. The only sure way to avoid violating the law is to refrain from picketing, leafleting, or oral advocacy altogether. Scienter cannot save so vague a statute as this.

A statute is vague when the conduct it forbids is not ascertainable. See Chicago v. Morales, 527 U.S. 41, 56, 144 L. Ed. 2d 67, 119 S. Ct. 1849 (1999). "[People] of common intelligence cannot be required to guess at the meaning of the enactment." Winters v. New York, 333 U.S. 507, 515, 92 L. Ed. 840, 68 S. Ct. 665 (1948). The terms "oral protest, education, or counseling" are at least as imprecise as criminal prohibitions on speech the Court has declared void for vagueness in past decades. In Coates v. Cincinnati, 402 U.S. 611, 29 L. Ed. 2d 214, 91 S. Ct. 1686 (1971), the Court encountered little difficulty in striking down a municipal ordinance making it a criminal offense for "three or more persons to assemble . . . on any of the sidewalks . . . and there conduct themselves in a manner annoying to persons passing by . . . ." Ibid. The Court held the ordinance to be unconstitutionally vague because "it subjected the exercise of the right of assembly to an unascertainable standard, and [was] unconstitutionally broad because it authorized the punishment of constitutionally protected conduct." Id. at 614. Vagueness led to overbreadth as well in Houston v. Hill, 482 U.S. 451, 96 L. Ed. 2d 398, 107 S. Ct. 2502 (1987), where the Court invalidated an ordinance making it "unlawful for any person to . . . in any manner oppose . . . or interrupt any policeman in the execution of his duty." Id. at 455. The "sweeping" restriction, the Court reasoned, placed citizens at risk of arrest for exercising their [775] "freedom . . . to oppose or challenge police action," a right "by which we distinguish a free nation from a police state." Id. at 462-463.

The requirement of specificity for statutes that impose criminal sanctions on public expression was established well before Coates and Hill, of course. In Carlson v. California, 310 U.S. 106, 84 L. Ed. 1104, 60 S. Ct. 746 (1940), a unanimous Court invalidated an ordinance prohibiting individuals from carrying or displaying any sign or banner or from picketing near a place of business "for the purpose of inducing or influencing, or attempting to induce or influence, any person to refrain from entering any such works, or factory, or place of business, or employment." Id. at 109. The statute employed imprecise language, providing citizens with no guidance as to whether particular expressive activities fell within its reach.

The Court found that the "sweeping and inexact terms of the ordinance disclose the threat to freedom of speech inherent in its existence," a result at odds with the guarantees of the First Amendment. Id. at 112.

Rather than adhere to this rule, the Court turns it on its head, stating the statute's overbreadth is "a virtue, not a vice." Ante, at 26. The Court goes even further, praising the statute's "prophylactic approach; it forbids all unwelcome demonstrators to come closer than eight feet." Ante, at 24. Indeed, in the Court's view, "bright-line prophylactic rules may be the best way to provide protection" to those individuals unwilling to hear a fellow citizen's message in a public forum. Ante, at 25. The Court is quite wrong. Overbreadth is a constitutional flaw, not a saving feature. Sweeping within its ambit even more protected speech does not save a criminal statute invalid in its essential reach and design. The Court, moreover, cannot meet the concern that the statute is vague; for neither the Colorado courts nor established legal principles offer satisfactory guidance in interpreting the statute's imprecisions. III.[776] Even aside from the erroneous, most disturbing assumptions that the statute is content neutral, viewpoint neutral, and neither vague nor overbroad, the Court falls into further serious error when it turns to the time, place, and manner rules set forth in Ward.

An essential requirement under Ward is that the regulation in question not "burden substantially more speech than necessary to further the government's legitimate interests." 491 U.S. at 799. As we have seen, however, Colorado and the Court attempt to justify the law on just the opposite assumption.

I have explained already how the statute is a failed attempt to make the enactment appear content neutral, a disguise for the real concern of the legislation. The legislature may as well have enacted a statute subjecting "oral protest, education, or counseling near abortion clinics" to criminal penalty. Both the State and the Court attempt to sidestep the enactment's obvious content-based restriction by praising the statute's breadth, by telling us all topics of conversation, not just discourse on abortion, are banned within the statutory proscription. The saving feature the Court tries to grasp simply creates additional free speech infirmity. Our precedents do not permit content censoring to be cured by taking even more protected speech within a statute's reach. The statute before us, as construed by the majority, would do just that. If it indeed proscribes "oral protest, education, or counseling" on all subjects across the board, it by definition becomes "substantially broader than necessary to achieve the government's interest." Id. at 800.

The whimsical, arbitrary nature of the statute's operation is further demonstration of a restriction upon more speech than necessary. The happenstance of a dental office being located in a building brings the restricted-speech zone into play. If the same building also houses an organization dedicated, [777] say, to environmental issues, a protest against the group's policies would be barred. Yet if, on the next block there were a public interest enterprise in a building with no health care facility, the speech would be unrestricted. The statute is a classic example of a proscription not narrowly tailored and resulting in restrictions of far more speech than necessary to achieve the legislature's object. The first time, place, and manner requirement of Ward cannot be satisfied.

Assuming Colorado enacted the statute to respond to incidents of disorderly and unlawful conduct near abortion clinics, there were alternatives to restricting speech. It is beyond dispute that pinching or shoving or hitting is a battery actionable under the criminal law and punishable as a crime. State courts have also found an actionable tort when there is a touching, done in an offensive manner, of an object closely identified with the body, even if it is not clothing or the body itself. See, e.g., Fisher v. Carrousel Motor Hotel, Inc., 424 S.W.2d 627, 630 (Tex. 1967) ("Personal indignity is the essence of an action for battery; and consequently the defendant is liable not only for contacts which do actual physical harm, but also for those which are offensive and insulting" (citing Prosser, Insult & Outrage, 44 Calif. L. Rev. 40 (1956)). The very statute before us, in its other parts, includes a provision aimed at ensuring access to health care facilities. The law imposes criminal sanctions upon any person who "knowingly obstructs, detains, hinders, impedes, or blocks another person's entry to or exit from a health care facility." Colo. Rev. Stat. § 18-9-122(2) (1999). With these means available to ensure access, the statute's overreaching in the regulation of speech becomes again apparent.

The majority insists the statute aims to protect distraught women who are embarrassed, vexed, or harassed as they attempt to enter abortion clinics. If these are punishable acts, they should be prohibited in those terms. In the course of praising Colorado's approach, the majority does not pause to tell us why, in its view, substantially less restrictive means [778] cannot be employed to ensure citizens access to health care facilities or to prevent physical contact between citizens. The Court's approach is at odds with the rigor demanded by Ward. See 491 U.S. at 799 ("Government may not regulate expression in such a manner that a substantial portion of the burden on speech does not serve to advance its goals").

There are further errors in the Court's novel, prophylactic analysis. The prophylactic theory seems to be based on a supposition that most citizens approaching a health care facility are unwilling to listen to a fellow citizen's message and that face-to-face communications will lead to lawless behavior within the power of the State to punish. These premises have no support in law or in fact. And even when there is authority to adopt preventive measures, of course, the First Amendment does not allow a speech prohibition in an imprecise or overly broad statute. Cf. Thornhill v. Alabama, 310 U.S. 88, 105, 84 L. Ed. 1093, 60 S. Ct. 736 (1940) ("The power and the duty of the State to take adequate steps to preserve the peace and to protect the privacy, the lives, and the property of its residents cannot be doubted. But no clear and present danger of destruction of life or property, or invasion of the right of privacy, or breach of the peace can be thought to be inherent in the activities of every person who approaches the premises of an employer and publicizes the facts of a labor dispute involving the latter"). The Court places our free speech traditions in grave jeopardy by licensing legislatures to adopt "bright-line prophylactic rules . . . to provide protection" to unwilling listeners in a quintessential public forum. Ante, at 25.

The Court's lack of concern with the statute's flaws is explained in part by its disregard of the importance of free discourse and the exchange of ideas in a traditional public forum. Our precedents have considered the level of protection afforded speech in specific locations, but the rules formulated in those decisions are not followed today. "To ascertain what limits, if any, may be placed on protected speech," our precedents instruct "we have often focused on [779] the 'place' of that speech, considering the nature of the forum the speaker seeks to employ. The standards by which limitations on speech must be evaluated 'differ depending on the character of the property at issue.'" Frisby v. Schultz, 487 U.S. at 479 (quoting Perry Ed. Assn. v. Perry Local Educators' Assn., 460 U.S. 37, 44, 74 L. Ed. 2d 794, 103 S. Ct. 948 (1983)). The quoted language was part of our holding in an important free speech case; and it is a holding the majority disregards.

Frisby upheld a municipal ordinance restricting targeted picketing in residential areas. The primary purpose of the ordinance, and a reason the Court sustained it, was to protect and preserve the tranquility of private homes. The private location at which respondents sought to engage in their expressive activities was stressed throughout the Court's opinion. See 487 U.S. at 483 ("We construe the ban to be a limited one; only focused picketing taking place solely in front of a particular residence is prohibited"). "Although in many locations," the Court reasoned, "we expect individuals to avoid speech they do not want to hear, the home is different. 'That we are often "captives" outside the sanctuary of the home and subject to objectionable speech . . . does not mean we must be captives everywhere.'" Id. at 484 (quoting Rowan v. Post Office Dept., 397 U.S. at 738).

The Colorado law does not seek to protect private residences. Nor does the enactment impose a place restriction upon expressive activity undertaken on property, such as fairgrounds, designated for limited, special purposes. See, e.g., Heffron v. International Soc. for Krishna Consciousness, Inc., 452 U.S. 640, 655, 69 L. Ed. 2d 298, 101 S. Ct. 2559 (1981). The statute applies to public streets and sidewalks, traditional public fora which "'time out of mind, have been used for purposes of assembly, communicating thoughts between citizens, and discussing public questions.'" See Boos, 485 U.S. at 318 (quoting Hague v. Committee for Industrial Organization, 307 U.S. 496, 515, 59 S. Ct. 954, 83 L. Ed. 1423 (1939) (opinion of Roberts, J.)). Given our traditions with respect to open discussion in public fora, this statute, [780] which sweeps so largely on First Amendment freedoms, cannot be sustained.

The statute fails a further test under Ward, for it does not "'leave open ample alternative channels for communication of the information.'" 491 U.S. at 791 (quoting Clark v. Community for Creative Non-Violence, 468 U.S. 288, 293, 82 L. Ed. 2d 221, 104 S. Ct. 3065 (1984)). Frisby again instructs us. A second reason we sustained the ordinance banning targeted residential picketing was because "ample alternative" avenues for communication remained open:

"'Protestors have not been barred from the residential neighborhoods. They may enter such neighborhoods, alone or in groups, even marching . . . . They may go door-to-door to proselytize their views. They may distribute literature in this manner . . . or through the mails. They may contact residents by telephone, short of harassment.'" 487 U.S. at 483-484 (quoting Brief for Appellants in No. 87-168, O. T. 1987, pp. 41-42).

The residential picketing ordinance, the Court concluded, "permitted the more general dissemination of a message" to the targeted audience. 487 U.S. at 483. The same conclusion cannot be reached here. Door-to-door distributions or mass mailing or telephone campaigns are not effective alternative avenues of communication for petitioners. They want to engage in peaceful face-to-face communication with individuals the petitioners believe are about to commit a profound moral wrong. Without the ability to interact in person, however momentarily, with a clinic patron near the very place where a woman might elect to receive an abortion, the statute strips petitioners of using speech in the time, place, and manner most vital to the protected expression.

In addition to leaving petitioners without adequate means of communication, the law forecloses peaceful leafleting, a mode of speech with deep roots in our Nation's history and [781] traditions. In an age when vast resources and talents are commanded by a sophisticated media to shape opinions on limitless subjects and ideas, the distribution of leaflets on a sidewalk may seem a bit antiquated. This case proves the necessity for the traditional mode of speech. It must be remembered that the whole course of our free speech jurisprudence, sustaining the idea of open public discourse which is the hallmark of the American constitutional system, rests to a significant extent on cases involving picketing and leafleting. Our foundational First Amendment cases are based on the recognition that citizens, subject to rare exceptions, must be able to discuss issues, great or small, through the means of expression they deem best suited to their purpose. It is for the speaker, not the government, to choose the best means of expressing a message. "The First Amendment," our cases illustrate, "protects [citizens'] right not only to advocate their cause but also to select what they believe to be the most effective means for so doing." Meyer v. Grant, 486 U.S. 414, 424, 100 L. Ed. 2d 425, 108 S. Ct. 1886 (1988). The Court's conclusion that Colorado's 8-foot no-approach zone protects citizens' ability to leaflet or otherwise engage in peaceful protest is untenable.

Given the Court's holding, it is necessary to recall our cases protecting the right to protest and hand out leaflets. In Lovell v. City of Griffin, 303 U.S. 444, 82 L. Ed. 949, 58 S. Ct. 666 (1938), the Court invalidated an ordinance forbidding the distribution of literature of any kind without the written permission of a city official. "The liberty of the press," the Court explained, "is not confined to newspapers and periodicals." Id. at 452. "It necessarily embraces pamphlets and leaflets. These indeed have been historic weapons in the defense of liberty, as the pamphlets of Thomas Paine and others in our own history abundantly attest. The press in its historic connotation comprehends every sort of publication which affords a vehicle of information and opinion." Ibid.

In Schneider v. State (Town of Irvington), 308 U.S. 147, 84 L. Ed. 155, 60 S. Ct. 146 (1939), reinforcing Lovell, the Court struck down a series of [782] municipal ordinances prohibiting the distribution of handbills on public streets on the rationale of preventing littering. Schneider made clear that while citizens may not enjoy a right to force an unwilling person to accept a leaflet, they do have a protected right to tender it. The Court stressed a basic First Amendment precept: "The streets are natural and proper places for the dissemination of information and opinion; and one is not to have the exercise of his liberty of expression in appropriate places abridged on the plea that it may exercised in some other place." 308 U.S. at 163. The words of the Court more than a half century ago demonstrate the necessity to adhere to those principles today:

"Municipal authorities, as trustees for the public, have the duty to keep their communities' streets open and available for movement of people and property, the primary purpose to which the streets are dedicated. So long as legislation to this end does not abridge the constitutional liberty of one rightfully upon the street to impart information through speech or the distribution of literature, it may lawfully regulate the conduct of those using the streets. For example, a person could not exercise this liberty by taking his stand in the middle of a crowded street, contrary to traffic regulations, and maintain his position to the stoppage of all traffic; a group of distributors could not insist upon a constitutional right to form a cordon across the street and to allow no pedestrian to pass who did not accept a tendered leaflet; nor does the guarantee of freedom of speech or of the press deprive a municipality of power to enact regulations against throwing literature broadcast in the streets. Prohibition of such conduct would not abridge the constitutional liberty since such activity bears no necessary relationship to the freedom to speak, write, print or distribute information or opinion.

"This court has characterized the freedom of speech and that of the press as fundamental personal rights and [783] liberties. The phrase is not an empty one and was not lightly used. It reflects the belief of the framers of the Constitution that exercise of the rights lies at the foundation of free government by free men. It stresses, as do many opinions of this court, the importance of preventing the restriction of enjoyment of these liberties.

"In every case, therefore, where legislative abridgment of the rights is asserted, the courts should be astute to examine the effect of the challenged legislation. Mere legislative preferences or beliefs respecting matters of public convenience may well support regulation directed at other personal activities, but be insufficient to justify such as diminishes the exercise of rights so vital to the maintenance of democratic institutions. And so, as cases arise, the delicate and difficult task falls upon the courts to weigh the circumstances and to appraise the substantiality of the reasons advanced in support of the regulation of the free enjoyment of the rights." 308 U.S. at 160-161 (footnote omitted).

After Lovell and Schneider the Court gave continued, explicit definition to our custom and practice of free and open discourse by picketing and leafleting. In Thornhill v. Alabama, 310 U.S. 88, 84 L. Ed. 1093, 60 S. Ct. 736 (1940), the Court considered a First Amendment challenge to a statute prohibiting "loitering or picketing" near "the premises or place of business of any . . . firm, corporation, or association of people, engaged in a lawful business." Id. at 91. Petitioner was arrested, charged, and convicted of violating the statute by engaging in peaceful picketing in front of a manufacturing plant. Id. at 94-95. The Court invalidated the Alabama statute. The breadth of Alabama's speech restriction was one reason for ruling it invalid on its face, just as it should be for the statute we consider today:

"[Alabama Code §] 3448 has been applied by the state courts so as to prohibit a single individual from walking [784] slowly and peacefully back and forth on the public sidewalk in front of the premises of an employer, without speaking to anyone, carrying a sign or placard on a staff above his head stating only the fact that the employer did not employ union men affiliated with the American Federation of Labor; the purpose of the described activity was concededly to advise customers and prospective customers of the relationship existing between the employer and its employees and thereby to induce such customers not to patronize the employer." Id. at 98-99 (footnote omitted).

The statute, in short, prohibited "whatever the means used to publicize the facts of a labor dispute, whether by printed sign, by pamphlet, by word of mouth or otherwise . . . so long as it occurs in the vicinity of the scene of the dispute." Id. at 101. The Court followed these observations with an explication of fundamental free speech principles I would have thought controlling in the present case:

"It does not follow that the State in dealing with the evils arising from industrial disputes may impair the effective exercise of the right to discuss freely industrial relations which are matters of public concern. A contrary conclusion could be used to support abridgment of freedom of speech and of the press concerning almost every matter of importance to society.

"The range of activities proscribed by § 3448, whether characterized as picketing or loitering or otherwise, embraces nearly every practicable, effective means whereby those interested – including the employees directly affected – may enlighten the public on the nature and causes of a labor dispute. The safeguarding of these means is essential to the securing of an informed and educated public opinion with respect to a matter which is of public concern. It may be that effective exercise [785] of the means of advancing public knowledge may persuade some of those reached to refrain from entering into advantageous relations with the business establishment which is the scene of the dispute. Every expression of opinion on matters that are important has the potentiality of inducing action in the interests of one rather than another group in society. But the group in power at any moment may not impose penal sanctions on peaceful and truthful discussion of matters of public interest merely on a showing that others may thereby be persuaded to take action inconsistent with its interests." Id. at 104.

Carlson v. California, 310 U.S. 106, 84 L. Ed. 1104, 60 S. Ct. 746 (1940), is in accord. In the course of reversing Carlson's conviction for engaging in a peaceful protest near a construction project in Shasta County, California, the Court declared that a citizen's right to "publicize the facts of a labor dispute in a peaceful way through appropriate means, whether by pamphlet, by word of mouth or by banner, must now be regarded as within that liberty of communication which is secured to every person by [the First Amendment through] the Fourteenth Amendment against abridgment by a State." Id. at 113.

The principles explained in Thornhill and Carlson were reaffirmed a few years later in the context of speech on religious matters when an individual sought to advertise a meeting of the Jehovah's Witnesses by engaging in a door-to-door distribution of leaflets. Martin v. City of Struthers, 319 U.S. 141, 87 L. Ed. 1313, 63 S. Ct. 862 (1943). The petitioner was convicted under a city ordinance which prohibited individuals from "distributing handbills, circulars or other advertisements" to private residences. Id. at 142. The Court invalidated the ordinance, reinforcing the vital idea today's Court ignores:

"While door to door distributers of literature may be either a nuisance or a blind for criminal activities, they may also be useful members of society engaged in the [786] dissemination of ideas in accordance with the best tradition of free discussion. The widespread use of this method of communication by many groups espousing various causes attests its major importance. 'Pamphlets have proved most effective instruments in the dissemination of opinion. And perhaps the most effective way of bringing them to the notice of individuals is their distribution at the homes of the people.'" Id. at 145 (quoting Schneider, 308 U.S. at 164).

The Court's more recent precedents honor the same principles: Government cannot foreclose a traditional medium of expression. In City of Ladue v. Gilleo, 512 U.S. 43, 129 L. Ed. 2d 36, 114 S. Ct. 2038 (1994), we considered a challenge to a municipal ordinance prohibiting, inter alia, "such absolutely pivotal speech as [the display of] a sign protesting an imminent governmental decision to go to war." Id. at 54. Respondent had placed a sign in a window of her home calling "For Peace in the Gulf." Id. at 46. We invalidated the ordinance, finding that the local government "had almost completely foreclosed a venerable means of communication that is both unique and important." Id. at 54. The opinion, which drew upon Lovell, Martin, and Schneider, was also careful to note the importance of the restriction on place imposed by the ordinance in question: "Displaying a sign from one's own residence often carries a message quite distinct from placing the same sign someplace else, or conveying the same text or picture by other means." 512 U.S. at 56. So, too, did we stress the importance of preserving the means citizens use to express messages bearing on important public debates. See id. at 57 ("Residential signs are an unusually cheap and convenient form of communication[,] especially for persons of modest means or limited mobility . . . ").

A year later in McIntyre v. Ohio Elections Comm'n, 514 U.S. 334, 131 L. Ed. 2d 426, 115 S. Ct. 1511 (1995), we once more confirmed the privileged status peaceful leafleting enjoys in our free speech tradition. Ohio prohibited anonymous leafleting in connection with [787] election campaigns. Invalidating the law, we observed as follows: "'Anonymous pamphlets, leaflets, brochures and even books have played an important role in the progress of mankind.'" Id. at 341 (quoting Talley v. California, 362 U.S. 60, 64, 4 L. Ed. 2d 559, 80 S. Ct. 536 (1960)). We rejected the State's claim that the restriction was needed to prevent fraud and libel in its election processes. Ohio had other laws in place to achieve these objectives. 514 U.S. at 350. The case, we concluded, rested upon fundamental free speech principles:

"Indeed, the speech in which Mrs. McIntyre engaged – handing out leaflets in the advocacy of a politically controversial viewpoint – is the essence of First Amendment expression. That this advocacy occurred in the heat of a controversial referendum vote only strengthens the protection afforded to Mrs. McIntyre's expression: Urgent, important, and effective speech can be no less protected than impotent speech, lest the right to speak be relegated to those instances when it is least needed. No form of speech is entitled to greater consti-tutional protection than Mrs. McIntyre's." Id. at 347 (citations omitted).

Petitioners commenced the present suit to challenge a statute preventing them from expressing their views on abortion through the same peaceful and vital methods approved in Lovell, Schneider, Thornhill, Carlson, and McIntyre. Laws punishing speech which protests the lawfulness or morality of the government's own policy are the essence of the tyrannical power the First Amendment guards against. We must remember that, by decree of this Court in discharging our duty to interpret the Constitution, any plea to the government to outlaw some abortions will be to no effect. See Planned Parenthood of Southeastern Pa. v. Casey, 505 U.S. 833, 120 L. Ed. 2d 674, 112 S. Ct. 2791 (1992). Absent the ability to ask the government to intervene, citizens who oppose abortion must seek to convince their fellow citizens of the moral imperative [788] of their cause. In a free society protest serves to produce stability, not to undermine it. "The right to speak freely and to promote diversity of ideas and programs is therefore one of the chief distinctions that sets us apart from totalitarian regimes." Terminiello v. Chicago, 337 U.S. 1, 4, 93 L. Ed. 1131, 69 S. Ct. 894 (1949). As Justice Brandeis observed: "[The framers] recognized the risks to which all human institutions are subject. But they knew that order cannot be secured merely through fear of punishment for its infraction; that it is hazardous to discourage thought, hope and imagination; that fear breeds repression; that repression breeds hate; that hate menaces stable government; that the path of safety lies in the opportunity to discuss freely supposed grievances and proposed remedies; and that the fitting remedy for evil counsels is good ones. Believing in the power of reason as applied through public discussion, they eschewed silence coerced by law – the argument of force in its worst form." Whitney v. California, 274 U.S. 357, 375-376, 71 L. Ed. 1095, 47 S. Ct. 6411 (1927) (concurring opinion).

The means of expression at stake here are of controlling importance. Citizens desiring to impart messages to women considering abortions likely do not have resources to use the mainstream media for their message, much less resources to locate women contemplating the option of abortion. Lacking the aid of the government or the media, they seek to resort to the time honored method of leafleting and the display of signs. Nowhere is the speech more important than at the time and place where the act is about to occur. As the named plaintiff, Leila Jeanne Hill, explained, "I engage in a variety of activities designed to impart information to abortion-bound women and their friends and families . . . ." App. 49. "In my many years of sidewalk counseling I have seen a number of [these] women change their minds about aborting their unborn children as a result of my sidewalk counseling, and God's grace." Id. at 51. [789]

When a person is walking at a hurried pace to enter a building, a solicitor who must stand still eight feet away cannot know whether the person can be persuaded to accept the leaflet or not. Merely viewing a picture or brief message on the outside of the leaflet might be critical in the choice to receive it. To solicit by pamphlet is to tender it to the person. The statute ignores this fact. What the statute restricts is one person trying to communicate to another, which ought to be the heart of civilized discourse.

Colorado's excuse, and the Court's excuse, for the serious burden imposed upon the right to leaflet or to discuss is that it occurs at the wrong place. Again, Colorado and the Court have it just backwards. For these protestors the 100-foot zone in which young women enter a building is not just the last place where the message can be communicated. It likely is the only place. It is the location where the Court should expend its utmost effort to vindicate free speech, not to burden or suppress it.

Perhaps the leaflet will contain a picture of an unborn child, a picture the speaker thinks vital to the message. One of the arguments by the proponents of abortion, I had thought, was that a young woman might have been so uninformed that she did not know how to avoid pregnancy. The speakers in this case seek to ask the same uninformed woman, or indeed any woman who is considering an abortion, to understand and to contemplate the nature of the life she carries within her. To restrict the right of the speaker to hand her a leaflet, to hold a sign, or to speak quietly is for the Court to deny the neutrality that must be the first principle of the First Amendment. In this respect I am in full agreement with JUSTICE SCALIA's explanation of the insult the Court gives when it tells us these grave moral matters can be discussed just as well through a bullhorn. It would be remiss, moreover, not to observe the profound difference a leaflet can have in a woman's decisionmaking process. [790] Consider the account of one young woman who testified before the Colorado Senate:

"Abortion is a major decision. Unfortunately, most women have to make this decision alone. I did and I know that I am not the only one. As soon as I said the word 'pregnant,' he was history, never to be heard of, from again. I was scared and all alone. I was too embarrassed to ask for help. If this law had been in effect then, I would not have got any information at all and gone through with my abortion because the only people that were on my side were the people at the abortion clinic. They knew exactly how I was feeling and what to say to make it all better. In my heart, I knew abortion was wrong, but it didn't matter. I had never taken responsibility for my actions so why start then. One of the major reasons I did not go through with my scheduled abortion was the picture I was given while I was pregnant. This was the first time I had ever seen the other side of the story. I think I speak for a lot of women, myself included, when I say abortion is the only way out because of [sic] it's all I knew. In Sex Education, I was not taught about adoption or the fetus or anything like that. All I learned about was venereal diseases and abortion. The people supplying the pamphlet helped me make my choice. I got an informed decision, I got information from both sides, and I made an informed decision that my son and I could both live with. Because of this picture I was given, right there, this little boy got a chance at life that he would never have had." Id. at 167-168.

There are, no doubt, women who would testify that abortion was necessary and unregretted. The point here is simply that speech makes a difference, as it must when acts of lasting significance and profound moral consequence are being contemplated. The majority reaches a contrary conclusion [791] only by disregarding settled free speech principles. In doing so it delivers a grave wound to the First Amendment as well as to the essential reasoning in the joint opinion in Casey, a concern to which I now turn.

IV. In Planned Parenthood of Southeastern Pa. v. Casey, the Court reaffirmed its prior holding that the Constitution protects a woman's right to terminate her pregnancy in its early stages. The joint opinion in Casey considered the woman's liberty interest and principles of stare decisis, but took care to recognize the gravity of the personal decision: "[Abortion] is an act fraught with consequences for others: for the woman who must live with the implications of her decision; for the persons who perform and assist in the procedure; for the spouse, family, and society which must confront the knowledge that these procedures exist, procedures some deem nothing short of an act of violence against innocent human life; and, depending on one's beliefs, for the life or potential life that is aborted." 505 U.S. at 852.

The Court now strikes at the heart of the reasoned, careful balance I had believed was the basis for the joint opinion in Casey. The vital principle of the opinion was that in defined instances the woman's decision whether to abort her child was in its essence a moral one, a choice the State could not dictate. Foreclosed from using the machinery of government to ban abortions in early term, those who oppose it are remitted to debate the issue in its moral dimensions. In a cruel way, the Court today turns its back on that balance. It in effect tells us the moral debate is not so important after all and can be conducted just as well through a bullhorn from an 8-foot distance as it can through a peaceful, face-to-face exchange of a leaflet. The lack of care with which the Court sustains the Colorado statute reflects a most troubling abdication of our responsibility to enforce the First Amendment.

[792] There runs through our First Amendment theory a concept of immediacy, the idea that thoughts and pleas and petitions must not be lost with the passage of time. In a fleeting existence we have but little time to find truth through discourse. No better illustration of the immediacy of speech, of the urgency of persuasion, of the preciousness of time, is presented than in this case. Here the citizens who claim First Amendment protection seek it for speech which, if it is to be effective, must take place at the very time and place a grievous moral wrong, in their view, is about to occur. The Court tears away from the protesters the guarantees of the First Amendment when they most need it. So committed is the Court to its course that it denies these protesters, in the face of what they consider to be one of life's gravest moral crises, even the opportunity to try to offer a fellow citizen a little pamphlet, a handheld paper seeking to reach a higher law.

I dissent.

Incitements and Threats

Unprotected speech that prompts violence or causes harm

Focal Cases:
Brandenburg v. Ohio, 395 U.S. 444 (1969)
Planned Parenthood v. American Coalition of Life Activists, 290 F.3d 1058 (9th Cir. 2002)

S ince the 1940s, the Supreme Court has created a set of categories establishing varying degrees
of constitutional protection for different speech based upon the presumed First Amendment
value of each type of expression. In 1942, the Court noted:

There are certain well-defined and narrowly limited classes of speech, the prevention and
punishment of which have never been thought to raise any constitutional problem. These
include the lewd and obscene, the profane, the libelous, and the insulting or "fighting
words" – those which by their very utterance inflict injury or tend to incite an immediate
breach of the peace. It has been well observed that such utterances are no essential part of
any exposition of ideas, and are of such slight social value as a step to truth that any
benefit that may be derived from them is clearly out-weighed by the social interest in
order and morality.[1]

This chapter examines the Court's treatment of the disfavored speech categories of criminal
conspiracy,[2] incitement,[3] threats[4] and fighting words.[5] Subsequent chapters will explore the
jurisprudence of hate speech, unpopular expression and obscenity. Speech that falls squarely
within any of these categories is not fully protected because the Supreme Court has determined
that these types of speech are not central to "the freedom of speech" shielded by the First
Amendment. The Court instead has found that these categories of speech cause real harms and
contribute little or no value to society or to the marketplace of ideas. However, the Court's
decisions also demonstrate that these categories must be carefully and narrowly drawn "with the
commands of the First Amendment clearly in mind" to insure that properly protected speech is

---

[1] Chaplinsky v. New Hampshire, 315 U.S. 568, 572 (1942).
[2] Scales v. United States, 367 U.S. 203 (1961).
[3] Brandenburg v. Ohio, 395 U.S. 444 (1969).
[4] Watts v. United States, 394 U.S. 705 (1969).
[5] Chaplinsky v. New Hampshire, 315 U.S. 568 (1942).

not infringed.[6] The Court has said it is particularly crucial to prevent government from punishing these categories of speech for illicit motives, especially when the sanctioned expression is political (as occurs in many cases in this chapter).[7]

BAD OR DANGEROUS SPEECH

For nearly a century, the Court has struggled to determine when speech is sufficiently dangerous or disruptive that it may be suppressed to protect the public peace, tranquility and safety.[8] At the start of the 20th Century, the Court applied a vague "bad tendency" test to allow government sanctions for any expression that had the slightest tendency to cause harm to the public welfare or public morals.[9] During the World War I era, however, the Court searched for a more rigorous principle to determine when the First Amendment should prevent government from punishing political and anti-war protests.

The Clear and Present Danger Test

In 1919, the Supreme Court adopted Justice Oliver Wendell Holmes' clear and present danger approach to protect the right of citizens to criticize government.[10] In *Schenck v. United States*, Holmes distinguished between protected advocacy of ideas and unprotected incitement of harm. "The question in every case is whether the words used are used in such circumstances and are of such a nature as to create a clear and present danger that they will bring about the substantive evils that Congress has a right to prevent. It is a question of proximity and degree," Holmes wrote.[11]

Although the clear and present danger test attempted to limit government suppression to situations in which the harm was great, certain and immediate, the test's focus on the probable effects of speech afforded government officials broad latitude to suppress speech they disliked. Under the clear and present danger test, the Supreme Court affirmed espionage convictions for peaceful protest of World War I.[12] The Court also upheld severe penalties under sedition and criminal anarchy laws for publishing, teaching or advising the value of overturning the existing government.[13] For fifty years the Court relied on the malleable clear and present danger standard, using it in the Red Scare of the 1950s and '60s to uphold punishment under the Smith Act for mere membership in the American Communist Party.[14]

The *Brandenburg* Test

Yet members of the Court also worked to reshape the test to reduce the power of government to penalize disfavored political groups, abstract doctrine or hyperbole.[15] In 1969, the Court in *Brandenburg v. Ohio* held that government could not constitutionally punish simple

---

[6] Watts v. United States, 394 U.S. 705, 707 (1969).

[7] NAACP v. Claiborne Hardware, 458 U.S. 886, 915 (1982).

[8] *See, e.g.,* ZECHARIAH CHAFEE, FREE SPEECH IN THE UNITED STATES (1941).

[9] Gitlow v. New York, 268 U.S. 652 (1925).

[10] Schenck v. United States, 249 U.S. 47 (1919).

[11] 249 U.S. at 52.

[12] *See, e.g.,* Abrams v. United States, 250 U.S. 616 (1919); Schenck v. United States, 249 U.S. 47 (1919); Frohwerk v. United States, 249 U.S. 204 (1919); Debs v. United States, 249 U.S. 211 (1919).

[13] Gitlow v. New York, 268 U.S. 652 (1925).

[14] Dennis v. United States, 341 U.S. 494 (1951); Scales v. United States, 367 U.S. 203 (1961). *See also* Whitney v. California, 274 U.S. 357 (1927); Kent Greenawalt, *Speech and Crime*, 1980 AM. B. FOUND. RES. J. 645 (1980).

[15] Noto v. United States, 367 U.S. 290 (1961); Yates v. United States, 354 U.S. 298 (1957); Watts v. United States, 394 U.S. 705 (1969).

advocacy of illegal activity.[16] In overturning the conviction of a Ku Klux Klan leader for making anti-Semitic and racist comments during a televised KKK rally of about a dozen people, the Court protected the right of people to assemble to advocate social, political and economic change. "Mere advocacy of the use of force or violence does not remove speech from the protection of the First Amendment," the Court said.[17]

Speech advocating change or unpopular ideas is protected by the First Amendment, the Court said, unless it 1) intends and 2) is likely to incite 3) imminent violence or illegal activity. In what has been called the incitement, the imminent harm or the *Brandenburg* test, the Court established that criticism of government or advocacy of radical ideas may be punished only when speakers intentionally incite immediate illegal activity. Speakers illegally incite when they go beyond discussion of strategies to explicitly encourage and support immediate violence.

For the past three decades, the Supreme Court has relied heavily on the *Brandenburg* test to restrict the power of government to punish advocacy or criticism of government. In 2002, however, Justice John Paul Stevens suggested that *Brandenburg* does not establish the legal limits for all types of advocacy.[18] In a brief opinion opposing denial of *cert.* in a case overturning a 15-year jail term for providing advice to an Arizona street gang, Justice Stevens re-opened the door to the clear and present danger test.

While the requirement that the consequence be "imminent" is justified with respect to mere advocacy, the same justification does not necessarily adhere to some speech that performs a teaching function. As our cases have long identified, the First Amendment does not prevent restrictions on speech that have "clear support in public danger." Long range planning of criminal enterprises – which may include oral advice, training exercises and perhaps the preparation of written materials – involves speech that should not be glibly characterized as mere "advocacy" and certainly may create significant public danger. Our cases have not yet considered whether, and if so to what extent, the First Amendment protects such instructional speech.[19]

THREATENING SPEECH

If the Supreme Court has failed to develop clear definitions and bright-line distinctions to guide First Amendment jurisprudence in advocacy and incitement cases, the Court's record is even less definitive when it comes to determining when government may penalize threats that arise purely through speech or assembly. Lower courts rely primarily upon the shaky guidance of *Brandenburg* and *Watts v. United States*[20] to decide the level of constitutional protection provided to what some perceive to be threats.

In the Supreme Court's only direct look at an anti-threat statute, the Supreme Court in 1969 overturned the conviction of an 18-year-old war protester for threatening the life of the President, in violation of federal law. The Court in *Watts* said the young man's comments were political hyperbole rather than a true threat of physical violence. The Court reasoned that the man's statement that, if drafted, the president is "the first man I want to get in my sights," had to be interpreted in the context of the political rally at which it occurred. In that context, the statement

---

[16] 395 U.S. 444 (1969).
[17] 395 U.S. at 447.
[18] Stewart v. McCoy, 123 S. Ct. 468 (2002).
[19] 123 S. Ct. at 469-70 (internal citations omitted).
[20] 394 U.S. 705 (1969).

expressed political opposition to the president and constituted protected political speech not a punishable threat. However, the Supreme Court's decision failed either to establish the boundary between protected political opposition and true threats or to fully outline the permissible government limits on true threats.

In 2003, however, the Supreme Court said the state of Virginia could constitutionally ban cross burning as a particularly virulent means to threaten or intimidate.[21] The Court in *Virginia v. Black* defined punishable threats as statements meant to communicate a serious intent to commit an illegal act of violence against a specific individual or group. Such threats may be punished, the Court said, even if the speaker does not intend to take action because the harm from threats extends beyond the possibility of real violence to the engendering of fear and the very real disruption that fear creates.

Prior to this 2003 ruling, lower courts looked to two seemingly contradictory Supreme Court assembly and protest cases for guidance in disputes involving apparent threats. In 1982, in *NAACP v. Claiborne Hardware*, the Court said the First Amendment protected explicit statements condoning violent retribution against opponents of a Civil Rights boycott because the statements were directed to a general audience in a public gathering and failed to incite illegal action.[22] Noting that the comments did not target a specific individual or individuals, did not stir a violent response from the audience and arose in the context of the historically nonviolent Civil Rights movement, the Supreme Court found the statement that "necks [of opponents] would be broken" was emotionally charged political rhetoric, not a true threat. Yet, twelve years later, in *Madsen v. Women's Health Center*, the Court said well crafted laws designed to limit protests outside abortion clinics could constitutionally prohibit threats "however communicated."[23]

Determining whether speech is threatening or merely emotionally charged requires objective scrutiny of the event taken as a whole.[24] Lower courts have relied heavily on case facts to establish the parameters of unprotected threats. In general, words lose First Amendment protection if they are threatening on their face and under the circumstances in which they are spoken.[25] Under developing standards, it appears a statement may be punished as a true threat if 1) the speaker intends to threaten or intimidate a specific individual or individuals, 2) a reasonable person would foresee the statement as likely to communicate a serious threat of harm by the speaker to those specific individuals, and 3) the context does not mitigate the threatening nature of the statement.

FIGHTING WORDS

Another category of low-value speech that threatens violence is what the Supreme Court calls fighting words. The fighting words doctrine developed from the Court's 1942 opinion in *Chaplinsky v. New Hampshire*.[26] In *Chaplinsky*, the Court affirmed the conviction of a Jehovah's Witness for calling a city marshal a racketeer and a fascist. The Court upheld a narrow reading of the state law to prohibit fighting words, which the Court later defined as "those personally abusive

---

[21] Virginia v. Black, 123 S.Ct. 1536 (2003).

[22] 458 U.S. 886 (1982).

[23] 512 U.S. 753, 753 (1994).

[24] United States v. Gilbert, 884 F.2d 454, 457 (9th Cir. 1989); United States v. Gordon, 974 F.2d 1110, 1117 (9th Cir. 1992); United States v. Orozco-Santillan, 903 F.2d 1262, 1266 (9th Cir. 1990); United States v. Merrill, 746 F.2d 458 (9th Cir. 1984); Roy v. United States, 416 F.2d 874, 877 (9th Cir. 1969); United States v. Carrier, 672 F.2d 300, 306 (2d Cir. 1982); Melugin v. Hames, 38 F.3d 1478 (9th Cir. 1994); United States v. Khorrami, 895 F.2d 1186, 1192 (7th Cir. 1990).

[25] United States v. Kelner, 534 F.2d 1010, 1027 (2d Cir. 1976).

[26] Chaplinsky v. New Hampshire, 315 U.S. 568 (1942).

epithets which, when addressed to the ordinary citizen, are, as a matter of common knowledge, inherently likely to provoke violent reaction."[27]

In the view of the Court, fighting words do not induce reasoned response or argument but, by their very nature, provoke a reasonable person to fight. Thus, fighting words are more like action than speech; they involve face-to-face confrontations in which words constitute a type of verbal assault. As such, they may be regulated. Nevertheless, the Supreme Court has found statutes that prohibit abusive or oppositional speech to be unconstitutionally overbroad.[28]

The Court has distinguished fighting words – words that incite an immediate breach of the peace – from protected speech that is merely offensive or provocative. The Supreme Court has said regulation of fighting words may not limit speech that is merely offensive because speech "may indeed best serve its high purpose when it induces a condition of unrest, creates dissatisfaction with conditions as they are, or even stirs people to anger."[29]

HECKLER'S VETO

Recognizing that freedom of speech may be most valuable when it is unpopular or confrontational, the Court has shaped a doctrine to prevent the objections of hostile audiences from silencing speakers who do not intentionally incite violence.[30] In striking down the conviction of a racist speaker whose audience became violent, the Court in *Terminiello v. City of Chicago* said a "function of free speech under our system of government is to invite dispute."[31] A speaker who prompts disagreement must be protected from the tyranny of the majority, the Court said, and the force of law must constrain the heckler in the audience not the speaker.

TERRORIST SPEECH AND ASSOCIATION

The highly ambiguous distinctions required in the above cases have fueled observations that the Supreme Court's protection of free speech is variable and responsive to social conditions.[32] For example, Frederick Siebert wrote in 1952: "Freedom contracts and the enforcement of restraints increases as the stresses on the stability of the government and of the structure of society increase. ... How much freedom we shall enjoy will depend on how widespread are the threats and the feeling of insecurity and instability."[33]

Today the stresses on government and social stability are high. In the wake of the bombing of the Murrah Federal Building in Oklahoma City in 1995, the shooting of students at Columbine (Colorado) High School in 1999 and the destruction of New York City's World Trade Center on Sept. 11, 2001, there is growing national concern with public safety and increased fear of terrorism. In this social context, the courts have been asked to review the constitutionality of laws intended to reduce threats to national security.[34] At issue are 1) the permissible extent of government

---

[27] Cohen v. California, 403 U.S. 15, 20 (1971). *See also* Chaplinsky at 572.

[28] *See, e.g.,* Gooding v. Wilson, 405 U.S. 518 (1972); Houston v. Hill, 482 U.S. 451 (1987).

[29] Terminiello v. City of Chicago, 337 U.S. 1, 4 (1949).

[30] Feiner v. New York, 340 U.S. 315 (1951); Gregory v. City of Chicago, 394 U.S. 111 (1969).

[31] 337 U.S. at 4.

[32] *See, e.g.,* MARGARET A. BLANCHARD, REVOLUTIONARY SPARKS (1992); LEE BOLLINGER, THE TOLERANT SOCIETY (1986); ZECHARIAH CHAFEE, FREE SPEECH IN THE UNITED STATES (1941).

[33] FREDERICK S. SIEBERT, FREEDOM OF THE PRESS IN ENGLAND 1476-1776 10, 13 (1952).

[34] *See, e.g.,* ACLU Foundation of California v. Barr, (D.C. Cir. 1991); United States v. Squillacote, 221 F.3d 542 (4th Cir. 2000); Boim v. Quranic Literacy Inc., 291 F.3d 1000 (7th Cir. 2002). *See also* Antiterrorism and Effective Death Penalty Act, Pub. L. No. 104-132, 110 Stat. 1214 et seq. (1996); Illegal Immigration and Reform and

investigation of uncharged suspects and 2) the proper distinction between punishable acts of terrorist conspiracy and constitutionally protected rights of association with or support for sometimes radical and often unpopular political groups. These are difficult tasks. No precise test differentiates valid government investigations from harassment and intimidation of individuals or groups based solely on their unpopular ideas.[35]

In 1991, for example, the Court of Appeals for the District of Columbia reversed the dismissal of a First Amendment challenge to government surveillance brought by eight alien residents in the United States. In deciding that a legitimate question existed about whether the government's electronic surveillance was permissible, the court said government would not violate the First Amendment by investigating a threat that "was not so immediate as to permit punitive measures against the utterer" but would run afoul of the constitution by investigating vague and general threats from groups whose "only menace was rhetorical and ideological."[36]

In addition, no bright line differentiates intellectual exploration of terrorist ideas from substantive conspiracy. It is not always clear whether an individual is an innocent supporter or a knowing accomplice with a group that may at times engage in illegal activity.[37] Thus, in 2002 the Court of Appeals for the Seventh Circuit allowed a lawsuit to proceed to determine whether Quranic Literacy in fact knowingly funded illegal activity by Hamas.[38] The court said liability would turn on the fact that although "violence has no sanctuary in the First Amendment, and the use of weapons, gunpowder, and gasoline may not constitutionally masquerade under the guise of 'advocacy,' ... liability may not be imposed merely because an individual belonged to a group, some members of which committed acts of violence."[39]

Clearly, a boundary exists. Criminal conspiracy is illegal; so is terrorism. Thus far, however, the U.S. Supreme Court has not determined when anti-terrorism laws conflict with the First Amendment.[40]

To gain insight into how the courts have wrestled with the difficult distinctions presented in the area of speech that provokes violence, you will read excerpts from the U.S. Supreme Court's ruling in *Brandenburg v. Ohio*[41] and the entire decision of the Court of Appeals for the Ninth Circuit in *Planned Parenthood v. American Coalition of Life Activists*.[42] Some additional cases that will enhance your understanding of incitement, threats and fighting words are listed below.

- *Houston v. Hill*, 482 U.S. 451 (1987) (striking as overbroad a statute prohibiting speech that interrupts police officer's performance of duty).
- *Watts v. United States*, 394 U.S. 705 (1969) (overturning conviction for threatening President).
- *Scales v. United States*, 367 U.S. 203 (1961) (affirming conviction under Smith Act for membership in the Communist party).

Immigrant Responsibility Act, Pub. L. No. 104-208, 110 Stat. 3009-546 (1996); Foreign Intelligence Surveillance Act , 50 U.S.C. §§ 1801-1811(1991).

[35] *See, e.g.*, United States v. Squillacote, 221 F.3d 542, 544 (4th Cir. 2000).

[36] ACLU Foundation of California v. Barr, 952 Fed.2d 457 (1991) (internal citation omitted). *See also* Alliance to End Repression v. City of Chicago, 742 F.2d 1007 (7th Cir. 1984).

[37] *See, e.g.*, Boim v. Quranic Literacy Inc., 291 F.3d 1000, 1007 (7th Cir. 2002).

[38] The U.S. government has designated Hamas a foreign terrorist organization.

[39] 291 F.3d at 1023.

[40] *But see* Reno v. American-Arab Anti-Discrimination Committee, 525 U.S. 471 (1999).

[41] 395 U.S. 444 (1969).

[42] 290 F.3d 1058 (9th Cir. 2002).

- *Yates v. United States*, 354 U.S. 298 (1957) (reversing conviction under Smith Act for Communist advocacy).
- *Dennis v. United States*, 341 U.S. 494 (1951) (affirming conviction under Smith Act for Communist advocacy).
- *Terminiello v. Chicago*, 337 U.S. 1 (1949) (overturning breach of peace conviction)
- *Chaplinsky v. New Hampshire*, 315 U.S. 568 (1942) (affirming conviction for fighting words)
- *Whitney v. California*, 274 U.S. 357 (1927) (affirming conviction under state criminal syndicalism law).
- *Gitlow v. New York*, 268 U.S. 652 (1925) (affirming conviction under state criminal anarchy law).
- *Abrams v. United States*, 250 U.S. 616 (1919) (affirming conviction for criminal conspiracy under the Espionage Act).

READING THE SPEECH HARM CASES

The following questions will assist your focused reading of the following cases.

- How significant are the facts of *Brandenburg* to the Court's decision?
- How well does *Brandenburg* distinguish abstract advocacy and unprotected incitement?
- Does *Brandenburg* establish a requirement of *imminent* lawless action before any advocacy speech falls outside the purview of the First Amendment?
- Does *Brandenburg* unequivocally replace the clear and present danger standard?
- Who bears the burden of proof in *Planned Parenthood*?
- Does *Planned Parenthood* invoke the reasonable person standard to determine whether a true threat exists? If not, what is the standard?
- How do the majority and the dissents in *Planned Parenthood* differ in their definition of proscribable threats?
- How does the *Planned Parenthood* majority differentiate the value and harm of the Nuremburg Files website itself and the Wanted Posters?
- On which U.S. Supreme Court precedents does *Planned Parenthood* rely, and how does it apply these precedents?
- Does the *Planned Parenthood* majority confine its decision to the facts in this case or does the Ninth Circuit establish a more general rule of law?
- What effect, if any, does the fact that the Nuremburg Files were distributed over the Internet have on the court's ruling?
- What test does the court suggest in *Planned Parenthood* by using the "burdens no more speech than necessary" language?
- Must a threat be explicit, overt or precise to lose constitutional protection?

Brandenburg v. Ohio
395 U.S. 444
(1969)
(Excerpts only. Most footnotes omitted.)

Author's Note: The state of Ohio convicted a Ku Klux Klan leader under the Ohio Criminal Syndicalism statute for "advocat[ing] . . . the duty, necessity, or propriety of crime, sabotage, violence, or unlawful methods of terrorism as a means of accomplishing industrial or political reform" and for "voluntarily assembl[ing] with any society, group, or assemblage of persons formed to teach or advocate the doctrines of criminal syndicalism. He was fined $ 1,000 and sentenced to one to 10 years in prison. challenged the constitutionality of law.

JUDGES: Warren, Black, Douglas, Harlan, Brennan, Stewart, White, Marshall

PER CURIAM

OPINION: [445] The record shows that a man, identified at trial as the appellant, telephoned an announcer-reporter on the staff of a Cincinnati television station and invited him to come to a Ku Klux Klan "rally" to be held at a farm in Hamilton County. With the cooperation of the organizers, the reporter and a cameraman attended the meeting and filmed the events. Portions of the films were later broadcast on the local station and on a national network.

...One film showed 12 hooded figures, some of whom carried firearms. They were gathered around a large wooden cross, which they burned. No one was present [446] other than the participants and the newsmen who made the film. Most of the words uttered during the scene were incomprehensible when the film was projected, but scattered phrases could be understood that were derogatory of Negroes and, in one instance, of Jews.[1]

---

[1] The significant portions that could be understood were:
"How far is the nigger going to – yeah."
"This is what we are going to do to the niggers."
"A dirty nigger."
"Send the Jews back to Israel."
"Let's give them back to the dark garden."
"Save America."
"Let's go back to constitutional betterment."
"Bury the niggers."
"We intend to do our part."
"Give us our state rights."
"Freedom for the whites."
"Nigger will have to fight for every inch he gets from now on."

Another scene on the same film showed the appellant, in Klan regalia, making a speech. The speech, in full, was as follows:

"This is an organizers' meeting. We have had quite a few members here today which are -- we have hundreds, hundreds of members throughout the State of Ohio. I can quote from a newspaper clipping from the Columbus, Ohio Dispatch, five weeks ago Sunday morning. The Klan has more members in the State of Ohio than does any other organization. We're not a revengent organization, but if our President, our Congress, our Supreme Court, continues to suppress the white, Caucasian race, it's possible that there might have to be some revengeance taken.

"We are marching on Congress July the Fourth, four hundred thousand strong. From there we are dividing into two groups, one group to march on St. Augustine, Florida, the other group to march into Mississippi. Thank you."

[447] The second film showed six hooded figures one of whom, later identified as the appellant, repeated a speech very similar to that recorded on the first film. The reference to the possibility of "revengeance" was omitted, and one sentence was added: "Personally, I believe the nigger should be returned to Africa, the Jew returned to Israel." Though some of the figures in the films carried weapons, the speaker did not.

... [The Court's prior] decisions have fashioned the principle that the constitutional guarantees of free speech and free press do not permit a State to forbid or proscribe advocacy of the use of force or of law violation except where such advocacy is directed to inciting or producing imminent lawless action and is likely to incite or produce such action. ... [448] "The mere abstract teaching . . . of the moral propriety or even moral necessity for a resort to force and violence, is not the same as preparing a group for violent action and steeling it to such action." A statute which fails to draw this distinction impermissibly intrudes upon the freedoms guaranteed by the First and Fourteenth Amendments. It sweeps within its condemnation speech which our Constitution has immunized from govern-mental control.

Measured by this test, Ohio's Criminal Syndicalism Act cannot be sustained. The Act punishes persons who "advocate or teach the duty, necessity, or propriety" of violence "as a means of accomplishing industrial or political reform"; or who publish or circulate or display any book or paper containing such advocacy; or who "justify" the commission of violent acts "with intent to exemplify, spread or advocate the propriety of the doctrines of criminal syndicalism"; or who "voluntarily assemble" with a group formed "to teach or advocate the doctrines of criminal syndicalism." Neither the indictment nor the trial judge's instructions to the jury in any way refined the statute's bald definition of the crime [449] in terms of mere advocacy not distinguished from incitement to imminent lawless action.

Accordingly, we are here confronted with a statute which, by its own words and as applied, purports to punish mere advocacy and to forbid, on pain of criminal punishment, assembly with others merely to advocate the described type of action. Such a statute falls within the condemnation of the First and Fourteenth Amendments.

... [450] CONCUR: MR. JUSTICE DOUGLAS, concurring.

While I join the opinion of the Court, I desire to enter a caveat. The "clear and present danger" test ... adumbrated by Mr. Justice Holmes ... said:

"The question in every case is whether the words used are used in such circumstances and are of such a nature as to create a clear and present danger that they will bring about the substantive evils that Congress has a right to prevent. It is a question of proximity and degree."

... [452] Mr. Justice Holmes, though never formally abandoning the "clear and present danger" test, moved closer to the First Amendment ideal when he said in dissent in Gitlow v. New York, 268 U.S. 652, 673:

"Every idea is an incitement. It offers itself for belief and if believed it is acted on unless some other belief outweighs it or some failure of energy stifles the movement at its birth. The only difference between the expression of an opinion and an incitement in the narrower sense is the speaker's enthusiasm for the result. Eloquence may set fire to reason. But whatever may be thought of the redundant discourse before us it had no chance of starting a present conflagration. If in the long run the beliefs expressed in proletarian dictatorship are destined to be accepted by the dominant forces of the community, the only meaning of free speech is that they should be given their chance and have their way."

We have never been faithful to the philosophy of that dissent. ...[454] My own view is quite different. I see no place in the regime of the First Amendment for any "clear and present danger" test. ... [456] The line between what is permissible and not subject to control and what may be made impermissible and subject to regulation is the line between ideas and overt acts.

Planned Parenthood v. American Coalition of Life Activists
290 F.3d 1058
(9th Cir. 2002)

JUDGES: Before: Mary M. Schroeder, Chief Judge, and Stephen Reinhardt, Alex Kozinski, Diarmuid F. O'Scannlain, Pamela Ann Rymer, Andrew J. Kleinfeld, Michael Daly Hawkins, Barry G. Silverman, Kim McLane Wardlaw, Marsha S. Berzon, and Johnnie B. Rawlinson, Circuit Judges.

OPINION: [1062] RYMER, Circuit Judge:

For the first time we construe what the Freedom of Access to Clinics Entrances Act (FACE), 18 U.S.C. § 248, means by "threat of force." FACE gives aggrieved persons a right of action against whoever by "threat of force . . . intentionally . . . intimidates . . . any person because that person is or has been . . . providing reproductive health services." 18 U.S.C. § 248(a)(1) and (c)(1)(A). This requires

that we define "threat of force" in a way that comports with the First Amendment, and it raises the question whether the conduct that occurred here falls within the category of unprotected speech.

Four physicians, Dr. Robert Crist, Dr. Warren M. Hern, Dr. Elizabeth Newhall, and Dr. James Newhall, and two health clinics that provide medical services to women including abortions, Planned Parenthood of the Columbia/Willamette, Inc. (PPCW) and the Portland Feminist Women's Health Center (PFWHC), brought suit under FACE[1]

---

[1] We refer collectively to the plaintiffs as "physicians" unless reference to a particular party is required. In addition to FACE, the case went to trial on claims that the same conduct violated the Racketeer Influenced and Corrupt Organizations

claiming that they were targeted with threats by the American Coalition of Life Activists (ACLA), Advocates for Life Ministries (ALM), and numerous individuals.[2] Three threats remain at issue: the Deadly Dozen "GUILTY" poster which identifies Hern and the Newhalls among ten others; the Crist "GUILTY "poster with Crist's name, addresses and photograph; and the" Nuremberg Files," which is a compilation about those whom the ACLA anticipated one day might be put on trial for crimes against humanity. The "GUILTY" posters identifying specific physicians were circulated in the wake of a series of "WANTED" and "unWANTED" posters that had identified other doctors who performed abortions before they were murdered.

Although the posters do not contain a threat on their face, the district court held that context could be considered. It defined a threat under FACE in accordance with our" true threat" jurisprudence, as a statement made when" a reasonable person would foresee that the statement would be interpreted by those to whom the maker communicates the statement as a serious expression of intent to harm. "Applying this definition, the court denied ACLA's motion for summary judgment in a published opinion. Planned Parenthood [1063] of the Columbia/Willamette, Inc. v. ACLA (PPCW II), 23 F. Supp. 2d 1182 (D. Or. 1998).[3] The jury returned a verdict in physicians' favor, and the court enjoined ACLA from publishing the posters or providing other materials with the specific intent to threaten Crist, Hern, Elizabeth Newhall, James Newhall, PPCW, or the Health Center. Planned Parenthood of the Columbia/Willamette, Inc. v. ACLA (PPCW III), 41 F. Supp. 2d 1130 (D. Or. 1999). ACLA timely appealed.

A panel of this court reversed. In its view, the standard adopted by the district court allowed the jury to find ACLA liable for putting the doctors in harm's way by singling them out for the attention of unrelated but violent third parties, conduct which is

protected by the First Amendment, rather than for authorizing or directly threatening harm itself, which is not. Planned Parenthood of the Columbia /Willamette, Inc. v. ACLA (PPCW IV), 244 F.3d 1007 (9th Cir.), reh'g en banc granted, 268 F.3d 908 (9th Cir. 2001). The panel decided that it should evaluate the record independently to determine whether ACLA's statements could reasonably be construed as saying that ACLA, or its agents, would physically harm doctors who did not stop performing abortions. Having done so, the panel found that the jury's verdict could not stand.

We reheard the case en banc because these issues are obviously important. We now conclude that it was proper for the district court to adopt our long-standing law on" true threats" to define a "threat" for purposes of FACE. FACE itself requires that the threat of force be made with the intent to intimidate. Thus, the jury must have found that ACLA made statements to intimidate the physicians, reasonably foreseeing that physicians would interpret the statements as a serious expression of ACLA's intent to harm them because they provided reproductive health services. Construing the facts in the light most favorable to physicians, the verdict is supported by substantial evidence. ACLA was aware that a "wanted"-type poster would likely be interpreted as a serious threat of death or bodily harm by a doctor in the reproductive health services community who was identified on one, given the previous pattern of "WANTED" posters identifying a specific physician followed by that physician's murder. The same is true of the posting about these physicians on that part of the "Nuremberg Files" where lines were drawn through the names of doctors who provided abortion services and who had been killed or wounded. We are independently satisfied that to this limited extent, ACLA's conduct amounted to a true threat and is not protected speech.

As we see no reversible error on liability or in the equitable relief that was granted, we affirm. However, we remand for consideration of whether the punitive damages award comports with due process.

I. The facts are fully set out in the district court's order granting injunctive relief, PPWC III, 41 F. Supp. 2d at 1131-1155, and we shall not belabor them. In sum:

On March 10, 1993, Michael Griffin shot and killed Dr. David Gunn as he entered an abortion clinic in Pensacola, Florida. Before this, a "WANTED" and an "unWANTED" poster with Gunn's name, photograph, address and other personal information were published. The "WANTED" poster describes Gunn as an abortionist and invites participation by prayer and [1064] fasting, by

---

Act (RICO), 18 U.S.C. § 1962 (except that ACLA was alleged to be the RICO enterprise and was not a defendant on this claim), and on claims that the defendants conspired to violate FACE and RICO. As each claim turns on whether there were true threats without constitutional protection, the appeal and our opinion focus only on FACE.

[2] Michael Bray, Andrew Burnett, David A. Crane, Timothy Paul Dreste, Joseph L. Foreman, Stephen P. Mears, Monica Migliorino Miller, Catherine Ramey, Dawn Marie Stover, Donald Treshman, and Charles Wysong. We refer to them collectively as "ACLA."

[3] The court had previously denied ACLA's motion to dismiss pursuant to Federal Rule of Civil Procedure 12(b)(6). Planned Parenthood of the Columbia/Willamette, Inc. v. ACLA (PPCW I), 945 F. Supp. 1355 (D. Or. 1996).

writing and calling him and sharing a willingness to help him leave his profession, and by asking him to stop doing abortions; the "unWANTED "poster states that he kills children at designated locations and "to defenseless unborn babies Gunn in [sic] heavily armed and very dangerous." After Gunn's murder, Bray and Paul Hill (a non-party who was later convicted of murdering a different doctor) prepared a statement supporting Griffin's acquittal on a justifiable homicide theory, which ALM, Burnett, Crane, Dodds, Foreman, McMillan, Ramey and Stover joined.

On August 21, 1993, Dr. George Patterson, who operated the clinic where Gunn worked, was shot to death. A"WANTED" poster had been circulated prior to his murder, indicating where he performed abortions and that he had Gunn perform abortions for his Pensacola clinic.

In July 1994, Dr. John Bayard Britton was murdered by Paul Hill after being named on an "unWANTED" poster that Hill helped to prepare. One gives Britton's physical description together with his home and office addresses and phone numbers, and charges "crimes against humanity"; another also displays his picture and states that "he is considered armed and extremely dangerous to women and children. Pray that he is soon apprehended by the love of Jesus!!!" In addition to these items, a third version of the Britton "unWANTED" poster lists personal achievements and Britton's" crimes against humanity," also warning that "John Bayard Britton is considered armed and extremely dangerous, especialy[sic] to women and children." ALM, Bray, Burnett, Crane, McMillan, Ramey and Stover signed a petition supporting Hill.

Many pro-life activists in Operation Rescue condemned these acts of violence. As a result, ALM, Bray, Burnett, Crane, Foreman, McMillan, Ramey and Stover, who espoused a "pro-force" point of view, split off to form ACLA. Burnett observed, "if someone was to condemn any violence against abortion, they probably wouldn't have felt comfortable working with us." Organizational meetings were held in the spring of 1994, and ACLA's first event was held in August 1994. ACLA is based in Portland, Oregon, as is ALM. ALM publishes Life Advocate, a magazine that is distributed nationally and advocates the use of force to oppose the delivery of abortion services. Except for Bray, who authored A Time to Kill and served time in federal prison for conspiring to bomb ten clinics, the individual defendants were directors of ACLA and actively involved in its affairs. ALM commissioned and published Bray's book, noting that

it "shows the connection between the [justifiable homicide] position and clinic destruction and the shootings of abortionists." Wysong and ACLA also drafted and circulated a "Contract on the Abortion Industry," having deliberately chosen that language to allude to mafia hit contracts.

ACLA presented the Deadly Dozen poster during a January 25, 1995 press conference at the March for Life event in Washington, D.C. Bray, Burnett, Crane, Dodds, Foreman, McMillan, Murch, Ramey, Stover, Treshman and Wysong were there; Dreste later ratified the poster's release. This poster is captioned "GUILTY" at the top (which meant the same thing to Crane, who drafted it, as "wanted"), beneath which in slightly smaller print the poster indicates" OF CRIMES AGAINST HUMANITY." The poster continues: "Abortion was provided as a choice for East European and Jewish women by the (Nazi) National Socialist Regime, and was prosecuted during the Nuremberg Trials (1945-46) under Allied Control Order No. 10 as a 'war crime.'" Under the heading "THE DEADLY DOZEN," the poster identifies thirteen doctors of whom James Newhall, Elizabeth Newhall, [1065] and Warren Hern are three. The poster provides Hern's residence and the home address of James Newhall and Elizabeth Newhall; it also lists the name and home address of Dr. George Kabacy, a doctor who provided abortions at PPCW. It offers a "$5,000 REWARD" "for information leading to arrest, conviction and revocation of license to practice medicine." At the bottom the poster bears the legend" ABOR-TIONIST" in large, bold typeface. The day after the Deadly Dozen poster was released, the FBI offered protection to doctors identified on it and advised them to wear bulletproof vests and take other security precautions, which they did. Knowing this, ALM reprinted the poster in the March 1995 edition of its magazine Life Advocate under a cover with the "grim reaper" holding a scythe; Murch printed it in his newsletter Salt & Light; and ACLA republished the Deadly Dozen poster at events in August 1995 and January 1996.

ACLA released the Crist poster along with five others in August 1995 at the old federal courthouse in St. Louis where the Dred Scott decision had been handed down. Burnett, Crane, Dreste, McMillan, Ramey, Stover and Wysong attended the event. Three of the posters identify doctors; the others identify reproductive health care clinics, one of which was a Planned Parenthood affiliate where Crist worked. The Crist poster has "GUILTY" in large bold letters at the top followed by "OF CRIMES AGAINST HUMANITY" in smaller font. It also gives his home and work addresses; states

"Please write, leaflet or picket his neighborhood to expose his blood guilt"; offers a "$ 500 REWARD" "to any ACLA organization that successfully persuades Crist to turn from his child killing through activities within ACLA guidelines"; and has "ABORTIONIST" in large bold type at the bottom.

At its January 1996 conference, ACLA displayed the Deadly Dozen poster, held a "White Rose Banquet "to honor prisoners convicted of anti-abortion violence, and introduced ALM's Paul deParrie to unveil the "Nuremberg Files." ACLA sent a hard copy of some of the Files to Neal Horsley (a nonparty) to post on the internet, and ACLA's name appeared on the Nuremberg Files website opened in January 1997. Approximately 200 people are listed under the label" ABORTIONISTS: the shooters," and 200 more are listed under Files for judges, politicians, law enforcement, spouses, and abortion rights supporters. Crist, Hern and the Newhalls are listed in the "abortionists" section, which bears the legend: "Black font (working); Greyed-out Name (wounded); Strikethrough (fatality)." The names of Gunn, Patterson and Britton are struck through.

By January 1995 ACLA knew the effect that "WANTED," "unWANTED," or "GUILTY" posters had on doctors named in them. For example, in a September 1993 issue of Life Advocate which reported that an "unwanted "poster was being prepared for Britton, ALM remarked of the Gunn murder that it "sent shock waves of fear through the ranks of abortion providers across the country. As a result, many more doctors quit out of fear for their lives, and the ones who are left are scared stiff." Of another doctor who decided to quit performing abortions after circulation of a "Not Wanted" poster, Bray wrote that "it is clear to all who possess faculties capable of inductive analysis: he was bothered and afraid." Wysong also stated: "Listening to what abortionists said, abortionists who have quit the practice who are no longer killing babies but are now pro-life. They said the two things they feared the most were being sued for malpractice and having their picture put on a poster." And Burnett testified with respect to the [1066] danger that "wanted" or "guilty" posters pose to the lives of those who provide abortions: "I mean, if I was an abortionist, I would be afraid."

By January 1995 the physicians knew about the Gunn, Patterson and Britton murders and the posters that preceded each. Hern was terrified when his name appeared on the Deadly Dozen poster; as he put it: "The fact that wanted posters about these doctors had been circulated, prior to their assassination, and that the – that the posters, then, were followed by the doctor's assassination,

emphasized for me the danger posed by this document, the Deadly Dozen List, which meant to me that – that, as night follows day, that my name was on this wanted poster . . . and that I would be assassinated, as had the other doctors been assassinated." Hern interpreted the poster as meaning "Do what we tell you to do, or we will kill you. And they do." Crist was "truly frightened, "and stopped practicing medicine for a while out of fear for his life. Dr. Elizabeth Newhall interpreted the Deadly Dozen poster as saying that if she didn't stop doing abortions, her life was at risk. Dr. James Newhall was "severely frightened" in light of the "clear pattern" of a wanted poster and a murder when there was "another wanted poster with my name on it."

The jury found for plaintiffs on all claims except for Bray and Treshman on the RICO claims.[4] The district court then considered equitable relief. It found that each defendant used intimidation as a means of interfering with the provision of reproductive health services; that each independently and as a co-conspirator published and distributed the Deadly Dozen poster, the Crist poster, and the Nuremberg Files; and that each acted with malice and specific intent in communicating true threats to kill, assault or do bodily harm to each of the plaintiffs to intimidate them from engaging in legal medical practices and procedures. The court found that the balance of hardships weighed "over-whelmingly" in plaintiffs' favor. It also found that the defendants' actions were not protected speech under the First Amendment. Accordingly, it issued a permanent injunction restraining defendants from threatening, with the specific intent to do so, any of the plaintiffs in violation of FACE; from publishing or distributing the Deadly Dozen poster and the Crist poster with specific intent to threaten the plaintiffs; from providing additional material concerning plaintiffs, with a specific intent to threaten, to the Nuremberg Files or similar web site; and from publishing or distributing the personally identifying information about the plaintiffs in the Files with a specific intent to threaten. The court also required defendants to turn over materials that are not in compliance with the injunction except for one copy

---

[4] On the FACE claims, the jury awarded $ 39,656 to Crist, $ 14,429 to Hern, $ 15,797.98 to Elizabeth Newhall, $ 375 to James Newhall, $ 405,834.86 to PPCW, and $ 50,243 to PFWHC from each defendant as compensatory damages and $ 14.5 million to Crist, $ 13 million to Hern, $ 14 million to Elizabeth Newhall, $ 14 million to James Newhall, $ 29.5 million to PPCW, and $ 23.5 million to PFWHC in punitive damages. On the RICO claims (after trebling), Crist was awarded $ 892,260; Hern, $ 324,657; Elizabeth Newhall, $ 355,454; James Newhall, $ 8,442; PPCW $ 9,131,280; and PFWHC, $ 1,130,466.

of anything included in the record, which counsel was permitted to retain.

II. Before turning to the merits, we must consider the standard of review because ACLA contends that in a free speech case it is de novo. Relying on Bose Corp. v. Consumers Union of United States, Inc., 466 U.S. 485, 80 L. Ed. 2d 502, 104 S. Ct. 1949 (1984), ACLA submits that we must first determine for ourselves [1067] whether its speech is classic protected speech or is a "true threat "by reviewing the entire record.

Physicians assert that the standard of review for which ACLA contends comes from libel cases, but that threat cases are different; the more searching review of the record incumbent upon courts in libel cases, they urge, is inapposite to threat cases. They also point out that we have decided all of our threats cases without engaging in de novo review of the factual record. See, e.g., United States v. Gilbert, 884 F.2d 454, 457 (9th Cir. 1989) (Gilbert II) ("Viewed as a whole, and using the contextual analysis we have used for other statutes, a rational trier of fact could find a threat."); United States v. Gordon, 974 F.2d 1110, 1117 (9th Cir. 1992) ("Although some of the factual circumstances surrounding the incident suggest a contrary result, the jury acted reasonably[in finding that] the threats were serious."); United States v. Orozco-Santillan, 903 F.2d 1262, 1266 (9th Cir. 1990) ("[A] rational jury could conclude that Orozco-Santillan's statement . . . was a threat."); see also United States v. Hoff, 22 F.3d 222, 224 (9th Cir. 1994) (reviewing for clear error conviction for intimidating forest ranger).

We do not entirely agree with either side. It is true that our threats cases have been decided without conducting a de novo review of the factual record, but the issue was not squarely presented in any of those cases. For this reason, we cannot take it as definitively resolved.

In Bose (a defamation action arising out of a publication about loudspeaker systems), the Court confronted an apparent conflict between Federal Rule of Civil Procedure 52(a), providing that findings of fact shall not be set aside unless clearly erroneous, and its rule in cases raising First Amendment issues that "an appellate court has an obligation to 'make an independent examination of the whole record' in order to make sure that 'the judgment does not constitute a forbidden intrusion on the field of free expression.'" Bose, 466 U.S. at 498-99 (quoting New York Times Co. v. Sullivan, 376 U.S. 254, 284, 11 L. Ed. 2d 686, 84 S. Ct. 710-86 (1964)). The Court noted that it had previously exercised independent judgment on questions such as whether particular remarks are "fighting words,"

Street v. New York, 394 U.S. 576, 592, 22 L. Ed. 2d 572, 89 S. Ct. 1354 (1969), and whether, as a matter of constitutional law, a motion picture is obscene. Jenkins v. Georgia, 418 U.S. 153, 159, 41 L. Ed. 2d 642, 94 S. Ct. 2750-61 (1974). In this connection, the Court observed that in Jenkins it had rejected the notion that a jury finding (there of obscenity) "is insulated from review so long as the jury was properly instructed and there is some evidence to support its findings"; rather, substantive constitutional limitations govern. Bose, 466 U.S. at 506-07. Therefore, it concluded, appellate judges must themselves determine whether the record establishes the constitutional facts required for showing actual malice with convincing clarity in a case governed by New York Times. This obligation does not, however, extend to any evidence that is not germane to the actual malice (or core constitutional fact) determination. Id. at 514 n.31.

The Court revisited the issue in Harte-Hanks Communications, Inc. v. Connaughton, 491 U.S. 657, 105 L. Ed. 2d 562, 109 S. Ct. 2678 (1989). Harte-Hanks was a libel action against a newspaper, also governed by New York Times. The court of appeals had affirmed a judgment against the paper without attempting to make an independent evaluation of the credibility of conflicting oral testimony concerning the facts underlying the jury's finding of actual malice. Certiorari was granted to consider whether the appellate [1068] court's analysis was consistent with Bose. Harte-Hanks conceded that when conducting the independent review required by New York Times and Bose, a reviewing court should properly hesitate to disregard a jury's opportunity to observe live testimony and assess witness credibility, but contended that the Supreme Court had nevertheless rejected the trial court's credibility determination in Bose. Justice Stevens, writing for the Court in both Bose and Harte-Hanks, noted that this was not correct; he explained that in Bose the Court had accepted the trial court's determination that the author of the report at issue did not provide credible testimony, but had been unwilling to infer actual malice from the finding. Id. at 689 n.35. The Harte-Hanks Court went on to review the entire record, holding that given the instructions, the jury's answers to special interrogatories, and the facts that were not in dispute, the jury must have found certain testimony incredible and that from these findings, considered with the undisputed evidence, it followed that the paper acted with actual malice and that the evidence was sufficient to support such a finding.

The same rule was reiterated in Hurley v. Irish-American Gay, Lesbian and Bisexual Group of

Boston, 515 U.S. 557, 132 L. Ed. 2d 487, 115 S. Ct. 2338 (1995), a First Amendment case involving a parade permit. As the Court explained: "This obligation rests upon us simply because the reaches of the First Amendment are ultimately defined by the facts it is held to embrace, and we must thus decide for ourselves whether a given course of con-duct falls on the near or far side of the line of constitutional protection." Id. at 567.

We have discussed the issue a number of times, in connection with threats in United States v. Merrill, 746 F.2d 458 (9th Cir. 1984), United States v. Gilbert (Gilbert I), 813 F.2d 1523 (9th Cir. 1987), Melugin v. Hames, 38 F.3d 1478 (9th Cir. 1994), and Lovell v. Poway United School Dist., 90 F.3d 367 (9th Cir. 1996), and in defamation actions in Newton v. National Broadcasting Co., 930 F.2d 662 (9th Cir. 1990), Eastwood v. National Enquirer, Inc., 123 F.3d 1249 (9th Cir. 1997), and Hoffman v. Capital Cities/ABC, Inc., 255 F.3d 1180 (9th Cir. 2001).

Merrill was prosecuted for mailing injurious articles through the mail (letters with live .22 caliber rim fire bullets, some with the words "Kill Reagan," some with pornographic playing cards) and for threatening the life of the President in violation of 18 U.S.C. § 871. ACLA relies on that part of Merrill where we considered the obscenity conviction under the Bose standard of review. We interpreted Bose and Smith v. United States, 431 U.S. 291, 52 L. Ed. 2d 324, 97 S. Ct. 1756 (1977), as allowing deferential (sufficiency of the evidence) review of findings about contemporary community standards and the offensiveness of the material, but as requiring more extensive review of the district court's findings that Miller's letters lacked serious political value. Smith, 431 U.S. at 305 (whether a work lacks serious literary, artistic, political, or scientific value for purposes of an obscenity prosecution is a "determination . . . particularly amenable to appellate review"). However, we did not apply heightened review to the threats conviction. Instead, we stated:

Whether any given form of written or oral expression constitutes a true threat for the statute's [§ 871] purposes is a question for the trier of fact under all of the circumstances. Roy v. United States, 416 F.2d [874,] 877-78 [(9th Cir. 1969)]. A few cases may be so clear that they can be resolved as a matter of law, e.g., Watts v. United States, 394 U.S. 705, 22 L. Ed. 2d 664, 89 S. Ct. 1399 (1969) (conditional statement made at [1069] political rally which provoked listeners' laughter was merely "political hyperbole," and question should not have gone to jury), but most cases arising under this statute present widely varying fact patterns that should be left to the trier of fact. United States v. Carrier, 672 F.2d [300,] 306 [(2d Cir. 1982)].

Merrill, 746 F.2d at 462-63. Under this standard we held that the district judge was not clearly erroneous in finding that the letters constituted an objectively serious threat to harm the President.

We followed Merrill in Gilbert I, 813 F.2d at 1529-30. Gilbert was charged with violating the Fair Housing Act, 42 U.S.C. § 3631(b) and (c), by mailing menacing flyers to intimidate the director of an adoption organization responsible for the placement and adoption of black and Asian children from aiding minority children's occupancy of dwellings in Kootenai County. Noting that whether expression is a true threat is for the trier of fact, we recognized that "whether any given form of written expression can supply the requisite intent requirement is a question for the trier of fact." Gilbert I, 813 F.2d at 1529. Thus, "it is a jury question whether actions and communications are clearly outside the ambit of first amendment protection." Id. at 1530. And following the Seventh Circuit's lead in United States v. Khorrami, 895 F.2d 1186, 1192 (7th Cir. 1990), we held in Melugin that "the issue whether the prosecution has shown a 'true threat' is a question of fact for the jury, not a question of law for the court." Melugin, 38 F.3d at 1485.

Lovell was a § 1983 action in which a student was suspended for allegedly threatening to shoot a teacher. We acknowledged that "different standards are sometimes used when reviewing district court cases in which the court adjudged the constitutionality of a restriction on speech," and that a de novo review of the facts is conducted when a restriction is upheld. Lovell, 90 F.3d at 370.

Newton was a defamation action brought by Wayne Newton (a public figure) against NBC. It was tried to a jury, which found actual malice. The appeal caused us specifically to consider how "to strike the proper balance between our constitutional (Seventh Amendment) deference to the fact finder and our constitutional duty to safeguard First Amendment values" in light of Bose and Harte-Hanks. Newton, 930 F.2d at 666. We observed that the "independent examination of the record" contemplated by Bose is "'not equivalent to a "de novo" review of the ultimate judgment itself,'" where the reviewing court makes an "original appraisal of all the evidence to decide whether or not judgment should be entered for the plaintiff." Id. at 670 n.10 (quoting Bose, 466 U.S. at 514 n.31). However, we also noted that as a general rule, we have conducted de novo review of the record when a restriction on speech has been upheld. Id. (citing Daily Herald Co. v. Munro, 838 F.2d 380, 383 (9th Cir. 1988)). We then read Bose and Harte-Hanks as creating a "credibility exception" to the New York Times rule of independent review, such that we give "special deference" to credibility determinations but conduct "a more searching review of other evidence "germane to the actual malice determination. 930 F.2d at 671, 672.

Eastwood was another defamation action in which we engaged in an independent review of actual malice. We thought that the jury was properly instructed, but in conducting the review we explained that "it is not enough for us to determine that a reasonable jury could have found for the plaintiff – a kind of sufficiency-of-the-evidence test, permitting us to affirm even though we would have reached a different conclusion. Rather, 'First Amendment [1070] questions of "constitutional fact" compel [us to conduct a] de novo review.' We ourselves must be convinced that the defendant acted with malice," even though we defer to the jury on questions of credibility. Eastwood, 123 F.3d at 1252 (citations omitted). See also Hoffman, 255 F.3d at 1186 (relying on Eastwood).

It is not easy to discern a rule from these cases that can easily be applied in a threats case where, by definition, a true threat is constitutionally unprotected. Indeed, FACE on its face requires that "threat of force" be defined and applied consistent with the First Amendment. Perhaps this explains why we have treated threat cases differently, explicitly holding that the question of whether there is a true threat is for the jury.

We conclude that the proper definition of a "threat" for purposes of FACE is a question of law that we review de novo. If it were clear that neither the Deadly Dozen nor the Crist poster, or the Nuremberg Files, was a threat as properly defined, the case should not have gone to the jury and summary judgment should have been granted in ACLA's favor. If there were material facts in dispute or it was not clear that the posters were protected expression instead of true threats, the question whether the posters and the Files amount to a "threat of force" for purposes of the statute was for the trier of fact. Assuming that the district court correctly defined "threat" and properly instructed the jury on the elements of liability pursuant to the statute, our review is for substantial evidence supporting the historical facts (including credibility determinations) and the elements of statutory liability (including intent). We review the district court's findings with respect to injunctive relief for clear error and its conclusions of law de novo. However, while we normally review the scope of injunctive relief for abuse of discretion, we will scrutinize the relief granted in this case to determine whether the challenged provisions of the injunction burden no more speech than necessary to achieve its goals.

Madsen v. Women's Health Ctr., Inc., 512 U.S. 753, 765, 114 S. Ct. 2516 (1994).

Given that the verdict for physicians and the injunctive relief granted in their favor restrict speech, we review the record independently in order to satisfy ourselves that the posters and the Files constitute a "true threat "such that they lack First Amendment protection. We will consider the undisputed facts as true, and construe the historical facts, the findings on the statutory elements, and all credibility determinations in favor of the prevailing party. In this way we give appropriate deference to the trier of fact, here both the jury and the district judge, yet assure that evidence of the core constitutional fact – a true threat – falls within the unprotected category and is narrowly enough bounded as a matter of constitutional law.

III. ACLA[5] argues that the First Amendment requires reversal because liability was based on political speech that constituted neither an incitement to imminent lawless action nor a true threat. It suggests that the key question for us to consider is whether these posters can be considered [1071] "true threats" when, in fact, the posters on their face contain no explicitly threatening language. Further, ACLA submits that classic political speech cannot be converted into non-protected speech by a context of violence that includes the independent action of others.

Physicians[6] counter that this threats case must be analyzed under the settled threats law of this circuit. Following precedent, it was proper for the jury to take context into account. They point out that the

---

[5] Treshman and Miller filed a separate brief. We treat their arguments with ACLA's, as each adopts the others' brief. An amicus curiae brief in support of reversal was also submitted on behalf of The Thomas Jefferson Center for the Protection of Free Expression. Paul deParrie submitted a pro se, non-party-in-interest brief challenging the permanent injunction entered by the district court, and an amicus brief in opposition to reconsideration of the panel opinion.

[6] Amicus briefs in support of affirmance were submitted on behalf of the American Medical Association; seventeen United States Senators and forty-two United States Representatives; the State of Connecticut; the Anti-Defamation League, the American Jewish Committee, and Hadassah, the Women's Zionist Organization of America, Inc.; Feminist Majority Foundation, Center for Reproductive Law and Policy, National Abortion and Reproductive Rights Action League and NARAL Foundation, National Abortion Federation, National Coalition of Abortion Providers, National Organization for Women Foundation, NOW Legal Defense and Education Fund, National Women's Health Foundation, Northwest Women's Law Center, Physicians for Reproductive Choice and Health, and Women's Law Project; and the ACLU Foundation of Oregon, Inc.

district court limited evidence of antiabortion violence to evidence tending to show knowledge of a particular defendant, and maintain that the objective standard on which the jury was instructed comports both with Ninth Circuit law and congressional intent. As the First Amendment does not protect true threats of force, physicians conclude, ACLA's speech was not protected.

A.   We start with the statute under which this action arises. Section 248(c)(1)(A) gives a private right of action to any person aggrieved by reason of the conduct prohibited by subsection (a). Subsection (a)(1) provides:

(a) . . . Whoever–

(1) by force or threat of force or by physical obstruction, intentionally injures, intimidates or interferes with or attempts to injure, intimidate or interfere with any person because that person is or has been, or in order to intimidate such person or any other person or any class of persons from, obtaining or providing reproductive health services . . . shall be subject to the   . . .   civil remedies provided in subsection (c) . . . . 18 U.S.C. § 248(a)(1).

The statute also provides that "nothing in this section shall be construed   . . .   to prohibit any expressive conduct (including peaceful picketing or other peaceful demonstration) protected from legal prohibition by the First Amendment to the Constitution." 18 U.S.C. § 248(d)(1).

FACE does not define "threat," although it does provide that "the term 'intimidate' means to place a person in reasonable apprehension of bodily harm to him-or herself or to another." 18 U.S.C. § 248(e)(3). Thus, the first task is to define "threat" for purposes of the Act. This requires a definition that comports with the First Amendment, that is, a "true threat."

The Supreme Court has provided benchmarks, but no definition.

Brandenburg v. Ohio, 395 U.S. 444, 447, 23 L. Ed. 2d 430, 89 S. Ct. 1827, 48 Ohio Op. 2d 320 (1969), makes it clear that the First Amendment protects speech that advocates violence, so long as the speech is not directed to inciting or producing imminent lawless action and is not likely to incite or produce such action. So do Hess v. Indiana, 414 U.S. 105, 38 L. Ed. 2d 303, 94 S. Ct. 326 (1973) (overturning disorderly conduct conviction of antiwar protestor who yelled "We'll take [1072] the fucking street later (or again)"), and NAACP v. Claiborne Hardware Co., 458 U.S. 886, 73 L. Ed. 2d 1215, 102 S. Ct. 3409 (1982). If ACLA had merely endorsed or encouraged the violent actions of others, its speech would be protected.

However, while advocating violence is protected, threatening a person with violence is not. In Watts v. United States, 394 U.S. 705 (1969), the Court explicitly distinguished between political hyperbole, which is protected, and true threats, which are not. Considering how to construe a statute which prohibited "knowingly and willfully . . . (making) any threat to take the life of or to inflict bodily harm upon the President," the Court admonished that any statute which criminalizes a form of pure speech "must be interpreted with the commands of the First Amendment clearly in mind. What is a threat must be distinguished from what is constitutionally protected speech." Id. at 705, 707. In that case, an 18-year old war protester told a discussion group of other young people at a public rally on the Washington Monument grounds: "They always holler at us to get an education. And now I have already received my draft classification as 1-A and I have got to report for my physical this Monday coming. I am not going. If they ever make me carry a rifle the first man I want to get in my sights is L.B.J." Id. at 706. His audience laughed. Taken in context, and given the conditional nature of the statement and the reaction of the listeners, the Court concluded that the speech could not be interpreted other than as "a kind of very crude offensive method of stating a political opposition to the President." Id. at 708. Accordingly, it ordered judgment entered for Watts.

ACLA's position is that the posters, including the Nuremberg Files, are protected political speech under Watts, and cannot lose this character by context. But this is not correct. The Court itself considered context and determined that Watts's statement was political hyperbole instead of a true threat because of context. Id. at 708. Beyond this, ACLA points out that the posters contain no language that is a threat. We agree that this is literally true. Therefore, ACLA submits, this case is really an incitement case in disguise. So viewed, the posters are protected speech under Brandenburg and Claiborne, which ACLA suggests is the closest analogue. We disagree that Claiborne is closely analogous.

In March 1966 black citizens in Claiborne County made a list of demands for racial equality and integration. Unsatisfied by the response, several hundred black persons at a meeting of the local National Association for the Advancement of Colored People (NAACP) voted to place a boycott on white merchants in the area. The boycott continued until October 1969. During this period, stores were watched and the names of persons who violated the boycott were read at meetings of the NAACP at the First Baptist Church, and published in a local paper called "Black-Times." These persons were branded as traitors to the black cause, were called demeaning names, and were socially ostracized. A few incidents of violence occurred.

Birdshot was fired at the houses of two boycott violators; a brick was thrown through a windshield; and a flower garden was damaged. None of the victims ceased trading with white merchants. Six other incidents of arguably unlawful conduct occurred. White business owners brought suit against the NAACP and Charles Evers, its field secretary, along with other individuals who had participated in the boycott, for violating Mississippi state laws on malicious interference with a business, antitrust, and illegal boycott. Plaintiffs pursued several theories of liability: participating in management of the [1073] boycott; serving as an "enforcer" or monitor; committing or threatening acts of violence, which showed that the perpetrator wanted the boycott to succeed by coercion when it could not succeed by persuasion; and as to Evers, threatening violence against boycott breakers, and as to the NAACP because he was its field secretary when he committed tortious and constitutionally unprotected acts. Damages for business losses during the boycott and injunctive relief were awarded.

The Court held that there could be no recovery based on intimidation by threats of social ostracism, because offensive and coercive speech is protected by the First Amendment. "The use of speeches, marches, and threats of social ostracism cannot provide the basis for a damages award. But violent conduct is beyond the pale of constitutional protection." 458 U.S. at 933. There was some evidence of violence, but the violence was not pervasive as it had been in Milk Wagon Drivers Union Local 753 v. Meadowmoor Dairies, Inc., 312 U.S. 287, 85 L. Ed. 836, 61 S. Ct. 552 (1941). Accordingly, the Court made clear that only losses proximately caused by unlawful conduct could be recovered. Further, civil liability could not be imposed consistent with the First Amendment solely on account of an individual's association with others who have committed acts of violence; he must have incited or authorized them himself.

For the same reasons the Court held that liability could not be imposed on Evers for his participation in the boycott itself, or for his threats of vilification or ostracism. However, the merchants also sought damages from Evers for his speeches. He gave one in April 1966, and two others in April 1969. In the first, he told his audience that they would be watched and that blacks who traded with white merchants would be answerable to him; he also said that any "uncle toms" who broke the boycott would "have their necks broken "by their own people. In his April 19, 1969 speech, Evers stated that boycott violators would be "disciplined" by their own people and warned that the Sheriff could not sleep with boycott

violators at night. And on April 21, Evers gave another speech to several hundred people calling for a total boycott of white-owned businesses and saying: "If we catch any of you going in any of them racist stores, we're gonna break your damn neck." The Court concluded that the "emotionally charged rhetoric" of Evers's speeches was within the bounds of Brandenberg. It was not followed by violence, and there was no evidence -- apart from the speeches themselves -- that Evers authorized, ratified, or directly threatened violence. "If there were other evidence of his authorization of wrongful conduct, the references to discipline in the speeches could be used to corroborate that evidence." Claiborne, 458 U.S. at 929. As there was not, the findings were constitutionally inadequate to support the damages judgment against him and, in turn, the NAACP.

Claiborne, of course, did not arise under a threats statute. The Court had no need to consider whether Evers's statements were true threats of force within the meaning of a threats statute; it held only that his speeches did not incite illegal activity, thus could not have caused business losses and could not be the basis for liability to white merchants. As the opinion points out, there was no context to give the speeches (including the expression "break your neck") the implication of authorizing or directly threatening unlawful conduct. To the extent there was any intimidating overtone, Evers's rhetoric was extemporaneous, surrounded by statements supporting non-violent action, and primarily of the social ostracism sort. No specific individuals were targeted. For all that appears, "the break your neck" comments were hyperbolic [1074] vernacular. Certainly there was no history that Evers or anyone else associated with the NAACP had broken anyone's neck who did not participate in, or opposed, this boycott or any others. Nor is there any indication that Evers's listeners took his statement that boycott breakers' "necks would be broken" as a serious threat that their necks would be broken; they kept on shopping at boycotted stores.

Thus, Watts was the only Supreme Court case that discussed the First Amendment in relation to true threats before we first confronted the issue. Apart from holding that Watts's crack about L.B.J. was not a true threat, the Court set out no standard for determining when a statement is a true threat that is unprotected speech under the First Amendment. Shortly after Watts was rendered, we had to decide in Roy v. United States, 416 F.2d 874 (9th Cir. 1969), whether a Marine Corps private made a true threat for purposes of 18 U.S.C. § 871 against the President, who was coming to his base the next day, by saying: "I am going to get him." We adopted a "reasonable speaker" test. As it has come to be articulated, the test is:

Whether a particular statement may properly be considered to be a threat is governed by an objective standard – whether a reasonable person would foresee that the statement would be interpreted by those to whom the maker communicates the statement as a serious expression of intent to harm or assault. United States v. Orozco-Santillan, 903 F.2d 1262, 1265 (9th Cir. 1990).

We have applied this test to threats statutes that are similar to FACE, see, e.g., United States v. Gilbert (Gilbert II), 884 F.2d 454, 457 (9th Cir. 1989) (Fair Housing Act banning threat of force to intimidate person based on race and housing practices, 42 U.S.C. § 3631); United States v. Mitchell, 812 F.2d 1250, 1255 (9th Cir. 1987) (threats against the President, 18 U.S.C. § 871); Merrill, 746 F.2d at 462-63 (same); United States v. Gordon, 974 F.2d 1110, 1117 (9th Cir. 1992) (threat to kill a former President, 18 U.S.C. § 879); Orozco-Santillan, 903 F.2d at 1265 (threats to assault a law enforcement officer with intent to intimidate, 18 U.S.C. § 115); Melugin, 38 F.3d at 1483-84 (threat to influence judicial proceeding under Alaska state law); McCalden v. California Library Ass'n, 955 F.2d 1214, 1222 (9th Cir. 1990) (threat to disrupt conference under California's Unruh Act); and Lovell, 90 F.3d at 371 (9th Cir. 1996) (§ 1983 action involving threat to shoot teacher). Other circuits have, too.[7] We see no reason not [1075] to apply the same test to FACE.[8]

---

[7] See, e.g., United States v. Whiffen, 121 F.3d 18, 20-21 (1st Cir. 1997) (statement is threat under 18 U.S.C. § 875(c) if reasonable person would foresee that it would be interpreted as expression of intent to harm); United States v. Sovie, 122 F.3d 122, 125 (2d Cir. 1997) (Second Circuit approach to threats, adopted in United States v. Kelner, 534 F.2d 1020 (2d Cir. 1976), is objective test and requires assessing whether a reasonable recipient of statement would construe it as threat in light of context); United States v. Kosma, 951 F.2d 549, 556-57 (3d Cir. 1991) (statement is threat under 18 U.S.C. § 871 if reasonable person would foresee that it would be interpreted as expression of intent to harm); United States v. Darby, 37 F.3d 1059, 1066 (4th Cir. 1994) (statement is threat under 18 U.S.C. § 875(c) if reasonable person would interpret the statement as threat); United States v. Morales, 272 F.3d 284, 287 (5th Cir. 2001) (statement is threat under 18 U.S.C. § 875(c) if recipient placed in reasonable fear of bodily harm); United States v. Landham, 251 F.3d 1072, 1080 (6th Cir. 2001) (statement is threat under 18 U.S.C. § 875(c) if reasonable recipient of message would interpret it as expression of intent to harm); United States v. Hartbarger, 148 F.3d 777, 782-83 (7th Cir. 1998) (cross burning is threat under 42 U.S.C. § 3631 because the reasonable person would foresee that it would be interpreted as expression of intent to harm); United States v. Hart, 212 F.3d 1067, 1072 (8th Cir. 2000) (placing Ryder truck in driveway of abortion clinic is

Under our cases, a threat is "an expression of an intention to inflict evil, injury, or damage on another." Gilbert II, 884 F.2d at 457; Orozco-Santillan, 903 F.2d at 1265. "Alleged threats should be considered in light of their entire factual context, including the surrounding events and reaction of the listeners." Orozco-Santillan, 903 F.2d at 1265; see also Mitchell, 812 F.2d at 1255 (citing Watts, 394 U.S. at 708; Merrill, 746 F.2d at 462; Roy, 416 F.2d at 876). "'The fact that a threat is subtle does not make it less of a threat.'" Orozco-Santillan, 903 F.2d at 1265 (quoting Gilbert II, 884 F.2d at 457). A true threat, that is one "where a reasonable person would foresee that the listener will believe he will be subjected to physical violence upon his person, is unprotected by the first amendment." Id. (citing Merrill, 746 F.2d at 462).

It is not necessary that the defendant intend to, or be able to carry out his threat; the only intent requirement for a true threat is that the defendant intentionally or knowingly communicate the threat. Orozco-Santillan, 903 F.2d at 1265 n.3; Gilbert II, 884 F.2d at 456-57; Mitchell, 812 F.2d at 1256 (upholding § 871 conviction of defendant with no capacity to carry out threat); Roy, 416 F.2d at 877.[9] Other circuits are in accord.[10] Nevertheless, we are

---

threat under FACE because, in light of entire factual context, person would reasonably conclude that the act expresses an intent to harm); United States v. Magleby, 241 F.3d 1306, 1311-13 (10th Cir. 2001) (cross burning is threat under the Fair Housing Act, 42 U.S.C. § 3631, because reasonable person would foresee that it would be interpreted as expression of intent to harm); United States v. Callahan, 702 F.2d 964, 965-66 (11th Cir. 1983) (statement is threat under 18 U.S.C. § 871 if reasonable person would construe statement as expression of intent to harm); Metz v. Dep't of Treasury, 780 F.2d 1001, 1002 (Fed. Cir. 1986) (threat evaluated by reasonable listener considering numerous factors).

Although all now apply an objective standard, several circuits have a "reasonable listener" test while others have a" reasonable speaker" test as we do. The difference does not appear to matter much because all consider context, including the effect of an allegedly threatening statement on the listener.
[8] Both the House and Senate specifically referred to Gilbert's interpretation of the Fair Housing Act's threat provision in adopting FACE's quite similar text. H. Rep. No. 103-306, at n.19 (1993); S. Rep. No. 103-117, at 29 (1993).
[9] We have held that 18 U.S.C. § 876, which criminalizes knowingly mailing any communication containing a threat to injure, is a specific intent crime. United States v. Twine, 853 F.2d 676 (9th Cir. 1988); United States v. King, 122 F.3d 808 (9th Cir. 1997). However, we were not defining "threat" or considering what a true threat is, and we made it clear that specific intent or ability to carry out the threat is not an essential element. King, 122 F.3d at 810 (quoting Twine, 853 F.2d at 681 n.4).
[10] See, e.g., United States v. Francis, 164 F.3d 120, 123 (2d Cir. 1999) (rejecting addition of substantive intent

urged to adopt a subjective intent requirement for FACE. In particular, amicus ACLU Foundation of Oregon, Inc., advocates a subjective intent component to "require evidence, albeit circumstantial or inferential in many cases, that the speaker actually intended to induce fear, intimidation, or terror; namely, that the speaker intended to threaten. If a person did not [1076] intend to threaten or intimidate (i.e., did not intend that his or her statement be understood as a threat), then the speech should not be considered to be a 'true threat,' unprotected by the First Amendment." However, this much is subsumed within the statutory standard of FACE itself, which requires that the threat of force be made with the intent to intimidate. The "requirement of intent to intimidate serves to insulate the statute from unconstitutional application to protected speech. " Gilbert I, 813 F.2d at 1529 (construing the Fair Housing Act's threat provision, 42 U.S.C. § 3631, which is essentially the same as FACE's). No reason appears to engraft another intent requirement onto the statute, because whether or not the maker of the threat has an actual intention to carry it out," an apparently serious threat may cause the mischief or evil toward which the statute was in part directed." Gilbert II, 884 F.2d at 458 (quoting Roy, 416 F.2d at 877).

The dissents would change the test, either to require that the speaker actually intend to carry out the threat or be in control of those who will, or to make it inapplicable when the speech is public rather than private. However, for years our test has focused on what a reasonable speaker would foresee the listener's reaction to be under the circumstances, and that is where we believe it should remain. See Madsen, 512 U.S. at 773 (noting that "threats . . . however communicated, are proscribable under the First Amendment, and indicating that display of signs "that could be interpreted as threats or veiled threats" could be prohibited). Threats are outside the First Amendment to "protect [] individuals from the fear of violence, from the disruption that fear engenders, and from the possibility that the threatened violence will occur." R.A.V. v. City of St. Paul, Minn., 505 U.S. 377, 388, 120 L. Ed. 2d 305, 112 S. Ct. 2538 (1992). This purpose is not served by

hinging constitutionality on the speaker's subjective intent or capacity to do (or not to do) harm. Rather, these factors go to how reasonably foreseeable it is to a speaker that the listener will seriously take his communication as an intent to inflict bodily harm. This suffices to distinguish a "true threat" from speech that is merely frightening. Thus, no reasonable speaker would foresee that a patient would take the statement "You have cancer and will die within six months," or that a pedestrian would take a warning "Get out of the way of that bus," as a serious expression of intent to inflict bodily harm; the harm is going to happen anyway.

Neither do we agree that threatening speech made in public is entitled to heightened constitutional protection just because it is communicated publicly rather than privately. As Madsen indicates, threats are unprotected by the First Amendment "however communicated." Madsen, 512 U.S. at 753.[11]

[1077] Therefore, we hold that "threat of force" in FACE means what our settled threats law says a true threat is: a statement which, in the entire context and under all the circumstances, a reasonable person would foresee would be interpreted by those to whom the statement is communicated as a serious expression of intent to inflict bodily harm upon that person. So defined, a threatening statement that violates FACE is unprotected under the First Amendment.

B. Although ACLA does not believe we should reach this point, if we do it submits that no claim was made out even under "true threats" cases. First, it argues that other threats cases were criminal actions against someone who made a real threat directly to

---

requirement to objective test); United States v. Miller, 115 F.3d 361, 363-64 (6th Cir. 1997) (same); United States v. Aman, 31 F.3d 550, 553-56 (7th Cir. 1994) (same); United States v. Patrick, 117 F.3d 375, 377 (8th Cir. 1997) (same); United States v. Martin, 163 F.3d 1212, 1215-16 (10th Cir. 1998) (same). But see United States v. Patillo, 438 F.2d 13, 15 (4th Cir. 1971) (including subjective intent element in § 871). The Fourth Circuit has abandoned this approach in its other true threat cases.

[11] Judge Reinhardt chides us for failing to accord public speech more protection than private speech. He misses the point. Threats, in whatever forum, may be independently proscribed without implicating the First Amendment. See e.g., Schenk v. Pro-Choice Network of Western New York, 519 U.S. 357, 373, 137 L. Ed. 2d 1, 117 S. Ct. 855 (1997) (so indicating in case involving public protest against abortion providers); Madsen, 512 U.S. at 774 (same); Kelner, 534 F.2d 1020 (JDL press conference in connection with public demonstration about the Palestine Liberation Organization and its leader); Hart, 212 F.3d 1067 (public protest against abortion providers).
Nor does Bauer v. Sampson, 261 F.3d 775 (9th Cir. 2001), turn on a public/private distinction, as Judge Kozinski's dissent suggests. No heightened scrutiny was given to the professor's speech on account of the fact that it had to do with a campus debate. Rather, the Orozco-Santillan test was applied, and we concluded that even though there was some violent content to his writings and cartoons, in the context of the underground campus newspaper in which they appeared, they would be perceived as hyperbole instead of as a serious expression of intent to inflict bodily harm.

others, not political speech as is the case here. It contrasts what it calls "a threat plus context" present in United States v. Dinwiddie, 76 F.3d 913 (8th Cir. 1996), and in other out-of-circuit cases,[12] with the absence of a direct threat in this case. However, our cases do not require that the maker of the threat personally cause physical harm to the listener. In Orozco-Santillan, we made it clear that the speaker did not need to be able to carry out the threat. Likewise in Mitchell, the speaker could not possibly have done so. In Gilbert, the threatening letter mentions neither the intended victim nor who would carry out the threat. No case to our knowledge has imposed such a requirement,[13] and we decline to now. It is the making of the threat with intent to intimidate – not the implementation of it – that violates FACE.

We do not understand Dinwiddie to hold anything different. Dinwiddie was also a civil suit under FACE. Mrs. Dinwiddie made comments to Crist outside his clinic, warning" Robert, remember Dr. Gunn . . . This could happen to you . . . He is not in the world anymore. Whoever sheds man's blood, by man his blood shall be shed." 76 F.3d at 917. She

also said: [1078] "You have not seen violence yet until you see what we do to you." Id. Writing for the Eighth Circuit, Judge Richard S. Arnold explained that in applying FACE's prohibition on using "threats of force," courts or juries must differentiate between "true threats" and protected speech. The alleged threat must be analyzed in light of its entire factual context to determine whether the recipient of the alleged threat could reasonably conclude that it expresses a determination or intent to injure presently or in the future. As outlined in the opinion, the Eighth Circuit considers a number of factors when deciding whether statements constitute threats of force: the reaction of the recipient and of other listeners, whether the threat was communicated directly to its victim, whether the maker of the threat had made similar statements to the victim in the past, and whether the victim had reason to believe that the maker had a propensity to engage in violence, but the list is not exhaustive and the presence or absence of any of these things is not dispositive. Id. at 925. The court concluded that although Mrs. Dinwiddie did not specifically say to Dr. Crist, "I am going to injure you," the statements in context, and Crist's reaction to them, show that they were "threats of force" that "intimidated" Crist. The court also noted that the fact that Mrs. Dinwiddie did not specifically say to Crist that she would injure him does not mean that her comments were not "threats of force." Id. at 925 n.9. Accordingly, the court upheld an injunction ordering Mrs. Dinwiddie to stop violating FACE (which, as it pointed out, would have a de minimis effect on her ability to express herself) and approved the injunction's nationwide scope.

ACLA also maintains that "context" means the direct circumstances surrounding delivery of the threat, or evidence sufficient to resolve ambiguity in the words of the statement – not two weeks of testimony as occurred here in the district court. Otherwise, ACLA submits, FACE is facially invalid. However, none of our cases has limited "context "to explaining ambiguous words, or to delivery. We, and so far as we can tell, other circuits as well, consider the whole factual context and "all of the circumstances," Merrill, 746 F.2d at 462, in order to determine whether a statement is a true threat. ACLA points to United States v. Kelner, 534 F.2d 1020 (2d Cir. 1976), but the Second Circuit's view is not to the contrary, as we noted in Lovell. Lovell, 90 F.3d at 372. The defendant in Kelner, who threatened to assassinate Yasser Arafat during a radio broadcast that also contained protected political expression, argued that this insulated his threat from prosecution; the court observed that this was not the case "so long as the threat on its face and in the circumstances in which it is made is so unequivocal, unconditional,

---

[12] It relies on United States v. Viefhaus, 168 F.3d 392 (10th Cir. 1999) (threat that bomb will be activated in 15 preselected major cities); United States v. Schiefen, 139 F.3d 638 (8th Cir. 1998) (personal letter sent to judge); United States v. Khorrami, 895 F.2d 1186 (7th Cir. 1990) (telephone calls and wanted posters sent directly to Jewish National Fund stating "death to the Fucking JNF"); United States v. Cooper, 865 F.2d 83 (4th Cir. 1989) (scoping out areas in Washington, D.C. to blow Rajiv Gandhi's brains out); United States v. Kosma, 951 F.2d 549 (3d Cir. 1991) (threat that 21 guns are going to put bullets through President Reagan's heart and brain); United States v. Kelner, 534 F.2d 1020 (2d Cir. 1976) (statement over radio that people are trained who are out now and intend to make sure that Arafat is assassinated); United States v. Sovie, 122 F.3d 122 (2d Cir. 1997) (reiterating Second Circuit test that "true threat" is one that "on its face and in the circumstances in which it is made is so unequivocal, unconditional, immediate and specific as to the person threatened, as to convey a gravity of purpose and imminent prospect of execution"); United States v. Fulmer, 108 F.3d 1486 (1st Cir. 1997) (silver bullets are coming; considered in context, appeared to be a threat).

[13] To the contrary, in Viefhaus, for example, the threat consisted of a hotline message from an unnamed person that violent acts would be executed by unnamed persons. In Khorrami, the purveyor of a "Crimes Against Humanity" poster made no statement that he would be the one to implement the threat. And in United States v. Bellrichard, 994 F.2d 1318 (8th Cir. 1993), letters warned that God or unnamed parties would kill the addressees. The same is true of Kelner, where the court noted that it was not necessary under § 875(c) (prescribing a communication containing a threat) for the government to prove that Kelner had a specific intent or a present ability to carry out his threat. 534 F.2d at 1023.

immediate and specific as to the person threatened, as to convey a gravity of purpose and imminent prospect of execution." Kelner, 534 F.2d at 1027. In Kelner as well as in Lovell, the threatening statement was considered in context to determine if it were a true threat or not. See United States v. Malik, 16 F.3d 45, 50 (2d Cir. 1994) (once there is sufficient extrinsic evidence to show that an ordinary and reasonable recipient would interpret letter as threat, case should go to the jury).

Indeed, context is critical in a true threats case and history can give meaning to the medium. Use of Ryder trucks – which the Eighth Circuit found to be a true threat in United States v. Hart, 212 F.3d 1067 (8th Cir. 2000) – is an example that is strikingly similar to the use of "wanted"-type posters in this case. Hart, who was a known anti-abortion activist, parked two Ryder trucks in the driveways of an abortion clinic. He was prosecuted and convicted of violating FACE. The court held that Hart had threatened the [1079] clinic to intimidate it by using Ryder trucks, because a Ryder truck had been used in the Oklahoma City bombing of the Murrah Federal Building. Hart knew the clinicians knew this and would fear for their lives. Thus, use of the Ryder truck was a true threat. Like the poster format here, the Ryder truck in Hart was a symbol of something beyond the vehicle: there, a devastating bomb; in this case, murder.[14]

ACLA's contention that allowing consideration of context beyond the direct circumstances surrounding delivery of the words themselves creates a facial invalidity in FACE and the Hobbs Act is unavailing. Of the courts to consider the constitu-tionality of threats statutes, including the United States Supreme Court in Watts, all have upheld constitutionality and ACLA points to none that has disallowed consideration of context.[15] This makes sense, because without context, a burning cross or dead rat mean nothing. In any event, the requirement of intent to intimidate cures whatever risk there might be of overbreadth.

Nor does consideration of context amount to viewpoint discrimination, as ACLA contends. ACLA's theory appears to be that because the posters did not contain any threat on their face, the views of

[14] See also, e.g., United States v. Magleby, 241 F.3d 1306 (10th Cir. 2001) (cross burning).

[15] See, e.g., United States v. Weslin, 156 F.3d 292 (2d Cir. 1998); United States v. Wilson, 154 F.3d 658 (7th Cir. 1998); United States v. Bird, 124 F.3d 667 (5th Cir. 1997); Hoffman v. Hunt, 126 F.3d 575 (4th Cir. 1997); Terry v. Reno, 322 U.S. App. D.C. 124, 101 F.3d 1412 (D.C. Cir. 1996); United States v. Soderna, 82 F.3d 1370 (7th Cir. 1996); Dinwiddie, 76 F.3d 913; Cheffer v. Reno, 55 F.3d 1517 (11th Cir. 1995).

abortion foes are chilled more than the views of abortion-right proponents because of the random acts of violence committed by some people against abortion providers. However, FACE itself is viewpoint neutral. See, e.g., United States v. Weslin, 156 F.3d 292, 296-97 (2d Cir. 1998); United States v. Wilson, 154 F.3d 658, 663 (7th Cir. 1998) ("The Act punishes anyone who engages in the prohibited conduct, irrespective of the person's viewpoint and does not target any message based on content. 'The Access Act thus does not play favorites: it protects from violent or obstructive activity not only abortion clinics, but facilities providing pre-pregnancy and pregnancy counseling services, as well as facilities counseling alternatives to abortion.'") (quoting Terry v. Reno, 101 F.3d 1412, 1419 (D.C. Cir. 1996)). Moreover, ACLA could not be liable under FACE unless it made a true threat with the intent to intimidate physicians. Thus it is making a threat to intimidate that makes ACLA's conduct unlawful, not its viewpoint.

Because of context, we conclude that the Crist and Deadly Dozen posters are not just a political statement. Even if the Gunn poster, which was the first "WANTED" poster, was a purely political message when originally issued, and even if the Britton poster were too, by the time of the Crist poster, the poster format itself had acquired currency as a death threat for abortion providers. Gunn was killed after his poster was released; Britton was killed after his poster was released; and Patterson was killed after his poster was released. Knowing this, and knowing the fear generated among those in the reproductive health services community who were singled out for identification on a "wanted"-type poster, ACLA deliberately identified Crist on a "GUILTY" poster and intentionally put the names of Hern and the Newhalls on the Deadly Dozen "GUILTY" poster to intimidate them. This goes well beyond the political message (regardless of what one thinks of it) [1080] that abortionists are killers who deserve death too.

The Nuremberg Files are somewhat different. Although they name individuals, they name hundreds of them. The avowed intent is "collecting dossiers on abortionists in anticipation that one day we may be able to hold them on trial for crimes against humanity." The web page states: "One of the great tragedies of the Nuremberg trials of Nazis after WWII was that complete information and documented evidence had not been collected so many war criminals went free or were only found guilty of minor crimes. We do not want the same thing to happen when the day comes to charge abortionists with their crimes. We anticipate the day when these people will be charged in PERFECTLY LEGAL COURTS once the tide of this nation's opinion turns against child-killing (as it surely will)." However offensive or disturbing this might be to those listed in the Files, being offensive and provocative is protected under the First Amendment. But, in two critical respects, the Files go further. In addition to listing judges, politicians and law enforcement personnel, the Files separately categorize "Abortionists" and list the names of individuals who provide abortion services, including, specifically, Crist, Hern, and both Newhalls. Also, names of abortion providers who have been murdered because of their activities are lined through in black, while names of those who have been wounded are highlighted in grey. As a result, we cannot say that it is clear as a matter of law that listing Crist, Hern, and the Newhalls on both the Nuremberg Files and the GUILTY posters is purely protected, political expression.

Accordingly, whether the Crist Poster, the Deadly Dozen poster, and the identification of Crist, Hern, Dr. Elizabeth Newhall and Dr. James Newhall in the Nuremburg Files as well as on "wanted"-type posters, constituted true threats was properly for the jury to decide.

C. ACLA next argues that the true threat instructions require reversal because they permitted consideration of motive, history of violence including the violent actions of others, and the defendants' subjective motives as part of context. We have already explained why it is proper for the whole factual context and all the circumstances bearing on a threat to be considered. The court also instructed the jury to consider evidence presented by the defense of non-violence and permissive exercise of free speech. That the contextual facts may have included the violent actions of others does not infect the instruction, because the issue is whether a reasonable person should have foreseen that the Crist Guilty Poster, the Deadly Dozen Poster, and the Nuremberg Files, would be interpreted as a serious threat of harm by doctors who provide abortions and were identified on them.

ACLA also contends that the district court employed the wrong standard of intent, allowing the jury to find in physicians' favor regardless of ACLA's subjective intent. The court instructed: "A statement is a 'true threat' when a reasonable person making the statement would foresee that the statement would be interpreted by those to whom it is communicated as a serious expression of an intent to bodily harm or assault." This language is taken from Orozco-Santillan, 903 F.2d at 1265, is an accurate statement of our law, and is faithful to the objective standard we use for determining whether a

statement is a true threat. For reasons we have already explained, we decline to read into FACE (or the Hobbs Act) a specific intent to threaten violence or to commit unlawful acts in addition to the intent to intimidate which the statute itself requires.

[1081] ACLA additionally faults the court for failing to provide any standard of intent because the elements instruction merely states that FACE is violated by "a threat of force to intimidate or interfere with, or attempt to intimidate or interfere with" physicians' ability to provide reproductive health services. As best we can tell, this boils down to a complaint that the instruction did not say "in order to" between" threat of force" and "to intimidate." However, this is the plain import of the instruction.

ACLA further suggests that the conspiracy instruction, combined with the "attempt to intimidate" instruction, could have resulted in liability for an "attempt to threaten" without proof of an actual threat.[16] We do not see how, because the jury had to find a true threat before reaching any other FACE or RICO issues. ACLA also posits that the standard form instruction, "if you find a defendant was a member of a conspiracy, that defendant is responsible for what other conspirators said or did to carry out the conspiracy, whether or not that defendant knew what they said or did," had the effect in this case of violating the rule of Claiborne that one cannot be held accountable for the speech of others by reason of mere association, absent ratification or adoption of it. However, the jury was instructed that a person does not become a

---

16 ACLA argues more broadly that no claim for conspiracy to violate FACE exists, but we decline to consider the issue because it is raised for the first time on appeal. Los Angeles News Serv. v. Reuters Television Int'l Ltd., 149 F.3d 987, 996 (9th Cir. 1998). It had every opportunity to assert this view in the district court before judgment, having moved to dismiss, for summary judgment, and for judgment as a matter of law as well as having objected to proposed instructions (but not on conspiracy). Failing to raise the issue until now, absent any exceptional circumstances or change in the law, prejudices both the plaintiffs and the process. Considerable time and resources were devoted to litigating these claims to verdict. In any event, we cannot see that substantial injustice occurred. FACE came into being in part because of "organized," "concerted" campaigns by "groups" to disrupt access to reproductive health services, S. Rep. No. 103-117, at 6-7 (1993), and the instruction effectively channeled the jury away from finding defendants liable for mere association and instead required it to find that each defendant threatened physicians intending to intimidate them or willfully joined with others to do so. See Madsen v. Women's Health Center, Inc., 512 U.S. 753, 776 (1994) (freedom of association protected by First Amendment does not extend to joining with others for the purpose of depriving third parties of their lawful rights).

conspirator merely by associating with one or more persons who are conspirators; rather, one becomes a member of a conspiracy by willfully participating in an unlawful plan with the intent to advance or further some object or purpose of it. There is no right to associate with others to engage in activities that are unlawful and unprotected by the First Amendment, as the making of true threats to intimidate providers of reproductive health services is. Madsen, 512 U.S. at 776 (upholding injunction restraining abortion protestors acting in concert with defendants). The Seventh Circuit had occasion to consider (and reject) a similar argument made by abortion protestors who had been convicted of conspiring to violate FACE in United States v. Wilson, 154 F.3d 658, 666-67 (7th Cir. 1998). It explained that the Supreme Court in Claiborne was referring to individuals who were engaging in a peaceful protest and thus were properly exercising their First Amendment rights, whereas FACE is aimed at those who themselves intend to intimidate and thereby deprive others of their lawful rights. As in Wilson, we are not persuaded that the instructions allowed any defendant in this case to be found liable for threats to intimidate for [1082] which he or she was not responsible. They either participated in making them, or agreed that they should be made.

Finally, we note that the jury was instructed that "even speech that is coercive may be protected if the speaker refrains from violence or from making a true threat. Moreover, the mere abstract teaching of the moral propriety or even moral necessity for resort to force and violence is protected speech under the First Amendment." It was reminded that "plaintiffs' claims are based only on the three statements I have listed for you," and that it should determine the case as to each defendant and each claim separately. Accordingly, the court did not abuse its discretion in formulating the instructions, nor was the jury incorrectly instructed as a matter of law on true threats or the elements of FACE.[17]

---

[17] ACLA cites other errors in the Hobbs Act and RICO instructions but offers no authority in support. Neither does it indicate that any objection on these issues was preserved. Its argument on appeal is not developed. In any event, the instructions appear to track model instructions and are not obviously wrong. For these reasons, we do not discuss these challenges and summarily reject them.
ACLA also contends that the court compromised its right to a fair trial by telling the jury that the United States Supreme Court has declared that women have a constitutional right to abortion, and no one is permitted to violate the law because of their views about abortion. It objected on the ground that the charge was "death to us" but makes no substantial

D. ACLA joins in Treshman's assertion that the court erroneously admitted prejudicial evidence by permitting: an FBI agent and two federal marshals to testify that the FBI and the Justice Department considered ACLA's two posters to be "serious threats"; references to non-party violence; introduction of defendants' arrests; physicians' counsel to tell the jury about Bray's invocations of the Fifth Amendment through a summary of his deposition; references to actions of certain defendants and non-parties on the abortion debate and to such things as the signing of "Defensive Action petitions" by five or six of the individual defendants; an exhibit with Rev. Sullivan's hearsay opinion that ACLA is a "cancer" which pro-lifers must "cut out immediately" before it" destroys the pro-life movement" to remain in the exhibit books; and by permitting deposition summaries to be introduced. ACLA recognizes that evidentiary rulings are normally reviewed for an abuse of discretion, but argues that in cases raising First Amendment issues appellate courts must independently examine the record for evidentiary errors which penalize political speech or allow "a forbidden intrusion on the field of free expression." Milkovich v. Lorain Journal Co., 497 U.S. 1, 17, 111 L. Ed. 2d 1, 110 S. Ct. 2695 (1990) (citation omitted). We decline ACLA's invitation to review evidentiary rulings de novo. No case of which we are aware suggests that the obligation to examine the record independently extends so far. Nor do we believe that appellate judges should retry cases, as ACLA's proposal would have us do. Accordingly, we review the district court's evidentiary rulings in this case, as we do evidentiary rulings in all cases, for abuse of discretion. None appears.

Testimony about the law enforcement officers' response to the Crist and Deadly Dozen "GUILTY" posters had some tendency to show the physicians' state of mind when they found out they were named on "wanted"-type posters, as well as to show the knowledge and intent of ACLA in distributing the posters regardless [1083] of the reaction they precipitated. Both are non-hearsay purposes. No testimony was allowed about what officers thought the posters meant. That FBI agents and United States Marshals advised physicians to take security precautions relates to how Crist, Hern, and the Newhalls perceived their own safety. The court admonished the jury that it should not conclude that these agencies had decided that the threats were "true threats." We assume that the jury followed the court's

---

argument on appeal why there was reversible error on this account. We summarily reject this argument as well.

limiting instruction, Ortiz-Sandoval v. Gomez, 81 F.3d 891, 899-900 (9th Cir. 1996), which cured whatever potential there may have been for an unduly prejudicial effect from admission of this testimony.

ACLA's knowledge of prior violence and its effect on reproductive health services providers bore directly on its intent to intimidate physicians, and was limited by the district court to that relevant purpose. Bray's invocation of the Fifth Amendment was not improperly admitted as to him in a civil trial. SEC v. Colello, 139 F.3d 674, 677 (9th Cir. 1998). Coconspirator statements were admissible so long as they were connected to the conspiracy and the jury found that the statements were made in furtherance of it. The same is true of the Defensive Action petitions, which were clearly admissible against those defendants who signed them and as to others with whom the signatories were conspiring. Speech does not become inadmissible to show context or intent simply because standing alone it is protected. Wisconsin v. Mitchell, 508 U.S. 476, 489, 124 L. Ed. 2d 436, 113 S. Ct. 2194-90 (1993) (First Amendment does not prohibit evidentiary use of speech to show motive or intent); Dinwiddie, 76 F.3d at 918, 925, n.10 (although advocacy of view that violence is justifiable is protected, it was appropriate for district court to consider plaintiff's awareness of defendant's advocacy of lethal force in determining whether defendant intimidated him with threats of force). Terry Sullivan was at the Chicago meeting that led to the founding of ACLA, and to the extent that he expressed any opinion about how ACLA was undermining a commitment to nonviolence, it was part of what happened at the time, was relevant to show that ACLA knew how its actions were being interpreted, and was within the district court's discretion to admit once Sullivan's testimony had laid a foundation. Neither Sullivan nor Flip Benham was available to testify at trial; as both had been examined at a deposition, their former testimony was not excluded by the hearsay rule, Fed. R. Evid. 804(b), and its presentation in the form of summaries was within the court's discretion under Rule 611(a). Oostendorp v. Khanna, 937 F.2d 1177, 1180 (7th Cir. 1991) (requiring deposition summaries not an abuse of discretionary authority to regulate conduct of civil trials); Walker v. Action Indus., Inc., 802 F.2d 703, 712 (4th Cir. 1986) (same); Kinglsey v. Baker/Beech-Nut Corp., 546 F.2d 1136, 1141 (5th Cir. 1977) (same); MANUAL FOR COMPLEX LITIGATION, Third, § 22.331 (1995).[18]

[1084] E.   ACLA also joins Treshman's argument that mistrials should have been granted because a juror objected to use of the word "abortionist"; the judge made a remark about Bill Clinton in admonishing a witness to tell the truth; jurors were invited to watch a criminal sentencing proceeding; three jurors had a conversation with one of the physicians during a lunch hour; and physicians' counsel likened defendants to the Oklahoma City and World Trade Center bombers and Islamic terrorists during his closing. We are asked to review the record de novo on this issue as well, although ACLA acknowledges that the normal standard for refusing to grant mistrials is abuse of discretion. We decline to change our standard, and see no reversible error.

When a juror informed the court that the defense's use of the term "abortionist" was becoming distracting, the district court instructed the jury that "it is perfectly legal, and proper, and within any free speech right, for one group, that is opposing another group, to refer to them in the terms they choose. And it's clear the pro-life people, traditionally, I believe, call abortion providers abortionists. So, there should not be any adverse reaction to these people using the lingo and terminology of their protest." The jurors all responded that they could live with that, and keep an open mind with respect to all the evidence. There was no objection to the process, and no abuse of discretion on account of taking no further action. Similarly, after learning of a chance encounter in the courthouse elevator between Elizabeth Newhall and three jurors in the presence of defense counsel, the court inquired whether the jurors had discussed anything substantive and whether their judgment would be impaired by the contact. They responded negatively and the court acted within its discretion in taking no further action. The court also instructed

---

[18] After noting that the decision to admit deposition testimony at all is within the sound discretion of the district court, Judge Flaum explained in Oostendorp:

It follows that the court may control the manner in which deposition testimony is presented; indeed, trial courts are charged to "exercise reasonable control" over the mode and order of interrogating witnesses and presenting evidence so as to (1) make the interrogation and presentation effective for the ascertainment of the truth [and to] avoid needless consumption of time . . . Fed. R. Evid. 611(a). The district court adopted its rule to serve these objectives, and we agree that requiring deposition summaries can be a reasonable means of implementing the mandate of Rule 611. We therefore conclude that the district court's requirement was not an abuse of its discretionary authority to regulate the conduct of civil trials. Oostendorp, 937 F.2d at 1179-1180. We hold only, for these reasons, that the district court did not abuse its discretion in requiring summaries in lieu of transcripts. As there was no challenge along the lines of Judge Berzon's dissent to the particular summaries that were presented, we have no occasion to consider whether the court did or did not err in receiving them.

that anything the jury may have seen or heard when the court was not in session is not evidence, and that the case was to be decided solely on the evidence received at trial. Finally, ACLA fails to explain why allowing the jurors to watch two sentencing proceedings was objectionable or prejudicial, and we cannot see how it was.

The judge himself recognized that his Clinton reference was inappropriate. He apologized to the jury about it, and explained that the court was attempting to suggest to the witness that she should just go ahead and answer a question. (The witness had remarked to counsel after being impeached with a prior inconsistent statement under oath, "I am not sure what you mean by truthful.") The judge told jurors to put his comment out of their minds, permitted the defense to re-open direct examination to allow the witness to explain her prior answer, and told the jury again in his final instructions that any remarks of his were not to be taken as an indication of how much weight to give the testimony of any witness. Whatever the impropriety, it was cured.

As might be expected, closing argument was robust on both sides; the court gave all counsel considerable latitude. Images of famous and infamous figures alike were evoked. The district judge was in the best position to decide whether any particular reference went too far. The court reminded [1085] the jury that counsels' statements were not evidence, and we cannot say that the defense was so prejudiced by the argument that a mistrial should have been granted.

F. Having concluded that "threat of force" was properly defined and that no trial error requires reversal, we consider whether the core constitutional fact – a true threat – exists such that the Crist and Deadly Dozen Posters, and the Nuremberg Files as to Crist, Hern, and the Newhalls, are without First Amendment protection. The task in this case does not seem dramatically different from determining that the issue should have gone to the jury and that the jury was properly instructed under FACE. Nevertheless, we review the evidence on true threats independently.

The true threats analysis turns on the poster pattern. Neither the Crist poster nor the Deadly Dozen poster contains any language that is overtly threatening. Both differ from prior posters in that the prior posters were captioned "WANTED" while these are captioned "GUILTY." The text also differs somewhat, but differences in caption or words are immaterial because the language itself is not what is threatening. Rather, it is use of the "wanted"-type format in the context of the poster pattern – poster followed by murder – that constitutes the threat.

Because of the pattern, a "wanted"-type poster naming a specific doctor who provides abortions was perceived by physicians, who are providers of reproductive health services, as a serious threat of death or bodily harm. After a "WANTED" poster on Dr. David Gunn appeared, he was shot and killed. After a "WANTED" poster on Dr. George Patterson appeared, he was shot and killed. After a "WANTED" poster on Dr. John Britton appeared, he was shot and killed. None of these "WANTED" posters contained threatening language, either. Neither did they identify who would pull the trigger. But knowing this pattern, knowing that unlawful action had followed "WANTED" posters on Gunn, Patterson and Britton, and knowing that "wanted"-type posters were intimidating and caused fear of serious harm to those named on them, ACLA published a "GUILTY" poster in essentially the same format on Dr. Crist and a Deadly Dozen "GUILTY" poster in similar format naming Dr. Hern, Dr. Elizabeth Newhall and Dr. James Newhall because they perform abortions. Physicians could well believe that ACLA would make good on the threat. One of the other doctors on the Deadly Dozen poster had in fact been shot before the poster was published. This is not political hyperbole. Nor is it merely "vituperative, abusive, and inexact." Watts, 394 U.S. at 708 (comparing language used in political arena to language used in labor disputes). In the context of the poster pattern, the posters were precise in their meaning to those in the relevant community of reproductive health service providers. They were a true threat.

The posters are a true threat because, like Ryder trucks or burning crosses, they connote something they do not literally say, yet both the actor and the recipient get the message. To the doctor who performs abortions, these posters meant "You're Wanted or You're Guilty; You'll be shot or killed." This was reinforced by the scorecard in the Nuremberg Files. The communication was not conditional or casual. It was specifically targeted. Crist, Hern, and the Newhalls, who performed abortions, were not amused. Cf. Watts, 394 U.S. at 708 (no true threat in political speech that was conditional, extemporaneous, and met with laughter); Claiborne, 458 U.S. at 928 (spontaneous and emotional [1086] appeal in extemporaneous speech protected when lawless action not incited).

The "GUILTY" posters were publicly distributed, but personally targeted. While a privately communicated threat is generally more likely to be taken seriously than a diffuse public one, this cannot be said of a threat that is made publicly but is about a specifically identified doctor and is in the same format that had previously resulted in the death of three doctors who had also been publicly, yet specifically, targeted. There were no individualized threats in Brandenberg, Watts or Claiborne. However, no one putting Crist, Hern, and the Newhalls on a "wanted"-type poster, or participating in selecting these particular abortion providers for such a poster or publishing it, could possibly believe anything other than that each would be seriously worried about being next in line to be shot and killed. And they were seriously worried.

As a direct result of having a "GUILTY" poster out on them, physicians wore bullet-proof vests and took other extraordinary security measures to protect themselves and their families. ACLA had every reason to foresee that its expression of intent to harm (the "GUILTY" poster identifying Crist, Hern, Elizabeth Newhall and James Newhall by name and putting them in the File that tracks hits and misses) would elicit this reaction. Physicians' fear did not simply happen; ACLA intended to intimidate them from doing what they do.

This is the point of the statute and is conduct that we are satisfied lacks any protection under the First Amendment.

Violence is not a protected value. Nor is a true threat of violence with intent to intimidate. ACLA may have been staking out a position for debate when it merely advocated violence as in Bray's A Time to Kill, or applauded it, as in the Defense Action petitions. Likewise, when it created the Nuremberg Files in the abstract, because the First Amendment does not preclude calling people demeaning or inflammatory names, or threatening social ostracism or vilification to advocate a political position. Claiborne, 458 U.S. at 903, 909-12. But, after being on "wanted"-type posters, Dr. Gunn, Dr. Patterson, and Dr. Britton can no longer participate in the debate. By replicating the poster pattern that preceded the elimination of Gunn, Patterson and Britton, and by putting Crist, Hern, and the Newhalls in an abortionists' File that scores fatalities, ACLA was not staking out a position of debate but of threatened demise. This turns the First Amendment on its head.

Like "fighting words," true threats are proscribable. We therefore conclude that the judgment of liability in physicians' favor is constitutionally permissible.

IV. ACLA submits that the damage award must be reversed or limited to the compensatory damages because the punitive award amounts to judgment without notice contrary to BMW of North America, Inc. v. Gore, 517 U.S. 559, 134 L. Ed. 2d 809, 116 S. Ct. 1589 (1996). We have since discussed the subject in depth in In re Exxon Valdez, 270 F.3d 1215, 1241

(9th Cir. 2001). Although our review is de novo, the district court should be given the opportunity to evaluate the punitive damages award and to make findings with respect to its propriety. Therefore, we vacate the award of punitive damages and remand for the district court to consider in the first instance whether the award is appropriate in light of Exxon Valdez.

V. After trial, the district court found that each defendant used intimidation as a means of interfering with the provision of reproductive health services and acted [1087] with malice and with specific intent in threatening physicians. It found that physicians remain threatened by ACLA's threats, and have no adequate remedy at law. The court concluded that physicians had proved by clear and convincing evidence that each defendant acting independently and as a co-conspirator prepared and published the Deadly Dozen Poster, the Crist Poster, and the Nuremberg Files with specific intent to make true threats to kill or do bodily harm to physicians, and to intimidate them from engaging in legal medical practices. It "totally rejected the defendants' attempts to justify their actions as an expression of opinion or as a legitimate and lawful exercise of free speech in order to dissuade the plaintiffs from providing abortion services." PPCW III, 41 F. Supp. 2d at 1154. Applying Madsen's standard, the court found that ACLA's actions were not protected under the First Amendment. Accordingly, it permanently enjoined each of the defendants, their agents, and all persons in active concert with any of them who receive actual notice, from threatening, with the specific intent to do so, Crist, Hern, Dr. Elizabeth Newhall, Dr. James Newhall, PPCW and PFWHC in violation of FACE; publishing, republishing, reproducing or distributing the Deadly Dozen Poster, or the Crist poster, or their equivalent, with specific intent to threaten physicians, PPCW or PFWHC; and from providing additional material concerning Crist, Hern, either Newhall, PPCW or PFWHC to the Nuremberg Files or any mirror web site with a specific intent to threaten, as well as from publishing the personally identifying information about them in the Nuremberg Files with a specific intent to threaten. The court also ordered ACLA to turn over possession of materials that are not in compliance with the injunction.

ACLA complains principally about the restraint on possessing the posters. Pointing to Stanley v. Georgia, 394 U.S. 557, 567, 22 L. Ed. 2d 542, 89 S. Ct. 1243 (1969), where the Court observed that "the State may no more prohibit mere possession of obscene matter on the ground that it may lead to antisocial conduct than it may prohibit possession of chemistry books on the ground that they may lead to the manufacture of homemade spirits, "ACLA contends that the injunction treats the posters worse than obscenity. However, the posters in this case are quite different from a book; the "wanted"-type posters themselves – not their ideological content – are the tool for threatening physicians. In this sense the posters' status is more like conduct than speech. Cf. United States v. O'Brien, 391 U.S. 367, 376, 20 L. Ed. 2d 672, 88 S. Ct. 1673-82 (1968) (explaining distinction between speech and conduct, and holding that expressive aspect of conduct does not exempt it from warranted regulation). The First Amendment interest in retaining possession of the threatening posters is de minimis, while ACLA's continued possession of them constitutes part of the threat. The court heard all the evidence, which included testimony that some defendants obstructed justice and ignored injunctions. Accordingly, we cannot say that the turn-over order was broader than necessary to assure that this particular threat will not be used again.

ACLA also suggests that the injunction is an improper prior restraint on speech because it prohibits dissemination of the posters. It is not. The Supreme Court has rejected the notion that all injunctions which incidentally affect expression are prior restraints. Madsen, 512 U.S. at 764 n.2; Schenck v. Pro- Choice Network of Western New York, 519 U.S. 357, 374 n.6 (1997). Like Madsen and Schenck, the injunction here was not issued because of the content of ACLA's [1088] expression, but because of prior unlawful conduct.

The terms of the injunction are finely tuned and exceedingly narrow. Only threats or use of the posters or their equivalent with the specific intent to threaten Crist, Hern, either Newhall, PPCW or PFWHC are prohibited. Only personal information about these particular persons may not be used in the Nuremberg Files with the specific intent to threaten them. This leaves huge room for ACLA to express its views. n19[19]

CONCLUSION: A "threat of force" for purposes of FACE is properly defined in accordance with our long-standing test on" true threats," as "whether a reasonable person would foresee that the statement would be interpreted by those to whom the maker communicates the statement as a serious expression of intent to harm or assault." This, coupled with the statute's requirement of intent to intimidate, comports with the First Amendment.

We have reviewed the record and are satisfied that use of the Crist Poster, the Deadly Dozen Poster, and the individual plaintiffs' listing in the Nuremberg Files constitute a true threat. In three prior incidents, a "wanted"-type poster identifying a specific doctor who provided abortion services was circulated, and the doctor named on the poster was killed. ACLA and physicians knew of this, and both understood the significance of the particular posters specifically identifying each of them. ACLA realized that "wanted" or "guilty" posters had a threatening meaning that physicians would take seriously. In conjunction with the "guilty" posters, being listed on a Nuremberg Files scorecard for abortion providers impliedly threatened physicians with being next on a hit list. To this extent only, the Files are also a true threat. However, the Nuremberg Files are protected speech.

There is substantial evidence that these posters were prepared and disseminated to intimidate physicians from providing reproductive health services. Thus, ACLA was appropriately found liable for a true threat to intimidate under FACE.

Holding ACLA accountable for this conduct does not impinge on legitimate protest or advocacy. Restraining it from continuing to threaten these physicians burdens speech no more than necessary.

Therefore, we affirm the judgment in all respects but for punitive damages, as to which we remand.

AFFIRMED IN PART; VACATED AND REMANDED IN PART.

DISSENT: REINHARDT, Circuit Judge, with whom KOZINSKI, KLEINFELD, and BERZON, Circuit Judges, join, dissenting:

I concur fully in both Judge Kozinski's and Judge Berzon's dissents. The differences between the majority and dissenting opinions with respect to the First Amendment are clear. I write separately to emphasize one point: the majority rejects the concept that speech made in a political forum on issues of public concern warrants heightened scrutiny. See Majority Op. at 7116. This rejection, if allowed to stand, would significantly weaken the First Amendment protections we now enjoy. It is a fundamental tenet of First Amendment jurisprudence that political speech in a public arena is different from purely private speech directed at an individual. See NAACP v. Claiborne Hardware Co., 458 U.S. 886, 926-27 [1089] (1982); Watts v. United States, 394 U.S. 705, 708 (1969); New York Times Co. v. Sullivan, 376 U.S. 254, 270 (1964); Terminiello v. City of Chicago, 337 U.S. 1, 4, 93 L. Ed. 1131, 69 S. Ct. 894 (1949). Political speech, ugly or frightening as it may sometimes be, lies at the heart of our

---

[19] Assuming that he has standing, deParrie's challenges fail for most of the same reasons. The district court found that he was an employee and agent of ALM and it is proper for the injunction to apply to him as well. Fed. R. Civ. P. 65.

democratic process. Private threats delivered one-on-one do not. The majority's unwillingness to recognize the difference is extremely troublesome. For this reason alone, I would be compelled to dissent.

DISSENT: KOZINSKI, Circuit Judge, with whom Circuit Judges REINHARDT, O'SCANNLAIN, KLEINFELD and BERZON join, dissenting:

The majority writes a lengthy opinion in a vain effort to justify a crushing monetary judgment and a strict injunction against speech protected by the First Amendment. The apparent thoroughness of the opinion, addressing a variety of issues that are not in serious dispute, n1 masks the fact that the majority utterly fails to apply its own definition of a threat, and affirms the verdict and injunction when the evidence in the record does not support a finding that defendants threatened plaintiffs.[1]

After meticulously canvassing the case law, the majority correctly distills the following definition of a true threat: "a statement which, in the entire context and under all the circumstances, a reasonable person would foresee would be interpreted by those to whom the statement is communicated as a serious expression of intent to inflict bodily harm upon that person." Maj. op. at 7116-17 (emphasis added).[2] The emphasized language is crucial, because it is not illegal–and cannot be made so–merely to say things that would frighten or intimidate the listener. For example, when a doctor says, "You have cancer and will die within six months, "it is not a threat, even though you almost certainly will be frightened. Similarly, "Get out of the way of that bus" is not a threat, even though it is said in order to scare you into changing your behavior. By contrast, "If you don't stop performing abortions, I'll kill you" is a true threat and surely illegal.

The difference between a true threat and protected expression is this: A true threat warns of violence or other harm that the speaker controls. Thus, when a doctor tells a patient, "Stop smoking or you'll die of lung cancer," that is not a threat because the doctor obviously can't [1090] cause the harm to come about. Similarly, "If you walk in that neighborhood late at night, you're going to get mugged" is not a threat, unless it is clear that the speaker himself (or one of his associates) will be doing the mugging.

In this case, none of the statements on which liability was premised were overtly threatening. On the contrary, the two posters and the web page, by their explicit terms, foreswore the use of violence and advocated lawful means of persuading plaintiffs to stop performing abortions or punishing them for continuing to do so. Nevertheless, because context matters, the statements could reasonably be interpreted as an effort to intimidate plaintiffs into ceasing their abortion-related activities. If that were enough to strip the speech of First Amendment protection, there would be nothing left to decide. But the Supreme Court has told us that "speech does not lose its protected character . . . simply because it may embarrass others or coerce them into action." NAACP v. Claiborne Hardware Co., 458 U.S. 886, 910 (1982) (emphasis added). In other words, some forms of intimidation enjoy constitutional protection.

Only a year after Claiborne Hardware, we incorporated this principle into our circuit's true threat jurisprudence. Striking down as overbroad a Montana statute that made it a crime to communicate to another "a threat to . . . commit a criminal offense," we stated: "The mere fact that communication induces or 'coerces' action in others does not remove it from first amendment protection." Wurtz v. Risley, 719 F.2d 1438, 1441 (9th Cir. 1983) (quoting Claiborne Hardware, 458 U.S. at 911). We noted–referring to Claiborne Hardware again–that the statute criminalized pure speech designed to alter someone else's conduct, so that a "civil rights activist who states to a restaurant owner, 'if you don't desegregate this restaurant I am going to organize a boycott' could be punished for the mere statement, even if no action followed." 719 F.2d at 1442. Claiborne Hardware and Wurtz hold that statements that are intimidating, even coercive, are protected by the First Amendment, so long as the speaker does not threaten that he, or someone acting in concert with

---

[1] For example, it is clear that context may be taken into account in determining whether something is a true threat, an issue to which the majority devotes 16 pages. See Maj. op. at 7105-14, 7119-22. Nor is there a dispute that someone may be punished for uttering threats, even though he has no intent to carry them out, see id. at 7114-15, or that we defer to the fact finder on questions of historical fact in First Amendment cases, id. at 7099-7100.

[2] Although the majority's definition does not specify who is to inflict the threatened harm, use of the active verb "inflict "rather than a passive phrase, such as "will be harmed," strongly suggests that the speaker must indicate he will take an active role in the inflicting. Recent academic commentary supports the view that this requirement is an integral component of a "true threat" analysis. See Steven G. Gey, The Nuremberg Files and the First Amendment Value of Threats, 78 Tex. L. Rev. 541, 590 (2000) (part of what "separates constitutionally unprotected true threats from constitutionally protected Claiborne Hardware-style political intimidation is [that] the speaker communicates the intent to carry out the threat personally or to cause it to be carried out"); Jennifer E. Rothman, Freedom of Speech and True Threats, 25 Harv. J.L. & Pub. Pol'y 283, 289 (2001) ("determining what is a true threat [should] require[]proof that the speaker explicitly or implicitly suggest that he or his co-conspirators will be the ones to carry out the threat").

him, will resort to violence if the warning is not heeded.

The majority recognizes that this is the standard it must apply, yet when it undertakes the critical task of canvassing the record for evidence that defendants made a true threat–a task the majority acknowledges we must perform de novo, Maj. op at 7105–its opinion fails to come up with any proof that defendants communicated an intent to inflict bodily harm upon plaintiffs.

Buried deep within the long opinion is a single paragraph that cites evidence supporting the finding that the two wanted posters prepared by defendants constituted a true threat. Maj. op at 7121-22; see also id. at 7137-38 (same analysis). The majority does not point to any statement by defendants that they intended to inflict bodily harm on plaintiffs, nor is there any evidence that defendants took any steps whatsoever to plan or carry out physical violence against anyone. Rather, the majority relies on the fact that "the poster format itself had acquired currency as a death threat for abortion providers. Gunn was killed after his poster was released; Britton was killed after his poster was released; and Patterson was killed after his poster was released." Id. at 7121; see also id. at 7137-38. But neither Dr. Gunn nor Dr. Patterson was killed by anyone connected with the posters bearing their names. Planned Parenthood of the Columbia/Willamette, Inc. v. Am. Coalition [1091] of Life Activists, 41 F. Supp. 2d 1130, 1134-35 (D. Or. 1999). In fact, Dr. Patterson's murder may have been unrelated to abortion: He was killed in what may have been a robbery attempt five months after his poster was issued; the crime is unsolved and plaintiffs' counsel conceded that no evidence ties his murderer to any anti-abortion group. R.T. at 131, 1197.

The record reveals one instance where an individual–Paul Hill, who is not a defendant in this case–participated in the preparation of the poster depicting a physician, Dr. Britton, and then murdered him some seven months later. All others who helped to make that poster, as well as those who prepared the other posters, did not resort to violence. And for years, hundreds of other posters circulated, condemning particular doctors with no violence ensuing. See R.T. at 1775-76, 1783-84, 2487, 2828. There is therefore no pattern showing that people who prepare wanted-type posters then engage in physical violence. To the extent the posters indicate a pattern, it is that almost all people engaged in poster-making were non-violent.[3]

The majority tries to fill this gaping hole in the record by noting that defendants "knew the fear generated among those in the reproductive health services community who were singled out for identification on a 'wanted'-type poster." Maj. op at 7121. But a statement does not become a true threat because it instills fear in the listener; as noted above, many statements generate fear in the listener, yet are not true threats and therefore may not be punished or enjoined consistent with the First Amendment. See pp. 7144-46 supra. In order for the statement to be a threat, it must send the message that the speakers themselves–or individuals acting in concert with them–will engage in physical violence. The majority's own definition of true threat makes this clear. Yet the opinion points to no evidence that defendants who prepared the posters would have been understood by a reasonable listener as saying that they will cause the harm.

Plaintiffs themselves explained that the fear they felt came, not from defendants, but from being singled out for attention by abortion protesters across the country. For example, plaintiff Dr. Elizabeth Newhall testified, "I feel like my risk comes from being identified as a target. And . . . all the John Salvis in the world know who I am, and that's my concern."[4] Planned Parenthood of the Columbia/Willamette, Inc. v. Am. Coalition of Life Activists, No. CV-95-01671-JO, at 302 (D. Or. Jan. 8, 1999); see also id. at 290 ("Up until January of '95, I felt relatively diluted by the – you know, in the pool of providers of abortion services. I didn't feel particularly visible to the people who were – you know, to the John Salvis of the world, you know. I sort of felt one of a big, big group."). Likewise, Dr.

---

[3] The majority so much as admits that the Nuremberg Files website does not constitute a threat because of the large

number of people listed there. Maj. op. at 7122. The majority does point out that doctors were listed separately, and that the names of doctors who were killed or wounded were stricken or greyed out, id. at 7122, but does not explain how this supports the inference that the posting of the website in any way indicated that defendants intended to inflict bodily harm on plaintiffs. At most, the greying out and strikeouts could be seen as public approval of those actions, and approval of past violence by others cannot be made illegal consistent with the First Amendment. See Hess v. Indiana, 414 U.S. 105, 108-09 (1973); Brandenburg v. Ohio, 395 U.S. 444, 447 (1969); Edwards v. South Carolina, 372 U.S. 229, 237, 9 L. Ed. 2d 697, 83 S. Ct. 680-38 (1963); Noto v. United States, 367 U.S. 290, 297, 6 L. Ed. 2d 836, 81 S. Ct. 1517-99 (1961).

[4] In December 1994, John Salvi killed two clinic workers and wounded five others in attacks on two clinics in Brookline, Massachusetts; Salvi later fired shots at a clinic in Norfolk, Virginia before he was apprehended. See Planned Parenthood, 41 F. Supp. 2d at 1135-36. Salvi is not a defendant in this case and, as far as the record reveals, was not engaged in the preparation of any posters.

Warren Martin Hern, another plaintiff, testified that when he heard he was on the list, "I was terrified. It's hard to describe the feeling that – that you are on a list of people to – who have been [1092] brought to public attention in this way. I felt that this was a – a list of doctors to be killed." Planned Parenthood, No. CV-95-01671-JO, at 625 (Jan. 11, 1999).

From the point of view of the victims, it makes little difference whether the violence against them will come from the makers of the posters or from unrelated third parties; bullets kill their victims regardless of who pulls the trigger. But it makes a difference for the purpose of the First Amendment. Speech – especially political speech, as this clearly was–may not be punished or enjoined unless it falls into one of the narrow categories of unprotected speech recognized by the Supreme Court: true threat, Watts v. United States, 394 U.S. 705, 707 (1969), incitement, Brandenburg v. Ohio, 395 U.S. 444, 447 (1969), conspiracy to commit criminal acts, Scales v. United States, 367 U.S. 203, 229, 6 L. Ed. 2d 782, 81 S. Ct. 1469 (1961), fighting words, Chaplinsky v. New Hampshire, 315 U.S. 568, 572, 86 L. Ed. 1031, 62 S. Ct. 766-73 (1942), etc.

Even assuming that one could somehow distill a true threat from the posters themselves, the majority opinion is still fatally defective because it contradicts the central holding of Claiborne Hardware: Where the speaker is engaged in public political speech, the public statements themselves cannot be the sole proof that they were true threats, unless the speech directly threatens actual injury to identifiable individuals. Absent such an unmistakable, specific threat, there must be evidence aside from the political statements themselves showing that the public speaker would himself or in conspiracy with others inflict unlawful harm. 458 U.S. at 932-34. The majority cites not a scintilla of evidence – other than the posters themselves – that plaintiffs or someone associated with them would carry out the threatened harm.

Given this lack of evidence, the posters can be viewed, at most, as a call to arms for other abortion protesters to harm plaintiffs. However, the Supreme Court made it clear that under Brandenburg, encouragement or even advocacy of violence is protected by the First Amendment: "Mere advocacy of the use of force or violence does not remove speech from the protection of the First Amendment." Claiborne Hardware, 458 U.S. at 927 (citing Brandenburg, 395 U.S. at 447) (emphasis in the original).[5] Claiborne Hardware in fact goes much

farther; it cautions that where liability is premised on "politically motivated" activities, we must" examine critically the basis on which liability was imposed." 458 U.S. at 915. As the Court explained, "Since respondents would impose liability on the basis of a public address – which predominantly contained highly charged political rhetoric lying at the core of the First Amendment – we approach this suggested basis for liability with extreme care." 458 U.S. at 926-27. This is precisely what the majority does not do; were it to do so, it would have no choice but to reverse.

The activities for which the district court held defendants liable were unquestionably of a political nature. There is no allegation that any of the posters in this case disclosed private information improperly obtained. We must therefore assume that the information in the posters was obtained from public sources. All defendants did was reproduce this public information in a format designed to convey a political viewpoint and to achieve political goals. The "Deadly Dozen" posters and the "Nuremberg Files" dossiers were unveiled at political rallies staged for the purpose of protesting Roe v. Wade, 410 U.S. 113, 35 L. Ed. 2d 147, 93 S. Ct. 705 (1973). Similarly, defendants presented the poster of Dr. Crist at a rally held on the steps of the St. Louis federal court-house, [1093] where the Dred Scott decision was handed down, in order to draw a parallel between "blacks being declared property and unborn children being denied their right to live." Planned Parenthood, CV-95-01671-JO, at 2677 (Jan. 22, 1999). The Nuremberg Files website is clearly an expression of a political point of view. The posters and the website are designed both to rally political support for the views espoused by defendants, and to intimidate plaintiffs and others like them into desisting abortion-related activities. This political agenda may not be to the liking of many people – political dissidents are often unpopular – but the speech, including the intimidating message, does not constitute a direct threat because there is no evidence other than the speech itself that the speakers intend to resort to physical violence if their threat is not heeded.

In determining whether the record here supports a finding of true threats, not only the reasoning but also the facts of Claiborne Hardware are highly relevant. Claiborne Hardware arose out of a seven-year effort (1966 to 1972) to obtain racial justice in Claiborne County, Mississippi. Claiborne Hardware, 458 U.S. at 898. The campaign employed a variety of tactics, one among them being the boycotting of

---

[5] Under Brandenburg, advocacy can be made illegal if it amounts to incitement. But incitement requires an immediacy of action that simply does not exist here, which is doubtless why plaintiffs did not premise their claims on an incitement theory.

white merchants. Id. at 900. The boycott and other concerted activities were organ-ized by the NAACP, in the person of its Mississippi field secretary Charles Evers, as well as by other black organizations and leaders. Id. at 898-900.

In order to persuade or coerce recalcitrant blacks to join the boycott, the organizers resorted to a variety of enforcement mechanisms. These included the posting of store watchers outside the boycotted stores. These watchers, also known as "Black Hats" or "Deacons," would "identify those who traded with the merchants." Id. at 903.[6] The names were collected and "read aloud at meetings at the First Baptist Church and published in a local black newspaper." Id. at 909. Evers made several speeches containing threats – including those of physical violence – against the boycott violators. Id. at 900 n.28, 902, 926-27. In addition, a number of violent acts–including shots fired at individuals' homes–were committed against the boycott breakers. Id. at 904-06.

The lawsuit that culminated in the Claiborne Hardware opinion was brought against scores of individuals and several organizations, including the NAACP. The state trial court found defendants liable in damages and entered "a broad permanent injunction," which prohibited the defen-dants from engaging in virtually all activities associated with the boycott, including picketing and using store watchers. Id. at 893. The Mississippi Supreme Court affirmed, finding liability based on a variety of state law theories, some of which had as their gravamen the use of force or threat of force by those engaged in the boycott. Id. at 894-95.

The United States Supreme Court began its opinion in Claiborne Hardware by noting that "the term 'concerted action' encompasses unlawful conspiracies and constitutionally protected assemblies" and that "certain joint activities have a 'chameleon-like' character." Id. at 888. The Claiborne County boycott, the Court noted, "had such a character; it included elements of criminality and elements of majesty." Id. The Court concluded [1094] that the state courts had erred in ascribing to all boycott organizers illegal acts – including violence and threats of violence – of some of the activists. The fact that certain activists engaged in such unlawful conduct, the Court held, could not be attributed to the other boycott organizers, unless it could be shown that the latter had personally committed or authorized the unlawful acts. Id. at 932-34.

---

[6] It would appear that in the small Mississippi community in Claiborne County, black residents knew each other on sight.

In the portion of Claiborne Hardware that is most relevant to our case, id. at 927-32, the Court dealt with the liability of the NAACP as a result of certain speeches made by Charles Evers. In these speeches, Evers seemed to threaten physical violence against blacks who refused to abide by the boycott, saying that: the boycott organizers knew the identity of those members of the black community who violated the boycott, id. at 900 n.28; discipline would be taken against the violators, id. at 902, 927; "if we catch any of you going in any of them racist stores, we're gonna break your damn neck," id. at 902; "the Sheriff could not sleep with boycott violators at night" in order to protect them, id.; "blacks who traded with white merchants would be answerable to him," id. at 900 n.28 (emphasis in the original).

These statements, the Supreme Court recognized, "might have been understood as inviting an unlawful form of discipline or, at least, as intending to create a fear of violence whether or not improper discipline was specifically intended." Id. at 927 (emphasis added). Noting that such statements might not be constitutionally protected, the Court proceeded to consider various exceptions to the rule that speech may not be prohibited or punished.

The Court concluded that the statements in question were not "fighting words" under the rule of Chaplinsky v. New Hampshire, 315 U.S. 568, 572-73 (1942); nor were they likely to cause an immediate panic, under the rule of Schenck v. United States, 249 U.S. 47, 52, 63 L. Ed. 470, 39 S. Ct. 247, 17 Ohio L. Rep. 149 (1919) ("The most stringent protection of free speech would not protect a man in falsely shouting fire in a theater and causing a panic."). 458 U.S. at 927. Nor was the speech in question an incitement under Brandenburg v. Ohio, 395 U.S. 444 (1969), because it resulted in no immediate harm to anyone. 458 U.S. at 927-28. The Court also cited, and found inapplicable, its one case that had held "true threats" were not constitutionally protected, Watts v. United States, 394 U.S. 705, 705 (1969). 458 U.S. at 928 n.71. The mere fact that the statements could be understood "as intending to create a fear of violence," 458 U.S. at 927, was insufficient to make them "true threats" under Watts.

The Court then considered the theory that the speeches themselves – which suggested violence against boycott violators – might constitute authorization or encouragement of unlawful activity, but flatly rejected it. 458 U.S. at 929. The Court noted that the statements were part of the" emotionally charged rhetoric of Charles Evers' speeches," and therefore could not be viewed as authorizing lawless action, even if they literally did so: "Strong and effective extemporaneous rhetoric cannot be nicely channeled in purely dulcet phrases. An advocate must [1095] be free to stimulate his audience with spontaneous and emotional appeals for unity and action in a common cause. When such appeals do not incite lawless action, they must be regarded as protected speech." 458 U.S. at 928. Absent "evidence – apart from the speeches themselves – that Evers authorized . . . violence" against the boycott breakers, neither he nor the NAACP could be held liable for, or enjoined from, speaking. 458 U.S. at 929. In other words, even when public speech sounds menacing, even when it expressly calls for violence, it cannot form the basis of liability unless it amounts to incitement or directly threatens actual injury to particular individuals.

While set in a different time and place, and involving a very different political cause, Claiborne Hardware bears remarkable similarities to our case:

Like Claiborne Hardware, this case involves a concerted effort by a variety of groups and individuals in pursuit of a common political cause. Some of the activities were lawful, others were not. In both cases, there was evidence that the various players communicated with each other and, at times, engaged in concerted action. The Supreme Court, however, held that mere association with groups or individuals who pursue unlawful conduct is an insufficient basis for the imposition of liability, unless it is shown that the defendants actually participated in or authorized the illegal conduct.

Both here and in Claiborne Hardware, there were instances of actual violence that followed heated rhetoric. The Court made clear, however, that unless the violence follows promptly after the speeches, thus meeting the stringent Brandenburg standard for incitement, no liability could be imposed on account of the speech.

The statements on which liability was premised in both cases were made during the course of political rallies and had a coercive effect on the intended targets. Yet the Supreme Court held in Claiborne Hardware that coercion alone could not serve as the basis for liability, because it had not been shown – by evidence aside from the political speeches themselves – that defendants or their agents were involved in or authorized actual violence.

In Claiborne Hardware, the boycott organizers gathered facts – the identity of those who violated the boycott – and publicized them to the community by way of speeches and a newspaper. As in our case, this ostentatious gathering of information, and publication thereof, were intended to put pressure on those whose names were publicized, and perhaps put them in fear that they will become objects of violence by members of the community. Yet the

Supreme Court held that this could not form the basis for liability.

To the extent Claiborne Hardware differs from our case, the difference makes ours a far weaker case for the imposition of liability. To begin with, Charles Evers's speeches in Claiborne Hardware explicitly threatened physical violence. Referring to the boycott violators, Evers repeatedly went so far as to say that [1096] "we," presumably including himself, would "break your damn neck." 458 U.S. at 902. In our case, the defendants never called for violence at all, and certainly said nothing suggesting that they personally would be involved in any violence against the plaintiffs.

Another difference between the two cases is that the record in Claiborne Hardware showed a concerted action between the boycott organizers, all of whom operated within close physical proximity in a small Mississippi county. By contrast, there is virtually no evidence that defendants had engaged in any concerted action with any of the other individuals who prepared "wanted" posters in the past.[7]

The most striking difference between the two cases is that one of Evers's speeches in Claiborne Hardware, which expressly threatened violence against the boycott violators, was in fact followed by violence; he then made additional speeches, again referring to violence against boycott breakers. 458 U.S. at 900 (April 1966 speech), 902 (April 1969 speeches).[8] By contrast, the record here contains no evidence that violence was committed against any

---

[7] The closest connection the district court could find between defendants and any of these individuals was a visit paid by two defendants, Andrew Burnett and Catherine Ramey, to John Burt, a maker of such posters. At that meeting, they "discussed 'wanted' posters." Planned Parenthood, 41 F. Supp. 2d at 1135. The district court did not find that defendants participated in the preparation of Burt's posters, nor that they otherwise engaged in concerted activities with other abortion protesters.

[8] On April 1, 1966, Evers made a speech "directed to all 8,000-plus black residents of Claiborne County," where he said that "blacks who traded with white merchants would be answerable to him" and that "any 'uncle toms' who broke the boycott would 'have their necks broken' by their own people." Claiborne Hardware, 458 U.S. at 900 n.28 (emphasis in the original). Later that year, violence was, indeed, committed against blacks who refused to join the boycott. Id. at 928. In April 1969, Evers reiterated his message in two other speeches, saying that "boycott violators would be 'disciplined' by their own people "and that "'If we catch any of you going in any of them racist stores, we're gonna break your damn neck.'" Id. at 902.

doctor after his name appeared on defendants' posters or web page.[9]

The opinion's effort to distinguish Claiborne Hardware does not bear scrutiny. The majority claims that in Claiborne Hardware, "there was no context to give the speeches (including the expression 'break your neck') the implication of . . . directly threatening unlawful conduct. " Maj. op. at 7111. As explained above, the majority is quite wrong on this point, see pp. 7093 supra, but it doesn't matter anyway: Evers's statements were threatening on their face. Not only did he speak of breaking necks and inflicting "discipline, "he used the first person plural "we" to indicate that he himself and those associated with him would be doing the neck-breaking, 458 U.S. at 902, and he said that "blacks who traded with [1097] white merchants would be answerable to him," id. at 900 n.28 (emphasis in the original).

It is possible – as the majority suggests – that Evers's statements were "hyperbolic vernacular," Maj. op. at 7111,[10] but the trier of fact in that case found otherwise. The Supreme Court nevertheless held that the statements ought to be treated as hyperbole because of their political content. By any measure, the statements in our case are far less threatening on their face, yet the majority chooses to defer to the jury's determination that they were true threats.

---

[9] The majority mentions that "one of the . . . doctors on the Deadly Dozen poster had in fact been shot before the poster was published." Maj. op. at 7138. The physician in question, Dr. Tiller, was shot and wounded in August 1993, a year and a half before the Deadly Dozen poster was unveiled. Planned Parenthood, 41 F. Supp. 2d at 1131-32, 1135. The majority does not explain how including Dr. Tiller's name on the Deadly Dozen poster contributed to the poster's threatening message. To the extent it is relevant at all, inclusion of Dr. Tiller's name cuts the other way because it goes counter to the supposed pattern that the majority is at such pains to establish, namely that listing of a name on a poster was followed by violence against that person. As to Dr. Tiller, that order is obviously reversed.

[10] In support of this claim, the majority states that there was no "indication that Evers's listeners took his statement that boycott breakers' 'necks would be broken' as a serious threat that their necks would be broken; they kept on shopping at boycotted stores." Maj. op. at 7111. The majority extrapolates this conclusion from only four out of ten incidents of boycott-related violence cited in Claiborne Hardware. See 458 U.S. at 904-06. Although these were the four incidents about which the most information was available–perhaps because these four particular victims were not afraid to lodge a complaint or to come forward and testify–they alone are hardly sufficient to support a conclusion that Evers's audience largely ignored his warnings.

The majority also relies on the fact that the posters here "were publicly distributed, but personally targeted." Maj. op. at 7138. But the threats in Claiborne Hardware were also individually targeted. Store watchers carefully noted the names of blacks who entered the boycotted stores, and those names were published in a newspaper and read out loud at the First Baptist Church, where Evers delivered his speeches. 458 U.S. at 903-04. When speaking of broken necks and other discipline, Evers was quite obviously referring to those individuals who had been identified as defying the boycott; in fact, he stated explicitly that he knew their identity and that they would be answerable to him. Id. at 900 n.28. The majority's opinion simply cannot be squared with Claiborne Hardware.

Claiborne Hardware ultimately stands for the proposition that those who would punish or deter protected speech must make a very substantial showing that the speech stands outside the umbrella of the First Amendment. This message was reinforced recently by the Supreme Court in Ashcroft v. Free Speech Coalition, 152 L. Ed. 2d 403, 122 S. Ct. 1389, 2002 WL 552476 (U.S. Apr. 16, 2002), where the government sought to prohibit simulated child pornography without satisfying the stringent requirements of Miller v. California, 413 U.S. 15, 37 L. Ed. 2d 419, 93 S. Ct. 2607 (1973). The Court rejected this effort, even though the government had earnestly argued that suppression of the speech would advance vital legitimate governmental interests, such as avoiding the exploitation of real children and punishing producers of real child pornography. See 152 L. Ed. 2d 403, id. at *11-*13; see also 152 L. Ed. 2d 403, id. at *16 (Thomas, J., concurring in the judgment); 152 L. Ed. 2d 403, id. at *17-*18 (O'Connor, J., concurring in the judgment in part and dissenting in part); 152 L. Ed. 2d 403, id. at *21 (Rehnquist, C. J., dissenting). The Court held that the connection between the protected speech and the harms in question is simply too "contingent and indirect" to warrant suppression. 152 L. Ed. 2d 403, Id. at *10; see also 152 L. Ed. 2d 403, id. at *12 ("The Government has shown no more than a remote connection between speech that might encourage thoughts or impulses and any resulting child abuse."). As Judge Berzon notes in her inspired dissent, defendants' speech, on its face, is political speech on an issue that is at the cutting edge of moral and political debate in our society, see Berzon Dissent at 7167, and political speech lies far closer to the core of the First Amendment than does simulated child pornography." The right to [1098] think is the beginning of freedom, and speech must be protected from the government because speech is the beginning of thought." Free Speech Coalition, 152 L. Ed. 2d 403, 2002 WL 552476, at *12. If political speech is to be deterred or punished, the rationale of Free Speech Coalition requires a far more robust and direct connection to unlawful conduct than these plaintiffs have offered or the majority has managed to demonstrate. The evidence that, despite their explicitly non-threatening language, the Deadly Dozen poster and the Nuremberg Files website were true threats is too "contingent and indirect" to satisfy the standard of Free Speech Coalition.

The cases on which the majority relies do not support its conclusion. United States v. Hart, 212 F.3d 1067 (8th Cir. 2000), is a case where the communication did not merely threaten harm in the future, but was itself perceived as dangerous. The defendant there parked two Ryder trucks in the driveway of an abortion clinic, as close to the building as possible. Hart, 212 F.3d at 1069, 1072. Given the association of Ryder trucks with the Oklahoma City bombing, and the timing and location of the incident, the trucks could reasonably be suspected of containing explosives. They were much like mailing a parcel containing a ticking clock or an envelope leaking white powder. The threat in Hart came not from the message itself, but from the potentially dangerous medium used to deliver it.

To make Hart even remotely analogous to our case, the defendant there would have had to be picketing abortion clinics with a placard depicting a Ryder truck. We know that the Eighth Circuit would not have permitted the imposition of liability in that situation because of the careful manner in which it circumscribed its holding. The court noted that the trucks were parked in a driveway of the abortion clinic, near the entrance, rather than on the street, and that the incident was timed to coincide with a visit by the President to the area, which heightened security concerns. Id. at 1072. In light of these facts, a reasonable person could believe that the trucks might be filled with explosives, which would not have been the case, had defendant merely carried a placard with a picture of a Ryder truck. In our case, the defendants merely displayed posters at locations nowhere near the plaintiffs' homes or workplaces. The threat, if any there was, came not from the posters themselves, but from the effect they would have in rousing others to take up arms against the plaintiffs. Hart has no relevance whatsoever to our case.

Nor does United States v. Dinwiddie, 76 F.3d 913 (8th Cir. 1996), a case involving repeated face-to-face confrontations between the defendant and the targets of her harangues, help the majority. Dinwiddie, a pro-life activist, stood outside Dr. Crist's abortion clinic and shouted various threats through a bullhorn, making it clear that she herself intended to carry them out. As Dinwiddie told one of Dr. Crist's co-workers: "You have not seen violence yet until you see what we do to you." Id. at 925 (emphasis added). Where the speaker directly confronts her target and expressly states that she is among those who will carry out the violence, it is hardly surprising when the court finds that there has been a true threat.[11] [1099] We have recognized that statements communicated directly to the target are much more likely to be true threats than those, as here, communicated as part of a public protest. Our caselaw also instructs that, in deciding whether the coercive speech is protected, it makes a big difference whether it is contained in a private communication – a face-to-face confrontation, a telephone call, a dead fish wrapped in newspaper[12] – or is made during the course of public discourse. The reason for this distinction is obvious: Private speech is aimed only at its target. Public speech, by contrast, seeks to move public opinion and to encourage those of like mind. Coercive speech that is part of public discourse enjoys far greater protection than identical speech made in a purely private context. We stated this clearly in McCalden v. Cal. Library Ass'n, 955 F.2d 1214 (9th Cir. 1990), where, relying on Brandenburg, Claiborne Hardware and Wurtz, we allowed" public speeches advocating violence" substantially more leeway under the First Amendment than "privately communicated threats." McCalden, 955 F.2d at 1222.[13]

---

[11] Even then, Dinwiddie is instructive for the restraint it exercised in granting relief. Dinwiddie was not subjected to a crushing and punitive award of damages, and the injunction against her was narrowly drawn and carefully tailored to accommodate her legitimate interests, including her interest in free expression. She was not banned from all speech of a certain kind, but only from speech that expressly violates the Freedom of Access to Clinic Entrances Act or is delivered through a bullhorn within 500 feet of an abortion clinic. Dinwiddie, 76 F.3d at 928-29. The Eighth Circuit emphasized that "the types of activity that the injunction would proscribe are quite narrow," and that Dinwiddie would be free to "carry signs, distribute literature, and speak at a reasonable volume even when she is within 500 feet of an abortion clinic." Id. By contrast, the injunction in our case indefinitely bars defendants from publishing, reproducing, distributing (and even owning) the posters, the website or anything similar, anywhere in the United States. Planned Parenthood, 41 F. Supp. 2d at 1155-56.

[12] See The Godfather (Paramount Pictures 1972).

[13] In my dissent from the failure to take McCalden en banc, I argued that this distinction was inapposite in McCalden because the statement involved–a warning by Holocaust survivors that they will disrupt an exhibit by a Holocaust revisionist with a demonstration–could not be characterized as a threat, even if communicated in private. McCalden, 955 F.2d at 1229 (Kozinski, J., dissenting from denial of rehearing en banc). I did not, of course, disagree with McCalden's

We reaffirmed the importance of the public-private distinction in Melugin v. Hames, 38 F.3d 1478 (9th Cir. 1994). Finding a death threat communicated to a magistrate judge by mail to be a "true threat," we expressly distinguished between "the 'threat' in Watts against President Johnson [which] was made during a public political rally opposing the Vietnam War" and defendant's threats, which "were directed in a private communication to a state judicial officer with the intent to obtain an immediate jury trial." Id. at 1484 (footnote omitted) (emphasis added).

In Bauer v. Sampson, 261 F.3d 775 (9th Cir. 2001), two members of today's majority emphasized the importance of the public character of speech in deciding whether it constitutes a "true threat." Bauer involved a college professor who published an underground campus newsletter containing threatening criticism of the college's board of trustees.[14] Noting that "expression involving a matter of public concern enjoys robust First Amendment protection," the opinion states that "although [the] writings have some violent content," the fact that they were made "in an underground campus newspaper in the [1100] broader context of especially contentious campus politics" rendered them a "hyperbole" and not a "true threat." Id. at 783-84.[15] The majority seems perfectly willing to

---

holding that public statements are entitled to more protection than private ones.

[14] These writings included a reference to a "two-ton slate of polished granite" that defendant "hoped to drop "on the college president; a comment that "no decent person could resist the urge to go postal" at a meeting of the board; a fantasy description of a funeral for one of the trustees; and creating "a satisfying acronym: MAIM" from the college president's name. Bauer, 261 F.3d at 780.

[15] In fact, no prior case in our circuit has ever found statements charged with political content and delivered in a public arena to be true threats. See, in addition to the cases already cited, Lovell v. Poway Unified Sch. Dist., 90 F.3d 367 (9th Cir. 1996) (finding a" true threat" where a student directly threatened to kill the school counselor in her own office); United States v. Gordon, 974 F.2d 1110 (9th Cir. 1992) (imposing liability where defendant entered former President Reagan's house and, when apprehended, repeatedly asserted his wish to kill the President); United States v. Orozco-Santillan, 903 F.2d 1262 (9th Cir. 1990) (holding that defendant's statements to an INS agent, delivered face-to-face and by phone, that the agent "will pay" for defendant's arrest, were "true threats"); United States v. Gilbert, 884 F.2d 454 (9th Cir. 1989) (finding a true "threat" where a white supremacist mailed a threatening letter and several posters directly to the founder of an adoption agency that placed minority children with white families); United States v. Mitchell, 812 F.2d 1250 (9th Cir. 1987) (finding a "true threat" where defendant, when questioned by customs officials and

---

have this court treat expressly violent statements by Charles Evers and Roy Bauer as hyperbole, but to hold the entirely nonviolent statements by defendants to be true threats.

Finally, a word about the remedy. The majority affirms a crushing liability verdict, including the award of punitive damages, in addition to the injunction.[16] An injunction against political speech is bad enough, but the liability verdict will have a far more chilling effect. Defendants will be destroyed financially by a huge debt that is almost certainly not dischargeable in bankruptcy; it will haunt them for the rest of their lives and prevent them from ever again becoming financially self-sufficient. The Supreme Court long ago recognized that the fear of financial ruin can have a seriously chilling effect on all manner of speech, and will surely cause other speakers to hesitate, lest they find themselves at the mercy of a local jury. See N.Y. Times Co. v. Sullivan, 376 U.S. 254, 277-79, 11 L. Ed. 2d 686, 84 S. Ct. 710 (1964). The lesson of what a local jury has done to defendants here will not be lost on others who would engage in heated political rhetoric in a wide variety of causes.

In that regard, a retrospective liability verdict is far more damaging than an injunction; the latter at least gives notice of what is prohibited and what is not. The fear of liability for damages, and especially punitive damages, puts the speaker at risk as to what a jury might later decide is a true threat, and how vindictive it might feel towards the speaker and his cause. In this case, defendants said nothing remotely threatening, yet they find themselves crucified financially. Who knows what other neutral statements a jury might imbue with a menacing meaning based on the activities of unrelated parties. In such circumstances, it is especially important for an appellate court to perform its constitutional function of reviewing the record to ensure that the speech in question clearly falls into one of the narrow [1101] categories that is unprotected by the First Amendment. The majority fails to do this.

While today it is abortion protesters who are singled out for punitive treatment, the precedent set by this court—the broad and uncritical deference to the judgment of a jury—will haunt dissidents of all political stripes for many years to come. Because this is contrary to the principles of the First Amendment

---

Secret Service agents in isolation, repeatedly-threatened to kill President Reagan); United States v. Merrill, 746 F.2d 458, 460 (9th Cir. 1984) (finding a "true threat "where defendant mailed to several individuals "letters [with] macabre and bloody depictions of President Reagan along with the words 'Kill Reagan'"); Roy v. United States, 416 F.2d 874,

as explicated by the Supreme Court in Claiborne Hardware and its long-standing jurisprudence stemming from Brandenburg v. Ohio, I respectfully dissent.

---

876 & n.6 (9th Cir. 1969) (finding that a statement by a marine to the telephone operator that he is" going to get" arriving President Johnson constitutes a threat, but suggesting that its decision could have been different if the "words were stated in a political . . . context").

[16] Although the majority remands the award of punitive damages, such award is affirmed unless grossly disproportionate. See In re Exxon Valdez, 270 F.3d 1215, 1241 (9th Cir. 2001).

BERZON, Circuit Judge, with whom REINHARDT, KOZINSKI, and KLEINFELD, Circuit Judges, join, and O'SCANNLAIN, Circuit Judge, joins as to Part III only, dissenting:

This case is proof positive that hard cases make bad law, and that when the case is very hard – meaning that competing legal and moral imperatives pull with impressive strength in opposite directions – there is the distinct danger of making very bad law.

The majority opinion in this case suitably struggles with the difficult First Amendment issues before us concerning whether the posters and website at issue are or are not First Amendment protected speech. The legal standard the majority applies, however, is, in my view, insufficiently cognizant of underlying First Amendment values, for reasons that are largely explained in Judge Kozinski's dissent, and for additional reasons that I develop below.

Moreover, the majority, in an offhand way, also decides two evidentiary issues that, I can say with some confidence, would not be decided so summarily, and would probably not be decided in the same way, were this a less wrenching case on its facts. Keeping one's eyes on the broader picture is not always easy when people's lives – in this case the lives of medical professionals – are being severely disrupted because they are performing constitutionally protected activities in a perfectly lawful manner at the behest of people who want their services and are entitled to have them. As judges, though, we need to recognize that we are not writing for this day and place only, and that rulings that appear peripheral in the present context will take on great significance as applied in another.

I.   The First Amendment and True Threats

1.   Clarifying the issue: The reason this is a hard First Amendment case becomes somewhat obscured in all the factual detail and quotation of precedent that we as judges engage in. The essential problem – one that, as far as I am aware, is unique in the plethora of "threat" cases and perhaps more generally in First Amendment jurisprudence – is that the speech for which the defendants are being held liable in damages and are enjoined from reiterating in the future is, on its face, clearly, indubitably, and quintessentially the kind of communication that is fully protected by the First Amendment.

The point is not simply that the two posters and the Nuremberg files contain no explicit threats that take them outside the free speech umbrella. We are not talking simply about ambiguous or implicit threats that depend on context for their meaning, such as the Ryder trucks in United States v. Hart, 212 F.3d 1067 (8th Cir. 2000). Rather, the pivotal issue for me is that what the communications in this case do contain has all the attributes that numerous cases and commentators have identified as core factors underlying the special protection accorded communication under our Constitution.

[1102] The posters and website are all public presentations on a matter of current moral and political importance; they provide information to the public on that matter and propose a – peaceful, legal – course of action; and they were presented with explicit reference to great moral and political controversies of the past. Cases that are a virtual First Amendment "greatest hits" establish that these kinds of expressions – those that provide information to the public (particularly when directed at publicly-available media), publish opinions on matters of public controversy, and urge others to action – are the kinds of speech central to our speech-protective regime, and remain so even when the message conveyed is, in substance, form, or both, anathema to some or all of the intended audience. See, e.g., Garrison v. Louisiana, 379 U.S. 64, 74, 13 L. Ed. 2d 125, 85 S. Ct. 209-75 (1964) ("Speech concerning public affairs is more than self-expression; it is the essence of self-government."); Roth v. United States, 354 U.S. 476, 484, 1 L. Ed. 2d 1498, 77 S. Ct. 1304, 14 Ohio Op. 2d 331 (1957) (The First Amendment "was fashioned to assure unfettered interchange of ideas for the bringing about of political and social changes desired by the people."); New York Times Co. v. Sullivan, 376 U.S. 254, 266 (1964) (The First Amendment "attempts to secure the widest possible dissemination of information from diverse and antagonistic sources."); Id. at 271 ("The constitutional protection does not turn upon the truth, popularity, or social utility of the ideas and beliefs which are offered."); Thornhill v. Alabama, 310 U.S. 88, 102, 84 L. Ed. 1093, 60 S. Ct. 736 (1940) ("Freedom of discussion, if it would fulfill its historic function in this nation, must embrace all issues about which information is needed or appropriate to enable the members of society to cope with the exigencies of their period."); Thomas v. Collins, 323 U.S. 516,

537, 89 L. Ed. 430, 65 S. Ct. 315 (1945) ("'Free trade in ideas' means free trade in the opportunity to persuade to action, not merely to describe facts."); Terminiello v. City of Chicago, 337 U.S. 1, 4 (1949) (Speech "may indeed best serve its high purpose when it induces a condition of unrest, creates dissatisfaction with conditions as they are, or even stirs people to anger. Speech is often provocative and challenging. It may strike at prejudices and preconceptions and have profound unsettling effects as it presses for acceptance of an idea.").

Tested against these most basic premises, there can be no doubt that the documents upon which the damages judgment and injunction in this case were based were, on their face, "expressions of grievance and protest on one of the major public issues of our time," and, as such, documents that "would seem clearly to qualify for . . . constitutional protection." New York Times, 376 U.S. at 271. The posters and website could not and would not have been proscribed, as "true threats" or otherwise, had there been no (1) history of similar – although not at all identical – publications put out by other people that were followed by murders – by other people, not members of either of the two defendant organizations – of health professionals who performed abortions; and (2) repeated advocacy by these defendants of the proposition that violence against abortion providers can be morally justified, advocacy that all concede was, standing alone, itself protected by the First Amendment. See Brandenburg v. Ohio, 395 U.S. 444, 447-48 (1969) ("The mere abstract teaching . . . of the moral propriety or even moral necessity for a resort to force and violence, is not the same as preparing a group for violent action and steeling it to such action.") (quoting Noto v. United States, 367 U.S. 290, 297-98 [1103] (1961)).[1] The precise question before us is therefore whether that context is sufficient to turn a set of communications that contain speech at the core of the First Amendment's protections into speech that can be proscribed pursuant to an injunction and compensated for through damages.

2. An analogy: Stated in those terms, the issue bears a close resemblance to that faced by the courts with regard to First Amendment limitations on

defamation actions, beginning with New York Times Co. v. Sullivan. Like "true threats," false speech has long been understood as a category of communication that contains few of the attributes that trigger constitutional speech protection and so great a likelihood of harming others that we refer to the speech as being beyond the protection of the First Amendment. See R.A.V. v. City of St. Paul, 505 U.S. 377, 383 (1992). Like "true threats," false, defamatory speech can severely disrupt peoples' lives, both by affecting them emotionally (as does apprehension of danger) and by impairing their social ties, their professional activities, and their ability to earn a living (as does the perceived need to protect oneself from physical harm).

The Supreme Court since the 1960s has developed a set of discrete principles designed not to provide false speech with constitutional protection, but to erect, on an ascending scale depending upon the perceived value of the particular kind of speech to the common dialogue that the First Amendment is designed to foster, doctrinal protections within defamation law that minimize self-censorship of truthful speech. Those protections are based upon realistic assessment of the vagaries of litigation and the fear of crippling damages liability.[2]

For example, New York Times observed that "allowance of the defense of truth . . . does not mean that only false speech will be deterred," because "under such a rule, would-be critics of official conduct may be deterred from voicing their criticism, even though it is believed to be true and even though it is in fact true, because of doubt whether it can be proved in court or fear of the expense of having to do so." 376 U.S. at 279; see also Gertz v. Robert Welch, Inc., 418 U.S. 323, 342, 41 L. Ed. 2d 789, 94 S. Ct. 2997 (1974) ("To assure to the freedoms of speech and press that 'breathing space' essential to their fruitful exercise . . . this Court has extended a measure of strategic protection to defamatory falsehood.") (internal citation omitted). Without a federal constitutional requirement focusing on the speaker's state of mind with regard to the truth of what he was saying (as well as careful scrutiny by the courts of any jury verdict based purely upon speech), the Court concluded, there would be a distinct danger that fear of defamation liability would "dampen[]the vigor and limit[]the variety of public debate," to the detriment of First Amendment values.

---

[1] In so stating – and elsewhere in this opinion – I do not address the constitutional viability of a cause of action for putting another in harm's way by publicizing information that makes it easier for known or suspected potential assailants to find an intended victim. There was no such cause of action in this case, as Judge Kozinski observes, and I express no view upon whether or under what circumstances such a cause of action could be stated under the law, including under the First Amendment.

---

[2] Similarly, the First Amendment's overbreadth doctrine extends some protection to speech that is without First Amendment value in order to limit self-censorship of speech that does possess this value. See Massachusetts v. Oakes, 491 U.S. 576, 581, 105 L. Ed. 2d 493, 109 S. Ct. 2633 (1989).

Id. The problem has been treated as one of balancing the very real injury caused by unwarranted [1104] damage to reputation against the dangers to the system of free expression worked by rules of liability that are easy to misperceive or to misapply in particular instances. And the Court's answer to this problem has, as noted, been far from unitary. Instead, the balance has been struck with regard to subcategories of defamation cases, according to the nature of the communication, the nature of the parties and, to some degree, the purpose of the speech.[3] Our problem here is similar. Any "true threats "within the three communications at issue were encased in documents and public events that promoted – at least for those listeners not "in the know" – precisely the kind of "debate on public issues [that] should be uninhibited, robust, and wide-open, and that . . . may well include vehement, caustic, and sometimes unpleasantly sharp attacks . . ." New York Times, 376 U.S. at 270. True, the targeted medical professionals and clinics were not public officials, but they were engaged in activities that the defendants, rightly or wrongly, regarded as both morally reprehensible and a matter for eventual governmental proscription through the political process (presumably through a constitutional amendment). Moreover, as both the majority and Judge Kozinski recognize, the posters and website remained core First Amendment speech even though – quite aside from any coded threat of physical harm – they exposed the targeted plaintiffs to other, nonviolent but still extremely disturbing, interference with their daily lives (in the form of unwanted public exposure and inflammatory rhetoric directed at them, their families, and their customers, both at home and

at work) and even if they induced fear in the plaintiffs that people unconnected with the defendants might harm them.[4]

Under these circumstances, the question for me becomes devising standards that, like the constitutional defamation standards that vary with the strength of the protection of the communication, rely not on an unitary "true threats" standard, as does the majority, but on considerations that lessen the danger of mistaken court verdicts and resulting self-censorship to a greater or lesser degree depending upon the nature of the speech in question and the role of speech of that nature in the scheme of the First Amendment.[5] [1105]

3. Some constitutional parameters: Judge Kozinski, in his dissent, makes one important suggestion toward this end with which, for all the reasons already canvassed, I fully agree: He suggests that "statements communicated directly to the target are much more likely to be true threats than those, as here, communicated as part of a public protest." Kozinski dissent at 7162. As a first cut at separating out the kinds of allegedly threatening communications that are central to First Amendment values and therefore must be tested by particularly stringent criteria before they can be prohibited, these two criteria – the public nature of the presentation and content addressing a public issue (which can include matters of social or economic as well as political import for the individuals involved, see Bartnicki v. Vopper, 532 U.S. 514, 535, 149 L. Ed. 2d 787, 121 S. Ct. 1753 (2001); Thornhill, 310 U.S. at 102-03) – are critical.

In a rare instance, a threat uttered in the course of a public political protest might conceivably exceed the bounds of protected speech. United States v. Kelner, 534 F.2d 1020 (2d Cir. 1976), is illustrative. (I am not aware of any case in this circuit in which a defendant was, as in Kelner, punished or held liable for a threat uttered in the course of public protest activity – a gap in itself telling with regard to the

---

[3] See New York Times, 376 U.S. at 279-80 (a public official may not recover damages "for a defamatory falsehood relating to his official conduct unless he proves that the statement was made with 'actual malice' - that is, with knowledge that it was false or with reckless disregard of whether it was false or not"); Curtis Publ'g Co. v. Butts, 388 U.S. 130, 164, 18 L. Ed. 2d 1094, 87 S. Ct. 1975 (1967) (opinion of Warren, C. J., concurring in the result) (New York Times standard applies to defamation cases brought by public figures); Gertz, 418 U.S. at 347-49 (New York Times standard not required for cases brought by private figure plaintiffs; instead, the states may only not "impose liability without fault" for the defamation of a private figure plaintiff - although a different standard may apply if" the substance of the defamatory statement [does not] make[]substantial danger to reputation apparent" - but the states "may not permit recovery of presumed or punitive damages" without proof of actual malice); Dun & Bradstreet, Inc. v. Greenmoss Builders, Inc., 472 U.S. 749, 761, 86 L. Ed. 2d 593, 105 S. Ct. 2939 (1985) (opinion of Powell, J.) (states may allow private figure plaintiffs to recover, without proof of actual malice, presumed or punitive damages for defamatory speech "involving no matters of public concern.").

[4] I discuss below the constitutional importance of the latter requirement - that any proscribed threat communicate the intention of the speaker or his or her agents.

[5] I note that there is one way in which the speech here differs from defamation: False, defamatory speech, even on matters of public concern, does not have any significant First Amendment value. R.A.V., 505 U.S. at 383. Although "true threats" also lack such value as a general matter, a "true threat" that includes only facially-protected speech nonetheless does have First Amendment value, because it not only is threatening but also has another meaning – the literal, facially-protected meaning – which here falls within the heart of First Amendment speech. For this and other reasons, the categories of defamatory speech and the rules applicable to them cannot rigidly determine the analysis applicable in threats cases.

importance and novelty of this case.) In Kelner, a member of the Jewish Defense League stated at a press conference held in New York just before Yassir Arafat was scheduled to be in the city that "We have people who have been trained and who are out now and who intend to make sure that Arafat and his lieutenants do not leave this country alive . . . . We are planning to assassinate Mr. Arafat . . . . Everything is planned in detail . . . . It's going to come off." Id. at 1021. The press conference was broadcast on television that evening.[6] Id. The Second Circuit upheld the defendant's conviction for uttering the threat, over the objection that the speech was simply an extreme statement of opposition to Mr. Arafat, protected under the First Amendment as hyperbolic public discussion of a public issue. Id. at 1024-28.

In doing so, the Second Circuit recognized that where the asserted threat "is made in the midst of what may be other protected political expression," courts must be vigilant to permit liability or conviction only in circumstances in which the danger to free expression is minimal; where that is the case, "the threat itself may affront such important social interests that it is punishable." Id. at 1027. The criteria the Second Circuit suggested to police the dividing line were that" the threat on its face and in the circumstances in which it is made is so unequivocal, unconditional, immediate and specific as to the person threatened, as to convey a gravity of purpose and imminent prospect of execution." Id. Measured against these criteria, Kelner held that, although politically motivated and designed to convey a public position of protest to Mr. Arafat's [1106] policies, the speech in question was not protected speech. Id. at 1028.

Kelner's criteria for adjudging the protection accorded alleged threats uttered in the course of public communications on public issues seem appropriate to me – and, as I show below, consistent with NAACP v. Claiborne Hardware Co., 458 U.S. 886 (1982) – with one exception, an addition, and some explication:

First, the exception: I would not include the imminence or immediacy of the threatened action as a prerequisite to finding a true threat delivered as part of a public speech, if all of the other factors were

[6] During the press conference, Mr. Kelner, the defendant, "was seated in military fatigues behind a desk with a .38 caliber' police special' in front of him," next to "another man . . . dressed in military fatigues." Id. The gun and uniform seem to me simply a prop and costume designed to enhance the communication of seriousness of purpose, not proof that the defendant was involved contemporaneously in actual violence.

present. The immediacy requirement calls to mind the standard the Supreme Court erected for proscription of inciting speech in Brandenburg. But as the majority can be read to recognize and as Judge Kozinski well explains, the separate constitutional category of unprotected speech for threats does not include statements that induce fear of violence by third parties.

Where there is no threat, explicit or implicit, that the speaker or someone under his or her control intends to harm someone, a statement inducing fear of physical harm must be either (1) a prediction or warning of injury, or (2) an inducement or encouragement of someone else to cause the injury. The former is, as Judge Kozinski suggests, clearly entitled to protection under the First Amendment as either informative or persuasive speech. The latter kind of statement may or may not be protected. Whether it is or not must be governed by the strict inducement standard of Brandenburg if the more than fifty years of contentious development of the protection of advocacy of illegal action is not to be for naught. See Brandenburg, 395 U.S. at 447-48 (overruling Whitney v. California, 274 U.S. 357, 71 L. Ed. 1095, 47 S. Ct. 641 (1927), and holding that "the constitutional guarantees of free speech and free press do not permit a State to forbid or proscribe advocacy of the use of force or of law violation except where such advocacy is directed to inciting or producing imminent lawless action and is likely to incite or produce such action"); see also 395 U.S. at 450-454 (Douglas, J., concurring) (recounting the history of the "clear and present danger" doctrine for adjudging the constitutionality of restrictions upon advocacy of illegal action).

One can, however, justify a somewhat different standard for judging the constitutionality of a restriction upon threats than for a restriction upon inducement of violence or other illegal action. There is a difference for speech-protective purposes between a statement that one oneself intends to do something and a statement encouraging or advocating that someone else do it. The latter will result in harmful action only if someone else is persuaded by the advocacy. If there is adequate time for that person to reflect, any harm will be due to another's considered act. The speech itself, in that circumstance, does not create the injury, although it may make it more likely. The Supreme Court has essentially decided that free expression would be too greatly burdened by anticipatory squelching of advocacy which can work harm only indirectly if at all. See Kelner, 534 F.2d at 1027 n.9 ("Short of [advocacy that is close, direct, effective and instantaneous in its impact] the community must satisfy itself with punishment of the one who committed the violation of law or attempted to do so, not punishment of the person who communicated with him about it.") (quoting Thomas Emerson, The System of Freedom of Expression 404-05 (1970)); see also Ashcroft v. Free Speech Coalition, 152 L. Ed. 2d 403, 122 S. Ct. 1389, 1403 (2002) (because "the Court's First Amendment cases draw vital distinctions between words and [1107] deeds," the government may not punish speech because it increases the chance that someone other than the speaker will commit an unlawful act).

A true threat, in contrast, implies a firmness of purpose by the person speaking, not mediated through anyone else's rational or emotional reaction to the speech. Threatening speech thereby works directly the harms of apprehension and disruption, whether the apparent resolve proves bluster or not and whether the injury is threatened to be immediate or delayed. Further, the social costs of a threat can be heightened rather than dissipated if the threatened injury is promised for some fairly ascertainable time in the future – the "specific" prong – for then the apprehension and disruption directly caused by the threat will continue for a longer rather than a shorter period. So, while I would police vigorously the line between inducement and threats – as the jury instructions in this case did,[7] although the majority opinion is less clear on this point – I would, where true threats are alleged, not require a finding of immediacy of the threatened harm.

Second, the addition: Although this court's cases on threats have not generally set any state of mind requirements, I would add to the Kelner requirements for proscribable threats in the public protest context the additional consideration whether the defendant subjectively intended the specific victims to understand the communication as an unequivocal threat that the speaker or his agents or coconspirators would physically harm them.[8] Especially where the

plaintiffs in such circumstances are relying only on surrounding context and are doing so to overcome the literal import of the words spoken, impairment of free public debate on public issues through self-censorship is a distinct possibility unless there is convincing proof that the literal meaning of the words was not what the defendants intended to convey.

The subjective intent requirement for alleged threats delivered in the course of public protest comports with Supreme Court precedent, both directly and by analogy. Although the Supreme Court has yet to outline fully the constitutional limitations applicable to proscription of threats, in its most direct look at the subject the Court expressed "grave doubts" that a person could be liable for threatening expression solely on the basis of an objective standard. Watts v. United States, 394 U.S. 705, 707-08 (1969). A few months later, in Brandenburg, the Court held that in an incitement case, the plaintiff or the government must not only prove that a statement "is likely to incite or produce" [1108] imminent lawless action, but must also prove that the statement "is directed to inciting or producing" such action. 395 U.S. at 447. This latter requirement is a subjective intent prerequisite, as it turns the speaker's liability in an incitement case on how the speaker intends others to understands his words. See also Hess v. Indiana, 414 U.S. 105, 109 (1973) (speech cannot be punished when no evidence exists that "words were intended to produce" imminent disorder).

With regard to this subjective intent requirement, there is no meaningful distinction between incitement cases and threat cases such as this one – that is, cases involving public protest speech, especially where the alleged threat, on its face, consisted entirely of advocacy. The First Amendment protects advocacy statements that are likely to produce imminent violent action, so long as the statements are not directed at producing such action. To do otherwise would be to endanger the First Amendment protection accorded advocacy of political change by holding speakers responsible for an impact they did not intend.

Similarly, a purely objective standard for judging the protection accorded such speech would chill speakers from engaging in facially protected public protest speech that some might think, in context, will be understood as a true threat although not intended

---

[7] The jury in this case was instructed that "the mere abstract teaching of the moral propriety or even moral necessity for a resort to force and violence is protected speech under the First Amendment, "and that "you are not to consider any evidence that the three statements allegedly 'incite' violence against plaintiffs."

[8] In Kelner, the jury was instructed that it needed to find that "Kelner 'intended the words as a threat against Yassir Arafat and his lieutenants.'" 534 F.2d at 1025. The Kelner court rejected a different intent requirement, namely, an intent to carry out the threatened action. Id. at 1025-27. The majority erroneously concludes that the dissenters would require that to find a "true threat," the speaker must have had the latter sort of intent – that is, the speaker must "actually intend to carry out the threat." See Majority Op. at 7115. To the contrary, there has been no intimation in either dissent that the speaker need have the intention, or the ability, to do so.

Rather, I propose the inclusion of a "specific intent" requirement with regard to the speaker's intent to threaten – that is, a requirement that the judge or jury determine whether the speaker intended to place the listener in fear of danger from the speaker or his agents.

as such. Unsure of whether their rough and tumble protected speech would be interpreted by a reasonable person as a threat, speakers will silence themselves rather than risk liability. Even though the Supreme Court has stated that protected political speech "is often vituperative, abusive, and inexact," speakers wishing to take advantage of these protected rhetorical means may be fearful of doing so under the majority's purely objective approach. Watts, 394 U.S. at 708; see also Rogers v. United States, 422 U.S. 35, 47, 45 L. Ed. 2d 1, 95 S. Ct. 2091 (1975) (Marshall, J., concurring).[9]

[1109] When the district court issued the injunction against the defendants, the court, for reasons it does not explain, relied on a different definition of threat than the one it instructed the jury to use. In contrast to the definition relied upon by the jury, the definition used for purposes of the injunction correctly incorporated the subjective intent requirement mandated by the First Amendment. Planned Parenthood of the Columbia/Willamette, Inc. v. American Coalition of Life Advocates, 41 F. Supp. 2d 1130, 1155 n.1 (D. Or. 1999). In addition, the district court found that the defendants did intend to threaten. As a result, the injunction comes close to conforming on its face to the dictates of the First Amendment. The injunction still falls short, however, because the district court did not state that a threat must be unequivocal, nor did it find the posters to be unequivocal threats. As I explain below, any definition of threats that does not include the unequivocal requirement provides too little protection for public political speech.[10]

Third, the explication: "Unequivocal" cannot mean literal: Ryder trucks, in the United States in the 1990s, and burning crosses, in the United States in the twentieth and twenty-first centuries, have unambiguous meanings that the individuals targeted will be hurt (at least unless they do what the perpetrator of the threat wants them to do, whether it be stop performing abortions or move out of town).

---

[9] The majority opinion does not appear to embrace any such subjective intent standard as a constitutional requirement, but does suggest that any such requirement was met here through the instruction on FACE's statutory elements. The jury, however, was specifically instructed several times, quite emphatically, that there is no subjective intent requirement in adjudging whether or not a statement is a "true threat." In closing argument, counsel for plaintiffs also informed the jury that subjective intent was not relevant. Further, in a separate instruction devoted to the case's various intent issues, the trial judge reminded the jury that it did have to find some form of intent when it considered the RICO charges against the defendants and when it considered punitive damages, but did not state that the jury had to find intent when considering whether the defendants violated FACE.
The very next instruction concerned the FACE cause of action and stated, ungrammatically and nearly incoherently, that the plaintiffs must prove that the defendant "made the threat of force to intimidate ... the plaintiff's ... ability to ... provide reproductive health services." Although "intimidate" was defined, correctly, as "place a person in reasonable apprehension of bodily harm," the FACE instruction left out the statute's clear motive or purpose requirement – that to be liable the defendant must act "because that person is or has been, or in order to intimidate such person ... from ... providing reproductive health services," 18 U.S.C. § 248(a)(1), substituting a confused and confusing locution. A jury specifically and repeatedly admonished not to take into account the defendants' subjective intent would not likely understand the obscure FACE instruction as a requirement that it should do so. There was also a RICO cause of action with separate elements. While the RICO instruction required, in addition to a true threat, an "intent of depriving a plaintiff of his or her ... protected right to provide abortion services," that is not equivalent to requiring an intent to communicate that the speaker or his or her confederates would physically injure the plaintiff.

[10] Part of the injunction fails to comply with the First Amendment for an additional reason. The injunction not only prevents the defendants from further distributing the posters, it also prevents them from possessing the posters or their equivalents. In effect, this latter part of the injunction regulates the type of written materials that the defendants may possess in the privacy of their homes, directly contradicting the Supreme Court's holding in Stanley v. Georgia, 394 U.S. 557 (1969):
If the First Amendment means anything, it means that a State has no business telling a man, sitting alone in his own house, what books he may read or what films he may watch. Our whole constitutional heritage rebels at the thought of giving government the power to control men's minds. Id. at 565; see also Free Speech Coalition, 122 S. Ct. at 1403 ("First Amendment freedoms are most in danger when the government seeks to control thought ....").
The majority nonetheless upholds the injunction against possession of the posters, distinguishing Stanley on the basis that "the posters in this case are quite different from a book; the 'wanted'-type posters themselves – not their ideological content – are the tool for threatening physicians. In this sense, the posters' status is more like conduct than speech." Majority Op. at 7141. But, whatever else they may be, the posters are speech – they express ideas through the use of words and pictures.
The majority also asserts that the "First Amendment interest in retaining possession of the threatening posters is de minimis, while ACLA's continued possession of them constitutes part of the threat." Id. at 7141. This summation ignores the fact that the posters do have First Amendment value – they express ideas about one of the most contentious political and moral issues of our time. And confined to the defendants' homes, the posters do not place anyone in apprehension of danger or disrupt their lives; they only influence "the moral content of [the defendants'] thoughts." Stanley, 394 U.S. at 565. As such, the First Amendment value of the posters is not outweighed by any competing considerations.

Instead, "unequivocal" means to me unambiguous, given the context. As such, the requirement is essentially a heightened burden of proof, requiring that a threatening meaning be clearly and convincingly apparent. And in determining whether that proof standard has been met, I would continue to apply the objective standard the majority embraces, based on our cases, in determining whether the speech in fact communicates an intent to harm specific individuals.

[1110] This case, I repeat, is uniquely difficult because to perceive a threat, one must disregard the actual language used and rely on context to negate the ordinary meaning of the communication. Further, the actual language is, in its own right, core First Amendment speech, speech that to a naive reader communicates protected information and ideas. So the crux of the plaintiffs' cause of action (once one accepts that only statements that evince an intention by the speaker or his or her agents to carry out the threat can be actionable) is really an assertion that the defendants were using Aesopian language or could be understood as doing so, and that the context in which the speech must be viewed provides the necessary evidence of the defendants' true, albeit coded, meaning.[11]

The first set of contextual evidence involves the poster/murder/poster/murder pattern the majority principally relies upon. Had the murders – or any murders, or any serious violence – been committed by the defendants and had the plaintiffs known that, the inference from the poster/murder pattern that the publication by them of posters similar to those previously followed by a murder might be a strong one.[12] The inference would be stronger had the defendants also put out the earlier posters and had the plaintiffs known that. Neither is the case.

Plaintiffs' main submission to fill this gap was extensive evidence concerning the defendants' opinions condoning the use of violence against medical professionals who perform abortions, including general statements to that effect and particular statements concerning the people who murdered the doctors depicted on the previous posters, stating that their actions were justified and that they should be acquitted. Plaintiffs' closing argument, for example, went on for pages and pages

about defendants' meetings and writings concerning the "justifiability of the use of force."

This evidence is certainly of some pertinence as to what the defendants may have intended to do.[13] It is more likely that someone who believes in violence would intentionally threaten to commit it. It is also pertinent to what persons in the plaintiffs' position – that is, persons involved in the abortion controversy and alert to the division of opinion within it – would likely understand concerning defendants' communication. Individuals who believe in violence are not only more likely to threaten to commit it but also actually to commit it, and so defendants' views might well influence plaintiffs' perception of their speech. And since the defendants would know that, defendants' public statements approving the use of violence against doctors who perform abortion are relevant to whether reasonable speakers in defendants' position would expect their communications to be understood as threats.

[1111] At the same time, heavy reliance on evidence of this kind raises profound First Amendment issues of its own. One cannot read plaintiffs' closing argument in this case without fearing that the jury was being encouraged to hold the defendants liable for their abstract advocacy of violence rather than for the alleged coded threats in the posters and website, the instructions to the jury to the contrary notwithstanding. And while advocacy evidence may make both an intent to threaten and a perception that there was a threat more likely, that is not unequivocally so. People do not always practice what they preach, as the stringent incitement standard recognizes. If we are serious about protecting advocacy of positions such as defendants' sanctioning of violence, as we are constrained to be, then permitting that protected speech to be the determinative "context" for holding other facially protected, public protest speech – the posters and website in this case – to be a "true threat" seems to me simply unacceptable under the First Amendment.

Finally, I note that the approach I've outlined here fully comports with Claiborne Hardware. Claiborne Hardware applied an "extreme care" standard in determining "liability on the basis of a public address

---

[11] The term "Aesopian language" developed in Tsarist Russia to refer to language that, like Aesop's fables, disguises the true meaning of speech by the use of metaphors, symbols and analogies, in order to avoid censorship.

[12] One defendant had been convicted of serious violence some years before the posters and website were published, so I except him from this part of the discussion.

[13] I note that on the instructions actually given to the jury, it is not easy to perceive the pertinence of much of this evidence. In particular, apart from extensive evidence of defendants' public statements concerning violence against abortion providers, there was also a great deal of evidence concerning their statements in meetings among anti-abortion activists. The jury was instructed that although speech can be a "true threat" no matter what defendants' subjective intent, that intent is nonetheless pertinent context. I am not sure I see why, but since I would make subjective intent directly relevant, the point is not of great importance to this dissent.

– which predominantly contained highly charged political rhetoric." 458 U.S. at 926-927. It went on to note that "in the passionate atmosphere in which the speeches were delivered, they might have been understood as inviting an unlawful form of discipline or, at least, as intending to create a fear of violence whether or not improper discipline was specifically intended." Id. at 927 (emphasis added). After reviewing the actual words used in context, however, the Court concluded that "Evers' addresses did not exceed the bounds of protected speech." Id. at 929. As I read the opinion, it held, essentially, that the supposed threats were not on their face unequivocal and were not made unequivocal by any contextual factors. So here.

I would therefore hold that under the special rules I would apply to public protest speech such as that in this case, plaintiffs' judgment cannot stand because, after a proper review of the record, we would have to conclude that there was no unequivocal, unconditional[14] and specific threat.[15]

II. Federal Law Enforcement Officers' Testimony Regarding Threats

I also disagree with the majority's conclusion that permitting law enforce-ment officers to testify as to their opinions about the meaning and import of the posters at issue was within the district court's discretion. The government may not seek to persuade a jury that certain speech contains characteristics that place it outside the realm of constitutionally protected speech by providing in testimony, as opposed to in a criminal indictment, its "nonjudicial determination" on the ultimate legal [1112] issue to be decided. Hill v. Rolleri, 615 F.2d 886, 890 (9th Cir. 1980).

The district court permitted the officers to repeat in testimony the warnings that the officers gave the plaintiffs after the release of the posters, purportedly in order to show the plaintiffs' state-of-mind in response to the posters. Under this rationale, the testimony had very little, if any, relevance to the issues before the jury, and, especially in light of the

First Amendment concerns the testimony raises, the resulting prejudice greatly outweighed its minimal probative value. The district court, therefore, abused its discretion in failing to exclude this testimony under Fed. R. Evid. 403.[16]

1. The testimony: The district court permitted the plaintiffs to call to testify an FBI agent, with 25 years experience, and two United States Marshals, one with 26 years and the other with 14 years experience. The following testimony was given:

"I told her that I was in receipt of threat information in the form of a flyer."

"That I had received a copy of a list called the Deadly Dozen List, which listed 13 doctors, who perform abortions, and that it was threatening in nature . . . ."

"I told her that I thought that her teachers, the teachers of her children, should know about this threat, as well, in order to maintain the security of the children."

"I told her that the children should be aware of – of the threat."

"I told him that he was on a threat list..."

"I told her that if she received additional threats or wanted protection, these were the numbers to contact . . . ."

"And we discussed the reasons we believed that the threat was serious . . . . We discussed the escalation in the incidents over the prior couple of years. We talked about the murder of Dr. Gunn in Florida. We talked about shootings involving Dr. Tiller in Kansas. We talked about shootings involving Dr. Christ. We talked about Michael Bray and his affiliation with the American Coalition of Life Advocates."

"Well, because of the nature of the threats, and – I asked Dr. Hern to – he had a bulletproof vest. I thought it would be a good thing if he wore that."

(emphases added). The testimony not only revealed the individual law enforcement officers' opinions of the meaning of the posters, but also informed the jury about the opinion of "headquarters," as follows:

"I told him . . . that I had been given instructions to notify – to immediately notify him, so that he could take some personal precautions for his safety."

"I was contacted by my headquarters in Washington, D.C. . . . I advised her that the

---

[14] "Unconditional" refers to the degree of determination contained in the threat, not whether it is "conditioned" in the sense that the target could avoid the harm by bowing to the speaker's will.

[15] I note as well that the majority, while it articulated a de novo review standard with respect to the true threat standard it did apply, did not in fact review the record with an eye to First Amendment concerns such as those I have discussed, nor did it include the intent issue within its review. (Actual malice, a state of mind standard, is precisely the issue upon which the Supreme Court has closely scrutinized the record in defamation cases. See, e.g., Harte-Hanks Communications, Inc. v. Connaughton, 491 U.S. 657, 686 (1989)).

[16] Rule 403 provides:
Although relevant, evidence may be excluded if its probative value is substantially outweighed by the danger of unfair prejudice, confusion of the issues, or misleading the jury, or by considerations of undue delay, waste of time, or needless presentation of cumulative evidence.

Marshal's Service was offering her protection, because her name appeared on the list, and stated that if she wanted protection, I would forward the request to our headquarters, who would then forward it to the Department of Justice."

"I was directed by my headquarters to immediately contact Dr. Warren Hern, because he was listed on the – the document. But, additionally, I was directed to contact all of the clinics in the district of Colorado." The officer further testified that he did contact all of the clinics in Colorado.

[1113] "Headquarters was taking this threat very seriously."

"I explained to Dr. Hern that Michael Bray had been a conspirator in – or involved in a conspiracy to blow up several abortion clinics. And because of his affiliation, in addition to the other things we discussed, that my headquarters believed that this was [a] serious threat, and something that – that we had to act on immediately." (emphases added).

My major concern here involves the First Amendment repercussions of allowing testimony by government employees as to the government's opinion concerning whether speech is outside the First Amendment's protections. In keeping with traditional Rule 403 analysis, however, I first explain why the testimony did not serve to elucidate any of the issues properly before the jury and then turn to the prejudicial effect the testimony had on the defendants' First Amendment rights.

2. Basic Rule 403 analysis: The majority holds the law enforcement testimony probative because it has "some tendency to show the physicians' state of mind when they found out they were named on 'wanted'-type posters . . . ." Majority Op. at 7127. Under the definition of a true threat that the majority uses (and under the one I would adopt, see Part I, supra) the plaintiffs' state of mind is relevant only to the extent that it tends to show "whether a reasonable person would foresee" that the plaintiffs would interpret the posters as threats. Majority Op. at 7112. The officers' testimony concerning the warnings muddled rather than illuminated the inquiry into the question how a reasonable lay person would understand the posters, as that testimony revealed the officers' reaction to the posters, not the plaintiffs'. The true threat standard focuses on how "those to whom the maker communicates the statement" would "interpret" it, not on the government's determination of whether a threat was made. See id. So the officers' reaction to the posters is largely irrelevant. Further, to the extent the testimony did tend to show the plaintiffs' state of mind, it suggested what the plaintiffs' reaction may have been to the officers' warnings or to the combination of learning about the posters and

receiving the warnings, not simply to the posters themselves.

During the testimony of one of the officers, the district court instructed the jury to consider the testimony only for what it revealed about the state of mind of the recipient of the warnings and not to take the testimony as an "administrative decision" that the posters constituted true threats. To the extent that the officers' testimony did bear on any pertinent issue – which, as I indicated above, is little if at all – the court's limiting instruction did not do much to maintain the jury's focus on this issue, as the court did not repeat the instruction when each of the law enforcement officers testified, nor did the court instruct the jury on this issue before deliberations, despite the defendants' request that the court do so.

It is unlikely that a jury can put aside the opinions of an FBI agent and United States Marshals – and their headquarters – as to the nature of the speech and instead focus solely on how those opinions bore on the plaintiffs' state of mind. See United States v. Gutierrez, 995 F.2d 169, 172 (9th Cir. 1993) ("The expert testimony of a law enforcement officer . . . often carries an aura of special reliability and trustworthiness.") (quoting United States v. Espinosa, 827 F.2d 604, 613 (9th Cir. 1987)). On traditional evidentiary grounds alone, such testimony should not be admitted in threats cases.

3. First Amendment-related prejudice: Turning now to the issue I find most troubling, [1114] the First Amendment ramifications of the law enforcement officers' testimony:

Admitting testimony by law enforcement officers as to whether certain speech has the primary characteristic of an unprotected category (for instance, is a serious threat, or is obscene, or is false) allows the government not only to prohibit or burden that category of speech (true threats, obscenity, defamation), but also persuasively to shape the jury's determination of what speech falls into the unprotected category. The obvious risk is that the government will use its "aura of special reliability and trustworthiness," Gutierrez, 995 F.2d at 172, to describe as undeserving of constitutional protection speech that in fact is only unpopular with the government. In Watts, the Court looked to the reaction of those to whom the speech was directed to determine how the speech should be taken. 394 U.S. at 708. Had the Secret Service run to the President to inform him of Watts' speech and warn him of the "threat," the Secret Service's reaction, and the President's resulting fear, presumably would not have been allowed to override the reaction of the actual audience to the speech.

Furthermore, the officers' testimony here quite naturally tended to blur the lines between various categories of speech – true threats, incitement, and perhaps some form of "putting in harm's way" – and therefore risked a jury finding of liability for speech that may not fall within the "threat" category as narrowly defined for First Amendment purposes. The officers testified that they told the plaintiffs the speech was a threat and one that should be taken seriously, but there is no indication that the officers distinguished between a" true" threat – a threat of violence by the speaker – and speech warning that a third party would harm the plaintiffs or speech containing a threatening quality because of its tendency to incite others or to put the plaintiffs in harm's way. Nor did the district court instruct the jury that the officers might use the term "threat" in a way that differed from the type of "threat" that does not receive constitutional protection.

The majority also concludes that the district court properly admitted the officers' testimony "to show the knowledge and intent of ACLA in distributing the posters regardless of the reaction they precipitated." Majority Op. at 7127. Testimony as to the statements made by the officers to the plaintiffs has little relevance to the intent and knowledge of the defendants. And, more importantly, the same First Amendment concerns come into play here: Under this rationale, if federal law enforcement officials dislike certain speech, they can take a substantial step towards rendering it unprotected by expressing publicly the view that such speech is threatening, because if the speaker then repeats the speech he does so with knowledge of the reaction it precipitated.

To the extent that our law allows law enforcement officers otherwise to testify directly on ultimate factual and legal questions that the jury must decide, we should draw the line at permitting the use of this persuasive aura in testimony that certain speech is of such a nature that it is undeserving of constitutional protection. Permitting such testimony cannot be reconciled with the role of the First Amendment to protect freedom of speech from suppression by the government.

III. Deposition Summaries

The majority approves – quite in passing – the district court's insistence that the parties submit as evidence summaries of deposition testimony, not the testimony itself. Majority Op. at 7128. As I read [1115] Federal Rule of Civil Procedure 32, which governs the admission of deposition testimony, it does not permit the substitution of summaries for actual testimony. Nor is there anything in the Federal Rules of Evidence or this court's case law to the contrary. Rather, it is a fundamental precept of our system for ascertaining facts that a jury is entitled to

learn what a witness actually said, rather than an inexact rendition presented by counsel (and probably initially drafted by paralegals).

Language can be subtle, ambiguous and malleable. Paraphrases, as any judge reading lawyers' briefs knows, are no substitute for quotation of the actual words spoken by a witness. As often as not, a check of the transcript will reveal that the language the witness actually spoke, in context, may well mean something other than what counsel has represented.

That does not mean that counsel is lying, but that shades of meaning can be critical. "As the childhood game of 'telephone' well demonstrates, words change significantly in the course of their re-telling by third parties." United States v. Pena-Espinoza, 47 F.3d 356, 364 (9th Cir. 1995) (Reinhardt, J., dissenting). Indeed, the game of "telephone "requires only that a listener repeat the exact language that he or she heard; a summary, in contrast, necessarily requires the more subjective choice of different words to convey the general idea communicated by the original language. "There is simply no way to summarize the contents of a transcript without offering to some degree a subjective view of their meaning and import." Id. Because that is so, summaries of witnesses' testimony are likely to distort the import of the actual testimony given and so impede the jury's search for truth.

Our legal system recognizes, in various contexts, that the same set of words may frequently lend itself to more than one reasonable interpretation. See, e.g., Chevron U.S.A., Inc. v. Nat'l Res. Def. Council, Inc., 467 U.S. 837, 81 L. Ed. 2d 694, 104 S. Ct. 2778 (1984). There is no reason to believe that a lawyer will not adopt the interpretation most favorable to his or her client, so long as the interpretation is reasonable, even if not perhaps the most reasonable. See United States v. Leon-Reyes, 177 F.3d 816, 820 (9th Cir. 1999) ("Summaries are normally prepared by an interested party and therefore may not be completely accurate or may be tainted with the preparing party's bias."). In our adversary system, it is the role of the trier of fact – not the advocate – ultimately to determine the meaning of witness testimony.

Further, access to the actual language a witness used – even on a cold record – is often essential to determining the witness's credibility and hence the weight, if any, to be accorded the testimony. Equivocations, hesitations, and internal contradictions may all be smoothed over by summaries that purport to extract the content of a witness's testimony. Requiring counsel to summarize testimony without allowing the trier of fact to have access to the testimony itself necessarily precludes the trier of fact from properly exercising his or her truth-determining role.

The record here provides concrete examples of various ways in which summaries can distort the import of the actual testimony and thereby impair the truth-ascertaining process. For instance, the summary of Michael Dodds' deposition condensed inaccurately the testimony he gave. The summary stated:

The other physician, on the Deadly Dozen List, from Dodds' region, Dr. Douglas Karpen, is from the Houston, Texas, area. Dodds believes that defendant Donald Treshman provided that name.

What Dodds actually said in his deposition regarding the source of Karpen's name for [1116] the Deadly Dozen list was "I don't know."[17]

The deposition of Roy McMillan provides an example of testimony that could reasonably be interpreted in either of two ways, but the summary provided the jury with only one interpretation. The summary stated:

As for the additional murder of Mr. Barrett [Dr. Britton's escort], McMillan felt that if it was, quote, right for one person, it would be right for someone else, end quote.

A look at McMillan's deposition transcript (which the defendants introduced in rebuttal) sheds a somewhat different light on the quotation included in the summary. In his deposition, McMillan was first asked about a petition in support of Michael Griffin, who killed Dr. Gunn, and then asked about "the second petition which was for Mr. Hill," who killed Mr. Barrett and Dr. Britton. The testimony went as follows:

[Answer:] This is identical – pretty much identical to the one that was circulated about the first abortionist's termination. And this was – this, the second one was regarding Paul Hill.

Question, and this one was put out by Michael Bray, is that right?

Answer, I am not sure who put it out, but I concurred that if it was right for one person, it would be right for someone else.

Thus, it appears that McMillan likely meant that if a petition in support of Griffin was right, so too was a petition in support of Hill. Either way, the interpretation should have been left entirely to the jury. (It is quite unlikely that this difference in meaning could have substantively affected the verdict, but that conclusion would require a separate inquiry.)

Finally, the record here also contains summary language that although technically accurate may nonetheless have conveyed a subtly different, but potentially important, sense of the speaker or of the events described from the testimony itself. The summary of Dawn Stover's deposition began with the sentence:

Dawn Stover is the associate director of defendant Advocates for Life Ministries.

Here is the excerpt from Stover's deposition transcript:

Question, are you still the associate director of Advocates for Life Ministries? Answer, I would guess that, but I have been inactive for so long that – I am still affiliated. I still talk to a couple of people in Advocates, but I don't do any directing and haven't done any directing for years. So – and having a title has never been that big of an issue. Question, was that ever a paid position? Answer, no. Question, so you don't know whether or not your status is currently associate director in terms of the eyes of the organization? Answer, I honestly don't know how they would perceive me as.   I don't know, just because I have been inactive for so long, but they may still.

Certainly, the jury reasonably could have found from Stover's testimony that she "is the associate director "of Advocates for Life Ministries, as the summary stated. At the same time, however, the jury might have considered Stover's current role in the organization as quite different depending on which of the above versions of her testimony they heard. One set of words rarely conveys precisely the same meaning as a second, truncated version.

The majority today pays no heed to all these "dangers of witnesses summarizing [1117] oral testimony." United States v. Baker, 10 F.3d 1374, 1412 (9th Cir. 1993), overruled on other grounds by United States v. Nordby, 225 F.3d 1053, 1059 (9th Cir. 2000), and instead notes, without qualification, only that the presentation of deposition testimony "in the form of summaries was within the court's discretion under Rule 611(a)," Majority Op. at 7128. The very first mandate of Rule 611(a), however, requires the trial court to "make the interrogation and presentation [of evidence] effective for the ascertainment of truth." Fed. R. Evid. 611(a)(1).[18] For all the reasons just discussed, substituting

---

[17] The district court did not allow Treshman to respond in his closing argument to the plaintiffs' argument based on the summaries because the actual transcripts were not in evidence.

[18] Rule 611(a) provides in its entirety:
The court shall exercise reasonable control over the mode and order of interrogating witnesses and presenting evidence so as to (1) make the interrogation and presentation effective for the ascertainment of the truth, (2) avoid needless consumption of time, and (3) protect witnesses from harassment or undue embarrassment.

summaries of testimony for a word-for-word transcript itself can hardly serve as an" effective" mode "for the ascertainment of truth." See id.

Moreover, it is Fed. R. Civ. Proc. 32, not Rule 611(a) of the Rules of Evidence, that directly, and with particularity, governs the presentation of deposition testimony. As I read it, Rule 32 decidedly does not permit courts to authorize the use of summaries in place of actual testimony.

Rule 32 begins with this general provision:

At the trial . . . any part or all of a deposition, so far as admissible under the rules of evidence applied as though the witness were then present and testifying, may be used . . . .

Rule 32(a) (emphasis added); see also Rule 32(b) ("Objection may be made at the trial or hearing to receiving in evidence any deposition or part thereof for any reason which would require the exclusion of the evidence if the witness were then present and testifying."). A witness who is "present and testifying" is doing just that – "testifying," not providing capsule versions of his or her testimony. And using "any part or all of a deposition" does not equate to using a paraphrased, condensed version of a deposition, any more than a course syllabus directing students to read" Hamlet" intends to subsume within that directive the Classic Comics version of "Hamlet."

Rule 32 also specifically addresses the "Form of Presentation" of deposition testimony, giving no indication that a district court may admit a summary of deposition testimony in lieu of the testimony itself. The pertinent section states, in relevant part:

Except as otherwise directed by the court, a party offering deposition testimony pursuant to this rule may offer it in stenographic or nonstenographic form, but, if in nonstenographic form, the party shall also provide the court with a transcript of the portions so offered.

Rule 32(c) (emphasis added). The rule therefore clearly anticipates the admission of stenographic or nonstenographic forms of testimony, not summaries.[19] Although [1118] Rule 32(c) does apply

"except as otherwise directed by the court," this caveat is most sensibly read to give the court discretion to direct either stenographic or non-stenographic presentation of deposition testimony, not to permit the presentation as "evidence" of summaries that approximate but do not reproduce the language the witness used in any form.

Bolstering this conclusion regarding Rule 32(c), Rule 28 provides for the taking of depositions in foreign countries "pursuant to a letter of request," and expressly grants the district court the discretion to admit the response to such a letter even if it is not a "verbatim transcript" of the testimony or if it exhibits "any similar departure from the requirements for depositions taken within the United States under these rules." See Rule 28(b). The assumption quite obviously underlying Rule 28 is that any report of testimony other than a" verbatim transcript" is a "departure from the requirements for depositions taken within the United States under these rules."

More generally, Rule 32 demonstrates an overall preference for the presentation of testimony in the manner that, to the extent practical, best provides the jury with complete information concerning the witness's demeanor. Rule 32(a), for example, clearly favors live testimony over deposition evidence by limiting the use of depositions to three situations: when an adverse party is the deponent; for impeachment purposes; or when the deponent is not available to testify at trial. Rule 32(a)(1)-(3). By so doing, the rule reflects the historical belief that live testimony better enables the jury to adjudge the credibility of a witness and therefore to determine the weight and import ascribed to the witness's testimony. Deposition testimony is itself only second-best.

When the rules do allow the admission of deposition testimony in a jury trial, Rule 32(c) permits a party in some instances to insist upon the presentation of testimony in "nonstenographic form," allowing the jury to hear and/or see the testimony as it was given. Rule 32(c) ("On request of any party in a case tried before a jury, deposition testimony

---

[19] The rules make clear that "nonstenographic" refers to audio or visual recording. See, e.g., Rule 32 Advisory Comm. Note: ("This new subdivision [c] . . . is included in view of the increased opportunities for video-recording and audio-recording of depositions under revised Rule 30(b)."); Fed. R. Civ. Proc. 30(b)(2) ("Any party may arrange for a transcription to be made from the recording of a deposition taken by non-stenographic means."); Rule 30 Advisory Comm. Note ("The primary change in subdivision (b) is that parties will be authorized to record deposition testimony by nonstenographic means without first having to obtain permission of the court or agreement from other counsel.");

Rule 30 Advisory Comm. Note ("A party choosing to record a deposition only by videotape or audiotape should understand that a transcript will be required by Rule 26(a)(3)(B) and Rule 32(c) if the deposition is later to be offered as evidence at trial . . . ."); Rule 26(a)(3) ("[A] party must provide . . . the following information regarding the evidence that it may present at trial . . . : (B) the designation of those witnesses whose testimony is expected to be presented by means of a deposition and, if not taken stenographically, a transcript of the pertinent portions of the deposition testimony.").

offered other than for impeachment purposes shall be presented in nonstenographic form, if available, unless the court for good cause orders otherwise.") (emphasis added). Rule 32(c), by favoring audio and video recordings over the reading of a cold transcript, therefore establishes a preference for testimony that is the most like live testimony. Under this scheme, the presentation of deposition testimony in stenographic form is third-best.

Such presentation, however, at least allows the jury to hear or read the actual words used by the witness. Deposition summaries, unless accompanied by a transcript of the testimony, deprive the jury of even this opportunity. With Rule 32's clear preference for live testimony, or for testimony most resembling it, it makes little sense to think the rule tacitly allows for this new, fourth-best, form of evidence, so far removed from the in-person live testimony for which it is a substitute. I conclude that Fed. R. Civ. Proc. Rule 32 withholds from district courts the authority to require the substitution of summaries of deposition testimony for the testimony itself, where truth and falsity are at issue, and that the general language of Fed. R. Evid. Rule 611 [1119] cannot override that determination.

There is nothing in our case law to the contrary. We have, while expressing great caution, allowed summaries of evidence in narrow circumstances, but never as a complete substitute for actual transcripts on material matters of historical fact.

For instance, in Leon-Reyes, 177 F.3d at 820, a perjury case, we held that the district court did not abuse its discretion in allowing the use of summaries of testimony from a prior trial in which the defendant had allegedly committed perjury, emphasizing that the district court instructed the jury to consider the summaries only for determining the materiality of the false statements and not for the truth of the witnesses' underlying testimony. Pena-Espinoza, 47 F.3d at 360, permitted – although making clear that it did "not wish to condone such procedures" – admission of summaries prepared by the prosecution of telephone call transcripts. The court specifically noted that:

The transcripts themselves were in evidence and the jury had them to examine during deliberations; the ruling expressly permitted defense counsel to require a reading of the full transcript on cross-examination and to dispute the veracity of the readers' summaries.

Id. Similarly, Baker, 10 F.3d at 1411-12, found district court discretion pursuant to Fed. R. Evid. 611(a) to permit a government witness to present summary testimony and a chart estimating, on the basis of testimony at trial, the value of narcotics transactions. Critically, the district court made clear

to the jury that the testimony and chart did not constitute evidence:

The [district] court instructed the jury that the summary testimony and exhibits were not evidence, did not represent an opinion of the court or the prosecution on the credibility of witnesses, and were to be disregarded to the extent the jury found them conflicting with the testimony and evidence received at trial.

Id. at 1411. As in Pena-Espinoza, the Baker court emphasized that this court is "not blind to the dangers of witnesses summarizing oral testimony" and that "such summaries should be admitted under Rule 611(a) only in exceptional cases." Id. at 1412.

Thus, when this court has upheld the admission of summary evidence under the abuse of discretion standard, we have done so not as a substitute for transcript evidence on matters of historical fact, but either on issues other than the truth of the matter testified to or as an assistance to the jury, while also including the actual transcripts in the record for the use of the jury or reviewing courts. And none of our cases discuss the provisions of Fed. R. Civ. Proc. Rule 32, because none of them involved deposition summaries as opposed to summaries of other forms of evidence.[20]

This is not a case in which the parties reached any agreement as to the summaries presented, so I do not consider whether such an agreement would be permissible. Nor did the defendants agree to the use of summaries at all; instead, they maintained a continuing objection to this procedure. And the district court did not review or [1120] revise the summaries after receiving objections prepared by the defendants, as it had originally planned to do. Cf. Leon-Reyes, 177 F.3d at 820 ("Summaries . . . must be scrutinized by the trial court to ensure that they are accurate, complete, not unduly prejudicial, limited to the relevant issues, and confined by appropriate jury instructions.").

The district court did allow the defendants to present counter-summaries, colored with argument, and, in rebuttal, to introduce excerpts from the transcripts. Such an adversarial procedure, however, does not ensure that the jury will have before it the evidence necessary to informed decision-making.

---

[20] Although the Fourth, Fifth, and Seventh Circuits have generally approved the use of deposition summaries for the oral presentation of deposition evidence, I have found no case in which it is clear that the pertinent portions of the transcripts were not also admitted as evidence and available for jury review. See Oostendorp v. Khanna, 937 F.2d 1177, 1179-80 (7th Cir. 1991); Walker v. Action Indus., Inc., 802 F.2d 703, 712 (4th Cir. 1986); Kingsley v. Baker/Beech-Nut Corp., 546 F.2d 1136, 1141 (5th Cir. 1977) (deposition transcripts definitely admitted as evidence).

The party responsible for summarizing the testimony may have little reason to move for the admission of the underlying testimony, precisely because that party may prefer its summary to the testimony itself. Likewise, the adverse party will, hopefully, point out blatant inconsistencies between the summary and the testimony, but may choose otherwise to avoid providing the jury with testimony that largely supports a summary introduced by the other side.

Nevertheless, the fact remains that the jury must have the opportunity to review the actual evidence – the transcripts of the testimony – when deliberating as to the meaning of testimony. It is nonsensical to expect the jury to determine the credibility of witnesses and testimony, the special province of the jury, without providing the jury with access to that testimony. Just as we, as judges, do not read attorneys' paraphrases of statutes when we try to discover what the legislature meant, see Fed. R. App. Proc. Rule 28(f), jurors cannot sensibly evaluate the meaning and credibility of words without knowing what those words are.

One final note: The majority presumably finds that the district court has the discretion under Rule 611(a) to require deposition summaries in lieu of the testimony itself in order to "avoid needless consumption of time." Rule 611(a)(2). Because the presentation of deposition summaries, without the agreement of the parties and the admission of the corresponding excerpts, is not "effective for the ascertainment of truth," Rule 611(a)(1), the consumption of time caused by the presentation of actual testimony is not "needless." Moreover, by providing an additional issue for the parties to dispute, the use of summaries is just as likely to increase as to decrease the time spent by counsel and by the court.

I recognize that district courts can and should reasonably limit the amount of time expended on the presentation of deposition testimony. This authority does not, however, give trial courts the discretion to replace such testimony entirely with a Reader's Digest Condensed Books version.[21]

IV. Conclusion As waves of fervent protest movements have ebbed and flowed, the courts have been called upon to delineate and enforce the line between protected speech and communications that are both of little or no value as information, expression of opinion or persuasion of others, and are of considerable harm to others. This judicial task has never been an easy one, as it can require – as here – recognizing the right of [1121] protesting groups to question deeply held societal notions of what is morally, politically, economically, or socially correct and what is not. The defendants here pose a special challenge, as they vehemently condone the view that murdering abortion providers – individuals who are providing medical services protected by the Constitution – is morally justified.

But the defendants have not murdered anyone, and for all the reasons I have discussed, neither their advocacy of doing so nor the posters and website they published crossed the line into unprotected speech. If we are not willing to provide stringent First Amendment protection and a fair trial to those with whom we as a society disagree as well as those with whom we agree – as the Supreme Court did when it struck down the conviction of members of the Ku Klux Klan for their racist, violence-condoning speech in Brandenburg – the First Amendment will become a dead letter. Moreover, the next protest group – which may be a new civil rights movement or another group eventually vindicated by acceptance of their goals by society at large – will (unless we cease fulfilling our obligation as judges to be evenhanded) be censored according to the rules applied to the last. I do not believe that the defendants' speech here, on this record and given two major erroneous evidentiary rulings, crossed the line into unprotected speech. I therefore dissent. [21]

---

[21] I do not address whether the use of deposition summaries in this case was harmless error, see Cerrato v. San Francisco Cmty. Coll. Dist., 26 F.3d 968, 974 (9th Cir. 1994) ("The harmless error standard in civil cases is whether the jury's verdict is more probably than not untainted by the error."), because the majority does not so hold.

Chapter

7

Hate Speech

Protected speech that demeans and excludes

Focal case:
R.A.V. v. City of St. Paul, 505 U.S. 377 (1992)

As mentioned in the previous chapter, the U.S. Supreme Court recognizes hate speech as a category of low value speech that does not warrant full First Amendment protection. The Court has not explicitly defined hate speech, but the category appears to encompass speech that demeans or discriminates against individuals based on race, color, gender, national origin, age, sexual orientation or other inherent characteristics or deeply held convictions, such as religious belief. Laws targeting hate speech have been criticized as unconstitutional attempts to legislate civility and enforce political correctness.

Several scholars have argued to the contrary that biased speech does more than offend; like threats or fighting words, hate speech is inherently harmful to those targeted and to social cohesion generally.[1] According to these scholars, name-calling, epithets and hate-filled diatribes not only fail to contribute to enlightened discourse and to the enhancement of social well-being, they silence their targets and harm the marketplace of ideas the First Amendment is designed to protect. Hate speech does not convey abstract principles; it acts to debase, threaten and intimidate. From this perspective, hate speech abuses the powerless and embodies systemic discrimination that violates the constitutional principle of equal protection under the law.

Despite some expressions of sympathy for these views, the Supreme Court has suggested that biased speech falls outside constitutional protection only when it is directed at and intended to immediately threaten or harm a specific individual or individuals. Thus, to be constitutional, laws targeting hate speech essentially must pass the *Brandenburg* test. Courts consistently have overturned statutes that sanction racist, sexist, anti-Semitic or otherwise deeply offensive speech

---

[1] *See, e.g.,* Richard Delgado, *Words that Wound: A Tort Action for Racial Insults, Epithets, and Name-Calling,* 17 HARV. CIV. RTS. -CIV. LIB. L. REV. 133 (1982); Mari Matsuda, *Public Response to Racist Speech: Considering the Victim's Story,* 87 MICH. L. REV. 2320 (1989); Charles Lawrence III, *If He Hollers Let Him Go: Regulating Racist Speech on Campus,* 1990 DUKE L. J. 431 (1990); Kenneth Karst, *Boundaries and Reasons: Freedom of Expression and the Subordination of Groups,* 1990 U. ILL. L. REV. 95 (1990); Nadine Strossen, *Regulating Racist Speech on Campus,* 1990 DUKE L. J. 484 (1990); Kent Greenawalt, *Insults and Epithets: Are They Protected Speech,* 42 RUTGERS L. REV. 287 (1990).

7.1

that does not threaten imminent violence. [2] Moreover, in its 1992 ruling in *RAV v. St. Paul*, the U.S. Supreme Court struck down a city anti-bias law as unconstitutionally content-based because it discriminatorily punished only certain types of hate speech. [3]

The year after *RAV v. St. Paul*, however, the Supreme Court upheld a state hate-crime statute that increased the punishment for crimes when the victim was targeted because of race, religion, color, disability, sexual orientation, national origin or ancestry. [4] Under the statute, a Wisconsin jury had doubled, to four years, the jail term of a black male convicted of aggravated battery in the racially motivated beating of a white boy. The attacker said the law violated the First Amendment because it punished him for offensive speech and ideas. The Wisconsin Supreme Court agreed. A unanimous U.S. Supreme Court reversed. In *Wisconsin v. Mitchell*, the Court dismissed claims that the law unconstitutionally chilled protected speech and ruled that the law constitutionally punished illegal conduct and appropriately reflected the increased harm inflicted on society by bias-motivated crimes. [5]

Then, in 2003, a deeply divided Supreme Court ruled that a state may ban cross burning that constitutes a true threat but may not define all cross burning as illegal intimidation. [6] A majority of the Court agreed that the state of Virginia could constitutionally prohibit cross burning that is intended to intimidate, but only four justices said the state could define *all* cross burning as an act of intimidation. In fact, three justices voted to strike down the law in its entirety. They said a law that targeted only the intimidation caused by cross burning and not other forms of symbolic threats was an unconstitutional form of viewpoint discrimination. In contrast, Justice Thomas said the First Amendment had no bearing on the statute because the law targeted acts of intimidation and violence, not speech. The ruling blurred the already fuzzy distinction between illegal conduct and threats, on one hand, and protected expression, on the other.

Most of the cases in this area of the law have not reached the U.S. Supreme Court. However, the following court rulings will enhance your understanding of the status of anti-hate speech laws.

- *Virginia v. Black*, 2003 U.S. LEXIS 2715 (April 7, 2003) (upholding state ban on cross burning that intimidates and rejecting statutory assumption that all cross burning intends to intimidate).
- *Dambrot v. Central Michigan University*, 55 F.3d 1177 (6th Cir. 1995) (striking university speech code).
- *Iota XI Chapter of Sigma Chi Fraternity v. George Mason University*, 993 F.2d 386 (4th Cir. 1993) (reversing sanctions for fraternity "ugly woman" contest).
- *UWM Post v. Board of Regents of the University of Wisconsin*, 774 F. Supp. 1163 (E.D. Wis. 1991) (striking university speech code).
- *Doe v. University of Michigan*, 721 F. Supp. 853 (E.D. Mich. 1989) (striking university speech code).
- *Collin v. Smith*, 578 F.2d 1197 (7th Cir. 1978) (striking city racial slur ordinance).
- *Skokie v. National Socialist Party*, 373 N.E. 2d 21 (1978) (striking city racial slur ordinance).

---

[2] *See, e.g.,* R.A.V. v. City of St. Paul, 505 U.S. 377 (1992); Collin v. Smith, 578 F.2d 1197 (7th Cir. 1978); Skokie v. National Socialist Party, 373 N.E. 2d 21 (1978); Doe v. University of Michigan, 721 F. Supp. 853 (E.D. Mich. 1989); UWM Post v. Board of Regents of the University of Wisconsin, 774 F. Supp. 1163 (E.D. Wis. 1991); Iota XI Chapter of Sigma Chi Fraternity v. George Mason University, 993 F.2d 386 (4th Cir. 1993); Dambrot v. Central Michigan University, 55 F.3d 1177 (6th Cir. 1995).

[3] R.A.V. v. City of St. Paul, 505 U.S. 377 (1992).

[4] Wisconsin v. Mitchell, 508 U.S. 476 (1993).

[5] 508 U.S. at 487-488.

[6] Virginia v. Black, 2003 U.S. Lexis 2715 (April 7, 2003).

READING *R.A.V. v. ST. PAUL*

As you read the Supreme Court's only ruling dealing directly with a hate speech ordinance, consider the following questions.

- Does the Court rely upon the facts of the case or abstract principles to reach its decision?
- Does the Court presume that the law is valid or invalid at the outset?
- In reviewing the law, is the text of the law, the effect of the speech upon a reasonable person (e.g., the threat standard), the likelihood of the speech to prompt violence (e.g., *Brandenburg*) or some other concern key to the Court's ruling?
- How does the Court determine whether the law targets protected speech or unprotected conduct?
- What interests does the Court balance and how? Does the Court give fair consideration to the harms of hate speech?
- What general rule of law does the Court establish in this case?
- Under the precedent established here, what would be necessary for a hate speech law to be constitutional?
- What do the separate opinions indicate about the clarity and predictability of the Court's hate speech jurisprudence?

R. A. V. v. City of St. Paul
505 U.S. 377
(1992)

JUDGES: SCALIA, J., delivered the opinion of the Court, in which REHNQUIST, C. J., and KENNEDY, SOUTER, and THOMAS, JJ., joined. WHITE, J., filed an opinion concurring in the judgment, in which BLACKMUN and O'CONNOR, JJ., joined, and in which STEVENS, J., joined except as to Part I-A. BLACKMUN, J., filed an opinion concurring in the judgment. STEVENS, J., filed an opinion concurring in the judgment, in Part I of which WHITE and BLACKMUN, JJ., joined.

OPINION: [379] JUSTICE SCALIA delivered the opinion of the Court.

In the predawn hours of June 21, 1990, petitioner and several other teenagers allegedly assembled crudely made cross by taping together broken chair legs. They then allegedly burned the cross inside the fenced yard of a black family that lived across the street from the house where petitioner was staying. Although this conduct could have been punished [380] under any of a number of laws,[1] one of the two provisions under which respondent city of St. Paul chose to charge petitioner (then a juvenile) was the St. Paul Bias-Motivated Crime Ordinance, St. Paul, Minn., Legis. Code § 292.02 (1990), which provides:

"Whoever places on public or private property a symbol, object, appellation, characterization or graffiti, including, but not limited to, a burning cross or Nazi swastika, which one knows or has reasonable grounds to know arouses anger, alarm or resentment in others on the basis of race, color, creed, religion or gender commits disorderly conduct and shall be guilty of a misdemeanor."

Petitioner moved to dismiss this count on the ground that the St. Paul ordinance was substantially overbroad and impermissibly content based and therefore facially invalid under the First Amendment.[2] The trial court granted this motion, but the Minnesota Supreme Court reversed. That court rejected petitioner's overbreadth claim because, as construed in prior Minnesota cases, see, e.g., In re Welfare of S. L. J., 263 N.W.2d 412 (Minn. 1978), the modifying phrase "arouses anger, alarm or resentment in others" limited the reach of the ordinance to conduct that amounts to "fighting words," i.e., "conduct that itself inflicts injury or

---

[1] The conduct might have violated Minnesota statutes carrying significant penalties. See, e.g., Minn. Stat. § 609.713(1) (1987) (providing for up to five years in prison for terroristic threats); § 609.563 (arson) (providing for up to five years and a $10,000 fine, depending on the value of the property intended to be damaged); § 609.595 (Supp. 1992) (criminal damage to property) (providing for up to one year and a $ 3,000 fine, depending upon the extent of the damage to the property).

[2] Petitioner has also been charged, in Count I of the delinquency petition, with a violation of Minn. Stat. § 609.2231(4) (Supp. 1990) (racially motivated assaults). Petitioner did not challenge this count.

tends to incite immediate violence . . ." In re Welfare of R. A. V., 464 N.W.2d 507, 510 (Minn. 1991) (citing Chaplinsky [381] v. New Hampshire, 315 U.S. 568, 572, 86 L. Ed. 1031, 62 S. Ct. 766 (1942)), and therefore the ordinance reached only expression "that the first amendment does not protect," 464 N.W.2d at 511. The court also concluded that the ordinance was not impermissibly content based because, in its view, "the ordinance is a narrowly tailored means toward accomplishing the compelling governmental interest in protecting the community against bias-motivated threats to public safety and order." Ibid. We granted certiorari, 501 U.S. 1204 (1991).

In construing the St. Paul ordinance, we are bound by the construction given to it by the Minnesota court. Posadas de Puerto Rico Associates v. Tourism Co. of Puerto Rico, 478 U.S. 328, 339, 92 L. Ed. 2d 266, 106 S. Ct. 2968 (1986); New York v. Ferber, 458 U.S. 747, 769, n.24, 73 L. Ed. 2d 1113, 102 S. Ct. 3348 (1982); Terminiello v. Chicago, 337 U.S. 1, 4, 93 L. Ed. 1131, 69 S. Ct. 894 (1949). Accordingly, we accept the Minnesota Supreme Court's authoritative statement that the ordinance reaches only those expressions that constitute "fighting words" within the meaning of Chaplinsky. 464 N.W.2d at 510-511. Petitioner and his amici urge us to modify the scope of the Chaplinsky formulation, thereby invalidating the ordinance as "substantially overbroad," Broadrick v. Oklahoma, 413 U.S. 601, 610, 37 L. Ed. 2d 830, 93 S. Ct. 2908 (1973). We find it unnecessary to consider this issue. Assuming, arguendo, that all of the expression reached by the ordinance is proscribable under the "fighting words" doctrine, we nonetheless conclude that the ordinance is facially unconstitutional in that it prohibits other-wise permitted speech solely on the basis of the subjects the speech addresses.[3]

---

[3] Contrary to JUSTICE WHITE's suggestion, post, 505 U.S. at 397-398, n.1, petitioner's claim is "fairly included" within the questions presented in the petition for certiorari, see this Court's Rule 14.1(a). It was clear from the petition and from petitioner's other filings in this Court (and in the courts below) that his assertion that the St. Paul ordinance "violates overbreadth . . . principles of the First Amendment," Pet. for Cert., was not just a technical "overbreadth" claim – i.e., a claim that the ordinance violated the rights of too many third parties – but included the contention that the ordinance was "overbroad" in the sense of restricting more speech than the Constitution permits, even in its application to him, because it is content based.

An important component of petitioner's argument is, and has been all along, that narrowly construing the ordinance to cover only "fighting words" cannot cure this fundamental defect. Id., at 12, 14, 15-16. In his briefs in this Court, petitioner argued that a narrowing construction was ineffective because (1) its boundaries were vague, Brief for Petitioner 26, and because (2) denominating particular expression a "fighting word" because of the impact of its ideological content upon the audience is inconsistent with the

The First Amendment generally prevents government from proscribing speech, see, e.g., Cantwell v. Connecticut, 310 U.S. 296, 309-311, 84 L. Ed. 1213, 60 S. Ct. 900 (1940), or even expressive conduct, see, e.g., Texas v. Johnson, 491 U.S. 397, 406, 105 L. Ed. 2d 342, 109 S. Ct. 2533 (1989), because of disapproval of the ideas expressed. Content-based regulations are presumptively invalid. Simon & Schuster, Inc. v. Members of N. Y. State Crime Victims Bd., 502 U.S. 105, 115, 116 L. Ed. 2d 476, 112 S. Ct. 501 (1991); id., at 124 (KENNEDY, J., concurring in judgment); Consolidated Edison Co. of N. Y. v. Public Serv. Comm'n of N. Y., 447 U.S. 530, 536, 65 L. Ed. 2d 319, 100 S. Ct. 2326 (1980); Police Dept. of Chicago v. Mosley, 408 U.S. 92, 95, 33 L. Ed. 2d 212, 92 S. Ct. 2286 (1972).

From 1791 to the present, however, our society, like other free but civilized societies, has permitted restrictions upon the content of speech in a [383] few limited areas, which are "of such slight social value as a step to truth that any benefit that may be derived from them is clearly outweighed by the social interest in order and morality." Chaplinsky, 315 U.S. at 572. We have recognized that "the freedom of speech" referred to by the First Amendment does not include a freedom to disregard these traditional limitations. See, e.g., Roth v. United States, 354 U.S. 476, 1 L. Ed. 2d 1498, 77 S. Ct. 1304 (1957) (obscenity); Beauharnais v. Illinois, 343 U.S. 250, 96 L. Ed. 919, 72 S. Ct. 725 (1952) (defamation); Chaplinsky v. New Hampshire, supra ("'fighting' words"); see generally Simon & Schuster, 502 U.S. at 124 (KENNEDY, J., concurring in judgment).

Our decisions since the 1960s have narrowed the scope of the traditional categorical exceptions for defamation, see New York Times Co. v. Sullivan, 376 U.S. 254, 11 L. Ed. 2d 686, 84 S. Ct. 710 (1964); Gertz v. Robert Welch, Inc., 418 U.S. 323, 41 L. Ed. 2d 789, 94 S. Ct. 2997 (1974); see generally Milkovich v. Lorain Journal Co., 497 U.S. 1, 13-17, 111 L. Ed. 2d 1, 110 S. Ct. 2695 (1990), and for obscenity, see Miller v. California, 413 U.S.

First Amendment, Reply Brief for Petitioner 5; id., at 13 ("[The ordinance] is overbroad, viewpoint discriminatory and vague as 'narrowly construed'") (emphasis added).

At oral argument, counsel for petitioner reiterated this second point: "It is . . . one of my positions, that in [punishing only some fighting words and not others], even though it is a subcategory, technically, of unprotected conduct, [the ordinance] still is picking out an opinion, a disfavored message, and making that clear through the State." Tr. of Oral Arg. 8. In resting our judgment upon this contention, we have not departed from our criteria of what is "fairly included" within the petition. See Arkansas Electric Cooperative Corp. v. Arkansas Pub. Serv. Comm'n, 461 U.S. 375, 382, n.6, 76 L. Ed. 2d 1, 103 S. Ct. 1905 (1983); Brown v. Socialist Workers '74 Campaign Comm., 459 U.S. 87, 94, n.9 (1982); Eddings v. Oklahoma, 455 U.S. 104, 113, n.9, 71 L. Ed. 2d 1, 102 S. Ct. 869 (1982); see generally R. Stern, E. Gressman, & S. Shapiro, Supreme Court Practice 361 (6th ed. 1986).

15, 37 L. Ed. 2d 419, 93 S. Ct. 2607 (1973), but a limited categorical approach has remained an important part of our First Amendment jurisprudence.

We have sometimes said that these categories of expression are "not within the area of constitutionally protected speech," Roth, 352 U.S. at 483; Beauharnais, supra, at 266; Chaplinsky, supra, at 571-572, or that the "protection of the First Amendment does not extend" to them, Bose Corp. v. Consumers Union of United States, Inc., 466 U.S. 485, 504, 80 L. Ed. 2d 502, 104 S. Ct. 1949 (1984); Sable Communications of Cal., Inc. v. FCC, 492 U.S. 115, 124, 106 L. ed. 2d 93, 109 S. Ct. 2829 (1989). Such statements must be taken in context, however, and are no more literally true than is the occasionally repeated shorthand characterizing obscenity "as not being speech at all," Sunstein, Pornography and the First Amendment, 1986 Duke L. J. 589, 615, n.46.

What they mean is that these areas of speech can, consistently with the First Amendment, be regulated because of their constitutionally proscribable content (obscenity, defamation, etc.) – not that they are categories of speech entirely invisible to the Constitution, so that they may be made the vehicles for [384] content discrimination unrelated to their distinctively proscribable content. Thus, the government may proscribe libel; but it may not make the further content discrimination of proscribing only libel critical of the government. We recently acknowledged this distinction in Ferber, 458 U.S. at 763, where, in upholding New York's child pornography law, we expressly recognized that there was no "question here of censoring a particular literary theme . . ." See also id., at 775 (O'CONNOR, J., concurring) ("As drafted, New York's statute does not attempt to suppress the communication of particular ideas").

Our cases surely do not establish the proposition that the First Amendment imposes no obstacle whatsoever to regulation of particular instances of such proscribable expression, so that the government "may regulate [them] freely," post, 505 U.S. at 400 (WHITE, J., concurring in judgment). That would mean that a city council could enact an ordinance prohibiting only those legally obscene works that contain criticism of the city government or, indeed, that do not include endorsement of the city government. Such a simplistic, all-or-nothing-at-all approach to First Amendment protection is at odds with common sense and with our jurisprudence as well.[4] It is [385] not true that "fighting words" have

at most a "de minimis" expressive content, ibid., or that their content is in all respects "worthless and undeserving of constitutional protection," post, 505 U.S. at 401; sometimes they are quite expressive indeed. We have not said that they constitute "no part of the expression of ideas," but only that they constitute "no essential part of any exposition of ideas." Chaplinsky, 315 U.S. at 572 (emphasis added).

The proposition that a particular instance of speech can be proscribable on the basis of one feature (e.g., obscenity) but not on the basis of another (e.g., opposition to the city government) is commonplace and has found application in many contexts. We have long held, for example, that nonverbal expressive activity can be banned because of the action it entails, but not because of the ideas it expresses – so that burning a flag in violation of an ordinance against outdoor fires would be punishable, whereas burning a flag in violation of an ordinance against dishonoring the flag is not. See Johnson, 491 U.S. at 406-407. See also Barnes v. Glen Theatre, Inc., 501 U.S. 560, 569-570, 115 L. Ed. 2d 504, 111 S. Ct. 2456 (1991) (plurality opinion); id., at 573-574 (SCALIA, J., concurring in judgment); id., at 581-582 (SOUTER, J., concurring in judgment); United

---

[4] JUSTICE WHITE concedes that a city council cannot prohibit only those legally obscene works that contain criticism of the city government, post, 505 U.S. at 406, but asserts that to be the consequence, not of the First Amendment, but of the Equal Protection Clause. Such content-based discrimination would not, he asserts, "be rationally related to a legitimate government interest." Ibid. But of course the only reason that government interest is not a "legitimate" one is that it violates the First Amendment. This Court itself has occasionally fused the First Amendment into the Equal Protection Clause in this fashion, but at least with the acknowledgment (which JUSTICE WHITE cannot afford to make) that the First Amendment underlies its analysis. See Police Dept. of Chicago v. Mosley, 408 U.S. 92, 95, 33 L. Ed. 2d 212, 92 S. Ct. 2286 (1972) (ordinance prohibiting only nonlabor picketing violated the Equal Protection Clause because there was no "appropriate governmental interest" supporting the distinction inasmuch as "the First Amendment means that government has no power to restrict expression because of its message, its ideas, its subject matter, or its content"); Carey v. Brown, 447 U.S. 455, 65 L. Ed. 2d 263, 100 S. Ct. 2286 (1980). See generally Simon & Schuster, Inc. v. Members of N. Y. State Crime Victims Bd., 502 U.S. 105, 124, 116 L. Ed. 2d 476, 112 S. Ct. 501 (1991) (KENNEDY, J., concurring in judgment). JUSTICE STEVENS seeks to avoid the point by dismissing the notion of obscene antigovernment speech as "fantastical," post, 505 U.S. at 418, apparently believing that any reference to politics prevents a finding of obscenity. Unfortunately for the purveyors of obscenity, that is obviously false. A shockingly hardcore pornographic movie that contains a model sporting a political tattoo can be found, "taken as a whole, [to] lack serious literary, artistic, political, or scientific value," Miller v. California, 413 U.S. 15, 24, 37 L. Ed. 2d 419, 93 S. Ct. 2607 (1973) (emphasis added). Anyway, it is easy enough to come up with other illustrations of a content-based restriction upon "unprotected speech" that is obviously invalid: the antigovernment libel illustration mentioned earlier, for one. See 505 U.S. at 384. And of course the concept of racist fighting words is, unfortunately, anything but a "highly speculative hypothetical," post, 505 U.S. at 419.

[386] States v. O'Brien, 391 U.S. 367, 376-377, 20 L. Ed. 2d 672, 88 S. Ct. 1673 (1968).

Similarly, we have upheld reasonable "time, place, or manner" restrictions, but only if they are "justified without reference to the content of the regulated speech." Ward v. Rock Against Racism, 491 U.S. 781, 791, 105 L. Ed. 2d 661, 109 S. Ct. 2746 (1989) (internal quotation marks omitted); see also Clark v. Community for Creative Non-Violence, 468 U.S. 288, 298, 82 L. Ed. 2d 221, 104 S. Ct. 3065 (1984) (noting that the O'Brien test differs little from the standard applied to time, place, or manner restrictions). And just as the power to proscribe particular speech on the basis of a noncontent element (e.g., noise) does not entail the power to proscribe the same speech on the basis of a content element; so also, the power to proscribe it on the basis of one content element (e.g., obscenity) does not entail the power to proscribe it on the basis of other content elements.

In other words, the exclusion of "fighting words" from the scope of the First Amendment simply means that, for purposes of that Amendment, the unprotected features of the words are, despite their verbal character, essentially a "nonspeech" element of communication. Fighting words are thus analogous to a noisy sound truck: Each is, as Justice Frankfurter recognized, a "mode of speech," Niemotko v. Maryland, 340 U.S. 268, 282, 95 L. Ed. 267, 71 S. Ct. 325 (1951) (opinion concurring in result); both can be used to convey an idea; but neither has, in and of itself, a claim upon the First Amendment. As with the sound truck, however, so also with fighting words: The government may not regulate use based on hostility – or favoritism – towards the underlying message expressed. Compare Frisby v. Schultz, 487 U.S. 474, 101 L. Ed. 2d 420, 108 S. Ct. 2495 (1988) (upholding, against facial challenge, a content-neutral ban on targeted residential picketing), with Carey v. Brown, 447 U.S. 455, 65 L. Ed. 2d 263, 100 S. Ct. 2286 (1980) (invalidating a ban on residential picketing that exempted labor picketing).[5]

[387] The concurrences describe us as setting forth a new First Amendment principle that prohibition of constitutionally proscribable speech cannot be "underinclusive," post, 505 U.S. at 402 (WHITE, J., concurring in judgment) – a First

Amendment "absolutism" whereby "within a particular 'proscribable' category of expression, . . . a government must either proscribe all speech or no speech at all," post, 505 U.S. at 419 (STEVENS, J., concurring in judgment). That easy target is of the concurrences' own invention. In our view, the First Amendment imposes not an "underinclusiveness" limitation but a "content discrimination" limitation upon a State's prohibition of proscribable speech. There is no problem whatever, for example, with a State's prohibiting obscenity (and other forms of proscribable expression) only in certain media or markets, for although that prohibition would be "underinclusive," it would not discriminate on the basis of content. See, e.g., Sable Communications, 492 U.S. at 124-126 (upholding 47 U. S. C. § 223(b)(1), which prohibits obscene telephone communications).

Even the prohibition against content discrimination that we assert the First Amendment requires is not absolute. It applies differently in the context of proscribable speech than in the area of fully protected speech. The rationale of the general prohibition, after all, is that content discrimination "raises the specter that the Government may effectively drive certain ideas or viewpoints from the marketplace," Simon & Schuster, 502 U.S. at 116; Leathers v. Medlock, 499 U.S. 439, 448, 113 L. Ed. 2d 494, 111 S. Ct. 1438 (1991); FCC v. League of Women Voters of Cal., 468 U.S. 364, 383-384, 82 L. Ed. 2d 278, 104 S. Ct. 3106 (1984); Consolidated Edison Co., 447 U.S. at 536; Police Dept. of Chicago v. Mosley, [388] 408 U.S. at 95-98. But content discrimination among various instances of a class of proscribable speech often does not pose this threat.

When the basis for the content discrimination consists entirely of the very reason the entire class of speech at issue is proscribable, no significant danger of idea or viewpoint discrimination exists. Such a reason, having been adjudged neutral enough to support exclusion of the entire class of speech from First Amendment protection, is also neutral enough to form the basis of distinction within the class. To illustrate: A State might choose to prohibit only that obscenity which is the most patently offensive in its prurience – i.e., that which involves the most lascivious displays of sexual activity. But it may not prohibit, for example, only that obscenity which includes offensive political messages. See Kucharek v. Hanaway, 902 F.2d 513, 517 (CA7 1990), cert. denied, 498 U.S. 1041, 112 L. Ed. 2d 702, 111 S. Ct. 713 (1991).

And the Federal Government can criminalize only those threats of violence that are directed against the president, see 18 U. S. C. § 871 – since the reasons why threats of violence are outside the First Amendment (protecting individuals from the fear of violence, from the disruption that fear engenders, and from the possibility that the threatened violence will

---

[5] Although JUSTICE WHITE asserts that our analysis disregards "established principles of First Amendment law," post, 505 U.S. at 415, he cites not a single case (and we are aware of none) that even involved, much less considered and resolved, the issue of content discrimination through regulation of "unprotected" speech – though we plainly recognized that as an issue in New York v. Ferber, 458 U.S. 747, 73 L. Ed. 2d 1113, 102 S. Ct. 3348 (1982). It is of course contrary to all traditions of our jurisprudence to consider the law on this point conclusively resolved by broad language in cases where the issue was not presented or even envisioned.

occur) have special force when applied to the person of the President. See Watts v. United States, 394 U.S. 705, 707, 22 L. Ed. 2d 664, 89 S. Ct. 1399 (1969) (upholding the facial validity of § 871 because of the "overwhelming interest in protecting the safety of [the] Chief Executive and in allowing him to perform his duties without interference from threats of physical violence"). But the Federal Government may not criminalize only those threats against the President that mention his policy on aid to inner cities.

And to take a final example (one mentioned by JUSTICE STEVENS, post, 505 U.S. at 421-422), a State may choose to regulate price advertising in one industry but not in others, because the risk of fraud (one of the characteristics of commercial speech that justifies depriving it of full First Amendment protection, see Virginia [389] State Bd. of Pharmacy v. Virginia Citizens Consumer Council, Inc., 425 U.S. 748, 771-772, 48 L. Ed. 2d 346, 96 S. Ct. 1817 (1976)) is in its view greater there. Cf. Morales v. Trans World Airlines, Inc., 504 U.S. 374, 119 L. Ed. 2d 157, 112 S. Ct. 2031 (1992) (state regulation of airline advertising); Ohralik v. Ohio State Bar Assn., 436 U.S. 447, 56 L. Ed. 2d 444, 98 S. Ct. 1912 (1978) (state regulation of lawyer advertising). But a State may not prohibit only that commercial advertising that depicts men in a demeaning fashion. See, e.g., Los Angeles Times, Aug. 8, 1989, section 4, p. 6, col. 1.

Another valid basis for according differential treatment to even a content-defined subclass of proscribable speech is that the subclass happens to be associated with particular "secondary effects" of the speech, so that the regulation is "justified without reference to the content of the . . . speech," Renton v. Playtime Theatres, Inc., 475 U.S. 41, 48, 89 L. Ed. 2d 29, 106 S. Ct. 925 (1986) (quoting, with emphasis, Virginia State Bd. of Pharmacy, 425 U.S. at 771); see also Young v. American Mini Theatres, Inc., 427 U.S. 50, 71, n.34, 49 L. Ed. 2d 310, 96 S. Ct. 2440 (1976) (plurality opinion); id., at 80-82 (Powell, J., concurring); Barnes, 501 U.S. at 586 (SOUTER, J., concurring in judgment). A State could, for example, permit all obscene live performances except those involving minors.

Moreover, since words can in some circumstances violate laws directed not against speech but against conduct (a law against treason, for example, is violated by telling the enemy the Nation's defense secrets), a particular content-based sub-category of a proscribable class of speech can be swept up incidentally within the reach of a statute directed at conduct rather than speech. See id., at 571 (plurality opinion); id., at 577 (SCALIA, J., concurring in judgment); id., at 582 (SOUTER, J., concurring in judgment); FTC v. Superior Court Trial Lawyers Assn., 493 U.S. 411, 425-432, 107 L. Ed. 2d 851,

110 S. Ct. 768 (1990); O'Brien, 391 U.S. at 376-377. Thus, for example, sexually derogatory "fighting words," among other words, may produce a violation of Title VII's general prohibition against sexual discrimination in employment practices, 42 U. S. C. § 2000e-2; 29 CFR § 1604.11 (1991). See also 18 [390] U. S. C. § 242; 42 U. S. C. §§ 1981, 1982. Where the government does not target conduct on the basis of its expressive content, acts are not shielded from regulation merely because they express a discriminatory idea or philosophy.

These bases for distinction refute the proposition that the selectivity of the restriction is "even arguably 'conditioned upon the sovereign's agreement with what a speaker may intend to say.'" Metromedia, Inc. v. San Diego, 453 U.S. 490, 555, 69 L. Ed. 2d 800, 101 S. Ct. 2882 (1981) (STEVENS, J., dissenting in part) (citation omitted). There may be other such bases as well. Indeed, to validate such selectivity (where totally proscribable speech is at issue) it may not even be necessary to identify any particular "neutral" basis, so long as the nature of the content discrimination is such that there is no realistic possibility that official suppression of ideas is afoot. (We cannot think of any First Amendment interest that would stand in the way of a State's prohibiting only those obscene motion pictures with blue-eyed actresses.) Save for that limitation, the regulation of "fighting words," like the regulation of noisy speech, may address some offensive instances and leave other, equally offensive, instances alone. See Posadas de Puerto Rico, 478 U.S. at 342-343.[6]

---

[6] JUSTICE STEVENS cites a string of opinions as supporting his assertion that "selective regulation of speech based on content" is not presumptively invalid. Post, 505 U.S. at 421-422. Analysis reveals, however, that they do not support it. To begin with, three of them did not command a majority of the Court, Young v. American Mini Theatres, Inc., 427 U.S. 50, 63-73, 49 L. Ed. 2d 310, 96 S. Ct. 2440 (1976) (plurality opinion); FCC v. Pacifica Foundation, 438 U.S. 726, 744-748, 57 L. Ed. 2d 1073, 98 S. Ct. 3026 (1978) (plurality opinion); Lehman v. Shaker Heights, 418 U.S. 298, 41 L. Ed. 2d 770, 94 S. Ct. 2714 (1974) (plurality opinion), and two others did not even discuss the First Amendment, Morales v. Trans World Airlines, Inc., 504 U.S. 374, 119 L. Ed. 2d 157, 112 S. Ct. 2031 (1992); Jacob Siegel Co. v. FTC, 327 U.S. 608, 90 L. Ed. 888, 66 S. Ct. 758 (1946). In any event, all that their contents establish is what we readily concede: that presumptive invalidity does not mean invariable invalidity, leaving room for such exceptions as reasonable and viewpoint-neutral content-based discrimination in non-public forums, see Lehman, 418 U.S. at 301-304; see also Cornelius v. NAACP Legal Defense & Ed. Fund, Inc., 473 U.S. 788, 806, 87 L. Ed. 2d 567, 105 S. Ct. 3439 (1985), or with respect to certain speech by government employees, see Broadrick v. Oklahoma, 413 U.S. 601, 37 L. Ed. 2d 830, 93 S. Ct. 2908 (1973); see also Civil Service Comm'n v. Letter Carriers, 413 U.S. 548, 564-567, 37 L. Ed. 2d 796, 93 S. Ct. 2880 (1973).

[391] Applying these principles to the St. Paul ordinance, we conclude that, even as narrowly construed by the Minnesota Supreme Court, the ordinance is facially unconstitutional. Although the phrase in the ordinance, "arouses anger, alarm or resentment in others," has been limited by the Minnesota Supreme Court's construction to reach only those symbols or displays that amount to "fighting words," the remaining, unmodified terms make clear that the ordinance applies only to "fighting words" that insult, or provoke violence, "on the basis of race, color, creed, religion or gender."

Displays containing abusive invective, no matter how vicious or severe, are permissible unless they are addressed to one of the specified disfavored topics. Those who wish to use "fighting words" in connection with other ideas – to express hostility, for example, on the basis of political affiliation, union membership, or homosexuality – are not covered. The First Amendment does not permit St. Paul to impose special prohibitions on those speakers who express views on disfavored subjects. See Simon & Schuster, 502 U.S. at 116; Arkansas Writers' Project, Inc. v. Ragland, 481 U.S. 221, 229-230, 95 L. Ed. 2d 209, 107 S. Ct. 1722 (1987).

In its practical operation, moreover, the ordinance goes even beyond mere content discrimination, to actual viewpoint discrimination. Displays containing some words – odious racial epithets, for example – would be prohibited to proponents of all views. But "fighting words" that do not themselves invoke race, color, creed, religion, or gender aspersions upon a person's mother, for example – would seemingly be usable ad libitum in the placards of those arguing in favor of racial, color, etc., tolerance and equality, but could not be used by those speakers' opponents. One could hold up a sign saying, for example, that all "anti-Catholic [392] bigots" are misbegotten; but not that all "papists" are, for that would insult and provoke violence "on the basis of religion." St. Paul has no such authority to license one side of a debate to fight freestyle, while requiring the other to follow Marquis of Queensberry rules.

What we have here, it must be emphasized, is not a prohibition of fighting words that are directed at certain persons or groups (which would be facially valid if it met the requirements of the Equal Protection Clause); but rather, a prohibition of fighting words that contain (as the Minnesota Supreme Court repeatedly emphasized) messages of "bias motivated" hatred and in particular, as applied to this case, messages "based on virulent notions of racial supremacy." 464 N.W.2d at 508, 511. One must wholeheartedly agree with the Minnesota Supreme Court that "it is the responsibility, even the obligation, of diverse communities to confront such notions in whatever form they appear," id., at 508, but the manner of that confrontation cannot consist of selective limitations upon speech. St. Paul's brief asserts that a general "fighting words" law would not meet the city's needs because only a content-specific measure can communicate to minority groups that the "group hatred" aspect of such speech "is not condoned by the majority." Brief for Respondent 25. The point of the First Amendment is that majority preferences must be expressed in some fashion other than silencing speech on the basis of its content.

Despite the fact that the Minnesota Supreme Court and St. Paul acknowledge that the ordinance is directed at expression of group hatred, JUSTICE STEVENS suggests that this "fundamentally misreads" the ordinance. Post, 505 U.S. at 433. It is directed, he claims, not to speech of a particular content, but to particular "injuries" that are "qualitatively different" from other injuries. Post, 505 U.S. at 424. This is wordplay. What makes the anger, fear, sense of dishonor, etc., produced by violation of this ordinance distinct from the anger, fear, sense of dishonor, etc., produced by other fighting words is [393] nothing other than the fact that it is caused by a distinctive idea, conveyed by a distinctive message.

The First Amendment cannot be evaded that easily. It is obvious that the symbols which will arouse "anger, alarm or resentment in others on the basis of race, color, creed, religion or gender" are those symbols that communicate a message of hostility based on one of these characteristics. St. Paul concedes in its brief that the ordinance applies only to "racial, religious, or gender-specific symbols" such as "a burning cross, Nazi swastika or other instrumentality of like import." Brief for Respondent 8. Indeed, St. Paul argued in the Juvenile Court that "the burning of a cross does express a message and it is, in fact, the content of that message which the St. Paul Ordinance attempts to legislate." Memorandum from the Ramsey County Attorney to the Honorable Charles A. Flinn, Jr., dated July 13, 1990, in In re Welfare of R. A. V., No. 89-D-1231 (Ramsey Cty. Juvenile Ct.), p. 1, reprinted in App. to Brief for Petitioner C-1.

The content-based discrimination reflected in the St. Paul ordinance comes within neither any of the specific exceptions to the First Amendment prohibition we discussed earlier nor a more general exception for content discrimination that does not threaten censorship of ideas. It assuredly does not fall within the exception for content discrimination based on the very reasons why the particular class of speech at issue (here, fighting words) is proscribable. As explained earlier, see supra, 505 U.S. at 386, the reason why fighting words are categorically excluded from the protection of the First Amendment is not that their content communicates any particular idea, but that their content embodies a particularly intolerable (and socially unnecessary) mode of expressing whatever idea the speaker wishes to convey.

St. Paul has not singled out an especially offensive mode of expression – it has not, for example, selected for prohibition only those fighting words that communicate ideas in a threatening (as opposed to a merely obnoxious) manner. Rather, it has proscribed fighting [394] words of whatever manner that communicate messages of racial, gender, or religious intolerance. Selectivity of this sort creates the possibility that the city is seeking to handicap the expression of particular ideas. That possibility would alone be enough to render the ordinance presumptively invalid, but St. Paul's comments and concessions in this case elevate the possibility to a certainty.

St. Paul argues that the ordinance comes within another of the specific exceptions we mentioned, the one that allows content discrimination aimed only at the "secondary effects" of the speech, see Renton v. Playtime Theatres, Inc., 475 U.S. 41, 89 L. Ed. 2d 29, 106 S. Ct. 925 (1986). According to St. Paul, the ordinance is intended, "not to impact on [sic] the right of free expression of the accused," but rather to "protect against the victimization of a person or persons who are particularly vulnerable because of their membership in a group that historically has been discriminated against." Brief for Respondent 28. Even assuming that an ordinance that completely proscribes, rather than merely regulates, a specified category of speech can ever be considered to be directed only to the secondary effects of such speech, it is clear that the St. Paul ordinance is not directed to secondary effects within the meaning of Renton. As we said in Boos v. Barry, 485 U.S. 312, 99 L. Ed. 2d 333, 108 S. Ct. 1157 (1988), "Listeners' reactions to speech are not the type of 'secondary effects' we referred to in Renton." Id., at 321. "The emotive impact of speech on its audience is not a 'secondary effect.'" Ibid. See also id., at 334 (opinion of Brennan, J.).[7]

[395] It hardly needs discussion that the ordinance does not fall within some more general exception permitting all selectivity that for any reason is beyond the suspicion of official suppression of ideas. The statements of St. Paul in this very case afford

---

[7] St. Paul has not argued in this case that the ordinance merely regulates that subclass of fighting words which is most likely to provoke a violent response. But even if one assumes (as appears unlikely) that the categories selected may be so described, that would not justify selective regulation under a "secondary effects" theory. The only reason why such expressive conduct would be especially correlated with violence is that it conveys a particularly odious message; because the "chain of causation" thus necessarily "runs through the persuasive effect of the expressive component" of the conduct, Barnes v. Glen Theatre, Inc., 501 U.S. 560, 586, 115 L. Ed. 2d 504, 111 S. Ct. 2456 (1991) (SOUTER, J., concurring in judgment), it is clear that the St. Paul ordinance regulates on the basis of the "primary" effect of the speech – i.e., its persuasive (or repellant) force.

ample basis for, if not full confirmation of, that suspicion.

Finally, St. Paul and its amici defend the conclusion of the Minnesota Supreme Court that, even if the ordinance regulates expression based on hostility towards its protected ideological content, this discrimination is nonetheless justified because it is narrowly tailored to serve compelling state interests. Specifically, they assert that the ordinance helps to ensure the basic human rights of members of groups that have historically been subjected to discrimination, including the right of such group members to live in peace where they wish. We do not doubt that these interests are compelling, and that the ordinance can be said to promote them. But the "danger of censorship" presented by a facially content-based statute, Leathers v. Medlock, 499 U.S. at 448, requires that that weapon be employed only where it is "necessary to serve the asserted [compelling] interest," Burson v. Freeman, 504 U.S. 191, 199, 119 L. Ed. 2d 5, 112 S. Ct. 1846 (1992) (plurality opinion) (emphasis added); Perry Ed. Assn. v. Perry Local Educators' Assn., 460 U.S. 37, 45, 74 L. Ed. 2d 794, 103 S. Ct. 948 (1983).

The existence of adequate content-neutral alternatives thus "undercuts significantly" any defense of such a statute, Boos v. Barry, 485 U.S. at 329, casting considerable doubt on the government's protestations that "the asserted justification is in fact an accurate description of the purpose and effect of the law," Burson, 504 U.S. at 213 (KENNEDY, J., concurring). See Boos, 485 U.S. at 324-329; cf. Minneapolis Star & Tribune Co. v. Minnesota Comm'r of Revenue, 460 U.S. 575, 586-587, 103 S. Ct. 1365, 75 L. Ed. 2d 295 (1983). The dispositive question in this case, therefore, is whether content discrimination is reasonably necessary to achieve St. Paul's compelling [396] interests; it plainly is not. An ordinance not limited to the favored topics, for example, would have precisely the same beneficial effect. In fact the only interest distinctively served by the content limitation is that of displaying the city council's special hostility towards the particular biases thus singled out.[8] That is precisely what the First Amendment forbids. The politicians of St. Paul are entitled to express that hostility – but not through the means of imposing unique limitations upon speakers who (however benightedly) disagree.

Let there be no mistake about our belief that burning a cross in someone's front yard is reprehensible. But St. Paul has sufficient means at its disposal to prevent such behavior without adding the First Amendment to the fire.

The judgment of the Minnesota Supreme Court is reversed, and the case is remanded for proceedings not inconsistent with this opinion. It is so ordered.

CONCUR: [397] JUSTICE WHITE, with whom JUSTICE BLACKMUN and JUSTICE O'CONNOR join, and with whom JUSTICE STEVENS joins except as to Part I-A, concurring in the judgment.

I agree with the majority that the judgment of the Minnesota Supreme Court should be reversed. However, our agreement ends there.

This case could easily be decided within the contours of established First Amendment law by holding, as petitioner argues, that the St. Paul ordinance is fatally overbroad because it criminalizes not only unprotected expression but expression protected by the First Amendment. See Part II, infra. Instead, "finding it unnecessary" to consider the questions upon which we granted review,[1] ante, 505

JUSTICE WHITE and JUSTICE STEVENS are therefore quite mistaken when they seek to convert the Burson plurality's passing comment that "the First Amendment does not require States to regulate for problems that do not exist," id., at 207, into endorsement of the revolutionary proposition that the suppression of particular ideas can be justified when only those ideas have been a source of trouble in the past. Post, 505 U.S. at 405 (WHITE, J., concurring in judgment); post, 505 U.S. at 434 (STEVENS, J., concurring in judgment).
[8] A plurality of the Court reached a different conclusion with regard to the Tennessee anti-electioneering statute considered earlier this Term in Burson v. Freeman, 504 U.S. 191, 119 L. Ed. 2d 5, 112 S. Ct. 1846 (1992). In light of the "logical connection" between electioneering and the State's compelling interest in preventing voter intimidation and election fraud – an inherent connection borne out by a "long history" and a "widespread and time-tested consensus," id., at 206, 208, n.10, 211 – the plurality concluded that it was faced with one of those "rare cases" in which the use of a facially content-based restriction was justified by interests unrelated to the suppression of ideas, id., at 211; see also id., at 213 (KENNEDY, J., concurring).

[1] The Court granted certiorari to review the following questions:
"1. May a local government enact a content-based, 'hate-crime' ordinance prohibiting the display of symbols, including a Nazi swastika or a burning cross, on public or private property, which one knows or has reason to know arouses anger, alarm, or resentment in others on the basis of race, color, creed, religion, or gender without violating overbreadth and vagueness principles of the First Amendment to the United States Constitution?
"2. Can the constitutionality of such a vague and substantially overbroad content-based restraint of expression be saved by a limiting construction, like that used to save the vague and overbroad content-neutral laws, restricting its application to 'fighting words' or 'imminent lawless action?'" Pet. for Cert. It has long been the rule of this Court that "only the questions set forth in the petition, or fairly included therein, will be considered by the Court." This Court's Rule 14.1(a). This Rule has served to focus the issues presented for review. But the majority reads the Rule so expansively that any First Amendment theory would appear to be "fairly included" within the questions quoted above.
Contrary to the impression the majority attempts to create through its selective quotation of petitioner's briefs, see ante,

U.S. at 381, the [398] Court holds the ordinance facially unconstitutional on a ground that was never presented to the Minnesota Supreme Court, a ground that has not been briefed by the parties before this Court, a ground that requires serious departures from the teaching of prior cases and is inconsistent with the plurality opinion in Burson v. Freeman, 504 U.S. 191, 119 L. Ed. 2d 5, 112 S. Ct. 1846 (1992), which was joined by two of the five Justices in the majority in the present case.

This Court ordinarily is not so eager to abandon its precedents. Twice within the past month, the Court has declined to overturn longstanding but controversial decisions on questions of constitutional law. See Allied-Signal, Inc. v. Director, Division of Taxation, 504 U.S. 768, 119 L. Ed. 2d 533, 112 S. Ct. 2251 (1992); Quill Corp. v. North Dakota, 504 U.S. 298, 119 L. Ed. 2d 91, 112 S. Ct. 1904 (1992). In each case, we had the benefit of full briefing on the critical issue, so that the parties and amici had the opportunity to apprise us of the impact of a change in the law. And in each case, the Court declined to abandon its precedents, invoking the principle of stare decisis. Allied-Signal, Inc., 504 U.S. at 783-786; Quill Corp., 504 U.S. at 317-318.

But in the present case, the majority casts aside long-established First Amendment doctrine without the benefit of briefing and adopts an untried theory. This is hardly a judicious way of proceeding, and the Court's reasoning in reaching its result is transparently wrong.

[399] This Court's decisions have plainly stated that expression falling within certain limited categories so lacks the values the First Amendment was designed to protect that the Constitution affords no protection to that expression. Chaplinsky v. New Hampshire, 315 U.S. 568, 86 L. Ed. 1031, 62 S. Ct. 766 (1942), made the point in the clearest possible terms:

"There are certain well-defined and narrowly limited classes of speech, the prevention and punishment of which have never been thought to

---

505 U.S. at 381-382, n.3, petitioner did not present to this Court or the Minnesota Supreme Court anything approximating the novel theory the majority adopts today. Most certainly petitioner did not "reiterate" such a claim at argument; he responded to a question from the bench, Tr. of Oral Arg. 8. Previously, this Court has shown the restraint to refrain from deciding cases on the basis of its own theories when they have not been pressed or passed upon by a state court of last resort. See, e.g., Illinois v. Gates, 462 U.S. 213, 217-224, 76 L. Ed. 2d 527, 103 S. Ct. 2317 (1983).
Given this threshold issue, it is my view that the Court lacks jurisdiction to decide the case on the majority rationale. Cf. Arkansas Electric Cooperative Corp. v. Arkansas Pub. Serv. Comm'n, 461 U.S. 375, 382, n.6, 76 L. Ed. 2d 1, 103 S. Ct. 1905 (1983). Certainly the preliminary jurisdictional and prudential concerns are sufficiently weighty that we would never have granted certiorari had petitioner sought review of a question based on the majority's decisional theory.

raise any Constitutional problem. . . . It has been well observed that such utterances are no essential part of any exposition of ideas, and are of such slight social value as a step to truth that any benefit that may be derived from them is clearly outweighed by the social interest in order and morality." Id., at 571-572.

See also Bose Corp. v. Consumers Union of United States, Inc., 466 U.S. 485, 504, 80 L. Ed. 2d 502, 104 S. Ct. 1949 (1984) (citing Chaplinsky).

Thus, as the majority concedes, see ante, 505 U.S. at 383-384, this Court has long held certain discrete categories of expression to be proscribable on the basis of their content. For instance, the Court has held that the individual who falsely shouts "fire" in a crowded theater may not claim the protection of the First Amendment. Schenck v. United States, 249 U.S. 47, 52, 63 L. Ed. 470, 39 S. Ct. 247 (1919). The Court has concluded that neither child pornography nor obscenity is protected by the First Amendment. New York v. Ferber, 458 U.S. 747, 764, 73 L. Ed. 2d 1113, 102 S. Ct. 3348 (1982); Miller v. California, 413 U.S. 15, 20, 37 L. Ed. 2d 419, 93 S. Ct. 2607 (1973); Roth v. United States, 354 U.S. 476, 484-485, 1 L. Ed. 2d 1498, 77 S. Ct. 1304 (1957). And the Court has observed that, "leaving aside the special considerations when public officials [and public figures] are the target, a libelous publication is not protected by the Constitution." Ferber, 458 U.S. at 763 (citations omitted).

[400] All of these categories are content based. But the Court has held that the First Amendment does not apply to them because their expressive content is worth-less or of de minimis value to society. Chaplinsky, 315 U.S. at 571-572. We have not departed from this principle, emphasizing repeatedly that, "within the confines of [these] given classifications, the evil to be restricted so overwhelmingly outweighs the expressive interests, if any, at stake, that no process of case-by-case adjudication is required." Ferber, 458 U.S. at 763-764; Bigelow v. Virginia, 421 U.S. 809, 819, 44 L. Ed. 2d 600, 95 S. Ct. 2222 (1975). This categorical approach has provided a principled and narrowly focused means for distinguishing between expression that the government may regulate freely and that which it may regulate on the basis of content only upon a showing of compelling need.[2]

Today, however, the Court announces that earlier Courts did not mean their repeated statements that certain categories of expression are "not within the area of constitutionally protected speech." Roth, 354

U.S. at 483. See ante, 505 U.S. at 383, citing Beauharnais v. Illinois, 343 U.S. 250, 266, 96 L. Ed. 919, 72 S. Ct. 725 (1952); Chaplinsky, 315 U.S. at 571-572; Bose Corp., 466 U.S. at 504; Sable Communications of Cal., Inc. v. FCC, 492 U.S. 115, 124, 106 L. Ed. 2d 93, 109 S. Ct. 2829 (1989). The present Court submits that such clear statements "must be taken in context" and are not "literally true." Ante, 505 U.S. at 383.

To the contrary, those statements meant precisely what they said: The categorical approach is a firmly entrenched part of our First Amendment jurisprudence. Indeed, the Court in Roth reviewed the guarantees of freedom of expression in effect at the time of the ratification of the Constitution and concluded, "In light of this history, it is apparent that the unconditional phrasing of the First Amendment was [401] not intended to protect every utterance." 354 U.S. at 482-483.

In its decision today, the Court points to "nothing . . . in this Court's precedents warranting disregard of this longstanding tradition." Burson, 504 U.S. at 216 (SCALIA, J., concurring in judgment); Allied-Signal, Inc., 504 U.S. at 783. Nevertheless, the majority holds that the First Amendment protects those narrow categories of expression long held to be undeserving of First Amendment protection – at least to the extent that lawmakers may not regulate some fighting words more strictly than others because of their content. The Court announces that such content-based distinctions violate the First Amendment because "the government may not regulate use based on hostility – or favoritism – towards the underlying message expressed." Ante, 505 U.S. at 386. Should the government want to criminalize certain fighting words, the Court now requires it to criminalize all fighting words.

To borrow a phrase: "Such a simplistic, all-or-nothing-at-all approach to First Amendment protection is at odds with common sense and with our jurisprudence as well." Ante, 505 U.S. at 384. It is inconsistent to hold that the government may proscribe an entire category of speech because the content of that speech is evil, Ferber, 458 U.S. at 763-764; but that the government may not treat a subset of that category differently without violating the First Amendment; the content of the subset is by definition worthless and undeserving of constitutional protection.

The majority's observation that fighting words are "quite expressive indeed," ante, 505 U.S. at 385, is no answer. Fighting words are not a means of exchanging views, rallying supporters, or registering a protest; they are directed against individuals to provoke violence or to inflict injury. Chaplinsky, 315 U.S. at 572. Therefore, a ban on all fighting words or on a subset of the fighting words category would restrict only the social evil of hate speech, without

---

[2] "In each of these areas, the limits of the unprotected category, as well as the unprotected character of particular communications, have been determined by the judicial evaluation of special facts that have been deemed to have constitutional significance." Bose Corp. v. Consumers Union of United States, Inc., 466 U.S. 485, 504-505, 80 L. Ed. 2d 502, 104 S. Ct. 1949 (1984).

creating the danger of driving viewpoints from the marketplace. See ante, 505 U.S. at 387.

[402] Therefore, the Court's insistence on inventing its brand of First Amendment underinclusiveness puzzles me.[3] The over-breadth doctrine has the redeeming virtue of attempting to avoid the chilling of protected expression, Broadrick v. Oklahoma, 413 U.S. 601, 612, 37 L. Ed. 2d 830, 93 S. Ct. 2908 (1973); Osborne v. Ohio, 495 U.S. 103, 112, n.8, 109 L. Ed. 2d 98, 110 S. Ct. 1691 (1990); Brockett v. Spokane Arcades, Inc., 472 U.S. 491, 503, 86 L. Ed. 2d 394, 105 S. Ct. 2794 (1985); Ferber, 458 U.S. at 772, but the Court's new "underbreadth" creation serves no desirable function. Instead, it permits, indeed invites, the continuation of expressive conduct that in this case is evil and worthless in First Amendment terms, see Ferber, 458 U.S. at 763-764; Chaplinsky, 315 U.S. at 571-572, until the city of St. Paul cures the underbreadth by adding to its ordinance a catchall phrase such as "and all other fighting words that may constitutionally be subject to this ordinance."

Any contribution of this holding to First Amendment jurisprudence is surely a negative one, since it necessarily signals that expressions of violence, such as the message of intimidation and racial hatred conveyed by burning a cross on someone's lawn, are of sufficient value to outweigh the social interest in order and morality that has traditionally placed such fighting words outside the First Amendment.[4] Indeed, by characterizing fighting words as a form of "debate", ante, 505 U.S. at 392, the majority legitimates hate speech as a form of public discussion.

[403] Furthermore, the Court obscures the line between speech that could be regulated freely on the basis of content (i.e., the narrow categories of expression falling outside the First Amendment) and that which could be regulated on the basis of content only upon a showing of a compelling state interest (i.e., all remaining expression). By placing fighting words, which the Court has long held to be valueless, on at least equal constitutional footing with political discourse and other forms of speech that we have deemed to have the greatest social value, the majority devalues the latter category. See Burson v.

Freeman, 504 U.S. at 196; Eu v. San Francisco Cty. Democratic Central Comm., 489 U.S. 214, 222-223, 103 L. Ed. 2d 271, 109 S. Ct. 1013 (1989).

In a second break with precedent, the Court refuses to sustain the ordinance even though it would survive under the strict scrutiny applicable to other protected expression. Assuming, arguendo, that the St. Paul ordinance is a content-based regulation of protected expression, it nevertheless would pass First Amendment review under settled law upon a showing that the regulation "'is necessary to serve a compelling state interest and is narrowly drawn to achieve that 2nd.'" Simon & Schuster, Inc. v. Members of N. Y. State Crime Victims Bd., 502 U.S. 105, 118, 116 L. Ed. 2d 476, 112 S. Ct. 501 (1991) (quoting Arkansas Writers' Project, Inc. v. Ragland, 481 U.S. 221, 231, 95 L. Ed. 2d 209, 107 S. Ct. 1722 (1987)). St. Paul has urged that its ordinance, in the words of the majority, "helps to ensure the basic human rights of members of groups that have historically been subjected to discrimination . . . ." Ante, 505 U.S. at 395. The Court expressly concedes that this interest is compelling and is promoted by the ordinance. Ibid. Nevertheless, the Court treats strict scrutiny analysis as irrelevant to the constitutionality of the legislation:

"The dispositive question . . . is whether content discrimination is reasonably necessary to achieve St. Paul's compelling interests; it plainly is not. An ordinance not [404] limited to the favored topics, for example, would have precisely the same beneficial effect." Ante, 505 U.S. at 395-396.

Under the majority's view, a narrowly drawn, content-based ordinance could never pass constitutional muster if the object of that legislation could be accomplished by banning a wider category of speech. This appears to be a general renunciation of strict scrutiny review, a fundamental tool of First Amendment analysis.[5]

---

[3] The assortment of exceptions the Court attaches to its rule belies the majority's claim, see ante, 505 U.S. at 387, that its new theory is truly concerned with content discrimination. See Part I-C, infra (discussing the exceptions).

[4] This does not suggest, of course, that cross burning is always unprotected. Burning a cross at a political rally would almost certainly be protected expression. Cf. Brandenburg v. Ohio, 395 U.S. 444, 445, 23 L. Ed. 2d 430, 89 S. Ct. 1827 (1969). But in such a context, the cross burning could not be characterized as a "direct personal insult or an invitation to exchange fisticuffs," Texas v. Johnson, 491 U.S. 397, 409, 105 L. Ed. 2d 342, 109 S. Ct. 2533 (1989), to which the fighting words doctrine, see Part II, infra, applies.

[5] The majority relies on Boos v. Barry, 485 U.S. 312, 99 L. Ed. 2d 333, 108 S. Ct. 1157 (1988), in arguing that the availability of content-neutral alternatives "'undercuts significantly'" a claim that content-based legislation is "'necessary to serve the asserted [compelling] interest.'" Ante, 505 U.S. at 395 (quoting Boos, 485 U.S. at 329, and Burson v. Freeman, 504 U.S. 191, 199, 119 L. Ed. 2d 5, 112 S. Ct. 1846 (1992) (plurality opinion)). Boos does not support the majority's analysis. In Boos, Congress already had decided that the challenged legislation was not necessary, and the Court pointedly deferred to this choice. 485 U.S. at 329. St. Paul lawmakers have made no such legislative choice.

Moreover, in Boos, the Court held that the challenged statute was not narrowly tailored because a less restrictive alternative was available. Ibid. But the Court's analysis today turns Boos inside out by substituting the majority's policy judgment that a more restrictive alternative could adequately serve the compelling need identified by St. Paul lawmakers. The result would be: (a) a statute that was not tailored to fit the need identified by the government; and (b) a greater restriction on fighting words, even though the Court clearly believes that

This abandonment of the doctrine is inexplicable in light of our decision in Burson v. Freeman, 504 U.S. 191, 119 L. Ed. 2d 5, 112 S. Ct. 1846 (1992), which was handed down just a month ago.[6] In Burson, seven of the eight participating Members of the Court agreed that the strict scrutiny standard applied in a case involving a First Amendment challenge to a content-based statute. See id., at 198 (plurality opinion); id., at 217 (STEVENS, J., [405] dissenting).[7] The statute at issue prohibited the solicitation of votes and the display or distribution of campaign materials within 100 feet of the entrance to a polling place. The plurality concluded that the legislation survived strict scrutiny because the State had asserted a compelling interest in regulating electioneering near polling places and because the statute at issue was narrowly tailored to accomplish that goal. Id., at 208-210.

Significantly, the statute in Burson did not proscribe all speech near polling places; it restricted only political speech. Id., at 197. The Burson plurality, which included THE CHIEF JUSTICE and JUSTICE KENNEDY, concluded that the distinction between types of speech required application of strict scrutiny, but it squarely rejected the proposition that the legislation failed First Amendment review because it could have been drafted in broader, content-neutral terms:

"States adopt laws to address the problems that confront them. The First Amendment does not require States to regulate for problems that do not exist." Id., at 207 (emphasis added).

This reasoning is in direct conflict with the majority's analysis in the present case, which leaves two options to lawmakers attempting to regulate expressions of violence: (1) enact a sweeping prohibition on an entire class of speech (thereby requiring "regulation for problems that do not exist"); or (2) not legislate at all.

Had the analysis adopted by the majority in the present case been applied in Burson, the challenged election law would have failed constitutional review, for its content-based distinction between political and nonpolitical speech could not have been

characterized as "reasonably necessary," ante, [406] at 395, to achieve the State's interest in regulating polling place premises.[8]

As with its rejection of the Court's categorical analysis, the majority offers no reasoned basis for discarding our firmly established strict scrutiny analysis at this time. The majority appears to believe that its doctrinal revisionism is necessary to prevent our elected lawmakers from prohibiting libel against members of one political party but not another and from enacting similarly preposterous laws. Ante, 505 U.S. at 384. The majority is misguided.

Although the First Amendment does not apply to categories of unprotected speech, such as fighting words, the Equal Protection Clause requires that the regulation of unprotected speech be rationally related to a legitimate government interest. A defamation statute that drew distinctions on the basis of political affiliation or "an ordinance prohibiting only those legally obscene works that contain criticism of the city government," ibid., would unquestionably fail national-basis review.[9]

[407] Turning to the St. Paul ordinance and assuming, arguendo, as the majority does, that the ordinance is not constitutionally overbroad (but see Part II, infra), there is no question that it would pass equal protection review. The ordinance proscribes a subset of "fighting words," those that injure "on the basis of race, color, creed, religion or gender." This selective regulation reflects the city's judgment that harms based on race, color, creed, religion, or gender are more pressing public concerns than the harms

---

fighting words have protected expressive content. Ante, 505 U.S. at 384-385.

[6] Earlier this Term, seven of the eight participating Members of the Court agreed that strict scrutiny analysis applied in Simon & Schuster, Inc. v. Members of N. Y. State Crime Victims Bd., 502 U.S. 105, 116 L. Ed. 2d 476, 112 S. Ct. 501 (1991), in which we struck down New York's "Son of Sam" law, which required "that an accused or convicted criminal's income from works describing his crime be deposited in an escrow account." Id., at 108.

[7] The Burson dissenters did not complain that the plurality erred in applying strict scrutiny; they objected that the plurality was not sufficiently rigorous in its review. 504 U.S. at 225-226 (STEVENS, J., dissenting).

[8] JUSTICE SCALIA concurred in the judgment in Burson, reasoning that the statute, "though content based, is constitutional [as] a reasonable, viewpoint-neutral regulation of a nonpublic forum." Id., at 214. However, nothing in his reasoning in the present case suggests that a content-based ban on fighting words would be constitutional were that ban limited to nonpublic fora. Taken together, the two opinions suggest that, in some settings, political speech, to which "the First Amendment 'has its fullest and most urgent application,'" is entitled to less constitutional protection than fighting words. Eu v. San Francisco Cty. Democratic Central Comm., 489 U.S. 214, 223, 103 L. Ed. 2d 271, 109 S. Ct. 1013 (1989) (quoting Monitor Patriot Co. v. Roy, 401 U.S. 265, 272, 28 L. Ed. 2d 35, 91 S. Ct. 621 (1971)).

[9] The majority is mistaken in stating that a ban on obscene works critical of government would fail equal protection review only because the ban would violate the First Amendment. Ante, 505 U.S. at 384-385, n.4. While decisions such as Police Dept. of Chicago v. Mosley, 408 U.S. 92, 33 L. Ed. 2d 212, 92 S. Ct. 2286 (1972), recognize that First Amendment principles may be relevant to an equal protection claim challenging distinctions that impact on protected expression, id., at 95-99, there is no basis for linking First and Fourteenth Amendment analysis in a case involving unprotected expression. Certainly, one need not resort to First Amendment principles to conclude that the sort of improbable legislation the majority hypothesizes is based on senseless distinctions.

caused by other fighting words. In light of our Nation's long and painful experience with discrimination, this determination is plainly reasonable. Indeed, as the majority concedes, the interest is compelling. Ante, 505 U.S. at 395.

The Court has patched up its argument with an apparently nonexhaustive list of ad hoc exceptions, in what can be viewed either as an attempt to confine the effects of its decision to the facts of this case, see post, 505 U.S. at 415 (BLACKMUN, J., concurring in judgment), or as an effort to anticipate some of the questions that will arise from its radical revision of First Amendment law.

For instance, if the majority were to give general application to the rule on which it decides this case, today's decision would call into question the constitutionality of the statute making it illegal to threaten the life of the President. 18 U. S. C. § 871. See Watts v. United States, 394 U.S. 705, 22 L. Ed. 2d 664, 89 S. Ct. 1399 (1969) (per curiam). Surely, this statute, by singling out certain threats, incorporates a content-based distinction; it indicates that the government especially disfavors threats against the President as opposed to threats against all others.[10] [408] See ante, 505 U.S. at 391. But because the Government could prohibit all threats and not just those directed against the President, under the Court's theory, the compelling reasons justifying the enactment of special legislation to safeguard the President would be irrelevant, and the statute would fail First Amendment review.

To save the statute, the majority has engrafted the following exception onto its newly announced First Amendment rule: Content-based distinctions may be drawn within an unprotected category of speech if the basis for the distinctions is "the very reason the entire class of speech at issue is proscribable." Ante, 505 U.S. at 388. Thus, the argument goes, the statute making it illegal to threaten the life of the President is constitutional, "since the reasons why threats of violence are outside the First Amendment (protecting individuals from the fear of violence, from the disruption that fear engenders, and from the possibility that the threatened violence will occur) have special force when applied to the person of the President." Ibid. The exception swallows the majority's rule. Certainly, it should apply to the St. Paul ordinance, since "the reasons why [fighting words] are outside the First Amendment . . . have special force when applied to [groups that have historically been subjected to discrimination]."

To avoid the result of its own analysis, the Court suggests that fighting words are simply a mode of communication, rather than a content-based category, and that the St. Paul ordinance has not singled out a particularly objectionable mode of communication. Ante, 505 U.S. at 386, 393. Again, the majority confuses the issue. A prohibition on fighting words is not a time, place, or manner restriction; it is a ban on a class of speech that conveys an overriding message of personal injury and imminent violence, Chaplinsky, 315 U.S. at 572, a message that is at its ugliest when directed against groups [409] that have long been the targets of discrimination. Accordingly, the ordinance falls within the first exception to the majority's theory.

As its second exception, the Court posits that certain content-based regulations will survive under the new regime if the regulated subclass " happens to be associated with particular 'secondary effects' of the speech . . .," ante, 505 U.S. at 389, which the majority treats as encompassing instances in which "words can . . . violate laws directed not against speech but against conduct . . .," ibid.[11] Again, there is a simple explanation for the Court's eagerness to craft an exception to its new First Amendment rule: Under the general rule the Court applies in this case, Title VII hostile work environment claims would suddenly be unconstitutional. Title VII of the Civil Rights Act of 1964 makes it unlawful to discriminate "because of [an] individual's race, color, religion, sex, or national origin," 42 U. S. C. § 2000e-2(a)(1), and the regulations covering hostile workplace claims forbid "sexual harassment," which includes "unwelcome sexual advances, requests for sexual favors, and other verbal or physical conduct of a sexual nature" that create "an intimidating, hostile, or offensive working environment," 29 CFR 1604.11(a) (1991).

The regulation does not prohibit workplace harassment generally; it focuses on what the majority would characterize as the "disfavored topic" of sexual harassment. Ante, 505 U.S. at 391. In this way, Title VII is similar to the St. Paul ordinance that the majority condemns because it "imposes special prohibitions on those speakers who express views on disfavored subjects." Ibid. Under the broad principle the Court uses to decide the present case, [410] hostile work environment claims based on sexual harassment should fail First Amendment review; because a general ban on harassment in the workplace would cover the problem of sexual harassment, any attempt to proscribe the subcategory of sexually harassing expression would violate the First Amendment.

---

[10] Indeed, such a law is content based in and of itself because it distinguishes between threatening and non-threatening speech.

[11] The consequences of the majority's conflation of the rarely used secondary effects standard and the O'Brien test for conduct incorporating "speech" and "nonspeech" elements, see generally United States v. O'Brien, 391 U.S. 367, 376-377, 20 L. Ed. 2d 672, 88 S. Ct. 1673 (1968), present another question that I fear will haunt us and the lower courts in the aftermath of the majority's opinion.

Hence, the majority's second exception, which the Court indicates would insulate a Title VII hostile work environment claim from an underinclusiveness challenge because "sexually derogatory 'fighting words' . . . may produce a violation of Title VII's general prohibition against sexual discrimination in employment practices." Ante, 505 U.S. at 389. But application of this exception to a hostile work environ-ment claim does not hold up under close examination.

First, the hostile work environment regulation is not keyed to the presence or absence of an economic quid pro quo, Meritor Savings Bank, F. S. B. v. Vinson, 477 U.S. 57, 65, 91 L. Ed. 2d 49, 106 S. Ct. 2399 (1986), but to the impact of the speech on the victimized worker. Consequently, the regulation would no more fall within a secondary effects exception than does the St. Paul ordinance. Ante, 505 U.S. at 394. Second, the majority's focus on the statute's general prohibition on discrimination glosses over the language of the specific regulation governing hostile working environment, which reaches beyond any "incidental" effect on speech. United States v. O'Brien, 391 U.S. 367, 376, 20 L. Ed. 2d 672, 88 S. Ct. 1673 (1968). If the relationship between the broader statute and specific regulation is sufficient to bring the Title VII regulation within O'Brien, then all St. Paul need do to bring its ordinance within this exception is to add some prefatory language concerning discrimination generally.

As to the third exception to the Court's theory for deciding this case, the majority concocts a catchall exclusion to protect against unforeseen problems, a concern that is heightened here given the lack of briefing on the majority's decisional theory. This final exception would apply in cases in which "there is no realistic possibility that official suppression of ideas is afoot." Ante, 505 U.S. at 390. As I have demonstrated, [411] this case does not concern the official suppression of ideas. See 505 U.S. at 401. The majority discards this notion out of hand. Ante, 505 U.S. at 395.

As I see it, the Court's theory does not work and will do nothing more than confuse the law. Its selection of this case to rewrite First Amendment law is particularly inexplicable, because the whole problem could have been avoided by deciding this case under settled First Amendment principles.

Although I disagree with the Court's analysis, I do agree with its conclusion: The St. Paul ordinance is unconstitutional. However, I would decide the case on overbreadth grounds.

We have emphasized time and again that overbreadth doctrine is an exception to the established principle that "a person to whom a statute may constitutionally be applied will not be heard to challenge that statute on the ground that it may conceivably be applied unconstitutionally to others, in other situations not before the Court." Broadrick v. Oklahoma, 413 U.S. at 610; Brockett v. Spokane Arcades, Inc., 472 U.S. at 503-504. A defendant being prosecuted for speech or expressive conduct may challenge the law on its face if it reaches protected expression, even when that person's activities are not protected by the First Amendment. This is because "the possible harm to society in permitting some unprotected speech to go unpunished is outweighed by the possibility that protected speech of others may be muted." Broadrick, 413 U.S. at 612; Osborne v. Ohio, 495 U.S. at 112, n.8; New York v. Ferber, 458 U.S. at 768-769; Schaumburg v. Citizens for a Better Environment, 444 U.S. 620, 634, 63 L. Ed. 2d 73, 100 S. Ct. 826 (1980); Gooding v. Wilson, 405 U.S. 518, 521, 31 L. Ed. 2d 408, 92 S. Ct. 1103 (1972).

However, we have consistently held that, because overbreadth analysis is "strong medicine," it may be invoked to strike an entire statute only when the overbreadth of the statute is not only "real, but substantial as well, judged in relation to the statute's plainly legitimate sweep," Broadrick, [412] 413 U.S. at 615, and when the statute is not susceptible to limitation or partial invalidation, id., at 613; Board of Airport Comm'rs of Los Angeles v. Jews for Jesus, Inc., 482 U.S. 569, 574, 96 L. Ed. 2d 500, 107 S. Ct. 2568 (1987). "When a federal court is dealing with a federal statute challenged as overbroad, it should . . . construe the statute to avoid constitutional problems, if the statute is subject to a limiting construction." Ferber, 458 U.S. at 769, n.24. Of course, "[a] state court is also free to deal with a state statute in the same way." Ibid. See, e.g., Osborne, 495 U.S. at 113-114.

Petitioner contends that the St. Paul ordinance is not susceptible to a narrowing construction and that the ordinance therefore should be considered as written, and not as construed by the Minnesota Supreme Court. Petitioner is wrong. Where a state court has interpreted a provision of state law, we cannot ignore that interpretation, even if it is not one that we would have reached if we were construing the statute in the first instance. Ibid.; Kolender v. Dawson, 461 U.S. 352, 355, 75 L. Ed. 2d 903, 103 S. Ct. 1855 (1983); Hoffman Estates v. Flipside, Hoffman Estates, Inc., 455 U.S. 489, 494, n.5, 71 L. Ed. 2d 362, 102 S. Ct. 1186 (1982).[12]

---

[12] Petitioner can derive no support from our statement in Virginia v. American Booksellers Assn., Inc., 484 U.S. 383, 397, 98 L. Ed. 2d 782, 108 S. Ct. 636 (1988), that "the statute must be 'readily susceptible' to the limitation; we will not rewrite a state law to conform it to constitutional requirements." In American Booksellers, no state court had construed the language in dispute. In that instance, we certified a question to the state court so that it would have an opportunity to provide a narrowing interpretation. Ibid. In

Of course, the mere presence of a state court interpretation does not insulate a statute from overbreadth review. We have stricken legislation when the construction supplied by the state court failed to cure the overbreadth problem. [413] See, e.g., Lewis v. New Orleans, 415 U.S. 130, 132-133, 39 L. Ed. 2d 214, 94 S. Ct. 970 (1974); Gooding, 405 U.S. at 524-525. But in such cases, we have looked to the statute as construed in determining whether it contravened the First Amendment. Here, the Minnesota Supreme Court has provided an authoritative construction of the St. Paul anti-bias ordinance. Consideration of petitioner's overbreadth claim must be based on that interpretation.

I agree with petitioner that the ordinance is invalid on its face. Although the ordinance as construed reaches categories of speech that are constitutionally unprotected, it also criminalizes a substantial amount of expression that – however repugnant – is shielded by the First Amendment.

In attempting to narrow the scope of the St. Paul anti-bias ordinance, the Minnesota Supreme Court relied upon two of the categories of speech and expressive conduct that fall outside the First Amendment's protective sphere: words that incite "imminent lawless action," Brandenburg v. Ohio, 395 U.S. 444, 449, 23 L. Ed. 2d 430, 89 S. Ct. 1827 (1969), and "fighting" words, Chaplinsky v. New Hampshire, 315 U.S. at 571-572. The Minnesota Supreme Court erred in its application of the Chaplinsky fighting words test and consequently interpreted the St. Paul ordinance in a fashion that rendered the ordinance facially overbroad.

In construing the St. Paul ordinance, the Minnesota Supreme Court drew upon the definition of fighting words that appears in Chaplinsky – words "which by their very utterance inflict injury or tend to incite an immediate breach of the peace." Id., at 572. However, the Minnesota court was far from clear in identifying the "injuries" inflicted by the expression that St. Paul sought to regulate. Indeed, the Minnesota court emphasized (tracking the language of the ordinance) that "the ordinance censors only those displays that one knows or should know will create anger, alarm or resentment based on racial, ethnic, gender or religious bias." In re Welfare of R. A. V., 464 N.W.2d 507, 510 (1991). I [414] therefore understand the court to have ruled that St. Paul may constitutionally prohibit expression that "by its very utterance" causes "anger, alarm or resentment."

Our fighting words cases have made clear, however, that such generalized reactions are not sufficient to strip expression of its constitutional protection. The mere fact that expressive activity causes hurt feelings, offense, or resentment does not render the expression unprotected. See United States v. Eichman, 496 U.S. 310, 319, 110 L. Ed. 2d 287, 110 S. Ct. 2404 (1990); Texas v. Johnson, 491 U.S. 397, 409, 414, 105 L. Ed. 2d 342, 109 S. Ct. 2533 (1989); Hustler Magazine, Inc. v. Falwell, 485 U.S. 46, 55-56, 99 L. Ed. 2d 41, 108 S. Ct. 876 (1988); FCC v. Pacifica Foundation, 438 U.S. 726, 745, 57 L. Ed. 2d 1073, 98 S. Ct. 3026 (1978); Hess v. Indiana, 414 U.S. 105, 107-108, 38 L. Ed. 2d 303, 94 S. Ct. 326 (1973); Cohen v. California, 403 U.S. 15, 20, 29 L. Ed. 2d 284, 91 S. Ct. 1780 (1971); Street v. New York, 394 U.S. 576, 592, 22 L. Ed. 2d 572, 89 S. Ct. 1354 (1969); Terminiello v. Chicago, 337 U.S. 1, 93 L. Ed. 1131, 69 S. Ct. 894 (1949).

In the First Amendment context, "criminal statutes must be scrutinized with particular care; those that make unlawful a substantial amount of constitutionally protected conduct may be held facially invalid even if they also have legitimate application." Houston v. Hill, 482 U.S. 451, 459, 96 L. Ed. 2d 398, 107 S. Ct. 2502 (1987) (citation omitted). The St. Paul anti-bias ordinance is such a law. Although the ordinance reaches conduct that is unprotected, it also makes criminal expressive conduct that causes only hurt feelings, offense, or resentment, and is protected by the First Amendment. Cf. Lewis, 415 U.S. at 132.[13]

The ordinance is therefore fatally overbroad and invalid on its face.

[415] Today, the Court has disregarded two established principles of First Amendment law without providing a coherent replacement theory. Its decision is an arid, doctrinaire interpretation, driven by the frequently irresistible impulse of judges to tinker with the First Amendment. The decision is mischievous at best and will surely confuse the lower courts. I join the judgment, but not the folly of the opinion.

Erznoznik v. Jacksonville, 422 U.S. 205, 216, 45 L. Ed. 2d 125, 95 S. Ct. 2268 (1975), the other case upon which petitioner principally relies, we observed not only that the ordinance at issue was not "by its plain terms . . . easily susceptible of a narrowing construction," but that the state courts had made no effort to restrict the scope of the statute when it was challenged on overbreadth grounds.

---

[13] Although the First Amendment protects offensive speech, Johnson v. Texas, 491 U.S. at 414, it does not require us to be subjected to such expression at all times, in all settings. We have held that such expression may be proscribed when it intrudes upon a "captive audience." Frisby v. Schultz, 487 U.S. 474, 484-485, 101 L. Ed. 2d 420, 108 S. Ct. 2495 (1988); FCC v. Pacifica Foundation, 438 U.S. 726, 748-749, 57 L. Ed. 2d 1073, 98 S. Ct. 3026 (1978). And expression may be limited when it merges into conduct. United States v. O'Brien, 391 U.S. 367, 20 L. Ed. 2d 672, 88 S. Ct. 1673 (1968); cf. Meritor Savings Bank, F. S. B. v. Vinson, 477 U.S. 57, 65, 91 L. Ed. 2d 49, 106 S. Ct. 2399 (1986). However, because of the manner in which the Minnesota Supreme Court construed the St. Paul ordinance, those issues are not before us in this case.

JUSTICE BLACKMUN, CONCURRING in the judgment.

I regret what the Court has done in this case. The majority opinion signals one of two possibilities: It will serve as precedent for future cases, or it will not. Either result is disheartening.

In the first instance, by deciding that a State cannot regulate speech that causes great harm unless it also regulates speech that does not (setting law and logic on their heads), the Court seems to abandon the categorical approach, and inevitably to relax the level of scrutiny applicable to content-based laws. As JUSTICE WHITE points out, this weakens the traditional protections of speech. If all expressive activity must be accorded the same protection, that protection will be scant. The simple reality is that the Court will never provide child pornography or cigarette advertising the level of protection customarily granted political speech. If we are forbidden to categorize, as the Court has done here, we shall reduce protection across the board. It is sad that in its effort to reach a satisfying result in this case, the Court is willing to weaken First Amendment protections.

In the second instance is the possibility that this case will not significantly alter First Amendment jurisprudence but, instead, will be regarded as an aberration – a case where the Court manipulated doctrine to strike down an ordinance whose premise it opposed, namely, that racial threats and verbal assaults are of greater harm than other fighting words. I fear that the Court has been distracted from its [416] proper mission by the temptation to decide the issue over "politically correct speech" and "cultural diversity," neither of which is presented here. If this is the meaning of today's opinion, it is perhaps even more regrettable.

I see no First Amendment values that are compromised by a law that prohibits hoodlums from driving minorities out of their homes by burning crosses on their lawns, but I see great harm in preventing the people of Saint Paul from specifically punishing the race-based fighting words that so prejudice their community.

I concur in the judgment, however, because I agree with JUSTICE WHITE that this particular ordinance reaches beyond fighting words to speech protected by the First Amendment.

JUSTICE STEVENS, with whom JUSTICE WHITE and JUSTICE BLACKMUN join as to Part I, concurring in the judgment.

Conduct that creates special risks or causes special harms may be prohibited by special rules. Lighting a fire near an ammunition dump or a gasoline storage tank is especially dangerous; such behavior may be punished more severely than burning trash in a vacant lot. Threatening someone because of her race or religious beliefs may cause particularly severe trauma or touch off a riot, and threatening a high public official may cause substantial social disruption; such threats may be punished more severely than threats against someone based on, say, his support of a particular athletic team. There are legitimate, reasonable, and neutral justifications for such special rules.

This case involves the constitutionality of one such ordinance. Because the regulated conduct has some communicative content – a message of racial, religious, or gender hostility – the ordinance raises two quite different First Amendment questions. Is the ordinance "overbroad" because [417] it prohibits too much speech? If not, is it "underbroad" because it does not prohibit enough speech?

In answering these questions, my colleagues today wrestle with two broad principles: first, that certain "categories of expression [including 'fighting words'] are 'not within the area of constitutionally protected speech,'" ante, 505 U.S. at 400 (WHITE, J., concurring in judgment); and second, that "content-based regulations [of expression] are presumptively invalid," ante, 505 U.S. at 382 (majority opinion). Although in past opinions the Court has repeated both of these maxims, it has – quite rightly – adhered to neither with the absolutism suggested by my colleagues. Thus, while I agree that the St. Paul ordinance is unconstitutionally overbroad for the reasons stated in Part II of JUSTICE WHITE's opinion, I write separately to suggest how the allure of absolute principles has skewed the analysis of both the majority and JUSTICE WHITE's opinions.

Fifty years ago, the Court articulated a categorical approach to First Amendment jurisprudence.

"There are certain well-defined and narrowly limited classes of speech, the prevention and punishment of which have never been thought to raise any Constitutional problem. . . . It has been well observed that such utterances are no essential part of any exposition of ideas, and are of such slight social value as a step to truth that any benefit that may be derived from them is clearly outweighed by the social interest in order and morality." Chaplinsky v. New Hampshire, 315 U.S. 568, 571-572, 86 L. Ed. 1031, 62 S. Ct. 766 (1942).

We have, as JUSTICE WHITE observes, often described such categories of expression as "not within the area of constitutionally protected speech." Roth v. United States, 354 U.S. 476, 483, 1 L. Ed. 2d 1498, 77 S. Ct. 1304 (1957).

[418] The Court today revises this categorical approach. It is not, the Court rules, that certain "categories" of expression are "unprotected," but rather that certain "elements" of expression are wholly "proscribable." To the Court, an expressive act, like a chemical compound, consists of more than one element. Although the act may be regulated because it contains a proscribable element, it may not be regulated on the basis of another

(nonproscribable) element it also contains. Thus, obscene antigovernment speech may be regulated because it is obscene, but not because it is antigovernment. Ante, 505 U.S. at 384. It is this revision of the categorical approach that allows the Court to assume that the St. Paul ordinance proscribes only fighting words, while at the same time concluding that the ordinance is invalid because it imposes a content-based regulation on expressive activity.

As an initial matter, the Court's revision of the categorical approach seems to me something of an adventure in a doctrinal wonderland, for the concept of "obscene antigovernment" speech is fantastical. The category of the obscene is very narrow; to be obscene, expression must be found by the trier of fact to "appeal to the prurient interest, . . . depict or describe, in a patently offensive way, sexual conduct, [and], taken as a whole, lack serious literary, artistic, political, or scientific value." Miller v. California, 413 U.S. 15, 24, 37 L. Ed. 2d 419, 93 S. Ct. 2607 (1973) (emphasis added). "Obscene anti-government" speech, then, is a contra-diction in terms: If expression is anti-government, it does not "lack serious . . . political . . . value" and cannot be obscene.

The Court attempts to bolster its argument by likening its novel analysis to that applied to restrictions on the time, place, or manner of expression or on expressive conduct. It is true that loud speech in favor of the Republican Party can be regulated because it is loud, but not because it is pro-Republican; and it is true that the public burning of the American flag can be regulated because it involves public burning and not because it involves the flag. But these analogies [419] are inapposite. In each of these examples, the two elements (e.g., loudness and pro-Republican orientation) can coexist; in the case of "obscene antigovernment" speech, however, the presence of one element ("obscenity") by definition means the absence of the other. To my mind, it is unwise and unsound to craft a new doctrine based on such highly speculative hypotheticals.

I am, however, even more troubled by the second step of the Court's analysis – namely, its conclusion that the St. Paul ordinance is an unconstitutional content-based regulation of speech. Drawing on broadly worded dicta, the Court establishes a near-absolute ban on content-based regulations of expression and holds that the First Amendment prohibits the regulation of fighting words by subject matter. Thus, while the Court rejects the "all-or-nothing-at-all" nature of the categorical approach, ante, 505 U.S. at 384, it promptly embraces an absolutism of its own: Within a particular "proscribable" category of expression, the Court holds, a government must either proscribe all speech

or no speech at all.[1] This aspect of the Court's ruling fundamentally misunderstands the role and constitutional status of content-based regulations on speech, conflicts with the very nature of First Amendment jurisprudence, and disrupts well-settled principles of First Amendment law.

[420] Although the Court has, on occasion, declared that content-based regulations of speech are "never permitted," Police Dept. of Chicago v. Mosley, 408 U.S. 92, 99, 33 L. Ed. 2d 212, 92 S. Ct. 2286 (1972), such claims are overstated. Indeed, in Mosley itself, the Court indicated that Chicago's selective proscription of nonlabor picketing was not per se unconstitutional, but rather could be upheld if the city demonstrated that nonlabor picketing was "clearly more disruptive than [labor] picketing." Id., at 100. Contrary to the broad dicta in Mosley and elsewhere, our decisions demonstrate that content-based distinctions, far from being presumptively invalid, are an inevitable and indispensable aspect of a coherent understanding of the First Amendment.

This is true at every level of First Amendment law. In broadest terms, our entire First Amendment jurisprudence creates a regime based on the content of speech. The scope of the First Amendment is determined by the content of expressive activity: Although the First Amendment broadly protects "speech," it does not protect the right to "fix prices, breach contracts, make false warranties, place bets with bookies, threaten, [or] extort." Schauer, Categories and the First Amendment: A Play in Three Acts, 34 Vand. L. Rev. 265, 270 (1981). Whether an agreement among competitors is a violation of the Sherman Act or protected activity under the Noerr-Pennington doctrine[2] hinges upon the content of the agreement. Similarly, "the line between permissible advocacy and impermissible incitement to crime or violence depends, not merely on the setting in which the speech occurs, but also on exactly what the speaker had to say." Young v.

---

[1] The Court disputes this characterization because it has crafted two exceptions, one for "certain media or markets" and the other for content discrimination based upon "the very reason that the entire class of speech at issue is proscribable." Ante, 505 U.S. at 388. These exceptions are, at best, ill defined. The Court does not tell us whether, with respect to the former, fighting words such as cross burning could be proscribed only in certain neighborhoods where the threat of violence is particularly severe, or whether, with respect to the second category, fighting words that create a particular risk of harm (such as a race riot) would be proscribable. The hypothetical and illusory category of these two exceptions persuades me that either my description of the Court's analysis is accurate or that the Court does not in fact mean much of what it says in its opinion.

[2] See Mine Workers v. Pennington, 381 U.S. 657, 14 L. Ed. 2d 626, 85 S. Ct. 1585 (1965); Eastern Railroad Presidents Conference v. Noerr Motor Freight, Inc., 365 U.S. 127, 5 L. Ed. 2d 464, 81 S. Ct. 523 (1961).

American Mini Theatres, Inc., 427 U.S. 50, 66, 49 L. Ed. 2d 310, 96 S. Ct. 2440 (1976) (plurality opinion); see also Musser v. Utah, 333 U.S. 95, 100-103, 92 L. Ed. 562, 68 S. Ct. 397 (1948) (Rutledge, J., dissenting).

[421] Likewise, whether speech falls within one of the categories of "unprotected" or "proscribable" expression is determined, in part, by its content. Whether a magazine is obscene, a gesture a fighting word, or a photograph child pornography is determined, in part, by its content. Even within categories of protected expression, the First Amendment status of speech is fixed by its content. New York Times Co. v. Sullivan, 376 U.S. 254, 11 L. Ed. 2d 686, 84 S. Ct. 710 (1964), and Dun & Bradstreet, Inc. v. Greenmoss Builders, Inc., 472 U.S. 749, 86 L. Ed. 2d 593, 105 S. Ct. 2939 (1985), establish that the level of protection given to speech depends upon its subject matter: Speech about public officials or matters of public concern receives greater protection than speech about other topics. It can, therefore, scarcely be said that the regulation of expressive activity cannot be predicated on its content: Much of our First Amendment jurisprudence is premised on the assumption that content makes a difference.

Consistent with this general premise, we have frequently upheld content-based regulations of speech. For example, in Young v. American Mini Theatres, the Court upheld zoning ordinances that regulated movie theaters based on the content of the films shown. In FCC v. Pacifica Foundation, 438 U.S. 726, 57 L. Ed. 2d 1073, 98 S. Ct. 3026 (1978) (plurality opinion), we upheld a restriction on the broadcast of specific indecent words. In Lehman v. Shaker Heights, 418 U.S. 298, 41 L. Ed. 2d 770, 94 S. Ct. 2714 (1974) (plurality opinion), we upheld a city law that permitted commercial advertising, but prohibited political advertising, on city buses. In Broadrick v. Oklahoma, 413 U.S. 601, 37 L. Ed. 2d 830, 93 S. Ct. 2908 (1973), we upheld a state law that restricted the speech of state employees, but only as concerned partisan political matters. We have long recognized the power of the Federal Trade Commission to regulate misleading advertising and labeling, see, e.g., Jacob Siegel Co. v. FTC, 327 U.S. 608, 90 L. Ed. 888, 66 S. Ct. 758 (1946), and the National Labor Relations Board's power to regulate an employer's election-related speech on the basis of its content, see, e.g., NLRB v. Gissel Packing Co., 395 U.S. 575, 616-618, 23 L. Ed. 2d 547, 89 S. Ct. 1918 (1969). [422] It is also beyond question that the Government may choose to limit advertisements for cigarettes, see 15 U. S. C. §§ 1331-1340,[3] but not for cigars; choose to regulate airline advertising, see Morales v. Trans World Airlines, Inc., 504 U.S. 374, 119 L. Ed. 2d 157, 112 S. Ct. 2031 (1992), but not bus advertising; or choose to monitor solicitation by lawyers, see Ohralik v. Ohio State Bar Assn., 436 U.S. 447, 56 L. Ed. 2d 444, 98 S. Ct. 1912 (1978), but not by doctors.

All of these cases involved the selective regulation of speech based on content – precisely the sort of regulation the Court invalidates today. Such selective regulations are unavoidably content based, but they are not, in my opinion, "presumptively invalid." As these many decisions and examples demonstrate, the prohibition on content-based regulations is not nearly as total as the Mosley dictum suggests.

Disregarding this vast body of case law, the Court today goes beyond even the overstatement in Mosley and applies the prohibition on content-based regulation to speech that the Court had until today considered wholly "unprotected" by the First Amendment – namely, fighting words. This new absolutism in the prohibition of content-based regulations severely contorts the fabric of settled First Amendment law.

Our First Amendment decisions have created a rough hierarchy in the constitutional protection of speech. Core political speech occupies the highest, most protected position; commercial speech and nonobscene, sexually explicit speech are regarded as a sort of second-class expression; obscenity and fighting words receive the least protection of all. Assuming that the Court is correct that this last class of speech is not wholly "unprotected," it certainly does not follow that fighting words and obscenity receive the same sort of protection afforded core political speech. Yet in ruling that proscribable speech cannot be regulated based on subject [423] matter, the Court does just that.[4] Perversely, this gives fighting words greater protection than is afforded commercial speech. If Congress can prohibit false advertising directed at airline passengers without also prohibiting false advertising directed at bus passengers and if a city can prohibit political advertisements in its buses while allowing

_____

[3] See also Packer Corp. v. Utah, 285 U.S. 105, 76 L. Ed. 643, 52 S. Ct. 273 (1932) (Brandeis, J.) (upholding a statute that prohibited the advertisement of cigarettes on billboards and streetcar placards).

[4] The Court states that the prohibition on content-based regulations "applies differently in the context of proscribable speech" than in the context of other speech, ante, 505 U.S. at 387, but its analysis belies that claim. The Court strikes down the St. Paul ordinance because it regulates fighting words based on subject matter, despite the fact that, as demonstrated above, we have long upheld regulations of commercial speech based on subject matter. The Court's self-description is inapt: By prohibiting the regulation of fighting words based on its subject matter, the Court provides the same protection to fighting words as is currently provided to core political speech.

other advertisements, it is ironic to hold that a city cannot regulate fighting words based on "race, color, creed, religion or gender" while leaving unregulated fighting words based on "union membership . . . or homosexuality." Ante, 505 U.S. at 391. The Court today turns First Amendment law on its head: Communication that was once entirely unprotected (and that still can be wholly proscribed) is now entitled to greater protection than commercial speech – and possibly greater protection than core political speech. See Burson v. Freeman, 504 U.S. 191, 195, 196, 119 L. Ed. 2d 5, 112 S. Ct. 1846 (1992).

Perhaps because the Court recognizes these perversities, it quickly offers some ad hoc limitations on its newly extended prohibition on content-based regulations. First, the Court states that a content-based regulation is valid "when the basis for the content discrimination consists entirely of the very reason the entire class of speech . . . is proscribable." Ante, 505 U.S. at 388. In a pivotal passage, the Court writes:

"The Federal Government can criminalize only those threats of violence that are directed against the President, see 18 U. S. C. § 871 – since the reasons why [424] threats of violence are outside the First Amendment (protecting individuals from the fear of violence, from the disruption that fear engenders, and from the possibility that the threatened violence will occur) have special force when applied to the . . . President." Ibid.

As I understand this opaque passage, Congress may choose from the set of unprotected speech (all threats) to proscribe only a subset (threats against the President) because those threats are particularly likely to cause "fear of violence," "disruption," and actual "violence."

Precisely this same reasoning, however, compels the conclusion that St. Paul's ordinance is constitutional. Just as Congress may determine that threats against the President entail more severe consequences than other threats, so St. Paul's City Council may determine that threats based on the target's race, religion, or gender cause more severe harm to both the target and to society than other threats. This latter judgment – that harms caused by racial, religious, and gender-based invective are qualitatively different from that caused by other fighting words – seems to me eminently reasonable and realistic.

Next, the Court recognizes that a State may regulate advertising in one industry but not another because "the risk of fraud (one of the characteristics . . . that justifies depriving [commercial speech] of full First Amendment protection . . .)" in the regulated industry is "greater" than in other industries. Ibid. Again, the same reasoning demonstrates the constitutionality of St. Paul's ordinance. "One of the characteristics that justifies" the constitutional status of fighting words is that such words "by their very

utterance inflict injury or tend to incite an immediate breach of the peace." Chaplinsky, 315 U.S. at 572. Certainly a legislature that may determine that the risk of fraud is greater in the legal [425] trade than in the medical trade may determine that the risk of injury or breach of peace created by race-based threats is greater than that created by other threats.

Similarly, it is impossible to reconcile the Court's analysis of the St. Paul ordinance with its recognition that "a prohibition of fighting words that are directed at certain persons or groups . . . would be facially valid." Ante, 505 U.S. at 392 (emphasis deleted).

A selective proscription of unprotected expression designed to protect "certain persons or groups" (for example, a law proscribing threats directed at the elderly) would be constitutional if it were based on a legitimate determination that the harm created by the regulated expression differs from that created by the unregulated expression (that is, if the elderly are more severely injured by threats than are the nonelderly). Such selective protection is no different from a law prohibiting minors (and only minors) from obtaining obscene publications. See Ginsberg v. New York, 390 U.S. 29, 20 L. Ed. 2d 195, 88 S. Ct. 1274 (1968). St. Paul has determined – reasonably in my judgment – that fighting-word injuries "based on race, color, creed, religion or gender" are qualitatively different and more severe than fighting-word injuries based on other characteristics. Whether the selective proscription of proscribable speech is defined by the protected target ("certain persons or groups") or the basis of the harm (injuries "based on race, color, creed, religion or gender") makes no constitutional difference: What matters is whether the legislature's selection is based on a legitimate, neutral, and reasonable distinction.

In sum, the central premise of the Court's ruling – that "content-based regulations are presumptively invalid" – has simplistic appeal, but lacks support in our First Amendment jurisprudence. To make matters worse, the Court today extends this overstated claim to reach categories of hitherto unprotected speech and, in doing so, wreaks havoc in an area of settled law.

Finally, although the Court recognizes [426] exceptions to its new principle, those exceptions undermine its very conclusion that the St. Paul ordinance is unconstitutional. Stated directly, the majority's position cannot withstand scrutiny.

Although I agree with much of JUSTICE WHITE's analysis, I do not join Part I-A of his opinion because I have reservations about the "categorical approach" to the First Amendment. These concerns, which I have noted on other occasions, see, e.g., New York v. Ferber, 458 U.S. 747, 778, 73 L. Ed. 2d 1113, 102 S. Ct. 3348 (1982) (opinion concurring in judgment), lead me to find JUSTICE WHITE's response to the Court's analysis unsatisfying.

Admittedly, the categorical approach to the First Amendment has some appeal: Either expression is protected or it is not – the categories create safe harbors for governments and speakers alike. But this approach sacrifices subtlety for clarity and is, I am convinced, ultimately unsound. As an initial matter, the concept of "categories" fits poorly with the complex reality of expression. Few dividing lines in First Amendment law are straight and unwavering, and efforts at categorization inevitably give rise only to fuzzy boundaries. Our definitions of "obscenity," see, e.g., Marks v. United States, 430 U.S. 188, 198, 51 L. Ed. 2d 260, 97 S. Ct. 990 (1977) (STEVENS, J., concurring in part and dissenting in part), and "public forum," see, e.g., United States Postal Service v. Council of Greenburgh Civic Assns., 453 U.S. 114, 126-131, 69 L. Ed. 2d 517, 101 S. Ct. 2676 (1981); id., at 136-140 (Brennan, J., concurring in judgment); id., at 147-151 (Marshall, J., dissenting); id., at 152-154 (STEVENS, J., dissenting) (all debating the definition of "public forum"), illustrate this all too well. The quest for doctrinal certainty through the definition of categories and subcategories is, in my opinion, destined to fail.

Moreover, the categorical approach does not take seriously the importance of context. The meaning of any expression and the legitimacy of its regulation can only be determined [427] in context.[5] Whether, for example, a picture or a sentence is obscene cannot be judged in the abstract, but rather only in the context of its setting, its use, and its audience. Similarly, although legislatures may freely regulate most nonobscene child porno-graphy, such pornography that is part of "a serious work of art, a documentary on behavioral problems, or a medical or psychiatric teaching device" may be entitled to constitutional protection; the "question whether a specific act of communication is protected by the First Amendment always requires some consideration of both its content and its context." Ferber, 458 U.S. at 778 (STEVENS, J., concurring in judgment); see also Smith v. United States, 431 U.S. 291, 311-321, 52 L. Ed. 2d 324, 97 S. Ct. 1756 (1977) (STEVENS, J., dissenting). The categorical approach sweeps too broadly when it declares that all such expression is beyond the protection of the First Amendment.

Perhaps sensing the limits of such an all-or-nothing approach, the Court has applied its analysis less categorically than its doctrinal statements suggest. The Court has recognized intermediate

categories of speech (for example, for indecent nonobscene speech and commercial speech) and geographic categories of speech (public fora, limited public fora, nonpublic fora) entitled to varying levels of protection. The Court has also stringently delimited the categories of unprotected speech. While we once declared that "libelous utterances [are] not . . . within the area of constitutionally protected speech," Beauharnais v. Illinois, 343 U.S. 250, 266, 96 L. Ed. 919, 72 S. Ct. 725 (1952), our rulings in New York Times Co. v. Sullivan, 376 U.S. 254, 11 L. Ed. 2d 686, 84 S. Ct. 710 (1964); Gertz v. Robert Welch, Inc., 418 U.S. 323, 41 L. Ed. 2d 789, 94 S. Ct. 2997 (1974), and Dun & Bradstreet, Inc. v. Greenmoss Builders, Inc., 472 U.S. 749, 86 L. Ed. 2d 593, 105 S. Ct. 2939 (1985), have substantially qualified this [428] broad claim.

Similarly, we have consistently construed the "fighting words" exception set forth in Chaplinsky narrowly. See, e.g., Houston v. Hill, 482 U.S. 451, 96 L. Ed. 2d 398, 107 S. Ct. 2502 (1987); Lewis v. New Orleans, 415 U.S. 130, 39 L. Ed. 2d 214, 94 S. Ct. 970 (1974); Cohen v. California, 403 U.S. 15, 29 L. Ed. 2d 284, 91 S. Ct. 1780 (1971). In the case of commercial speech, our ruling that "the Constitution imposes no . . . restraint on government [regulation] as respects purely commercial advertising," Valentine v. Chrestensen, 316 U.S. 52, 54, 86 L. Ed. 1262, 62 S. Ct. 920 (1942), was expressly repudiated in Virginia Bd. of Pharmacy v. Virginia Citizens Consumer Council, Inc., 425 U.S. 748, 48 L. Ed. 2d 346, 96 S. Ct. 1817 (1976). In short, the history of the categorical approach is largely the history of narrowing the categories of unprotected speech.

This evolution, I believe, indicates that the categorical approach is unworkable and the quest for absolute categories of "protected" and "unprotected" speech ultimately futile. My analysis of the faults and limits of this approach persuades me that the categorical approach presented in Part I-A of JUSTICE WHITE's opinion is not an adequate response to the novel "underbreadth" analysis the Court sets forth today.

As the foregoing suggests, I disagree with both the Court's and part of JUSTICE WHITE's analysis of the constitutionality of the St. Paul ordinance. Unlike the Court, I do not believe that all content-based regulations are equally infirm and presumptively invalid; unlike JUSTICE WHITE, I do not believe that fighting words are wholly unprotected by the First Amendment. To the contrary, I believe our decisions establish a more complex and subtle analysis, one that considers the content and context of the regulated speech, and the nature and scope of the restriction on speech. Applying this analysis and assuming, arguendo, (as the Court does) that the St. Paul ordinance is not overbroad, I conclude that such a selective, subject-

---

[5] "A word," as Justice Holmes has noted, "is not a crystal, transparent and unchanged, it is the skin of a living thought and may vary greatly in color and content according to the circumstances and the time in which it is used." Towne v. Eisner, 245 U.S. 418, 425, 62 L. Ed. 372, 38 S. Ct. 158 (1918); see also Jacobellis v. Ohio, 378 U.S. 184, 201, 12 L. Ed. 2d 793, 84 S. Ct. 1676 (1964) (Warren, C. J., dissenting).

matter regulation on proscribable speech is constitutional.

[429] Not all content-based regulations are alike; our decisions clearly recognize that some content-based restrictions raise more constitutional questions than others. Although the Court's analysis of content-based regulations cannot be reduced to a simple formula, we have considered a number of factors in determining the validity of such regulations.

First, as suggested above, the scope of protection provided expressive activity depends in part upon its content and character. We have long recognized that when government regulates political speech or "the expression of editorial opinion on matters of public importance," FCC v. League of Women Voters of Cal., 468 U.S. 364, 375-376, 82 L. Ed. 2d 278, 104 S. Ct. 3106 (1984), "First Amendment protection is 'at its zenith,'" Meyer v. Grant, 486 U.S. 414, 425, 100 L. Ed. 2d 425, 108 S. Ct. 1886 (1988). In comparison, we have recognized that "commercial speech receives a limited form of First Amendment protection," Posadas de Puerto Rico Associates v. Tourism Co. of Puerto Rico, 478 U.S. 328, 340, 92 L. Ed. 2d 266, 106 S. Ct. 2968 (1986), and that "society's interest in protecting [sexually explicit films] is of a wholly different, and lesser, magnitude than [its] interest in untrammeled political debate," Young v. American Mini Theatres, 427 U.S. at 70; see also FCC v. Pacifica Foundation, 438 U.S. 726, 57 L. Ed. 2d 1073, 98 S. Ct. 3026 (1978). The character of expressive activity also weighs in our consideration of its constitutional status. As we have frequently noted, "the government generally has a freer hand in restricting expressive conduct than it has in restricting the written or spoken word." Texas v. Johnson, 491 U.S. 397, 406, 105 L. Ed. 2d 342, 109 S. Ct. 2533 (1989); see also United States v. O'Brien, 391 U.S. 367, 20 L. Ed. 2d 672, 88 S. Ct. 1673 (1968).

The protection afforded expression turns as well on the context of the regulated speech. We have noted, for example, that "any assessment of the precise scope of employer expression, of course, must be made in the context of its labor relations setting . . . [and] must take into account the economic dependence of the employees on their employers." NLRB v. Gissel Packing Co., 395 U.S. at 617. Similarly, the distinctive character of a university environment, see [430] Widmar v. Vincent, 454 U.S. 263, 277-280, 70 L. Ed. 2d 440, 102 S. Ct. 269 (1981) (STEVENS, J., concurring in judgment), or a secondary school environment, see Hazelwood School Dist. v. Kuhlmeier, 484 U.S. 260, 98 L. Ed. 2d 592, 108 S. Ct. 562 (1988), influences our First Amendment analysis. The same is true of the presence of a "'captive audience [, one] there as a matter of necessity, not of choice.'" Lehman v.

Shaker Heights, 418 U.S. at 302 (citation omitted).[6] Perhaps the most familiar embodiment of the relevance of context is our "fora" jurisprudence, differentiating the levels of protection afforded speech in different locations.

The nature of a contested restriction of speech also informs our evaluation of its constitutionality. Thus, for example, "any system of prior restraints of expression comes to this Court bearing a heavy presumption against its constitutional validity." Bantam Books, Inc. v. Sullivan, 372 U.S. 58, 70, 9 L. Ed. 2d 584, 83 S. Ct. 631 (1963). More particularly to the matter of content-based regulations, we have implicitly distinguished between restrictions on expression based on subject matter and restrictions based on viewpoint, indicating that the latter are particularly pernicious. "If there is a bedrock principle underlying the First Amendment, it is that the Government may not prohibit the expression of an idea simply because society finds the idea itself offensive or disagreeable." Texas v. Johnson, 491 U.S. at 414. "Viewpoint discrimination is censorship in its purest form," Perry Ed. Assn. v. Perry Local Educators' Assn., 460 U.S. 37, 62, 74 L. Ed. 2d 794, 103 S. Ct. 948 (1983) (Brennan, J., dissenting), and requires particular scrutiny, in part because such regulation often indicates a legislative effort to skew public debate on an issue, see, e.g., Schacht v. United States, 398 U.S. 58, 63, 26 L. Ed. 2d 44, 90 S. Ct. 1555 (1970). "Especially where . . . the legislature's suppression of speech suggests an attempt [431] to give one side of a debatable public question an advantage in expressing its views to the people, the First Amendment is plainly offended." First Nat. Bank of Boston v. Bellotti, 435 U.S. 765, 785-786, 55 L. Ed. 2d 707, 98 S. Ct. 1407 (1978).

Thus, although a regulation that on its face regulates speech by subject matter may in some instances effectively suppress particular viewpoints, see, e.g., Consolidated Edison Co. of N. Y. v. Public Serv. Comm'n of N. Y., 447 U.S. 530, 546-547, 65 L. Ed. 2d 319, 100 S. Ct. 2326 (1980) (STEVENS, J., concurring in judgment), in general, viewpoint-based restrictions on expression require greater scrutiny than subject-matter-based restrictions.[7]

Finally, in considering the validity of content-based regulations we have also looked more broadly

---

[6] Cf. In re Chase, 468 F.2d 128, 139-140 (CA7 1972) (Stevens, J., dissenting) (arguing that defendant who, for reasons of religious belief, refused to rise and stand as the trial judge entered the courtroom was not subject to contempt proceedings because he was not present in the courtroom "as a matter of choice").

[7] Although the Court has sometimes suggested that subject-matter-based and viewpoint-based regulations are equally problematic, see, e.g., Consolidated Edison Co. of N. Y. v. Public Serv. Comm'n of N. Y., 447 U.S. at 537, our decisions belie such claims.

at the scope of the restrictions. For example, in Young v. American Mini Theatres, 427 U.S. at 71, we found significant the fact that "what [was] ultimately at stake [was] nothing more than a limitation on the place where adult films may be exhibited." Similarly, in FCC v. Pacifica Foundation, the Court emphasized two dimensions of the limited scope of the FCC ruling. First, the ruling concerned only broadcast material which presents particular problems because it "confronts the citizen . . . in the privacy of the home"; second, the ruling was not a complete ban on the use of selected offensive words, but rather merely a limitation on the times such speech could be broadcast. 438 U.S. at 748-750.

All of these factors play some role in our evaluation of content-based regulations on expression. Such a multifaceted analysis cannot be conflated into two dimensions. Whatever the allure of absolute doctrines, it is just too simple to declare expression "protected" or "unprotected" or to proclaim a regulation "content based" or "content neutral." [432] In applying this analysis to the St. Paul ordinance, I assume, arguendo – as the Court does – that the ordinance regulates only fighting words and therefore is not overbroad. Looking to the content and character of the regulated activity, two things are clear. First, by hypothesis the ordinance bars only low-value speech, namely, fighting words. By definition such expression constitutes "no essential part of any exposition of ideas, and [is] of such slight social value as a step to truth that any benefit that may be derived from [it] is clearly outweighed by the social interest in order and morality." Chaplinsky, 315 U.S. at 572. Second, the ordinance regulates "expressive conduct [rather] than . . . the written or spoken word." Texas v. Johnson, 491 U.S. at 406.

Looking to the context of the regulated activity, it is again significant that the ordinance (by hypothesis) regulates only fighting words. Whether words are fighting words is determined in part by their context. Fighting words are not words that merely cause offense; fighting words must be directed at individuals so as to "by their very utterance inflict injury." By hypothesis, then, the St. Paul ordinance restricts speech in confrontational and potentially violent situations. The case at hand is illustrative. The cross burning in this case – directed as it was to a single African-American family trapped in their home – was nothing more than a crude form of physical intimidation. That this cross burning sends a message of racial hostility does not automatically endow it with complete constitutional protection.[8]

[433] Significantly, the St. Paul ordinance regulates speech not on the basis of its subject matter or the viewpoint expressed, but rather on the basis of the harm the speech causes. In this regard, the Court fundamentally misreads the St. Paul ordinance. The Court describes the St. Paul ordinance as regulating expression "addressed to one of [several] specified disfavored topics," ante, 505 U.S. at 391 (emphasis supplied), as policing "disfavored subjects," ibid. (emphasis supplied), and as "prohibiting . . . speech solely on the basis of the subjects the speech addresses," ante, 505 U.S. at 381 (emphasis supplied). Contrary to the Court's suggestion, the ordinance regulates only a subcategory of expression that causes injuries based on "race, color, creed, religion or gender," not a subcategory that involves discussions that concern those characteristics.[9] The ordinance, as construed by the Court, criminalizes expression that "one knows . . . [by its very utterance inflicts injury on] others on the basis of race, color, creed, religion or [434] gender." In this regard, the ordinance resembles the child pornography law at issue in Ferber, which in effect singled out child pornography because those publications caused far greater harms than pornography involving adults.

Moreover, even if the St. Paul ordinance did regulate fighting words based on its subject matter, such a regulation would, in my opinion, be constitutional. As noted above, subject-matter-based regulations on commercial speech are widespread and largely unproblematic. As we have long

---

8 The Court makes much of St. Paul's description of the ordinance as regulating "a message." Ante, 505 U.S. at 393. As always, however, St. Paul's argument must be read in context: "Finally, we ask the Court to reflect on the 'content' of the 'expressive conduct' represented by a 'burning cross.' It is no

less than the first step in an act of racial violence. It was and unfortunately still is the equivalent of [the] waving of a knife before the thrust, the pointing of a gun before it is fired, the lighting of the match before the arson, the hanging of the noose before the lynching. It is not a political statement, or even a cowardly statement of hatred. It is the first step in an act of assault. It can be no more protected than holding a gun to a victim's head. It is perhaps the ultimate expression of 'fighting words.'" App. to Brief for Petitioner C-6.
9 The Court contends that this distinction is "wordplay," reasoning that "what makes [the harms caused by race-based threats] distinct from [the harms] produced by other fighting words is . . . the fact that [the former are] caused by a distinctive idea." Ante, 505 U.S. at 392-393 (emphasis added). In this way, the Court concludes that regulating speech based on the injury it causes is no different from regulating speech based on its subject matter. This analysis fundamentally miscomprehends the role of "race, color, creed, religion [and] gender" in contemporary American society. One need look no further than the recent social unrest in the Nation's cities to see that race-based threats may cause more harm to society and to individuals than other threats. Just as the statute prohibiting threats against the President is justifiable because of the place of the President in our social and political order, so a statute prohibiting race-based threats is justifiable because of the place of race in our social and political order. Although it is regrettable that race occupies such a place and is so incendiary an issue, until the Nation matures beyond that condition, laws such as St. Paul's ordinance will remain reasonable and justifiable.

recognized, subject-matter regulations generally do not raise the same concerns of government censorship and the distortion of public discourse presented by viewpoint regulations. Thus, in upholding subject-matter regulations we have carefully noted that viewpoint-based discrimination was not implicated. See Young v. American Mini Theatres, 427 U.S. at 67 (emphasizing "the need for absolute neutrality by the government," and observing that the contested statute was not animated by "hostility for the point of view" of the theaters); FCC v. Pacifica Foundation, 438 U.S. at 745-746 (stressing that "government must remain neutral in the marketplace of ideas"); see also FCC v. League of Women's Voters of Cal., 468 U.S. at 412-417 (STEVENS, J., dissenting); Metromedia, Inc. v. San Diego, 453 U.S. 490, 554-555, 69 L. Ed. 2d 800, 101 S. Ct. 2882 (1981) (STEVENS, J., dissenting in part). Indeed, some subject-matter restrictions are a functional necessity in contemporary governance: "The First Amendment does not require States to regulate for problems that do not exist." Burson v. Freeman, 504 U.S. at 207.

Contrary to the suggestion of the majority, the St. Paul ordinance does not regulate expression based on viewpoint. The Court contends that the ordinance requires proponents of racial intolerance to "follow the Marquis of Queensberry rules" while allowing advocates of racial tolerance to "fight freestyle." The law does no such thing.

[435] The Court writes:

"One could hold up a sign saying, for example, that all 'anti-Catholic bigots' are misbegotten; but not that all 'papists' are, for that would insult and provoke violence 'on the basis of religion.'" Ante, 505 U.S. at 391-392.

This may be true, but it hardly proves the Court's point. The Court's reasoning is asymmetrical. The response to a sign saying that "all [religious] bigots are misbegotten" is a sign saying that "all advocates of religious tolerance are misbegotten." Assuming such signs could be fighting words (which seems to me extremely unlikely), neither sign would be banned by the ordinance for the attacks were not "based on . . . religion" but rather on one's beliefs about tolerance. Conversely (and again assuming such signs are fighting words), just as the ordinance would prohibit a Muslim from hoisting a sign claiming that all Catholics were misbegotten, so the

ordinance would bar a Catholic from hoisting a similar sign attacking Muslims.

The St. Paul ordinance is evenhanded. In a battle between advocates of tolerance and advocates of intolerance, the ordinance does not prevent either side from hurling fighting words at the other on the basis of their conflicting ideas, but it does bar both sides from hurling such words on the basis of the target's "race, color, creed, religion or gender. To extend the Court's pugilistic metaphor, the St. Paul ordinance simply bans punches "below the belt" – by either party. It does not, therefore, favor one side of any debate.[10]

[436] Finally, it is noteworthy that the St. Paul ordinance is, as construed by the Court today, quite narrow. The St. Paul ordinance does not ban all "hate speech," nor does it ban, say, all cross burnings or all swastika displays. Rather it only bans a subcategory of the already narrow category of fighting words. Such a limited ordinance leaves open and protected a vast range of expression on the subjects of racial, religious, and gender equality. As construed by the Court today, the ordinance certainly does not "'raise the specter that the Government may effectively drive certain ideas or viewpoints from the marketplace.'" Ante, 505 U.S. at 387. Petitioner is free to burn a cross to announce a rally or to express his views about racial supremacy, he may do so on private property or public land, at day or at night, so long as the burning is not so threatening and so directed at an individual as to "by its very [execution] inflict injury." Such a limited proscription scarcely offends the First Amendment.

In sum, the St. Paul ordinance (as construed by the Court) regulates expressive activity that is wholly proscribable and does so not on the basis of viewpoint, but rather in recognition of the different harms caused by such activity. Taken together, these several considerations persuade me that the St. Paul ordinance is not an unconstitutional content-based regulation of speech. Thus, were the ordinance not overbroad, I would vote to uphold it.

---

[10] Cf. FCC v. League of Women Voters of Cal., 468 U.S. 364, 418, 82 L. Ed. 2d 278, 104 S. Ct. 3106 (1984) (STEVENS, J., dissenting) ("In this case . . . the regulation applies . . . to a defined class of . . . licensees [who] represent heterogeneous points of view. There is simply no sensible basis for considering this regulation a viewpoint restriction – or . . . to condemn it as 'content-based' – because it applies equally to station owners of all shades of opinion").

Chapter

8

Offensive Speech and Unpopular Association

Protection for profanity and bigotry

Focal cases:
Cohen v. California, 403 U.S. 15 (1971)
Hurley v. Irish-American Gay, Lesbian & Bisexual Group, 515 U.S. 557 (1995)

T he Supreme Court has clearly and consistently established that the First Amendment protects the right to express unpopular or offensive ideas.[1] The Court has reasoned that the benefits of such speech far exceed its costs to an open marketplace of ideas. The Court fundamentally asserts that the candid exchange of extreme, radical, vulgar and even repulsive views is vital to the search for truth advanced by the First Amendment. Thus, government efforts to eliminate unpopular or offensive speech strike at the heart of the First Amendment and constitute the very essence of censorship.[2]

OFFENSIVE LANGUAGE

In 1971 the Supreme Court said in *Cohen v. California*[3] that even the most profane language does not fall into one of the narrow categories of proscribed expression and may not be punished merely because it offends. The Court said Paul Cohen's conviction for wearing a jacket bearing the popular anti-war slogan, "Fuck the Draft," in the halls of a Los Angeles courthouse was unconstitutional.

Writing for the Court, Justice Harlan noted that "while the particular four-letter word being litigated here is perhaps more distasteful than most others of its genre, it is nevertheless often true that one man's vulgarity is another's lyric."[4] The Court reasoned that specific terminology was a

---

[1] *But see* Bethel School District v. Fraser, 478 U.S. 675 (1986) (denying public school student right to use profanity in school sponsored forum).

[2] Young v. American Mini Theatres, Inc., 427 U.S. 50, 64 (1976) ; Police Department of the City of Chicago v. Mosley, 408 U.S. 92, 96 (1972).

[3] Cohen v. California, 403 U.S. 15 (1971).

[4] 403 U.S. at 25.

matter of personal choice and style that conveyed much more than the substance of the message transmitted. The Court recognized that language functions on many levels and incorporates both emotional and cognitive content. Indeed, to borrow a concept from Marshal McLuhan, the manner of expression *is* the message because distasteful or offensive language transmits "inexpressible emotions" that often is impossible to communicate through more polite phrases. [5]

UNPOPULAR ASSOCIATIONS

Sometimes unpopular and highly disturbing ideas are communicated without the use of coarse language. Sometimes, in fact, ideas that are highly offensive to the majority of citizens can be conveyed without a single word. Visualize a burning cross surrounded by a crowd of white cloaked and hooded figures. Imagine a park filled with individuals wearing military uniforms emblazoned with swastikas. Consider a group of intellectuals dressed in black gathered beneath a red flag bearing a hammer and sickle. These iconic images of the Ku Klux Klan, Nazism and Communism wordlessly express intolerance or challenge deeply held mainstream American ideologies.

However, the First Amendment's assembly clause – upon which the Court has built the concept of freedom of association – protects the right of each of these groups to assemble peaceably. [6] Constitutional protection for freedom of association advances the notion that each individual has the right to join together with like-minded people to develop common expressive interests without government interference. Freedom of association protects the formation of unpopular groups from suppression by the majority.[7] It does not protect knowing involvement in a group's illegal activities (*scienter*).[8] The right of free association creates a shield against public hostility, persecution, harassment, threats, reprisals or interference with the right of groups to coalesce for even the most offensive reasons. To this end, the Court has interpreted the right of free association to incorporate an element of privacy that protects citizens from mandatory disclosure of their affiliations[9] and defends associations from compulsory publication of their memberships.[10]

Yet, from the 1950s to the '70s, amid pervasive fears of Nazism and Communism, the Supreme Court upheld a variety of government actions that limited the freedom of individuals associated with Communism, Marxism or nations with whom the United States was at war.[11]

---

[5] 403 U.S. at 26.

[6] Note that the assembly clause has been relatively neglected by First Amendment scholars. *See, e.g.,* JEROME A. BARRON & C. THOMAS DIENES, FIRST AMENDMENT LAW IN A NUTSHELL (2d 2000) (including no references to the assembly clause in the extensive index). *But see* Victor Brudney, *Association, Advocacy, and The First Amendment,* 4 WM. & MARY BILL OF RTS. J. 1 (1995); *Note: State Power And Discrimination By Private Clubs: First Amendment Protection For Nonexpressive Associations,* 104 HARV. L. REV. 1835 (1991); Heather R. Henthorne, *Resident Aliens And The First Amendment: The Need for Judicial Recognition of Full Free Speech and Association Rights,* 39 CATH. U.L. REV. 595 (1990); Stephen E. Gottlieb, *Rebuilding The Right of Association: The Right to Hold a Convention as a Test Case,* 11 HOFSTRA L. REV. 191, (Fall, 1982); Andy Pearson, *The Anti-Terrorism and Effective Death Penalty Act of 1996: A Return to Guilt By Association,* 24 WM. MITCHELL L. REV. 1185 (1998).

[7] *See, e.g.,* Keyishian v. Bd. of Regents of the Univ. of the State of NY, 385 U.S. 589 (1967) (rejecting government power to deny faculty status to members of Communist Party); Wieman v. Updegraff, 344 U.S. 183 (1952) (striking down state law requiring loyalty [anti-Communist] oath from state employees); Joint Anti-Fascist Refugee Committee v. McGrath, 341 U.S. 123 (1951) (reversing lower courts and requiring review of merits of constitutional challenge to Attorney General's designation of organization as Communist).

[8] *See, e.g.,* Scales v. United States, 367 U.S. 203 (1961); Elfbrandt v. Russell, 384 U.S. 11 (1966).

[9] *See, e.g.,* Shelton v Tucker, 364 US 479 (1960) (finding unconstitutional a state statute requiring public school teachers to disclose all organizational memberships).

[10] *See, e.g.,* Gibson v. Florida Legislative Investigation Committee, 372 U.S. 539 (1963); Bates v. City of Little Rock, 361 U.S. 516 (1960); *NAACP v. Alabama,* 357 U.S. 449 (1958).

[11] *See, e.g.,* Kleindienst v. Mandel, 408 U.S. 753 (1972) (finding constitutional the exclusion of a foreign Marxist economist invited to speak at several prestigious U.S. academic institutions); Scales v. United States, 367 U.S. 203 (1961) (affirming constitutionality of conviction for Communist Party membership); Communist Party of the

Thus, during times of social strain, the right of assembly or association has not consistently prevented harassment or sanctions for guilt by association.[12]

The right to freely associate also is limited to some degree by constitutional concern with equality. Although an important element of the right of free association is the right not to associate,[13] the Court sometimes has held that the Constitution requires organizations to admit or accommodate individuals they would prefer to exclude.[14] The Court has affirmed the right of truly private, intimate or selective associations not to admit individuals or groups whose ideas or behaviors violate or interfere with the goals of the group.[15] Exclusions based on race and gender, however, are suspect, and the Court has found them unconstitutional when they do not directly advance the group's primary mission.

THE RIGHT TO BE HEARD

The First Amendment's assembly clause also guarantees speakers some right to be heard by an assembled group because freedom of speech means little if no one is listening. (See related discussions of the right to gather on public property in Chap. 5 and the doctrine against heckler's veto in Chap. 6.) However, any right to be heard is bounded by conflicting interests, including the right to privacy and the right of individuals to be free from harassment. Consequently, the Court on occasion has affirmed the right of unwilling listeners to be free from verbal assault even in a public forum.[16]

READING THE CASES

In addition to the two cases highlighted in this chapter, the following cases provide a more extensive foundation for understanding the rather complex and contradictory Court rulings on the First Amendment freedom of association.

- *PGA Tour v. Martin*, 532 U.S. 661 (2001) (upholding Americans with Disabilities Act requirement that PGA accommodate handicap of qualified golfer).

United States v. Subversive Activities Control Bd., 367 U.S. 1 (1961) (affirming constitutionality of federal requirement that Communist Party register as a subversive organization); Carlson v. Landon, 342 U.S. 524 (1952) (allowing indefinite detention of alien Communist Party members pending final determination of their deportability); Amer. Communications Ass'n v. Douds, 339 U.S. 382 (1950) (upholding constitutionality of federal requirement that union organizers swear they are not Communists); Ludecke v. Watkins, 335 U.S. 160 (1948) (affirming constitutionality of deportation of legal German residents in U.S.); Korematsu v. United States, 323 US 214 (1944) (affirming constitutionality of interment of legal Japanese residents in U.S.).

[12] *See, e.g.,* Reno v. American Arab Anti-Discrimination Committee, 525 U.S. 471 (1999) (rejecting selective enforcement claim as grounds for court intervention in INS deportation proceeding); Younger v. Harris, 401 U.S. 37 (1971) (refusing to enjoin prosecution under state syndicalism statute for distribution of pamphlets of the Progressive labor party).

[13] *See, e.g.,* Wooley v. Maynard, 430 U.S. 705 (1977).

[14] *See, e.g.,* PGA Tour v Martin, 532 U.S. 661 (2001) (upholding Americans with Disabilities Act requirement that PGA accommodate handicap of qualified golfer); Bd. of Directors of Rotary Int'l v. Rotary Club of Duarte, 481 U.S. 537 (1987) (upholding constitutionality of state requirement that organization admit females because gender is unrelated to the nature of the association); Minnesota Dept. of Human Rts v. U.S. Jaycees, 468 U.S. 609 (1984) (ruling that state requirement that women be admitted did not unconstitutionally infringe the freedom of association); Healy v. James, 408 U.S. 169 (1972) (finding a state university may not constitutionally deny recognition of student [SDS] association because of disagreement with the association's goals).

[15] *See, e.g.,* Boy Scouts of America v. Dale, 530 U.S. 640 (2000) (ruling Boy Scouts to be a private organization with a right to exclude gay members); Hurley v. Irish-American Gay, Lesbian & Bisexual Group, 515 U.S. 557 (1995) (finding St. Patrick's Day parade is a private association that constitutionally may exclude group based on sexual orientation).

[16] *See, e.g.,* Hill v. Colorado, 530 U.S. 703 (2000). *But see* Watchtower Bible & Tract Soc'y of N.Y., Inc. v. Vill. of Stratton, 122 S. Ct. 2080 (2002).

- *Boy Scouts of America v. Dale*, 530 U.S. 640 (2000) (ruling Boy Scouts to be a private organization with a right to exclude gay members).
- *Bd. of Directors of Rotary Int'l v. Rotary Club of Duarte*, 481 U.S. 537 (1987) (upholding constitutionality of state requirement that organization admit females because gender is unrelated to the nature of the association).
- *Wooley v. Maynard*, 430 U.S. 705 (1977) (striking mandated state motto on license plates).
- *Kleindienst v. Mandel*, 408 U.S. 753 (1972) (finding constitutional the exclusion of a foreign Marxist economist invited to speak at several prestigious U.S. academic institutions).
- *Keyishian v. Bd. of Regents of the Univ. of the State of NY*, 385 U.S. 589 (1967) (rejecting government power to deny faculty status to members of Communist Party).
- *NAACP v. Alabama*, 357 U.S. 449 (1958) (protecting NAACP membership list from mandatory disclosure).
- *Wieman v. Updegraff*, 344 U.S. 183 (1952) (striking down state law requiring loyalty [anti-Communist] oath from state employees).
- *Carlson v. Landon*, 342 U.S. 524 (1952) (allowing indefinite detention of alien Communist Party members pending final determination of their deportability).
- *Ludecke v. Watkins*, 335 U.S. 160 (1948) (affirming constitutionality of deportation of legal German residents in U.S.).
- *Korematsu v. United States*, 323 US 214 (1944) (affirming constitutionality of detention of legal Japanese residents in U.S.).

While reading the suggested cases and the two focus cases that follow, consider the following questions.

- Are there boundaries beyond which legal offensive speech may not go?
- How does the Court apply the speech/action dichotomy to offensive speech?
- What is the basis of the dissent in *Cohen*?
- Whose constitutional rights are at issue in *Hurley* and what are they?
- What facts does the Court rely upon to determine that the Council's action in *Hurley* is constitutional?
- Who bears the burden of proof in the two cases?
- In both cases, what interests does the Court balance and how?
- Does the Court adequately consider the harms of offensive speech or associational exclusion?
- In either case, does the Court provide a clear test or rule to determine when offensive speech or mandatory association is constitutional?
- What does *Hurley* indicate about the clarity and predictability of the Court's definition of a right of association?

Cohen v. California
403 U.S. 15
(1971)

JUDGES: Harlan, J., delivered the opinion of the Court, in which Douglas, Brennan, Stewart, and Marshall, JJ., joined. Blackmun, J., filed a dissenting opinion, in which Burger, C. J., and Black, J., joined, and in which White, J., joined in part.

OPINION: [15] MR. JUSTICE HARLAN delivered the opinion of the Court.

This case may seem at first blush too inconsequential to find its way into our books, but the issue it presents is of no small constitutional significance.

[16] Appellant Paul Robert Cohen was convicted in the Los Angeles Municipal Court of violating that part of California Penal Code § 415 which prohibits "maliciously and willfully disturb[ing] the peace or quiet of any neighborhood or person . . . by . . . offensive conduct . . . ."[1] He was given 30 days' imprisonment. The facts upon which his conviction rests are detailed in the opinion of the Court of Appeal of California, Second Appellate District, as follows:

"On April 26, 1968, the defendant was observed in the Los Angeles County Courthouse in the corridor outside of division 20 of the municipal court wearing a jacket bearing the words 'Fuck the Draft' which were plainly visible. There were women and children present in the corridor. The defendant was arrested. The defendant testified that he wore the jacket knowing that the words were on the jacket as a means of informing the public of the depth of his feelings against the Vietnam War and the draft.

"The defendant did not engage in, nor threaten to engage in, nor did anyone as the result of his conduct [17] in fact commit or threaten to commit any act of violence. The defendant did not make any loud or unusual noise, nor was there any evidence that he

uttered any sound prior to his arrest." 1 Cal. App. 3d 94, 97-98, 81 Cal. Rptr. 503, 505 (1969).

In affirming the conviction the Court of Appeal held that "offensive conduct" means "behavior which has a tendency to provoke others to acts of violence or to in turn disturb the peace," and that the State had proved this element because, on the facts of this case, "it was certainly reasonably foreseeable that such conduct might cause others to rise up to commit a violent act against the person of the defendant or attempt to forcibly remove his jacket." 1 Cal. App. 3d, at 99-100, 81 Cal. Rptr., at 506. The California Supreme Court declined review by a divided vote.[2] We brought the case here, postponing the consideration of the question of our jurisdiction over this appeal to a hearing of the case on the merits. 399 U.S. 904. We now reverse.

[1] The question of our jurisdiction need not detain us long. Throughout the proceedings below, Cohen consistently [18] claimed that, as construed to apply to the facts of this case, the statute infringed his rights to freedom of expression guaranteed by the First and Fourteenth Amendments of the Federal Constitution. That contention has been rejected by the highest California state court in which review could be had. Accordingly, we are fully satisfied that Cohen has properly invoked our jurisdiction by this appeal. 28 U.S.C. § 1257 (2); Dahnke-Walker Milling Co. v. Bondurant, 257 U.S. 282 (1921).

I.   In order to lay hands on the precise issue which this case involves, it is useful first to canvass various matters which this record does not present. [2] [3]The conviction quite clearly rests upon the asserted offensiveness of the words Cohen used to convey his message to the public. The only "conduct" which the State sought to punish is the fact of communication. Thus, we deal here with a

---

[1] The statute provides in full:

"Every person who maliciously and willfully disturbs the peace or quiet of any neighborhood or person, by loud or unusual noise, or by tumultuous or offensive conduct, or threatening, traducing, quarreling, challenging to fight, or fighting, or who, on the public streets of any unincorporated town, or upon the public highways in such unincorporated town, run any horse race, either for a wager or for amusement, or fire any gun or pistol in such unincorporated town, or use any vulgar, profane, or indecent language within the presence or hearing of women or children, in a loud and boisterous manner, is guilty of a misdemeanor, and upon conviction by any Court of competent jurisdiction shall be punished by fine not exceeding two hundred dollars, or by imprisonment in the County Jail for not more than ninety days, or by both fine and imprisonment, or either, at the discretion of the Court."

[2] The suggestion has been made that, in light of the supervening opinion of the California Supreme Court in In re Bushman, 1 Cal. 3d 767, 463 P. 2d 727 (1970), it is "not at all certain that the California Court of Appeal's construction of § 415 is now the authoritative California construction." Post, at 27 (BLACKMUN, J., dissenting). In the course of the Bushman opinion, Chief Justice Traynor stated:

"[One] may . . . be guilty of disturbing the peace through 'offensive' conduct [within the meaning of § 415] if by his actions he willfully and maliciously incites others to violence or engages in conduct likely to incite others to violence. (People v. Cohen (1969) 1 Cal. App. 3d 94, 101, [81 Cal. Rptr. 503].)" 1 Cal. 3d, at 773, 463 P. 2d, at 730.
We perceive no difference of substance between the Bushman construction and that of the Court of Appeal, particularly in light of the Bushman court's approving citation of Cohen.

conviction resting solely upon "speech," cf. Stromberg v. California, 283 U.S. 359 (1931), not upon any separately identifiable conduct which allegedly was intended by Cohen to be perceived by others as expressive of particular views but which, on its face, does not necessarily convey any message and hence arguably could be regulated without effectively repressing Cohen's ability to express himself. Cf. United States v. O'Brien, 391 U.S. 367 (1968). Further, the State certainly lacks power to punish Cohen for the underlying content of the message the inscription conveyed. At least so long as there is no showing of an intent to incite disobedience to or disruption of the draft, Cohen could not, consistently with the First and Fourteenth Amendments, be punished for asserting the evident position on the inutility or immorality of the draft his jacket reflected. Yates v. United States, 354 U.S. 298 (1957).

[*19*] [4] [5] Appellant's conviction, then, rests squarely upon his exercise of the "freedom of speech" protected from arbitrary governmental interference by the Constitution and can be justified, if at all, only as a valid regulation of the manner in which he exercised that freedom, not as a permissible prohibition on the substantive message it conveys. This does not end the inquiry, of course, for the First and Fourteenth Amendments have never been thought to give absolute protection to every individual to speak whenever or wherever he pleases, or to use any form of address in any circumstances that he chooses. In this vein, too, however, we think it important to note that several issues typically associated with such problems are not presented here.

[6]In the first place, Cohen was tried under a statute applicable throughout the entire State. Any attempt to support this conviction on the ground that the statute seeks to preserve an appropriately decorous atmosphere in the courthouse where Cohen was arrested must fail in the absence of any language in the statute that would have put appellant on notice that certain kinds of otherwise permissible speech or conduct would nevertheless, under California law, not be tolerated in certain places. See Edwards v. South Carolina, 372 U.S. 229, 236-237, and n. 11 (1963). Cf. Adderley v. Florida, 385 U.S. 39 (1966). No fair reading of the phrase "offensive conduct" can be said sufficiently to inform the ordinary person that distinctions between certain locations are thereby created.[3]

---

[3] It is illuminating to note what transpired when Cohen entered a courtroom in the building. He removed his jacket and stood with it folded over his arm. Meanwhile, a policeman sent the presiding judge a note suggesting that Cohen be held in contempt of court. The judge declined to do so and Cohen was arrested by the officer only after he emerged from the courtroom. App. 18-19.

[7] In the second place, as it comes to us, this case cannot be said to fall within those relatively few categories of [20] instances where prior decisions have established the power of government to deal more comprehensively with certain forms of individual expression simply upon a showing that such a form was employed. This is not, for example, an obscenity case. Whatever else may be necessary to give rise to the States' broader power to prohibit obscene expression, such expression must be, in some significant way, erotic. Roth v. United States, 354 U.S. 476 (1957). It cannot plausibly be maintained that this vulgar allusion to the Selective Service System would conjure up such psychic stimulation in anyone likely to be confronted with Cohen's crudely defaced jacket.

[8] [9] This Court has also held that the States are free to ban the simple use, without a demonstration of additional justifying circumstances, of so-called "fighting words," those personally abusive epithets which, when addressed to the ordinary citizen, are, as a matter of common knowledge, inherently likely to provoke violent reaction. Chaplinsky v. New Hampshire, 315 U.S. 568 (1942). While the four-letter word displayed by Cohen in relation to the draft is not uncommonly employed in a personally provocative fashion, in this instance it was clearly not "directed to the person of the hearer." Cantwell v. Connecticut, 310 U.S. 296, 309 (1940). No individual actually or likely to be present could reasonably have regarded the words on appellant's jacket as a direct personal insult. Nor do we have here an instance of the exercise of the State's police power to prevent a speaker from intentionally provoking a given group to hostile reaction. Cf. Feiner v. New York, 340 U.S. 315 (1951); Terminiello v. Chicago, 337 U.S. 1 (1949). There is, as noted above, no showing that anyone who saw Cohen was in fact violently aroused or that appellant intended such a result.

[*21*] [10] [11] [12]Finally, in arguments before this Court much has been made of the claim that Cohen's distasteful mode of expression was thrust upon unwilling or unsuspecting viewers, and that the State might therefore legitimately act as it did in order to protect the sensitive from otherwise unavoidable exposure to appellant's crude form of protest. Of course, the mere presumed presence of unwitting listeners or viewers does not serve automatically to justify curtailing all speech capable of giving offense. See, e.g., Organization for a Better Austin v. Keefe, 402 U.S. 415 (1971). While this Court has recognized that government may properly act in many situations to prohibit intrusion into the privacy of the home of unwelcome views and ideas which cannot be totally banned from the public dialogue, e.g., Rowan v. Post Office Dept., 397 U.S. 728 (1970), we have at the same time consistently stressed that "we are often 'captives' outside the

sanctuary of the home and subject to objectionable speech. " Id., at 738. The ability of government, consonant with the Constitution, to shut off discourse solely to protect others from hearing it is, in other words, dependent upon a showing that substantial privacy interests are being invaded in an essentially intolerable manner. Any broader view of this authority would effectively empower a majority to silence dissidents simply as a matter of personal predilections.

[13] [14] In this regard, persons confronted with Cohen's jacket were in a quite different posture than, say, those subjected to the raucous emissions of sound trucks blaring outside their residences. Those in the Los Angeles courthouse could effectively avoid further bombardment of their sensibilities simply by averting their eyes. And, while it may be that one has a more substantial claim to a recognizable privacy interest when walking through a courthouse corridor than, for example, strolling through Central Park, surely it is nothing like the interest in [22] being free from unwanted expression in the confines of one's own home. Cf. Keefe, supra. Given the subtlety and complexity of the factors involved, if Cohen's "speech" was otherwise entitled to constitutional protection, we do not think the fact that some unwilling "listeners" in a public building may have been briefly exposed to it can serve to justify this breach of the peace conviction where, as here, there was no evidence that persons powerless to avoid appellant's conduct did in fact object to it, and where that portion of the statute upon which Cohen's conviction rests evinces no concern, either on its face or as construed by the California courts, with the special plight of the captive auditor, but, instead, indiscriminately sweeps within its prohibitions all "offensive conduct" that disturbs "any neighborhood or person." Cf. Edwards v. South Carolina, supra.[4]

II.   [15] Against this background, the issue flushed by this case stands out in bold relief. It is whether California can excise, as "offensive conduct," one particular scurrilous epithet from the public discourse, either upon the theory of the court below that its use is inherently likely to cause violent reaction or upon a more general assertion that the

States, acting as guardians of public morality, [23] may properly remove this offensive word from the public vocabulary.

[16] [17] [18] The rationale of the California court is plainly untenable. At most it reflects an "undifferentiated fear or apprehension of disturbance [which] is not enough to overcome the right to freedom of expression." Tinker v. Des Moines Indep. Community School Dist., 393 U.S. 503, 508 (1969). We have been shown no evidence that substantial numbers of citizens are standing ready to strike out physically at whoever may assault their sensibilities with execrations like that uttered by Cohen. There may be some persons about with such lawless and violent proclivities, but that is an insufficient base upon which to erect, consistently with constitutional values, a governmental power to force persons who wish to ventilate their dissident views into avoiding particular forms of expression. The argument amounts to little more than the self-defeating proposition that to avoid physical censorship of one who has not sought to provoke such a response by a hypothetical coterie of the violent and lawless, the States may more appropriately effectuate that censorship themselves. Cf. Ashton v. Kentucky, 384 U.S. 195, 200 (1966); Cox v. Louisiana, 379 U.S. 536, 550-551 (1965).

[19] Admittedly, it is not so obvious that the First and Fourteenth Amendments must be taken to disable the States from punishing public utterance of this unseemly expletive in order to maintain what they regard as a suitable level of discourse within the body politic.[5] We [24] think, however, that examination and reflection will reveal the shortcomings of a contrary viewpoint.

[20] At the outset, we cannot overemphasize that, in our judgment, most situations where the State has

---

[4] In fact, other portions of the same statute do make some such distinctions. For example, the statute also prohibits disturbing "the peace or quiet . . . by loud or unusual noise" and using "vulgar, profane, or indecent language within the presence or hearing of women or children, in a loud and boisterous manner." See n. 1, supra. This second-quoted provision in particular serves to put the actor on much fairer notice as to what is prohibited. It also buttresses our view that the "offensive conduct" portion, as construed and applied in this case, cannot legitimately be justified in this Court as designed or intended to make fine distinctions between differently situated recipients.

---

[5] The amicus urges, with some force, that this issue is not properly before us since the statute, as construed, punishes only conduct that might cause others to react violently. However, because the opinion below appears to erect a virtually irrebuttable presumption that use of this word will produce such results, the statute as thus construed appears to impose, in effect, a flat ban on the public utterance of this word. With the case in this posture, it does not seem inappropriate to inquire whether any other rationale might properly support this result. While we think it clear, for the reasons expressed above, that no statute which merely proscribes "offensive conduct" and has been construed as broadly as this one was below can subsequently be justified in this Court as discriminating between conduct that occurs in different places or that offends only certain persons, it is not so unreasonable to seek to justify its full broad sweep on an alternate rationale such as this. Because it is not so patently clear that acceptance of the justification presently under consideration would render the statute overbroad or unconstitutionally vague, and because the answer to appellee's argument seems quite clear, we do not pass on the contention that this claim is not presented on this record.

a justifiable interest in regulating speech will fall within one or more of the various established exceptions, discussed above but not applicable here, to the usual rule that governmental bodies may not prescribe the form or content of individual expression. Equally important to our conclusion is the constitutional backdrop against which our decision must be made. The constitutional right of free expression is powerful medicine in a society as diverse and populous as ours. It is designed and intended to remove governmental restraints from the arena of public discussion, putting the decision as to what views shall be voiced largely into the hands of each of us, in the hope that use of such freedom will ultimately produce a more capable citizenry and more perfect polity and in the belief that no other approach would comport with the premise of individual dignity and choice upon which our political system rests. See Whitney v. California, 274 U.S. 357, 375-377 (1927) (Brandeis, J., concurring). [21] [22] To many, the immediate consequence of this freedom may often appear to be only verbal tumult, discord, and [25] even offensive utterance. These are, however, within established limits, in truth necessary side effects of the broader enduring values which the process of open debate permits us to achieve. That the air may at times seem filled with verbal cacophony is, in this sense not a sign of weakness but of strength. We cannot lose sight of the fact that, in what otherwise might seem a trifling and annoying instance of individual distasteful abuse of a privilege, these fundamental societal values are truly implicated. That is why "wholly neutral futilities . . . come under the protection of free speech as fully as do Keats' poems or Donne's sermons," Winters v. New York, 333 U.S. 507, 528 (1948) (Frankfurter, J., dissenting), and why "so long as the means are peaceful, the communication need not meet standards of acceptability," Organization for a Better Austin v. Keefe, 402 U.S. 415, 419 (1971).

Against this perception of the constitutional policies involved, we discern certain more particularized considerations that peculiarly call for reversal of this conviction. First, the principle contended for by the State seems inherently boundless. How is one to distinguish this from any other offensive word? Surely the State has no right to cleanse public debate to the point where it is grammatically palatable to the most squeamish among us. Yet no readily ascertainable general principle exists for stopping short of that result were we to affirm the judgment below. For, while the particular four-letter word being litigated here is perhaps more distasteful than most others of its genre, it is nevertheless often true that one man's vulgarity is another's lyric. Indeed, we think it is largely because governmental officials cannot make principled distinctions in this area that the

Constitution leaves matters of taste and style so largely to the individual.

[23] [24] Additionally, we cannot overlook the fact, because it [26] is well illustrated by the episode involved here, that much linguistic expression serves a dual communicative function: it conveys not only ideas capable of relatively precise, detached explication, but otherwise inexpressible emotions as well. In fact, words are often chosen as much for their emotive as their cognitive force. We cannot sanction the view that the Constitution, while solicitous of the cognitive content of individual speech, has little or no regard for that emotive function which, practically speaking, may often be the more important element of the overall message sought to be communicated. Indeed, as Mr. Justice Frankfurter has said, "one of the prerogatives of American citizenship is the right to criticize public men and measures – and that means not only informed and responsible criticism but the freedom to speak foolishly and without moderation." Baumgartner v. United States, 322 U.S. 665, 673-674 (1944).

Finally, and in the same vein, we cannot indulge the facile assumption that one can forbid particular words without also running a substantial risk of suppressing ideas in the process. Indeed, governments might soon seize upon the censorship of particular words as a convenient guise for banning the expression of unpopular views. We have been able, as noted above, to discern little social benefit that might result from running the risk of opening the door to such grave results.

[25] It is, in sum, our judgment that, absent a more particularized and compelling reason for its actions, the State may not, consistently with the First and Fourteenth Amendments, make the simple public display here involved of this single four-letter expletive a criminal offense. Because that is the only arguably sustainable rationale for the conviction here at issue, the judgment below must be   Reversed.

DISSENT: [27] MR. JUSTICE BLACKMUN, with whom THE CHIEF JUSTICE and MR. JUSTICE BLACK join.

I dissent, and I do so for two reasons:

1.   Cohen's absurd and immature antic, in my view, was mainly conduct and little speech. See Street v. New York, 394 U.S. 576 (1969); Cox v. Louisiana, 379 U.S. 536, 555 (1965); Giboney v. Empire Storage Co., 336 U.S. 490, 502 (1949). The California Court of Appeal appears so to have described it, 1 Cal. App. 3d 94, 100, 81 Cal. Rptr. 503, 507, and I cannot characterize it otherwise. Further, the case appears to me to be well within the sphere of Chaplinsky v. New Hampshire, 315 U.S. 568 (1942), where Mr. Justice Murphy, a known champion of First Amendment freedoms, wrote for a unanimous bench. As a consequence, this Court's

agonizing over First Amendment values seems misplaced and unnecessary.

2. I am not at all certain that the California Court of Appeal's construction of § 415 is now the authoritative California construction. The Court of Appeal filed its opinion on October 22, 1969. The Supreme Court of California declined review by a four-to-three vote on December 17. See 1 Cal. App. 3d, at 104. A month later, on January 27, 1970, the State Supreme Court in another case construed § 415, evidently for the first time. In re Bushman, 1 Cal. 3d 767, 463 P. 2d 727. Chief Justice Traynor, who was among the dissenters to his court's refusal to take Cohen's case, wrote the majority opinion. He held that § 415 "is not unconstitutionally vague and overbroad" and further said:

"That part of Penal Code section 415 in question here makes punishable only willful and malicious conduct that is violent and endangers public safety and order or that creates a clear and present danger that others will engage in violence of that nature.
[28]   ". . . [It] does not make criminal any nonviolent act unless the act incites or threatens to incite others to violence . . . ." 1 Cal. 3d, at 773-774, 463 P. 2d, at 731.

Cohen was cited in *Bushman,* 1 Cal. 3d, at 773, 463 P. 2d, at 730, but I am not convinced that its description there and Cohen itself are completely consistent with the "clear and present danger" standard enunciated in *Bushman.* Inasmuch as this Court does not dismiss this case, it ought to be remanded to the California Court of Appeal for reconsideration in the light of the subsequently rendered decision by the State's highest tribunal in *Bushman.*

MR. JUSTICE WHITE concurs in Paragraph 2 of MR. JUSTICE BLACKMUN'S dissenting opinion.

Hurley v. Irish-American Gay, Lesbian and Bisexual Group of Boston
515 U.S. 557
(1995)
(Excerpts only. Footnotes omitted.)

Author's Note: In 1947, the City of Boston awarded authority to organize its annual St. Patrick's Day-Evacuation Day Parade to a Boston veterans council that determined participants each year. In 1992, the council refused to allow the Irish-American Gay, Lesbian and Bisexual Group of Boston to participate in the parade, but a court order allowed the group to march. When the council again refused GLIB's application in 1993, the group sued, contending that the denial violated the First Amendment and state law prohibiting discrimination based on sexual orientation. The trial court agreed with GLIB and held that GLIB's inclusion would not infringe the council's First Amendment rights because the parade lacked any expressive purpose. The U.S. Supreme Court unanimously reversed.

JUDGES: SOUTER, J., delivered the opinion for a unanimous Court.

[559] The issue in this case is whether Massachusetts may require private citizens who organize a parade to include among the marchers a group imparting a message the organizers do not wish to convey. We hold that such a mandate violates the First Amendment.

... [562] The [lower] court found that the Council had no written criteria and employed no particular procedures for admission, voted on new applications in batches, had occasionally admitted groups who simply showed up at the parade without having submitted an application, and did "not generally inquire into the specific messages or views of each applicant." The court consequently rejected the Council's contention that the parade was "private" (in the sense of being exclusive), holding instead that "the lack of genuine selectivity in choosing participants and sponsors demonstrates that the Parade is a public event." It found the parade to be "eclectic," containing a wide variety of "patriotic, commercial, political, moral, artistic, religious, athletic, public service, trade union, and eleemosynary themes," as well as conflicting messages. While noting that the Council had indeed excluded the Ku Klux Klan and ROAR (an anti-busing group), it attributed little significance to these facts, concluding ultimately that "the only common theme among the participants and sponsors is their public involvement in the Parade."

The court rejected the Council's assertion that the exclusion of "groups with sexual themes merely formalized [the fact] that the Parade expresses traditional religious and social values," and found the Council's "final position [to be] that GLIB would be excluded because of its values and its message, *i.e.,* its members' sexual orientation." ... [563] The court rejected the notion that GLIB's admission would trample on the Council's First Amendment rights since the court understood that constitutional protection of any interest in expressive association would "require focus on a specific message, theme, or group" absent from the parade.

The court held that because the statute did not mandate inclusion of GLIB but only prohibited discrimination based on sexual orientation, any infringement on the Council's right to expressive association was only "incidental" and "no greater than necessary to accomplish the statute's legitimate purpose" of eradicating discrimination. Accordingly, it ruled that "GLIB is entitled to participate in the Parade on the same terms and conditions as other participants."

...The Supreme Judicial Court of Massachusetts affirmed. ... [565] The court rejected petitioners' further challenge to the law as overbroad, holding that it does not, on its face, regulate speech, does not let public officials examine the content of speech, and would not be interpreted as reaching speech. Finally, the court rejected the challenge that the public accommo-dations law was unconstitutionally vague, holding that this case did not present an issue of speech and that the law gave persons of [565] ordinary intelligence a reasonable opportunity to know what was prohibited.

Justice Nolan dissented. In his view, the Council "does not need a narrow or distinct theme or message in its parade for it to be protected under the First Amendment." First, he wrote, even if the parade had no message at all, GLIB's particular message could not be forced upon it. Second, according to Justice Nolan, the trial judge clearly erred in finding the parade devoid of expressive purpose. He would have held that the Council, like any expressive association, cannot be barred from excluding applicants who do not share the views the Council wishes to advance. Under either a pure speech or associational theory, the State's purpose of eliminating discrimination on the basis of sexual orientation, according to the dissent, could be achieved by more narrowly drawn means, such as ordering admission of individuals regardless of sexual preference, without taking the further step of prohibiting the Council from editing the views expressed in their parade. ... [566] We granted certiorari to determine whether the requirement to admit a parade contingent expressing a message not of the private organizers' own choosing violates the First Amendment. We hold that it does and reverse.

... While the guarantees of free speech and equal protection guard only against encroachment by the government and "erect no shield against merely private conduct," respondents originally argued that the Council's conduct was not purely private, but had the character of state action. ... [T]hey "do not press that issue here." In this Court, then, their claim for inclusion in the parade rests solely on the Massachusetts public accommodations law.

[567] There is no corresponding concession from the other side, however, and certainly not to the state

courts' characterization of the parade as lacking the element of expression for purposes of the First Amendment. Accordingly, our review of petitioners' claim that their activity is indeed in the nature of protected speech carries with it a constitutional duty to conduct an independent examination of the record as a whole, without deference to the trial court. This obligation rests upon us simply because the reaches of the First Amendment are ultimately defined by the facts it is held to embrace, and we must thus decide for ourselves whether a given course of conduct falls on the near or far side of the line of constitutional protection.

... [568] If there were no reason for a group of people to march from here to there except to reach a destination, they could make the trip without expressing any message beyond the fact of the march itself. Some people might call such a procession a parade, but it would not be much of one. ... [W]e use the word "parade" to indicate marchers who are making some sort of collective point, not just to each other but to bystanders along the way. Indeed, a parade's dependence on watchers is so extreme that nowadays, as with Bishop Berkeley's celebrated tree, "if a parade or demonstration receives no media coverage, it may as well not have happened." Parades are thus a form of expression, not just motion, and the inherent expressiveness of marching to make a point explains our cases involving protest marches.

... [569] The protected expression that inheres in a parade is not limited to its banners and songs, however, for the Constitution looks beyond written or spoken words as mediums of expression. Noting that "symbolism is a primitive but effective way of communicating ideas," our cases have recognized that the First Amendment shields such acts as saluting a flag (and refusing to do so), wearing an armband to protest a war, displaying a red flag, and even "marching, walking or parading" in uniforms displaying the swastika. As some of these examples show, a narrow, succinctly articulable message is not a condition of constitutional protection, which if confined to expressions conveying a "particularized message," would never reach the unquestionably shielded painting of Jackson Pollock, music of Arnold Schoenberg, or Jabberwocky verse of Lewis Carroll.

Not many marches, then, are beyond the realm of expressive parades, and the South Boston celebration is not one of them. ... To be sure, we agree with the state courts that in spite of excluding some applicants, the Council is rather lenient in admitting participants. But a private speaker does not forfeit constitutional protection simply by combining multifarious voices, or by failing to edit their themes to isolate an exact message as the exclusive [570] subject matter of the speech. Nor, under our precedent, does First Amendment protection require a speaker to generate, as an original matter, each item featured in the communication. Cable operators, for example, are engaged in protected speech activities even when they only select programming originally produced by others. For that matter, the presentation of an edited compilation of speech generated by other persons is a staple of most newspapers' opinion pages, which, of course, fall squarely within the core of First Amendment security, as does even the simple selection of a paid noncommercial advertisement for inclusion in a daily paper. The selection of contingents to make a parade is entitled to similar protection.

Respondents' participation as a unit in the parade was equally expressive. GLIB was formed for the very purpose of marching in it, as the trial court found, in order to celebrate its members' identity as openly gay, lesbian, and bisexual descendants of the Irish immigrants, to show that there are such individuals in the community, and to support the like men and women who sought to march in the New York parade. The organization distributed a fact sheet describing the members' intentions, and the record otherwise corroborates the expressive nature of GLIB's participation. In 1993, members of GLIB marched behind a shamrock-strewn banner with the simple inscription "Irish American Gay, Lesbian and Bisexual Group of Boston." GLIB understandably seeks to communicate its ideas as part of the existing parade, rather than staging one of its own.

[571] The Massachusetts public accommodations law under which respondents brought suit ... [572] today prohibits discrimination on the basis of "race, color, religious creed, national origin, sex, sexual orientation . . ., deafness, blindness or any physical or mental disability or ancestry" in "the admission of any person to, or treatment in any place of public accommodation, resort or amusement." Provisions like these are well within the State's usual power to enact when a legislature has reason to believe that a given group is the target of discrimination, and they do not, as a general matter, violate the First or Fourteenth Amendments. Nor is this statute unusual in any obvious way, since it does not, on its face, target speech or discriminate on the basis of its content, the focal point of its prohibition being rather on the act of discriminating against individuals in the provision of publicly available goods, privileges, and services on the proscribed grounds.

In the case before us, however, the Massachusetts law has been applied in a peculiar way. Its enforcement does not address any dispute about the participation of openly gay, lesbian, or bisexual individuals in various units admitted to the parade. Petitioners disclaim any intent to exclude homosexuals as such, and no individual member of

GLIB claims to have been excluded from parading as a member of any group that the Council has approved to march. Instead, the disagreement goes to the admission of GLIB as its own parade unit carrying its own banner. Since every participating unit affects the message conveyed by the private organizers, the state courts' application of the statute produced an order essentially requiring petitioners to alter the expressive content [573] of their parade. Although the state courts spoke of the parade as a place of public accommodation, once the expressive character of both the parade and the marching GLIB contingent is understood, it becomes apparent that the state courts' application of the statute had the effect of declaring the sponsors' speech itself to be the public accommodation. Under this approach any contingent of protected individuals with a message would have the right to participate in petitioners' speech, so that the communication produced by the private organizers would be shaped by all those protected by the law who wished to join in with some expressive demonstration of their own. But this use of the State's power violates the fundamental rule of protection under the First Amendment, that a speaker has the autonomy to choose the content of his own message.

"Since *all* speech inherently involves choices of what to say and what to leave unsaid," one important manifestation of the principle of free speech is that one who chooses to speak may also decide "what not to say." Although the State may at times "prescribe what shall be orthodox in commercial advertising" by requiring the dissemination of "purely factual and uncontroversial information," outside that context it may not compel affirmance of a belief with which the speaker disagrees. Indeed this general rule, that the speaker has the right to tailor the speech, applies not only to expressions of value, opinion, or endorsement, but equally to statements of fact the speaker would rather avoid, [574] subject, perhaps, to the permissive law of defamation. Nor is the rule's benefit restricted to the press, being enjoyed by business corporations generally and by ordinary people engaged in unsophisticated expression as well as by professional publishers. Its point is simply the point of all speech protection, which is to shield just those choices of content that in someone's eyes are misguided, or even hurtful.

Petitioners' claim to the benefit of this principle of autonomy to control one's own speech is as sound as the South Boston parade is expressive. Rather like a composer, the Council selects the expressive units of the parade from potential participants, and though the score may not produce a particularized message, each contingent's expression in the Council's eyes comports with what merits celebration on that day. Even if this view gives the Council credit for a more considered judgment than it actively made, the Council clearly decided to exclude a message it did not like from the communication it chose to make, and that is enough to invoke its right as a private speaker to shape its expression by speaking on one subject while remaining silent on another. The message it disfavored is not difficult to identify. Although GLIB's point (like the Council's) is not wholly articulate, a contingent marching behind the organization's banner would at least bear witness to the fact that some Irish are gay, lesbian, or bisexual, and the presence of the organized marchers would suggest their view that people of their sexual orientations have as much claim to unqualified social acceptance as heterosexuals and indeed as members of parade units organized around other identifying characteristics. The parade's organizers may not believe these facts about Irish sexuality to be so, or they may object to unqualified [575] social acceptance of gays and lesbians or have some other reason for wishing to keep GLIB's message out of the parade. But whatever the reason, it boils down to the choice of a speaker not to propound a particular point of view, and that choice is presumed to lie beyond the government's power to control.

... Respondents contend ... that admission of GLIB to the parade would not threaten the core principle of speaker's autonomy because the Council, like a cable operator, is merely "a conduit" for the speech of participants in the parade "rather than itself a speaker." But this metaphor is not apt here, because GLIB's participation would likely be perceived as having resulted from the Council's customary determination about a unit admitted to the parade, that its message was worthy of presentation and quite possibly of support as well. A newspaper, similarly, "is more than a passive receptacle or conduit for news, comment, and advertising," and we have held that "the choice of material . . . and the decisions made as to limitations on the size and content . . . and treatment of public issues . . .– whether fair or unfair – constitute the exercise of editorial control and judgment" upon which the State can not intrude. ... [576] Thus, when dissemination of a view contrary to one's own is forced upon a speaker intimately connected with the communication advanced, the speaker's right to autonomy over the message is compromised.

... [577] [I]n the context of an expressive parade, as with a protest march, the parade's overall message is distilled from the individual presentations along the way, and each unit's expression is perceived by spectators as part of the whole. ... True, the size and success of petitioners' parade makes it an enviable vehicle for the dissemination of GLIB's views, but that fact, [578] without more, would fall far short of supporting a claim that petitioners enjoy an abiding monopoly of access to spectators. Considering that GLIB presumably would have had a fair shot (under

neutral criteria developed by the city) at obtaining a parade permit of its own, respondents have not shown that petitioners enjoy the capacity to "silence the voice of competing speakers" ... . Nor has any other legitimate interest been identified in support of applying the Massachusetts statute in this way to expressive activity like the parade.

The statute, Mass. Gen. Laws § 272:98 (1992), is a piece of protective legislation that announces no purpose beyond the object both expressed and apparent in its provisions, which is to prevent any denial of access to (or discriminatory treatment in) public accommodations on proscribed grounds, including sexual orientation. On its face, the object of the law is to ensure by statute for gays and lesbians desiring to make use of public accommodations what the old common law promised to any member of the public wanting a meal at the inn, that accepting the usual terms of service, they will not be turned away merely on the proprietor's exercise of personal preference. When the law is applied to expressive activity in the way it was done here, its apparent object is simply to require speakers to modify the content of their expression to whatever extent beneficiaries of the law choose to alter it with messages of their own. But in the absence of some further, legitimate end, this object is merely to allow exactly what the general rule of speaker's autonomy forbids.

... [579] Having availed itself of the public thoroughfares "for purposes of assembly [and] communicating thoughts between citizens," the Council is engaged in a use of the streets that has "from ancient times, been a part of the privileges, immunities, rights, and liberties of citizens." Our tradition of free speech commands that a speaker who takes to the street corner to express his views in this way should be free from interference by the State based on the content of what he says. The very idea that a noncommercial speech restriction be used to produce thoughts and statements acceptable to some groups or, indeed, all people, grates on the First Amendment, for it amounts to nothing less than a proposal to limit speech in the service of orthodox expression. The Speech Clause has no more certain antithesis. While the law is free to promote all sorts of conduct in place of harmful behavior, it is not free to interfere with speech for no better reason than promoting an approved message or discouraging a disfavored one, however enlightened either purpose may strike the government.

... [580] *New York State Club Assn.* is also instructive by the contrast it provides. There, we turned back a facial challenge to a state anti-discrimination statute on the assumption that the expressive associational character of a dining club with over 400 members could be sufficiently attenuated to permit application of the law even to such a private organization, but we also recognized that the State did not prohibit exclusion of those whose views were at odds with positions espoused by the general club memberships. In other words, although the association provided public benefits to which a State could ensure equal access, it was also engaged in expressive activity; compelled access to the benefit, which was upheld, did not trespass on the organization's message itself. If we were to analyze this case strictly along those lines, GLIB would lose.

Assuming the parade to be large enough and a source of benefits (apart from its expression) that would generally justify a mandated access provision, GLIB could [581] nonetheless be refused admission as an expressive contingent with its own message just as readily as a private club could exclude an applicant whose manifest views were at odds with a position taken by the club's existing members. ...

Obscenity and Indecency

Limiting the reach of the First Amendment

Focal case:
Miller v. California, 413 U.S. 15 (1973)

A s the discussion in the preceding chapters indicates, the Supreme Court repeatedly has held that "all ideas having even the slightest redeeming social importance – unorthodox ideas, controversial ideas, even ideas hateful to the prevailing climate of opinion" – have full First Amendment protection unless they conflict with a narrow set of more important constitutional values.[1] Despite this broad declaration, the Supreme Court – since at least 1931 – has not required government laws banning obscenity to pass any of the speech protective First Amendment tests. Instead, the Court has held that "obscenity is not within the area of constitutionally protected speech or press."[2] The Supreme Court has reasoned that obscenity is of so little utility and is so harmful to society that it is not part of "the freedom of speech" protected by the First Amendment.[3] Moreover, the Court has said, properly tailored anti-obscenity laws protect the public morals, health and safety.

First Amendment scholar Harry Kalven has said the Court has built its obscenity jurisprudence upon four legs: 1) incitement – obscenity incites anti-social acts; 2) advocacy – obscenity prompts psychological excitement that encourages sexual aggression; 3) disgust – obscenity disgusts individuals with normal sexual attitudes; and 4) morality – obscenity arouses improper and unhealthy sexual interests.[4] Other scholars suggest the Court's approach to obscenity reflects a belief that obscenity resembles an action rather than a form of expression.[5] Extending this logic, some feminist scholars contend that obscenity constitutes a punishable act of violence

---

[1] Roth v. United States, 354 U.S. 476, 480-81 (1957).

[2] Roth, 354 U.S. at 483. *See also* Near v. Minnesota, 283 U.S. 697 (1931).

[3] *See* Miller v. California, 413 U.S. 15, 23 (1975).

[4] Harry Kalven, *The Metaphysics of the Law of Obscenity*, 1960 Sup. Ct. Rev. 1 (1960).

[5] *See* Frederick Schauer, *Speech and 'Speech' – Obscenity and 'Obscenity': An Exercise in the Interpretation of Constitutional Language*, 67 GEO. L.J. 899 (1979).

and subjugation against women that violates equal protection and infringes women's fundamental civil liberties.[6]

The Court has not consistently articulated its justifications for finding strict anti-obscenity laws constitutional. Instead, having placed obscenity outside the protection of the First Amendment, the Court has worked to develop a clear definition of the types of expression that are legally obscene. This is no easy task. From the start, the definitional approach to obscenity generated profound disagreement among the justices and produced many divided opinions.[7]

OBSCENITY

The Court's most recent obscenity test, established in 1973 in *Miller v. California*, defines illegal obscenity as any expression

1.   the average person, applying contemporary community standards, would find appeals to prurient interests,
2.   that depicts in a patently offensive way specific sexual or excretory conduct or organs (as prohibited by the applicable law), and
3.   that, when taken as a whole, lacks serious literary, artistic, political or scientific value.[8]

Sexually offensive expression that does not satisfy all three prongs of the test receives some First Amendment protection.

Obscenity is distinguished from other explicit sexual expression through its emphasis on prurience. According to the Supreme Court, obscenity disgusts and debases the average person;[9] obscenity goes beyond overt depictions of nudity, sex and excretion to corrupt the public morals by encouraging an unnatural or excessive interest in these topics.[10] The Court has said prurient speech does not simply express normal sexual desires; it appeals to people in an "uneasy . . . itching, morbid or lascivious" way.[11] Similarly, as the second prong of the *Miller* test indicates, obscenity encompasses only patently "hard core" sexual materials that depict or describe in an extremely offensive manner conduct expressly prohibited by state law.[12]

In addition to definitional problems, courts have struggled to determine how to properly determine and apply the *Miller* test's "contemporary community standard." This prong of the test necessarily requires juries to apply local standards because the Court in *Miller* said any "national community standard" to determine obscenity would be ineffective and overly censorious.[13] Yet global communications, particularly the Internet, challenge the concept that communications relate to any particular locale. An inherent trait of the Internet is its universality: universal access, universal content and universal audience,[14] and the absence of geographic limits to the Internet makes defining "community" both tenuous and arbitrary.

---

[6] *See* ANDREA DWORKIN AND CATHERINE MACKINNON, PORNOGRAPHY AND CIVIL RIGHTS: A NEW DAY FOR WOMEN'S EQUALITY (1988).

[7] *See* Interstate Circuit, Inc. v. Dallas, 390 U.S. 676, 705 n.1 (1968) (noting that the 13 obscenity rulings in the previous decade had produced 55 separate opinions).

[8] Miller v. California, 413 U.S. 15 (1973).

[9] Miller, 413 U.S. at 25.

[10] *See* Miller, 413 U.S. at 17 (defining prurience as "a shameful or morbid interest in nudity, sex, or excretion, which goes substantially beyond customary limits of candor in description or representation of such matters and is matter which is utterly without redeeming social importance").

[11] Brockett v. Spokane Arcades, Inc., 472 U.S. 491, 496 (1985) (finding that material that provokes "only normal, healthy sexual desires" is not prurient).

[12] Miller, 413 U.S. at 27.

[13] *See* Miller, 413 U.S. at 30.

[14] *See* Eileen Candia, *Comment, The Information Super Highway - Caution - Road Blocks Ahead: Is the Use of Filtering Technology to Prevent Access to 'Harmful' Sites Constitutional?*, 9 TEMP. POL. & CIV. RTS. L. REV. 85, 96 (1999).

INDECENT NOT OBSCENE

When sexually explicit material does not meet the *Miller* standard, when it is *not* legally obscene, it generally is protected. However, the distinction between unprotected obscene material and protected sexual explicitness turns on the facts in each case; no bright line establishes the boundary.[15] According to the Supreme Court, "The normal definition of 'indecent' merely refers to nonconformance with accepted standards of morality."[16] Vulgar sexual expression and innuendo are indecent.[17]

Historically, the Court has said indecent, lewd and graphic sexual material is protected expression *unless* if it involves broadcasts over the public airwaves to susceptible children[18] (See Chap. 12 on media distinctions), threats to public safety[19] or minors engaged in sexual activity.[20] Thus, in 1978 in *FCC v. Pacifica*, the Court held that the Federal Communications Commission had the authority to fine broadcasters for disseminating "vulgar," "offensive," and "shocking" material. The landmark ruling involved the 2 p.m. radio broadcast of a George Carlin monologue satirizing an FCC regulation establishing seven "words you couldn't say on the public airwaves."[21] Asserting that children were likely to hear the monologue, which involved frequent repetition of the seven "Filthy Words," the Court upheld the FCC's power to levy fines for indecent speech. The Court reasoned that the "utterances [were] no essential part of any exposition of ideas and [were] of such slight social value as a step to truth that any benefit that may be derived from them is clearly outweighed by the social interest in order and morality."[22]

More recently, a plurality of the Supreme Court in 2000 applied intermediate scrutiny to uphold a public decency ordinance that prohibited public nudity, including nude dancing.[23] Five justices acknowledged that nude dancing, performed as entertainment, enjoyed some First Amendment protection, but the plurality reasoned that the city had the authority and power to address the negative secondary effects of nude dancing, which included violence, sexual harassment, drunkenness, prostitution and sexually transmitted diseases. The Court said the city's important interest in protecting the public health and safety outweighed the First Amendment protection afforded nude dancing.

ADDRESSING SECONDARY EFFECTS

The Supreme Court's protection of indecent expression has been far from absolute, in part because the Court has accepted arguments that indecent materials, and the establishments that sell or present them, cause substantial harms to society.[24] The Court believes a link exists among indecent materials, the "adult" businesses that sell them and an array of social ills, including

---

[15] Rollin M. Perkins & Ronald N. Boyce, *Criminal Law* 471 (3d ed. 1982).

[16] FCC v. Pacifica Found., 438 U.S. 726, 740 (1978).

[17] Pacifica, 438 U.S. at 729; Communications Act of 1934, ch. 652, 301, 48 Stat. 1081, as amended, 47 U.S.C. 151 et seq. (1994); 18 U.S.C. 1464 (1994) (establishing fines and or imprisonment for utterance of "any obscene, indecent, or profane language by means of radio communication").

[18] Pacifica, 438 U.S. 726 (1978).

[19] Erie v. Pap's A.M., 529 U.S. 277 (2000).

[20] Reno v. American Civil Liberties Union, 521 U.S. 844 (1997) (finding unconstitutional Communications Decency Act of 1996 ban on Internet transmissions of indecent material); United States v. Playboy Entertainment Group, 120 U.S. 1878 (2000). *See also* Fox v. United States, 248 F.3d 394 (5th Cir. 2001), vacated and remanded, 535 U.S. 1014 (2002) (rejecting First Amendment challenge to CIPA); United States v. Bunnell, 2002 U.S. Dist. LEXIS 8319 (D. Maine 2002) (rejecting First Amendment protection against child pornography prosecution for sutdent's course-related possession of materials).

[21] Pacifica, 438 U.S. at 729.

[22] Pacifica, 438 U.S. at 746 (internal citation omitted).

[23] Erie v. Pap's A.M., 529 U.S. 277 (2000).

[24] *See, e.g.,* FCC v. Pacifica, 438 U.S. 726 (1978); Erie v. Pap's A.M., 529 U.S. 277 (2000).

increased crime, decreased property values, erosion of community character and reduction in retail business.

Based on these secondary effects, the Court long has upheld zoning and land-use regulations that do not ban but strictly control and severely limit the location of "adult" businesses.[25] The Court generally has ruled that laws that target adult businesses based on the subject matter of their business are content-neutral time, place and manner regulations if the law's "predominate concerns" are with reducing the deleterious secondary effects of such establishments.[26] To justify such laws, the Court has said, government may demonstrate its substantial, non-speech related interest with any evidence that is "reasonably believed to be relevant."[27]

In 2002, for example, the Supreme Court allowed the city of Los Angeles to defend a city ordinance that prohibited multiple adult businesses in any building.[28] Both lower courts had granted summary judgment to the bookstore and video arcade that challenged the law's premise that two adult businesses at one location increased crime. Upon review, however, a plurality of the Supreme Court said the ordinance was not facially unconstitutional because the city could reasonably rely on a six-year-old police study to support its argument that the single occupancy rule advanced a substantial interest in reducing crime. The Court remanded the case for intermediate scrutiny review to determine whether the law was narrowly tailored to advance the city's interest.

APPLYING ANTI-RACKETEERING LAWS TO ADULT BUSINESSES

The federal government and a number of states also have used laws designed to target organized crime to increase the penalties imposed upon adult businesses found guilty of selling obscenity. Federal and state Racketeer Influenced and Corrupt Organizations (RICO) statutes that permit government seizure of all assets related to an organized pattern of illegal activity (generally defined as two or more illegal acts)[29] have been used to seize the equipment and publications of adult businesses even when much of the material does not meet the *Miller* obscenity standard.

Thus, in 1989, the Supreme Court upheld the constitutionality of an Indiana statute that permitted prosecutors to define repeated distribution of obscene materials (normally a misdemeanor offense) as racketeering (a felony).[30] The Court held, however, that the *pretrial* seizure of the contents of an adult bookstore was an unconstitutional prior restraint. Then, in 1993, in *Alexander v. United States*, the Court upheld a six-year prison term, a fine of $100,000, and the forfeiture of $9 million and all business assets as constitutional punishment for the sale of obscene materials.[31] The owner of several adult bookstores and video arcades in Minnesota had been found guilty under the federal RICO act of selling four obscene magazines and three obscene videotapes. The Supreme Court said the massive forfeiture was not an unconstitutional prior restraint but a permissible criminal punishment that did not impose government censorship or unduly chill First Amendment rights. Only four justices believed the First Amendment prohibited government confiscation of the storeowner's constitutionally protected indecent materials.

---

[25] *See, e.g.,* Young v. American Mini Theatres, Inc., 427 U.S. 50 (1976); Renton v. Playtime Theatres, Inc., 475 U.S. 41 (1986).

[26] Renton, 475 U.S. at 47.

[27] Renton, 475 U.S. at 51-52.

[28] City of Los Angeles v. Alameda Books, Inc., 535 U.S. 425 (2002).

[29] *See, e.g.,* 18 USCS 1961 et seq.

[30] Ft. Wayne Books v. Indiana, 489 U.S. 46 (1989).

[31] 509 U.S. 544 (1993).

PROTECTING MINORS

Transporting obscene material across state lines – whether by post, by car, or by e-mail – has been a federal crime since the early 1800s.[32] In the 1990s, however, Congress enacted a number of laws making it a crime to transmit either obscene or indecent material over the Internet to minors.[33] In 1997, the Supreme Court struck down the first federal ban on transmission of indecent material over the Internet.[34] Despite strongly affirming government authority to prohibit the delivery of obscenity, the majority of the Court found the Communication Decency Act's ban on Internet transport of indecency unconstitutionally vague and overbroad. The Court agreed that protection of children from harmful material was an important government objective but reiterated that this goal could not be achieved at the expense of limiting adults to only that sexual expression that is "fit for children."[35] Lower courts, however, have ruled that the First Amendment does not protect possession of child pornography even for journalistic or scholarly purposes.[36]

CONTEMPORARY COMMUNITY STANDARDS

In 2002, the Supreme Court grappled with how to apply the *Miller* community standard requirement to online indecency when it vacated and remanded an appeals court decision that found the federal Child Online Protection Act (COPA) unconstitutionally required the application of a national community standard.[37] Congress enacted COPA to protect minors from online dissemination of sexually explicit materials. In upholding an injunction against the application of COPA, the Court of Appeals for the Third Circuit said the law unconstitutionally burdened protected speech because it required every web publisher to abide by the most restrictive and conservative state community standards to avoid both civil and criminal liability.[38]

Yet the Supreme Court lifted the injunction and said the difficult application of a community standard to the online environment was not sufficient to render the law unconstitutional. In fact, two members of the Court said a national community standard is both constitutional and necessary "for any reasonable regulation of Internet obscenity."[39] The Supreme Court remanded the case, asking the circuit court to apply strict scrutiny to determine whether COPA was unconstitutionally vague.

The role of the Internet also was central in another 2002 Supreme Court decision, this time striking down provisions of the federal Child Pornography Prevention Act of 1996 that prohibited Internet dissemination of "virtual child pornography."[40] The Court in *Ashcroft v. Free Speech Coalition*

---

[32] *See, e.g.,* An Act for the Suppression of Trade in, and Circulation of, Obscene Literature and Articles of Immoral Use, 17 Stat. 598 (1873) (The Comstock Act); Rowan v. Post Office, 397 U.S. 728 (1970); ApolloMedia v. Reno, 526 U.S. 1061 (1999).

[33] *See, e.g.,* J. Krause, *Can Anyone Stop Internet Porn?* 88 A.B.A. J. 56 (2002); Communications Decency Act, Telecommunications Act of 1996, Pub. L. No. 104-104 § 502, 110 Stat. 56.; Child Online Protection Act of 1998, Pub. L. No. 105-277, Div. C, Title XIV, § 1402, 112 Stat. 2681-736 (codified at 47 U.S.C. § 231 (2000)); Child Internet Protection Act of 2000, 47 U.S.C. § 254(h)(6)(B)(i) (2001); Child Pornography Prevention Act, Pub. L. No. 104-208, Title I, § 121, 110 Stat. 3009, 3009-26 to 3009-31 (1996) (amending 18 U.S.C. §§ 2241, 2243, 2251, 2252, 2256, 42 U.S.C. § 2000aa, and adding 18 U.S.C. § 2252A).

[34] Reno v. American Civil Liberties Union, 521 U.S. 844 (1997).

[35] Butler *v.* Michigan, 352 U.S. 380, 383 (1957); Denver Area Educ. Telcoms. Consortium v. FCC, 518 U.S. 727, 759 (1996); United States *v.* Playboy Entertainment Group, Inc., 529 U.S. 803, 814 (2000); Ashcroft v. Free Speech Coalition, 535 U.S. 234, 422 (2002).

[36] *See* United States v. Matthews, 209 F.3d 338 (4th Cir. 2000); United States v. Bunnell, 2002 U.S. Dist. LEXIS 8319 (D. Maine 2002).

[37] Ashcroft v. ACLU, 535 U.S. 564 (2002).

[38] ACLU v. Reno, 217 F.3d 162, 177 (3d Cir. 2000).

[39] Ashcroft, 535 U.S. at 789 (O'Connor, J., concurring), and 791 (Breyer, J., concurring) .

[40] 535 U.S. 234 (2002).

said virtual child pornography – or sexual images presented as child pornography that do not involve real minors (think of adults *appearing* as minors or of animated films, etc.) – is distinguishable from real child pornography, which may be banned without regard to whether it has redeeming value. The Court reiterated its profound concern about the potential harm of real child pornography but said virtual online child pornography was constitutionally protected because it neither involved children in pornographic activity nor encouraged sexual abuse of minors. In addition, the Court said the government had failed to show that the law narrowly targeted only materials "harmful" to non-consenting adults and minors.[41]

PUBLIC SUBSIDIES OF INDECENCY

While government attempts to prevent online access to indecent material appear to be unconstitutional, the Supreme Court has held that the Constitution does not prohibit government from refusing to give subsidies or to purchase certain expressive materials because of their indecent content. In 1998, for example, the Supreme Court held in *National Endowment for the Arts v. Finley* that the NEA could constitutionally consider decency and respect for diverse public attitudes when awarding federal grants to support works of arts.[42] The Court rejected a facial challenge to the law and said that, when acting as patron, government allocation of public funds is necessarily selective. The Court said the NEA decency rule permitted government to consider aesthetics and "general standards of decency" but did not prevent government funding of indecent art.[43] In addition, the Court said the rule posed little risk of government censorship of indecent art because there was no agreement over what constitutes indecency.

The Supreme Court stopped short of broadly endorsing the decency rule, however. Instead, the Court said an applicant who could show that the NEA invidiously "manipulated" funding to suppress or eliminate "certain ideas or viewpoints from the marketplace" might successfully challenge the rule.[44] In solitary dissent, Justice Souter said the decency rule clearly imposed unconstitutional viewpoint discrimination against protected expression.

In 2003, the Supreme Court similarly ruled that a federal law requiring public libraries to block Internet access to indecency or forfeit federal funding was constitutional.[45] After finding that public libraries do not constitute public forums, the Court in *United States v. American Library Association* found the Children's Internet Protection Act's screening requirement advanced the libraries' core mission of enhancing learning. The Court applied rational scrutiny and said its precedents clearly established that government may make content-based distinctions in determining its allocation of speech subsidies.[46]

READING THE LAW ON OBSCENITY AND INDECENCY

Despite nearly a decade of efforts to establish a clear standard to separate punishable obscenity from protected speech about sex, the Supreme Court has failed to fully clarify or settle this area of the law. Reading *Miller v. California* and the suggested cases that follow will greatly increase your understanding of this topic.

- *Ashcroft v. Free Speech Coalition*, 535 U.S. 234 (2002) (ban on virtual child pornography unconstitutional).

---

[41] Nicole I. Khoury, *Note: United States v. Playboy: Children and Sexually Explicit Material: Whose Problem Is It?*, 22 U. TOL. L. REV. 431, 431 (2002).

[42] 524 U.S. 569 (1998). *See also* Pico v. Island Trees School District, 474 F. Supp. 387 (1979).

[43] NEA, 514 U.S. at 576.

[44] NEA, 514 U.S. at 587.

[45] United States v. American Library Assoc., 123 S.Ct. 2297 (2003).

[46] *See* Arkansas Educational Television commission v. Forbes, 523 U.S. 666 (1998); National Endowment for the Arts v. Finley, 524 U.S. 569 (1998).

- *NEA v. Finley*, 524 U.S. 569 (1998)(decency provision in government funding of arts constitutional).
- *Reno v. ACLU*, 521 U.S. 844 (1997) (Communications Decency Act ban on Internet transmissions of indecent material unconstitutional).
- *Denver Area Educational Telecommunications Consortium, Inc. v. FCC*, 518 U.S. 727 (1996) (FCC-supported ban on cable leased-access indecency constitutional).
- *Alexander v. United States*, 509 U.S. 544 (1993) (application of RICO to confiscate indecency constitutional).
- *Barnes v. Glen Theatre*, 501 U.S. 560 (1991) (anti-nudity law constitutional).
- *Renton v. Playtime Theatres*, 475 U.S. 41 (1986) (zoning law eliminating adult businesses from church, school, park and residential areas constitutional).
- *Jenkins v. Georgia*, 418 U.S. 153 (1974) (the film "Carnal Knowledge" not obscene under *Miller* standard).
- *Roth v. United States*, 354 U.S. 476 (1957) (ban on mailing obscenity constitutional).

The following questions are designed to help you read *Miller v. California* from a critical perspective.

- What law is challenged in this case and by whom?
- What rationale(s) does the Court provide to justify its exclusion of obscenity from constitutional protection?
- How does the Court apply the concept of overbreadth in this decision?
- What characteristics of the law raise vagueness concerns for the Court?
- Does the Court examine the intent, the text or the effect of the statute to determine the law's constitutionality?
- Under this precedent, is material with "serious artistic value" protected regardless of its prurience?
- What is the "contemporary community" whose standards dictate what is obscene?
- What "safeguards" does the Court require when regulations target obscenity?
- Must an individual reasonably know that materials are obscene to suffer prosecution?
- What are the primary objections raised by Justices Douglas and Brennan in their dissents?

Miller v. California
413 U.S. 15
(1973)

JUDGES: Burger, C. J., delivered the opinion of the Court, in which White, Blackmun, Powell, and Rehnquist, JJ., joined. Douglas, J., filed a dissenting opinion. Brennan, J., filed a dissenting opinion, in which Stewart and Marshall, JJ., joined.

OPINION: [16] MR. CHIEF JUSTICE BURGER delivered the opinion of the Court.

This is one of a group of "obscenity-pornography" cases being reviewed by the Court in a re-examination of standards enunciated in earlier cases involving what Mr. Justice Harlan called "the intractable obscenity problem." *Interstate Circuit,* *Inc. v. Dallas*, 390 U.S. 676, 704 (1968) (concurring and dissenting).

[1A] Appellant conducted a mass mailing campaign to advertise the sale of illustrated books, euphemistically called "adult" material. After a jury trial, he was convicted of violating California Penal Code § 311.2 (a), a misdemeanor, by knowingly distributing obscene matter,[1] [17] and the Appellate

---

[1] At the time of the commission of the alleged offense, which was prior to June 25, 1969, §§ 311.2 (a) and 311 of the California Penal Code read in relevant part:

"§ 311.2 Sending or bringing into state for sale or distribution; printing, exhibiting, distributing or possessing within state

Department, Superior Court of California, County of Orange, summarily affirmed the judgment without opinion. Appellant's conviction was specifically [18] based on his conduct in causing five unsolicited advertising brochures to be sent through the mail in an envelope addressed to a restaurant in Newport Beach, California. The envelope was opened by the manager of the restaurant and his mother. They had not requested the brochures; they complained to the police.

[1B] The brochures advertise four books entitled "Intercourse," "Man-Woman," "Sex Orgies Illustrated," and "An Illustrated History of Pornography," and a film entitled "Marital Intercourse." While the brochures contain some descriptive printed material, primarily they consist of

---

"(a) Every person who knowingly: sends or causes to be sent, or brings or causes to be brought, into this state for sale or distribution, or in this state prepares, publishes, prints, exhibits, distributes, or offers to distribute, or has in his possession with intent to distribute or to exhibit or offer to distribute, any obscene matter is guilty of a misdemeanor...."
"§ 311. Definitions
"As used in this chapter:
"(a) 'Obscene' means that to the average person, applying contemporary standards, the predominant appeal of the matter, taken as a whole, is to prurient interest, i.e., a shameful or morbid interest in nudity, sex, or excretion, which goes substantially beyond customary limits of candor in description or representation of such matters and is matter which is utterly without redeeming social importance.
"(b) 'Matter' means any book, magazine, newspaper, or other printed or written material or any picture, drawing, photograph, motion picture, or other pictorial representation or any statute or other figure, or any recording, transcription or mechanical, chemical or electrical reproduction or any other articles, equipment, machines or materials.
"(c) 'Person' means any individual, partnership, firm, association, corporation, or other legal entity.
"(d) 'Distribute' means to transfer possession of, whether with or without consideration.
"(e) 'Knowingly' means having knowledge that the matter is obscene."
Section 311 (e) of the California Penal Code, *supra*, was amended on June 25, 1969, to read as follows:
"(e) 'Knowingly' means being aware of the character of the matter."
Cal. Amended Stats. 1969, c. 249, § 1, p. 598. Despite appellant's contentions to the contrary, the record indicates that the new § 311 (e) was not applied *ex post facto* to his case, but only the old § 311 (e) as construed by state decisions prior to the commission of the alleged offense. See *People v. Pinkus*, 256 Cal. App. 2d 941, 948-950, 63 Cal. Rptr. 680, 685-686 (App. Dept., Superior Ct., Los Angeles, 1967); *People v. Campise*, 242 Cal. App. 2d 905, 914, 51 Cal. Rptr. 815, 821 (App. Dept., Superior Ct., San Diego, 1966). Cf. *Bouie v. City of Columbia*, 378 U.S. 347 (1964). Nor did § 311.2, *supra*, as applied, create any "direct, immediate burden on the performance of the postal functions," or infringe on congressional commerce powers under Art. I, § 8, cl. 3. *Roth v. United States*, 354 U.S. 476, 494 (1957), quoting *Railway Mail Assn. v. Corsi*, 326 U.S. 88, 96 (1945). See also *Mishkin v. New York*, 383 U.S. 502, 506 (1966); *Smith v. California*, 361 U.S. 147, 150-152 (1959).

---

pictures and drawings very explicitly depicting men and women in groups of two or more engaging in a variety of sexual activities, with genitals often prominently displayed.

I   [2] This case involves the application of a State's criminal obscenity statute to a situation in which sexually explicit materials have been thrust by aggressive sales action upon unwilling recipients who had in no way indicated any desire to receive such materials. This Court has recognized that the States have a legitimate interest in prohibiting dissemination or exhibition of obscene material[2] [19] when the mode of dissemination carries with it a significant danger of offending the sensibilities of unwilling recipients or of exposure to juveniles. *Stanley v. Georgia*, 394 U.S. 557, 567 (1969); *Ginsberg v. New York*, 390 U.S. 629, 637-643 (1968); *Interstate Circuit, Inc. v. Dallas, supra*, at 690; *Redrup v. New York*, 386 U.S. 767, 769 (1967); *Jacobellis v. Ohio*, 378 U.S. 184, 195 (1964). See *Rabe v. Washington*, 405 U.S. 313, 317 (1972) (BURGER, C. J., concurring); *United States v. Reidel*, 402 U.S. 351, 360-362 (1971) (opinion of MARSHALL, J.); *Joseph Burstyn, Inc. v. Wilson*, 343 U.S. 495, 502 (1952); *Breard v. Alexandria*, 341 U.S. 622, 644-645 (1951); *Kovacs v. Cooper*, 336 U.S. 77, 88-89 (1949); *Prince v. Massachusetts*, 321 U.S. 158, 169-170 (1944). Cf. *Butler v. Michigan*, 352 U.S. 380, 382-383 (1957); *Public Utilities Comm'n v. Pollak*, 343 U.S. 451, 464-465 (1952). It is in this context that we are called [20] on to define the standards which must be used to identify obscene

---

[2] This Court has defined "obscene material" as "material which deals with sex in a manner appealing to prurient interest," *Roth v. United States, supra*, at 487, but the *Roth* definition does not reflect the precise meaning of "obscene" as traditionally used in the English language. Derived from the Latin *obscaenus, ob*, to, plus *caenum*, filth, "obscene" is defined in the Webster's Third New International Dictionary (Unabridged 1969) as "1a: disgusting to the senses . . . b: grossly repugnant to the generally accepted notions of what is appropriate . . . 2: offensive or revolting as countering or violating some ideal or principle." The Oxford English Dictionary (1933 ed.) gives a similar definition, "offensive to the senses, or to taste or refinement; disgusting, repulsive, filthy, foul, abominable, loathsome."
The material we are discussing in this case is more accurately defined as "pornography" or "pornographic material." "Pornography" derives from the Greek (*porne*, harlot, and *graphos*, writing). The word now means "1: a description of prostitutes or prostitution 2: a depiction (as in writing or painting) of licentiousness or lewdness: a portrayal of erotic behavior designed to cause sexual excitement." Webster's Third New International Dictionary, *supra*. Pornographic material which is obscene forms a sub-group of all "obscene" expression, but not the whole, at least as the word "obscene" is now used in our language. We note, therefore, that the words "obscene material," as used in this case, have a specific judicial meaning which derives from the *Roth* case, i.e., obscene material "which deals with sex." *Roth, supra*, at 487. See also ALI Model Penal Code § 251.4 (l) "Obscene Defined." (Official Draft 1962.)

material that a State may regulate without infringing on the First Amendment as applicable to the States through the Fourteenth Amendment.

The dissent of MR. JUSTICE BRENNAN reviews the background of the obscenity problem, but since the Court now undertakes to formulate standards more concrete than those in the past, it is useful for us to focus on two of the landmark cases in the somewhat tortured history of the Court's obscenity decisions. In *Roth* v. *United States*, 354 U.S. 476 (1957), the Court sustained a conviction under a federal statute punishing the mailing of "obscene, lewd, lascivious or filthy . . ." materials. The key to that holding was the Court's rejection of the claim that obscene materials were protected by the First Amendment. Five Justices joined in the opinion stating:

"All ideas having even the slightest redeeming social importance – unorthodox ideas, controversial ideas, even ideas hateful to the prevailing climate of opinion – have the full protection of the [First Amendment] guaranties, unless excludable because they encroach upon the limited area of more important interests. But implicit in the history of the First Amendment is the rejection of obscenity as utterly without redeeming social importance . . . . This is the same judgment expressed by this Court in *Chaplinsky* v. *New Hampshire*, 315 U.S. 568, 571-572:

"'. . . There are certain well-defined and narrowly limited classes of speech, the prevention and punishment of which have never been thought to raise any Constitutional problem. *These include the lewd and obscene . . . . It has been well observed that such utterances are no essential part of any exposition of ideas, and are of such slight social* [21] *value as a step to truth that any benefit that may be derived from them is clearly outweighed by the social interest in order and morality. . . .*' [Emphasis by Court in *Roth* opinion.]

"We hold that obscenity is not within the area of constitutionally protected speech or press." 354 U.S., at 484-485 (footnotes omitted).

Nine years later, in *Memoirs* v. *Massachusetts*, 383 U.S. 413 (1966), the Court veered sharply away from the *Roth* concept and, with only three Justices in the plurality opinion, articulated a new test of obscenity. The plurality held that under the *Roth* definition

"as elaborated in subsequent cases, three elements must coalesce: it must be established that (a) the dominant theme of the material taken as a whole appeals to a prurient interest in sex; (b) the material is patently offensive because it affronts contemporary community standards relating to the description or representation of sexual matters; and

(c) the material is utterly without redeeming social value." *Id.*, at 418.

The sharpness of the break with *Roth*, represented by the third element of the *Memoirs* test and emphasized by MR. JUSTICE WHITE's dissent, *id.*, at 460-462, was further underscored when the *Memoirs* plurality went on to state:

"The Supreme Judicial Court erred in holding that a book need not be 'unqualifiedly worthless before it can be deemed obscene.' A book cannot be proscribed unless it is found to be *utterly* without redeeming social value." *Id.*, at 419 (emphasis in original).

While *Roth* presumed "obscenity" to be "utterly without redeeming social importance," *Memoirs* required [22] that to prove obscenity it must be affirmatively established that the material is "*utterly* without redeeming social value." Thus, even as they repeated the words of *Roth*, the *Memoirs* plurality produced a drastically altered test that called on the prosecution to prove a negative, *i.e.*, that the material was "*utterly* without redeeming social value" – a burden virtually impossible to discharge under our criminal standards of proof. Such considerations caused Mr. Justice Harlan to wonder if the "*utterly* without redeeming social value" test had any meaning at all. See *Memoirs* v. *Massachusetts, id.*, at 459 (Harlan, J., dissenting). See also *id.*, at 461 (WHITE, J., dissenting); *United States* v. *Groner*, 479 F.2d 577, 579-581 (CA5 1973).

[3] Apart from the initial formulation in the *Roth* case, no majority of the Court has at any given time been able to agree on a standard to determine what constitutes obscene, pornographic material subject to regulation under the States' police power. See, *e.g., Redrup* v. *New York*, 386 U.S., at 770-771. We have seen "a variety of views among the members of the Court unmatched in any other course of constitutional adjudication." *Interstate Circuit, Inc.* v. *Dallas*, 390 U.S., at 704-705 (Harlan, J., concurring and dissenting) (footnote omitted).[3] This is not remarkable, for in the area [23] of freedom of speech and press the courts must always remain sensitive to any infringement on genuinely serious

---

[3] In the absence of a majority view, this Court was compelled to embark on the practice of summarily reversing convictions for the dissemination of materials that at least five members of the Court, applying their separate tests, found to be protected by the First Amendment. *Redrup* v. *New York*, 386 U.S. 767 (1967). Thirty-one cases have been decided in this manner. Beyond the necessity of circumstances, however, no justification has ever been offered in support of the *Redrup* "policy." See *Walker* v. *Ohio*, 398 U.S. 434-435 (1970) (dissenting opinions of BURGER, C. J., and Harlan, J.). The *Redrup* procedure has cast us in the role of an unreviewable board of censorship for the 50 States, subjectively judging each piece of material brought before us.

literary, artistic, political, or scientific expression. This is an area in which there are few eternal verities.

The case we now review was tried on the theory that the California Penal Code § 311 approximately incorporates the three-stage *Memoirs* test, *supra*. But now the *Memoirs* test has been abandoned as unworkable by its author,[4] and no Member of the Court today supports the *Memoirs* formulation.

II [4A][5][6] [7] This much has been categorically settled by the Court, that obscene material is unprotected by the First Amendment. *Kois* v. *Wisconsin*, 408 U.S. 229 (1972); *United States* v. *Reidel*, 402 U.S., at 354; *Roth* v. *United States, supra*, at 485.[5] "The First and Fourteenth Amendments have never been treated as absolutes [footnote omitted]." *Breard* v. *Alexandria*, 341 U.S., at 642, and cases cited. See *Times Film Corp.* v. *Chicago*, 365 U.S. 43, 47-50 (1961); *Joseph Burstyn, Inc.* v. *Wilson*, 343 U.S., at 502. We acknowledge, however, the inherent dangers of undertaking to regulate any form of expression. State statutes designed to regulate obscene materials must be [24] carefully limited. See *Interstate Circuit, Inc.* v. *Dallas, supra*, at 682-685. As a result, we now confine the permissible scope of such regulation to works which depict or describe sexual conduct. That conduct must be specifically defined by the applicable state law, as written or authoritatively construed.[6] A state offense must also be limited to works which, taken as a whole, appeal to the prurient interest in sex, which portray sexual conduct in a patently offensive way, and which, taken as a whole, do not have serious literary, artistic, political, or scientific value.

---

[4] See the dissenting opinion of MR. JUSTICE BRENNAN in *Paris Adult Theatre I* v. *Slaton, post*, p. 73.

[5] As Mr. Chief Justice Warren stated, dissenting, in *Jacobellis* v. *Ohio*, 378 U.S. 184, 200 (1964):
"For all the sound and fury that the *Roth* test has generated, it has not been proved unsound, and I believe that we should try to live with it – at least until a more satisfactory definition is evolved. No government – be it federal, state, or local – should be forced to choose between repressing all material, including that within the realm of decency, and allowing unrestrained license to publish any material, no matter how vile. There must be a rule of reason in this as in other areas of the law, and we have attempted in the *Roth* case to provide such a rule."

[6] As Mr. Chief Justice Warren stated, dissenting, in *Jacobellis* v. *Ohio*, 378 U.S. 184, 200 (1964):
"For all the sound and fury that the *Roth* test has generated, it has not been proved unsound, and I believe that we should try to live with it – at least until a more satisfactory definition is evolved. No government – be it federal, state, or local – should be forced to choose between repressing all material, including that within the realm of decency, and allowing unrestrained license to publish any material, no matter how vile. There must be a rule of reason in this as in other areas of the law, and we have attempted in the *Roth* case to provide such a rule."

[8A][9A] The basic guidelines for the trier of fact must be: (a) whether "the average person, applying contemporary community standards" would find that the work, taken as a whole, appeals to the prurient interest, *Kois* v. *Wisconsin, supra*, at 230, quoting *Roth* v. *United States, supra*, at 489; (b) whether the work depicts or describes, in a patently offensive way, sexual conduct specifically defined by the applicable state law; and (c) whether the work, taken as a whole, lacks serious literary, artistic, political, or scientific value. We do not adopt as a constitutional standard the "*utterly* without redeeming social value" test of *Memoirs* v. *Massachusetts*, [25] 383 U.S., at 419; that concept has never commanded the adherence of more than three Justices at one time.[7] See *supra*, at 21. If a state law that regulates obscene material is thus limited, as written or construed, the First Amendment values applicable to the States through the Fourteenth Amendment are adequately protected by the ultimate power of appellate courts to conduct an independent review of constitutional claims when necessary. See *Kois* v. *Wisconsin, supra*, at 232; *Memoirs* v. *Massachusetts, supra*, at 459-460 (Harlan, J., dissenting); *Jacobellis* v. *Ohio*, 378 U.S., at 204 (Harlan, J., dissenting); *New York Times Co.* v. *Sullivan*, 376 U.S. 254, 284-285 (1964); *Roth* v. *United States, supra*, at 497-498 (Harlan, J., concurring and dissenting).

[9B][10] [11] We emphasize that it is not our function to propose regulatory schemes for the States. That must await their concrete legislative efforts. It is possible, however, to give a few plain examples of what a state statute could define for regulation under part (b) of the standard announced in this opinion, *supra*:

(a) Patently offensive representations or descriptions of ultimate sexual acts, normal or perverted, actual or simulated.

(b) Patently offensive representations or descriptions of masturbation, excretory functions, and lewd exhibition of the genitals.

[12A][13][14][15A] Sex and nudity may not be exploited without limit by films or pictures exhibited or sold in places of public accommodation any more than live sex and nudity can [26] be exhibited or sold without limit in such public places.[8] At a minimum,

---

[7] "A quotation from Voltaire in the flyleaf of a book will not constitutionally redeem an otherwise obscene publication . . . ." *Kois* v. *Wisconsin*, 408 U.S. 229, 231 (1972). See *Memoirs* v. *Massachusetts*, 383 U.S. 413, 461 (1966) (WHITE, J., dissenting). We also reject, as a constitutional standard, the ambiguous concept of "social importance." See *id.*, at 462 (WHITE, J., dissenting).

[8] Although we are not presented here with the problem of regulating lewd public conduct itself, the States have greater power to regulate nonverbal, physical conduct than to suppress depictions or descriptions of the same behavior. In *United States* v. *O'Brien*, 391 U.S. 367, 377 (1968), a case not dealing with obscenity, the Court held a State regulation of

prurient, patently offensive depiction or description of sexual conduct must have serious literary, artistic, political, or scientific value to merit First Amendment protection. See *Kois* v. *Wisconsin, supra,* at 230-232; *Roth* v. *United States, supra,* at 487; *Thornhill* v. *Alabama,* 310 U.S. 88, 101-102 (1940). For example, medical books for the education of physicians and related personnel necessarily use graphic illustrations and descriptions of human anatomy. In resolving the inevitably sensitive questions of fact and law, we must continue to rely on the jury system, accompanied by the safeguards that judges, rules of evidence, presumption of innocence, and other protective features provide, as we do with rape, murder, and a host of other offenses against society and its individual members.[9]

[12B][15B] MR. JUSTICE BRENNAN, author of the opinions of the Court, or the plurality opinions, in *Roth* v. *United States, supra; Jacobellis* v. *Ohio, supra; Ginzburg* v. *United* [27] *States,* 383 U.S. 463 (1966), *Mishkin* v. *New York,* 383 U.S. 502 (1966); and *Memoirs* v. *Massachusetts, supra,* has abandoned his former position and now maintains that no formulation of this Court, the Congress, or the States can adequately distinguish obscene material unprotected by the First Amendment from protected expression, *Paris Adult Theatre I* v. *Slaton, post,* p. 73 (BRENNAN, J., dissenting). Paradoxically, MR. JUSTICE BRENNAN indicates that suppression of unprotected obscene material is permissible to avoid exposure to unconsenting adults, as in this case, and to juveniles, although he gives no indication of how the division between protected and nonprotected materials may be drawn with greater precision for these purposes than for regulation of commercial exposure to consenting adults only. Nor does he indicate where in the Constitution he finds the authority to distinguish between a willing "adult" one month past the state law age of majority and a willing "juvenile" one month younger.

[16][17A] Under the holdings announced today, no one will be subject to prosecution for the sale or exposure of obscene materials unless these materials depict or describe patently offensive "hard core" sexual conduct specifically defined by the regulating state law, as written or construed. We are satisfied that these specific prerequisites will provide fair notice to a dealer in such materials that his public and commercial activities may bring prosecution. See *Roth* v. *United States, supra,* at 491-492. Cf. *Ginsberg* v. *New York,* 390 U.S., at 643.[10] If [28] the inability to define regulated materials with ultimate, god-like precision altogether removes the power of the States or the Congress to regulate, then "hard core" pornography may be exposed without limit to the juvenile, the passerby, and the consenting adult alike, as, indeed, MR. JUSTICE DOUGLAS contends. As to MR. JUSTICE DOUGLAS' position, see *United States* v. *Thirty-seven Photographs,* 402 U.S. 363, 379-380 (1971) (Black, J., joined by DOUGLAS, J., dissenting); *Ginzburg* v. *United States, supra,* at 476, 491-492 (Black, J., and DOUGLAS, J., dissenting); *Jacobellis* v. *Ohio, supra,* at 196 (Black, J., joined by DOUGLAS, J., concurring); *Roth, supra,* at 508-514 (DOUGLAS, J., dissenting). In this belief, however, MR. JUSTICE DOUGLAS now stands alone.

[17B] MR. JUSTICE BRENNAN also emphasizes "institutional stress" in justification of his change of view. Noting that "the number of obscenity cases on our docket gives ample testimony to the burden that has been placed upon this Court," he quite rightly remarks that the examination of contested materials "is hardly a source of edification to the members of this Court." *Paris Adult* [29]

---

conduct which itself embodied both speech and nonspeech elements to be "sufficiently justified if . . . it furthers an important or substantial governmental interest; if the governmental interest is unrelated to the suppression of free expression; and if the incidental restriction on alleged First Amendment freedoms is no greater than is essential to the furtherance of that interest." See *California* v. *LaRue,* 409 U.S. 109, 117-118 (1972).

[9] The mere fact juries may reach different conclusions as to the same material does not mean that constitutional rights are abridged. As this Court observed in *Roth* v. *United States,* 354 U.S., at 492 n. 30, "it is common experience that different juries may reach different results under any criminal statute. That is one of the consequences we accept under our jury system. Cf. *Dunlop* v. *United States,* 165 U.S. 486, 499-500."

[10] As MR. JUSTICE BRENNAN stated for the Court in *Roth* v. *United States, supra,* at 491-492:
"Many decisions have recognized that these terms of obscenity statutes are not precise. [Footnote omitted.] This Court, however, has consistently held that lack of precision is not itself offensive to the requirements of due process. '. . . The Constitution does not require impossible standards'; all that is required is that the language 'conveys sufficiently definite warning as to the proscribed conduct when measured by common understanding and practices. . . .' *United States* v. *Petrillo,* 332 U.S. 1, 7-8. These words, applied according to the proper standard for judging obscenity, already discussed, give adequate warning of the conduct proscribed and mark ' . . . boundaries sufficiently distinct for judges and juries fairly to administer the law . . . . That there may be marginal cases in which it is difficult to determine the side of the line on which a particular fact situation falls is no sufficient reason to hold the language too ambiguous to define a criminal offense. . . .' *Id.,* at 7. See also *United States* v. *Harriss,* 347 U.S. 612, 624, n. 15; *Boyce Motor Lines, Inc.* v. *United States,* 342 U.S. 337, 340; *United States* v. *Ragen,* 314 U.S. 513, 523-524; *United States* v. *Wurzbach,* 280 U.S. 396; *Hygrade Provision Co.* v. *Sherman,* 266 U.S. 497; *Fox* v. *Washington,* 236 U.S. 273; *Nash* v. *United States,* 229 U.S. 373."

Theatre I v. *Slaton, post,* at 92, 93. He also notes, and we agree, that "uncertainty of the standards creates a continuing source of tension between state and federal courts . . . ." "The problem is . . . that one cannot say with certainty that material is obscene until at least five members of this Court, applying inevitably obscure standards, have pronounced it so." *Id.,* at 93, 92.

It is certainly true that the absence, since *Roth,* of a single majority view of this Court as to proper standards for testing obscenity has placed a strain on both state and federal courts. But today, for the first time since *Roth* was decided in 1957, a majority of this Court has agreed on concrete guidelines to isolate "hard core" pornography from expression protected by the First Amendment. Now we may abandon the casual practice of *Redrup* v. *New York,* 386 U.S. 767 (1967), and attempt to provide positive guidance to federal and state courts alike.

[18][19] This may not be an easy road, free from difficulty. But no amount of "fatigue" should lead us to adopt a convenient "institutional" rationale – an absolutist, "anything goes" view of the First Amendment – because it will lighten our burdens.[11] "Such an abnegation of judicial supervision in this field would be inconsistent with our duty to uphold the constitutional guarantees." *Jacobellis* v. *Ohio, supra,* at 187-188 (opinion of BRENNAN, J.). Nor should we remedy "tension between state and federal courts" by arbitrarily depriving the States of a power reserved to them under the Constitution, a power which they have enjoyed and exercised continuously from before the adoption of the First Amendment to this day. See *Roth* v. *United States, supra,* at 482-485. "Our duty admits of no 'substitute for facing up [30] to the tough individual problems of constitutional judgment involved in every obscenity case.' [*Roth* v. *United States, supra,* at 498]; see *Manual Enterprises, Inc.* v. *Day,* 370 U.S. 478, 488 (opinion of Harlan, J.) [footnote omitted]." *Jacobellis* v. *Ohio, supra,* at 188 (opinion of BRENNAN, J.).

III   [20A][21] Under a National Constitution, fundamental First Amendment limitations on the powers of the States do not vary from community to community, but this does not mean that there are, or should or can be, fixed, uniform national standards of precisely what appeals to the "prurient interest" or is "patently offensive." These are essentially questions of fact, and our Nation is simply too big and too diverse for this Court to reasonably expect that such standards could be articulated for all 50 States in a single formulation, even assuming the prerequisite consensus exists. When triers of fact are asked to decide whether "the average person, applying contemporary community standards" would

consider certain materials "prurient," it would be unrealistic to require that the answer be based on some abstract formulation. The adversary system, with lay jurors as the usual ultimate factfinders in criminal prosecutions, has historically permitted triers of fact to draw on the standards of their community, guided always by limiting instructions on the law. To require a State to structure obscenity proceedings around evidence of a *national* "community standard" would be an exercise in futility.

As noted before, this case was tried on the theory that the California obscenity statute sought to incorporate the tripartite test of *Memoirs.* This, a "national" standard of First Amendment protection enumerated by a plurality of this Court, was correctly regarded at the time of trial as limiting state prosecution under the controlling case [31] law. The jury, however, was explicitly instructed that, in determining whether the "dominant theme of the material as a whole . . . appeals to the prurient interest" and in determining whether the material "goes substantially beyond customary limits of candor and affronts contemporary community standards of decency," it was to apply "contemporary community standards of the State of California."

[22A] During the trial, both the prosecution and the defense assumed that the relevant "community standards" in making the factual determination of obscenity were those of the State of California, not some hypothetical standard of the entire United States of America. Defense counsel at trial never objected to the testimony of the State's expert on community standards[12] or to the instructions of the trial judge on "statewide" standards. On appeal to the Appellate Department, Superior Court of California, County of Orange, appellant for the first time contended that application of state, rather than national, standards violated the First and Fourteenth Amendments.

[22B][23] We conclude that neither the State's alleged failure to offer evidence of "national standards," nor the trial court's charge that the jury consider state community standards, were constitutional errors. Nothing in the First Amendment requires that a jury must consider hypothetical and unascertainable "national standards" when attempting to determine whether certain materials are obscene as a matter [32] of fact. Mr.

---

[11] We must note, in addition, that any assumption concerning the relative burdens of the past and the probable burden under the standards now adopted is pure speculation.

[12] The record simply does not support appellant's contention, belatedly raised on appeal, that the State's expert was unqualified to give evidence on California "community standards." The expert, a police officer with many years of specialization in obscenity offenses, had conducted an extensive statewide survey and had given expert evidence on 26 occasions in the year prior to this trial. Allowing such expert testimony was certainly not constitutional error. Cf. *United States* v. *Augenblick,* 393 U.S. 348, 356 (1969).

Chief Justice Warren pointedly commented in his dissent in *Jacobellis* v. *Ohio, supra*, at 200:

"It is my belief that when the Court said in *Roth* that obscenity is to be defined by reference to 'community standards,' it meant community standards – not a national standard, as is sometimes argued. I believe that there is no provable 'national standard' . . . . At all events, this Court has not been able to enunciate one, and it would be unreasonable to expect local courts to divine one."

[24][25A][26][27A] It is neither realistic nor constitutionally sound to read the First Amendment as requiring that the people of Maine or Mississippi accept public depiction of conduct found tolerable in Las Vegas, or New York City.[13] [33] See *Hoyt* v. *Minnesota*, 399 U.S. 524-525 (1970) (BLACKMUN, J., dissenting); *Walker* v. *Ohio*, 398 U.S. 434 (1970) (BURGER, C. J., dissenting); *id.*, at 434-435 (Harlan, J., dissenting); *Cain* v. *Kentucky*, 397 U.S. 319 (1970) (BURGER, C. J., dissenting); *id.*, at 319-320 (Harlan, J., dissenting); *United States* v. *Groner*, 479 F.2d, at 581-583; O'Meara & Shaffer, Obscenity in The Supreme Court: A Note on *Jacobellis* v. *Ohio*, 40 Notre Dame Law. 1, 6-7 (1964). See also *Memoirs* v. *Massachusetts*, 383 U.S., at 458 (Harlan, J., dissenting); *Jacobellis* v. *Ohio, supra*, at 203-204 (Harlan, J., dissenting); *Roth* v. *United States, supra*,

---

[13] In *Jacobellis* v. *Ohio*, 378 U.S. 184 (1964), two Justices argued that application of "local" community standards would run the risk of preventing dissemination of materials in some places because sellers would be unwilling to risk criminal conviction by testing variations in standards from place to place. *Id.*, at 193-195 (opinion of BRENNAN, J., joined by Goldberg, J.). The use of "national" standards, however, necessarily implies that materials found tolerable in some places, but not under the "national" criteria, will nevertheless be unavailable where they are acceptable. Thus, in terms of danger to free expression, the potential for suppression seems at least as great in the application of a single nationwide standard as in allowing distribution in accordance with local tastes, a point which Mr. Justice Harlan often emphasized. See *Roth* v. *United States*, 354 U.S., at 506. Appellant also argues that adherence to a "national standard" is necessary "in order to avoid unconscionable burdens on the free flow of interstate commerce." As noted *supra*, at 18 n. 1, the application of domestic state police powers in this case did not intrude on any congressional powers under Art. I, § 8, cl. 3, for there is no indication that appellant's materials were ever distributed interstate. Appellant's argument would appear without substance in any event. Obscene material may be validly regulated by a State in the exercise of its traditional local power to protect the general welfare of its population despite some possible incidental effect on the flow of such materials across state lines. See, *e.g.*, *Head* v. *New Mexico Board*, 374 U.S. 424 (1963); *Huron Portland Cement Co.* v. *Detroit*, 362 U.S. 440 (1960); *Breard* v. *Alexandria*, 341 U.S. 622 (1951); *H. P. Hood & Sons* v. *Du Mond*, 336 U.S. 525 (1949); *Southern Pacific Co.* v. *Arizona*, 325 U.S. 761 (1945); *Baldwin* v. *G. A. F. Seelig, Inc.*, 294 U.S. 511 (1935); *Sligh* v. *Kirkwood*, 237 U.S. 52 (1915).

at 505-506 (Harlan, J., concurring and dissenting). People in different States vary in their tastes and attitudes, and this diversity is not to be strangled by the absolutism of imposed uniformity. As the Court made clear in *Mishkin* v. *New York*, 383 U.S., at 508-509, the primary concern with requiring a jury to apply the standard of "the average person, applying contemporary community standards" is to be certain that, so far as material is not aimed at a deviant group, it will be judged by its impact on an average person, rather than a particularly susceptible or sensitive person – or indeed a totally insensitive one. See *Roth* v. *United States, supra*, at 489. Cf. the now discredited test in *Regina* v. *Hicklin*, [1868] L. R. 3 Q. B. 360. We hold that the requirement that the jury evaluate the materials with reference to "contemporary [34] standards of the State of California" serves this protective purpose and is constitutionally adequate.[14]

IV [25B][27B][28][29][30][31A]The dissenting Justices sound the alarm of repression. But, in our view, to equate the free and robust exchange of ideas and political debate with commercial exploitation of obscene material demeans the grand conception of the First Amendment and its high purposes in the historic struggle for freedom. It is a "misuse of the great guarantees of free speech and free press . . . ." *Breard* v. *Alexandria*, 341 U.S., at 645. The First Amendment protects works which, taken as a whole, have serious literary, artistic, political, or scientific value, regardless of whether the government or a majority of the people approve of the ideas these works represent. "The protection given speech and press was fashioned to assure unfettered interchange of *ideas* for the bringing about of [35] political and social changes desired by the people," *Roth* v. *United*

---

[14] Appellant's jurisdictional statement contends that he was subjected to "double jeopardy" because a Los Angeles County trial judge dismissed, before trial, a prior prosecution based on the same brochures, but apparently alleging exposures at a different time in a different setting. Appellant argues that once material has been found not to be obscene in one proceeding, the State is "collaterally estopped" from ever alleging it to be obscene in a different proceeding. It is not clear from the record that appellant properly raised this issue, better regarded as a question of procedural due process than a "double jeopardy" claim, in the state courts below. Appellant failed to address any portion of his brief on the merits to this issue, and appellee contends that the question was waived under California law because it was improperly pleaded at trial. Nor is it totally clear from the record before us what collateral effect the pretrial dismissal might have under state law. The dismissal was based, at least in part, on a failure of the prosecution to present affirmative evidence required by state law, evidence which was apparently presented in this case. Appellant's contention, therefore, is best left to the California courts for further consideration on remand. The issue is not, in any event, a proper subject for appeal. See *Mishkin* v. *New York*, 383 U.S. 502, 512-514 (1966).

States, supra, at 484 (emphasis added). See *Kois* v. *Wisconsin*, 408 U.S., at 230-232; *Thornhill* v. *Alabama*, 310 U.S., at 101-102. But the public portrayal of hard-core sexual conduct for its own sake, and for the ensuing commercial gain, is a different matter.[15]

[31B] There is no evidence, empirical or historical, that the stern 19th century American censorship of public distribution and display of material relating to sex, see *Roth* v. *United States, supra*, at 482-485, in any way limited or affected expression of serious literary, artistic, political, or scientific ideas. On the contrary, it is beyond any question that the era following Thomas Jefferson to Theodore Roosevelt was an "extraordinarily vigorous period," not just in economics and politics, but in *belles lettres* and in "the outlying fields of social and political philosophies."[16] We do not see the harsh hand [36] of censorship of ideas – good or bad, sound or unsound – and "repression" of political liberty lurking in every state regulation of commercial exploitation of human interest in sex.

[32] MR. JUSTICE BRENNAN finds "it is hard to see how state-ordered regimentation of our minds can ever be forestalled." *Paris Adult Theatre I* v. *Slaton, post*, at 110 (BRENNAN, J., dissenting). These doleful anticipations assume that courts cannot distinguish commerce in ideas, protected by the First Amendment, from commercial exploitation of obscene material. Moreover, state regulation of hard-core pornography so as to make it unavailable to nonadults, a regulation which MR. JUSTICE BRENNAN finds constitutionally permissible, has all the elements of "censorship" for adults; indeed even more rigid enforcement techniques may be called for with such dichotomy of regulation. See *Interstate Circuit, Inc.* v. *Dallas*, 390 U.S., at 690.[17]

One can concede that the "sexual revolution" of recent years may have had useful byproducts in striking layers of prudery from a subject long irrationally kept from needed ventilation. But it does not follow that no regulation of patently offensive "hard core" materials is needed or permissible; civilized people do not allow unregulated access to heroin because it is a derivative of medicinal morphine.

[4B][8B][20B] In sum, we (a) reaffirm the *Roth* holding that obscene material is not protected by the First Amendment; (b) hold that such material can be regulated by the States, subject to the specific safeguards enunciated [37] above, without a showing that the material is "*utterly* without redeeming social value"; and (c) hold that obscenity is to be determined by applying "contemporary community standards," see *Kois* v. *Wisconsin, supra*, at 230, and *Roth* v. *United States, supra*, at 489, not "national standards." The judgment of the Appellate Department of the Superior Court, Orange County, California, is vacated and the case remanded to that court for further proceedings not inconsistent with the First Amendment standards established by this opinion. See *United States* v. *12 200-ft. Reels of Film, post*, at 130 n. 7.

Vacated and remanded.

---

[17] "We have indicated . . . that because of its strong and abiding interest in youth, a State may regulate the dissemination to juveniles of, and their access to, material objectionable as to them, but which a State clearly could not regulate as to adults. *Ginsberg* v. *New York*, . . . [390 U.S. 629 (1968)]." *Interstate Circuit, Inc.* v. *Dallas*, 390 U.S. 676, 690 (1968) (footnote omitted).

DISSENT: MR. JUSTICE DOUGLAS, DISSENTING.

I.   Today we leave open the way for California[1] to send a man to prison for distributing brochures that advertise books and a movie under freshly written standards defining obscenity which until today's decision were never the part of any law. The Court has worked hard to define obscenity and concededly has failed. In *Roth* v. *United States*, 354 U.S. 476, it ruled that "[obscene material is material which deals with sex in a manner appealing to prurient interest." *Id.*, at 487. Obscenity, it was said, was rejected by the First Amendment because it is "utterly without redeeming [38] social importance."

---

[15] In the apt words of Mr. Chief Justice Warren, appellant in this case was "plainly engaged in the commercial exploitation of the morbid and shameful craving for materials with prurient effect. I believe that the State and Federal Governments can constitutionally punish such conduct. That is all that these cases present to us, and that is all we need to decide." *Roth* v. *United States, supra*, at 496 (concurring opinion).

[16] See 2 V. Parrington, Main Currents in American Thought *ix et seq.* (1930). As to the latter part of the 19th century, Parrington observed "A new age had come and other dreams – the age and the dreams of a middle-class sovereignty . . . . From the crude and vast romanticisms of that vigorous sovereignty emerged eventually a spirit of realistic criticism, seeking to evaluate the worth of this new America, and discover if possible other philosophies to take the place of those which had gone down in the fierce battles of the Civil War." *Id.*, at 474. Cf. 2 S. Morison, H. Commager & W. Leuchtenburg, The Growth of the American Republic 197-233 (6th ed. 1969); Paths of American Thought 123-166, 203-290 (A. Schlesinger & M. White ed. 1963) (articles of Fleming, Lerner, Morton & Lucia White, E. Rostow, Samuelson, Kazin, Hofstadter); and H. Wish, Society and Thought in Modern America 337-386 (1952).

---

[1] California defines "obscene matter" as "matter, taken as a whole, the predominant appeal of which to the average person, applying contemporary standards, is to prurient interest, i.e., a shameful or morbid interest in nudity, sex, or excretion; and is matter which taken as a whole goes substantially beyond customary limits of candor in description or representation of such matters; and is matter which taken as a whole is utterly without redeeming social importance." Calif. Penal Code § 311 (a).

Id., at 484. The presence of a "prurient interest" was to be determined by "contemporary community standards." *Id.*, at 489. That test, it has been said, could not be determined by one standard here and another standard there, *Jacobellis* v. *Ohio*, 378 U.S. 184, 194, but "on the basis of a national standard." *Id.*, at 195. My Brother STEWART in *Jacobellis* commented that the difficulty of the Court in giving content to obscenity was that it was "faced with the task of trying to define what may be indefinable." *Id.*, at 197.

In *Memoirs* v. *Massachusetts*, 383 U.S. 413, 418, the *Roth* test was elaborated to read as follows: "Three elements must coalesce: it must be established that (a) the dominant theme of the material taken as a whole appeals to a prurient interest in sex; (b) the material is patently offensive because it affronts contemporary community standards relating to the description or representation of sexual matters; and (c) the material is utterly without redeeming social value."

In *Ginzburg* v. *United States*, 383 U.S. 463, a publisher was sent to prison, not for the kind of books and periodicals he sold, but for the manner in which the publications were advertised. The "leer of the sensualist" was said to permeate the advertisements. *Id.*, at 468. The Court said, "Where the purveyor's sole emphasis is on the sexually provocative aspects of his publications, that fact may be decisive in the determination of obscenity." *Id.*, at 470. As Mr. Justice Black said in dissent, " . . . Ginzburg . . . is now finally and authoritatively condemned to serve five years in prison for distributing printed matter about sex which neither Ginzburg nor anyone else could possibly have known to be criminal." *Id.*, at 476. That observation by Mr. Justice Black is underlined by the fact that the *Ginzburg* decision was five to four.

[39] A further refinement was added by *Ginsberg* v. *New York*, 390 U.S. 629, 641, where the Court held that "it was not irrational for the legislature to find that exposure to material condemned by the statute is harmful to minors."

But even those members of this Court who had created the new and changing standards of "obscenity" could not agree on their application. And so we adopted a *per curiam* treatment of so-called obscene publications that seemed to pass constitutional muster under the several constitutional tests which had been formulated. See *Redrup* v. *New York*, 386 U.S. 767. Some condemn it if its "dominant tendency might be to 'deprave or corrupt' a reader." [2] Others look not to the content of the book but to whether it is advertised "'to appeal to the

erotic interests of customers.'"[3] Some condemn only "hardcore pornography"; but even then a true definition is lacking. It has indeed been said of that definition, "I could never succeed in [defining it] intelligibly," but "I know it when I see it."[4]

Today we would add a new three-pronged test: "(a) whether 'the average person, applying contemporary community standards' would find that the work, taken as a whole, appeals to the prurient interest, . . . (b) whether the work depicts or describes, in a patently offensive way, sexual conduct specifically defined by the applicable state law, and (c) whether the work, taken as a whole, lacks serious literary, artistic, political, or scientific value."

Those are the standards we ourselves have written into the Constitution.[5] Yet how under these vague tests can [40] we sustain convictions for the sale of an article prior to the time when some court has declared it to be obscene?

Today the Court retreats from the earlier formulations of the constitutional test and undertakes to make new definitions. This effort, like the earlier ones, is earnest and well intentioned. The difficulty is that we do not deal with constitutional terms, since "obscenity" is not mentioned in the Constitution or Bill of Rights. And the First Amendment makes no such exception from "the press" which it undertakes to protect nor, as I have said on other occasions, is an exception necessarily implied, for there was no recognized exception to the free press at the time the Bill of Rights was adopted which treated "obscene" publications differently from other types of papers, magazines, and books. So there are no constitutional guidelines for deciding what is and what is not

---

[2] *Roth* v. *United States*, 354 U.S. 476, 502 (opinion of Harlan, J.).

[3] *Ginzburg* v. *United States*, 383 U.S. 463, 467.
[4] *Jacobellis* v. *Ohio*, 378 U.S. 184, 197 (STEWART, J., concurring).
[5] At the conclusion of a two-year study, the U.S. Commission on Obscenity and Pornography determined that the standards we have written interfere with constitutionally protected materials:
"Society's attempts to legislate for adults in the area of obscenity have not been successful. Present laws prohibiting the consensual sale or distribution of explicit sexual materials to adults are extremely unsatisfactory in their practical application. The Constitution permits material to be deemed 'obscene' for adults only if, as a whole, it appeals to the 'prurient' interest of the average person, is 'patently offensive' in light of 'community standards,' and lacks 'redeeming social value.' These vague and highly subjective aesthetic, psychological and moral tests do not provide meaningful guidance for law enforcement officials, juries or courts. As a result, law is inconsistently and sometimes erroneously applied and the distinctions made by courts between prohibited and permissible materials often appear indefensible. Errors in the application of the law and uncertainty about its scope also cause interference with the communication of constitutionally protected materials." Report of the Commission on Obscenity and Pornography 53 (1970).

"obscene." The Court is at large because we deal with tastes and standards of literature. What shocks me may [41] be sustenance for my neighbor. What causes one person to boil up in rage over one pamphlet or movie may reflect only his neurosis, not shared by others. We deal here with a regime of censorship which, if adopted, should be done by constitutional amendment after full debate by the people.

Obscenity cases usually generate tremendous emotional outbursts. They have no business being in the courts. If a constitutional amendment authorized censorship, the censor would probably be an administrative agency. Then criminal prosecutions could follow as, if, and when publishers defied the censor and sold their literature. Under that regime a publisher would know when he was on dangerous ground. Under the present regime – whether the old standards or the new ones are used – the criminal law becomes a trap. A brand new test would put a publisher behind bars under a new law improvised by the courts after the publication. That was done in *Ginzburg* and has all the evils of an *ex post facto* law.

My contention is that until a civil proceeding has placed a tract beyond the pale, no criminal prosecution should be sustained. For no more vivid illustration of vague and uncertain laws could be designed than those we have fashioned. As Mr. Justice Harlan has said:

"The upshot of all this divergence in viewpoint is that anyone who undertakes to examine the Court's decisions since *Roth* which have held particular material obscene or not obscene would find himself in utter bewilderment." *Interstate Circuit, Inc.* v. *Dallas*, 390 U.S. 676, 707.

In *Bouie* v. *City of Columbia*, 378 U.S. 347, we upset a conviction for remaining on property after being asked to leave, while the only unlawful act charged by the statute was entering. We held that the defendants had received no "fair warning, at the time of their conduct" [42] while on the property "that the act for which they now stand convicted was rendered criminal" by the state statute. *Id.*, at 355. The same requirement of "fair warning" is due here, as much as in *Bouie*. The latter involved racial discrimination; the present case involves rights earnestly urged as being protected by the First Amendment. In any case – certainly when constitutional rights are concerned – we should not allow men to go to prison or be fined when they had no "fair warning" that what they did was criminal conduct.

II.   If a specific book, play, paper, or motion picture has in a civil proceeding been condemned as obscene and review of that finding has been completed, and thereafter a person publishes, shows, or displays that particular book or film, then a vague law has been made specific. There would remain the underlying question whether the First Amendment

allows an implied exception in the case of obscenity. I do not think it does[6] and my views [43] on the issue have been stated over and over again.[7] But at least a criminal prosecution brought at that juncture would not violate the time-honored void-for-vagueness test.[8]

No such protective procedure has been designed by California in this case. Obscenity – which even we cannot define with precision – is a hodge-podge. To send [44] men to jail for violating standards they cannot understand, construe, and apply is a

---

[6] It is said that "obscene" publications can be banned on authority of restraints on communications incident to decrees restraining unlawful business monopolies or unlawful restraints of trade, *Sugar Institute* v. *United States*, 297 U.S. 553, 597, or communications respecting the sale of spurious or fraudulent securities. *Hall* v. *Geiger-Jones Co.*, 242 U.S. 539, 549; *Caldwell* v. *Sioux Falls Stock Yards Co.*, 242 U.S. 559, 567; *Merrick* v. *Halsey & Co.*, 242 U.S. 568, 584. The First Amendment answer is that whenever speech and conduct are brigaded – as they are when one shouts "Fire" in a crowded theater – speech can be outlawed. Mr. Justice Black, writing for a unanimous Court in *Giboney* v. *Empire Storage Co.*, 336 U.S. 490, stated that labor unions could be restrained from picketing a firm in support of a secondary boycott which a State had validly outlawed. Mr. Justice Black said: "It rarely has been suggested that the constitutional freedom for speech and press extends its immunity to speech or writing used as an integral part of conduct in violation of a valid criminal statute. We reject the contention now." *Id.*, at 498.

[7] See *United States* v. *12 200-ft. Reels of Film, post*, p. 123; *United States* v. *Orito, post*, p. 139; *Kois* v. *Wisconsin*, 408 U.S. 229; *Byrne* v. *Karalexis*, 396 U.S. 976, 977; *Ginsberg* v. *New York*, 390 U.S. 629, 650; *Jacobs* v. *New York*, 388 U.S. 431, 436; *Ginzberg* v. *United States*, 383 U.S. 463, 482; *Memoirs* v. *Massachusetts*, 383 U.S. 413, 424; *Bantam Books, Inc.* v. *Sullivan*, 372 U.S. 58, 72; *Times Film Corp.* v. *Chicago*, 365 U.S. 43, 78; *Smith* v. *California*, 361 U.S. 147, 167; *Kingsley Pictures Corp.* v. *Regents*, 360 U.S. 684, 697; *Roth* v. *United States*, 354 U.S. 476, 508; *Kingsley Books, Inc.* v. *Brown*, 354 U.S. 436, 446; *Superior Films, Inc.* v. *Department of Education*, 346 U.S. 587, 588; *Gelling* v. *Texas*, 343 U.S. 960.

[8] The Commission on Obscenity and Pornography has advocated such a procedure:

"*The Commission recommends the enactment, in all jurisdictions which enact or retain provisions prohibiting the dissemination of sexual materials to adults or young persons, of legislation authorizing prosecutors to obtain declaratory judgments as to whether particular materials fall within existing legal prohibitions ....*

"A declaratory judgment procedure ... would permit prosecutors to proceed civilly, rather than through the criminal process, against suspected violations of obscenity prohibition. If such civil procedures are utilized, penalties would be imposed for violation of the law only with respect to conduct occurring after a civil declaration is obtained. The Commission believes this course of action to be appropriate whenever there is any existing doubt regarding the legal status of materials; where other alternatives are available, the criminal process should not ordinarily be invoked against persons who might have reasonably believed, in good faith, that the books or films they distributed were entitled to constitutional protection, for the threat of criminal sanctions might otherwise deter the free distribution of constitutionally protected material." Report of the Commission on Obscenity and Pornography 63 (1970).

monstrous thing to do in a Nation dedicated to fair trials and due process.

III.   While the right to know is the corollary of the right to speak or publish, no one can be forced by government to listen to disclosure that he finds offensive. That was the basis of my dissent in *Public Utilities Comm'n* v. *Pollak*, 343 U.S. 451, 467, where I protested against making streetcar passengers a "captive" audience. There is no "captive audience" problem in these obscenity cases. No one is being compelled to look or to listen. Those who enter newsstands or bookstalls may be offended by what they see. But they are not compelled by the State to frequent those places; and it is only state or governmental action against which the First Amendment, applicable to the States by virtue of the Fourteenth, raises a ban.

The idea that the First Amendment permits government to ban publications that are "offensive" to some people puts an ominous gloss on freedom of the press. That test would make it possible to ban any paper or any journal or magazine in some benighted place. The First Amendment was designed "to invite dispute," to induce "a condition of unrest," to "create dissatisfaction with conditions as they are," and even to stir "people to anger." *Terminiello* v. *Chicago*, 337 U.S. 1, 4. The idea that the First Amendment permits punishment for ideas that are "offensive" to the particular judge or jury sitting in judgment is astounding.

No greater leveler of speech or literature has ever been designed. To give the power to the censor, as we do today, is to make a sharp and radical break with the traditions of a free society. The First Amendment was not fashioned as a vehicle for [45] dispensing tranquilizers to the people. Its prime function was to keep debate open to "offensive" as well as to "staid" people. The tendency throughout history has been to subdue the individual and to exalt the power of government. The use of the standard "offensive" gives authority to government that cuts the very vitals out of the First Amendment.[9] As is intimated by the Court's opinion,

---

[9] Obscenity law has had a capricious history:

"The white slave traffic was first exposed by W. T. Stead in a magazine article, 'The Maiden Tribute.' The English law did absolutely nothing to the profiteers in vice, but put Stead in prison for a year for writing about an indecent subject. When the law supplies no definite standard of criminality, a judge in deciding what is indecent or profane may consciously disregard the sound test of present injury, and proceeding upon an entirely different theory may condemn the defendant because his words express ideas which are thought liable to cause bad future consequences. Thus musical comedies enjoy almost unbridled license, while a problem play is often forbidden because opposed to our views of marriage. In the same way, the law of blasphemy has been used against Shelley's *Queen Mab* and the decorous promulgation of

the materials before us may be garbage. But so is much of what is said in political campaigns, in the daily press, on TV, or over the radio. By reason of the First Amendment – and solely because of it – speakers and publishers have not been threatened or subdued because their thoughts and ideas may be "offensive" to some.

The standard "offensive" is unconstitutional in yet another way. In *Coates* v. *City of Cincinnati*, 402 U.S. 611, we had before us a municipal ordinance that made it a crime for three or more persons to assemble on a street and conduct themselves "in a manner annoying to persons [46] passing by." We struck it down, saying: "If three or more people meet together on a sidewalk or street corner, they must conduct themselves so as not to annoy any police officer or other person who should happen to pass by. In our opinion this ordinance is unconstitutionally vague because it subjects the exercise of the right of assembly to an unascertainable standard, and unconstitutionally broad because it authorizes the punishment of constitutionally protected conduct.

"Conduct that annoys some people does not annoy others. Thus, the ordinance is vague, not in the sense that it requires a person to conform his conduct to an imprecise but comprehensive normative standard, but rather in the sense that no standard of conduct is specified at all." *Id.*, at 614.

How we can deny Ohio the convenience of punishing people who "annoy" others and allow California power to punish people who publish materials "offensive" to some people is difficult to square with constitutional requirements.

If there are to be restraints on what is obscene, then a constitutional amendment should be the way of achieving the end. There are societies where religion and mathematics are the only free segments. It would be a dark day for America if that were our destiny. But the people can make it such if they choose to write obscenity into the Constitution and define it.

We deal with highly emotional, not rational, questions. To many the Song of Solomon is obscene. I do not think we, the judges, were ever given the constitutional power to make definitions of obscenity. If it is to be defined, let the people debate and decide by a constitutional amendment what they want to ban as obscene and what standards they want the legislatures and the courts to apply. Perhaps the people will decide that the path towards a mature,

---

pantheistic ideas, on the ground that to attack religion is to loosen the bonds of society and endanger the state. This is simply a roundabout modern method to make heterodoxy in sex matters and even in religion a crime." Z. Chafee, Free Speech in the United States 151 (1942).

integrated society requires [47] that all ideas competing for acceptance must have no censor. Perhaps they will decide otherwise. Whatever the choice, the courts will have some guidelines. Now we have none except our own predilections.

MR. JUSTICE BRENNAN, with whom MR. JUSTICE STEWART and MR. JUSTICE MARSHALL join, DISSENTING.

In my dissent in *Paris Adult Theatre I* v. *Slaton, post*, p. 73, decided this date, I noted that I had no occasion to consider the extent of state power to regulate the distribution of sexually oriented material to juveniles or the offensive exposure of such material to unconsenting adults. In the case before us, appellant was convicted of distributing obscene matter in violation of California Penal Code § 311.2, on the basis of evidence that he had caused to be mailed unsolicited brochures advertising various books and a movie. I need not now decide whether a statute might be drawn to impose, within the requirements of the First Amendment, criminal penalties for the precise conduct at issue here. For it is clear that under my dissent in *Paris Adult Theatre I*, the statute under which the prosecution was brought is unconstitutionally overbroad, and therefore invalid on its face.* "The transcendent value to all society of constitutionally protected expression is deemed to justify allowing 'attacks on overly broad statutes with no requirement that the person making the attack demonstrate that his own conduct could not be regulated by a statute drawn with the requisite narrow specificity.'" *Gooding* v. *Wilson*, 405 U.S. 518, 521 (1972), quoting [48] from *Dombrowski* v. *Pfister*, 380 U.S. 479, 486 (1965). See also *Baggett* v. *Bullitt*, 377 U.S. 360, 366 (1964); *Coates* v. *City of Cincinnati*, 402 U.S. 611, 616 (1971); *id.*, at 619-620 (WHITE, J., dissenting); *United States* v. *Raines*, 362 U.S. 17, 21-22 (1960); *NAACP* v. *Button*, 371 U.S. 415, 433 (1963). Since my view in *Paris Adult Theatre I* represents a substantial departure from the course of our prior decisions, and since the state courts have as yet had no opportunity to consider whether a "readily apparent construction suggests itself as a vehicle for rehabilitating the [statute] in a single prosecution," *Dombrowski* v. *Pfister, supra*, at 491, I would reverse the judgment of the Appellate Department of the Superior Court and remand the case for proceedings not inconsistent with this opinion. See *Coates* v. *City of Cincinnati, supra*, at 616.

---

* Cal. Penal Code § 311.2 (a) provides that "Every person who knowingly: sends or causes to be sent, or brings or causes to be brought, into this state for sale or distribution, or in this state prepares, publishes, prints, exhibits, distributes, or offers to distribute, or has in his possession with intent to distribute or to exhibit or offer to distribute, any obscene matter is guilty of a misdemeanor."

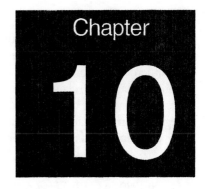
Commercial Speech

Shifting First Amendment protection

Focal cases:
Central Hudson Gas and Electric Corp. v. Public Service Commission of New York, 447 U.S. 557 (1980)
Greater New Orleans Broadcasting Association v. United States, 527 U.S. 173 (1999)

For three decades beginning in the 1940s, the Supreme Court considered advertising generally to be an element of commerce[1] rather than a part of "the freedom of speech" protected by the First Amendment.[2] Under this view, the Court continues to protect the important government interest in accurately informed consumer choice by upholding laws that punish false or fraudulent commercial messages.[3] But in the mid-1970s, the Court recognized that truthful commercial speech did more than propose commercial transactions; it contributed valuable information to citizens and to the marketplace of ideas.[4] Since then, the Court has refined its commercial speech doctrine[5] and granted non-misleading commercial speech increasing First Amendment protection.[6]

---

[1] The Constitution's Commerce Clause grants Congress authority to regulate commerce.

[2] *See* Valentine v. Christensen, 316 U.S. 52 (1942); Beard v. Alexander, 341 U.S. 622 (1951). *But see* New York Times v. Sullivan, 376 U.S. 254 (1964) (extending First Amendment protection to political content in Civil Rights ad); Pittsburgh Press Co. v. Pittsburgh Comm. on Human Relations, 413 U.S. 376, 389 (1973) (suggesting the First Amendment might protect legal commercial speech).

[3] *See, e.g.,* Illinois v. Telemarketing Associates, 123 S.Ct. 1829 (2003); Kozinski & Banner, *The Anti-History and Pre-History of Commercial Speech*, 71 TEXAS L. REV. 747 (1993).

[4] *See, e.g.,* Bigelow v. Virginia, 421 U.S. 809 (1975); Virginia State Board of Pharmacy v. Virginia Citizens Consumer Council, 425 U.S. 1817 (1976).

[5] *See, e.g.,* Michael Hoefges and Milagros Rivera-Sanchez, *Vice Advertising under the Supreme Court's Commercial Speech Doctrine: The Shifting Central Hudson Analysis*, 22 HASTINGS COMM/ENT 343 (2000) (noting that the Court for two decades has "tinkered" with its review of commercial speech).

[6] *See* Virginia State Board of Pharmacy v. Virginia Citizens Consumer Council, 425 U.S. 748 (1976); Bates v. State Bar of Ariz., 433 U.S. 350 (1977); Carey v. Population Services Int'l, 431 U.S. 678 (1977); Linmark Assoc. v. Willingboro, 431 U.S. 85 (1977); Central Hudson Gas & Elec. Corp. v. Public Serv. Comm'n of N.Y., 447 U.S. 557 (1980); United States v. Edge Broadcasting Co., 509 U.S. 418 (1993); Rubin v. Coors Brewing Co., 514 U.S. 476 (1995); 44 Liquormart, Inc. v. Rhode Island, 517 U.S. 484 (1996); Greater New Orleans Broadcasting Assoc. v. United States, 527 U.S. 173 (1999);. *But see* Posadas de Puerto Rico v. Tourism Co., 478 U.S. 328 (1986).

At the same time, however, the Court repeatedly has said commercial speech is not full value speech and does not warrant full First Amendment protection.[7] The Court justified reduced protection of commercial speech by asserting that common sense differences exist between commercial and noncommercial speech, that courts can readily determine and punish the falsity of commercial speech claims, and that the profit motive makes commercial speech more hardy and resilient in the face of government regulation.[8] As a result, the Court has allowed government to regulate commercial speech "in a variety of ways and for a variety of reasons" far more easily than government could censor other forms of protected speech.[9]

MODERN COMMERCIAL SPEECH TEST

In 1980, in *Central Hudson Gas and Electric Corp. v. Public Service Commission of New York*, the Supreme Court established a four-part, intermediate-level test to determine when laws directed at truthful commercial speech are constitutional.[10] The *Central Hudson* test requires government to show that regulation of commercial speech is carefully crafted to achieve important government objectives while limiting the harm to free speech interests.[11] Under the *Central Hudson* test, it is constitutional for government to regulate commercial speech

1. that is not misleading and relates to lawful activities *if*
2. the regulation "directly advances"
3. a "substantial" government interest and
4. the regulation is "not more extensive than necessary" to achieve its goals.[12]

Both the Court and a number of legal scholars have said the *Central Hudson* test is virtually indistinguishable from the intermediate scrutiny test established in *United States v. O'Brien*.[13] The *Central Hudson* test accordingly has been criticized as unnecessary, based on a false value distinction between commercial and noncommercial speech[14] and too imprecise to yield consistent court decisions.[15] Nevertheless, it remains the foundation of modern commercial speech jurisprudence.

Applying the Central Hudson Test

Several recent Supreme Court decisions indicate that the Court continues to struggle with the *Central Hudson* test and the degree to which the Constitution should protect truthful commercial speech. These problems have been most apparent when the Court has reviewed government restrictions on "vice" products and services, such as tobacco, alcohol and gambling. In 1993, for example, the Court upheld a ban on broadcast advertisements by state-run lotteries, finding a complete ban on such ads in non-lottery states to be a "reasonable" means to "directly" protect the objectives of both lottery and non-lottery states in reducing the ill effects of gambling.[16] The Court justified its ruling in *United States v. Edge Broadcasting Company* by restating its historical view

---

[7] *See, e.g.*, Central Hudson, 447 U.S. at 573.

[8] 44 Liquormart, 517 U.S. at 492 (citing Bates v. State Bar of Ariz., 443 U.S. 350 (1977)).

[9] 44 Liquormart, 517 U.S. at 522 (Thomas, J., concurring).

[10] Central Hudson, 447 U.S. 557 (1980).

[11] 447 U.S. at 566.

[12] 447 U.S. at 566.

[13] 391 U.S. 376 (1968). *See, e.g.*, Central Hudson, 447 U.S. at 376-77; San Francisco Arts & Athletics, Inc. v. U.S. Olympic Comm., 483 U.S. 522, 537 n. 16 (1987) (calling the two tests "substantially similar"); Bd. of Trustees of the State Univ. of N.Y. v. Fox, 492 U.S. 469, 478 (1989) (calling the tests "similar"); R. Randall Kelso, *Three Years Hence: An Update on Filling Gaps in the Supreme Court's Approach to Constitutional Review of Legislation*, 36 S. TEX. L.REV. 1, 34 (1995) (referring to "tortured" distinction among tests of mid-level review).

[14] *See, e.g.*, Daniel E. Troy, *Advertising: Not "Low Value" Speech*, 16 YALE J. ON REG. 85 (1999).

[15] *See, e.g.*, Phillip B. Kurland, Posadas de Pureto Rico: *"Twas Strange, 'Twas Passing Strange, 'Twas Pitiful, 'Twas Wondrous Pitiful,"* 1986 S. CT. REV. 1 (1986); Susan Dente Ross, *Reconstructing First Amendment Doctrine: The 1990s [R]Evolution of the Central Hudson and O'Brien Tests*, 23:4 COMM/ENT 101 (2002).

[16] Edge Broadcasting, 509 U.S. at 429, 428, 426.

that commercial speech occupies "a subordinate position ... in the scale of First Amendment values."[17]

But three years later the Court unanimously struck down a state ban on alcohol price advertisements and directly attacked previous rationales for reduced constitutional protection of commercial speech.[18] In *44 Liquormart v. Rhode Island*, the Court said:

Regulations that suppress the truth are no less troubling because they target objectively verifiable information, nor are they less effective because they aim at durable messages. As a result, neither the 'greater objectivity' nor the 'greater hardiness' of truthful, non-misleading commercial speech justifies reviewing its complete suppression with added deference.[19]

The Court said the Constitution is particularly hostile to outright bans on speech – even commercial speech – because "the First Amendment directs us to be especially skeptical of regulations that seek to keep people in the dark for what the government perceives to be their own good."[20]

In *44 Liquormart*, the Court applied the *Central Hudson* test to require a "searching" examination of the ban's fit with the government's asserted goals, a careful evaluation of whether "less burdensome alternatives" existed and a rigorous determination of whether "alternative channels permit[ted] communication of the restricted speech."[21] The Court ruled the ban was both overbroad and ill-conceived to directly advance the governmental goals.

In 1999, a unanimous Court expressly rejected the idea that advertising automatically receives reduced constitutional protection. In *Greater New Orleans Broadcasting Association v. United States*,[22] the Court struck down a federal ban on broadcast ads for private casino gambling in states where such gambling was legal. The Court said all commercial speech regulations are constitutionally suspect unless they advance and protect consumer interests because the Constitution forbids government to impose its judgment on which truthful information should reach the public. In addition, government distinctions among speakers (in this case private vs. public casino owners) must rest upon "sound reasons" that relate directly to the government's regulatory interest because such distinctions tend to manipulate consumer opinion and choice.[23]

Then, in 2001, the Court struck down a Massachusetts law that prohibited most billboards and point-of-purchase advertisements for tobacco products to reduce use of tobacco by minors.[24] The Court's fractured decision comprised five separate opinions in which the justices struggled with how to determine whether the First Amendment prohibited such a regulation.[25] A majority of the Court found the ban directly and materially advanced the state's important interest in reducing teen-age smoking. However, the Court said, the "broad sweep of the regulations" unconstitutionally restricted adults' access to information and was not narrowly tailored to the state's interest.[26] Three justices argued that strict scrutiny should protect truthful advertising of legal products from government regulation.

Recent Supreme Court rulings on commercial speech indicate that today "the mere fact that messages propose commercial transactions does not in and of itself dictate the constitutional

---

[17] Id. at 430 (1993).

[18] 44 Liquormart, 517 U.S. at 501 (1996).

[19] Id. (internal citations omitted).

[20] 517 U.S. at 503.

[21] 517 U.S. at 529, 531.

[22] 527 U.S. 173 (1999).

[23] 527 U.S. at 193.

[24] Lorillard Tobacco v. Reilly, 535 U.S. 525 (2001).

[25] 535 U.S. at 554.

[26] 535 U.S. at 561.

analysis."[27] Rather, a strong majority of the Court has determined that most advertising regulation should be subjected to heightened scrutiny. Evidence of the existence of less speech-intrusive strategies to achieve government objectives generally renders laws targeting truthful commercial speech unconstitutional.

REGULATING ADS AND SOLICITATION BY LICENSED PROFESSIONALS

The Supreme Court, however, has said states have increased power to regulate advertisements by doctors and lawyers. The Court has expressed concerns that self-promotion by these professionals may easily mislead or pressure potential clients and sully the reputation of the profession. In 1978, for example, the Court said the Constitution permits states to ban in-person solicitation of clients by lawyers because such solicitation is primarily a business transaction.[28] In general, the Court has said print advertisements do not present the same coercive threat as face-to-face appeals, so the Court held that a complete ban on newspaper advertising for routine legal services violated the First Amendment.[29] However, states may punish lawyers who fail to fully disclose fees and conditions of service in newspaper ads[30] and may prohibit lawyers from sending mail solicitations to traumatized accident victims.[31]

CONTROLLING DECEPTIVE ADS

Although the Supreme Court has increasingly protected truthful commercial speech, the Court steadfastly has maintained that deceptive and misleading advertising may be prohibited and sanctioned without raising First Amendment concerns. For example, in 2003, the Supreme Court ruled tha the First Amendment does not prevent state fraud prosecution for false and misleading claims in charitable telephone solicitations.[32]

Federal and state laws that regulate false advertising are supplemented by Federal Trade Commission rules and guidelines and self-regulation by the advertising industry. The Federal Trade Commission was established by Congress to "protect the public from unfair and deceptive acts and practices in the advertising and marketing of goods and services."[33] According to the FTC, an ad is deceptive if it 1) makes a claim or omits information 2) that is material to the consumer decision to purchase, 3) that is likely to mislead a reasonable consumer, and 4) that causes harm. The FTC focuses on the first and third parts of the test, accepting that any deceptive claims or omissions that mislead consumers are, by definition, material and cause harm.

The FTC wields its power through advisory opinions, industry guidelines, policy statements, rules and adjudication. FTC advisory opinions respond to advertiser queries and provide informed, but not binding, legal advice. FTC guides for an array of industries provide legally enforceable detailed descriptions of what practices are deceptive and how to avoid them. FTC policy statements – also enforceable by the FTC and the federal courts – provide broader guidance across industries on such topics as endorsements, testimonials, substantiation or product comparisons. For example, the FTC policy on substantiation requires advertisers to have a reasonable basis for objective claims they make about their product or service. The FTC's Trade Regulation Rules are enacted through a formal process of proposals, hearings and comment. FTC rules have the force of law and carry civil fines of up to $11,000 for each violation.

---

[27] 44 Liquormart at 501.

[28] Ohralik v. Ohio State Bar Association, 436 U.S. 447 (1978).

[29] Bates, 443 U.S. 350 (1977).

[30] Zauderer v. Office of Disciplinary Counsel of the Supreme Court of Ohio, 471 U.S. 626 (1985).

[31] Florida Bar v. Went For It, Inc., 515 U.S. 618 (1995).

[32] Illinois v. Telemarketing Associates, 123 S.Ct. 1829 (2003).

[33] 16 C.F.R. Sec. 0.1 (1999).

The FTC investigates complaints and enforces its guidelines, policies and regulations either through its administrative authority or by taking suspected violators to federal court. Advertisers who wish to avoid adjudication may sign FTC-initiated consent decrees that require them to stop certain ads or practices. Under consent decrees, advertisers do not admit liability. Before a proposed consent decree becomes final, however, the FTC allows 60 days for public comment.

If an advertiser does not sign a consent decree, the FTC may initiate administrative adjudication. Here an FTC administrative law judge hears the case and issues a statement of findings and conclusions of law. The judge either imposes a cease and desist order on the advertiser or dismisses the complaint. The judge's decision may be appealed to the full FTC, whose decision may be appealed to the federal court of appeals and then the U.S. Supreme Court.

Alternately, the FTC may take the case directly to federal court to seek an injunction to stop the advertising. Courts may fine advertisers who violate federal statutes or FTC regulations and may require advertisers to pay damages to injured consumers. In rare cases, the FTC may ask the Justice Department to pursue criminal charges against a deceptive advertiser.

A number of advertising industry organizations also oversee advertising practices in an attempt to self-regulate and increase the truthfulness and credibility of advertising claims. The National Advertising Division of the Better Business Bureau and its review units are the leading advertising industry self-regulator. They monitor ads, investigate complaints, publish findings and issue recommendations to advertisers. Compliance with NAD advice is voluntary but the negative publicity about deceptive practices strongly influences advertisers.

LIABILITY FOR DECEPTIVE OR HARMFUL PROMOTIONS

While advertising agencies and others who produce marketing claims may be held legally liable for false or deceptive claims, publishers historically have been protected from liability. Magazine and newspaper publishers generally are not liable for harmful advertising they publish because they lack *scienter* and are viewed merely as the vehicle for the messages of the advertisers. However, in 1992 a federal circuit court of appeals upheld a damage award of $4.3 million in damages from *Soldier of Fortune* magazine for the contract killing and shooting arranged in response to a "gun for hire" classified ad the magazine published.[34] The court said the magazine was liable because it knowingly published an ad that a reasonable person would recognize posed an unreasonable risk of harm. That same year, another federal court of appeals allowed a civil liability lawsuit in a triple-murder contract killing to proceed against Paladin Enterprises, publishers of the book *Hit Man*, which promoted itself as a how-to guide for hiring a killer or committing murder. The court said the First Amendment in no way protects speech – commercial or otherwise – that aids and abets crime.[35]

READING THE COMMERCIAL SPEECH CASES

This chapter and the cases that follow focus on modern commercial speech jurisprudence and contemporary standards for punishing deceptive advertising. The cases in the following list provide the foundation for greater understanding of the development of this area of the law and the evolution of contemporary commercial speech jurisprudence.

- *Greater New Orleans Broadcasting Assoc. v. United States*, 527 U.S. 173 (1999) (ban on gambling ads unconstitutional).
- *44 Liquormart, Inc. v. Rhode Island*, 517 U.S. 484 (1996) (ban on alcohol price ads unconstitutional).

---

[34] Braun v. Soldier of Fortune, 968 F.2d 110 (11th Cir. 1992).
[35] Rice v. Paladin Enters., 128 F.3d 233 (4th Cir. 1997); cert. denied, 523 U.S. 1074 (1998).

- *Rubin v. Coors Brewing Co.*, 514 U.S. 476 (1995) (ban on alcohol content labeling unconstitutional).
- *United States v. Edge Broadcasting Co.*, 509 U.S. 418 (1993) (federal ban on lottery ads constitutional).
- *Posadas de Puerto Rico Assocs. v. Tourism Co.*, 478 U.S. 328, 345-346 (1986) (upholding ban on gambling ads because the power to ban the activity itself logically includes power to regulate promotion of that activity).
- *Virginia State Board of Pharmacy v. Virginia Citizens Consumer Council*, 425 U.S. 1817 (1976) (ban on price ads for prescription drugs unconstitutional).
- *Bigelow v. Virginia*, 421 U.S. 809 (1975) (ban on abortion ads unconstitutional).
- *Valentine v. Chrestensen*, 316 U.S. 52 (1942) (commercial speech has no First Amendment protection).

As you read the two focal cases below, consider these questions.

- Does the Court's four-part test in *Central Hudson* "elevate" the protection of commercial speech to equal that of noncommercial speech?
- To what extent is the speech in these two cases purely commercial?
- Where or how does the Court draw the line between commercial and noncommercial speech?
- To what extent does the Court consider any informational value of the commercial speech in reaching its decisions?
- What does *Greater New Orleans* indicate about "the greater includes the lesser" reasoning adopted by the Court in *Posadas v. Puerto Rico*?
- Does the Court distinguish commercial speech about "vice" products from other commercial speech and treat it differently?
- Compare the Court's application of the *Central Hudson* test in the two cases and identify any ways in which it may have changed.

Central Hudson Gas & Electric Corp. v. Public Service Commission of New York
447 U.S. 557
(1980)

PRIOR HISTORY: Appeal From The Court Of Appeals Of New York.

JUDGES: POWELL, J., delivered the opinion of the Court, in which BURGER, C. J., and STEWART, WHITE, and MARSHALL, JJ., joined. BRENNAN, J., filed an opinion concurring in the judgment,. BLACKMUN, J., and STEVENS, J., filed opinions concurring in the judgment, in which BRENNAN, J., joined. REHNQUIST, J., filed a dissenting opinion.

OPINION: [558] MR. JUSTICE POWELL.
[1A]   This case presents the question whether a regulation of the Public Service Commission of the State of New York violates the First and Fourteenth Amendments because it completely bans promotional advertising by an electrical utility.

I.   In December 1973, the Commission, appellee here, ordered electric utilities in New York State to cease all advertising that "[promotes] the use of electricity." App. to Juris. [559] Statement 31a. The order was based on the Commission's finding that "the interconnected utility system in New York State does not have sufficient fuel stocks or sources of supply to continue furnishing all customer demands for the 1973-1974 winter." Id., at 26a.

Three years later, when the fuel shortage had eased, the Commission requested comments from the public on its proposal to continue the ban on promotional advertising. Central Hudson Gas & Electric Corp., the appellant in this case, opposed the ban on First Amendment grounds. App. A10. After reviewing the public comments, the Commission extended the prohibition in a Policy Statement issued on February 25, 1977.

The Policy Statement divided advertising expenses "into two broad categories: promotional – advertising intended to stimulate the purchase of utility services – and institutional and informational, a broad category inclusive of all advertising not clearly intended to promote sales."[1] App. to Juris. Statement 35a. The Commission declared all promotional advertising contrary to the national policy of conserving energy. It acknowledged that the ban is not a perfect vehicle for conserving energy. For example, the Commission's order prohibits promotional advertising to develop consumption during periods when demand for electricity is low. By limiting growth in "off-peak" consumption, the ban limits the "beneficial side effects" of such growth in terms of more efficient use of existing power plants. Id., at 37a. And since oil dealers are not under the Commission's jurisdiction and [560] thus remain free to advertise, it was recognized that the ban can achieve only "piecemeal conservationism." Still, the Commission adopted the restriction because it was deemed likely to "result in some dampening of unnecessary growth" in energy consumption. Ibid.

The Commission's order explicitly permitted "informational" advertising designed to encourage "shifts of consumption" from peak demand times to periods of low electricity demand. Ibid. (emphasis in original). Informational advertising would not seek to increase aggregate consumption, but would invite a leveling of demand throughout any given 24-hour period. The agency offered to review "specific proposals by the companies for specifically described [advertising] programs that meet these criteria." Id., at 38a.

When it rejected requests for rehearing on the Policy Statement, the Commission supplemented its rationale for the advertising ban. The agency observed that additional electricity probably would be more expensive to produce than existing output. Because electricity rates in New York were not then based on marginal cost,[2] the Commission feared that additional power would be priced below the actual cost of generation. The additional electricity would be subsidized by all consumers through generally

higher rates. Id., at 57a-58a. The state agency also thought that promotional advertising would give "misleading signals" to the public by appearing to encourage energy consumption at a time when conservation is needed. Id., at 59a.

Appellant challenged the order in state court, arguing that the Commission had restrained commercial speech in violation of the First and Fourteenth Amendments.[3] The Commission's [561] order was upheld by the trial court and at the intermediate appellate level.[4] The New York Court of Appeals affirmed. It found little value to advertising in "the noncompetitive market in which electric corporations operate." Consolidated Edison Co. v. Public Service Comm'n, 47 N. Y. 2d 94, 110, 390 N. E. 2d 749, 757 (1979). Since consumers "have no choice regarding the source of their electric power," the court denied that "promotional advertising of electricity might contribute to society's interest in 'informed and reliable' economic decision making." Ibid. The court also observed that by encouraging consumption, promotional advertising would only exacerbate the current energy situation. Id., at 110, 390 N. E. 2d, at 758. The court concluded that the governmental interest in the prohibition outweighed the limited constitutional value of the commercial speech at issue. We noted probable jurisdiction, 444 U.S. 962 (1979), and now reverse.

II. [2] The Commission's order restricts only commercial speech, that is, expression related solely to the economic interests of the speaker and its audience. Virginia Pharmacy Board v. Virginia Citizens Consumer Council, 425 U.S. 748, 762 (1976); Bates v. State Bar of Arizona, 433 U.S. 350, 363-364 (1977); Friedman v. Rogers, 440 U.S. 1, 11 (1979). The First Amendment, as applied to the States through the Fourteenth Amendment, protects commercial speech from unwarranted governmental regulation. Virginia Pharmacy Board, 425 U.S., at 761-762. Commercial expression not only serves the economic interest of the speaker, but also assists consumers and furthers the societal interest in the fullest possible [562] dissemination of information. In applying the First Amendment to this area, we have rejected the "highly paternalistic" view that government has complete power to suppress or regulate commercial speech. "[People] will perceive their own best interests if only they are well enough informed, and . . . the best means to that end

---

[1] The dissenting opinion attempts to construe the Policy Statement to authorize advertising that would result "in a net energy savings" even if the advertising encouraged consumption of additional electricity. Post, at 604-605. The attempted construction fails, however, since the Policy Statement is phrased only in terms of advertising that promotes "the purchase of utility services" and "sales" of electricity. Plainly, the Commission did not intend to permit advertising that would enhance net energy efficiency by increasing consumption of electrical services.

[2] "Marginal cost" has been defined as the "extra or incremental cost of producing an extra unit of output." P. Samuelson, Economics 463 (10th ed. 1976) (emphasis in original).

[3] Central Hudson also alleged that the Commission's order reaches beyond the agency's statutory powers. This argument was rejected by the New York Court of Appeals, Consolidated Edison Co. v. Public Service Comm'n, 47 N. Y. 2d 94, 102-104, 390 N. E. 2d 749, 752-754 (1979), and was not argued to this Court.

[4] Consolidated Edison Co. v. Public Service Comm'n, 63 App. Div. 2d 364, 407 N. Y. S. 2d 735 (1978); App. to Juris. Statement 22a (N. Y. Sup. Ct., Feb. 17, 1978).

is to open the channels of communication, rather than to close them. . . ." Id., at 770; see Linmark Associates, Inc. v. Willingboro, 431 U.S. 85, 92 (1977). Even when advertising communicates only an incomplete version of the relevant facts, the First Amendment presumes that some accurate information is better than no information at all. Bates v. State Bar of Arizona, supra, at 374.

[3A][4] Nevertheless, our decisions have recognized "the 'commonsense' distinction between speech proposing a commercial transaction, which occurs in an area traditionally subject to government regulation, and other varieties of speech. " Ohralik v. Ohio State Bar Assn., 436 U.S. 447, 455-456 (1978); see Bates v. State Bar of Arizona, supra, at 381; see also Jackson & Jeffries, Commercial Speech: Economic Due Process and the First Amendment, 65 Va. L. Rev. 1, 38-39 (1979).[5] The

[563] Constitution therefore accords a lesser protection to commercial speech than to other constitutionally guaranteed expression. 436 U.S., at 456, 457. The protection available for particular commercial expression turns on the nature both of the expression and of the governmental interests served by its regulation.

[3B][5] The First Amendment's concern for commercial speech is based on the informational function of advertising. See First National Bank of Boston v. Bellotti, 435 U.S. 765, 783 (1978). Consequently, there can be no constitutional objection to the suppression of commercial messages that do not accurately inform the public about lawful activity. The government may ban forms of communication more likely to deceive the public than to inform it, Friedman v. Rogers, supra, at 13, 15-16; Ohralik v. Ohio State Bar Assn., supra, at 464-465, or [564] commercial speech related to illegal activity, Pittsburgh Press Co. v. Human Relations Comm'n, 413 U.S. 376, 388 (1973).[6]

[6] If the communication is neither misleading nor related to unlawful activity, the government's power is more circumscribed. The State must assert a substantial interest to be achieved by restrictions on commercial speech. Moreover, the regulatory technique must be in proportion to that interest. The limitation on expression must be designed carefully to achieve the State's goal. Compliance with this requirement may be measured by two criteria. First, the restriction must directly advance the state interest involved; the regulation may not be sustained if it provides only ineffective or remote support for the government's purpose. Second, if the governmental interest could be served as well by a more limited restriction on commercial speech, the excessive restrictions cannot survive.

Under the first criterion, the Court has declined to uphold regulations that only indirectly advance the state interest involved. In both Bates and Virginia Pharmacy Board, the Court concluded that an advertising ban could not be imposed to protect the ethical or performance standards of a profession. The

---

[5] In an opinion concurring in the judgment, MR. JUSTICE STEVENS suggests that the Commission's order reaches beyond commercial speech to suppress expression that is entitled to the full protection of the First Amendment. See post, at 580-581. We find no support for this claim in the record of this case. The Commission's Policy Statement excluded "institutional and informational" messages from the advertising ban, which was restricted to all advertising "clearly intended to promote sales." App. to Juris. Statement 35a. The complaint alleged only that the "prohibition of promotional advertising by Petitioner is not reasonable regulation of Petitioner's commercial speech. . . ." Id., at 70a. Moreover, the state-court opinions and the arguments of the parties before this Court also viewed this litigation as involving only commercial speech. Nevertheless, the concurring opinion of MR. JUSTICE STEVENS views the Commission's order as suppressing more than commercial speech because it would outlaw, for example, advertising that promoted electricity consumption by touting the environmental benefits of such uses. See post, at 581. Apparently the opinion would accord full First Amendment protection to all promotional advertising that includes claims "relating to . . . questions frequently discussed and debated by our political leaders." Ibid. Although this approach responds to the serious issues surrounding our national energy policy as raised in this case, we think it would blur further the line the Court has sought to draw in commercial speech cases. It would grant broad constitutional protection to any advertising that links a product to a current public debate. But many, if not most, products may be tied to public concerns with the environment, energy, economic policy, or individual health and safety. We rule today in Consolidated Edison Co. v. Public Service Comm'n, ante, p. 530, that utilities enjoy the full panoply of First Amendment protections for their direct comments on public issues. There is no reason for providing similar constitutional protection when such statements are made only in the context of commercial transactions. In that context, for example, the State retains the power to "[insure] that the stream of commercial information [flows] cleanly as well as freely." Virginia Pharmacy Board v. Virginia Citizens Consumer Council, 425 U.S. 748, 772 (1975). This Court's decisions on commercial expression have rested on the premise that such speech, although meriting some protection, is of less constitutional moment than other forms of speech. As we stated in Ohralik, the failure to

distinguish between commercial and noncommercial speech "could invite dilution, simply by a leveling process, of the force of the [First] Amendment's guarantee with respect to the latter kind of speech." 436 U.S., at 456.

[6] In most other contexts, the First Amendment prohibits regulation based on the content of the message. Consolidated Edison Co. v. Public Service Comm'n, ante, at 537-540. Two features of commercial speech permit regulation of its content. First, commercial speakers have extensive knowledge of both the market and their products. Thus, they are well situated to evaluate the accuracy of their messages and the lawfulness of the underlying activity. Bates v. State Bar of Arizona, 433 U.S. 350, 381 (1977). In addition, commercial speech, the offspring of economic self-interest, is a hardy breed of expression that is not "particularly susceptible to being crushed by overbroad regulation." Ibid.

Court noted in Virginia Pharmacy Board that "[the] advertising ban does not directly affect professional standards one way or the other." 425 U.S., at 769. In Bates, the Court overturned an advertising prohibition that was designed to protect the "quality" of a lawyer's work. [565] "Restraints on advertising . . . are an ineffective way of deterring shoddy work." 433 U.S., at 378.[7]

[7][8A][9A] The second criterion recognizes that the First Amendment mandates that speech restrictions be "narrowly drawn." In re Primus, 436 U.S. 412, 438 (1978).[8] The regulatory technique may extend only as far as the interest it serves. The State cannot regulate speech that poses no danger to the asserted state interest, see First National Bank of Boston v. Bellotti, supra, at 794-795, nor can it completely suppress information when narrower restrictions on expression would serve its interest as well. For example, in Bates the Court explicitly did not "foreclose the possibility that some limited supplementation, by way of warning or disclaimer or the like, might be required" in promotional materials. 433 U.S., at 384. See Virginia Pharmacy Board, supra, at 773. And in Carey v. Population Services International, 431 U.S. 678, 701-702 (1977), we held that the State's "arguments . . . do not justify the total suppression of advertising concerning contraceptives." This holding left open the possibility that [566] the State could implement more carefully drawn restrictions. See id., at 712 (POWELL, J., concurring in part and in judgment); id., at 716-717 (STEVENS, J., concurring in part and in judgment).[9]

---

[7] In Linmark Associates, Inc. v. Willingboro, 431 U.S. 85, 95-96 (1977), we observed that there was no definite connection between the township's goal of integrated housing and its ban on the use of "For Sale" signs in front of houses

[8] This analysis is not an application of the "overbreadth" doctrine. The latter theory permits the invalidation of regulations on First Amendment grounds even when the litigant challenging the regulation has engaged in no constitutionally protected activity. E.g., Kunz v. New York, 340 U.S. 290 (1951).
The overbreadth doctrine derives from the recognition that unconstitutional restriction of expression may deter protected speech by parties not before the court and thereby escape judicial review. Broadrick v. Oklahoma, 413 U.S. 601, 612-613 (1973); see Note, The First Amendment Overbreadth Doctrine, 83 Harv. L. Rev. 844, 853-858 (1970). This restraint is less likely where the expression is linked to "commercial well-being" and therefore is not easily deterred by "overbroad regulation." Bates v. State Bar of Arizona, supra, at 381. In this case, the Commission's prohibition acts directly against the promotional activities of Central Hudson, and to the extent the limitations are unnecessary to serve the State's interest, they are invalid.

[9] We review with special care regulations that entirely suppress commercial speech in order to pursue a nonspeech-related policy. In those circumstances, a ban on speech could screen from public view the underlying governmental policy. See Virginia Pharmacy Board, 425 U.S., at 780, n. 8

[8B][9B][10] In commercial speech cases, then, a four-part analysis has developed. At the outset, we must determine whether the expression is protected by the First Amendment. For commercial speech to come within that provision, it at least must concern lawful activity and not be misleading. Next, we ask whether the asserted governmental interest is substantial. If both inquiries yield positive answers, we must determine whether the regulation directly advances the governmental interest asserted, and whether it is not more extensive than is necessary to serve that interest.

III. [1B] We now apply this four-step analysis for commercial speech to the Commission's arguments in support of its ban on promotional advertising.

A   The Commission does not claim that the expression at issue either is inaccurate or relates to unlawful activity. Yet the New York Court of Appeals questioned whether Central Hudson's advertising is protected commercial speech. Because appellant holds a monopoly over the sale of electricity in its service area, the state court suggested that the Commission's order restricts no commercial speech of any worth. The court stated that advertising in a "noncompetitive market" [567] could not improve the decisionmaking of consumers. 47 N. Y. 2d, at 110, 390 N. E. 2d, at 757. The court saw no constitutional problem with barring commercial speech that it viewed as conveying little useful information.

This reasoning falls short of establishing that appellant's advertising is not commercial speech protected by the First Amendment. Monopoly over the supply of a product provides no protection from competition with substitutes for that product. Electric utilities compete with suppliers of fuel oil and natural gas in several markets, such as those for home heating and industrial power. This Court noted the existence of interfuel competition 45 years ago, see West Ohio Gas Co. v. Public Utilities Comm'n, 294 U.S. 63, 72 (1935). Each energy source continues to offer peculiar advantages and disadvantages that may influence consumer choice. For consumers in those competitive markets, advertising by utilities is just as valuable as advertising by unregulated firms.[10]

Even in monopoly markets, the suppression of advertising reduces the information available for consumer decisions and thereby defeats the purpose

---

(STEWART, J., concurring). Indeed, in recent years this Court has not approved a blanket ban on commercial speech unless the expression itself was flawed in some way, either because it was deceptive or related to unlawful activity.

[10] Several commercial speech decisions have involved enterprises subject to extensive state regulation. E.g., Friedman v. Rogers, 440 U.S. 1, 4-5 (1979) (optometrists); Bates v. State Bar of Arizona, 433 U.S. 350 (1977) (lawyers); Virginia Pharmacy Board v. Virginia Citizens Consumer Council, supra, at 750-752 (pharmacists).

of the First Amendment. The New York court's argument appears to assume that the providers of a monopoly service or product are willing to pay for wholly ineffective advertising. Most businesses – even regulated monopolies – are unlikely to underwrite promotional advertising that is of no interest or use to consumers. Indeed, a monopoly enterprise legitimately may wish to inform the public that it has developed new services or terms of doing business. A consumer may need information to aid his decision whether or not to use the monopoly service at all, or how much of the service he should purchase. In the absence of factors that would distort the decision to advertise, we [568] may assume that the willingness of a business to promote its products reflects a belief that consumers are interested in the advertising.[11] Since no such extraordinary conditions have been identified in this case, appellant's monopoly position does not alter the First Amendment's protection for its commercial speech.

B   The Commission offers two state interests as justifications for the ban on promotional advertising. The first concerns energy conservation. Any increase in demand for electricity – during peak or off-peak periods – means greater consumption of energy. The Commission argues, and the New York court agreed, that the State's interest in conserving energy is sufficient to support suppression of advertising designed to increase consumption of electricity. In view of our country's dependence on energy resources beyond our control, no one can doubt the importance of energy conservation. Plainly, therefore, the state interest asserted is substantial.

The Commission also argues that promotional advertising will aggravate inequities caused by the failure to base the utilities' rates on marginal cost. The utilities argued to the Commission that if they could promote the use of electricity in periods of low demand, they would improve their utilization of generating capacity. The Commission responded that promotion of off-peak consumption also would increase consumption during peak periods. If peak demand were to rise, the absence of marginal cost rates would mean that the rates charged for the additional power would not reflect the true costs of expanding production. Instead, the extra costs would [569] be borne by all consumers through higher overall rates. Without promotional advertising, the Commission stated, this inequitable turn of events

would be less likely to occur. The choice among rate structures involves difficult and important questions of economic supply and distributional fairness.[12] The State's concern that rates be fair and efficient represents a clear and substantial governmental interest.

C   Next, we focus on the relationship between the State's interests and the advertising ban. Under this criterion, the Commission's laudable concern over the equity and efficiency of appellant's rates does not provide a constitutionally adequate reason for restricting protected speech. The link between the advertising prohibition and appellant's rate structure is, at most, tenuous. The impact of promotional advertising on the equity of appellant's rates is highly speculative. Advertising to increase off-peak usage would have to increase peak usage, while other factors that directly affect the fairness and efficiency of appellant's rates remained constant. Such conditional and remote eventualities simply cannot justify silencing appellant's promotional advertising.

In contrast, the State's interest in energy conservation is directly advanced by the Commission order at issue here. There is an immediate connection between advertising and demand for electricity. Central Hudson would not contest the advertising ban unless it believed that promotion would increase its sales. Thus, we find a direct link between the state interest in conservation and the Commission's order.

D   We come finally to the critical inquiry in this case: whether the Commission's complete suppression of speech ordinarily protected by the First Amendment is no more extensive than [570] necessary to further the State's interest in energy conservation. The Commission's order reaches all promotional advertising, regardless of the impact of the touted service on overall energy use. But the energy conservation rationale, as important as it is, cannot justify suppressing information about electric devices or services that would cause no net increase in total energy use. In addition, no showing has been made that a more limited restriction on the content of promotional advertising would not serve adequately the State's interests.

Appellant insists that but for the ban, it would advertise products and services that use energy efficiently. These include the "heat pump," which both parties acknowledge to be a major improvement in electric heating, and the use of electric heat as a "backup" to solar and other heat sources. Although the Commission has questioned the efficiency of electric heating before this Court, neither the Commission's Policy Statement nor its order denying rehearing made findings on this issue. In the absence of authoritative findings to the contrary, we must credit as within the realm of

---

[11] There may be a greater incentive for a utility to advertise if it can use promotional expenses in determining its rate of return, rather than pass those costs on solely to shareholders. That practice, however, hardly distorts the economic decision whether to advertise. Unregulated businesses pass on promotional costs to consumers, and this Court expressly approved the practice for utilities in West Ohio Gas Co. v. Public Utilities Comm'n, 294 U.S. 63, 72 (1935).

[12] See W. Jones, Regulated Industries 191-287 (2d ed. 1976).

possibility the claim that electric heat can be an efficient alternative in some circumstances.

The Commission's order prevents appellant from promoting electric services that would reduce energy use by diverting demand from less efficient sources, or that would consume roughly the same amount of energy as do alternative sources. In neither situation would the utility's advertising endanger conservation or mislead the public. To the extent that the Commission's order suppresses speech that in no way impairs the State's interest in energy conservation, the Commission's order violates the First and Fourteenth Amendments and must be invalidated. See First National Bank of Boston v. Bellotti, 435 U.S. 765 (1978).

The Commission also has not demonstrated that its interest in conservation cannot be protected adequately by more limited regulation of appellant's commercial expression. To further [571] its policy of conservation, the Commission could attempt to restrict the format and content of Central Hudson's advertising. It might, for example, require that the advertisements include information about the relative efficiency and expense of the offered service, both under current conditions and for the foreseeable future. Cf. Banzhaf v. FCC, 132 U. S. App. D. C. 14, 405 F.2d 1082 (1968), cert. denied sub nom. Tobacco Institute, Inc. v. FCC, 396 U.S. 842 (1969).[13] In the absence of a showing that more limited speech regulation would be ineffective, we cannot approve the complete suppression of Central Hudson's advertising.[14]

IV. [11] Our decision today in no way disparages the national interest in energy conservation. We accept without reservation the argument that conservation, as well as the development of alternative energy sources, is an imperative national goal. Administrative bodies empowered to regulate electric utilities have the authority – and indeed the duty – to take appropriate action to further this goal. When, however, such action involves [572] the

suppression of speech, the First and Fourteenth Amendments require that the restriction be no more extensive than is necessary to serve the state interest. In this case, the record before us fails to show that the total ban on promotional advertising meets this requirement.[15]

Accordingly, the judgment of the New York Court of Appeals is Reversed.

CONCUR BY: BRENNAN; BLACKMUN; STEVENS

MR. JUSTICE BRENNAN, concurring in the judgment.

One of the major difficulties in this case is the proper characterization of the Commission's Policy Statement. I find it impossible to determine on the present record whether the Commission's ban on all "promotional" advertising, in contrast to "institutional and informational" advertising, see ante, at 559, is intended to encompass more than "commercial speech." I am inclined to think that MR. JUSTICE STEVENS is correct that the Commission's order prohibits more than mere proposals to engage in certain kinds of commercial transactions, and therefore I agree with his conclusion that the ban surely violates the First and Fourteenth Amendments. But even on the assumption that the Court is correct that the Commission's order reaches only commercial speech, I agree with MR. JUSTICE BLACKMUN that "[no] differences between commercial speech and other protected speech justify suppression of commercial speech in order to influence public conduct through manipulation of the availability of information." Post, at 578.

Accordingly, with the qualifications implicit in the preceding [573] paragraph, I join the opinions of MR. JUSTICE BLACKMUN and MR. JUSTICE STEVENS concurring in the judgment.

MR. JUSTICE BLACKMUN, with whom MR. JUSTICE BRENNAN joins, concurring in the judgment.

I agree with the Court that the Public Service Commission's ban on promotional advertising of electricity by public utilities is inconsistent with the First and Fourteenth Amendments. I concur only in the Court's judgment, however, because I believe the test now evolved and applied by the Court is not consistent with our prior cases and does not

---

[13] The Commission also might consider a system of previewing advertising campaigns to insure that they will not defeat conservation policy. It has instituted such a program for approving "informational" advertising under the Policy Statement challenged in this case. See supra, at 560. We have observed that commercial speech is such a sturdy brand of expression that traditional prior restraint doctrine may not apply to it. Virginia Pharmacy Board v. Virginia Citizens Consumer Council, 425 U.S., at 771-772, n. 24. And in other areas of speech regulation, such as obscenity, we have recognized that a prescreening arrangement can pass constitutional muster if it includes adequate procedural safeguards. Freedman v. Maryland, 380 U.S. 51 (1965).

[14] In view of our conclusion that the Commission's advertising policy violates the First and Fourteenth Amendments, we do not reach appellant's claims that the agency's order also violated the Equal Protection Clause of the Fourteenth Amendment, and that it is both overbroad and vague.

---

[15] The Commission order at issue here was not promulgated in response to an emergency situation. Although the advertising ban initially was prompted by critical fuel shortage in 1973, the Commission makes no claim that an emergency now exists. We do not consider the powers that the State might have over utility advertising in emergency circumstances. See State v. Oklahoma Gas & Electric Co., 536 P. 2d 887, 895-896 (Okla. 1975).

provide adequate protection for truthful, non-misleading, non-coercive commercial speech.

The Court asserts, ante, at 566, that "a four-part analysis has developed" from our decisions concerning commercial speech. Under this four-part test a restraint on commercial "communication [that] is neither misleading nor related to unlawful activity" is subject to an intermediate level of scrutiny, and suppression is permitted whenever it "directly advances" a "substantial" governmental interest and is "not more extensive than is necessary to serve that interest." Ante, at 564 and 566. I agree with the Court that this level of intermediate scrutiny is appropriate for a restraint on commercial speech designed to protect consumers from misleading or coercive speech, or a regulation related to the time, place, or manner of commercial speech. I do not agree, however, that the Court's four-part test is the proper one to be applied when a State seeks to suppress information about a product in order to manipulate a private economic decision that the State cannot or has not regulated or outlawed directly.

Since the Court, without citing empirical data or other authority, finds a "direct link" between advertising and energy consumption, it leaves open the possibility that the State may suppress advertising of electricity in order to lessen demand for electricity. I, of course, agree with the Court that, [574] in today's world, energy conservation is a goal of paramount national and local importance. I disagree with the Court, however, when it says that suppression of speech may be a permissible means to achieve that goal. MR. JUSTICE STEVENS appropriately notes: "The justification for the regulation is nothing more than the expressed fear that the audience may find the utility's message persuasive. Without the aid of any coercion, deception, or misinformation, truthful communi-cation may persuade some citizens to consume more electricity than they otherwise would." Post, at 581.

The Court recognizes that we have never held that commercial speech may be suppressed in order to further the State's interest in discouraging purchases of the underlying product that is advertised. Ante, at 566, n. 9. Permissible restraints on commercial speech have been limited to measures designed to protect consumers from fraudulent, misleading, or coercive sales techniques.[1] Those designed to deprive consumers

of information about products or services that are legally offered for sale consistently have been invalidated.[2]

I seriously doubt whether suppression of information concerning the availability and price of a legally offered product is ever a permissible way for the State to "dampen" demand for or use of the product. Even though "commercial" speech is involved, such a regulatory measure strikes at the heart of the First Amendment. This is because it is a covert attempt [575] by the State to manipulate the choices of its citizens, not by persuasion or direct regulation, but by depriving the public of the information needed to make a free choice. As the Court recognizes, the State's policy choices are insulated from the visibility and scrutiny that direct regulation would entail and the conduct of citizens is molded by the information that government chooses to give them. Ante, at 566, n. 9 ("We review with special care regulations that entirely suppress commercial speech in order to pursue a nonspeech-related policy. In those circumstances, a ban on speech could screen from public view the underlying governmental policy"). See Rotunda, The Commercial Speech Doctrine in the Supreme Court, 1976 U. Ill. Law Forum 1080, 1080-1083.

If the First Amendment guarantee means anything, it means that, absent clear and present danger, government has no power to restrict expression because of the effect its message is likely to have on the public. See generally Comment, First Amendment Protection for Commercial Advertising: The New Constitutional Doctrine, 44 U. Chi. L. Rev. 205, 243-251 (1976). Our cases indicate that this guarantee applies even to commercial speech. In Virginia Pharmacy Board v. Virginia Consumer Council, 425 U.S. 748 (1976), we held that Virginia could not pursue its goal of encouraging the public to patronize the "professional pharmacist" (one who provided individual attention and a stable pharmacist-customer relationship) by "keeping the public in ignorance of the entirely lawful terms that competing pharmacists are offering." Id., at 770. We noted that our decision left the State free to pursue its goal of maintaining high standards among its pharmacists by "[requiring] whatever professional standards it wishes of its pharmacists." Ibid.

We went on in Virginia Pharmacy Board to discuss the types of regulation of commercial speech that, due to the "commonsense differences"

---

[1] See Friedman v. Rogers, 440 U.S. 1, 10 (1979) (Court upheld a ban on practice of optometry under a trade name as a permissible requirement that commercial information "'appear in such a form . . . as [is] necessary to prevent its being deceptive,'" quoting from Virginia Pharmacy Board v. Virginia Consumer Council, 425 U.S. 748, 772, n. 24 (1976)); Ohralik v. Ohio State Bar Assn., 436 U.S. 447 (1978).

[2] See Bates v. State Bar of Arizona, 433 U.S. 350 (1977); Carey v. Population Services International, 431 U.S. 678, 700-702 (1977); Linmark Associates, Inc. v. Willingboro, 431 U.S. 85 (1977); Virginia Pharmacy Board v. Virginia Consumer Council, 425 U.S. 748 (1976); Bigelow v. Virginia, 421 U.S. 809 (1975).

between this form of speech and other forms, are or may be constitutionally permissible. We indicated that government may impose reasonable "time, [576] place, and manner" restrictions, and that it can deal with false, deceptive, and misleading commercial speech. We noted that the question of advertising of illegal transactions and the special problems of the electronic broadcast media were not presented.

Concluding with a restatement of the type of restraint that is not permitted, we said: "What is at issue is whether a State may completely suppress the dissemination of concededly truthful information about entirely lawful activity, fearful of that information's effect upon its disseminators and its recipients. . . . [We] conclude that the answer to this [question] is in the negative." Id., at 773.

Virginia Pharmacy Board did not analyze the State's interests to determine whether they were "substantial." Obviously, preventing professional dereliction and low quality health care are "substantial," legitimate, and important state goals. Nor did the opinion analyze the ban on speech to determine whether it "directly [advanced], " ante, at 566, 569, these goals. We also did not inquire whether a "more limited regulation of ... commercial expression," ante, at 570, would adequately serve the State's interests. Rather, we held that the State "may not [pursue its goals] by keeping the public in ignorance." 425 U.S., at 770. (Emphasis supplied.)

Until today, this principle has governed. In Linmark Associates, Inc. v. Willingboro, 431 U.S. 85 (1977), we considered whether a town could ban "For Sale" signs on residential property to further its goal of promoting stable, racially integrated housing. We did note that the record did not establish that the ordinance was necessary to enable the State to achieve its goal. The holding of Linmark, however, was much broader.[3] We stated: "The constitutional defect in this ordinance, however, [577] is far more basic. The Township Council here, like the Virginia Assembly in Virginia Pharmacy Bd., acted to prevent its residents from obtaining certain information . . . which pertains to sales activity in Willingboro. . .

---

[3] In my view, the Court today misconstrues the holdings of both Virginia Pharmacy Board and Linmark Associates by implying that those decisions were based on the fact that the restraints were not closely enough related to the governmental interests asserted. See ante, at 564-565, and n. 7. Although the Court noted the lack of substantial relationship between the restraint and the governmental interest in each of those cases, the holding of each clearly rested on a much broader principle.

. The Council has sought to restrict the free flow of these data because it fears that otherwise homeowners will make decisions inimical to what the Council views as the homeowners' self-interest and the corporate interest of the township: they will choose to leave town. The Council's concern, then, was not with any commercial aspect of "For Sale" signs – with offerors communicating offers to offerees – but with the substance of the information communicated to Willingboro citizens." Id., at 96.

The Court in Linmark resolved beyond all doubt that a strict standard of review applies to suppression of commercial information, where the purpose of the restraint is to influence behavior by depriving citizens of information. The Court followed the strong statement above with an explicit adoption of the standard advocated by Mr. Justice Brandeis in his concurring opinion in Whitney v. California, 274 U.S. 357, 377 (1927): "If there be time to expose through discussion the falsehood and fallacies, to avert the evil by the processes of education, the remedy to be applied is more speech, not enforced silence. Only an emergency can justify repression." 431 U.S., at 97.

Carey v. Population Services International, 431 U.S. 678, 700-702 (1977), also applied to content-based restraints on commercial speech the same standard of review we have applied to other varieties of speech. There the Court held that a ban on advertising of contraceptives could not be justified [578] by the State's interest in avoiding "'legitimation' of illicit sexual behavior" because the advertisements could not be characterized as "'directed to inciting or producing imminent lawless action and . . . likely to incite or produce such action,'" id., at 701, quoting Brandenburg v. Ohio, 395 U.S. 444, 447 (1969).

Our prior references to the "'commonsense differences'" between commercial speech and other speech "'suggest that a different degree of protection is necessary to insure that the flow of truthful and legitimate commercial information is unimpaired.'" Linmark Associates, 431 U.S., at 98, quoting Virginia Pharmacy Board, 425 U.S., at 771-772, n. 24. We have not suggested that the "commonsense differences" between commercial speech and other speech justify relaxed scrutiny of restraints that suppress truthful, nondeceptive, noncoercive commercial speech. The differences articulated by the Court, see ante, at 564, n. 6, justify a more permissive approach to regulation of the manner of commercial speech for the purpose of protecting consumers from deception or coercion, and these differences explain why doctrines designed to prevent "chilling" of protected speech are inapplicable to commercial speech. No differences between commercial speech and other protected speech justify suppression of commercial speech in order to influence public conduct through manipulation of the availability of information. The Court stated in Carey v. Population Services International:

"Appellants suggest no distinction between commercial and noncommercial speech that would render these discredited arguments meritorious when offered to justify prohibitions on commercial speech. On the contrary, such arguments are clearly directed not at any commercial aspect of the prohibited advertising but at the ideas conveyed and form of expression – the core of First Amendment values." 431 U.S., at 701, n. 28 (emphasis added).

[579] It appears that the Court would permit the State to ban all direct advertising of air conditioning, assuming that a more limited restriction on such advertising would not effectively deter the public from cooling its homes. In my view, our cases do not support this type of suppression. If a governmental unit believes that use or overuse of air conditioning is a serious problem, it must attack that problem directly, by prohibiting air conditioning or regulating thermostat levels. Just as the Commonwealth of Virginia may promote professionalism of pharmacists directly, so too New York may not promote energy conservation "by keeping the public in ignorance." Virginia Pharmacy Board, 425 U.S., at 770.

MR. JUSTICE STEVENS, with whom MR. JUSTICE BRENNAN joins, concurring in the judgment.

Because "commercial speech" is afforded less constitutional protection than other forms of speech,[1] it is important that the commercial speech concept not be defined too broadly lest speech deserving of greater constitutional protection be inadvertently suppressed. The issue in this case is whether New York's prohibition on the promotion of the use of electricity through advertising is a ban on nothing but commercial speech.

In my judgment one of the two definitions the Court uses in addressing that issue is too broad and the other may be somewhat too narrow. The Court first describes commercial speech as "expression related solely to the economic interests of the speaker and its audience." Ante, at 561. Although it is not entirely clear whether this definition uses the subject matter of the speech or the motivation of the speaker as the limiting factor, it seems clear to me that it encompasses speech that is entitled to the maximum protection afforded by the First Amendment. Neither a labor leader's exhortation to

[580] strike, nor an economist's dissertation on the money supply, should receive any lesser protection because the subject matter concerns only the economic interests of the audience. Nor should the economic motivation of a speaker qualify his constitutional protection; even Shakespeare may have been motivated by the prospect of pecuniary reward. Thus, the Court's first definition of commercial speech is unquestionably too broad.[2]

The Court's second definition refers to "'speech proposing a commercial transaction.'" Ante, at 562. A saleman's solicitation, a broker's offer, and a manufacturer's publication of a price list or the terms of his standard warranty would unquestionably fit within this concept[3] Presumably, the definition is intended to encompass advertising that advises possible buyers of the availability of specific products at specific prices and describes the advantages of purchasing such items. Perhaps it also extends to other communications that do little more than make the name of a product or a service more familiar to the general public. Whatever the precise contours of the concept, and perhaps it is too early to enunciate an exact formulation, I am persuaded that it should not include the entire range of communication that is embraced within the term "promotional advertising."

This case involves a governmental regulation that completely bans promotional advertising by an electric utility. This ban encompasses a great deal more than mere proposals to engage in certain kinds of commercial transactions. It prohibits all advocacy of the immediate or future use of electricity. [581] It curtails expression by an informed and interested group of persons of their point of view on questions relating to the production and consumption of electrical energy – questions frequently discussed and debated by our political leaders. For example, an electric company's advocacy of the use of electric heat for environmental reasons, as opposed to wood-burning stoves, would seem to fall squarely within New York's promotional advertising ban and also within the bounds of maximum First Amendment protection. The breadth of the ban thus exceeds the

---

[1] See Ohralik v. Ohio State Bar Assn., 436 U.S. 447, 456, quoted ante, at 563, n. 5. Cf. Smith v. United States, 431 U.S. 291, 318 (STEVENS, J., dissenting).

[2] See Farber, Commercial Speech and First Amendment Theory, 74 Nw. U. L. Rev. 372, 382-383 (1979):
"Economic motivation could not be made a disqualifying factor [from maximum protection] without enormous damage to the first amendment. Little purpose would be served by a first amendment which failed to protect newspapers, paid public speakers, political candidates with partially economic motives and professional authors." (Footnotes omitted.)

[3] See id., at 386-387.

boundaries of the commercial speech concept, however that concept may be defined.[4]

The justification for the regulation is nothing more than the expressed fear that the audience may find the utility's message persuasive. Without the aid of any coercion, deception, or misinformation, truthful communication may persuade some citizens to consume more electricity than they otherwise would. I assume that such a consequence would be undesirable and that government may therefore prohibit and punish the unnecessary or excessive use of electricity. But if the perceived harm associated with greater electrical usage is not sufficiently serious to justify direct regulation, surely it does not constitute the kind of clear and present danger that can justify the suppression of speech.

[582] Although they were written in a different context, the words used by Mr. Justice Brandeis in his concurring opinion in Whitney v. California, 274 U.S. 357, 376-377, explain my reaction to the prohibition against advocacy involved in this case:

"But even advocacy of violation, however reprehensible morally, is not a justification for denying free speech where the advocacy falls short of incitement and there is nothing to indicate that the advocacy would be immediately acted on. The wide difference between advocacy and incitement, between preparation and attempt, between assembling and conspiracy, must be borne in mind. In order to support a finding of clear and present danger it must be shown either that immediate serious violence was to be expected or was advocated, or that the past conduct furnished reason to believe that such advocacy was then contemplated.

"Those who won our independence by revolution were not cowards. They did not fear political change. They did not exalt order at the cost of liberty. To courageous, self-reliant men, with confidence in the power of free and fearless reasoning applied through the processes of popular government, no danger flowing from speech can be deemed clear and present, unless the incidence of the evil apprehended is so imminent that it may befall before there is opportunity for full discussion. If there be time to expose through discussion the falsehood and fallacies, to avert the evil by the processes of education, the remedy to be applied is more speech, not enforced silence. Only an emergency can justify repression. Such must be the rule if authority is to be reconciled with freedom. Such, in my opinion, is the command of the Constitution." (Footnote omitted.)[5]

[583] In sum, I concur in the result because I do not consider this to be a "commercial speech" case. Accordingly, I see no need to decide whether the Court's four-part analysis, ante, at 566, adequately protects commercial speech – as properly defined – in the face of a blanket ban of the sort involved in this case.

MR. JUSTICE REHNQUIST, dissenting.

The Court today invalidates an order issued by the New York Public Service Commission designed to promote a policy that has been declared to be of critical national concern. The order was issued by the Commission in 1973 in response to the Mideastern oil embargo crisis. It prohibits electric corporations "from promoting the use of electricity through the use of advertising, subsidy payments . . . , or employee incentives." State of New York Public Service Commission, Case No. 26532 (Dec. 5, 1973), App. to Juris. Statement 31a (emphasis added). Although the immediate crisis created by the oil embargo has subsided, the ban on promotional advertising remains in effect. The regulation was re-examined by the New York Public Service Commission in 1977. Its constitutionality was subsequently upheld by the New York Court of Appeals, which concluded that

---

[4] The utility's characterization of the Commission's ban in its complaint as involving commercial speech clearly does not bind this Court's consideration of the First Amendment issues in this new and evolving area of constitutional law. Nor does the Commission's intention not to suppress "institutional and informational" speech insure that only "commercial speech" will be suppressed. The blurry line between the two categories of speech has the practical effect of requiring that the utilities either refrain from speech that is close to the line, or seek advice from the Public Service Commission. But the Commission does not possess the necessary expertise in dealing with these sensitive free speech questions; and, in any event, ordinarily speech entitled to maximum First Amendment protection may not be subjected to a prior clearance procedure with a government agency.

---

[5] Mr. Justice Brandeis quoted Lord Justice Scrutton's comment in King v. Secretary of State for Home Affairs ex parte O'Brien, [1923] 2 K. B. 361, 382: "'You really believe in freedom of speech, if you are willing to allow it to men whose opinions seem to you wrong and even dangerous. . . .'" 274 U.S., at 377, n. 4. See also Young v. American Mini Theatres, Inc., 427 U.S. 50, 63 (opinion of STEVENS, J.).

the paramount national interest in energy conservation justified its retention.[1]

[584] The Court's asserted justification for invalidating the New York law is the public interest discerned by the Court to underlie the First Amendment in the free flow of commercial information. Prior to this Court's recent decision in Virginia Pharmacy Board v. Virginia Citizens Consumer Council, 425 U.S. 748 (1976), however, commercial speech was afforded no protection under the First Amendment whatsoever. See, e.g., Breard v. Alexandria, 341 U.S. 622 (1951); Valentine v. Chrestensen, 316 U.S. 52 (1942). Given what seems to me full recognition of the holding of Virginia Pharmacy Board that commercial speech is entitled to some degree of First Amendment protection, I think the Court is nonetheless incorrect in invalidating the carefully considered state ban on promotional advertising in light of pressing national and state energy needs.

The Court's analysis in my view is wrong in several respects. Initially, I disagree with the Court's conclusion that the speech of a state-created monopoly, which is the subject of a comprehensive regulatory scheme, is entitled to protection under the First Amendment. I also think that the Court errs here in failing to recognize that the state law is most accurately viewed as an economic regulation and that the speech involved (if it falls within the scope of the First Amendment at all) occupies a significantly more subordinate position in the hierarchy of First Amendment values than the Court gives it today. Finally, the Court in reaching its decision improperly substitutes its own judgment for that of the State in deciding how a proper ban on promotional advertising should be drafted. With regard to this latter point, the Court adopts as its final part of a four-part test a "no more [585] extensive than necessary" analysis that will unduly impair a state legislature's ability to adopt legislation reasonably designed to promote interests that have always been rightly thought to be of great importance to the State.

I.   In concluding that appellant's promotional advertising constitutes protected speech, the Court reasons that speech by electric utilities is valuable to consumers who must decide whether to use the monopoly service or turn to an alternative energy source, and if they decide to use the service how much of it to purchase. Ante, at 567. The Court in so doing "[assumes] that the willingness of a business to promote its products reflects a belief that consumers are interested in the advertising." Ante, at 568. The Court's analysis ignores the fact that the monopoly here is entirely state-created and subject to an extensive state regulatory scheme from which it derives benefits as well as burdens.

While this Court has stated that the "capacity [of speech] for informing the public does not depend upon the identity of its source," First National Bank of Boston v. Bellotti, 435 U.S. 765, 777 (1978), the source of the speech nevertheless may be relevant in determining whether a given message is protected under the First Amendment.[2] When the source of the speech is a state-created monopoly such as this, traditional First Amendment concerns, if they come into play at all, certainly do not justify the broad interventionist role adopted by the Court today. In Consolidated Edison Co. v. [586] Public Service Comm'n, ante, at 549-550, MR. JUSTICE BLACKMUN observed: "A public utility is a state-created monopoly. See, e.g., N. Y. Pub. Serv. Law § 68 (McKinney 1955); Jones, Origins of the Certificate of Public Convenience and Necessity; Developments in the States 1870-1920, 79 Colum. L. Rev. 426, 458-461 (1979); Comment, Utility Rates, Consumers, and the New York State Public Service Commission, 39 Albany L. Rev. 707, 709-714 (1975). Although monopolies generally are against the public policies of the United States and of the State of New York, see, e.g., N. Y. Gen. Bus. Law § 340 (McKinney 1968 and Supp. 1979-1980), . . . utilities are permitted to operate as monopolies because of a determination by the State that the public interest is better served by protecting them from competition. See 2 A. Kahn, The Economics of Regulation 113-171 (1971). "This exceptional grant of power to private enterprises justifies extensive oversight on the part of the State to protect the ratepayers

---

[1] The New York Court of Appeals stated: "In light of current exigencies, one of the policies of any public service legislation must be the conservation of our vital and irreplaceable resources. The Legislature has but recently imposed upon the commission a duty 'to encourage all persons and corporations . . . to formulate and carry out long-range programs . . . [for] the preservation of environmental values and the conservation of natural resources' (Public Service Law, § 5, subd. 2). Implicit in this amendment is a legislative recognition of the serious situation which confronts our State and Nation. More important, conservation of resources has become an avowed legislative policy embodied in the commission's enabling act (see also, Matter of New York State Council of Retail Merchants v. Public Serv. Comm. of State of N. Y., 45 N. Y. 2d 661, 673-674)." Consolidated Edison Co. v. Public Service Comm'n, 47 N. Y. 2d 94, 102-103, 390 N. E. 2d 749, 753 (1979).

[2] In Brown v. Glines, 444 U.S. 348 (1980), for example, we recently upheld Air Force regulations that imposed restrictions on the free speech and petition rights of Air Force personnel. See also, e.g., Parker v. Levy, 417 U.S. 733 (1974) (commissioned officer may be prohibited from publicly urging enlisted personnel to disobey orders that might send them into combat); Snepp v. United States, 444 U.S. 507 (1980) (employees of intelligence agency may be required to submit publications relating to agency activity for prepublication review by the agency).

from exploitation of the monopoly power through excessive rates and other forms of overreaching. . . . New York law gives its Public Service Commission plenary supervisory powers over all property, real and personal, 'used or to be used for or in connection with or to facilitate the . . . sale or furnishing of electricity for light, heat or power.' N. Y. Pub. Serv. Law §§ 2 (12) and 66 (1) (McKinney 1955)."

Thus, although First National Bank of Boston v. Bellotti, supra, holds that speech of a corporation is entitled to some First Amendment protection, it by no means follows that a utility with monopoly power conferred by a State is also entitled to such protection.

The state-created monopoly status of a utility arises from the unique characteristics of the services that a utility provides. As recognized in Cantor v. Detroit Edison Co., 428 U.S. 579, 595-596 (1976), "public utility regulation typically [587] assumes that the private firm is a natural monopoly and that public controls are necessary to protect the consumer from exploitation." The consequences of this natural monopoly in my view justify much more wide-ranging supervision and control of a utility under the First Amendment than this Court held in Bellotti to be permissible with regard to ordinary corporations. Corporate status is generally conferred as a result of a State's determination that the corporate characteristics "enhance its efficiency as an economic entity." First National Bank of Boston v. Bellotti, supra, at 825-826 (REHNQUIST, J., dissenting). A utility, by contrast, fulfills a function that serves special public interests as a result of the natural monopoly of the service provided. Indeed, the extensive regulations governing decisionmaking by public utilities suggest that for purposes of First Amendment analysis, a utility is far closer to a state-controlled enterprise than is an ordinary corporation.[3] Accordingly, I think a State has

broad discretion in determining the statements that a utility may make in that such statements emanate from the entity created by the State to provide important and unique public services. And a state regulatory body charged with the oversight of these types of services may reasonably decide to impose on the utility a special duty to conform its conduct to [588] the agency's conception of the public interest. Thus I think it is constitutionally permissible for it to decide that promotional advertising is inconsistent with the public interest in energy conservation. I also think New York's ban on such advertising falls within the scope of permissible state regulation of an economic activity by an entity that could not exist in corporate form, say nothing of enjoy monopoly status, were it not for the laws of New York.[4]

II.   This Court has previously recognized that although commercial speech may be entitled to First Amendment protection, that protection is not as extensive as that accorded to the advocacy of ideas. Thus, we stated in Ohralik v. Ohio State Bar Assn., 436 U.S. 447, 455-456 (1978): "Expression concerning purely commercial transactions has come within the ambit of the Amendment's protection [589] only recently. In rejecting the notion that such speech 'is wholly outside the protection of the First Amendment,' Virginia Pharmacy, supra, at 761, we were careful not to hold 'that it is wholly undifferentiable from other forms' of speech. 425 U.S., at 771, n. 24. We have not discarded the 'common-sense' distinction

---

[3] In this regard the New York Court of Appeals stated: "Public utilities, from the earliest days in this State, have been regulated and franchised to serve the commonweal. Our policy is 'to withdraw the unrestricted right of competition between corporations occupying . . . the public streets . . . and supplying the public with their products or utilities which are well nigh necessities' (People ex rel. New York Edison Co. v. Willcox, 207 N. Y. 86, 99; Matter of New York Elec. Lines Co., 201 N. Y. 321). The realities of the situation all but dictate that a utility be granted monopoly status (see People ex rel. New York Elec. Lines Co. v. Squire, 107 N. Y. 593, 603-605). To protect against abuse of this superior economic position extensive governmental regulation has been deemed a necessary coordinate (see People ex rel. New York Edison Co. v. Willcox, supra, at pp. 93-94)." 47 N. Y. 2d, at 109-110, 390 N. E. 2d, at 757.

[4] The Commission's restrictions on promotional advertising are grounded in its concern that electric utilities fulfill their obligation under the New York Public Service Law to provide "adequate" service at "just and reasonable" rates. N. Y. Pub. Serv. Law § 65 (1) (McKinney 1955). The Commission, under state law, is required to set reasonable rates. N. Y. Pub. Serv. Law §§ 66 (2) and 72 (McKinney 1955); § 66 (12) (McKinney Supp. 1979). The Commission has also been authorized by the legislature to prescribe "such reasonable improvements [in electric utilities' practices] as will best promote the public interest. . . ." § 66 (2). And in the performance of its duties the Commission is required to "encourage all persons and corporations subject to its jurisdiction to formulate and carry out long-range programs, individually or cooperatively, for the performance of their public service responsibilities with economy, efficiency, and care for the public safety, the preservation of environmental values, and the conservation of natural resources." N. Y. Pub. Serv. Law § 5 (2) (McKinney Supp. 1979). Here I think it was quite reasonable for the State Public Service Commission to conclude that the ban on promotional advertising was necessary to prevent utilities from using their broad state-conferred monopoly power to promote their own economic well-being at the expense of the state interest in energy conservation – an interest that could reasonably be found to be inconsistent with the promotion of greater profits for utilities.

between speech proposing a commercial transaction, which occurs in an area traditionally subject to government regulation, and other varieties of speech. Ibid. To require a parity of constitutional protection for commercial and noncommercial speech alike could invite dilution, simply by a leveling process, of the force of the Amendment's guarantee with respect to the latter kind of speech. Rather than subject the First Amendment to such a devitalization, we instead have afforded commercial speech a limited measure of protection, commensurate with its subordinate position in the scale of First Amendment values, while allowing modes of regulation that might be impermissible in the realm of noncommercial expression." (Footnote omitted.)

The Court's decision today fails to give due deference to this subordinate position of commercial speech. The Court in so doing returns to the bygone era of Lochner v. New York, 198 U.S. 45 (1905), in which it was common practice for this Court to strike down economic regulations adopted by a State based on the Court's own notions of the most appropriate means for the State to implement its considered policies.

I had thought by now it had become well established that a State has broad discretion in imposing economic regulations. As this Court stated in Nebbia v. New York, 291 U.S. 502, 537 (1934):

"[There] can be no doubt that upon proper occasion and by appropriate measures the state may regulate a business in any of its aspects. . . . [590] "So far as the requirement of due process is concerned, and in the absence of other constitutional restriction, a state is free to adopt whatever economic policy may reasonably be deemed to promote public welfare, and to enforce that policy by legislation adapted to its purpose. The courts are without authority either to declare such policy, or, when it is declared by the legislature, to override it. If the laws passed are seen to have a reasonable relation to a proper legislative purpose, and are neither arbitrary nor discriminatory, the requirements of due process are satisfied, and judicial determination to that effect renders a court functus officio. . . . [It] does not lie with the courts to determine that the rule is unwise."

And Mr. Justice Black, writing for the Court, observed more recently in Ferguson v. Skrupa, 372 U.S. 726, 730 (1963): "The doctrine . . . that due process authorizes courts to hold laws unconstitutional when they believe the legislature has acted unwisely – has long since been discarded. We have returned to the original constitutional proposition that courts do not substitute their social and economic beliefs for the judgment of legislative bodies, who are elected to pass laws."

The State of New York has determined here that economic realities require the grant of monopoly status to public utilities in order to distribute efficiently the services they provide, and in granting utilities such status it has made them subject to an extensive regulatory scheme. When the State adopted this scheme and when its Public Service Commission issued its initial ban on promotional advertising in 1973, commercial speech had not been held to fall within the scope of the First Amendment at all. Virginia Pharmacy Board v. Virginia Citizens Consumer Council, 425 U.S. 748 (1976), however, subsequently accorded commercial speech a limited measure of First Amendment protection.

[591] The Court today holds not only that commercial speech is entitled to First Amendment protection, but also that when it is protected a State may not regulate it unless its reason for doing so amounts to a "substantial" governmental interest, its regulation "directly advances" that interest, and its manner of regulation is "not more extensive than necessary" to serve the interest. Ante, at 566. The test adopted by the Court thus elevates the protection accorded commercial speech that falls within the scope of the First Amendment to a level that is virtually indistinguishable from that of noncommercial speech. I think the Court in so doing has effectively accomplished the "devitalization" of the First Amendment that it counseled against in Ohralik. I think it has also, by labeling economic regulation of business conduct as a restraint on "free speech," gone far to resurrect the discredited doctrine of cases such as Lochner and Tyson & Brother v. Banton, 273 U.S. 418 (1927). New York's order here is in my view more akin to an economic regulation to which virtually complete deference should be accorded by this Court.

I doubt there would be any question as to the constitutionality of New York's conservation effort if the Public Service Commission had chosen to raise the price of electricity, see, e.g., Sunshine Anthracite Coal Co. v. Adkins, 310 U.S. 381 (1940); Old Dearborn Distributing Co. v. Seagram-Distillers Corp., 299 U.S. 183 (1936), to condition its sale on specified terms, see, e.g., Nebbia v. New York, supra, at 527-528, or to restrict its production, see, e.g., Wickard v. Filburn, 317 U.S. 111 (1942). In terms of constitutional values, I think that such controls are virtually indistinguishable from the State's ban on promotional advertising.

An ostensible justification for striking down New York's ban on promotional advertising is that this Court has previously "rejected the 'highly paternalistic' view that government has complete power to suppress or regulate commercial speech. '[People] will perceive their own best interests if [592] only they are well enough informed and . . . the best means to that end is to open the channels of communication, rather than to close them. . . .'"

Ante, at 562. Whatever the merits of this view, I think the Court has carried its logic too far here.

The view apparently derives from the Court's frequent reference to the "marketplace of ideas," which was deemed analogous to the commercial market in which a laissez-faire policy would lead to optimum economic decisionmaking under the guidance of the "invisible hand." See, e.g., Adam Smith, Wealth of Nations (1776). This notion was expressed by Mr. Justice Holmes in his dissenting opinion in Abrams v. United States, 250 U.S. 616, 630 (1919), wherein he stated that "the best test of truth is the power of the thought to get itself accepted in the competition of the market. . . ." See also, e.g., Consolidated Edison v. Public Service Comm'n, ante, at 534; J. Mill, On Liberty (1858); J. Milton, Areopagitica, A Speech for the Liberty of Unlicensed Printing (1644).

While it is true that an important objective of the First Amendment is to foster the free flow of information, identification of speech that falls within its protection is not aided by the metaphorical reference to a "marketplace of ideas." There is no reason for believing that the marketplace of ideas is free from market imperfections any more than there is to believe that the invisible hand will always lead to optimum economic decisions in the commercial market. See, e.g., Baker, Scope of the First Amendment, Freedom of Speech, 25 UCLA L. Rev. 964, 967-981 (1978). Indeed, many types of speech have been held to fall outside the scope of the First Amendment, thereby subject to governmental regulation, despite this Court's references to a marketplace of ideas. See, e.g., Chaplinsky v. New Hampshire, 315 U.S. 568 (1942) (fighting words); Beauharnais v. Illinois, 343 U.S. 250 (1952) (group libel); Roth v. United States, 354 U.S. 476 (1957) (obscenity). It also has been held that the government has [593] a greater interest in regulating some types of protected speech than others. See, e.g., FCC v. Pacifica Foundation, 438 U.S. 726 (1978) (indecent speech); Virginia Pharmacy Board v. Virginia Citizens Consumer Council, supra (commercial speech). And as this Court stated in Gertz v. Robert Welch, Inc., 418 U.S. 323, 344, n. 9 (1974): "Of course, an opportunity for rebuttal seldom suffices to undo [the] harm of a defamatory falsehood. Indeed the law of defamation is rooted in our experience that the truth rarely catches up with a lie." The Court similarly has recognized that false and misleading commercial speech is not entitled to any First Amendment protection. See, e.g., ante, at 566.

The above examples illustrate that in a number of instances government may constitutionally decide that societal interests justify the imposition of restrictions on the free flow of information. When the question is whether a given commercial message is protected, I do not think this Court's determination that the information will "assist" consumers justifies judicial invalidation of a reasonably drafted state restriction on such speech when the restriction is designed to promote a concededly substantial state interest. I consequently disagree with the Court's conclusion that the societal interest in the dissemination of commercial information is sufficient to justify a restriction on the State's authority to regulate promotional advertising by utilities; indeed, in the case of a regulated monopoly, it is difficult for me to distinguish "society" from the state legislature and the Public Service Commission. Nor do I think there is any basis for concluding that individual citizens of the State will recognize the need for and act to promote energy conservation to the extent the government deems appropriate, if only the channels of communication are left open.[5] Thus, even if I were [594] to agree that commercial speech is entitled to some First Amendment protection, I would hold here that the State's decision to ban promotional advertising, in light of the substantial state interest at stake, is a constitutionally permissible exercise of its power to adopt regulations designed to promote the interests of its citizens.

The plethora of opinions filed in this case highlights the doctrinal difficulties that emerge from this Court's decisions granting First Amendment protection to commercial speech. My Brother STEVENS, quoting Mr. Justice Brandeis in Whitney v. California, 274 U.S. 357, 376-377 (1927), includes Mr. Justice Brandeis' statement that "[those] who won our independence by revolution

---

[5] Although the Constitution attaches great importance to freedom of speech under the First Amendment so that individuals will be better informed and their thoughts and ideas will be uninhibited, it does not follow that "people will perceive their own best interests," or that if they do they will act to promote them. With respect to governmental policies that do not offer immediate tangible benefits and the success of which depends on incremental contributions by all members of society, such as would seem to be the case with energy conservation, a strong argument can be made that while a policy may be in the longrun interest of all members of society, some rational individuals will perceive it to their own shortrun advantage to not act in accordance with that policy. When the regulation of commercial speech is at issue, I think this is a consideration that the government may properly take into account. As was observed in Townsend v. Yeomans, 301 U.S. 441, 451 (1937), "the legislature, acting within its sphere, is presumed to know the needs of the people of the State." This observation in my view is applicable to the determination of the State Public Service Commission here.

were not cowards. They did not fear political change. They did not exalt order at the cost of liberty." Ante, at 582. MR. JUSTICE BLACKMUN, in his separate opinion, joins only in the Court's judgment because he believes that the Court's opinion "does not provide adequate protection for truthful, non-misleading, non-coercive commercial speech." Ante, at 573. Both MR. JUSTICE STEVENS, ante, at 582, and MR. JUSTICE BLACKMUN, ante, at 577, would apply the following formulation by Mr. Justice Brandeis of the clear-and-present-danger test to the regulation of speech at issue in this case: "If there be time to expose through discussion the falsehood [595] and fallacies, to avert the evil by the processes of education, the remedy to be applied is more speech, not enforced silence. Only an emergency can justify repression." Whitney v. California, supra, at 377 (concurring opinion).

Although the Court today does not go so far as to adopt this position, its reasons for invalidating New York's ban on promotional advertising make it quite difficult for a legislature to draft a statute regulating promotional advertising that will satisfy the First Amendment requirements established by the Court in this context. See Part III, infra.

Two ideas are here at war with one another, and their resolution, although it be on a judicial battlefield, will be a very difficult one. The sort of "advocacy" of which Mr. Justice Brandeis spoke was not the advocacy on the part of a utility to use more of its product. Nor do I think those who won our independence, while declining to "exalt order at the cost of liberty," would have viewed a merchant's unfettered freedom to advertise in hawking his wares as a "liberty" not subject to extensive regulation in light of the government's substantial interest in attaining "order" in the economic sphere.

While I agree that when the government attempts to regulate speech of those expressing views on public issues, the speech is protected by the First Amendment unless it presents "a clear and present danger" of a substantive evil that the government has a right to prohibit, see, e.g., Schenck v. United States, 249 U.S. 47, 52 (1919), I think it is important to recognize that this test is appropriate in the political context in light of the central importance of such speech to our system of self-government. As observed in Buckley v. Valeo, 424 U.S. 1, 14 (1976): "Discussion of public issues and debate on the qualifications of candidates are integral to the operation of the system of government established by our Constitution. The First Amendment affords the broadest protection to [596] such political expression in order 'to assure [the] unfettered interchange of ideas for the bringing

about of political and social changes desired by the people.'"

And in Garrison v. Louisiana, 379 U.S. 64, 74-75 (1964), this Court stated that "speech concerning public affairs is more than self-expression; it is the essence of self-government."

The First Amendment, however, does not always require a clear and present danger to be present before the government may regulate speech. Although First Amendment protection is not limited to the "exposition of ideas" on public issues, see, e.g., Winters v. New York, 333 U.S. 507, 510 (1948) – both because the line between the informing and the entertaining is elusive and because art, literature, and the like may contribute to important First Amendment interests of the individual in freedom of speech – it is well established that the government may regulate obscenity even though its does not present a clear and present danger. Compare, e.g., Paris Adult Theatre I v. Slaton, 413 U.S. 49, 57-58 (1973), with Brandenburg v. Ohio, 395 U.S. 444, 447 (1969). Indecent speech, at least when broadcast over the airwaves, also may be regulated absent a clear and present danger of the type described by Mr. Justice Brandeis and required by this Court in Brandenburg. FCC v. Pacifica Foundation, 438 U.S. 726 (1978). And in a slightly different context this Court declined to apply the clear-and-present-danger test to a conspiracy among members of the press in violation of the Sherman Act because to do so would "degrade" that doctrine. Associated Press v. United States, 326 U.S. 1, 7 (1945). Nor does the Court today apply the clear-and-present-danger test in invalidating New York's ban on promotional advertising. As noted above, in these and other contexts the Court has clearly rejected the notion that there must be a free "marketplace of ideas."

If the complaint of those who feel the Court's opinion does not go far enough is that the "only test of truth is its ability [597] to get itself accepted in the marketplace of ideas" – the test advocated by Thomas Jefferson in his first inaugural address, and by Mr. Justice Holmes in Abrams v. United States, 250 U.S. 616, 630 (1919) (dissenting opinion) – there is no reason whatsoever to limit the protection accorded commercial speech to "truthful, nonmisleading, noncoercive" speech. See ante, at 573 (BLACKMUN, J., concurring in judgment). If the "commercial speech" is in fact misleading, the "marketplace of ideas" will in time reveal that fact. It may not reveal it sufficiently soon to avoid harm to numerous people, but if the reasoning of Brandeis and Holmes is applied in this context, that was one of the risks we took in protecting free speech in a democratic society.

Unfortunately, although the "marketplace of ideas" has a historically and sensibly defined context in the world of political speech, it has virtually none in the realm of business transactions. Even so staunch a defender of the First Amendment as Mr. Justice Black, in his dissent in Breard v. Alexandria, 341 U.S., at 650, n., stated: "Of course I believe that the present ordinance could constitutionally be applied to a 'merchant' who goes from door to door 'selling pots.'"

And yet, with the change in solicitation and advertising techniques, the line between what Central Hudson did here and the peddler selling pots in Alexandria a generation ago is difficult, if not impossible to fix. Doubtless that was why Mr. Justice Black joined the unanimous opinion of the Court in Valentine v. Chrestensen, 316 U.S., at 54, in which the Court stated: "This court has unequivocally held that the streets are proper places for the exercise of the freedom of communicating information and disseminating opinion and that, though the states and municipalities may appropriately regulate the privilege in the public interest, they may not unduly burden or proscribe its employment in these public [598] thoroughfares. We are equally clear that the Constitution imposes no such restraint on government as respects purely commercial advertising. Whether, and to what extent, one may promote or pursue a gainful occupation in the streets, to what extent such activity shall be adjudged a derogation of the public right of user, are matters for legislative judgment." (Emphasis added.)

I remain of the view that the Court unlocked a Pandora's Box when it "elevated" commercial speech to the level of traditional political speech by according it First Amendment protection in Virginia Pharmacy Board v. Virginia Citizens Consumer Council, 425 U.S. 748 (1976). The line between "commercial speech," and the kind of speech that those who drafted the First Amendment had in mind, may not be a technically or intellectually easy one to draw, but it surely produced far fewer problems than has the development of judicial doctrine in this area since Virginia Pharmacy Board. For in the world of political advocacy and its marketplace of ideas, there is no such thing as a "fraudulent" idea: there may be useless proposals, totally unworkable schemes, as well as very sound proposals that will receive the imprimatur of the "marketplace of ideas" through our majoritarian system of election and representative government. The free flow of information is important in this context not because it will lead to the discovery of any objective "truth," but because it is essential to our system of self-government.

The notion that more speech is the remedy to expose falsehood and fallacies is wholly out of place in the commercial bazaar, where if applied logically the remedy of one who was defrauded would be merely a statement, available upon request, reciting the Latin maxim "caveat emptor." But since "fraudulent speech" in this area is to be remediable under Virginia Pharmacy Board, supra, the remedy of one defrauded is a lawsuit or an agency proceeding based on common-law notions of fraud that are separated by a world of difference [599] from the realm of politics and government. What time, legal decisions, and common sense have so widely severed, I declined to join in Virginia Pharmacy Board, and regret now to see the Court reaping the seeds that it there sowed. For in a democracy, the economic is subordinate to the political, a lesson that our ancestors learned long ago, and that our descendants will undoubtedly have to relearn many years hence.

III.　　　The Court concedes that the state interest in energy conservation is plainly substantial, ante, at 568, as is the State's concern that its rates be fair and efficient. Ante, at 569. It also concedes that there is a direct link between the Commission's ban on promotional advertising and the State's interest in conservation. Ibid. The Court nonetheless strikes down the ban on promotional advertising because the Commission has failed to demonstrate, under the final part of the Court's four-part test, that its regulation is no more extensive than necessary to serve the State's interest. Ante, at 569-571. In reaching this conclusion, the Court conjures up potential advertisements that a utility might make that conceivably would result in net energy savings. The Court does not indicate that the New York Public Service Commission has in fact construed its ban on "promotional" advertising to preclude the dissemination of information that clearly would result in a net energy savings, nor does it even suggest that the Commission has been confronted with and rejected such an advertising proposal.[6] The final part of the Court's test [600] thus leaves room for so many hypothetical "better" ways that any ingenious lawyer will surely seize on one of them to secure the invalidation of what the state agency actually did. As MR. JUSTICE BLACKMUN observed in Illinois Elections Bd. v. Socialist Workers Party, 440 U.S. 173, 188-189

---

6 Indeed appellee in its brief states: "[Neither] Central Hudson nor any other party made an attempt before the Commission to demonstrate or argue for a specific advertising strategy that would avoid the difficulties that the Commission found inherent in electric utility promotional advertising. The Commission, therefore, continued to enforce its ban on promotion which it had instituted in 1973." Brief for Appellee 15. The Court makes no attempt to address this statement, or to explain why, when no state body has addressed the issue, the Court should nonetheless resolve it by invalidating the state regulation.

(1979) (concurring opinion): "A judge would be unimaginative indeed if he could not come up with something a little less 'drastic' or a little less 'restrictive' in almost any situation, and thereby enable himself to vote to strike legislation down."

Here the Court concludes that the State's interest in energy conservation cannot justify a blanket ban on promotional advertising. In its statement of the facts, the Court observes that the Commission's ban on promotional advertising is not "a perfect vehicle for conserving energy." It states: "[The] Commission's order prohibits promotional advertising to develop consumption during periods when demand for electricity is low. By limiting growth in 'off-peak' consumption, the ban limits the 'beneficial side effects' of such growth in terms of more efficient use of existing powerplants. [App. to Juris. Statement] 37a." Ante, at 559.

The Court's analysis in this regard is in my view fundamentally misguided because it fails to recognize that the beneficial side effects of "more efficient use" may be inconsistent with the goal of energy conservation. Indeed, the Commission explicitly found that the promotion of off-peak consumption would impair conservation efforts.[7] The Commission stated: "Increased off-peak generation, ... while conferring [601] some beneficial side effects, also consumes valuable energy resources and, if it is the result of increased sales, necessarily creates incremental air pollution and thermal discharges to waterways. More important, any increase in off-peak generation from most of the major companies producing electricity in this State would not, at this time, be produced from coal or nuclear resources, but would require the use of oil-fired generating facilities. The increased requirement for fuel oil to serve the incremental off-peak load created by promotional advertising would aggravate the nation's already unacceptably high level of dependence on foreign sources of supply and would, in addition, frustrate rather than encourage conservation efforts." App. to Juris. Statement 37a.[8]

The Court also observes, as the Commission acknowledged, that the ban on promotional advertising can achieve only "piecemeal conservationism" because oil dealers are not under the Commission's jurisdiction, and they remain free to advertise. Until I have mastered electrical engineering and marketing, I am not prepared to contradict by virtue of my judicial office those who assume that the ban will be successful in making a substantial contribution to conservation efforts. [602] And I doubt that any of this Court's First Amendment decisions justify striking down the Commission's order because more steps toward conservation could have been made. This is especially true when, as here, the Commission lacks authority over oil dealers.

The Court concludes that the Commission's ban on promotional advertising must be struck down because it is more extensive than necessary: it may result in the suppression of advertising by utilities that promotes the use of electrical devices or services that cause no net increase in total energy use. The Court's reasoning in this regard, however, is highly speculative. The Court provides two examples that it claims support its conclusion. It first states that both parties acknowledge that the "heat pump" will be "a major improvement in electric heating," and that but for the ban the utilities would advertise this type of "energy [efficient]" product.[9] The New York Public Service Commission, however, considered the merits of the heat pump and concluded that it would most likely result in an overall increase in electric energy consumption. The Commission stated:

"[Installation] of a heat pump means also installation of central air-conditioning. To this extent, promotion of off-peak electric space heating involves promotion of on-peak summer air-conditioning as well as on-peak usage [603] of electricity for water heating. And the price of electricity to

---

[7] In making this finding, the Commission distinguished "between promotional advertising designed to shift existing consumption from peak to off-peak hours and advertising designed to promote additional consumption during off-peak hours." App. to Juris. Statement 58a, n. 2. It proscribed only the latter. Ibid.

[8] And in denying appellant's petition for rehearing, the Commission again stated: "While promotion of off-peak usage, particularly electric space heating, is touted by some as desirable because it might increase off-peak usage and thereby improve a summer-peaking company's load factor, we are convinced that off-peak promotion, especially in the context of imperfectly structured electric rates, is inconsistent with the public interest, even if it could be divorced in the public mind from promoting electric usage generally. As we pointed out in our Policy Statement,

increases in generation, even off-peak generation, at this time, requires the burning of scarce oil resources. This increased requirement for fuel oil aggravates the nation's already high level of dependence on foreign sources of supply." Id., at 58a (footnotes omitted).

[9] As previously discussed, however, it does not follow that because a product is "energy efficient" it is also consistent with the goal of energy conservation. Thus, with regard to the heat pump, counsel for appellees stated at oral argument that "Central Hudson says there are some [heat pumps] without air conditioning, but . . . they have never advised us of that." Tr. of Oral Arg. 32-33. The electric heat pump, he continued, "normally [carries] with it air conditioning in the summer, and the commission found that this would result in air conditioning that would not otherwise happen." Id., at 33. This is but one example of the veritable Sargasso Sea of difficult nonlegal issues that we wade into by adopting a rule that requires judges to evaluate highly complex and often controversial questions arising in disciplines quite foreign to ours.

most consumers in the State does not now fully reflect the much higher marginal costs of on-peak consump-tion in summer peaking markets. In these circum-stances, there would be a subsidization of consumption on-peak, and consequently, higher rates for all consumers." App. to Juris. Statement 58a.

Subsidization of peak consumption not only may encourage the use of scarce energy resources during peak periods, but also may lead to larger reserve generating capacity requirements for the State.

The Court next asserts that electric heating as a backup to solar and other heat may be an efficient alternative energy source. Ante, at 570. The Court fails to establish, however, that an advertising proposal of this sort was properly presented to the Commission. Indeed, the Court's concession that the Commission did not make findings on this issue suggests that the Commission did not even consider it. Nor does the Court rely on any support for its assertion other than the assertion of appellant. Rather, it speculates that "[in] the absence of authoritative findings to the contrary, we must credit as within the realm of possibility the claim that electric heat can be an efficient alternative in some circumstances." Ibid.[10]

Ordinarily it is the role of the State Public Service Commission to make factual determinations con-cerning whether a device or service will result in a net energy savings and, if so, whether and to what extent state law permits dissemination of information about the device or service. Otherwise, [604] as here, this Court will have no factual basis for its assertions. And the State will never have an opportunity to consider the issue and thus to construe its law in a manner consistent with the Federal Constitution. As stated in Barrows v. Jackson, 346 U.S. 249, 256-257 (1953): "It would indeed be undesirable for this Court to consider every conceivable situation which might possibly arise in the application of complex and comprehensive legislation. Nor are we so ready to frustrate the expressed will of Congress or that of the state legislatures. Cf. Southern Pacific Co. v. Gallagher, 306 U.S. 167, 172."

I think the Court would do well to heed the admonition in Barrows here. The terms of the order of the New York Public Service Commission in my view indicate that advertising designed to promote net savings in energy use does not fall within the scope of the ban. The order prohibits electric corporations "from promoting the use of electricity through the use of advertising, subsidy payments ..., or employee incentives." App. to Juris. Statement 31a (emphasis added). It is not clear to me that advertising that is likely to result in net savings of energy is advertising that "[promotes] the use of electricity," nor does the Court point to any language in the Commission order that suggests it has adopted this construction. Rather, it would seem more accurate to characterize such advertising as designed to "discourage" the use of electricity.[11] Indeed, I think it is quite likely that the Commission [605] would view advertising that would clearly result in a net savings in energy as consistent with the objectives of its order and therefore permissible.[12] The Commission, for example, has authorized the dissemination of information that would result in shifts in electrical energy demand, thereby reducing the demand for electricity during peak periods. Id., at 37a.[13] It has also indicated a willingness to consider at least some other types of "specific proposals" submitted by utilities. Id., at 37a-38a. And it clearly permits informational as opposed to promotional dissemination of information. Id., at 43a-46a. Even if the

---

[10] Even assuming the Court's speculation is correct, it has shown too little. For the regulation to truly be "no more extensive than necessary," it must be established that a more efficient energy source will serve only as a means for saving energy, rather than as an inducement to consume more energy because the cost has decreased or because other energy using products will be used in conjunction with the more efficient one.

[11] This characterization is supported by the reasoning of the New York Court of Appeals, which stated: "[Promotional] advertising . . . seeks . . . to encourage the increased consumption of electricity, whether during peak hours or off-peak hours. Thus, not only does such communication lack any beneficial informative content, but it may be affirmatively detrimental to the society. . . . Conserving diminishing resources is a matter of vital State concern and increased use of electrical energy is inimical to our interests. Promotional advertising, if permitted, would only serve to exacerbate the crisis." 47 N. Y. 2d, at 110, 390 N. E. 2d, at 757-758.

[12] At oral argument counsel for appellant conceded that the ban would not apply to utility advertising promoting the nonuse of electricity. Tr. of Oral Arg. 6. Indeed, counsel stated: "If the use reduces the amount of electricity used, it is not within the ban. The promotional ban is defined as anything which might be expected to increase the use of electricity." Ibid. And counsel for appellee stated that "the only thing that is involved here is the promotion by advertising of electric usage." Id., at 30. "And if a showing can be made that promotion in fact is going to conserve energy," counsel for appellee continued, "which . . . has never been made to us, the commission's order says we are ready to relax our ban, we're not interested in banning for the sake of banning it. We think that is basically a bad idea, if we can avoid it. In gas, we have been relaxing it as more gas has become available." Id., at 40.

[13] By contrast, as previously discussed, the Public Serv. Comm'n does not permit the promotion of off-peak consumption alone. Supra, at 600-601, and n. 8.

Commission were ultimately to reject the view that its ban on promotional advertising does not include advertising that results in net energy savings, I think the Commission should at least be given an opportunity to consider it.

It is in my view inappropriate for the Court to invalidate the State's ban on commercial advertising here, based on its speculation that in some cases the advertising may result in a net savings in electrical energy use, and in the cases in which it is clear a net energy savings would result from utility advertising, the Public Service Commission would apply its [606] ban so as to proscribe such advertising. Even

assuming that the Court's speculation is correct, I do not think it follows that facial invalidation of the ban is the appropriate course. As stated in Parker v. Levy, 417 U.S. 733, 760 (1974), "even if there are marginal applications in which a statute would infringe on First Amendment values, facial invalidation is inappropriate if the 'remainder of the statute . . . covers a whole range of easily identifiable and constitutionally proscribable . . . conduct. . . .' CSC v. Letter Carriers, 413 U.S. 548, 580-581 (1973). " This is clearly the case here.

For the foregoing reasons, I would affirm the judgment of the New York Court of Appeals.

Greater New Orleans Broadcasting Assoc. v. United States
527 U.S. 173
(1999)
(Excerpts only. Footnotes omitted.)

PRIOR HISTORY: On writ of certiorari to the United States Court of Appeals for the Fifth Circuit.

JUDGES: STEVENS, J., delivered the opinion of the Court, in which REHNQUIST, C. J., and O'CONNOR, SCALIA, KENNEDY, SOUTER, GINSBURG, and BREYER, JJ., joined. REHNQUIST, C. J., filed a concurring opinion. THOMAS, J., filed an opinion concurring in the judgment.

OPINION: [176] JUSTICE STEVENS.

Federal law prohibits some, but by no means all, broadcast advertising of lotteries and casino gambling. In United States v. Edge Broadcasting Co., 509 U.S. 418, 125 L. Ed. 2d 345, 113 S. Ct. 2696 (1993), we upheld the constitutionality of 18 U.S.C. § 1304 as applied to broadcast advertising of Virginia's lottery by a radio station located in North Carolina, where no such lottery was authorized. Today we hold that § 1304 may not be applied to advertisements of private casino gambling that are broadcast by radio or television stations located in Louisiana, where such gambling is legal.

Through most of the 19th and the first half of the 20th centuries, Congress adhered to a policy that not only discouraged the operation of lotteries and similar schemes, but forbade the dissemination of information concerning such enterprises by use of the mails, even when the lottery in question was chartered by a state legislature. ... [177]

Congress extended its restrictions on lottery-related information to broadcasting as communications technology made that practice both possible and profitable. It enacted the statute at issue in this case as § 316 of the Communications Act of 1934, 48 Stat. 1088. Now codified at 18 U.S.C.

§ 1304 ("Broadcasting lottery information"), the statute prohibits radio and television broadcasting, by any station for which a license is required, of "any advertisement of or information concerning any lottery, gift enterprise, or similar scheme, offering prizes dependent in whole or in part upon lot or chance, or any list of the prizes drawn or awarded by means of any such lottery, gift enterprise, or scheme, whether said list contains any part or all of such prizes."

The statute provides that each day's prohibited broadcasting constitutes a separate offense punishable by a fine, imprisonment for not more than one year, or both. Ibid. Although § 1304 is a criminal statute, the Solicitor General informs us that, in practice, the provision traditionally has been enforced by the Federal Communications Commission (FCC), which imposes administrative sanctions on radio and television licensees for violations of the agency's implementing regulation.

... [178] During the second half of this century, Congress dramatically narrowed the scope of the broadcast prohibition in § 1304. The first inroad was minor: In 1950, certain not-for-profit fishing contests were exempted as "innocent pastimes . . . far removed from the reprehensible type of gambling activity which it was paramount in the congressional mind to forbid." S. Rep. No. 2243, 81st Cong., 2d Sess., p. 2 (1950); see Act of Aug. 16, 1950, ch. 722, 64 Stat. 451, 18 U.S.C. § 1305.

...With subsequent modifications, [an] amendment now exempts advertisements of State-conducted lotteries from the nationwide postal restrictions in §§ 1301 and 1302, and from the broadcast restriction in § 1304, when "broadcast by a radio or television station licensed to a location in . . . a State which conducts such a lottery." §

1307(a)(1)(B); see also §§ 1307(a)(1)(A), (b)(1). The § 1304 broadcast restriction remained in place, however, for stations licensed in States that do not conduct lotteries. In Edge, we held that this remaining restriction on broadcasts from nonlottery States, such as North Carolina, supported the "laws against gambling" in those jurisdictions and properly advanced the "congressional policy of balancing the interests of lottery and nonlottery States." 509 U.S. at 428.

In 1988, Congress enacted two additional statutes that significantly curtailed the coverage of § 1304. First, the Indian Gaming Regulatory Act (IGRA), 25 U.S.C. § 2701 et seq., authorized Native American tribes to conduct various forms of gambling – including casino gambling – pursuant to tribal-state compacts if the State permits [179] such gambling "for any purpose by any person, organization, or entity." § 2710(d)(1)(B). The IGRA also exempted "any gaming conducted by an Indian tribe pursuant to" the Act from both the postal and transportation restrictions in 18 U.S.C. §§ 1301-1302, and the broadcast restriction in § 1304. 25 U.S.C. § 2720. Second, the Charity Games Advertising Clarification Act of 1988, 18 U.S.C. § 1307(a)(2), extended the exemption from §§ 1301-1304 for state-run lotteries to include any other lottery, gift enterprise, or similar scheme – not prohibited by the law of the State in which it operates – when conducted by: (i) any governmental organization; (ii) any not-for-profit organization; or (iii) a commercial organization as a promotional activity "clearly occasional and ancillary to the primary business of that organization." There is no dispute that the exemption in § 1307(a)(2) applies to casinos conducted by State and local governments. And, unlike the 1975 broadcast exemption for advertisements of and information concerning State-conducted lotteries, the exemptions in both of these 1988 statutes are not geographically limited; they shield messages from § 1304's reach in States that do not authorize such gambling as well as those that do.

... [180] These exemptions make the scope of § 3702's advertising prohibition somewhat unclear, but the prohibition is not limited to broadcast media and does not depend on the location of a broadcast station or other disseminator of promotional materials. Thus, unlike the uniform federal antigambling policy that prevailed in 1934 when 18 U.S.C. § 1304 was enacted, federal statutes now accommodate both pro-gambling and antigambling segments of the national polity.

Petitioners are an association of Louisiana broadcasters and its members who operate FCC-licensed radio and television stations in the New Orleans metropolitan area. But for the threat of sanctions pursuant to § 1304 and the FCC's companion regulation, petitioners would broadcast promotional advertisements for gaming available at private, for-profit casinos that are lawful and regulated in both Louisiana and neighboring Mississippi. According to an FCC official, however, "under appropriate conditions, some broadcast signals from Louisiana broadcasting stations may be heard [181] in neighboring states including Texas and Arkansas," 3 Record 628, where private casino gambling is unlawful.

Petitioners brought this action against the United States and the FCC in the District Court for the Eastern District of Louisiana, praying for a declaration that § 1304 and the FCC's regulation violate the First Amendment as applied to them, and for an injunction preventing enforcement of the statute and the rule against them. After noting that all parties agreed that the case should be decided on their cross-motions for summary judgment, the District Court ruled in favor of the Government. 866 F. Supp. 975, 976 (1994). The Court applied the standard for assessing commercial speech restrictions set out in Central Hudson Gas & Elec. Corp. v. Public Serv. Comm'n of N. Y., 447 U.S. 557, 566, 65 L. Ed. 2d 341, 100 S. Ct. 2343 (1980), and concluded that the restrictions at issue adequately advanced the Government's "substantial interest (1) in protecting the interest of nonlottery states and (2) in reducing participation in gambling and thereby minimizing the social costs associated therewith." 866 F. Supp. at 979. The Court pointed out that federal law does not prohibit the broadcast of all information about casinos, such as advertising that promotes a casino's amenities rather than its "gaming aspects," and observed that advertising for state-authorized casinos in Louisiana and Mississippi was actually "abundant." Id. at 980.

A divided panel of the Court of Appeals for the Fifth Circuit agreed with the District Court's application of Central Hudson, and affirmed the grant of summary judgment to the Government. 69 F.3d 1296, 1298 (1995). ... The majority relied heavily on our decision in Posadas de Puerto Rico Associates v. Tourism Co. of P. R., 478 U.S. 328, 92 L. Ed. 2d 266, 106 S. Ct. 2968 (1986), see 69 F.3d at 1300-1302, and endorsed the theory that, because gambling is in a category of "vice activity" that can be banned altogether, "advertising of gambling can lay no greater claim on constitutional protection than the underlying activity," id. at 1302. In dissent, Chief Judge Politz contended that the many exceptions to the original prohibition in § 1304 – and that section's conflict with the policies of States that had legalized gambling – precluded justification of the restriction by either an interest in supporting anti-casino state policies or "an independent federal interest in discouraging public participation in commercial gambling." Id. at 1303-1304.

... The majority recognized [183] that at least part of the Central Hudson inquiry had "become a tougher standard for the state to satisfy," id. at 338, but held that § 1304's restriction on speech sufficiently advanced the asserted governmental interests and was not "broader than necessary to control participation in casino gambling," id. at 340. ... We now reverse.

In a number of cases involving restrictions on speech that is "commercial" in nature, we have employed Central Hudson's four-part test to resolve First Amendment challenges ... In this analysis, the Government bears the burden of identifying a substantial interest and justifying the challenged restriction. ... The four parts of the Central Hudson test are not entirely discrete. All are important and, to a certain extent, interrelated: [184] Each raises a relevant question that may not be dispositive to the First Amendment inquiry, but the answer to which may inform a judgment concerning the other three. Partly because of these intricacies, petitioners as well as certain judges, scholars, and amici curiae have advocated repudiation of the Central Hudson standard and implementation of a more straightforward and stringent test for assessing the validity of governmental restrictions on commercial speech. ... It is, however, an established part of our constitutional jurisprudence that we do not ordinarily reach out to make novel or unnecessarily broad pronouncements on constitutional issues when a case can be fully resolved on a narrower ground. ... In this case, there is no need to break new ground. Central Hudson, as applied in our more recent commercial speech cases, provides an adequate basis for decision.

All parties to this case agree that the messages petitioners wish to broadcast constitute commercial speech, and that these broadcasts would satisfy the first part of the Central Hudson test: Their content is not misleading and concerns lawful activities, i.e., private casino gambling in Louisiana and Mississippi. As well, the proposed commercial messages would convey information – whether taken favorably or unfavorably by the audience – about an activity that is the subject of intense public debate in many communities. In addition, petitioners' broadcasts presumably would disseminate [185] accurate information as to the operation of market competitors, such as pay-out ratios, which can benefit listeners by informing their consumption choices and fostering price competition. Thus, even if the broadcasters' interest in conveying these messages is entirely pecuniary, the interests of, and benefit to, the audience may be broader. ...

The second part of the Central Hudson test asks whether the asserted governmental interest served by the speech restriction is substantial. The Solicitor General identifies two such interests: (1) reducing the social costs associated with "gambling" or "casino gambling," and (2) assisting States that "restrict gambling" or "prohibit casino gambling" within their own borders. Underlying Congress' statutory scheme, the Solicitor General contends, is the judgment that gambling contributes to corruption and organized crime; underwrites bribery, narcotics trafficking, and other illegal conduct; imposes a regressive tax on the poor; and "offers a false but sometimes irresistible hope of financial advancement." Brief for Respondents 15-16. With respect to casino gambling, the Solicitor General states that many of the associated social costs stem from "pathological" or "compulsive" gambling by approximately 3 million Americans, whose behavior is primarily associated with "continuous play" games, such as slot machines. He also observes that compulsive gambling has grown along with the expansion of legalized gambling nationwide, leading to billions of dollars in economic costs; injury and loss to these [186] gamblers as well as their families, communities, and government; and street, white-collar, and organized crime. Id. at 16-20.

We can accept the characterization of these two interests as "substantial," but that conclusion is by no means self-evident. No one seriously doubts that the Federal Government may assert a legitimate and substantial interest in alleviating the societal ills recited above, or in assisting like-minded States to do the same. Cf. Edge, 509 U.S. at 428. But in the judgment of both the Congress and many state legislatures, the social costs that support the suppression of gambling are offset, and sometimes outweighed, by countervailing policy considerations, primarily in the form of economic benefits. Despite its awareness of the potential [187] social costs, Congress has not only sanctioned casino gambling for Indian tribes through tribal-state compacts, but has enacted other statutes that reflect approval of state legislation that authorizes a host of public and private gambling activities. See, e.g., 18 U.S.C. §§ 1307, 1953(b); 25 U.S.C. §§ 2701-2702, 2710(d); 28 U.S.C. § 3704(a). ... [T]he federal policy of discouraging gambling in general, and casino gambling in particular, is now decidedly equivocal.

Of course, it is not our function to weigh the policy arguments on either side of the nationwide debate over whether and to what extent casino and other forms of gambling should be legalized. Moreover, enacted congressional policy and "governmental interests" are not necessarily equivalents for purposes of commercial speech analysis. See Bolger, 463 U.S. at 70-71. But we cannot ignore Congress' unwillingness to adopt a single national policy that consistently endorses either interest asserted by the Solicitor General. See Edenfield, 507 U.S. at 768; 44 Liquormart, 517 U.S. at 531 (O'CONNOR, J., concurring in the judgment).

Even though the Government has identified substantial interests, when we consider both their quality and the information sought to be suppressed, the crosscurrents in the scope and application of § 1304 become more difficult for the Government to defend.

The third part of the Central Hudson test asks whether the speech restriction directly and materially advances the asserted governmental interest. "This burden is not satisfied by mere speculation or conjecture; rather, a governmental body seeking to sustain a restriction on commercial speech must demonstrate that the harms it recites are real and that its restriction will in fact alleviate them to a material degree." Edenfield, 507 U.S. at 770-771. Consequently, "the regulation may not be sustained if it provides only ineffective or remote support for the government's purpose." Central Hudson, 447 U.S. at 564. We have observed that "this requirement is critical; otherwise, 'a State could with ease restrict commercial speech in the service of other objectives that could not themselves justify a burden on commercial expression.'" Rubin, 514 U.S. at 487, quoting Edenfield, 507 U.S. at 771.

The fourth part of the test complements the direct-advancement inquiry of the third, asking whether the speech restriction is not more extensive than necessary to serve the interests that support it. The Government is not required to employ the least restrictive means conceivable, but it must demonstrate narrow tailoring of the challenged regulation to the asserted interest – "a fit that is not necessarily perfect, but reasonable; that represents not necessarily the single best disposition but one whose scope is in proportion to the interest served." Fox, 492 U.S. at 480 (internal quotation marks omitted); see 44 Liquormart, 517 U.S. at 529, 531 (O'CONNOR, J., concurring in judgment). ...

As applied to petitioners' case, § 1304 cannot satisfy these standards. With regard to the first asserted interest – [189] alleviating the social costs of casino gambling by limiting demand – ... it does not necessarily follow that the Government's speech ban has directly and materially furthered the asserted interest. While it is no doubt fair to assume that more advertising would have some impact on overall demand for gambling, it is also reasonable to assume that much of that advertising would merely channel gamblers to one casino rather than another. More important, any measure of the effectiveness of the Government's attempt to minimize the social costs of gambling cannot ignore Congress' simultaneous encouragement of tribal casino gambling, which may well be growing at a rate exceeding any increase in gambling or compulsive gambling that private casino advertising could produce. See n. 5, supra. And, as the Court of Appeals recognized, the Government fails to "connect casino gambling and compulsive gambling with broadcast advertising for casinos" – let alone broadcast advertising for non-Indian commercial casinos. 149 F.3d at 339.

We need not resolve the question whether any lack of evidence in the record fails to satisfy the standard of proof under Central Hudson, however, because the flaw in the Government's case is more fundamental: The operation of § 1304 and its attendant regulatory regime is so pierced by exemptions and inconsistencies that the Government cannot hope to exonerate it. ...

The FCC's interpretation and application of §§ 1304 and 1307 underscore the statute's infirmity. Attempting to enforce the underlying purposes and policy of the statute, the FCC has permitted broadcasters to tempt viewers with claims of "Vegas-style excitement" at a commercial "casino," if "casino" is part of the establishment's proper name and the advertisement can be taken to refer to the casino's amenities, [191] rather than directly promote its gaming aspects. While we can hardly fault the FCC in view of the statute's focus on the suppression of certain types of information, the agency's practice is squarely at odds with the governmental interests asserted in this case.

From what we can gather, the Government is committed to prohibiting accurate product information, not commercial enticements of all kinds, and then only when conveyed over certain forms of media and for certain types of gambling – indeed, for only certain brands of casino gambling – and despite the fact that messages about the availability of such gambling are being conveyed over the airwaves by other speakers. ... [T]he Government presents no convincing reason for pegging its speech ban to the identity of the owners or operators of the advertised casinos. ... [192]

Ironically, the most significant difference identified by the Government between tribal and other classes of casino gambling is that the former are "heavily regulated." Brief for Respondents 38. If such direct regulation provides a basis for believing that the social costs of gambling in tribal casinos are sufficiently mitigated to make their advertising tolerable, one would have thought that Congress might have at least experimented with comparable regulation before abridging the speech rights of federally unregulated casinos. While Congress' failure to institute such direct regulation of private casino gambling does not necessarily compromise the constitutionality of § 1304, it does undermine the asserted justifications for the restriction before us. See Rubin, 514 U.S. at 490-491. There surely are practical and nonspeech-related forms of regulation – including a prohibition or supervision of gambling on credit; limitations on the use of cash machines on casino premises; controls on admissions; pot or betting limits; location restrictions; and licensing requirements – that could more directly and effectively alleviate some of the social costs of casino gambling.

...[193] [T]he power to prohibit or to regulate particular conduct does not necessarily include the power to prohibit or regulate speech about that conduct. 44 Liquormart, 517 U.S. at 509-511 (opinion of STEVENS, J.); see id. at 531-532 (O'CONNOR, J., concurring in judgment); Rubin, 514 U.S. at 483, n. 2. It is well settled that the First Amendment mandates closer scrutiny of government restrictions on speech than of its regulation of commerce alone. Fox, 492 U.S. at 408. And to the extent that the purpose and operation of federal law distinguishes among information about tribal, governmental, and private casinos based on the identity of their owners or operators, the Government presents no sound reason why such lines bear any meaningful relationship to the particular interest asserted: minimizing casino gambling and its social costs by way of a (partial) broadcast ban. Discovery Network, 507 U.S. at 424, 428. Even under the degree of scrutiny that we have [194] applied in commercial speech cases, decisions that select among speakers conveying virtually identical messages are in serious tension with the principles undergirding the First Amendment. Cf. Carey v. Brown, 447 U.S. 455, 465, 65 L. Ed. 2d 263, 100 S. Ct. 2286 (1980); First Nat. Bank of Boston v. Bellotti, 435 U.S. 765, 777, 784-785, 55 L. Ed. 2d 707, 98 S. Ct. 1407 (1978).

The second interest asserted by the Government – the derivative goal of "assisting" States with policies that disfavor private casinos – adds little to its case. We cannot see how this broadcast restraint, ambivalent as it is, might directly and adequately further any state interest in dampening consumer demand for casino gambling if it cannot achieve the same goal with respect to the similar federal interest.

Furthermore, even assuming that the state policies on which the Federal Government seeks to embellish are more coherent and pressing than their federal counterpart, § 1304 sacrifices an intolerable amount of truthful speech about lawful conduct when compared to all of the policies at stake and the social ills that one could reasonably hope such a ban to eliminate. ... Congress' choice here was neither a rough [195] approximation of efficacy, nor a reasonable accommodation of competing State and private interests. Rather, the regulation distinguishes among the indistinct, permitting a variety of speech that poses the same risks the Government purports to fear, while banning messages unlikely to cause any harm at all. Considering the manner in which § 1304 and its exceptions operate and the scope of the speech it proscribes, the Government's second asserted interest provides no more convincing basis for upholding the regulation than the first.

Accordingly, respondents cannot overcome the presumption that the speaker and the audience, not the Government, should be left to assess the value of accurate and nonmisleading information about lawful conduct. ... [T]he broadcast prohibition in 18 U.S.C. § 1304 and 47 CFR § 73.1211 (1998) violates the [196] First Amendment. The judgment of the Court of Appeals is therefore ... Reversed.

... [197] JUSTICE THOMAS, concurring in the judgment.

I continue to adhere to my view that "in cases such as this, in which the government's asserted interest is to keep legal users of a product or service ignorant in order to manipulate their choices in the marketplace," the Central Hudson test should not be applied because "such an 'interest' is per se illegitimate and can no more justify regulation of 'commercial speech' than it can justify regulation of 'noncommercial' speech." 44 Liquormart, Inc. v. Rhode Island, 517 U.S. 484, 518, 134 L. Ed. 2d 711, 116 S. Ct. 1495 (1996) (concurring in part and concurring in the judgment).

Chapter 11

Political Speech

The First Amendment's primary concern

Focal cases:
Buckley v. Valeo, 424 U.S. 1 (1976)
Burson v. Freeman, 504 U.S. 191 (1992)
Federal Election Commission v. Colorado Republican Federal Campaign Committee, 533 U.S. 431 (2001)

The U.S. Supreme Court long has held that political speech occupies the most central and hallowed position in First Amendment values because the ability of citizens to openly discuss and criticize government is vital to the democratic process.[1] In 1964, for example, the Court said, "[T]he central meaning of the First Amendment" is the principle that "debate on public issues should be uninhibited, robust and wide-open."[2] Alexander Meiklejohn has suggested that the Court's reasoning rests on the premise that "self-government can exist only insofar as the voters acquire the intelligence, integrity, sensitivity and generous devotion to the general welfare" that comes about through uninhibited exchange of ideas.[3]

Thus, the Court in 1966 said:

Whatever differences may exist about interpretations of the First Amendment, there is practically universal agreement that a major purpose of that Amendment was to protect the free discussion of governmental affairs. This of course includes discussions of candidates, structures and forms of government, the manner in which government is operated or should be operated, and all such matters relating to political processes.[4]

The Court has said that "the First Amendment has its fullest and most urgent application"[5] to political speech, including campaign spending, political association,[6] campaigning, access to the

---

[1] *See, e.g.,* National Endowment for the Arts v. Finley, 524 U.S. 569, 597 (1998) (Scalia, J., concurring); Eu v. San Francisco Cty. Democratic Cent. Comm. (1989); Boos v. Barry, 485 U.S. 312, 318 (1988); Brown v. Hartlage, 456 U.S. 45, 52-54 (1982); Mills v. Alabama, 384 U.S. 214, 218-19 (1966).

[2] New York Times v. Sullivan, 376 U.S. 254, 270 & 273 (1964).

[3] Alexander Meiklejohn, "The First Amendment is and Absolute," 1961 SUP. CT. REV. 245, 255 (1961).

[4] Mills v. Alabama, 384 U.S. 214, 218-19 (1966).

[5] Monitor Patriot Co. v. Roy, 401 U.S. 265, 272 (1971).

[6] *See* NAACP v. Alabama, 357 U.S. 449, 460 (1958) (acknowledging that "[e]ffective advocacy of both public and private points of view, particularly controversial ones, is undeniably enhanced by group association").

ballot, political advertising and the role of the media in the broad exchange of political information. Thus, government restrictions on political speech must pass the most exacting strict scrutiny. Yet the fundamental rights of political involvement and self-governance sometimes give way to compelling state interests in avoiding political corruption or coercion of voters. In recent years, for example, the Court has been asked to consider the constitutionality of federal and state campaign finance reforms, FCC political broadcasting requirements, and statutory restrictions on candidate speech.

CAMPAIGN FINANCE RESTRICTIONS

For more than a quarter century, the Supreme Court has attempted to apply its ruling in *Buckley v. Valeo*[7] to establish clear, predictable standards for constitutionally acceptable limits on campaign finance. However, some observers say *Buckley*'s "political compromise" has failed to achieve anything "even approaching a coherent jurisprudence" in this area.[8]

In *Buckley*, the Court acknowledged the critical importance and interconnection of funding and political speech. The Court, however, distinguished between campaign expenditures and campaign contributions, viewing the first as related to the personal expressive rights of candidates or other individuals and the second as tied to contributors' speech. Based on that dichotomy, the Court's *per curiam* decision held that federal expenditure limits unconstitutionally infringed candidates' rights to speak freely. In contrast, the Court said, limits on contributions constitutionally advanced the substantial government interest in addressing both real and perceived campaign corruption, only incidentally harmed supporters' ability to associate with a candidate and left ample alternative means for supporters to express their candidate preferences.

Under the *Buckley* standard, the Court struck down a state statute prohibiting banks from financing political discussion of referendum proposals that did not materially affect their own business.[9] The Court reasoned that the categorical ban unconstitutionally infringed the right of banks to actively participate in political issues because the state had failed to show that the law was necessary to protect citizen confidence in the electoral process. In contrast, the Court upheld the constitutionality of a state law requiring corporations to spend only specifically designated funds to influence the outcome of state elections.[10] Although the law infringed the political expressive activity of corporations, the Court said the statute was narrowly tailored to prevent political corruption and to assure that corporate political spending reflected the wishes of corporation constituents. In another decision, the Court found constitutional a state statute imposing *Buckley*-type limits on contributions to *state* political candidates.[11]

In 1996, the Court held that a Federal Election Campaign Act limit on political party expenditures violated the party's First Amendment rights.[12] In *Colorado Republican Federal Campaign Committee v. Federal Election Commission*, the Court said the government could not constitutionally prevent the Colorado Republican Party from sponsoring ads to support its candidate for the U.S. Senate.[13] However, the justices failed to agree on whether the law was invalid because the political party had an autonomous constitutional right to spend money on its own political speech, the party's spending was protected as an extension of the candidate's right to unlimited political spending, or all limits on campaign contributions and expenditures were facially unconstitutional

---

[7] 424 U.S. 1 (1976).

[8] Robert F. Bauer, "Going Nowhere, Slowly: The Long Struggle over Campaign Finance Reform and Some attempts at Explanation and Alternatives," 51 CATH. U.L. REV. 741, 750 & 749 (2002).

[9] First Nat'l Bank of Boston v. Bellotti, 435 U.S. 765 (1978).

[10] Austin v. Michigan State Chamber of Commerce, 494 U.S. 652 (1990).

[11] Nixon v. Shrink Missouri Government PAC, 528 U.S. 377 (2000).

[12] Colorado Republican Fed'l Campaign Comm. v. Federal Election Comm'n, 518 U.S. 604 (1996).

[13] *But see* Federal Election Comm'n v. Beaumont, 123 S.Ct. 2200 (2003) (refusing to apply strict scrutiny and finding constitutional application to a nonprofit political advocacy group of the ban on political contributions).

because they directly abridged core political expressive and associational rights.[14] The Supreme Court revisited that question, and that case, in 2001. In *Colorado Republican II*, the Court upheld limits on party expenditures that were coordinated with candidates. The Court said, "There is no significant functional difference between a party's coordinated expenditure and a direct party contribution to the candidate. ... Coordinated expenditures of money donated to a party are tailor-made to undermine contribution limits."[15]

In 2003, the Court again upheld the law's ban on political contributions as a constitutional means to avoid election tampering that does not unduly harm the free speech interests of political advocacy groups, such as Right to Life.[16]

CAMPAIGN SPEECH

Although political campaigning is of utmost importance to the democratic process, the Court has found that other competing interests – or the First Amendment interests of other parties – sometimes are equally compelling.

For example, three years before *Buckley*, the Court said the Democratic National Committee did not have a First Amendment right to express its political views on television if broadcasters chose not to sell the committee advertising time.[17] The Court said the Constitution protected the right of broadcasters to make content decisions. Only two justices advanced the idea that the First Amendment provided an affirmative right of access to enable individuals to participate in public discussion.

Yet, the Court later held that the Federal Election Campaign Act's requirement that broadcasters provide "reasonable access" for federal political candidates was a constitutional means to enhance the exchange of information critical to the democratic process.[18] Six justices interpreted the Communications Act of 1934 to impose a limited right of reasonable access to licensed broadcast media for legitimate federal political candidates. However, that limited right of access does not force a public television station to include an independent presidential candidate in a televised pre-election debate.[19] The Court said that although public television receives federal funding, it is not a public forum. As a consequence, the First Amendment empowers public television journalists to impose reasonable, objective, content-neutral criteria to determine whom to include in political debates.

The Supreme Court generally has disfavored direct limits on candidate speech. In 1982, the Court struck down a state law prohibiting candidates from making promises to voters in exchange for their votes.[20] The Court said the state could not address its compelling interest in reducing political corruption with a broad, paternalistic law that excluded entire subjects from campaign discussion. In a unanimous decision, the Court said the law unconstitutionally abridged the free speech of candidates and chilled political debate. Twenty years later, the Court invalidated a state law that severely restricted the permissible speech of state judicial candidates.[21] The Court said the law's ban on expression of views on disputed legal or political issues was not narrowly tailored and the state's asserted interest in an impartial court system was not compelling.

---

[14] *See also* Federal Election Comm'n v. National Conservative Political Action Comm., 470 U.S. 480, 497 (1985) (ruling unconstitutional FECA rules limiting individual expenditures not coordinated with a candidate's campaign).

[15] Federal Election Comm'n v. Colorado Republican Fed'l Campaign Comm., 33 U.S. 431, 464 (2001).

[16] Federal Election Comm'n v. Beaumont, 123 S.Ct. 2200 (2003).

[17] CBS v. Democratic Nat'l Comm., 412 U.S. 94 (1973). *See also* Chap. 12 discussion of broadcaster rights and responsibilities.

[18] CBS v. Federal Communications Comm., 453 U.S. 367 (1981).

[19] Arkansas Educational Television Comm'n v. Forbes, 532 U.S. 666 (1998).

[20] Brown v. Hartlage, 456 U.S. 45 (1982).

[21] Republican Party of Minnesota v. White, 122 S. Ct. 2528 (2002).

The Supreme Court also generally has found laws that limit voters' ability to initiate petitions to be invalid. The Court has struck down a state law making it a crime to pay others to circulate political petitions,[22] another state law prohibiting the distribution of anonymous campaign literature[23] and a third state law requiring petition circulators to be registered voters and to wear name tags.[24] In each of these cases, the Court reasoned that the law directly and excessively infringed core political expression without directly advancing the state's compelling interest in fair, informed elections. The Court said the ban on paid petition circulators limited the number of people distributing petitions and, therefore, reduced the number of people who would receive the message. The ban on anonymous literature was only tangentially related to the state's interest in eliminating false and fraudulent campaign claims, and the mandated disclosure of authorship chilled political speech without materially increasing the useful information provided to voters. The registration and name-badge requirements limited and discouraged political participation while only tenuously advancing the state's interest in preventing fraud in the initiative process.

However, a majority of the court upheld a state law prohibiting voter solicitation or distribution of campaign literature within 100 feet of the polls.[25] The Court said the law was an appropriate accommodation of the conflicting fundamental rights of free speech and secret ballot. Even under strict scrutiny review, a plurality of justices said the law's content-based restriction on core political expression in a public forum imposed only a slight infringement on First Amendment rights. Moreover, they said the law was narrowly tailored to advance the state's compelling interest in eliminating voter intimidation and election fraud and in insuring the legitimacy and integrity of citizens' fundamental right to vote. The three dissenting justices said the law was a thinly veiled attempt by the state to censor election-day campaigning.

BALLOTS AND POLITICAL PRIMARIES

The Court generally has distinguished between laws that control the election process and laws that dictate party procedures, finding the first valid and the second unconstitutional. In 1997, for example, the Supreme Court upheld a state law prohibiting a candidate from appearing on the ballot as the nominee of more than one party.[26] Although the law effectively limited the ability of small political parties to endorse candidates, the Court said the law reduced voter confusion caused by multi-party endorsements on the ballot and did not severely burden the right of minor political parties to associate with favored candidates. In another decision, the Court said a state law prohibiting write-in voting in general elections did not violate voters' First Amendment rights.[27] Because the state provided a variety of ways for candidate names to be included on the ballot, the Court said the law was a presumptively valid means to control factionalism in general elections that only slightly infringed the associational rights of voters and candidates.

However, the Court has decided that state laws prohibiting party endorsement of primary candidates and banning single-party primary ballots violate the First Amendment rights of political parties. The Court held that a state law that imposed limits on the organization of political parties and banned party endorsement of primary candidates violated both the free speech and the free association rights of the parties.[28] The Court said the law directly infringed the party's ability to express political views and hampered the ability of voters to receive significant political information. Another state law allowing all voters, regardless of party affiliation, to vote for any

---

[22] Meyer v. Grant, 486 U.S. 414 (1988).

[23] McIntyre v. Ohio Elections Comm'n, 514 U.S. 334 (1995).

[24] Buckley v. American Constitutional Law Foundation, 525 U.S. 182 (1999).

[25] Burson v. Freeman, 504 U.S. 191 (1992).

[26] Timmons v. Twin Cities Area New Party, 520 U.S. 351 (1997).

[27] Burdick v. Takushi, 504 U.S. 428 (1992).

[28] Eu v. San Francisco County Democratic Central Comm., 489 U.S. 214 (1989).

candidate in primary elections that determined party candidates for the general election was found unconstitutional.[29] The Court said the "blanket" primary system violated the right of political parties not to associate with non-party members and to control their candidate selection process.

In addition, a state law requiring independent presidential candidates who wished to appear on the general election ballot to file a statement of candidacy six months prior to the general election unconstitutionally infringed the First Amendment rights of the candidate and his or her supporters.[30] The Court said the law placed an unacceptable burden on the ability of voters to associate effectively with late-emerging candidates. Moreover, the law's primary effect was to limit the field of candidates in the general election.

READING THE POLITICAL SPEECH CASES

This chapter and the cases that follow outline the jurisprudence of political speech. The cases in the list below offer greater development of this area of the law.

- *Nixon v. Shrink Missouri Government PAC*, 528 U.S. 377 (2000) (affirms state campaign contribution limits).
- *California Democratic Party v. Jones*, 530 U.S. 567 (2000) (affirms political party right of free association).
- *Buckley v. American Constitutional Law Foundation*, 525 U.S. 182 (1999) (strikes state restrictions on people who circulate ballot initiatives).
- *Arkansas Educational Television Commission v. Forbes*, 523 U.S. 666 (1998) (affirms right of public TV to exclude candidate from televised presidential debate).
- *Timmons v. Twin Cities Area New Party*, 520 U.S. 351 (1997) (affirms state ban on individual appearing as candidate for multiple parties on ballot).
- *McIntyre v. Ohio Elections Commission*, 514 U.S. 334 (1995) (strikes ban on anonymous campaign literature).
- *Burdick v. Takushi*, 504 U.S. 428 (1992) (strikes state ban on write-in votes).
- *Austin v. Michigan State Chamber of Commerce*, 494 U.S. 652 (1990) (affirms state limit on corporate campaign spending).
- *Eu v. San Francisco County Democratic Central Committee*, 489 U.S. 214 (1989) (strikes state ban on endorsement of party candidate).
- *Meyer v. Grant*, 486 U.S. 414 (1988) (strikes state law punishing citizen ballot initiatives).
- *Anderson v. Celebrezze*, 460 U.S. 780 (1983) (strikes state requirement for independent presidential candidates to file statement).
- *Brown v. Hartlage*, 456 U.S. 45 (1982) (strikes state ban on candidate campaign promises).
- *Columbia Broadcasting System v. Federal Communications Commission*, 453 U.S. 367 (1981) (affirms reasonable candidate access rule).
- *First National Bank v. Bellotti*, 435 U.S. 765 (1978) (strikes ban on certain business expenditures to influence referendums).
- *Columbia Broadcasting System v. Democratic National Committee*, 412 U.S. 94 (1973) (no First Amendment right to purchase editorial ad time).
- *Mills v. Alabama*, 384 U.S. 214 (1966) (strikes criminal law against newspaper election-day candidate endorsements).

These questions should help guide your reading and assist you in focusing on the key elements of these decisions.

---

[29] California Democratic Party v. Jones, 530 U.S. 566 (2000).
[30] Anderson v. Celebrezze, 460 U.S. 780 (1983).

- When is spending money in support of political candidates or causes speech and when is it conduct?
- On what basis does the Court in *Buckley v. Valeo* distinguish contributions from spending?
- How carefully does the Court match the "fit" of the campaign finance restrictions in *Buckley* to their objectives?
- Do the spending or contributions limits unconstitutionally favor some candidates or speakers? Why?
- Why does the Court view the ban at issue in *Burson v. Freeman* as content based?
- What evidence does the Court examine to scrutinize the tailoring of the polling place ban to the government's compelling interest?
- Does the Court modify its *Buckley* distinction between contributions and expenditures in *Colorado Republican II*?
- In the Court's view, what is the particular significance of "coordinated" expenditures?
- What, if any, unique First Amendment functions does the Court believe political parties perform in elections?
- What test does the Court apply in *Colorado Republican II* and how does it define and apply the test's various prongs?
- How does the dissent in *Colorado Republican II* describe the Court's protection of core political speech?
- What are the dissent's central points of disagreement with the majority opinion and judgment?

Buckley v. Valeo
424 U.S. 1
(1976)
(Excerpts only. Footnotes omitted.)

Author's Note: Key provisions of the Federal Election Campaign Act of 1971 limiting individual political contributions and independent expenditures "to a clearly identified candidate" in any election to $1,000, with an overall annual limitation of $25,000; imposing limits on candidate and political party campaign expenditures; mandating disclosure of contributions or expenditures above a certain threshold; and establishing a system of public funding for the presidential campaign are challenged as unconstitutional violations of free speech and association.

OPINION: [6] PER CURIAM.

These appeals present constitutional challenges to the key provisions of the Federal Election Campaign Act of 1971, (Act) and related provisions of the Internal Revenue Code of 1954, all as amended in 1974.

The Court of Appeals, in sustaining the legislation in large part against various constitutional challenges, viewed it as "by far the most comprehensive reform legislation [ever] passed by Congress concerning the election of the President, Vice-President, and members of Congress." 171 U.S. App. D.C. 172, 82, 519 F. 2d 821, 831 (1975). The statutes at issue summarized in broad terms, contain the following provisions: (8a) individual political contributions are limited to $1,000 to any single candidate per election, with an overall annual limitation of $25,000 by any contributor; independent expenditures by individuals and groups "relative to a clearly identified candidate" are limited to $1,000 a year; campaign spending by candidates for various federal offices and spending for national conventions by political parties are subject to prescribed limits; (b) contributions and expenditures above certain threshold levels must be reported and publicly disclosed; (c) a system for public funding of Presidential campaign activities is established by Subtitle H of the Internal Revenue Code; and (d) a Federal Election Commission is established to administer and enforce the legislation. [7]

... The complaint sought both a [9] declaratory judgment that the major provisions of the Act were unconstitutional and an injunction against enforcement of those provisions. ... [10]

On plenary review, a majority of the Court of Appeals rejected, for the most part, appellants' constitutional attacks. The court found "a clear and compelling interest," 171 U.S. App. D.C., at 192, 519 F. 2d, at 841, in preserving the integrity of the electoral process. On that basis, the court upheld, with one exception, the substantive provisions of the Act with respect to contributions, expenditures, and disclosure.

... [11] In this Court, appellants argue that the Court of Appeals failed to give this legislation the critical scrutiny demanded under accepted First Amendment and equal protection principles. In appellants' view, limiting the use of money for political purposes constitutes a restriction on communication violative of the First Amendment, since virtually all meaningful political communications in the modern setting involve the expenditure of money. ... [12]

The intricate statutory scheme adopted by Congress to regulate federal election campaigns includes restrictions [13] on political contributions and expenditures that apply broadly to all phases of and all participants in the election process. The major contribution and expenditure limitations in the Act prohibit individuals from contributing more than $25,000 in a single year or more than $1,000 to any single candidate for an election campaign and from spending more than $1,000 a year "relative to a clearly identified candidate." Other provisions restrict a candidate's use of personal and family resources in his campaign and limit the overall amount that can be spent by a candidate in campaigning for federal office. ...

The constitutional power of Congress to regulate federal elections is well established and is not questioned by any of the parties in this case. Thus, the critical [14] constitutional questions presented here go not to the basic power of Congress to legislate in this area, but to whether the specific legislation that Congress has enacted interferes with First Amendment freedoms or invidiously discriminates against non-incumbent candidates and minor parties in contravention of the Fifth Amendment. ...

The Act's contribution and expenditure limitations operate in an area of the most fundamental First Amendment activities. Discussion of public issues and debate on the qualifications of candidates are integral to the operation of the system of government established by our Constitution. The First Amendment affords the broadest protection to such political expression in order "to assure [the] unfettered interchange of ideas for the bringing about of political and social changes desired by the people." Roth v. United States, 354 U.S. 476, 484 (1957). Although First Amendment protections are not confined to "the exposition of ideas," Winters v. New York, 333 U.S. 507, 510 (1948), "there is practically universal agreement that a major purpose of that Amendment was to protect the free discussion of governmental affairs,... of course includ[ing] discussions of candidates...." Mills v. Alabama, 384 U.S. 214, 218 (1966). This no more than reflects our "profound national commitment to the principle that debate on public issues should be uninhibited, robust, and wide-open," New York Times Co. v. Sullivan, 376 U.S. 254, 270 (1964). In a republic where the people are sovereign, the ability of the citizenry to make informed choices among [15] candidates for office is essential, for the identities of those who are elected will inevitably shape the course that we follow as a nation. As the Court observed in Monitor Patriot Co. v. Roy, 401 U.S. 265, 272 (1971), "it can hardly be doubted that the constitutional guarantee has its fullest and most urgent application precisely to the conduct of campaigns for political office."

The First Amendment protects political association as well as political expression. The constitutional right of association explicated in NAACP v. Alabama, 357 U.S. 449, 460 (1958), stemmed from the Court's recognition that "[e]ffective) advocacy of both public and private points of view, particularly controversial ones, is undeniably enhanced by group association." Subsequent decisions have made clear that the First and Fourteenth Amendments guarantee "freedom to associate with others for the common advancement of political beliefs and ideas,'" a freedom that encompasses "'[t]he right to associate with the political party of one's choice.'" Kusper v. Pontikes, 414 U.S. 51, 56, 57 (1973), quoted in Cousins v. Wigoda, 419 U.S. 477, 487 (1975).

... Appellees contend that what the Act regulates is conduct, and that its effect on speech and association is incidental at most. Appellants respond that contributions and expenditures are at the very core of political speech, and that the Act's limitations thus constitute restraints on First Amendment liberty that are both gross and direct.

In upholding the constitutional validity of the Act's contribution and expenditure provisions on the ground [16] that those provisions should be viewed as regulating conduct not speech, the Court of Appeals relied upon United States v. O'Brien, 391 U.S. 367 (1968). ... We cannot share the view that the present Act's contribution and expenditure limitations are comparable to the restrictions on conduct upheld in O'Brien. The expenditure of money simply cannot be equated with such conduct as destruction of a draft card. Some forms of communication made possible by the giving and spending of money involve speech alone, some involve conduct primarily, and some involve a combination of the two. Yet this Court has never suggested that the dependence of a communication on the expenditure of money operates itself to introduce a nonspeech element or to reduce the exacting scrutiny required by the First Amendment. See Bigelow v. Virginia, 421 U.S. 809, [17] 820 (1975); New York Times Co. v. Sullivan, supra, at 266. For example, in Cox v. Louisiana, 379 U.S. 559 (1965), the Court contrasted picketing and parading with a newspaper comment and a telegram by a citizen to a public official. The parading and picketing activities were said to constitute conduct "intertwined with expression and association," whereas the newspaper comment and the telegram were described as a "pure form of expression" involving "free speech alone" rather than "expression mixed with particular conduct." Id., at 563-564.

Even if the categorization of the expenditure of money as conduct were accepted, the limitations challenged here would not meet the O'Brien test because the governmental interests advanced in support of the Act involve "suppressing communication." The interests served by the Act include restricting the voices of people and interest groups who have money to spend and reducing the overall scope of federal election campaigns. Although the Act does not focus on the ideas expressed by persons or groups subjected to its regulations, it is aimed in part at equalizing the relative ability of all voters to affect electoral outcomes by placing a ceiling on expenditures for political expression by citizens and groups. Unlike O'Brien, where the Selective Service System's administrative interest in the preservation of draft cards was wholly unrelated to their use as a means of communication, it is beyond dispute that the interest in regulating the alleged "conduct" of giving or spending money "arises in some measure because the communication allegedly integral to the conduct is itself thought to be harmful." 391 U.S. at 382.

Nor can the Act's contribution and expenditure limitations be sustained, as some of the parties suggest, by reference to the constitutional principles reflected in ... [18] the proposition that the government may adopt reasonable time, place, and manner regulations, which do not discriminate among speakers or ideas, in order to further an important governmental interest unrelated to the restriction of communication. ... [T]he present Act's contribution and expenditure limitations impose direct quantity restrictions on political communication and association by persons, groups, candidates, and political parties in addition to any

reasonable time, place, and manner regulations otherwise imposed. [19]

A restriction on the amount of money a person or group can spend on political communication during a campaign necessarily reduces the quantity of expression by restricting the number of issues discussed, the depth of their exploration, and the size of the audience reached. This is because virtually every means of communicating ideas in today's mass society requires the expenditure of money. The distribution of the humblest handbill or leaflet entails printing, paper, and circulation costs. Speeches and rallies generally necessitate hiring a hall and publicizing the event. The electorate's increasing dependence on television, radio, and other mass media for news and information has made these expensive modes of communication indispensable instruments of effective political speech.

The expenditure limitations contained in the Act represent substantial rather than merely theoretical restraints on the quantity and diversity of political speech. The $1,000 ceiling on spending "relative to a clearly identified candidate," 18 U.S.C. § 608 (e)(1) (1970 ed., Supp. IV), would appear to exclude all citizens and groups except candidates, political parties, and the institutional press from any significant use of the most [20] effective modes of communication. Although the Act's limitations on expenditures by campaign organizations and political parties provide substantially greater room for discussion and debate, they would have required restrictions in the scope of a number of past congressional and Presidential campaigns and would operate to constrain campaigning by candidates who raise sums in excess of the spending ceiling.

By contrast with a limitation upon expenditures for political expression, a limitation upon the amount that any one person or group may contribute to a candidate or political committee entails only a marginal restriction upon the contributor's ability to engage in free [21] communication. A contribution serves as a general expression of support for the candidate and his views, but does not communicate the underlying basis for the support. The quantity of communication by the contributor does not increase perceptibly with the size of his contribution, since the expression rests solely on the undifferentiated, symbolic act of contributing. At most, the size of the contribution provides a very rough index of the intensity of the contributor's support for the candidate. A limitation on the amount of money a person may give to a candidate or campaign organization thus involves little direct restraint on his political communication, for it permits the symbolic expression of support evidenced by a contribution but does not in any way infringe the contributor's freedom to discuss candidates and issues. While contributions may result in political expression if spent by a candidate or an association to present views to the voters, the transformation of contributions into political debate involves speech by someone other than the contributor.

Given the important role of contributions in financing political campaigns, contribution restrictions could have a severe impact on political dialogue if the limitations prevented candidates and political committees from amassing the resources necessary for effective advocacy. There is no indication, however, that the contribution limitations imposed by the Act would have any dramatic adverse effect on the funding of campaigns and political associations. The overall effect of the Act's [22] contribution ceilings is merely to require candidates and political committees to raise funds from a greater number of persons and to compel people who would otherwise contribute amounts greater than the statutory limits to expend such funds on direct political expression, rather than to reduce the total amount of money potentially available to promote political expression.

The Act's contribution and expenditure limitations also impinge on protected associational freedoms. Making a contribution, like joining a political party, serves to affiliate a person with a candidate. In addition, it enables like-minded persons to pool their resources in furtherance of common political goals. The Act's contribution ceilings thus limit one important means of associating with a candidate or committee, but leave the contributor free to become a member of any political association and to assist personally in the association's efforts on behalf of candidates. And the Act's contribution limitations permit associations and candidates to aggregate large sums of money to promote effective advocacy. By contrast, the Act's $1,000 limitation on independent expenditures "relative to a clearly identified candidate" precludes most associations from effectively amplifying the voice of their adherents, the original basis for the recognition of First Amendment protection of the freedom of association. See NAACP v. Alabama, 357 U.S. at 460. The Act's constraints on the ability of independent associations and candidate campaign organizations to expend resources on political expression "is simultaneously an interference with the freedom of [their] adherents," Sweezy v. New Hampshire, 354 U.S. 234, 250 (1957) (plurality opinion). See Cousins v. [23] Wigoda, 419 U.S. at 487-488; NAACP v. Button, 371 U.S. 415, 431 (1963).

In sum, although the Act's contribution and expenditure limitations both implicate fundamental First Amendment interests, its expenditure ceilings impose significantly more severe restrictions on protected freedoms of political expression and association than do its limitations on financial contributions. ... [24]

[T]he primary First Amendment problem raised by the Act's contribution limitations is their restriction of one aspect of the contributor's freedom of political association. [25] ... In view of the fundamental nature of the right to associate, governmental "action which may have the effect of curtailing the freedom to associate is subject to the closest scrutiny." NAACP v. Alabama, supra, at 460-461. Yet, it is clear that "[n]either the right to associate nor the right to participate in political activities is absolute." CSC v. Letter Carriers, 413 U.S. 548, 567 (1973). Even a "'significant interference' with protected rights of political association" may be sustained if the State demonstrates a sufficiently important interest and employs means closely drawn to avoid unnecessary abridgment of associational freedoms. Cousins v. Wigoda, supra, at 488; NAACP v. Button, supra, at 438; Shelton v. Tucker, supra, at 488. ... [26]

It is unnecessary to look beyond the Act's primary purpose – to limit the actuality and appearance of corruption resulting from large individual financial contributions – in order to find a constitutionally sufficient justification for the $1,000 contribution limitation. Under a system of private financing of elections, a candidate lacking immense personal or family wealth must depend on financial contributions from others to provide the resources necessary to conduct a successful campaign. The increasing importance of the communications media and sophisticated mass-mailing and polling operations to effective campaigning make the raising of large sums of money an ever more essential ingredient of an effective candidacy. To the extent that large contributions are given to secure political quid pro quo's from current and potential office holders, the integrity of our system of [27] representative democracy is undermined. Although the scope of such pernicious practices can never be reliably ascertained, the deeply disturbing examples surfacing after the 1972 election demonstrate that the problem is not an illusory one.

Of almost equal concern as the danger of actual quid pro quo arrangements is the impact of the appearance of corruption stemming from public awareness of the opportunities for abuse inherent in a regime of large individual financial contributions. ... Congress could legitimately conclude that the avoidance of the appearance of improper influence "is also critical... if confidence in the system of representative Government is not to be eroded to a disastrous extent." ... [28]

The Act's $1,000 contribution limitation focuses precisely on the problem of large campaign contributions – the narrow aspect of political association where the actuality and potential for corruption have been identified – while leaving persons free to engage in independent political expression, to associate actively through volunteering their services, and to assist to a limited but nonetheless substantial extent in supporting candidates and committees with financial resources. Significantly, the [29] Act's contribution limitations in themselves do not undermine to any material degree the potential for robust and effective discussion of candidates and campaign issues by individual citizens, associations, the institutional press, candidates, and political parties. ...

We find that, under the rigorous standard of review established by our prior decisions, the weighty interests served by restricting the size of financial contributions to political candidates are sufficient to justify the limited effect upon First Amendment freedoms caused by the $1,000 contribution ceiling. ... [30]

[A]ppellants argue that the contribution limitations work such an invidious discrimination between incumbents [31] and challengers that the statutory provisions must be declared unconstitutional on their face. In considering this contention, it is important at the outset to note that the Act applies the same limitations on contributions to all candidates regardless of their present occupations, ideological views, or party affiliations. ... [32]

There is no such evidence to support the claim that the contribution limitations in themselves discriminate against major-party challengers to incumbents. Challengers can and often do defeat incumbents in federal elections. Major-party challengers in federal elections are usually men and women who are well known and influential in their community or State. Often such challengers are themselves incumbents in important local, state, or federal offices. Statistics in the record indicate that major-party challengers as well as incumbents are capable of raising large sums for campaigning. Indeed, a small but nonetheless significant number of challengers have in recent elections outspent their incumbent rivals. And, to the extent that incumbents generally are more likely than challengers to attract very large contributions, the Act's $1,000 ceiling has the practical effect of benefiting challengers as a class. Contrary to the broad generalization [33] drawn by the appellants, the practical impact of the contribution ceilings in any given election will clearly depend upon the amounts in excess of the ceilings that, for various reasons, the candidates in that election would otherwise have received and the utility of these additional amounts to the candidates. To be sure, the limitations may have a significant effect on particular challengers or incumbents, but the record provides no basis for predicting that such

adventitious factors will invariably and invidiously benefit incumbents as a class. Since the danger of corruption and the appearance of corruption apply with equal force to challengers and to incumbents, Congress had ample justification for imposing the same fundraising constraints upon both.

The charge of discrimination against minor-party and independent candidates is more troubling, but the record provides no basis for concluding that the Act invidiously disadvantages such candidates. As noted above, the Act on its face treats all candidates equally with regard to contribution limitations. And the restriction would appear to benefit minor-party and independent candidates relative to their major-party opponents because major-party candidates receive far more money in large contributions. Although there is some [34] force to appellants' response that minor-party candidates are primarily concerned with their ability to amass the resources necessary to reach the electorate rather than with their funding position relative to their major-party opponents, the record is virtually devoid of support for the claim that the $1,000 contribution limitation will have a serious effect on the initiation and scope of minor-party and independent candidacies. Moreover, any attempt [35] to exclude minor parties and independents en masse from the Act's contribution limitations overlooks the fact that minor-party candidates may win elective office or have a substantial impact on the outcome of an election. ... [39]

The Act's expenditure ceilings impose direct and substantial restraints on the quantity of political speech. The most drastic of the limitations restricts individuals and groups, including political parties that fail to place a candidate on the ballot, to an expenditure of $1,000 "relative to a clearly identified candidate during a calendar year." § 608 (e)(1). Other expenditure ceilings limit spending by candidates, § 608 (a), their campaigns, § 608 (c), and political parties in connection with election campaigns, § 608 (f). It is clear that a primary effect of these expenditure limitations is to restrict the quantity of campaign speech by individuals, groups, and candidates. The restrictions, while neutral as to the ideas expressed, limit political expression "at the core of our electoral process and of the First Amendment freedoms." Williams v. Rhodes, 393 U.S. 23, 32 (1968).

... The plain effect of [the limits] is to [40] prohibit all individuals, who are neither candidates nor owners of institutional press facilities, and all groups, except political parties and campaign organizations, from voicing their views "relative to a clearly identified candidate" through means that entail aggregate expenditures of more than $1,000 during a calendar year. The provision, for example, would make it a federal criminal offense for a person or association to place a single one-quarter page advertisement "relative to a clearly identified candidate" in a major metropolitan newspaper. ... [44]

We turn then to the basic First Amendment question – whether [the expenditure limit] even as thus narrowly and explicitly construed, impermissibly burdens the constitutional right of free expression. ... [T]he constitutionality of § 608 (e)(1) turns on whether the governmental interests advanced in its support satisfy the exacting scrutiny applicable to [45] limitations on core First Amendment rights of political expression.

We find that the governmental interest in preventing corruption and the appearance of corruption is inadequate to justify § 608 (e)(1)'s ceiling on independent expenditures. First, assuming, arguendo, that large independent expenditures pose the same dangers of actual or apparent quid pro quo arrangements as do large contributions, § 608 (e)(1) does not provide an answer that sufficiently relates to the elimination of those dangers. Unlike the contribution limitations' total ban on the giving of large amounts of money to candidates, § 608 (e)(1) prevents only some large expenditures. So long as persons and groups eschew expenditures that in express terms advocate the election or defeat of a clearly identified candidate, they are free to spend as much as they want to promote the candidate and his views. ... Yet no substantial societal interest would be served by a loophole-closing provision designed to check corruption that permitted unscrupulous persons and organizations to expend unlimited sums of money in order to obtain improper influence over candidates for elective office. Cf. Mills v. Alabama, 384 U.S. at 220.

Second, quite apart from the shortcomings of § 608 (e) [46] (1) in preventing any abuses generated by large independent expenditures, the independent advocacy restricted by the provision does not presently appear to pose dangers of real or apparent corruption comparable to those identified with large campaign contributions. ... [47] § 608(e)(1) limits expenditures for express advocacy of candidates made totally independently of the candidate and his campaign. Unlike contributions, such independent expenditures may well provide little assistance to the candidate's campaign and indeed may prove counterproductive. The absence of prearrangement and coordination of an expenditure with the candidate or his agent not only undermines the value of the expenditure to the candidate, but also alleviates the danger that expenditures will be given as a quid pro quo for improper commitments from the candidate. Rather than preventing circumvention of the contribution limitations, § 608 (e)(1) severely restricts all independent advocacy despite its substantially diminished potential for abuse.

While the independent expenditure ceiling thus fails to serve any substantial governmental interest in stemming [48] the reality or appearance of corruption in the electoral process, it heavily burdens core First Amendment expression. For the First Amendment right to "'speak one's mind... on all public institutions'" includes the right to engage in "'vigorous advocacy' no less than 'abstract discussion.'" New York Times Co. v. Sullivan, 376 U.S. at 269, quoting Bridges v. California, 314 U.S. 252, 270 (1941), and NAACP v. Button, 371 U.S. at 429. Advocacy of the election or defeat of candidates for federal office is no less entitled to protection under the First Amendment than the discussion of political policy generally or advocacy of the passage or defeat of legislation.

It is argued, however, that the ancillary governmental interest in equalizing the relative ability of individuals and groups to influence the outcome of elections serves to justify the limitation on express advocacy of the election or defeat of candidates imposed by § 608 (e)(1)'s expenditure ceiling. But the concept that government may restrict the speech of some elements of our society in [49] order to enhance the relative voice of others is wholly foreign to the First Amendment, which was designed "to secure 'the widest possible dissemination of information from diverse and antagonistic sources,'" and "'to assure unfettered interchange of ideas for the bringing about of political and social changes desired by the people.'" New York Times Co. v. Sullivan, supra, at 266, 269, quoting Associated Press v. United States, 326 U.S. 1, 20 (1945), and Roth v. United States, 354 U.S. at 484. The First Amendment's protection against governmental abridgment of free expression cannot properly be made to depend on a person's financial ability to engage in public discussion. Cf. Eastern R. Conf. v. Noerr Motors, 365 U.S. 127, 139 (1961). ... [50] For the reasons stated, we conclude that § 608 (e)(1)'s independent expenditure limitation is unconstitutional under the First Amendment.

... [58] In sum, the provisions of the Act that impose a $1,000 limitation on contributions to a single candidate, § 608 (b)(1), a $5,000 limitation on contributions by a political committee to a single candidate, § 608 (b)(2), and a $25,000 limitation on total contributions by an individual during any calendar year, § 608 (b)(3), are constitutionally valid. These limitations, along with the disclosure provisions, constitute the Act's primary weapons against the reality or appearance of improper influence stemming from the dependence of candidates on large campaign contributions. The contribution ceilings thus serve the basic governmental interest in safeguarding the integrity of the electoral process without directly impinging upon the rights of individual citizens and candidates to engage in political debate and discussion. By contrast, the First Amendment requires the invalidation of the Act's independent expenditure ceiling, § 608 (e)(1), its limitation on a candidate's expenditures from his own personal funds, § 608 (a), and its ceilings on overall campaign expenditures, § 608 (c). These provisions place substantial and direct restrictions [59] on the ability of candidates, citizens, and associations to engage in protected political expression, restrictions that the First Amendment cannot tolerate.

Burson v. Freeman
504 U.S. 191
(1992)
(Excerpts only. Footnotes omitted.)

Author's Note: A candidate challenges a Tennessee law that prohibits the solicitation of votes and the display or distribution of campaign materials within 100 feet of the entrance to a polling place, asserting that the law unconstitutionally abridges her ability to communicate with voters. The State Supreme Court struck down the law as too crude a mechanism for advancing the state's compelling interest in protecting the right to a secret ballot and the fairness of elections.

PRIOR HISTORY: On writ of certiorari to the Supreme Court of Tennessee, Middle Division.

JUDGES: BLACKMUN, J., announced the judgment of the Court and delivered an opinion, in which REHNQUIST, C. J., and WHITE and KENNEDY, JJ., joined. KENNEDY, J., filed a concurring opinion. SCALIA, J., filed an opinion concurring in the judgment. STEVENS, J., filed a dissenting opinion, in which O'CONNOR and SOUTER, JJ., joined. THOMAS, J., took no part in the consideration or decision of the case.

OPINION: [193] MR. JUSTICE BLACKMUN.

Twenty-six years ago, this Court, in a majority opinion written by Justice Hugo L. Black, struck down a state law that made it a crime for a newspaper editor to publish an editorial on election day urging readers to vote in a particular way. *Mills v. Alabama*, 384 U.S. 214, 16 L. Ed. 2d 484, 86 S. Ct. 1434 (1966). While the Court did not hesitate to denounce the statute as an "obvious and flagrant abridgment" of First Amendment rights, *id.*, at 219, it was quick to point out that its holding "in no way involved the extent of a State's power to regulate conduct in and around the polls in order to maintain peace, order and decorum there," *id.*, at 218.

Today, we confront the issue carefully left open in *Mills*. The question presented is whether a provision of the Tennessee Code, which prohibits the solicitation of votes and the display or distribution of campaign materials within 100 feet of the entrance to a polling place, violates the First and Fourteenth Amendments.

The State of Tennessee has carved out an election-day "campaign-free zone" through § 2-7-111(b) of its election code. That section reads in pertinent part:

"Within the appropriate boundary as established in subsection (a) [100 feet from the entrances], and the building in which the polling place is located, the display of campaign posters, signs or other campaign materials, distribution of campaign materials, and solicitation of votes for or against any person or political party or position [194] on a question are prohibited." Tenn. Code Ann. § 2-7-111(b) (Supp. 1991).

Violation of § 2-7-111(b) is a Class C misdemeanor punishable by a term of imprisonment not greater than 30 days or a fine not to exceed $50, or both. Tenn. Code Ann. §§ 2-19-119 and 40-35-111(e)(3) (1990).

Respondent Mary Rebecca Freeman has been a candidate for office in Tennessee. ... Asserting that §§ 2-7-111(b) and 2-19-119 limited her ability to communicate with voters, respondent brought a facial challenge to these statutes in Davidson County Chancery Court. She sought a declaratory judgment that the provisions were unconstitutional under both the United States and the Tennessee Constitutions. She also sought a permanent injunction against their enforcement. ...

The Tennessee Supreme Court, by a 4-to-1 vote, ... held that § 2-7-111(b) was content based "because it regulates a specific subject matter, the solicitation of votes and the display or distribution of campaign materials, and a certain category of speakers, campaign workers." *Id.*, at 213. The court then held that such a content-based statute could not be upheld unless (i) the burden placed on free speech rights is justified by a compelling state interest and (ii) the means chosen bear a substantial relation to that interest and are the least intrusive to achieve the State's goals. While the Tennessee Supreme Court found that the State unquestionably had shown a compelling interest in banning solicitation of voters and distribution of campaign materials within the polling place itself, it concluded that the State had not shown a compelling interest in regulating the premises around the polling place. Accordingly, the court held that the 100-foot limit was not narrowly tailored to protect the demonstrated interest. The court also held that the statute was not the least restrictive means to serve the State's interests.

... We now reverse the Tennessee Supreme Court's judgment that the statute violates the First Amendment of the United States Constitution. ...

[196] The Tennessee statute implicates three central concerns in our First Amendment jurisprudence: regulation of political speech, regulation of speech in a public forum, and regulation based on the content of the speech. The speech restricted by § 2-7-111(b) obviously is political speech. "Whatever differences may exist about interpretations of the First Amendment, there is practically universal agreement that a major purpose of that Amendment was to protect the free discussion of governmental affairs." *Mills* v. *Alabama*, 384 U.S. at 218. "For speech concerning public affairs is more than self-expression; it is the essence of self-government." *Garrison* v. *Louisiana*, 379 U.S. 64, 74-75, 13 L. Ed. 2d 125, 85 S. Ct. 209 (1964). Accordingly, this Court has recognized that "the First Amendment 'has its fullest and most urgent application' to speech uttered during a campaign for political office." ...

The second important feature of § 2-7-111(b) is that it bars speech in quintessential public forums. These forums include those places "which by long tradition or by government fiat have been devoted to assembly and debate," such as parks, streets, and sidewalks. *Perry Ed. Assn.* v. *Perry Local Educators' Assn.*, 460 U.S. 37, 45, 74 L. Ed. 2d 794, 103 S. Ct. 948 (1983). "Such use [197] of the streets and public places has, from ancient times, been a part of the privileges, immunities, rights, and liberties of citizens." *Hague* v. *CIO*, 307 U.S. 496, 515, 83 L. Ed. 1423, 59 S. Ct. 954 (1939) (opinion of Roberts, J.). At the same time, however, expressive activity, even in a quintessential public forum, may interfere with other important activities for which the property is used. Accordingly, this Court has held that the government may regulate the time, place, and manner of the expressive activity, so long as such restrictions are content neutral, are narrowly tailored to serve a significant governmental interest, and leave open ample alternatives for communication. ...

The Tennessee restriction under consideration, however, is not a facially content-neutral time, place, or manner restriction. Whether individuals may exercise their free speech rights near polling places depends entirely on whether their speech is related to a political campaign. The statute does not reach other categories of speech, such as commercial solicitation, distribution, and display.

This Court has held that the First Amendment's hostility to content-based regulation extends not only to a restriction on a particular viewpoint, but also to a prohibition of public discussion of an entire topic. ...

[198] As a facially content-based restriction on political speech in a public forum, § 2-7-111(b) must be subjected to exacting scrutiny: The State must show that the "regulation is necessary to serve a compelling state interest and that it is narrowly drawn to achieve that end." ... Despite the ritualistic ease with which we state this now familiar standard, its announcement does not allow us to avoid the truly difficult issues involving the First Amendment. ... This case presents us with a particularly difficult reconciliation: the accommodation of the right to engage in political discourse with the right to vote – a right at the heart of our democracy.

[199] ... [T]his Court has concluded that a State has a compelling interest in protecting voters from confusion and undue influence. See *Eu*, 489 U.S. at 228-229. The Court also has recognized that a State "indisputably has a compelling interest in preserving the integrity of its election process." *Id.*, at 231. The Court thus has "upheld generally applicable and evenhanded restrictions that protect the integrity and reliability of the electoral process itself." *Anderson* v. *Celebrezze*, 460 U.S. 780, 788, n. 9, 75 L. Ed. 2d 547, 103 S. Ct. 1564 (1983) (collecting cases). In other words, it has recognized that a State has a compelling interest in ensuring that an individual's right to vote is not undermined by fraud in the election process.

To survive strict scrutiny, however, a State must do more than assert a compelling state interest – it must demonstrate that its law is necessary to serve the asserted interest. [200] While we readily acknowledge that a law rarely survives such scrutiny, an examination of the evolution of election reform, both in this country and abroad, demonstrates the necessity of restricted areas in or around polling places.

... [206] [A]n examination of the history of election regulation in this country reveals a persistent battle against two evils: voter intimidation and election fraud. After an unsuccessful experiment with an unofficial ballot system, all 50 States, together with numerous other Western democracies, settled on the same solution: a secret ballot secured in part by a restricted zone around the voting compartments. We find that this widespread and time-tested consensus demonstrates that some restricted zone is necessary in order to serve the States' compelling interests in preventing voter intimidation and election fraud.

Respondent and the dissent advance three principal challenges to this conclusion. First, respondent argues that restricted zones are overinclusive because States could secure these same compelling interests with statutes that make it a misdemeanor to interfere with an election or to use violence or intimidation to prevent voting. See, *e.g.*, Tenn. Code Ann. §§ 2-19-101 and 2-19-115 (Supp. 1991). We are not persuaded. Intimidation and interference laws fall short of serving a State's compelling interests because they "deal [207] with only the most blatant and specific attempts" to impede elections. Cf. *Buckley* v. *Valeo*, 424 U.S. 1, 28, 46 L. Ed. 2d 659, 96 S. Ct. 612 (1976) (existence of bribery statute does not preclude need for limits on contributions to political campaigns). Moreover, because law enforcement officers generally are barred from the vicinity of the polls to avoid any appearance of coercion in the electoral process, see Tenn. Code Ann. § 2-7-103 (1985), many acts of interference would go undetected. These undetected or less than blatant acts may nonetheless drive the voter away before remedial action can be taken.

Second, respondent and the dissent argue that Tennessee's statute is underinclusive because it does not restrict other types of speech, such as charitable and commercial solicitation or exit polling, within the 100-foot zone. We agree that distinguishing among types of speech requires that the statute be subjected to strict scrutiny. We do not, however, agree that the failure to regulate all speech renders the statute fatally underinclusive. In fact, as one early commentator pointed out, allowing members of the general public access to the polling place makes it more difficult for political machines to buy off all the monitors. See Wigmore 52. But regardless of the need for such additional monitoring, there is, as summarized above, ample evidence that political candidates have used campaign workers to commit voter intimidation or electoral fraud. In contrast, there is simply no evidence that political candidates have used other forms of solicitation or exit polling to commit such electoral abuses. States adopt laws to address the problems that confront them. The First Amendment does not require States to regulate for problems that do not exist.

Finally, the dissent argues that we confuse history with necessity. Yet the dissent concedes that a secret ballot was necessary to cure electoral abuses. Contrary to the dissent's contention, the link between ballot secrecy and some restricted zone surrounding the voting area is not merely timing – it is common sense. The only way to preserve the [208] secrecy of the ballot is to limit access to the area around the voter. Accordingly, we hold that *some* restricted zone around the voting area is necessary to secure the State's compelling interest.

The real question then is *how large* a restricted zone is permissible or sufficiently tailored.

Respondent and the dissent argue that Tennessee's 100-foot boundary is not narrowly drawn to achieve the State's compelling interest in protecting the right to vote. We disagree.

As a preliminary matter, the long, uninterrupted, and prevalent use of these statutes makes it difficult for States to come forward with the sort of proof the dissent wishes to require. The majority of these laws were adopted originally in the 1890's, long before States engaged in extensive legislative hearings on election regulations. The prevalence of these laws, both here and abroad, then encouraged their re-enactment without much comment. The fact that these laws have been in effect for a long period of time also makes it difficult for the States to put on witnesses who can testify as to what would happen without them. Finally, it is difficult to isolate the exact effect of these laws on voter intimidation and election fraud. Voter intimidation and election fraud are successful precisely because they are difficult to detect.

Furthermore, because a government has such a compelling interest in securing the right to vote freely and effectively, this Court never has held a State "to the burden of demonstrating empirically the objective effects on political stability that [are] produced" by the voting regulation in question. [209] *Munro* v. *Socialist Workers Party*, 479 U.S. 189, 195, 93 L. Ed. 2d 499, 107 S. Ct. 533 (1986). Elections vary from year to year, and place to place. It is therefore difficult to make specific findings about the effects of a voting regulation. Moreover, the remedy for a tainted election is an imperfect one. Rerunning an election would have a negative impact on voter turnout. Thus, requiring proof that a 100-foot boundary is perfectly tailored to deal with voter intimidation and election fraud "would necessitate that a State's political system sustain some level of damage before the legislature could take corrective action. Legislatures, we think, should be permitted to respond to potential deficiencies in the electoral process with foresight rather than reactively, provided that the response is reasonable and does not *significantly impinge* on constitutionally protected rights." *Id.*, at 195-196 (emphasis added).

[210] We do not think that the minor geographic limitation prescribed by § 2-7-111(b) constitutes such a significant impingement. Thus, we simply do not view the question whether the 100-foot boundary line could be somewhat tighter as a question of "constitutional dimension." *Id.*, at 197. Reducing the boundary to 25 feet, as suggested by the Tennessee Supreme Court, 802 S.W.2d at 214, is a difference only in degree, not a less restrictive alternative in kind. *Buckley* v. *Valeo*, 424 U.S. at 30. As was pointed out in the dissenting opinion in the Tennessee Supreme Court, it "takes approximately 15 seconds to walk 75 feet." 802 S.W.2d at 215.

The State of Tennessee has decided that these last 15 seconds before its citizens enter the polling place should be their own, as free from interference as possible. We do not find that this is an unconstitutional choice.

At some measurable distance from the polls, of course, governmental regulation of vote solicitation could effectively become an impermissible burden akin to the statute struck down in *Mills* v. *Alabama*, 384 U.S. 214, 16 L. Ed. 2d 484, 86 S. Ct. 1434 (1966). ... In conclusion, we reaffirm that it is the rare case in which we have held that a law survives strict scrutiny. This, however, is such a rare case. Here, the State, as recognized administrator of elections, has asserted that the exercise of free speech rights conflicts with another fundamental right, the right to cast a ballot in an election free from the taint of intimidation and fraud. A long history, a substantial consensus, and simple common sense show that some restricted zone around polling places is necessary to protect that fundamental right. Given the conflict between these two rights, we hold that requiring solicitors to stand 100 feet from the entrances to polling places does not constitute an unconstitutional compromise.

The judgment of the Tennessee Supreme Court is reversed, and the case is remanded for further proceedings not inconsistent with this opinion. *It is so ordered.*

Federal Election Commission v. Colorado Republican Federal Campaign Committee
533 U.S. 431
(2001)

PRIOR HISTORY: On writ of certiorari to the United States Court of Appeals for the Tenth Circuit.

JUDGES: SOUTER, J., delivered the opinion of the Court, in which STEVENS, O'CONNOR, GINSBURG, and BREYER, JJ., joined. THOMAS, J., filed a dissenting opinion, in which SCALIA and KENNEDY, JJ., joined, and in which REHNQUIST, C. J., joined as to Part II.

OPINION: [437] MR. JUSTICE SOUTER.

[1A]In *Colorado Republican Federal Campaign Comm.* v. *Federal Election Comm'n*, 518 U.S. 604, 135 L. Ed. 2d 795, 116 S. Ct. 2309 (1996) (*Colorado I*), we held that spending limits set by the Federal Election Campaign Act were unconstitutional as applied to the Colorado Republican Party's independent expenditures in connection with a senatorial campaign. We remanded for consideration of the party's claim that all limits on expenditures by a political party in connection with congressional campaigns are facially unconstitutional and thus unenforceable even as to spending coordinated with a candidate. Today we reject that facial challenge to the limits on parties' coordinated expenditures.

I.   We first examined the Federal Election Campaign Act of 1971 in *Buckley* v. *Valeo*, 424 U.S. 1, 46 L. Ed. 2d 659, 96 S. Ct. 612 (1976) *(per curiam)*, where we held that the Act's limitations on contributions to a candidate's election campaign were generally constitutional, but that limitations on election expenditures were not. Id. at 12-59. Later cases have respected this line between contributing and spending. See, *e.g.*, *Nixon* v. *Shrink Missouri Government PAC*, 528 U.S. 377, 386-388, 145 L. Ed. 2d 886, 120 S. Ct. 897 (2000); *Colorado I, supra,* at 610, 614-615; *Federal Election* [438] *Comm'n* v. *Massachusetts Citizens for Life, Inc.*, 479 U.S. 238, 259-260, 93 L. Ed. 2d 539, 107 S. Ct. 616 (1986).

The simplicity of the distinction is qualified, however, by the Act's provision for a functional, not formal, definition of "contribution," which includes "expenditures made by any person in cooperation, consultation, or concert, with, or at the request or suggestion of, a candidate, his authorized political committees, or their agents," 2 U.S.C. § 441a(a)(7)(B)(i).[1] Expenditures coordinated with a candidate, that is, are contributions under the Act.

The Federal Election Commission originally took the position that any expenditure by a political party in connection with a particular election for federal office was presumed to be coordinated with the party's candidate. See *Federal Election Comm'n* v. *Democratic Senatorial Campaign Comm.*, 454 U.S. 27, 28-29, n. 1, 70 L. Ed. 2d 23, 102 S. Ct. 38 (1981); Brief for Petitioner 6-7. The Commission thus operated on the assumption that all expenditure limits imposed on political parties were, in essence, contribution limits and therefore constitutional. Brief for Respondent in *Colorado I*, O.T. 1995, No. 95-

---

[1] "Contribution" is otherwise defined as "any gift, subscription, loan, advance, or deposit of money or anything of value made by any person for the purpose of influencing any election for Federal office"; or "the payment by any person of compensation for the personal services of another person which are rendered to a political committee without charge for any purpose." 2 U.S.C. § 431(8). The Act defines "expenditure" as "any purchase, payment, distribution, loan, advance, deposit, or gift of money or anything of value, made by any person for the purpose of influencing any election for Federal office." § 431(9)(A)(i). A "written contract, promise, or agreement to make an expenditure" also counts as an expenditure. § 431(9)(A)(ii).

489, pp. 28-30. Such limits include 2 U.S.C. § 441a(d)(3), which provides that in elections for the United States Senate, each national or state party committee[2] is [439] limited to spending the greater of $20,000 (adjusted for inflation, § 441a(c)) or two cents multiplied by the voting age population of the State in which the election is held, § 441a(d)(3)(A).[3]

Colorado I was an as-applied challenge to § 441a(d)(3) (which we spoke of as the Party Expenditure Provision), occasioned by the Commission's enforcement action against the Colorado Republican Federal Campaign Committee (Party) for exceeding the campaign spending limit through its payments for radio advertisements attacking Democratic Congressman and senatorial candidate Timothy Wirth. *Colorado I, supra,* at 612-613. The Party defended in part with the claim that the party expenditure limitations violated the First Amendment, and the principal opinion in *Colorado I* agreed that the limitations were unconstitutional as applied to the advertising expenditures at issue. Unlike the Commission, the Members of the Court who joined the principal opinion thought the payments were "independent expenditures" as that term had been used in our prior cases, owing to the facts that the Party spent the money before selecting its own senatorial candidate and without any arrangement with potential nominees. *Colorado I,* 518 U.S. at 613-614 (opinion of BREYER, J.).

The Party's broader claim remained: that although prior decisions of this Court had upheld the constitutionality of limits on coordinated expenditures by political speakers [440] other than parties, the congressional campaign expenditure limitations on parties themselves are facially unconstitutional, and so are incapable of reaching party spending even when coordinated with a candidate. Id. at 623-626.[4] We remanded that facial challenge, which had not been fully briefed or

considered below. *Ibid.* On remand the District Court held for the Party, 41 F. Supp. 2d 1197 (1999), and a divided panel of the Court of Appeals for the Tenth Circuit affirmed, 213 F.3d 1221 (2000).[5] We granted certiorari to resolve the question left open by *Colorado I,* see 531 U.S. 923 (2000), and we now reverse.

II. [2] Spending for political ends and contributing to political candidates both fall within the First Amendment's protection of speech and political association. *Buckley,* 424 U.S. at 14-23. But ever since we first reviewed the 1971 Act, we have understood that limits on political expenditures deserve closer scrutiny than restrictions on political contributions. *Ibid;* see also, *e.g., Shrink Missouri,* 528 U.S. at 386-388; *Colorado I, supra,* at 610, 614-615; *Massachusetts Citizens for Life,* 479 U.S. at 259-260. Restraints on expenditures generally curb more expressive and associational activity than limits on contributions do. *Shrink Missouri, supra,* at 386-388; *Colorado I, supra,* at 615; *Buckley,* 424 U.S. at 19-23. A further reason for the distinction is that limits on contributions [441] are more clearly justified by a link to political corruption than limits on other kinds of unlimited political spending are (corruption being understood not only as *quid pro quo* agreements, but also as undue influence on an officer holder's judgment, and the appearance of such influence, *Shrink Missouri, supra,* at 388-389). At least this is so where the spending is not coordinated with a candidate or his campaign. *Colorado I, supra,* at 615; *Buckley,* 424 U.S. at 47. In *Buckley* we said that:

"unlike contributions, . . . independent expenditures may well provide little assistance to the candidate's campaign and indeed may prove counterproductive. The absence of prearrangement and coordination of an expenditure with the candidate or his agent not only undermines the value of the expenditure to the candidate, but also alleviates the danger that expenditures will be given as a *quid pro quo* for improper commitments from the candidate." *Ibid.*

Given these differences, we have routinely struck down limitations on independent expenditures by candidates, other individuals, and groups, see *Federal Election Comm'n* v. *National Conservative Political Action Comm.,* 470 U.S. 480, 490-501, 84 L. Ed. 2d 455, 105 S. Ct. 1459 (1985) (political action committees); *Buckley, supra,* at 39-58

---

[2] A political party's "national committee" is the "organization which, by virtue of the bylaws of a political party, is responsible for the day-to-day operation of such political party at the national level, as determined by the [Federal Election] Commission." § 431(14). A "state committee" fills the same role at the state level. § 431(15).

[3] The same limits apply to campaigns for House of Representatives from States entitled to only one Representative. § 441a(d)(3)(A). For other States, the limit on party expenditures in connection with House campaigns is $10,000 preadjustment. § 441a(d)(3)(B). As adjusted for inflation, the 2000 Senate limits ranged from $67,560 to $1,636,438; House limits ranged from $33,780 to $67,560. 26 FEC Record 14-15 (Mar. 2000).
The FEC reads the Act to permit parties to make campaign contributions within the otherwise-applicable contribution limits, in addition to the expenditures permitted by § 441a(d). See n. 16, *infra.*

[4] The limits applicable to presidential campaigns were not at issue in *Colorado I,* 518 U.S. 604, 610-611, 135 L. Ed. 2d 795, 116 S. Ct. 2309 (1996), and are not at issue here, Brief for Respondent 49, n. 30.

---

[5] Along with its constitutional claim, the Party argued to the District Court that the Party Expenditure Provision's application to independent expenditures was not severable from the other possible applications of the provision, a nonconstitutional basis for resolving the case that the *Colorado I* principal opinion suggested should be explored on remand. *Colorado I, supra,* at 625-626. The District Court rejected the nonseverability argument, 41 F. Supp. 2d at 1207, and the Party did not renew it on appeal, 213 F.3d at 1225, n. 3.

(individuals, groups, candidates, and campaigns),[6] while repeatedly upholding contribution limits, see *Shrink Missouri, supra* (contributions by political action [442] committees); *California Medical Assn. v. Federal Election Comm'n,* 453 U.S. 182, 193-199, 69 L. Ed. 2d 567, 101 S. Ct. 2712 (1981) (contributions by individuals and associations); *Buckley, supra,* at 23-36 (contributions by individuals, groups, and political committees).[7]

The First Amendment line between spending and donating is easy to draw when it falls between independent expenditures by individuals or political action committees (PACs) without any candidate's approval (or wink or nod), and contributions in the form of cash gifts to candidates. See, *e.g., Shrink Missouri, supra,* at 386-388; *Buckley, supra,* at 19-23.[8] But facts speak less clearly once the

independence of [443] the spending cannot be taken for granted, and money spent by an individual or PAC according to an arrangement with a candidate is therefore harder to classify. As already seen, Congress drew a functional, not a formal, line between contributions and expenditures when it provided that coordinated expenditures by individuals and nonparty groups are subject to the Act's contribution limits, 2 U.S.C. § 441a(a)(7)(B)(i); *Colorado I,* 518 U.S. at 611. In *Buckley,* the Court acknowledged Congress's functional classification, 424 U.S. at 46-47, and n. 53, and observed that treating coordinated expenditures as contributions "prevents attempts to circumvent the Act through prearranged or coordinated expenditures amounting to disguised contributions," id. at 47. *Buckley,* in fact, enhanced the significance of this functional treatment by striking down independent expenditure limits on First Amendment grounds while upholding limitations on contributions (by individuals and nonparty groups), as defined to include coordinated expenditures, id. at 23-59.[9]

Colorado I addressed the FEC's effort to stretch the functional treatment of coordinated expenditures further than the plain application of the statutory definition. As we said, the FEC argued that parties and candidates are coupled so closely that all of a party's expenditures on an election campaign are coordinated with its candidate; because *Buckley* had treated some coordinated expenditures like contributions [444] and upheld their limitation, the argument went, the Party Expenditure Provision should stand as applied to all party election spending. See Brief for Respondent in *Colorado I,* O.T. 1995, No. 95-489, pp. 28-30; see also *Colorado I, supra,* at 619-623. *Colorado I* held otherwise, however, the principal opinion's view being that some party expenditures could be seen as "independent" for constitutional purposes. 518 U.S. at 614. The principal opinion found no reason to see these expenditures as more likely to serve or be seen as instruments of corruption than independent expenditures by anyone else. So there was no justification for subjecting party election spending

---

[6] The expenditure limits invalidated in *Buckley* applied to candidates and their campaigns, and to "persons." See *Buckley,* 424 U.S. at 39- 40, 51, 54, 58. "Person" was defined as "an individual, partnership, committee, association, corporation, or any other organization or group of persons." 18 U.S.C. § 591(g) (1970 ed., Supp. IV); see also *Buckley,* 424 U.S. at 144-235 (appendix reprinting then-current Act). Although this language is broad enough to cover political parties, id. at 19, and n. 19, 39, parties with a candidate on the ballot were covered instead by the special Party Expenditure Provision, which was not challenged on First Amendment grounds, id. at 58, n. 66.

[7] The contribution limits at issue in *Buckley* applied to "persons" ("person" again defined as "an individual, partnership, committee, association, corporation or any other organization or group of persons," id. at 23). Certain groups (referred to under current law as "multicandidate political committees") that registered with the FEC and met other qualifications, including making contributions to five or more candidates for federal office, were subject to a higher limit. Id. at 35.
The current contribution limits appear in 2 U.S.C. § 441a(a). They provide that "persons" (still broadly defined, see § 431(11)) may contribute no more than $1,000 to a candidate "with respect to any election for Federal office," $5,000 to any political committee in any year, and $20,000 to the national committees of a political party in any year. § 441a(a)(1). Individuals are limited to a yearly contribution total of $25,000. § 441a(a)(3). "Multicandidate political committees" are limited to a $5,000 contribution to a candidate "with respect to any election," $5,000 to any political committee in any year, and $15,000 to the national committees of a political party in any year. § 441a(a)(2). Unlike the party expenditure limits, these contribution limits are not adjusted for inflation.
[8] The Party does not challenge the constitutionality of limits on cash contributions from parties to candidates, Brief for Respondent 49, n. 31, which, on the FEC's reading of the Act, are imposed on parties by the generally applicable contribution limits of 2 U.S.C. § 441a(a), see n. 16, *infra.* And the Party, unlike JUSTICE THOMAS, *post,* at 1 (dissenting opinion), does not call for the overruling of *Buckley.* Nor does the FEC ask us to revisit *Buckley*'s general approach to expenditure limits, although some have argued that such limits could be justified in light of post-*Buckley* developments in campaign finance, see, *e.g.,* Blasi, Free Speech and the Widening Gyre of Fundraising, 94 Colum. L. Rev. 1281

(1994); cf. *Nixon* v. *Shrink Missouri,* 528 U.S. 377, 409, 145 L. Ed. 2d 886, 120 S. Ct. 897 (2000) (KENNEDY, J., dissenting) ("I would leave open the possibility that Congress, or a state legislature, might devise a system in which there are some limits on both expenditures and contributions, thus permitting officeholders to concentrate their time and efforts on official duties rather than on fundraising"); id. at 405 (BREYER, J., concurring) ("Suppose *Buckley* denies the political branches sufficient leeway to enact comprehensive solutions to the problems posed by campaign finance. If so, like JUSTICE KENNEDY, I believe the Constitution would require us to reconsider *Buckley*").
[9] As noted, n. 6, *supra,* the Party Expenditure Provision itself was not challenged on First Amendment grounds in *Buckley, supra,* at 58, n. 66.

across the board to the kinds of limits previously invalidated when applied to individuals and nonparty groups. The principal opinion observed that "the independent expression of a political party's views is 'core' First Amendment activity no less than is the independent expression of individuals, candidates, or other political committees." Id. at 616. Since the FEC did not advance any other convincing reason for refusing to draw the independent-coordinated line accepted since *Buckley*, see *National Conservative Political Action Comm.*, 470 U.S. at 497-498; *Buckley, supra*, at 46-47, that was the end of the case so far as it concerned independent spending. *Colorado I, supra*, at 617-623.

But that still left the question whether the First Amendment allows coordinated election expenditures by parties to be treated functionally as contributions, the way coordinated expenditures by other entities are treated. *Colorado I* found no justification for placing parties at a disadvantage when spending independently; but was there a case for leaving them entirely free to coordinate unlimited spending with candidates when others could not? The principal opinion in *Colorado I* noted that coordinated expenditures "share some of the constitutionally relevant features of independent expenditures." 518 U.S. at 624. But it also observed that "many [party coordinated expenditures] are . . . virtually indistinguishable [445] from simple contributions." *Ibid.* Coordinated spending by a party, in other words, covers a spectrum of activity, as does coordinated spending by other political actors. The issue in this case is, accordingly, whether a party is otherwise in a different position from other political speakers, giving it a claim to demand a generally higher standard of scrutiny before its coordinated spending can be limited. The issue is posed by two questions: does limiting coordinated spending impose a unique burden on parties, and is there reason to think that coordinated spending by a party would raise the risk of corruption posed when others spend in coordination with a candidate? The issue is best viewed through the positions developed by the Party and the Government in this case.

III.   The Party's argument that its coordinated spending, like its independent spending, should be left free from restriction under the *Buckley* line of cases boils down to this: because a party's most important speech is aimed at electing candidates and is itself expressed through those candidates, any limit on party support for a candidate imposes a unique First Amendment burden. See Brief for Respondent 26-31. The point of organizing a party, the argument goes, is to run a successful candidate who shares the party's policy goals. Id. at 26. Therefore, while a campaign contribution is only one of several ways that individuals and nonparty groups speak and associate politically, see *Shrink Missouri*, 528 U.S. at 386-387; *Buckley*, 424 U.S. at 20-22, financial support of candidates is essential to the nature of political parties as we know them. And coordination with a candidate is a party's natural way of operating, not merely an option that can easily be avoided. Brief for Respondent 26. Limitation of any party expenditure coordinated with a candidate, the Party contends, is therefore a serious, rather than incidental, imposition on the party's speech and associative purpose, and that justifies a stricter level of scrutiny than we have applied [446] to analogous limits on individuals and nonparty groups. But whatever level of scrutiny is applied, the Party goes on to argue, the burden on a party reflects a fatal mismatch between the effects of limiting coordinated party expenditures and the prevention of corruption or the appearance of it. Brief for Respondent 20-22, 25-32; see also 213 F.3d at 1227.

[3A] The Government's argument for treating coordinated spending like contributions goes back to *Buckley*. There, the rationale for endorsing Congress's equation of coordinated expenditures and contributions was that the equation "prevents attempts to circumvent the Act through prearranged or coordinated expenditures amounting to disguised contributions." 424 U.S. at 47. The idea was that coordinated expenditures are as useful to the candidate as cash, and that such "disguised contributions" might be given "as a *quid pro quo* for improper commitments from the candidate" (in contrast to independent expenditures, which are poor sources of leverage for a spender because they might be duplicative or counterproductive from a candidate's point of view). *Ibid.* In effect, therefore, *Buckley* subjected limits on coordinated expenditures by individuals and nonparty groups to the same scrutiny it applied to limits on their cash contributions. The standard of scrutiny requires the limit to be "'closely drawn' to match a 'sufficiently important interest,' . . . though the dollar amount of the limit need not be 'fine tuned,'" *Shrink Missouri, supra*, at 387-388 (quoting *Buckley, supra*, at 25, 30).

The Government develops this rationale a step further in applying it here. Coordinated spending by a party should be limited not only because it is like a party contribution, but for a further reason. A party's right to make unlimited expenditures coordinated with a candidate would induce individual and other nonparty contributors to give to the party in order to finance coordinated spending for a favored candidate beyond the contribution limits binding on them. The [447] Government points out that a degree of circumvention is occurring under present law (which allows unlimited independent spending and some coordinated spending). Individuals and nonparty groups who have reached the limit of direct contributions to a candidate give to a party with the understanding that the contribution to the party will produce increased party spending for the candidate's benefit. The Government argues that if coordinated spending were unlimited, circumvention would increase: because coordinated spending is as effective as direct contributions in supporting a candidate, an increased opportunity for coordinated spending would aggravate the use of a party to funnel money to a candidate from individuals and nonparty groups, who would thus bypass the contribution limits that *Buckley* upheld. IV. [1B] Each of the competing positions is plausible at first blush. Our evaluation of the arguments, however, leads us to reject the Party's claim to suffer a burden unique in any way that should make a categorical difference under the First Amendment. On the other side, the Government's contentions are ultimately borne out by evidence, entitling it to prevail in its characterization of party coordinated spending as the functional equivalent of contributions.

A   In assessing the Party's argument, we start with a word about what the Party is not saying. First, we do not understand the Party to be arguing that the line between independent and coordinated expenditures is conceptually unsound when applied to a political party instead of an individual or other association. See, *e.g.*, Brief for Respondent 29 (describing "independent party speech"). Indeed, the good sense of recognizing the distinction between independence and coordination was implicit in the principal opinion in *Colorado I*, which did not accept the notion of a "metaphysical 448] identity" between party and candidate, 518 U.S. at 622-623, but rather decided that some of a party's expenditures could be understood as being independent and therefore immune to limitation just as an individual's independent expenditure would be, id. at 619-623.

Second, we do not understand the Party to be arguing that associations in general or political parties in particular may claim a variety of First Amendment protection that is different in kind from the speech and associational rights of their members.[10] The Party's point, rather, is best

understood as a factual one: coordinated spending is essential to parties because "a party and its candidate are joined at the hip," Brief for Respondent 31, owing to the very conception of the party as an organization formed to elect candidates. Parties, thus formed, have an especially strong working relationship with their candidates, id. at 26, and the speech this special relationship facilitates is much more effective than independent speech, id. at 29.

[449] There are two basic arguments here. The first turns on the relationship of a party to a candidate: a coordinated relationship between them so defines a party that it cannot function as such without coordinated spending, the object of which is a candidate's election. We think political history and political reality belie this argument. The second argument turns on the nature of a party as uniquely able to spend in ways that promote candidate success. We think that this argument is a double-edged sword, and one hardly limited to political parties.

1   The assertion that the party is so joined at the hip to candidates that most of its spending must necessarily be coordinated spending is a statement at odds with the history of nearly 30 years under the Act. It is well to remember that ever since the Act was amended in 1974, coordinated spending by a party committee in a given race has been limited by the provision challenged here (or its predecessor). See 18 U.S.C. § 608(f) (1970 ed., Supp. IV); see also *Buckley*, 424 U.S. at 194 (reprinting then-effective Party Expenditure Provision). It was not until 1996 and the decision in *Colorado I* that any spending was allowed above that amount, and since then only independent spending has been unlimited. As a consequence, the Party's claim that coordinated spending beyond the limit imposed by the Act is essential to its very function as a party amounts implicitly to saying that for almost three decades political parties have not been functional or have been functioning in systematic violation of the law. The Party, of course, does not in terms make either statement, and we cannot accept either implication. There is no question about the closeness of candidates to parties and no doubt that the Act affected parties' roles and their exercise of power. But the political scientists who have weighed in on this litigation observe that "there is little evidence to suggest that coordinated party spending limits

---

[10] We have repeatedly held that political parties and other associations derive rights from their members. *E.g.*, *Norman v. Reed*, 502 U.S. 279, 288, 116 L. Ed. 2d 711, 112 S. Ct. 698 (1992); *Tashjian v. Republican Party of Conn.*, 479 U.S. 208, 214-215, 93 L. Ed. 2d 514, 107 S. Ct. 544 (1986); *Roberts v. United States Jaycees*, 468 U.S. 609, 622-623, 82 L. Ed. 2d 462, 104 S. Ct. 3244 (1984); *NAACP v. Alabama ex rel. Patterson*, 357 U.S. 449, 459-460, 2 L. Ed. 2d 1488, 78 S. Ct. 1163 (1958); *Sweezy v. New Hampshire*, 354 U.S. 234, 250, 1 L. Ed. 2d 1311, 77 S. Ct. 1203 (1957). While some commentators have assumed that associations' rights are also limited to the rights of the individuals who belong to them, *e.g.*, Supreme Court, 1996 Term, Leading Cases, Associational Rights of Political Parties, 111 Harv. L. Rev. 197, 315, n. 50 (1977), that view has been subject to debate, see, *e.g.*, Gottlieb, Fleshing Out the Right of Association, 49 Albany L. Rev. 825, 826, 836-837 (1985); see generally Issacharoff, Private Parties with Public Purposes, 101 Colum. L. Rev 274 (2001). There is some language in our cases supporting the position that parties' rights are more than

the sum of their members' rights, *e.g.*, *California Democratic Party v. Jones*, 530 U.S. 567, 575, 147 L. Ed. 2d 502, 120 S. Ct. 2402 (2000) (referring to the "special place" the First Amendment reserves for the process by which a political party selects a standard bearer); *Timmons v. Twin Cities Area New Party*, 520 U.S. 351, 373, 137 L. Ed. 2d 589, 117 S. Ct. 1364 (1997) (STEVENS, J., dissenting), but we have never settled upon the nature of any such difference and have no reason to do so here.

adopted by Congress have frustrated the ability of political [450] parties to exercise their First Amendment rights to support their candidates," and that "in reality, political parties are dominant players, second only to the candidates themselves, in federal elections." Brief for Paul Allen Beck et al. as *Amici Curiae* 5-6. For the Party to claim after all these years of strictly limited coordinated spending that unlimited coordinated spending is essential to the nature and functioning of parties is in reality to assert just that "metaphysical identity," 518 U.S. at 623, between freespending party and candidate that we could not accept in *Colorado I*.[11]

2   There is a different weakness in the seemingly unexceptionable premise that parties are organized for the purpose of electing candidates, Brief for Respondent 26 ("Parties exist precisely to elect candidates that share the goals of their party"), so that imposing on the way parties serve that function is uniquely burdensome. The fault here is not so much metaphysics as myopia, a refusal to see how the power of money actually works in the political structure.

When we look directly at a party's function in getting and spending money, it would ignore reality to think that the party role is adequately described by speaking generally of [451] electing particular candidates. The money parties spend comes from contributors with their own personal interests. PACs, for example, are frequent party contributors who (according to one of the Party's own experts) "do not pursue the same objectives in electoral politics," that parties do. App. 180 (statement of Professor Anthony Corrado). PACs "are most concerned with advancing their narrow interests" and therefore "provide support to candidates who share their views, regardless of party affiliation." *Ibid.* In fact, many PACs naturally express their narrow interests by contributing to both parties during the same electoral cycle,[12] and

sometimes even directly to two competing candidates in the same election, L. Sabato, PAC Power, Inside the World of Political Action Committees 88 (1984).[13] Parties [452] are thus necessarily the instruments of some contributors whose object is not to support the party's message or to elect party candidates across the board, but rather to support a specific candidate for the sake of a position on one, narrow issue, or even to support any candidate who will be obliged to the contributors.[14]

Parties thus perform functions more complex than simply electing candidates; whether they like it or not, they act as agents for spending on behalf of those who seek to produce obligated officeholders. It is this party role, which functionally unites parties

---

[11] To say that history and common sense make us skeptical that parties are uniquely incapacitated by the challenged limitations is not to deny that limiting parties' coordinated expenditures while permitting unlimited independent expenditures prompts parties to structure their spending in a way that they would not otherwise choose to do. See *post*, at 6-7. And we acknowledge below, *infra*, at 17-19, that limiting coordinated expenditures imposes some burden on parties' associational efficiency. But the very evidence cited by the dissent suggests that it is nonetheless possible for parties, like individuals and nonparty groups, to speak independently. *E.g.*, App. 218 (statement of Professor Anthony Corrado) ("It is likely that parties will allocate an increasing amount of money to independent expenditure efforts in the future"); id. at 159 (affidavit of Donald K. Bain, Chairman of the Colorado Republican Federal Campaign Committee) (describing ability to make independent expenditures as "welcome").

[12] As former Senator Paul Simon explained, "I believe people contribute to party committees on both sides of the aisle for the same reason that Federal Express does, because they want favors. There is an expectation that giving to party committees helps you legislatively." App. 270. See also id. at 269-270 (recounting debate over a bill favored by Federal Express during which a colleague exclaimed "we've got to pay attention to who is buttering our bread"). The FEC's public records confirm that Federal Express's PAC (along with many others) contributed to both major parties in recent elections. See, *e.g.*, FEC Disclosure Report, Search Results for Federal Express Political Action Committee (June 20, 2001), http:// herndon1.sdrdc.com/ cgi-bin/com_supopp/C00068692; FEC Disclosure Report, Search Results for Association of Trial Lawyers of America Political Action Committee (June 20, 2001), http://herndon1.sdrdc.com/cgi-bin/com_supopp/ C00024521; FEC Disclosure Report, Search Results for Philip Morris Companies, Inc., Political Action Committee (June 20, 2001), http://herndon1.sdrdc.com/cgi-bin/com_supopp/C00089136; FEC Disclosure Report Search Results for American Medical Association Political Action Committee (June 20, 2001), http:// herndon1.sdrdc.com/cgi- bin/com_supopp/ C00000422; FEC Disclosure Report, Search Results for Letter Carriers Political Action Fund (June 20, 2001), http:// herndon1.sdrdc.com/cgi-bin/com_supopp/C00023580.

[13] For example, the PACs associated with AOL Time Warner Inc. and Philip Morris Companies, Inc., both made contributions to the competing 2000 Senate campaigns of George Allen and Charles Robb. See FEC Disclosure Report, Search Results for AOL Time Warner Inc. Political Action Committee (June 20, 2001), http:// herndon1.sdrdc.com/cgi-bin/com_supopp/C00339291; FEC Disclosure Report, Search Results for Philip Morris Companies, Inc., Political Action Committee (June 20, 2001), http:// herndon1.sdrdc.com/cgi-bin/com_supopp/C00089136.

[14] We have long recognized Congress's concern with this reality of political life. For example, in *United States* v. *Automobile Workers*, 352 U.S. 567 (1957), Justice Frankfurther recounted Senator Robinson's explanation for the Federal Corrupt Practices Act's restriction of corporate campaign contributions:
"We all know . . . that one of the great political evils of the time is the apparent hold on political parties which business interests and certain organizations seek and sometimes obtain by reason of liberal campaign contributions. Many believe that when an individual or association of individuals makes large contributions for the purpose of aiding candidates of political parties in winning the elections, they expect, and sometimes demand, and occasionally, at least, receive, consideration by the beneficiaries of their contributions which not infrequently is harmful to the general public interest." Id. at 576 (quoting 65 Cong. Rec. 9507-9508 (1924)).

with other self-interested political actors, that the Party Expenditure Provision targets. This party role, accordingly, provides good reason to view limits on coordinated spending by parties through the same lens applied to such spending by donors, like PACs, that can use parties as conduits for contributions meant to place candidates under obligation. [453]

3   Insofar as the Party suggests that its strong working relationship with candidates and its unique ability to speak in coordination with them should be taken into account in the First Amendment analysis, we agree. It is the accepted understanding that a party combines its members' power to speak by aggregating contributions and broadcasting messages more widely than individual contributors generally could afford to do, and the party marshals this power with greater sophistication than individuals generally could, using such mechanisms as speech coordinated with a candidate. In other words, the party is efficient in generating large sums to spend and in pinpointing effective ways to spend them. Cf. *Colorado I*, 518 U.S. at 637 (THOMAS, J., concurring in judgment and dissenting in part) ("Political associations allow citizens to pool their resources and make their advocacy more effective").

[1C] [3B] It does not, however, follow from a party's efficiency in getting large sums and spending intelligently that limits on a party's coordinated spending should be scrutinized under an unusually high standard, and in fact any argument from sophistication and power would cut both ways. On the one hand, one can seek the benefit of stricter scrutiny of a law capping party coordinated spending by emphasizing the heavy burden imposed by limiting the most effective mechanism of sophisticated spending. And yet it is exactly this efficiency culminating in coordinated spending that (on the Government's view) places a party in a position to be used to circumvent contribution limits that apply to individuals and PACs, and thereby to exacerbate the threat of corruption and apparent corruption that those contribution limits are aimed at reducing. As a consequence, what the Party calls an unusual burden imposed by regulating its spending is not a simple premise for arguing for tighter scrutiny of limits on a party; it is the premise for a question pointing in [454] the opposite direction. If the coordinated spending of other, less efficient and perhaps less practiced political actors can be limited consistently with the Constitution, why would the Constitution forbid regulation aimed at a party whose very efficiency in channeling benefits to candidates threatens to undermine the contribution (and hence coordinated spending) limits to which those others are unquestionably subject?

4   [1D][4A] The preceding question assumes that parties enjoy a power and experience that sets them apart from other political spenders. But in fact

the assumption is too crude. While parties command bigger spending budgets than most individuals, some individuals could easily rival party committees in spending. Rich political activists crop up, and the United States has known its Citizens Kane. Their money speaks loudly, too, and they are therefore burdened by restrictions on its use just as parties are. And yet they are validly subject to coordinated spending limits, *Buckley*, 424 U.S. at 46-47, and so are PACs, id. at 35-36, 46-47, which may amass bigger treasuries than most party members can spare for politics.[15]

[1E] [4B] Just as rich donors, media executives, and PACs have the means to speak as loudly as parties do, they would also have the capacity to work effectively in tandem with a candidate, just as a party can do. While a candidate has no way of coordinating spending with every contributor, there is nothing hard about coordinating with someone with a fortune to donate, any more than a candidate would have difficulty in coordinating spending with an inner circle of personal political associates or with his own family. Yet all of them are [455] subject to coordinated spending limits upheld in *Buckley, supra,* at 53, n. 59. A party, indeed, is now like some of these political actors in yet another way: in its right under *Colorado I* to spend money in support of a candidate without legal limit so long as it spends independently. A party may spend independently every cent it can raise wherever it thinks its candidate will shine, on every subject and any viewpoint.

[1F] A party is not, therefore, in a unique position. It is in the same position as some individuals and PACs, as to whom coordinated spending limits have already been held valid, *Buckley, supra,* at 46-47; and, indeed, a party is better off, for a party has the special privilege the others do not enjoy, of making coordinated expenditures up to the limit of the Party Expenditure Provision.[16]

5   The Party's arguments for being treated differently from other political actors subject to limitation on political spending under the Act do not pan out. Despite decades of limitation on coordinated spending, parties have not been rendered useless. In reality, parties continue to organize to elect candidates, and also function for the benefit of

---

[15] By noting that other political actors are validly burdened by limitations on their coordinated spending, we do not mean to take a position as to the wisdom of policies that promote one source of campaign funding or another. Cf. Brief for Respondent 27, n. 17 (citing academic support for expanding the role of parties in campaign finance).

[16] This is the position of the FEC in the aftermath of *Colorado I*: that a party committee may make coordinated expenditures up to the amount of its expenditure limit, in addition to the amount of direct contributions permitted by the generally applicable contribution limit. Brief for Petitioner 5-6, and n. 3.

donors whose object is to place candidates under obligation, a fact that parties cannot escape. Indeed, parties' capacity to concentrate power to elect is the very capacity that apparently opens them to exploitation as channels for circumventing contribution and coordinated spending limits binding on other political players. And some of these players could marshal the same power and sophistication for the same electoral objectives as political parties themselves.

[456] [1G] [3C] [5A] We accordingly apply to a party's coordinated spending limitation the same scrutiny we have applied to the other political actors, that is, scrutiny appropriate for a contribution limit, enquiring whether the restriction is "closely drawn" to match what we have recognized as the "sufficiently important" government interest in combating political corruption. *Shrink Missouri*, 528 U.S. at 387-388 (quoting *Buckley, supra*, at 25, 30).[17] With the standard thus settled, the issue remains whether adequate evidentiary grounds exist to sustain the limit under that standard, on the theory that unlimited coordinated spending by a party raises the risk of corruption (and its appearance) through circumvention of valid contribution limits. Indeed, all members of the Court agree that circumvention is a valid theory of corruption; the remaining bone of contention is evidentiary.[18] [5B][457]

B   [1H] Since there is no recent experience with unlimited coordinated spending, the question is

whether experience under the present law confirms a serious threat of abuse from the unlimited coordinated party spending as the Government contends. Cf. *Burson* v. *Freeman*, 504 U.S. 191, 208, 119 L. Ed. 2d 5, 112 S. Ct. 1846 (1992) (opinion of Blackmun, J.) (noting difficulty of mustering evidence to support long-enforced statutes). It clearly does. Despite years of enforcement of the challenged limits, substantial evidence demonstrates how candidates, donors, and parties test the limits of the current law, and it shows beyond serious doubt how contribution limits would be eroded if inducement to circumvent them were enhanced by declaring parties' coordinated spending wide open.[19]

[458] Under the Act, a donor is limited to $2,000 in contributions to one candidate in a given election cycle. The same donor may give as much as another $20,000 each year to a national party committee supporting the candidate.[20] What a realist would expect to occur has occurred. Donors give to the party with the tacit understanding that the favored candidate will benefit. See App. 247 (Declaration of Robert Hickmott, former Democratic fundraiser and National Finance Director for Timothy Wirth's Senate campaign) ("We . . . told contributors who had made the maximum allowable contribution to the Wirth campaign but who wanted to do more that they could raise money for the DSCC so that we could get our maximum [Party Expenditure Provision] allocation from the DSCC"); id. at 274 (declaration of Timothy Wirth) ("I understood that when I raised

---

[17] Whether a different characterization, and hence a different type of scrutiny, could be appropriate in the context of an as-applied challenge focused on application of the limit to specific expenditures is a question that, as JUSTICE THOMAS notes, *post*, at 4, n. 2, we need not reach in this facial challenge. Cf. Brief for Petitioner at 9, n. 5 (noting that the FEC has solicited comments regarding possible criteria for identifying coordinated expenditures).

The Party appears to argue that even if the Party Expenditure Provision is justified with regard to coordinated expenditures that amount to no more than payment of the candidate's bills, the limitation is facially invalid because of its potential application to expenditures that involve more of the party's own speech. Brief for Respondent 48-49. But the Party does not tell us what proportion of the spending falls in one category or the other, or otherwise lay the groundwork for its facial overbreadth claim. Cf. *Broadrick* v. *Oklahoma*, 413 U.S. 601, 37 L. Ed. 2d 830, 93 S. Ct. 2908 (1973) (overbreadth must be substantial to trigger facial invalidation).

[18] Apart from circumvention, the FEC also argues that the Party Expenditure Provision is justified by a concern with *quid pro quo* arrangements and similar corrupting relationships between candidates and parties themselves, see Brief for Petitioner 33-38. We find no need to reach that argument because the evidence supports the long-recognized rationale of combating circumvention of contribution limits designed to combat the corrupting influence of large contributions to candidates from individuals and nonparty groups. The dissent does not take issue with this justification as a theoretical matter. See also 213 F.3d 1221, 1232 (CA10 2000) (Court of Appeals acknowledging circumvention as a possible "avenue of abuse").

[19] In *Colorado I*, the principal opinion suggested that the Party Expenditure Provision was not enacted out of "a special concern about the potentially 'corrupting' effect of party expenditures, but rather for the constitutionally insufficient purpose of reducing what [Congress] saw as wasteful and excessive campaign spending." *Colorado I*, 518 U.S. at 618. That observation was relevant to our examination of the Party Expenditure Provision as applied to independent expenditures, see id. at 617-618, limits on which were invalidated with regard to other political actors in *Buckley* in part because they were justified by concern with wasteful campaign spending, *Buckley*, 424 U.S. at 57. Our point in *Colorado I* was that there was no evidence that Congress had a special motivation regarding parties that would justify limiting their independent expenditures after similar limits imposed on other spenders had been invalidated. As for the Party Expenditure Provision's application to coordinated expenditures, on the other hand, the evidence discussed in the text suggests that the anti-circumvention rationale that justifies other coordinated expenditure limits, see *Buckley, supra*, at 46-47, is at work here as well. The dissent ignores this distinction, *post*, at 11-12, but neither the dissent nor the Party seriously argues that Congress was not concerned with circumvention of contribution limits using parties as conduits. All acknowledge that Congress enacted other measures prompted by just that concern. See *post*, at 18; Brief for Respondent 41-42 ("FECA provides interlocking multi-layered provisions designed to prevent circumvention").

[20] See n. 7, *supra*; see generally Federal Election Commission, Campaign Guide for Congressional Candidates and Committees 10 (1999).

funds for the DSCC, the donors expected that I would receive the amount of their donations multiplied by a certain number that the DSCC had determined in advance, assuming the DSCC has raised other funds"); id. at 166 (declaration of Leon G. Billings, former Executive Director of the Democratic Senatorial Campaign Committee (DSCC)) ("People often contribute to party committees because they have given the maximum amount to a candidate, and want to help the candidate indirectly by contributing to the party"); id. at 99-100 (fundraising letter from Congressman Wayne Allard, dated Aug. 27, 1996, explaining to contributor that "you are at the limit of what you can directly contribute to my campaign," but "you can further help my campaign by assisting the Colorado Republican Party").[21]

[459] Although the understanding between donor and party may involve no definite commitment and may be tacit on the donor's part, the frequency of the practice and the volume of money involved has required some manner of informal bookkeeping by the recipient. In the Democratic Party, at least, the method is known as "tallying," a system that helps to connect donors to candidates through the accommodation of a party. See App. 246-247 (Hickmott declaration) ("[The tally system] is an informal agreement between the DSCC and the candidates' campaigns that if you help the DSCC raise contributions, we will turn around and help your campaign"); id. at 268 (declaration of former Senator Paul Simon) ("Donors would be told the money they contributed could be credited to any Senate candidate. The callers would make clear that this was not a direct contribution, but it was fairly close to direct"); id. at 165-166 (Billings declaration) ("There appeared to be an understanding between the DSCC and the Senators that the amount of money they received from the DSCC was related to how much they raised for the Committee").[22]

Such is the state of affairs under the current law, which requires most party spending on a candidate's behalf to be [460] done independently, and thus less desirably from the point of view of a donor and his favored candidate. If suddenly every dollar of spending could be coordinated with the candidate, the inducement to circumvent would almost certainly intensify. Indeed, if a candidate could be assured that donations through a party could result in funds passed through to him for spending on virtually identical items as his own campaign funds, a candidate enjoying the patronage of affluent contributors would have a strong incentive not merely to direct donors to his party, but to promote circumvention as a step toward reducing the number of donors requiring time-consuming cultivation. If a candidate could arrange for a party committee to foot his bills, to be paid with $20,000 contributions to the party by his supporters, the number of donors necessary to raise $1,000,000 could be reduced from 500 (at $2,000 per cycle) to 46 (at $2,000 to the candidate and $20,000 to the party, without regard to donations outside the election year).[23] [461]

---

quotations attest. See also n. 23, *infra*. And the fact that the parties may not fund sure losers, stressed by the dissent (*post*, at 15), is irrelevant. The issue is what would become of contribution limits if parties could use unlimited coordinated spending to funnel contributions to those serious contenders who are favored by the donors.

[23] Any such dollar-for-dollar pass-through would presumably be too obvious to escape the special provision on earmarking, 2 U.S.C. § 441a(a)(8), see *infra*, at 27. But the example illustrates the undeniable inducement to more subtle circumvention.

The same enhanced value of coordinated spending that could be expected to promote greater circumvention of contribution limits for the benefit of the candidate-fundraiser would probably enhance the power of the fundraiser to use circumvention as a tactic to increase personal power and a claim to party leadership. The affluent nominee can already do this to a limited extent, by directing donations to the party and making sure that the party knows who raised the money, and that the needier candidates who receive the benefit of party spending know whom to thank. The candidate can thus become a player beyond his own race, and the donor's influence is multiplied. See generally App. 249 (Hickmott declaration) ("Incumbents who were not raising money for themselves because they were not up for reelection would sometimes raise money for other Senators, or for challengers. They would send $20,000 to the DSCC and ask that this be entered on another candidate's tally. They might do this, for example, if they were planning to run for a leadership position and wanted to obtain the support of the Senators they assisted"). If the effectiveness of party spending could be enhanced by limitless coordination, the ties of straitened candidates to prosperous ones and, vicariously, to large donors would be reinforced as well. Party officials who control distribution of coordinated expenditures would obviously form an additional link in this chain. See id. at 164, 168 (Billings declaration) ("[The DSCC's three-member Executive Committee] basically made the decisions as to how to distribute the money.... Taking away the limits on

---

[21] Contrary to the dissent's suggestion, *post*, at 14, we are not closing our eyes to District Court findings rejecting this record evidence. After alluding to the evidence cited above, 41 F. Supp. 2d 1197, 1203-1204 (Colo. 1999), and concluding that it did not support theories of corruption that we do not address here, see id. at 1211; n. 18, *supra*, the District Court mistakenly concluded that *Colorado I* had rejected the anti-circumvention rationale as a matter of law, 41 F. Supp. 2d at 1211, n. 9. We explain below, *infra*, at 28-30, why *Colorado I*'s rejection of the anti-circumvention rationale in the context of limits applied to independent party expenditures does not control the outcome of this case.

[22] The dissent dismisses this evidence as describing "legal" practices. *Post*, at 15-16. The dissent may be correct that the FEC considers tallying legal, see Reply Brief for Petitioner 9, n. 3, but one thing is clear: tallying is a sign that contribution limits are being diluted and could be diluted further if the floodgates were open. Why, after all, does a party bother to tally? The obvious answer is that it wants to know who gets the benefit of the contributions to the party, as the record

V.   [1I] While this evidence rules out denying the potential for corruption by circumvention, the Party does try to minimize the threat. It says that most contributions to parties are small, with negligible corrupting momentum to be carried through the party conduit. Brief for Respondent 14. But some contributions are not small; they can go up to $20,000, 2 U.S.C. § 441a(a)(1)(B),[24] and the record shows that even under present law substantial donations turn the parties into matchmakers whose special meetings and receptions give the donors the chance to get their points across to the candidates.[25] The Party again discounts the threat of outflanking contribution limits on individuals and nonparty groups by stressing that incumbent candidates give more excess campaign funds to parties than parties spend on coordinated expenditures. Brief for Respondent 34. But the fact that parties may do well for themselves off incumbents does not defuse concern over circumvention; if contributions to a party were not used as a funnel from donors to candidates, there would be no reason for using the tallying system the way the witnesses have described it.

[462] Finally, the Party falls back to claiming that, even if there is a threat of circumvention, the First Amendment demands a response better tailored to that threat than a limitation on spending, even coordinated spending. Brief for Respondent 46-48. The Party has two suggestions.

First, it says that better crafted safeguards are in place already, in particular the earmarking rule of § 441a(a)(8), which provides that contributions that "are in any way earmarked or otherwise directed through an intermediary or conduit to [a] candidate" are treated as contributions to the candidate. The Party says that this provision either suffices to address any risk of circumvention or would suffice if clarified to cover practices like tallying. Brief for Respondent 42, 47; see also 213 F.2d at 1232. This position, however, ignores the practical difficulty of identifying and directly combating circumvention under actual political conditions. Donations are made to a party by contributors who favor the party's candidates in races that affect them; donors are (of course) permitted to express their views and preferences to party officials; and the party is permitted (as we have held it must be) to spend money in its own right. When this is the environment for contributions going into a general party treasury, and candidate-fundraisers are rewarded with something less obvious than dollar-for-dollar pass-throughs (distributed through contributions and party spending), circumvention is obviously very hard to trace. The earmarking provision, even if it dealt directly with tallying, would reach only the most clumsy attempts to pass contributions through to candidates. To treat the earmarking provision as the outer limit of acceptable tailoring would disarm any serious effort to limit the corrosive effects of what Chief Judge Seymour called "'understandings' regarding what donors give what amounts to the party, which candidates are to receive what funds from the party, and what interests particular donors are seeking to promote," 213 F.3d at 1241 (dissenting opinion); see also Briffault, Political Parties and Campaign Finance Reform, [463] 100 Colum. L. Rev 620, 652 (2000) (describing "web of relations linking major donors, party committees, and elected officials").[26]

The Party's second preferred prescription for the threat of an end run calls for replacing limits on coordinated expenditures by parties with limits on contributions to parties, the latter supposedly imposing a lesser First Amendment burden. Brief for Respondent 46-48. The Party thus invokes the general rule that contribution limits take a lesser First Amendment toll, expenditure limits a greater one. That was one strand of the reasoning in Buckley itself, which rejected the argument that limitations on independent expenditures by individuals, groups, and candidates were justifiable in order to avoid circumvention of contribution limitations. Buckley, 424 U.S. at 44. It was also one strand of the logic of the Colorado I principal opinion in rejecting the Party Expenditure Provision's application to independent party expenditures. 518 U.S. at 617.[27]

In each of those cases, however, the Court's reasoning contained another strand. The analysis ultimately turned on the understanding that the expenditures at issue were not potential alter egos for contributions, but were independent and therefore functionally true expenditures, qualifying for the

---

coordinated expenditures would result in a fundamental transferal of power to certain individual Senators").

[24] In 1996, 46 percent of itemized (over $200) individual contributions to the Democratic national party committees and 15 percent of such contributions to the Republican national party committees were $10,000 or more. Biersack & Haskell, Spitting on the Umpire: Political Parties, the Federal Election Campaign Act, and the 1996 Campaigns, in Financing the 1996 Election 155, 160 (J. Green ed. 1999).

[25] For example, the DSCC has established exclusive clubs for the most generous donors, who are invited to special meetings and social events with Senators and candidates. App. 254-255 (Hickmott declaration).

[26] The Party's argument for relying on better earmarking enforcement, accepted by the dissent, post, at 18, would invite a corresponding attack on all contribution limits. As we said in Buckley, 424 U.S. at 27-28, and Shrink Missouri, 528 U.S. at 390, the policy supporting contribution limits is the same as for laws against bribery. But we do not throw out the contribution limits for unskillful tailoring; prohibitions on bribery, like the earmarking provision here, address only the "most blatant and specific" attempts at corruption, id. at 28.

[27] The dissent therefore suggests, post, at 19, and the District Court mistakenly concluded, see discussion n. 21, supra, that Colorado I disposed of the tailoring question for purposes of this case.

most demanding First Amendment scrutiny employed in *Buckley. Colorado I, supra,* at 617; *Buckley, supra,* at 44-47. Thus, in *Colorado I* we could not assume, "absent [464] convincing evidence to the contrary," that the Party's independent expenditures formed a link in a chain of corruption-by-conduit. 518 U.S. at 617. "The absence of prearrangement and coordination of an expenditure with the candidate or his agent not only undermines the value of the expenditure to the candidate, but also alleviates the danger that expenditures will be given as a *quid pro quo* for improper commitments from the candidate," *Buckley, supra,* at 47; therefore, "the constitutionally significant fact" in *Colorado I* was "the lack of coordination between the candidate and the source of the expenditure," 518 U.S. at 617.

Here, however, just the opposite is true. There is no significant functional difference between a party's coordinated expenditure and a direct party contribution to the candidate, and there is good reason to expect that a party's right of unlimited coordinated spending would attract increased contributions to parties to finance exactly that kind of spending.[28] Coordinated expenditures of money donated to a party are tailor-made to undermine contribution limits. Therefore the choice here is not, as in *Buckley* and *Colorado I,* between a limit on pure contributions and pure expenditures.[29] The choice is between limiting contributions and [465] limiting expenditures whose special value as expenditures is also the source of their power to corrupt. Congress is entitled to its choice.

* * *

We hold that a party's coordinated expenditures, unlike expenditures truly independent, may be restricted to minimize circumvention of contribution limits. We therefore reject the Party's facial challenge and, accordingly, reverse the judgment of the United States Court of Appeals for the Tenth Circuit.

It is so ordered.

DISSENT: JUSTICE THOMAS, with whom JUSTICE SCALIA and JUSTICE KENNEDY join, and with whom THE CHIEF JUSTICE joins as to Part II, dissenting.

The Party Expenditure Provision, 2 U.S.C. § 441a(d)(3), severely limits the amount of money that a national or state committee of a political party can spend in coordination with its own candidate for the Senate or House of Representatives. See, *ante,* at 3, and n. 3. Because this provision sweeps too broadly, interferes with the party-candidate relationship, and has not been proved necessary to combat corruption, I respectfully dissent.

I.   As an initial matter, I continue to believe that *Buckley* v. *Valeo,* 424 U.S. 1, 46 L. Ed. 2d 659, 96 S. Ct. 612 (1976) *(per curiam),* should be overruled. See *Nixon* v. *Shrink Missouri Government PAC,* 528 U.S. 377, 410, 145 L. Ed. 2d 886, 120 S. Ct. 897 (2000) (THOMAS, J., dissenting); *Colorado Republican Federal Campaign Comm.* v. *Federal Election Comm'n,* 518 U.S. 604, 631, 135 L. Ed. 2d 795, 116 S. Ct. 2309 (1996) *(Colorado I)* (THOMAS, J., concurring in judgment and dissenting in part). "Political speech is the primary object of First Amendment protection," *Shrink Missouri, supra,* at 410-411 (THOMAS, J., dissenting); see also *Eu* v. *San Francisco County Democratic Central* [466] *Comm.,* 489 U.S. 214, 223, 103 L. Ed. 2d 271, 109 S. Ct. 1013 (1989); *Mills* v. *Alabama,* 384 U.S. 214, 218, 16 L. Ed. 2d 484, 86 S. Ct. 1434 (1966), and it is the lifeblood of a self-governing people, see *Shrink Missouri, supra,* at 405 (KENNEDY, J., dissenting) ("Political speech in the course of elections [is] the speech upon which democracy depends"). I remain baffled that this Court has extended the most generous First Amendment safeguards to filing lawsuits, wearing profane jackets, and exhibiting drive-in movies with

---

[28] The dissent notes a superficial tension between this analysis and our recent statement in *Bartnicki* v. *Vopper,* 532 U.S. (2001), that "it would be quite remarkable to hold that speech by a law-abiding [entity] can be suppressed in order to deter conduct by a non-law-abiding third party," id. at __ (slip op., at 14). Unlike *Bartnicki,* there is no clear dichotomy here between law abider and lawbreaker. The problem of circumvention is a systemic one, accomplished only through complicity between donor and party.

[29] Also, again, contrast *Bartnicki,* where the gulf between the First Amendment implications of two enforcement options was clear. We rejected the decision to penalize disclosure of lawfully obtained information of public interest instead of vigorously enforcing prohibitions on intercepting private conversations. *Ibid.*

nudity,[1] but has offered only tepid protection to the core speech and associational rights that our Founders sought to defend.

In this case, the Government does not attempt to argue that the Party Expenditure Provision satisfies strict scrutiny, see *Perry Ed. Assn.* v. *Perry Local Educators' Assn.*, 460 U.S. 37, 45, 74 L. Ed. 2d 794, 103 S. Ct. 948 (1983) (providing that, under strict scrutiny, a restriction on speech is constitutional only if it is narrowly tailored to serve a compelling governmental interest). Nor could it. For the reasons explained in my separate opinions in *Colorado I*, *supra*, at 641-644, and *Shrink Missouri*, *supra*, at 427-430, the campaign financing law at issue fails strict scrutiny.

II. We need not, however, overrule *Buckley* and apply strict scrutiny in order to hold the Party Expenditure Provision unconstitutional. Even under *Buckley*, which described the requisite scrutiny as "exacting" and "rigorous," 424 U.S. at 16, 29, the regulation cannot pass constitutional muster. In practice, *Buckley* scrutiny has meant that restrictions on contributions by individuals and political committees do not violate the First Amendment so long as they are "closely drawn" to match a "sufficiently important" government interest, *Shrink Missouri*, *supra*, at 387-389; see also *Buckley*, *supra*, at 58, but that restrictions on independent expenditures [467] are constitutionally invalid, see *Buckley*, *supra*, at 58-59; see also *Federal Election Comm'n* v. *National Conservative Political Action Comm.*, 470 U.S. 480, 501, 84 L. Ed. 2d 455, 105 S. Ct. 1459 (1985). The rationale for this distinction between contributions and independent expenditures has been that, whereas ceilings on contributions by individuals and political committees "entail only a marginal restriction" on First Amendment interests, *Buckley*, 424 U.S. at 20, limitations on independent expenditures "impose significantly more severe restrictions on protected freedoms of political expression and association." Id. at 23.

A The Court notes this existing rationale and attempts simply to treat coordinated expenditures by political parties as equivalent to contributions by individuals and political committees. Thus, at least implicitly, the Court draws two conclusions: coordinated expenditures are no different from contributions, and political parties are no different from individuals and political committees. Both conclusions are flawed.

1 The Court considers a coordinated expenditure to be an "'expenditure made by any person in cooperation, consultation, or concert, with, or at the request or suggestion of, a candidate, his

authorized political committees, or their agents.'" *Ante*, at 2 (quoting 2 U.S.C. § 441a(a)(7)(B)(i)). This definition covers a broad array of conduct, some of which is akin to an independent expenditure. At one extreme, to be sure, are outlays that are "virtually indistinguishable from simple contributions." *Colorado I*, 518 U.S. at 624 (opinion of BREYER, J.). An example would be "a donation of money with direct payment of a candidate's media bills." *Ibid.* But toward the other end of the spectrum are expenditures that largely resemble, and should be entitled to the same protection as, independent expenditures. [468] Take, for example, a situation in which the party develops a television advertising campaign touting a candidate's record on education, and the party simply "consults," 2 U.S.C. § 441a(a)(7)(B)(i), with the candidate on which time slot the advertisement should run for maximum effectiveness. I see no constitutional difference between this expenditure and a purely independent one. In the language of *Buckley*, the advertising campaign is not a mere "general expression of support for the candidate and his views," but a communication of "the underlying basis for the support." 424 U.S. at 21. It is not just "symbolic expression," *ibid.* but a clear manifestation of the party's most fundamental political views. By restricting such speech, the Party Expenditure Provision undermines parties' "freedom to discuss candidates and issues," *ibid.* and cannot be reconciled with our campaign finance jurisprudence.

2 Even if I were to ignore the breadth of the statutory text, and to assume that all coordinated expenditures are functionally equivalent to contributions,[2] I still would strike down the Party Expenditure Provision. The source of the "contribution" at issue is a political party, not an individual or a political committee, as in *Buckley* and *Shrink Missouri*. [469] Restricting contributions by individuals and political committees may, under *Buckley*, entail only a "marginal restriction," *Buckley*, *supra*, at 20, but the same cannot be said about limitations on political parties.

---

[1] *NAACP* v. *Button*, 371 U.S. 415, 444, 9 L. Ed. 2d 405, 83 S. Ct. 328 (1963); *Cohen* v. *California*, 403 U.S. 15, 26, 29 L. Ed. 2d 284, 91 S. Ct. 1780 (1971); *Erznoznik* v. *Jacksonville*, 422 U.S. 205, 208-215, 45 L. Ed. 2d 125, 95 S. Ct. 2268 (1975).

[2] The Court makes this very assumption. See *ante*, at 29 ("There is no significant functional difference between a party's coordinated expenditure and a direct party contribution to the candidate"). To the extent the Court has not defined the universe of coordinated expenditures and leaves open the possibility that there are such expenditures that would not be functionally identical to direct contributions, the constitutionality of the Party Expenditure Provision as applied to such expenditures remains unresolved. See, *e.g.*, *ante*, at 21, n. 17. At oral argument, the Government appeared to suggest that the Party Expenditure Provision might not reach expenditures that are not functionally identical to contributions. See Tr. of Oral Arg. 15 (stating that the purpose of the Party Expenditure Provision is simply to prevent someone "from making contributions in the form of paying the candidate's bills").

Political parties and their candidates are "inextricably intertwined" in the conduct of an election. *Colorado I, supra,* at 630 (KENNEDY, J., concurring in judgment and dissenting in part). A party nominates its candidate; a candidate often is identified by party affiliation throughout the election and on the ballot; and a party's public image is largely defined by what its candidates say and do. See, *e.g., California Democratic Party* v. *Jones,* 530 U.S. 567, 575, 147 L. Ed. 2d 502, 120 S. Ct. 2402 (2000) ("Some political parties -- such as President Theodore Roosevelt's Bull Moose Party, the La Follette Progressives of 1924, the Henry Wallace Progressives of 1948, and the George Wallace American Independent Party of 1968 – are virtually inseparable from their nominees (and tend not to outlast them"); see also M. Zak, Back to Basics for the Republican Party 1 (2000) (noting that the Republican Party has been identified as the "Party of Lincoln"). Most importantly, a party's success or failure depends in large part on whether its candidates get elected. Because of this unity of interest, it is natural for a party and its candidate to work together and consult with one another during the course of the election. See, *e.g.,* App. 137 (declaration of Herbert E. Alexander, Director of the Citizens' Research Foundation at the University of Southern California). Indeed, "it would be impractical and imprudent . . . for a party to support its own candidates without some form of 'cooperation' or 'consultation.'" See *Colorado I,* 518 U.S. at 630 (KENNEDY, J., concurring in judgment and dissenting in part). "Candidates are necessary to make the party's message known and effective, and vice versa." Id. at 629. Thus, the ordinary means for a party to provide support is to make coordinated expenditures, see, *e.g.,* App. 137-138 (declaration of Herbert E. Alexander), as the Government itself maintained just five years ago, see [470] Brief for Respondent in *Colorado I,* O. T. 1995, No. 95-489, p. 27 (contending that Congress had made an "empirical judgment that party officials will as a matter of course consult with the party's candidates before funding communications intended to influence the outcome of a federal election"); see also FEC Advisory Opinion 1985-14, CCH Fed. Election Camp. Fin. Guide P5819, p. 11,186, n. 4 (1985) ("Party political committees are incapable of making independent expenditures").

As the District Court explained, to break this link between the party and its candidates would impose "additional costs and burdens to promote the party message." 41 F. Supp. 2d 1197, 1210 (Colo. 1999). This observation finds full support in the record. See, *e.g.,* App. 218 (statement of Anthony Corrado, Associate Professor of Government, Colby College) (explaining that, to ensure that expenditures were

independent, party organizations had to establish legally separate entities, which in turn had to "rent and furnish an office, hire staff, and pay other administrative costs," as well as "engage additional consulting services" and "duplicate many of the functions already being undertaken by other party offices"); id. at 52 (statement by Federal Election Commission admitting that national party established separate entities that made independent expenditures); id. at 217 (statement of Anthony Corrado) (explaining that reliance on independent expenditures would increase fundraising demands on party organizations because independent expenditures are less effective means of communication); id. at 219 ("Independent expenditures do not qualify for the lowest unit rates on the purchase of broadcasting time"); App. in No. 99-1211 (CA10), p. 512 (report of Frank J. Sorauf, professor at University of Minnesota, and Jonathan S. Krasno, professor at Princeton University) (noting inefficiency of independent expenditures).

Establishing and maintaining independence also tends to create voter confusion and to undermine the candidate that the party sought to support. App. 220 (statement of Anthony Corrado); App. in No. 99-1211 (CA10), at 623-624 [471] deposition of John Heubusch); App. 159 (affidavit of Donald K. Bain) ("Our communications can be more focused, understandable, and effective if the Party and its candidates can work together"). Finally, because of the ambiguity in the term "coordinated expenditure," the Party Expenditure Provision chills permissible speech as well. See, *e.g.,* id. at 159-160 (affidavit of Donald K. Bain). Thus, far from being a mere "marginal" restraint on speech, *Buckley,* 424 U.S. at 20, the Party Expenditure Provision has restricted the party's most natural form of communication; has precluded parties "from effectively amplifying the voice of their adherents," id. at 22; and has had a "stifling effect on the ability of the party to do what it exists to do."[3] *Colorado I,* 518 U.S. at 630

---

[3] The Court contends that, notwithstanding this burden, "it is nonetheless *possible* for parties, like individuals and nonparty groups, to speak independently." *Ante,* at 15, n. 11 (emphasis added). That is correct, but it does not render the restriction constitutional. If Congress were to pass a law imposing a $1,000 tax on every political newspaper editorial, the law would surely constitute an unconstitutional restraint on speech, even though it would still be *possible* for newspapers to print such editorials.

The Court's holding presents an additional First Amendment problem. Because of the close relationship between parties and candidates, lower courts will face a difficult, if not insurmountable, task in trying to determine whether particular party expenditures are in fact coordinated or independent. As the American Civil Liberties Union points out, "even if such an inquiry is feasible, it inevitably would involve an intrusive and constitutionally troubling investigation of the inner

(KENNEDY, J., concurring in judgment and dissenting in part).

The Court nevertheless concludes that these concerns of inhibiting party speech are rendered "implausible" by the nearly 30 years of history in which coordinated spending has been statutorily limited. *Ante*, at 14. Without a single citation to the record, the Court rejects the assertion "that for almost three decades political parties have not been functional [472] or have been functioning in systematic violation of the law." *Ibid.* I am unpersuaded by the Court's attempts to downplay the extent of the burden on political parties' First Amendment rights. First, the Court does not examine the record or the findings of the District Court, but instead relies wholly on the "observations" of the "political scientists" who happen to have written an *amicus* brief in support of the petitioner. *Ibid.* I find more convincing, and more relevant, the record evidence that the parties have developed, which, as noted above, indicates that parties have suffered as a result of the Party Expenditure Provision.[4] See, *supra*, at 6-7. Second, we have never before upheld a limitation on speech simply because speakers have coped with the limitation for 30 years. See, *e.g.*, *Bartnicki* v. *Vopper*, 532 U.S. ___, ___ (2001) (slip op., at 1-2) (holding unconstitutional under the First Amendment restrictions on the disclosure of the contents of an illegally intercepted communication, even though federal law had prohibited such disclosure for 67 years). And finally, if the passage of time were relevant to the constitutional inquiry, I would wonder why the Court adopted [473] a "30-year" rule rather than the possible countervailing "200-year" rule. For nearly 200 years, this country had congressional elections without limitations on coordinated expenditures by political parties.

---

workings of political parties." Brief for American Civil Liberties Union et al. as *Amici Curiae* 18.

[4] Moreover, were I to depart from the record, as does the Court, I could consider sources suggesting that parties in fact have lost power in recent years. See, *e.g.*, M. Wattenberg, The Decline of American Political Parties, 1952-1996, p. 174 (1998) (indicating that percentage of voters who identify with a party has declined while percentage of split tickets has increased); Maisel, American Political Parties: Still Central to a Functioning Democracy?, in American Political Parties: Decline or Resurgence?, 103, 107-111 (J. Cohen, R. Fleisher, & P. Kantor eds. 2001) (describing weaknesses of modern political parties). I also could explore how political parties have coped with the restrictions on coordinated expenditures. As JUSTICE KENNEDY has explained, "the Court has forced a substantial amount of political speech underground, as contributors and candidates devise ever more elaborate methods of avoiding contribution limits." *Nixon* v. *Shrink Missouri Government PAC*, 528 U.S. 377, 406, 145 L. Ed. 2d 886, 120 S. Ct. 897 (2000) (dissenting opinion). Perhaps political parties have survived, not because the regulation at issue imposes less than a substantial burden on speech, but simply because the parties have found "underground" alternatives for communication.

Nowhere does the Court suggest that these elections were not "functional," *ante*, at 14, or that they were marred by corruption.

The Court's only other response to the argument that parties are linked to candidates and that breaking this link would impose significant costs on speech is no response at all. The Court contends that parties are not organized simply to "elect particular candidates" as evidenced by the fact that many political action committees donate money to both parties and sometimes even opposing candidates. *Ante*, at 15. According to the Court, "parties are thus necessarily the instruments of some contributors whose object is not to support the party's message or to elect party candidates across the board." Id. at 16-17. There are two flaws in the Court's analysis. First, no one argues that a party's role is merely to get particular candidates elected. Surely, among other reasons, parties also exist to develop and promote a platform. See, *e.g.*, Brief for Respondent 23.

The point is simply that parties and candidates have shared interests, that it is natural for them to work together, and that breaking the connection between parties and their candidates inhibits the promotion of the party's message. Second, the mere fact that some donors contribute to both parties and their candidates does not necessarily imply that the donors control the parties or their candidates. It certainly does not mean that the parties are mere "instruments" or "agents," *ante*, at 17, of the donors. Indeed, if a party receives money from donors on both sides of an issue, how can it be a tool of both donors? If the Green Party were to receive a donation from an industry that pollutes, would the Green Party necessarily become, through no choice of its own, an instrument of the polluters? The Court proffers no evidence that parties have become pawns of wealthy contributors. [474] Parties might be the target of the speech of donors, but that does not suggest that parties are influenced (let alone improperly influenced) by the speech. Thus, the Court offers no explanation for why political parties should be treated the same as individuals and political committees.

B   But even if I were to view parties' coordinated expenditures as akin to contributions by individuals and political committees, I still would hold the Party Expenditure Provision constitutionally invalid. Under *Shrink Missouri*, a contribution limit is constitutional only if the Government demonstrates that the regulation is "closely drawn" to match a "sufficiently important interest." 528 U.S. at 387-388 (quoting *Buckley*, *supra*, at 25) (internal quotation marks omitted). In this case, there is no question that the Government has asserted a sufficient interest, that of preventing corruption. See *Shrink Missouri*, *supra*, at 388 ("'The prevention of corruption and the appearance of corruption' was found to be a 'constitutionally sufficient justification'") (quoting *Buckley, supra,* at 25-26). The question is whether the Government has demonstrated both that coordinated expenditures by parties give rise to corruption and that the restriction is "closely drawn" to curb this corruption. I believe it has not.

1   As this Court made clear just last Term, "we have never accepted mere conjecture as adequate to carry a First Amendment burden." *Shrink Missouri,* 528 U.S. at 392. Some "quantum of empirical evidence [is] needed to satisfy heightened judicial scrutiny of legislative judgments." Id. at 391. Precisely how much evidence is required will "vary up or down with the novelty and plausibility of the justification raised." *Ibid.* Today, the Court has jettisoned this evidentiary requirement.

[475] Considering that we have never upheld an expenditure limitation against political parties, I would posit that substantial evidence is necessary to justify the infringement of parties' First Amendment interests. But we need not accept this high evidentiary standard to strike down the Party Expenditure Provision for want of evidence. Under the least demanding evidentiary requirement, the Government has failed to carry its burden, for it has presented no evidence at all of corruption or the perception of corruption. The Government does not, and indeed cannot, point to any congressional findings suggesting that the Party Expenditure Provision is necessary, or even helpful, in reducing corruption or the perception of corruption. In fact, this Court has recognized that "Congress wrote the Party Expenditure Provision not so much because of a special concern about the potentially 'corrupting' effect of party expenditures, but rather for the constitutionally insufficient purpose of reducing what it saw as wasteful and excessive campaign spending."[5] *Colorado I,* 518 U.S. at 618. See also *ibid.* ("Rather than indicating a special fear of the corruptive influence of political parties, the legislative history demonstrates Congress' general desire to enhance what was seen as an important and legitimate role for political parties in American elections").

Without explanation, the Court departs from this earlier, well-considered understanding of the Party Expenditure Provision. Were there any evidence of corruption in the [476] record that the parties have since developed, such a departure might be justified. But as the District Court found, "the facts which [the] FEC contends support its position . . . do not establish that the limit on party coordinated expenditures is necessary to prevent corruption or the appearance thereof." 41 F. Supp. 2d at 1211. Indeed, "none of the FEC's examples [of alleged corruption] involves coordinated expenditures." *Ibid.* See also App. in No. 99-1211 (CA10), at 346 (declaration of Herbert E. Alexander) ("In the decades since 1974, when coordinated expenditures were allowed for both presidential and congressional campaigns, there has not been any dispute relating to them, no charges of corruption or the appearance thereof . . . "); id. at 430 (statement of Anthony Corrado) ("There is no academic analysis or scholarly study conducted to date that demonstrates that parties are corrupted by the federally regulated contributions, the so-called 'hard-money funds,' they receive from donors. None of the studies of party finance or party coordinated spending contends that these funds are corruptive or generate the appearance of corruption in the political process"); id. at 624 (deposition of John Heubusch) (testifying that, in his experience, political party spending was not a source of corruption of Members of the United States Senate).[6]

The dearth of evidence is unsurprising in light of the unique relationship between a political party and its candidates: "The very aim of a political party is to influence its candidate's stance on issues and, if the candidate takes office or is reelected, his votes." *Colorado I,* 518 U.S. at [477] 646 (THOMAS, J., concurring in judgment and dissenting in part). If coordinated expenditures help achieve this aim, the achievement "does not . . . constitute 'a subversion of the political process.'" *Ibid.* (quoting *Federal Election Comm'n,* 470 U.S. at 497). It is simply the essence of our Nation's party system of government. One can speak of an individual citizen or a political action committee corrupting or coercing a candidate, but "what could it mean for a party to 'corrupt' its candidate or to exercise 'coercive' influence over him?" 470 U.S. at 646.

---

[5] The Court contends that I "ignore [a] distinction," *ante,* at 23, n.19: Whereas Congress may not have been concerned with corruption insofar as independent expenditures were implicated, Congress was concerned with corruption insofar as coordinated expenditures were implicated. This "distinction" must have been lost on Congress as well, which made no finding that the Party Expenditure Provision serves different purposes for different expenditures. It also was lost on the Court in *Colorado I,* which stated in no uncertain terms that Congress was not motivated by "the potentially 'corrupting' effect of party expenditures." *Colorado I,* 518 U.S. at 618.

---

[6] In *Missouri Republican Party* v. *Lamb,* 227 F.3d 1070 (2000), the Eighth Circuit held that the State of Missouri's restrictions on contributions by political parties violated the First Amendment. In accord with the Tenth Circuit in this case, the Eighth Circuit concluded that "the record is wholly devoid of any evidence that limiting parties' campaign contributions will either reduce corruption or measurably decrease the number of occasions on which limitations on individuals' campaign contributions are circumvented." Id. at 1073.

Apparently unable to provide an answer to this question, the Court relies upon an alternative theory of corruption. According to the Court, the Party Expenditure Provision helps combat circumvention of the limits on individual donors' contributions, which limits are necessary to reduce corruption by those donors.[7] See *ante*, at 17-20. The primary problem with this contention, however, is that it too is plainly contradicted by the findings of the District Court, see 41 F. Supp. 2d at 1211, and the overwhelming evidence in the record, see, *supra*, at 11.[8] And this contention is particularly surprising in light of *Colorado I*, in which we discussed the same opportunity for corruption through circumvention, and, far from finding it dispositive, concluded [478] that any opportunity for corruption was "at best, attenuated." 518 U.S. at 616.

Without addressing the District Court's determination or reflecting on this Court's understanding in *Colorado I*, the Court today asserts that its newfound position is supported by "substantial evidence." The best evidence the Court can come up with, however, is the Democratic Senatorial Campaign Committee's (DSCC) use of the "tally system," which "connects donors to candidates through the accommodation of a party." *Ante*, at 24. The tally system is not evidence of corruption-by-circumvention. In actuality, the DSCC is not acting as a mere conduit, allowing donors to contribute money in excess of the legal limits. The DSCC instead has allocated money based on a number of factors, including "the financial strength of the campaign," "what [the candidate's] poll numbers looked like," and "who had the best chance of winning or who needed the money most." App. 250-251 (declaration of Robert Hickmott, former Democratic fundraiser and National Finance Director for Timothy Wirth's Senate campaign); see also App. in No. 99-1211 (CA10), at 430 (statement of Anthony Corrado) ("When parties are deciding whether to spend funds on behalf of a candidate, they chiefly examine the competitiveness of the district or race, the political situation of the incumbent, and the strength of the party contender's candidacy"); id. at

563 (deposition of Donald Bain) (stating that the party generally did not support someone who has a safe seat or is clearly not going to win). As the District Court found, "the primary consideration in allocating funds is which races are marginal – that is which races are ones where party money could be the difference between winning and losing." 41 F. Supp. 2d at 1203. "Maintaining party control over seats is paramount to the parties' pursuits." *Ibid.;* see also App. in No. 99-1211 (CA10), at 483 (stating that primary goal of legislative campaign committees is "to win or maintain control of the chamber and the powers of the majority legislative party"). The [479] "bottom line" of the tally system is that "some candidates get back more money than they raise, and others get back less." App. 250 (declaration of Robert Hickmott).

Moreover, the Court does not explain how the tally system could constitute evidence of corruption. Both the initial contribution to the party and the subsequent expenditure by the party on the candidate are currently legal. In essence, the Court is asserting that it is corrupt for parties to do what is legal to enhance their participation in the political process. Each step in the process is permitted, but the combination of those steps, the Court apparently believes, amounts to corruption sufficient to silence those who wish to support a candidate. In my view, the First Amendment demands a more coherent explication of the evidence of corruption.[9]

Finally, even if the tally system were evidence of corruption-through-circumvention, it is only evidence of what is occurring under the current system, not of additional "corruption" that would arise in the absence of the Party Expenditure Provision. The Court speculates that, if we invalidated the Party Expenditure Provision, "the inducement to circumvent would almost certainly intensify." *Ante*, at 25. But that is nothing more than supposition, which is insufficient under our precedents to sustain a restriction on First Amendment interests. See *Shrink Missouri*, 528 U.S. at 392 ("We have never accepted mere conjecture as adequate to carry a First Amendment burden"). See also *United States* v. *Playboy Entertainment Group, Inc.*, 529 U.S. 803, 822, 146 L. Ed. 2d 865, 120 S. Ct. 1878 (2000) (concluding that the government "must present more than anecdote and supposition"). And it is weak supposition at that. The Court does not contend that [480] the DSCC's alleged efforts to channel money through the tally system were

---

[7] The Court does not argue that the Party Expenditure Provision is necessary to reduce the perception of corruption. Nor could the record sustain such an argument. See 41 F. Supp. 2d 1197, 1211 (Colo. 1999).

[8] Contrary to the Court's suggestion, *ante*, at 24, n. 21, the District Court did not simply conclude that "*Colorado I* had rejected the anti-circumvention rationale as a matter of law." Instead, the District Court first concluded there was no evidence of corruption, 41 F. Supp. 2d at 1211. Only after the District Court made this factual finding did it, in a footnote, cite *Colorado I* to support the legal conclusion. See 41 F. Supp. 2d at 1211, n. 9 ("Moreover, if the skirting of contribution limits is the issue with which the FEC is concerned . . . there are more tailored means of addressing such a concern than limiting the coordinated expenditure limits" (citing *Colorado I*)).

---

[9] Ironically, earlier this Term, this Court was less willing to uphold a speech restriction based on inference of circumvention. See, *e.g.*, *Bartnicki* v. *Vopper*, 532 U.S. ___, ___ (2001) (slip op., at 14-20) (holding unconstitutional the prohibition on disclosure of illegally intercepted conversation even though the initial step in the disclosure process, the interception, was illegal and harmful to those whose privacy was invaded).

restricted in any way by the Party Expenditure Provision. On the contrary, the Court suggests that a donation to the DSCC was increased by the party; in other words, the candidate got more than the initial donation. See *ante,* at 23 (quoting declaration of Timothy Wirth) ("'I understood that when I raised funds for the DSCC, the donors expected that I would receive the amount of their donations *multiplied* by a certain number that the DSCC had determined in advance, *assuming the DSCC has raised other funds*'" (emphasis added)). Because I am unpersuaded by weak speculation ungrounded in any evidence, I disagree with the Court's conclusion that the Party Expenditure Provision furthers the Government interest of reducing corruption.[10] [481]

2   Even if the Government had presented evidence that the Party Expenditure Provision affects corruption, the statute still would be unconstitutional, because there are better tailored alternatives for addressing the corruption. In addition to bribery laws and disclosure laws, see *Shrink Missouri, supra,* at 428 (THOMAS, J., dissenting), the Government has two options that would not entail the restriction of political parties' First Amendment rights.

First, the Government could enforce the earmarking rule of 2 U.S.C. § 441a(a)(8), under which contributions that "are in any way earmarked or otherwise directed through an intermediary or conduit to [a] candidate" are treated as contributions to the candidate. Vigilant enforcement of this provision is a precise response to the Court's circumvention concerns. If a donor contributes

$2,000 to a candidate (the maximum donation in an election cycle), he cannot direct the political party to funnel another dime to the candidate without confronting the Federal Election Campaign Act's civil and criminal penalties, see 2 U.S.C. § 437g(a)(6)(C) (civil); § 437g(d) (criminal).

According to the Court, reliance on this earmarking provision "ignores the practical difficulty of identifying and directly combating circumvention" and "would reach only the most clumsy attempts to pass contributions through to candidates." *Ante,* at 27, 28. The Court, however, does not cite any evidence to support this assertion. Nor does it articulate what failed steps the Government already has taken. Nor does it explain why the burden that the Government allegedly would have to bear in uncovering circumvention justifies the infringement of political parties' First Amendment rights. In previous cases, we have not been so willing to overlook such failures. See, *e.g., Bartnicki* 532 U.S. at   (slip op., at 15-16) ("There is no empirical evidence to support the assumption that the prohibition against disclosures reduces the number of illegal interceptions").

[482] In any event, there is a second, well-tailored option for combating corruption that does not entail the reduction of parties' First Amendment freedoms. The heart of the Court's circumvention argument is that, whereas individuals can donate only $2,000 to a candidate in a given election cycle, they can donate $20,000 to the national committees of a political party, an amount that is allegedly large enough to corrupt the candidate. See *ante,* at 18. If indeed $20,000 is enough to corrupt a candidate (an assumption that seems implausible on its face and is, in any event, unsupported by any evidence), the proper response is to lower the cap. That way, the speech restriction is directed at the source of the alleged corruption – the individual donor – and not the party. "The normal method of deterring unlawful conduct is to impose an appropriate punishment on the person who engages in it." *Bartnicki,* 532 U.S. at

(slip op., at 14). "It would be quite remarkable to hold that speech by a law-abiding [entity] can be suppressed in order to deter conduct by a non-law-abiding third party." *Ibid.* The Court takes that unorthodox path today, a decision that is all the more remarkable considering that the controlling opinion in *Colorado I* expressly rejected it just five years ago. 518 U.S. at 617 ("We could understand how Congress, were it to conclude that the potential for evasion of the individual limits was a serious matter, might decide to change the statute's limitations on contributions to political parties. But we do not believe that the risk of corruption present here could justify the 'markedly greater burden on basic

---

[10] The other "evidence" on which the Court relies is less compelling than the tally system. The Court presents four quotations, two of which do not even support the proposition that donations are funneled through parties to candidates. See *ante,* at 23 (quoting declaration of Leon G. Billings, former Executive Director of the DSCC); *ante,* at 24. These comments simply reflect the obvious fact that a candidate benefits when his party receives money. Neither comment suggests that the candidate is aided through the surreptitious laundering of money, as opposed to issue advertisements, get-out-the-vote campaigns, and independent expenditures. The other two quotations are somewhat suspect in that they are made by Timothy Wirth, who was the object of the negative advertisements giving rise to this lawsuit, and by his national finance director. See *ante,* at 23 (quoting App. 274 (declaration of Timothy Wirth)); App. 247 (declaration of Robert Hickmott, former Democratic fundraiser and National Finance Director for Timothy Wirth's Senate campaign). Moreover, neither Wirth nor his finance director described how donations were actually treated by the DSCC, either in general or in Wirth's particular case; instead Wirth and his finance director simply reflected on their understandings of how the money would be used in Wirth's election. As noted above, the District Court found that "the primary consideration in allocating funds is which races are marginal." 41 F. Supp. 2d at 1203. And the evidence in the record supports this finding. See *supra,* at 13.

freedoms caused by' the statute's limitations on *expenditures*" (citations omitted)).

In my view, it makes no sense to contravene a political party's core First Amendment rights because of what a third party might unlawfully try to do. Instead of broadly restricting political parties' speech, the Government should have pursued better-tailored alternatives for combating the alleged corruption.

Media Distinctions

The medium's effect on First Amendment protection

Focal cases:
Miami Herald v. Tornillo, 418 U.S. 241 (1974)
Red Lion Broadcasting v. FCC, 395 U.S. 367 (1967)
Turner Broadcasting v. FCC, 512 U.S. 622 (1994)
Denver Area Educational Telecommunications Consortium v. FCC, 518 U.S. 727 (1996)
Reno v. ACLU, 521 U.S. 844 (1997)

Historically, the Supreme Court has distinguished the level of First Amendment protection given different communications media on the grounds that each medium poses novel threats to society and affords unique speech opportunities. The Court has given the greatest constitutional protection to print media, the form of press that existed when the framers drafted the Constitution. In contrast, when the telegraph and telephone emerged, the Court viewed them not as members of "the press" protected by the First Amendment but as vehicles of commerce, carriers of information.[1] As such, these common carriers were subject to the government's power to regulate commerce.[2] Motion pictures suffered long from the stigma of being nothing more than entertainment (something substantially less important than "the freedom of speech" protected by the First Amendment). When radio, broadcasting, cable and each subsequent technology of communication emerged, the Court confronted anew the question of whether the technology and its content should be regulated commerce or protected free speech and press.[3]

At times, the Court has viewed "the press" expansively. In 1938, for example, the Court said, "The press in its historic connotation comprehends every sort of publication which affords a vehicle of information and opinion."[4] More often, however, the Court has categorized the press, looking at the unique impact of each medium to permit government to apply different regulations to each. For example, in 1949 the Court upheld the right of a city to regulate amplified broadcasts

---

[1] *See* ITHIEL DE SOLA POOL, TECHNOLOGIES OF FREEDOM (1983).

[2] U.S. Const. art. 1, § 8.

[3] *See, e.g,.* Burstyn v. Wilson, 343 U.S. 495 (1952).

[4] Lovell v. Griffin, 303 U.S. 444, 452 (1938).

from trucks roving through town. [5] The Court said amplified messages cannot be equated with "the exchange of ideas by speech or paper" because amplified "words ... may have all the effect of force" and create "an unwilling listener ... [who] is practically helpless to escape this interference."[6] In his concurring opinion, Justice Jackson concluded, "The moving picture screen, the radio, the newspaper, the handbill, the sound truck and the street corner orator have differing natures, values, abuses and dangers. Each, in my view, is a law unto itself."[7]

The power of government to treat media differently is limited, however. The Supreme Court consistently has said government must provide a strong justification to support regulatory distinctions among media and among different members of a specific medium.[8] In *Minneapolis Star & Tribune v. Minnesota*, for example, the Court said the state had failed to demonstrate a sufficiently strong government interest to justify a tax imposed on ink and paper that applied only to the largest newspapers. Accordingly, the Court viewed the tax as an unconstitutional form of government discrimination or coercion. Regulatory distinctions may not hide censorial intent. Thus, the Court said:

"[D]ifferential treatment, unless justified by some special characteristic of the press, suggests that the goal of the regulation is not unrelated to suppression of expression, and such a goal is presumptively unconstitutional. Differential taxation of the press, then, places such a burden on the interests protected by the First Amendment that we cannot countenance such treatment unless the State asserts a counterbalancing interest of compelling importance that it cannot achieve without differential taxation."[9]

When adequately justified, medium-specific regulations may respond to economic traits as well as inherent characteristics of different media. In recent years, for example, growth of media conglomerates and concentration of ownership place unprecedented power in the hands of a few individuals to amplify or stifle the voices of various speakers and groups. Sometimes this power corresponds to near-monopoly control of crucial parts of the communication delivery system, what economists call a bottleneck. For example, local telephone company ownership of the last mile of the telephone lines and cable company control of the cable grid potentially enable these owners to prevent other telephone and cable operators from reaching customers. When competition is squelched, possibly diverse content from a variety of sources does not reach consumers. At times, the Court argues that this ability to limit communication undermines First Amendment goals and requires government intervention. At other times, the Court is unwilling to allow government to regulate media infrastructure because such regulation often affects media content.[10]

NEWSPAPERS

As the original and ultimate form of "the press," newspapers and other print forms of non-prurient communication stand at the pinnacle of constitutional protection. Like political speech, which occupies the heart of free speech, newspapers embody the soul of the constitutional premise that the press performs a fundamental democratic function. In 1936, for example, the Supreme Court described the goal of the First Amendment as the preservation of an untrammeled press as a vital source of public information. "The newspapers, magazines and other journals of the country, it is safe to say, have shed and continue to shed, more light on the public and business

---

[5] Kovacs v. Cooper, 336 U.S. 77 (1949).

[6] 336 U.S. at 87, 83, 86-7.

[7] 336 U.S. at 97 (Jackson, J., concurring) .

[8] *See, e.g.*, Minneapolis Star & Tribune Co. v. Minnesota Commissioner of Revenue, 460 U.S. 575 (1983).

[9] Id. at 585.

[10] Miami Herald v. Tornillo, 418 U.S. 241 (1974); Red Lion Broadcasting v. FCC, 395 U.S. 367 (1967). *See also* Jerome Barron, *Access to the Press – A New First Amendment Right*, 80 HARV. L. REV. 1641 (1967).

affairs of the nation than any other instrumentality of publicity; and since informed public opinion is the most potent of all restraints upon misgovernment, the suppression or abridgement of the publicity afforded by a free press cannot be regarded otherwise than with grave concern."[11]

The Court has gone so far as to describe the freedom of the press as the "freedom to publish,"[12] and the freedom of the press from prior restraints, licensing, and targeted taxes and fees is nearly inviolate. According to the Supreme Court, "The power of a privately owned newspaper to advance its own political, social, and economic views is bounded by only two factors: first, the acceptance of a sufficient number of readers – and hence advertisers – to assure financial success; and, second, the journalistic integrity of its editors and publishers."[13]

However, in 1974 the Court examined press autonomy in light of the dramatic decline in newspaper competition and the growing consolidation of both newspaper and multi-media ownership.[14] The issue in *Miami Herald v. Tornillo* was whether a state could constitutionally require a newspaper to publish a response to a political attack. The underlying question, though, was whether one-newspaper communities so severely impeded the ability of newspapers to provide diverse content and fulfill their constitutional role that government could step in to mandate access for individuals whose views were excluded. The argument pitted a newspaper's editorial autonomy against balanced, fair and responsible coverage of political candidates. The Court concluded that even when the political coverage of a monopoly newspaper distorts political discussion and disfavors one candidate, the First Amendment expressly prohibits government from requiring newspapers to print specific content.

Any government dictate that newspapers cover certain topics or provide space for certain speakers sounded alarms that such laws would give preferential treatment to those favored by government. In addition, government-imposed newspaper content would necessarily impinge the ability of newspapers to print the content of their choosing because newspapers have limited space. Thus, rather than increase exchange of political opinions, a right-to-reply statute might discourage newspapers from taking stands against candidates for fear of triggering an obligation to provide response space. Finally, the Court seemed to echo press critic A. J. Liebling's famous comment that "in America, freedom of the press is guaranteed only to those who own one." The Court said that allowing monopoly newspapers a free hand to exclude certain speakers did not prevent those speakers from starting their own newspapers, or handing our flyers, or standing on a soap box in the town square to disseminate their messages.

The Court historically has viewed newspaper freedom from the perspective of the rights of private owners of presses – the publisher and editors – rather than the interests of readers or the broad objectives of a democratic state. Press owners are free to publish what they like, subject only to punishment after the fact for speech-related violations including libel, obscenity and false advertising. Newspaper owners also are free to distribute their publications using the public streets and sidewalks, subject only to reasonable laws of general application that apply even-handedly to anyone using these public ways in a similar fashion.[15]

BROADCASTING

Ownership is at the base of distinctions between print media and broadcasting. Whereas print media are privately owned, operated and controlled, broadcast stations are licensed by government to use segments of the public airwaves. The Communications Act of 1934 granted licensing authority to the federal government, now administered through the Federal Communication

---

[11] Grosjean v. American Press Co., 297 U.S. 233, 250 (1936).

[12] Associated Press v. United States, 326 U.S. 1, 20 (1945).

[13] Columbia Broadcasting System, Inc. v. Democratic National Committee, 412 U.S. 94, 117 (1973).

[14] Miami Herald v. Tornillo, 418 U.S. 241 (1974).

[15] Lakewood v. Plain Dealer, 486 U.S. 750 (1988); Cincinnati v. Discovery Network, 507 U.S. 410 (1993).

Commission.[16] Fair and equitable licensing is intended to stop broadcasters from interfering with each other's signals and to assure efficient use of the broadcast spectrum to achieve the "public interest, convenience and necessity."[17]

An FCC license does not grant ownership *per se* but grants stations the privilege to operate as a public trustee using the public airwaves to disseminate content. [18] That, at least, is the theory. Broadcast licenses are exclusive; the grant of a license to one applicant excludes other potential broadcasters from that portion of the spectrum. Thus, licensing both prevents unsuccessful applicants from reaching their target audience and potentially limits the diversity of ideas reaching the audience.

Historically, FCC licensees paid a very modest fee for their monopolization of an extremely lucrative slice of the electromagnetic spectrum. The licensing process is fairly routine: In exchange for a low annual fee, successful applicants receive an eight-year license that is almost automatically renewed. The FCC will not consider competing applications to an existing licensee unless the licensee has run seriously afoul of FCC regulations during the previous license term. When there are competing applications for the same license, the FCC since 1996[19] has auctioned licenses off to the highest bidder. Congress believed auctions would allow government to collect a more reasonable amount for valuable spectrum allocations and would eliminate the constant litigation that arose from the FCC's prior process of awarding licenses on the basis of perceived merit. Auctions have not been entirely smooth or successful. The FCC has not collected the full amounts bid,[20] and unsuccessful bidders have challenged the FCC process.[21]

FCC licensing also raises First Amendment concerns because licensing may truncate or distort the marketplace of ideas. One response is the emergence on un-used or under-used spectrum of stations operating without a license – so-called pirate stations. Pirate stations are illegal, and the FCC can fine them and/or seize their equipment. Yet, late in the 20th Century, pirate stations proliferated as independent, alternate voices to the nearly uniform content spawned by the increasingly centralized, corporate world of commercial broadcasting. In fact, in 2000, the FCC encouraged the creation of low-power stations to compete with full-power commercial broadcasters.[22] But the National Association of Broadcasters, the powerful lobbying group of commercial broadcasting, nipped that in the bud. Under intense pressure from NAB, Congress passed the Radio Preservation Act of 2000 to severely restrict the number of low power stations.[23]

FCC ownership limits are another mechanism designed to counterbalance the exclusionary impact of licensing. For at least three decades, the FCC restricted the number and diversity of media properties a single individual or organization could own. Throughout that time, the FCC argued tenaciously that ownership limits served the public interest by diversifying control of broadcasting and providing a greater breadth of views to the audience. Yet the FCC and Congress vacillated on how much restriction of broadcast ownership was appropriate. FCC ownership rules and federal laws shifted as the government lurched from periods of more invasive regulation to periods of deregulation. Those who endorse the economic theory of regulation argue that such shifts in regulation respond to the power of lobby groups, particularly the NAB, to obtain favorable regulation.

---

[16] 47 U.S.C. §303 and §307(b).

[17] 47 U.S.C. §§ 302(a), 307(d).

[18] *See* In the Matter of Principles for Reallocation of Spectrum to Encourage the Development of Telecommunications Technologies for the New Millennium, 14 F.C.C. Rcd. 19868 (1999).

[19] The Telecommunications Act, Public Law 104-104, 104th Cong., 2d Sess. (Feb. 1996).

[20] FCC v. NextWave Personal Communications, 123 S. Ct. 832 (2003) (rejects FCC authority to revoke licenses for non-timely payment).

[21] U.S. Airwaves Inc. v. FCC , Nos. 98-1266 and 98-1267, petitions denied (D.C. Cir. , Nov. 21, 2000)

[22] In the Matter of Creation of Low Power Radio Services, 15 F.C.C. Rcd. 2205 (2000).

[23] H.R. 3439, 106th Cong., 2d Sess. (2000).

In the late 20th and early 21st centuries, the federal government was in a deregulatory phase. In 1996, Congress passed the sweeping Telecommunications Act,[24] which reduced limits on multiple-media ownership, consolidation of media ownership in a single community and national TV ownership. The act permits an individual to own as many TV stations as they wish so long as the stations do not reach more than 35 percent of the nation's total viewing audience. As applied, the law also allows one individual to own multiple newspapers and broadcast stations in a single market. The law also required the FCC to review its ownership limits every two years to determine whether they advanced the public interest. In 2002, after a federal court of appeals roundly rejected the FCC's ownership rules,[25] the FCC began to consider formally whether it should eliminate the ownership rules.[26] Following a brief round of poorly publicized public hearings around the United States, the FCC eliminated most of its ownership regulations in June 2003.

Broadcast Content Regulations

For decades, broadcast regulation extended far beyond licensing and ownership restrictions. Virtually from the inception of the medium, the Supreme Court accepted greater government regulation of broadcasting than print because broadcasting presents peculiar problems. These problems reach beyond the chaos of signal overlap and the scarcity of spectrum capacity. The Court has expressed concern that auditory and visual broadcast messages are pervasive and intrusive; they cannot effectively be pre-screened by the audience, and they are uniquely accessible to young children. Although the Communications Act of 1934 expressly prohibits the FCC from censoring broadcast content, it simultaneously requires the FCC to assure that broadcasters operate in the "public interest, convenience and necessity." This tension has enabled the FCC and Congress to impose content standards and coverage requirements on broadcasters to *advance*, not abridge, First Amendment goals. In the name of public interest objectives, current federal law and FCC regulations dictate the amount and nature of broadcast advertising (particularly about "vice" products or services and during children's programming), mandate access and equal time for federal political candidates, determine permissible broadcast times for "indecent" adult programming, limit and require identification of violent content, and impose content standards on children's programming, among other things.

The FCC has the power to levy fines and to threaten the licenses of broadcasters who violate these rules. Courts have upheld such fines and said they do not constitute government censorship.[27] Some media critics say the FCC uses this power too sparingly or inequitably. FCC fines often represent only a small percentage of the profits generated by the sanctioned programming. For example, a Pueblo, Colorado, radio station that broadcast Eminem's "The Real Slim Shady" more than 400 times received a $7,000 fine in 2001. The radio station said it had tried, but evidently failed, to edit out all the portions of the song the FCC would find indecent. The honor for racking up the largest indecency fines in FCC history, however, goes to "The Howard Stern Show." Indecency in that show cost Infinity Broadcasting more than $1.7 million in a settlement for pennies on the dollar of total fines assessed against the show.

Much FCC regulation rests on the premise that audience interests take priority over the editorial autonomy of broadcasters. In fact, the Supreme Court has said the Constitution protects some right for the public to receive information vital to the effective functioning of democracy. Thus, the Court has upheld both a federal statute mandating "reasonable access" to broadcast

---

[24] Public Law 104-104, 104th Cong., 2d Sess. (Feb. 1996).

[25] Sinclair Broadcast Group v. FCC, 284 F.3d 148 (D.C. Cir. 2002); Fox Television Stations Inc. v. FCC, 280 F.3d 1027 (D.C. Cir. 2002).

[26] In the Matter of Cross-Ownership of Broadcast Stations and Newspapers, 16 F.C.C.R. 17283 (2002).

[27] *See, e.g.,* Action for Children's Television v. FCC, 58 F.3d 654 (D.C. Cir. 1995); South Fork Broadcasting Corp. v. Federal Communications Commission, 59 F.3d 1249, (D.C.Cir. 1995).

outlets for federal political candidates[28] and the Communication Act Section 315 requirement that stations must provides equal (non-news) time to all legally qualified federal candidates.[29] However, the public interest standard does not supplant the editorial control of broadcasters, and it does not provide an enforceable right of access to electronic media.

This premise has led to increasing broadcaster freedom. In 2000, for example, the U.S. Court of Appeals for the District of Columbia Circuit ordered the FCC to eliminate two rules that required stations to notify and provide free time to candidates when broadcasters carried personal attacks on them or aired editorial endorsements of their opponents.[30] While broadcasters are free to reject advertisements they do not wish to air,[31] they are not entirely free to advertise "vice" products. In 1971, for example, Congress prohibited broadcast advertisements for cigarettes.[32] Although federal law does not prohibit broadcast ads for distilled beverages, public pressure has led broadcasters to shun such advertisements. However, a 1999 U.S. Supreme Court ruling freed broadcasters to run ads for gambling in states where gambling is legal.[33]

CABLE

From the inception of cable television systems in the 1940s until 1984, cable grew primarily in response to unique community demands for television delivery in areas not suited to receive over-the-air television via antennas. During those early years, cable – then called community area television or CATV – was simply a physical extension of broadcast television. Its role as a First Amendment-protected communications medium was unclear. To CATV households, cable television was the exact equivalent of broadcast television. To the FCC and the courts, however, CATV did not embody the traits of broadcasters – most notably use of the scarce public airwaves – that justified government regulation.

As cable systems multiplied, however, citizens and community planners became increasingly interested in the unique potential of this medium to serve educational, governmental and entertainment goals. Cable's programming capacity far exceeded the limited number of broadcast channels available and promised a heretofore unimagined diversity of content. In light of this vision of cable as a communications panacea, Congress enacted the Cable Communications Policy Act of 1984 to encourage and enable growth of cable systems.[34] The Cable Act was the result of compromise between vehement lobbying by the cable industry to enable cable expansion and the nation's cities, which wanted to maintain their authority to impose unique and sometimes impractical franchise conditions upon local cable operators. The Cable Act established the FCC as the primary government authority over cable technology and mandated *national* regulatory standards while granting cities limited power to award local franchises and collect franchise fees.

Cable flourished, and broadcasters, who feared cable's competitive assault on their viewers and advertisers, vigorously lobbied Congress. Consumers also complained of run-away cable fees, poor service and broken promises. In the first major swing of seesawing regulation, Congress in 1992 passed the Cable Television Consumer Protection and Competition Act to strictly regulate the fees and conditions of cable service.[35] In addition to its more stringent government regulation of cable, the law encouraged increased competition among cable providers and prohibited cities from awarding monopoly cable franchises.

---

[28] Columbia Broadcasting System v. FCC, 453 U.S. 567 (1981).

[29] Red Lion Broadcasting v. FCC, 395 U.S. 367 (1969).

[30] In the Matter of Repeal or Modification of the Personal Attack and Political Editorial Rules, 15 F.C.C. R. 20697 (2000); Radio Television News Directors Association v. FCC, 229 F.3d 269 (2000).

[31] CBS v. Democratic National Committee (1973).

[32] 15 U.S.C. Sec. 1335.

[33] Greater New Orleans Broadcasting v. United States, 527 U.S. 173 (1999).

[34] 47 U.S.C. §§ 601-639.

[35] 106 Stat. 1460 (1992); 47 U.S.C.S. § 543 (1996).

The Telecommunications Act of 1996[36] went a step further, deregulating telephone companies and direct broadcast satellite TV providers to allow them to enter the cable market. However, based on the rather faulty assumption that effective cable competition existed or was on the horizon, the Telecommunications Act again deregulated cable, phasing out government oversight of cable fees in favor of market-driven pricing. In effect, the 1996 act also eliminated a ban on cable ownership of wireless cable or satellite master antenna television systems, two competitive forms of home video delivery. FCC rules continue to limit multi-system cable operators to 30 percent of the nation's cable subscribers and impose restrictions on the number of channels MSOs can dedicate to their own programming.

Cable competition did not emerge in most communities in the last years of the century. Media mergers proliferated; cable competitors did not enter the market; telephone moved into other more lucrative markets, such as Internet delivery; and direct broadcast TV did not catch on. So, direct broadcast TV providers lobbied Congress for additional deregulation on the grounds that existing laws impeded their entry into cable. Congress obligingly amended the Telecommunications Act in 1999 to allow direct broadcasters to carry local stations, but a single cable provider for home video remained the norm in most non-urban U.S. communities in 2003.

Cable Content Regulations

Many of the content rules that apply to over-the-air television apply to cable programmers as well. Candidate access and equal time rules apply, but cable systems have greater freedom to broadcast indecent (adult, non-obscene) content during daytime hours.

Cable-specific regulations responded in large part to fear that cable's superior capacity and picture quality would lead to the demise of broadcast television. Thus, rules and regulations dating back nearly 40 years require cable systems to carry local broadcast stations. Although cable operators repeatedly challenged these "must-carry" rules as a violation of their First Amendment rights,[37] courts have said the rules do not unduly infringe cable operators' editorial autonomy and constitutionally limit cable's ability to prevent broadcasters from reaching consumers. In two separate rulings in *Turner Broadcasting System v. FCC*, the U.S. Supreme Court said must-carry rules are a narrowly tailored, content-neutral means to protect the vital constitutional function served by local broadcast television.[38]

In two highly divided and complex decisions, the Court ruled that although cable operators engage in protected First Amendment speech, the must-carry rules caused only insignificant abridgement of their editorial freedom because cable systems could expand to include desired programming. Even if must-carry rules favor broadcast content over cable content, the Court said, that preference is permissible because it does not reflect government support for any specific content and responds to the unique economic and technological traits of cable – especially its monopolization of the home video delivery market. Must-carry rules apply to all except the very smallest cable systems.

Based on the fear of monopoly control of the home video market, courts earlier had ruled that cities could not grant an exclusive contract to one cable provider.[39] Cable competition is essential to the content diversity so vital to First Amendment interests.[40]

At one time, cable operators were required by law to set aside channels for public, educational and governmental access.[41] PEG access no longer is required, but most systems provide public,

---

[36] 110 Stat. 56 (1996); 47 U.S.C. §§ 251 et seq. (1996).
[37] *See, e.g.,* Quincy Cable v. FCC, 768 F.2d 1434 (1985).
[38] 512 U.S. 622 (1994); 520 U.S. 180 (1997).
[39] Preferred Communications v. Los Angeles, 13 F.3d 1327 (9th Cir. 1994); *cert. den'd,* 512 U.S. 1235 (1994).
[40] *See, e.g.,* Preferred Communications v. Los Angeles, 476 U.S. 488 (1986).
[41] Cable Television Report and Order, 36 F.C.C. 2d 143 (1972).

educational and governmental channels as a negotiated part of their franchise contract with local authorities. The Cable Act of 1984 does require cable systems with more than thirty-five channels to offer leased-access channels for rent by commercial programmers. Leased-access channels are intended to increase the diversity of programming reaching consumers by allowing video programmers who do not operate cable systems to gain access to cable homes.

Cable operators have limited control over the content of PEG and leased-access channels, are prohibited from censoring these channels, and are required to afford the widest possible access to the broadest diversity of programmers and information sources. For example, cable operators may not prohibit indecent programming on access channels, and they generally are not liable for legal violations that arise from programming on leased-access channels. However, in 1996 the Supreme Court ruled that cable operators may adopt policies that segregate, scramble or limit the time during which adult programming will be carried.[42]

In a case that pitted the First Amendment interests of cable operators, cable programmers, and audience members against each other, the Court suggested that the judiciary should use a light and responsive touch when regulating shifting technologies. The Court's context-specific cable jurisprudence provided scant guidance to lower courts that struggled with the extent to which cable operators could legally create "safe havens" to protect children viewers from sexually explicit programming, for example. Then in 2000, the Supreme Court ruled that mandatory scrambling by cable operators of sexually explicit programming was unconstitutional.[43] The Court said government-imposed scrambling unconstitutionally singled out disfavored content, was not supported by a compelling government interest and was not the least intrusive means to achieve government goals. The editorial authority of cable operators on PEG and leased-access channels remains unclear.

NEW TECHNOLOGIES AND NEW ENTRANTS INTO EXISTING MARKETS

Proliferating digital technologies and deregulation at the close of the 20th Century created an unprecedented complexity of communications media and players. Cable operators were providing broadband Internet connections that afforded ultra-fast connections but limited flexibility in service providers. Telephone companies, long regulated as nondiscriminatory common carriers of other people's content, were originating information content, offering video through wireless cable and even operating cable systems. Telephone, cable, broadcast, publishing, music and film companies converged into giant, multi-media conglomerates that owned media systems, services and products from development through global marketing to at-home delivery of everything from cookbooks to classic films.

Clearly the regulatory challenges at the turn of the century were daunting. The potential for new technology to afford more universal access to consumers and greater capacity for more diverse programming was balanced by a fear of monopoly control of an unprecedented breadth of communication. For the most part, the U.S. Supreme Court remained on the sidelines waiting for the dust to settle while lower courts struggled to determine the degree of First Amendment protection to be afforded emerging technologies.

The Supreme Court did decide a handful of indecency cases (See Chap. 9.) that shed some light on the high court's view of the Internet. In *Reno v. American Civil Liberties Union*, the Supreme Court in 1997 sketched its constitutional perspective of the Internet.[44] In striking down the 1996 Communications Decency Act's ban on Internet transmission of indecency, the Court said the prohibition unconstitutionally stifled protected speech and was both vague and overbroad. The Court recognized the important government interest in shielding children from sexually explicit

---

[42] Denver Area Educ. Telecommunications Consortium v. FCC, 518 U.S. 727 (1996).

[43] United States v. Playboy Entertainment Group, 529 U.S. 803 (2000).

[44] 521 U.S. 844 (1997).

material but said a blanket government restriction on a specific class of protected speech was highly suspect. Reiterating the concept that each medium raises unique constitutional issues, the Court distinguished the Internet from broadcasting. Unlike broadcasting – which is licensed, involves scarce, public airwaves and is readily accessible to children – the Internet presents no clear justification for reduced First Amendment protection. Indeed, the Court said, because Internet access requires sophistication and navigational skill, children and other users are less likely to inadvertently confront objectionable content on the Internet than through broadcasting. The Court suggested technological means might further reduce the threat to children while protecting the Internet as a potentially rich source of diverse information from a full panoply of speakers.

When Congress obliged by passing the Children's Internet Protection Act, which required public schools and libraries to install filtering software on computers to block children's access to Internet pornography, the Supreme Court upheld the law against a constitutional challenge.[45]

Other Issues

Fear of harm to children is but one of several concerns prompting federal laws aimed at new technologies. In the wake of the Sept. 11, 2001, attacks, the federal government – both in Congress and through the executive branch – adopted a wave of regulations to improve the nation's protection against and responsiveness to acts of terrorism. First among these was the lengthy USA PATRIOT Act of 2001, which included broad provisions to expand the ability of government investigators to tap into email and other personal computer transmissions and to access computerized financial records without a search warrant and without notifying the individual under surveillance.[46] One section of the USA Patriot Act requires Internet service providers to divulge the confidential electronic communications of clients and a broad range of customer records – including sources of payment made by a customer, such as credit card and bank account information. Early in 2003, members of Congress were considering a sequel to the PATRIOT Act that proposed to radically increase the government's power to secretly gather intelligence and conduct surveillance by telephone and online.[47]

The federal government also invested millions of dollars to enhance its ability to protect the security of the information it gathers and stores on computers. In 2002, Congress enacted the Homeland Security Act, part of which broadly revised government information security polices and information sharing practices. The so-called Federal Information Security Management Act of 2002 requires all federal agencies to implement information security systems especially for computerized data. Another provision of the Homeland Security Act encourages the sharing and secrecy of critical national infrastructure information, including information related to information technology, telecommunications systems and "virtual" infrastructure. The Cyber Security Research and Development Act dedicated nearly $900 million in federal funds for computer and network security research. Another federally funded research project, called World Infrastructure Security Environment, focused on the development of more effective privacy filters, methods to mask the identity of individuals under government surveillance, and automatic data deletion functions. A separate privacy-oriented law, the Health Insurance Portability and Accountability Act of 1996 that took effect in April 2003, encouraged electronic data sharing among health-care providers but mandated security and confidentiality safeguards for health information.

Congress also enacted an electronic-commerce law to increase the ability of government agencies to share information electronically with the public.[48] The law provided $345 million over

---

[45] United States v. American Library Association, 123 S.Ct. 2297 (2003).

[46] The Uniting and Strengthening America by Providing Appropriate Tools Required To Intercept and Obstruct Terrorism Act of 2001, Pub. L. No. 107-56, 115 Stat. 272 (2001).

[47] Domestic Security Enhancement Act of 2003 (so-called USA PATRIOT Act II).

[48] Electronic Government Act of 2002.

four years to update government Internet sites, to require federal courts to post their opinions online, and to increase federal tax filing via the Internet. At the same time, however, increasing consumer protection concerns spawned a rash of legislation targeting Internet investing and banking, online shopping, identity theft and spam advertising.

Heightened concern with technological invasion of personal privacy, for example, led Congress to enact a law strictly limiting the dissemination of unwanted faxes and to consider a similar law to prevent unsolicited commercial email.[49] Congress also passed a statute allowing Americans to register with the FCC to prevent calls from telemarketers.[50] However, the national association of telemarketers promptly challenged the law as an unconstitutional infringement of their right to free speech.[51]

Proliferating regulation targeting new technologies reflected a fundamental paradox: The greater the popularity and ubiquity of new communications technologies, the greater their potential to erode significant citizen interests in security, privacy, accurate information, and solitude, to name but a few of the most dominant concerns. Courts reviewing regulations of new technologies are faced with the Herculean task of determining – as technologies develop and are adopted into society – the proper balance between unfettered freedom of expression and constraint of the potentially deleterious effects of invasive technologies.[52]

ADDITIONAL CASE READINGS

Beyond the case and case excerpts referenced in and attached to this chapter, you will gain insights into the distinctions the Court has drawn among the media and how it has determined when those distinctions are constitutionally acceptable by reading the following cases.

- *Sinclair Broadcast Group v. Federal Communications Commission*, 284 F.3d 148 (D.C. Cir. 2002) (affirms FCC authority to establish local ownership rules).
- *Fox Television Stations Inc. v. Federal Communications Commission*, 280 F.3d 1027 (D.C. Cir. 2002) (strikes broadcast/cable ownership rules).
- *American Library Association v. United States*, 201 F. Supp. 2d 401 (E.D. Pa. 2002) (strikes Children's Internet Protection Act).
- *Turner Broadcasting System v. Federal Communications Commission*, 520 U.S. 180 (1997) (affirms must-carry rules).
- *Leathers v. Medlock*, 499 U.S. 439 (1991) (affirms state application of sales tax to cable but not other media).
- *Preferred Communications v. Los Angeles*, 476 U.S. 488 (1986) (strikes monopoly cable franchises).
- *Quincy Cable v. Federal Communications Commission*, 768 F.2d 1434 (D.C. Cir. 1985) (strikes must-carry rules).
- *Federal Communications Commission v. League of Women Voters*, 468 U.S. 364 (1984) (strikes ban on broadcast editorializing).
- *Minneapolis Star & Tribune Co. v. Minnesota Commissioner of Revenue*, 460 U.S. 575 (1983).
- *Columbia Broadcasting System v. Federal Communications Commission*, 453 U.S. 567 (1981) (affirms candidate right of reasonable access to broadcasting).
- *Columbia Broadcasting System v. Democratic National Committee*, 412 U.S. 94 (1973) (denies advertisers right of access to broadcasting).

---

[49] *See* FCC Rules Implementing the Telephone Consumer Protection Act of 1991, FCC 03-152 (CG Docket No. 02-278) (July 3, 2003); 2003 H.R. 2525, 108th Cong., 1st Sess. (June 18, 2003).

[50] Telemarketing Sales Rule, 2003 H.R. 395, Pub. Law No. 108-10, 16 C.F.R. 310.4 (March 11, 2003).

[51] *See* Paul Tharp, *Dialing up a lawsuit*, THE N.Y. POST (July 7, 2003).

[52] *See* ITHIEL DE SOLA POOL, TECHNOLOGIES OF FREEDOM (1983).

- *Burstyn v. Wilson*, 343 U.S. 495 (1952)(strikes law banning sacrilegious films).
- *Kovacs v. Cooper*, 336 U.S. 77 (1949) (affirms time, place, manner regulations of soundtrucks).
- *Lovell v. Griffin*, 303 U.S. 444, 452 (1938) (strikes ban on pamphlet distribution).

As you read the following cases and excerpts, consider these questions.

- How and why might these decisions differ if they involved a different medium of communication?
- How does the Court in *Miami Herald v. Tornillo* weigh the virtual elimination of competing newspapers in its decision?
- Is a right to reply statute content based or content neutral? Why?
- What constitutional problems does the Court believe arise from forcing newspapers to grant a right of reply?
- How does the Court handle the claim that a right to reply statute does not constrain the newspaper's freedom of speech?
- How does the Court in *Red Lion Broadcasting v. FCC* reconcile the apparent tension between the "public interest" doctrine for broadcasters and the explicit prohibition on government control of broadcast content?
- Identify the key justifications the Court names for lessened First Amendment protection against broadcast regulation.
- Whose First Amendment rights are of pre-eminent concern to the Court in *Red Lion* and why?
- How does the Court characterize the First Amendment role and status of cable in *Turner Broadcasting v. FCC*?
- Whose First Amendment interests are implicated by the must-carry regulations, and which interests take precedence in the Court's decision?
- On what basis does the Court conclude that must-carry regulations are content neutral?
- What, if any, clear First Amendment standard for review of cable regulation does the Court articulate in *Denver Area Educational Telecommunications Consortium v. FCC*?
- What test does the Court apply in *Denver* and how does it justify this choice?
- To what degree does the Court apply public forum law to the regulation of cable and why?
- What are the unique First Amendment functions or values of the Internet, according to the Court in *ACLU v. Reno*?
- Whose First Amendment rights does the Court believe are most directly implicated when government regulates the Internet and why?
- What test does the Court suggest should apply to regulation of Internet speech, and what does this say about the Court's view of the constitutional value of this new medium?

Miami Herald Publishing Co. v. Tornillo
418 U.S. 241
(1974)

PRIOR HISTORY: Appeal from the Supreme Court of Florida.

JUDGES: BURGER, C. J., delivered the opinion for a unanimous Court. BRENNAN, J., filed a concurring statement, in which REHNQUIST, J., joined. WHITE, J., filed a concurring opinion.

OPINION: [243]MR. CHIEF JUSTICE BURGER delivered the opinion of the Court.

[1] The issue in this case is whether a state statute granting a political candidate a right to equal space to reply to criticism and attacks on his record by a newspaper violates the guarantees of a free press. I.   In the fall of 1972, appellee, Executive Director of the Classroom Teachers Association, apparently a teachers' collective-bargaining agent, was a candidate for the Florida House of Representatives. On September 20, 1972, and again on September 29, 1972, appellant printed editorials critical of appellee's candidacy.[1] In [244] response to these editorials appellee demanded that appellant print verbatim his replies, defending the role of the Classroom Teachers Association and the organization's accomplishments for the citizens of Dade County. Appellant declined to print the appellee's replies, and appellee brought suit in Circuit Court, Dade County, seeking declaratory and injunctive relief and actual and punitive damages in excess of $5,000. The action was premised on Florida Statute § 104.38 (1973), a "right of reply" statute which provides that if a candidate for nomination or election is assailed regarding his personal character or official record by any newspaper, the candidate has the right to demand that the newspaper print, free of cost to the candidate, any reply the candidate may make to the newspaper's charges. The reply must appear in as conspicuous a place and in the same kind of type as the charges which prompted the reply, provided it does not take up more space than the charges. Failure to comply with the statute constitutes a first-degree misdemeanor.[2]

[245] Appellant sought a declaration that § 104.38 was unconstitutional. After an emergency hearing requested by appellee, the Circuit Court denied injunctive relief because, absent special circumstances, no injunction could properly issue against the commission of a crime, and held that § 104.38 was unconstitutional as an infringement on the freedom of the press under the First and Fourteenth Amendments to the Constitution. 38 Fla. Supp. 80 (1972). The Circuit Court concluded that dictating what a newspaper must print was no different from dictating what it must not print. The

---

[1] The text of the September 20, 1972, editorial is as follows:
"The State's Laws And Pat Tornillo
"LOOK who's upholding the law!
"Pat Tornillo, boss of the Classroom Teachers Association and candidate for the State Legislature in the Oct. 3 runoff election, has denounced his opponent as lacking 'the knowledge to be a legislator, as evidenced by his failure to file a list of contributions to and expenditures of his campaign as required by law.'
"Czar Tornillo calls 'violation of this law inexcusable.'
"This is the same Pat Tornillo who led the CTA strike from February 19 to March 11, 1968, against the school children and taxpayers of Dade County. Call it whatever you will, it was an illegal act against the public interest and clearly prohibited by the statutes.
"We cannot say it would be illegal but certainly it would be inexcusable of the voters if they sent Pat Tornillo to Tallahassee to occupy the seat for District 103 in the House of Representatives."
The text of the September 29, 1972, editorial is as follows:
"FROM the people who brought you this – the teacher strike of '68 – come now instructions on how to vote for responsible government, i.e., against Crutcher Harrison and Ethel Beckham, for Pat Tornillo. The tracts and blurbs and bumper stickers pile up daily in teachers' school mailboxes amidst continuing pouts that the School Board should be delivering all this at your expense. The screeds say the strike is not an issue. We say maybe it wouldn't be were it not a part of a continuation of disregard of any and all laws the CTA might find aggravating. Whether in defiance of zoning laws at CTA Towers, contracts and laws during the strike, or more recently state prohibitions against soliciting campaign funds amongst teachers, CTA says fie and try and sue us – what's good for CTA is good for CTA and that is natural law. Tornillo's law, maybe. For years now he has been kicking the public shin to call attention to his shakedown statesmanship. He and whichever acerbic proxy is in alleged office have always felt their private ventures so chock-full of public weal that we should leap at the chance to nab the tab, be it half the Glorious Leader's salary or the dues check off or anything else except perhaps mileage on the staff hydrofoil. Give him public office, says Pat, and he will no doubt live by the Golden Rule. Our translation reads that as more gold and more rule."

[2] "104.38 Newspaper assailing candidate in an election; space for reply – If any newspaper in its columns assails the personal character of any candidate for nomination or for election in any election, or charges said candidate with malfeasance or misfeasance in office, or otherwise attacks his official record, or gives to another free space for such purpose, such newspaper shall upon request of such candidate immediately publish free of cost any reply he may make thereto in as conspicuous a place and in the same kind of type as the matter that calls for such reply, provided such reply does not take up more space than the matter replied to. Any person or firm failing to comply with the provisions of this section shall be guilty of a misdemeanor of the first degree, punishable as provided in § 775.082 or § 775.083."

Circuit Judge viewed the statute's vagueness as serving "to restrict and stifle protected expression." Id., at 83. Appellee's cause was dismissed with prejudice.

On direct appeal, the Florida Supreme Court reversed, holding that § 104.38 did not violate constitutional guarantees. 287 So. 2d 78 (1973).[3] It held that free speech was enhanced and not abridged by the Florida right-of-reply statute, which in that court's view, furthered the "broad societal interest in the free flow of information to the public." Id., at 82. It also held that the statute is [246] not impermissibly vague; the statute informs "those who are subject to it as to what conduct on their part will render them liable to its penalties." Id., at 85.[4] Civil remedies, including damages, were held to be available under this statute; the case was remanded to the trial court for further proceedings not inconsistent with the Florida Supreme Court's opinion.

We postponed consideration of the question of jurisdiction to the hearing of the case on the merits. 414 U.S. 1142 (1974).

II. [2] Although both parties contend that this Court has jurisdiction to review the judgment of the Florida Supreme Court, a suggestion was initially made that the judgment of the Florida Supreme Court might not be "final" under 28 U. S. C. § 1257.[5] In North Dakota State Pharmacy Bd. v. Snyder's Stores, 414 U.S. 156 (1973), we reviewed a judgment of the North Dakota Supreme Court, under which the case had been remanded so that further state proceedings could be conducted respecting Snyder's application for a permit to operate a drug store. We held that to be a final judgment for purposes of our jurisdiction. Under the principles of finality enunciated in Snyder's Stores, the judgment of [247] the Florida Supreme Court in this case is ripe for review by this Court.[6]

III. A   The challenged statute creates a right to reply to press criticism of a candidate for nomination or election. The statute was enacted in 1913, and this is only the second recorded case decided under its provisions.[7]

Appellant contends the statute is void on its face because it purports to regulate the content of a newspaper in violation of the First Amendment. Alternatively it is urged that the statute is void for vagueness since no editor could know exactly what words would call the statute into operation. It is also contended that the statute fails to distinguish between critical comment which is and which is not defamatory.

B   The appellee and supporting advocates of an enforceable right of access to the press vigorously argue that [248] government has an obligation to ensure that a wide variety of views reach the public.[8] The contentions of access proponents will be set out in some detail.[9] It is urged that at the time the First Amendment to the Constitution[10] was ratified in 1791 as part of our Bill of Rights the press was broadly representative of the people it was serving. While many of the newspapers were intensely partisan and narrow in their views, the press collectively presented a broad range of opinions to readers. Entry into publishing was inexpensive; pamphlets and books provided meaningful alternatives to the organized press for the expression of unpopular ideas and often treated events and expressed views not covered by conventional

---

[3] The Supreme Court did not disturb the Circuit Court's holding that injunctive relief was not proper in this case even if the statute were constitutional. According to the Supreme Court neither side took issue with that part of the Circuit Court's decision. 287 So. 2d, at 85.

[4] The Supreme Court placed the following limiting construction on the statute:
"[We] hold that the mandate of the statute refers to 'any reply' which is wholly responsive to the charge made in the editorial or other article in a newspaper being replied to and further that such reply will be neither libelous nor slanderous of the publication nor anyone else, nor vulgar nor profane." Id., at 86.

[5] Appellee's Response to Appellant's Jurisdictional Statement and Motion to Affirm the Judgment Below or, in the Alternative, to Dismiss the Appeal 4-7.

[6] Both appellant and appellee claim that the uncertainty of the constitutional validity of § 104.38 restricts the present exercise of First Amendment rights. Brief for Appellant 41; Brief for Appellee 79. Appellant finds urgency for the present

consideration of the constitutionality of the statute in the upcoming 1974 elections. Whichever way we were to decide on the merits, it would be intolerable to leave unanswered, under these circumstances, an important question of freedom of the press under the First Amendment; an uneasy and unsettled constitutional posture of § 104.38 could only further harm the operation of a free press. Mills v. Alabama, 384 U.S. 214, 221-222 (1966) (DOUGLAS, J., concurring). See also Organization for a Better Austin v. Keefe, 402 U.S. 415, 418 n. (1971).

[7] In its first court test the statute was declared unconstitutional. State v. News-Journal Corp., 36 Fla. Supp. 164 (Volusia County Judge's Court, 1972). In neither of the two suits, the instant action and the News-Journal action, has the Florida Attorney General defended the statute's constitutionality.

[8] See generally Barron, Access to the Press – A New First Amendment Right, 80 Harv. L. Rev. 1641 (1967).

[9] For a good overview of the position of access advocates see Lange, The Role of the Access Doctrine in the Regulation of the Mass Media: A Critical Review and Assessment, 52 N. C.L. Rev. 1, 8-9 (1973) (hereinafter Lange).

[10] "Congress shall make no law respecting an establishment of religion, or prohibiting the free exercise thereof; or abridging the freedom of speech, or of the press; or of the right of the people peaceably to assemble, and to petition the Government for a redress of grievances."

newspapers.[11] A true marketplace of ideas existed in which there was relatively easy access to the channels of communication.

Access advocates submit that although newspapers of the present are superficially similar to those of 1791 the press of today is in reality very different from that known in the early years of our national existence. In the past half century a communications revolution has seen the introduction of radio and television into our lives, the promise of a global community through the [249] use of communications satellites, and the specter of a "wired" nation by means of an expanding cable television network with two-way capabilities. The printed press, it is said, has not escaped the effects of this revolution. Newspapers have become big business and there are far fewer of them to serve a larger literate population.[12] Chains of newspapers, national newspapers, national wire and news services, and one-newspaper towns,[13] are the dominant features of a press that has become noncompetitive and enormously powerful and influential in its capacity to manipulate popular opinion and change the course of events. Major metropolitan newspapers have collaborated to establish news services national in scope.[14] Such national news organizations provide syndicated "interpretive reporting" as well as syndicated features and commentary, all of which can serve as part of the new school of "advocacy journalism."

The elimination of competing newspapers in most of our large cities, and the concentration of control of media that results from the only newspaper's being owned by the same interests which own a television station and a radio station, are important components of this trend toward [250] concentration of control of outlets to inform the public.

The result of these vast changes has been to place in a few hands the power to inform the American people and shape public opinion.[15] Much of the editorial opinion and commentary that is printed is that of syndicated columnists distributed nationwide and, as a result, we are told, on national and world issues there tends to be a homogeneity of editorial opinion, commentary, and interpretive analysis. The abuses of bias and manipulative reportage are, likewise, said to be the result of the vast accumulations of unreviewable power in the modern media empires. In effect, it is claimed, the public has lost any ability to respond or to contribute in a meaningful way to the debate on issues. The monopoly of the means of communication allows for little or no critical analysis of the media except in professional journals of very limited readership.

"This concentration of nationwide news organizations – like other large institutions – has grown increasingly remote from and unresponsive to the popular constituencies on which they depend and which depend on them." Report of the Task Force in Twentieth Century Fund Task Force Report for a National News Council, A Free and Responsive Press 4 (1973).

Appellee cites the report of the Commission on Freedom of the Press, chaired by Robert M. Hutchins, in which it was stated, as long ago as 1947, that "[the] right of free [251] public expression has . . . lost its earlier reality." Commission on Freedom of the Press, A Free and Responsible Press 15 (1947).

The obvious solution, which was available to dissidents at an earlier time when entry into publishing was relatively inexpensive, today would be to have additional newspapers. But the same economic factors which have caused the disappearance of vast numbers of metropolitan newspapers,[16] have made entry into the marketplace of ideas served by the print media almost impossible. It is urged that the claim of newspapers to be "surrogates for the public" carries with it a concomitant fiduciary obligation to account for that stewardship.[17] From this premise it is reasoned that

---

[11] See Commission on Freedom of the Press, A Free and Responsible Press 14 (1947) (hereinafter sometimes Commission).

[12] Commission 15. Even in the last 20 years there has been a significant increase in the number of people likely to read newspapers. Bagdikian, Fat Newspapers and Slim Coverage, Columbia Journalism Review 15, 16 (Sept./Oct. 1973).

[13] "Nearly half of U.S. daily newspapers, representing some three-fifths of daily and Sunday circulation, are owned by newspaper groups and chains, including diversified business conglomerates. One-newspaper towns have become the rule, with effective competition operating in only 4 percent of our large cities." Background Paper by Alfred Balk in Twentieth Century Fund Task Force Report for a National News Council, A Free and Responsive Press 18 (1973).

[14] Report of the Task Force in Twentieth Century Fund Task Force Report for a National News Council, A Free and Responsive Press 4 (1973).

[15] "Local monopoly in printed news raises serious questions of diversity of information and opinion. What a local newspaper does not print about local affairs does not see general print at all. And, having the power to take initiative in reporting and enunciation of opinions, it has extraordinary power to set the atmosphere and determine the terms of local consideration of public issues." B. Bagdikian, The Information Machines 127 (1971).

[16] The newspapers have persuaded Congress to grant them immunity from the antitrust laws in the case of "failing" newspapers for joint operations. 84 Stat. 466, 15 U. S. C. § 1801 et seq.

[17] "Freedom of the press is a right belonging, like all rights in a democracy, to all the people. As a practical matter, however, it can be exercised only by those who have effective access to the press. Where financial, economic, and technological conditions limit such access to a small minority, the exercise of that right by that minority takes on fiduciary or quasi-fiduciary characteristics." A. MacLeish in W. Hocking, Freedom of the Press 99 n. 4 (1947)(italics omitted).

the only effective way to insure fairness and accuracy and to provide for some accountability is for government to take affirmative action. The First Amendment interest of the public in being informed is said to be in peril because the "marketplace of ideas" is today a monopoly controlled by the owners of the market.

Proponents of enforced access to the press take comfort from language in several of this Court's decisions which suggests that the First Amendment acts as a sword as well as a shield, that it imposes obligations on the owners of the press in addition to protecting the press from government regulation. In Associated Press v. United States, 326 U.S. 1, 20 (1945), the Court, in [252] rejecting the argument that the press is immune from the antitrust laws by virtue of the First Amendment, stated:

"The First Amendment, far from providing an argument against application of the Sherman Act, here provides powerful reasons to the contrary. That Amendment rests on the assumption that the widest possible dissemination of information from diverse and antagonistic sources is essential to the welfare of the public, that a free press is a condition of a free society. Surely a command that the government itself shall not impede the free flow of ideas does not afford non-governmental combinations a refuge if they impose restraints upon that constitutionally guaranteed freedom. Freedom to publish means freedom for all and not for some. Freedom to publish is guaranteed by the Constitution, but freedom to combine to keep others from publishing is not. Freedom of the press from governmental interference under the First Amendment does not sanction repression of that freedom by private interests." (Footnote omitted.)

In New York Times Co. v. Sullivan, 376 U.S. 254, 270 (1964), the Court spoke of "a profound national commitment to the principle that debate on public issues should be uninhibited, robust, and wide-open." It is argued that the "uninhibited, robust" debate is not "wide-open" but open only to a monopoly in control of the press. Appellee cites the plurality opinion in Rosenbloom v. Metromedia, Inc., 403 U.S. 29, 47, and n. 15 (1971), which he suggests seemed to invite experimentation by the States in right-to-access regulation of the press.[18]

[253] Access advocates note that MR. JUSTICE DOUGLAS a decade ago expressed his deep concern regarding the effects of newspaper monopolies: "Where one paper has a monopoly in an area, it seldom presents two sides of an issue. It too often hammers away on one ideological or political line using its monopoly position not to educate people, not to promote debate, but to inculcate in its readers one philosophy, one attitude – and to make money."

"The newspapers that give a variety of views and news that is not slanted or contrived are few indeed. And the problem promises to get worse . . . ." The Great Rights 124-125, 127 (E. Cahn ed. 1963).

They also claim the qualified support of Professor Thomas I. Emerson, who has written that "[a] limited right of access to the press can be safely enforced," [254] although he believes that "[government] measures to encourage a multiplicity of outlets, rather than compelling a few outlets to represent everybody, seems a preferable course of action." T. Emerson, The System of Freedom of Expression 671 (1970).

IV.   However much validity may be found in these arguments, at each point the implementation of a remedy such as an enforceable right of access necessarily calls for some mechanism, either governmental or consensual.[19] If it is governmental coercion, this at once brings about a confrontation with the express provisions of the First Amendment and the judicial gloss on that Amendment developed over the years.[20]

---

[18] "If the States fear that private citizens will not be able to respond adequately to publicity involving them, the solution lies in the direction of ensuring their ability to respond, rather than in stifling public discussion of matters of public concern.[*]

"[*]Some states have adopted retraction statutes or right-of-reply statutes . . . .

"One writer, in arguing that the First Amendment itself should be read to guarantee a right of access to the media not limited to a right to respond to defamatory falsehoods, has suggested several ways the law might encourage public discussion. Barron, Access to the Press – A New First Amendment Right, 80 Harv. L. Rev. 1641, 1666-1678 (1967). It is important to recognize that the private individual often desires press exposure either for himself, his ideas, or his causes. Constitutional adjudication must take into account the individual's interest in access to the press as well as the individual's interest in preserving his reputation, even though libel actions by their nature encourage a narrow view of the individual's interest since they focus only on situations where the individual has been harmed by undesired press attention. A constitutional rule that deters the press from covering the ideas or activities of the private individual thus conceives the individual's interest too narrowly."

[19] The National News Council, an independent and voluntary body concerned with press fairness, was created in 1973 to provide a means for neutral examination of claims of press inaccuracy. The Council was created following the publication of the Twentieth Century Fund Task Force Report for a National News Council, A Free and Responsive Press. The background paper attached to the Report dealt in some detail with the British Press Council, seen by the author of the paper as having the most interest to the United States of the European press councils.

[20] Because we hold that § 104.38 violates the First Amendment's guarantee of a free press we have no occasion

The Court foresaw the problems relating to government-enforced access as early as its decision in Associated Press v. United States, supra. There it carefully contrasted the private "compulsion to print" called for by the Association's bylaws with the provisions of the District Court decree against appellants which "does not compel AP or its members to permit publication of anything which their 'reason' tells them should not be published." 326 U.S., at 20 n. 18. In Branzburg v. Hayes, 408 U.S. 665, 681 (1972), we emphasized that the cases then [255] before us "involve no intrusions upon speech or assembly, no prior restraint or restriction on what the press may publish, and no express or implied command that the press publish what it prefers to withhold." In Columbia Broadcasting System, Inc. v. Democratic National Committee, 412 U.S. 94, 117 (1973), the plurality opinion as to Part III noted: "The power of a privately owned newspaper to advance its own political, social, and economic views is bounded by only two factors: first, the acceptance of a sufficient number of readers – and hence advertisers – to assure financial success; and, second, the journalistic integrity of its editors and publishers."

An attitude strongly adverse to any attempt to extend a right of access to newspapers was echoed by other Members of this Court in their separate opinions in that case. Id., at 145 (STEWART, J., concurring); id., at 182 n. 12 (BRENNAN, J., joined by MARSHALL, J., dissenting). Recently, while approving a bar against employment advertising specifying "male" or "female" preference, the Court's opinion in Pittsburgh Press Co. v. Human Relations Comm'n, 413 U.S. 376, 391 (1973), took pains to limit its holding within narrow bounds: "Nor, a fortiori, does our decision authorize any restriction whatever, whether of content or layout, on stories or commentary originated by Pittsburgh Press, its columnists, or its contributors. On the contrary, we reaffirm unequivocally the protection afforded to editorial judgment and to the free expression of views on these and other issues, however controversial."

Dissenting in Pittsburgh Press, MR. JUSTICE STEWART, joined by MR. JUSTICE DOUGLAS, expressed the view that no "government agency – local, state, or federal – can tell [256] a newspaper in advance what it can print and what it cannot." Id., at 400. See Associates & Aldrich Co. v. Times Mirror Co., 440 F.2d 133, 135 (CA9 1971).

[3] We see that beginning with Associated Press, supra, the Court has expressed sensitivity as to whether a restriction or requirement constituted the compulsion exerted by government on a newspaper

to consider appellant's further argument that the statute is unconstitutionally vague.

to print that which it would not otherwise print. The clear implication has been that any such a compulsion to publish that which "'reason' tells them should not be published" is unconstitutional. A responsible press is an undoubtedly desirable goal, but press responsibility is not mandated by the Constitution and like many other virtues it cannot be legislated.

[4] Appellee's argument that the Florida statute does not amount to a restriction of appellant's right to speak because "the statute in question here has not prevented the Miami Herald from saying anything it wished"[21] begs the core question. Compelling editors or publishers to publish that which "'reason' tells them should not be published" is what is at issue in this case. The Florida statute operates as a command in the same sense as a statute or regulation forbidding appellant to publish specified matter. Governmental restraint on publishing need not fall into familiar or traditional patterns to be subject to constitutional limitations on governmental powers. Grosjean v. American Press Co., 297 U.S. 233, 244-245 (1936). The Florida statute exacts a penalty on the basis of the content of a newspaper. The first phase of the penalty resulting from the compelled printing of a reply is exacted in terms of the cost in printing and composing time and materials and in taking up space that could be devoted to other material the newspaper may have preferred to print. It is correct, as appellee contends, that a newspaper is not subject to the [257] finite technological limitations of time that confront a broadcaster but it is not correct to say that, as an economic reality, a newspaper can proceed to infinite expansion of its column space to accommodate the replies that a government agency determines or a statute commands the readers should have available.[22]

[5] Faced with the penalties that would accrue to any newspaper that published news or commentary arguably within the reach of the right-of-access statute, editors might well conclude that the safe course is to avoid controversy. Therefore, under the operation of the Florida statute, political and electoral coverage would be blunted or

---

[21] Brief for Appellee 5.

[22] "However, since the amount of space a newspaper can devote to 'live news' is finite, [*] if a newspaper is forced to publish a particular item, it must as a practical matter, omit something else.

"[*] The number of column inches available for news is predetermined by a number of financial and physical factors, including circulation, the amount of advertising, and, increasingly, the availability of newsprint. . . ." Note, 48 Tulane L. Rev. 433, 438 (1974) (one footnote omitted). Another factor operating against the "solution" of adding more pages to accommodate the access matter is that "increasingly subscribers complain of bulky, unwieldy papers." Bagdikian, Fat Newspapers and Slim Coverage, Columbia Journalism Review 19 (Sept./Oct. 1973).

reduced.[23] Government-enforced right of access inescapably "dampens the vigor and limits the variety of public debate," New York Times Co. v. Sullivan, 376 U.S., at 279. The Court, in Mills v. Alabama, 384 U.S. 214, 218 (1966), stated: "[There] is practically universal agreement that a major purpose of [the First] Amendment was to protect the free discussion of governmental affairs. This of course includes discussions of candidates. . . ."

[258] [6] Even if a newspaper would face no additional costs to comply with a compulsory access law and would not be forced to forgo publication of news or opinion by the inclusion of a reply, the Florida statute fails to clear the barriers of the First Amendment because of its intrusion into the function of editors. A newspaper is more than a passive receptacle or conduit for news, comment, and advertising. [24] The choice of material to go into a newspaper, and the decisions made as to limitations on the size and content of the paper, and treatment of public issues and public officials – whether fair or unfair – constitute the exercise of editorial control and judgment. It has yet to be demonstrated how governmental regulation of this crucial process can be exercised consistent with First Amendment guarantees of a free press as they have evolved to this time. Accordingly, the judgment of the Supreme Court of Florida is reversed.

It is so ordered.

CONCUR: MR. JUSTICE BRENNAN, with whom MR. JUSTICE REHNQUIST joins, concurring.

I join the Court's opinion which, as I understand it, addresses only "right of reply" statutes and implies no view upon the constitutionality of "retraction" statutes affording plaintiffs able to prove defamatory falsehoods a statutory action to require publication of a retraction. [259] See generally Note, Vindication of the Reputation of a Public Official, 80 Harv. L. Rev. 1730, 1739-1747 (1967).

CONCUR: MR. JUSTICE WHITE, concurring.

The Court today holds that the First Amendment bars a State from requiring a newspaper to print the reply of a candidate for public office whose personal character has been criticized by that newspaper's editorials. According to our accepted jurisprudence,

the First Amendment erects a virtually insurmountable barrier between government and the print media so far as government tampering, in advance of publication, with news and editorial content is concerned. New York Times Co. v. United States, 403 U.S. 713 (1971). A newspaper or magazine is not a public utility subject to "reasonable" governmental regulation in matters affecting the exercise of journalistic judgment as to what shall be printed. Cf. Mills v. Alabama, 384 U.S. 214, 220 (1966). We have learned, and continue to learn, from what we view as the unhappy experiences of other nations where government has been allowed to meddle in the internal editorial affairs of newspapers. Regardless of how beneficent-sounding the purposes of controlling the press might be, we prefer "the power of reason as applied through public discussion"[1] and remain intensely skeptical about those measures that would allow government to insinuate itself into the editorial rooms of this Nation's press.

"Whatever differences may exist about interpretations of the First Amendment, there is practically universal agreement that a major purpose of that Amendment was to protect the free discussion of governmental affairs. This of course includes discussions of candidates, structures and forms of [260] government, the manner in which government is operated or should be operated, and all such matters relating to political processes. The Constitution specifically selected the press . . . to play an important role in the discussion of public affairs. Thus the press serves and was designed to serve as a powerful antidote to any abuses of power by governmental officials and as a constitutionally chosen means for keeping officials elected by the people responsible to all the people whom they were selected to serve. Suppression of the right of the press to praise or criticize governmental agents and to clamor and contend for or against change . . . muzzles one of the very agencies the Framers of our Constitution thoughtfully and deliberately selected to improve our society and keep it free." Mills v. Alabama, supra, at 218-219.

Of course, the press is not always accurate, or even responsible, and may not present full and fair debate on important public issues. But the balance struck by the First Amendment with respect to the press is that society must take the risk that occasionally debate on vital matters will not be comprehensive and that all viewpoints may not be expressed. The press would be unlicensed because, in Jefferson's words, "[where] the press is free, and

---

[23] See the description of the likely effect of the Florida statute on publishers, in Lange 70-71.

[24] "[Liberty] of the press is in peril as soon as the government tries to compel what is to go into a newspaper. A journal does not merely print observed facts the way a cow is photographed through a plate-glass window. As soon as the facts are set in their context, you have interpretation and you have selection, and editorial selection opens the way to editorial suppression. Then how can the state force abstention from discrimination in the news without dictating selection?"

---

[1] Whitney v. California, 274 U.S. 357, 375 (1927) (Brandeis, J., concurring).

every man able to read, all is safe."[2] Any other accommodation – any other system that would supplant private control of the press with the heavy hand of government intrusion – would make the government the censor of what the people may read and know.

To justify this statute, Florida advances a concededly important interest of ensuring free and fair elections by means of an electorate informed about the issues. But [261] prior compulsion by government in matters going to the very nerve center of a newspaper – the decision as to what copy will or will not be included in any given edition – collides with the First Amendment. Woven into the fabric of the First Amendment is the unexceptionable, but nonetheless timeless, sentiment that "liberty of the press is in peril as soon as the government tries to compel what is to go into a newspaper." 2 Z. Chafee, Government and Mass Communications 633 (1947).

The constitutionally obnoxious feature of § 104.38 is not that the Florida Legislature may also have placed a high premium on the protection of individual reputational interests; for government certainly has "a pervasive and strong interest in preventing and redressing attacks upon reputation." Rosenblatt v. Baer, 383 U.S. 75, 86 (1966). Quite the contrary, this law runs afoul of the elementary First Amendment proposition that government may not force a newspaper to print copy which, in its journalistic discretion, it chooses to leave on the newsroom floor. Whatever power may reside in government to influence the publishing of certain narrowly circumscribed categories of material, see, e.g., Pittsburgh Press Co. v. Human Relations Comm'n, 413 U.S. 376 (1973); New York Times Co. v. United States, 403 U.S., at 730 (WHITE, J., concurring), we have never thought that the First Amendment permitted public officials to dictate to the press the contents of its news columns or the slant of its editorials.

But though a newspaper may publish without government censorship, it has never been entirely free from liability for what it chooses to print. See ibid. Among other things, the press has not been wholly at liberty to publish falsehoods damaging to individual reputation. At least until today, we have cherished the average citizen's [262] reputation interest enough to afford him a fair chance to vindicate himself in an action for libel characteristically provided by state law. He has been unable to force the press to tell his side of the story or to print a retraction, but he has had at least the opportunity to win a judgment if he has been able to prove the falsity of the damaging publication, as well as a fair chance to recover reasonable damages for his injury.

Reaffirming the rule that the press cannot be forced to print an answer to a personal attack made by it, however, throws into stark relief the cones-quences of the new balance forged by the Court in the companion case also announced today. Gertz v. Robert Welch, Inc., post, p. 323, goes far toward eviscerating the effectiveness of the ordinary libel action, which has long been the only potent response available to the private citizen libeled by the press. Under Gertz, the burden of proving liability is immeasurably increased, proving damages is made exceedingl more difficult, and vindicating reputation by merely proving falsehood and winning a judg-ment to that effect are wholly foreclosed. Needlessly, in my view, the Court trivializes and denigrates the interest in reputation by removing virtually all the protection the law has always afforded.

Of course, these two decisions do not mean that because government may not dictate what the press is to print, neither can it afford a remedy for libel in any form. Gertz itself leaves a putative remedy for libel intact, albeit in severely emaciated form; and the press certainly remains liable for knowing or reckless falsehoods under New York Times Co. v. Sullivan, 376 U.S. 254 (1964), and its progeny, however improper an injunction against publication might be.

One need not think less of the First Amendment to sustain reasonable methods for allowing the average citizen [263] to redeem a falsely tarnished reputation. Nor does one have to doubt the genuine decency, integrity, and good sense of the vast majority of professional journalists to support the right of any individual to have his day in court when he has been falsely maligned in the public press. The press is the servant, not the master, of the citizenry, and its freedom does not carry with it an unrestricted hunting license to prey on the ordinary citizen.

"In plain English, freedom carries with it responsibility even for the press; freedom of the press is not a freedom from responsibility for its exercise." "Without . . . a lively sense of responsibility a free press may readily become a powerful instrument of injustice." Pennekamp v. Florida, 328 U.S. 331, 356, 365 (1946) (Frankfurter, J., concurring) (footnote omitted).

To me it is a near absurdity to so deprecate individual dignity, as the Court does in Gertz, and to leave the people at the complete mercy of the press, at least in this stage of our history when the press, as the majority in this case so well documents, is steadily becoming more powerful and much less likely to be deterred by threats of libel suits.

---

[2] Letter to Col. Charles Yancey in 14 The Writings of Thomas Jefferson 384 (Lipscomb ed. 1904).

Red Lion Broadcasting System v. Federal Communications Commission
395 U.S. 367
(1969)
(Excerpts only. Footnotes omitted.)

PRIOR HISTORY: Certiorari to the United States Court of Appeals for the District of Columbia Circuit.

JUDGES: Warren, Black, Harlan, Brennan, Stewart, White, Marshall; Douglas took no part in the Court's decision.

OPINION: [369] MR. JUSTICE WHITE delivered the opinion of the unanimous Court.

The Federal Communications Commission has for many years imposed on radio and television broadcasters the requirement that discussion of public issues be presented on broadcast stations, and that each side of those issues must be given fair coverage. This is known as the fairness doctrine, which originated very early in the history of broadcasting and has maintained its present outlines for some time. It is an obligation whose content has been defined in a long series of FCC rulings in particular cases, and which is distinct from the statutory [370] requirement of § 315 of the Communications Act that equal time be allotted all qualified candidates for public office. Two aspects of the fairness doctrine, relating to personal attacks in the context of controversial public issues and to political editorializing, were codified more precisely in the form of FCC regulations in 1967. The two cases before us now, which were decided separately below, challenge the constitutional and statutory bases of the doctrine and component rules. Red Lion [371] involves the application of the fairness doctrine to a particular broadcast, and RTNDA arises as an action to review the FCC's 1967 promulgation of the personal attack and political editorializing regulations, which were laid down after the Red Lion litigation had begun.

The Red Lion Broadcasting Company is licensed to operate a Pennsylvania radio station, WGCB. On November 27, 1964, WGCB carried a 15-minute broadcast by the Reverend Billy James Hargis as part of a "Christian Crusade" series. A book by Fred J. Cook entitled "Goldwater – Extremist on the Right" was discussed by Hargis, who said that Cook had been fired by a newspaper for making false charges against city officials; that Cook had then worked for a Communist-affiliated publication; that he had defended Alger Hiss and attacked J. Edgar Hoover and the Central Intelligence Agency; and that he had now written a "book to smear and destroy Barry Goldwater." When Cook heard of the broadcast he [372] concluded that he had been personally attacked and demanded free reply time, which the station refused. After an exchange of letters among Cook, Red Lion, and the FCC, the FCC declared that the Hargis broadcast constituted a personal attack on Cook; that Red Lion had failed to meet its obligation under the fairness doctrine as expressed in Times-Mirror Broadcasting Co., 24 P & F Radio Reg. 404 (1962), to send a tape, transcript, or summary of the broadcast to Cook and offer him reply time; and that the station must provide reply time whether or not Cook would pay for it. On review in the Court of Appeals for the District of Columbia Circuit, the [373] FCC's position was upheld as constitutional and otherwise proper. 127 U. S. App. D. C. 129, 381 F.2d 908 (1967). ... [375]

Believing that the specific application of the fairness doctrine in Red Lion ... [serves to]enhance rather than abridge the freedoms of speech and press protected by the First Amendment, we hold them valid and constitutional. ... The history of the emergence of the fairness doctrine and of the related legislation shows that the Commission's action in the Red Lion case did not exceed its authority, and that in adopting the new regulations the Commission was implementing congressional policy rather than embarking on a frolic of its own.

Before 1927, the allocation of frequencies was left entirely to the private sector, and the result was chaos. [376] It quickly became apparent that broadcast frequencies constituted a scarce resource whose use could be regulated and rationalized only by the Government. Without government control, the medium would be of little use because of the cacophony of competing voices, none of which could be clearly and predictably heard. Consequently, the Federal Radio Commission was established [377] to allocate frequencies among competing applicants in a manner responsive to the public "convenience, interest, or necessity."

Very shortly thereafter the Commission expressed its view that the "public interest requires ample play for the free and fair competition of opposing views, and the commission believes that the principle applies . . . to all discussions of issues of importance to the public." Great Lakes Broadcasting Co., 3 F. R. C. Ann. Rep. 32, 33 (1929), rev'd on other grounds, 59 App. D. C. 197, 37 F.2d 993, cert. dismissed, 281

U.S. 706 (1930). This doctrine was applied through denial of license renewals or construction permits, both by the FRC, Trinity Methodist Church, South v. FRC, 61 App. D. C. 311, 62 F.2d 850 (1932), cert. denied, 288 U.S. 599 (1933), and its successor FCC, Young People's Association for the Propagation of the Gospel, 6 F. C. C. 178 (1938). After an extended period during which the licensee was obliged not only to cover and to cover fairly the views of others, but also to refrain from expressing his own personal views, Mayflower Broadcasting Corp., 8 F. C. C. 333 (1940), the latter limitation on the licensee was abandoned and the doctrine developed into its present form.

There is a twofold duty laid down by the FCC's decisions and described by the 1949 Report on Editorializing by Broadcast Licensees, 13 F. C. C. 1246 (1949). The broadcaster must give adequate coverage to public issues, United Broadcasting Co., 10 F. C. C. 515 (1945), and coverage must be fair in that it accurately reflects the opposing views. New Broadcasting Co., 6 P & F Radio Reg. 258 (1950). This must be done at the broadcaster's own expense if sponsorship is unavailable. Cullman Broadcasting Co., 25 P & F Radio Reg. 895 (1963). [378] Moreover, the duty must be met by programming obtained at the licensee's own initiative if available from no other source. John J. Dempsey, 6 P & F Radio Reg. 615 (1950); see Metropolitan Broadcasting Corp., 19 P & F Radio Reg. 602 (1960); The Evening News Assn., 6 P & F Radio Reg. 283 (1950). The Federal Radio Commission had imposed these two basic duties on broadcasters since the outset, Great Lakes Broadcasting Co., 3 F. R. C. Ann. Rep. 32 (1929), rev'd on other grounds, 59 App. D. C. 197, 37 F.2d 993, cert. dismissed, 281 U.S. 706 (1930); Chicago Federation of Labor v. FRC, 3 F. R. C. Ann. Rep. 36 (1929), aff'd, 59 App. D. C. 333, 41 F.2d 422 (1930); KFKB Broadcasting Assn. v. FRC, 60 App. D. C. 79, 47 F.2d 670 (1931), and in particular respects the personal attack rules and regulations at issue here have spelled them out in greater detail.

When a personal attack has been made on a figure involved in a public issue, both the doctrine of cases such as Red Lion and Times-Mirror Broadcasting Co., 24 P & F Radio Reg. 404 (1962), and also the 1967 regulations at issue in RTNDA require that the individual attacked himself be offered an opportunity to respond. Likewise, where one candidate is endorsed in a political editorial, the other candidates must themselves be offered reply time to use personally or through a spokesman. These obligations differ from the general fairness requirement that issues be presented, and presented with coverage of competing views, in that the broadcaster does not have the option of presenting the attacked party's side himself or choosing a third party to represent that side. But

insofar as there is an obligation of the broadcaster to see that both sides are presented, and insofar as that is an affirmative obligation, the personal attack doctrine and regulations do not differ from the preceding fairness doctrine. ... [379]

The statutory authority of the FCC to promulgate these regulations derives from the mandate to the "Commission from time to time, as public convenience, interest, or necessity requires" to promulgate "such rules and regulations and prescribe such restrictions and conditions . . . as may be necessary to carry out the provisions of this chapter . . . ." 47 U. S. C. § 303 and § 303 (r). ... [380] This mandate to the FCC to assure that broadcasters operate in the public interest is a broad one, a power "not niggardly but expansive," National Broadcasting Co. v. United States, 319 U.S. 190, 219 (1943), whose validity ... is broad enough to encompass these regulations. ...

Congress, in 1959, announced that the phrase "public interest," which had been in the Act since 1927, imposed a duty on broadcasters to discuss both sides of controversial public issues. In other words, the amendment vindicated the FCC's general view that the fairness doctrine inhered in the public interest standard. ... [381] Thirty years of consistent administrative construction left undisturbed by Congress until 1959, when that construction was expressly accepted, reinforce the natural conclusion that the public interest language of the Act authorized the Commission to require licensees to use their stations for discussion of public issues, and that the FCC is free to implement this requirement by reasonable rules and regulations which fall short of abridgment of the freedom of speech and press, and of the censorship proscribed by § 326 of the Act.

... [383] "[B]roadcast frequencies are limited and, therefore, they have been necessarily considered a public trust. Every licensee who is fortunate in obtaining a license is mandated to operate in the public interest and has assumed the obligation of presenting important public questions fairly and without bias." S. Rep. No. 562, 86th Cong., 1st Sess., 8-9 (1959). See also, specifically adverting to Federal Communications Commission doctrine, id., at 13.

... [385] When the Congress ratified the FCC's implication of a fairness doctrine in 1959 it did not, of course, approve every past decision or pronouncement by the Commission on this subject, or give it a completely free hand for the future. The statutory authority does not go so far. But we cannot say that when a station publishes personal attacks or endorses political candidates, it is a misconstruction of the public interest standard to require the station to offer time for a response rather than to leave the response entirely within the control of the station which has attacked either the candidacies or the men who wish to reply in their own defense. When a broadcaster grants time to a political candidate, Congress itself requires that equal time be offered to his opponents. It would exceed our competence to hold that the Commission is unauthorized by the statute to employ a similar device where personal attacks or political editorials are broadcast by a radio or television station.

In light of the fact that the "public interest" in broadcasting clearly encompasses the presentation of vigorous debate of controversial issues of importance and concern to the public; the fact that the FCC has rested upon that language from its very inception a doctrine that these issues must be discussed, and fairly; and the fact that Congress has acknowledged that the analogous provisions of § 315 are not preclusive in this area, and knowingly preserved the FCC's complementary efforts, we think the fairness doctrine and its component personal attack and political editorializing regulations are a legitimate exercise of congressionally delegated authority. ... [386] .We cannot say that the FCC's declaratory ruling in Red Lion , or the regulations at issue in RTNDA, are beyond the scope of the congressionally conferred power to assure that stations are operated by those whose possession of a license serves "the public interest."

The broadcasters challenge the fairness doctrine and its specific manifestations in the personal attack and political editorial rules on conventional First Amendment grounds, alleging that the rules abridge their freedom of speech and press. Their contention is that the First Amendment protects their desire to use their allotted frequencies continuously to broadcast whatever they choose, and to exclude whomever they choose from ever using that frequency. No man may be prevented from saying or publishing what he thinks, or from refusing in his speech or other utterances to give equal weight to the views of his opponents. This right, they say, applies equally to broadcasters.

Although broadcasting is clearly a medium affected by a First Amendment interest, United States v. Paramount Pictures, Inc., 334 U.S. 131, 166 (1948), differences in the characteristics of new media justify differences in the First Amendment standards applied to them. Joseph [387] Burstyn, Inc. v. Wilson, 343 U.S. 495, 503 (1952). For example, the ability of new technology to produce sounds more raucous than those of the human voice justifies restrictions on the sound level, and on the hours and places of use, of sound trucks so long as the restrictions are reasonable and applied without discrimination. Kovacs v. Cooper, 336 U.S. 77 (1949).

Just as the Government may limit the use of sound-amplifying equipment potentially so noisy that it drowns out civilized private speech, so may the Government limit the use of broadcast equipment. The right of free speech of a broadcaster, the user of a sound truck, or any other individual does not embrace a right to snuff out the free speech of others. Associated Press v. United States, 326 U.S. 1, 20 (1945).

When two people converse face to face, both should not speak at once if either is to be clearly understood. But the range of the human voice is so limited that there could be meaningful communications if half the people in the United States were talking and the other half listening. Just as clearly, half the people might publish and the other half read. But the reach of radio signals is [388] incomparably greater than the range of the human voice and the problem of interference is a massive reality. The lack of know-how and equipment may keep many from the air, but only a tiny fraction of those with resources and intelligence can hope to communicate by radio at the same time if intelligible communication is to be had, even if the entire radio spectrum is utilized in the present state of commercially acceptable technology.

It was this fact, and the chaos which ensued from permitting anyone to use any frequency at whatever power level he wished, which made necessary the enactment of the Radio Act of 1927 and the Communications Act of 1934, as the Court has noted at length before. National Broadcasting Co. v. United States, 319 U.S. 190, 210-214 (1943). It was this reality which at the very least necessitated first the division of the radio spectrum into portions reserved respectively for public broadcasting and for other important radio uses such as amateur operation, aircraft, police, defense, and navigation; and then the subdivision of each portion, and assignment of specific frequencies to individual users or groups of users. Beyond this, however, because the frequencies reserved for public broadcasting were limited in number, it was essential for the Government to tell some applicants that they could not broadcast at all because there was room for only a few.

Where there are substantially more individuals who want to broadcast than there are frequencies to allocate, it is idle to posit an unabridgeable First Amendment right to broadcast comparable to the right of every individual to speak, write, or publish. If 100 persons want broadcast [389] licenses but there are only 10 frequencies to allocate, all of them may have the same "right" to a license; but if there is to be any effective communication by radio, only a few can be licensed and the rest must be barred from the airwaves. It would be strange if the First Amendment, aimed at protecting and furthering communications, prevented the Government from making radio communication possible by requiring licenses to broadcast and by limiting the number of licenses so as not to overcrowd the spectrum.

This has been the consistent view of the Court. Congress unquestionably has the power to grant and deny licenses and to eliminate existing stations. FRC v. Nelson Bros. Bond & Mortgage Co., 289 U.S. 266 (1933). No one has a First Amendment right to a license or to monopolize a radio frequency; to deny a station license because "the public interest" requires it "is not a denial of free speech." National Broadcasting Co. v. United States, 319 U.S. 190, 227 (1943).

By the same token, as far as the First Amendment is concerned those who are licensed stand no better than those to whom licenses are refused. A license permits broadcasting, but the licensee has no constitutional right to be the one who holds the license or to monopolize a radio frequency to the exclusion of his fellow citizens. There is nothing in the First Amendment which prevents the Government from requiring a licensee to share his frequency with others and to conduct himself as a proxy or fiduciary with obligations to present those views and voices which are representative of his community and which would otherwise, by necessity, be barred from the airwaves.

... [390] Because of the scarcity of radio frequencies, the Government is permitted to put restraints on licensees in favor of others whose views should be expressed on this unique medium. But the people as a whole retain their interest in free speech by radio and their collective right to have the medium function consistently with the ends and purposes of the First Amendment. It is the right of the viewers and listeners, not the right of the broadcasters, which is paramount. See FCC v. Sanders Bros. Radio Station, 309 U.S. 470, 475 (1940); FCC v. Allentown Broadcasting Corp., 349 U.S. 358, 361-362 (1955); 2 Z. Chafee, Government and Mass Communications 546 (1947). It is the purpose of the First Amendment to preserve an uninhibited marketplace of ideas in which truth will ultimately prevail, rather than to countenance monopolization of that market, whether it be by the Government itself or a private licensee. Associated Press v. United States, 326 U.S. 1, 20 (1945); New York Times Co. v. Sullivan, 376 U.S. 254, 270 (1964); Abrams v. United States, 250 U.S. 616, 630 (1919) (Holmes, J., dissenting). "Speech concerning public affairs is more than self-expression; it is the essence of self-government." Garrison v. Louisiana, 379 U.S. 64, 74-75 (1964). See Brennan, The Supreme Court and the Meiklejohn Interpretation of the First Amendment, 79 Harv. L. Rev. 1 (1965). It is the right of the public to receive suitable access to social, political, esthetic, moral, and other ideas and experiences which is crucial here. That right may not constitutionally be abridged either by Congress or by the FCC.

... [391] As we have said, the First Amendment confers no right on licensees to prevent others from broadcasting on "their" frequencies and no right to an unconditional monopoly of a scarce resource which the Government has denied others the right to use. ... Nor can we say that it is inconsistent with the First Amendment goal of producing an informed public capable of conducting its own affairs to require a broadcaster to permit answers to personal attacks occurring in the course of discussing controversial issues, or to require that the political opponents of those endorsed by the station be given a chance to communicate with the public. Otherwise, station owners and a few networks would have unfettered power to make time available only to the highest bidders, to communicate only their own views on public issues, people and candidates, and to permit on the air only those with whom they agreed. There is no sanctuary in the First Amendment for unlimited private censorship operating in a medium not open to all. "Freedom of the press from governmental interference under the First Amendment does not sanction repression of that freedom by private interests." Associated Press v. United States, 326 U.S. 1, 20 (1945).

... [394] It does not violate the First Amendment to treat licensees given the privilege of using scarce radio frequencies as proxies for the entire community, obligated to give suitable time and attention to matters of great public concern. To condition the granting or renewal of licenses on a willingness to present representative community views on controversial issues is consistent with the ends and purposes of those constitutional provisions forbidding the abridgment of freedom of speech and freedom of the press. Congress need not stand idly by and permit those with licenses to ignore the problems which beset the people or to exclude from the airways anything but their own views of fundamental questions. The statute, long administrative practice, and cases are to this effect.

Licenses to broadcast do not confer ownership of designated frequencies, but only the temporary privilege of using them. 47 U. S. C. § 301. ... [396] We need not and do not now ratify every past and future decision by the FCC with regard to programming. There is no question here of the Commission's refusal to permit the broadcaster to carry a particular program or to publish his own views; of a discriminatory refusal to require the licensee to broadcast certain views which have been denied access to the airwaves; of government censorship of a particular program contrary to § 326; or of the official government view dominating public broadcasting. Such questions would raise more serious First Amendment issues. But we do hold that the Congress and the Commission do not violate the First Amendment when they require a radio or television station to give reply time to answer personal attacks and political editorials.

It is argued that even if at one time the lack of available frequencies for all who wished to use them justified the Government's choice of those who would best serve the public interest by acting as proxy for those who would present differing views, or by giving the latter access directly to broadcast facilities, this condition no longer prevails so that continuing control is not justified. To this there are several answers.

Scarcity is not entirely a thing of the past. Advances [397] in technology, such as microwave transmission, have led to more efficient utilization of the frequency spectrum, but uses for that spectrum have also grown apace. Portions of the spectrum must be reserved for vital uses unconnected with human communication, such as radio-navigational aids used by aircraft and vessels. Conflicts have even emerged between such vital functions as defense preparedness and experimentation in methods of averting midair collisions through radio warning devices. ... [398] Comparative hearings between competing applicants for broadcast spectrum space are by no means a thing of the past. The radio spectrum has become so congested that at times it has been necessary to suspend new applications. The very high frequency television spectrum is, in the country's major markets, almost entirely occupied, although space reserved for ultra high frequency television transmission, which is a relatively recent development as a commercially viable alternative, has not yet been completely filled.

[399] The rapidity with which technological advances succeed one another to create more efficient use of spectrum space on the one hand, and to create new uses for that space by ever growing numbers of people on the other, makes it unwise to speculate on the future allocation of that space. It is enough to say that the resource is one of considerable

and growing importance whose scarcity impelled its regulation by an agency authorized by Congress. Nothing in this record, or in our own researches, convinces us that the resource is no longer one for which there are more immediate and potential uses than can be accommodated, and for which wise planning is essential. ... [400] Even where there are gaps in spectrum utilization, the fact remains that existing broadcasters have often attained their present position because of their initial government selection in competition with others before new technological advances opened new opportunities for further uses. Long experience in broadcasting, confirmed habits of listeners and viewers, network affiliation, and other advantages in program procurement give existing broadcasters a substantial advantage over new entrants, even where new entry is technologically possible. These advantages are the fruit of a preferred position conferred by the Government. Some present possibility for new entry by competing stations is not enough, in itself, to render unconstitutional the Government's effort to assure that a broadcaster's programming ranges widely enough to serve the public interest.

In view of the scarcity of broadcast frequencies, the Government's role in allocating those frequencies, and the legitimate claims of those unable without governmental assistance to gain access to those frequencies for expression of their views, we hold the regulations and [401] ruling at issue here are both authorized by statute and constitutional. The judgment of the Court of Appeals in Red Lion is affirmed and that in RTNDA reversed and the causes remanded for proceedings consistent with this opinion.

It is so ordered.

Not having heard oral argument in these cases, MR. JUSTICE DOUGLAS took no part in the Court's decision.

Turner Broadcasting System v. Federal Communications Commission
512 U.S. 622
(1994)
(Excerpts only. Footnotes omitted.)

PRIOR HISTORY: On appeal from the United States District Court for the District of Columbia.

JUDGES: KENNEDY, J., announced the judgment of the Court and delivered the opinion for a unanimous Court with respect to Part I, the opinion of the Court with respect to Parts II-A and II-B, in which REHNQUIST, C. J., and BLACKMUN, O'CONNOR, SCALIA, SOUTER, THOMAS, and

GINSBURG, JJ., joined, the opinion of the Court with respect to Parts II-C, II-D, and III-A, in which REHNQUIST, C. J., and BLACKMUN, STEVENS, and SOUTER, JJ., joined, and an opinion with respect to Part III-B, in which REHNQUIST, C. J., and BLACKMUN and SOUTER, JJ., joined. BLACKMUN, J., filed a concurring opinion. STEVENS, J., filed an opinion concurring in part and concurring in the judgment. O'CONNOR, J., filed an opinion concurring in part and dissenting in part, in which SCALIA and GINSBURG, JJ., joined, and in Parts I and III of which THOMAS, J., joined. GINSBURG, J., filed an opinion concurring in part and dissenting in part.

OPINION: [626] MR. JUSTICE KENNEDY announced the judgment of the Court and delivered the opinion of the Court, except as to Part III-B.

Sections 4 and 5 of the Cable Television Consumer Protection and Competition Act of 1992 require cable television systems to devote a portion of their channels to the transmission of local broadcast television stations. This case presents the question whether these provisions abridge the freedom of speech or of the press, in violation of the First Amendment.

The United States District Court for the District of Columbia granted summary judgment for the United States, [627] holding that the challenged provisions are consistent with the First Amendment. Because issues of material fact remain unresolved in the record as developed thus far, we vacate the District Court's judgment and remand the case for further proceedings.

The role of cable television in the Nation's communications system has undergone dramatic change over the past 45 years. Given the pace of technological advancement and the increasing convergence between cable and other electronic media, the cable industry today stands at the center of an ongoing telecommunications revolution with still undefined potential to affect the way we communicate and develop our intellectual resources.

... Broadcast and cable television are distinguished by the different technologies through which they reach viewers. Broadcast stations radiate electromagnetic signals from a central transmitting antenna. These signals can be captured, in turn, by any television set within the antenna's range. Cable systems, by contrast, rely upon a physical, point-to-point [628] connection between a transmission facility and the television sets of individual subscribers. Cable systems make this connection much like telephone companies, using cable or optical fibers strung aboveground or buried in ducts to reach the homes or businesses of subscribers. The construction of this physical infrastructure entails the use of public rights-of-way and easements and often results in the disruption of traffic on streets and other public property. As a result, the cable medium may depend for its very existence upon express permission from local governing authorities. See generally *Community Communications Co. v. Boulder*, 660 F.2d 1370, 1377-1378 (CA10 1981).

Cable technology affords two principal benefits over broadcast. First, it eliminates the signal interference sometimes encountered in over-the-air broadcasting and thus gives viewers undistorted reception of broadcast stations. Second, it is capable of transmitting many more channels than are available through broadcasting, giving subscribers access to far greater programming variety. More than half of the cable systems in operation today have a capacity to carry between 30 and 53 channels. 1994 Television and Cable Factbook I-69. And about 40 percent of cable subscribers are served by systems with a capacity of more than 53 channels. *Ibid.* Newer systems can carry hundreds of channels, and many older systems are being upgraded with fiber optic rebuilds and digital compression technology to increase channel capacity. See, *e.g.*, Cablevision Systems Adds to Rapid Fiber Growth in Cable Systems, Communications Daily, pp. 6-7 (Feb. 26, 1993).

The cable television industry includes both cable operators (those who own the physical cable network and transmit the cable signal to the viewer) and cable programmers (those who produce television programs and sell or license them to cable operators). In some cases, cable operators have acquired ownership of cable programmers, and vice versa. Although cable operators may create some of their own programming, [629] most of their programming is drawn from outside sources. These outside sources include not only local or distant broadcast stations, but also the many national and regional cable programming networks that have emerged in recent years, such as CNN, MTV, ESPN, TNT, C-Span, The Family Channel, Nickelodeon, Arts and Entertainment, Black Entertainment Television, CourtTV, The Discovery Channel, American Movie Classics, Comedy Central, The Learning Channel, and The Weather Channel. Once the cable operator has selected the programming sources, the cable system functions, in essence, as a conduit for the speech of others, transmitting it on a continuous and unedited basis to subscribers. See Brenner, Cable Television and the Freedom of Expression, 1988 Duke L. J. 329, 339 ("For the most part, cable personnel do not review any of the material provided by cable networks. . . . Cable systems have no conscious control over program services provided by others"). ... [630]

On October 5, 1992, Congress overrode a Presidential veto to enact the Cable Television Consumer Protection and Competition Act of 1992, Pub. L. 102-385, 106 Stat. 1460 (1992 Cable Act or Act). ... At issue in this case is the constitutionality of the so-called must-carry provisions, contained in §§ 4 and 5 of the Act, which require cable operators to carry the signals of a specified number of local broadcast television stations.

Section 4 requires carriage of "local commercial television stations," defined to include all full power television broadcasters, other than those qualifying as "noncommercial educational" stations under § 5, that operate within the same television market as the cable system. § 4, 47 U.S.C. §§ 534(b)(1)(B), (h)(1)(A) (1988 ed., Supp. IV). Cable systems with more than 12 active channels, and more than 300 subscribers, are required to set aside up to one-third of their channels for commercial broadcast stations that request carriage. § 534(b)(1)(B). Cable systems with more than 300 subscribers, but only 12 or fewer active channels, must [631] carry the signals of three commercial broadcast stations. § 534(b)(1)(A).

If there are fewer broadcasters requesting carriage than slots made available under the Act, the cable operator is obligated to carry only those broadcasters who make the request. If, however, there are more requesting broadcast stations than slots available, the cable operator is permitted to choose which of these stations it will carry. § 534(b)(2). The broadcast signals carried under this provision must be transmitted on a continuous, uninterrupted basis, § 534(b)(3), and must be placed in the same numerical channel position as when broadcast over the air. § 534(b)(6). Further, subject to a few exceptions, a cable operator may not charge a fee for carrying broadcast signals in fulfillment of its must-carry obligations. § 534(b)(10).

Section 5 of the Act imposes similar requirements regarding the carriage of local public broadcast television stations, [632] referred to in the Act as local "noncommercial educational television stations." 47 U.S.C. § 535(a) (1988 ed., Supp. IV). ... Taken together, therefore, §§ 4 and 5 subject all but the smallest cable systems nationwide to must-carry obligations, and confer must-carry privileges on all full power broadcasters operating within the same television market as a qualified cable system.

... In brief, Congress found that the physical characteristics of cable transmission, compounded by the increasing [633] concentration of economic power in the cable industry, are endangering the ability of over-the-air broadcast television stations to compete for a viewing audience and thus for necessary operating revenues. Congress determined that regulation of the market for video programming was necessary to correct this competitive imbalance.

In particular, Congress found that over 60 percent of the households with television sets subscribe to cable, § 2(a)(3), and for these households cable has replaced over-the-air broadcast television as the primary provider of video programming. § 2(a)(17). This is so, Congress found, because "most subscribers to cable television systems do not or cannot maintain antennas to receive broadcast television services, do not have input selector switches to convert from a cable to antenna reception system, or cannot otherwise receive broadcast television services." *Ibid.* In addition, Congress concluded that due to "local franchising requirements and the extraordinary expense of constructing more

than one cable television system to serve a particular geographic area," the overwhelming majority of cable operators exercise a monopoly over cable service. § 2(a)(2). "The result," Congress determined, "is undue market power for the cable operator as compared to that of consumers and video programmers." *Ibid.*

According to Congress, this market position gives cable operators the power and the incentive to harm broadcast competitors. The power derives from the cable operator's ability, as owner of the transmission facility, to "terminate the retransmission of the broadcast signal, refuse to carry new signals, or reposition a broadcast signal to a disadvantageous channel position." § 2(a)(15). The incentive derives from the economic reality that "cable television systems and broadcast television stations increasingly compete for television advertising revenues." § 2(a)(14). By refusing carriage of broadcasters' signals, cable operators, as a practical matter, can reduce the number of households that have [634] access to the broadcasters' programming, and thereby capture advertising dollars that would otherwise go to broadcast stations. § 2(a)(15).

Congress found, in addition, that increased vertical integration in the cable industry is making it even harder for broadcasters to secure carriage on cable systems, because cable operators have a financial incentive to favor their affiliated programmers. § 2(a)(5). Congress also determined that the cable industry is characterized by horizontal concentration, with many cable operators sharing common ownership. This has resulted in greater "barriers to entry for new programmers and a reduction in the number of media voices available to consumers." § 2(a)(4).

In light of these technological and economic conditions, Congress concluded that unless cable operators are required to carry local broadcast stations, "there is a substantial likelihood that . . . additional local broadcast signals will be deleted, repositioned, or not carried," § 2(a)(15); the "marked shift in market share" from broadcast to cable will continue to erode the advertising revenue base which sustains free local broadcast television, §§ 2(a)(13)-(14); and that, as a consequence, "the economic viability of free local broadcast television and its ability to originate quality local programming will be seriously jeopardized." § 2(a)(16).

Soon after the Act became law, appellants filed these five consolidated actions in the United States District Court for the District of Columbia against the United States and the Federal Communications Commission (hereinafter referred to collectively as the Government), challenging the constitutionality of the must-carry provisions. Appellants, plaintiffs below, are numerous cable programmers and cable operators. ... Although the Government had not asked for summary judgment, the District Court, in a divided opinion, granted summary judgment in favor of the Government and the other intervenor-defendants, ruling that the must-carry provisions are consistent with the First Amendment. 819 F. Supp. 32 (DC 1993).

The court found that in enacting the must-carry provisions, Congress employed "its regulatory powers over the economy to impose order upon a market in dysfunction." Id., at 40. The court characterized the 1992 Cable Act as "simply industry-specific antitrust and fair trade practice regulatory legislation," ibid., and said that the must-carry requirements "are essentially economic regulation designed to create competitive balance in the video industry as a whole, and to redress the effects of cable operators' anti-competitive practices." Ibid. The court rejected appellants' contention that the must-carry requirements warrant strict scrutiny as a content-based regulation, concluding that both the commercial and public broadcast provisions "are, in intent as well as form, unrelated (in all but the most recondite sense) to the content of any messages that [the] cable operators, broadcasters, and programmers have in contemplation to deliver." Ibid. The court proceeded to sustain the must-carry provisions under the intermediate standard of scrutiny set forth in United States v. O'Brien, 391 U.S. 367, 20 L. Ed. 2d 672, 88 S. Ct. 1673 (1968), concluding that the preservation of local broadcasting is an important governmental interest, and that the must-carry provisions are sufficiently tailored to serve that interest. 819 F. Supp. at 45-47.

Judge Williams dissented. He acknowledged the "very real problem" that "cable systems control access 'bottlenecks' to an important communications medium," id., at 57, but concluded that Congress may not address that problem [636] by extending access rights only to broadcast television stations. In his view, the must-carry rules are content based, and thus subject to strict scrutiny, because they require cable operators to carry speech they might otherwise choose to exclude, and because Congress' decision to grant favorable access to broadcast programmers rested "in part, but quite explicitly, on a finding about their content." Id., at 58. Applying strict scrutiny, Judge Williams determined that the interests advanced in support of the law are inadequate to justify it. While assuming "as an abstract matter" that the interest in preserving access to free television is compelling, he found "no evidence that this access is in jeopardy." Id., at 62. Likewise, he concluded that the rules are insufficiently tailored to the asserted interest in programming diversity because cable operators "now carry the vast majority of local stations," and thus to the extent the rules have any effect at all, "it will be

only to replace the mix chosen by cablecasters – whose livelihoods depend largely on satisfying audience demand – with a mix derived from congressional dictate." Id., at 61.

There can be no disagreement on an initial premise: Cable programmers and cable operators engage in and transmit speech, and they are entitled to the protection of the speech and press provisions of the First Amendment. Leathers v. Medlock, 499 U.S. 439, 444, 113 L. Ed. 2d 494, 111 S. Ct. 1438 (1991). Through "original programming or by exercising editorial discretion over which stations or programs to include in its repertoire," cable programmers and operators "seek to communicate messages on a wide variety of topics and in a wide variety of formats." Los Angeles v. Preferred Communications, Inc., 476 U.S. 488, 494, 90 L. Ed. 2d 480, 106 S. Ct. 2034 (1986). By requiring cable systems to set aside a portion of their channels for local broadcasters, [637] the must-carry rules regulate cable speech in two respects: The rules reduce the number of channels over which cable operators exercise unfettered control, and they render it more difficult for cable programmers to compete for carriage on the limited channels remaining. Nevertheless, because not every interference with speech triggers the same degree of scrutiny under the First Amendment, we must decide at the outset the level of scrutiny applicable to the must-carry provisions.

We address first the Government's contention that regulation of cable television should be analyzed under the same First Amendment standard that applies to regulation of broadcast television. It is true that our cases have permitted more intrusive regulation of broadcast speakers than of speakers in other media. Compare Red Lion Broadcasting Co. v. FCC, 395 U.S. 367, 23 L. Ed. 2d 371, 89 S. Ct. 1794 (1969) (television), and National Broadcasting Co. v. United States, 319 U.S. 190, 87 L. Ed. 1344, 63 S. Ct. 997 (1943) (radio), with Miami Herald Publishing Co. v. Tornillo, 418 U.S. 241, 41 L. Ed. 2d 730, 94 S. Ct. 2831 (1974) (print), and Riley v. National Federation of Blind of N.C., Inc., 487 U.S. 781, 101 L. Ed. 2d 669, 108 S. Ct. 2667 (1988) (personal solicitation). But the rationale for applying a less rigorous standard of First Amendment scrutiny to broadcast regulation, whatever its validity in the cases elaborating it, does not apply in the context of cable regulation.

The justification for our distinct approach to broadcast regulation rests upon the unique physical limitations of the broadcast medium. ... Although courts and commentators have criticized the scarcity rationale since its inception, we have declined to question its continuing validity as support for our broadcast jurisprudence, see FCC v. League of Women Voters, supra, at 376, n. 11, and see no reason to do so here. The broadcast [639] cases are inapposite in the present context because cable television does not suffer from the inherent limitations that characterize the broadcast medium. Indeed, given the rapid advances in fiber optics and digital compression technology, soon there may be no practical limitation on the number of speakers who may use the cable medium. Nor is there any danger of physical interference between two cable speakers attempting to share the same channel. In light of these fundamental technological differences between broadcast and cable transmission, application of the more relaxed standard of scrutiny adopted in *Red Lion* and the other broadcast cases is inapt when determining the First Amendment validity of cable regulation. ...

This is not to say that the unique physical characteristics of cable transmission should be ignored when determining the constitutionality of regulations affecting cable speech. They should not. See *infra*, at 32-33. But whatever relevance these physical characteristics may have in the evaluation of particular cable regulations, they do not require the alteration of settled principles of our First Amendment jurisprudence.

Although the Government acknowledges the substantial technological differences between broadcast and cable, ... [i]t asserts that the foundation of our broadcast jurisprudence is not the physical limitations of the electromagnetic spectrum, but rather the "market dysfunction" that characterizes the broadcast market. ... [640] While we agree that the cable market suffers certain structural impediments, ... the mere assertion of dysfunction or failure in a speech market, without more, is not sufficient to shield a speech regulation from the First Amendment standards applicable to nonbroadcast media.

By a related course of reasoning, the Government and some appellees maintain that the must-carry provisions are nothing more than industry-specific antitrust legislation, and thus warrant rational basis scrutiny under this Court's "precedents governing legislative efforts to correct market failure in a market whose commodity is speech," such as *Associated Press* v. *United States*, 326 U.S. 1, 89 L. Ed. 2013, 65 S. Ct. 1416 (1945), and *Lorain Journal Co.* v. *United States*, 342 U.S. 143, 96 L. Ed. 162, 72 S. Ct. 181 (1951). See Brief for Federal Appellees 17. This contention is unavailing. *Associated Press* and *Lorain Journal* both involved actions against members of the press brought under the Sherman Antitrust Act, a law of general application. But while the enforcement of a generally applicable law may or may not be subject to heightened scrutiny under the First Amendment, ... laws that single out the press, or certain elements thereof, for special treatment "pose a particular danger of abuse by the State,"...

and so are always [641] subject to at least some degree of heightened First Amendment scrutiny. ... Because the must-carry provisions impose special obligations upon cable operators and special burdens upon cable programmers, some measure of heightened First Amendment scrutiny is demanded.

At the heart of the First Amendment lies the principle that each person should decide for him or herself the ideas and beliefs deserving of expression, consideration, and adherence. Our political system and cultural life rest upon this ideal. See *Leathers* v. *Medlock*, 499 U.S. at 449 (citing *Cohen* v. *California*, 403 U.S. 15, 24, 29 L. Ed. 2d 284, 91 S. Ct. 1780 (1971)); *West Virginia Bd. of Ed.* v. *Barnette*, 319 U.S. 624, 638, 640-642, 87 L. Ed. 1628, 63 S. Ct. 1178 (1943). Government action that stifles speech on account of its message, or that requires the utterance of a particular message favored by the Government, contravenes this essential right. Laws of this sort pose the inherent risk that the Government seeks not to advance a legitimate regulatory goal, but to suppress unpopular ideas or information or manipulate the public debate through coercion rather than persuasion. These restrictions "raise the specter that the Government may effectively drive certain ideas or viewpoints from the marketplace." *Simon & Schuster, Inc.* v. *Members of the New York State Crime Victims Bd.*, 502 U.S. 105, 116, 116 L. Ed. 2d 476, 112 S. Ct. 501 (1991).

For these reasons, the First Amendment, subject only to narrow and well-understood exceptions, does not countenance governmental control over the content of messages expressed by private individuals. ... [642] Our precedents thus apply the most exacting scrutiny to regulations that suppress, disadvantage, or impose differential burdens upon speech because of its content. ... Laws that compel speakers to utter or distribute speech bearing a particular message are subject to the same rigorous scrutiny. ... In contrast, regulations that are unrelated to the content of speech are subject to an intermediate level of scrutiny ... because in most cases they pose a less substantial risk of excising certain ideas or viewpoints from the public dialogue.

Deciding whether a particular regulation is content-based or content-neutral is not always a simple task. ... [643] As a general rule, laws that by their terms distinguish favored speech from disfavored speech on the basis of the ideas or views expressed are content-based. ... By contrast, laws that confer benefits or impose burdens on speech without reference to the ideas or views expressed are in most instances content-neutral.

Insofar as they pertain to the carriage of full power broadcasters, the must-carry rules, on their face, impose burdens and confer benefits without reference to the content of speech. n6 Although the provisions interfere with cable operators' [644] editorial discretion by compelling them to offer carriage to a certain minimum number of broadcast stations, the extent of the interference does not depend upon the content of the cable operators' programming. The rules impose obligations upon all operators, save those with fewer than 300 subscribers, regardless of the programs or stations they now offer or have offered in the past. Nothing in the Act imposes a restriction, penalty, or burden by reason of the views, programs, or stations the cable operator has selected or will select. The number of channels a cable operator must set aside depends only on the operator's channel capacity, see 47 U.S.C. §§ 534(b)(1), 535(b)(2)-(3) (1988 ed., Supp. IV); hence, an operator cannot avoid or mitigate its obligations under the Act by altering the programming it offers to subscribers. Cf. *Miami Herald Publishing Co.* v. *Tornillo*, 418 U.S. at 256-257 (newspaper may avoid access obligations by refraining from speech critical of political candidates).

The must-carry rules also require carriage, under certain limited circumstances, of low power broadcast stations. 47 U.S.C. § 534(c); see n. 2, *supra*. Under the Act, a low power station may become eligible for carriage only if, among other things, the FCC determines that the station's programming "would address local news and informational needs which are not being adequately served by full power television broadcast stations because of the geographic distance of such full power stations from the low power station's community of license." § 534(h)(2)(B). We recognize that this aspect of § 4 appears to single out certain low-power broadcasters for special benefits on the basis of content. Because the District Court did not address whether these particular provisions are content-based, and because the parties make only the most glancing reference to the operation of, and justifications for, 'the low-power broadcast provisions, we think it prudent to allow the District Court to consider the content-neutral or content-based character of this provision in the first instance on remand.

In a similar vein, although a broadcast station's eligibility for must-carry is based upon its geographic proximity to a qualifying cable system, § 534(h)(1)(C)(i), the Act permits the FCC to grant must-carry privileges upon request to otherwise ineligible broadcast stations. In acting upon these requests, the FCC is directed to give "attention to the value of localism" and, in particular, to whether the requesting station "provides news coverage of issues of concern to such community . . . or coverage of sporting and other events of interest to the community." § 534(h)(1)(C)(ii). Again, the District Court did not address this provision, but may do so on remand. [645]

The must-carry provisions also burden cable programmers by reducing the number of channels for which they can compete. But, again, this burden is unrelated to content, for it extends to all cable programmers irrespective of the programming they choose to offer viewers. Cf. *Boos, supra*, at 319 (individuals may picket in front of a foreign embassy so long as their picket signs are not critical of the foreign government). And finally, the privileges conferred by the must-carry provisions are also unrelated to content. The rules benefit all full power broadcasters who request carriage–be they commercial or noncommercial, independent or network-affiliated, English or Spanish language, religious or secular. The aggregate effect of the rules is thus to make every full power commercial and noncommercial broadcaster eligible for must-carry, provided only that the broadcaster operates within the same television market as a cable system.

It is true that the must-carry provisions distinguish between speakers in the television programming market. But they do so based only upon the manner in which speakers transmit their messages to viewers, and not upon the messages they carry: Broadcasters, which transmit over the airwaves, are favored, while cable programmers, which do not, are disfavored. Cable operators, too, are burdened by the carriage obligations, but only because they control access to the cable conduit. So long as they are not a subtle means of exercising a content preference, speaker distinctions of this nature are not presumed invalid under the First Amendment. ...[646]

Our review of the Act and its various findings persuades us that Congress' overriding objective in enacting must-carry was not to favor programming of a particular subject matter, viewpoint, or format, but rather to preserve access to free television programming for the 40 percent of Americans without cable. ... [647]

By preventing cable operators from refusing carriage to broadcast television stations, the must-carry rules ensure that broadcast television stations will retain a large enough potential audience to earn necessary advertising revenue – or, in the case of noncommercial broadcasters, sufficient viewer contributions, see § 2(a)(8)(B) – to maintain their continued operation. In so doing, the provisions are designed to guarantee the survival of a medium that has become a vital part of the Nation's communication system, and to ensure that every individual with a television set can obtain access to free television programming.

This overriding congressional purpose is unrelated to the content of expression disseminated by cable and broadcast speakers. ... The design and operation of the challenged provisions confirm that the purposes underlying the enactment of the must-carry scheme are unrelated to the content of speech. The rules, as mentioned, confer must-carry rights on all full power broadcasters, irrespective of the content of their programming. They do not require or prohibit the carriage of particular ideas or points of view. They do not penalize cable operators or programmers because of the content of their programming. They do not compel cable operators to affirm points of view with which they disagree. They do not produce any net decrease in the amount of available speech. And they leave cable operators free to carry whatever programming they wish on all channels not subject to must-carry requirements. [648]

Appellants and the dissent make much of the fact that, in the course of describing the purposes behind the Act, Congress referred to the value of broadcast programming. In particular, Congress noted that broadcast television is "an important source of local news[,] public affairs programming and other local broadcast services critical to an informed electorate," § 2(a)(11); see also § 2(a)(10), and that noncommercial television "provides educational and informational programming to the Nation's citizens." § 2(a)(8). We do not think, however, that such references cast any material doubt on the content-neutral character of must-carry. That Congress acknowledged the local orientation of broadcast programming and the role that noncommercial stations have played in educating the public does not indicate that Congress regarded broadcast programming as *more* valuable than cable programming. Rather, it reflects nothing more than the recognition that the services provided by broadcast television have some intrinsic value and, thus, are worth preserving against the threats posed by cable. See 819 F. Supp. at 44 ("Congress' solicitousness for local broadcasters' material simply rests on its assumption that they have as much to say of interest or value as the cable programmers who service a given geographic market audience").

... [649] In short, Congress' acknowledgment that broadcast television stations make a valuable contribution to the Nation's communications system does not render the must-carry scheme content-based. The scope and operation of the challenged provisions make clear, in our view, that Congress designed the must-carry provisions not to promote speech of a particular content, but to prevent cable operators from exploiting their economic power to the detriment of broadcasters, and thereby to ensure that all Americans, especially those unable to subscribe to cable, have access to free television programming – whatever its content.

We likewise reject the suggestion ... that the must-carry rules are content-based because the preference for broadcast stations "*automatically* entails content requirements." 819 F. Supp. at 58. It is true that broadcast programming, unlike cable

programming, is subject to certain limited content restraints imposed by statute and FCC regulation. But it does not follow that Congress mandated cable carriage of broadcast television stations as a means of ensuring that particular [650] programs will be shown, or not shown, on cable systems.

... [652] [G]iven the minimal extent to which the FCC and Congress actually influence the programming offered by broadcast stations, it would be difficult to conclude that Congress enacted must-carry in an effort to exercise content control over what subscribers view on cable television. In a regime where Congress or the FCC exercised more intrusive control over the content of broadcast programming, an argument similar to [this] might carry greater weight. But in the present regulatory system, those concerns are without foundation.

In short, the must-carry provisions are not designed to favor or disadvantage speech of any particular content. Rather, they are meant to protect broadcast television from what Congress determined to be unfair competition by cable systems. In enacting the provisions, Congress sought to preserve the existing structure of the Nation's broadcast television medium while permitting the concomitant expansion and development of cable television, and, in particular, to ensure that broadcast television remains available as a source of video programming for those without cable. Appellants' ability to hypothesize a content-based purpose for these provisions rests on little more than speculation and does not cast doubt upon the content-neutral character of must-carry. Cf. *Arizona* v. *California,* 283 U.S. 423, 455-457, 75 L. Ed. 1154, 51 S. Ct. 522 (1931). Indeed, "it is a familiar principle of constitutional law that this Court will not strike down an otherwise constitutional statute on the basis of an alleged illicit legislative motive." [653]

Appellants advance three additional arguments to support their view that the must-carry provisions warrant strict scrutiny. In brief, appellants contend that the provisions (1) compel speech by cable operators, (2) favor broadcast programmers over cable programmers, and (3) single out certain members of the press for disfavored treatment. None of these arguments suffices to require strict scrutiny in the present case. ...

[656] Although a daily newspaper and a cable operator both may enjoy monopoly status in a given locale, the cable operator exercises far greater control over access to the relevant medium. A daily newspaper, no matter how secure its local monopoly, does not possess the power to obstruct readers' access to other competing publications – whether they be weekly local newspapers, or daily newspapers published in other cities. Thus, when a newspaper asserts exclusive control over its own

news copy, it does not thereby prevent other newspapers from being distributed to willing recipients in the same locale.

The same is not true of cable. When an individual subscribes to cable, the physical connection between the television set and the cable network gives the cable operator bottleneck, or gatekeeper, control over most (if not all) of the television programming that is channeled into the subscriber's home. Hence, simply by virtue of its ownership of the essential pathway for cable speech, a cable operator can prevent its subscribers from obtaining access to programming it chooses to exclude. A cable operator, unlike speakers in other media, can thus silence the voice of competing speakers with a mere flick of the switch.

[657] The potential for abuse of this private power over a central avenue of communication cannot be overlooked. ... The First Amendment's command that government not impede the freedom of speech does not disable the government from taking steps to ensure that private interests not restrict, through physical control of a critical pathway of communication, the free flow of information and ideas. ... Second, appellants urge us to apply strict scrutiny because the must-carry provisions favor one set of speakers (broadcast programmers) over another (cable programmers). Appellants maintain that as a consequence of this speaker preference, some cable programmers who would have secured carriage in the absence of must-carry may now be dropped. Relying on language in *Buckley* v. *Valeo*, 424 U.S. 1, 46 L. Ed. 2d 659, 96 S. Ct. 612 (1976), appellants contend that such a regulation is presumed invalid under the First Amendment because the government may not "restrict the speech of some elements of our society in order to enhance the relative voice of others." *Id.*, at 48-49.

[658] ... Our holding in *Buckley* does not support appellants' broad assertion that all speaker-partial laws are presumed invalid. Rather, it stands for the proposition that speaker-based laws demand strict scrutiny when they reflect the Government's preference for the substance of what the favored speakers have to say (or aversion to what the disfavored speakers have to say). ... *Buckley* thus stands for the proposition that laws favoring some speakers over others demand strict scrutiny when the legislature's speaker preference reflects a content preference.

The question here is whether Congress preferred broadcasters over cable programmers based on the content of programming [659] each group offers. The answer, as we explained above ... is no. Congress granted must-carry privileges to broadcast stations on the belief that the broadcast television industry is in economic peril due to the physical characteristics of cable transmission and the economic incentives facing the cable industry. Thus, the fact that the provisions benefit broadcasters and not cable

programmers does not call for strict scrutiny under our precedents.

Finally, appellants maintain that strict scrutiny applies because the must-carry provisions single out certain members of the press – here, cable operators – for disfavored treatment. ... Regulations that discriminate among media, or among different speakers within a single medium, often present serious First Amendment concerns. ... [660] It would be error to conclude, however, that the First Amendment mandates strict scrutiny for any speech regulation that applies to one medium (or a subset thereof) but not others. ... Rather, laws of this nature are "constitutionally suspect only in certain circumstances." ... But such heightened scrutiny is unwarranted when the differential treatment is "justified by some special [661] characteristic of" the particular medium being regulated.

The must-carry provisions, as we have explained above, are justified by special characteristics of the cable medium: the bottleneck monopoly power exercised by cable operators and the dangers this power poses to the viability of broadcast television. Appellants do not argue, nor does it appear, that other media – in particular, media that transmit video programming such as MMDS and SMATV – are subject to bottleneck monopoly control, or pose a demonstrable threat to the survival of broadcast television. It should come as no surprise, then, that Congress decided to impose the must-carry obligations upon cable operators only.

In addition, the must-carry provisions are not structured in a manner that carries the inherent risk of undermining First Amendment interests. The regulations are broad-based, applying to almost all cable systems in the country, rather than just a select few. ... For these reasons, the must-carry rules do not call for strict scrutiny.

In sum, the must-carry provisions do not pose such inherent dangers to free expression, or present such potential for censorship or manipulation, as to justify application of the most exacting level of First Amendment scrutiny. We agree [662] with the District Court that the appropriate standard by which to evaluate the constitutionality of must-carry is the intermediate level of scrutiny applicable to content-neutral restrictions that impose an incidental burden on speech. See *Ward* v. *Rock Against Racism*, 491 U.S. 781, 105 L. Ed. 2d 661, 109 S. Ct. 2746 (1989); *United States* v. *O'Brien*, 391 U.S. 367, 20 L. Ed. 2d 672, 88 S. Ct. 1673 (1968).

Under *O'Brien*, a content-neutral regulation will be sustained if "it furthers an important or substantial governmental interest; if the governmental interest is unrelated to the suppression of free expression; and if the incidental restriction on alleged First Amendment freedoms is no greater than is essential to the furtherance of that interest." *Id.*, at 377.

To satisfy this standard, a regulation need not be the least speech-restrictive means of advancing the Government's interests. "Rather, the requirement of narrow tailoring is satisfied 'so long as the . . . regulation promotes a substantial government interest that would be achieved less effectively absent the regulation.'" *Ward, supra,* at 799 (quoting *United States* v. *Albertini,* 472 U.S. 675, 689, 86 L. Ed. 2d 536, 105 S. Ct. 2897 (1985)). Narrow tailoring in this context requires, in other words, that the means chosen do not "burden substantially more speech than is necessary to further the government's legitimate interests." *Ward, supra,* at 799.

Congress declared that the must-carry provisions serve three interrelated interests: (1) preserving the benefits of free, over-the-air local broadcast television, (2) promoting the widespread dissemination of information from a multiplicity of sources, and (3) promoting fair competition in the market for television programming. S. Rep. No. 102-92, p. 58, (1991); H. R. Rep. No. 102-6 28, 63 (1992); 1992 Cable Act, §§ 2(a)(8), (9), and (10). None of these interests is related to the "suppression of free expression," *O'Brien,* 391 U.S. at 377, or to the content of any speakers' messages. And [663] viewed in the abstract, we have no difficulty concluding that each of them is an important governmental interest. *Ibid.*

In the Communications Act of 1934, Congress created a system of free broadcast service and directed that communications facilities be licensed across the country in a "fair, efficient, and equitable" manner. Communications Act of 1934, § 307(b), 48 Stat. 1083, 47 U.S.C. § 307(b). Congress designed this system of allocation to afford each community of appreciable size an over-the-air source of information and an outlet for exchange on matters of local concern. ... [T]he importance of local broadcasting outlets "can scarcely be exaggerated, for broadcasting is demonstrably a principal source of information and entertainment for a great part of the Nation's population." The interest in maintaining the local broadcasting structure does not evaporate simply because cable has come upon the scene. Although cable and other technologies have ushered in alternatives to broadcast television, nearly 40 percent of American households still rely on broadcast stations as their exclusive source of television programming. ... "[P]rotecting noncable households from loss of regular television broadcasting service due to competition from cable systems" is an important federal interest.

Likewise, assuring that the public has access to a multiplicity of information sources is a governmental purpose of the highest order, for it promotes values central to the First Amendment. Indeed, "'it has long been a basic tenet of national communications policy that "the widest possible dissemination of information from diverse and antagonistic sources is essential to the welfare of the public."'" ... Finally, the Government's interest in eliminating restraints on fair competition is always substantial, even when the individuals or entities subject to particular regulations are engaged in expressive activity protected by the First Amendment. See *Lorain Journal Co.* v. *United States,* 342 U.S. 143, 96 L. Ed. 162, 72 S. Ct. 181 (1951); *Associated Press* v. *United States, supra;* cf. *FTC* v. *Superior Court Trial Lawyers Assn.,* 493 U.S. 411, 431-432, 107 L. Ed. 2d 851, 110 S. Ct. 768 (1990).

... [I]n applying *O'Brien* scrutiny we must ask first whether the Government has adequately shown that the economic [665] health of local broadcasting is in genuine jeopardy and in need of the protections afforded by must-carry. Assuming an affirmative answer to the foregoing question, the Government still bears the burden of showing that the remedy it has adopted does not "burden substantially more speech than is necessary to further the government's legitimate interests." *Ward,* 491 U.S. at 799. On the state of the record developed thus far, and in the absence of findings of fact from the District Court, we are unable to conclude that the Government has satisfied either inquiry. ...

[666] The Government's assertion that the must-carry rules are necessary to protect the viability of broadcast television rests on two essential propositions: (1) that unless cable operators are compelled to carry broadcast stations, significant numbers of broadcast stations will be refused carriage on cable systems; and (2) that the broadcast stations denied carriage will either deteriorate to a substantial degree or fail altogether. ... [667] Without a more substantial elaboration in the District Court of the predictive or historical evidence upon which Congress relied, or the introduction of some additional evidence to establish that the dropped or repositioned broadcasters would be at serious risk of financial difficulty, we cannot determine whether the threat to broadcast television is real enough to overcome the challenge to the provisions made by these appellants. We think it significant, for instance, that the parties have not presented any evidence that local broadcast stations have fallen into bankruptcy, turned in their broadcast licenses, curtailed their broadcast operations, or suffered a serious reduction in operating revenues as a result of their being dropped from, or otherwise disadvantaged by, cable systems.

The paucity of evidence indicating that broadcast television is in jeopardy is not the only deficiency in this record. Also lacking are any findings concerning the actual effects of [668] must-carry on the speech of cable operators and cable programmers – *i.e.,* the extent to which cable operators will, in fact, be forced to make changes in their current or anticipated programming selections; the degree to which cable programmers will be dropped from cable systems to make room for local broadcasters; and the extent to which cable operators can satisfy their must-carry obligations by devoting previously unused channel capacity to the carriage of local broadcasters. The answers to these and perhaps other questions are critical to the narrow tailoring step of the *O'Brien* analysis, for unless we know the extent to which the must-carry provisions in fact interfere with protected speech, we cannot say whether they suppress "substantially more speech than . . . necessary" to ensure the viability of broadcast television. *Ward,* 491 U.S. at 799. Finally, the record fails to provide any judicial findings concerning the availability and efficacy of "constitutionally acceptable less restrictive means" of achieving the Government's asserted interests. See *Sable Communications,* 492 U.S. at 129.

In sum, because there are genuine issues of material fact still to be resolved on this record, we hold that the District Court erred in granting summary judgment in favor of the Government. See *Anderson* v. *Liberty Lobby, Inc.,* 477 U.S. 242, 250, 91 L. Ed. 2d 202, 106 S. Ct. 2505 (1986). Because of the unresolved factual questions, the importance of the issues to the broadcast and cable industries, and the conflicting conclusions that the parties contend are to be drawn from the statistics and other evidence presented, we think it necessary to permit the parties to develop a more thorough factual record, and to allow the District Court to resolve any factual disputes remaining, before passing upon the constitutional validity of the challenged provisions.

The judgment below is vacated, and the case is remanded for further proceedings consistent with this opinion.

It is so ordered.

CONCUR BY: BLACKMUN; STEVENS (In Part); O'CONNOR (In Part); GINSBURG (In Part)

[669] JUSTICE BLACKMUN, concurring.

I join JUSTICE KENNEDY's opinion, which aptly identifies and analyzes the First Amendment concerns and principles that should guide consideration of free speech issues in the expanding cable industry. I write to emphasize the paramount importance of according substantial deference to the predictive judgments of Congress ... particularly where, as here, that legislative body has compiled an extensive record in the course of reaching its judgment. Nonetheless, the standard for summary judgment is high, and no less so when First Amendment values are at stake and the issue is of far-reaching importance. Because in this case there

remain a few unresolved issues of material fact, a remand is appropriate. ...

JUSTICE STEVENS, concurring in part and concurring in the judgment.

As JUSTICE KENNEDY has ably explained, the "overriding congressional purpose" of the challenged must-carry provisions of the 1992 Cable Act is to "guarantee the survival of a medium that has become a vital part of the Nation's communication system," a purpose that is "unrelated to the content of expression." ... While I agree with most of JUSTICE KENNEDY's reasoning, ... I part ways with him on the appropriate disposition of this case. In my view the District Court's judgment sustaining the must-carry provisions should be affirmed. ... Economic measures are always subject to second-guessing; they rest on inevitably provisional and uncertain forecasts about the future effect of legal rules in complex conditions. Whether Congress might have accomplished its goals more efficiently through other means; whether it correctly interpreted emerging trends in the protean communications industry; and indeed whether must-carry is actually imprudent as a matter of policy will remain matters of debate long after the 1992 Act has been repealed or replaced by successor legislation. But the question for us is merely whether *Congress* could fairly conclude that cable operators' monopoly position threatens the continued viability of broadcast television and that must-carry is an appropriate means of minimizing that risk. [671]

As JUSTICE KENNEDY recognizes, ... findings by the Congress, particularly those emerging from such sustained deliberations, merit special respect from this Court. Accorded proper deference, the findings ... are sufficient to sustain the must-carry provisions against facial attack. ... [672]

An industry need not be in its death throes before Congress may act to protect it from economic harm threatened by a monopoly. The mandatory access mechanism that Congress fashioned ... is a simple and direct means of dealing with the dangers posed by cable operators' exclusive control of what is fast becoming the preeminent means of transferring video signals to homes. ... [673] While additional evidence might cast further light on the efficacy and wisdom of the must-carry provisions, additional evidence is not necessary to resolve the question of their facial constitutionality.

... [674] The must-carry provisions may ultimately prove an ineffective or needlessly meddlesome means of achieving Congress' legitimate goals. However, such a conclusion could be confidently drawn, if ever, only after the must-carry scheme has been tested by experience. On its face, that scheme is rationally calculated to redress the dangers that Congress discerned after its lengthy investigation of the relationship between the cable and broadcasting industries.

It is thus my view that we should affirm the judgment of the District Court. Were I to vote to affirm, however, no disposition of this appeal would command the support of a majority of the Court. An accommodation is therefore necessary. ... Accordingly, because I am in substantial agreement with JUSTICE KENNEDY's analysis of the case, I concur in the judgment vacating and remanding for further   proceedings.

DISSENT BY: O'CONNOR (In Part); GINSBURG (In Part)

DISSENT: JUSTICE O'CONNOR, with whom JUSTICE SCALIA and JUSTICE GINSBURG join, and with whom JUSTICE THOMAS joins as to Parts I and III, concurring in part and dissenting in part.

There are only so many channels that any cable system can carry. If there are fewer channels than programmers who want to use the system, some programmers will have to be dropped. In the must-carry provisions of the Cable [675] Television Consumer Protection and Competition Act of 1992, ... Congress made a choice: By reserving a little over one-third of the channels on a cable system for broadcasters, it ensured that in most cases it will be a cable programmer who is dropped and a broadcaster who is retained. The question presented in this case is whether this choice comports with the commands of the First Amendment.

The 1992 Cable Act implicates the First Amendment rights of two classes of speakers. First, it tells cable operators which programmers they must carry, and keeps cable operators from carrying others that they might prefer. Though cable operators do not actually originate most of the programming they show, the Court correctly holds that they are, for First Amendment purposes, speakers. ... Selecting which speech to retransmit is, as we know from the example of publishing houses, movie theaters, bookstores, and Reader's Digest, no less communication than is creating the speech in the first place.

Second, the Act deprives a certain class of video programmers – those who operate cable channels rather than broadcast stations – of access to over one-third of an entire medium. Cable programmers may compete only for those channels that are not set aside by the must-carry provisions. A cable programmer that might otherwise have been carried may well be denied access in favor of a broadcaster that is less appealing to the viewers but is favored by the must-carry rules. It is as if the government ordered all movie theaters to reserve at least one-third of their screening for films made by American production

companies, or required all bookstores to devote one-third of their shelf space to nonprofit publishers. As the Court explains ..., cable programmers and [676] operators stand in the same position under the First Amendment as do the more traditional media.

Under the First Amendment, it is normally not within the government's power to decide who may speak and who may not, at least on private property or in traditional public fora. The government does have the power to impose content-neutral time, place, and manner restrictions, but this is in large part precisely because such restrictions apply to all speakers. Laws that treat all speakers equally are relatively poor tools for controlling public debate, and their very generality creates a substantial political check that prevents them from being unduly burdensome. Laws that single out particular speakers are substantially more dangerous, even when they do not draw explicit content distinctions. ...

I agree with the Court that some speaker-based restrictions – those genuinely justified without reference to content – need not be subject to strict scrutiny. But looking at the statute at issue, I cannot avoid the conclusion that its preference for broadcasters over cable programmers is justified with reference to content. The findings ... which I must assume state the justifications for the law, make this clear. ... [677]

Similar justifications are reflected in the operative provisions of the Act. ... Preferences for diversity of viewpoints, for localism, for educational programming, and for news and public affairs all make reference to content. They may not reflect hostility to particular points of view, or a desire to suppress certain subjects because they are controversial or offensive. They may be quite benignly motivated. But benign motivation, we have consistently held, is not enough to avoid the need for strict scrutiny of content-based justifications. ... The First Amendment does more than just bar government from intentionally suppressing speech of which it disapproves. It also generally [678] prohibits the government from excepting certain kinds of speech from regulation because it thinks the speech is especially valuable. ...

This is why the Court is mistaken in concluding that the interest in diversity – in "access to a multiplicity" of "diverse and antagonistic sources" – is content neutral. Indeed, the interest is not "related to the *suppression* of free expression," ... but that is not enough for content neutrality. The interest in giving a tax break to religious, sports, or professional magazines ... is not related to the suppression of speech; the interest in giving labor picketers an exemption from a general picketing ban ... is not related to the suppression of speech. But they are both related to the *content* of speech – to its communicative impact. The interest in ensuring access to a multiplicity of diverse and antagonistic sources of information, no matter how praiseworthy, is directly tied to the content of what the speakers will likely say.

The Court dismisses the findings quoted above by speculating that they do not reveal a preference for certain kinds of content; rather, the Court suggests, the findings show "nothing more than the recognition that the services provided by broadcast television have some intrinsic value and, thus, are worth preserving against the threats posed by [679] cable." ... I cannot agree. ... The controversial judgment at the heart of the statute is not that broadcast television has some value – obviously it does – but that broadcasters should be preferred over cable programmers. ... To say in the face of the findings that the must-carry rules "impose burdens and confer benefits without reference to the content of speech"... cannot be correct, especially in light of the care with which we must normally approach speaker-based restrictions. ...

It may well be that Congress also had other, content-neutral, purposes in mind when enacting the statute. ... But when a content-based justification appears on the statute's face, we cannot ignore it because another, content-neutral justification is present.

Content-based speech restrictions are generally unconstitutional unless they are narrowly tailored to a compelling state interest. ... This is an exacting test. It is not enough that the goals of the law be legitimate, or reasonable, or even praiseworthy. There must be some pressing public necessity, some essential value that has to be preserved; and even then the law must restrict as little speech as possible to serve the goal.

The interest in localism, either in the dissemination of opinions held by the listeners' neighbors or in the reporting of events that have to do with the local community, cannot be described as "compelling" for the purposes of the compelling state interest test. ...[681] The interests in public affairs programming and educational programming seem somewhat weightier, though it is a difficult question whether they are compelling enough to justify restricting other sorts of speech. But even assuming arguendo that the Government could set some channels aside for educational or news programming, the Act is insufficiently tailored to this goal. ... Even if the Government can restrict entertainment in order to benefit supposedly more valuable speech, I do not think the restriction can extend to other speech that is as valuable as the speech being benefited. In the rare circumstances where the government may draw content-based distinctions to serve its goals, the restrictions must serve the goals a good deal more precisely than this.

Finally, my conclusion that the must-carry rules are content based leads me to conclude that they are an impermissible restraint on the cable operators' editorial discretion as well as on the cable programmers' speech. ... [*682] Even if I am mistaken about the must-carry provisions being content based, however, in my view they fail content-neutral scrutiny as well. Assuming arguendo that the provisions are justified with reference to the content-neutral interests in fair competition and preservation of free television, they nonetheless restrict too much speech that does not implicate these interests.

Sometimes, a cable system's choice to carry a cable programmer rather than a broadcaster may be motivated by anticompetitive impulses, or might lead to the broadcaster going out of business. ... That some speech within a broad category causes harm, however, does not justify restricting the whole category.

... The must-carry provisions are fatally overbroad, even under a content-neutral analysis: They disadvantage cable programmers even if the operator has no anticompetitive motives, and even if the broadcaster that would have to be dropped to make room for the cable programmer would survive without cable access.

... The question is not whether there will be control over who gets to speak over cable – the question is who will have this control. Under the FCC's view, the answer is Congress, acting within relatively broad limits. Under my [684] view, the answer is the cable operator. ... I have no doubt that there is danger in having a single cable operator decide what millions of subscribers can or cannot watch. And I have no ... doubt that Congress can act to relieve this danger. ... Congress can encourage the creation of new media, such as inexpensive satellite broadcasting, or fiber-optic networks with virtually unlimited channels, or even simple devices that would let people easily switch from cable to over-the-air broadcasting. And of course Congress can subsidize broadcasters that it thinks provide especially valuable programming.

... Congress might also conceivably obligate cable operators to act as common carriers for some of their channels, with those channels being open to all through some sort of lottery system or timesharing arrangement. Setting aside any possible Takings Clause issues, it stands to reason that if Congress may demand that telephone companies operate as common carriers, it can ask the same of cable companies; such an approach would not suffer from the defect of preferring one speaker to another. [685]

But the First Amendment as we understand it today rests on the premise that it is government power, rather than private power, that is the main threat to free expression; and as a consequence, the

Amendment imposes substantial limitations on the Government even when it is trying to serve concededly praiseworthy goals. Perhaps Congress can to some extent restrict, even in a content-based manner, the speech of cable operators and cable programmers. But it must do so in compliance with the constitutional requirements, requirements that were not complied with here. Accordingly, I would reverse the judgment below.

JUSTICE GINSBURG, concurring in part and dissenting in part.

... I conclude that Congress' "must-carry" regime, which requires cable operators to set aside just over one-third of their channels for local broadcast stations, reflects an unwarranted content-based preference and hypothesizes a risk to local stations that remains imaginary. ...

The "must-carry" rules Congress has ordered do not differentiate on the basis of "viewpoint," and therefore do not fall in the category of speech regulation that Government must avoid most assiduously. ... The rules, however, do reflect a content preference, and on that account demand close scrutiny.

The Court has identified as Congress' "overriding objective in enacting must-carry," the preservation of over-the-air [686] television service for those unwilling or unable to subscribe to cable, and has remanded the case for further airing centered on that allegedly overriding, content-neutral purpose. ... But an intertwined or even discrete content-neutral justification does not render speculative, or reduce to harmless surplus, Congress' evident plan to advance local programming. ...

As Circuit Judge Williams stated: "Congress rested its decision to promote [local broadcast] stations in part, but quite explicitly, on a finding about their content – that they were 'an important source of local news and public affairs programming and other local broadcast services critical to an informed electorate.'" Moreover, as Judge Williams persuasively explained, "[the] facts do not support an inference that over-the-air TV is at risk" ...; "whatever risk there may be in the abstract has completely failed to materialize. ... The paucity of evidence indicating that broadcast television is in jeopardy," if it persists on remand, should impel an ultimate judgment for the petitioners.

Denver Area Educational Telecommunications Consortium v. Federal Communications Commission
518 U.S. 727
(1996)
(Excerpts only. Footnotes omitted.)

PRIOR HISTORY: On Writs of Certiorari to the United States Court of Appeals for the District of Columbia Circuit.

JUDGES: BREYER, J., announced the judgment of the Court and delivered the opinion of the Court with respect to Part III, in which STEVENS, O'CONNOR, KENNEDY, SOUTER, and GINSBURG, JJ., joined, an opinion with respect to Parts I, II, and V, in which STEVENS, O'CONNOR, and SOUTER, JJ., joined, and an opinion with respect to Parts IV and VI, in which STEVENS and SOUTER, JJ., joined. STEVENS, J., and SOUTER, J., filed concurring opinions. O'CONNOR, J., filed an opinion concurring in part and dissenting in part. KENNEDY, J., filed an opinion concurring in part, concurring in the judgment in part, and dissenting in part, in which GINSBURG, J., joined. THOMAS, J., filed an opinion concurring in the judgment in part and dissenting in part, in which REHNQUIST, C. J., and SCALIA, J., joined.

OPINION: [732] MR. JUSTICE BREYER

These cases present First Amendment challenges to three statutory provisions that seek to regulate the broadcasting of "patently offensive" sex-related material on cable television. Cable Television Consumer Protection and Competition Act of 1992 (1992 Act or Act), 106 Stat. 1486, §§ 10(a), 10(b), and 10(c), 47 U.S.C. §§ 532(h), 532(j), and note following § 531. The provisions apply to programs broadcast over cable on what are known as "leased access channels" and "public, educational, or governmental channels." Two of the provisions essentially permit a cable system operator to prohibit the broadcasting of "programming" that the "operator reasonably believes describes or depicts sexual or excretory activities or organs in a patently offensive manner." 1992 [733] Act, § 10(a); see § 10(c). ...

We conclude that the first provision – that *permits* the operator to decide whether or not to broadcast such programs on *leased* access channels – is consistent with the First Amendment. The second provision, that *requires* leased channel operators to segregate and to block that programming, and the third provision, applicable to public, educational, and governmental channels, violate the First Amendment, for they are not appropriately tailored to achieve the basic, legitimate objective of protecting children from exposure to "patently offensive" material.

Cable operators typically own a physical cable network used to convey programming over several dozen cable channels into subscribers' houses. ... [734] A "leased channel" is a channel that federal law requires a cable system operator to reserve for commercial lease by unaffiliated third parties. About 10 to 15 percent of a cable system's channels would typically fall into this category. See 47 U.S.C. § 532(b). "Public, educational, or governmental channels" (which we shall call "public access" channels) are channels that, over the years, local governments have required cable system operators to set aside for public, educational, or governmental purposes as part of the consideration an operator gives in return for permission to install cables under city streets and to use public rights-of-way. ...

In 1992, in an effort to control sexually explicit programming conveyed over access channels, Congress enacted the three provisions before us. The first two provisions relate to leased channels. The first says:

"This subsection shall permit a cable operator to enforce prospectively a written and published policy of prohibiting programming that the cable operator reasonably believes describes or depicts sexual or excretory activities or organs in a patently offensive manner as measured by contemporary community standards." 1992 Act, § 10(a)(2), 106 Stat. 1486. [735]

The second provision, applicable only to leased channels, requires cable operators to segregate and to block similar programming if they decide to permit, rather than to prohibit, its broadcast. ... The regulations require the cable operators to place this material on a single channel and to block it (say, by scrambling). They also require the system operator to provide access to the blocked channel "within 30 days" of a subscriber's written request for access and to reblock it within 30 days of a subscriber's request to do so. 47 CFR § 76.701(c) (1995).

The third provision is similar to the first provision, but applies only to public access channels. The relevant statutory section instructs the FCC to promulgate regulations that will

"enable a cable operator of a cable system to prohibit the use, on such system, of any channel capacity of any public, educational, or governmental access facility for any programming which contains obscene material, sexually explicit conduct, or material soliciting or promoting unlawful conduct." 1992 Act, § 10(c), 106 Stat. 1486. [736] ...

The upshot is, as we said at the beginning, that the federal law before us (the statute as implemented through regulations) now *permits* cable operators

either to allow or to forbid the transmission of "patently offensive" sex-related materials over both leased and public access channels, and *requires* those operators, at a minimum, to segregate and to block transmission of that same material on leased channels. ... [737]

We turn initially to the provision that *permits* cable system operators to prohibit "patently offensive" (or "indecent") programming transmitted over leased access channels. 1992 Act, § 10(a). ...

We recognize that the First Amendment, the terms of which apply to governmental action, ordinarily does not itself throw into constitutional doubt the decisions of private citizens to permit, or to restrict, speech – and this is so *ordinarily* even where those decisions take place within the framework of a regulatory regime such as broadcasting. Were that not so, courts might have to face the difficult, and potentially restrictive, practical task of deciding which, among any number of private parties involved in providing a program (for example, networks, station owners, program editors, and program producers), is the "speaker" whose rights may not be abridged, and who is the speech-restricting "censor." Furthermore, as this Court has held, the editorial function itself is an aspect of "speech," see *Turner*, 512 U.S. at 636, and a court's decision that a private party, say, the station owner, is a "censor," could itself interfere [738] with that private "censor's" freedom to speak as an editor. Thus, not surprisingly, this Court's First Amendment broadcasting cases have dealt with governmental efforts to *restrict*, not governmental efforts to provide or to maintain, a broadcaster's freedom to pick and to choose programming. ... [739]

JUSTICES KENNEDY and THOMAS would have us decide these cases simply by transferring and applying literally categorical standards this Court has developed in other contexts. For JUSTICE KENNEDY, leased access [740] channels are like a common carrier, cable cast is a protected medium, strict scrutiny applies, § 10(a) fails this test, and, therefore, § 10(a) is invalid. *Post*, at 796-801, 805-807. For JUSTICE THOMAS, the case is simple because the cable operator who owns the system over which access channels are broadcast, like a bookstore owner with respect to what it displays on the shelves, has a predominant First Amendment interest. *Post*, at 816-817, 822-824. Both categorical approaches suffer from the same flaws: They import law developed in very different contexts into a new and changing environment, and they lack the flexibility necessary to allow government to respond to very serious practical problems without sacrificing the free exchange of ideas the First Amendment is designed to protect.

The history of this Court's First Amendment jurisprudence, however, is one of continual development, as the Constitution's general command that "Congress shall make no law . . . abridging the freedom of speech, or of the press," has been applied to new circumstances requiring different adaptations of prior principles and precedents. The essence of that protection is that Congress may not regulate speech except in cases of extraordinary need and with the exercise of a degree of care that we have not elsewhere required. ... At the same time, our cases have not left Congress or the States powerless to address the most serious problems. ...

Over the years, this Court has restated and refined these basic First Amendment principles, adopting them more particularly to the balance of competing interests and the special [741] circumstances of each field of application. ...This tradition teaches that the First Amendment embodies an overarching commitment to protect speech from government regulation through close judicial scrutiny, thereby enforcing the Constitution's constraints, but without imposing judicial formulas so rigid that they become a straitjacket that disables government from responding to serious problems. This Court, in different contexts, has consistently held that government may directly regulate speech to address extraordinary problems, where its regulations are appropriately tailored to resolve those problems without imposing an unnecessarily great restriction on speech. JUSTICES KENNEDY and THOMAS would have us further declare which, among the many applications of the general approach that this Court has developed over the years, we are applying here. But no definitive choice among competing [742] analogies (broadcast, common carrier, bookstore) allows us to declare a rigid single standard, good for now and for all future media and purposes. That is not to say that we reject all the more specific formulations of the standard – they appropriately cover the vast majority of cases involving government regulation of speech. Rather, aware as we are of the changes taking place in the law, the technology, and the industrial structure related to telecommunications, ... we believe it unwise and unnecessary definitively to pick one analogy or one specific set of words now.

... We therefore think it premature to answer the broad questions that JUSTICES KENNEDY and THOMAS raise in their efforts to find a definitive analogy, deciding, for example, the extent to which private property can be designated a public forum...; whether public access channels are a public forum...; whether the Government's viewpoint neutral decision to limit a public forum is subject to the same scrutiny as a selective exclusion from a pre-existing public forum...; whether exclusion from common carriage must for all purposes be treated like exclusion from a public forum...; and whether the interests of the owners of communications [743] media always

subordinate the interests of all other users of a medium....

Rather than decide these issues, we can decide these cases more narrowly, by closely scrutinizing § 10(a) to assure that it properly addresses an extremely important problem, without imposing, in light of the relevant interests, an unnecessarily great restriction on speech. The importance of the interest at stake here – protecting children from exposure to patently offensive depictions of sex; the accommodation of the interests of programmers in maintaining access channels and of cable operators in editing the contents of their channels; the similarity of the problem and its solution to those at issue in *Pacifica, supra;* and the flexibility inherent in an approach that *permits* private cable operators to make editorial decisions, lead us to conclude that § 10(a) is a sufficiently tailored response to an extraordinarily important problem.

First, the provision before us comes accompanied with an extremely important justification, one that this Court has often found compelling – the need to protect children from exposure to patently offensive sex-related material. ... Second, the provision arises in a very particular context – congressional *permission* for cable operators to regulate programming that, but for a previous Act of Congress, would have had no path of access to cable channels free of an operator's control. The First Amendment interests involved are therefore complex, and require a balance between those interests served by the access requirements themselves (increasing the availability of avenues of expression to programmers who otherwise would not have them), H. R. Rep. No. 98-934, at 31-36, and the disadvantage to the First Amendment interests of cable operators and other programmers (those to whom the cable operator would have assigned [744] the channels devoted to access). ...Third, the problem Congress addressed here is remarkably similar to the problem addressed by the FCC in *Pacifica*, and the balance Congress struck is commensurate with the balance we approved there.

In *Pacifica* this Court considered a governmental ban of a radio broadcast of "indecent" materials. ... The Court found this ban constitutionally permissible primarily because "broadcasting is uniquely accessible to children" and children were likely listeners to the program there at issue – an afternoon radio broadcast. 438 U.S. at 749-750. In addition, the Court wrote, "the broadcast media have established a uniquely pervasive presence in the lives of all Americans," *id.,* at 748, "patently offensive, indecent material . . . confronts the citizen, not only in public, but also in the privacy of the home," generally without sufficient prior warning to allow the recipient to avert his or her eyes or ears, *ibid.;* and "adults who feel the need may purchase tapes and records or go to theaters and nightclubs" to hear similar performances, *id.*, at 750, n. 28.

All these factors are present here. ... [745] There is nothing to stop "adults who feel the need" from finding similar programming elsewhere, say, on tape or in theaters. In fact, the power of cable systems to control home program viewing is not absolute. Over-the-air broadcasting and direct broadcast satellites already provide alternative ways for programmers to reach the home and are likely to do so to a greater extent in the near future. ... [T]he permissive nature of § 10(a) means that it likely restricts speech less than, not more than, the ban at issue in *Pacifica*. The provision removes a restriction as to [746] some speakers – namely, cable operators. See *supra*, at 743. Moreover, although the provision does create a risk that a program will not appear, that risk is not the same as the certainty that accompanies a governmental ban. In fact, a glance at the programming that cable operators allow on their own (non-access) channels suggests that this distinction is not theoretical, but real. See App. 393 (regular channel broadcast of Playboy and "Real Sex" programming). Finally, the provision's permissive nature brings with it a flexibility that allows cable operators, for example, not to ban broadcasts, but, say, to rearrange broadcast times, better to fit the desires of adult audiences while lessening the risks of harm to children. See First Report and Order P31, 8 FCC Rcd, at 1003 (interpreting the Act's provisions to allow cable operators broad discretion over what to do with offensive materials). In all these respects, the permissive nature of the approach taken by Congress renders this measure appropriate as a means of achieving the underlying purpose of protecting children. ... [747]

The existence of this complex balance of interests persuades us that the permissive nature of the provision, coupled with its viewpoint-neutral application, is a constitutionally permissible way to protect children from the type of sexual material that concerned Congress, while accommodating both the First Amendment interests served by the access requirements and those served in restoring to cable operators a degree of the editorial control that Congress removed in 1984.

Our basic disagreement with JUSTICE KENNEDY is narrow. Like him, we believe that we must scrutinize § 10(a) with the greatest care. Like JUSTICES KENNEDY and THOMAS, we believe that the interest of protecting children that § 10(a) purports to serve is compelling. But we part company with JUSTICE ... KENNEDY's focus on categorical analysis[, which] forces him to disregard the cable system operators' interests. *Post*, at 805-806. We, on the other hand, recognize that in the context of cable broadcast that involves an access requirement (here, its partial removal), and unlike in most cases where we have explicitly required "narrow tailoring," the expressive interests of cable operators do play a legitimate role. Cf. *Turner*, 512 U.S. at 636-637. While we cannot agree with JUSTICE THOMAS that *everything* turns on the rights of the cable owner, see *post*, at 823-824, we also cannot agree with JUSTICE KENNEDY that we must ignore the expressive interests of cable operators altogether. ... [748]

Petitioners and JUSTICE KENNEDY, see *post*, at 797-798, 803-804, argue that the opposite result is required. ... The Court's distinction in *Turner* ... between cable and broadcast television relied on the inapplicability of the spectrum scarcity problem to cable. See 512 U.S. at 637-641. While that distinction was relevant in *Turner* to the justification for structural regulations at issue there (the "must carry" rules), it has little to do with a case that involves the effects of television viewing on children. Those effects are the result of how parents and children view television programming, and how pervasive and intrusive that programming is. In that respect, cable and broadcast television differ little, if at all. See *supra*, at 744-745. JUSTICE KENNEDY would have us decide that *all* common carriage exclusions are subject to the highest scrutiny, see *post*, at 796-799, and then decide these cases on the basis of categories that provide imprecise analogies rather than on the basis of a more contextual assessment, consistent with our First Amendment tradition, of assessing whether Congress carefully and appropriately addressed a serious problem.

[749] ... For three reasons, however, it is unnecessary, indeed, unwise, for us definitively to decide whether or how to apply the public forum doctrine to leased access channels. First, while it may be that content-based exclusions from the right to use common carriers could violate the First Amendment, see *post*, at 796-800 (opinion of KENNEDY, J.), it is not at all clear that the public forum doctrine should be imported wholesale into the area of common carriage regulation. As discussed above, we are wary of the notion that a partial analogy in one context, for which we have developed doctrines, can compel a full range of decisions in such a new and changing area. See *supra*, at 739-743. Second, it is plain from this Court's cases that a public forum "may be created for a limited purpose." ... [750] Our cases have not yet determined, however, that government's decision to dedicate a public forum to one type of content or another is necessarily subject to the highest level of scrutiny. Must a local government, for example, show a compelling state interest if it builds a band shell in the park and dedicates it solely to classical music (but not to jazz)? The answer is not obvious. ... But, at a minimum, these cases do not require us to answer it. Finally, and most important, the effects of Congress' decision on the interests of programmers, viewers, cable operators, and children

are the same, whether we characterize Congress' decision as one that limits access to a public forum, discriminates in common carriage, or constrains speech because of its content. If we consider this particular limitation of indecent television programming acceptable as a constraint on speech, we must no less accept the limitation it places on access to the claimed public forum or on use of a common carrier.

Consequently, if one wishes to view the permissive provisions before us through a "public forum" lens, one should view those provisions as *limiting* the otherwise totally open nature of the forum that leased access channels provide for communication of other than patently offensive sexual material – taking account of the fact that the limitation was imposed in light of experience gained from maintaining a *totally* open "forum." One must still ask whether the First Amendment forbids the limitation. But unless a label alone were to make a critical First Amendment difference (and we think here it does not), the features of these cases that we have already discussed – the Government's interest in protecting children, the "permissive" aspect of the statute, and the nature of the medium – sufficiently justify the "limitation" on the availability of this forum. ...[753]

For the reasons discussed, we conclude that § 10(a) is consistent with the First Amendment. ...

[760] The statute's third provision, as implemented by FCC regulation, is similar to its first provision, in that it too *permits* a cable operator to prevent transmission of "patently offensive" programming, in this case on public access channels. 1992 Act, § 10(c); 47 CFR § 76.702 (1995). But there are four important differences.

The first is the historical background. As JUSTICE KENNEDY points out, see *post*, at 788-790, cable operators have traditionally agreed to reserve channel capacity for public, governmental, and educational channels as part of the consideration they give municipalities that award them cable franchises. See H. R. Rep. No. 98-934, at 30. In the terms preferred by JUSTICE THOMAS, see *post*, at 827-828, the requirement to reserve capacity for public access channels is similar to the reservation of a public easement, or a dedication [761] of land for streets and parks, as part of a municipality's approval of a subdivision of land. Cf. *post*, at 793-794 (opinion of KENNEDY, J.). Significantly, these are channels over which cable operators have not historically exercised editorial control. H. R. Rep. No. 98-934, *supra*, at 30. Unlike § 10(a) therefore, § 10(c) does not restore to cable operators editorial rights that they once had, and the countervailing First Amendment interest is nonexistent, or at least much diminished. See also *post*, at 792-793 (opinion of KENNEDY, J.).

The second difference is the institutional background that has developed as a result of the historical difference. When a "leased channel" is made available by the operator to a private lessee, the lessee has total control of programming during the leased time slot. See 47 U.S.C. § 532(c)(2). Public access channels, on the other hand, are normally subject to complex supervisory systems of various sorts, often with both public and private elements. See § 531(b) (franchising authorities "may require rules and procedures for the use of the [public access] channel capacity"). Municipalities generally provide in their cable franchising agreements for an access channel manager, who is most commonly a non-profit organization, but may also be the municipality, or, in some instances, the cable system owner. ... [762] Access channel activity and management are partly financed with public funds – through franchise fees or other payments pursuant to the franchise agreement, or from general municipal funds ... – and are commonly subject to supervision by a local supervisory board. ...

This system of public, private, and mixed nonprofit elements, through its supervising boards and nonprofit or governmental access managers, can set programming policy and approve or disapprove particular programming services. And this system can police that policy by, for example, requiring indemnification by programmers, certification of compliance with local standards, time segregation, adult content advisories, or even by prescreening individual programs. ... [763] Whether these locally accountable bodies prescreen programming, promulgate rules for the use of public access channels, or are merely available to respond when problems arise, the upshot is the same: There is a locally accountable body capable of addressing the problem, should it arise, of patently offensive programming broadcast to children, making it unlikely that many children will in fact be exposed to programming considered patently offensive in that community. ...

Third, the existence of a system aimed at encouraging and securing programming that the community considers valuable strongly suggests that a "cable operator's veto" is less likely necessary to achieve the statute's basic objective, protecting children, than a similar veto in the context of leased channels. Of course, the system of access managers and supervising boards can make mistakes, which the operator might in some cases correct with its veto power. Balanced against this potential benefit, however, is the risk that the veto itself may be mistaken; and its use, or threatened use, could prevent the presentation of programming, that, though borderline, is not "patently offensive" to its targeted audience. ... And this latter threat must bulk large within a system that already has publicly accountable systems for maintaining responsible programs.

Finally, our examination of the legislative history and the record before us is consistent with what common sense suggests, namely that the public/nonprofit programming control systems now in place would normally avoid, minimize, or [764] eliminate any child-related problems concerning "patently offensive" programming. We have found anecdotal references to what seem isolated instances of potentially indecent programming, some of which may well have occurred on leased, not public access, channels. ... But these few examples do not necessarily indicate a significant nationwide pattern. ... [765] Moreover, comments submitted to the FCC undermine any suggestion that prior to 1992 there were significant problems of indecent programming on public access channels. ... At most, we have found borderline examples as to which people's judgment may differ, perhaps acceptable in some communities but not others, of the type that petitioners fear the law might prohibit. ...[766] It is difficult to see how such borderline examples could show a compelling need, nationally, to protect children from significantly harmful materials. ... In the absence of a factual basis substantiating the harm and the efficacy of its proposed cure, we cannot assume that the harm exists or that the regulation redresses it. ...

The upshot, in respect to the public access channels, is a law that could radically change present programming-related relationships among local community and nonprofit supervising boards and access managers, which relationships are established through municipal law, regulation, and contract. In doing so, it would not significantly restore editorial rights of cable operators, but would greatly increase the risk that certain categories of programming (say, borderline offensive programs) will not appear. At the same time, given present supervisory mechanisms, the need for this particular provision, aimed directly at public access channels, is not obvious. Having carefully reviewed the legislative history of the Act, the proceedings before the FCC, the record below, and the submissions of the parties and *amici* here, we conclude that the Government cannot sustain its burden of showing that § 10(c) is necessary to protect children or that it is appropriately tailored to secure that end. ... Consequently, we find that this third provision violates the First Amendment.

... [768] For these reasons, the judgment of the Court of Appeals is affirmed insofar as it upheld § 10(a); the judgment of the Court of Appeals is reversed insofar as it upheld § 10(b) and § 10(c). *It is so ordered*.

CONCURBY: STEVENS; SOUTER; O'CONNOR (In Part); KENNEDY (In Part); THOMAS (In Part)

CONCUR: JUSTICE STEVENS, concurring.

The difference between § 10(a) and § 10(c) is the difference between a permit and a prohibition. The former restores the freedom of cable operators to reject indecent programs; the latter requires local franchising authorities to reject such programs. While I join the Court's opinion, I add these comments to emphasize the difference between the two provisions and to endorse the analysis in Part III-B of JUSTICE KENNEDY's opinion even though I do not think it necessary to characterize the public access channels as public fora. Like JUSTICE SOUTER, I am convinced that it would be unwise to take a categorical approach to the resolution of novel First Amendment questions arising in an industry as dynamic as this.

... [769] Section 10(a) is ... best understood as a limitation on the amount of speech that the Federal Government has spared from the censorial control of the cable operator, rather than a direct prohibition against the communication of speech that, in the absence of federal intervention, would flow freely. I do not agree, however, that § 10(a) established a public forum. Unlike sidewalks and parks, the Federal Government created leased access channels in the course of its legitimate regulation of the communications industry. In so doing, it did not establish an entirely open forum, but rather restricted access to certain speakers, namely unaffiliated programmers able to lease the air time. By facilitating certain speech that cable operators would not otherwise carry, the leased access channels operate like the must-carry rules...

When the Federal Government opens cable channels that would otherwise be left entirely in private hands, it deserves more deference than a rigid application of the public forum doctrine would allow. At this early stage in the regulation of this developing industry, Congress should not be put to an all or nothing-at-all choice in deciding whether to open certain cable channels to programmers who would otherwise lack the resources to participate in the marketplace of ideas.

Just as Congress may legitimately limit access to these channels to unaffiliated programmers, I believe it may also limit, within certain reasonable bounds, the extent of the access [770] that it confers upon those programmers. If the Government had a reasonable basis for concluding that there were already enough classical musical programs or cartoons being telecast – or, perhaps, even enough political debate – I would find no First Amendment objection to an open access requirement that was extended on an impartial basis to all but those particular subjects. A contrary conclusion would ill-serve First Amendment values by dissuading the Government from creating access rights altogether.

Of course, the fact that the Federal Government may be entitled to some deference in regulating access for cable programmers does not mean that it may evade First Amendment constraints by selectively choosing which speech should be excepted from private control. If the Government spared all speech but that communicated by Republicans from the control of the cable operator, for example, the First Amendment violation would be plain. [771] ...

Even though it is often difficult to determine whether a given access restriction impermissibly singles out certain ideas for repression, in this case I find no basis for concluding that § 10(a) is a species of viewpoint discrimination. ... Nor can it be argued that indecent programming has no outlet other than leased access channels, and thus that the exclusion of such speech from special protection is designed to prohibit its communication altogether. ... [772]

In sum, § 10(a) constitutes a reasonable, viewpoint-neutral limitation on a federally created access right for certain cable programmers. Accordingly, I would affirm the judgment of the Court of Appeals as to this provision.

As both JUSTICE BREYER and JUSTICE KENNEDY have explained, the public, educational, and governmental access channels that are regulated by § 10(c) are not creations of the Federal Government. They owe their existence to contracts forged between cable operators and local cable franchising authorities. ...[773] What is of critical importance to me, however, is that if left to their own devices, [cable] authorities may choose to carry some programming that the Federal Government has decided to restrict. As I read § 10(c), ... [i]t would inject federally authorized private censors into forums from which they might otherwise be excluded, and it would therefore limit local forums that might otherwise be open to all constitutionally protected speech.

Section 10(c) operates as a direct restriction on speech that, in the absence of federal intervention, might flow freely.... The Federal Government has no more entitlement to restrict the power of a local authority to disseminate materials on channels of its own creation, then it has to restrict the power of cable operators to do so on channels that they own. ...When the Government [774] acts to suppress directly the dissemination of such speech, however, it may not rely solely on speculation and conjecture. ...Given the direct nature of the restriction on speech that § 10(c) imposes, the Government has failed to carry its burden of justification. Accordingly, I agree that the judgment of the Court of Appeals with respect to § 10(c) should be reversed.

JUSTICE SOUTER, concurring.

JUSTICE KENNEDY's separate opinion stresses the worthy point that First Amendment values generally are well served by categorizing speech protection according to the respective characters of the expression, its context, and the restriction at issue. Reviewing speech regulations under fairly strict categorical rules keeps the starch in the standards for those moments when the daily politics cries loudest for limiting what may be said. JUSTICE KENNEDY sees no warrant in these cases for anything but a categorical and rule-based approach applying a fixed level of scrutiny, the strictest, to judge the content-based provisions of §§ 10(a), (b), and (c), and he accordingly faults the principal opinion [775] for declining to decide the precise doctrinal categories that should govern the issue at hand. The value of the categorical approach generally to First Amendment security prompts a word to explain why I join the Court's unwillingness to announce a definitive categorical analysis in this case.

Neither the speech nor the limitation at issue here may be categorized simply by content. ... Nor does the fact that we deal in these cases with cable transmission necessarily suggest that a simple category subject [776] to a standard level of scrutiny ought to be recognized at this point. ... [S]ettling upon a definitive level-of-scrutiny rule of review for so complex a category would require a subtle judgment; but there is even more to be considered, enough more to demand a subtlety tantamount to prescience.

All of the relevant characteristics of cable are presently in a state of technological and regulatory flux. Recent and far-reaching legislation not only affects the technical feasibility of parental control over children's access to undesirable material ... but portends fundamental changes in the competitive structure of the industry and, therefore, the ability of individual entities to act as bottlenecks to the free flow of information... . As cable and telephone companies begin their competition for control over the single wire that will carry both their services, we can hardly settle rules for review of regulation on the assumption that cable will remain a separable and useful category of First Amendment scrutiny. And as broadcast, cable, and the cybertechnology of the Internet and the World Wide Web approach the day of using a common receiver, we can [777] hardly assume that standards for judging the regulation of one of them will not have immense, but now unknown and unknowable, effects on the others.

Accordingly, in charting a course that will permit reasonable regulation in light of the values in competition, we have to accept the likelihood that the media of communication will become less categorical and more protean. Because we cannot be confident that for purposes of judging speech restrictions it will continue to make sense to distinguish cable from other technologies, and because we know that changes in these regulated technologies will enormously alter the structure of regulation itself, we should be shy about saying the final word today about what will be accepted as reasonable tomorrow. In my own ignorance I have to accept the real possibility that "if we had to decide today . . . just what the First Amendment should mean in cyberspace, . . . we would get it fundamentally wrong." ...

The upshot of appreciating the fluidity of the subject that Congress must regulate is simply to accept the fact that not every nuance of our old standards will necessarily do for the new technology, and that a proper choice among existing doctrinal categories is not obvious. Rather than definitively settling the issue now, JUSTICE BREYER wisely reasons by direct analogy rather than by rule. ... [778] [T]hat means it will take some time before reaching a final method of review for cases like these. ... Maybe the judicial obligation ... can itself be captured by a much older rule, familiar to every doctor of medicine: "First, do no harm."

DISSENT BY: O'CONNOR (In Part); KENNEDY (In Part); THOMAS (In Part)

DISSENT: [779] JUSTICE O'CONNOR, concurring in part and dissenting in part.

I agree that § 10(a) is constitutional and that § 10(b) is unconstitutional... . I find the features shared by § 10(a), which covers leased access channels, and § 10(c), which covers public access channels, to be more significant than the differences. For that reason, I would find that § 10(c) also withstands constitutional scrutiny.

Both §§ 10(a) and 10(c) serve an important governmental interest: the well-established compelling interest of protecting children from exposure to indecent material. ... Cable television, like broadcast television, is a medium that is uniquely accessible to children ..., and, of course, children have equally easy access to public access channels as to leased access channels. By permitting a cable operator to prevent transmission of patently offensive sex-related programming, §§ 10(a) and 10(c) further the interest of protecting children. Furthermore, both provisions are permissive. Neither presents an outright ban on a category of speech. ...

[780] The distinctions upon which the Court relies in deciding that § 10(c) must fall while § 10(a) survives are not, in my view, constitutionally significant. ... I am not persuaded that the difference in the origin of the access channels is sufficient to justify upholding § 10(a) and striking down § 10(c).

The interest in protecting children remains the same, whether on a leased access channel or a public access channel, and allowing the cable operator the option of prohibiting the transmission of indecent speech seems a constitutionally permissible means of addressing that interest. Nor is the fact that public access programming may be subject to supervisory systems in addition to the cable operator ... sufficient in my mind to render § 10(c) so ill tailored to its goal as to be unconstitutional.

Given the compelling interest served by § 10(c), its permissive nature, and its fit within our precedent, I would hold § 10(c), like § 10(a), constitutional.

JUSTICE KENNEDY, with whom JUSTICE GINSBURG joins, concurring in part, concurring in the judgment in part, and dissenting in part.

The plurality opinion, insofar as it upholds § 10(a) of the 1992 Cable Act, is adrift. The opinion treats concepts such as public forum, broadcaster, and common carrier as mere labels rather than as categories with settled legal significance; [781] it applies no standard, and by this omission loses sight of existing First Amendment doctrine. When confronted with a threat to free speech in the context of an emerging technology, we ought to have the discipline to analyze the case by reference to existing elaborations of constant First Amendment principles. This is the essence of the case-by-case approach to ensuring protection of speech under the First Amendment, even in novel settings. Rather than undertake this task, however, the plurality just declares that, all things considered, § 10(a) seems fine. I think the implications of our past cases for these cases are clearer than the plurality suggests, and they require us to hold § 10(a) invalid. ... [782]

Congress singles out one sort of speech for vulnerability to private censorship in a context where content-based discrimination is not otherwise permitted. The plurality at least recognizes this as state action. ... The plurality balks at taking the next step, however, which is to advise us what standard it applies to determine whether the state action conforms to the First Amendment. Sections 10(a) and (c) disadvantage non-obscene, indecent programming, a protected category of expression ... on the basis of its content. The Constitution in general does not tolerate content-based restriction of, or discrimination against, speech. ... In the [783] realm of speech and expression, the First Amendment envisions the citizen shaping the government, not the reverse. ... We therefore have given "the most exacting scrutiny to regulations that suppress, disadvantage, or impose differential burdens upon speech because of its content."

Sections 10(a) and (c) are unusual. They do not require direct action against speech, but do authorize a cable operator to deny the use of its property to certain forms of speech. As a general matter, a private person may exclude certain speakers from his or her property without violating the First Amendment, ... and if §§ 10(a) and (c) were no more than affirmations of this principle they might be unremarkable. Access channels, however, are property of the cable operator, dedicated or otherwise reserved for programming of other speakers or the government. A public access channel is a public forum, and laws requiring leased access channels create common-carrier obligations. When the government identifies certain speech on the basis of its content as vulnerable to exclusion from a common carrier or public forum, strict scrutiny applies. These laws cannot survive this exacting review. However compelling Congress' interest in shielding children from indecent programming, the provisions in this case are not drawn with enough care to withstand scrutiny under our precedents.

... [784] I do think it necessary, however, to decide what standard applies to discrimination against indecent programming on cable access channels in the present state of the industry. We owe at least that much to public and leased access programmers whose speech is put at risk nationwide by these laws. ... [U]se of a standard does not foreclose consideration of context. Indeed, if strict scrutiny is an instance of "judicial formulas so rigid that they become a straitjacket that disables government from responding to serious problems,"... this is a grave indictment of our First Amendment jurisprudence, which relies on strict scrutiny in a number of settings where context is important. ... [S]trict scrutiny ... does not disable government from addressing serious problems [785] but does ensure that the solutions do not sacrifice speech to a greater extent than necessary. ...

[T]he creation of standards and adherence to them, even when it means affording protection to speech unpopular or distasteful, is the central achievement of our First Amendment jurisprudence. Standards are the means by which we state in advance how to test a law's validity, rather than letting the height of the bar be determined by the apparent exigencies of the day. They also provide notice and fair warning to those who must predict how the courts will respond to attempts to suppress their speech. Yet formulations like strict scrutiny, used in a number of constitutional settings to ensure that the inequities of the moment are subordinated to commitments made for the long run, ... mean little if they can be watered down whenever they seem too strong. They mean still less if they can be ignored altogether when considering a case not on all fours with what we have seen before.

... The straightforward issue here is whether the Government can deprive certain speakers, on the basis of the content of their speech, of protections afforded [786] all others. There is no reason to discard our existing First Amendment jurisprudence in answering this question.

... The plurality cannot bring itself to apply strict scrutiny, yet realizes it cannot decide these cases without uttering some sort of standard; so it has settled for synonym. ... All we know about the substitutes is that they are inferior to their antecedents. ... These restatements have unfortunate consequences. The first is to make principles intended to protect speech easy to manipulate. ... Second, the plurality's exercise in pushing around synonyms for the words of our usual standards will sow confusion in the courts bound by our precedents. ... [787] This is why comparisons and analogies to other areas of our First Amendment case law become a responsibility, rather than the luxury the plurality considers them to be. The comparisons provide discipline to the Court and guidance for others, and give clear content to our standards – all the things I find missing in the plurality's opinion. The novelty and complexity of these cases is a reason to look for help from other areas of our First Amendment jurisprudence, not a license to wander into uncharted areas of the law with no compass other than our own opinions about good policy.

Another troubling aspect of the plurality's approach is its suggestion that Congress has more leeway than usual to enact restrictions on speech where emerging technologies are concerned, because we are unsure what standard should be used to assess them. ... If the plurality is concerned about technology's direction, it ought to begin by allowing speech, not suppressing it. ... [790]

My principal concern is with public access channels (the P of PEG). These are the channels open to programming by members of the public. ... [791] Public access channels meet the definition of a public forum. We have recognized two kinds of public fora. ... They provide groups and individuals who generally have not had access to the electronic media with the opportunity to become sources of information in the electronic marketplace [792] of ideas."

It is important to understand that public access channels are public fora created by local or state governments in the cable franchise. ... [T]he editorial discretion of a cable operator is a function of the cable franchise it receives from local government. ... [793] In providing public access channels under their franchise agreements, cable operators therefore are not exercising their own First Amendment rights. They serve as conduits for the speech of others. ... Section 10(c) thus restores no power of editorial discretion over public access channels that the cable operator once had; the discretion never existed. It vests the cable operator with a power under federal law, defined by reference to the content of speech, to override the franchise agreement and undercut the public forum the agreement creates. ...

We need not decide here any broad issue whether private property can be declared a public forum by simple governmental decree. That is not what happens in the creation of public access channels. Rather, in return for granting cable operators easements to use public rights-of-way [794] for their cable lines, local governments have bargained for a right to use cable lines for public access channels. ... [I]t seems to me clear that when a local government contracts to use private property for public expressive activity, it creates a public forum.

Treating access channels as public fora ... defines the First Amendment rights of speakers seeking to use the channels. When property has been dedicated to public expressive activities, by tradition or government designation, access is protected by the First Amendment. Regulations of speech content in a designated public forum, whether of limited or unlimited character, are "subject to the highest scrutiny" and "survive only if they are narrowly drawn to achieve a compelling state interest." ...

Leased access channels, as distinct from public access channels, are those the cable operator must set aside for unaffiliated [795] programmers who pay to transmit shows of their own without the cable operator's creative assistance or editorial approval. In my view, strict scrutiny also applies to § 10(a)'s authorization to cable operators to exclude indecent programming from these channels. ... [796]

Laws requiring cable operators to provide leased access are the practical equivalent of making them common carriers, analogous in this respect to telephone companies: They are obliged to provide a conduit for the speech of others. ... [797] ... We have held that a law precluding a common carrier from transmitting protected speech is subject to strict scrutiny, ... but we have not had occasion to consider the standard for reviewing a law, such as § 10(a), permitting a carrier in its discretion to exclude specified speech.

Laws removing common-carriage protection from a single form of speech based on its content should be reviewed under the same standard as content-based restrictions on speech in a public forum. ... A common-carriage [798] mandate ... serves the same function as a public forum. It ensures open, nondiscriminatory access to the means of communication. ... [T]he leased access provisions were narrowly drawn structural regulations of private industry ... to enhance the free flow and diversity of information available to the public without governmental intrusion into decisions about program content. ... The functional equivalence of designating a public forum and mandating common carriage suggests the same scrutiny should be applied

to attempts in either setting to impose content discrimination by law. Under our precedents, the scrutiny is strict. ... [800]

Except in instances involving well-settled categories of proscribable speech, ... strict scrutiny is the baseline rule for reviewing any content-based discrimination against speech. ... The question remains whether a dispensation from strict scrutiny might be appropriate because § 10(a) restores in part an editorial discretion once exercised by the cable operator over speech occurring on its property. This is where public-forum doctrine gives guidance. Common-carrier requirements of leased access are little different in function from designated public forums, and no different standard of review should apply. It is not that the functional equivalence of leased access channels to designated public forums [801] compels strict scrutiny; rather, it simply militates against recognizing an exception to the normal rule. ...

If Government has a freer hand to draw content-based distinctions in limiting a forum than in excluding someone from it, the First Amendment would be a dead letter in designated public forums; every exclusion could be recast as a limitation. ... The power to limit or redefine forums for a specific legitimate purpose ... does not allow the government to exclude certain speech or speakers from them for any reason at all. ... [802]

I do not foreclose the possibility that the Government could create a forum limited to certain topics or to serving the special needs of certain speakers or audiences without its actions being subject to strict scrutiny. ... This is not the correct analogy. These cases are more akin to the Government's creation of a band shell in which all types of music might be performed except for rap music. The provisions here are content-based discriminations in the strong sense of suppressing a certain form of expression that the Government dislikes or otherwise wishes to exclude on account of its effects, and there is no justification for anything but strict scrutiny here.

Giving government free rein to exclude speech it dislikes by delimiting public forums (or common-carriage provisions) would have pernicious effects in the modern age. Minds are [803] not changed in streets and parks as they once were. To an increasing degree, the more significant interchanges of ideas and shaping of public consciousness occur in mass and electronic media. ... The extent of public entitlement to participate in those means of communication may be changed as technologies change; and in expanding those entitlements the Government has no greater right to discriminate on suspect grounds than it does when it effects a ban on speech against the backdrop of the entitlements to which we have been more accustomed. It contravenes the First Amendment to give

Government a general license to single out some categories of speech for lesser protection so long as it stops short of viewpoint discrimination.

The Government ... argues the nature of the speech in question – indecent broadcast (or cable cast) – is subject to the lower standard of review. ... We already have rejected the application of this lower broadcast standard of review to infringements on the liberties of cable operators, even though they control an important communications [804] medium.

...

Other than the few categories of expression that can be proscribed, ... we have been reluctant to mark off new categories of speech for diminished constitutional protection. Our hesitancy reflects [805] skepticism about the possibility of courts drawing principled distinctions to use in judging governmental restrictions on speech and ideas, ... a concern heightened here by the inextricability of indecency from expression. ... Indecency often is inseparable from the ideas and viewpoints conveyed, or separable only with loss of truth or expressive power. Under our traditional First Amendment jurisprudence, factors perhaps justifying some restriction on indecent cable programming may all be taken into account without derogating this category of protected speech as marginal.

At a minimum, the proper standard for reviewing §§ 10(a) and (c) is strict scrutiny. The plurality gives no reason why it should be otherwise. I would hold these enactments unconstitutional because they are not narrowly tailored to serve a compelling interest.

The Government has no compelling interest in restoring a cable operator's First Amendment right of editorial discretion. ... [806] Congress does have, however, a compelling interest in protecting children from indecent speech. ... This interest is substantial enough to justify some regulation of indecent speech even under, I will assume, the indecency standard used here.

Sections 10(a) and (c) nonetheless are not narrowly tailored to protect children from indecent programs on access channels. First, to the extent some operators may allow indecent programming, children in localities those operators serve will be left unprotected. Partial service of a compelling interest is not narrow tailoring. ... Put another way, the [807] interest in protecting children from indecency only at the caprice of the cable operator is not compelling. Perhaps Congress drafted the law this way to avoid the clear constitutional difficulties of banning indecent speech from access channels, but the First Amendment does not permit this sort of ill fit between a law restricting speech and the interest it is said to serve.

Second, to the extent cable operators prohibit indecent programming on access channels, not only

children but adults will be deprived of it. ... It matters not that indecent programming might be available on the operator's other channels. The Government has no legitimate interest in making access channels pristine. ... When applying strict scrutiny, we will not assume plausible alternatives will fail to protect compelling interests; there must be some basis in the record, in legislative findings or otherwise, establishing the law enacted as the least restrictive means. ... There is none here.

Sections 10(a) and (c) present a classic case of discrimination against speech based on its content. There are legitimate reasons why the Government might wish to regulate or even restrict the speech at issue here, but §§ 10(a) and (c) are not drawn to address those reasons with the precision the First Amendment requires. ... [810]

[G]iving the Government the benefit of the doubt when it restricts speech, is an unusual approach to the First Amendment, to put it mildly. Worse, it ignores evidence of industry structure that should cast doubt on the plurality's sanguine view of the probable fate of programming considered "indecent" under § 10(a). ... [812] In agreement with the plurality's analysis of § 10(b) of the Act, insofar as it applies strict scrutiny, I join [that part] of its opinion. ... I dissent from the judgment of the Court insofar as it upholds the constitutionality of § 10(a).

JUSTICE THOMAS, joined by THE CHIEF JUSTICE and JUSTICE SCALIA, concurring in the judgment in part and dissenting in part.

I agree with the principal opinion's conclusion that § 10(a) is constitutionally permissible, but I disagree with its conclusion that §§ 10(b) and (c) violate the First Amendment. For many years, we have failed to articulate how, and to what extent, the First Amendment protects cable operators, programmers, and viewers from state and federal regulation. I think it is time we did so, and I cannot go along with JUSTICE BREYER's assiduous attempts to avoid addressing that issue openly.

The text of the First Amendment makes no distinctions among print, broadcast, and cable media, but we have done so. ... [813] Our First Amendment distinctions between media, dubious from their infancy, placed cable in a doctrinal wasteland in which regulators and cable operators alike could not be sure whether cable was entitled to the substantial First Amendment protections afforded the print media or was [814] subject to the more onerous obligations shouldered by the broadcast media. ... Over time, however, we have drawn closer to recognizing that cable operators should enjoy the same First Amendment rights as the non-broadcast media. ... [815] [C]able operators are generally entitled to much the same First Amendment protection as the print media. ...[816] [W]hen there is a conflict, a programmer's asserted right to transmit over an operator's cable system must give way to the operator's editorial discretion. ... [T]he programmer's right to compete for channel space [817] is derivative of, and subordinate to, the operator's editorial discretion. ... Viewers have a general right to see what a willing operator transmits, but ... they certainly have no right to force an unwilling operator to speak. ...

None of the petitioners in these cases are cable operators; they are all cable viewers or access programmers or their representative organizations. ... It is not intuitively obvious that the First Amendment protects the interests petitioners assert, and neither petitioners nor the plurality have adequately explained the source or justification of those asserted rights. ... [818]

In the process of deciding not to decide on a governing standard, JUSTICE BREYER purports to discover in our cases an expansive, general principle permitting government to "directly regulate speech to address extraordinary problems, where its regulations are appropriately tailored to resolve those problems without imposing an unnecessarily great restriction on speech."... This heretofore unknown standard is facially subjective and openly invites balancing of asserted speech interests to a degree not ordinarily permitted. ... [E]ven if the plurality's balancing test were an appropriate standard, it could only be applied to protect speech interests that, under the circumstances, are themselves protected by the First Amendment. But ... JUSTICE BREYER never explains whether (and if so, how) a programmer's ordinarily unprotected interest in affirmative transmission of its programming acquires constitutional significance on leased and public access channels. ... [820]

As I read the [relevant] provisions, they provide leased and public access programmers with an expansive and federally enforced statutory right to transmit virtually any programming over access channels, limited only by the bounds of decency. It is no doubt true that once programmers have been given, rightly or wrongly, the ability to speak on access channels, the First Amendment continues to protect programmers from certain government intrusions. Certainly, under our current jurisprudence, Congress could not impose a total ban on the transmission of indecent programming. ... At the same time, however, the Court has not recognized, as entitled to full constitutional protection, statutorily created speech rights that directly conflict with the constitutionally protected private speech rights of another person or entity. ...

There is no getting around the fact that leased and public access are a type of forced speech. ... [821] [F]ederal access requirements are subject to some form of heightened scrutiny. ... Under that view, content neutral governmental impositions on an operator's editorial discretion may be sustained only if they further an important governmental interest unrelated to the suppression of free speech and are no greater than is essential to further the asserted interest. Of course, the analysis I joined ... would have required strict scrutiny. ...

Petitioners must concede that cable access is not a constitutionally required entitlement and that the right they claim to leased and public access has, by definition, been governmentally created at the expense of cable operators' editorial [822] discretion. Just because the Court has apparently accepted, for now, the proposition that the Constitution permits some degree of forced speech in the cable context does not mean that the beneficiaries of a government-imposed forced speech program enjoy additional First Amendment protections beyond those normally afforded to purely private speakers.

... The question petitioners pose is whether §§ 10(a) and (c) are improper restrictions on their free speech rights, but ...the proper question is whether the leased and public access requirements (with §§ 10(a) and (c)) are improper restrictions on the *operators'* free speech rights. In my view, the constitutional presumption properly runs in favor of the operators' editorial discretion, and that discretion may not be burdened without a compelling reason for doing so. ... It is one thing to compel an operator to carry leased and public access speech, ... but it is another thing altogether to say that the First Amendment forbids Congress to give back part of the operators' editorial discretion, which all recognize as fundamentally protected, in favor of a broader access right. ... [823] [O]perators' journalistic freedom ... is infringed, whether the challenged restrictions be content neutral or content based.

Because the access provisions are part of a scheme that restricts the free speech rights of cable operators and expands the speaking opportunities of access programmers, who have no underlying constitutional right to speak through the cable medium, I do not believe that access programmers can challenge the scheme, or a particular part of it, as an abridgment of their "freedom of speech." Outside the public forum doctrine, ... government intervention that grants access programmers an opportunity to speak that they would not otherwise enjoy – and which does not directly limit programmers' underlying speech rights – cannot be an abridgment of the same programmers' First Amendment rights, even if the new speaking opportunity is content based.

The permissive nature of §§ 10(a) and (c) is important in this regard. ... §§ 10(a) and (c) do not burden a programmer's right to seek access for its indecent programming on an operator's system. Rather, they merely restore part of the editorial discretion an operator would have absent government regulation without burdening the programmer's underlying speech rights.

[824] The First Amendment challenge, if one is to be made, must come from the party whose constitutionally protected freedom of speech has been burdened. Viewing the federal access requirements as a whole, it is the cable operator, not the access programmer, whose speech rights have been infringed. Consequently, it is the operator, and not the programmer, whose speech has arguably been infringed by these provisions. ... [P]etitioners in these cases cannot reasonably assert that the Court should strictly scrutinize the provisions at issue in a way that maximizes their ability to speak over leased and public access channels and, by necessity, minimizes the operators' discretion.

It makes no difference that the leased access restrictions may take the form of common carrier obligations. ... [825] Labeling leased access a common carrier scheme has no real First Amendment consequences. It simply does not follow from common carrier status that cable operators may not, with Congress' blessing, decline to carry indecent speech on their leased access channels. Common carriers are private entities and may, consistent with the First Amendment, exercise editorial discretion in the absence of a specific statutory prohibition. ... [T]he fact that the leased access provisions impose a form of common carrier obligation on cable operators does not alter my view that Congress' leased access scheme burdens the constitutionally protected speech rights of cable operators in order [826] to expand the speaking opportunities of access programmers, but does not independently burden the First Amendment rights of programmers or viewers. ...

I do not agree with petitioners' ... assertion that public access channels are public fora. We have said that government may designate public property for use by the public as a place for expressive activity and that, so designated, that property becomes a public forum. ... [827] Cable systems are not public property. Cable systems are privately owned and privately managed, and petitioners point to no case in which we have held that government may designate private property as a public forum. ... [828]

It may be true, as petitioners argue, that title is not dispositive of the public forum analysis, but the nature of the regulatory restrictions placed on cable operators by local franchising authorities is not consistent with the kinds of governmental property interests we have said may be formally dedicated as public fora. ... [N]othing in the record suggests that local franchising authorities take any formal easement or other property interest in those channels that would permit the government to designate that property as a public forum.

[829] Similarly, assertion of government control over private property cannot justify designation of that property as a public forum. ... [W]e have never even hinted that regulatory control, and particularly direct regulatory control over a private entity's First Amendment speech rights, could justify creation of a public forum. Properly construed, our cases have limited the government's ability to declare a public forum to property the government owns outright, or in which the government holds a significant property interest consistent with the communicative purpose of the forum to be designated. ... [830]

Thus, even were I inclined to view public access channels as public property, which I am not, the numerous additional obligations imposed on the cable operator in managing and operating the public access channels convince me that these channels share few, if any, of the basic characteristics of a public forum. As I have already indicated, public access requirements, in my view, are a regulatory restriction on the exercise of cable operators' editorial discretion, not a transfer of a sufficient property interest in the channels to support a designation of that property as a public forum. Public access channels are not public fora, and, therefore, petitioners' attempt to redistribute cable speech rights in their favor must fail. For this reason, and the other reasons articulated earlier, I would sustain both § 10(a) and § 10(c).

Most sexually oriented programming appears on premium or pay-per-view channels that are naturally blocked from nonpaying customers by market forces..., and it is only governmental intervention in the first instance that requires access channels, on which indecent programming may appear, to be made part of the basic cable package. Section 10(b) does nothing more than adjust the nature of government-imposed leased access requirements [832] in order to emulate the market forces that keep indecent programming primarily on premium channels (without permitting the operator to charge subscribers for that programming).

Unlike §§ 10(a) and (c), § 10(b) clearly implicates petitioners' free speech rights. Though § 10(b) by no means bans indecent speech, it clearly places content-based restrictions on the transmission of private speech by requiring cable operators to block and segregate indecent programming that the operator has agreed to carry. Consequently, § 10(b) must be subjected to strict scrutiny and can be upheld only if it furthers a compelling governmental interest by the least restrictive means available. ... The parties agree that Congress has a "compelling interest in protecting the physical and psychological well-being of minors" and that its interest "extends to shielding minors from the influence of [indecent speech] that is not obscene by adult standards." ...

Because § 10(b) is narrowly tailored to achieve that well-established compelling interest, I would uphold it. I therefore dissent from the Court's decision to the contrary. ... [836]

Given the limited scope of § 10(b) as a default setting, I see nothing constitutionally infirm about Congress' decision to permit the cable operator 30 days to unblock or reblock the segregated channel.

Petitioners also claim that § 10(b) and its implementing regulations are impermissibly underinclusive because they apply only to leased access programming. ... [837] In arguing that Congress could not impose a blocking requirement without also imposing that requirement on public access and no-naccess channels, petitioners fail to allege, much less argue, that doing so would further Congress' compelling interest. While it is true that indecent programming appears on non-access channels, that programming appears almost exclusively on "per-program or per channel services that subscribers must specifically request in advance,

in the same manner as under the blocking approach mandated by section 10(b)." ... In contrast to these premium services, leased access channels are part of the basic cable package, and the segregation and blocking scheme Congress imposed does nothing more than convert sexually oriented leased access programming into a free "premium service." ... [838] [I]f the segregation and blocking scheme established by Congress is narrowly tailored to achieve a compelling governmental interest, it does not become constitutionally suspect merely because Congress did not extend the same restriction to other channels on which there was less of a perceived problem (and perhaps no compelling interest).

The United States has carried its burden of demonstrating that § 10(b) and its implementing regulations are narrowly tailored to satisfy a compelling governmental interest. Accordingly, I would affirm the judgment of the Court of Appeals in its entirety.

Reno v. American Civil Liberties Union
521 U.S. 844
(1997)
(Excerpts only. Footnotes omitted.)

Author's Note: Part of the Telecommunications Act of 1996, the Communications Decency Act, prohibits the knowing transmission to minors of "indecent" or "patently offensive" communications over the Internet. Congress enacted the law to protect children from sexually explicit materials. A three-judge district court struck down the law as a violation of the First Amendment. On expedited review, the Supreme Court agreed, and its decision offers some insight into how the Court perceives the First Amendment status of the Internet.

PRIOR HISTORY: On appeal from the United States District Court for the Eastern District of Pennsylvania.

JUDGES: STEVENS, J., delivered the opinion of the Court, in which SCALIA, KENNEDY, SOUTER, THOMAS, GINSBURG, and BREYER, JJ., joined. O'CONNOR, J., filed an opinion concurring in the judgment in part and dissenting in part, in which REHNQUIST, C. J., joined.

OPINION: [849] MR. JUSTICE STEVENS delivered the opinion of the Court.

... The District Court made extensive findings of fact.... Because those findings provide the underpinnings for the legal issues, we begin with a summary of the undisputed facts. ...

The Internet is an international network of interconnected computers. It is the outgrowth of what began in 1969 as a [850] military program called "ARPANET," which was designed to enable computers operated by the military, defense contractors, and universities conducting defense-related research to communicate with one another by redundant channels even if some portions of the network were damaged in a war. While the ARPANET no longer exists, it provided an example for the development of a number of civilian networks that, eventually linking with each other, now enable tens of millions of people to communicate with one another and to access vast amounts of information from around the world. The Internet is "a unique and wholly new medium of worldwide human communication."

The Internet has experienced "extraordinary growth." The number of "host" computers – those that store information and relay communications – increased from about 300 in 1981 to approximately 9,400,000 by the time of the trial in 1996. Roughly 60% of these hosts are located in the United States. About 40 million people used the Internet at the time of trial, a number that is expected to mushroom to 200 million by 1999.

Individuals can obtain access to the Internet from many different sources, generally hosts themselves or entities with a host affiliation. Most colleges and universities provide access for their students and faculty; many corporations provide their employees with access through an office network; many communities and local libraries provide free access; and an increasing number of storefront "computer coffee shops" provide access for a small hourly fee. Several major national "online services" such as America Online, CompuServe, the Microsoft Network, and Prodigy offer access to their own extensive proprietary networks as well as a link to the much larger resources of the Internet. These commercial [851] online services had almost 12 million individual subscribers at the time of trial.

Anyone with access to the Internet may take advantage of a wide variety of communication and information retrieval methods. These methods are constantly evolving and difficult to categorize precisely. But, as presently constituted, those most relevant to this case are electronic mail ("e-mail"), automatic mailing list services ("mail exploders," sometimes referred to as "listservs"), "newsgroups," "chat rooms," and the "World Wide Web." All of these methods can be used to transmit text; most can transmit sound, pictures, and moving video images. Taken together, these tools constitute a unique medium – known to its users as "cyberspace" – located in no particular geographical location but available to anyone, anywhere in the world, with access to the Internet.

E-mail enables an individual to send an electronic message – generally akin to a note or letter – to another individual or to a group of addressees. The message is generally stored electronically, sometimes waiting for the recipient to check her "mailbox" and sometimes making its receipt known through some type of prompt. A mail exploder is a sort of e-mail group. Subscribers can send messages to a common e-mail address, which then forwards the message to the group's other subscribers. Newsgroups also serve groups of regular participants, but these postings may be read by others as well. There are thousands of such groups, each serving to foster an exchange of information or opinion on a particular topic running the gamut from, say, the music of Wagner to Balkan politics to AIDS prevention to the Chicago Bulls. About 100,000 new messages are posted every day. In most newsgroups, postings are automatically purged at regular intervals. In addition to posting a message that can be read later, two or more individuals wishing to communicate more immediately can enter a chat room to engage in real-time dialogue – in other words, by typing messages to one another that appear almost immediately on [852] the others' computer screens. The District Court found that at any given time "tens of thousands of users are engaging in conversations on a huge range of subjects." It is "no exaggeration to conclude that the content on the Internet is as diverse as human thought."

The best known category of communication over the Internet is the World Wide Web, which allows users to search for and retrieve information stored in remote computers, as well as, in some cases, to communicate back to designated sites. In concrete terms, the Web consists of a vast number of documents stored in different computers all over the world. Some of these documents are simply files containing information. However, more elaborate documents, commonly known as Web "pages," are also prevalent. Each has its own address – "rather like a telephone number." Web pages frequently contain information and sometimes allow the viewer to communicate with the page's (or "site's") author. They generally also contain "links" to other documents created by that site's author or to other (generally) related sites. Typically, the links are either blue or underlined text – sometimes images.

Navigating the Web is relatively straightforward. A user may either type the address of a known page or enter one or more keywords into a commercial "search engine" in an effort to locate sites on a subject of interest. A particular Web page may contain the information sought by the "surfer," or, through its links, it may be an avenue to other documents located anywhere on the Internet. Users generally explore a given Web page, or move to another, by clicking a computer "mouse" on one of the page's icons or links. Access to most Web pages is freely available, but some allow access only to those who have purchased the right from a [853] commercial provider. The Web is thus comparable, from the readers' viewpoint, to both a vast library including millions of readily available and indexed publications and a sprawling mall offering goods and services.

From the publishers' point of view, it constitutes a vast platform from which to address and hear from a world-wide audience of millions of readers, viewers, researchers, and buyers. Any person or organization with a computer connected to the Internet can "publish" information. Publishers include government agencies, educational institutions, commercial entities, advocacy groups, and individuals. Publishers may either make their material available to the entire pool of Internet users, or confine access to a selected group, such as those willing to pay for the privilege. "No single organization controls any membership in the Web, nor is there any centralized point from which individual Web sites or services can be blocked from the Web."

... [854] Though [sexually explicit] material is widely available, users seldom encounter such content accidentally. "A document's title or a description of the document will usually appear before the document itself . . . and in many cases the user will receive detailed information about a site's content before he or she need take the step to access the document. Almost all sexually explicit images are preceded by warnings as to the content." For that reason, the "odds are slim" that a user would enter a sexually explicit site by accident. Unlike communications received by radio or television, "the receipt of information on the Internet requires a series of affirmative steps more deliberate and directed than merely turning a dial. A child requires some sophistication and some ability to read to retrieve material and thereby to use the Internet unattended."

Systems have been developed to help parents control the material that may be available on a home computer with Internet [855] access. A system may either limit a computer's access to an approved list of sources that have been identified as containing no adult material, it may block designated inappropriate sites, or it may attempt to block messages containing identifiable objectionable features. "Although parental control software currently can screen for certain suggestive words or for known sexually explicit sites, it cannot now screen for sexually explicit images." Nevertheless, the evidence indicates that "a reasonably effective method by which parents can prevent their children from accessing sexually explicit and other material which parents may believe is inappropriate for their children will soon be available." ...

The problem of age verification differs for different uses of the Internet. ... The Government offered no evidence that there was a reliable way to screen recipients and participants in such fora for [856] age. Moreover, even if it were technologically feasible to block minors' access to newsgroups and chat rooms containing discussions of art, politics or other subjects that potentially elicit "indecent" or "patently offensive" contributions, it would not be possible to block their access to that material and "still allow them access to the remaining content, even if the overwhelming majority of that content was not indecent."

Technology exists by which an operator of a Web site may condition access on the verification of requested information such as a credit card number or an adult password. Credit card verification is only feasible, however, either in connection with a commercial transaction in which the card is used, or by payment to a verification agency. Using credit card possession as a surrogate for proof of age would impose costs on non-commercial Web sites that would require many of them to shut down. For that reason, at the time of the trial, credit card verification was "effectively unavailable to a substantial number of Internet content providers."... Moreover, the imposition of such a requirement "would completely

bar adults who do not have a credit card and lack the resources to obtain one from accessing any blocked material."

Commercial pornographic sites that charge their users for access have assigned them passwords as a method of age verification. The record does not contain any evidence concerning the reliability of these technologies. Even if passwords are effective for commercial purveyors of indecent material, the District Court found that an adult password requirement would impose significant burdens on noncommercial sites, both because they would discourage users from accessing their sites and because the cost of creating and [857] maintaining such screening systems would be "beyond their reach." ...

The Telecommunications Act of 1996, Pub. L. 104-104, 110 Stat. 56, was an unusually important legislative enactment. As stated on the first of its 103 pages, its primary purpose was to reduce regulation and encourage "the rapid deployment of new telecommunications technologies." The major components of the statute have nothing to do with the Internet; they were designed to promote competition in the local telephone service market, the multichannel video market, [858] and the market for over-the-air broadcasting. The Act includes seven Titles, six of which are the product of extensive committee hearings and the subject of discussion in Reports prepared by Committees of the Senate and the House of Representatives. By contrast, Title V – known as the "Communications Decency Act of 1996" (CDA) – contains provisions that were either added in executive committee after the hearings were concluded or as amendments offered during floor debate on the legislation. An amendment offered in the Senate was the source of the two statutory provisions challenged in this case. They are informally described [859] as the "indecent transmission" provision and the "patently offensive display" provision. ...

The first, 47 U.S.C. A. § 223(a) (Supp. 1997), prohibits the knowing transmission of obscene or indecent messages to any recipient under 18 years of age. ... The second provision, § 223(d), prohibits the knowing sending or displaying of patently offensive messages in a manner that is available to a person under 18 years of age.

... [860] The breadth of these prohibitions is qualified by two affirmative defenses. See § 223(e)(5). One covers those who take "good faith, reasonable, effective, and appropriate actions" to restrict access by minors to the prohibited communications. § 223(e)(5)(A). The other covers those who [861] restrict access to covered material by requiring certain designated forms of age proof, such as a verified credit card or an adult identification number or code. § 223(e)(5)(B).

On February 8, 1996, immediately after the President signed the statute, 20 plaintiffs filed suit against the Attorney General of the United States and the Department of Justice challenging the constitutionality of §§ 223(a)(1) and 223(d). A week later, based on his conclusion that the term "indecent" was too vague to provide the basis for a criminal prosecution, District Judge Buckwalter entered a temporary restraining order against enforcement of § 223(a)(1)(B)(ii) insofar as it applies to indecent communications. A second suit was then filed by 27 additional plaintiffs, the two cases [862] were consolidated, and a three-judge District Court ... entered a preliminary injunction against enforcement of both of the challenged provisions. ... [864] The judgment of the District Court enjoins the Government from enforcing the prohibitions in § 223(a)(1)(B) insofar as they relate to "indecent" communications, but expressly preserves the Government's right to investigate and prosecute the obscenity or child pornography activities prohibited therein. The injunction against enforcement of §§ 223(d)(1) and (2) is unqualified because those provisions contain no separate reference to obscenity or child pornography.

... [866] Relying on the premise that "of all forms of communication" broadcasting had received the most limited First Amendment protection,... the Court concluded that the ease with which children may obtain access to broadcasts [867] ... justified special treatment of indecent broadcasting. ... [867] The CDA's broad categorical prohibitions are not limited to particular times and are not dependent on any evaluation by an agency familiar with the unique characteristics of the Internet. ... Finally, the Commission's order applied to a medium which as a matter of history had "received the most limited First Amendment protection," ... in large part because warnings could not adequately protect the listener from unexpected program content. The Internet, however, has no comparable history. Moreover, the District Court found that the risk of encountering indecent material by accident is remote because a series of affirmative steps is required to access specific material.

... According to the Government, the CDA is constitutional because [868] it constitutes a sort of "cyberzoning" on the Internet. But the CDA applies broadly to the entire universe of cyberspace. And the purpose of the CDA is to protect children from the primary effects of "indecent" and "patently offensive" speech, rather than any "secondary" effect of such speech. Thus, the CDA is a content-based blanket restriction on speech, and, as such, cannot be "properly analyzed as a form of time, place, and manner regulation." ...

In *Southeastern Promotions, Ltd.* v. *Conrad,* 420 U.S. 546, 557, 43 L. Ed. 2d 448, 95 S. Ct. 1239 (1975), we observed that "each medium of expression . . . may present its own problems." Thus, some of our cases have recognized special justifications for regulation of the broadcast media that are not applicable to other speakers. ... In these cases, the Court relied on the history of extensive government regulation of the broadcast medium ...; the scarcity of available frequencies at its inception ...; and its "invasive" nature. ...

Those factors are not present in cyberspace. Neither before nor after the enactment of the CDA have the vast democratic fora of the Internet been subject to the type [869] of government supervision and regulation that has attended the broadcast industry. Moreover, the Internet is not as "invasive" as radio or television. The District Court specifically found that "communications over the Internet do not 'invade' an individual's home or appear on one's computer screen unbidden. Users seldom encounter content 'by accident.'" 929 F. Supp. at 844 (finding 88). It also found that "almost all sexually explicit images are preceded by warnings as to the content," and cited testimony that "'odds are slim' that a user would come across a sexually explicit sight by accident." *Ibid.*

We distinguished *Pacifica* in *Sable,* 492 U.S. at 128, on just this basis. In *Sable,* a company engaged in the business of offering sexually oriented prerecorded telephone messages (popularly known as "dial-a-porn") challenged the constitutionality of an amendment to the Communications Act that imposed a blanket prohibition on indecent as well as obscene interstate commercial telephone messages. We held that the statute was constitutional insofar as it applied to obscene messages but invalid as applied to indecent messages. In attempting to justify the complete ban and criminalization of indecent commercial telephone messages, the Government relied on *Pacifica,* arguing that the ban was necessary to prevent children from gaining access to such messages. We agreed that "there is a compelling interest in protecting the physical and psychological well-being of minors" which extended to shielding them from indecent messages that are not obscene by adult standards, 492 U.S. at [870] 126, but distinguished our "emphatically narrow holding" in *Pacifica* because it did not involve a complete ban and because it involved a different medium of communication, *id.,* at 127. We explained that "the dial-it medium requires the listener to take affirmative steps to receive the communication." *Id.,* at 127-128. "Placing a telephone call," we continued, "is not the same as turning on a radio and being taken by surprise by an indecent message." *Id.,* at 128.

Finally, unlike the conditions that prevailed when Congress first authorized regulation of the broadcast spectrum, the Internet can hardly be considered a "scarce" expressive commodity. It provides relatively unlimited, low-cost capacity for communication of all kinds. The Government estimates that "as many as 40 million people use the Internet today, and that figure is expected to grow to 200 million by 1999." This dynamic, multifaceted category of communication includes not only traditional print and news services, but also audio, video, and still images, as well as interactive, real-time dialogue. Through the use of chat rooms, any person with a phone line can become a town crier with a voice that resonates farther than it could from any soapbox. Through the use of Web pages, mail exploders, and newsgroups, the same individual can become a pamphleteer. As the District Court found, "the content on the Internet is as diverse as human thought." 929 F. Supp. at 842 (finding 74). We agree with its conclusion that our cases provide no basis for qualifying the level of First Amendment scrutiny that should be applied to this medium.

Regardless of whether the CDA is so vague that it violates the Fifth Amendment, the many ambiguities concerning the scope of its coverage render it problematic for purposes of the First Amendment. ... [871] This uncertainty undermines the likelihood that the CDA has been carefully tailored to the congressional goal of protecting minors from potentially harmful materials.

... [874] We are persuaded that the CDA lacks the precision that the First Amendment requires when a statute regulates the content of speech. In order to deny minors access to potentially harmful speech, the CDA effectively suppresses a large amount of speech that adults have a constitutional right to receive and to address to one another. That burden on adult speech is unacceptable if less restrictive alternatives would be at least as effective in achieving the legitimate purpose that the statute was enacted to serve. ... [875]

The District Court was correct to conclude that the CDA effectively resembles the ban on "dial-a-porn" invalidated in *Sable.* 929 F. Supp. 824, 854. In *Sable,* 492 U.S. at 129, this Court rejected the argument that we should defer to the congressional judgment that nothing less than a total ban would be effective in preventing enterprising youngsters from gaining access to indecent communications. *Sable* thus made clear that the mere fact that a statutory regulation of speech was enacted for the important purpose of protecting children from exposure to sexually explicit material does not foreclose inquiry into its validity. As we pointed out last [876] Term, that inquiry embodies an "over-arching commitment" to make sure that Congress has designed its statute to accomplish its purpose "without imposing an

unnecessarily great restriction on speech." *Denver,* 518 U.S. at (slip op., at 11).

... Given the size of the potential audience for most messages, in the absence of a viable age verification process, the sender must be charged with knowing that one or more minors will likely view it. Knowledge that, for instance, one or more members of a 100-person chat group will be minor – and therefore that it would be a crime to send the group an indecent message – would surely burden communication among adults.

The District Court found that at the time of trial existing technology did not include any effective method for a sender to prevent minors from obtaining access to its communications on the Internet without also denying access to adults. The Court found no effective way to determine the age of a user who is accessing material through e-mail, mail exploders, newsgroups, or chat rooms. 929 F. Supp. at 845 (findings 90-94). As a practical matter, the Court also found [877] that it would be prohibitively expensive for noncommercial – as well as some commercial – speakers who have Web sites to verify that their users are adults. *Id.,* at 845-848 (findings 95-116). These limitations must inevitably curtail a significant amount of adult communication on the Internet. By contrast, the District Court found that "despite its limitations, currently available *user-based* software suggests that a reasonably effective method by which *parents* can prevent their children from accessing sexually explicit and other material which *parents* may believe is inappropriate for their children will soon be widely available." *Id.,* at 842 (finding 73) (emphases added).

The breadth of the CDA's coverage is wholly unprecedented. ... [878] It is at least clear that the strength of the Government's interest in protecting minors is not equally strong throughout the coverage of this broad statute. Under the CDA, a parent allowing her 17-year-old to use the family computer to obtain information on the Internet that she, in her parental judgment, deems appropriate could face a lengthy prison term. See 47 U.S.C. A. § 223(a)(2) (Supp. 1997). Similarly, a parent who sent his 17-year-old college freshman information on birth control via e-mail could be incarcerated even though neither he, his child, nor anyone in their home community, found the material "indecent" or "patently offensive," if the college town's community thought otherwise. [879]

The breadth of this content-based restriction of speech imposes an especially heavy burden on the Government to explain why a less restrictive provision would not be as effective as the CDA. It has not done so. The arguments in this Court have referred to possible alternatives such as requiring that indecent material be "tagged" in a way that facilitates parental control of material coming into their homes, making exceptions for messages with artistic or educational value, providing some tolerance for parental choice, and regulating some portions of the Internet – such as commercial web sites – differently than others, such as chat rooms. Particularly in the light of the absence of any detailed findings by the Congress, or even hearings addressing the special problems of the CDA, we are persuaded that the CDA is not narrowly tailored if that requirement has any meaning at all. ...

The Government first contends that, even though the CDA effectively censors discourse on many of the Internet's modalities – such as chat groups, newsgroups, and mail exploders – it is nonetheless constitutional because it provides a "reasonable opportunity" for speakers to engage in the restricted speech on the World Wide Web. ... [*880] The Government's position is equivalent to arguing that a statute could ban leaflets on certain subjects as long as individuals are free to publish books. In invalidating a number of laws that banned leafletting on the streets *regardless of* their content – we explained that "one is not to have the exercise of his liberty of expression in appropriate places abridged on the plea that it may be exercised in some other place." ...

Because both sections prohibit the dissemination of indecent messages only to persons known to be under 18, the Government argues, it does not require transmitters to "refrain from communicating indecent material to adults; they need only refrain from disseminating such materials to persons they know to be under 18." Brief for Appellants 24. This argument ignores the fact that most Internet for a – including chat rooms, newsgroups, mail exploders, and the Web – are open to all comers. The Government's assertion that the knowledge requirement somehow protects the communications of adults is therefore untenable. Even the strongest reading of the "specific person" requirement of § 223(d) cannot save the statute. It would confer broad powers of censorship, in the form of a "heckler's veto," upon any opponent of indecent speech who might simply log on and inform the would-be discoursers that his 17-year-old child – a "specific person . . . under 18 years of age," 47 U.S.C. A. § 223(d)(1)(A) (Supp. 1997) – would be present. [881] ...

The Government's three remaining arguments focus on the defenses provided in § 223(e)(5). ... [T]he Government suggests that "tagging" provides a defense that saves the constitutionality of the Act. The suggestion assumes that transmitters may encode their indecent communications in a way that would indicate their contents, thus permitting recipients to block their reception with appropriate software. It is the requirement that the good faith action must be "effective" that makes this defense illusory. The Government recognizes that its proposed screening software does not currently exist. Even if it did, there is no way to know whether a potential recipient will actually block the encoded material. Without the impossible knowledge that every guardian in America is screening for the "tag," the transmitter could not reasonably rely on its action to be "effective."

For its second and third arguments concerning defenses – which we can consider together – the Government relies on ... the transmitter [to have] restricted access by requiring use of a verified credit card or adult identification. Such verification is not only technologically available but actually is used by commercial providers of sexually explicit material. These providers, therefore, would be protected by the defense. Under the findings of the District Court, however, it is not economically feasible for most noncommercial speakers to employ such verification. Accordingly, this defense would not significantly [882] narrow the statute's burden on noncommercial speech. Even with respect to the commercial pornographers that would be protected by the defense, the Government failed to adduce any evidence that these verification techniques actually preclude minors from posing as adults. Given that the risk of criminal sanctions "hovers over each content provider, like the proverbial sword of Damocles," the District Court correctly refused to rely on unproven future technology to save the statute. The Government thus failed to prove that the proffered defense would significantly reduce the heavy burden on adult speech produced by the prohibition on offensive displays.

We agree with the District Court's conclusion that the CDA places an unacceptably heavy burden on protected speech, and that the defenses do not constitute the sort of "narrow tailoring" that will save an otherwise patently invalid unconstitutional provision. In *Sable,* 492 U.S. at 127, we remarked that the speech restriction at issue there amounted to "'burning the house to roast the pig.'" The CDA, casting a far darker shadow over free speech, threatens to torch a large segment of the Internet community. ... [885]

[T]he Government asserts that – in addition to its interest in protecting children – its "equally significant" interest in fostering the growth of the Internet provides an independent basis for upholding the constitutionality of the CDA. Brief for Appellants 19. The Government apparently assumes that the unregulated availability of "indecent" and "patently offensive" material on the Internet is driving countless citizens away from the medium because of the risk of exposing themselves or their children to harmful material.

We find this argument singularly unpersuasive. The dramatic expansion of this new marketplace of ideas contradicts the factual basis of this contention. The record demonstrates that the growth of the Internet has been and continues to be phenomenal. As a matter of constitutional tradition, in the absence of evidence to the contrary, we presume that governmental regulation of the content of speech is more likely to interfere with the free exchange of ideas than to encourage it. The interest in encouraging freedom of expression in a democratic society outweighs any theoretical but unproven benefit of censorship.

For the foregoing reasons, the judgment of the district court is affirmed. *It is so ordered.*

CONCUR BY: O'CONNOR (In Part)
DISSENT BY: O'CONNOR (In Part)

[886] JUSTICE O'CONNOR, with whom THE CHIEF JUSTICE joins, concurring in the judgment in part and dissenting in part.

I write separately to explain why I view the Communications Decency Act of 1996 (CDA) as little more than an attempt by Congress to create "adult zones" on the Internet. Our precedent indicates that the creation of such zones can be constitutionally sound. Despite the soundness of its purpose, however, portions of the CDA are unconstitutional because they stray from the blueprint our prior cases have developed for constructing a "zoning law" that passes constitutional muster.

Appellees bring a facial challenge to three provisions of the CDA. ... None of these provisions purports to keep indecent (or patently offensive) material away from adults, who have a First Amendment right to obtain this speech. ... Thus, the undeniable purpose of the CDA is to segregate indecent material on the Internet into certain areas that minors cannot access. ... [887]

The creation of "adult zones" is by no means a novel concept. ... [888] [A] zoning law is valid if (i) it does not unduly restrict adult access to the material; and (ii) minors have no First Amendment right to read or view the banned material. As applied to the Internet as it exists in 1997, the "display" provision and some applications of the "indecency transmission" and "specific person" provisions fail to adhere to the first of these limiting principles by restricting adults' access to protected materials in certain circumstances. Unlike the Court, however, I would invalidate the provisions only in those circumstances.

Our cases make clear that a "zoning" law is valid only if adults are still able to obtain the regulated speech. If they cannot, the law does more than simply keep children away from speech they have no right to obtain — it interferes with the rights of adults to obtain constitutionally protected speech and effectively "reduces the adult population . . . to reading only what is fit for children." ... The First

Amendment does not tolerate such interference. [889] ... If the law does not unduly restrict adults' access to constitutionally protected speech, however, it may be valid. ...

[T]he Court has previously only considered laws that operated in the physical world, a world that with two characteristics that make it possible to create "adult zones": geography and identity. ... [T]he twin characteristics of geography and identity enable the establishment's proprietor to prevent children from entering the establishment, but to let adults inside.

The electronic world is fundamentally different. Because it is no more than the interconnection of electronic pathways, cyberspace allows speakers and listeners to mask their identities. [890] Cyberspace undeniably reflects some form of geography; chat rooms and Web sites, for example, exist at fixed "locations" on the Internet. Since users can transmit and receive messages on the Internet without revealing anything about their identities or ages, ... however, it is not currently possible to exclude persons from accessing certain messages on the basis of their identity.

Cyberspace differs from the physical world in another basic way: Cyberspace is malleable. Thus, it is possible to construct barriers in cyberspace and use them to screen for identity, making cyberspace more like the physical world and, consequently, more amenable to zoning laws. This transformation of cyberspace is already underway. ... Internet speakers (users who post material on the Internet) have begun to zone cyberspace itself through the use of "gateway" technology. Such technology requires Internet users to enter information about themselves – perhaps an adult identification number or a credit card number – before they can access certain areas of cyberspace, ... much like a bouncer checks a person's driver's license before admitting him to a nightclub. Internet users who access information have not attempted to zone cyberspace itself, but have tried to limit their own power to access information in cyberspace, much as a parent controls what her children watch on television by installing a lock box. ... [891]

Despite this progress, the transformation of cyberspace is not complete. Although gateway technology has been available on the World Wide Web for some time now, ... it is not available to *all* Web speakers ... and is just now becoming technologically feasible for chat rooms and USENET newsgroups. ... Gateway technology is not ubiquitous in cyberspace, and because without it "there is no means of age verification," cyberspace still remains largely unzoned – and unzoneable. ...

Although the prospects for the eventual zoning of the Internet appear promising, I agree with the Court that we must evaluate the constitutionality of the CDA as it applies to the Internet as it exists today. ... Given the present state of cyberspace, I agree with the Court that the "display" provision cannot pass muster. Until gateway technology is available throughout cyberspace, and it is not in 1997, a speaker cannot be reasonably assured that the speech he displays will reach only adults because it is impossible to confine speech to an "adult zone." Thus, the only way for a speaker to avoid liability under the CDA is to refrain completely from using indecent speech. But this [892] forced silence impinges on the First Amendment right of adults to make and obtain this speech and, for all intents and purposes, "reduces the adult population [on the Internet] to reading only what is fit for children." ...

The "indecency transmission" and "specific person" provisions present a closer issue, for they are not unconstitutional in all of their applications. As discussed above, the "indecency transmission" provision makes it a crime to transmit knowingly an indecent message to a person the sender knows is under 18 years of age. ... The "specific person" provision proscribes the same conduct ... .

So construed, both provisions are constitutional as applied to a conversation involving only an adult and one or more minors. ... Restricting what the adult may say to the minors in no way restricts the adult's ability to communicate with other adults. He is not prevented from [893] speaking indecently to other adults in a chat room (because there are no other adults participating in the conversation) and he remains free to send indecent e-mails to other adults.

... If a minor enters a chat room otherwise occupied by adults, the CDA effectively requires the adults in the room to stop using indecent speech. If they did not, they could be prosecuted under the "indecency transmission" and "specific person" provisions for any indecent statements they make to the group, since they would be transmitting an indecent message to specific persons, one of whom is a minor. ... The CDA is therefore akin to a law that makes it a crime for a bookstore owner to sell pornographic magazines to anyone once a minor enters his store. Even assuming such a law might be constitutional in the physical world as a reasonable alternative to excluding minors completely from the store, the absence of any means of excluding minors from chat rooms in cyberspace restricts the rights of adults to engage in indecent speech in those rooms. The "indecency transmission" and "specific person" provisions share this defect.

But these two provisions do not infringe on adults' speech in *all* situations. And as discussed below, I do not find that the provisions are overbroad in the sense that they restrict minors' access to a substantial amount of speech that minors have the right to read and view. ... [894] I agree with the Court that the provisions are overbroad in that they cover any and all communications between adults and minors, regardless of how many adults might be part of the audience to the communication.

This conclusion does not end the matter, however. Where, as here, "the parties challenging the statute are those who desire to engage in protected speech that the overbroad statute purports to punish . . . the statute may forthwith be declared invalid to the extent that it reaches too far, but otherwise left intact." ... I would therefore sustain the "indecency transmission" and "specific person" provisions to the extent they [895] apply to the transmission of Internet communications where the party initiating the communication knows that all of the recipients are minors.

Whether the CDA substantially interferes with the First Amendment rights of minors, and thereby runs afoul of the second characteristic of valid zoning laws, presents a closer question. ... The Court neither "accepts nor rejects" the argument that the CDA is facially overbroad because it substantially interferes with the First Amendment rights of minors. ... I would reject it. ... [896]

In my view, the universe of speech constitutionally protected as to minors but banned by the CDA – *i.e.*, the universe of material that is "patently offensive," but which nonetheless has some redeeming value for minors or does not appeal to their prurient interest – is a very small one. ... That the CDA might deny minors the right to obtain material that has some "value" ... is largely beside the point. ... Accordingly, in my view, the CDA does not burden a substantial amount of minors' constitutionally protected speech.

Thus, the constitutionality of the CDA as a zoning law hinges on the extent to which it substantially interferes with the First Amendment rights of adults. Because the rights [897] of adults are infringed only by the "display" provision and by the "indecency transmission" and "specific person" provisions as applied to communications involving more than one adult, I would invalidate the CDA only to that extent. Insofar as the "indecency transmission" and "specific person" provisions prohibit the use of indecent speech in communications between an adult and one or more minors, however, they can and should be sustained. The Court reaches a contrary conclusion, and from that holding that I respectfully dissent.

Expression in Schools

The influence of educational goals on speakers

Focal cases:
Tinker v. Des Moines Independent School District, 393 U.S. 503 (1969)
Bethel School District v. Fraser, 478 U.S. 675 (1986)
Hazelwood School District v. Kuhlmeier, 484 U.S. 260 (1988)
Board of Regents of the University of Wisconsin v. Southworth, 529 U.S. 217 (2000)

T wo centuries ago, Horace Mann, who is widely recognized as the initiator of public schooling in America, suggested public education could strengthen democracy by uniting children from all classes and instilling in them the foundational concepts of self-governance. Throughout the 19th century, public schools emerged with school officials acting *in loco parentis*[1] to train future citizens and develop the workforce demanded by the burgeoning industrial complex in America. Conceived as a means to develop a cohesive society, the public schools were the natural site for inculcating social norms and values.[2] Thus, in 1998, President Bill Clinton said, "Schools do more than train children's minds. They also help to nurture their souls by reinforcing the values they learn at home and in their communities."[3]

At the turn of the 20th Century, however, John Dewey had promoted a different view of public education. His revolutionary concept of child-centered learning focused less on strict obedience to authority and more on experiential learning. Dewey suggested that public schools

---

[1] William Westmiller, *Losing All Hope ... In loco parentis*, 44 Libertarian Enterprise (April 21, 1999) *available at* http://www.webleyweb.com/tle/libe44-19990421-09.html (*in loco parentis* is the legal doctrine holding that officials have all the rights and powers of parents while children are in their custody).

[2] *See, e.g.*, Ambach v. Norwick 441 U.S. 68 (1979) (adopting the authoritarian perspective of public education).

[3] Quote *available at* http://www.ed.gov/Speeches/08-1995/religion.html. *See also* Richard W. Riley, U.S. Secretary of Education, *Religious Expression in Public Schools available at* http://www.ed.gov/Speeches/08-1995/religion.html.

should function as exhilarating laboratories of the real world rather than as tools of indoctrination.[4] Education, in Dewey's progressive view, is not preparation for life; education is life itself.[5]

Today, progressive education continues to flourish alongside and interwoven with the more authoritarian model endorsed by Mann. Americans continue to disagree on whether the paramount value of public schools is the inculcation of socially appropriate civic behavior or the freedom for students to experiment widely with diverse ideas and their expression.[6] The two models differ markedly in their view of free expression in public schools. The authoritarian model would limit free speech to advance discipline, training and other educational objectives. The progressive model would encourage free speech as an opportunity for students to experience the effects of robust disagreement. Consequently, the value of uninhibited free speech in the public schools remains unclear. The uncertainty grows when school expression involves religion and schools must determine whether student prayer, for example, is impermissible government "establishment" or protected individual free "exercise" of religion.[7]

PARAMOUNT CONCERNS

Throughout most of the 20th Century, the U.S. Supreme Court grappled with the power of public schools and universities to control speech and association on their campuses and at their activities.[8] The Court's school expression cases do not form a clear, coherent whole because different cases rest upon different facets of the educational experience, the goals of administrators or the freedom of students.

A primary focus throughout this body of law, however, is the Court's concern for what it deems to be schools' primary mission: educating students. While the mission of lower schools and universities may be the same, however, the Court has acknowledged that the mechanisms for educating youngsters and adults often must be quite different. Thus, the free speech rights of public-school students are "not automatically coextensive with the rights of adults."[9] While a university's mission "is well served if students have the means to engage in dynamic discussions of philosophical, religious, scientific, social and political subjects,"[10] public schools – even high schools – have no duty "affirmatively to promote particular student speech."[11] In fact, public school officials often have an obligation to control expression in the schools to ensure a supportive educational environment relatively free of disruptions.[12]

In this light, the Court has varied the power of school authorities to control lewd, vulgar, offensive, ungrammatical or even religious speech with the context in which the speech occurs.

---

[4] *See, e.g.,* Bd. of Educ. Island Trees Union Free School v. Pico, 457 U.S. 853 (1982) (adopting the progressive perspective of public education).

[5] John Dewey, *Attributed Comment,* in J. BARTLETT & J. KAPLAN, eds., BARTLETT'S FAMILIAR QUOTATIONS 577 (16th 1992).

[6] John Merrow, *In Schools We Trust,* The Merrow Report on PBS (1997) *available at* http://www.pbs.org/merrow/tv/trust/index.html.

[7] *See, e.g.,* Santa Fe Independent School Dist. v. Doe, 530 U.S. 290 (2000).

[8] Waugh v. Mississippi, 237 U.S. 589 (1915); Meyer v. Nebraska, 262 U.S. 390 (1923); Pierce v. Society of Sisters, 268 U.S. 510 (1925); Hamilton v. Regents of the University of California, 293 U.S. 245 (1934); Minersville School District v. Gobitis, 310 U.S. 586 (1940); West Virginia State Board of Education v. Barnette, 319 U.S. 624 (1943); Shelton v. Tucker, 364 U.S. 479 (1948); Keyishian v. Board of Regents, 385 U.S. 589 (1967); Tinker v. Des Moines Independent Community School District, 393 U.S. 503 (1969); Healy v. James, 408 U.S. 169 (1972); Papish v. Board of Curators of the University of Missouri, 410 U.S. 667 (1973); Widmar v. Vincent, 454 U.S. 263 (1981); Board of Education v. Pico, 457 U.S. 853 (1982); Perry Education Association v. Perry Local Educators' Association, 460 U.S. 37 (1983); Wallace v. Jaffree, 472 U.S. 38 (1985).

[9] Bethel School Dist. v. Fraser, 478 U.S. 675, 683 (1986).

[10] Bd. of Regents, Univ. of Wisc. v. Southworth, 529 U.S. 217, 233 (2000).

[11] Hazelwood at 270-271.

[12] Edwards v. Aguillard 482 U.S. 578 (1987); Tinker v. Des Moines 393 U.S. 503, 509 (1969).

- First, youth. Public schools have far greater ability to censor student expression than do universities because of the age and maturity of the students involved. [13] Thus, in 1986, the Court in *Bethel School District v. Fraser* upheld punishment of a high-school student for a speech laced with sexual innuendo on the grounds that the school had a responsibility to eliminate inappropriate language from school-sponsored activities that involved sensitive youngsters.[14] On a university campus, however, student expression cannot be shut off simply because it fails to conform with prevailing standards of decency.[15]

- Second, school curriculum. Schools enjoy greater authority over speech related to the school's curriculum than extra-curricular speech.[16] School-sponsored speech likely to reach young children is most susceptible to school control because of the power of such speech to undermine the educational mission of the school.[17] Accordingly, in *Hazelwood School District v. Kuhlmeier*, the Supreme Court in 1988 affirmed the right of high school authorities to eliminate stories on teen-age pregnancy and divorce from the student newspaper because the newspaper could "fairly be characterized as part of the school curriculum."[18] The Supreme Court has not yet examined the extent to which a school's control over its curriculum may permit control of the expression of teachers, faculty or administrators.

- Finally, educational environment. Public schools have the authority to prevent or punish student speech on school grounds when that speech materially or substantially disrupts educational activities or violates other students' rights.[19] However, the Court's 1969 landmark case, *Tinker v. Des Moines Independent Community School District*, established that public-school students do not shed their constitutional rights when they pass through the schoolhouse gates.[20] In fact, the Court said, high-school students could not constitutionally be sanctioned for the silent, non-disruptive wearing of black armbands in protest of the Vietnam war.

MANDATED SPEECH

In schools, as elsewhere, the Supreme Court has distinguished between the power of schools to mandate, to permit or to prohibit speech. In one of the early school expression cases, students challenged the public school requirement that they stand, salute the flag and recite the pledge of allegiance during the school day. Although this practice continues in many schools today, the Court in 1943 said it was unconstitutional for school officials to *require* students to say the pledge.[21] The Court also limited the ability of states to mandate the inclusion of religious content in the curriculum. In 1987, the Court struck down a Louisiana law requiring public schools that teach evolution to teach "creation science" as well. [22] The Court also has struck down state laws that require schools to post the Ten Commandments[23] or permit a moment of silence for voluntary

---

[13] *See, e.g.,* Hazelwood v. Kuhlmeier, 484 U.S. 260, 271, n. 7 (1988).

[14] 478 U.S. 675 (1986).

[15] Papish v. Bd. of Curators of the Univ. of Missouri, 410 U.S. 667 (1973) (per curiam) (remanding for application of the First Amendment a lower court ruling upholding university expulsion of student for "indecent speech" in the university newspaper).

[16] *See, e.g.,* Bethel School Dist. v. Fraser, 478 U.S. 675 (1986); Hazelwood v. Kuhlmeier, 484 U.S. 260 (1988); Bd. of Regents, Univ. of Wisc. v. Southworth, 529 U.S. 217 (2000).

[17] *See, e.g,* Widmar v. Vincent, 454 U.S. 263, 274 (1981); Bethel School Dist. v. Fraser, 478 U.S. 675 (1986).

[18] 484 U.S. 260, 271 (1988).

[19] Tinker v. Des Moines, 393 U.S. 503, 509 (1969). *See also* SDS Healy v. James, 408 U.S. 169 (1972) (limiting the power of universities to ban non-violent student organizations).

[20] Tinker at 506.

[21] West Virginia St. Bd. of Ed. v. Barnette, 319 U.S. 624 (1943).

[22] Edwards v. Aguillard 482 U.S. 578 (1987).

[23] Stone v. Graham, 449 U.S. 39 (1980) (per curiam).

prayer.[24] Yet, in 2001 the Supreme Court refused to impose an injunction or to grant *certiorari* in a case brought by Virginia public school students against the state's mandated moment of silence at the start of school.[25]

Student Expression or School-Sponsored Speech

Hazelwood v. Kuhlmeier established that high school newspapers generally are part of the school curriculum and hence are subject to control and oversight by school officials. This is not true of university student newspapers.[26] In 2001, the U.S. Court of Appeals for the Sixth Circuit flatly rejected application of the *Hazelwood* standard to university student publications and said the university student press should be viewed as a limited public forum. The appeals court said Kentucky State University's concern with "quality" could not constitutionally justify either its refusal to distribute the student yearbook or its transfer of the student publications adviser after she refused to censor material in the student newspaper. This strong affirmation of the First Amendment rights of the university student press follows other lower courts rulings that university officials may not withdraw or reduce funding to student publications or withhold student activities fees in an attempt to control, manipulate or punish past or future content.[27]

In 2003, the U.S. Court of Appeals for the Seventh Circuit was poised to review the earlier decision of three of its members who rejected application of *Hazelwood* to university student media and held that universities may not censor student press by withholding services or funds.[28] Student editors of the *Innovator* newspaper at Governors State University in Illinois sued the public university and its administrators after the dean of student affairs halted printing of the paper in response to articles and letters to the editor critical of the university. In its initial decision, three members of the court said, "The Supreme Court's restrictive First Amendment standard in *Hazelwood* sprang from its premise that the special circumstances of a secondary school environment permit school authorities to exercise greater control over expression by students than the First Amendment would otherwise permit. However, the judicial deference the Supreme Court found necessary in the high school setting – and in the factual context of *Hazelwood* – is inappropriate for a university setting."[29] Then the full court voted to vacate the ruling and to set the case for rehearing *en banc*.

The line demarcating student speech that schools must not infringe from school-sponsored speech and curriculum the schools control is contextual. In general, the Court distinguishes between activities that bear the imprimatur of the school, and hence should reflect and advance the school's mission, and activities in and around schools that a reasonable person would recognize to be unaffiliated with the school. In considering the views of the reasonable person, the Court considers the age of the students involved. The Court also recognizes that student attendance is virtually mandatory at many public school events (particularly graduations, school assemblies or even sports events), and these captive audience members should be protected from inappropriate speech.

---

[24] Wallace v. Jaffree, 472 U.S. 38 (1985).

[25] Brown v. Gilmore, 533 U.S. 1301 (2001), 534 U.S. 996 (2001).

[26] Hazelwood, 484 U.S. at 273 n.7; Board of Regents of the Univ. of Wisconsin Sys. v. Southworth, 529 U.S. 217 (2000) (Souter, J., concurring); Kincaid v. Gibson, 236 F.2d 342 (6th Cir. 2001)(en banc). *See also* Schiff v. Williams, 477 F.2d 456(4th Cir. 1973); Leuth v. St. Clair County Comm. College, 732 F.Supp. 1410 (E.D.Mich.1990). *But see* Hosty v. Carter, 2003 U.S. App. LEXIS 13195 (7th Cir. 2003), vacating 325 F.3d 1945 (7th Cir. 2003) and granting rehearing *en banc*.

[27] Schiff v. Williams, 477 F.2d 456 (4th Cir. 1973); Leuth v. St. Clair County Comm. College, 732 F.Supp. 1410 (E.D.Mich.1990); Kincaid v. Gibson, 236 F.3d 342 (6th Cir. 2001)(en banc).

[28] Hosty v. Carter, 325 F.3d 945 (7th Cir. 2003), 2003 U.S. App. LEXIS 13195 (7th Cir. 2003).

[29] Hosty, 325 F.3d at *9.

The Court demonstrated the distinction between student expression and school-sponsored speech in two cases involving religious expression at school activities or on school grounds. In the first of the two cases, *Santa Fe Independent School District v. Doe*,[30] the Court in 2000 struck down a Texas high school policy providing for student-led prayers before football games. Here, the Court said, the non-sectarian invocation by a student-elected chaplain bore the unmistakable endorsement of the school and constituted unconstitutional establishment of religion. In the second case, *Good News Club v. Milford Central School*,[31] the Court in 2001 said the New York public school could not constitutionally prohibit a club from using its facility after hours simply because the club was religious. The Supreme Court said the school's refusal to permit the religious club to meet in an empty classroom immediately after school on an equal footing with other non-school organizations amounted to unconstitutional viewpoint discrimination.[32] Even middle-school children, the Court said, would recognize that the club's endorsement of religion was not part of the school's curriculum. In this decision and others involving the distribution of university student fees,[33] the Court reasoned that when school policies or funds establish limited public forums, schools generally may not discriminate against religious expression.

POTENTIAL DISRUPTION

In *Tinker*, the Supreme Court established that students should not be prevented from engaging in non-disruptive speech. Accordingly, school speech and dress codes are disfavored under the First Amendment because they tend to interfere with protected speech, often based on viewpoint or vague concerns about social propriety. However, some courts have upheld anti-harassment codes when schools establish a concrete basis – such as a history of disruption and interference with the rights of other students – for rules that narrowly target clothing or speech that poses a well-founded likelihood of disruption.[34] Other cases, though, have found similar regulations unconstitutional.[35]

Courts are divided on the ability of schools to establish dress and hate-speech codes in part because of the age of the students involved and in part because of the specific environment in the particular school. Federal courts, though not the Supreme Court, generally have concluded that universities may not discipline students for speech that is non-disruptive but that may constitute sexual or racial harassment.[36] Public schools, however, appear to have greater leeway. In 2002, for example, the U.S. Court of Appeals for the Third Circuit upheld portions of a public school's racial harassment policy, which sanctioned both speech and clothing.[37] The court of appeals struck down sanctions on dress and speech that caused "ill will" but upheld broad prohibitions on racially harassing speech because the school had identified a specific and concrete association between

---

[30] 530 U.S. 290 (2000).

[31] 533 U.S. 98 (2001).

[32] *See also* Hills v. Scottsdale Unified School District, 2003 U.S. App. LEXIS 10255 (9th Cir. May 22, 2003)

[33] *See, e.g.*, Board of Regents of the University of Wisconsin v. Southworth, 529 U.S. 217 (2000); Rosenberger v. Rector & Visitors, University of Virginia, 515 U.S. 819 (1995).

[34] *See, also*, See, e.g., King v. Saddleback Junior College Dist., 445 F. 2d 932 (9th Cir.), *cert. den'd*, 404 U.S. 979 (1971); Gfell v. Rickelman, 441 F. 2d 444 (6th Cir. 1971); Ferrell v. Dallas Independent School Dist., 392 F. 2d 697 (5th Cir.), *cert. den'd*, 393 U.S. 856 (1968).

[35] *See, e.g.*, Richards v. Thurston, 424 F. 2d 1281 (1st Cir. 1970); Breen v. Kahl, 419 F. 2d 1034 (7th Cir. 1969), *cert. den'd*, 398 U.S. 937 (1970).

[36] *See, e.g.*, Dambrot v. Central Michigan University, 55 F.3d 1177 (6th Cir. 1995); UWM Post, Inc. v. Board of Regents of University of Wisconsin System, 774 F. Supp. 1163 (E.D. Wis. 1991); Doe v. University of Michigan, 721 F. Supp. 852 (E.D. Mich. 1989); Iota XI Chapter of Sigma Chi Fraternity v. George Mason University, 993 F.2d 386 (4th Cir. 1993).

[37] Sypniewski v. Warren Hills Reg'l Bd. of Educ. 307 F.3d 243 (3d. Cir. 2002) *cert. den'd* Warren Hills Reg'l Bd. v. Sypniewski, 2003 U.S. LEXIS 3721 (2003).

certain words and symbols (notably the Confederate flag[38]) and a well-founded fear of genuine disruption and substantial interference with school operations and the rights of students.

The Supreme Court denied *cert.* in that case as well as another in which the Court of Appeals for the Sixth Circuit affirmed the authority of high-school officials to punish a student for wearing Marilyn Manson T-shirts.[39] The court held that the school had the authority to sanction messages displayed on T-shirts that violated the school's "common core of values that include ... human dignity and worth, ... self respect and responsibility." The Court of Appeals for the Sixth Circuit held that student dress falls within the purview of school authorities not only when it meets the *Tinker* standard of disruption but also when it threatens curricular values or school image. [40]

FACULTY EXPRESSION

The Supreme Court has recognized a close link between the First Amendment freedom to explore ideas in the classroom and the freedom of faculty members to teach without inhibition and to express their views about school curriculum and policies.[41] In a number of cases, the Court resoundingly rejected "the theory" that public teachers constitutionally may be subjected to limits on their free speech or association in exchange for the benefits of public employment.[42] In 1968, for example, the Court struck down the dismissal of a public school teacher who had criticized the local school board and said, "The public employee surely can associate, and speak freely and petition openly, and he is protected by the First Amendment from retaliation for doing so."[43] In 2003, the Supreme Court denied *cert.* to a First Amendment appeal brought by a graduate student seeking to force the university to give him a passing grade on a master's thesis to which he added a page of excoriating comments about the school and its faculty after his graduate committee had approved the work.[44] The lower court had deferred to the judgment of school officials to determine grades.

As the civil rights and the anti-war movements of the 1960s and '70s enveloped university campuses and infiltrated school buildings across the country,[45] the Supreme Court repeatedly said the academic freedom of teachers and the open exchange of ideas in classrooms were of paramount importance in a free society and of "special concern [to] the First Amendment."[46] In this vein, the Court struck down laws that limited discussion of novel or controversial ideas or that prohibited the teaching of unpopular subjects.[47]

Freedom to teach controversial topics in public schools, however, does not permit states to mandate the teaching of Biblical creationism or to prohibit the teaching of evolution because the

---

[38] *See* West v. Derby Unified School Dist, 206 F.3d 1358 (10th Cir.) *cert. den'd* 531 U.S. 825 (2000); Phillips v. Anderson County School District, 987 F. Supp. 488 (D.S.C. 1997); Melton v. Young, 465 F.2d 1332 (6th Cir. 1972).

[39] Boroff v. Van Wert City Board of Education,220 F.3d 465 (6th Cir. 2000), *cert. den'd* 532 U.S. 920 (2001).

[40] *But see* Saxe v. State Coll. Area Sch. Dist., 240 F.3d 200, 207 (3d Cir. 2001) (holding that school speech codes must meet the *Tinker* standard).

[41] *See, e.g.,* Wieman v. Updegraff, 344 U.S. 183 (1952); Shelton v. Tucker, 364 U.S. 479 (1960); Keyishian v. Board of Regents, 385 U.S. 589 (1967); Rosenberger v. Rector and Visitors of Univ. of Va., 515 U.S. 819 (1995).

[42] *See, e.g.,* Keyishian v. Board of Regents, 385 U.S. 589, 605-606 (1967); Wieman v. Updegraff, 344 U.S. 183 (1952); Slochower v. Board of Education, 350 U.S. 551 (1956); Cramp v. Board of Public Instruction, 368 U.S. 278 (1961); Baggett v. Bullitt, 377 U.S. 360 (1964); Shelton v. Tucker, 364 U.S. 479 (1960; Beilan v. Board of Education, 357 U.S. 399, 405 (1958).

[43] Pickering v. Bd. of Ed., 391 U.S. 563, 574-75 (1968).

[44] Brown v. Li, 308 F.3d 939 (9th Cir. 2002), *cert. den'd* 123 S.Ct. 1488 (2003).

[45] *See, e.g.,* Tinker v. Des Moines Ind. School Dist., 393 U.S. 503 (1969).

[46] *See, e.g.,* Keyishian v. Board of Regents of University of New York, 385 U.S. 589, 603 (1967); Healy v. James, 408 U.S. 169, 180-181 (1972); Shelton, 364 U.S. 479, 487 (1960).

[47] *See,* Shelton, 364 U.S. 479; Epperson v. Arkansas, 393 U.S. 97 (1968).

Court said such edicts amount to government establishment of religion.[48] Moreover, the Supreme Court has indicated in *dicta* that schools and universities may incidentally inhibit the freedom of expression of school employees when they select speakers or establish curriculum.[49] Thus, the Court of Appeals for the Ninth Circuit upheld the authority of a Los Angeles high school to prevent a teacher from creating a hallway bulletin board whose message challenged the official school awareness campaign on gay and lesbian issues.[50]

STUDENT PRIVACY AND SAFETY

The Family Educational Rights and Privacy Act of 1974, usually called the Buckley Amendment,[51] protects the privacy of sensitive student educational files by limiting access to students over 18, the legal guardians of student minors or school officials on a "need to know" basis. In contrast, the Federal Crime Awareness and Campus Security Act of 1990[52] and amendments to the Higher Education Act require disclosure of campus crime statistics and the results of campus judicial proceedings.

Tension exists between the two laws in terms of the proper balance of student privacy and public safety and knowledge of campus crime. Public schools and universities withhold grades, health information, student disciplinary records and even individually identifiable student law enforcement records on the grounds that release would threaten federal funding to the institution. FERPA permits schools to release general directory information and physical statistics on athletes.

Courts have found that FERPA does not apply to all information held by schools or produced in schools. For example, the Supreme Court in 2002 ruled that peer grading, in which students swapped work and noted each other's grades, did not violate FERPA because the items did not constitute educational records until the teacher collected and recorded students' grades.[53] In the early 1990s, at least two federal district courts rejected the U.S. Department of Education's position that campus police reports that name individual students as victims, suspects or witnesses are educational records subject to privacy under the law.[54] In contrast, the U.S. Court of Appeals for the Sixth Circuit concluded in 2002 that personally identifiable university disciplinary records *were* educational records protected by the privacy provisions of FERPA.[55] The appeals court upheld a permanent injunction against the release of student disciplinary records by Miami University and The Ohio State University.

Generally, the courts have held that government sanctions, not private lawsuits, are the proper response to violations of privacy under FERPA.[56] The Supreme Court most recently reiterated this point when it rejected a lawsuit brought against Gonzaga University by a male student who objected to the school's release of personal information as part of Washington State's teacher certification process. The student had been denied teacher certification after Gonzaga released data about his alleged sexual misconduct toward a female undergraduate.

---

[48] *See, e.g.,* Edwards v. Aguillard, 482 U.S. 578 (1987).

[49] Arkansas Educational Television Commission v. Forbes, 523 U.S. 666, 674 (1998).

[50] Downs v. Los Angeles Unified School District, 228 F.3d 1003 (9th Cir. 2000).

[51] 20 U.S.C. sec. 1232g (1994, Supp. IV 1998 & Supp. V 1999).

[52] 20 U.S.C. 1092 (1994 & Supp. IV 1998).

[53] Owasso Independent School District v. Falvo, 534 U.S. 426 (2002).

[54] *See* Student Press Law Center v. Alexander, 778 F. Supp. 1227 (D. D.C. 1991); Bauer v. Kincaid, 759 F. Supp. 575 (W.D. Mo. 1991).

[55] United States v. Miami Univ., 294 F.3d 797 (6th Cir. 2002) (affirming summary judgment).

[56] *See, e.g.,* Gonzaga University v. Doe, 122 S.Ct. 2268 (2002).

ADDITIONAL CASE READINGS

This chapter indicates that the law of school expression is highly fact-specific. Its doctrines are narrow, and its precedents sometimes conflict. Moreover, tension exists between laws enacted specifically to advance the privacy of students and those designed to increase awareness of crime on campus or to inform the public about the operation of public universities (For more on open records, see Chap. 17.) Reading the cases that follow and those suggested below will provide added insight into how the courts view the rights and freedoms of students, faculty and administrators.

- *Hosty v. Carter*, 325 F.3d 945 (7th Cir. 2003) (rejecting application of *Hazelwood* to university publication).
- *Board of Regents, University of Wisconsin v. Southworth*, 529 U.S. 217, 233 (2000) (requiring universities to distribute student fees non-discriminatorily among accredited organizations).
- *Santa Fe Independent School District v. Doe*, 530 U.S. 290 (2000) (rejecting school policy of student-led prayers before school events).
- *Dambrot v. Central Michigan University*, 55 F.3d 1177 (6th Cir. 1995) (striking university speech code).
- *Rosenberger v. Rector & Visitors, University of Virginia*, 515 U.S. 819 (1995).
- *Hazelwood v. Kuhlmeier*, 484 U.S. 260 (1988) (affirming authority of school to control content of high school publication).
- *Edwards v. Aguillard*, 482 U.S. 578 (1987) (rejecting school mandate to teach creationism).
- *Bethel School District v. Fraser*, 478 U.S. 675, 683 (1986) (affirming right of public school authorities to sanction student sexual innuendo during school function).
- *Board of Education, Island Trees Union Free School v. Pico*, 457 U.S. 853 (1982) (denying school authority to remove library books based on content).
- *Healy v. James*, 408 U.S. 169 (1972) (limiting the authority of universities to ban non-violent student organizations based on viewpoint).
- *Tinker v. Des Moines Independent Community School District*, 393 U.S. 503 (1969) (affirming student right to engage in non-disruptive protest in school).
- *Keyishian v. Board of Regents*, 385 U.S. 589 (1967) (rejecting anti-communist loyalty oath by teachers).
- *West Virginia State Board of Education v. Barnette*, 319 U.S. 624 (1943) (striking mandatory flag salute).

Consider the following questions as you read of these excerpts and cases.

- Do the dissenters differ from the majority on a point of law, educational philosophy or both?
- How does the majority of the Court distinguish the primary mission of public schools from the mission of universities?
- What test is established in *Tinker* and when should it be applied?
- In *Tinker*, how does the Court define the boundaries of school authority? In *Fraser*? *Hazelwood*? *Southworth*?
- How does the Court determine when a case involves official government speech or student expression?
- Under these cases, what constitutes a public forum?
- What restrictions apply to government behavior in school-based public forums?
- How does the Court determine which precedents or areas of law to apply in school expression cases?

Tinker v. Des Moines Independent Community School District
393 U.S. 503
(1969)
(Excerpts only. Footnotes omitted.)

Author's Note: A Des Moines school policy prohibited students from wearing armbands to school. Three high school and junior high students, aware of the policy, war black armbands to express opposition to the Vietnam conflict and were suspended. The students sued, seeking an injunction to stop enforcement of the policy. The district court upheld the policy as reasonable, and an evenly divided court of appeals, sitting *en banc,* affirmed.

PRIOR HISTORY: Certiorari to the United States Court of Appeals for the Eighth Circuit.

JUDGES: Warren, Black, Douglas, Harlan, Brennan, Stewart, White, Fortas, Marshall.

OPINION: FORTAS

...[505] I. The District Court recognized that the wearing of an armband for the purpose of expressing certain views is the type of symbolic act that is within the Free Speech Clause of the First Amendment. See *West Virginia* v. *Barnette,* 319 U.S. 624 (1943); *Stromberg* v. *California,* 283 U.S. 359 (1931). Cf. *Thornhill* v. *Alabama,* 310 U.S. 88 (1940); *Edwards* v. *South Carolina,* 372 U.S. 229 (1963); *Brown* v. *Louisiana,* 383 U.S. 131 (1966). As we shall discuss, the wearing of armbands in the circumstances of this case was entirely divorced from actually or potentially disruptive conduct by those participating in it. It was closely akin to "pure speech" [506] which, we have repeatedly held, is entitled to comprehensive protection under the First Amendment. Cf. *Cox* v. *Louisiana,* 379 U.S. 536, 555 (1965); *Adderley* v. *Florida,* 385 U.S. 39 (1966).

First Amendment rights, applied in light of the special characteristics of the school environment, are available to teachers and students. It can hardly be argued that either students or teachers shed their constitutional rights to freedom of speech or expression at the schoolhouse gate. This has been the unmistakable holding of this Court for almost 50 years. ... [507]

On the other hand, the Court has repeatedly emphasized the need for affirming the comprehensive authority of the States and of school officials, consistent with fundamental constitutional safeguards, to prescribe and control conduct in the schools. ... Our problem lies in the area where students in the exercise of First Amendment rights collide with the rules of the school authorities.

The problem posed by the present case... [508] does not concern aggressive, disruptive action

or even group demonstrations. Our problem involves direct, primary First Amendment rights akin to "pure speech."

The school officials banned and sought to punish petitioners for a silent, passive expression of opinion, unaccompanied by any disorder or disturbance on the part of petitioners. There is here no evidence whatever of petitioners' interference, actual or nascent, with the schools' work or of collision with the rights of other students to be secure and to be let alone. Accordingly, this case does not concern speech or action that intrudes upon the work of the schools or the rights of other students. ... Outside the classrooms, a few students made hostile remarks to the children wearing armbands, but there were no threats or acts of violence on school premises.

The District Court concluded that the action of the school authorities was reasonable because it was based upon their fear of a disturbance from the wearing of the armbands. But, in our system, undifferentiated fear or apprehension of disturbance is not enough to overcome the right to freedom of expression. Any departure from absolute regimentation may cause trouble. Any variation from the majority's opinion may inspire fear. Any word spoken, in class, in the lunchroom, or on the campus, that deviates from the views of another person may start an argument or cause a disturbance. But our Constitution says we must take this risk...; and our history says that it is this sort of hazardous freedom -- this kind of openness -- that is [509] the basis of our national strength and of the independence and vigor of Americans who grow up and live in this relatively permissive, often disputatious, society.

In order for the State in the person of school officials to justify prohibition of a particular expression of opinion, it must be able to show that its action was caused by something more than a mere desire to avoid the discomfort and unpleasantness that always accompany an unpopular viewpoint. Certainly where there is no finding and no showing that engaging in the forbidden conduct would "materially and substantially interfere with the requirements of appropriate discipline in the operation of the school," the prohibition cannot be sustained. Burnside v. Byars, 363 F.2d 744, 749 (5th Cir. 1966).

... [T]he record fails to yield evidence that the school authorities had reason to anticipate that the wearing of the armbands would substantially interfere with the work of the school or impinge upon the rights of other students. ... [510] On the contrary, the action of the school authorities appears to have been based upon an urgent wish to avoid the controversy which might result from the expression, even by the silent symbol of armbands, of opposition to this Nation's part in the conflagration in Vietnam. It is revealing, in this respect, that the meeting at which the school principals decided to issue the contested regulation was called in response to a student's statement to the journalism teacher in one of the schools that he wanted to write an article on Vietnam and have it published in the school paper. (The student was dissuaded.)

It is also relevant that the school authorities did not purport to prohibit the wearing of all symbols of political or controversial significance. The record shows that students in some of the schools wore buttons relating to national political campaigns, and some even wore the Iron Cross, traditionally a symbol of Nazism. ... Instead, a particular symbol – black armbands worn to exhibit opposition to this Nation's involvement [511] in Vietnam – was singled out for prohibition. Clearly, the prohibition of expression of one particular opinion, at least without evidence that it is necessary to avoid material and substantial interference with schoolwork or discipline, is not constitutionally permissible.

In our system, state-operated schools may not be enclaves of totalitarianism. School officials do not possess absolute authority over their students. Students in school as well as out of school are "persons" under our Constitution. They are possessed of fundamental rights, which the State must respect, just as they themselves must respect their obligations to the State. In our system, students may not be regarded as closed-circuit recipients of only that which the State chooses to communicate. They may not be confined to the expression of those sentiments that are officially approved. In the absence of a specific showing of constitutionally valid reasons to regulate their speech, students are entitled to freedom of expression of their views.

... [512] The principle of these cases is not confined to the supervised and ordained discussion which takes place in the classroom. The principal use to which the schools are dedicated is to accommodate students during prescribed hours for the purpose of certain types of activities. Among those activities is personal intercommunication among the students. This is not only an inevitable part of the process of attending school; it is also an important part of the educational process. A student's rights, therefore, do not embrace merely the classroom hours. When he is in the cafeteria, or on the playing field, or on [513] the campus during the authorized hours, he may express his opinions, even on controversial subjects like the conflict in Vietnam, if he does so without "materially and substantially interfer[ing] with the requirements of appropriate discipline in the operation of the school" and without colliding with the rights of others. ... But conduct by the student, in class or out of it, which for any reason – whether it stems from time, place, or type of behavior – materially disrupts class work or involves substantial disorder or invasion of the rights of others is, of course, not immunized by the constitutional guarantee of freedom of speech.

Under our Constitution, free speech is not a right that is given only to be so circumscribed that it exists in principle but not in fact. Freedom of expression would not truly exist if the right could be exercised only in an area that a benevolent government has provided as a safe haven for crackpots. ... [W]e do not confine the permissible exercise of First Amendment rights to a telephone booth or the four corners of a pamphlet, or to supervised and ordained discussion in a school classroom.

If a regulation were adopted by school officials forbidding discussion of the Vietnam conflict, or the expression by any student of opposition to it anywhere on school property except as part of a prescribed classroom exercise, it would be obvious that the regulation would violate the constitutional rights of students, at least if it could not be justified by a showing that the students' activities would materially and substantially disrupt the work and discipline of the school. [514]...

In the circumstances of the present case, the prohibition of the silent, passive "witness of the armbands," as one of the children called it, is no less offensive to the Constitution's guarantees. ...

CONCUR BY: STEWART; WHITE

MR. JUSTICE STEWART, concurring.

Although I agree with much of what is said in the Court's opinion, and with its judgment in this case, I [515] cannot share the Court's uncritical assumption that, school discipline aside, the First Amendment rights of children are co-extensive with those of adults. ... I continue to hold the view [that] ... "a State may permissibly determine that, at least in some precisely delineated areas, a child – like someone in a captive audience – is not possessed of that full capacity for individual choice which is the presupposition of First Amendment guarantees." *Ginsberg* v. *New York*, 390 U.S. 629, 649-650 (concurring in result).

MR. JUSTICE WHITE, concurring.

While I join the Court's opinion, I deem it appropriate to note, first, that the Court continues to recognize a distinction between communicating by words and communicating by acts or conduct which sufficiently impinges on some valid state interest. ...

DISSENT BY: BLACK; HARLAN

MR. JUSTICE BLACK, dissenting.

The Court's holding in this case ushers in what I deem to be an entirely new era in which the power to control pupils by the elected "officials of state supported public schools . . ." in the United States is in ultimate effect transferred to the Supreme Court. The Court brought [516] this particular case here on a petition for certiorari urging that the First and Fourteenth Amendments protect the right of school pupils to express their political views all the way "from kindergarten through high school." Here the constitutional right to "political expression" asserted was a right to wear black armbands during school hours and at classes in order to demonstrate to the other students that the petitioners were mourning because of the death of United States soldiers in Vietnam and to protest that war which they were against. ...

[*517] [T]he crucial ... questions are whether students and teachers may use the schools at their whim as a platform for the exercise of free speech – "symbolic" or "pure" – and whether the courts will allocate to themselves the function of deciding how the pupils' school day will be spent. While I have always believed that under the First and Fourteenth Amendments neither the State nor the Federal Government has any authority to regulate or censor the content of speech, I have never believed that any person has a right to give speeches or engage in demonstrations where he pleases and when he pleases. ...

While the record does not show that any of these armband students shouted, used profane language, or were violent in any manner, detailed testimony by some of them shows their armbands caused comments, warnings by other students, the poking of fun at them, and a warning by an older football player that other, non-protesting students had better let them alone. There is also evidence that a teacher of mathematics had his lesson period practically "wrecked" chiefly by disputes with Mary Beth Tinker, who wore her armband for her "demonstration." [518] Even a casual reading of the record shows that this armband did divert students' minds from their regular lessons, and that talk, comments, etc., made John Tinker "self-conscious" in attending school with his armband. While the absence of obscene remarks or boisterous and loud disorder perhaps justifies the Court's statement that the few armband students did not actually "disrupt" the class work, I think the record overwhelmingly shows that the armbands did exactly what the elected school officials and principals foresaw they would, that is, took the students' minds off their class work and diverted them to thoughts about the highly emotional subject of the Vietnam war. And I repeat that if the time has come when pupils of state-supported schools, kindergartens, grammar schools, or high schools, can defy and flout orders of school officials to keep their minds on their own schoolwork, it is the beginning of a new revolutionary era of permissiveness in this country fostered by the judiciary. ...

[519] There was at one time a line of cases holding "reasonableness" as the court saw it to be the test of a "due process" violation. ... [We] totally repudiated the old reasonableness-due process test, the doctrine that judges have the power to hold laws unconstitutional upon the belief of judges that they "shock the conscience" or that they are [520] "unreasonable," "arbitrary," "irrational," "contrary to fundamental 'decency,'" or some other such flexible term without precise boundaries. I have many times expressed my opposition to that concept on the ground that it gives judges power to strike down any law they do not like. If the majority of the Court today, by agreeing to the opinion of my Brother Fortas, is resurrecting that old reasonableness-due process test, I think the constitutional change should be plainly, unequivocally, and forthrightly stated for the benefit of the bench and bar. It will be a sad day for the country, I believe... .

[521] I deny, therefore, that it has been the "unmistakable holding of this Court for almost 50 years" that "students" and "teachers" take with them into the "schoolhouse gate" constitutional rights to "freedom of speech or expression." ... The truth is that a teacher of kindergarten, grammar school, or high school pupils no more carries into a school with him a complete right to freedom of speech and expression than an anti-Catholic or anti-Semite carries with him a complete freedom of [522] speech and religion into a Catholic church or Jewish synagogue. Nor does a person carry with him into the United States Senate or House, or into the Supreme Court, or any other court, a complete constitutional right to go into those places contrary to their rules and speak his mind on any subject he pleases. It is a myth to say that any person has a constitutional right to say what he pleases, where he pleases, and when he pleases. Our Court has decided precisely the opposite. ...

In my view, teachers in state-controlled public schools are hired to teach there. ...[C]ertainly a teacher is not paid to go into school and teach subjects the State does not hire him to teach as a part of its selected curriculum. Nor are public school students sent to the schools at public expense to broadcast political or any other views to educate and inform the public. The original idea of schools, which I do not believe is yet abandoned as worthless or out of date, was that children had not yet reached the point of experience and wisdom which enabled them to teach all of their elders. It may be that the Nation has outworn the old-fashioned slogan that "children are to be seen not heard," but one may, I hope, be permitted to harbor the thought that taxpayers send children to school on the premise that at their age they need to learn, not teach.

... [523] Iowa's public schools ... are operated to give students an opportunity to learn, not to talk politics by actual speech, or by "symbolic" [524] speech. And, as I have pointed out before, the record amply shows that public protest in the school classes against the Vietnam war "distracted from that singleness of purpose which the State [here Iowa] desired to exist in its public educational institutions."... It was, of course, to distract the attention of other students that some students insisted up to the very point of their own suspension from school that they were determined to sit in school with their symbolic armbands.

Change has been said to be truly the law of life but sometimes the old and the tried and true are worth holding. The schools of this Nation have undoubtedly contributed to giving us tranquility and to making us a more law-abiding people. Uncontrolled and uncontrollable liberty is an enemy to domestic peace. We cannot close our eyes to the fact that some of the country's greatest problems are crimes committed by the youth, too many of school age. School discipline, like parental discipline, is an integral and important part of training our children to be good citizens – to be better citizens. Here a very small number of students have crisply and summarily [525] refused to obey a school order designed to give pupils who want to learn the opportunity to do so. One does not need to be a prophet or the son of a prophet to know that after the Court's holding today some students in Iowa schools and indeed in all schools will be ready, able, and willing to defy their teachers on practically all orders. This is the more unfortunate for the schools since groups of students all over the land are already running loose, conducting break-ins, sit-ins, lie-ins, and smash-ins. Many of these student groups, as is all too familiar to all who read the newspapers and watch the television news programs, have already engaged in rioting, property seizures, and destruction. They have picketed schools to force

students not to cross their picket lines and have too often violently attacked earnest but frightened students who wanted an education that the pickets did not want them to get. Students engaged in such activities are apparently confident that they know far more about how to operate public school systems than do their parents, teachers, and elected school officials. It is no answer to say that the particular students here have not yet reached such high points in their demands to attend classes in order to exercise their political pressures. Turned loose with lawsuits for damages and injunctions against their teachers as they are here, it is nothing but wishful thinking to imagine that young, immature students will not soon believe it is their right to control the schools rather than the right of the States that collect the taxes to hire the teachers for the benefit of the pupils. This case, therefore, wholly without constitutional reasons in my judgment, subjects all the public schools in the country to the whims and caprices of their loudest-mouthed, but maybe not their brightest, students. I, for one, am not fully persuaded that school pupils are wise enough... . I wish, therefore, wholly to disclaim any purpose on my part to hold that the Federal Constitution compels the teachers, parents, and elected school officials to surrender control of the American public school system to public school students. I dissent.

MR. JUSTICE HARLAN, dissenting.

I certainly agree that state public school authorities in the discharge of their responsibilities are not wholly exempt from the requirements of the Fourteenth Amendment respecting the freedoms of expression and association. At the same time I am reluctant to believe that there is any disagreement between the majority and myself on the proposition that school officials should be accorded the widest authority in maintaining discipline and good order in their institutions. To translate that proposition into a workable constitutional rule, I would, in cases like this, cast upon those complaining the burden of showing that a particular school measure was motivated by other than legitimate school concerns – for example, a desire to prohibit the expression of an unpopular point of view, while permitting expression of the dominant opinion.

Finding nothing in this record which impugns the good faith of respondents in promulgating the armband regulation, I would affirm the judgment below.

Bethel School District v.. Fraser
478 U.S. 675
(1986)
(Excerpts only. Footnotes omitted.)

Author's Note: A Bethel High School rule prohibited obscene speech on campus. Before a student assembly, a student shared his proposed speech laced with sexual innuendos with three teachers, two of whom advised him the speech might cause problems but neither said it violated school rules. The student presented the speech to an audience of 600 students, including some 14 year olds. Teachers said some students responded enthusiastically; others were "bewildered" or "embarrassed." The speaker was suspended and eliminated from consideration as a graduation speaker. The student sued.

PRIOR HISTORY: Certiorari to the United States Court of Appeals for the Ninth Circuit.

JUDGES: BURGER, C. J., delivered the opinion of the Court, in which WHITE, POWELL, REHNQUIST, and O'CONNOR, JJ., joined. BRENNAN, J., filed an opinion concurring in the judgment. BLACKMUN, J., concurred in the result. MARSHALL, J., and STEVENS, J., filed dissenting opinions.

OPINION: [677] CHIEF JUSTICE BURGER.

We granted certiorari to decide whether the First Amendment prevents a school district from disciplining a high school student for giving a lewd speech at a school assembly.

...[679] The District Court held that the school's sanctions violated respondent's right to freedom of speech under the First Amendment to the United States Constitution, that the school's disruptive-conduct rule is unconstitutionally vague and overbroad, and that the removal of respondent's name from the graduation speaker's list violated the Due Process Clause of the Fourteenth Amendment. ... The District Court ... enjoined the School District from preventing respondent from speaking at the commencement ceremonies. Respondent, who had been elected graduation speaker by a write-in vote of his classmates, delivered a speech at the commencement ceremonies on June 8, 1983.

The Court of Appeals for the Ninth Circuit affirmed ..., holding that respondent's speech was indistinguishable from the protest armband in *Tinker* v. *Des Moines Independent Community School Dist.*, 393 U.S. 503 (1969). The court explicitly rejected the School District's argument that the speech, unlike the passive conduct of wearing a black armband, had a disruptive effect on the educational process. The Court of [680] Appeals

also rejected the School District's argument that it had an interest in protecting an essentially captive audience of minors from lewd and indecent language in a setting sponsored by the school, reasoning that the School District's "unbridled discretion" to determine what discourse is "decent" would "increase the risk of cementing white, middle-class standards for determining what is acceptable and proper speech and behavior in our public schools."... Finally, the Court of Appeals rejected the School District's argument that, incident to its responsibility for the school curriculum, it had the power to control the language used to express ideas during a school-sponsored activity.

We granted certiorari... . We reverse.

... The marked distinction between the political "message" of the armbands in *Tinker* and the sexual content of respondent's speech in this case seems to have been given little weight by the Court of Appeals. In upholding the students' right to engage in a nondisruptive, passive expression of a political viewpoint in *Tinker*, this Court was careful to note that the case did "not concern speech or action that intrudes upon the work of the schools or the rights of other students." ... [681]

... [T]he objectives of public education [are] the "[inculcation of] fundamental values necessary to the maintenance of a democratic political system."

These fundamental values of "habits and manners of civility" essential to a democratic society must, of course, include tolerance of divergent political and religious views, even when the views expressed may be unpopular. But these "fundamental values" must also take into account consideration of the sensibilities of others, and, in the case of a school, the sensibilities of fellow students. The undoubted freedom to advocate unpopular and controversial views in schools and classrooms must be balanced against the society's countervailing interest in teaching students the boundaries of socially appropriate behavior. Even the most heated political discourse in a democratic society requires consideration for the personal sensibilities of the other participants and audiences.

... [682]The First Amendment guarantees wide freedom in matters of adult public discourse. ... It does not follow, however, that simply because the use of an offensive form of expression may not be prohibited to adults making what the speaker considers a political point, the same latitude must be permitted to children in a public school. ... Surely it is a highly appropriate function of public school education to prohibit the use of vulgar and offensive terms in public discourse. Indeed, the "fundamental values necessary to the maintenance of a democratic political system" disfavor the use of terms of debate highly offensive or highly threatening to others. Nothing in the Constitution prohibits the states from insisting that certain modes of expression are inappropriate and subject to sanctions. The inculcation of these values is truly the "work of the schools." ... The determination of what manner of speech in the classroom or in school assembly is inappropriate properly rests with the school board.

The process of educating our youth for citizenship in public schools is not confined to books, the curriculum, and the civics class; schools must teach by example the shared values of a civilized social order. ... The schools, as instruments of the state, may determine that the essential lessons of civil, mature conduct cannot be conveyed in a school that tolerates lewd, indecent, or offensive speech and conduct such as that indulged in by this confused boy.

The pervasive sexual innuendo in Fraser's speech was plainly offensive to both teachers and students – indeed to any mature person. ... [684] This Court's First Amendment jurisprudence has acknowledged limitations on the otherwise absolute interest of the speaker in reaching an unlimited audience where the speech is sexually explicit and the audience may include children. ... [T]he obvious concern on the part of parents, and school authorities acting *in loco parentis*, [is] to protect children – especially in a captive audience – from exposure to sexually explicit, indecent, or lewd speech. We have also recognized an interest in protecting minors from exposure to vulgar and offensive spoken language. ... [685]

We hold that petitioner School District acted entirely within its permissible authority in imposing sanctions upon Fraser in response to his offensively lewd and indecent speech. Unlike the sanctions imposed on the students wearing armbands in *Tinker*, the penalties imposed in this case were unrelated to any political viewpoint. The First Amendment does not prevent the school officials from determining that to permit a vulgar and lewd speech such as respondent's would undermine the school's basic educational mission. A high school assembly or classroom is no place for a sexually explicit monologue directed towards an unsuspecting audience of teenage students. Accordingly, it was perfectly appropriate for the school to disassociate itself to make the point to the pupils that vulgar speech and lewd conduct is wholly inconsistent with the "fundamental values" of public [686] school education. ...

[687] The judgment of the Court of Appeals for the Ninth Circuit is *Reversed*.

JUSTICE BLACKMUN concurs in the result.

CONCUR BY: JUSTICE BRENNAN, concurring in the judgment.

Respondent gave the following speech at a high school assembly in support of a candidate for student government office:

"'I know a man who is firm – he's firm in his pants, he's firm in his shirt, his character is firm – but most . . . of all, his belief in you, the students of Bethel, is firm.

"'Jeff Kuhlman is a man who takes his point and pounds it in. If necessary, he'll take an issue and nail it to the wall. He doesn't attack things in spurts – he drives hard, pushing and pushing until finally – he succeeds.

"'Jeff is a man who will go to the very end – even the climax, for each and every one of you.

"'So vote for Jeff for A. S. B. vice-president – he'll never come between you and the best our high school can be.'"

The Court, referring to these remarks as "obscene," "vulgar," "lewd," and "offensively lewd," concludes that school officials properly punished respondent for uttering the speech. Having read the full text of respondent's remarks, I find it difficult to believe that it is the same speech the Court describes. To my mind, the most that can be said about respondent's speech – and all that need be said – is that in light of the discretion school officials have to teach high school students how to conduct civil and effective public discourse, and to prevent disruption of school educational activities, it was [688] not unconstitutional for school officials to conclude, under the circumstances of this case, that respondent's remarks exceeded permissible limits. Thus, while I concur in the Court's judgment, I write separately to express my understanding of the breadth of the Court's holding.

The Court today reaffirms the unimpeachable proposition that students do not "'shed their constitutional rights to freedom of speech or expression at the schoolhouse gate.'" ... [T]he language respondent used is far removed from the very narrow class of "obscene" speech which the Court has held is not protected by the First Amendment. ... It is true, however, that the State has interests in teaching high school students how to conduct civil and effective public discourse and in avoiding disruption of educational school activities. Thus, the Court holds that under certain circumstances, high school students may properly be reprimanded for giving a speech at a high school assembly which school officials conclude disrupted the school's educational [689] mission. Respondent's speech may well have been protected had he given it in school but under different circumstances, where the school's legitimate interests in teaching and maintaining civil public discourse were less weighty.

In the present case, school officials sought only to ensure that a high school assembly proceed in an orderly manner. There is no suggestion that school officials attempted to regulate respondent's speech because they disagreed with the views he sought to express. Nor does this case involve an attempt by school officials to ban written materials they consider "inappropriate" for high school students, or to limit what students should hear, read, or learn about. Thus, the Court's holding concerns only the authority that school officials have to restrict a high school student's use of disruptive language in a speech given to a high school assembly.

The authority school officials have to regulate such speech by high school students is not limitless. Under the circumstances of this case, however, I believe that school officials did not violate the First Amendment in determining that respondent should be disciplined for the disruptive language he used while addressing a high school assembly. Thus, I concur in the judgment reversing the decision of the Court of Appeals.

DISSENT BY: MARSHALL; STEVENS

JUSTICE MARSHALL, dissenting.

I agree with the principles that JUSTICE BRENNAN sets out in his opinion concurring in the judgment. I dissent from the Court's decision, however, because in my view the School District failed to demonstrate that respondent's remarks were indeed disruptive. ... [S]chool administration must be given wide latitude to determine what forms of conduct are inconsistent with the school's educational mission; nevertheless, where speech is involved, we may not unquestioningly accept a teacher's or administrator's assertion that certain pure speech interfered with education. Here the School District, despite a clear opportunity to do so, failed to bring in evidence sufficient to convince either of the two lower courts that education at Bethel School was disrupted by respondent's speech. I therefore see no reason to disturb the Court of Appeals' judgment.

[691] JUSTICE STEVENS, dissenting.

"Frankly, my dear, I don't give a damn."

When I was a high school student, the use of those words in a public forum shocked the Nation. Today Clark Gable's four-letter expletive is less offensive than it was then. Nevertheless, I assume that high school administrators may prohibit the use of that word in classroom discussion and even in extracurricular activities that are sponsored by the school and held on school premises. For I believe a

school faculty must regulate the content as well as the style of student speech in carrying out its educational mission. It does seem to me, however, that if a student is to be punished for using offensive speech, he is entitled to fair notice of the scope of the prohibition and the consequences of its violation. [692] The interest in free speech protected by the First Amendment and the interest in fair procedure protected by the Due Process Clause of the Fourteenth Amendment combine to require this conclusion.

This respondent was an outstanding young man with a fine academic record. ... This fact ... indicates that he was probably in a better position to determine whether an audience composed of 600 of his contemporaries would be offended by the use of a four-letter word – or a sexual metaphor – than is a group of judges who are at least two generations and 3,000 miles away from the scene of the crime.

The fact that the speech may not have been offensive to his audience – or that he honestly believed that it would be inoffensive – does not mean that he had a constitutional right to deliver it. For the school – not the student – must prescribe the rules of conduct in an educational institution. But it [693] does mean that he should not be disciplined for speaking frankly in a school assembly if he had no reason to anticipate punitive consequences. ... [695] At best, the rule is sufficiently ambiguous that without a further explanation or construction it could not advise the reader of the student handbook that the speech would be forbidden. ... [T]he teachers' responses certainly did not give him any better notice of the likelihood of discipline than did the student handbook itself. In my opinion, therefore, the most difficult question is whether the speech was so obviously offensive that an intelligent high school student must be presumed to have realized that he would be punished for giving it. [696]

... It seems fairly obvious that respondent's speech would be inappropriate in certain classroom and formal social settings. On the other hand, in a locker room or perhaps in a school corridor the metaphor in the speech might be regarded as rather routine comment. If this be true, and if respondent's audience consisted almost entirely of young people with whom he conversed on a daily basis, can we – at this distance – confidently assert that he must have known that the school administration would punish him for delivering it?

For three reasons, I think not. First, it seems highly unlikely that he would have decided to deliver the speech if he had known that it would result in his suspension and disqualification from delivering the school commencement address. Second, I believe a strong presumption in favor of free expression should apply whenever an issue of this kind is arguable. Third, because the Court has adopted the policy of applying contemporary community standards in evaluating expression with sexual connotations, this Court should defer to the views of the district and circuit judges who are in a much better position to evaluate this speech than we are.

I would affirm the judgment of the Court of Appeals.

Hazelwood School District v. Kuhlmeier
484 U.S. 260
(1988)

PRIOR HISTORY: On Writ of Certiorari to the United States Court of Appeals for the Eighth Circuit.

JUDGES: WHITE, J., delivered the opinion of the Court, in which REHNQUIST, C. J., and STEVENS, O'CONNOR, and SCALIA, JJ., joined. BRENNAN, J., filed a dissenting opinion, in which MARSHALL and BLACKMUN, JJ., joined.

OPINION: [262] JUSTICE WHITE delivered the opinion of the Court.

This case concerns the extent to which educators may exercise editorial control over the contents of a high school newspaper produced as part of the school's journalism curriculum.

I.   Petitioners are the Hazelwood School District in St. Louis County, Missouri; various school officials; Robert Eugene Reynolds, the principal of Hazelwood East High School; and Howard Emerson, a teacher in the school district. Respondents are three former Hazelwood East students who were staff members of Spectrum, the school newspaper. They contend that school officials violated their First Amendment rights by deleting two pages of articles from the May 13, 1983, issue of Spectrum.

Spectrum was written and edited by the Journalism II class at Hazelwood East. The newspaper was published every three weeks or so during the 1982-1983 school year. More than 4,500 copies of the newspaper were distributed during that year to students, school personnel, and members of the community.

The Board of Education allocated funds from its annual budget for the printing of Spectrum. These funds were supplemented by proceeds from sales of the newspaper. The printing expenses during the 1982-1983 school year totaled $ 4,668.50; revenue from sales was $ 1,166.84. The other costs associated with the newspaper – such as supplies, textbooks, [263] and a portion of the journalism teacher's salary – were borne entirely by the Board.

The Journalism II course was taught by Robert Stergos for most of the 1982-1983 academic year. Stergos left Hazelwood East to take a job in private industry on April 29, 1983, when the May 13 edition of Spectrum was nearing completion, and petitioner Emerson took his place as newspaper adviser for the remaining weeks of the term.

The practice at Hazelwood East during the spring 1983 semester was for the journalism teacher to submit page proofs of each Spectrum issue to Principal Reynolds for his review prior to publication. On May 10, Emerson delivered the proofs of the May 13 edition to Reynolds, who objected to two of the articles scheduled to appear in that edition. One of the stories described three Hazelwood East students' experiences with pregnancy; the other discussed the impact of divorce on students at the school.

Reynolds was concerned that, although the pregnancy story used false names "to keep the identity of these girls a secret," the pregnant students still might be identifiable from the text. He also believed that the article's references to sexual activity and birth control were inappropriate for some of the younger students at the school. In addition, Reynolds was concerned that a student identified by name in the divorce story had complained that her father "wasn't spending enough time with my mom, my sister and I" prior to the divorce, "was always out of town on business or out late playing cards with the guys," and "always argued about everything" with her mother. *App. to Pet. for Cert. 38.* Reynolds believed that the student's parents should have been given an opportunity to respond to these remarks or to consent to their publication. He was unaware that Emerson had deleted the student's name from the final version of the article.

Reynolds believed that there was no time to make the necessary changes in the stories before the scheduled press run [264] and that the newspaper would not appear before the end of the school year if printing were delayed to any significant extent. He concluded that his only options under the circumstances were to publish a four-page newspaper instead of the planned six-page newspaper, eliminating the two pages on which the offending stories appeared, or to publish no newspaper at all. Accordingly, he directed

Emerson to withhold from publication the two pages containing the stories on pregnancy and divorce.[1] He informed his superiors of the decision, and they concurred.

Respondents subsequently commenced this action in the United States District Court for the Eastern District of Missouri seeking a declaration that their First Amendment rights had been violated, injunctive relief, and monetary damages. After a bench trial, the District Court denied an injunction, holding that no First Amendment violation had occurred. 607 F. Supp. 1450 (1985).

The District Court concluded that school officials may impose restraints on students' speech in activities that are "'an integral part of the school's educational function'" – including the publication of a school-sponsored newspaper by a journalism class – so long as their decision has "'a substantial and reasonable basis.'" Id., at 1466 (quoting Frasca v. Andrews, 463 F. Supp. 1043, 1052 (EDNY 1979)). The court found that Principal Reynolds' concern that the pregnant students' anonymity would be lost and their privacy invaded was "legitimate and reasonable," given "the small number of pregnant students at Hazelwood East and several identifying characteristics that were disclosed in the article." 607 F. Supp., at 1466. The court held that Reynolds' action was also justified "to avoid the impression that [the school] endorses [265] the sexual norms of the subjects" and to shield younger students from exposure to unsuitable material. Ibid. The deletion of the article on divorce was seen by the court as a reasonable response to the invasion of privacy concerns raised by the named student's remarks. Because the article did not indicate that the student's parents had been offered an opportunity to respond to her allegations, said the court, there was cause for "serious doubt that the article complied with the rules of fairness which are standard in the field of journalism and which were covered in the textbook used in the Journalism II class." Id., at 1467. Furthermore, the court concluded that Reynolds was justified in deleting two full pages of the newspaper, instead of deleting only the pregnancy and divorce stories or requiring that those stories be modified to address his concerns, based on his "reasonable belief that he had to make an immediate decision and that there was no time to make modifications to the articles in question." Id., at 1466.

---

[1] The two pages deleted from the newspaper also contained articles on teenage marriage, runaways, and juvenile delinquents, as well as a general article on teenage pregnancy. Reynolds testified that he had no objection to these articles and that they were deleted only because they appeared on the same pages as the two objectionable articles.

The Court of Appeals for the Eighth Circuit reversed. 795 F. 2d 1368 (1986). The court held at the outset that Spectrum was not only "a part of the school adopted curriculum," id., at 1373, but also a public forum, because the newspaper was "intended to be and operated as a conduit for student viewpoint." Id., at 1372. The court then concluded that Spectrum's status as a public forum precluded school officials from censoring its contents except when "'necessary to avoid material and substantial interference with school work or discipline ... or the rights of others.'" Id., at 1374 (quoting Tinker v. Des Moines Independent Community School Dist., 393 U.S. 503, 511 (1969)).

The Court of Appeals found "no evidence in the record that the principal could have reasonably forecast that the censored articles or any materials in the censored articles would have materially disrupted class work or given rise to substantial disorder in the school." 795 F. 2d, at 1375. School officials were entitled to censor the articles on the ground that [266] they invaded the rights of others, according to the court, only if publication of the articles could have resulted in tort liability to the school. The court concluded that no tort action for libel or invasion of privacy could have been maintained against the school by the subjects of the two articles or by their families. Accordingly, the court held that school officials had violated respondents' First Amendment rights by deleting the two pages of the newspaper.

We granted certiorari, 479 U.S. 1053 (1987), and we now reverse.

II.   [7] Students in the public schools do not "shed their constitutional rights to freedom of speech or expression at the schoolhouse gate." Tinker, supra, at 506. They cannot be punished merely for expressing their personal views on the school premises – whether "in the cafeteria, or on the playing field, or on the campus during the authorized hours," 393 U.S., at 512-513 – unless school authorities have reason to believe that such expression will "substantially interfere with the work of the school or impinge upon the rights of other students." Id., at 509.

[8] We have nonetheless recognized that the First Amendment rights of students in the public schools "are not automatically coextensive with the rights of adults in other settings," Bethel School District No. 403 v. Fraser, 478 U.S. 675, 682 (1986), and must be "applied in light of the special characteristics of the school environment." Tinker, supra, at 506; cf. New Jersey v. T. L. O., 469 U.S. 325, 341-343 (1985). A school need not tolerate student speech that is inconsistent with its "basic educational mission," Fraser, supra, at 685, even though the government could not censor similar speech outside the school. Accordingly, we held in Fraser that a student could be disciplined for

having delivered a speech that was "sexually explicit" but not legally obscene at an official school assembly, because the school was entitled to "disassociate itself" from the speech in a manner [267] that would demonstrate to others that such vulgarity is "wholly inconsistent with the 'fundamental values' of public school education." 478 U.S., at 685-686. We thus recognized that "[t]he determination of what manner of speech in the classroom or in school assembly is inappropriate properly rests with the school board," id., at 683, rather than with the federal courts. It is in this context that respondents' First Amendment claims must be considered.

A   [1B] [9] [10] We deal first with the question whether Spectrum may appropriately be characterized as a forum for public expression. The public schools do not possess all of the attributes of streets, parks, and other traditional public forums that "time out of mind, have been used for purposes of assembly, communicating thoughts between citizens, and discussing public questions." Hague v. CIO, 307 U.S. 496, 515 (1939). Cf. Widmar v. Vincent, 454 U.S. 263, 267-268, n. 5 (1981). Hence, school facilities may be deemed to be public forums only if school authorities have "by policy or by practice" opened those facilities "for indiscriminate use by the general public," Perry Education Assn. v. Perry Local Educators' Assn., 460 U.S. 37, 47 (1983), or by some segment of the public, such as student organizations. Id., at 46, n. 7 (citing Widmar v. Vincent). If the facilities have instead been reserved for other intended purposes, "communicative or otherwise," then no public forum has been created, and school officials may impose reasonable restrictions on the speech of students, teachers, and other members of the school community. 460 U.S., at 46, n. 7. "The government does not create a public forum by inaction or by permitting limited discourse, but only by intentionally opening a nontraditional forum for public discourse." Cornelius v. NAACP Legal Defense & Educational Fund, Inc., 473 U.S. 788, 802 (1985). [268]

[1C] The policy of school officials toward Spectrum was reflected in Hazelwood School Board Policy 348.51 and the Hazelwood East Curriculum Guide. Board Policy 348.51 provided that "[s]chool sponsored publications are developed within the adopted curriculum and its educational implications in regular classroom activities." App. 22. The Hazelwood East Curriculum Guide described the Journalism II course as a "laboratory situation in which the students publish the school newspaper applying skills they have learned in Journalism I." Id., at 11. The lessons that were to be learned from the Journalism II course, according to the

Curriculum Guide, included development of journalistic skills under deadline pressure, "the legal, moral, and ethical restrictions imposed upon journalists within the school community," and "responsibility and acceptance of criticism for articles of opinion." Ibid. Journalism II was taught by a faculty member during regular class hours. Students received grades and academic credit for their performance in the course.

School officials did not deviate in practice from their policy that production of Spectrum was to be part of the educational curriculum and a "regular classroom activit[y]." The District Court found that Robert Stergos, the journalism teacher during most of the 1982-1983 school year, "both had the authority to exercise and in fact exercised a great deal of control over Spectrum." 607 F. Supp., at 1453. For example, Stergos selected the editors of the newspaper, scheduled publication dates, decided the number of pages for each issue, assigned story ideas to class members, advised students on the development of their stories, reviewed the use of quotations, edited stories, selected and edited the letters to the editor, and dealt with the printing company. Many of these decisions were made without consultation with the Journalism II students. The District Court thus found it "clear that Mr. Stergos was the final authority with respect to almost every aspect of the production and publication of Spectrum, including its content." Ibid. Moreover, after [269] each Spectrum issue had been finally approved by Stergos or his successor, the issue still had to be reviewed by Principal Reynolds prior to publication. Respondents' assertion that they had believed that they could publish "practically anything" in Spectrum was therefore dismissed by the District Court as simply "not credible." Id., at 1456. These factual findings are amply supported by the record, and were not rejected as clearly erroneous by the Court of Appeals.

The evidence relied upon by the Court of Appeals in finding Spectrum to be a public forum, see 795 F. 2d, at 1372-1373, is equivocal at best. For example, Board Policy 348.51, which stated in part that "[s]chool sponsored student publications will not restrict free expression or diverse viewpoints within the rules of responsible journalism," also stated that such publications were "developed within the adopted curriculum and its educational implications." App. 22. One might reasonably infer from the full text of Policy 348.51 that school officials retained ultimate control over what constituted "responsible journalism" in a school-sponsored newspaper. Although the State-ment of Policy published in the September 14, 1982, issue of Spectrum declared that

"Spectrum, as a student-press publication, accepts all rights implied by the First Amendment," this statement, understood in the context of the paper's role in the school's curriculum, suggests at most that the administration will not interfere with the students' exercise of those First Amendment rights that attend the publication of a school-sponsored newspaper. It does not reflect an intent to expand those rights by converting a curricular newspaper into a public forum.[2] Finally, [270] that students were permitted to exercise some authority over the contents of Spectrum was fully consistent with the Curriculum Guide objective of teaching the Journalism II students "leadership responsibilities as issue and page editors." *App. 11.*

A decision to teach leadership skills in the context of a classroom activity hardly implies a decision to relinquish school control over that activity. In sum, the evidence relied upon by the Court of Appeals fails to demonstrate the "clear intent to create a public forum," Cornelius, 473 U.S., at 802, that existed in cases in which we found public forums to have been created. See *id.,* at 802-803 (citing Widmar v. Vincent, 454 U.S., at 267; Madison School District v. Wisconsin Employment Relations Comm'n, 429 U.S. 167, 174, n. 6 (1976); Southeastern Promotions, Ltd. v. Conrad, 420 U.S. 546, 555 (1975)). School officials did not evince either "by policy or by practice," Perry Education Assn., 460 U.S., at 47, any intent to open the pages of Spectrum to "indiscriminate use," ibid., by its student reporters and editors, or by the student body generally. Instead, they "reserve[d] the forum for its intended purpos[e]," *id.,* at 46, as a supervised learning experience for journalism students. Accordingly, school officials were entitled to regulate the contents of Spectrum in any reasonable manner. Ibid. It is this standard, rather than our decision in Tinker, that governs this case.

B   [2B] The question whether the First Amendment requires a school to tolerate particular student speech – the question that we addressed in Tinker – is different from the question whether the

First Amendment requires a school affirmatively [271] to promote particular student speech. The former question addresses educators' ability to silence a student's personal expression that happens to occur on the school premises. The latter question concerns educators' authority over school-sponsored publications, theatrical productions, and other expressive activities that students, parents, and members of the public might reasonably perceive to bear the imprimatur of the school. These activities may fairly be characterized as part of the school curriculum, whether or not they occur in a traditional classroom setting, so long as they are supervised by faculty members and designed to impart particular knowledge or skills to student participants and audiences.[3]

[2C] [3B] Educators are entitled to exercise greater control over this second form of student expression to assure that participants learn whatever lessons the activity is designed to teach, that readers or listeners are not exposed to material that may be inappropriate for their level of maturity, and that the views of the individual speaker are not erroneously attributed to the school. Hence, a school may in its capacity as publisher of a school newspaper or producer of a school play "disassociate itself," Fraser, 478 U.S., at 685, not only from speech that would "substantially interfere with [its] work ... or impinge upon the rights of other students," Tinker, 393 U.S., at 509, but also from speech that is, for example, ungrammatical, poorly written, inadequately researched, biased or prejudiced, vulgar or profane, or unsuitable for immature audiences.[4] A school must be able to set high standards for [272] the student speech that is disseminated under its auspices – standards that may be higher than those demanded by some

[2] The Statement also cited Tinker v. Des Moines Independent Community School Dist., 393 U.S. 503 (1969), for the proposition that "[o]nly speech that 'materially and substantially interferes with the requirements of appropriate discipline' can be found unacceptable and therefore be prohibited." *App. 26.* This portion of the Statement does not, of course, even accurately reflect our holding in Tinker. Furthermore, the Statement nowhere expressly extended the Tinker standard to the news and feature articles contained in a school-sponsored newspaper. The dissent apparently finds as a fact that the Statement was published annually in Spectrum; however, the District Court was unable to conclude that the Statement appeared on more than one occasion. In any event, even if the Statement says what the dissent believes that it says, the evidence that school officials never intended to designate Spectrum as a public forum remains overwhelming.

[3] The distinction that we draw between speech that is sponsored by the school and speech that is not is fully consistent with Papish v. University of Missouri Board of Curators, 410 U.S. 667 (1973) (per curiam), which involved an off-campus "underground" newspaper that school officials merely had allowed to be sold on a state university campus.

[4] The dissent perceives no difference between the First Amendment analysis applied in Tinker and that applied in Fraser. We disagree. The decision in Fraser rested on the "vulgar," "lewd," and "plainly offensive" character of a speech delivered at an official school assembly rather than on any propensity of the speech to "materially disrup[t] class work or involv[e] substantial disorder or invasion of the rights of others." 393 U.S., at 513. Indeed, the Fraser Court cited as "especially relevant" a portion of Justice Black's dissenting opinion in Tinker "'disclaim[ing] any purpose ... to hold that the Federal Constitution compels the teachers, parents, and elected school officials to surrender control of the American public school system to public school students.'" 478 U.S., at 686 (quoting 393 U.S., at 526). Of course, Justice Black's observations are equally relevant to the instant case.

newspaper publishers or theatrical producers in the "real" world – and may refuse to disseminate student speech that does not meet those standards. In addition, a school must be able to take into account the emotional maturity of the intended audience in determining whether to disseminate student speech on potentially sensitive topics, which might range from the existence of Santa Claus in an elementary school setting to the particulars of teenage sexual activity in a high school setting. A school must also retain the authority to refuse to sponsor student speech that might reasonably be perceived to advocate drug or alcohol use, irresponsible sex, or conduct otherwise inconsistent with "the shared values of a civilized social order," Fraser, supra, at 683, or to associate the school with any position other than neutrality on matters of political controversy. Otherwise, the schools would be unduly constrained from fulfilling their role as "a principal instrument in awakening the child to cultural values, in preparing him for later professional training, and in helping him to adjust normally to his environment." Brown v. Board of Education, 347 U.S. 483, 493 (1954).

[2D][3C][11A][12A] Accordingly, we conclude that the standard articulated in Tinker for determining when a school may punish student expression need not also be the standard for determining when a school may refuse to lend its name and resources to the dissemination [273] of student expression.[5] Instead, we hold that educators do not offend the First Amendment by exercising editorial control over the style and content of student speech in school-sponsored expressive activities so long as their actions are reasonably related to legitimate pedagogical concerns.[6]

[11B][3D][12B][3E][12C] This standard is consistent with our oft-expressed view that the education of the Nation's youth is primarily the responsibility of parents, teachers, and state and local school officials, and not of federal judges. See, e.g., Board of Education of Hendrick Hudson Central School Dist. v. Rowley, 458 U.S. 176, 208 (1982); Wood v. Strickland, 420 U.S. 308, 326 (1975); Epperson v. Arkansas, 393 U.S. 97, 104 (1968). It is only when the decision to censor a school-sponsored publication, theatrical production, or other vehicle of student expression has no valid educational purpose that the First Amendment is so "directly and sharply implicate[d]," ibid., as to require judicial intervention to protect students' constitutional rights.[7] [274]

III.   [12D][4B] [5B] [6B] We also conclude that Principal Reynolds acted reasonably in requiring the deletion from the May 13 issue of Spectrum of the pregnancy article, the divorce article, and the remaining articles that were to appear on the same pages of the newspaper.

[4C]The initial paragraph of the pregnancy article declared that "[a]ll names have been changed to keep the identity of these girls a secret." The principal concluded that the students' anonymity was not adequately protected, however, given the other identifying information in the article and the small number of pregnant students at the school. Indeed, a teacher at the school credibly testified that she could positively identify at least one of the girls and possibly all three. It is likely that many students at Hazelwood East would have been at least as successful in identifying the girls. Reynolds therefore could reasonably have feared that the article violated whatever pledge of anonymity had been given to the pregnant students. In addition, he could reasonably have been concerned that the article was not sufficiently sensitive to the privacy interests of the students' boyfriends and parents, who were discussed in the article but who were given no opportunity to consent to its publication or to offer a response. The article did not contain graphic accounts of sexual activity. The girls did comment in the article, however, concerning their sexual histories and their use or nonuse of birth control. It was not unreasonable for the principal to have concluded

---

[5] We therefore need not decide whether the Court of Appeals correctly construed Tinker as precluding school officials from censoring student speech to avoid "invasion of the rights of others," 393 U.S., at 513, except where that speech could result in tort liability to the school.

[6] We reject respondents' suggestion that school officials be permitted to exercise prepublication control over school-sponsored publications only pursuant to specific written regulations. To require such regulations in the context of a curricular activity could unduly constrain the ability of educators to educate. We need not now decide whether such regulations are required before school officials may censor publications not sponsored by the school that students seek to distribute on school grounds. See Baughman v. Freienmuth, 478 F. 2d 1345 (CA4 1973); Shanley v. Northeast Independent School Dist., Bexar Cty., Tex., 462 F. 2d 960 (CA5 1972); Eisner v. Stamford Board of Education, 440 F. 2d 803 (CA2 1971).

[7] A number of lower federal courts have similarly recognized that educators' decisions with regard to the content of school-sponsored newspapers, dramatic productions, and other expressive activities are entitled to substantial deference. See, e.g., Nicholson v. Board of Education, Torrance Unified School Dist., 682 F. 2d 858 (CA9 1982); Seyfried v. Walton, 668 F. 2d 214 (CA3 1981); Trachtman v. Anker, 563 F. 2d 512 (CA2 1977), cert. denied, 435 U.S. 925 (1978); Frasca v. Andrews, 463 F. Supp. 1043 (EDNY 1979). We need not now decide whether the same degree of deference is appropriate with respect to school-sponsored expressive activities at the college and university level.

that such frank talk was inappropriate in a school-sponsored publication distributed to 14-year-old freshmen [275] and presumably taken home to be read by students' even younger brothers and sisters.

[5C] The student who was quoted by name in the version of the divorce article seen by Principal Reynolds made comments sharply critical of her father. The principal could reasonably have concluded that an individual publicly identified as an inattentive parent – indeed, as one who chose "playing cards with the guys" over home and family – was entitled to an opportunity to defend himself as a matter of journalistic fairness. These concerns were shared by both of Spectrum's faculty advisers for the 1982-1983 school year, who testified that they would not have allowed the article to be printed without deletion of the student's name.[8]

[6C] Principal Reynolds testified credibly at trial that, at the time that he reviewed the proofs of the May 13 issue during an extended telephone conversation with Emerson, he believed that there was no time to make any changes in the articles, and that the newspaper had to be printed immediately or not at all. It is true that Reynolds did not verify whether the necessary modifications could still have been made in the articles, and that Emerson did not volunteer the information that printing could be delayed until the changes were made. We nonetheless agree with the District Court that the decision to excise the two pages containing the problematic articles was reasonable given the particular circumstances of this case. These circumstances included the very recent [276] replacement of Stergos by Emerson, who may not have been entirely familiar with Spectrum editorial and production procedures, and the pressure felt by Reynolds to make an immediate decision so that students would not be deprived of the newspaper altogether.

[4D] [5D] [6D] In sum, we cannot reject as unreasonable Principal Reynolds' conclusion that neither the pregnancy article nor the divorce article was suitable for publication in Spectrum. Reynolds could reasonably have concluded that the students who had written and edited these articles had not sufficiently mastered those portions of the Journalism II curriculum that pertained to the treatment of controversial issues and personal attacks, the need to protect the privacy of individuals whose most intimate concerns are to be revealed in the newspaper, and "the legal, moral, and ethical restrictions imposed upon journalists within [a] school community" that includes adolescent subjects and readers. Finally, we conclude that the principal's decision to delete two pages of Spectrum, rather than to delete only the offending articles or to require that they be modified, was reasonable under the circumstances

as he understood them. Accordingly, no violation of First Amendment rights occurred.[9]

The judgment of the Court of Appeals for the Eighth Circuit is therefore *Reversed*.

DISSENT BY: [277] JUSTICE BRENNAN, with whom JUSTICE MARSHALL and JUSTICE BLACKMUN join, dissenting.

When the young men and women of Hazelwood East High School registered for Journalism II, they expected a civics lesson. Spectrum, the newspaper they were to publish, "was not just a class exercise in which students learned to prepare papers and hone writing skills, it was a . . . forum established to give students an opportunity to express their views while gaining an appreciation of their rights and responsibilities under the First Amendment to the United States Constitution. ..." 795 F. 2d 1368, 1373 (CA8 1986). "[A]t the beginning of each school year," *id.*, at 1372, the student journalists published a Statement of Policy – tacitly approved each year by school authorities – announcing their expectation that "Spectrum, as a student-press publication, accepts all rights implied by the First Amendment. ... Only speech that 'materially and substantially interferes with the requirements of appropriate discipline' can be found unacceptable and therefore prohibited." *App. 26* (quoting Tinker v. Des Moines Independent Community School Dist., 393 U.S. 503, 513 (1969)). The school board itself affirmatively guaranteed the students of Journalism II an atmosphere conducive to fostering such an appreciation and exercising the full panoply

---

[8] The reasonableness of Principal Reynolds' concerns about the two articles was further substantiated by the trial testimony of Martin Duggan, a former editorial page editor of the St. Louis Globe Democrat and a former college journalism instructor and newspaper adviser. Duggan testified that the divorce story did not meet journalistic standards of fairness and balance because the father was not given an opportunity to respond, and that the pregnancy story was not appropriate for publication in a high school newspaper because it was unduly intrusive into the privacy of the girls, their parents, and their boyfriends. The District Court found Duggan to be "an objective and independent witness" whose testimony was entitled to significant weight. 607 F. Supp. 1450, 1461 (ED Mo. 1985).

[9] It is likely that the approach urged by the dissent would as a practical matter have far more deleterious consequences for the student press than does the approach that we adopt today. The dissent correctly acknowledges "[t]he State's prerogative to dissolve the student newspaper entirely." Post, at 287. It is likely that many public schools would do just that rather than open their newspapers to all student expression that does not threaten "materia[l] disrup[tion of] class work" or violation of "rights that are protected by law," post, at 289, regardless of how sexually explicit, racially intemperate, or personally insulting that expression otherwise might be.

of rights associated with a free student press.[1] "School sponsored student publications," it vowed, "will not restrict free expression or diverse viewpoints within the rules of responsible journalism." *App. 22* (Board Policy 48.51).

[278] This case arose when the Hazelwood East administration breached its own promise, dashing its students' expectations. The school principal, without prior consultation or explanation, excised six articles – comprising two full pages – of the May 13, 1983, issue of Spectrum. He did so not because any of the articles would "materially and substantially interfere with the requirements of appropriate discipline," but simply because he considered two of the six "inappropriate, personal, sensitive, and unsuitable" for student consumption. 795 F. 2d, at 1371.

In my view the principal broke more than just a promise. He violated the First Amendment's prohibitions against censorship of any student expression that neither disrupts class work nor invades the rights of others, and against any censorship that is not narrowly tailored to serve its purpose.

I. Public education serves vital national interests in preparing the Nation's youth for life in our increasingly complex society and for the duties of citizenship in our democratic Republic. See Brown v. Board of Education, 347 U.S. 483, 493 (1954). The public school conveys to our young the information and tools required not merely to survive in, but to contribute to, civilized society. It also inculcates in tomorrow's leaders the "fundamental values necessary to the maintenance of a democratic political system . . . ." Ambach v. Norwick, 441 U.S. 68, 77 (1979). All the while, the public educator nurtures students' social and moral development by transmitting to them an official dogma of "'community values.'" Board of Education v. Pico, 457 U.S. 853, 864 (1982) (plurality opinion) (citation omitted).

The public educator's task is weighty and delicate indeed. It demands particularized and supremely subjective choices among diverse curricula, moral values, and political stances to teach or inculcate in students, and among various methodologies for doing so. Accordingly, we have traditionally reserved [279] the "daily

operation of school systems" to the States and their local school boards. Epperson v. Arkansas, 393 U.S. 97, 104 (1968); see Board of Education v. Pico, supra, at 863-864. We have not, however, hesitated to intervene where their decisions run afoul of the Constitution. *See, e.g.*, Edwards v. Aguillard, 482 U.S. 578 (1987) (striking state statute that forbade teaching of evolution in public school unless accompanied by instruction on theory of "creation science"); Board of Education v. Pico, supra (school board may not remove books from library shelves merely because it disapproves of ideas they express); Epperson v. Arkansas, supra (striking state-law prohibition against teaching Darwinian theory of evolution in public school); West Virginia Board of Education v. Barnette, 319 U.S. 624 (1943) (public school may not compel student to salute flag); Meyer v. Nebraska, 262 U.S. 390 (1923) (state law prohibiting the teaching of foreign languages in public or private schools is unconstitutional).

Free student expression undoubtedly sometimes interferes with the effectiveness of the school's pedagogical functions. Some brands of student expression do so by directly preventing the school from pursuing its pedagogical mission: The young polemic who stands on a soapbox during calculus class to deliver an eloquent political diatribe interferes with the legitimate teaching of calculus. And the student who delivers a lewd endorsement of a student-government candidate might so extremely distract an impressionable high school audience as to interfere with the orderly operation of the school. See Bethel School Dist. No. 403 v. Fraser, 478 U.S. 675 (1986). Other student speech, however, frustrates the school's legitimate pedagogical purposes merely by expressing a message that conflicts with the school's, without directly interfering with the school's expression of its message: A student who responds to a political science teacher's question with the retort, "socialism is good," subverts the school's inculcation of the message that capitalism is better. [280] Even the maverick who sits in class passively sporting a symbol of protest against a government policy, cf. Tinker v. Des Moines Independent Community School Dist., 393 U.S. 503 (1969), or the gossip who sits in the student commons swapping stories of sexual escapade could readily muddle a clear official message condoning the government policy or condemning teenage sex. Likewise, the student newspaper that, like Spectrum, conveys a moral position at odds with the school's official stance might subvert the administration's legitimate inculcation of its own perception of community values.

---

[1] The Court suggests that the passage quoted in the text did not "exten[d] the Tinker standard to the news and feature articles contained in a school-sponsored newspaper" because the passage did not expressly mention them. Ante, at 269, n. 2. It is hard to imagine why the Court (or anyone else) might expect a passage that applies categorically to "a student-press publication," composed almost exclusively of "news and feature articles," to mention those categories expressly. Understandably, neither court below so limited the passage.

If mere incompatibility with the school's pedagogical message were a constitutionally sufficient justification for the suppression of student speech, school officials could censor each of the students or student organizations in the foregoing hypotheticals, converting our public schools into "enclaves of totalitarianism," *id.*, at 511, that "strangle the free mind at its source," West Virginia Board of Education v. Barnette, supra, at 637. The First Amendment permits no such blanket censorship authority. While the "constitutional rights of students in public school are not automatically coextensive with the rights of adults in other settings," Fraser, supra, at 682, students in the public schools do not "shed their constitutional rights to freedom of speech or expression at the schoolhouse gate," Tinker, supra, at 506. Just as the public on the street corner must, in the interest of fostering "enlightened opinion," Cantwell v. Connecticut, 310 U.S. 296, 310 (1940), tolerate speech that "tempt[s] [the listener] to throw [the speaker] off the street," *id.*, at 309, public educators must accommodate some student expression even if it offends them or offers views or values that contradict those the school wishes to inculcate.

In Tinker, this Court struck the balance. We held that official censorship of student expression – there the suspension of several students until they removed their armbands protesting the Vietnam war – is unconstitutional unless the [281] speech "materially disrupts class work or involves substantial disorder or invasion of the rights of others. ..." 393 U.S., at 513. School officials may not suppress "silent, passive expression of opinion, unaccompanied by any disorder or disturbance on the part of" the speaker. *Id.*, at 508. The "mere desire to avoid the discomfort and unpleasantness that always accompany an unpopular viewpoint," *id.*, at 509, or an unsavory subject, Fraser, supra, at 688-689 (BRENNAN, J., concurring in judgment), does not justify official suppression of student speech in the high school.

This Court applied the Tinker test just a Term ago in Fraser, supra, upholding an official decision to discipline a student for delivering a lewd speech in support of a student-government candidate. The Court today casts no doubt on Tinker's vitality. Instead it erects a taxonomy of school censorship, concluding that Tinker applies to one category and not another. On the one hand is censorship "to silence a student's personal expression that happens to occur on the school premises." *Ante*, at 271. On the other hand is censorship of expression that arises in the context of "school-sponsored ... expressive activities that students, parents, and members of the public might reasonably perceive to bear the imprimatur of the school." *Ibid.*

The Court does not, for it cannot, purport to discern from our precedents the distinction it creates. One could, I suppose, readily characterize the students' symbolic speech in Tinker as "personal expression that happens to [have] occur[red] on school premises," although Tinker did not even hint that the personal nature of the speech was of any (much less dispositive) relevance. But that same description could not by any stretch of the imagination fit Fraser's speech. He did not just "happen" to deliver his lewd speech to an ad hoc gathering on the playground. As the second paragraph of Fraser evinces, if ever a forum for student expression was "school-sponsored," Fraser's was:[282]

"Fraser ... delivered a speech nominating a fellow student for student elective office. Approximately 600 high school students ... attended the assembly. Students were required to attend the assembly or to report to the study hall. The assembly was part of a school-sponsored educational program in self-government." Fraser, 478 U.S., at 677 (emphasis added).

Yet, from the first sentence of its analysis, see *id.*, at 680, Fraser faithfully applied Tinker.

Nor has this Court ever intimated a distinction between personal and school-sponsored speech in any other context. Particularly telling is this Court's heavy reliance on Tinker in two cases of First Amendment infringement on state college campuses. See Papish v. University of Missouri Board of Curators, 410 U.S. 667, 671, n. 6 (1973) (per curiam); Healy v. James, 408 U.S. 169, 180, 189, and n. 18, 191 (1972). One involved the expulsion of a student for lewd expression in a newspaper that she sold on campus pursuant to university authorization, see Papish, *supra*, at 667-668, and the other involved the denial of university recognition and concomitant benefits to a political student organization, see Healy, supra, at 174, 176, 181-182. Tracking Tinker's analysis, the Court found each act of suppression unconstitutional. In neither case did this Court suggest the distinction, which the Court today finds dispositive, between school-sponsored and incidental student expression.

II.   Even if we were writing on a clean slate, I would reject the Court's rationale for abandoning Tinker in this case. The Court offers no more than an obscure tangle of three excuses to afford educators "greater control" over school-sponsored speech than the Tinker test would permit: the public educator's prerogative to control curriculum; the pedagogical interest in shielding the high school audience from objectionable viewpoints and sensitive topics; and the school's need [283] to dissociate itself from student expression. *Ante*, at 271. None of the excuses, once disentangled, supports the distinction that the Court draws. Tinker fully addresses the first concern; the second is illegitimate; and the third is readily achievable through less oppressive means.

A   The Court is certainly correct that the First Amendment permits educators "to assure that participants learn whatever lessons the activity is designed to teach. ... " *Ante*, at 271. That is, however, the essence of the Tinker test, not an excuse to abandon it. Under Tinker, school officials may censor only such student speech as would "materially disrup[t]" a legitimate curricular function. Manifestly, student speech is more likely to disrupt a curricular function when it arises in the context of a curricular activity − one that "is designed to teach" something − than when it arises in the context of a non-curricular activity. Thus, under Tinker, the school may constitutionally punish the budding political orator if he disrupts calculus class but not if he holds his tongue for the cafeteria. See Consolidated Edison Co. v. Public Service Comm'n of New York, 447 U.S. 530, 544-545 (1980) (STEVENS, J., concurring in judgment). That is not because some more stringent standard applies in the curricular context. (After all, this Court applied the same standard whether the students in Tinker wore their armbands to the "classroom" or the "cafeteria." 393 U.S., at 512.) It is because student speech in the non-curricular context is less likely to disrupt materially any legitimate pedagogical purpose.

I fully agree with the Court that the First Amendment should afford an educator the prerogative not to sponsor the publication of a newspaper article that is "ungrammatical, poorly written, inadequately researched, biased or prejudiced," or that falls short of the "high standards for . . . student speech that is disseminated under [the school's] auspices. ..." *Ante*, at 271-272. But we need not abandon Tinker [284] to reach that conclusion; we need only apply it. The enumerated criteria reflect the skills that the curricular newspaper "is designed to teach." The educator may, under Tinker, constitutionally "censor" poor grammar, writing, or research because to reward such expression would "materially disrup[t]" the newspaper's curricular purpose.

The same cannot be said of official censorship designed to shield the audience or dissociate the sponsor from the expression. Censorship so motivated might well serve (although, as I demonstrate infra, at 285-289, cannot legitimately serve) some other school purpose. But it in no way furthers the curricular purposes of a student newspaper, unless one believes that the purpose of the school newspaper is to teach students that the press ought never report bad news, express unpopular views, or print a thought that might upset its sponsors. Unsurprisingly, Hazelwood East claims no such pedagogical purpose.

The Court relies on bits of testimony to portray the principal's conduct as a pedagogical lesson to Journalism II students who "had not sufficiently mastered those portions of the ... curriculum that pertained to the treatment of controversial issues and personal attacks, the need to protect the privacy of individuals ..., and 'the legal, moral, and ethical restrictions imposed upon journalists. ...'" *Ante*, at 276. In that regard, the Court attempts to justify censorship of the article on teenage pregnancy on the basis of the principal's judgment that (1) "the [pregnant] students' anonymity was not adequately protected," despite the article's use of aliases; and (2) the judgment that "the article was not sufficiently sensitive to the privacy interests of the students' boyfriends and parents. ..." *Ante*, at 274. Similarly, the Court finds in the principal's decision to censor the divorce article a journalistic lesson that the author should have given the father of one student an "opportunity to defend himself" against her charge that (in the Court's words) he "chose [285] 'playing cards with the guys' over home and family. ..." *Ante*, at 275.

But the principal never consulted the students before censoring their work. "[T]hey learned of the deletions when the paper was released. ..." 795 F. 2d, at 1371. Further, he explained the deletions only in the broadest of generalities. In one meeting called at the behest of seven protesting Spectrum staff members (presumably a fraction of the full class), he characterized the articles as "'too sensitive' for 'our immature audience of readers,'" 607 F. Supp. 1450, 1459 (ED Mo. 1985), and in a later meeting he deemed them simply "inappropriate, personal, sensitive and unsuitable for the newspaper," ibid. The Court's supposition that the principal intended (or the protesters understood) those generalities as a lesson on the nuances of journalistic responsibility is utterly incredible. If he did, a fact that neither the District Court nor the Court of Appeals found, the lesson was lost on all but the psychic Spectrum staffer.

B   The Court's second excuse for deviating from precedent is the school's interest in shielding an impressionable high school audience from material whose substance is "unsuitable for immature audiences." *Ante*, at 271 (footnote omitted). Specifically, the majority decrees that we must afford educators authority to shield high school students from exposure to "potentially sensitive topics" (like "the particulars of teen-age sexual activity") or unacceptable social viewpoints (like the advocacy of "irresponsible se[x] or conduct otherwise inconsistent with 'the shared values of a civilized social order'") through school-sponsored student activities. *Ante*, at 272 (citation omitted).

Tinker teaches us that the state educator's undeniable, and undeniably vital, mandate to inculcate moral and political values is not a general warrant to act as "thought police" stifling discussion of all but state-approved topics and advocacy of all [286] but the official position. See also Epperson v. Arkansas, 393 U.S. 97 (1968); Meyer v. Nebraska, 262 U.S. 390 (1923). Otherwise educators could transform students into "closed-circuit recipients of only that which the State chooses to communicate," Tinker, 393 U.S., at 511, and cast a perverse and impermissible "pall of orthodoxy over the classroom," Keyishian v. Board of Regents, 385 U.S. 589, 603 (1967). Thus, the State cannot constitutionally prohibit its high school students from recounting in the locker room "the particulars of [their] teen-age sexual activity," nor even from advocating "irresponsible se[x]" or other presumed abominations of "the shared values of a civilized social order." Even in its capacity as educator the State may not assume an Orwellian "guardianship of the public mind," Thomas v. Collins, 323 U.S. 516, 545 (1945) (Jackson, J., concurring).

The mere fact of school sponsorship does not, as the Court suggests, license such thought control in the high school, whether through school suppression of disfavored viewpoints or through official assessment of topic sensitivity.[2] The former would constitute unabashed and unconstitutional viewpoint [287] discrimination, see Board of Education v. Pico, 457 U.S., at 878-879 (BLACKMUN, J., concurring in part and concurring in judgment), as well as an impermissible infringement of the students' "'right to receive information and ideas,'" id., at 867 (plurality opinion) (citations omitted); see First National Bank v. Bellotti, 435

U.S. 765, 783 (1978).[3] Just as a school board may not purge its state-funded library of all books that "'offen[d] [its] social, political and moral tastes,'" 457 U.S., at 858-859 (plurality opinion) (citation omitted), school officials may not, out of like motivation, discriminatorily excise objectionable ideas from a student publication. The State's prerogative to dissolve the student newspaper entirely (or to limit its subject matter) no more entitles it to dictate which viewpoints students may express on its pages, than the State's prerogative to close down the schoolhouse entitles it to prohibit the non-disruptive expression of antiwar sentiment within its gates.

Official censorship of student speech on the ground that it addresses "potentially sensitive topics" is, for related reasons, equally impermissible. I would not begrudge an educator the authority to limit the substantive scope of a school-sponsored publication to a certain, objectively definable topic, such as literary criticism, school sports, or an overview of the school year. Unlike those determinate limitations, "potential topic sensitivity" is a vaporous nonstandard – like "'public welfare, peace, safety, health, decency, good order, morals or convenience,'" Shuttlesworth v. Birmingham, 394 U.S. 147, 150 (1969), or "'general welfare of citizens,'" Staub v. Baxley, 355 U.S. 313, 322 (1958) – that invites manipulation to achieve ends that cannot permissibly be achieved through blatant viewpoint discrimination and chills student speech to which school officials might not [288] object. In part because of those dangers, this Court has consistently condemned any scheme allowing a state official boundless discretion in licensing speech from a particular forum. See, e.g., Shuttlesworth v. Birmingham, supra, at 150-151, and n. 2; Cox v. Louisiana, 379 U.S. 536, 557-558 (1965); Staub v. Baxley, supra, at 322-324.

The case before us aptly illustrates how readily school officials (and courts) can camouflage viewpoint discrimination as the "mere" protection of students from sensitive topics. Among the grounds that the Court advances to uphold the principal's censorship of one of the articles was the potential sensitivity of "teenage sexual activity." Ante, at 272. Yet the District Court specifically found that the principal "did not, as a matter of principle, oppose discussion of said topi[c] in Spectrum." 607 F. Supp., at 1467. That much is also clear from the same principal's approval of the "squeal law" article on the same page, dealing

---

[2] The Court quotes language in Bethel School Dist. No. 403 v. Fraser, 478 U.S. 675 (1986), for the proposition that "'[t]he determination of what manner of speech in the classroom or in school assembly is inappropriate properly rests with the school board.'" Ante, at 267 (quoting 478 U.S., at 683). As the discussion immediately preceding that quotation makes clear, however, the Court was referring only to the appropriateness of the manner in which the message is conveyed, not of the message's content. See, e.g., Fraser, 478 U.S., at 683 ("[T]he 'fundamental values necessary to the maintenance of a democratic political system' disfavor the use of terms of debate highly offensive or highly threatening to others"). In fact, the Fraser Court coupled its first mention of "society's . . . interest in teaching students the boundaries of socially appropriate behavior," with an acknowledgment of "[t]he undoubted freedom to advocate unpopular and controversial views in schools and classrooms," id., at 681 (emphasis added). See also id., at 689 (BRENNAN, J., concurring in judgment) ("Nor does this case involve an attempt by school officials to ban written materials they consider 'inappropriate' for high school students" (citation omitted)).

[3] Petitioners themselves concede that "'[c]ontrol over access'" to Spectrum is permissible only if "'the distinctions drawn . . . are viewpoint neutral.'" Brief for Petitioners 32 (quoting Cornelius v. NAACP Legal Defense & Educational Fund, Inc., 473 U.S. 788, 806 (1985)).

forthrightly with "teenage sexuality," "the use of contraceptives by teenagers," and "teenage pregnancy," *App. 4-5.* If topic sensitivity were the true basis of the principal's decision, the two articles should have been equally objectionable. It is much more likely that the objectionable article was objectionable because of the viewpoint it expressed: It might have been read (as the majority apparently does) to advocate "irresponsible sex." *See ante,* at 272.

C   The sole concomitant of school sponsorship that might conceivably justify the distinction that the Court draws between sponsored and non-sponsored student expression is the risk "that the views of the individual speaker [might be] erroneously attributed to the school." *Ante,* at 271. Of course, the risk of erroneous attribution inheres in any student expression, including "personal expression" that, like the armbands in Tinker, "happens to occur on the school premises," ante, at 271. Nevertheless, the majority is certainly correct that indicia of school sponsorship increase the likelihood [289] of such attribution, and that state educators may therefore have a legitimate interest in dissociating themselves from student speech.

But "'[e]ven though the governmental purpose be legitimate and substantial, that purpose cannot be pursued by means that broadly stifle fundamental personal liberties when the end can be more narrowly achieved.'" Keyishian v. Board of Regents, 385 U.S., at 602 (quoting Shelton v. Tucker, 364 U.S. 479, 488 (1960)). Dissociative means short of censorship are available to the school. It could, for example, require the student activity to publish a disclaimer, such as the "Statement of Policy" that Spectrum published each school year announcing that "[a]ll ... editorials appearing in this newspaper reflect the opinions of the Spectrum staff, which are not necessarily shared by the administrators or faculty of Hazelwood East," *App. 26*; or it could simply issue its own response clarifying the official position on the matter and explaining why the student position is wrong. Yet, without so much as acknowledging the less oppressive alternatives, the Court approves of brutal censorship.

III.   Since the censorship served no legitimate pedagogical purpose, it cannot by any stretch of the imagination have been designed to prevent "materia[l] disrup[tion of] class work," Tinker, 393 U.S., at 513. Nor did the censorship fall within the category that Tinker described as necessary to prevent student expression from "inva[ding] the rights of others," *ibid.* If that term is to have any content, it must be limited to rights that are protected by law. "Any yardstick less exacting than

[that] could result in school officials curtailing speech at the slightest fear of disturbance," 795 F. 2d, at 1376, a prospect that would be completely at odds with this Court's pronouncement that the "undifferentiated fear or apprehension of disturbance is not enough [even in the public school context] to overcome the right to freedom of expression." [290] Tinker, *supra,* at 508. And, as the Court of Appeals correctly reasoned, whatever journalistic impropriety these articles may have contained, they could not conceivably be tortious, much less criminal. See 795 F. 2d, at 1375-1376.

Finally, even if the majority were correct that the principal could constitutionally have censored the objectionable material, I would emphatically object to the brutal manner in which he did so. Where "[t]he separation of legitimate from illegitimate speech calls for more sensitive tools" Speiser v. Randall, 357 U.S. 513, 525 (1958); see Keyishian v. Board of Regents, *supra,* at 602, the principal used a paper shredder. He objected to some material in two articles, but excised six entire articles. He did not so much as inquire into obvious alternatives, such as precise deletions or additions (one of which had already been made), rearranging the layout, or delaying publication. Such unthinking contempt for individual rights is intolerable from any state official. It is particularly insidious from one to whom the public entrusts the task of inculcating in its youth an appreciation for the cherished democratic liberties that our Constitution guarantees.

IV.   The Court opens its analysis in this case by purporting to reaffirm Tinker's time-tested proposition that public school students "do not 'shed their constitutional rights to freedom of speech or expression at the schoolhouse gate.'" *Ante,* at 266 (quoting Tinker, *supra,* at 506). That is an ironic introduction to an opinion that denudes high school students of much of the First Amendment protection that Tinker itself prescribed. Instead of "teach[ing] children to respect the diversity of ideas that is fundamental to the American system," Board of Education v. Pico, 457 U.S., at 880 (BLACKMUN, J., concurring in part and concurring in judgment), and "that our Constitution is a living reality, not parchment preserved under glass," Shanley v. Northeast Independent School Dist., Bexar Cty., Tex., 462 F. 2d 960, 972 (CA5 [291] 1972), the Court today "teach[es] youth to discount important principles of our government as mere platitudes." West Virginia Board of Education v. Barnette, 319 U.S., at 637. The young men and women of Hazelwood East expected a civics lesson, but not the one the Court teaches them today.

I dissent.

Board of Regents of the University of Wisconsin System v. Southworth
529 U.S. 217
(2000)
(Excerpts only. Footnotes omitted.)

Author's Note: A group of University of Wisconsin students challenged the use of mandatory student activity fees to support student organizations that promote political or ideological ideas with which they disagree. Registered Student Organizations (RSOs) receive funding from student fees either through allocations from student government, the Associated Students of Madison (ASM), or through a general referendum of the student population. The University argued that the controversial speech advances its educational mission, but the lower courts struck down the student fee program as impermissible compelled speech.

PRIOR HISTORY: On Writ of Certiorari to the United States Court of Appeals for the Seventh Circuit.

JUDGES: KENNEDY, J., delivered the opinion of the Court, in which REHNQUIST, C. J., and O'CONNOR, SCALIA, THOMAS, and GINSBURG, JJ., joined. SOUTER, J., filed an opinion concurring in the judgment, in which STEVENS and BREYER, JJ., joined.

OPINION: [220] JUSTICE KENNEDY delivered the opinion of the Court.
... [221] We reverse. The First Amendment permits a public university to charge its students an activity fee used to fund a program to facilitate extracurricular student speech if the program is viewpoint neutral. We do not sustain, however, the student referendum mechanism of the University's program, which appears to permit the exaction of fees in violation of the viewpoint neutrality principle. As to that aspect of the program, we remand for further proceedings.
...[222] In the University's [223] view, the activity fees "enhance the educational experience" of its students by "promoting extracurricular activities," "stimulating advocacy and debate on diverse points of view," enabling "participation in political activity," "promoting student participation in campus administrative activity," and providing "opportunities to develop social skills, " all consistent with the University's mission. ... [T]he fee supports extracurricular endeavors pursued by the University's registered student organizations or RSO's. To qualify for RSO status students must organize as a not-for-profit group, limit membership

primarily to students, and agree to undertake activities related to student life on campus. During the 1995-1996 school year, 623 groups had RSO status on the Madison campus. ... As one would expect, the expressive activities undertaken by RSO's are diverse in range and content, from displaying posters and circulating newsletters throughout the campus, to hosting campus debates and guest speakers, and to what can best be described as political lobbying. ... [224] The University acknowledges that, in addition to providing campus services (e.g., tutoring and counseling), ... RSO's engage in political and ideological expression.
... "[T]he process for reviewing and approving allocations for funding is administered in a viewpoint-neutral fashion," and that the University does not use the fee program for "advocating a particular point of view." ...[225] [The] stipulation regarding the program's viewpoint neutrality does not extend to the referendum process.
... RSO's, as a general rule, do not receive lump-sum cash distributions. Rather, RSO's obtain funding support on a reimbursement basis by submitting receipts or invoices to the University. Guidelines identify expenses appropriate for reimbursement. Permitted expenditures include, in the main, costs for printing, postage, office supplies, and use of University facilities and equipment. Materials printed with student fees must contain a disclaimer that the views expressed are not those of the ASM. The University also reimburses RSO's for fees arising from membership in "other related and non-profit organizations."
...RSO's may not receive reimbursement for "gifts, donations, and contributions," the costs of legal services, or for "activities which are politically partisan or religious in nature." ... A separate policy statement on [] funding states that an RSO can receive funding if it "does not have a primarily [226] political orientation (i.e. is not a registered political group)." The same policy adds that an RSO "shall not use [student fees] for any lobbying purposes." ...
The University's Student Organization Handbook has guidelines for regulating the conduct and activities of RSO's. In addition to obligating RSO's to adhere to the fee program's rules and regulations, the guidelines establish procedures authorizing any student to complain to the University that an RSO is

in noncompliance. An extensive investigative process is in place to evaluate and remedy violations. The University's policy includes a range of sanctions for noncompliance, including probation, suspension, or termination of RSO status.

... In March 1996, ... [227] [r]espondents alleged, *inter alia*, that imposition of the segregated fee violated their rights of free speech, free association, and free exercise under the First Amendment. They contended the University must grant them the choice not to fund those RSO's that engage in political and ideological expression offensive to their personal beliefs. Respondents requested both injunctive and declaratory relief. On cross-motions for summary judgment, the District Court ruled in their favor, declaring the University's segregated fee program invalid. ... The District Court decided the fee program compelled students "to support political and ideological activity with which they disagree" in violation of respondents' First Amendment rights to freedom of speech and association. ... The District Court's order enjoined the board of regents from using segregated fees to fund any RSO engaging in political or ideological speech.

... As the District Court had done, the Court of Appeals found our compelled speech precedents controlling. ... [I]t concluded that the program was not germane to the University's mission, did not further a vital policy of the University, and imposed too much of a burden on respondents' free speech rights. ... [T]he students here have a First Amendment interest in not being compelled to contribute to an organization whose expressive activities conflict with their own personal beliefs. It added that [228] protecting the objecting students' free speech rights was "of heightened concern" ... because "if the university cannot discriminate in the disbursement of funds, it is imperative that students not be compelled to fund organizations which engage in political and ideological activities – that is the only way to protect the individual's rights." The Court of Appeals extended the District Court's order and enjoined the board of regents from requiring objecting students to pay that portion of the fee used to fund RSO's engaged in political or ideological expression.

Three members of the Court of Appeals dissented from the denial of the University's motion for rehearing en banc. In their view, the panel opinion overlooked the "crucial difference between a requirement to pay money to an organization that explicitly aims to subsidize one viewpoint to the exclusion of other viewpoints ... and a requirement to pay a fee to a group that creates a viewpoint-neutral forum, as is true of the student activity fee here."

Other courts addressing First Amendment challenges to similar student fee programs have reached conflicting results. These conflicts, together with the importance of the issue presented, led us to grant certiorari. 526 U.S. 1038 (1999). We reverse the judgment of the Court of Appeals. [229]

The case we decide here, however, does not raise the issue of the government's right, or, to be more specific, the state-controlled University's right, to use its own funds to advance a particular message. The University's whole justification for fostering the challenged expression is that it springs from the initiative of the students, who alone give it purpose and content in the course of their extracurricular endeavors. ... If the challenged speech here were financed by tuition dollars and the University and its officials were responsible for its content, the case might be evaluated on the premise that the government itself is the speaker. That is not the case before us.

The University of Wisconsin exacts the fee at issue for the sole purpose of facilitating the free and open exchange of ideas by, and among, its students. We conclude the objecting students may insist upon certain safeguards with respect to the expressive activities which they are required to support. Our public forum cases are instructive here by close [230] analogy. This is true even though the student activities fund is not a public forum in the traditional sense of the term and despite the circumstance that those cases most often involve a demand for access, not a claim to be exempt from supporting speech. The standard of viewpoint neutrality found in the public forum cases provides the standard we find controlling. We decide that the viewpoint neutrality requirement of the University program is in general sufficient to protect the rights of the objecting students. The student referendum aspect of the program for funding speech and expressive activities, however, appears to be inconsistent with the viewpoint neutrality requirement.

We must begin by recognizing that the complaining students are being required to pay fees which are subsidies for speech they find objectionable, even offensive. ... [231] [S]tudents who attend the University cannot be required to pay subsidies for the speech of other students without some First Amendment protection. ... It infringes on the speech and beliefs of the individual to be required, by this mandatory student activity fee program, to pay subsidies for the objectionable speech of others without any recognition of the State's corresponding duty to him or her. Yet recognition must be given as well to the important and substantial purposes of the

University, which seeks to facilitate a wide range of speech.

... [232] The speech the University seeks to encourage in the program before us is distinguished not by discernable limits but by its vast, unexplored bounds. To insist upon asking what speech is germane would be contrary to the very goal the University seeks to pursue. It is not for the Court to say what is or is not germane to the ideas to be pursued in an institution of higher learning.

Just as the vast extent of permitted expression makes the test of germane speech inappropriate for intervention, so too does it underscore the high potential for intrusion on the First Amendment rights of the objecting students. It is all but inevitable that the fees will result in subsidies to speech which some students find objectionable and offensive to their personal beliefs. If the standard of germane speech is inapplicable, then, it might be argued the remedy is to allow each student to list those causes which he or she will or will not support. If a university decided that its students' First Amendment interests were better protected by some type of optional or refund system it would be free to do so. We decline to impose a system of that sort as a constitutional requirement, however. The restriction could be so disruptive and expensive that the program to support extracurricular speech would be ineffective. The First Amendment does not require the University to put the program at risk.

[233] The University may determine that its mission is well served if students have the means to engage in dynamic discussions of philosophical, religious, scientific, social, and political subjects in their extracurricular campus life outside the lecture hall. If the University reaches this conclusion, it is entitled to impose a mandatory fee to sustain an open dialogue to these ends.

The University must provide some protection to its students' First Amendment interests, however. The proper measure, and the principal standard of protection for objecting students, we conclude, is the requirement of viewpoint neutrality in the allocation of funding support. Viewpoint neutrality was the obligation to which we gave substance in Rosenberger v. Rector and Visitors of Univ. of Va., 515 U.S. 819, 132 L. Ed. 2d 700, 115 S. Ct. 2510 (1995). There the University of Virginia feared that any association with a student newspaper advancing religious viewpoints would violate the Establishment Clause. We rejected the argument, holding that the school's adherence to a rule of viewpoint neutrality in administering its student fee program would prevent "any mistaken impression that the student newspapers speak for the University." While Rosenberger was concerned with the rights a student has to use an extracurricular speech program already in place, today's case considers the antecedent question,

acknowledged but unresolved in Rosenberger: whether a public university may require its students to pay a fee which creates the mechanism for the extracurricular speech in the first instance. When a university requires its students to pay fees to support the extracurricular speech of other students, all in the interest of open discussion, it may not prefer some viewpoints to others. There is symmetry then in our holding here and in Rosenberger: Viewpoint neutrality is the justification for requiring the student to pay the fee in the first instance and for ensuring the integrity of the program's operation once the funds have been collected. We conclude that the University of Wisconsin may sustain [234] the extracurricular dimensions of its programs by using mandatory student fees with viewpoint neutrality as the operational principle.

... Our decision ought not to be taken to imply that in other instances the University, its agents or employees, or – of [235] particular importance – its faculty, are subject to the First Amendment analysis which controls in this case. Where the University speaks, either in its own name through its regents or officers, or in myriad other ways through its diverse faculties, the analysis likely would be altogether different. The Court has not held, or suggested, that when the government speaks the rules we have discussed come into play. When the government speaks, for instance to promote its own policies or to advance a particular idea, it is, in the end, accountable to the electorate and the political process for its advocacy. If the citizenry objects, newly elected officials later could espouse some different or contrary position.

In the instant case, the speech is not that of the University or its agents. It is not, furthermore, speech by an instructor or a professor in the academic context, where principles applicable to government speech would have to be considered.

It remains to discuss the referendum aspect of the University's program. While the record is not well developed on the point, it appears that by majority vote of the student body a given RSO may be funded or defunded. It is unclear to us what protection, if any, there is for viewpoint neutrality in this part of the process. To the extent the referendum substitutes majority determinations for viewpoint neutrality it would undermine the constitutional protection the program requires. The whole theory of viewpoint neutrality is that minority views are treated with the same respect as are majority views. Access to a public forum, for instance, does not depend upon majoritarian consent. That principle is controlling here. A remand is necessary and appropriate to [236] resolve this point; and the case in all events must be reexamined in light of the principles we have discussed.

The judgment of the Court of Appeals is reversed, and the case is remanded for further proceedings consistent with this opinion. In this Court the parties shall bear their own costs.

It is so ordered.

CONCUR BY: JUSTICE SOUTER, with whom JUSTICE STEVENS and JUSTICE BREYER join, concurring in the judgment.

The majority today validates the University's student activity fee after recognizing a new category of First Amendment interests and a new standard of viewpoint neutrality protection. I agree that the University's scheme is permissible, but do not believe that the Court should take the occasion to impose a cast-iron viewpoint neutrality requirement to uphold it. Instead, I would hold that the First Amendment interest claimed by the student respondents (hereinafter Southworth) here is simply insufficient to merit protection by anything more than the viewpoint neutrality already accorded by the University, and I would go no further.

... The question before us is thus properly cast not as whether viewpoint neutrality is required, but whether Southworth has a claim to relief from this specific viewpoint neutral scheme. Two sources of law might be considered in answering this question.

The first comprises First Amendment and related cases grouped under the umbrella of academic freedom. Such law might be implicated by the University's proffered rationale, that the grant scheme funded by the student activity fee is an integral element in the discharge of its educational mission. Our understanding of academic freedom has included not merely liberty from restraints on thought, expression, and association in the academy, but also the idea that universities and schools should have the freedom to make decisions about how and what to teach. ... Some of the opinions in our books emphasize broad conceptions of academic freedom that if accepted by the Court might seem to clothe the University with an immunity to any challenge to regulations made or obligations imposed in the discharge of its educational mission. ... [238]

Our other cases on academic freedom thus far have dealt with more limited subjects, and do not compel the conclusion that the objecting university student is without a First Amendment claim here. While we have spoken in terms of a wide protection for the academic freedom [239] and autonomy that bars legislatures (and courts) from imposing conditions on the spectrum of subjects taught and viewpoints expressed in college teaching ..., we have never held that universities lie entirely beyond the reach of students' First Amendment rights. Thus our prior cases do not go so far as to control the result in this one, and going beyond those cases would be out of order, simply because the University has not litigated on grounds of academic freedom. As to that freedom and university autonomy, then, it is enough to say that protecting a university's discretion to shape its educational mission may prove to be an important consideration in First Amendment analysis of objections to student fees.

The second avenue for addressing Southworth's claim to a pro rata refund or the total abolition of the student activity fee is to see how closely the circumstances here resemble instances of governmental speech mandates found to require relief. As a threshold matter, it is plain that this case falls far afield of those involving compelled or controlled speech, apart from subsidy schemes. ...[240] [T]he clear connection between fee payer and offensive speech that loomed large in our decisions in the union and bar cases is simply not evident here. Second, Southworth's objection has less force than it might otherwise carry because the challenged fees support a government [241] program that aims to broaden public discourse. ... [O]ur cases do suggest that under the First Amendment the government may properly use its tax revenue to promote general discourse. ... [242] And we have recognized the same principle outside of the sphere of government spending as well. ...The same consideration goes against the fee payer's speech objection to the scheme here.

Third, our prior compelled speech and compelled funding cases are distinguishable on the basis of the legitimacy of governmental interest. No one disputes the University's assertion that some educational value is derived from the activities supported by the fee.

... Finally, the weakness of Southworth's claim is underscored by its setting within a university, whose students are inevitably required to support the expression of personally [243] offensive viewpoints in ways that cannot be thought constitutionally objectionable unless one is prepared to deny the University its choice over what to teach. No one disputes that some fraction of students' tuition payments may be used for course offerings that are ideologically offensive to some students, and for paying professors who say things in the university forum that are radically at odds with the politics of particular students. Least of all does anyone claim that the University is somehow required to offer a spectrum of courses to satisfy a viewpoint neutrality requirement. The University need not provide junior years abroad in North Korea as well as France, instruct in the theory of plutocracy as well as democracy, or teach Nietzsche as well as St. Thomas. Since uses of tuition payments (not optional for anyone who wishes to stay in college) may fund offensive speech far more obviously than the student activity fee does, it is difficult to see how the activity fee could present a stronger argument for a refund.

In sum, I see no basis to provide relief from the scheme being administered, would go no further, and respectfully concur in the judgment.

Chapter

14

Libel

The First Amendment and defamatory speech

Focal cases:
New York Times v. Sullivan, 376 U.S. 254 (1964)
Zeran v. America Online, 129 F.3d 327 (4ᵗʰ Cir. 1997)

Defamation, the focus of libel law, is the dissemination of information that harms an individual's reputation. Until the 1960s, libel law was controlled by common law. Precedents clearly established that because defamation plays "no essential part of any exposition of ideas,"[1] it falls outside "the area of constitutionally protected speech."[2] Thus, common law protected personal reputation rather than the right to criticize or verbally attack individuals. To win a suit prior to 1964, a libel plaintiff had to prove only that a statement that would harm his personal reputation was published about him. The allegedly defamatory statement was presumed to be false, and, to avoid paying damages, the defendant bore the burden of proving that the statement was in fact true. The common law imposed a principle of strict liability: falsity and damages were presumed; fault by the publisher, author or speaker was irrelevant. Media defendants in libel suits who could not convincingly prove the truth of their statements lost.

ORIGINS OF THE ACTUAL MALICE STANDARD
Then, in 1964, the Supreme Court revolutionized the field of libel. In a case involving minor errors in a *New York Times* advertisement detailing racial abuse of civil rights activists by Southern officials, the Supreme Court said libel suits enjoyed "no talismanic immunity from constitutional limitations."[3] The Court in *New York Times v. Sullivan* said the "central meaning" of the First Amendment was to protect "debate on public issues [that] include[s] vehement, caustic and sometimes unpleasantly sharp attacks on government and public officials."[4] Such debate necessarily includes speech that may include errors that harm the reputations of government officers.

---

[1] Chaplinsky v. New Hampshire, 315 U.S. 568, 572 (1942).
[2] Beauharnais v. Illinois, 343 U.S. 250, 266 (1952).
[3] New York Times v. Sullivan, 376 U.S. 254, 269 (1964).
[4] 376 U.S. at 270.

To provide the vital "breathing room" needed for citizens to freely discuss and criticize government officials, the Court shifted the burden of proof from the media defendant to the public official plaintiffs.[5] The Court extended constitutional protection to defamation of government officials by eliminating the common-law doctrine that defamatory statements presumptively result in awards and by requiring government officials to prove the falsity of defamatory statements.

To win a libel suit against the media, the Court said, public officials need to prove more than mere publication of defamatory material. Instead, public officials must prove, convincingly, both that the libelous statement was false and that the media were significantly at fault. The Court imposed a new standard of fault – called actual malice (see below) – on government official plaintiffs and said the heightened burden was necessary to fulfill the constitutional presumption that discussion of government officials should be unfettered and robust.

ELEMENTS OF DEFAMATION

In civil libel suits, a plaintiff sues a defendant to obtain damages to compensate for the harm caused by defamatory comments or publications. Plaintiffs bear the responsibility of proving to a jury that they deserve compensation. Following *New York Times v. Sullivan* and its progeny,[6] most plaintiffs in civil libel suits must prove five things:
Publication
Identification
Defamation
Falsity
Fault

Publication

Under libel law, *publication* occurs when *one* person other than the author and the subject of the material sees or hears the information. When defamation is disseminated via mass media, the plaintiff does not have to prove that a sizeable audience received the message; publication is presumed in these cases.[7] Re-distribution or re-publication of a libel also constitutes publication under the law. However, libel law ties liability to a defendant's prior knowledge of the libelous content, or *scienter*.

Mere distributors of others' messages, such as bookstores, libraries, telephone common carriers or online service providers who do not originate the content in question, are not legally responsible for libel they disseminate.[8] The Telecommunications Policy Act of 1996 explicitly extended this exemption from liability to online service providers, even if the OSP edits content to eliminate obscene or otherwise objectionable material.[9] Congress said OSP protection from liability was vital because the virtual impossibility of effectively screening millions of online messages otherwise would lead online providers to take measures to protect themselves from libel that would unavoidably reduce freedom of expression online.[10] The Supreme Court has denied *cert.*

---

[5] 376 U.S. at 279-80.

[6] 376 U.S. 254 (1964); Garrison v. Louisiana 379 U.S. 64 (1964); Curtis Pub. Co. v. Butts, 388 U.S. 130 (1967); Rosenbloom v. Metromedia, 403 U.S. 29 (1971); Gertz v. Welch, 418 U.S. 323 (1974); Herbert v. Lando, 441 U.S. 153 (1979); Dun & Bradstreet v. Greenmoss Builders, 472 U.S. 749 (1985); Philadelphia Newspapers v. Hepps, 475 U.S. 767 (1986); Harte-Hanks Communications v. Connaughton, 491 U.S. 657 (1989).

[7] *Restatement (2d) of Torts* § 559 (e).

[8] Telecommunications Policy Act of 1996, 47 U.S.C. § 230.

[9] 47 U.S.C. § 230 © (1). *See* Batzel v. smith, 2003 U.S. App. LEXIS 12736 (9th Cir. 2003).

[10] *See* Zeran v. America Online, 129 F.3d 327 (4th Cir. 1997), *cert. den'd*, 524 U.S. 937 (1998). *See also* Blumenthal v. Drudge, 992 F. Supp. 44, 52 (D.D.C. 1998) (ruling that 47 U.S.C. § 230 forbids imposition of publisher liability on service provider for exercising its editorial and self-regulatory functions).

in at least two cases in which a U.S. Circuit Court of Appeals upheld this provision and ruled that America Online was not liable for defamatory language posted by users of its online service.[11]

Identification

Libel plaintiffs must also show that the information published was "of or concerning" them.[12] *Identification* of the plaintiff in association with the defamatory language does not need to be explicit; the individual does not have to be identified by name. In fact, identification can be taken from the context of more than one story, or it can arise through insufficient disguise of an individual in a fictional account or when an individual – such as Susan Smith of Seattle–shares a common name with other people. Identification occurs under the law if only one person identifies the plaintiff as the subject of the defamation. However, to determine whether the plaintiff's reputation was actually harmed, courts generally consider the number of people who reasonably identified the individual.

In general, the requirement of identification prevents large groups from suing for libel. Under what is informally known as the rule of 25, it is presumed that members of groups of more than 25 are not identified. However, this presumption can be overcome. Courts have accepted identification of individual members in groups of about 15 to 25 members.[13]

Defamation

Defamation, as mentioned before, consists of statements that, in their ordinary meaning to a reasonable person, inflict "hatred, ridicule or contempt" upon someone.[14] Defamation occurs when any message – oral, written, broadcast or digital – lowers the reputation of someone (or some thing) in the eyes of another. Defamation arises in news, editorials, opinion columns,[15] cartoons, caricatures, advertisements[16] and even altered or out-of-context photographs. Living individuals, businesses, business products and even vegetables can be libeled. A judge must determine whether the statements are legally *capable* of constituting libel; generally a jury determines whether the statements did, in fact, defame the individual.

Some words, on their face, are clearly defamatory. To accuse someone of a crime, or incompetence, or immorality, or of spreading a communicable disease is libel *per se*. In contrast, libel *per quod* arises when seemingly innocent statements become libelous when the message is combined with the external knowledge of audience members. For example, if a story reports that George Ingraham is the father of a daughter born to Alice Smith and readers know that George Ingraham is single or is married to Mary Ingraham, that is libel *per quod.*[17] Perhaps because of its more limited impact and its more tenuous fault, some courts make it more difficult for plaintiffs to win suits for libel *per quod.*

Libel can be overt – as in calling someone a thief – or it can arise through insinuation and innuendo. However, the allegedly libelous statement must be taken in context.[18] Thus, what might appear to be defamatory may be protected humor, fair comment, hyperbole or parody.[19] Statements of "pure opinion," for example, are immune to libel. In 1990, the Supreme Court in

---

[11] Ben Ezra, Weinstein, & Co. v. America Online, 206 F.3d 980 (10th Cir. 2000), *cert. den'd*, 2000 U.S. LEXIS 5157 (U.S. Oct. 2, 2000) (America Online acted solely as an interactive computer service provider and therefore is immune from suit); Zeran v. America Online, 129 F.3d 327 (4th Cir. 1997), *cert. den'd*, 524 U.S. 937 (1998).

[12] *Restatement (2d) of Torts* § 564.

[13] *Restatement (2d) of Torts* § 564A (c).

[14] *Restatement (2d) of Torts* §§ 559 (e), 563 (c), 614.

[15] *But see* Milkovich v. Lorain Journal, 497 U.S. 1 (1990) (protecting "pure opinion" on issues of public concern).

[16] New York Times v. Sullivan, 376 U.S. 254 (1964).

[17] *See, e.g.,* Karrigan v. Valentine, 339 P.2d 52 (Kan. 1959).

[18] *Restatement (2d) of Torts* §563 (d).

[19] *See, e.g.,* Greenbelt Cooperative Pub. Ass'n. v. Bresler, 398 U.S. 6 (1970).

Milkovich v. Lorain Journal ruled that the First Amendment protects statements of personal opinion that are reasonably derived from either accurately stated or widely known facts.[20] However, *Milkovich* stops far short of protecting all apparent statements of opinion. To earn protection from libel, statements of opinion must not suggest, assert or "imply a false assertion of fact" and must reflect an accurate and complete assessment of the facts on which the opinion is based.[21] Thus, to gain protection as "pure opinion," comments may not contain unfounded statements that are susceptible to being proven true or false.

The distinction between implied fact and pure opinion is not absolute or clear.[22] Courts often make the determination by examining the totality of circumstances, which – in addition to determining whether the statement can be factually verified – includes scrutiny of the ordinary meaning of the phrases, the journalistic and social contexts of the comments,[23] and the "general tenor" or tone of the piece taken as a whole.[24] In general, vague terms expressing judgment or emotion are more likely to be viewed as opinion than are precise, objective labels. Thus, to call someone a loathsome creep is likely to be opinion; to label the same individual a lying thief likely is not. However, while calling someone a loathsome toad would be subject to factual verification (and found to be false because she is *not* actually a toad), such a comment likely would be understood and protected as "hyperbolic language."[25]

Falsity

Some libel plaintiffs can win a lawsuit without proving *falsity*. As will be discussed below, all libel plaintiffs are not equal under the law. In *New York Times v. Sullivan*, the Supreme Court said the First Amendment requires government officials to bear a heavy burden before they can win a libel suit because, in a democracy, citizens and media must be given the greatest possible freedom to discuss the failings and foibles of those in government.[26] To protect this freedom of speech, government officials must prove that the libelous statement was made with "actual malice – that is, with knowledge that [the statement] was false or with reckless disregard of whether it was false or not."[27] Actual malice, as a term of law, is *not* simply bias or ill will or negligence. Actual malice means the libelous statement was either a "calculated falsehood"[28] or was published with "serious doubts as to [its] truth."[29]

In subsequent rulings, the Court said the Constitution also protects robust public discussion of prominent, non-government leaders of public movements and, to a lesser degree, discussion of private individuals enmeshed in issues of public concern or general public interest.[30] As plaintiffs, individuals in these categories must prove falsity to win a libel suit. Only private individuals defamed in the course of discussion of purely private matters do not have to prove falsity.[31] When a private person is defamed, the common law presumption of falsity remains intact, and the defendant – not the plaintiff – generally bears the burden to prove that the defamatory statement is true.

---

[20] 497 U.S. 1 (1990).

[21] 497 U.S. at 18.

[22] *See* Rodriguez v. Panayiotou (George Michael), 314 F.3d 979 (9th Cir. 2002) (finding singer's criticism of arresting officer is not protected as pure opinion).

[23] *See* Ollman v. Evans, 750 F.2d 970 (D.C. Cir. 1984).

[24] 497 U.S. at 21.

[25] 497 U.S. at 21.

[26] 376 U.S. 254 (1964).

[27] 376 U.S. at 279-80, 297.

[28] Garrison v. Louisiana, 379 U.S. 64, 75 (1964).

[29] St. Amant v. Thompson, 390 U.S. 727, 731 (1968).

[30] *See, e.g.,* Philadelphia Newspapers v. Hepps, 475 U.S. 767 (1986); Dun & Bradstreet v. Greenmoss Builders, 472 U.S. 749 (1985); Rosenbloom v. Metromedia, 403 U.S. 29 (1971).

[31] Dun & Bradstreet v. Greenmoss Builders, 472 U.S. 749 (1985).

To prove either truth or falsity in court requires a preponderance of direct, explicit evidence to demonstrate that the essence of the libelous comments is either true or false. Every detail of every statement need not be false to prove falsity. Instead, it is sufficient that the evidence demonstrates that the gist of the statement is substantially untrue or generally inaccurate.

Fault

The level of *fault* that must be proven in a libel suit depends upon the public/private status of the individual, the degree to which the libel involved a public controversy or matter of public concern, and the type of damages sought by the plaintiff.

The Actual Malice Standard

When the Court established the *New York Times* actual malice standard of fault in 1964, it said public officials suing media for libel must prove media acted with knowledge of falsity or reckless disregard for truth.[32] Proving that a newspaper disseminated information it knew to be false often requires examining the state of mind of the journalists as well as the decision-making processes that preceded publication.[33] The Court has accepted this intrusion into the editorial process.[34] However, knowledge of falsity also can be established by showing that a journalist completely fabricated facts.[35]

In many cases, plaintiffs seek to demonstrate that media behaved recklessly rather than with absolute knowledge that the information was false. Reckless disregard for the truth is more than mere divergence from professional standards of care. Reckless disregard arises when a journalist bases a story upon the unverified statements of unknown or unreliable sources.[36] Distorted or biased selection of facts[37] or dissemination of statements that are so improbable that "only a reckless man would have put them in circulation" also contributes to a finding of reckless disregard.[38] Again, determining recklessness usually involves inquiry into the editorial process.

Expanding the Actual Malice Standard of Fault

The Court in *New York Times* applied the actual malice standard only to defamation involving public officials' official conduct.[39] The Court said open criticism of the official conduct of government officers was so vital to democracy that libel damages could not be allowed to chill this speech by punishing inadvertent errors. Later in 1964, however, the Court included discussion of "anything [that] might touch an official's fitness for office" under the constitutional protection of the actual malice standard.[40] In subsequent years, the Court found that the First Amendment also protected discussion and criticism of non-elected officials, candidates for public office, and individuals whose position "would invite public scrutiny and discussion of the person holding it."[41] Thus, plaintiffs in these groups had to show that the defamation occurred due to actual malice. Then the Court said public figures – individuals who enjoy general fame and notoriety or who are "intimately involved in the resolution of important public questions" – also must prove actual

---

[32] 376 U.S. 254 (1964).

[33] Herbert v. Lando, 441 U.S. 153 (1979).

[34] Ibid.

[35] Cantrell v. Forest City Pub. Co., 419 U.S. 245 (1974). *But see* Masson v. New Yorker Magazine, 501 U.S. 496 (1991) (allowing some editorial discretion over direct quotations).

[36] *See* Curtis Pub. Co. v. Butts, 388 U.S. 130 (1967).

[37] Harte-Hanks v. Connaughton, 491 U.S. 657 (1989).

[38] St. Amant v. Thompson, 390 U.S. 727, 732 (1968).

[39] 376 U.S. 254 (1964).

[40] Garrison v. Louisiana, 379 U.S. 64, 77.

[41] Rosenblatt v. Baer, 383 U.S 75, 85 (1966).

malice.[42] Finally, in 1971, the Court said even private figures who are libeled in relation to matters of public concern must prove this heightened level of fault.[43]

Private figures vs. public figures or officials

Three years later, however, the Supreme Court backtracked a bit and said the public status of the plaintiff, not the public interest in the speech, determined the standard of fault that must be proven. In *Gertz v. Welch*, the Court rejected a blanket requirement that all libel plaintiffs prove actual malice and established a hierarchy of libel plaintiffs with varying requirements of fault.[44] The Court in *Gertz* ruled that a prominent civil rights attorney was a private figure, more vulnerable to injury and more deserving of recompense than public figures or government officials. The Court ruled that as a private plaintiff, Gertz did not need to prove either falsity or actual malice. Instead, private libel plaintiffs only need to prove some degree of media negligence, a lesser standard than actual malice, to win. Negligence generally occurs when someone employs less than the standard, professional level of care. If private figure plaintiffs seek punitive damages, however, the Court said they must prove actual malice.

In *Gertz*, the Court directed states to determine what standard of fault they would require private figures to prove in libel suits, but the Court said states could not impose the abandoned standard of strict liability. The Court said the standard of fault should be tied to: 1) the ease of the individual's access to media to "counteract false statements" and 2) the degree to which the individual (through seeking government office or attempting to affect public policy) voluntarily exposed herself to "closer public scrutiny."[45] Thus, the Court distinguished among private individuals, public figures and public officials.

Under *Gertz* and subsequent rulings, the Court defined private figures as people who do not meet the standards for either public officials or public figures. Public officials serve a visible, public function; they generally are elected to office or fill a government position of some authority. However, different jurisdictions vary in how lofty a post in government an individual must hold before she becomes a public official who must prove actual malice.

In *Gertz*, the Court identified two types of public figures who must prove actual malice in libel suits.[46] First, all-purpose public figures have either pervasive power and influence or widespread fame and notoriety; the few individuals in this category generally are household names across the nation. Second, limited-purpose public figures voluntarily inject themselves into public controversies with a desire to affect the outcome, and they become public figures only in that context.[47] Individuals rarely become limited-purpose public figures unintentionally; private figures must purposefully enter into a public controversy to shed their libel protection as private persons. However, the judgment that an individual constitutes a limited-purpose public figure is not clear-cut, and some courts consider the ease of the individual's access to media as well as the public significance of the issue with which the libel is associated to determine whether someone constitutes a public figure.[48]

In 1986, the Supreme Court seemed to revert to a position it had abandoned more than a decade earlier and ruled that a private person suing the media for libel must prove both falsity and fault when the "allegedly defamatory speech is of public concern."[49] In *Philadelphia Newspapers v. Hepps*, the Court failed to define "matters of public concerns," but it referred analogously to discussion of public affairs, a seemingly expansive category of speech. Other courts have defined

---

[42] Curtis Publishing Co. v. Butts, 388 U.S. 130 (1967).

[43] Rosenbloom v. Metromedia, 403 U.S. 29 (1971).

[44] Gertz v. Welch, 418 U.S. 323 (1974).

[45] 418 U.S. at 344.

[46] 418 U.S. 323 (1974).

[47] *See* Hutchinson v. Proxmire, 443 U.S. 111 (1979).

[48] *See, e.g.,* Time v. Firestone, 424 U.S. 448 (1976).

[49] Philadelphia Newspapers v. Hepps, 475 U.S. 767, 779 (1986)(Brennan, J., concurring).

matters of public concern more narrowly to mean something beyond mere newsworthiness. At a minimum, matters of public concern must be of interest to people beyond the circle of participants. However, the Court said in *Hepps* that when the balance between private reputation and broad discussion of matters of public concern is uncertain, "we believe that the Constitution requires us to tip [] in favor of protecting true speech. To ensure that true speech on matters of public concern is not deterred, we hold that the common-law presumption that defamatory speech is false cannot stand... ."[50]

The obligations of parties to libel suits and the ultimate verdicts depend upon the important yet unclear line between public figures and private individuals. Libel rulings are further complicated by the fact that limited public figure status *may* disappear with time if the issue that prompted that status is no longer of public concern.

DAMAGES

People who are defamed seek different restitution or compensation. Some want only to have the error corrected and to have their reputation repaired to the degree that is possible. For these individuals, a correction, retraction or apology is often adequate.[51] Some sixty percent of the states have retraction statutes that limit media liability following prompt and thorough retraction or correction. While the laws differ broadly, some require plaintiffs to pursue apologies or corrections before bringing a lawsuit.

Many people who believe they have been defamed pursue the matter in court, and more than half win damages from media companies.[52] However, plaintiffs and defendants alike often are unhappy with the results and the expensive, time-consuming and publicity laden process.[53] A number of associations, including scholars, government officials and attorneys, have examined alternatives to the legal process and proposed reforms in libel law. None of the numerous proposals, which focus on simplifying the process, eliminating or reducing monetary awards to actual costs, mandating arbitration or prohibiting suits by public officials or other groups, has been broadly implemented. No generally acceptable solution has been found to the sometimes-excessive damage awards meted out by sympathetic juries.

Libel plaintiffs may sue for four types of damages: presumed damages, actual damages, special damages, and/or punitive damages. To receive money for presumed damages, which are not documented but are simply assumed to result when reputation is harmed, public figures, public officials, and some private figures must prove actual malice. Only private figures whose defamation is unrelated to matters of public concern need not prove actual malice to gain presumed damages.

Plaintiffs must prove they suffered actual injuries to obtain actual damages, but they do not have to document the costs of these injuries. Instead, actual damages are assigned by a jury to compensate individuals for the pain, shame, emotional and psychological strain, and humiliation of defamation as well as for monetary loss. Because many of these harms cannot be quantified, plaintiffs seek vastly different amounts for comparatively similar harms. In most cases, a jury determines the amount it believes the individual deserves. Judges and appellate courts often modify the monetary awards set by juries.

Special damages, in contrast, are limited to the amount of specific, documented financial losses a plaintiff can prove resulted from the libel. Special damages compensate directly for and are

---

[50] 475 U.S. at 777.

[51] BEZANSON, R.P., CRANBERG, G. & SOLOSKI, J. LIBEL LAW AND THE PRESS (1987) (reporting that three-fourths of the interviewed libel litigants would have been satisfied with a correction, apology, or retraction).

[52] *See* SOLOSKI, J. & BEZANSON, R.P. (eds.) REFORMING LIBEL LAW (1992).

[53] *See* BEZANSON, R.P., CRANBERG, G. & SOLOSKI, J. LIBEL LAW AND THE PRESS (1987).

equal to the precise amount of monetary loss. In trade libel suits and, in some states, in cases of libel *per quod*, special damages are the only type of damages that can be awarded.

Punitive damages are designed to punish the bad behavior of the publisher of the defamation rather than to compensate the plaintiff for the harm done. Punitive damages often amount to millions of dollars. Only private figures defamed in relation to private concerns are not required to prove actual malice to win punitive awards. The Supreme Court has ruled that "grossly excessive" punitive awards that are not reasonably related to the egregiousness of the defendant's behavior and the amount of the harm suffered by the plaintiff may violate the Constitution.[54]

The following table summarizes the level of proof required for different types of plaintiffs to obtain various types of damages.

Prominence	Compensatory Damages	Presumed/Punitive Damages
Private person/private speech	Fault	Negligence
Private person/public concern	Negligence & falsity	Actual malice & falsity
Public figure/private speech	Negligence & falsity	Actual malice & falsity
Public figure/public concern	Actual malice & falsity	Actual malice & falsity
Public official/private speech	Negligence & falsity	Actual malice & falsity
Public official/official fitness	Actual malice & falsity	Actual malice & falsity

STATE LAWS ON LIBEL

Lawsuits are extremely costly in time, money and resources, and many people assert that libel suits are among the most serious problems facing U.S. media today.[55] While most libel suits are brought by individuals seeking to restore their reputation and correct misinformation published about them, some libel suits seek to punish and stifle public criticism. Land developers, major corporations and non-profit organizations including the Church of Scientology and the Liberty Lobby, a conservative political group, have brought libel suits in an attempt to limit investigative reporting.

These suits, called SLAPP suits, or Strategic Lawsuits Against Public Participation, chill public discussion and generally stop public criticism of the plaintiffs, at least while the sometimes lengthy cases are pending. Some states, concerned about the use of the judicial system for strategic gain rather than for correction of a wrong, adopted procedures to eliminate these suits from the system early in the process.

Some states have increased the burden of libel suits on their courts by adopting statutes called veggie libel laws that prohibit publication of intentional falsehoods about fruits, vegetables and other perishable foods produced in the state. Suits under these laws and product disparagement or trade libel suits generally require the plaintiff to prove ill will or actual malice as well as loss of business or income.[56]

Nearly half of the states have criminal libel laws that enable the state to bring libel charges against an individual. These statutes are rarely used because most states believe people have adequate remedies for libel under civil law. The Supreme Court supported this position in 1966 when it unanimously overturned a criminal libel conviction for communications "calculated to create disturbances of the peace."[57] However, criminal cases arise on occasion, and they allow the state to correct major harms to the public or to the reputation of large groups. Criminal libel also

---

[54] BMW of N. Am. v. Gore, 517 U.S. 559 (1996).

[55] *See, e.g.*, Smolla, R.A. & Garetner, M.J. *The Annenberg Libel Reform Proposal: The Case for Enactment*, 31 WILLIAM AND MARY LAW REVIEW 25 (1989); SMOLLA, R.A. *The Annenberg Libel Reform Proproposal*, in SOLOSKI, J. & BEZANSON, R.P. (eds.) REFORMING LIBEL LAW (1992).

[56] *Restatement (2d) of Torts* §§ b23A (d), 626; Bose Corp. v. Consumers Union of United States, 466 U.S. 485 (1984).

[57] *See, e.g.*, Ashton v. Kentucky, 384 U.S. 195, 198 (1966).

allows prosecution for libeling the dead (something clearly not available under civil law) and can impose jail terms as well as fines upon those found guilty.

LIBEL PROTECTIONS AND DEFENSES

Truth

Although the burden of proof in most libel cases today rests with the plaintiff, defendants may choose to present affirmative defenses in order to end a lawsuit quickly with a dismissal or summary judgment. Truth is an absolute defense in libel suits, but few defendants use this defense because truth is notoriously difficult to determine, no less to prove.

Two rules, with limited application, reflect judicial recognition that truth is uncertain and error is human. A few states have established what is called the innocent construction rule. Under this rule, statements cannot legally be defamatory if their meaning is innocent "given their natural and obvious" usage.[58] Some courts also have adopted the single mistake rule, which provides a defense against libel when a report indicates that an individual has made a single business mistake. Under this rule, for example, if a food writer reports that a vegetarian restaurant included beef stock in its soup on Tuesday, this likely would not be defamatory – even if false – so long as it did not imply a pattern of dishonest business practices.

Privilege

Many media communications that contain defamatory language are protected by what is know as qualified privilege. This protection is an extension of the absolute protection the Constitution provides for members of Congress to speak openly on the floor of the House and Senate without fear of lawsuit.[59] This absolute privilege, as it is now called, prevents the speaker from being sued for any defamatory content in her communications during the official proceedings of Congress. Absolute privilege today applies to a wide array of official communications from the legislative, judicial and executive branches at any level of government – national to local. Absolute privilege attaches to virtually anyone participating in or testifying before a legislative session. It also protects virtually all communication during official judicial proceedings, be they in the courtroom or the grand jury chamber. The official statements and publications of executive branch administrators, mayors, governors and the president also are absolutely protected. As broad as absolute privilege is, it does not protect unofficial comments, discussion outside the official government proceedings or information shared during recesses in the sessions outlined above.

Qualified privilege effectively extends immunity from libel prosecution to the broadcast or publication of accurate, thorough, fair reports of official government proceedings and records – the public record.[60] In general, protection attaches to reports that indicate the official source of the information. This protection from lawsuits embraces coverage of meetings of the local town council and the U.S. Senate, grand jury indictments and witness testimony, court filings in civil complaints[61] and jury verdicts in criminal trials, and police reports and executive branch actions. The privilege given to reports of legally closed records or of communications during legally closed proceedings is uncertain. In addition, qualified reporting privilege is conditional; it can be lost when a report is inaccurate or malicious.

---

[58] See Kyu Ho Youm, *The Innocent Construction Rule: Ten Years After Modification,* 14 COMM. & THE LAW 49 (1992). *See,also.,* Chapski v. Copley Press, 92 Ill. 2d 344, 352 (1982) (statement not actionable per se if it can reasonably be construed as having innocent interpretation or as referring to person other than plaintiff).

[59] U.S. Constitution, Art. 1, § 1.

[60] *Restatement (2d) of Torts,* § 611.

[61] Note, however, that some states do not consider civil filings privileged until some official judicial action has occurred in the case.

Neutral Reportage

An extremely limited number of courts allows a defense of neutral reportage,[62] which permits reporters to accurately report newsworthy statements of significant public interest made by prominent, reputable public figures or public officials without fear of libel.[63] This protection exists even when the reporter doubts the truth of the statements she reports as long as the report is fair and balanced. The theory behind this very limited protection is that charges about newsworthy public controversies made by prominent figures are, regardless of their truth, newsworthy and of value to the public.

Fair Comment

Fair Comment and criticism is a common-law defense intended to encourage open, opinionated discussion of topics of public concern. Although the name suggests otherwise, the comment does not have to be fair to gain common-law protection. Instead, it must be fair to comment or criticize because the individual, event or object has held itself up for public scrutiny. Fair comment, like the constitutional protection for opinion, requires that the statement include a fair exposition of the facts underlying the author's opinion so that readers may make an independent evaluation of the value of the author's opinion.

Consent

Few individuals directly consent to the publication of defamatory comments about themselves. However, the common law recognizes and a few courts accept implied consent as a libel defense. Implied consent occurs when someone responds, on the record, to defamatory assertions and both the assertions and the response are published in the same story. Implied consent may also arise when the defamed individual shares the defamatory charges with others.

Right of Reply

The right of reply defense does not apply to the original defamation. Instead, this defense arises when an individual who is libeled replies in kind. This common law defense permits people to respond to defamation with a defamatory statement of similar proportion without opening themselves up to a libel suit. This defense may also protect the media who carry both the original and the reply charges from suit.

Statutes of Limitations and Jurisdiction

Statutes of limitations require lawsuits to be filed within a certain period from the alleged offense.[64] Limits on how long a plaintiff can wait to initiate a suit are designed to assure that evidence will be fresh and witnesses' or experts' memories will be reliable. In libel cases, the statute of limitations varies among states but generally does not exceed two years. Differences in the period during which a libel suit may be filed sometimes encourage plaintiffs to "shop" for a hospitable jurisdiction in which to bring a lawsuit. For example, if an individual who lives in Portland, Oregon, is defamed by the *Oregonian*, she has one year to file suit in Oregon. However, she may decide to bring suit in the neighboring state of Washington, where the statute of limitations is two years, if the *Oregonian* regularly circulates there.

---

[62] *Restatement (2nd) of Torts*, § 611.

[63] *See, e.g.,* Edwards v. Nat'l Audubon Society, 556 F.2d 113 (2nd Cir. 997); Price v. Viking Penguin, 881 F.2d 1426 (8th Cir. 1989).

[64] *See* Van Buskirk v. N.Y. Times Co., 325 F.3d 87 (2nd Cir. 2003) (applying N.Y. one-year statute of limitations to online posting).

In 2003, the Supreme Court denied *certiorari* on the question of libel jurisdiction related to the Internet. Based on the assumption that the Internet may be said to circulate in all 50 states, plaintiffs brought suit in Virginia against two Connecticut newspapers, their editors and two reporters for news stories posted online about Connecticut prisoners held in Virginia jails that allegedly defamed a Virginia warden.[65] In dismissing the suit, the U.S. Court of Appeals for the Fourth Circuit said court jurisdiction over out-of-state individuals who post information on the Internet is tied directly to the intent of those posting the information. The court said that unless the individuals "manifest an intent to aim their websites or the posted articles at [an] audience" in the non-residential state, that state has no authority to decide the case.[66]

ADDITIONAL CASE READINGS

The cases mentioned below and those that follow will increase your understanding of the important and complex field of libel law.

- *Young v. New Haven Advocate*, 315 F.3d 256 (4th Cir. 2002) (rejecting Virginia courts' jurisdiction for libel posted online by Connecticut newspaper).
- *Ben Ezra, Weinstein, & Co. v. America Online*, 206 F.3d 980 (10th Cir. 2000) (affirming America Online's immunity from liability as an online service provider).
- *Masson v. New Yorker Magazine* (1991) (finding that intentional manipulation of quotations does not constitute actual malice).
- *Milkovich v. Lorain Journal* (1990) (rejecting categorical protection from libel for statements of opinion).
- *Harte-Hanks Communications v. Connaughton*, 491 U.S. 657 (1989) (affirming public figure libel award upon finding actual malice).
- *Philadelphia Newspapers v. Hepps*, 475 U.S. 767 (1986) (requiring private figure libel plaintiff to prove falsity in defamation involving matter of public concern).
- *Dun & Bradstreet v. Greenmoss Builders*, 472 U.S. 749 (1985) (rejecting actual malice requirement for presumed or punitive damages when libel involves purely private speech).
- *Woolston v. Reader's Digest*, 443 U.S. 157 (1979) (finding that citation for contempt does not constitute a public controversy or create public figure status).
- *Hutchinson v. Proxmire*, 443 U.S. 111 (1979) (finding recipient of "Golden Fleece" award not a public figure for libel purposes).
- *Herbert v. Lando*, 441 U.S. 153 (1979) (First Amendment does not bar inquiry into editorial process in determining requisite fault in libel case).
- *Time, Inc. v. Firestone*, 424 U.S. 448 (1976) (rejecting public figure libel status for wealthy divorcee).
- *Gertz v. Welch*, 418 U.S. 323 (1974) (rejecting application of *New York Times'* actual malice to private figure).
- *Rosenbloom v. Metromedia*, 403 U.S. 29 (1971) (applying *New York Times'* actual malice to private figure when libel involved matter of public concern).
- *Greenbelt Cooperative Publishing Association v. Bresler*, 398 U.S. 6 (1970) (requiring application of *New York Times'* actual malice to public figure libel plaintiffs).

---

[65] Young v. New Haven Advocate, 315 F.3d 256 (4th Cir. 2002), *cert den'd* 2003 U.S. LEXIS 3743 (U.S., May 19, 2003). *See also* ALS Scan v. Digital Service Consultants, 293 F.3d 707 (4th Cir. 2002).

[66] 315 F.3d at 259. *See* Revell v. Lidov, 317 F.3d 467 (5th Cir. 2002) (finding Texas lacks jurisdiction over defamation posted from Mass. on N.Y. online bulletin board). *But see* Northwest Healthcare Alliance v. Healthgrades.com, 2002 U.S. App. LEXIS 21131 (4th Cir. 2002) (affirming Wash. state jurisdiction over libel by Del. corporation operating online out of Colorado). *See also* rulings in Australia and United Kingdom exerting jurisdiction over U.S. publications of Dow Jones (e.g. Dow Jones v. Gutnick and Harrods Ltd. v. Dow Jones).

- *Curtis Publishing Co. v. Butts*, 388 U.S. 130 (1967) (applying *New York Times*' actual malice to public figure libel plaintiffs).
- *Garrison v. Louisiana*, 379 U.S. 64 (1964) (applying *New York Times*' actual malice in criminal libel case involving criticism of official conduct of public officials).

Keeping the following questions in mind as you read the cases below will help you focus on the most salient aspects of these cases.

- How does the Supreme Court in *New York Times v. Sullivan* distinguish that case from libel precedents and justify its divergent decision in the case?
- What is the "central meaning" of the First Amendment and why is this important to the Court's decision?
- Attempt to reconcile the Supreme Court's position on the "value" of falsity with libel law.
- Does the Supreme Court consider the quantity of distribution of *The New York Times* in Montgomery, Ala., to determine whether the libel was "published"?
- Under current rulings, "should" the Alabama courts exercise jurisdiction in *New York Times v. Sullivan*?
- What constitutes "identification" in *New York Times v. Sullivan*? Is this libel "of and concerning" Sullivan or is it more generalized criticism of government?
- Do the falsehoods in *New York Times* go to the heart of the libel?
- Who bears the burden of proof in *New York Times* and why?
- Under the *New York Times* precedent, do government officials have to prove actual malice in all libel cases?
- What defenses are presented in *New York Times*?
- In *Zeran*, how does the court distinguish publishers and distributors, and what is the libel significance of this distinction?
- What interests does the court in *Zeran* say Congress sought to protect by eliminating libel liability for online service providers?
- How does this interest compare with the constitutionally protected interest in *New York Times*, and what do the two cases suggest about the contemporary limits of libel law?
- What differences, if any, does *Zeran* draw between online and traditional media liability for libel?

New York Times Co. v. Sullivan
376 U.S. 254
(1964)

PRIOR HISTORY: Certiorari to the Supreme Court of Alabama.

JUDGES: Warren, Black, Douglas, Clark, Harlan, Brennan, Stewart, White, Goldberg

OPINION: [256] MR. JUSTICE BRENNAN delivered the opinion of the Court.

We are required in this case to determine for the first time the extent to which the constitutional protections for speech and press limit a State's power to award damages in a libel action brought by a public official against critics of his official conduct.

Respondent L. B. Sullivan is one of the three elected Commissioners of the City of Montgomery, Alabama. He testified that he was "Commissioner of Public Affairs and the duties are supervision of the Police Department, Fire Department, Department of Cemetery and Department of Scales." He brought this civil libel action against the four individual petitioners, who are Negroes and Alabama clergymen, and against petitioner the New York Times Company, a New York corporation which publishes the New York Times, a daily newspaper. A jury in the Circuit Court of Montgomery County awarded him damages of $500,000, the full amount claimed, against all the petitioners, and the Supreme Court of Alabama affirmed. 273 Ala. 656, 144 So. 2d 25.

Respondent's complaint alleged that he had been libeled by statements in a full-page advertisement that was carried in the New York Times on March 29, 1960.[1] Entitled "Heed Their Rising Voices," the advertisement began by stating that "As the whole world knows by now, thousands of Southern Negro students are engaged in widespread non-violent demonstrations in positive affirmation of the right to live in human dignity as guaranteed by the U.S. Constitution and the Bill of Rights." It went on to charge that "in their efforts to uphold these guarantees, they are being met by an unprecedented wave of terror by those who would deny and negate that document which the whole world looks upon as setting the pattern for modern freedom. . . ." Succeeding [257] paragraphs purported to illustrate the "wave of terror" by describing certain alleged events. The text concluded with an appeal for funds for three purposes: support of the student movement, "the struggle for the right-to-vote," and the legal defense of Dr. Martin Luther King, Jr.,

leader of the movement, against a perjury indictment then pending in Montgomery.

The text appeared over the names of 64 persons, many widely known for their activities in public affairs, religion, trade unions, and the performing arts. Below these names, and under a line reading "We in the south who are struggling daily for dignity and freedom warmly endorse this appeal," appeared the names of the four individual petitioners and of 16 other persons, all but two of whom were identified as clergymen in various Southern cities. The advertisement was signed at the bottom of the page by the "Committee to Defend Martin Luther King and the Struggle for Freedom in the South," and the officers of the Committee were listed.

Of the 10 paragraphs of text in the advertisement, the third and a portion of the sixth were the basis of respondent's claim of libel. They read as follows:

Third paragraph: "In Montgomery, Alabama, after students sang 'My Country, 'Tis of Thee' on the State Capitol steps, their leaders were expelled from school, and truckloads of police armed with shotguns and tear-gas ringed the Alabama State College Campus. When the entire student body protested to state authorities by refusing to re-register, their dining hall was padlocked in an attempt to starve them into submission."

Sixth paragraph: "Again and again the Southern violators have answered Dr. King's peaceful protests with intimidation and violence. They have bombed his home almost killing his wife and child. They have [258] assaulted his person. They have arrested him seven times – for 'speeding,' 'loitering' and similar 'offenses.' And now they have charged him with 'perjury' – a felony under which they could imprison him for ten years. . . ."

Although neither of these statements mentions respondent by name, he contended that the word "police" in the third paragraph referred to him as the Montgomery Commissioner who supervised the Police Department, so that he was being accused of "ringing" the campus with police. He further claimed that the paragraph would be read as imputing to the police, and hence to him, the padlocking of the dining hall in order to starve the students into submission.[2] As to the sixth paragraph, he contended that since arrests are ordinarily made by the police, the statement "They have arrested

---

[1] A copy of the advertisement is printed in the Appendix.

[2] Respondent did not consider the charge of expelling the students to be applicable to him, since "that responsibility rests with the State Department of Education."

[Dr. King] seven times" would be read as referring to him; he further contended that the "They" who did the arresting would be equated with the "They" who committed the other described acts and with the "Southern violators." Thus, he argued, the paragraph would be read as accusing the Montgomery police, and hence him, of answering Dr. King's protests with "intimidation and violence," bombing his home, assaulting his person, and charging him with perjury. Respondent and six other Montgomery residents testified that they read some or all of the statements as referring to him in his capacity as Commissioner.

It is uncontroverted that some of the statements contained in the two paragraphs were not accurate descriptions of events, which occurred in Montgomery. Although Negro students staged a demonstration on the State Capitol steps, they sang the National Anthem and not "My [259] Country, 'Tis of Thee." Although nine students were expelled by the State Board of Education, this was not for leading the demonstration at the Capitol, but for demanding service at a lunch counter in the Montgomery County Courthouse on another day. Not the entire student body, but most of it, had protested the expulsion, not by refusing to register, but by boycotting classes on a single day; virtually all the students did register for the ensuing semester. The campus dining hall was not padlocked on any occasion, and the only students who may have been barred from eating there were the few who had neither signed a pre-registration application nor requested temporary meal tickets. Although the police were deployed near the campus in large numbers on three occasions, they did not at any time "ring" the campus, and they were not called to the campus in connection with the demonstration on the State Capitol steps, as the third paragraph implied. Dr. King had not been arrested seven times, but only four; and although he claimed to have been assaulted some years earlier in connection with his arrest for loitering outside a courtroom, one of the officers who made the arrest denied that there was such an assault.

On the premise that the charges in the sixth paragraph could be read as referring to him, respondent was allowed to prove that he had not participated in the events described. Although Dr. King's home had in fact been bombed twice when his wife and child were there, both of these occasions antedated respondent's tenure as Commissioner, and the police were not only not implicated in the bombings, but had made every effort to apprehend those who were. Three of Dr. King's four arrests took place before respondent became Commissioner. Although Dr. King had in fact been indicted (he was subsequently acquitted) on two counts of perjury, each of which carried a possible five-year sentence, respondent had nothing to do with procuring the indictment.

[260] Respondent made no effort to prove that he suffered actual pecuniary loss as a result of the alleged libel.[3] One of his witnesses, a former employer, testified that if he had believed the statements, he doubted whether he "would want to be associated with anybody who would be a party to such things that are stated in that ad," and that he would not re-employ respondent if he believed "that he allowed the Police Department to do the things that the paper say he did." But neither this witness nor any of the others testified that he had actually believed the statements in their supposed reference to respondent.

The cost of the advertisement was approximately $4800, and it was published by the Times upon an order from a New York advertising agency acting for the signatory Committee. The agency submitted the advertisement with a letter from A. Philip Randolph, Chairman of the Committee, certifying that the persons whose names appeared on the advertisement had given their permission. Mr. Randolph was known to the Times' Advertising Acceptability Department as a responsible person, and in accepting the letter as sufficient proof of authorization it followed its established practice. There was testimony that the copy of the advertisement which accompanied the letter listed only the 64 names appearing under the text, and that the statement, "We in the south . . . warmly endorse this appeal," and the list of names thereunder, which included those of the individual petitioners, were subsequently added when the first proof of the advertisement was received. Each of the individual petitioners testified that he had not authorized the use of his name, and that he had been unaware of its use until receipt of respondent's demand for a retraction. The manager of the Advertising Acceptability [261] Department testified that he had approved the advertisement for publication because he knew nothing to cause him to believe that anything in it was false, and because it bore the endorsement of "a number of people who are well known and whose reputation" he "had no reason to question." Neither he nor anyone else at the Times made an effort to confirm the accuracy of the advertisement, either by checking it against recent Times news stories relating to some of the described events or by any other means.

Alabama law denies a public officer recovery of punitive damages in a libel action brought on account of a publication concerning his official

---

[3] Approximately 394 copies of the edition of the Times containing the advertisement were circulated in Alabama. Of these, about 35 copies were distributed in Montgomery County. The total circulation of the Times for that day was approximately 650,000 copies.

conduct unless he first makes a written demand for a public retraction and the defendant fails or refuses to comply. Alabama Code, Tit. 7, § 914. Respondent served such a demand upon each of the petitioners. None of the individual petitioners responded to the demand, primarily because each took the position that he had not authorized the use of his name on the advertisement and therefore had not published the statements that respondent alleged had libeled him. The Times did not publish a retraction in response to the demand, but wrote respondent a letter stating, among other things, that "we ... are somewhat puzzled as to how you think the statements in any way reflect on you," and "you might, if you desire, let us know in what respect you claim that the statements in the advertisement reflect on you." Respondent filed this suit a few days later without answering the letter. The Times did, however, subsequently publish a retraction of the advertisement upon the demand of Governor John Patterson of Alabama, who asserted that the publication charged him with "grave misconduct and ... improper actions and omissions as Governor of Alabama and Ex-Officio Chairman of the State Board of Education of Alabama." When asked to explain why there had been a retraction for the Governor but not for respondent, the [262] Secretary of the Times testified: "We did that because we didn't want anything that was published by The Times to be a reflection on the State of Alabama and the Governor was, as far as we could see, the embodiment of the State of Alabama and the proper representative of the State and, furthermore, we had by that time learned more of the actual facts which the ad purported to recite and, finally, the ad did refer to the action of the State authorities and the Board of Education presumably of which the Governor is the ex-officio chairman ..." On the other hand, he testified that he did not think that "any of the language in there referred to Mr. Sullivan."

The trial judge submitted the case to the jury under instructions that the statements in the advertisement were "libelous per se" and were not privileged, so that petitioners might be held liable if the jury found that they had published the advertisement and that the statements were made "of and concerning" respondent. The jury was instructed that, because the statements were libelous per se, "the law ... implies legal injury from the bare fact of publication itself," "falsity and malice are presumed," "general damages need not be alleged or proved but are presumed," and "punitive damages may be awarded by the jury even though the amount of actual damages is neither found nor shown." An award of punitive damages – as distinguished from "general" damages, which are compensatory in nature – apparently requires proof of actual malice under Alabama law, and the judge

charged that "mere negligence or carelessness is not evidence of actual malice or malice in fact, and does not justify an award of exemplary or punitive damages." He refused to charge, however, that the jury must be "convinced" of malice, in the sense of "actual intent" to harm or "gross negligence and recklessness," to make such an award, and he also refused to require that a verdict for respondent differentiate between compensatory and punitive damages. The judge rejected petitioners' contention [263] that his rulings abridged the freedoms of speech and of the press that are guaranteed by the First and Fourteenth Amendments.

In affirming the judgment, the Supreme Court of Alabama sustained the trial judge's rulings and instructions in all respects. 273 Ala. 656, 144 So. 2d 25. It held that "where the words published tend to injure a person libeled by them in his reputation, profession, trade or business, or charge him with an indictable offense, or tend to bring the individual into public contempt," they are "libelous per se"; that "the matter complained of is, under the above doctrine, libelous per se, if it was published of and concerning the plaintiff"; and that it was actionable without "proof of pecuniary injury ..., such injury being implied." Id., at 673, 676, 144 So. 2d at 37, 41. It approved the trial court's ruling that the jury could find the statements to have been made "of and concerning" respondent, stating: "We think it common knowledge that the average person knows that municipal agents, such as police and firemen, and others, are under the control and direction of the city governing body, and more particularly under the direction and control of a single commissioner. In measuring the performance or deficiencies of such groups, praise or criticism is usually attached to the official in complete control of the body." Id., at 674-675, 144 So. 2d at 39. In sustaining the trial court's determination that the verdict was not excessive, the court said that malice could be inferred from the Times' "irresponsibility" in printing the advertisement while "the Times in its own files had articles already published which would have demonstrated the falsity of the allegations in the advertisement"; from the Times' failure to retract for respondent while retracting for the Governor, whereas the falsity of some of the allegations was then known to the Times and "the matter contained in the advertisement was equally false as to both parties"; and from the testimony of the Times' Secretary that, [264] apart from the statement that the dining hall was padlocked, he thought the two paragraphs were "substantially correct." Id., at 686-687, 144 So. 2d at 50-51. The court reaffirmed a statement in an earlier opinion that "There is no legal measure of damages in cases of this character." Id., at 686, 144 So. 2d at 50. It rejected petitioners' constitutional contentions with the brief statements that "The First Amendment of the U.S. Constitution does not protect libelous publications" and "The Fourteenth Amendment is directed against State action and not private action." Id., at 676, 144 So. 2d at 40.

[1]Because of the importance of the constitutional issues involved, we granted the separate petitions for certiorari of the individual petitioners and of the Times. 371 U.S. 946. We reverse the judgment. We hold that the rule of law applied by the Alabama courts is constitutionally deficient for failure to provide the safeguards for freedom of speech and of the press that are required by the First and Fourteenth Amendments in a libel action brought by a public official against critics of his official conduct.[4] [265] We further hold that under the proper safeguards the evidence presented in this case is constitutionally insufficient to support the judgment for respondent.

I. [2][3][4] We may dispose at the outset of two grounds asserted to insulate the judgment of the Alabama courts from constitutional scrutiny. The first is the proposition relied on by the State Supreme Court – that "The Fourteenth Amendment is directed against State action and not private action." That proposition has no application to this case. Although this is a civil lawsuit between private parties, the Alabama courts have applied a state rule of law, which petitioners claim to impose invalid restrictions on their constitutional freedoms of speech and press. It matters not that that law has been applied in a civil action and that it is common law only, though supplemented by statute. See, e.g., Alabama Code, Tit. 7, §§ 908-917. The test is not the form in which state power has been applied but, whatever the form, whether such power has in fact been exercised. See Ex parte Virginia, 100 U.S. 339, 346-347; American Federation of Labor v. Swing, 312 U.S. 321.

---

[4] Since we sustain the contentions of all the petitioners under the First Amendment's guarantees of freedom of speech and of the press as applied to the States by the Fourteenth Amendment, we do not decide the questions presented by the other claims of violation of the Fourteenth Amendment. The individual petitioners contend that the judgment against them offends the Due Process Clause because there was no evidence to show that they had published or authorized the publication of the alleged libel, and that the Due Process and Equal Protection Clauses were violated by racial segregation and racial bias in the courtroom. The Times contends that the assumption of jurisdiction over its corporate person by the Alabama courts overreaches the territorial limits of the Due Process Clause. The latter claim is foreclosed from our review by the ruling of the Alabama courts that the Times entered a general appearance in the action and thus waived its jurisdictional objection; we cannot say that this ruling lacks "fair or substantial support" in prior Alabama decisions. See Thompson v. Wilson, 224 Ala. 299, 140 So. 439 (1932); compare N. A. A. C. P. v. Alabama, 357 U.S. 449, 454-458.

The second contention is that the constitutional guarantees of freedom of speech and of the press are inapplicable here, at least so far as the Times is concerned, because the allegedly libelous statements were published as part of a paid, "commercial" advertisement. The argument relies on Valentine v. Chrestensen, 316 U.S. 52, where the Court held that a city ordinance forbidding street distribution of commercial and business advertising matter did not abridge the First Amendment freedoms, even as applied to a handbill having a commercial message on one side but a protest against certain official action on the other. The reliance is wholly misplaced. The Court in Chrestensen reaffirmed the constitutional protection for "the freedom of communicating [266] information and disseminating opinion"; its holding was based upon the factual conclusions that the handbill was "purely commercial advertising" and that the protest against official action had been added only to evade the ordinance.

[5][6] The publication here was not a "commercial" advertisement in the sense in which the word was used in Chrestensen. It communicated information, expressed opinion, recited grievances, protested claimed abuses, and sought financial support on behalf of a movement whose existence and objectives are matters of the highest public interest and concern. See N. A. A. C. P. v. Button, 371 U.S. 415, 435. That the Times was paid for publishing the advertisement is as immaterial in this connection as is the fact that newspapers and books are sold. Smith v. California, 361 U.S. 147, 150; cf. Bantam Books, Inc., v. Sullivan, 372 U.S. 58, 64, n. 6. Any other conclusion would discourage newspapers from carrying "editorial advertisements" of this type, and so might shut off an important outlet for the promulgation of information and ideas by persons who do not themselves have access to publishing facilities – who wish to exercise their freedom of speech even though they are not members of the press. Cf. Lovell v. Griffin, 303 U.S. 444, 452; Schneider v. State, 308 U.S. 147, 164. The effect would be to shackle the First Amendment in its attempt to secure "the widest possible dissemination of information from diverse and antagonistic sources." Associated Press v. United States, 326 U.S. 1, 20. To avoid placing such a handicap upon the freedoms of expression, we hold that if the allegedly libelous statements would otherwise be constitutionally protected from the present judgment, they do not forfeit that protection because they were published in the form of a paid advertisement.[5]

II. [267] Under Alabama law as applied in this case, a publication is "libelous per se" if the

---

[5] See American Law Institute, Restatement of Torts, § 593, Comment b (1938).

words "tend to injure a person ... in his reputation" or to "bring [him] into public contempt"; the trial court stated that the standard was met if the words are such as to "injure him in his public office, or impute misconduct to him in his office, or want of official integrity, or want of fidelity to a public trust... ." The jury must find that the words were published "of and concerning" the plaintiff, but where the plaintiff is a public official his place in the governmental hierarchy is sufficient evidence to support a finding that his reputation has been affected by statements that reflect upon the agency of which he is in charge. Once "libel per se" has been established, the defendant has no defense as to stated facts unless he can persuade the jury that they were true in all their particulars. Alabama Ride Co. v. Vance, 235 Ala. 263, 178 So. 438 (1938); Johnson Publishing Co. v. Davis, 271 Ala. 474, 494-495, 124 So. 2d 441, 457-458 (1960). His privilege of "fair comment" for expressions of opinion depends on the truth of the facts upon which the comment is based. Parsons v. Age-Herald Publishing Co., 181 Ala. 439, 450, 61 So. 345, 350 (1913).

Unless he can discharge the burden of proving truth, general damages are presumed, and may be awarded without proof of pecuniary injury. A showing of actual malice is apparently a prerequisite to recovery of punitive damages, and the defendant may in any event forestall a punitive award by a retraction meeting the statutory requirements. Good motives and belief in truth do not negate an inference of malice, but are relevant only in mitigation of punitive damages if the jury chooses to accord them weight. Johnson Publishing Co. v. Davis, supra, 271 Ala., at 495, 124 So. 2d, at 458.

[268] The question before us is whether this rule of liability, as applied to an action brought by a public official against critics of his official conduct, abridges the freedom of speech and of the press that is guaranteed by the First and Fourteenth Amendments.

[7][8] Respondent relies heavily, as did the Alabama courts, on statements of this Court to the effect that the Constitution does not protect libelous publications.[6] Those statements do not foreclose our inquiry here. None of the cases sustained the use of libel laws to impose sanctions upon expression critical of the official conduct of public officials. The dictum in Pennekamp v. Florida, 328 U.S. 331, 348-349, that "when the statements amount to

defamation, a judge has such remedy in damages for libel as do other public servants," implied no view as to what remedy might constitutionally be afforded to public officials. In Beauharnais v. Illinois, 343 U.S. 250, the Court sustained an Illinois criminal libel statute as applied to a publication held to be both defamatory of a racial group and "liable to cause violence and disorder." But the Court was careful to note that it "retains and exercises authority to nullify action which encroaches on freedom of utterance under the guise of punishing libel"; for "public men, are, as it were, public property," and "discussion cannot be denied and the right, as well as the duty, of criticism must not be stifled." Id., at 263-264, and n. 18.

In the only previous case that did present the question of constitutional limitations upon the power to award damages for libel of a public official, the Court was equally divided and the question was not decided. Schenectady Union Pub. Co. v. Sweeney, 316 U.S. 642. [269] In deciding the question now, we are compelled by neither precedent nor policy to give any more weight to the epithet "libel" than we have to other "mere labels" of state law. N. A. A. C. P. v. Button, 371 U.S. 415, 429. Like insurrection,[7] contempt,[8] advocacy of unlawful acts,[9] breach of the peace,[10] obscenity,[11] solicitation of legal business,[12] and the various other formulae for the repression of expression that have been challenged in this Court, libel can claim no talismanic immunity from constitutional limitations. It must be measured by standards that satisfy the First Amendment.

[9][10][11] The general proposition that freedom of expression upon public questions is secured by the First Amendment has long beensettled by our decisions. The constitutional safeguard, we have said, "was fashioned to assure people." Roth v. United States, 354 U.S. 476, 484. "The maintenance of the opportunity for free political discussion to the end that government may be responsive to the will of the people and that changes may be obtained by lawful means, an opportunity essential to the security of the Republic, is a fundamental principle of our constitutional system." Stromberg v. California, 283 U.S. 359, 369. "It is a prized American privilege to speak one's mind, although not always with perfect good taste, on all public institutions," Bridges v. California, 314 U.S. 252, 270, and this opportunity is to be afforded for "vigorous advocacy" no less than "abstract discussion." N. A. A. C. P. v. Button, 371 U.S. 415,

---

[6] Konigsberg v. State Bar of California, 366 U.S. 36, 49, and n. 10; Times Film Corp. v. City of Chicago, 365 U.S. 43, 48; Roth v. United States, 354 U.S. 476, 486-487; Beauharnais v. Illinois, 343 U.S. 250, 266; Pennekamp v. Florida, 328 U.S. 331, 348-349; Chaplinsky v. New Hampshire, 315 U.S. 568, 572; Near v. Minnesota, 283 U.S. 697, 715.

[7] Herndon v. Lowry, 301 U.S. 242.
[8] Bridges v. California, 314 U.S. 252; Pennekamp v. Florida, 328 U.S. 331.
[9] De Jonge v. Oregon, 299 U.S. 353.
[10] Edwards v. South Carolina, 372 U.S. 229.
[11] Roth v. United States, 354 U.S. 476.
[12] N. A. A. C. P. v. Button, 371 U.S. 415.

429. [270] The First Amendment, said Judge Learned Hand, "presupposes that right conclusions are more likely to be gathered out of a multitude of tongues, than through any kind of authoritative selection. To many this is, and always will be, folly; but we have staked upon it our all." United States v. Associated Press, 52 F. Supp. 362, 372 (D. C. S. D. N. Y. 1943). Mr. Justice Brandeis, in his concurring opinion in Whitney v. California, 274 U.S. 357, 375-376, gave the principle its classic formulation:

"Those who won our independence believed . . . that public discussion is a political duty; and that this should be a fundamental principle of the American government. They recognized the risks to which all human institutions are subject. But they knew that order cannot be secured merely through fear of punishment for its infraction; that it is hazardous to discourage thought, hope and imagination; that fear breeds repression; that repression breeds hate; that hate menaces stable government; that the path of safety lies in the opportunity to discuss freely supposed grievances and proposed remedies; and that the fitting remedy for evil counsels is good ones. Believing in the power of reason as applied through public discussion, they eschewed silence coerced by law – the argument of force in its worst form. Recognizing the occasional tyrannies of governing majorities, they amended the Constitution so that free speech and assembly should be guaranteed."

[12][13] Thus we consider this case against the background of a profound national commitment to the principle that debate on public issues should be uninhibited, robust, and wide-open, and that it may well include vehement, caustic, and sometimes unpleasantly sharp attacks on government and public officials. See Terminiello v. Chicago, 337 U.S. 1, 4; De Jonge v. Oregon, 299 U.S. 353, 365. [271] The present advertisement, as an expression of grievance and protest on one of the major public issues of our time, would seem clearly to qualify for the constitutional protection. The question is whether it forfeits that protection by the falsity of some of its factual statements and by its alleged defamation of respondent.

[14] Authoritative interpretations of the First Amendment guarantees have consistently refused to recognize an exception for any test of truth – whether administered by judges, juries, or administrative officials – and especially one that puts the burden of proving truth on the speaker. Cf. Speiser v. Randall, 357 U.S. 513, 525-526. The constitutional protection does not turn upon "the truth, popularity, or social utility of the ideas and beliefs which are offered." N. A. A. C. P. v. Button, 371 U.S. 415, 445. As Madison said, "Some degree of abuse is inseparable from the proper use of every thing; and in no instance is this more true than in that of the press." 4 Elliot's Debates on the Federal

Constitution (1876), p. 571. In Cantwell v. Connecticut, 310 U.S. 296, 310, the Court declared:

"In the realm of religious faith, and in that of political belief, sharp differences arise. In both fields the tenets of one man may seem the rankest error to his neighbor. To persuade others to his own point of view, the pleader, as we know, at times, resorts to exaggeration, to vilification of men who have been, or are, prominent in church or state, and even to false statement. But the people of this nation have ordained in the light of history, that, in spite of the probability of excesses and abuses, these liberties are, in the long view, essential to enlightened opinion and right conduct on the part of the citizens of a democracy."

That erroneous statement is inevitable in free debate, and that it must be protected if the freedoms of expression [272] are to have the "breathing space" that they "need . . . to survive," N. A. A. C. P. v. Button, 371 U.S. 415, 433, was also recognized by the Court of Appeals for the District of Columbia Circuit in Sweeney v. Patterson, 76 U.S. App. D. C. 23, 24, 128 F.2d 457, 458 (1942), cert. denied, 317 U.S. 678. Judge Edgerton spoke for a unanimous court which affirmed the dismissal of a Congressman's libel suit based upon a newspaper article charging him with anti-Semitism in opposing a judicial appointment. He said:

"Cases which impose liability for erroneous reports of the political conduct of officials reflect the obsolete doctrine that the governed must not criticize their governors ... . The interest of the public here outweighs the interest of appellant or any other individual. The protection of the public requires not merely discussion, but information. Political conduct and views, which some respectable people approve, and others condemn, are constantly imputed to Congressmen. Errors of fact, particularly in regard to a man's mental states and processes, are inevitable ... . Whatever is added to the field of libel is taken from the field of free debate."[13]

[15] Injury to official reputation affords no more warrant for repressing speech that would otherwise be free than does factual error. Where judicial officers are involved, this Court has held that concern for the dignity and [273] reputation of the courts does not justify the punishment as criminal

---

[13] See also Mill, On Liberty (Oxford: Blackwell, 1947), at 47: ". . . To argue sophistically, to suppress facts or arguments, to misstate the elements of the case, or misrepresent the opposite opinion . . . all this, even to the most aggravated degree, is so continually done in perfect good faith, by persons who are not considered, and in many other respects may not deserve to be considered, ignorant or incompetent, that it is rarely possible, on adequate grounds, conscientiously to stamp the misrepresentation as morally culpable; and still less could law presume to interfere with this kind of controversial misconduct."

contempt of criticism of the judge or his decision. Bridges v. California, 314 U.S. 252.

This is true even though the utterance contains "half-truths" and "misinformation." Pennekamp v. Florida, 328 U.S. 331, 342, 343, n. 5, 345. Such repression can be justified, if at all, only by a clear and present danger of the obstruction of justice. See also Craig v. Harney, 331 U.S. 367; Wood v. Georgia, 370 U.S. 375. If judges are to be treated as "men of fortitude, able to thrive in a hardy climate," Craig v. Harney, supra, 331 U.S., at 376, surely the same must be true of other government officials, such as elected city commissioners.[14] Criticism of their official conduct does not lose its constitutional protection merely because it is effective criticism and hence diminishes their official reputations.

[16] If neither factual error nor defamatory content suffices to remove the constitutional shield from criticism of official conduct, the combination of the two elements is no less inadequate. This is the lesson to be drawn from the great controversy over the Sedition Act of 1798, 1 Stat. 596, which first crystallized a national awareness of the central meaning of the First Amendment. See Levy, Legacy of Suppression (1960), at 258 et seq.; Smith, Freedom's Fetters (1956), at 426, 431, and passim. That statute made it a crime, punishable by a $5,000 fine and five years in prison, "if any person shall write, print, utter or publish . . . any false, scandalous and malicious [274] writing or writings against the government of the United States, or either house of the Congress ... , or the President ..., with intent to defame ... or to bring them, or either of them, into contempt or disrepute; or to excite against them, or either or any of them, the hatred of the good people of the United States." The Act allowed the defendant the defense of truth, and provided that the jury were to be judges both of the law and the facts. Despite these qualifications, the Act was vigorously condemned as unconstitutional in an attack joined in by Jefferson and Madison. In the famous Virginia Resolutions of 1798, the General Assembly of Virginia resolved that it "doth particularly protest against the palpable and alarming infractions of the Constitution, in the two late cases of the 'Alien and Sedition Acts,' passed at the last session of Congress... . [The Sedition Act] exercises ... a power not delegated by the

Constitution, but, on the contrary, expressly and positively forbidden by one of the amendments thereto – a power which, more than any other, ought to produce universal alarm, because it is levelled against the right of freely examining public characters and measures, and of free communication among the people thereon, which has ever been justly deemed the only effectual guardian of every other right." 4 Elliot's Debates, supra, pp. 553-554.

Madison prepared the Report in support of the protest. His premise was that the Constitution created a form of government under which "The people, not the government, possess the absolute sovereignty." The structure of the government dispersed power in reflection of the people's distrust of concentrated power, and of power itself at all levels. This form of government was "altogether different" from the British form, under which the Crown was sovereign and the people were subjects. "Is [275] it not natural and necessary, under such different circumstances," he asked, "that a different degree of freedom in the use of the press should be contemplated?" Id., pp. 569-570. Earlier, in a debate in the House of Representatives, Madison had said: "If we advert to the nature of Republican Government, we shall find that the censorial power is in the people over the Government, and not in the Government over the people." 4 Annals of Congress, p. 934 (1794).

Of the exercise of that power by the press, his Report said: "In every state, probably, in the Union, the press has exerted a freedom in canvassing the merits and measures of public men, of every description, which has not been confined to the strict limits of the common law. On this footing the freedom of the press has stood; on this foundation it yet stands ... ." 4 Elliot's Debates, supra, p. 570. The right of free public discussion of the stewardship of public officials was thus, in Madison's view, a fundamental principle of the American form of government.[15]

---

[14] The climate in which public officials operate, especially during a political campaign, has been described by one commentator in the following terms: "Charges of gross incompetence, disregard of the public interest, communist sympathies, and the like usually have filled the air; and hints of bribery, embezzlement, and other criminal conduct are not infrequent." Noel, Defamation of Public Officers and Candidates, 49 Col. L. Rev. 875 (1949).
For a similar description written 60 years earlier, see Chase, Criticism of Public Officers and Candidates for Office, 23 Am. L. Rev. 346 (1889).

[15] The Report on the Virginia Resolutions further stated: "It is manifestly impossible to punish the intent to bring those who administer the government into disrepute or contempt, without striking at the right of freely discussing public characters and measures; ... which, again, is equivalent to a protection of those who administer the government, if they should at any time deserve the contempt or hatred of the people, against being exposed to it, by free animadversions on their characters and conduct. Nor can there be a doubt ... that a government thus intrenched in penal statutes against the just and natural effects of a culpable administration, will easily evade the responsibility which is essential to a faithful discharge of its duty.
"Let it be recollected, lastly, that the right of electing the members of the government constitutes more particularly the essence of a free and responsible government. The value and efficacy of this right depends on the knowledge of the comparative merits and demerits of the candidates for public trust, and on the equal freedom, consequently, of examining

[276] Although the Sedition Act was never tested in this Court, n16 the attack upon its validity has carried the day in the court of history. Fines levied in its prosecution were repaid by Act of Congress on the ground that it was unconstitutional. See, e.g., Act of July 4, 1840, c. 45, 6 Stat. 802, accompanied by H. R. Rep. No. 86, 26th Cong., 1st Sess. (1840). Calhoun, reporting to the Senate on February 4, 1836, assumed that its invalidity was a matter "which no one now doubts." Report with Senate bill No. 122, 24th Cong., 1st Sess., p. 3. Jefferson, as President, pardoned those who had been convicted and sentenced under the Act and remitted their fines, stating: "I discharged every person under punishment or prosecution under the sedition law, because I considered, and now consider, that law to be a nullity, as absolute and as palpable as if Congress had ordered us to fall down and worship a golden image." Letter to Mrs. Adams, July 22, 1804, 4 Jefferson's Works (Washington ed.), pp. 555, 556. The invalidity of the Act has also been assumed by Justices of this Court. See Holmes, J., dissenting and joined by Brandeis, J., in Abrams v. United States, 250 U.S. 616, 630; Jackson, J., dissenting in Beauharnais v. Illinois, 343 U.S. 250, 288-289; Douglas, The Right of the People (1958), p. 47. See also Cooley, Constitutional Limitations (8th ed., Carrington, 1927), pp. 899-900; Chafee, Free Speech in the United States (1942), pp. 27-28. These views reflect a broad consensus that the Act, because of the restraint it imposed upon criticism of government and public officials, was inconsistent with the First Amendment.[16]

[17] There is no force in respondent's argument that the constitutional limitations implicit in the history of the Sedition Act apply only to Congress and not to the States. It is true that the First Amendment was originally addressed only to action by the Federal Government, and [277] that Jefferson, for one, while denying the power of Congress "to controul the freedom of the press," recognized such a power in the States. See the 1804 Letter to Abigail Adams quoted in Dennis v. United States, 341 U.S. 494, 522, n. 4 (concurring opinion). But this distinction was eliminated with the adoption of the Fourteenth Amendment and the application to the States of the First Amendment's restrictions. See, e.g., Gitlow v. New York, 268 U.S. 652, 666; Schneider v. State, 308 U.S. 147, 160; Bridges v. California, 314 U.S. 252, 268; Edwards v. South Carolina, 372 U.S. 229, 235.

[18] What a State may not constitutionally bring about by means of a criminal statute is likewise beyond the reach of its civil law of libel.[17] The fear of damage awards under a rule such as that invoked by the Alabama courts here may be markedly more inhibiting than the fear of prosecution under a criminal statute. See City of Chicago v. Tribune Co., 307 Ill. 595, 607, 139 N. E. 86, 90 (1923). Alabama, for example, has a criminal libel law which subjects to prosecution "any person who speaks, writes, or prints of and concerning another any accusation falsely and maliciously importing the commission by such person of a felony, or any other indictable offense involving moral turpitude," and which allows as punishment upon conviction a fine not exceeding $500 and a prison sentence of six months. Alabama Code, Tit. 14, § 350. Presumably a person charged with violation of this statute enjoys ordinary criminal-law safeguards such as the requirements of an indictment and of proof beyond a reasonable doubt. These safeguards are not available to the defendant in a civil action. The judgment awarded in this case – without the need for any proof of actual pecuniary loss – was one thousand times greater than the maximum fine provided by the Alabama criminal statute, and one hundred times greater than that provided by the Sedition Act. [278] And since there is no double-jeopardy limitation applicable to civil lawsuits, this is not the only judgment that may be awarded against petitioners for the same publication.[18] Whether or not a newspaper can survive a succession of such judgments, the pall of fear and timidity imposed upon those who would give voice to public criticism is an atmosphere in which the First Amendment freedoms cannot survive. Plainly the Alabama law of civil libel is "a form of regulation that creates hazards to protected freedoms markedly greater than those that attend reliance upon the criminal law." Bantam Books, Inc., v. Sullivan, 372 U.S. 58, 70.

[19] The state rule of law is not saved by its allowance of the defense of truth. A defense for erroneous statements honestly made is no less essential here than was the requirement of proof of guilty knowledge which, in Smith v. California, 361 U.S. 147, we held indispensable to a valid conviction of a bookseller for possessing obscene writings for sale. We said:

"For if the bookseller is criminally liable without knowledge of the contents, ... he will tend to restrict the books he sells to those he has inspected; and thus the State will have imposed a restriction upon the distribution of constitutionally protected as well as obscene literature ... . And the bookseller's

---

and discussing these merits and demerits of the candidates respectively." 4 Elliot's Debates, supra, p. 575.
[16] The Act expired by its terms in 1801.
[17] Cf. Farmers Union v. WDAY, 360 U.S. 525, 535.

---

[18] The Times states that four other libel suits based on the advertisement have been filed against it by others who have served as Montgomery City Commissioners and by the Governor of Alabama; that another $500,000 verdict has been awarded in the only one of these cases that has yet gone to trial; and that the damages sought in the other three total $2,000,000.

burden would become the public's burden, for by restricting him the public's access to reading matter would be restricted ... . [His] timidity in the face of his absolute criminal liability, thus would tend to restrict the public's access to forms of the printed word which the State could not constitutionally [279] suppress directly. The bookseller's self-censorship, compelled by the State, would be a censorship affecting the whole public, hardly less virulent for being privately administered. Through it, the distribution of all books, both obscene and not obscene, would be impeded." (361 U.S. 147, 153-154.)

A rule compelling the critic of official conduct to guarantee the truth of all his factual assertions – and to do so on pain of libel judgments virtually unlimited in amount – leads to a comparable "self-censorship." Allowance of the defense of truth, with the burden of proving it on the defendant, does not mean that only false speech will be deterred.[19] Even courts accepting this defense as an adequate safeguard have recognized the difficulties of adducing legal proofs that the alleged libel was true in all its factual particulars. See, e.g., Post Publishing Co. v. Hallam, 59 F. 530, 540 (C. A. 6th Cir. 1893); see also Noel, Defamation of Public Officers and Candidates, 49 Col. L. Rev. 875, 892 (1949). Under such a rule, would-be critics of official conduct may be deterred from voicing their criticism, even though it is believed to be true and even though it is in fact true, because of doubt whether it can be proved in court or fear of the expense of having to do so. They tend to make only statements which "steer far wider of the unlawful zone." Speiser v. Randall, supra, 357 U.S., at 526. The rule thus dampens the vigor and limits the variety of public debate. It is inconsistent with the First and Fourteenth Amendments.

[20] The constitutional guarantees require, we think, a federal rule that prohibits a public official from recovering damages for a defamatory falsehood relating to his official conduct unless he proves that the statement was made [280] with "actual malice" – that is, with knowledge that it was false or with reckless disregard of whether it was false or not. An oft-cited statement of a like rule, which has been adopted by a number of state courts,[20] is found in the Kansas case of Coleman v.

MacLennan, 78 Kan. 711, 98 P. 281 (1908). The State Attorney General, a candidate for re-election and a member of the commission charged with the management and control of the state school fund, sued a newspaper publisher for alleged libel in an article purporting to state facts relating to his official conduct in connection with a school-fund transaction. The defendant pleaded privilege and the trial judge, over the plaintiff's objection, instructed the jury that

"where an article is published and circulated among voters for the sole purpose of giving what the defendant [281] believes to be truthful information concerning a candidate for public office and for the purpose of enabling such voters to cast their ballot more intelligently, and the whole thing is done in good faith and without malice, the article is privileged, although the principal matters contained in the article may be untrue in fact and derogatory to the character of the plaintiff; and in such a case the burden is on the plaintiff to show actual malice in the publication of the article."

In answer to a special question, the jury found that the plaintiff had not proved actual malice, and a general verdict was returned for the defendant. On appeal the Supreme Court of Kansas, in an opinion by Justice Burch, reasoned as follows (78 Kan., at 724, 98 P., at 286):

"It is of the utmost consequence that the people should discuss the character and qualifications of candidates for their suffrages. The importance to the state and to society of such discussions is so vast, and the advantages derived are so great, that they more than counterbalance the inconvenience of private persons whose conduct may be involved, and occasional injury to the reputations of individuals must yield to the public welfare,

Salinger v. Cowles, 195 Iowa 873, 889, 191 N. W. 167, 174 (1922); Snively v. Record Publishing Co., 185 Cal. 565, 571-576, 198 P. 1 (1921); McLean v. Merriman, 42 S. D. 394, 175 N. W. 878 (1920). Applying the same rule to candidates for public office, see, e.g., Phoenix Newspapers v. Choisser, 82 Ariz. 271, 276-277, 312 P. 2d 150, 154 (1957); Friedell v. Blakely Printing Co., 163 Minn. 226, 230, 203 N. W. 974, 975 (1925). And see Chagnon v. Union-Leader Corp., 103 N. H. 426, 438, 174 A. 2d 825, 833 (1961), cert. denied, 369 U.S. 830.
The consensus of scholarly opinion apparently favors the rule that is here adopted. E.g., 1 Harper and James, Torts, § 5.26, at 449-450 (1956); Noel, Defamation of Public Officers and Candidates, 49 Col. L. Rev. 875, 891-895, 897, 903 (1949); Hallen, Fair Comment, 8 Tex. L. Rev. 41, 61 (1929); Smith, Charges Against Candidates, 18 Mich. L. Rev. 1, 115 (1919); Chase, Criticism of Public Officers and Candidates for Office, 23 Am. L. Rev. 346, 367-371 (1889); Cooley, Constitutional Limitations (7th ed., Lane, 1903), at 604, 616-628. But see, e.g., American Law Institute, Restatement of Torts, § 598, Comment a (1938) (reversing the position taken in Tentative Draft 13, § 1041 (2) (1936)); Veeder, Freedom of Public Discussion, 23 Harv. L. Rev. 413, 419 (1910).

---

[19] Even a false statement may be deemed to make a valuable contribution to public debate, since it brings about "the clearer perception and livelier impression of truth, produced by its collision with error." Mill, On Liberty (Oxford: Blackwell, 1947), at 15; see also Milton, Areopagitica, in Prose Works (Yale, 1959), Vol. II, at 561.

[20] E.g., Ponder v. Cobb, 257 N. C. 281, 299, 126 S.E.2d 67, 80 (1962); Lawrence v. Fox, 357 Mich. 134, 146, 97 N.W.2d 719, 725 (1959); Stice v. Beacon Newspaper Corp., 185 Kan. 61, 65-67, 340 P.2d 396, 400-401 (1959); Bailey v. Charleston Mail Assn., 126 W. Va. 292, 307, 27 S.E.2d 837, 844 (1943);

although at times such injury may be great. The public benefit from publicity is so great, and the chance of injury to private character so small, that such discussion must be privileged."

The court thus sustained the trial court's instruction as a correct statement of the law, saying:

"In such a case the occasion gives rise to a privilege, qualified to this extent: any one claiming to be defamed by the communication must show actual malice or go remediless. This privilege extends to a great variety of subjects, and includes matters of [282] public concern, public men, and candidates for office." 78 Kan., at 723, 98 P., at 285.

Such a privilege for criticism of official conduct[21] is appropriately analogous to the protection accorded a public official when he is sued for libel by a private citizen. In Barr v. Matteo, 360 U.S. 564, 575, this Court held the utterance of a federal official to be absolutely privileged if made "within the outer perimeter" of his duties. The States accord the same immunity to statements of their highest officers, although some differentiate their lesser officials and qualify the privilege they enjoy.[22] But all hold that all officials are protected unless actual malice can be proved. The reason for the official privilege is said to be that the threat of damage suits would otherwise "inhibit the fearless, vigorous, and effective administration of policies of government" and "dampen the ardor of all but the most resolute, or the most irresponsible, in the unflinching discharge of their duties." Barr v. Matteo, supra, 360 U.S., at 571. Analogous considerations support the privilege for the citizen-critic of government. It is as much his duty to criticize as it is the official's duty to administer. See Whitney v. California, 274 U.S. 357, 375 (concurring opinion of Mr. Justice Brandeis), quoted supra, p. 270. As Madison said, see supra, p. 275, "the censorial power is in the people over the Government, and not in the Government over the people." It would give public servants an unjustified preference over the public they serve, if critics of official conduct [283] did not have a fair equivalent of the immunity granted to the officials themselves.

We conclude that such a privilege is required by the First and Fourteenth Amendments.

III.   [21][22][23] We hold today that the Constitution delimits a State's power to award damages for libel in actions brought by public officials against critics of their official conduct.

Since this is such an action,[23] the rule requiring proof of actual malice is applicable. While Alabama law apparently requires proof of actual malice for an award of punitive damages,[24] where general damages are concerned malice is "presumed." Such a presumption is inconsistent [284] with the federal rule. "The power to create presumptions is not a means of escape from constitutional restrictions," Bailey v. Alabama, 219 U.S. 219, 239; "the showing of malice required for the forfeiture of the privilege is not presumed but is a matter for proof by the plaintiff ... ." Lawrence v. Fox, 357 Mich.

---

[21] The privilege immunizing honest misstatements of fact is often referred to as a "conditional" privilege to distinguish it from the "absolute" privilege recognized in judicial, legislative, administrative and executive proceedings. See, e.g., Prosser, Torts (2d ed., 1955), § 95.

[22] See 1 Harper and James, Torts, § 5.23, at 429-430 (1956); Prosser, Torts (2d ed., 1955), at 612-613; American Law Institute, Restatement of Torts (1938), § 591.

---

[23] We have no occasion here to determine how far down into the lower ranks of government employees the "public official" designation would extend for purposes of this rule, or otherwise to specify categories of persons who would or would not be included. Cf. Barr v. Matteo, 360 U.S. 564, 573-575. Nor need we here determine the boundaries of the "official conduct" concept. It is enough for the present case that respondent's position as an elected city commissioner clearly made him a public official, and that the allegations in the advertisement concerned what was allegedly his official conduct as Commissioner in charge of the Police Department. As to the statements alleging the assaulting of Dr. King and the bombing of his home, it is immaterial that they might not be considered to involve respondent's official conduct if he himself had been accused of perpetrating the assault and the bombing. Respondent does not claim that the statements charged him personally with these acts; his contention is that the advertisement connects him with them only in his official capacity as the Commissioner supervising the police, on the theory that the police might be equated with the "They" who did the bombing and assaulting. Thus, if these allegations can be read as referring to respondent at all, they must be read as describing his performance of his official duties.

[24] Johnson Publishing Co. v. Davis, 271 Ala. 474, 487, 124 So. 2d 441, 450 (1960). Thus, the trial judge here instructed the jury that "mere negligence or carelessness is not evidence of actual malice or malice in fact, and does not justify an award of exemplary or punitive damages in an action for libel."

The court refused, however, to give the following instruction which had been requested by the Times:

"I charge you ... that punitive damages, as the name indicates, are designed to punish the defendant, the New York Times Company, a corporation, and the other defendants in this case, ... and I further charge you that such punitive damages may be awarded only in the event that you, the jury, are convinced by a fair preponderance of the evidence that the defendant ... was motivated by personal ill will, that is actual intent to do the plaintiff harm, or that the defendant ... was guilty of gross negligence and recklessness and not of just ordinary negligence or carelessness in publishing the matter complained of so as to indicate a wanton disregard of plaintiff's rights."

The trial court's error in failing to require any finding of actual malice for an award of general damages makes it unnecessary for us to consider the sufficiency under the federal standard of the instructions regarding actual malice that were given as to punitive damages.

134, 146, 97 N.W.2d 719, 725 (1959).[25] Since the trial judge did not instruct the jury to differentiate between general and punitive damages, it may be that the verdict was wholly an award of one or the other. But it is impossible to know, in view of the general verdict returned. Because of this uncertainty, the judgment must be reversed and the case remanded. Stromberg v. California, 283 U.S. 359, 367-368; Williams v. North Carolina, 317 U.S. 287, 291-292; see Yates v. United States, 354 U.S. 298, 311-312; Cramer v. United States, 325 U.S. 1, 36, n. 45.

[24][25][26] Since respondent may seek a new trial, we deem that considerations of effective judicial administration require us to review the evidence in the present record to determine [285] whether it could constitutionally support a judgment for respondent. This Court's duty is not limited to the elaboration of constitutional principles; we must also in proper cases review the evidence to make certain that those principles have been constitutionally applied. This is such a case, particularly since the question is one of alleged trespass across "the line between speech unconditionally guaranteed and speech which may legitimately be regulated." Speiser v. Randall, 357 U.S. 513, 525. In cases where that line must be drawn, the rule is that we "examine for ourselves the statements in issue and the circumstances under which they were made to see . . . whether they are of a character which the principles of the First Amendment, as adopted by the Due Process Clause of the Fourteenth Amendment, protect." Pennekamp v. Florida, 328 U.S. 331, 335; see also One, Inc., v. Olesen, 355 U.S. 371; Sunshine Book Co. v. Summerfield, 355 U.S. 372. We must "make an independent examination of the whole record," Edwards v. South Carolina, 372 U.S. 229, 235, so as to assure ourselves that the judgment does not constitute a forbidden intrusion on the field of free expression.[26]

[25] Accord, Coleman v. MacLennan, supra, 78 Kan., at 741, 98 P., at 292; Gough v. Tribune-Journal Co., 75 Idaho 502, 510, 275 P.2d 663, 668 (1954).

[26] The Seventh Amendment does not, as respondent contends, preclude such an examination by this Court. That Amendment, providing that "no fact tried by a jury, shall be otherwise reexamined in any Court of the United States, than according to the rules of the common law," is applicable to state cases coming here. Chicago, B. & Q. R. Co. v. Chicago, 166 U.S. 226, 242-243; cf. The Justices v. Murray, 9 Wall. 274. But its ban on re-examination of facts does not preclude us from determining whether governing rules of federal law have been properly applied to the facts. "This Court will review the finding of facts by a State court . . . where a conclusion of law as to a Federal right and a finding of fact are so intermingled as to make it necessary, in order to pass upon the Federal question, to analyze the facts." Fiske v. Kansas, 274 U.S. 380, 385-386. See also Haynes v. Washington, 373 U.S. 503, 515-516.

[27][28][29][30] Applying these standards, we consider that the proof presented to show actual malice lacks the convincing [286] clarity which the constitutional standard demands, and hence that it would not constitutionally sustain the judgment for respondent under the proper rule of law. The case of the individual petitioners requires little discussion. Even assuming that they could constitutionally be found to have authorized the use of their names on the advertisement, there was no evidence whatever that they were aware of any erroneous statements or were in any way reckless in that regard. The judgment against them is thus without constitutional support.

[31][32] As to the Times, we similarly conclude that the facts do not support a finding of actual malice. The statement by the Times' Secretary that, apart from the padlocking allegation, he thought the advertisement was "substantially correct," affords no constitutional warrant for the Alabama Supreme Court's conclusion that it was a "cavalier ignoring of the falsity of the advertisement [from which] the jury could not have but been impressed with the bad faith of The Times, and its maliciousness inferable therefrom." The statement does not indicate malice at the time of the publication; even if the advertisement was not "substantially correct" – although respondent's own proofs tend to show that it was – that opinion was at least a reasonable one, and there was no evidence to impeach the witness' good faith in holding it.

The Times' failure to retract upon respondent's demand, although it later retracted upon the demand of Governor Patterson, is likewise not adequate evidence of malice for constitutional purposes. Whether or not a failure to retract may ever constitute such evidence, there are two reasons why it does not here. First, the letter written by the Times reflected a reasonable doubt on its part as to whether the advertisement could reasonably be taken to refer to respondent at all. Second, it was not a final refusal, since it asked for an explanation on this point – a request that respondent chose to ignore. Nor does the retraction upon the demand of the Governor supply the [287] necessary proof. It may be doubted that a failure to retract which is not itself evidence of malice can retroactively become such by virtue of a retraction subsequently made to another party. But in any event that did not happen here, since the explanation given by the Times' Secretary for the distinction drawn between respondent and the Governor was a reasonable one, the good faith of which was not impeached.

[33] Finally, there is evidence that the Times published the advertisement without checking its accuracy against the news stories in the Times' own files. The mere presence of the stories in the files does not, of course, establish that the Times "knew" the advertisement was false, since the state of mind

required for actual malice would have to be brought home to the persons in the Times' organization having responsibility for the publication of the advertisement. With respect to the failure of those persons to make the check, the record shows that they relied upon their knowledge of the good reputation of many of those whose names were listed as sponsors of the advertisement, and upon the letter from A. Philip Randolph, known to them as a responsible individual, certifying that the use of the names was authorized. There was testimony that the persons handling the advertisement saw nothing in it that would render it unacceptable under the Times' policy of rejecting advertisements containing "attacks of a personal character";[27] their failure to reject it on this ground was not unreasonable. We think [288] the evidence against the Times supports at most a finding of negligence in failing to discover the misstatements, and is constitutionally insufficient to show the recklessness that is required for a finding of actual malice. Cf. Charles Parker Co. v. Silver City Crystal Co., 142 Conn. 605, 618, 116 A.2d 440, 446 (1955); Phoenix Newspapers, Inc., v. Choisser, 82 Ariz. 271, 277-278, 312 P.2d 150, 154-155 (1957).

[34] We also think the evidence was constitutionally defective in another respect: it was incapable of supporting the jury's finding that the allegedly libelous statements were made "of and concerning" respondent. Respondent relies on the words of the advertisement and the testimony of six witnesses to establish a connection between it and himself. Thus, in his brief to this Court, he states:

"The reference to respondent as police commissioner is clear from the ad. In addition, the jury heard the testimony of a newspaper editor ... ; a real estate and insurance man ... ; the sales manager of a men's clothing store ... ; a food equipment man ... ; a service station operator ... ; and the operator of a truck line for whom respondent had formerly worked ... . Each of these witnesses stated that he associated the statements with respondent ... ." (Citations to record omitted.)

There was no reference to respondent in the advertisement, either by name or official position. A number of the allegedly libelous statements – the charges that the dining hall was padlocked and that Dr. King's home was bombed, his person assaulted,

and a perjury prosecution instituted against him – did not even concern the police; despite the ingenuity of the arguments which would attach this significance to the word "They," it is plain that these statements could not reasonably be read as accusing respondent of personal involvement in the acts [289] in question. The statements upon which respondent principally relies as referring to him are the two allegations that did concern the police or police functions: that "truckloads of police . . . ringed the Alabama State College Campus" after the demonstration on the State Capitol steps, and that Dr. King had been "arrested . . . seven times." These statements were false only in that the police had been "deployed near" the campus but had not actually "ringed" it and had not gone there in connection with the State Capitol demonstration, and in that Dr. King had been arrested only four times. The ruling that these discrepancies between what was true and what was asserted were sufficient to injure respondent's reputation may itself raise constitutional problems, but we need not consider them here.

Although the statements may be taken as referring to the police, they did not on their face make even an oblique reference to respondent as an individual. Support for the asserted reference must, therefore, be sought in the testimony of respondent's witnesses. But none of them suggested any basis for the belief that respondent himself was attacked in the advertisement beyond the bare fact that he was in overall charge of the Police Department and thus bore official responsibility for police conduct; to the extent that some of the witnesses thought respondent to have been charged with ordering or approving the conduct or otherwise being personally involved in it, they based this notion not on any statements in the advertisement, and not on any evidence that he had in fact been so involved, but solely on the unsupported assumption that, because of his official position, he must have been.[28] This reliance on the bare [290] fact of respondent's official position[29] was made explicit by the Supreme Court of Alabama. That court, in holding that the trial court "did not err in overruling the demurrer [of the Times] in the aspect that the

---

[27] The Times has set forth in a booklet its "Advertising Acceptability Standards." Listed among the classes of advertising that the newspaper does not accept are advertisements that are "fraudulent or deceptive," that are "ambiguous in wording and . . . may mislead," and that contain "attacks of a personal character." In replying to respondent's interrogatories before the trial, the Secretary of the Times stated that "as the advertisement made no attacks of a personal character upon any individual and otherwise met the advertising acceptability standards promulgated," it had been approved for publication.

[28] Respondent's own testimony was that "as Commissioner of Public Affairs it is part of my duty to supervise the Police Department and I certainly feel like it [a statement] is associated with me when it describes police activities." He thought that "by virtue of being Police Commissioner and Commissioner of Public Affairs," he was charged with "any activity on the part of the Police Department."
"When it describes police action, certainly I feel it reflects on me as an individual." He added that "It is my feeling that it reflects not only on me but on the other Commissioners and the community."
[29] Compare Ponder v. Cobb, 257 N. C. 281, 126 S.E.2d 67 (1962).

libelous [291] matter was not of and concerning the [plaintiff,]" based its ruling on the proposition that:

"We think it common knowledge that the average person knows that municipal agents, such as police and firemen, and others, are under the control and direction of the city governing body, and more particularly under the direction and control of a single commissioner. In measuring the performance or deficiencies of such groups, praise or criticism is usually attached to the official in complete control of the body." 273 Ala., at 674-675, 144 So.2d, at 39.

Grover C. Hall testified that to him the third paragraph of the advertisement called to mind "the City government – the Commissioners," and that "now that you ask it I would naturally think a little more about the police Commissioner because his responsibility is exclusively with the constabulary." It was "the phrase about starvation" that led to the association; "the other didn't hit me with any particular force."

Arnold D. Blackwell testified that the third paragraph was associated in his mind with "the Police Commissioner and the police force. The people on the police force." If he had believed the statement about the padlocking of the dining hall, he would have thought "that the people on our police force or the heads of our police force were acting without their jurisdiction and would not be competent for the position." "I would assume that the Commissioner had ordered the police force to do that and therefore it would be his responsibility."

Harry W. Kaminsky associated the statement about "truckloads of police" with respondent "because he is the Police Commissioner." He thought that the reference to arrests in the sixth paragraph "implicates the Police Department, I think, or the authorities that would do that – arrest folks for speeding and loitering and such as that." Asked whether he would associate with respondent a newspaper report that the police had "beat somebody up or assaulted them on the streets of Montgomery,"

He replied: "I still say he is the Police Commissioner and those men are working directly under him and therefore I would think that he would have something to do with it." In general, he said, "I look at Mr. Sullivan when I see the Police Department."

H. M. Price, Sr., testified that he associated the first sentence of the third paragraph with respondent because: "I would just automatically consider that the Police Commissioner in Montgomery would have to put his approval on those kind of things as an individual."

William M. Parker, Jr., testified that he associated the statements in the two paragraphs with "the Commissioners of the City of Montgomery," and since respondent "was the Police Commissioner," he "thought of him first." He told the examining counsel: "I think if you were the Police Commissioner I would have thought it was speaking of you."

Horace W. White, respondent's former employer, testified that the statement about "truck-loads of police" made him think of respondent "as being the head of the Police Department." Asked whether he read the statement as charging respondent himself with ringing the campus or having shotguns and tear-gas, he replied: "Well, I thought of his department being charged with it, yes, sir. He is the head of the Police Department as I understand it." He further said that the reason he would have been unwilling to re-employ respondent if he had believed the advertisement was "the fact that he allowed the Police Department to do the things that the paper say he did."

[35][38] This proposition has disquieting implications for criticism of governmental conduct. For good reason, "no court of last resort in this country has ever held, or even suggested, that prosecutions for libel on government have any place in the American system of jurisprudence." City of Chicago v. Tribune Co., 307 Ill. 595, 601, 139 N. E. 86, 88 [292] (1923). The present proposition would sidestep this obstacle by transmuting criticism of government, however impersonal it may seem on its face, into personal criticism, and hence potential libel, of the officials of whom the government is composed. There is no legal alchemy by which a State may thus create the cause of action that would otherwise be denied for a publication which, as respondent himself said of the advertisement, "reflects not only on me but on the other Commissioners and the community." Raising as it does the possibility that a good-faith critic of government will be penalized for his criticism, the proposition relied on by the Alabama courts strikes at the very center of the constitutionally protected area of free expression.[30] We hold that such a proposition may not constitutionally be utilized to establish that an otherwise impersonal attack on governmental operations was a libel of an official responsible for those operations. Since it was relied on exclusively here, and there was no other evidence to connect the statements with respondent, the evidence was constitutionally insufficient to support a finding that the statements referred to respondent.

[36][37] The judgment of the Supreme Court of Alabama is reversed and the case is remanded to that court for further proceedings not inconsistent with this opinion.

Reversed and remanded.

---

[30] Insofar as the proposition means only that the statements about police conduct libeled respondent by implicitly criticizing his ability to run the Police Department, recovery

[APPENDIX IN ORIGINAL.]

CONCUR BY: BLACK; GOLDBERG

CONCUR: [293] MR. JUSTICE BLACK, with whom MR. JUSTICE DOUGLAS joins, concurring.

I concur in reversing this half-million-dollar judgment against the New York Times Company and the four individual defendants. In reversing the Court holds that "the Constitution delimits a State's power to award damages for libel in actions brought by public officials against critics of their official conduct." Ante, p. 283. I base my vote to reverse on the belief that the First and Fourteenth Amendments not merely "delimit" a State's power to award damages to "public officials against critics of their official conduct" but completely prohibit a State from exercising such a power. The Court goes on to hold that a State can subject such critics to damages if "actual malice" can be proved against them. "Malice," even as defined by the Court, is an elusive, abstract concept, hard to prove and hard to disprove.

The requirement that malice be proved provides at best an evanescent protection for the right critically to discuss public affairs and certainly does not measure up to the sturdy safeguard embodied in the First Amendment. Unlike the Court, therefore, I vote to reverse exclusively on the ground that the Times and the individual defendants had an absolute, unconditional constitutional right to publish in the Times advertisement their criticisms of the Montgomery agencies and officials. I do not base my vote to reverse on any failure to prove that these individual defendants signed the advertisement or that their criticism of the Police Department was aimed at the plaintiff Sullivan, who was then the Montgomery City Commissioner having supervision of the city's police; for present purposes I assume these things were proved. Nor is my reason for reversal the size of the half-million-dollar judgment, large as it is. If Alabama has constitutional power to use its civil libel law to impose damages on the press for criticizing the way public officials perform or fail [294] to perform their duties, I know of no provision in the Federal Constitution which either expressly or impliedly bars the State from fixing the amount of damages. The half-million-dollar verdict does give dramatic proof, however, that state libel laws threaten the

___

is also precluded in this case by the doctrine of fair comment. See American Law Institute, Restatement of Torts (1938), § 607. Since the Fourteenth Amendment requires recognition of the conditional privilege for honest misstatements of fact, it follows that a defense of fair comment must be afforded for honest expression of opinion based upon privileged, as well as true, statements of fact. Both defenses are of course defeasible if the public official proves actual malice, as was not done here.

very existence of an American press virile enough to publish unpopular views on public affairs and bold enough to criticize the conduct of public officials. The factual background of this case emphasizes the imminence and enormity of that threat. One of the acute and highly emotional issues in this country arises out of efforts of many people, even including some public officials, to continue state-commanded segregation of races in the public schools and other public places, despite our several holdings that such a state practice is forbidden by the Fourteenth Amendment. Montgomery is one of the localities in which widespread hostility to desegregation has been manifested. This hostility has sometimes extended itself to persons who favor desegregation, particularly to so-called "outside agitators," a term which can be made to fit papers like the Times, which is published in New York. The scarcity of testimony to show that Commissioner Sullivan suffered any actual damages at all suggests that these feelings of hostility had at least as much to do with rendition of this half-million-dollar verdict as did an appraisal of damages.

Viewed realistically, this record lends support to an inference that instead of being damaged Commissioner Sullivan's political, social, and financial prestige has likely been enhanced by the Times' publication. Moreover, a second half-million-dollar libel verdict against the Times based on the same advertisement has already been awarded to another Commissioner. There a jury again gave the full amount claimed. There is no reason to believe that there are not more such huge verdicts lurking just around the corner for the Times or any other newspaper or broadcaster which [295] might dare to criticize public officials. In fact, briefs before us show that in Alabama there are now pending eleven libel suits by local and state officials against the Times seeking $5,600,000, and five such suits against the Columbia Broadcasting System seeking $1,700,000.

Moreover, this technique for harassing and punishing a free press – now that it has been show to be possible – is by no means limited to cases with racial overtones; it can be used in other fields where public feelings may make local as well as out-of-state newspapers easy prey for libel verdict seekers.

In my opinion the Federal Constitution has dealt with this deadly danger to the press in the only way possible without leaving the free press open to destruction – by granting the press an absolute immunity for criticism of the way public officials do their public duty. Compare Barr v. Matteo, 360 U.S. 564. Stopgap measures like those the Court adopts are in my judgment not enough. This record certainly does not indicate that any different verdict would have been rendered here whatever the Court had charged the jury about "malice," "truth," "good motives," "justifiable ends," or any other legal formulas which in theory would protect the press. Nor does the record indicate that any of these legalistic words would have caused the courts below to set aside or to reduce the half-million-dollar verdict in any amount.

I agree with the Court that the Fourteenth Amendment made the First applicable to the States.[1] This means to me that since the adoption of the Fourteenth Amendment a State has no more power than the Federal Government to use a civil libel law or any other law to impose damages for merely discussing public affairs and criticizing public officials. The power of the United [296] States to do that is, in my judgment, precisely nil. Such was the general view held when the First Amendment was adopted and ever since.[2] Congress never has sought to challenge this viewpoint by passing any civil libel law. It did pass the Sedition Act in 1798,[3] which made it a crime – "seditious libel" – to criticize federal officials or the Federal Government. As the Court's opinion correctly points out, however, ante, pp. 273-276, that Act came to an ignominious end and by common consent has generally been treated as having been a wholly unjustifiable and much to be regretted violation of the First Amendment. Since the First Amendment is now made applicable to the States by the Fourteenth, it no more permits the States to impose damages for libel than it does the Federal Government.

We would, I think, more faithfully interpret the First Amendment by holding that at the very least it leaves the people and the press free to criticize officials and discuss public affairs with impunity. This Nation of ours elects many of its important officials; so do the States, the municipalities, the counties, and even many precincts. These officials are responsible to the people for the way they perform their duties. While our Court has held that some kinds of speech and writings, such as "obscenity," Roth v. United States, 354 U.S. 476, and "fighting words," Chaplinsky v. New Hampshire, 315 U.S. 568, are not expression within the protection of the First Amendment,[4] freedom to discuss public affairs and public officials [297] is unquestionably, as the Court today holds, the kind

of speech the First Amendment was primarily designed to keep within the area of free discussion.

To punish the exercise of this right to discuss public affairs or to penalize it through libel judgments is to abridge or shut off discussion of the very kind most needed. This Nation, I suspect, can live in peace without libel suits based on public discussions of public affairs and public officials. But I doubt that a country can live in freedom where its people can be made to suffer physically or financially for criticizing their government, its actions, or its officials. "For a representative democracy ceases to exist the moment that the public functionaries are by any means absolved from their responsibility to their constituents; and this happens whenever the constituent can be restrained in any manner from speaking, writing, or publishing his opinions upon any public measure, or upon the conduct of those who may advise or execute it."[5] An unconditional right to say what one pleases about public affairs is what I consider to be the minimum guarantee of the First Amendment.[6]

I regret that the Court has stopped short of this holding indispensable to preserve our free press from destruction.

MR. JUSTICE GOLDBERG, with whom MR. JUSTICE DOUGLAS joins, concurring in the result.

The Court today announces a constitutional standard which prohibits "a public official from recovering damages for a defamatory falsehood relating to his official conduct unless he proves that the statement was made with [298] 'actual malice' – that is, with knowledge that it was false or with reckless disregard of whether it was false or not." Ante, at 279-280. The Court thus rules that the Constitution gives citizens and newspapers a "conditional privilege" immunizing non-malicious misstatements of fact regarding the official conduct of a government officer. The impressive array of

---

[1] See cases collected in Speiser v. Randall, 357 U.S. 513, 530 (concurring opinion).

[2] See, e.g., 1 Tucker, Blackstone's Commentaries (1803), 297-299 (editor's appendix). St. George Tucker, a distinguished Virginia jurist, took part in the Annapolis Convention of 1786, sat on both state and federal courts, and was widely known for his writings on judicial and constitutional subjects.

[3] Act of July 14, 1798, 1 Stat. 596.

[4] But see Smith v. California, 361 U.S. 147, 155 (concurring opinion); Roth v. United States, 354 U.S. 476, 508 (dissenting opinion).

[5] 1 Tucker, Blackstone's Commentaries (1803), 297 (editor's appendix); cf. Brant, Seditious Libel: Myth and Reality, 39 N. Y. U. L. Rev. 1.

[6] Cf. Meiklejohn, Free Speech and Its Relation to Self-Government (1948).

history[1] and precedent marshaled by the Court, however, confirms my belief that the Constitution affords greater protection than that provided by the Court's standard to citizen and press in exercising the right of public criticism.

In my view, the First and Fourteenth Amendments to the Constitution afford to the citizen and to the press an absolute, unconditional privilege to criticize official conduct despite the harm which may flow from excesses and abuses. The prized American right "to speak one's mind," cf. Bridges v. California, 314 U.S. 252, 270, about public officials and affairs needs "breathing space to survive," N. A. A. C. P. v. Button, 371 U.S. 415, 433. The right should not depend upon a probing by the jury of the motivation[2] of the citizen or press. The theory [299] of our Constitution is that every citizen may speak his mind and every newspaper express its view on matters of public concern and may not be barred from speaking or publishing because those in control of government think that what is said or written is unwise, unfair, false, or malicious. In a democratic society, one who assumes to act for the citizens in an executive, legislative, or judicial capacity must expect that his official acts will be commented upon and criticized. Such criticism cannot, in my opinion, be muzzled or deterred by the courts at the instance of public officials under the label of libel.

It has been recognized that "prosecutions for libel on government have [no] place in the American system of jurisprudence." City of Chicago v. Tribune Co., 307 Ill. 595, 601, 139 N. E. 86, 88. I fully agree. Government, however, is not an abstraction; it is made up of individuals – of governors responsible to the governed. In a democratic society where men are free by ballots to remove those in power, any statement critical of governmental action is necessarily "of and concerning" the governors and any statement critical of the governors' official conduct is necessarily "of and concerning" the government. If the rule that libel on government has no place in our Constitution is to have real meaning, then libel on the official conduct of the governors likewise can have no place in our Constitution.

We must recognize that we are writing upon a clean slate.[3] As the Court notes, although there have been [300] "statements of this Court to the effect that the Constitution does not protect libelous publications ... none of the cases sustained the use of libel laws to impose sanctions upon expression critical of the official conduct of public officials." Ante, at 268. We should be particularly careful, therefore, adequately to protect the liberties, which are embodied in the First and Fourteenth Amendments. It may be urged that deliberately and maliciously false statements have no conceivable value as free speech. That argument, however, is not responsive to the real issue presented by this case, which is whether that freedom of speech which all agree is constitutionally protected can be effectively safeguarded by a rule allowing the imposition of liability upon a jury's evaluation of the speaker's state of mind.

If individual citizens may be held liable in damages for strong words, which a jury finds false and maliciously motivated, there can be little doubt that public debate and advocacy will be constrained. And if newspapers, publishing advertisements dealing with public issues, thereby risk liability, there can also be little doubt that the ability of minority groups to secure publication of their views on public affairs and to seek support for their causes will be greatly diminished. Cf. Farmers Educational & Coop. Union v. WDAY, Inc., 360 U.S. 525, 530. The opinion of the Court conclusively demonstrates the chilling effect of the Alabama libel laws on First Amendment freedoms [301] in the area of race relations. The American Colonists were not willing, nor should we be, to take the risk that "men who

---

[1] I fully agree with the Court that the attack upon the validity of the Sedition Act of 1798, 1 Stat. 596, "has carried the day in the court of history," ante, at 276, and that the Act would today be declared unconstitutional. It should be pointed out, however, that the Sedition Act proscribed writings which were "false, scandalous and malicious." (Emphasis added.) For prosecutions under the Sedition Act charging malice, see, e.g., Trial of Matthew Lyon (1798), in Wharton, State Trials of the United States (1849), p. 333; Trial of Thomas Cooper (1800), in id., at 659; Trial of Anthony Haswell (1800), in id., at 684; Trial of James Thompson Callender (1800), in id., at 688.

[2] The requirement of proving actual malice or reckless disregard may, in the mind of the jury, add little to the requirement of proving falsity, a requirement which the Court recognizes not to be an adequate safeguard. The thought suggested by Mr. Justice Jackson in United States v. Ballard, 322 U.S. 78, 92-93, is relevant here: "As a matter of either practice or philosophy I do not see how we can separate an issue as to what is believed from considerations as to what is believable. The most convincing proof that one believes his statements is to show that they have been true in his experience. Likewise, that one knowingly falsified is best proved by showing that what he said happened never did happen." See note 4, infra.

[3] It was not until Gitlow v. New York, 268 U.S. 652, decided in 1925, that it was intimated that the freedom of speech guaranteed by the First Amendment was applicable to the States by reason of the Fourteenth Amendment. Other intimations followed. See Whitney v. California, 274 U.S. 357; Fiske v. Kansas, 274 U.S. 380. In 1931 Chief Justice Hughes speaking for the Court in Stromberg v. California, 283 U.S. 359, 368, declared: "It has been determined that the conception of liberty under the due process clause of the Fourteenth Amendment embraces the right of free speech." Thus we deal with a constitutional principle enunciated less than four decades ago, and consider for the first time the application of that principle to issues arising in libel cases brought by state officials.

injure and oppress the people under their administration [and] provoke them to cry out and complain" will also be empowered to "make that very complaint the foundation for new oppressions and prosecutions." The Trial of John Peter Zenger, 17 Howell's St. Tr. 675, 721-722 (1735) (argument of counsel to the jury). To impose liability for critical, albeit erroneous or even malicious, comments on official conduct would effectively resurrect "the obsolete doctrine that the governed must not criticize their governors." Cf. Sweeney v. Patterson, 76 U.S. App. D.C. 23, 24, 128 F.2d 457, 458.

Our national experience teaches that repressions breed hate and "that hate menaces stable government." Whitney v. California, 274 U.S. 357, 375 (Brandeis, J., concurring). We should be ever mindful of the wise counsel of Chief Justice Hughes:

"Imperative is the need to preserve inviolate the constitutional rights of free speech, free press and free assembly in order to maintain the opportunity for free political discussion, to the end that government may be responsive to the will of the people and that changes, if desired, may be obtained by peaceful means. Therein lies the security of the Republic, the very foundation of constitutional government." De Jonge v. Oregon, 299 U.S. 353, 365.

This is not to say that the Constitution protects defamatory statements directed against the private conduct of a public official or private citizen. Freedom of press and of speech insures that government will respond to the will of the people and that changes may be obtained by peaceful means. Purely private defamation has little to do with the political ends of a self-governing society. The imposition of liability for private defamation does not [302] abridge the freedom of public speech or any other freedom protected by the First Amendment.[4] This, of course, cannot be said "where public officials are concerned or where public matters are involved ... . One main function of the First Amendment is to ensure ample opportunity for the people to determine and resolve public issues. Where public matters are involved,

the doubts should be resolved in favor of freedom of expression rather than against it." Douglas, The Right of the People (1958), p. 41.

In many jurisdictions, legislators, judges and executive officers are clothed with absolute immunity against liability for defamatory words uttered in the discharge of their public duties. See, e.g., Barr v. Matteo, 360 U.S. 564; City of Chicago v. Tribune Co., 307 Ill., at 610, 139 N. E., at 91. Judge Learned Hand ably summarized the policies underlying the rule:

"It does indeed go without saying that an official, who is in fact guilty of using his powers to vent his spleen upon others, or for any other personal motive not connected with the public good, should not escape liability for the injuries he may so cause; and, if it were possible in practice to confine such complaints to the guilty, it would be monstrous to deny recovery. The justification for doing so is that it is impossible to know whether the claim is well founded until the [303] case has been tried, and that to submit all officials, the innocent as well as the guilty, to the burden of a trial and to the inevitable danger of its outcome, would dampen the ardor of all but the most resolute, or the most irresponsible, in the unflinching discharge of their duties. Again and again the public interest calls for action which may turn out to be founded on a mistake, in the face of which an official may later find himself hard put to it to satisfy a jury of his good faith. There must indeed be means of punishing public officers who have been truant to their duties; but that is quite another matter from exposing such as have been honestly mistaken to suit by anyone who has suffered from their errors. As is so often the case, the answer must be found in a balance between the evils inevitable in either alternative. In this instance it has been thought in the end better to leave unredressed the wrongs done by dishonest officers than to subject those who try to do their duty to the constant dread of retaliation ... .

"The decisions have, indeed, always imposed as a limitation upon the immunity that the official's act must have been within the scope of his powers; and it can be argued that official powers, since they exist only for the public good, never cover occasions where the public good is not their aim, and hence that to exercise a power dishonestly is necessarily to overstep its bounds. A moment's reflection shows, however, that that cannot be the meaning of the limitation without defeating the whole doctrine. What is meant by saying that the officer must be acting within his power cannot be more than that the occasion must be such as would have justified the act, if he had been using his power for any of the purposes on whose account it was vested in him. ..." Gregoire v. Biddle, 177 F.2d 579, 581.

---

[4] In most cases, as in the case at bar, there will be little difficulty in distinguishing defamatory speech relating to private conduct from that relating to official conduct. I recognize, of course, that there will be a gray area. The difficulties of applying a public-private standard are, however, certainly of a different genre from those attending the differentiation between a malicious and nonmalicious state of mind. If the constitutional standard is to be shaped by a concept of malice, the speaker takes the risk not only that the jury will inaccurately determine his state of mind but also that the jury will fail properly to apply the constitutional standard set by the elusive concept of malice. See note 2, supra.

[304] If the government official should be immune from libel actions so that his ardor to serve the public will not be dampened and "fearless, vigorous, and effective administration of policies of government" not be inhibited, Barr v. Matteo, supra, at 571, then the citizen and the press should likewise be immune from libel actions for their criticism of official conduct. Their ardor as citizens will thus not be dampened and they will be free "to applaud or to criticize the way public employees do their jobs, from the least to the most important."[5] If liability can attach to political criticism because it damages the reputation of a public official as a public official, then no critical citizen can safely utter anything but faint praise about the government or its officials. The vigorous criticism by press and citizen of the conduct of the government of the day by the officials of the day will soon yield to silence if officials in control of government agencies, instead of answering criticisms, can resort to friendly juries to forestall criticism of their official conduct.[6]

---

[5] MR. JUSTICE BLACK concurring in Barr v. Matteo, 360 U.S. 564, 577, observed that: "The effective functioning of a free government like ours depends largely on the force of an informed public opinion. This calls for the widest possible understanding of the quality of government service rendered by all elective or appointed public officials or employees. Such an informed understanding depends, of course, on the freedom people have to applaud or to criticize the way public employees do their jobs, from the least to the most important."

[6] See notes 2, 4, supra.

The conclusion that the Constitution affords the citizen and the press an absolute privilege for criticism of official conduct does not leave the public official without defenses against unsubstantiated opinions or deliberate misstatements. "Under our system of government, counterargument and education are the weapons available to expose these matters, not abridgment ... of free speech ... ." Wood v. Georgia, 370 U.S. 375, 389. The public [305] official certainly has equal if not greater access than most private citizens to media of communication. In any event, despite the possibility that some excesses and abuses may go unremedied, we must recognize that "the people of this nation have ordained in the light of history, that, in spite of the probability of excesses and abuses, [certain] liberties are, in the long view, essential to enlightened opinion and right conduct on the part of the citizens of a democracy." Cantwell v. Connecticut, 310 U.S. 296, 310. As Mr. Justice Brandeis correctly observed, "sunlight is the most powerful of all disinfectants."[7]

For these reasons, I strongly believe that the Constitution accords citizens and press an unconditional freedom to criticize official conduct. It necessarily follows that in a case such as this, where all agree that the allegedly defamatory statements related to official conduct, the judgments for libel cannot constitutionally be sustained.

---

[7] See Freund, The Supreme Court of the United States (1949), p. 61.

Zeran v. America Online
129 F.3d 327
(4th Cir. 1997)
(Excerpts only. Footnotes omitted.)

SUBSEQUENT HISTORY: Certiorari Denied June 22, 1998, 1998 U.S. LEXIS 4047.

PRIOR HISTORY: Appeal from the United States District Court for the Eastern District of Virginia, at Alexandria. T. S. Ellis, III, District Judge.

JUDGES: Before WILKINSON, Chief Judge, RUSSELL, Circuit Judge, and BOYLE, Chief United States District Judge for the Eastern District of North Carolina, sitting by designation.

OPINION: [328] Chief Judge Wilkinson wrote the opinion, in which Judge Russell and Chief Judge Boyle joined.

Kenneth Zeran brought this action against America Online, Inc. ("AOL"), arguing that AOL

unreasonably delayed in removing defamatory messages posted by an unidentified third party, refused to post retractions of those messages, and failed to screen for similar postings thereafter. The district court granted judgment for AOL on the grounds that the Communications Decency Act of 1996 ("CDA") – 47 U.S.C. § 230 – bars Zeran's claims. Zeran appeals, arguing that § 230 leaves intact liability for interactive computer service providers who possess notice of defamatory material posted through their services. He also contends that § 230 does not apply here because his claims arise from AOL's alleged negligence prior to the CDA's enactment. Section 230, however, plainly immunizes computer service providers like AOL from liability for information that originates with third parties. Furthermore, Congress clearly expressed its intent that § 230 apply to lawsuits, like Zeran's, instituted after the CDA's enactment. Accordingly, we affirm the judgment of the district court.

...[329] AOL is ... an interactive computer service. Much of the information transmitted over its network originates with the company's millions of subscribers. They may transmit information privately via electronic mail, or they may communicate publicly by posting messages on AOL bulletin boards, where the messages may be read by any AOL subscriber.

... On April 25, 1995, an unidentified person posted a message on an AOL bulletin board advertising "Naughty Oklahoma T-Shirts." The posting described the sale of shirts featuring offensive and tasteless slogans related to the April 19, 1995, bombing of the Alfred P. Murrah Federal Building in Oklahoma City. Those interested in purchasing the shirts were instructed to call "Ken" at Zeran's home phone number in Seattle, Washington. As a result of this anonymously perpetrated prank, Zeran received a high volume of calls, comprised primarily of angry and derogatory messages, but also including death threats. Zeran could not change his phone number because he relied on its availability to the public in running his business out of his home. Later that day, Zeran called AOL and informed a company representative of his predicament. The employee assured Zeran that the posting would be removed from AOL's bulletin board but explained that as a matter of policy AOL would not post a retraction. The parties dispute the date that AOL removed this original posting from its bulletin board.

On April 26, the next day, an unknown person posted another message advertising additional shirts with new tasteless slogans related to the Oklahoma City bombing. Again, interested buyers were told to call Zeran's phone number, to ask for "Ken," and to "please call back if busy" due to high demand. The angry, threatening phone calls intensified. Over the next four days, an unidentified party continued to post messages on AOL's bulletin board, advertising additional items including bumper stickers and key chains with still more offensive slogans. During this time period, Zeran called AOL repeatedly and was told by company representatives that the individual account from which the messages were posted would soon be closed. Zeran also reported his case to Seattle FBI agents. By April 30, Zeran was receiving an abusive phone call approximately every two minutes.

Meanwhile, an announcer for Oklahoma City radio station KRXO received a copy of the first AOL posting. On May 1, the announcer related the message's contents on the air, attributed them to "Ken" at Zeran's phone number, and urged the listening audience to call the number. After this radio broadcast, Zeran was inundated with death threats and other violent calls from Oklahoma City residents. Over the next few days, Zeran talked to both KRXO and AOL representatives. He also spoke to his local police, who subsequently surveilled his home to protect his safety. By May 14, after an Oklahoma City newspaper published a story exposing the shirt advertisements as a hoax and after KRXO made an on-air apology, the number of calls to Zeran's residence finally subsided to fifteen per day.

Zeran first filed suit on January 4, 1996, against radio station KRXO in the United States District Court for the Western District of Oklahoma. On April 23, 1996, he filed this separate suit against AOL in the same court. Zeran did not bring any action against the party who posted the offensive messages. After Zeran's suit against AOL was transferred to the Eastern District of Virginia pursuant to 28 U.S.C. § 1404(a), AOL answered Zeran's complaint and interposed 47 U.S.C. § 230 as an affirmative defense. [330] The district court granted AOL's motion [for summary judgment], and Zeran filed this appeal.

Because § 230 was successfully advanced by AOL in the district court as a defense to Zeran's claims, we shall briefly examine its operation here. Zeran seeks to hold AOL liable for defamatory speech initiated by a third party. He argued to the district court that once he notified AOL of the unidentified third party's hoax, AOL had a duty to remove the defamatory posting promptly, to notify its subscribers of the message's false nature, and to effectively screen future defamatory material. Section 230 entered this litigation as an affirmative defense pled by AOL. The company claimed that Congress immunized interactive computer service providers from claims based on information posted by a third party.

The relevant portion of § 230 states: "No provider or user of an interactive computer service shall be treated as the publisher or speaker of any information provided by another information content provider." 47 U.S.C. § 230(c)(1). By its plain language, § 230 creates a federal immunity to any cause of action that would make service providers liable for information originating with a third-party user of the service. Specifically, § 230 precludes courts from entertaining claims that would place a computer service provider in a publisher's role. Thus, lawsuits seeking to hold a service provider liable for its exercise of a publisher's traditional editorial functions – such as deciding whether to publish, withdraw, postpone or alter content – are barred.

The purpose of this statutory immunity is not difficult to discern. Congress recognized the threat that tort-based lawsuits pose to freedom of speech in the new and burgeoning Internet medium. The imposition of tort liability on service providers for the communications of others represented, for Congress, simply another form of intrusive government regulation of speech. Section 230 was enacted, in part, to maintain the robust nature of Internet communication and, accordingly, to keep government interference in the medium to a minimum. In specific statutory findings, Congress recognized the Internet and interactive computer services as offering "a forum for a true diversity of political discourse, unique opportunities for cultural development, and myriad avenues for intellectual activity." Id. § 230(a)(3). It also found that the Internet and interactive computer services "have flourished, to the benefit of all Americans, with a minimum of government regulation." Id. § 230(a)(4) (emphasis added). Congress further stated that it is "the policy of the United States . . . to preserve the vibrant and competitive free market that presently exists for the Internet and other interactive computer services, unfettered by Federal or State regulation." Id. § 230(b)(2) (emphasis added).

None of this means, of course, that the original culpable party who posts defamatory messages would escape accountability. While Congress acted to keep government regulation of the Internet to a minimum, it also found it to be the policy of the United States "to ensure vigorous enforcement of Federal criminal laws to deter and punish trafficking in obscenity, stalking, and harassment by means of computer." Id. § 230(b)(5). Congress made a policy choice, however, not to deter harmful online speech through the separate route of imposing tort liability on companies that serve as intermediaries [331] for other parties' potentially injurious messages.

Congress' purpose in providing the § 230 immunity was thus evident. Interactive computer services have millions of users. ... The amount of information communicated via interactive computer services is therefore staggering. The specter of tort liability in an area of such prolific speech would have an obvious chilling effect. It would be impossible for service providers to screen each of their millions of postings for possible problems. Faced with potential liability for each message republished by their services, interactive computer service providers might choose to severely restrict the number and type of messages posted. Congress considered the weight of the speech interests implicated and chose to immunize service providers to avoid any such restrictive effect.

Another important purpose of § 230 was to encourage service providers to self-regulate the dissemination of offensive material over their services. In this respect, § 230 responded to a New York state court decision, Stratton Oakmont, Inc. v.

Prodigy Servs. Co., 1995 N.Y. Misc. LEXIS 229, 1995 WL 323710 (N.Y. Sup. Ct. May 24, 1995). There, the plaintiffs sued Prodigy – an interactive computer service like AOL – for defamatory comments made by an unidentified party on one of Prodigy's bulletin boards. The court held Prodigy to the strict liability standard normally applied to original publishers of defamatory statements, rejecting Prodigy's claims that it should be held only to the lower "knowledge" standard usually reserved for distributors. The court reasoned that Prodigy acted more like an original publisher than a distributor both because it advertised its practice of controlling content on its service and because it actively screened and edited messages posted on its bulletin boards.

Congress enacted § 230 to remove the disincentives to self-regulation created by the Stratton Oakmont decision. Under that court's holding, computer service providers who regulated the dissemination of offensive material on their services risked subjecting themselves to liability, because such regulation cast the service provider in the role of a publisher. Fearing that the specter of liability would therefore deter service providers from blocking and screening offensive material, Congress enacted § 230's broad immunity "to remove disincentives for the development and utilization of blocking and filtering technologies that empower parents to restrict their children's access to objectionable or inappropriate online material." 47 U.S.C. § 230(b)(4). In line with this purpose, § 230 forbids the imposition of publisher liability on a service provider for the exercise of its editorial and self-regulatory functions.

Zeran argues, however, that the § 230 immunity eliminates only publisher liability, leaving distributor liability intact. Publishers can be held liable for defamatory statements contained in their works even absent proof that they had specific knowledge of the statement's inclusion. ... According to Zeran, interactive computer service providers like AOL are normally considered instead to be distributors, like traditional news vendors or book sellers. Distributors cannot be held liable for defamatory statements contained in the materials they distribute unless it is proven at a minimum that they have actual knowledge of the defamatory statements upon which liability is predicated. ...

Zeran contends that he provided AOL with sufficient notice of the defamatory statements appearing on the company's bulletin board. This notice is significant, says Zeran, because AOL could be held liable as a distributor only if it acquired knowledge of the defamatory statements' existence.

Because of the difference between these two forms of liability, Zeran contends that the term "distributor" carries a legally distinct meaning from the term "publisher." [332] Accordingly, he asserts that Congress' use of only the term "publisher" in § 230 indicates a purpose to immunize service providers only from publisher liability. He argues that distributors are left unprotected by § 230 and, therefore, his suit should be permitted to proceed against AOL. We disagree. ...

The terms "publisher" and "distributor" derive their legal significance from the context of defamation law. Although Zeran attempts to artfully plead his claims as ones of negligence, they are indistinguishable from a garden-variety defamation action. Because the publication of a statement is a necessary element in a defamation action, only one who publishes can be subject to this form of tort liability. ... Publication does not only describe the choice by an author to include certain information. In addition, both the negligent communication of a defamatory statement and the failure to remove such a statement when first communicated by another party – each alleged by Zeran here under a negligence label – constitute publication. ... In fact, every repetition of a defamatory statement is considered a publication. Keeton et al., supra, § 113, at 799.

In this case, AOL is legally considered to be a publisher. "Every one who takes part in the publication ... is charged with publication." Id. Even distributors are considered to be publishers for purposes of defamation law:

Those who are in the business of making their facilities available to disseminate the writings composed, the speeches made, and the information gathered by others may also be regarded as participating to such an extent in making the books, newspapers, magazines, and information available to others as to be regarded as publishers. They are intentionally making the contents available to others, sometimes without knowing all of the contents – including the defamatory content – and sometimes without any opportunity to ascertain, in advance, that any defamatory matter was to be included in the matter published. Id. at 803.

AOL falls squarely within this traditional definition of a publisher and, therefore, is clearly protected by § 230's immunity. ...

It is undoubtedly true that mere conduits, or distributors, are subject to a different standard of liability. As explained above, distributors must at a minimum have knowledge of the existence of a defamatory statement as a prerequisite to liability. But this distinction signifies only that different standards of liability may be applied within the larger publisher category, depending on the specific type of publisher concerned. ... To the extent that decisions ... utilize the terms "publisher" and "distributor" separately, the decisions correctly describe two different standards of liability. [They] do not, however, suggest that distributors are not also a type of publisher for purposes of defamation law.

Zeran simply attaches too much importance to the presence of the distinct notice element in distributor liability. The simple fact of notice surely cannot transform one from an original publisher to a distributor in the eyes of the law. To the contrary, once a computer service provider receives notice of a potentially defamatory posting, it is thrust into the role of a traditional publisher. The computer service provider must decide whether to publish, edit, or withdraw the posting. In this respect, Zeran seeks to impose liability on AOL for assuming the [333] role for which § 230 specifically proscribes liability – the publisher role.

Our view that Zeran's complaint treats AOL as a publisher is reinforced because AOL is cast in the same position as the party who originally posted the offensive messages. According to Zeran's logic, AOL is legally at fault because it communicated to third parties an allegedly defamatory statement. This is precisely the theory under which the original poster of the offensive messages would be found liable. If the original party is considered a publisher of the offensive messages, Zeran certainly cannot attach liability to AOL under the same theory without conceding that AOL too must be treated as a publisher of the statements.

Zeran next contends that interpreting § 230 to impose liability on service providers with knowledge of defamatory content on their services is consistent with the statutory purposes ... . Zeran fails, however, to understand the practical implications of notice liability in the interactive computer service context. Liability upon notice would defeat the dual purposes advanced by § 230 of the CDA. ... [L]iability upon notice reinforces service providers' incentives to restrict speech and abstain from self-regulation.

If computer service providers were subject to distributor liability, they would face potential liability each time they receive notice of a potentially defamatory statement – from any party, concerning any message. Each notification would require a careful yet rapid investigation of the circumstances surrounding the posted information, a legal judgment concerning the information's defamatory character, and an on-the-spot editorial decision whether to risk liability by allowing the continued publication of that information. Although this might be feasible for the traditional print publisher, the sheer number of postings on interactive computer services would create an impossible burden in the Internet context. ... Because service providers would be subject to liability only for the publication of information, and not for its removal, they would have a natural incentive simply to remove messages upon notification, whether the contents were defamatory or not. ... Thus, like strict liability, liability upon notice has a chilling effect on the freedom of Internet speech.

Similarly, notice-based liability would deter service providers from regulating the dissemination of offensive material over their own services. Any efforts by a service provider to investigate and screen material posted on its service would only lead to notice of potentially defamatory material more frequently and thereby create a stronger basis for liability. Instead of subjecting themselves to further possible lawsuits, service providers would likely eschew any attempts at self-regulation.

More generally, notice-based liability for interactive computer service providers would provide third parties with a no-cost means to create the basis for future lawsuits. Whenever one was displeased with the speech of another party conducted over an interactive computer service, the offended party could simply "notify" the relevant service provider, claiming the information to be legally defamatory. In light of the vast amount of speech communicated through interactive computer services, these notices could produce an impossible burden for service providers, who would be faced with ceaseless choices of suppressing controversial speech or sustaining prohibitive liability. Because the probable effects of distributor liability on the vigor of Internet speech and on service provider self-regulation are directly contrary to § 230's statutory purposes, we will not assume that Congress intended to leave liability upon notice intact.

Zeran finally contends that the interpretive canon favoring retention of common law principles unless Congress speaks directly to the issue counsels a restrictive reading of the [334] § 230 immunity here. ... This interpretive canon does not persuade us to reach a different result. Here, Congress has indeed spoken directly to the issue by employing the legally significant term "publisher," which has traditionally encompassed distributors and original publishers alike. ... [I]nterpreting § 230 to leave distributor liability in effect would defeat the two primary purposes of the statute and would certainly

"lessen the scope plainly intended" by Congress' use of the term "publisher."

Section 230 represents the approach of Congress to a problem of national and international dimension. The Supreme Court underscored this point in ACLU v. Reno, finding that the Internet allows "tens of millions of people to communicate with one another and to access vast amounts of information from around the world.[It] is 'a unique and wholly new medium of worldwide human communication.'" 117 S. Ct. at 2334 (citation omitted). Application of the canon invoked by Zeran here would significantly lessen Congress' power, derived from the Commerce Clause, to act in a field whose international character is apparent. While Congress allowed for the enforcement of "any State law that is consistent with [§ 230]," 47 U.S.C. § 230(d)(3), it is equally plain that Congress' desire to promote unfettered speech on the Internet must supersede conflicting common law causes of action. Section 230(d)(3) continues: "No cause of action may be brought and no liability may be imposed under any State or local law that is inconsistent with this section." With respect to federal-state preemption, the Court has advised: "When Congress has 'unmistakably . . . ordained,' that its enactments alone are to regulate a part of commerce, state laws regulating that aspect of commerce must fall. The result is compelled whether Congress' command is explicitly stated in the statute's language or implicitly contained in its structure and purpose."... Here, Congress' command is explicitly stated. Its exercise of its commerce power is clear and counteracts the caution counseled by the interpretive canon favoring retention of common law principles.

... Section 230 applies by its plain terms to complaints brought after the CDA became effective. ... Here, Zeran [335] did not file his complaint until over two months after § 230's immunity became effective. Thus, the statute's application in this litigation is in fact prospective. ... Here, Congress decided that free speech on the Internet and self-regulation of offensive speech were so important that § 230 should be given immediate, comprehensive effect.

... For the foregoing reasons, we affirm the judgment of the district court. AFFIRMED.

Privacy and Its Invasion

Harms from publicity and newsgathering

Focal cases:
Cox Broadcasting v. Cohn, 420 U.S. 469 (1975)
Bartnicki v. Vopper, 532 U.S. 514 (2001)

I n 1890, legal scholars Samuel Warren and Louis Brandeis suggested that U.S. law should
develop an "inviolate right of privacy against the exposures of the yellow press."[1] The authors
referred to a common-law understanding of privacy that provides for personal control of
information about oneself and protects the right to be left alone. Like trespass law that prevents
intrusion on personal property, they argued privacy law should prevent intrusion into personal
life and distribution of personal information. These ideas led eventually to the development of
four different torts for invasion of privacy in the United States.

CONSTITUTIONAL FOUNDATIONS

Before exploring those torts in detail, a more generalized discussion of privacy may be useful.
The foundations of a right to privacy are imbedded – though not explicitly mentioned – in
several parts of the U.S. Constitution, notably the First, Third, Fourth and Fifth Amendments.
Thus, in a 1965 decision overturning a state ban on sale of contraceptives, the Supreme Court
said the Constitution creates "zones of privacy."[2] The Court said the First Amendment's implicit
right of free association has a penumbra that protects intimate, personal privacy from
governmental intrusion.[3] In addition, the First Amendment protects the privacy of our
associations – intimate or political – by banning government from forcing us to disclose our
personal affiliations and memberships without a compelling reason.[4]

The Third and Fourth amendments protect the home as the greatest bastion of privacy. The
Third Amendment ban on quartering soldiers in private homes during peacetime protects the

---

[1] Warren, S. & Brandeis, L., *The Right of Privacy*, 4 HARV. L. REV. 193, 196 (1890).
[2] Griswold v. Connecticut, 381 U.S. 479, 484 (1965).
[3] Griswold, 381 U.S. 479.
[4] NAACP *v.* Alabama, 357 U.S. 449 (1958).

physical sanctity of the home from occupation. The Fourth Amendment's prohibition of unreasonable government search and seizure "affirms the right of the people to be secure in their persons, houses, papers and effects."[5] This guaranty protects against both physical and electronic intrusion into our homes,[6] and it prevents police from inviting third parties – including journalists – to accompany them on official business on private property.[7]

However, during times of national insecurity, war or the war on terrorism, these protections may be undermined by legislative, executive and judicial actions that place greater priority on protection of the state than protection of the individual.[8] Thus, the USA PATRIOT Act of 2001[9] adopted a broad definition of domestic terrorism that enables government surveillance and sneak and peek searches. The act undermines personal privacy by reducing the legal requirements imposed on government to obtain personal records and effects the government believes to be relevant to foreign intelligence, permitting expansive access to telephone and Internet usage records "relevant to an ongoing criminal investigation," and allowing covert searches of people's homes and offices.[10] Under the law, telephone companies, online service providers and libraries face unprecedented numbers of subpoenas and increased pressure to deliver personal information about customers even without subpoenas, according to some sources.[11] The quantity of covert surveillance of private citizens is kept secret even from Congress.[12]

Finally, to a more limited degree, the Fifth Amendment's guaranty against self-incrimination allows citizens to ensure government may not pry into their private lives.

The Court has acknowledged each of these constitutional protections for privacy but has said none of them establishes a broad, generalized right of privacy.

STATUTORY PRIVACY

Federal and state statutes as well as state constitutions establish some rights of privacy. Many laws detail rights of privacy related to specific types of information or conduct. For example, the federal Freedom of Information Act[13] establishes a statutory right of privacy in information that individuals must submit to government, such as personal tax filings (to be discussed in detail in Chap. 17).[14] In a ruling on the privacy provisions of FOIA, the Supreme Court noted that the act, tort law, and the Constitution each define personal privacy differently.[15] Among other things, open records laws generally enumerate the right of an individual to limit access to and make corrections to personal records held by government and some businesses.

The Supreme Court long has held personal communications through the mail to be private.[16] However, this privacy right arose from the constitutional establishment of the postal system and

---

[5] 381 U.S. at 484.

[6] *See, e.g.,* Kyllo v. United States, 533 U.S. 27 (2001) (warrantless police use of thermal-imaging device of private home violates constitution).

[7] *See* Wilson v. Layne, 526 U.S. 603 (1999).

[8] *See generally,* N. Chang, Silencing Political Dissent (2002).

[9] The full title of the act is the Uniting and Strengthening America by Providing Appropriate Tools Required to Intercept and Obstruct Terrorism Act, Pub. L. No. 107-56.

[10] USA PATRIOT Act §§ 213, 216, 215, amending 50 U.S.C. §§ 3103, 1862, 1863.

[11] N. Chang, Silencing Political Dissent 48-50 (2002).

[12] STATEMENT BY THE PRESIDENT upon signing into law H.R. 2883, the Intelligence Authorization Act for Fiscal Year 2002 (Dec. 28, 2001) available at http://www.fas.org/irp/congress/2001_rpt/hrep107-328.html.

[13] 5 U.S.C.S. 552.

[14] *See, e.g.,* Henke v. U.S. Dept. of Commerce, 83 F.3d 1453 (D.C. Cir. 1996); Doe v. Chao, 306 F.3d 170 (4th Cir. 2002).

[15] U.S. Dept. of Justice v. Reporters Committee for Freedom of Press, 489 U.S. 749 (1989).

[16] *See, e.g.,* United States v. Van Leeuwen, 347 U.S. 249 (1970); *Ex parte* Jackson, 96 U.S. 727 (1877).

did not extend to electronic communications as well.[17] So, legislation, including the Electronic Communications Privacy Act of 1986 and the Stored Communications Act,[18] protects private electronic messages from interception, regardless of the form in which the message is transmitted or stored.[19] In 2001, the U.S. Court of Appeals for the Ninth Circuit said it would be "senseless" for privacy law to protect telephone messages but not information stored on a secure web server.[20] In 2003, the First Circuit made the same point about stored e-mail messages. "It makes no ... sense that a private message expressed in a digitized voice recording stored in a voice mailbox should be protected from interception, but the same words expressed in an e-mail stored in an electronic post office pending delivery should not."[21]

Federal, state and common law all prohibit third parties from monitoring or recording personal communications by telephone, cell phone, e-mail or other electronic devices without consent.[22] It also is a crime in many states, and federally, to publicize information gained through illegal interceptions or wiretaps.[23] However, the Supreme Court ruled in 2001 in *Bartnicki v. Vopper* that the First Amendment protects the accurate disclosure of information gained from illegal interception of cell phone conversations about issues of legitimate public concern when the journalists were not parties to the illegal interception.[24]

Participants generally are free to record their own conversations, but a dozen states and common law prohibit the recording of private conversations without permission from all parties.[25] Federal Communications Commission regulations also require advance notification of recording to all participants.[26] A separate FCC rule, mandating notification of recordings intended for broadcast, does not apply when the recording equipment is visible to participants.

TORT PRIVACY

In addition to constitutional and statutory protection of privacy, four separate communicative torts of invasion of privacy have evolved. Individuals harmed by invasion of privacy seek redress through civil action. Sometimes individuals sue for more than one form of invasion of privacy.

1. Intrusion involves gathering information, particularly as in newsgathering, in a manner that violates an individual's seclusion.
2. Appropriation occurs through the unauthorized use of someone's likeness or identity for commercial gain in violation of a person's property interest in his own image.[27]

---

[17] *See, e.g.,* Olmstead v. United States, 277 U.S. 438 (1928).

[18] 18 U.S.C. §§ 2511, 2520 (2000).

[19] *See, e.g.,* Konop v. Hawaiian Airlines, 236 F.3d 1035 (9th Cir. 2001) (remanding for trial question of whether unauthorized access and transmission of information on a secure website violated the law).

[20] 266 F.3d at 1046.

[21] Blumofe v. Pharmatrak, 329 F.3d 9 (1st Cir. 2003) (remanding for further fact finding whether online pharmaceutical tracking firm intentionally violated Electronic Communications Privacy Act of 1986,. by collecting private information about online drug purchasers).

[22] *See,* Omnibus Crime Control and Safe Streets Act of 1968, 18 U.S.C.S. § 2511 (1) (a); Electronic Communications Privacy Act of 1986, 18 U.S.C.A. § 2510.

[23] 18 U.S.C.A. § 2511 (1) (c).

[24] Bartnicki v. Vopper, 532 U.S. 514 (2001). *See also,* Katz v. United States 389 U.S. 347 (1967) (finding government's warrantless eavesdropping on telephone booth unreasonable when a person has a legitimate expectation of privacy that society would recognize as reasonable).

[25] California, Delaware, Florida, Hawaii, Illinois, Maryland, Massachusetts, Minnesota, Montana, New Hampshire, Pennsylvania, and Washington.

[26] 47 C.F.R. §64.501, § 73.1206.

[27] *See* Zacchini v. Scripps-Howard Broadcasting Co., 433 U.S. 562 (1977) (awarding damages for unauthorized broadcast of performer's entire act).

3. False Light arises when publicity misrepresents someone in a way that hurts her personal comfort or happiness.[28]
4. Disclosure of private facts exists as a tort when private information that is not newsworthy and is (or would be) highly offensive to a reasonable person is widely publicized.[29]

Intrusion

The basic premise of the intrusion tort is that individuals have a right to be left alone where they have a legitimate expectation of privacy and to give consent for violations of this private sphere. The tort of intrusion occurs when someone trespasses, physically or electronically, into another person's private space.[30] Such intrusions include secret video or audio recordings, use of infrared or heat-sensing cameras and telephoto lenses, and long-distance audio surveillance. Intrusion occurs at the time of information gathering, regardless of whether the information is published.

The Supreme Court has said that the right to privacy "varies widely in different settings."[31] Privacy interests take on "special force" inside the home and in its immediate surroundings and are "far less important when strolling through Central Park."[32] In general, people do not have a legitimate expectation of privacy where their behaviors are visible or audible through normal daily behavior. Thus, individuals rarely have a legitimate expectation of privacy even at their own homes when the property is readily accessible or visible to the public from a public space. Employees generally have reduced privacy in the workplace and do not have a reasonable expectation of privacy in the contents of their work computers.[33]

People rarely enjoy a right of privacy in public places or even in quasi-public places, such as restaurants or shopping malls. However, the Court has recognized that the right to privacy may exist in a public forum when an individual has "the right to avoid unwelcome speech ... in confrontational settings."[34] Under this reasoning, the Court ruled that the right to privacy for women seeking abortions extended to the public sidewalks adjacent to clinics and overcame the First Amendment interests of individuals seeking to protest abortions or counsel the women.

Secret recordings may constitute intrusion, particularly in spaces with heightened privacy interests, such as homes, hospital rooms or medical helicopters.[35] Physical intrusion is also of

---

[28] *See* Time, Inc. v. Hill 385 U.S. 374 (1967) (applying actual malice standard to false light claim).

[29] *Restatement (2nd) of Torts*, § 652 D. *See* Cox Broadcasting Corp. v. Cohn, 420 U.S. 469 (1975) (disclosure of rape victim's name protected by the First Amendment); Landmark Communications v. Virginia (1978) (First Amendment protects newspaper disclosure of confidential information about judicial disciplinary process); Smith v. Daily Mail Pub. Co. (1979) (First Amendment generally protects truthful publication of legally obtained private information of public concern); Florida Star v. BJF, 491 U.S. 524 (1989) (damages for disclosure of private facts gained from legally obtained public record require showing of compelling government interest served); Butterworth v. Smith, 494 U.S. 624 (1990) (constitution bars state sanctions for disclosure of own grand jury testimony after grand jury has ended).

[30] Restatement (2nd) of Torts§ 652 B.

[31] Hill v. Colorado, 530 U.S. 703, 716 (2000).

[32] 530 U.S. at 715.

[33] *See, e.g.,* United States v. Angevine, 281 F.3d 1130 (10th Cir. 2002), *cert. den'd,* Angevine v. United States, 2002 U.S. LEXIS 6338 (U.S. Oct. 7, 2002); Leventhal v. Knapek, 266 F.3d 64 (2nd Cir. 2001). *See also* Thomas Greenberg, E-Mail and Voice Mail: Employee Privacy and the Federal Wiretap Statute, 44 Am. U. L. Rev. 219 (1994).

[34] Ibid.

[35] *See* Dietemann v. Time, Inc., 449 F.2d 245 (9th Cir. 1971) (awarding damages for intrusion for secret recordings by journalists in doctor's home). *But see* Medical Lab Management Consultants v. ABC, 306 F.3d 806

special concern in these private places. In a case prompted by the growing practice of journalist "ride-alongs" with police, the Supreme Court ruled that the practice violated the Fourth Amendment rights of homeowners.[36] Thus, when journalists accompany police onto private property without the consent of the property owners, their "intrusion into a private home" likely is not exempt from invasion of privacy and trespass claims. However, emergency officials may exercise control over private property briefly during an emergency if the property owner is not present, and owners give implied consent for journalists to be present when they talk to reporters inside their homes.

Electronic intrusion also may result from the inundation of personal and home computers by unsolicited bulk email. Some courts have ruled that spam constitutes a form of intrusion or trespass[37] that online service providers may prohibit.[38] Federal and state legislatures also have responded to citizen complaints by initiating legislation to eliminate and/or punish origination of bulk junk email. In 2001 alone, for example, Congress introduced eight bills addressing spam,[39] and by 2003 more than two-thirds of the states had passed some form of anti-spam law.[40]

A less visible form of electronic intrusion also has raised concerns in Congress and prompted litigation.[41] Many Internet web sites place cookies, or information gathering files, onto the computers of individuals who access their sites. These cookies then gather and store personal information about the computer users and about computer usage patterns without the knowledge of the computer users. This information often is used for marketing purposes and may be sold.

Generally, third parties are not liable for intrusion by others, even if they benefit from the intrusion. Thus, the Supreme Court refused in *Bartnicki v. Vopper* to hold media liable for broadcasting an innocently obtained tape of an illegally recorded private cell phone conversation.[42]

Appropriation

The tort of appropriation recognizes both an individual's right to avoid the ill effects that may arise when her name or image is used for commercial purposes and the individual's interest

---

(9th Cir. 2002) (affirming summary judgment in favor of American Broadcasting Co. against intrusion claim for covert videotaping during business tour).

[36] Wilson v. Layne, 526 U.S. 603 (1999).

[37] Restatement (2nd) of Torts §§ 252 and 892 A (5).

[38] *See, e.g.,* Verizon Online Servs. v. Ralsky, 203 F. Supp. 2d 601 (E.D. Va. 2002); America Online v. LCGM, 46 F. Supp. 2d 444 (E.D. Va. 1998); America Online v. IMS, 24 F. Supp. 2d 548 (E.D. Va. 1998); CompuServe v. Cyber Promotions, 962 F. Supp. 1015 (S.D. Ohio 1997).

[39] *See* Unsolicited Commercial Electronic Mail Act of 2001, H.R. 95, 107th Cong. (2001); Wireless Telephone Spam Protection Act, H.R. 113, 107th Cong. (2001); Anti-Spamming Act of 2001, H.R. 718, 107th Cong. (2001); Anti-Spamming Act of 2001, H.R. 1017, 107th Cong. (2001); Who Is E-Mailing Our Kids Act, H.R. 1846, 107th Cong. (2001); Protect Children From E-Mail Smut Act of 2001, H.R. 2472, 107th Cong. (2001); Netizens Protection Act of 2001, H.R. 3146, 107th Cong. (2001); "CAN SPAM" Act of 2001, S. 630, 107th Cong. (2001).

[40] *See also* David E. Sorkin, *Spam Laws: United States: State Laws,* at http://www.spamlaws.com /state/index.html (visited June 24, 2003) (listing thirty-four states that have passed some form of anti-spam legislation).

[41] *See, e.g.,* Consumer Internet Privacy Enhancement Act," H.R. 237, 107th Cong. (2001); The Online Privacy protection Act of 2001, H.R. 89, 107th Cong. (2001); Electronic Privacy Protection Act, H.R. 112, 107th Cong. (2001); Social Security Online Privacy Protection Act, H.R. 91, 107th Cong. (2001); Consumer Privacy Protection Act, S. 2606, 106th Cong. (2000). *See also* Blumofe v. Pharmatrak, 329 F.3d 9 (1st Cir. 2003); Doubleclick, 154 F. Supp. 2d 497 (S.D. N.Y. 2001); Intuit, 138 F. Supp. 2d 1272 (C.D. Cal. 2001); Chance v. Avenue A, 165 F. Supp. 2d 1153 (W.D. Wash. 2001).

[42] 532 U.S. 514 (2001).

in controlling the quantity and nature of publicity about herself.[43] The law provides for remedies when a commercial user "appropriates to his own use or benefit the name or likeness of another."[44] Virtually anyone may suffer humiliation from unwilling association with a commercial product, but it is primarily celebrities who have a legal interest in protecting and benefiting from the commercial value of their own name or photograph.

This latter interest is sometimes called the right of publicity. Undue publicity, as a form of misappropriation, is essentially a property based right designed to assure that the individual benefits from the commercial exploitation of his identity. The right protects both actual images of the celebrity and the use of look-alikes and sound-alikes, but it is recognized in fewer than half the states, and law in this area is far from settled.[45] As a property right, the right to publicity may – or may not – outlive the individual.[46]

The U.S. Supreme Court has heard only one case on appropriation. In 1977, the Court upheld a damage award to a circus performer for the news broadcast of his entire act.[47] More recently, the Court has denied *certiorari* to appeals in at least two cases where substantial damages were awarded to well-known singers whose voices were deliberately imitated in advertisements.[48]

State courts also struggle to define the limits of this right. For example, in New York, film director Spike Lee sued media megalith Viacom to prevent its TNN cable network from rebranding itself "Spike TV." In June 2003 both a trial court and a court of appeals agreed to prevent the cable network from using the name "Spike TV" until the court could hear Spike Lee's claim that the name change was an intentional attempt to mislead the public into thinking the director of "Do the Right Thing" was affiliated with the new "men's only" network.[49] In granting an injunction, the lower court said, "a celebrity can in fact establish a vested right in the use of only their first name or a surname."[50] The injunction was lifted in July when the parties agreed to an out-of-court settlements, the details of which have not been disclosed.[51]

Consent is a clear defense to appropriation law. However, consent may not be binding if it is not written, signed by the responsible individual, timely and for the image as it is used for commercial purposes. Subsequent alteration of images may eliminate consent as a defense.

The incidental use doctrine provides another defense to appropriation for the media. Under this doctrine, passing references to a real name or image in products sold for a profit do not constitute appropriation even if the user receives "incidental" commercial benefits from the use.[52] However, explicit or implied product endorsements do constitute appropriation.

Media sometimes respond to appropriation suits by claiming the material was used in a non-commercial, editorial way or was newsworthy, a term that is broadly defined by the courts.[53] If evidence indicates the material was newsworthy, the First Amendment protects the media. For

---

[43] *See* Solano v. Playgirl, 292 F.3d 1078 (9th Cir. 2002), *cert. den'd*, Playgirl v. Solano, 2002 U.S. LEXIS 8482 (U.S. Nov. 18, 2002) (remanding for trial on both aspects of appropriation).

[44] Restatement (2nd) of Torts, § 652 C. See also Restatement (2nd) of Torts, § 652 A and Restatement (3rd) of Unfair Competition, Chap. 4 § 46.

[45] *See* Solano v. Playgirl, 292 F.3d 1078 (9th Cir. 2002).

[46] Restatement (3rd) of Unfair Competition, Chap. 4 §§ 46-7.

[47] Zacchini v. Scripps Howard Broadcasting, 433 U.S. 562 (1977).

[48] Waits v. Frito-Lay, 978 F.2d 1093 (9th Cir. 1992), *cert. den'd*, 506 U.S. 1080 (1993); Midler v. Young & Rubicam, 944 F.2d 909 (9th Cir. 1991), *cert. den'd*, 503 U.S. 951 (1992).

[49] *News in Brief*, 229 NEW YORK L.J. 1 (June 20, 2003).

[50] Deroy Murdock, *Got Spike?*, National Review Online (June 26, 2003).

[51] Lee v. Viacom, No. 110080/2003 (N.Y. Sup. Ct. July 8, 2003).

[52] *See, e.g.*, Benavidez v. Anheuser-Busch, 873 F.2d 102 (5th Cir. 1989).

[53] *See, e.g.*, Hoffman v. Capital Cities/ABC, 225 F.3d 1180 (9th Cir. 2001).

example, in 1996 a federal court of appeals ruled that a sports card company's unauthorized use of the images of Major League Baseball players on their parody cards constituted social commentary protected by the First Amendment.[54]

In 2002, however, the U.S. Court of Appeals for the Ninth Circuit rejected a newsworthiness defense presented by *Playgirl* magazine. The court remanded for trial a claim of misappropriation and false light invasion of privacy brought against the magazine by actor Jose Solano, Jr., best known for his role as Manny Gutierrez on the syndicated television program "Baywatch."[55] Solano claimed he suffered humiliation and embarrassment as a result of use of his photograph on the magazine's cover beneath the headline, "TV Guys. PRIMETIME'S SEXY YOUNG STARS EXPOSED." The court of appeals directed the lower court to determine whether the cover falsely suggested Solano had posed nude for the magazine and whether he had indirectly consented to this commercial use of his image, among other issues.

False light

Jose Solano's false light claim against *Playgirl* indicates how photographs taken for one purpose, such as promotion of a television show, might reasonably misrepresent and harm an individual when they appear in another context, such as a sexually oriented magazine. However, the classic example of false light invasion of privacy arose when *Time* magazine fictionalized parts of a story about the hostage ordeal of the Hill family. While the family's capture by escaped convicts was newsworthy, the family claimed the story portrayed them to the public inaccurately and in a way that was highly offensive to a reasonable person. The Supreme Court, however, said this was insufficient to win damages. In newsworthy stories about matters of public interest, false light plaintiffs need to prove actual malice, the Court said.[56]

In providing media the added protection of the actual malice standard, the Court said it was concerned that damage awards would lead to self-censorship by the media and deprive the public of important, newsworthy information. Moreover, the Court said, "Exposure of the self to others in varying degrees is a concomitant of life in a civilized community. The risk of [media] exposure is an essential incident of life in a society which places a primary value on freedom of speech and the press."[57] Thus, the Supreme Court concluded, public figure plaintiffs and private figures placed in a false light in the context of newsworthy issues must bear a higher burden of proof to protect open public discourse. Courts differ on the degree of fault private figure false light plaintiffs must prove if the story is not newsworthy.

Disclosure of private facts

The element of public interest and legitimate public concern that justified the actual malice standard of fault for damages to the Hills also arises when plaintiffs sue for disclosure of private facts. In these suits, plaintiffs do not sue over misrepresentation or inaccuracy. Indeed, stories that prompt disclosure suits are true. Plaintiffs bring suits for the harm caused by publicizing intimate private facts about their lives to a large number of people.

Certainly, disclosure of truly private personal information violates the core concept of privacy. But what is truly private information? The Supreme Court has said two requirements must be met before information is truly private under this tort. First, the individual must have a legitimate expectation of privacy with regard to the facts. Second, society must view this

---

[54] Cardtoons v. Major League Baseball Players Association, 95 F.3d 959 (10th Cir. 1996).
[55] Solano v. Playgirl, 292 F.3d 1078 (9th Cir. 2002).
[56] Time, Inc. v. Hill, 385 U.S. 374 (1967).
[57] 385 U.S. at 388.

expectation of privacy as reasonable.[58] The first prong of the test is more than the subjective impression of the plaintiff; a legitimate expectation of privacy exists if society would find the expectation justified. The expectation of privacy in personal information, like the expectation of privacy in personal space, varies according to the specific nature of the information and how confidentially it is maintained. In general, the greater the intimacy, the lower the public significance, and the more secret the information, the greater is the legitimate expectation of privacy.[59]

Under the second prong, a reasonable expectation of privacy exists only when the information 1) is not of legitimate interest to the public and 2) its publication is highly offensive to a reasonable person.[60] Some scholars interpret the second prong to establish a tort of outrage. In this view, invasion of privacy occurs when publication of private facts is so unjustified that it affronts common decency and outrages a reasonable person.

In general, information that is either widely known or available or that is newsworthy does not meet the test for publicity of private facts.[61] Thus, in *Cox Broadcasting v. Cohn*, the Supreme Court ruled that media could not be held liable for obtaining the name of a rape victim from a public court proceeding and publicizing it in violation of state law.[62] The Court said no legitimate expectation of privacy exists in information that is widely available to the public, even if that information is offensive to a reasonable person. In another decision involving publicizing the name of a rape victim, the Court ruled that the First Amendment prevents punishment of the media for accurate dissemination of legally obtained information of public importance unless the plaintiff demonstrates that such punishment directly advances a compelling government interest.[63]

More recently, the Court held that the First Amendment even protects disclosure of illegally intercepted private conversations on matters of public importance.[64] In *Bartnicki v. Vopper*, an unidentified individual intercepted and taped a cell phone conversation between a teachers' union representative and its president about possible violence associated with a proposed teachers strike. The tape was given to the media and broadcast. In refusing to affirm an award of damages for disclosure of private facts, the Supreme Court noted that the media played no part in the illegal interception. The Court then balanced the competing interests in personal privacy and public awareness of matters of important public concern and ruled that liability could not be imposed for the truthful disclosure in this case.

Courts vary in their determinations of what information is sufficiently offensive to justify punishment for publicity of truly private facts. In general, however, offensiveness is narrowly defined. Disclosure of details related to sexual behavior, embarrassing communicable diseases, intimate correspondences, private family information and personal finances likely is offensive to a reasonable person.[65] The more sensitive, humiliating or salacious the fact, the more likely it is to qualify as highly offensive. However, newsworthiness, which is broadly defined, outweighs

---

[58] Katz v. United States 389 U.S. 347 (1967).

[59] *See, e.g,* Nixon v. Administrator of General Services, 433 U.S. 425 (1977) (rejecting former president's broad personal privacy claim as related to the records of his official conduct as president).

[60] Restatement (2nd) of Torts, § 652 D.

[61] Restatement (2nd) of Torts, § 652 D (b).

[62] *See,* Cox Broadcasting v. Cohn, 420 U.S. 469 (1975).

[63] Florida Star v. BJF, 491 U.S. 524 (1989).

[64] Bartnicki v. Vopper, 532 U.S. 514 (2001).

[65] Restatement (2nd) of Torts § 652 D (b), (g).

offensiveness. Even prurient details may at times be of sufficient public concern that they no longer qualify as truly private facts under the law.

DEFENSES

As noted above, the First Amendment protection for newsworthy information presents a significant impediment to many claims of invasion of privacy. The Supreme Court has been extremely reluctant to allow media to be found liable for dissemination of truthful information about matters of public concern, and the vast majority of information publicized by the media falls into this category. Courts also have recognized implied consent as a media defense against privacy suits. Courts generally accept that people give implied consent for use of photographs and personal information – such as name, age, and address – when they speak with reporters or participate in public events. However, consent is not certain unless a responsible party provides written consent for use of the particular information in a specific context.

INTENTIONAL INFLICTION OF EMOTIONAL HARM

The tort that arises from intentional infliction of emotional distress is closely related to the harm of disclosure of private facts, but the offense of intentional infliction of emotional distress results from intentionally or recklessly outrageous conduct on the part of the publisher rather than from the inherently sensitive nature of the information disclosed.[66] Intentional infliction of emotional distress often involves speech that violates common standards of decency and good taste. These tort suits, therefore, tend to run headlong into the First Amendment's protection for offensive speech, and few plaintiffs prevail against the media.

In the mid-1980s, well-known conservative minister Jerry Falwell brought the most famous case of intentional infliction of emotional harm against Larry Flynt's *Hustler* magazine.[67] *Hustler* had published a series of parody advertisements, and one suggested that Falwell's first sexual experience was while drunk, in an outhouse with his mother. Falwell sued, and the Supreme Court based its protection of *Hustler* upon the paramount value of open, uninhibited public discourse about public figures.

The Court acknowledged the outrageousness of the publication but noted its explicit labeling as ad parody. The Court ruled that outrageously offensive speech must be protected because outrageousness is an inherently subjective standard and applying it to limit free speech "would allow a jury to impose liability on the basis of jurors' tastes or views, or perhaps on the basis of their dislike of a particular expression"[68] The Constitution protects political parody, biting satire,and vicious debate on public issues – even if the speaker has bad motives and even if the speech inflicts substantial harm – because to do otherwise would unleash suppression of a broad and ambiguous category of speech, the Court said. The Court said public figures must prove *New York Times* actual malice to win suits for emotional distress.

PROMOTING VIOLENCE

Those seeking solutions to violence in society sometimes blame the media for teaching, modeling and inciting violent behavior. Clearly, media have effects in society, but First Amendment theory holds that the benefits of free exchange of information outweigh the potential harms of dangerous ideas. As a consequence, courts asked to determine the liability of media charged with negligent contribution to someone's death or injury often apply the stringent

---

[66] *Restatement (2nd) of Torts*, § 46. *See* Hustler v. Falwell, 485 U.S. 46 (1988) (requiring public figure to prove actual malice to win damages for intentional infliction of emotional distress).

[67] Hustler v. Falwell, 485 U.S. 46 (1988).

[68] 485 U.S. at 55.

Brandenburg incitement test, which requires both speaker intent to incite violence and the likelihood that imminent violence will result.[69]

At least one court has applied *Brandenburg* to hold that it does not protect explicit, detailed instructions on how to commit murder.[70] The U.S. Court of Appeals for the Fourth Circuit held in 1997 that *Brandenburg*'s protection of abstract advocacy of violence did not protect publishers of the book *Hit Man* from liability for murders committed according to its detailed how-to plan. In a similar case, another federal court of appeals affirmed the liability of a magazine for negligently publishing an ad that led to a contract killing.[71] The court said *Soldier of Fortune* magazine was liable because it reasonably should have foreseen the risk involved in publishing a "gun for hire" classified advertisement. Media rarely are found liable for physical harm absent such overt risks.

ADDITIONAL CASE READINGS

The following cases highlight the development of privacy law in the courts. Reading these cases will enhance your understanding of the history and direction of privacy law.

- *Blumofe v. Pharmatrak*, 329 F.3d 9 (1st Cir. 2003) (remanding question of whether clandestine online collection of personal data violates privacy).
- *United States v. Angevine*, 281 F.3d 1130 (10th Cir. 2002) (finding limited right of privacy in material on work computers).
- *Medical Lab Management Consultants v. ABC*, 306 F.3d 806 (9th Cir. 2002) (rejecting privacy claim for covert videotaping of business during invited tour).
- *Solano v. Playgirl*, 292 F.3d 1078 (9th Cir. 2002) (remanding false light and appropriation claim).
- *Verizon Online Services v. Ralsky*, 203 F. Supp. 2d 601 (E.D. Va. 2002) (finding unsolicited bulk email constitutes intrusion).
- *Kyllo v. United States*, 533 U.S. 27 (2001) (finding warrantless police thermal-imaging of home violates Fourth Amendment privacy right).
- *Konop v. Hawaiian Airlines*, 236 F.3d 1035 (9th Cir. 2001) (remanding question of whether unauthorized dissemination of information on a secure website violated privacy).
- *Hill v. Colorado*, 530 U.S. 703, 716 (2000) (finding privacy interest on public sidewalk).
- *Wilson v. Layne*, 526 U.S. 603 (1999) (ruling journalists accompanying police into home violates right of privacy).
- *Florida Star v. BJF*, 491 U.S. 524 (1989) (finding damages against media for disclosure of private facts legally obtained from public record require showing of compelling government interest).
- *Hustler v. Falwell*, 485 U.S. 46 (1988) (requiring public figure to prove actual malice for damage award in emotional distress suit).
- *Zacchini v. Scripps-Howard Broadcasting Co.*, 433 U.S. 562 (1977) (finding broadcast of performer's entire act constitutes appropriation).

---

[69] *See, e.g.*, Davidson v. Time Warner, 25 Media L. Rep. 1705 (S.D. Tex. 1997); Herceg v. Hustler Magazine, 814 F.2d 1017 (5th Cir. 1987); Olivia N. v. NBC, 178 Cal. Rptr. 888 (Cal. Ct. App. 1981); Zamora v. CBS, 480 F. Supp. 199 (S.D. Fla. 1979). *See also* Planned Parenthood of the Colombia/Willamette v. American Coalition of Life Activists, 290 F.3d 1058 (9th Cir. 2002) (applying the Brandenburg test to implied threats posted on a web site).

[70] Rice v. Paladin Enterprises, 128 F.3d 233 (4th Cir. 1997), *cert. den'd*, 523 U.S. 1074 (1998).

[71] Braun v. Soldier of Fortune Magazine, 968 F.2d 1110 (11th Cir. 1992), *cert. den'd*, 506 U.S. 1071 (1993).

- *Dietemann v. Time, Inc.*, 449 F.2d 245 (9th Cir. 1971) (finding intrusion for secret recordings in doctor's home).
- *Time, Inc. v. Hill*, 385 U.S. 374 (1967) (finding newsworthiness protects media from false light damages).
- *Griswold v. Connecticut*, 381 U.S. 479, 484 (1965) (striking state law banning contraceptives as violation of First Amendment privacy right).

The following questions should guide your reading of the cases below.
- Whose right of privacy is at issue in *Cox Broadcasting*?
- How does the Court in *Cox* narrow the broad ruling urged by the media?
- What are the harms to media, beyond monetary damages, the Court envisions from punishing publication?
- What is the rule articulated by the *Cox* majority?
- As expressed in his concurring opinion in *Cox*, what rule would Justice Douglas urge the Court to adopt?
- How does the majority in *Cox* define a matter of public interest?
- Why do the justices disagree on the proper level of scrutiny to apply to the anti-wiretapping laws at issue in *Bartnicki*?
- How does the Court in *Bartnicki* describe and weigh the competing interests?
- Does *Bartnicki* establish a new rule? If so, what?
- What conversations enjoy a legitimate right of privacy under the Court's ruling in *Bartnicki*?
- After *Bartnicki*, when is newsworthy information private?
- In *Bartnicki*, what are the primary points on which the majority and the dissent disagree?

Cox Broadcasting Corp. v. Cohn
420 U.S. 469
(1975)

PRIOR HISTORY: Appeal from the Supreme Court of Georgia.

JUDGES: WHITE, J., delivered the opinion of the Court, in BRENNAN, STEWART, MARSHALL, BLACKMUN, and POWELL, JJ., joined. POWELL, J., filed a concurring opinion. BURGER, C. J., concurred in the judgment. DOUGLAS, J., filed an opinion concurring in the judgment. REHNQUIST, J., filed a dissenting opinion.

OPINION: [471] MR. JUSTICE WHITE delivered the opinion of the Court.

[1A] The issue before us in this case is whether, consistently with the First and Fourteenth Amendments, a State may extend a cause of action for damages for invasion of privacy caused by the publication of the name of a deceased rape victim, which was publicly revealed in connection with the prosecution of the crime.

I. In August 1971, appellee's 17-year-old daughter was the victim of a rape and did not survive the incident. Six youths were soon indicted for murder and rape. Although there was substantial press coverage of the crime and of subsequent developments, the identity of the victim was not disclosed pending trial, perhaps because of Ga. Code Ann. § 26-9901 (1972),[1]

---

[1] "It shall be unlawful for any news media or any other person to print and publish, broadcast, televise, or disseminate through any other medium of public dissemination or cause to be printed and published, broadcast, televised, or disseminated in any newspaper, magazine, periodical or other publication published in this State or through any radio or television broadcast originating in the State the name or identity of any female who may have been raped or upon whom an assault with intent to commit rape may have been made. Any person or

which makes [472] it a misdemeanor to publish or broadcast the name or identity of a rape victim. In April 1972, some eight months later, the six defendants appeared in court. Five pleaded guilty to rape or attempted rape, the charge of murder having been dropped. The guilty pleas were accepted by the court, and the trial of the defendant pleading not guilty was set for a later date.

In the course of the proceedings that day, appellant Wassell,[2] a reporter covering the incident for his employer, learned the name of the victim from an examination of the indictments which were made available for his inspection in the courtroom.[3]

---

corporation violating the provisions of this section shall, upon conviction, be punished as for a misdemeanor."
Three other States have similar statutes. See Fla. Stat. Ann. §§ 794.03, 794.04 (1965 and Supp. 1974-1975); S. C. Code Ann. § 16-81 (1962); Wis. Stat. Ann. § 942.02 (1958). The Wisconsin Supreme Court upheld the constitutionality of a predecessor of § 942.02 in State v. Evjue, 253 Wis. 146, 33 N. W. 2d 305 (1948). The South Carolina statute was involved in Nappier v. Jefferson Standard Life Insurance Co., 322 F.2d 502, 505 (CA4 1963), but no constitutional challenge to the statute was made. In Hunter v. Washington Post, 102 Daily Washington L. Rptr. 1561 (1974), the District of Columbia Superior Court denied the defendant's motion for judgment on the pleadings based upon constitutional grounds in an action brought for invasion of privacy resulting from the defendant's publication identifying the plaintiff as a rape victim and giving her name, age, and address.
[2] Wassell was employed at the time in question as a news staff reporter for WSB-TV and had been so employed for the prior nine years. His function was to investigate newsworthy stories and make televised news reports. He was assigned the coverage of the trial of the young men accused of the rape and murder of Cynthia Cohn on the morning of April 10, 1972, the day it began, and had not been involved with the story previously. He was present during the entire hearing that day except for the first 30 minutes. App. 16-17.
[3] Wassell has described the way in which he obtained the information reported in the broadcast as follows:
"The information on which I prepared the said report was obtained from several sources. First, by personally attending and taking notes of the said trial and the subsequent transfer of four of the six defendants to the Fulton County Jail, I obtained personal knowledge of the events that transpired during the trial of this action and the said transfer of the defendants. Such personal observations and notes were the primary and almost exclusive source of the information upon which the said news report was based. Secondly, during a recess of the said trial, I approached the clerk of the court, who was sitting directly in front of the bench, and requested to see a copy of the indictments. In open court, I was handed the indictments, both the murder and the rape indictments, and was allowed to examine fully this document. As is shown by the said indictments . . . the name of the said Cynthia Cohn appears in clear type. Moreover, no attempt was made by the clerk or anyone else to withhold the name and identity of the

That the name of the [473] victim appears in the indictments and that the indictments were public records available for inspection are not disputed.[4] Later that day, Wassell broadcast over the facilities of station WSB-TV, a television station owned by appellant Cox Broadcasting Corp., a news report concerning [474] the court proceedings. The report named the victim of the crime and was repeated the following day.[5]

In May 1972, appellee brought an action for money damages against appellants, relying on § 26-9901 and claiming that his right to privacy had been invaded by the television broadcasts giving the name of his deceased daughter. Appellants admitted the broadcasts but claimed that they were privileged under both state law and the First and Fourteenth Amendments. The trial court, rejecting appellants' constitutional claims and holding that the Georgia statute gave a civil remedy to those injured by its violation, granted summary judgment to appellee as to liability, with the determination of damages to await trial by jury.

On appeal, the Georgia Supreme Court, in its initial opinion, held that the trial court had erred in construing § 26-9901 to extend a civil cause

---

victim from me or from anyone else and the said indictments apparently were available for public inspection upon request." Id., at 17-18
[4] The indictments are in pertinent part as follows:
"THE GRAND JURORS selected, chosen and sworn for the County of Fulton . . . in the name and behalf of the citizens of Georgia, charge and accuse [the defendants] with the offense of: –
"RAPE
"for that said accused, in the County of Fulton and State of Georgia, on the 18th day of August, 1971 did have carnal knowledge of the person of Cynthia Leslie Cohn, a female, forcibly and against her will . . . ." Id., at 22-23.
"THE GRAND JURORS selected, chosen and sworn for the County of Fulton . . . in the name and behalf of the citizens of Georgia, charge and accuse [the defendants] with the offense of: –
"MURDER
"for that said accused, in the County of Fulton and State of Georgia, on the 18th day of August, 1971 did while in the commission of the offense of Rape, a felony, upon the person of Cynthia Leslie Cohn, a female human being, cause her death by causing her to suffocate . . . ." Id., at 24-25.
[5] The relevant portion of the transcript of the televised report reads as follows:
"Six youths went on trial today for the murder-rape of a teenaged girl.
"The six Sandy Springs High School boys were charged with murder and rape in the death of seventeen year old Cynthia Cohn following a drinking party last August 18th.
"The tragic death of the high school girl shocked the entire Sandy Springs community. Today the six boys had their day in court." App. 19-20.

of action for invasion of privacy and thus found it unnecessary to consider the constitutionality of the statute. 231 Ga. 60, 200 S. E. 2d 127 (1973). The court went on to rule, however, that the complaint stated a cause of action "for the invasion of the appellee's right of privacy, or for the tort of public disclosure" – a "common law tort [existing] in this jurisdiction without the help of the statute that the trial judge in this case relied on." Id., at 62, 200 S. E. 2d, at 130. Although the privacy invaded was not that of the deceased victim, the father was held to have stated a [475] claim for invasion of his own privacy by reason of the publication of his daughter's name. The court explained, however, that liability did not follow as a matter of law and that summary judgment was improper; whether the public disclosure of the name actually invaded appellee's "zone of privacy," and if so, to what extent, were issues to be determined by the trier of fact. Also, "in formulating such an issue for determination by the fact-finder, it is reasonable to require the appellee to prove that the appellants invaded his privacy with wilflul or negligent disregard for the fact that reasonable men would find the invasion highly offensive." Id., at 64, 200 S. E. 2d, at 131. The Georgia Supreme Court did agree with the trial court, however, that the First and Fourteenth Amendments did not, as a matter of law, require judgment for appellants. The court concurred with the statement in Briscoe v. Reader's Digest Assn., Inc., 4 Cal. 3d 529, 541, 483 P. 2d 34, 42 (1971), that "the rights guaranteed by the First Amendment do not require total abrogation of the right to privacy. The goals sought by each may be achieved with a minimum of intrusion upon the other."

Upon motion for rehearing the Georgia court countered the argument that the victim's name was a matter of public interest and could be published with impunity by relying on § 26-9901 as an authoritative declaration of state policy that the name of a rape victim was not a matter of public concern. This time the court felt compelled to determine the constitutionality of the statute and sustained it as a "legitimate limitation on the right of freedom of expression contained in the First Amendment." The court could discern "no public interest or general concern about the identity of the victim of such a crime as will make the right to disclose the identity of the victim rise to the level of First Amendment protection." 231 Ga., at 68, 200 S. E. 2d, at 134.

[476] We postponed decision as to our jurisdiction over this appeal to the hearing on the merits. 415 U.S. 912 (1974). We conclude that the Court has jurisdiction, and reverse the judgment of the Georgia Supreme Court.

II. [2A][3A] Appellants invoke the appellate jurisdiction of this Court under 28 U. S. C. § 1257 (2) and, if that jurisdictional basis is found to be absent, through a petition for certiorari under 28 U.S.C. § 2103. Two questions concerning our jurisdiction must be resolved: (1) whether the constitutional validity of § 26-9901 was "drawn in question," with the Georgia Supreme Court upholding its validity, and (2) whether the decision from which this appeal has been taken is a "[final] judgment or decree."

A [2B] Appellants clearly raised the issue of the constitutionality of § 26-9901 in their motion for rehearing in the Georgia Supreme Court. In denying that motion that court held: "A majority of this court does not consider this statute to be in conflict with the First Amendment." 231 Ga., at 68, 200 S. E. 2d, at 134. Since the court relied upon the statute as a declaration of the public policy of Georgia that the disclosure of a rape victim's name was not to be protected expression, the statute was drawn in question in a manner directly bearing upon the merits of the action, and the decision in favor of its constitutional validity invokes this Court's appellate jurisdiction. Cf. Garrity v. New Jersey, 385 U.S. 493, 495-496 (1967).

B Since 1789, Congress has granted this Court appellate jurisdiction with respect to state litigation only after the highest state court in which judgment could be had has [477] rendered a "[final] judgment or decree." Title 28 U. S. C. § 1257 retains this limitation on our power to review cases coming from state courts. The Court has noted that "[considerations] of English usage as well as those of judicial policy" would justify an interpretation of the final-judgment rule to preclude review "where anything further remains to be determined by a State court, no matter how dissociated from the only federal issue that has finally been adjudicated by the highest court of the State." Radio Station WOW, Inc. v. Johnson, 326 U.S. 120, 124 (1945). But the Court there observed that the rule had not been administered in such a mechanical fashion and that there were circumstances in which there has been "a departure from this requirement of finality for federal appellate jurisdiction." Ibid.

[4A] These circumstances were said to be "very few," ibid.; but as the cases have unfolded, the Court has recurringly encountered situations in which the highest court of a State has finally determined the federal issue present in a particular case, but in which there are further proceedings in the lower state courts to come. There are now at least four categories of such cases in which the Court has treated the decision on the federal issue as a final judgment for the purposes of 28 U.S.C. § 1257 and has taken jurisdiction without awaiting the completion of the additional proceedings anticipated in the lower state courts. In most, if not all, of the cases in these categories, these additional proceedings would not require the decision of other federal questions that might also require review by the Court at a later date,[6] and immediate [478] rather than delayed review would be the best way to avoid "the mischief of economic waste and of delayed justice," Radio Station WOW, Inc. v. Johnson, supra, at 124, as well as precipitate interference with state litigation.[7] In the cases in the first two categories considered below, the federal issue would not be mooted or otherwise affected by the proceedings yet to be had because those proceedings have little substance, their outcome is certain, or they are wholly unrelated to the federal question. In the other two categories, however, the federal issue would be mooted if the petitioner or appellant seeking to bring the action here prevailed on the merits in the later state-court proceedings, but there is nevertheless [479] sufficient justification for immediate review of the federal question finally determined in the state courts.

[4B][5] In the first category are those cases in which there are further proceedings – even entire trials – yet to occur in the state courts but where for one reason or another the federal issue is conclusive or the outcome of further proceedings pre-ordained. In these circumstances, because the case is for all practical purposes concluded, the judgment of the state court on the federal issue is deemed final. In Mills v. Alabama, 384 U.S. 214 (1966), for example, a demurrer to a criminal complaint was sustained on federal constitutional grounds by a state trial court. The State Supreme Court reversed, remanding for jury trial. This Court took jurisdiction on the reasoning that the appellant had no defense other than his federal claim and could not prevail at trial on the facts or any non-federal ground. To dismiss the appeal "would not only be an inexcusable delay of the benefits Congress intended to grant by providing for appeal to this Court, but it would also result in a completely unnecessary waste of time and energy in judicial systems already troubled by delays due to congested dockets."Id., at 217-218 (footnote omitted).[8]

[480] Second, there are cases such as Radio Station WOW, supra, and Brady v. Maryland, 373 U.S. 83 (1963), in which the federal issue, finally decided by the highest court in the State, will survive and require decision regardless of the outcome of future state-court proceedings. In Radio Station WOW, the Nebraska Supreme Court directed the transfer of the properties of a federally licensed radio station and ordered an accounting, rejecting the claim that the transfer order would interfere with the federal license. The

---

[6] Eminent domain proceedings are of the type that may involve an interlocutory decision as to a federal question with another federal question to be decided later. "For in those cases the federal constitutional question embraces not only a taking, but a taking on payment of just compensation. A state judgment is not final unless it covers both aspects of that integral problem." North Dakota State Board of Pharmacy v. Snyder's Drug Stores, Inc., 414 U.S. 156, 163 (1973). See also Grays Harbor Co. v. Coats-Fordney Co., 243 U.S. 251, 256 (1917); Radio Station WOW, Inc. v. Johnson, 326 U.S. 120, 127 (1945).

[7] Gillespie v. United States Steel Corp., 379 U.S. 148 (1964), arose in the federal courts and involved the requirement of 28 U. S. C. § 1291 that judgments of district courts be final if they are to be appealed to the courts of appeals. In the course of deciding that the judgment of the District Court in the case had been final, the Court indicated its approach to finality requirements: "And our cases long have recognized that whether a ruling is 'final' within the meaning of § 1291 is frequently so close a question that decision of that issue either way can be supported with equally forceful arguments, and that it is impossible to devise a formula to resolve all marginal cases coming within what might well be called the 'twilight zone' of finality. Because of this difficulty this Court has held that the requirement of finality is to be given a 'practical rather than a technical construction.' Cohen v. Beneficial Industrial Loan Corp., [337 U.S. 541, 546]. See also Brown Shoe Co. v. United States, 370 U.S. 294, 306; Bronson v. Railroad Co., 2 Black 524, 531; Forgay v. Conrad, 6 How. 201, 203. Dickinson v. Petroleum Conversion Corp., 338 U.S. 507, 511, pointed out that in deciding the question of finality the most important competing considerations are 'the inconvenience and costs of piecemeal review on the one hand and the danger of denying justice by delay on the other.'" 379 U.S., at 152-153.

---

[8] Other cases from state courts where this Court's jurisdiction was sustained for similar reasons include: Organization for a Better Austin v. Keefe, 402 U.S. 415, 418 n. (1971); Construction Laborers v. Curry, 371 U.S. 542, 550-551 (1963); Pope v. Atlantic C. L. R. Co., 345 U.S. 379, 382 (1953); Richfield Oil Corp. v. State Board, 329 U.S. 69, 73-74 (1946). In the Richfield case the Court said with respect to finality:
"The designation given the judgment by state practice is not controlling. Dept. of Banking v. Pink, 317 U.S. 264, 268. The question is whether it can be said that 'there is nothing more to be decided' (Clark v. Williard, 292 U.S. 112, 118), that there has been 'an effective determination of the litigation.' Market Street Ry. Co. v. Railroad Commission, 324 U.S. 548, 551; see Radio Station WOW v. Johnson, 326 U.S. 120, 123-124. That question will be resolved not only by an examination of the entire record (Clark v. Williard, supra) but, where necessary, by resort to the local law to determine what effect the judgment has under the state rules of practice." Id., at 72.

federal issue was held reviewable here despite the pending accounting on the "presupposition . . . that the federal questions that could come here have been adjudicated by the State court, and that the accounting which remains to be taken could not remotely give rise to a federal question ... that may later come here...." 326 U.S., at 127. The judgment rejecting the federal claim and directing the transfer was deemed "dissociated from a provision for an accounting even though that is decreed in the same order." Id., at 126. Nothing that could happen in the course of the accounting, short of settlement of the case, would foreclose or make unnecessary decision on the federal question. Older cases in the Court had reached the same result on similar facts. Carondelet Canal & Nav. Co. v. Louisiana, 233 U.S. 362 (1914); Forgay v. Conrad, 6 How. 201 (1848). In the latter case, the Court, in an opinion by Mr. Chief Justice Taney, stated that the Court had not understood the final-judgment rule "in this strict and technical sense, but has given [it] a more liberal, and, as we think, a more reasonable construction, [481] and one more consonant to the intention of the legislature." Id., at 203.[9]

In the third category are those situations where the federal claim has been finally decided, with further proceedings on the merits in the state courts to come, but in which later review of the federal issue cannot be had, whatever the ultimate outcome of the case. Thus, in these cases, if the party seeking interim review ultimately prevails on the merits, the federal issue will be mooted; if he were to lose on the merits, however, the governing state law would not permit him again to present his federal claims for review. The Court has taken jurisdiction in these circumstances prior to completion of the case in the state courts. California v. Stewart, 384 U.S. 436 (1966) (decided with Miranda v. Arizona), epitomizes this category. There the state court reversed a conviction on federal constitutional grounds and remanded for a new trial. Although the State might have prevailed at trial, we granted its petition for certiorari and affirmed, explaining that the state judgment was "final" since an acquittal of the defendant at trial would preclude, under state law, an appeal by the State. Id., at 498 n. 71.

A recent decision in this category is North Dakota State Board of Pharmacy v. Snyder's Drug Stores, Inc., 414 U.S. 156 (1973), in which the Pharmacy Board rejected an application for a pharmacy operating permit relying on a state statute specifying ownership requirements which the applicant did not meet. The State Supreme [482] Court held the statute unconstitutional and remanded the matter to the Board for further consideration of the application, freed from the constraints of the ownership statute. The Board brought the case here, claiming that the statute was constitutionally acceptable under modern cases. After reviewing the various circumstances under which the finality requirement has been deemed satisfied despite the fact that litigation had not terminated in the state courts, we entertained the case over claims that we had no jurisdiction. The federal issue would not survive the remand, whatever the result of the state administrative proceedings. The Board might deny the license on state-law grounds, thus foreclosing the federal issue, and the Court also ascertained that under state law the Board could not bring the federal issue here in the event the applicant satisfied the requirements of state law except for the invalidated ownership statute. Under these circumstances, the issue was ripe for review.[10]

Lastly, there are those situations where the federal issue has been finally decided in the state courts with further proceedings pending in which the party seeking review here might prevail on the merits on nonfederal grounds, thus rendering unnecessary review of the federal issue by this Court, and where reversal of the state court on the federal issue would be preclusive of any further [483] litigation on the relevant cause of action rather than merely controlling the nature and character of, or determining the admissibility of evidence in, the state proceedings still to come. In these circumstances, if a refusal immediately to review the state-court decision might seriously erode federal policy, the Court has entertained and decided the federal issue, which itself has been finally determined by the state courts for purposes of the state litigation.

---

[9] In Brady v. Maryland, 373 U.S. 83 (1963), the Maryland courts had ordered a new trial in a criminal case but on punishment only, and the petitioner asserted here that he was entitled to a new trial on guilt as well. We entertained the case, saying that the federal issue was separable and would not be mooted by the new trial on punishment ordered in the state courts. Id., at 85 n. 1.

---

[10] Cohen v. Beneficial Industrial Loan Corp., 337 U.S. 541 (1949), was a diversity action in the federal courts in the course of which there arose the question of the validity of a state statute requiring plaintiffs in stockholder suits to post security for costs as a prerequisite to bringing the action. The District Court held the state law inapplicable, the Court of Appeals reversed, and this Court, after granting certiorari, held that the issue of security for costs was separable from and independent of the merits and that if review were to be postponed until the termination of the litigation, "it will be too late effectively to review the present order, and the rights conferred by the statute, if it is applicable, will have been lost, probably irreparably." Id., at 546.

In Construction Laborers v. Curry, 371 U.S. 542 (1963), the state courts temporarily enjoined labor union picketing over claims that the National Labor Relations Board had exclusive jurisdiction of the controversy. The Court took jurisdiction for two independent reasons. First, the power of the state court to proceed in the face of the preemption claim was deemed an issue separable from the merits and ripe for review in this Court, particularly "when postponing review would seriously erode the national labor policy requiring the subject matter of respondents' cause to be heard by the . . . Board, not by the state courts." Id., at 550. Second, the Court was convinced that in any event the union had no defense to the entry of a permanent injunction other than the preemption claim that had already been ruled on in the state courts. Hence the case was for all practical purposes concluded in the state tribunals.

In Mercantile National Bank v. Langdeau, 371 U.S. 555 (1963), two national banks were sued, along with others, in the courts of Travis County, Tex. The claim asserted was conspiracy to defraud an insurance company. The banks as a preliminary matter asserted that a special federal venue statute immunized them from suit in Travis County and that they could properly be sued only in another county. Although trial was still to be had and the banks might well prevail on the merits, the Court, relying on Curry, entertained the issue as a "separate [484] and independent matter, anterior to the merits and not enmeshed in the factual and legal issues comprising the plaintiff's cause of action." Id., at 558. Moreover, it would serve the policy of the federal statute "to determine now in which state court appellants may be tried rather than to subject them ... to long and complex litigation which may all be for naught if consideration of the preliminary question of venue is postponed until the conclusion of the proceedings." Ibid.

Miami Herald Publishing Co. v. Tornillo, 418 U.S. 241 (1974), is the latest case in this category.[11]

There a candidate for public office sued a newspaper for refusing, allegedly contrary to a state statute, to carry his reply to the paper's editorial critical of his qualifications. The trial court held the act unconstitutional, denying both injunctive relief and damages. The State Supreme Court reversed, sustaining the statute against the challenge based upon the First and Fourteenth Amendments and remanding the case for a trial and appropriate relief, including damages. The newspaper brought the case here. We sustained our jurisdiction, relying on the principles elaborated in the North Dakota case and observing:

"Whichever way we were to decide on the merits, it [485] would be intolerable to leave unanswered, under these circumstances, an important question of freedom of the press under the First Amendment; an uneasy and unsettled constitutional posture of § 104.38 could only further harm the operation of a free press. Mills v. Alabama, 384 U.S. 214, 221-222 (1966) (DOUGLAS, J., concurring). See also Organization for a Better Austin v. Keefe, 402 U.S. 415, 418 n. (1971)." 418 U.S., at 247 n. 6.[12]

[3B] [6A] [7A] In light of the prior cases, we conclude that we have jurisdiction to review the judgment of the Georgia Supreme Court rejecting the challenge under the First and Fourteenth Amendments to the state law authorizing damage suits against the press for publishing the name of a rape victim whose identity is revealed in the course of a public prosecution. The Georgia Supreme Court's judgment is plainly final on the federal issue and is not subject to further review in the state courts. Appellants will be liable for damages if the elements of the state cause of action are proved. They may prevail at trial on nonfederal grounds, it is true, but if the Georgia court erroneously upheld the statute, there should be no trial at all. Moreover, even if appellants prevailed at trial and made unnecessary further consideration of the constitutional question, there would remain in effect the unreviewed decision of the State Supreme Court that a civil action for publishing the name of a rape victim disclosed in a public judicial proceeding may go forward despite the First and Fourteenth Amendments.

---

[11] Meanwhile Hudson Distributors v. Eli Lilly, 377 U.S. 386 (1964), another case of this genre, had been decided. There a retailer sued to invalidate a state fair trade act as inconsistent with the federal antitrust laws and not saved by a federal statute authorizing state fair trade legislation under certain conditions. The defendant manufacturer cross-petitioned for enforcement of the state act against the plaintiff-retailer. The trial court struck down the statute, but a state appellate court reversed and remanded for trial on the cross-petition. The Ohio Supreme Court affirmed that decision. Relying on Curry and Mercantile National Bank v. Langdeau, 371 U.S. 555 (1963), this Court found the state-court judgment to be ripe for review, although the retailer might prevail at the trial. 377 U.S., at 389 n. 4.

[12] The import of the Court's holding in Tornillo is underlined by its citation of the concurring opinion in Mills v. Alabama. There, MR. JUSTICE DOUGLAS, joined by MR. JUSTICE BRENNAN, stated that even if the appellant had a defense and might prevail at trial, jurisdiction was properly noted in order to foreclose unwarranted restrictions on the press should the state court's constitutional judgment prove to be in error.

Delaying final [486] decision of the First Amendment claim until after trial will "leave unanswered ... an important question of freedom of the press under the First Amendment," "an uneasy and unsettled constitutional posture [that] could only further harm the operation of a free press." Tornillo, supra, at 247 n. 6. On the other hand, if we now hold that the First and Fourteenth Amendments bar civil liability for broadcasting the victim's name, this litigation ends. Given these factors – that the litigation could be terminated by our decision on the merits[13] and that a failure to decide the question now will leave the press in Georgia operating in the shadow of the civil and criminal sanctions of a rule of law and a statute the constitutionality of which is in serious doubt – we find that reaching the merits is consistent with the pragmatic approach that we have followed in the past in determining finality. [487] See Gillespie v. United States Steel Corp., 379 U.S. 148 (1964); Radio Station WOW, Inc. v. Johnson, 326 U.S., at 124; Mills v. Alabama, 384 U.S., at 221-222 (DOUGLAS, J., concurring).[14]

III. [6B][7B] Georgia stoutly defends both § 26-9901 and the State's common-law privacy action challenged here. Its claims are not without force, for powerful arguments can be made, and have been made, that however it may be ultimately defined, there is a zone of privacy surrounding every individual, a zone within which the State may protect him from intrusion by the press, with all its attendant publicity.[15] Indeed, the central thesis of the root article by Warren and Brandeis, The Right to Privacy, 4 Harv. L. Rev. 193, 196 (1890), was that the press was overstepping its prerogatives by publishing essentially private information and that there should be a remedy for the alleged abuses.[16]

[488][8] More compellingly, the century has experienced a strong tide running in favor of the so-called right of privacy. In 1967, we noted that "[it] has been said that a 'right of privacy' has been recognized at common law in 30 States plus the District of Columbia and by statute in

---

[13] MR. JUSTICE REHNQUIST, post, at 507-508, is correct in saying that this factor involves consideration of the merits in determining jurisdiction. But it does so only to the extent of determining that the issue is substantial and only in the context that if the state court's final decision on the federal issue is incorrect, federal law forecloses further proceedings in the state court. That the petitioner who protests against the state court's decision on the federal question might prevail on the merits on nonfederal grounds in the course of further proceedings anticipated in the state court and hence obviate later review of the federal issue here is not preclusive of our jurisdiction. Curry, Langdeau, North Dakota State Board of Pharmacy, California v. Stewart, 384 U.S. 436 (1966) (decided with Miranda v. Arizona, and Miami Herald Publishing Co. v. Tornillo, 418 U.S. 241 (1974), make this clear. In those cases, the federal issue having been decided, arguably wrongly, and being determinative of the litigation if decided the other way, the finality rule was satisfied. The author of the dissent, a member of the majority in Tornillo, does not disavow that decision. He seeks only to distinguish it by indicating that the First Amendment issue at stake there was more important and pressing than the one here. This seems to embrace the thesis of that case and of this one as far as the approach to finality is concerned, even though the merits and the avoidance doctrine are to some extent involved.

[14] In finding that we have appellate jurisdiction, we also take jurisdiction over any aspects of the case which would otherwise fall solely within our certiorari jurisdiction. See Flournoy v. Wiener, 321 U.S. 253, 263 (1944); Prudential Insurance Co. v. Cheek, 259 U.S. 530, 547 (1922); cf. Palmore v. United States, 411 U.S. 389, 397 n. 6 (1973); Mishkin v. New York, 383 U.S. 502, 512 (1966).

[15] See T. Emerson, The System of Freedom of Expression 544-562 (1970); Konvitz, Privacy and the Law: A Philosophical Prelude, 31 Law & Contemp. Prob. 272 (1966); Bloustein, Privacy as an Aspect of Human Dignity: An Answer to Dean Prosser, 39 N. Y. U. L. Rev. 962 (1964).

[16] "Of the desirability – indeed of the necessity – of some such protection [of the right of privacy], there can, it is believed, be no doubt. The press is overstepping in every direction the obvious bounds of propriety and of decency. Gossip is no longer the resource of the idle and of the vicious, but has become a trade, which is pursued with industry as well as effrontery. To satisfy a prurient taste the details of sexual relations are spread broadcast in the columns of the daily papers. To occupy the indolent, column upon column is filled with idle gossip, which can only be procured by intrusion upon the domestic circle. The intensity and complexity of life, attendant upon advancing civilization, have rendered necessary some retreat from the world, and man, under the refining influence of culture, has become more sensitive to publicity, so that solitude and privacy have become more essential to the individual; but modern enterprise and invention have, through invasions upon his privacy, subjected him to mental pain and distress, far greater than could be inflicted by mere bodily injury. Nor is the harm wrought by such invasions confined to the suffering of those who may be made the subjects of journalistic or other enterprise. In this, as in other branches of commerce, the supply creates the demand. Each crop of unseemly gossip, thus harvested, becomes the seed of more, and, in direct proportion to its circulation, results in a lowering of social standards and of morality. Even gossip apparently harmless, when widely and persistently circulated, is potent for evil. It both belittles and perverts. It belittles by inverting the relative importance of things, thus dwarfing the thoughts and aspirations of a people. When personal gossip attains the dignity of print, and crowds the space available for matters of real interest to the community, what wonder that the ignorant and thoughtless mistake its relative importance. Easy of comprehension, appealing to that weak side of human nature which is never wholly cast down by the misfortunes and frailties of our neighbors, no one can be surprised that it usurps the place of interest in brains capable of other things. Triviality destroys at once robustness of thought and delicacy of feeling. No enthusiasm can flourish, no generous impulse can survive under its blighting influence."

four States." Time, Inc. v. Hill, 385 U.S. 374, 383 n. 7. We there cited the 1964 edition of Prosser's Law of Torts. The 1971 edition of that same source states that "[in] one form or another, the right of privacy is by this time recognized and accepted in all but a very few jurisdictions." W. Prosser, Law of Torts 804 (4th ed.) (footnote omitted). Nor is it irrelevant [489] here that the right of privacy is no recent arrival in the jurisprudence of Georgia, which has embraced the right in some form since 1905 when the Georgia Supreme Court decided the leading case of Pavesich v. New England Life Ins. Co., 122 Ga. 190, 50 S. E. 68.

These are impressive credentials for a right of privacy,[17] but we should recognize that we do not have at issue here an action for the invasion of privacy involving the appropriation of one's name or photograph, a physical or other tangible intrusion into a private area, or a publication of otherwise private information that is also false although perhaps not defamatory. The version of the privacy tort now before us–termed in Georgia "the tort of public disclosure," 231 Ga., at 60, 200 S. E. 2d, at 130–is that in which the plaintiff claims the right to be free from unwanted publicity about his private affairs, which, although wholly true, would be offensive to a person of ordinary sensibilities. Because the gravamen of the claimed injury is the publication of information, whether true or not, the dissemination of which is embarrassing or otherwise painful to an individual, it is here that claims of privacy most directly confront the constitutional freedoms of speech and press. The face-off is apparent, and the appellants urge upon us the broad holding that the press may not be made criminally or civilly liable for publishing information that is neither false nor misleading but absolutely accurate, however damaging it may be to reputation or individual sensibilities.

[9][10A][11][12] It is true that in defamation actions, where the protected interest is personal reputation, the prevailing view is that truth is a defense;[18] and the message of New York [490] Times Co. v. Sullivan, 376 U.S. 254 (1964);

Garrison v. Louisiana, 379 U.S. 64 (1964); Curtis Publishing Co. v. Butts, 388 U.S. 130 (1967), and like cases is that the defense of truth is constitutionally required wher the subject of the publication is a public official or public figure. What is more, the defamed public official or public figure must prove not only that the publication is false but that it was knowingly so or was circulated with reckless disregard for its truth or falsity. Similarly, where the interest at issue is privacy rather than reputation and the right claimed is to be free from the publication of false or misleading information about one's affairs, the target of the publication must prove knowing or reckless falsehood where the materials published, although assertedly private, are "matters of public interest." Time, Inc. v. Hill, supra, at 387-388.[19]

[10B] The Court has nevertheless carefully left open the question whether the First and Fourteenth Amendments require that truth be recognized as a defense in a defamation action brought by a private person as distinguished from a public official or public figure. Garrison held that where criticism is of a public official and his conduct of public business, "the interest in private reputation is overborne [491] by the larger public interest, secured by the Constitution, in the dissemination of truth," 379 U.S., at 73 (footnote omitted), but recognized that "different interests may be involved where purely private libels, totally unrelated to public affairs, are concerned; therefore, nothing we say today is to be taken as intimating any views as to the impact of the constitutional guarantees in the discrete area of purely private libels." Id., at 72 n. 8. In similar fashion, Time, Inc. v. Hill, supra, expressly saved the question whether truthful publication of very private matters unrelated to public affairs could be constitutionally proscribed. 385 U.S., at 383 n. 7.

[13] Those precedents, as well as other considerations, counsel similar caution here. In this sphere of collision between claims of privacy and those of the free press, the interests on both sides are plainly rooted in the traditions and significant concerns of our society. Rather than address the broader question whether truthful publications

---

[17] See also Time, Inc. v. Hill, 385 U.S. 374, 404 (1967) (opinion of Harlan, J.); id., at 412-415 (Fortas, J., dissenting).

[18] See Restatement (Second) of Torts § 582 (Tent. Draft No. 20, Apr. 25, 1974); W. Prosser, Law of Torts § 116 (4th ed. 1971). Under the common law, truth was not a complete defense to prosecutions for criminal libel, although it was in civil actions. Several jurisdictions in this country have provided, however, that the defense of truth in civil actions requires a showing that the publication was made for good motives or for justifiable ends. See id., at 796-797.

---

[19] In another "false light" invasion of privacy case before us this Term, Cantrell v. Forest City Publishing Co., 419 U.S. 245, 250-251 (1974), we observed that we had, in that case, "no occasion to consider whether a State may constitutionally apply a more relaxed standard of liability for a publisher or broadcaster of false statements injurious to a private individual under a false-light theory of invasion of privacy, or whether the constitutional standard announced in Time, Inc. v. Hill applies to all false-light cases. Cf. Gertz v. Robert Welch, Inc., 418 U.S. 323."

may ever be subjected to civil or criminal liability consistently with the First and Fourteenth Amendments, or to put it another way, whether the State may ever define and protect an area of privacy free from unwanted publicity in the press, it is appropriate to focus on the narrower interface between press and privacy that this case presents, namely, whether the State may impose sanctions on the accurate publication of the name of a rape victim obtained from public records – more specifically, from judicial records which are maintained in connection with a public prosecution and which themselves are open to public inspection. We are convinced that the State may not do so.

In the first place, in a society in which each individual has but limited time and resources with which to observe at first hand the operations of his government, he relies necessarily upon the press to bring to him in convenient form the facts of those operations. Great responsibility [492] is accordingly placed upon the news media to report fully and accurately the proceedings of government, and official records and documents open to the public are the basic data of governmental operations. Without the information provided by the press most of us and many of our representatives would be unable to vote intelligently or to register opinions on the administration of government generally. With respect to judicial proceedings in particular, the function of the press serves to guarantee the fairness of trials and to bring to bear the beneficial effects of public scrutiny upon the administration of justice. See Sheppard v. Maxwell, 384 U.S. 333, 350 (1966).

Appellee has claimed in this litigation that the efforts of the press have infringed his right to privacy by broadcasting to the world the fact that his daughter was a rape victim. The commission of crime, prosecutions resulting from it, and judicial proceedings arising from the prosecutions, however, are without question events of legitimate concern to the public and consequently fall within the responsibility of the press to report the operations of government.

The special protected nature of accurate reports of judicial proceedings has repeatedly been recognized. This Court, in an opinion written by MR. JUSTICE DOUGLAS, has said:

"A trial is a public event. What transpires in the court room is public property. If a transcript of the court proceedings had been published, we suppose none would claim that the judge could punish the publisher for contempt. And we can see no difference though the conduct of the attorneys, of the jury, or even of the judge himself, may have reflected on the court. Those who see and hear what transpired can report it with impunity. There is no special perquisite of the judiciary which

enables [493] it, as distinguished from other institutions of democratic government, to suppress, edit, or censor events which transpire in proceedings before it." Craig v. Harney, 331 U.S. 367, 374 (1947) (emphasis added).

See also Sheppard v. Maxwell, supra, at 362-363; Estes v. Texas, 381 U.S. 532, 541-542 (1965); Pennekamp v. Florida, 328 U.S. 331 (1946); Bridges v. California, 314 U.S. 252 (1941).

[14] The developing law surrounding the tort of invasion of privacy recognizes a privilege in the press to report the events of judicial proceedings. The Warren and Brandeis article, supra, noted that the proposed new right would be limited in the same manner as actions for libel and slander where such a publication was a privileged communication: "the right to privacy is not invaded by any publication made in a court of justice ... and (at least in many jurisdictions) reports of any such proceedings would in some measure be accorded a like privilege."[20]

The Restatement of Torts, § 867, embraced an action for privacy.[21] Tentative Draft No. 13 of the Second Restatement of Torts, §§ 652A-652E, divides the privacy tort into four branches;[22] and with respect to the wrong of giving unwanted publicity about private life, the commentary [494] to § 652D states: "There is no liability when the defendant merely gives further publicity to information about the plaintiff which is already public. Thus there is no liability for giving publicity to facts about the plaintiff's life which are matters of public record . . . ."[23] The same is true of the separate tort of physically or otherwise intruding upon the seclusion or private affairs of another. Section 652B, Comment c, provides that "there is no liability for the examination of a public record concerning the plaintiff, or of documents which the plaintiff is required to keep and make available for public inspection."[24] According to this draft, ascertaining and publishing the contents of

---

[20] 4 Harv. L. Rev., at 216-217.

[21] Restatement of Torts § 867 (1939).

[22] Restatement (Second) of Torts §§ 652A-652E (Tent. Draft No. 13, Apr. 27, 1967). The four branches are: unreasonable intrusion upon the seclusion of another (§ 652B), appropriation of the other's name or likeness (§ 652C), unreasonable publicity given to the other's private life (§ 652D), and publicity which unreasonably places the other in a false light before the public (§ 652E). See § 652A. The same categorization is suggested in W. Prosser, Law of Torts § 117 (4th ed. 1971); Prosser, Privacy, 48 Calif. L. Rev. 383 (1960).

[23] Restatement (Second) of Torts, supra, § 652D, Comment c, at 114.

[24] Id., § 652B, Comment c, at 104.

public records are simply not within the reach of these kinds of privacy actions.[25]

[15][16][17] Thus even the prevailing law of invasion of privacy generally recognizes that the interests in privacy fade [495] when the information involved already appears on the public record. The conclusion is compelling when viewed in terms of the First and Fourteenth Amendments and in light of the public interest in a vigorous press. The Georgia cause of action for invasion of privacy through public disclosure of the name of a rape victim imposes sanctions on pure expression – the content of a publication – and not conduct or a combination of speech and nonspeech elements that might otherwise be open to regulation or prohibition. See United States v. O'Brien, 391 U.S. 367, 376-377 (1968). The publication of truthful information available on the public record contains none of the indicia of those limited categories of expression, such as "fighting" words, which "are no essential part of any exposition of ideas, and are of such slight social value as a step to truth that any benefit that may be derived from them is clearly outweighed by the social interest in order and morality." Chaplinsky v. New Hampshire, 315 U.S. 568, 572 (1942).

[18][19] By placing the information in the public domain on official court records, the State must be presumed to have concluded that the public interest was thereby being served. Public records by their very nature are of interest to those concerned with the administration of government, and a public benefit is performed by the reporting of the true contents of the records by the media. The freedom of the press to publish that information appears to us to be of critical importance to our type of government in which the citizenry is the final judge of the proper conduct of public business. In preserving that form of government the First and Fourteenth Amendments command nothing less than that the States may not impose sanctions on the publication of truthful information contained in official court records open to public inspection.

[496][20][21] We are reluctant to embark on a course that would make public records generally available to the media but forbid their publication if offensive to the sensibilities of the supposed reasonable man. Such a rule would make it very difficult for the media to inform citizens about the public business and yet stay within the law. The rule would invite timidity and self-censorship and very likely lead to the suppression of many items that would otherwise be published and that should be made available to the public. At the very least, the First and Fourteenth Amendments will not allow exposing the press to liability for truthfully publishing information released to the public in official court records. If there are privacy interests to be protected in judicial proceedings, the States must respond by means which avoid public documentation or other exposure of private information. Their political institutions must weigh the interests in privacy with the interests of the public to know and of the press to publish.[26] Once true information is disclosed in public court documents open to public inspection, the press cannot be sanctioned for publishing it. In this instance as in others reliance must rest upon the judgment of those who decide what to publish or broadcast. See Miami Herald Publishing Co. v. Tornillo, 418 U.S., at 258.

[1B][22A] Appellant Wassell based his televised report upon notes taken during the court proceedings and obtained the name of the victim from the indictments handed to him at his request during a recess in the hearing. Appellee has not contended that the name was obtained in an improper fashion or that it was not on an official court document open to public inspection. Under these circumstances, [497] the protection of freedom of the press provided by the First and Fourteenth Amendments bars the State of Georgia from making appellants' broadcast the basis of civil liability.[27] [22B] Reversed.

[25] See also W. Prosser, Law of Torts, supra, at 810-811. For decisions emphasizing as a defense to actions claiming invasion of privacy the fact that the invasion in question was derived from official records available to the public, see Hubbard v. Journal Publishing Co., 69 N. M. 473, 368 P. 2d 147 (1962) (information regarding sexual assault by a boy upon his younger sister derived from official juvenile-court records open to public inspection); Edmiston v. Time, Inc., 257 F.Supp. 22 (SDNY 1966) (fair and true report of court opinion); Bell v. Courier-Journal & Louisville Times Co., 402 S. W. 2d 84 (Ky. 1966); Lamont v. Commissioner of Motor Vehicles, 269 F.Supp. 880 (SDNY), aff'd, 386 F.2d 449 (CA2 1967), cert. denied, 391 U.S. 915 (1968); Frith v. Associated Press, 176 F.Supp. 671 (EDSC 1959); Meetze v. Associated Press, 230 S. C. 330, 95 S. E. 2d 606 (1956); Thompson v. Curtis Publishing Co., 193 F.2d 953 (CA3 1952); Garner v. Triangle Publications, 97 F.Supp. 546 (SDNY 1951); Berg v. Minneapolis Star & Tribune Co., 79 F.Supp. 957 (Minn. 1948).

MR. CHIEF JUSTICE BURGER concurs in the judgment.

CONCUR: MR. JUSTICE POWELL, concurring.

I join in the Court's opinion, as I agree with the holding and most of its supporting rationale.[1] My understanding of some of our decisions concerning the law of defamation, however, differs from that expressed in today's opinion. Accordingly, I think it appropriate to state separately my views.

I am in entire accord with the Court's determination that the First Amendment proscribes imposition of civil liability in a privacy action predicated on the truthful publication of matters contained in open judicial records. But my impression of the role of truth in defamation actions brought by private citizens differs from the Court's. The Court identifies as an "open" question the issue of "whether the First and Fourteenth Amendments require that truth be recognized as a defense in a defamation action brought by a private person as distinguished [498] from a public official or a public figure." Ante, at 490. In my view, our recent decision in Gertz v. Robert Welch, Inc., 418 U.S. 323 (1974), largely resolves that issue.

Gertz is the most recent of a line of cases in which this Court has sought to resolve the conflict between the State's desire to protect the reputational interests of its citizens and the competing commands of the First Amendment. In each of the many defamation actions considered in the 10 years following New York Times Co. v. Sullivan, 376 U.S. 254 (1964), state law provided that truth was a defense to the action.[2] Today's

opinion reiterates what we previously have recognized, see Garrison v. Louisiana, 379 U.S. 64, 74 (1964) – that the defense of truth is constitutionally required when the subject of the alleged defamation is a public figure. Ante, at 489-490. Indeed, even if not explicitly recognized, this determination is implicit in the Court's articulation of a standard of recovery that rests on knowing or [499] reckless disregard of the truth. I think that the constitutional necessity of recognizing a defense of truth is equally implicit in our statement of the permissible standard of liability for the publication or broadcast of defamatory statements whose substance makes apparent the substantial danger of injury to the reputation of a private citizen.

In Gertz we held that the First Amendment prohibits the States from imposing strict liability for media publication of allegedly false statements that are claimed to defame a private individual. While providing the required "breathing space" for First Amendment freedoms, the Gertz standard affords the States substantial latitude in compensating private individuals for wrongful injury to reputation.[3] "[So] long as they do not impose liability without fault, the States may define for themselves the appropriate standard of liability for a publisher or broadcaster of defamatory falsehood injurious to a private individual." 418 U.S., at 347. The requirement that the state standard of liability be related to the defendant's failure to avoid publication of "defamatory falsehood" limits the grounds on which a normal action for defamation can be brought. It is fair to say that if the statements are true, the standard contemplated by Gertz cannot be satisfied.

---

[26] We mean to imply nothing about any constitutional questions which might arise from a state policy not allowing access by the public and press to various kinds of official records, such as records of juvenile-court proceedings.

[27] Appellants have contended that whether they derived the information in question from public records or instead through their own investigation, the First and Fourteenth Amendments bar any sanctions from being imposed by the State because of the publication. Because appellants have prevailed on more limited grounds, we need not address this broader challenge to the validity of § 26-9901 and of Georgia's right of action for public disclosure.

[1] At the outset, I note my agreement that Miami Herald Publishing Co. v. Tornillo, 418 U.S. 241 (1974), supports the conclusion that the issue presented in this appeal is final for review. 28 U. S. C. § 1257.

[2] In Time, Inc. v. Hill, 385 U.S. 374 (1967), the Court considered a state cause of action that afforded protection against unwanted publicity rather than damage to reputation through the publication of false statements of fact. In such actions, however, the State also recognized that truth was an absolute defense against liability for publication of reports concerning newsworthy people or events. Id., at 383. The Court's abandonment of the "matter of general or public interest" standard as the determinative factor for

deciding whether to apply the New York Times malice standard to defamation litigation brought by private individuals, Gertz v. Robert Welch, Inc., 418 U.S. 323, 346 (1974); see also Rosenbloom v. Metromedia, Inc., 403 U.S. 29, 79 (1971) (MARSHALL, J., dissenting), calls into question the conceptual basis of Time, Inc. v. Hill. In neither Gertz nor our more recent decision in Cantrell v. Forest City Publishing Co., 419 U.S. 245 (1974), however, have we been called upon to determine whether a State may constitutionally apply a more relaxed standard of liability under a false-light theory of invasion of privacy. See id., at 250-251; Gertz, supra, at 348; ante, at 490 n. 19.

[3] Our recent opinions dealing with First Amendment limitations on state defamation actions all center around the common premise that while the Constitution requires that false ideas be corrected only by the competitive impact of other ideas, the First Amendment affords no constitutional protection for false statements of fact. See Gertz, supra, at 339-340. Beginning with this common assumption, the decisions of this Court have undertaken to identify a standard of care with respect to the truth of the published facts that will afford the required "breathing space" for First Amendment values.

In Gertz we recognized the need to establish a broad rule of general applicability, acknowledging that such an [500] approach necessarily requires treating alike cases that involve differences as well as similarities. Id., at 343-344. Of course, no rule of law is infinitely elastic. In some instances state actions that are denominated actions in defamation may in fact seek to protect citizens from injuries that are quite different from the wrongful damage to reputation flowing from false statements of fact. In such cases, the Constitution may permit a different balance to be struck. And, as today's opinion properly recognizes, causes of action grounded in a State's desire to protect privacy generally implicate interests that are distinct from those protected by defamation actions. But in cases in which the interests sought to be protected are similar to those considered in Gertz, I view that opinion as requiring that the truth be recognized as a complete defense.

MR. JUSTICE DOUGLAS, concurring in the judgment.

I agree that the state judgment is "final," and I also agree in the reversal of the Georgia court.* On the [501] merits, the case for me is on all fours with New Jersey State Lottery Comm'n v. United States, 491 F.2d 219 (CA3 1974), vacated and remanded, ante, p. 371. For the reasons I stated in my dissent from our disposition of that case, there is no power on the part of government to suppress or penalize the publication of "news of the day."

DISSENT: MR. JUSTICE REHNQUIST, dissenting.

Because I am of the opinion that the decision which is the subject of this appeal is not a "final" judgment or decree, as that term is used in 28 U. S. C. § 1257, I would dismiss this appeal for want of jurisdiction.

Radio Station WOW, Inc. v. Johnson, 326 U.S. 120 (1945), established that in a "very few" circumstances review of state-court decisions could be had in this Court even though something "further [remained] to be determined by a State court." Id., at 124. Over the years, however, and despite vigorous protest by Mr. Justice Harlan,[1] this

Court has steadily discovered new exceptions to the finality requirement, such that they can hardly any longer be described as "very few." Whatever may be the unexpressed reasons for this process of expansion, see, e. g., Hudson Distributors v. Eli Lilly, 377 U.S. 386, 401 (1964) (Harlan, J., dissenting), it has frequently been the subject of no more formal an express explanation than cursory citations to preceding cases in [502] the line. Especially is this true of cases in which the Court, as it does today, relies on Construction Laborers v. Curry, 371 U.S. 542 (1963).[2] Although the Court's opinion today does accord detailed consideration to this problem, I do not believe that the reasons it expresses can support its result.

I. The Court has taken what it terms a "pragmatic" approach to the finality problem presented in this case. In so doing, it has relied heavily on Gillespie v. United States Steel Corp., 379 U.S. 148 (1964). As the Court acknowledges, ante, at 478 n. 7, Gillespie involved 28 U. S. C. § 1291, which restricts the appellate jurisdiction of the federal courts of appeals to "final decisions of the district courts." Although acknowledging this distinction, the Court accords it no importance and adopts Gillespie's approach without any consideration of whether the finality requirement for this Court's jurisdiction over a "judgment or decree" of a state court is grounded on more serious concerns than is the limitation of court of appeals jurisdiction to final "decisions" of the district courts.[3] I believe that the underlying

v. Robert Welch, Inc., 418 U.S. 323, 355 (1974) (DOUGLAS, J., dissenting); Time, Inc. v. Hill, 385 U.S. 374, 398 (1967) (Black, J., concurring); id., at 401 (DOUGLAS, J., concurring); Garrison v. Louisiana, 379 U.S. 64, 80 (1964) (DOUGLAS, J., concurring). In this context, of course, "public affairs" must be broadly construed – indeed, the term may be said to embrace "any matter of sufficient general interest to prompt media coverage . . . ." Gertz v. Robert Welch, Inc., supra, at 357 n. 6(DOUGLAS, J., dissenting). By its now-familiar process of balancing and accommodating First Amendment freedoms with state or individual interests, the Court raises a specter of liability which must inevitably induce self-censorship by the media, thereby inhibiting the rough-and-tumble discourse which the First Amendment so clearly protects.

[1] See Construction Laborers v. Curry, 371 U.S. 542, 553 (1963); Mercantile National Bank v. Langdeau, 371 U.S. 555, 572 (1963); Hudson Distributors v. Eli Lilly, 377 U.S. 386, 395 (1964); Organization for a Better Austin v. Keefe, 402 U.S. 415, 420 (1971).

[2] See, e.g., American Radio Assn. v. Mobile S. S. Assn., 419 U.S. 215, 217 n. 1 (1974); Hudson Distributors v. Eli Lilly, supra, at 389 n. 4.

[3] The textual distinction between §§ 1291 and 1257, the former referring to "final decisions," while the latter refers

*While I join in the narrow result reached by the Court, I write separately to emphasize that I would ground that result upon a far broader proposition, namely, that the First Amendment, made applicable to the States through the Fourteenth, prohibits the use of state law "to impose damages for merely discussing public affairs. . . ." New York Times Co. v. Sullivan, 376 U.S. 254, 295 (1964) (Black, J., concurring). See also Cantrell v. Forest City Publ. Co., 419 U.S. 245, 254 (1974) (DOUGLAS, J., dissenting); Gertz

concerns are different, [503] and that the difference counsels a more restrictive approach when § 1257 finality is at issue.

According to Gillespie, the finality requirement is imposed as a matter of minimizing "the inconvenience and costs of piecemeal review." This proposition is undoubtedly sound so long as one is considering the administration of the federal court system. Were judicial efficiency the only interest at stake there would be less inclination to challenge the Court's resolution in this case, although, as discussed below, I have serious reservations that the standards the Court has formulated are effective for achieving even this single goal. The case before us, however, is an appeal from a state court, and this fact introduces additional interests which must be accommodated in fashioning any exception to the literal application of the finality requirement. I consider § 1257 finality to be but one of a number of congressional provisions reflecting concern that uncontrolled federal judicial interference with state administrative and judicial functions would have untoward consequences for our federal system.[4]

This is by no means a novel view of the § 1257 finality requirement. In Radio Station WOW, Inc. v. Johnson, 326 U.S., at 124, Mr. Justice Frankfurter's [504] opinion for the Court explained the finality requirement as follows:

"This requirement has the support of considerations generally applicable to good judicial administration. It avoids the mischief of economic waste and of delayed justice. Only in very few situations, where intermediate rulings may carry serious public consequences, has there been a departure from this requirement of finality for federal appellate jurisdiction. This prerequisite to review derives added force when the jurisdiction of this Court is invoked to upset the decision of a State court. Here we are in the realm of potential conflict between the courts of two different governments. And so, ever since 1789, Congress has granted this Court the power to intervene in State litigation only after 'the highest court of a State in which a decision in the suit could be had' has rendered a 'final judgment or decree.' § 237 of the Judicial Code, 28 U. S. C. § 344 (a). This requirement is not one of those technicalities to be easily scorned. It is an important factor in the smooth working of our federal system." (Emphasis added.)

In Republic Gas Co. v. Oklahoma, 334 U.S. 62, 67 (1948), Mr. Justice Frankfurter, speaking for the Court, again expressed this view:

"This prerequisite for the exercise of the appellate powers of this Court is especially pertinent when a constitutional barrier is asserted against a State court's decision on matters peculiarly of local concern. Close observance of this limitation upon the Court is not regard for a strangling technicality. History bears ample testimony that it is an important factor in securing harmonious State-federal relations."

[505] That comity and federalism are significant elements of § 1257 finality has been recognized by other members of the Court as well, perhaps most notably by Mr. Justice Harlan. See, e.g., Hudson Distributors v. Eli Lilly, 377 U.S., at 397-398 (dissenting); Mercantile National Bank v. Langdeau, 371 U.S. 555, 572 (1963) (dissenting). In the latter dissent, he argued that one basis of the finality rule was that it foreclosed "this Court from passing on constitutional issues that may be dissipated by the final outcome of a case, thus helping to keep to a minimum undesirable federal-state conflicts." One need cast no doubt on the Court's decision in such cases as Langdeau to recognize that Mr. Justice Harlan was focusing on a consideration which should be of significance in the Court's disposition of this case.

"Harmonious state-federal relations" are no less important today than when Mr. Justice Frankfurter penned Radio Station WOW and Republic Gas Co. Indeed, we have in recent years emphasized and re-emphasized the importance of comity and federalism in dealing with a related problem, that of district court interference with ongoing state judicial proceedings. See Younger v. Harris, 401 U.S. 37 (1971); Samuels v. Mackell, 401 U.S. 66 (1971). Because these concerns are important, and because they provide "added force" to § 1257's

---

to "final judgments or decrees," first appeared in the Evarts Act, Act of Mar. 3, 1891, 26 Stat. 826, which created the courts of appeals. Section 6 of that Act provided that courts of appeals should exercise appellate jurisdiction over "final decision" of the federal trial courts. The House version of the Act had referred to "final judgment or decree," 21 Cong. Rec. 3402 (1890), but the Senate Judiciary Committee changed the wording without formal explanation. See id., at 10218. Perhaps significance can be attached to the fact that under the House bill the courts of appeals would have been independent of the federal trial courts, being manned by full-time appellate judges; the Senate version, on the other hand, generally provided that court of appeals duties would be performed by the trial judges within each circuit. See § 3, 26 Stat. 827.

The first Judiciary Act, Act of Sept. 24, 1789, 1 Stat. 73, used the terms "judgment" and "decree" in defining the appellate jurisdiction of both the Supreme Court, § 25, and the original circuit courts. § 22.

[4] See, e.g., 28 U. S. C. § 1341 (limitation on power of district courts to enjoin state taxing systems); 28 U. S. C. § 1739 (requiring that state judicial proceedings be accorded full faith and credit in federal courts); 28 U. S. C. §§ 2253-2254 (prescribing various restrictions on federal habeas corpus for state prisoners); 28 U. S. C. § 2281 (three-judge district court requirement); 28 U. S. C. § 2283 (restricting power of federal courts to enjoin state-court proceedings).

finality requirement, I believe that the Court has erred by simply importing the approach of cases in which the only concern is efficient judicial administration.

II. But quite apart from the considerations of federalism which counsel against an expansive reading of our jurisdiction under § 1257, the Court's holding today enunciates a virtually formless exception to the finality requirement, one which differs in kind from those previously carved out. By contrast, Construction Laborers v. Curry, supra, [506] and Mercantile National Bank v. Langdeau, supra, are based on the understandable principle that where the proper forum for trying the issue joined in the state courts depends on the resolution of the federal question raised on appeal, sound judicial administration requires that such a question be decided by this Court, if it is to be decided at all, sooner rather than later in the course of the litigation. Organization for a Better Austin v. Keefe, 402 U.S. 415 (1971), and Mills v. Alabama, 384 U.S. 214 (1966), rest on the premise that where as a practical matter the state litigation has been concluded by the decision of the State's highest court, the fact that in terms of state procedure the ruling is interlocutory should not bar a determination by this Court of the merits of the federal question.

Still other exceptions, as noted in the Court's opinion, have been made where the federal question decided by the highest court of the State is bound to survive and be presented for decision here regardless of the outcome of future state-court proceedings, Radio Station WOW, supra; Brady v. Maryland, 373 U.S. 83 (1963), and for the situation in which later review of the federal issue cannot be had, whatever the ultimate outcome of the subsequent proceedings directed by the highest court of the State, California v. Stewart, 384 U.S. 436 (1966) (decided with Miranda v. Arizona); North Dakota State Board of Pharmacy v. Snyder's Drug Stores, Inc., 414 U.S. 156 (1973). While the totality of these exceptions certainly indicates that the Court has been willing to impart to the language "final judgment or decree" a great deal of flexibility, each of them is arguably consistent with the intent of Congress in enacting § 1257, if not with the language it used, and each of them is relatively workable in practice.

To those established exceptions is now added one so [507] formless that it cannot be paraphrased, but instead must be quoted: "Given these factors – that the litigation could be terminated by our decision on the merits and that a failure to decide the question now will leave the press in Georgia operating in the shadow of the civil

and criminal sanctions of a rule of law and a statute the constitutionality of which is in serious doubt – we find that reaching the merits is consistent with the pragmatic approach that we have followed in the past in determining finality." Ante, at 486.

There are a number of difficulties with this test. One of them is the Court's willingness to look to the merits. It is not clear from the Court's opinion, however, exactly how great a look at the merits we are to take. On the one hand, the Court emphasizes that if we reverse the Supreme Court of Georgia the litigation will end, ante, at 485-486, and it refers to cases in which the federal issue has been decided "arguably wrongly." Ante, at 486 n. 13. On the other hand, it claims to look to the merits "only to the extent of determining that the issue is substantial." Ibid. If the latter is all the Court means, then the inquiry is no more extensive than is involved when we determine whether a case is appropriate for plenary consideration; but if no more is meant, our decision is just as likely to be a costly intermediate step in the litigation as it is to be the concluding event. If, on the other hand, the Court really intends its doctrine to reach only so far as cases in which our decision in all probability will terminate the litigation, then the Court is reversing the traditional sequence of judicial decision-making. Heretofore, it has generally been thought that a court first assumed jurisdiction of a case, and then went on to decide the merits of the questions it presented. But henceforth in determining [508] our own jurisdiction we may be obliged to determine whether or not we agree with the merits of the decision of the highest court of a State.

Yet another difficulty with the Court's formulation is the problem of transposing to any other case the requirement that "failure to decide the question now will leave the press in Georgia operating in the shadow of the civil and criminal sanctions of a rule of law and a statute the constitutionality of which is in serious doubt." Ante, at 486. Assuming that we are to make this determination of "serious doubt" at the time we note probable jurisdiction of such an appeal, is it enough that the highest court of the State has ruled against any federal constitutional claim? If that is the case, then because § 1257 by other language imposes that requirement, we will have completely read out of the statute the limitation of our jurisdiction to a "final judgment or decree." Perhaps the Court's new standard for finality is limited to cases in which a First Amendment freedom is at issue. The language used by Congress, however, certainly provides no basis for preferring the First Amendment, as incorporated by the Fourteenth Amendment, to the various other Amendments, which are likewise "incorporated," or indeed for preferring any of the "incorporated" Amendments over the due process and equal protection provisions which are embodied literally in the Fourteenth Amendment.

Another problem is that in applying the second prong of its test, the Court has not engaged in any independent inquiry as to the consequences of permitting the decision of the Supreme Court of Georgia to remain undisturbed pending final state-court resolution of the case. This suggests that in order to invoke the benefit of today's rule, the "shadow" in which an appellant must stand need be neither deep nor wide. In this case nothing more is [509] at issue than the right to report the name of the victim of a rape. No hindrance of any sort has been imposed on reporting the fact of a rape or the circumstances surrounding it. Yet the Court unquestioningly places this issue on a par with the core First Amendment interest involved in Miami Herald Publishing Co. v. Tornillo, 418 U.S. 241 (1974), and Mills v. Alabama, supra, that of protecting the press in its role of providing uninhibited political discourse.[5]

But the greatest difficulty with the test enunciated today is that it totally abandons the principle that constitutional issues are too important to be decided save when absolutely necessary, and are to be avoided if there are grounds for decision of lesser dimension.[6] The long line of cases which established this rule makes clear that it is a principle primarily designed, not to benefit the lower courts, or state-federal relations, but rather to safeguard this Court's own process of constitutional adjudication.

"Considerations of propriety, as well as long-established practice, demand that we refrain from passing upon the constitutionality of an act of Congress unless obliged to do so in the proper performance of our judicial function, when the question is raised [510] by a party whose interests entitle him to raise it." Blair v. United States, 250 U.S. 273, 279 (1919).

"The Court will not 'anticipate a question of constitutional law in advance of the necessity of deciding it.' Liverpool, N. Y. & P. S. S. Co. v. Emigration Commissioners, 113 U.S. 33, 39;

Abrams v. Van Schaick, 293 U.S. 188; Wilshire Oil Co. v. United States, 295 U.S. 100. 'It is not the habit of the Court to decide questions of a constitutional nature unless absolutely necessary to a decision of the case.' Burton v. United States, 196 U.S. 283, 295." Ashwander v. Tennessee Valley Authority, 297 U.S. 288, 346-347 (1936) (Brandeis, J., concurring).

In this case there has yet to be an adjudication of liability against appellants, and unlike the appellant in Mills v. Alabama, they do not concede that they have no non-federal defenses. Nonetheless, the Court rules on their constitutional defense. Far from eschewing a constitutional holding in advance of the necessity for one, the Court construes § 1257 so that it may virtually rush out and meet the prospective constitutional litigant as he approaches our doors.

III. This Court is obliged to make preliminary determinations of its jurisdiction at the time it votes to note probable jurisdiction. At that stage of the proceedings, prior to briefing on the merits or oral argument, such determinations must of necessity be based on relatively cursory acquaintance with the record of the proceedings below. The need for an understandable and workable application of a jurisdictional provision such as § 1257 is therefore far greater than for a similar interpretation of statutes dealing with substantive law.[7] We, of course, retain [511] the authority to dismiss a case for want of a final judgment after having studied briefs on the merits and having heard oral argument, but I can recall not a single instance of such a disposition during the last three Terms of the Court. While in theory this may be explained

by saying that during these Terms we have never accorded plenary consideration to a § 1257 case which was not a "final judgment or decree," I would guess it just as accurate to say that after the Court has studied briefs and heard oral argument, it has an understandable tendency to proceed to a decision on the merits in preference to dismissing for want of jurisdiction. It is thus especially disturbing that the rule of this case, unlike the more workable and straightforward exceptions which the Court has previously formulated, will seriously compound the already difficult task of accurately determining, at a preliminary stage, whether an appeal from a state-court judgment is a "final judgment or decree."

A further aspect of the difficulties which the Court is generating is illustrated by a petition for certiorari recently filed in this Court, Time, Inc. v. Firestone, No. 74-944. The case was twice before the Florida Supreme Court. That court's first decision was rendered in December 1972; it rejected Time's First Amendment defense to a libel action, and remanded for further proceedings on

---

[5] As pointed out in Tornillo, 418 U.S., at 247 n. 6, not only did uncertainty about Florida's "right of reply" statute interfere with this important press function, but delay by this Court would have left the matter unresolved during the impending 1974 elections. In Mills, the Court observed that "there is practically universal agreement that a major purpose of [the First] Amendment was to protect the free discussion of governmental affairs." 384 U.S., at 218.
[6]

state-law issues. The second decision was rendered in 1974, and dealt with the state-law issues litigated on remand. Before this Court, Time seeks review of the First Amendment defense rejected by the Florida Supreme Court in December 1972. Under the Court's decision today, one could conclude that the 1972 judgment was itself a final decision from which review might [512] have been had. If it was, then petitioner Time is confronted by 28 U. S. C. § 2101 (c), which restricts this Court's jurisdiction over state civil cases to those in which review is sought within 90 days of the entry of a reviewable judgment.

I in no way suggest either my own or the Court's views on our jurisdiction over Time, Inc. v. Firestone. This example is simply illustrative of the difficulties which today's decision poses not only for this Court, but also for a prudent counsel who is faced with an adverse interlocutory ruling by a State's highest court on a federal issue asserted as a dispositive bar to further litigation. I suppose that such counsel would be unwilling to presume that this Court would flout both the meaning of words and the command of Congress by employing loose standards of finality to obtain jurisdiction, but strict ones to prevent its loss. He thus would

be compelled to judge his situation in light of today's formless, unworkable exception to the finality requirement. I would expect him frequently to choose to seek immediate review in this Court, solely as a matter of assuring that his federal contentions are not lost for want of timely filing. The inevitable result will be totally unnecessary additions to our docket and serious interruptions and delays of the state adjudicatory process.

Although unable to persuade my Brethren that we do not have in this case a final judgment or decree of the Supreme Court of Georgia, I nonetheless take heart from the fact that we are concerned here with an area in which "stare decisis has historically been accorded considerably less than its usual weight." Gonzalez v. Employees Credit Union, 419 U.S. 90, 95 (1974). I would dismiss for want of jurisdiction.

_____

[7] Cf. United States v. Sisson, 399 U.S. 267, 307 (1970): "Clarity is to be desired in any statute, but in matters of jurisdiction it is especially important. Otherwise the courts and the parties must expend great energy, not on the merits of dispute settlement, but on simply deciding whether a court has the power to hear a case."

Bartnicki v. Vopper
121 S. Ct. 1753
(2001)
(Excerpts only. Footnotes omitted.)

Author's Note: Contentious negotiations between a Pennsylvania teachers' union and the state board of education received extensive media coverage. During negotiations, the union negotiator and the president of the union talked about the board's intransigence and said dramatic action might be needed. During the cell phone conversation, the union president said, "…we're gonna have to go to their, their homes … To blow off their front porches …" A recording was made of the illegally intercepted call and anonymously provided to several media. After negotiations were settled, Vopper (a radio host) broadcast the tape. Other media repeatedly disclosed the contents of the conversation. Vopper sued for violation of federal anti-wiretapping laws that prohibit knowing dissemination of illegally obtained information. Bartnicki alleged the media knew, or should reasonably have known, that the private conversation was illegally obtained. The district court denied a media motion for summary

judgment on the grounds that they did not know the tape was obtained illegally and the broadcast was protected under the First Amendment. On appeal, the court found the anti-wiretapping statute content neutral but held it to be unconstitutionally overbroad and remanded for summary judgment in favor of the media. Another court of appeals, hearing a similar case, upheld the constitutionality of the anti-wiretapping statute. The Supreme Court granted *cert.* to resolve the conflict.

PRIOR HISTORY: On writs of certiorari to the United States Court of Appeals for the Third Circuit.

JUDGES: Stevens, J., delivered the opinion of the Court, in which OConnor, Kennedy, Souter, Ginsburg, and Breyer, JJ., joined. Breyer, J., filed a concurring opinion, in which OConnor, J., joined. Rehnquist, C.J., filed a dissenting opinion, in which Scalia and Thomas, JJ., joined.

OPINION: These cases raise an important question concerning what degree of protection, if any, the First Amendment provides to speech that discloses the contents of an illegally intercepted communication. That question is both novel and narrow. Despite the fact that federal law has prohibited such disclosures since 1934, this is the first time that we have confronted such an issue.

The suit at hand involves the repeated intentional disclosure of an illegally intercepted cellular telephone conversation about a public issue. The persons who made the disclosures did not participate in the interception, but they did know or at least had reason to know that the interception was unlawful. Accordingly, these cases present a conflict between interests of the highest order on the one hand, the interest in the full and free dissemination of information concerning public issues, and, on the other hand, the interest in individual privacy and, more specifically, in fostering private speech. ...[W]e are firmly convinced that the disclosures made by respondents in this suit are protected by the First Amendment. ...

Congress undertook to draft comprehensive legislation both authorizing the use of evidence obtained by electronic surveillance on specified conditions, and prohibiting its use otherwise. The ultimate result of those efforts was Title III of the Omnibus Crime Control and Safe Streets Act of 1968, 82 Stat. 211, entitled Wiretapping and Electronic Surveillance.

One of the stated purposes of that title was to protect effectively the privacy of wire and oral communications. Ibid. In addition to authorizing and regulating electronic surveillance for law enforcement purposes, Title III also regulated private conduct. One part of those regulations, 2511 (1), defined five offenses punishable by a fine of not more than $10,000, by imprisonment for not more than five years, or by both. Subsection (a) applied to any person who willfully intercepts ... any wire or oral communication. Subsection (b) applied to the intentional use of devices designed to intercept oral conversations; subsection (d) applied to the use of the contents of illegally intercepted wire or oral communications; and subsection (e) prohibited the unauthorized disclosure of the contents of interceptions that were authorized for law enforcement purposes. Subsection (c), the original version of the provision most directly at issue in this case, applied to any person who willfully discloses, or endeavors to disclose, to any other person the contents of any wire or oral communication, knowing or having reason to know that the information was obtained through the interception of a wire or oral communication in violation of this subsection. The oral communications protected by the Act were only those uttered by a person exhibiting an expectation that such communication is not subject to interception under circumstances justifying such expectation. 18 U.S.C. 2510(2).

As enacted in 1968, Title III did not apply to the monitoring of radio transmissions. In the Electronic Communications Privacy Act of 1986, 100 Stat. 1848, however, Congress enlarged the coverage of Title III to prohibit the interception of electronic as well as oral and wire communications. By reason of that amendment, as well as a 1994 amendment which applied to cordless telephone communications, 108 Stat. 4279, Title III now applies to the interception of conversations over both cellular and cordless phones. ...

The constitutional question before us ... is whether the application of these statutes in such circumstances violates the First Amendment.

In answering that question, we accept respondent's submission on three factual matters ...

First, respondents played no part in the illegal interception. Rather, they found out about the interception only after it occurred, and in fact never learned the identity of the person or persons who made the interception. Second, their access to the information on the tapes was obtained lawfully, even though the information itself was intercepted unlawfully by someone else. ... Third, the subject matter of the conversation was a matter of public concern. If the statements about the labor negotiations had been made in a public arena during a bargaining session, for example they would have been newsworthy. This would also be true if a third party had inadvertently overheard Bartnicki making the same statements to Kane when the two thought they were alone.

We agree with petitioners that 2511(1)(c), as well as its Pennsylvania analog, is in fact a content-neutral law of general applicability. ... In this case, the basic purpose of the statute at issue is to protec[t] the privacy of wire[, electronic,] and oral communications. The statute does not distinguish based on the content of the intercepted conversations, nor is it justified by reference to the content of those conversations. Rather, the communications at issue are singled out by virtue of the fact that they were illegally intercepted by virtue of the source, rather than the subject matter.

On the other hand, the naked prohibition against disclosures is fairly characterized as a regulation of pure speech. ... [I]t is the kind of speech that the First Amendment protects. As the majority below put it, [i]f the acts of disclosing and publishing information do not constitute speech, it is hard to imagine what does fall within that category, as distinct from the category of expressive conduct.

As a general matter, state action to punish the publication of truthful information seldom can satisfy constitutional standards. More specifically, this Court has repeatedly held that if a newspaper lawfully obtains truthful information about a matter of public significance then state officials may not constitutionally punish publication of the information, absent a need . . . of the highest order.

Accordingly, in New York Times Co. v. United States, 403 U.S. 713 (1971) (per curiam), the Court upheld the right of the press to publish information of great public concern obtained from documents stolen by a third party. In so doing, that decision resolved a conflict between the basic rule against prior restraints on publication and the interest in preserving the secrecy of information that, if disclosed, might seriously impair the security of the Nation. In resolving that conflict, the attention of every Member of this Court was focused on the character of the stolen documents contents and the consequences of public disclosure. Although the undisputed fact that the newspaper intended to publish information obtained from stolen documents was noted in Justice Harlan's dissent, neither the majority nor the dissenters placed any weight on that fact.

However, New York Times v. United States raised, but did not resolve the question whether, in cases where information has been acquired unlawfully by a newspaper or by a source, government may ever punish not only the unlawful acquisition but the ensuing publication as well. … Simply put, the issue here is this: Where the punished publisher of information has obtained the information in question in a manner lawful in itself but from a source who has obtained it unlawfully, may the government punish the ensuing publication of that information based on the defect in a chain? …

The Government identifies two interests served by the statute: first, the interest in removing an incentive for parties to intercept private conversations, and second, the interest in minimizing the harm to persons whose conversations have been illegally intercepted. We assume that those interests adequately justify the prohibition in 2511(1)(d) against the interceptor's own use of information that he or she acquired by violating 2511(1)(a), but it by no means follows that punishing disclosures of lawfully obtained information of public interest by one not involved in the initial illegality is an acceptable means of serving those ends. …

Privacy of communication is an important interest, and Title III's restrictions are intended to protect that interest, thereby encouraging the uninhibited exchange of ideas and information among private parties. Moreover, the fear of public disclosure of private conversations might well have a chilling effect on private speech.

In a democratic society privacy of communication is essential if citizens are to think and act creatively and constructively. Fear or suspicion that one's speech is being monitored by a stranger, even without the reality of such activity, can have a seriously inhibiting effect upon the willingness to voice critical and constructive ideas.

Accordingly, it seems to us that there are important interests to be considered on both sides of the constitutional calculus. In considering that balance, we acknowledge that some intrusions on privacy are more offensive than others, and that the disclosure of the contents of a private conversation can be an even greater intrusion on privacy than the interception itself. As a result, there is a valid independent justification for prohibiting such disclosures by persons who lawfully obtained access to the contents of an illegally intercepted message, even if that prohibition does not play a significant role in preventing such interceptions from occurring in the first place.

We need not decide whether that interest is strong enough to justify the application of 2511(c) to disclosures of trade secrets or domestic gossip or other information of purely private concern. In other words, the outcome of the case does not turn on whether 2511(1)(c) may be enforced with respect to most violations of the statute without offending the First Amendment. The enforcement of that provision in this case, however, implicates the core purposes of the First Amendment because it imposes sanctions on the publication of truthful information of public concern.

In this case, privacy concerns give way when balanced against the interest in publishing matters of public importance. As Warren and Brandeis stated in their classic law review article: The right of privacy does not prohibit any publication of matter which is of public or general interest. One of the costs associated with participation in public affairs is an attendant loss of privacy.

Exposure of the self to others in varying degrees is a concomitant of life in a civilized community. The risk of this exposure is an essential incident of life in a society which places a primary value on freedom of speech and of press. Freedom of discussion, if it would fulfill its historic function in this nation, must embrace all issues about which information is needed or appropriate to enable the members of society to cope with the exigencies of their period.

Our opinion in New York Times Co. v. Sullivan, 376 U.S. 254 (1964), reviewed many of the decisions that settled the general proposition that freedom of expression upon public questions is secured by the First Amendment. Those cases all relied on our profound national commitment to the principle that debate on public issues should be uninhibited, robust and wide-open. It was the overriding importance of that commitment that supported our holding that neither factual error nor defamatory content, nor a combination of the two, sufficed to remove the First Amendment shield from criticism of official conduct. We think it clear that parallel reasoning requires the conclusion that a stranger's illegal conduct does not suffice to remove the First Amendment shield from speech about a matter of public concern. The months of negotiations over the proper level of compensation for teachers at the Wyoming Valley West High School were unquestionably a matter of public concern, and respondents were clearly engaged in debate about that concern. ...

The judgment is affirmed. It is so ordered.

CONCUR: Justice Breyer, with whom Justice O'Connor joins, concurring.

I join the Court's opinion because I agree with its narrow holding, limited to the special circumstances present here: (1) the radio broadcasters acted lawfully (up to the time of final public disclosure); and (2) the information publicized involved a matter of unusual public concern, namely a threat of potential physical harm to others. I write separately to explain why, in my view, the Court's holding does not imply a significantly broader constitutional immunity for the media.

As the Court recognizes, the question before us, a question of immunity from statutorily imposed civil liability, implicates competing constitutional concerns. The statutes directly interfere with free expression in that they prevent the media from publishing information. At the same time, they help to protect personal privacy, an interest here that includes not only the right to be let alone but also the interest . . . in fostering private speech. Given these competing interests on both sides of the equation, the key question becomes one of proper fit.

I would ask whether the statutes strike a reasonable balance between their speech-restricting and speech-enhancing consequences. Or do they instead impose restrictions on speech that are disproportionate when measured against their corresponding privacy and speech-related benefits, taking into account the kind, the importance, and the extent of these benefits, as well as the need for the restrictions in order to secure those benefits? What this Court has called strict scrutiny with its strong presumption against constitutionality is

normally out of place where, as here, important competing constitutional interests are implicated.

The statutory restrictions before us directly enhance private speech. The statutes ensure the privacy of telephone conversations much as a trespass statute ensures privacy within the home. That assurance of privacy helps to overcome our natural reluctance to discuss private matters when we fear that our private conversations may become public. And the statutory restrictions consequently encourage conversations that otherwise might not take place.

At the same time, these statutes restrict public speech directly, deliberately, and of necessity. They include media publication within their scope not simply as a means, say, to deter interception, but also as an end. Media dissemination of an intimate conversation to an entire community will often cause the speakers serious harm over and above the harm caused by an initial disclosure to the person who intercepted the phone call. And the threat of that widespread dissemination can create a far more powerful disincentive to speak privately than the comparatively minor threat of disclosure to an interceptor and perhaps to a handful of others. Insofar as these statutes protect private communications against that widespread dissemination, they resemble laws that would award damages caused through publication of information obtained by theft from a private bedroom.

As a general matter, despite the statutes' direct restrictions on speech, the Federal Constitution must tolerate laws of this kind because of the importance of these privacy and speech-related objectives. Rather than broadly forbid this kind of legislative enactment, the Constitution demands legislative efforts to tailor the laws in order reasonably to reconcile media freedom with personal, speech-related privacy.

Nonetheless, looked at more specifically, the statutes, as applied in these circumstances, do not reasonably reconcile the competing constitutional objectives. Rather, they disproportionately interfere with media freedom. For one thing, the broadcasters here engaged in no unlawful activity other than the ultimate publication of the information another had previously obtained. They neither encouraged nor participated directly or indirectly in the interception. ...

For another thing, the speakers had little or no legitimate interest in maintaining the privacy of the particular conversation. That conversation involved a suggestion about blow[ing] off . . . front porches and do[ing] some work on some of these guys, thereby raising a significant concern for the safety of others. Where publication of private information constitutes a wrongful act, the law recognizes a privilege allowing the reporting of threats to public safety. Even where the danger may have passed by the time of publication, that fact cannot legitimize the speakers' earlier privacy expectation. Nor should editors, who must make a publication decision quickly, have to determine present or continued danger before publishing this kind of threat.

Further, the speakers themselves, the president of a teachers union and the union's chief negotiator, were limited public figures, for they voluntarily engaged in a public controversy. They thereby subjected themselves to somewhat greater public scrutiny and had a lesser interest in privacy than an individual engaged in purely private affairs.

This is not to say that the Constitution requires anyone, including public figures, to give up entirely the right to private communication, i.e., communication free from telephone taps or interceptions. But the subject matter of the conversation at issue here is far removed from that in situations where the media publicizes truly private matters.

Thus, in finding a constitutional privilege to publish unlawfully intercepted conversations of the kind here at issue, the Court does not create a public interest exception that swallows up the statutes privacy-protecting general rule. Rather, it finds constitutional protection for publication of intercepted information of a special kind. Here, the speakers legitimate privacy expectations are unusually low, and the public interest in defeating those expectations is unusually high. Given these circumstances, along with the lawful nature of respondent's behavior, the statute's enforcement would disproportionately harm media freedom.

...[W]e should avoid adopting overly broad or rigid constitutional rules, which would unnecessarily restrict legislative flexibility. I consequently agree with the Court's holding that the statutes as applied here violate the Constitution, but I would not extend that holding beyond these present circumstances.

DISSENT: Chief Justice Rehnquist, with whom Justice Scalia and Justice Thomas join, dissenting.

Technology now permits millions of important and confidential conversations to occur through a vast system of electronic networks. These advances, however, raise significant privacy concerns. We are placed in the uncomfortable position of not knowing who might have access to our personal and business e-mails, our medical and financial records, or our cordless and cellular telephone conversations. In an attempt to prevent some of the most egregious violations of privacy,

the United States, the District of Columbia, and 40 States have enacted laws prohibiting the intentional interception and knowing disclosure of electronic communications. The Court holds that all of these statutes violate the First Amendment insofar as the illegally intercepted conversation touches upon a matter of public concern, an amorphous concept that the Court does not even attempt to define. But the Court's decision diminishes, rather than enhances, the purposes of the First Amendment: chilling the speech of the millions of Americans who rely upon electronic technology to communicate each day.

Over 30 years ago, with Title III of the Omnibus Crime Control and Safe Streets Act of 1968, Congress recognized that the [t]remendous scientific and technological developments that have taken place in the last century have made possible today the widespread use and abuse of electronic surveillance techniques. As a result of these developments, privacy of communication is seriously jeopardized by these techniques of surveillance. No longer is it possible, in short, for each man to retreat into his home and be left alone. Every spoken word relating to each mans personal, marital, religious, political, or commercial concerns can be intercepted by an unseen auditor and turned against the speaker to the auditors advantage.

This concern for privacy was inseparably bound up with the desire that personal conversations be frank and uninhibited, not cramped by fears of clandestine surveillance and purposeful disclosure:

In a democratic society privacy of communication is essential if citizens are to think and act creatively and constructively. Fear or suspicion that ones speech is being monitored by a stranger, even without the reality of such activity, can have a seriously inhibiting effect upon the willingness to voice critical and constructive ideas.

To effectuate these important privacy and speech interests, Congress and the vast majority of States have proscribed the intentional interception and knowing disclosure of the contents of electronic communications.

The Court correctly observes that these are content-neutral law[s] of general applicability which serve recognized interests of the highest order: the interest in individual privacy and in fostering private speech. It nonetheless subjects these laws to the strict scrutiny normally reserved for governmental attempts to censor different viewpoints or ideas. There is scant support, either in precedent or in reason, for the Courts tacit application of strict scrutiny. ...

Here, Congress and the Pennsylvania Legislature have acted without reference to the content of the regulated speech. There is no intimation that these laws seek to suppress unpopular ideas or information or manipulate the public debate or that they distinguish favored speech from disfavored speech on the basis of the ideas or views expressed. ... As the concerns motivating strict scrutiny are absent, these content-neutral restrictions upon speech need pass only intermediate scrutiny.

The Court's attempt to avoid these precedents by reliance upon the Daily Mail string of newspaper cases is unpersuasive. In these cases, we held that statutes prohibiting the media from publishing certain truthful information ... violated the First Amendment. In so doing, we stated that if a newspaper lawfully obtains truthful information about a matter of public significance then state officials may not constitutionally punish publication of the information, absent a need to further a state interest of the highest order. Neither this Daily Mail principle nor any other aspect of these cases, however, justifies the Courts imposition of strict scrutiny here.

Each of the laws at issue in the Daily Mail cases regulated the content or subject matter of speech. This fact alone was enough to trigger strict scrutiny and suffices to distinguish these anti-disclosure provisions. But, as our synthesis of these cases in Florida Star made clear, three other unique factors also informed the scope of the Daily Mail principle.

First, the information published by the newspapers had been lawfully obtained from the government itself. ... Second, the information in each case was already publicly available, and punishing further dissemination would not have advanced the purported government interests of confidentiality. ...Third, these cases were concerned with the timidity and self-censorship which may result from allowing the media to be punished for publishing certain truthful information.

... The Daily Mail principle does not settle the issue whether, in cases where information has been acquired unlawfully by a newspaper or by a source, the government may ever punish not only the unlawful acquisition, but the ensuing publication as well.

Undaunted, the Court places an inordinate amount of weight upon the fact that the receipt of an illegally intercepted communication has not been criminalized. But this hardly renders those who knowingly receive and disclose such communications law-abiding, and it certainly does not bring them under the Daily Mail principle. The transmission of the intercepted communication from the eavesdropper to the third party is itself illegal; and where, as here, the third party then knowingly discloses that communication, another illegal act has been committed. The third party in this situation cannot be likened to the reporters in the Daily Mail cases, who lawfully obtained their information through consensual interviews or public documents.

These laws are content neutral; they only regulate information that was illegally obtained; they do not restrict republication of what is already in the public domain; they impose no special burdens upon the media; they have a scienter requirement to provide fair warning; and they promote the privacy and free speech of those using cellular telephones. It is hard to imagine a more narrowly tailored prohibition of the disclosure of illegally intercepted communications, and it distorts our precedents to review these statutes under the often fatal standard of strict scrutiny. These laws therefore should be upheld if they further a substantial governmental interest unrelated to the suppression of free speech, and they do.

Congress and the overwhelming majority of States reasonably have concluded that sanctioning the knowing disclosure of illegally intercepted communications will deter the initial interception itself, a crime which is extremely difficult to detect.

...The dry up the market theory, which posits that it is possible to deter an illegal act that is difficult to police by preventing the wrongdoer from enjoying the fruits of the crime, is neither novel nor implausible. It is a time-tested theory that undergirds numerous laws, such as the prohibition of the knowing possession of stolen goods. ...

The same logic applies here and demonstrates that the incidental restriction on alleged First Amendment freedoms is no greater than essential to further the interest of protecting the privacy of individual communications. Were there no prohibition on disclosure, an unlawful eavesdropper who wanted to disclose the conversation could anonymously launder the interception through a third party and thereby avoid detection. Indeed, demand for illegally obtained private information would only increase if it could be disclosed without repercussion. The law against interceptions, which the Court agrees is valid, would be utterly ineffectual without these anti-disclosure provisions.

... At base, the Court's decision to hold these statutes unconstitutional rests upon nothing more than the bald substitution of its own prognostications in place of the reasoned judgment of 41 legislative bodies and the United States Congress. ...

These statutes also protect the important interests of deterring clandestine invasions of privacy and preventing the involuntary broadcast of private communications. Over a century ago, Samuel Warren and Louis Brandeis recognized that [t]he intensity and complexity of life, attendant upon advancing civilization, have rendered necessary some retreat from the world, and man, under the refining influence of culture, has become more sensitive to publicity, so that solitude and privacy have become more essential to the individual. There is necessarily, and within suitably defined areas, a freedom not to speak publicly, one which serves the same ultimate end as freedom of speech in its affirmative aspect. One who speaks into a phone is surely entitled to assume that the words he utters into the mouthpiece will not be broadcast to the world.

These statutes undeniably protect this venerable right of privacy. Concomitantly, they further the First Amendment rights of the parties to the conversation. At the heart of the First Amendment lies the principle that each person should decide for himself or herself the ideas and beliefs deserving of expression, consideration, and adherence. By protecting the privacy of individual thought and expression, these statutes further the uninhibited, robust, and wide-open speech of the private parties. … [T]hese laws protect millions of people who communicate electronically on a daily basis. The chilling effect of the Court's decision upon these private conversations will surely be great. …

Although the Court recognizes and even extols the virtues of this right to privacy, these are mere words, overridden by the Court's newfound right to publish unlawfully acquired information of public concern. The Court concludes that the private conversation between Gloria Bartnicki and Anthony Kane is somehow a debate worthy of constitutional protection. Perhaps the Court is correct that [i]f the statements about the labor negotiations had been made in a public arena during a bargaining session, for example they would have been newsworthy. The point, however, is that Bartnicki and Kane had no intention of contributing to a public debate at all, and it is perverse to hold that another's unlawful interception and knowing disclosure of their conversation is speech worthy of constitutional protection.

The Constitution should not protect the involuntary broadcast of personal conversations. Even where the communications involve public figures or concern public matters, the conversations are nonetheless private and worthy of protection. Although public persons may have forgone the right to live their lives screened from public scrutiny in some areas, it does not and should not follow that they also have abandoned their right to have a private conversation without fear of it being intentionally intercepted and knowingly disclosed.

The Court's decision to hold inviolable our right to broadcast conversations of public importance enjoys little support in our precedents. … By no stretch of the imagination can the statutes at issue here be dubbed prior restraints. And the Court's parallel reasoning from other inapposite cases fails to persuade.

Surely the interest in individual privacy at its narrowest must embrace the right to be free from surreptitious eavesdropping on, and involuntary broadcast of, our cellular telephone conversations. The Court subordinates that right, not to the claims of those who themselves wish to speak, but to the claims of those who wish to publish the intercepted conversations of others. Congress' effort to balance the above claim to privacy against a marginal claim to speak freely is thereby set at naught.

Copyright

Protecting intellectual products and encouraging creativity

Focal cases:
Harper & Row Publishers v. Nation Enterprises, 471 U.S. 539 (1985)
Universal City Studios v. Corley, 273 F.3d 429 (2nd Cir. 2001)

I deas are valuable. That is a core tenet of the First Amendment and the fundamental premise of copyright and other laws protecting intellectual property. However, while the First Amendment promotes the broad dissemination of ideas to enhance the public good, copyrights, patents and trademarks limit distribution of original expression to encourage intellectual creativity and to protect the proprietary interests of the creator. As the Supreme Court said in 1975, "The immediate effect of our copyright law is to secure a fair return for an author's creative labor. But the ultimate aim is, by this incentive, to stimulate artistic creativity for the general public good."[1] The Court repeatedly has held that copyright law does not violate the First Amendment because it provides only a limited monopoly over the *form* of expression, not the ideas or facts contained therein, and it permits "fair use" of copyrighted material to advance the public interest in the open exchange of ideas.[2]

Intellectual, or immaterial, property laws emerge from Article I, Section 8, of the Constitution, which authorizes Congress "to promote the progress of science and useful arts by securing for limited times to authors and inventors the exclusive right to their respective writings and discoveries." Section 8 embraces the natural law presumption that individuals should benefit from the fruits of their intellect and reflects the economic concept that scarcity increases value and potential return to the owner. Intellectual property laws include patent law, trademark law and copyright law, which is the primary focus of this chapter.

Before delving into copyright law, the chapter briefly identifies the key components of patent and trademark law and misappropriation to clarify these closely related topics. Patent law protects practical, applied concepts and strategies. The works of inventors – designs, production processes

---

[1] Twentieth Century Music v. Aiken, 422 U.S. 151, 156 (1975).

[2] *See* Eldred v. Ashcroft, 537 U.S. 186 (2003); Harper & Row Publ. v. Nation Enterprises, 471 U.S. 539, 556, 560 (1985); Campbell v. Acuff-Rose Music, 510 U.S. 569 (1994).

or machinery – are protected by federal patent law, which provides 20 years of exclusive benefits to the creator.

TRADEMARKS

Trademarks – the identifying word, slogan, symbol or device of a given brand – are also protected by law. Trademark protection initially lasts five years, but trademarks may be renewed indefinitely in 10-year increments. Trademarks distinguish one cola, one paper tissue, one CD player from another to reduce consumer confusion, to identify the producer of the product and to create a brand identity. Thus, Coke® is not Pepsi®. Kleenex® is not Scott®. Sony Discman® is not, well Discman® is not any other CD player. Moreover, only GAP® products benefit from GAP® advertising.

Other areas of trademark law protect service marks, such as Days Inn®, and collective marks, such as the National Association of Broadcasters. But marks for these groups and services, as well as trademarks, can be abandoned or diluted to the point of becoming generic. If a trademark owner does not use a mark for two years, he loses ownership. Similarly, if trademark owners do not assure that the mark is used exclusively to identify their products, the mark can become generic and be adopted into the general language. Both Kleenex® and Xerox® have fought to retain ownership of their trademarks and to prevent general adoption of the marks to refer to paper tissues and photocopying respectively.

In 1996, Congress increased the value of trademarks by providing for trademark protection whenever any other product uses a famous or distinctive trademark to confuse or deceive consumers. Previously, trademarks owners could enforce the exclusivity of their marks only from use by similar or competing products.[3] A 2003 ruling of the Supreme Court narrowed the apparently expansive sweep of the '96 law. The Court unanimously rejected a summary judgment award to the owners of the Victoria's Secret® trademark in a dilution suit brought against Victor's Little Secret store and ruled that trademark dilution requires proof of actual harm when the marks are not identical.[4]

MISAPPROPRIATION

The common law of misappropriation of intangible property is designed to punish certain types of deception that lead to unfair competition. Misappropriation occurs only when there is a reasonable likelihood that a significant number of ordinary consumers are likely to be misled. Misappropriation cases may arise when an individual presents the work of someone else as her own, such as plagiarism, or, more rarely, when she presents her own work in such a way as to mislead consumers to believe it is another product. The first type of misappropriation occurs when broadcasters read excerpts from the local newspaper without permission.[5] The second type may be invoked when an author, seeking to capitalize on the success of the Harry Potter series, publishes a book of similar design under the title Harry Podter.

THE RIGHTS OF COPYRIGHT

Federal copyright law has protected the original works of authors – be they books, photographs, newspapers, movies, symphonies, software, plays or drawings – from unauthorized copying or performance since 1790. Copyright law became necessary and increasingly important as first the printing press, then records, radio, television, tapes, cable, CDs, DVDs, the Internet and all manner of digital transmission and duplication technologies threatened the ability of

---

[3] Federal Trademark Dilution Act of 1995, See 15 U.S.C. 1125 (c) (2000).

[4] Moseley v. Secret Catalogue, 537 U.S. 418 (2003).

[5] See Pottstown Daily News Publ. v. Pottstown Broadcasting, 247 F. Supp. 578 (E.D. Penn. 1965).

authors to control the use of their creative products and increased the ease and quality of copying.[6]

Copyright protects all "original works of authorship fixed in any tangible medium of expression."[7] Original, in the copyright sense, is not a qualitative judgment but rather reflects the need for the author to originate the work. In a snapshot, for example, originality may arise simply from the time of day and angle from which you chose to photograph the landscape.[8] Works are fixed, for copyright purposes, once they are created and kept in any way. Thus, downloading copyrighted material even temporarily onto the RAM of your home computer or placing it on an electronic bulletin board or on your web site most likely creates fixed copies of the original and constitutes copyright infringement.[9]

Copyright protects original expression, not the underlying facts or ideas.[10] Titles, slogans, utilitarian objects, mathematical equations and formulas, methods, systems and a variety of trivial things cannot be copyrighted. The Supreme Court in 1991 said originality requires at least some modicum of creativity, not just the expenditure of time and effort.[11] Consequently, original compilations, collective works and derivatives of copyrighted works may be copyrighted as long as the new work is sufficiently distinct and original.

Copyright owners exercise almost monopoly control over the copyrighted material for the duration of the copyright term. A copyright owner enjoys exclusive rights to:

1. distribute or publish the copyrighted work (including the right of first publication),
2. display the work publicly,
3. perform the work publicly,
4. reproduce or copy the work, and
5. create derivative works or adapt the work.

Copyright owners may divide their rights and allocate portions to other individuals. For example, a book's author generally signs over rights including the distribution rights to a publishing company. However, the specifics of the contract determine whether the book publisher thereby owns only the right to publish the work as a tangible book or also has the right to distribute the work online, on audiotape or on the Internet.[12]

COPYRIGHT INFRINGEMENT

Copyright holders may sue anyone who infringes any of their "exclusive rights." Injunctions imposed to limit harm while copyright infringement suits are litigated do not violate the First Amendment ban on prior restraint.

Direct infringement arises when an individual takes positive steps that result in illegal copying or use of copyrighted materials. Contributory infringement occurs when someone knowingly

---

[6] See I. Trotter Hardy, *Copyright Owners' Rights and Users' Privileges on the Internet: Computer RAM 'Copies': A Hit or a Myth?* 22 DAYTON L. REV. 423 (1997).

[7] 17 U.S.C. § 102.

[8] See Bleistein v. Donaldson Lithographing, 188 U.S. 239 (1903); Los Angeles News Service v. Tullo, 973 F.2d 791 (9th Cir. 1992).

[9] See, e.g., Playboy Enterprises v. Starware Publ. Corp., 900 F. Supp. 433 (S.D. Fla. 1995); Playboy Enterprises v. Frena, 839 F. Supp. 1552 (M.D. Fla. 1993).

[10] See Miller v. Universal City Studios, 650 F. 2d 1365 (5th Cir. 1981).

[11] See Feist Publications v. Telephone Service Co., 499 U.S. 340 (1991). The idea that copyright might be based on the investment of time and effort has been called the "sweat of the brow" argument. See also Key Publ. v. Chinatown Today, 945 F. 2d 509 (2nd Cir. 1991); Dastar Corp. v. Twentieth Century Fox Film Corp., 123 S. Ct. 2041 (2003) (unanimously refusing to apply Lanham Act to permit *de facto* enforcement of copyright provisions on product in public domain).

[12] See New York Times v. Tasini, 533 U.S. 483 (2001) (denying newspaper authority to redistribute freelancers' work online).

causes or facilitates infringement by another person. Courts generally have found contributory infringement when an individual knows, or reasonably should have known, that she provides the site, facility or means for infringement to occur,[13] and the service or equipment does not serve other legitimate purposes.[14] In the case of innocent distribution of copyright violations, the doctrine of vicarious liability holds that individuals who stand to benefit directly from copyright infringements they could reasonably have prevented may be held liable for the resulting infringements. Thus, online service supervisors who gain financially or otherwise from a user's infringement are vicariously liable.[15]

The courts determine copyright infringement based on whether:

- the plaintiff holds a valid copyright,
- the defendant had access to the copyrighted work prior to the alleged infringement, and
- the two works are substantially similar or the same.

Valid copyright exists regardless of whether the creator has officially registered the work with the Copyright Office in Washington, D.C., or provided notice of the copyright on the work. However, registration substantiates copyright ownership and notice undermines any claim that infringement occurred innocently, which often is claimed to mitigate financial awards.

Courts generally presume access to broadly distributed or widely available originals. In cases of lesser known works or works with limited distribution, however, the plaintiff must show that the defendant had timely access to the original. Similarly, in the era of digital replication and with literal duplication of an original, copying is presumed. However, when the copying is not exact, courts generally determine infringement by scrutinizing whether both the theme of the copy and the form of its expression are substantially similar to the original.

Liability for copyright infringement

Copyright law imposes strict liability on anyone who directly infringes copyrighted material, regardless of whether they knew the material was protected.[16] The law permits a waiver of minimum damages for direct infringement when a teacher, librarian, archivist, broadcaster or newspaper publisher reasonably believed their use was fair. Aside from those limited exceptions, however, even third-party distributors with no prior knowledge of the infringement and producers of equipment or services that aid infringement generally are strictly liable for violation of copyright.[17]

FAIR USE

Copyright law does provide for limited "fair use" of copyrighted materials during the copyright term. The fair use doctrine is designed to balance the author's right to reasonable compensation and control of the work against the public's interest in the broadest possible dissemination of information and ideas. Fair use permits limited, reasonable duplication of copyrighted materials without the copyright owner's consent for criticism and commentary, news reporting and teaching, and scholarship and research to advance the arts and sciences.[18] The

---

[13] *See* M. Jackson, *One Step Forward, Two Steps Back: An Historical Analysis of Copyright Liability*, 20 CARDOZO ARTS & ENT. L. J. 367, 392-400 (2002).

[14] Sony Corp. v. Universal City Studios, 464 U.S. 417, 442 (1984).

[15] *See, e.g.,* A&M Records v. Napster, 239 F.3d 1004 (9th Cir. 2001); A&M Records v. Napster, 114 F. Supp. 2d (N.D. Cal. 2000).

[16] 17 U.S.C. § 504 (c) (2).

[17] *See*, e.g., F. W. Woolworth v. Contemporary Arts, 334 U.S. 228 (1952); Sony Corp. v. Universal City Studios, 464 U.S. 417 (1984).

[18] Copyright Act of 1976, 17 U.S.C. § 107.

Supreme Court has said fair use should be productive and transform the original to express a new message.[19] To determine whether a use is "fair" under copyright law, courts examine:

1. the purpose and character of the use,
2. the nature of the copyrighted work,
3. the amount and substantiality of copied material as related to the totality of the work, and
4. the effect of the copying on the market for and the value of the original.

In deciding what constitutes fair use, courts weigh and balance all four considerations[20] but tend to give greatest weight to the potential of the copying to harm the financial benefits that will accrue to the author or owner of the copyright. Accordingly, non-commercial uses and uses that have little potential to undermine the market for the original copyrighted material are more likely to fall under the fair use doctrine than uses designed purely to make a profit and to compete with the original.

Purpose and character of use

Making a single copy of a copyrighted work for teaching and non-commercial research purposes or making multiple copies for one-time distribution to an entire class generally are protected uses. On the other hand, making even a single copy of an entire book for personal use and entertainment is not fair use. It hurts the market for the book. For the same reason, it is not fair use for MP3 or Napster to provide copies or to facilitate swapping of copyrighted music CDs even if the service is free and no one directly profits monetarily.[21] However, because the practice did not *not* harm the value of the original, the Supreme Court ruled that the use of VCRs to tape record entire television shows to shift the time of personal viewing is a protected fair use.[22]

Business uses of copyrighted materials are less likely to be protected. Intentional reproduction of copyrighted materials for internal distribution within a business is not fair use.[23] Nor is it fair use to commercially reproduce copyrighted articles for sale to students in course packs[24] or to record and copy segments of the evening news from television and sell the clips.[25] Both of these uses, courts concluded, are overtly commercial and very likely to impair the market for the original. It also is rare that reproducing copyrighted materials in purely commercial advertisements will constitute fair use.[26]

Yet, commercial purpose alone does not automatically exclude the use from the fair use doctrine. Newsworthiness and public interest in the material contribute to a finding of fair use. Thus, a commercial use intended to disseminate knowledge to the public through news reports or to inform the public through commentary, criticism or parody of the original work may qualify

---

[19] Campbell v. Acuff-Rose Music, 510 U.S. 569 (1994).

[20] *See also* 17 U.S.C. § 107.

[21] UMG Recordings v. MP3.com, Inc., 92 F. Supp. 2d 349 (S.D. N.Y. 2000); A&M Records v. Napster, 239 F.3d 1004 (9th Cir. 2001); A&M Records v. Napster, 114 F. Supp. 2d (N.D. Cal. 2000).

[22] Sony Corp. v. Universal City Studios, 464 U.S. 417 (1984). *See also* Recording Indus. Ass'n of America, Inc. v. Diamond Multimedia Sys., Inc., 180 F.3d 1072 (9th Cir. 1999), *affirm'g* 29 F. Supp. 2d 624 (C.D. Cal. 1998) (ruling that an MP3 player for computers is not an illegal device designed primarily for digital audio recording but is designed to enhance personal use by permitting time shifting).

[23] *See* American Geophysical Union v. Texaco, 60 F.3d 913 (2nd Cir. 1994).

[24] Basic Books v. Kinko's Graphics Corp., 758 F. Supp. 1522 (S.D. N.Y. 1991); Princeton University Press v. Michigan Document Service, 855 F. Supp. 905 (E.D. Mich. 1994), *affirm'd* Michigan Document Service v. Princeton University Press, 99 F.3d 1381 (6th Cir. 1996), *cert. den'd* 520 U.S. 1156 (1997).

[25] Pacific and Southern Co. v. Duncan, 744 F.2d 1490 (11th Cir. 1984).

[26] *See* Triangle Publications v. Knight-Ridder Newspapers, 626 F.2d 1171 (5th Cir. 1980) (finding fair use when copyrighted material appeared in ad comparing competing products).

as fair use.[27] However, even newsworthy use of copyrighted material may fail to be fair if it is intended to replace the original in the market.[28]

Nature of the copyrighted work

The second factor courts weigh to determine whether unauthorized use of copyrighted material is fair is the nature of the original. In this view, all works are not equally original and equally worthy of total monopoly control by the author. Works of less originality, e.g. factual databases or tables, are subject to greater fair use applications than are truly creative and original works of fiction, such as scripts, plays or novels. Thus, both the newsworthiness of the factual content and the inherently informational nature of news stories weigh in favor of a finding of fair use for borrowing from news reports. Similarly, fair use is more likely to be found when borrowing is from works that are not commercially available.

In contrast, borrowing segments of extremely short works, appropriating content from a commercial source for a competing commercial use, reprinting copies of consumable works, or publishing excerpts from an unpublished manuscript likely are not fair because each raises a significant likelihood of damaging the financial value and return of the original. Clearly, copying a consumable work, such as a workbook that accompanies a text, directly harms the market for the original. It is equally clear that copying and distributing portions of an unpublished work directly harms the ability of the copyright owner to determine the time and place of initial distribution and may well dramatically alter the commercial value of the owner's first publication rights.[29]

Amount and substantiality of original used

The determination of fair use hinges on the nature of the borrowing and whether the copied portion steals the heart or the gist of the original and, thereby, devalues the original.[30] This issue is often the core of suits involving parodies because parody requires sufficient borrowing of the key characteristics of the original to allow ready public recognition for humorous effect.[31] For example, when 2 Live Crew created a parody of Roy Orbison's "Pretty Woman," the parody used the original's opening line, melody and identifiable bass riff in its rather off-color, commercial rap version that also incorporated substantially new lyrics and music. Acknowledging that 2 Live Crew's parody borrowed the "heart" of the original for commercial gain, the Supreme Court nonetheless ruled unanimously that the use was fair because such borrowing is the essence of parody's commentary, the rap version significantly transformed the original, and the parody posed little if any potential harm to the original's market value.[32]

In 2002, the copyright holders of Margaret Mitchell's classic novel "Gone with the Wind" settled a copyright infringement suit they had brought against the publishers of a new work called "Wind Done Gone." A year earlier, the Court of Appeals for the Eleventh Circuit had overturned a lower court ruling imposing an injunction on distribution of Alice Randall's novel, which retold the original from the perspective of a slave at the plantation home of heroine Scarlett O'Hara.[33] The confidential settlement permits distribution of the work, labeled "An Unauthorized Parody," with payments to the original copyright holder.[34] Other creators, such as

---

[27] *See, e.g.,* Rosemont v. Random House, 366 F.2d 303 (2nd Cir. 1966); Campbell v. Acuff-Rose Music, 510 U.S. 569 (1994).

[28] *See* Harper & Row Publ. v. Nation Enterprises, 471 U.S. 539 (1985).

[29] *Ibid.*

[30] *Ibid.*

[31] *See* Campbell v. Acuff-Rose Music, 510 U.S. 569 (1994).

[32] *Ibid.*

[33] SunTrust Bank v. Houghton Mifflin 268 F.3d 1257 (11th Cir. 2001).

[34] *See* www.houghtonmifflinbooks.com/features/randall_url/may9pr.shtml.

Weird Al Yankovic, avoid such legal entanglement by obtaining prior permission from the copyright owner.

In a related area, the Supreme Court has yet to consider whether musical sampling, which digitally copies key phrases from many compositions to create a new work, constitutes fair use.[35] Clearly, however, when courts determine fair use, they do not use a precise mathematical calculus to evaluate the amount and substantiality of borrowing; there is no magic proportion of the total that may fairly be borrowed. However, in general, it is far less problematic to copy a few words, especially when those words do not constitute a complete segment or component of the whole, than to copy an entire book or several complete stanzas of a song.

Impact on the market for the original

The final consideration in deciding fair use is the effect the unauthorized borrowing has on the value of the original. Courts may presume market harm when, and only when, the copy is a commercial duplication of the original. In cases where the copy does not seek to replace the original and sufficiently transforms the original, a majority of the Supreme Court has said proof of adverse affect on the existing and potential market for the original is "the single most important element of fair use."[36] Proof of adverse impact alone overturns a claim of fair use in such cases. In contrast, inability to show any adverse impact on the market for the original may be sufficient to demonstrate that the use is fair. However, parodies may suppress market demand for the original without undermining a fair use claim so long as the parody does not supplant the original in the original market.[37]

COPYRIGHT DURATION

In 1998, the Copyright Term Extension Act increased the duration of copyright protection from the previous 50 years to 70 years after the author's death.[38] The benefits of copyright may be inherited when the copyright owner dies. When a company holds the copyright – which is usually the case in works for hire, or contract work – the copyright term is either 120 years from creation or 95 years from publication, whichever is shorter. The copyright term is also a maximum of 95 years for works copyrighted prior to the 1998 revision. At the end of the copyright term, the material enters the public domain, where it is available for general use by anyone.

To counterbalance the possibility that the extension of copyright terms might unduly limit public access to valuable materials, the 1998 act mandates periodic reviews of the law's impact on fair use and permits libraries to reproduce copyrighted works for scholarly and other legitimate purposes during the final 20 years of the copyright term if the works are no longer commercially available. Finally, the law exempts small businesses from paying royalties for playing copyrighted music broadcast over the radio, television or Internet.[39]

Nonetheless, a non-profit group that distributes free electronic versions of books in the public domain over the Internet; a company that reprints rare, out-of-print books in the public domain; individuals who sell and purchase relatively inexpensive music in the public domain; and a company that restores old films were among the plaintiffs[40] who challenged the copyright

---

[35] *But see* Grand Upright Music v. Warner Bros. Records, 780 F.Supp. 183 (S.D. N.Y. 1991) (ruling that digital sampling violates copyright).

[36] Harper & Row v. Nation, 471 U.S. 539, 566 (1985).

[37] Campbell v. Acuff Rose, 510 U.S. at 598 (Kennedy, J., concurring).

[38] Copyright Term Extension Act, amending 17 U.S.C. 302 (a).

[39] 17 U.S.C. § 110 (B).

[40] Eldred v. Reno, 239 F.3d 372, 374 (D.C. Cir. 2001).

revision, arguing that the extension of pre-existing copyrights violated their First Amendment right to gain access to original materials after a "limited time."[41] In *Eldred v. Ashcroft*, the Supreme Court applied rational review to hold that the Constitution clearly gives Congress power to expand the duration of copyrights to enhance the incentive for authors to create and distribute original works. The Court said it had long ago established that copyright does not violate the First Amendment. First Amendment concern lies far more with an author's freedom to speak than with any subsequent user's desire to appropriate the original author's words, the Court said.

TECHNOLOGICAL SHIFTS AND COPYRIGHT

The federal copyright statute enacted at the turn of the 20th Century operated until 1976,[42] when the law underwent a major revision, generally bringing U.S. copyright into line with international standards.[43] That law remains the foundation of U.S. copyright today, although in 1997 and 1998 Congress enacted amendments through the No Electronic Theft and the Digital Millennium Copyright.[44] These two laws increase liability for online copyright infringement, limit the liability of innocent online service providers, and increase penalties for the sale and distribution of technologies that assist copyright infringement. Part of the Digital Millennium Copyright Act exempts online service providers who act as mere conduits and only briefly cache copyrighted material or permit unsupervised user storage of information from monetary damages if they neither originate nor alter the infringing material.[45] However, once online service providers receive notice of a possible copyright infringement, they must promptly remove or block access to the material or become liable for contributory infringement.[46]

Separate provisions of the DMCA make it a crime to create, import, traffic, use, or distribute any technologies or devices that circumvent online controls and digital encryption designed to prevent unauthorized access to copyrighted works.[47] Liability exists even if these anti-encryption technologies do not lead to copyright infringement. Under these provisions, the U.S. Court of Appeals for the Second Circuit in 2001 upheld a district court injunction on the online distribution of software that circumvents anti-pirating encryption on DVDs.[48] In *Universal City Studios v. Corley*, the court rejected the defendant's claim that application of the ban to anti-encryption software unconstitutionally targeted protected speech and excessively burdened the constitutionally protected fair use of encrypted copyrighted materials. In rejecting these claims, the court of appeals noted that the Supreme Court has never said the First Amendment provides a right of fair use. Moreover, Congress carefully constructed the anti-trafficking provisions, which in part require the Library of Congress to periodically review the effect of the law on fair use, to prevent trafficking while protecting fair use.

In recent decisions, two federal appeals courts upheld temporary injunctions against online service providers that facilitate downloading and swapping of copyrighted music files.[49] Both

---

[41] 537 U.S. 186 (2003).

[42] Copyright Act of 1976, 17 U.S.C. 502-510.

[43] 17 U.S.C.A. § 101. Note, however, that the United States did not sign the international Berne Convention on copyright until 1988.

[44] No Electronic Theft Act, Pub. L. No. 105-147, 111 Stat. 2678 (1997), amending 17 U.S. C. 506 (a) (2); Digital Millennium Copyright Act, Pub. L. No. 105-304, 112 Stat. 2860 (1998).

[45] 17 U.S.C. 512 (2000).

[46] *See, e.g.,* A&M Records v. Napster, 239 F.3d 1004 (9th Cir. 2001); A&M Records v. Napster, 114 F. Supp. 2d (N.D. Cal. 2000).

[47] *See* 17 U.S.C. § 1201 (2000).

[48] *See* Universal City Studios v. Corley, 273 F.3d 429 (2nd Cir. 2001); Universal City Studios v. Reimerdes (Corley), 111 F. Supp. 2d 294 (S.D. N.Y. 2000).

[49] *See* In re Aimster Copyright Litigation, 2003 U.S. App. LEXIS 13229 (7th Cir. June 2003) (balancing knowledge and advocacy of infringing uses against reasonably probable actual and potential non-infringing uses

Aimster and Napster argued that their services were innocent transporters for the fair use of copyrighted material by others. The Recording Industry Association of America said these services, and others like them, facilitated copyright infringement and should be liable for contributory infringement. In 2001, the Ninth Circuit Court of Appeals agreed with RIAA and upheld an injunction against Napster because Napster knew its service could be used to violate copyright. Two years later, the Seventh Circuit Court of Appeals balanced the service provider's actual knowledge and advocacy of infringing uses against the reasonable probability of non-infringing uses to affirm an injunction against Aimster.

In June 2003, the RIAA moved its litigation to a new front. The association vowed to file thousands of civil lawsuits against individual music fans who directly infringe copyrights through personal sharing of digitized music files online.[50]

While new technologies do not require radical transformation of copyright law, they present new opportunities to copyright holders and potential violators of copyright and new challenges to the courts. In recent years, copyright litigation has increased dramatically as technologies enable faster, more perfect duplication and novel means of copyright protection. Difficulties in identifying those who directly infringe copyrights online pose new questions about contributory infringement and vicarious liability, and redistribution of copyrighted materials in different media raises new issues about what constitutes permissible republication of a work. For example, in 2001, the Supreme Court held that the rights granted by an author to the publisher of a collective work, such as a newspaper, do not automatically include the right to redistribute portions of the work online.[51]

ADDITIONAL CASE READINGS

Reading the cases in this list and those presented below will greatly enhance your understanding of the law of copyright and provide a more thorough overview of recent developments in the law.

- *Eldred v. Ashcroft*, 537 U.S. 186 (2003) (finding the Copyright Term Extension Act's extension of existing copyrights neither exceeds Congress' power nor violates the First Amendment).
- *In re Aimster Copyright Litigation*, 2003 U.S. App. LEXIS 13229 (7th Cir. June 2003) (balancing knowledge and advocacy of infringing uses against reasonably probable actual and potential non-infringing uses to affirm temporary injunction against potential contributory infringement by Aimster online service).
- *A&M Records v. Napster*, 239 F.3d 1004 (9th Cir. 2001) (holding Napster liable on grounds that knowledge of specific infringing uses of its service is sufficient to find contributory infringement).
- *Recording Industry Association of America v. Diamond Multimedia Systems*, 180 F.3d 1072 (9th Cir. 1999) (ruling that an MP3 player for computers is designed primarily to enhance personal use not to aid illegal digital audio recordings).

---

to affirm temporary injunction against potential contributory infringement by Aimster/Madster); A&M Records v. Napster, 239 F.3d 1004 (9th Cir. 2001), *affirm'g in part* 114 F. Supp. 2d 896 (N.D. Cal. 2000) (holding Napster liable on grounds that knowledge of specific infringing uses of its service is sufficient to find contributory infringement).

[50] *See* Laura Sydell, Programmers Aim to Evade File-Sharing Crackdown, National Public Radio (July 8, 2003) available at http://news.npr.org/index.html.

[51] *See* New York Times v. Tasini, 533 U.S. 483 (2001), *affirm'g* Tasini v. New York Times, 192 F.3d 356 (2nd Cir. 1999), 972 F. Supp. 804 (S.D. N.Y. 1997).

- *Princeton University Press v. Michigan Document Service*, 99 F.3d 1381 (6th Cir. 1996) (affirming finding of copyright infringement by copying service reproducing course packs).
- *Campbell v. Acuff-Rose Music*, 510 U.S. 569 (1994) (finding parody use of key elements of copyright protected song protected as fair use).
- *Feist Publications v. Telephone Service Co.*, 499 U.S. 340 (1991) (finding alphabetical telephone listings insufficiently original to be copyrightable).
- *Sony Corporation v. Universal City Studios*, 464 U.S. 417 (1984) (finding producer of VCRs is not liable for contributory infringement of television program copyrights).

The following questions should guide your reading of the cases below.

- What precedent or foundation does the Supreme Court offer for the fair-use test it applies in *Harper & Row Publishers v. Nation*?
- Who bears the burden of proof under the test articulated in *Harper & Row Publishers v. Nation*?
- What is a "reasonable and customary use" of copyrighted material and how does the Court distinguish it from The Nation's use in this case?
- How do the majority and the dissent differ in their description and application of the idea/expression dichotomy in copyright?
- To what degree does the Court apply public interest as a component in determining fair use?
- Does the Court make clear whether and when paraphrasing or summary may infringe copyright?
- Is the dissent in *Harper & Row Publishers v. Nation* accurate in its claim that the majority decision categorically excludes prepublication use from fair use?
- Is "bad intent" a component of the determination of fair use?
- Does the decision in *Harper & Row Publishers v. Nation* place greater priority on property rights or free speech?
- What analytical approach does the court apply in *Universal City Studios v. Corley* and what alternative strategy might it have adopted to resolve the case?
- How does the court define computer code for First Amendment purposes in *Universal City Studios v. Corley*?
- In *Universal City Studios v. Corley*, what is the unique trait of computer code that determines its First Amendment status?
- Under the court's analysis, who bears the burden of showing that the injunction and the statute are narrowly tailored? Why?
- Is the court's speech/function distinction reasonable?
- What are the effects of the analogies to encryption/decryption used by the court in *Universal City Studios v. Corley* to guide its reasoning?
- What evidence does the court provide to support claims of harm to film studios?

Harper & Row, Publishers, Inc. v. Nation Enterprises
471 U.S. 539
(1985)

PRIOR HISTORY: Certiorari To The United States Court Of Appeals For The Second Circuit.

JUDGES: O'CONNOR, J., delivered the opinion of the Court, in which BURGER, C. J., and BLACKMUN, POWELL, REHNQUIST, and STEVENS, JJ., joined. BRENNAN, J., filed a dissenting opinion, in which WHITE and MARSHALL, JJ., joined.

OPINION: [541] JUSTICE O'CONNOR delivered the opinion of the Court.

[1A] This case requires us to consider to what extent the "fair use" provision of the Copyright Revision Act of 1976 (hereinafter [542] the Copyright Act), 17 U. S. C. § 107, sanctions the unauthorized use of quotations from a public figure's unpublished manuscript. In March 1979, an undisclosed source provided The Nation Magazine with the unpublished manuscript of "A Time to Heal: The Autobiography of Gerald R. Ford." Working directly from the purloined manuscript, an editor of The Nation produced a short piece entitled "The Ford Memoirs – Behind the Nixon Pardon." The piece was timed to "scoop" an article scheduled shortly to appear in Time Magazine. Time had agreed to purchase the exclusive right to print prepublication excerpts from the copyright holders, Harper & Row Publishers, Inc. (hereinafter Harper & Row), and Reader's Digest Association, Inc. (hereinafter Reader's Digest). As a result of The Nation article, Time canceled its agreement. Petitioners brought a successful copyright action against The Nation. On appeal, the Second Circuit reversed the lower court's finding of infringement, holding that The Nation's act was sanctioned as a "fair use" of the copyrighted material. We granted certiorari, 467 U.S. 1214 (1984), and we now reverse.

I. In February 1977, shortly after leaving the White House, former President Gerald R. Ford contracted with petitioners Harper & Row and Reader's Digest, to publish his as yet unwritten memoirs. The memoirs were to contain "significant hitherto unpublished material" concerning the Watergate crisis, Mr. Ford's pardon of former President Nixon and "Mr. Ford's reflections on this period of history, and the morality and personalities involved." App. to Pet. for Cert. C-14 – C-15. In addition to the right to publish the Ford memoirs in book form, the agreement gave petitioners the exclusive right to license prepublication excerpts, known in the trade as "first serial rights." Two years later, as the memoirs were nearing completion, petitioners negotiated a prepublication licensing agreement with Time, a weekly news magazine. Time agreed to pay $25,000, $12,500 in advance and an [543] additional $12,500 at publication, in exchange for the right to excerpt 7,500 words from Mr. Ford's account of the Nixon pardon. The issue featuring the excerpts was timed to appear approximately one week before shipment of the full-length book version to bookstores. Exclusivity was an important consideration; Harper & Row instituted procedures designed to maintain the confidentiality of the manuscript, and Time retained the right to renegotiate the second payment should the material appear in print prior to its release of the excerpts.

Two to three weeks before the Time article's scheduled release, an unidentified person secretly brought a copy of the Ford manuscript to Victor Navasky, editor of The Nation, a political commentary magazine. Mr. Navasky knew that his possession of the manuscript was not authorized and that the manuscript must be returned quickly to his "source" to avoid discovery. 557 F.Supp. 1067, 1069 (SDNY 1983). He hastily put together what he believed was "a real hot news story" composed of quotes, paraphrases, and facts drawn exclusively from the manuscript. Ibid. Mr. Navasky attempted no independent commentary, research or criticism, in part because of the need for speed if he was to "make news" by "[publishing] in advance of publication of the Ford book." App. 416-417. The 2,250-word article, reprinted in the Appendix to this opinion, appeared on April 3, 1979. As a result of The Nation's article, Time canceled its piece and refused to pay the remaining $12,500.

Petitioners brought suit in the District Court for the Southern District of New York, alleging conversion, tortious interference with contract, and violations of the Copyright Act. After a 6-day bench trial, the District Judge found that "A Time to Heal" was protected by copyright at the time of The Nation publication and that respondents' use of the copyrighted material constituted an infringement under the Copyright Act, §§ 106(1), (2), and (3), protecting respectively the right to reproduce the work, the right to license preparation of derivative works, and the right of first distribution of [544] the copyrighted work to the public. App. to Pet. for Cert. C-29 – C-30. The District Court rejected respondents' argument that The Nation's piece was a "fair use" sanctioned by § 107 of the Act. Though billed as "hot news," the article contained no new facts. The magazine had "published its article for profit," taking "the heart" of "a soon-to-be published" work. This unauthorized use "caused the Time agreement to be aborted and thus diminished the value of the copyright." 557 F.Supp., at 1072. Although certain elements of the Ford memoirs, such as historical facts and memoranda, were not per se copyrightable, the District Court held that it was "the totality of these facts and memoranda collected together with Ford's reflections that made them of value to The Nation, [and] this . . . totality . . . is protected by the copyright laws." Id., at 1072-1073. The court awarded actual damages of $12,500.

A divided panel of the Court of Appeals for the Second Circuit reversed. The majority recognized that Mr. Ford's verbatim "reflections" were original "expression" protected by copyright. But it held that the District Court had erred in assuming the "coupling [of these reflections] with un-copyrightable fact transformed that information into a copyrighted 'totality.'" 723 F.2d 195, 205 (1983). The majority noted that copyright attaches to expression, not facts or ideas. It concluded that, to avoid granting a copyright monopoly over the facts underlying history and news, "'expression' [in such works must be confined] to its barest elements – the ordering and choice of the words them-selves." Id., at 204. Thus similarities between the original and the challenged work traceable to the copying or paraphrasing of uncopyrightable material, such as historical facts, memoranda and other public documents, and quoted remarks of third parties, must be disregarded in evaluating whether the second author's use was fair or infringing.

"When the uncopyrighted material is stripped away, the article in The Nation contains, at most, approximately [545] 300 words that are copyrighted. These remaining paragraphs and scattered phrases are all verbatim quotations from the memoirs, which had not appeared previously in other publications. They include a short segment of Ford's conversations with Henry Kissinger and several other individuals. Ford's impressionistic depictions of Nixon, ill with phlebitis after the resignation and pardon, and of Nixon's character, constitute the major portion of this material. It is these parts of the magazine piece on which [the court] must focus in [its] examination of the question whether there was a 'fair use' of copyrighted matter." Id., at 206.

Examining the four factors enumerated in § 107, see infra, at 547, n. 2, the majority found the purpose of the article was "news reporting," the original work was essentially factual in nature, the 300 words appropriated were insubstantial in relation to the 2,250-word piece, and the impact on the market for the original was minimal as "the evidence [did] not support a finding that it was the very limited use of expression per se which led to Time's decision not to print the excerpt." The Nation's borrowing of verbatim quotations merely "[lent] authenticity to this politically significant material ... complementing the reporting of the facts." 723 F.2d, at 208. The Court of Appeals was especially influenced by the "politically significant" nature of the subject matter and its conviction that it is not "the purpose of the Copyright Act to impede that harvest of knowledge so necessary to a democratic state" or "chill the activities of the press by forbidding a circumscribed use of copyrighted words." Id., at 197, 209.

II. [2] We agree with the Court of Appeals that copyright is intended to increase and not to impede the harvest of knowledge. But we believe the Second Circuit gave insufficient deference to the scheme established by the Copyright Act for [546] fostering the original works that provide the seed and substance of this harvest. The rights conferred by copyright are designed to assure contributors to the store of knowledge a fair return for their labors. Twentieth Century Music Corp. v. Aiken, 422 U.S. 151, 156 (1975).

Article I, § 8, of the Constitution provides: "The Congress shall have Power . . . to Promote the Progress of Science and useful Arts, by securing for limited Times to Authors and Inventors the exclusive Right to their respective Writings and Discoveries."

As we noted last Term: "[This] limited grant is a means by which an important public purpose may be achieved. It is intended to motivate the creative activity of authors and inventors by the provision of a special reward, and to allow the public access to the products of their genius after the limited period of exclusive control has expired." Sony Corp. of America v. Universal City Studios, Inc., 464 U.S. 417, 429 (1984). "The monopoly created by copyright thus rewards the individual author in order to benefit the public." Id., at 477 (dissenting opinion). This principle applies equally to works of fiction and nonfiction. The book at issue here, for example, was two years in the making, and began with a contract giving the author's copyright to the publishers in exchange for their services in producing and marketing the work. In preparing the book, Mr. Ford drafted essays and word portraits of public figures and participated in hundreds of taped interviews that were later distilled to chronicle his personal viewpoint. It is evident that the monopoly granted by copyright actively served its intended purpose of inducing the creation of new material of potential historical value.

[3] [4] Section 106 of the Copyright Act confers a bundle of exclusive rights to the owner of the copyright.[1] Under the Copyright [547] Act, these rights – to publish, copy, and distribute the author's work – vest in the author of an original work from the time of its creation. § 106. In practice, the author commonly sells his rights to publishers who offer royalties in exchange for their services in producing and marketing the author's work. The copyright owner's rights, however, are subject to certain statutory exceptions. §§ 107-118. Among these is § 107, which codifies the traditional privilege of other authors to make "fair use" of an earlier writer's work.[2] In addition, no author may copyright facts or ideas. § 102. The copyright is limited to those aspects of the work – termed "expression"– that display the stamp of the author's originality.

[5] Creation of a nonfiction work, even a compilation of pure fact, entails originality. See, e.g., Schroeder v. William Morrow & Co., 566 F.2d 3 (CA7 1977) (copyright in gardening directory); cf. Burrow-Giles Lithographic Co. v. Sarony, 111 U.S. 53, 58 (1884) (originator of a photograph may claim copyright in his work). The copyright holders of "A Time to Heal" complied with the relevant statutory notice and registration [548] procedures. See §§ 106, 401, 408; App. to Pet. for Cert. C-20. Thus there is no

dispute that the unpublished manuscript of "A Time to Heal," as a whole, was protected by § 106 from unauthorized reproduction. Nor do respondents dispute that verbatim copying of excerpts of the manuscript's original form of expression would constitute infringement unless excused as fair use. See 1 M. Nimmer, Copyright § 2.11[B], p. 2-159 (1984) (hereinafter Nimmer). Yet copyright does not prevent subsequent users from copying from a prior author's work those constituent elements that are not original – for example, quotations borrowed under the rubric of fair use from other copyrighted works, facts, or materials in the public domain – as long as such use does not unfairly appropriate the author's original contributions. Ibid.; A. Latman, Fair Use of Copyrighted Works (1958), reprinted as Study No. 14 in Copyright Law Revision Studies Nos. 14-16, prepared for the Senate Committee on the Judiciary, 86th Cong., 2d Sess., 7 (1960) (hereinafter Latman). Perhaps the controversy between the lower courts in this case over copyrightability is more aptly styled a dispute over whether The Nation's appropriation of unoriginal and uncopyrightable elements encroached on the originality embodied in the work as a whole. Especially in the realm of factual narrative, the law is currently unsettled regarding the ways in which uncopyrightable elements combine with the author's original contributions to form protected expression. Compare Wainwright Securities Inc. v. Wall Street Transcript Corp., 558 F.2d 91 (CA2 1977) (protection accorded author's analysis, structuring of material and marshaling of facts), with Hoehling v. Universal City Studios, Inc., 618 F.2d 972 (CA2 1980) (limiting protection to ordering and choice of words). See, e.g., 1 Nimmer § 2.11[D], at 2-164 – 2-165.

[1B] We need not reach these issues, however, as The Nation has admitted to lifting verbatim quotes of the author's original language totaling between 300 and 400 words and constituting some 13% of The Nation article. In using generous [549] verbatim excerpts of Mr. Ford's unpublished manuscript to lend authenticity to its account of the forthcoming memoirs, The Nation effectively arrogated to itself the right of first publication, an important marketable subsidiary right. For the reasons set forth below, we find that this use of the copyrighted manuscript, even stripped to the verbatim quotes conceded by The Nation to be copyrightable expression, was not a fair use within the meaning of the Copyright Act.

III. A   Fair use was traditionally defined as "a privilege in others than the owner of the copyright to use the copyrighted material in a reasonable manner without his consent." H. Ball, Law of Copyright and Literary Property 260 (1944)

---

[1] Section 106 provides in pertinent part:

"Subject to sections 107 through 118, the owner of copyright under this title has the exclusive rights to do and authorize any of the following:

"(1) to reproduce the copyrighted work in copies ... ;

"(2) to prepare derivative works based upon the copyrighted work;

"(3) to distribute copies ... of the copyrighted work to the public. ..."

[2] Section 107 states:

"Notwithstanding the provisions of section 106, the fair use of a copyrighted work ... for purposes such as criticism, comment, news reporting, teaching (including multiple copies for classroom use), scholarship, or research, is not an infringement of copyright. In determining whether the use made of a work in any particular case is a fair use the factors to be considered shall include –

"(1) the purpose and character of the use, including whether such use is of a commercial nature or is for nonprofit educational purposes;

"(2) the nature of the copyrighted work;

"(3) the amount and substantiality of the portion used in relation to the copyrighted work as a whole; and

"(4) the effect of the use upon the potential market for or value of the copyrighted work."

(hereinafter Ball). The statutory formulation of the defense of fair use in the Copyright Act reflects the intent of Congress to codify the common-law doctrine. 3 Nimmer § 13.05. Section 107 requires a case-by-case determination whether a particular use is fair, and the statute notes four nonexclusive factors to be considered. This approach was "intended to restate the [pre-existing] judicial doctrine of fair use, not to change, narrow, or enlarge it in any way." H. R. Rep. No. 94-1476, p. 66 (1976) (hereinafter House Report).

"[The] author's consent to a reasonable use of his copyrighted works [had] always been implied by the courts as a necessary incident of the constitutional policy of promoting the progress of science and the useful arts, since a prohibition of such use would inhibit subsequent writers from attempting to improve upon prior works and thus ... frustrate the very ends sought to be attained." Ball 260. Professor Latman, in a study of the doctrine of fair use commissioned by Congress for the revision effort, see Sony Corp. of America v. Universal City Studios, Inc., 464 U.S., at 462-463, n. 9 (dissenting opinion), summarized prior law as turning on the "importance [550] of the material copied or performed from the point of view of the reasonable copyright owner. In other words, would the reasonable copyright owner have consented to the use?" Latman 15.[3]

As early as 1841, Justice Story gave judicial recognition to the doctrine in a case that concerned the letters of another former President, George Washington.

"[A] reviewer may fairly cite largely from the original work, if his design be really and truly to use the passages for the purposes of fair and reasonable criticism. On the other hand, it is as clear, that if he thus cites the most important parts of the work, with a view, not to criticise, but to supersede the use of the original work, and substitute the review for it, such a use will be deemed in law a piracy." Folsom v. Marsh, 9 F. Cas. 342, 344-345 (No. 4,901) (CC Mass.)

As Justice Story's hypothetical illustrates, the fair use doctrine has always precluded a use that "[supersedes] the use of the original." Ibid. Accord, S. Rep. No. 94-473, p. 65 (1975) (hereinafter Senate Report).

[6A] Perhaps because the fair use doctrine was predicated on the author's implied consent to "reasonable and customary" use when he released his work for public consumption, fair use traditionally was not recognized as a defense to charges [551] of copying from an author's as yet unpublished works.[4] Under common-law copyright "the property of the author . . . in his intellectual creation [was] absolute until he voluntarily [parted] with the same. " American Tobacco Co. v. Werckmeister, 207 U.S. 284, 299 (1907); 2 Nimmer § 8.23, at 8-273. This absolute rule, however, was tempered in practice by the equitable nature of the fair use doctrine. In a given case, factors such as implied consent through de facto publication on performance or dissemination of a work may tip the balance of equities in favor of prepublication use. See Copyright Law Revision – Part 2: Discussion and Comments on Report of the Register of Copyrights on General Revision of the U.S. Copyright Law, 88th Cong., 1st Sess., 27 (H. R. Comm. Print 1963) (discussion suggesting works disseminated to the public in a form not constituting a technical "publication" should nevertheless be subject to fair use); 3 Nimmer § 13.05, at 13-62, n. 2. But it has never been seriously disputed that "the fact that the plaintiff's work is unpublished . . . is a factor tending to negate the defense of fair use." Ibid. Publication of an author's expression before he has authorized its dissemination seriously infringes the author's right to decide when and whether it will be made public, a factor not present in fair use of published

---

[3] Professor Nimmer notes: "[Perhaps] no more precise guide can be stated than Joseph McDonald's clever paraphrase of the Golden Rule: 'Take not from others to such an extent and in such a manner that you would be resentful if they so took from you.'" 3 Nimmer § 13.05[A], at 13-66, quoting McDonald, Non-infringing Uses, 9 Bull. Copyright Soc. 466, 467 (1962). This "equitable rule of reason," Sony Corp. of America v. Universal City Studios, Inc., 464 U.S., at 448, "permits courts to avoid rigid application of the copyright statute when, on occasion, it would stifle the very creativity which that law is designed to foster." Iowa State University Research Foundation, Inc. v. American Broadcasting Cos., 621 F.2d 57, 60 (CA2 1980). See generally L. Seltzer, Exemptions and Fair Use in Copyright 18-48 (1978).

[4] See Latman 7; Strauss, Protection of Unpublished Works (1957), reprinted as Study No. 29 in Copyright Law Revision Studies Nos. 29-31, prepared for the Senate Committee on the Judiciary, 86th Cong., 2d Sess., 4, n. 32 (1961) (citing cases); R. Shaw, Literary Property in the United States 67 (1950) ("[There] can be no 'fair use' of unpublished material"); Ball 260, n. 5 ("[The] doctrine of fair use does not apply to unpublished works"); A. Weil, American Copyright Law § 276, p. 115 (1917) (the author of an unpublished work "has, probably, the right to prevent even a 'fair use' of the work by others"). Cf. M. Flint, A User's Guide to Copyright para. 10.06 (1979) (United Kingdom) ("no fair dealing with unpublished works"); Beloff v. Pressdram Ltd., [1973] All E. R. 241, 263 (Ch. 1972) (same).

16.14

works.[5] [552] Respondents contend, however, that Congress, in including first publication among the rights enumerated in § 106, which are expressly subject to fair use under § 107, intended that fair use would apply in pari materia to published and unpublished works. The Copyright Act does not support this proposition.

The Copyright Act represents the culmination of a major legislative reexamination of copyright doctrine. See Mills Music, Inc. v. Snyder, 469 U.S. 153, 159-160 (1985); Sony Corp. of America v. Universal City Studios, Inc., 464 U.S., at 462-463, n. 9 (dissenting opinion). Among its other innovations, it eliminated publication "as a dividing line between common law and statutory protection," House Report, at 129, extending statutory protection to all works from the time of their creation. It also recognized for the first time a distinct statutory right of first publication, which had previously been an element of the common-law protections afforded unpublished works. The Report of the House Committee on the Judiciary confirms that "Clause (3) of section 106, establishes the exclusive right of publications. . . . Under this provision the copyright owner would have the right to control the first public distribution of an authorized copy . . . of his work." Id., at 62.

Though the right of first publication, like the other rights enumerated in § 106, is expressly made subject to the fair use provision of § 107, fair use analysis must always be tailored to the individual case. Id., at 65; 3 Nimmer § 13.05[A]. The [553] nature of the interest at stake is highly relevant to whether a given use is fair. From the beginning, those entrusted with the task of revision recognized the "overbalancing reasons to preserve the common law protection of undisseminated works until the author or his successor chooses to disclose them." Copyright Law Revision, Report of the Register of Copyrights on the General Revision of the U.S. Copyright Law, 87th Cong., 1st Sess., 41

---

[5] See, e.g., Wheaton v. Peters, 8 Pet. 591, 657 (1834) (distinguishing the author's common-law right to "obtain redress against anyone who . . . by improperly obtaining a copy [of his unpublished work] endeavors to realize a profit by its publication" from rights in a published work, which are prescribed by statute); Press Publishing Co. v. Monroe, 73 F. 196, 199 (CA2), writ of error dism'd, 164 U.S. 105 (1896); Stanley v. Columbia Broadcasting System, Inc., 35 Cal. 2d 653, 660-661, 221 P. 2d 73, 77-78 (1950) (en banc); Golding v. RKO Radio Pictures, Inc., 193 P. 2d 153, 162 (Cal. App. 1948) ("An unauthorized appropriation of [an unpublished work] is not to be neutralized on the plea that 'it is such a little one'"), aff'd, 35 Cal. 2d 690, 221 P. 2d 95 (1950); Fendler v. Morosco, 253 N.Y. 281, 291, 171 N. E. 56, 59 ("Since plaintiff had not published or produced her play, perhaps any use that others made of it might be unfair"), rehearing denied, 254 N.Y. 563, 173 N. E. 867 (1930).

(Comm. Print 1961). The right of first publication implicates a threshold decision by the author whether and in what form to release his work. First publication is inherently different from other § 106 rights in that only one person can be the first publisher; as the contract with Time illustrates, the commercial value of the right lies primarily in exclusivity. Because the potential damage to the author from judicially enforced "sharing" of the first publication right with unauthorized users of his manuscript is substantial, the balance of equities in evaluating such a claim of fair use inevitably shifts.

The Senate Report confirms that Congress intended the unpublished nature of the work to figure prominently in fair use analysis. In discussing fair use of photocopied materials in the classroom the Committee Report states: "A key, though not necessarily determinative, factor in fair use is whether or not the work is available to the potential user. If the work is 'out of print' and unavailable for purchase through normal channels, the user may have more justification for reproducing it.... The applicability of the fair use doctrine to unpublished works is narrowly limited since, although the work is unavailable, this is the result of a deliberate choice on the part of the copyright owner. Under ordinary circumstances, the copyright owner's 'right of first publication' would outweigh any needs of reproduction for classroom purposes." Senate Report, at 64.

Although the Committee selected photocopying of classroom materials to illustrate fair use, it emphasized that "the same [554] general standards of fair use are applicable to all kinds of uses of copyrighted material." Id., at 65. We find unconvincing respondents' contention that the absence of the quoted passage from the House Report indicates an intent to abandon the traditional distinction between fair use of published and unpublished works. It appears instead that the fair use discussion of photocopying of classroom materials was omitted from the final Report because educators and publishers in the interim had negotiated a set of guidelines that rendered the discussion obsolete. House Report, at 67. The House Report nevertheless incorporates the discussion by reference, citing to the Senate Report and stating: "The Committee has reviewed this discussion, and considers it still has value as an analysis of various aspects of the [fair use] problem." Ibid.

[6B] Even if the legislative history were entirely silent, we would be bound to conclude from Congress' characterization of § 107 as a "restatement" that its effect was to preserve existing law concerning fair use of unpublished works as of other types of protected works and not to "change, narrow, or enlarge it." Id., at 66. We conclude that the unpublished nature of a work is "[a] key, though not necessarily determinative, factor" tending to negate a defense of fair use. Senate Report, at 64. See 3 Nimmer § 13.05, at 13-62, n. 2; W. Patry, The Fair Use Privilege in Copyright Law 125 (1985) (hereinafter Patry).

[6C] We also find unpersuasive respondents' argument that fair use may be made of a soon-to-be-published manuscript on the ground that the author has demonstrated he has no interest in nonpublication. This argument assumes that the unpublished nature of copyrighted material is only relevant to letters or other confidential writings not intended for dissemination. It is true that common-law copyright was often enlisted in the service of personal privacy. See Brandeis & Warren, The Right to Privacy, 4 Harv. L. Rev. 193, 198-199 (1890). In its commercial guise, however, an author's right to choose when he will publish is no less deserving of protection. [555] The period encompassing the work's initiation, its preparation, and its grooming for public dissemination is a crucial one for any literary endeavor. The Copyright Act, which accords the copyright owner the "right to control the first public distribution" of his work, House Report, at 62, echos the common law's concern that the author or copyright owner retain control throughout this critical stage. See generally Comment, The Stage of Publication as a "Fair Use" Factor: Harper & Row, Publishers v. Nation Enterprises, 58 St. John's L. Rev. 597 (1984). The obvious benefit to author and public alike of assuring authors the leisure to develop their ideas free from fear of expropriation outweighs any short-term "news value" to be gained from premature publication of the author's expression. See Goldstein, Copyright and the First Amendment, 70 Colum. L. Rev. 983, 1004-1006 (1970) (The absolute protection the common law accorded to soon-to-be published works "[was] justified by [its] brevity and expedience"). The author's control of first public distribution implicates not only his personal interest in creative control but his property interest in exploitation of prepublication rights, which are valuable in themselves and serve as a valuable adjunct to publicity and marketing. See Belushi v. Woodward, 598 F.Supp. 36 (DC 1984) (successful marketing depends on coordination of serialization and release to public); Marks, Subsidiary Rights and Permissions, in What Happens in Book Publishing 230 (C. Grannis ed. 1967) (exploitation of subsidiary rights is necessary to financial success of new books). Under ordinary circumstances, the author's right to control the first public appearance of his undisseminated expression will outweigh a claim of fair use.

B Respondents, however, contend that First Amendment values require a different rule under the circumstances of this case. The thrust of the decision below is that "[the] scope of [fair use] is undoubtedly wider when the information [556] conveyed relates to matters of high public concern." Consumers Union of the United States, Inc. v. General Signal Corp., 724 F.2d 1044, 1050 (CA2 1983) (construing 723 F.2d 195 (1983) (case below) as allowing advertiser to quote Consumer Reports), cert. denied, 469 U.S. 823 (1984). Respondents advance the substantial public import of the subject matter of the Ford memoirs as grounds for excusing a use that would ordinarily not pass muster as a fair use – the piracy of verbatim quotations for the purpose of "scooping" the authorized first serialization. Respondents explain their copying of Mr. Ford's expression as essential to reporting the news story it claims the book itself represents. In respondents' view, not only the facts contained in Mr. Ford's memoirs, but "the precise manner in which [he] expressed himself [were] as newsworthy as what he had to say." Brief for Respondents 38-39. Respondents argue that the public's interest in learning this news as fast as possible outweighs the right of the author to control its first publication.

[7] The Second Circuit noted, correctly, that copyright's idea/expression dichotomy "[strikes] a definitional balance between the First Amendment and the Copyright Act by permitting free communication of facts while still protecting an author's expression." 723 F.2d, at 203. No author may copyright his ideas or the facts he narrates. 17 U. S. C. § 102(b). See, e.g., New York Times Co. v. United States, 403 U.S. 713, 726, n. (1971) (BRENNAN, J., concurring) (Copyright laws are not restrictions on freedom of speech as copyright protects only form of expression and not the ideas expressed); 1 Nimmer § 1.10[B][2]. As this Court long ago observed: "[The] news element – the information respecting current events contained in the literary production – is not the creation of the writer, but is a report of matters that ordinarily are publici juris; it is the history of the day." International News Service v. Associated Press, 248 U.S. 215, 234 (1918). But copyright assures those who write and publish factual narratives such as "A Time to Heal" that [557] they may at least enjoy the right to market the original expression contained therein as just compensation for their investment. Cf. Zacchini v. Scripps-Howard Broadcasting Co., 433 U.S. 562, 575 (1977).

Respondents' theory, however, would expand fair use to effectively destroy any expectation of copyright protection in the work of a public figure. Absent such protection, there would be little incentive to create or profit in financing such memoirs, and the public would be denied an important source of significant historical information. The promise of copyright would be an empty one if it could be avoided merely by dubbing the infringement a fair use "news report" of the book. See Wainwright Securities Inc. v. Wall Street Transcript Corp., 558 F.2d 91 (CA2 1977), cert. denied, 434 U.S. 1014 (1978).

[8A] [9A] Nor do respondents assert any actual necessity for circumventing the copyright scheme with respect to the types of works and users at issue here.[6] Where an author and publisher have invested extensive resources in creating an original work and are poised to release it to the public, no legitimate aim is served by pre-empting the right of first publication. The fact that the words the author has chosen to clothe his narrative may of themselves be "newsworthy" is not an independent justification for unauthorized copying of the author's expression prior to publication. To paraphrase another recent Second Circuit decision: "[Respondent] possessed an unfettered right to use any factual information revealed in [the memoirs] for the purpose of enlightening its audience, but it can claim [558] no need to 'bodily appropriate' [Mr. Ford's] 'expression' of that information by utilizing portions of the actual [manuscript]. The public interest in the free flow of information is assured by the law's refusal to recognize a valid copyright in facts. The fair use doctrine is not a license for corporate theft, empowering a court to ignore a copyright whenever it determines the underlying work contains material of possible public importance." Iowa State University Research Foundation, Inc. v. American Broadcasting Cos., Inc., 621 F.2d 57, 61 (1980) (citations omitted). Accord, Roy Export Co. Establishment v. Columbia Broadcasting System, Inc., 503 F.Supp. 1137 (SDNY 1980) ("newsworthiness" of material copied does not justify copying), aff'd, 672 F.2d 1095 (CA2), cert. denied, 459 U.S. 826 (1982); Quinto v. Legal Times of Washington, Inc., 506 F.Supp. 554 (DC 1981) (same).

[8B] In our haste to disseminate news, it should not be forgotten that the Framers intended copyright itself to be the engine of free expression. By establishing a marketable right to the use of one's expression, copyright supplies the economic incentive to create and disseminate ideas. This Court stated in Mazer v. Stein, 347 U.S. 201, 209 (1954): "The economic philosophy behind the clause empowering Congress to grant patents and copyrights is the conviction that encouragement of individual effort by personal gain is the best way to advance public welfare through the talents of authors and inventors in 'Science and useful Arts.'"

And again in Twentieth Century Music Corp. v. Aiken: "The immediate effect of our copyright law is to secure a fair return for an 'author's' creative labor. But the ultimate aim is, by this incentive, to stimulate [the creation of useful works] for the general public good." 422 U.S., at 156.

[559] It is fundamentally at odds with the scheme of copyright to accord lesser rights in those works that are of greatest importance to the public. Such a notion ignores the major premise of copyright and injures author and public alike. "[To] propose that fair use be imposed whenever the 'social value [of dissemination] . . . outweighs any detriment to the artist,' would be to propose depriving copyright owners of their right in the property precisely when they encounter those users who could afford to pay for it." Gordon, Fair Use as Market Failure: A Structural and Economic Analysis of the Betamax Case and its Predecessors, 82 Colum. L. Rev. 1600, 1615 (1982). And as one commentator has noted: "If every volume that was in the public interest could be pirated away by a competing publisher, . . . the public [soon] would have nothing worth reading." Sobel, Copyright and the First Amendment: A Gathering Storm?, 19 ASCAP Copyright Law Symposium 43, 78 (1971). See generally Comment, Copyright and the First Amendment; Where Lies the Public Interest?, 59 Tulane L. Rev. 135 (1984).

Moreover, freedom of thought and expression "includes both the right to speak freely and the right to refrain from speaking at all." Wooley v. Maynard, 430 U.S. 705, 714 (1977) (BURGER, C. J.). We do not suggest this right not to speak would sanction abuse of the copyright owner's monopoly as an instrument to suppress facts. But in the words of New York's Chief Judge Fuld:

"The essential thrust of the First Amendment is to prohibit improper restraints on the voluntary public expression of ideas; it shields the man who wants to speak or publish when others wish him to be quiet. There is necessarily, and within suitably defined areas, a concomitant freedom not to speak publicly, one which serves the same ultimate end as freedom of speech in its affirmative aspect." Estate of Hemingway v. Random House, Inc., 23 N.Y. 2d 341, 348, 244 N. E. 2d 250, 255 (1968).

---

[6] It bears noting that Congress in the Copyright Act recognized a public interest warranting specific exemptions in a number of areas not within traditional fair use, see, e.g., 17 U. S. C. § 115 (compulsory license for records); § 105 (no copyright in Government works). No such exemption limits copyright in personal narratives written by public servants after they leave Government service.

[560] Courts and commentators have recognized that copyright, and the right of first publication in particular, serve this countervailing First Amendment value. See Schnapper v. Foley, 215 U. S. App. D. C. 59, 667 F.2d 102 (1981), cert. denied, 455 U.S. 948 (1982); 1 Nimmer § 1.10[B], at 1-70, n. 24; Patry 140-142.

[10A] In view of the First Amendment protections already embodied in the Copyright Act's distinction between copyrightable expression and uncopyrightable facts and ideas, and the latitude for scholarship and comment traditionally afforded by fair use, we see no warrant for expanding the doctrine of fair use to create what amounts to a public figure exception to copyright. Whether verbatim copying from a public figure's manuscript in a given case is or is not fair must be judged according to the traditional equities of fair use.

IV. [11] [12] Fair use is a mixed question of law and fact. Pacific & Southern Co. v. Duncan, 744 F.2d 1490, 1495, n. 8 (CA11 1984). Where the district court has found facts sufficient to evaluate each of the statutory factors, an appellate court "need not remand for further factfinding . . . [but] may conclude as a matter of law that [the challenged use] [does] not qualify as a fair use of the copyrighted work." Id., at 1495. Thus whether The Nation article constitutes fair use under § 107 must be reviewed in light of the principles discussed above. The factors enumerated in the section are not meant to be exclusive: "[Since] the doctrine is an equitable rule of reason, no generally applicable definition is possible, and each case raising the question must be decided on its own facts." House Report, at 65. The four factors identified by Congress as especially relevant in determining whether the use was fair are: (1) the purpose and character of the use; (2) the nature of the copyrighted work; (3) the substantiality of the portion used in relation to the copyrighted work as [561] a whole; (4) the effect on the potential market for or value of the copyrighted work. We address each one separately.

[13] [14] Purpose of the Use. The Second Circuit correctly identified news reporting as the general purpose of The Nation's use. News reporting is one of the examples enumerated in § 107 to "give some idea of the sort of activities the courts might regard as fair use under the circumstances." Senate Report, at 61. This listing was not intended to be exhaustive, see ibid.; § 101 (definition of "including" and "such as"), or to single out any particular use as presumptively a "fair" use. The drafters resisted pressures from special interest groups to create presumptive

categories of fair use, but structured the provision as an affirmative defense requiring a case-by-case analysis. See H. R. Rep. No. 83, 90th Cong., 1st Sess., 37 (1967); Patry 477, n. 4. "[Whether] a use referred to in the first sentence of section 107 is a fair use in a particular case will depend upon the application of the determinative factors, including those mentioned in the second sentence." Senate Report, at 62. The fact that an article arguably is "news" and therefore a productive use is simply one factor in a fair use analysis.

We agree with the Second Circuit that the trial court erred in fixing on whether the information contained in the memoirs was actually new to the public. As Judge Meskill wisely noted, "[courts] should be chary of deciding what is and what is not news." 723 F.2d, at 215 (dissenting). Cf. Gertz v. Robert Welch, Inc., 418 U.S. 323, 345-346 (1974). "The issue is not what constitutes 'news,' but whether a claim of newsreporting is a valid fair use defense to an infringement of copyrightable expression." Patry 119. The Nation has every right to seek to be the first to publish information. But The Nation went beyond simply reporting uncopyrightable information and actively sought to exploit the headline value of its infringement, making a "news event" out of its unauthorized first publication of a noted figure's copyrighted expression.

[562][15] The fact that a publication was commercial as opposed to nonprofit is a separate factor that tends to weigh against a finding of fair use." [Every] commercial use of copyrighted material is presumptively an unfair exploitation of the monopoly privilege that belongs to the owner of the copyright." Sony Corp. of America v. Universal City Studios, Inc., 464 U.S., at 451. In arguing that the purpose of news reporting is not purely commercial, The Nation misses the point entirely. The crux of the profit/nonprofit distinction is not whether the sole motive of the use is monetary gain but whether the user stands to profit from exploitation of the copyrighted material without paying the customary price. See Roy Export Co. Establishment v. Columbia Broadcasting System, Inc., 503 F.Supp., at 1144; 3 Nimmer § 13.05[A][1], at 13-71, n. 25.3.

[16] [17A] [18] In evaluating character and purpose we cannot ignore The Nation's stated purpose of scooping the forthcoming hardcover and Time abstracts.[7] App. to Pet. for Cert. C-27. The

---

[7] The dissent excuses The Nation's unconsented use of an unpublished manuscript as "standard journalistic practice," taking judicial notice of New York Times articles regarding the memoirs of John Erlichman, John Dean's "Blind

Nation's use had not merely the incidental effect but the intended purpose of supplanting the copyright holder's commercially valuable right of first publication. See Meredith Corp. v. Harper & Row, Publishers, Inc., 378 F.Supp. 686, 690 (SDNY) (purpose of text was to compete with original), aff'd, 500 F.2d 1221 (CA2 1974). Also relevant to the "character" of the use is "the propriety of the defendant's conduct." 3 Nimmer § 13.05[A], at 13-72. "Fair use presupposes 'good faith' and 'fair dealing.'" Time Inc. v. Bernard Geis Associates, 293 F.Supp. 130, 146 (SDNY 1968), quoting [563] Schulman, Fair Use and the Revision of the Copyright Act, 53 Iowa L. Rev. 832 (1968). The trial court found that The Nation knowingly exploited a purloined manuscript. App. to Pet. for Cert. B-1, C-20 – C-21, C-28 – C-29. Unlike the typical claim of fair use, The Nation cannot offer up even the fiction of consent as justification. Like its competitor newsweekly, it was free to bid for the right of abstracting excerpts from "A Time to Heal." Fair use "distinguishes between 'a true scholar and a chiseler who infringes a work for personal profit.'" Wainwright Securities Inc. v. Wall Street Transcript Corp., 558 F.2d, at 94, quoting from Hearings on Bills for the General Revision of the Copyright Law before the House Committee on the Judiciary, 89th Cong., 1st Sess., ser. 8, pt. 3, p. 1706 (1966) (statement of John Schulman).

[17B][19] Nature of the Copyrighted Work. Second, the Act directs attention to the nature of the copyrighted work. "A Time to Heal" may be characterized as an unpublished historical narrative or autobiography. The law generally recognizes a greater need to disseminate factual works than works of fiction or fantasy. See Gorman, Fact or Fancy? The Implications for Copyright, 29 J. Copyright Soc. 560, 561 (1982).

"[Even] within the field of fact works, there are gradations as to the relative proportion of fact and fancy. One may move from sparsely embellished maps and directories to elegantly written biography. The extent to which one must permit expressive language to be copied, in order to assure dissemination of the underlying facts, will thus vary from case to case." Id., at 563.

Some of the briefer quotes from the memoirs are arguably necessary adequately to convey the facts; for example, Mr. Ford's characterization of the

White House tapes as the "smoking gun" is perhaps so integral to the idea expressed as to be inseparable from it. Cf. 1 Nimmer § 1.10[C]. But The Nation did not stop at isolated phrases and instead excerpted subjective descriptions and portraits of public figures whose power lies in the author's individualized expression. Such [564] use, focusing on the most expressive elements of the work, exceeds that necessary to disseminate the facts.

[6D] The fact that a work is unpublished is a critical element of its "nature." 3 Nimmer § 13.05[A]; Comment, 58 St. John's L. Rev., at 613. Our prior discussion establishes that the scope of fair use is narrower with respect to unpublished works. While even substantial quotations might qualify as fair use in a review of a published work or a news account of a speech that had been delivered to the public or disseminated to the press, see House Report, at 65, the author's right to control the first public appearance of his expression weighs against such use of the work before its release. The right of first publication encompasses not only the choice whether to publish at all, but also the choices of when, where, and in what form first to publish a work.

In the case of Mr. Ford's manuscript, the copyright holders' interest in confidentiality is irrefutable; the copyright holders had entered into a contractual undertaking to "keep the manuscript confidential" and required that all those to whom the manuscript was shown also "sign an agreement to keep the manuscript confidential." App. to Pet. for Cert. C-19 – C-20. While the copyright holders' contract with Time required Time to submit its proposed article seven days before publication, The Nation's clandestine publication afforded no such opportunity for creative or quality control. Id., at C-18. It was hastily patched together and contained "a number of inaccuracies." App. 300b-300c (testimony of Victor Navasky). A use that so clearly infringes the copyright holder's interests in confidentiality and creative control is difficult to characterize as "fair."

Amount and Substantiality of the Portion Used. Next, the Act directs us to examine the amount and substantiality of the portion used in relation to the copyrighted work as a whole. In absolute terms, the words actually quoted were an insubstantial portion of "A Time to Heal." The District Court, however, found that "[The] Nation took what was [565] essentially the heart of the book." 557 F.Supp., at 1072. We believe the Court of Appeals erred in overruling the District Judge's evaluation of the qualitative nature of the taking. See, e.g., Roy Export Co. Establishment v. Columbia Broadcasting System, Inc., 503 F.Supp., at 1145 (taking of 55 seconds out of 1 hour and 29-minute film

---

Ambition," and Bernstein and Woodward's "The Final Days" as proof of such practice. Post, at 590-593, and n. 14. Amici curiae sought to bring this alleged practice to the attention of the Court of Appeals for the Second Circuit, citing these same articles. The Court of Appeals, at Harper & Row's motion, struck these exhibits for failure of proof at trial, Record Doc. No. 19; thus they are not a proper subject for this Court's judicial notice.

deemed qualitatively substantial). A Time editor described the chapters on the pardon as "the most interesting and moving parts of the entire manuscript." Reply Brief for Petitioners 16, n. 8. The portions actually quoted were selected by Mr. Navasky as among the most powerful passages in those chapters. He testified that he used verbatim excerpts because simply reciting the information could not adequately convey the "absolute certainty with which [Ford] expressed himself," App. 303; or show that "this comes from President Ford," id., at 305; or carry the "definitive quality" of the original, id., at 306. In short, he quoted these passages precisely because they qualitatively embodied Ford's distinctive expression. [20] As the statutory language indicates, a taking may not be excused merely because it is insubstantial with respect to the infringing work. As Judge Learned Hand cogently remarked, "no plagiarist can excuse the wrong by showing how much of his work he did not pirate." Sheldon v. Metro-Goldwyn Pictures Corp., 81 F.2d 49, 56 (CA2), cert. denied, 298 U.S. 669 (1936). Conversely, the fact that a substantial portion of the infringing work was copied verbatim is evidence of the qualitative value of the copied material, both to the originator and to the plagiarist who seeks to profit from marketing someone else's copyrighted expression.

Stripped to the verbatim quotes,[8] the direct takings from the unpublished manuscript constitute at least 13% of the infringing [566] article. See Meeropol v. Nizer, 560 F.2d 1061, 1071 (CA2 1977) (copyrighted letters constituted less than 1% of infringing work but were prominently featured). The Nation article is structured around the quoted excerpts which serve as its dramatic focal points. See Appendix to this opinion, post, p. 570. In view of the expressive value of the excerpts and their key role in the infringing work, we cannot agree with the Second Circuit that the "magazine took a meager, indeed an infinitesimal amount of Ford's original language." 723 F.2d, at 209.

[21] [22] [23] Effect on the Market. Finally, the Act focuses on "the effect of the use upon the potential market for or value of the copyrighted work." This last factor is undoubtedly the single most important element of fair use.[9] See 3 Nimmer § 13.05[A], at 13-76, and cases cited therein. "Fair use, when properly applied, is limited to copying by others which [567] does not materially impair the marketability of the work which is copied." 1 Nimmer § 1.10[D], at 1-87. The trial court found not merely a potential but an actual effect on the market. Time's cancellation of its projected serialization and its refusal to pay the $12,500 were the direct effect of the infringement. The Court of Appeals rejected this fact-finding as clearly erroneous, noting that the record did not establish a causal relation between Time's non-performance and respondents' unauthorized publication of Mr. Ford's expression as opposed to the facts taken from the memoirs. We disagree. Rarely will a case of copyright infringement present such clear-cut evidence of actual damage. Petitioners assured Time that there would be no other authorized publication of any portion of the unpublished manuscript prior to April 23, 1979. Any publication of material from chapters 1 and 3 would permit Time to renegotiate its final payment. Time cited The Nation's article, which contained verbatim quotes from the unpublished manuscript, as a reason for its nonperformance.

With respect to apportionment of profits flowing from a copyright infringement, this Court has held that an infringer who commingles infringing and noninfringing elements "must abide the cones-quences, unless he can make a separation of the profits so as to assure to the injured party all that justly belongs to him." Sheldon v. Metro-Goldwyn Pictures Corp., 309 U.S. 390, 406 (1940). Cf. 17 U. S. C. § 504(b) (the infringer is required to prove

---

[8] See Appendix to this opinion, post, p. 570. The Court of Appeals found that only "approximately 300 words" were copyrightable but did not specify which words. The court's discussion, however, indicates it excluded from consideration those portions of The Nation's piece that, although copied verbatim from Ford's manuscript, were quotes attributed by Ford to third persons and quotations from Government documents. At oral argument, counsel for The Nation did not dispute that verbatim quotes and very close paraphrase could constitute infringement. Tr. of Oral Arg. 24-25. Thus the Appendix identifies as potentially infringing only verbatim quotes or very close paraphrase and excludes from consideration Government documents and words attributed to third persons. The Appendix is not intended to endorse any particular rule of copyrightability but is intended merely as an aid to facilitate our discussion.

[9] Economists who have addressed the issue believe the fair use exception should come into play only in those situations in which the market fails or the price the copyright holder would ask is near zero. See, e.g., T. Brennan, Harper & Row v. The Nation, Copyrightability and Fair Use, Dept. of Justice Economic Policy Office Discussion Paper 13-17 (1984); Gordon, Fair Use as Market Failure: A Structural and Economic Analysis of the Betamax Case and its Predecessors, 82 Colum. L. Rev. 1600, 1615 (1982). As the facts here demonstrate, there is a fully functioning market that encourages the creation and dissemination of memoirs of public figures. In the economists' view, permitting "fair use" to displace normal copyright channels disrupts the copyright market without a commensurate public benefit.

elements of profits attributable to other than the infringed work). Similarly, once a copyright holder establishes with reasonable probability the existence of a causal connection between the infringement and a loss of revenue, the burden properly shifts to the infringer to show that this damage would have occurred had there been no taking of copyrighted expression. See 3 Nimmer § 14.02, at 14-7 – 14-8.1. Petitioners established a prima facie case of actual damage that respondents failed to rebut. See Stevens Linen Associates, [568] Inc. v. Mastercraft Corp., 656 F.2d 11, 15 (CA2 1981). The trial court properly awarded actual damages and accounting of profits. See 17 U. S. C. § 504(b).

[24] More important, to negate fair use one need only show that if the challenged use "should become widespread, it would adversely affect the potential market for the copyrighted work." Sony Corp. of America v. Universal City Studios, Inc., 464 U.S., at 451 (emphasis added); id., at 484, and n. 36 (collecting cases) (dissenting opinion). This inquiry must take account not only of harm to the original but also of harm to the market for derivative works. See Iowa State University Research Foundation, Inc. v. American Broadcasting Cos., 621 F.2d 57 (CA2 1980); Meeropol v. Nizer, supra, at 1070; Roy Export v. Columbia Broadcasting System, Inc., 503 F.Supp., at 1146. "If the defendant's work adversely affects the value of any of the rights in the copyrighted work (in this case the adaptation [and serialization] right) the use is not fair." 3 Nimmer § 13.05[B], at 13-77 – 13-78 (footnote omitted).

It is undisputed that the factual material in the balance of The Nation's article, besides the verbatim quotes at issue here, was drawn exclusively from the chapters on the pardon. The excerpts were employed as featured episodes in a story about the Nixon pardon – precisely the use petitioners had licensed to Time. The borrowing of these verbatim quotes from the unpublished manuscript lent The Nation's piece a special air of authenticity – as Navasky expressed it, the reader would know it was Ford speaking and not The Nation. App. 300c. Thus it directly competed for a share of the market for prepublication excerpts. The Senate Report states:

"With certain special exceptions . . . a use that supplants any part of the normal market for a copyrighted work would ordinarily be considered an infringement." Senate Report, at 65.

[569] Placed in a broader perspective, a fair use doctrine that permits extensive prepublication quotations from an unreleased manuscript without the copyright owner's consent poses substantial potential for damage to the marketability of first serialization rights in general. "Isolated instances of minor infringements, when multiplied many times, become in the aggregate a major inroad on copyright that must be prevented." Ibid.

V. [1C] [9B] [10B] The Court of Appeals erred in concluding that The Nation's use of the copyrighted material was excused by the public's interest in the subject matter. It erred, as well, in overlooking the unpublished nature of the work and the resulting impact on the potential market for first serial rights of permitting unauthorized prepublication excerpts under the rubric of fair use. Finally, in finding the taking "infinitesimal," the Court of Appeals accorded too little weight to the qualitative importance of the quoted passages of original expression. In sum, the traditional doctrine of fair use, as embodied in the Copyright Act, does not sanction the use made by The Nation of these copyrighted materials. Any copyright infringer may claim to benefit the public by increasing public access to the copyrighted work. See Pacific & Southern Co. v. Duncan, 744 F.2d, at 1499-1500. But Congress has not designed, and we see no warrant for judicially imposing, a "compulsory license" permitting unfettered access to the unpublished copyrighted expression of public figures.

The Nation conceded that its verbatim copying of some 300 words of direct quotation from the Ford manuscript would constitute an infringement unless excused as a fair use. Because we find that The Nation's use of these verbatim excerpts from the unpublished manuscript was not a fair use, the judgment of the Court of Appeals is reversed, and the case is remanded for further proceedings consistent with this opinion.

It is so ordered.

[570] APPENDIX TO OPINION OF THE COURT

The portions of The Nation article which were copied verbatim from "A Time to Heal," excepting quotes from Government documents and quotes attributed by Ford to third persons, are identified in boldface in the text. See ante, at 562, n. 7. The corresponding passages in the Ford manuscript are footnoted.

THE FORD MEMOIRS
BEHIND THE NIXON PARDON

In his memoirs, A Time To Heal, which Harper & Row will publish in late May or early June, former President Gerald R. Ford says that the idea of giving a blanket pardon to Richard M. Nixon was raised before Nixon resigned from the Presidency by Gen. Alexander Haig, who was then the White House chief of staff.

Ford also writes that, but for a mis-understanding, he might have selected Ronald

Reagan as his 1976 running mate, that Washington lawyer Edward Bennett Williams, a Democrat, was his choice for head of the Central Intelligence Agency, that Nixon was the one who first proposed Rockefeller for Vice President, and that he regretted his "cowardice"[1] in allowing Rockefeller to remove himself from Vice Presidential contention. Ford also describes his often prickly relations with Henry Kissinger.

The Nation obtained the 655-page typescript before publication. Advance excerpts from the book will appear in Time in mid-April and in The Reader's Digest thereafter. Although the initial print order has not been decided, the figure is tentatively set at 50,000; it could change, depending upon the public reaction to the serialization.

Ford's account of the Nixon pardon contains significant new detail on the negotiations and considerations that surround [571] it. According to Ford's version, the subject was first broached to him by General Haig on August 1, 1974, a week before Nixon resigned. General Haig revealed that the newly transcribed White House tapes were the equivalent of the "smoking gun"[2] and that Ford should prepare himself to become President.

Ford was deeply hurt by Haig's revelation: "Over the past several months Nixon had repeatedly assured me that he was not involved in Watergate, that the evidence would prove his innocence, that the matter would fade from view."[3] Ford had believed him, but he let Haig explain the President's alternatives.

He could "ride it out"[4] or he could resign, Haig said. He then listed the different ways Nixon might resign and concluded by pointing out that Nixon could agree to leave in return for an agreement that the new President, Ford, would pardon him.[5] Although Ford said it would be improper for him to make any recommendation, he basically agreed with Haig's assessment and adds, "Because of his references to the pardon authority, I did ask Haig about the extent of a President's pardon power."[6]

"It's my understanding from a White House lawyer," Haig replied, "that a President does have authority to grant a pardon even before criminal action has been taken against an individual."

[572] But because Ford had neglected to tell Haig he thought the idea of a resignation conditioned on a pardon was improper, his press aide, Bob Hartmann, suggested that Haig might well have returned to the White House and told President Nixon that he had mentioned the idea and Ford seemed comfortable with it. "Silence implies assent."

Ford then consulted with White House special counsel James St. Clair, who had no advice one way or the other on the matter more than pointing out that he was not the lawyer who had given Haig the opinion on the pardon. Ford also discussed the matter with Jack Marsh, who felt that the mention of a pardon in this context was a "time bomb," and with Bryce Harlow, who had served six Presidents and who agreed that the mere mention of a pardon "could cause a lot of trouble."[7]

As a result of these various conversations, Vice President Ford called Haig and read him a written statement: "I want you to understand that I have no intention of recommending what the President should do about resigning or not resigning and that nothing we talked about yesterday afternoon should be given any consideration in whatever decision the President may wish to make."

Despite what Haig had told him about the "smoking gun" tapes, Ford told a Jackson, Mich., luncheon audience later in the day that the President was not guilty of an impeachable offense. "Had I said otherwise at that moment," he writes, "the whole house of cards might have collapsed."[8]

In justifying the pardon, Ford goes out of his way to assure the reader that "compassion for

---

[1] I was angry at myself for showing cowardice in not saying to the ultra-conservatives, "It's going to be Ford and Rockefeller, whatever the consequences." p. 496.

[2] [It] contained the so-called smoking gun. p. 3.

[3] [Over] the past several months Nixon had repeatedly assured me that he was not involved in Watergate, that the evidence would prove his inno-cence that the matter would fade from view. p. 7.

[4] The first [option] was that he could try to "ride it out" by letting impeachment take its natural course through the House and the Senate trial, fighting against conviction all the way. p. 4.

[5] Finally, Haig said that according to some on Nixon's White House staff, Nixon could agree to leave in return for an agreement that the new President – Gerald Ford – would pardon him. p. 5.

[6] Because of his references to pardon authority, I did ask Haig about the extent of a President's pardon power. pp. 5-6.

[7] Only after I had finished did [Bryce Harlow] let me know in no uncertain terms that he agreed with Bob and Jack, that the mere mention of the pardon option could cause a lot of trouble in the days ahead. p. 18.

[8] During the luncheon I repeated my assertion that the President was not guilty of an impeachable offense. Had I said otherwise at that moment, the whole house of cards might have collapsed. p. 21.

Nixon as an individual [573] hadn't prompted my decision at all."[9] Rather, he did it because he had "to get the monkey off my back one way or the other."[10]

The precipitating factor in his decision was a series of secret meetings his general counsel, Phil Buchen, held with Watergate Special Prosecutor Leon Jaworski in the Jefferson Hotel, where they were both staying at the time. Ford attributes Jaworski with providing some "crucial" information[11] – i.e., that Nixon was under investigation in ten separate areas, and that the court process could "take years."[12] Ford cites a memorandum from Jaworski's assistant, Henry S. Ruth Jr., as being especially persuasive. Ruth had written:

"If you decide to recommend indictment I think it is fair and proper to notify Jack Miller and the White House sufficiently in advance so that pardon action could be taken before the indictment." He went on to say: "One can make a strong argument for leniency and if President Ford is so inclined, I think he ought to do it early rather than late."

Ford decided that court proceedings against Nixon might take six years, that Nixon "would not spend time quietly in San Clemente,"[13] and "it would be virtually impossible for me to direct public attention on anything else."[14]

Buchen, Haig and Henry Kissinger agreed with him. Hartmann was not so sure.

[574] Buchen wanted to condition the pardon on Nixon agreeing to settle the question of who would retain custody and control over the tapes and Presidential papers that might be relevant to various Watergate proceedings, but Ford was reluctant to do that.

At one point a plan was considered whereby the Presidential materials would be kept in a vault at a Federal facility near San Clemente, but the vault would require two keys to open it. One would be retained by the General Services Administration, the other by Richard Nixon.

The White House did, however, want Nixon to make a full confession on the occasion of his pardon or, at a minimum, express true contrition. Ford tells of the negotiation with Jack Miller, Nixon's lawyer, over the wording of Nixon's statement. But as Ford reports Miller's response. Nixon was not likely to yield. "His few meetings with his client had shown him that the former President's ability to discuss Watergate objectively was almost nonexistent."[15]

The statement they really wanted was never forthcoming. As soon as Ford's emissary arrived in San Clemente, he was confronted with an ultimatum by Ron Zeigler, Nixon's former press secretary. "Lets get one thing straight immediately," Zeigler said. "President Nixon is not issuing any statement whatsoever regarding Watergate, whether Jerry Ford pardons him or not." Zeigler proposed a draft, which was turned down on the ground that "no statement would be better than that."[16] They went through three more drafts before they agreed on the statement Nixon finally made, which stopped far short of a full confession.

When Ford aide Benton Becker tried to explain to Nixon that acceptance of a pardon was an admission of guilt, he [575] felt the President wasn't really listening. Instead, Nixon wanted to talk about the Washington Redskins. And when Becker left, Nixon pressed on him some cuff links and a tiepin "out of my own jewelry box."

Ultimately, Ford sums up the philosophy underlying his decision as one he picked up as a student at Yale Law School many years before. "I learned that public policy often took precedence over a rule of law. Although I respected the tenet that no man should be above the law, public policy demanded that I put Nixon – and Watergate – behind us as quickly as possible."[17]

Later, when Ford learned that Nixon's phlebitis had acted up and his health was seriously impaired, he debated whether to pay the ailing former President a visit. "If I made the trip it would remind everybody of Watergate and the pardon. If I didn't,

---

[9] But compassion for Nixon as an individual hadn't prompted my decision at all. p. 266.

[10] I had to get the monkey off my back one way or another. p. 236.

[11] Jaworski gave Phil several crucial pieces of information. p. 246.

[12] And if the verdict was Guilty, one had to assume that Nixon would appeal. That process would take years. p. 248.

[13] The entire process would no doubt require years: a minimum of two, a maximum of six. And Nixon would not spend time quietly in San Clemente. p. 238.

[14] It would be virtually impossible for me to direct public attention on anything else. p. 239.

---

[15] But [Miller] wasn't optimistic about getting such a statement. His few meetings with his client had shown him that the former President's ability to discuss Watergate objectively was almost nonexistent. p. 246.

[16] When Zeigler asked Becker what he thought of it, Becker replied that no statement would be better than that. p. 251.

[17] Years before, at Yale Law School, I'd learned that public policy often took precedence over a rule of law. Although I respected the tenet that no man should be above the law, public policy demanded that I put Nixon – and Watergate – behind us as quickly as possible. p. 256.

people would say I lacked compassion."[18] Ford went:

He was stretched out flat on his back. There were tubes in his nose and mouth, and wires led from his arms, chest and legs to machines with orange lights that blinked on and off. His face was ashen, and I thought I had never seen anyone closer to death.[19]

The manuscript made available to The Nation includes many references to Henry Kissinger and other personalities who played a major role during the Ford years.

[576] On Kissinger. Immediately after being informed by Nixon of his intention to resign, Ford returned to the Executive Office Building and phoned Henry Kissinger to let him know how he felt. "Henry," he said, "I need you. The country needs you. I want you to stay. I'll do everything I can to work with you."[20]

"Sir," Kissinger replied, "it is my job to get along with you and not yours to get along with me."

"We'll get along," Ford said. "I know we'll get along." Referring to Kissinger's joint jobs as Secretary of State and National Security Adviser to the President, Ford said, "I don't want to make any change. I think it's worked out well, so let's keep it that way."[21]

Later Ford did make the change and relieved Kissinger of his responsibilities as National Security Adviser at the same time that he fired James Schlesinger as Secretary of Defense. Shortly thereafter, he reports, Kissinger presented him with a "draft" letter of resignation, which he said Ford could call upon at will if he felt he needed it to quiet dissent from conservatives who objected to Kissinger's role in the firing of Schlesinger.

On John Connally. When Ford was informed that Nixon wanted him to replace Agnew, he told the President he had "no ambition to hold office after January 1977."[22] Nixon replied that that was good since his own choice for his running mate in 1976 was John Connally. "He'd be excellent," observed Nixon. Ford says he had "no problem with that."

[577] On the Decision to Run Again. Ford was, he tells us, so sincere in his intention not to run again that he thought he would announce it and enhance his credibility in the country and the Congress, as well as keep the promise he had made to his wife, Betty.

Kissinger talked him out of it. "You can't do that. It would be disastrous from a foreign policy point of view. For the next two and a half years foreign governments would know that they were dealing with a lame-duck President. All our initiatives would be dead in the water, and I wouldn't be able to implement your foreign policy. It would probably have the same consequences in dealing with the Congress on domestic issues. You can't reassert the authority of the Presidency if you leave yourself hanging out on a dead limb. You've got to be an affirmative President."

On David Kennerly, the White House photographer. Schlesinger was arguing with Kissinger and Ford over the appropriate response to the seizure of the Mayaguez. At issue was whether airstrikes against the Cambodians were desirable; Schlesinger was opposed to bombings. Following a lull in the conversation, Ford reports, up spoke the 30-year-old White House photographer, David Kennerly, who had been taking pictures for the last hour.

"Has anyone considered," Kennerly asked, "that this might be the act of a local Cambodian commander who has just taken it into his own hands to stop any ship that comes by?" Nobody, apparently, had considered it, but following several seconds of silence, Ford tells us, the view carried the day. "Massive airstrikes would constitute overkill," Ford decided. "It would be far better to have Navy jets from the Coral Sea make surgical strikes against specific targets."[23]

[578] On Nixon's Character. Nixon's flaw, according to Ford, was "pride." "A terribly proud

---

[18] My staff debated whether or not I ought to visit Nixon at the Long Beach Hospital, only half an hour away. If I made the trip, it would remind eveyrone of Watergate and the pardon. If I didn't, people would say I lacked compassion. I ended their debate as soon as I found out it had begun. Of course I would go. p. 298.

[19] He was stretched out flat on his back. There were tubes in his nose and mouth, and wires led from his arms, chest and legs to machines with orange lights that blinked on and off. His face was ashen, and I thought I had never seen anyone closer to death. p. 299.

[20] "Henry," I said when he came on the line, "I need you. The country needs you. I want you to stay. I'll do everything I can to work with you." p. 46.

[21] "We'll get along," I said. "I know we can get along." We talked about the two hats he wore, as Secretary of State and National Security Adviser to the President. "I don't want to make any change," I said. "I think it's worked out well, so let's keep it that way." p. 46.

[22] I told him about my promise to Betty and said that I had no ambitions to hold office after January 1977. p. 155.

[23] Subjectively, I felt that what Kennerly had said made a lot of sense. Massive airstrikes would constitute overkill. It would be far better to have Navy jets from the Coral Sea make surgical strikes against specific targets in the vicinity of Kompong Som. p. 416.

16.24

man," writes Ford, "he detested weakness in other people. I'd often heard him speak disparagingly of those whom he felt to be soft and expedient. (Curiously, he didn't feel that the press was weak. Reporters, he sensed, were his adversaries. He knew they didn't like him, and he responded with reciprocal disdain.)"[24]

Nixon felt disdain for the Democratic leadership of the House, whom he also regarded as weak. According to Ford, "His pride and personal contempt for weakness had overcome his ability to tell the difference between right and wrong," [25] all of which leads Ford to wonder whether Nixon had known in advance about Watergate.

On hearing Nixon's resignation speech, which Ford felt lacked an adequate plea for forgiveness, he was persuaded that "Nixon was out of touch with reality." [26]

In February of last year, when The Washington Post obtained and printed advance excerpts from H. R. Haldeman's memoir, The Ends of Power, on the eve of its publication by Times Books, The New York Times called The Post's feat "a second-rate burglary."

The Post disagreed, claiming that its coup represented "first-rate enterprise" and arguing that it had burglarized nothing, that publication of the Haldeman memoir came under the Fair Comment doctrine long recognized by the [579] courts, and that "There is a fundamental journalistic principle here – a First Amendment principle that was central to the Pentagon Papers case."

In the issue of The Nation dated May 5, 1979, our special Spring Books number, we will discuss some of the ethical problems raised by the issue of disclosure.

DISSENT: JUSTICE BRENNAN, with whom JUSTICE WHITE and JUSTICE MARSHALL join, dissenting.

The Court holds that The Nation's quotation of 300 words from the unpublished 200,000-word manuscript of President Gerald R. Ford infringed the copyright in that manuscript, even though the quotations related to a historical event of undoubted significance – the resignation and pardon of President Richard M. Nixon. Although the Court pursues the laudable goal of protecting "the economic incentive to create and disseminate ideas," ante, at 558, this zealous defense of the copyright owner's prerogative will, I fear, stifle the broad dissemination of ideas and information copyright is intended to nurture. Protection of the copyright owner's economic interest is achieved in this case through an exceedingly narrow definition of the scope of fair use. The progress of arts and sciences and the robust public debate essential to an enlightened citizenry are ill served by

this constricted reading of the fair use doctrine. See 17 U. S. C. § 107. I therefore respectfully dissent.

I. A This case presents two issues. First, did The Nation's use of material from the Ford manuscript in forms other than direct quotation from that manuscript infringe Harper & Row's copyright. Second, did the quotation of approximately 300 words from the manuscript infringe the copyright because this quotation did not constitute "fair use" within the meaning [580] of § 107 of the Copyright Act. 17 U. S. C. § 107. The Court finds no need to resolve the threshold copyrightability issue. The use of 300 words of quotation was, the Court finds, beyond the scope of fair use and thus a copyright infringement.[1] Because I disagree with the Court's fair use holding, it is necessary for me to decide the threshold copyrightability question.

B "The enactment of copyright legislation by Congress under the terms of the Constitution is not based upon any natural right that the author has in his writings ... but upon the ground that the welfare of the public will be served and progress of science and useful arts will be promoted by securing to authors for limited periods the exclusive rights to their writings." H. R. Rep. No. 2222, 60th Cong., 2d Sess., 7 (1909). Congress thus seeks to define the rights included in copyright so as to serve the public welfare and not necessarily so as to maximize an author's control over his or her product. The challenge of copyright is to strike the "difficult balance between the interests of authors and inventors in the control and exploitation of their writings and discoveries on the one hand, and society's competing interest in the free flow of ideas, information, and commerce on the other hand." Sony Corp. of America v. Universal City Studios, Inc., 464 U.S. 417, 429 (1984).

The "originality" requirement now embodied in §102 of the Copyright Act is crucial to

---

[24] In Nixon's case, that flaw was pride. A terribly proud man, he detested weakness in other people. I'd often heard him speak disparagingly of those whom he felt to be soft and expedient. (Curiously, he didn't feel that the press was weak. Reporters, he sensed, were his adversaries. He knew they didn't like him, and he responded with reciprocal disdain.) p. 53.

[25] His pride and personal contempt for weakness had overcome his ability to tell the difference between right and wrong. p. 54.

[26] The speech lasted fifteen minutes, and at the end I was convinced Nixon was out of touch with reality. p. 57.

[1] In bypassing the threshold issue, the Court certainly does not intimate that The Nation's use of ideas and information other than the quoted material would constitute a violation of the copyright laws. At one point in its opinion the Court correctly states the governing principles with respect to the copy-rightability question. See ante, at 556 ("No author may copyright his ideas or the facts he narrates").

16.25

maintenance of the appropriate balance between these competing interests.[2] Properly interpreted [581] in the light of the legislative history, this section extends copyright protection to an author's literary form but permits free use by others of the ideas and information the author communicates. See S. Rep. No. 93-983, pp. 107-108 (1974) ("Copyright does not preclude others from using the ideas or information revealed by the author's work. It pertains to the literary ... form in which the author expressed intellectual concepts"); H. R. Rep. No. 94-1476, pp. 56-57 (1976) (same); New York Times Co. v. United States, 403 U.S. 713, 726, n. (1971) (BRENNAN, J., concurring) ("[The] copyright laws, of course, protect only the form of expression and not the ideas expressed"). This limitation of protection to literary form precludes any claim of copyright in facts, including historical narration.

"It is not to be supposed that the framers of the Constitution, when they empowered Congress 'to promote the progress of science and useful arts, by securing for limited times to authors and inventors the exclusive right to their respective writings and discoveries' (Const., Art I, § 8, par. 8), intended to confer upon one who might happen to be the first to report a historic event the exclusive right for any period to spread the knowledge of it." International News Service v. Associated Press, 248 U.S. 215, 234 (1918).

Accord, Rosemont Enterprises, Inc. v. Random House, Inc., 366 F.2d 303, 309 (CA2 1966), cert. denied, 385 U.S. 1009 (1967). See 1 Nimmer § 2.11[A], at 2-158.[3]

[582] The "promotion of science and the useful arts" requires this limit on the scope of an author's control. Were an author able to prevent subsequent authors from using concepts, ideas, or facts contained in his or her work, the creative process would wither and scholars would be forced into unproductive replication of the research of their predecessors. See Hoehling v. Universal City Studios, Inc., 618 F.2d 972, 979 (CA2 1980). This limitation on copyright also ensures consonance with our most important First Amendment values. Cf. Zacchini v. Scripps-Howard Broadcasting Co., 433 U.S. 562, 577, n. 13 (1977). Our "profound national commitment to the principle that debate on public issues should be uninhibited, robust, and wide-open," New York Times Co. v. Sullivan, 376 U.S. 254, 270 (1964), leaves no room for a statutory monopoly over information and ideas. "The arena of public debate would be quiet, indeed, if a politician could copyright his speeches or a philosopher his treatises and thus obtain a monopoly on the ideas they contained." Lee v. Runge, 404 U.S. 887, 893 (1971) (Douglas, J., dissenting from denial of certiorari). A broad dissemination of principles, ideas, and factual information is crucial to the robust public debate and informed citizenry that are "the essence of self-government." Garrison v. Louisiana, 379 U.S. 64, 74-75 (1964). And every citizen must be permitted freely to marshal ideas and facts in the advocacy of particular political choices.[4]

It follows that infringement of copyright must be based on a taking of literary form, as opposed to the ideas or information contained in a copyrighted work. Deciding whether an infringing appropriation of literary form has occurred is difficult for at least two reasons. First, the distinction between [583] literary form and information or ideas is often elusive in practice. Second, infringement must be based on a substantial appropriation of literary form. This determination is equally challenging. Not surprisingly, the test for infringement has defied precise formulation.[5] In

---

[2] Section 102(b) states: "In no case does copyright protection for an original work of authorship extend to any idea, procedure, process, system, method of operation, concept, principle, or discovery, regardless of the form in which it is described, explained, illustrated, or embodied in such work." 17 U. S. C. § 102(b). The doctrines of fair use, see 17 U. S. C. § 107, and substantial similarity, see 3 M. Nimmer, Copyright § 13.05 (1984) (hereinafter Nimmer), also function to accommodate these competing considerations. See generally Gorman, Fact or Fancy? The Implications for Copyright, 29 J. Copyright Soc. 560 (1982).

[3] By the same token, an author may not claim copyright in statements made by others and reported verbatim in the author's work. See Suid v. Newsweek Magazine, 503 F.Supp. 146, 148 (DC 1980); Rokeach v. Avco Embassy Pictures Corp., 197 USPQ 155, 161 (SDNY 1978).

[4] It would be perverse to prohibit government from limiting the financial resources upon which a political speaker may draw, see FEC v. National Conservative Political Action Committee, 470 U.S. 480 (1985), but to permit government to limit the intellectual resources upon which that speaker may draw.

[5] The protection of literary form must proscribe more than merely word-for-word appropriation of substantial portions of an author's work. Otherwise a plagiarist could avoid infringement by immaterial variations. Nichols v. Universal Pictures Corp., 45 F.2d 119, 121 (CA2 1930). The step beyond the narrow and clear prohibition of wholesale copying is, however, a venture onto somewhat uncertain terrain. Compare Hoehling v. Universal City Studios, Inc., 618 F.2d 972, 974 (CA2 1980), with Wainwright Securities Inc. v. Wall Street Transcript Corp., 558 F.2d 91 (CA2 1977). See also 1 Nimmer § 1.10B, at 1-73 – 1-74 ("It is the particular selection and arrangement of ideas, as well as a given specificity in the form of their expression, which warrants protection"); Chafee, Reflections on the Law of

general, though, the inquiry proceeds along two axes: how closely has the second author tracked the first author's particular language and structure of presentation; and how much of the first author's language and structure has the second author appropriated.[6]

In the present case the infringement analysis must be applied to a historical biography in which the author has chronicled the events of his White House tenure and commented on those events from his unique perspective. Apart from the quotations, virtually all of the material in The Nation's article indirectly recounted Mr. Ford's factual narrative of the Nixon resignation and pardon, his latter-day reflections on some events of his Presidency, and his perceptions of the personalities at the center of those events. See ante, at 570-579. No copyright can be claimed in this information qua information. Infringement would thus have to be based [584] on too close and substantial a tracking of Mr. Ford's expression of this information.[7]

The Language. Much of the information The Nation conveyed was not in the form of paraphrase at all, but took the form of synopsis of lengthy

---

Copyright: I, 45 Colum. L. Rev. 503, 513 (1945) ("[The] line . . . [lies] somewhere between the author's idea and the precise form in which he wrote it down. . . . [The] protection covers the 'pattern' of the work");
Gorman, supra, at 593 ("too literal and substantial copying and paraphrasing of . . . language").

[6] The inquiry into the substantiality of appropriation has a quantitative and a qualitative aspect.

[7] Neither the District Court nor the dissent in the Court of Appeals approached the question in this way. Despite recognizing that this material was not "per se copyrightable," the District Court held that the "totality of these facts and memoranda collected together with Mr. Ford's reflections . . . is protected by the copyright laws." 557 F.Supp. 1067, 1072-1073 (SDNY 1983). The dissent in the Court of Appeals signaled approval of this approach. 723 F.2d 195, 213-214 (CA2 1983) (Meskill, J., dissenting). Such an approach must be rejected. Copyright protection cannot be extended to factual information whenever that information is interwoven with protected expression (purportedly in this case Mr. Ford's reflections) into an expressive "totality." Most works of history or biography blend factual narrative and reflective or speculative commentary in this way. Precluding subsequent use of facts so presented cannot be squared with the specific legislative intent, expressed in both House and Senate Reports, that "[copyright] does not preclude others from using the . . . information revealed by the author's work." See S. Rep. No. 93-983, pp. 107-108 (1974); H. R. Rep. No. 94-1476, pp. 56-57 (1976). The core purposes of copyright would be thwarted and serious First Amendment concerns would arise. An author could obtain a monopoly on narration of historical events simply by being the first to discuss them in a reflective or analytical manner.

discussions in the Ford manuscript.[8] In the course of this summary presentation, The [585] Nation did use occasional sentences that closely resembled language in the original Ford manuscript.[9] But

---

[8] For example, the Ford manuscript expends several hundred words discussing relations between Mr. Ford and Ronald Reagan in the weeks before the Republican Convention of 1976: "About a month before the convention, my aides had met with Reagan's representatives to discuss the need for party unity. And they had reached an agreement. At the end of the Presidential balloting, the winner would go to the loser's hotel suite and congratulate his opponent for waging a fine campaign. Together, they would appear at a press conference and urge all Republicans to put aside their differences and rally behind the ticket. That was the only way we could leave Kansas City with a hope of victory. When it appeared I was going to win, Sears contacted Cheney and refined the scenario. He insisted on two conditions. The first was that I had to see Reagan alone; there could be no aides from either camp in the room. Secondly, under no circumstances should I offer him the nomination to be Vice President. Reagan had said all along that he wasn't interested in the job. He had meant what he said. If I tried to talk him out of it, he would have to turn me down, and that would be embarrassing because it would appear that he was refusing to help the GOP. When Cheney relayed those conditions to me, I agreed to go along with them. I would need Reagan's assistance in the fall campaign. It would be stupid to anger him or his followers at this moment.
"Later I was told that just before my arrival at the Californian's hotel, one of his closest advisors, businessman Justin Dart, had urged him to say yes if I asked him to be my running mate, Regardless of anything he'd said before, Dart had insisted, it was his patriotic duty to accept the number two post. Finally, according to Dart, Reagan had agreed. But at the time, no one mentioned this new development to me. Had I been aware of the Dart-Reagan conversation, would I have chosen him? I can't say for sure – I thought his challenge had been divisive, and that it would probably hurt the party in the fall campaign; additionally, I resented some of the things that he'd been saying about me and my Administration's policies – but I certainly would have considered him." App. 628-629. The Nation encapsulated this discussion in the following sentence: "Ford also writes that, but for a misunderstanding, he might have selected Ronald Reagan as his 1976 running mate." Id., at 627. In most other instances, a single sentence or brief paragraph in The Nation's article similarly conveys the gist of a discussion in the Ford manuscript that runs into the hundreds of words. See generally Addendum B to Defendant's Post-Trial Memorandum, id., at 627-704.

[9] For example, at one point The Nation's article reads: "Ford told a Jackson, Mich., luncheon audience later in the day that the President was not guilty of an impeachable offense." Ante, at 572. The portion of the Ford manuscript discussed stated: "Representative Thad Cochran . . . escorted me to a luncheon at the Jackson Hilton Hotel. During the luncheon I repeated my assertion that the President was not guilty of an impeachable offense." App. 649. In several other places the language in The Nation's article parallels Mr. Ford's original expression to a similar degree. Compare ante, at 570-579, with App. 627-704.

these linguistic similarities are insufficient to constitute an infringement for three reasons. First, some leeway must be given to subsequent authors seeking to convey facts because those "wishing to express the ideas contained in a factual work [586] often can choose from only a narrow range of expression." Landsberg v. Scrabble Crossword Game Players, Inc., 736 F.2d 485, 488 (CA9 1984). Second, much of what The Nation paraphrased was material in which Harper & Row could claim no copyright.[10] Third, The Nation paraphrased nothing approximating the totality of a single paragraph, much less a chapter or the work as a whole. At most The Nation paraphrased disparate isolated sentences from the original. A finding of infringement based on paraphrase generally requires far more close and substantial a tracking of the original language than occurred in this case. See, e.g., Wainwright Securities Inc. v. Wall Street Transcript Corp., 558 F.2d 91 (CA2 1977).

The Structure of Presentation. The article does not mimic Mr. Ford's structure. The information The Nation presents is drawn from scattered sections of the Ford work and does not appear in the sequence in which Mr. Ford presented it.[11] Some of The Nation's discussion of the pardon does roughly track the order in which the Ford manuscript presents information about the pardon. With respect to this similarity, however, Mr. Ford has done no more than present the facts [587] chronologically and cannot claim infringement when a subsequent author similarly presents the facts of history in a chronological manner. Also, it is difficult to suggest that a 2,000-word article could bodily appropriate the structure of a 200,000-

word book. Most of what Mr. Ford created, and most of the history he recounted, were simply not represented in The Nation's article.[12]

When The Nation was not quoting Mr. Ford, therefore, its efforts to convey the historical information in the Ford manuscript did not so closely and substantially track Mr. Ford's language and structure as to constitute an appropriation of literary form.

II. The Nation is thus liable in copyright only if the quotation of 300 words infringed any of Harper & Row's exclusive rights under § 106 of the Act. Section 106 explicitly makes the grant of exclusive rights "[subject] to section 107 through 118." 17 U. S. C. § 106. Section 107 states: "Notwithstanding the provisions of section 106, the fair use of a copyrighted work . . . for purposes such as criticism, comment, news reporting, teaching (including multiple copies for classroom use), scholarship or research, is not an infringement of copyright." The question here is whether The Nation's [588] quotation was a noninfringing fair use within the meaning of § 107.

Congress "eschewed a rigid, bright-line approach to fair use." Sony Corp. of America v. Universal City Studios, Inc., 464 U.S., at 449, n. 31. A court is to apply an "equitable rule of reason" analysis, id., at 448, guided by four statutorily prescribed factors:

"(1) the purpose and character of the use, including whether such use is of a commercial nature or is for nonprofit educational purposes;

"(2) the nature of the copyrighted work;

"(3) the amount and substantiality of the portion used in relation to the copyrighted work as a whole; and

"(4) the effect of the use upon the potential market for or value of the copyrighted work." 17 U. S. C. § 107.

These factors are not necessarily the exclusive determinants of the fair use inquiry and do not mechanistically resolve fair use issues;

---

[10] Often the paraphrasing was of statements others had made to Mr. Ford. E.g., ante, at 571 ("He could 'ride it out' or he could resign, Haig said"). See generally ante, at 570-579. No copyright can be asserted in the verbatim representation of such statements of others. 17 U. S. C. § 102. See Suid v. Newsweek Magazine, 503 F.Supp., at 148; Rokeach v. Avco Embassy Pictures Corp., 197 USPQ, at 161. Other paraphrased material came from Government documents in which no copyright interest can be claimed. For example, the article quotes from a memorandum prepared by Henry S. Ruth, Jr., in his official capacity as assistant to Watergate Special Prosecutor Leon Jaworski. See ante, at 573. This document is a work of the United States Government. See 17 U. S. C. § 105.

[11] According to an exhibit Harper & Row introduced at trial the pages in the Ford manuscript that correspond to consecutive sections of the article are as follows: 607-608, 401, 44, 496, 1, 2-3, 4, 8, 7, 4-5, 5, 5-6, 8, 14, 15, 16, 16, 18, 19, 21, 266, 236, 246, 248, 249, 238-239, 239, 243, 245, 246, 250, 250-251, 251, 252, 253, 254, 256, 298, 299, 46, 494, 537, 155-156, 216, 415, 416, 416, 53-54, 57. See App. to Pet. for Cert. E-1 to E-41.

[12] In one sense The Nation "copied" Mr. Ford's selection of facts because it reported on only those facts Mr. Ford chose to select for presentation. But this tracking of a historian's selection of facts generally should not supply the basis for a finding of infringement. See Myers v. Mail & Express Co., 36 Copyright Off. Bull. 478 (SDNY 1919) (L. Hand, J.). To hold otherwise would be to require a second author to duplicate the research of the first author so as to avoid reliance on the first author's judgment as to what facts are particularly pertinent. "'It is just such wasted effort that the proscription against the copyright of ideas and facts . . . are designed to prevent.'" Miller v. Universal City Studios, Inc., 650 F.2d 1365, 1371 (CA5 1981), quoting Rosemont Enterprises, Inc. v. Random House, Inc., 366 F.2d 303, 310 (CA2 1966). See Gorman, 29 J. Copyright Soc., at 594-595.

"no generally applicable definition is possible, and each case raising the question must be decided on its own facts." H. R. Rep. No. 94-1476, at 65. See also id., at 66 ("[The] endless variety of situations and combinations of circumstances that can arise in particular cases precludes the formulation of exact rules in the statute"); S. Rep. No. 94-473, p. 62 (1975). The statutory factors do, however, provide substantial guidance to courts undertaking the proper fact-specific inquiry.

With respect to a work of history, particularly the memoirs of a public official, the statutorily prescribed analysis cannot properly be conducted without constant attention to copyright's crucial distinction between protected literary form and unprotected information or ideas. The question must always be: Was the subsequent author's use of literary form a fair use within the meaning of § 107, in light of the purpose for the use, the nature of the copyrighted work, the amount of literary form used, and the effect of this use of literary form on the value of or market for the original?

[589] Limiting the inquiry to the propriety of a subsequent author's use of the copyright owner's literary form is not easy in the case of a work of history. Protection against only substantial appropriation of literary form does not ensure historians a return commensurate with the full value of their labors. The literary form contained in works like "A Time to Heal" reflects only a part of the labor that goes into the book. It is the labor of collecting, sifting, organizing, and reflecting that predominates in the creation of works of history such as this one. The value this labor produces lies primarily in the information and ideas revealed, and not in the particular collocation of words through which the information and ideas are expressed. Copyright thus does not protect that which is often of most value in a work of history, and courts must resist the tendency to reject the fair use defense on the basis of their feeling that an author of history has been deprived of the full value of his or her labor. A subsequent author's taking of information and ideas is in no sense piratical because copyright law simply does not create any property interest in information and ideas.

The urge to compensate for subsequent use of information and ideas is perhaps understandable. An inequity seems to lurk in the idea that much of the fruit of the historian's labor may be used without compensation. This, however, is not some unforeseen byproduct of a statutory scheme intended primarily to ensure a return for works of the imagination. Congress made the affirmative choice that the copyright laws should apply in this way: "Copyright does not preclude others from using the ideas or information revealed by the author's work. It pertains to the literary . . . form in

which the author expressed intellectual concepts." H. R. Rep. No. 94-1476, at 56-57. This distinction is at the essence of copyright. The copyright laws serve as the "engine of free expression," ante, at 558, only when the statutory monopoly does not choke off multifarious indirect uses and consequent broad dissemination of information and ideas. To ensure the progress of arts and sciences and the integrity [590] of First Amendment values, ideas and information must not be freighted with claims of proprietary right.[13]

In my judgment, the Court's fair use analysis has fallen to the temptation to find copyright violation based on a minimal use of literary form in order to provide compensation for the appropriation of information from a work of history. The failure to distinguish between information and literary form permeates every aspect of the Court's fair use analysis and leads the Court to the wrong result in this case. Application of the statutorily prescribed analysis with attention to the distinction between information and literary form leads to a straightforward finding of fair use within the meaning of § 107.

The Purpose of the Use. The Nation's purpose in quoting 300 words of the Ford manuscript was, as the Court acknowledges, news reporting. See ante, at 561. The Ford work contained information about important events of recent history. Two principals, Mr. Ford and General Alexander Haig, were at the time of The Nation's publication in 1979 widely thought to be candidates for the Presidency. That The Nation objectively reported the information in the Ford manuscript without independent commentary in no way diminishes the conclusion that it was reporting news. A typical newsstory differs from an editorial precisely in that it presents newsworthy information in a straightforward and unelaborated manner. Nor does the source of the information render The Nation's article any less a news report. Often books and manuscripts, solicited and unsolicited, are [591] the subject matter of news reports. E.g., New York Times Co. v. United States, 403 U.S. 713 (1971).

---

[13] This congressional limitation on the scope of copyright does not threaten the production of history. That this limitation results in significant diminution of economic incentives is far from apparent. In any event noneconomic incentives motivate much historical research and writing. For example, former public officials often have great incentive to "tell their side of the story." And much history is the product of academic scholarship. Perhaps most importantly, the urge to preserve the past is as old as humankind.

Frequently the manuscripts are unpublished at the time of the news report.[14]

Section 107 lists news reporting as a prime example of fair use of another's expression. Like criticism and all other purposes Congress explicitly approved in § 107, news reporting informs the public; the language of § 107 makes clear that Congress saw the spread of knowledge and information as the strongest justification for a properly limited appropriation of expression. The Court of Appeals was therefore correct to conclude that the purpose of The Nation's use — dissemination of the information contained in the quotations of Mr. Ford's work — furthered the public interest. 723 F.2d 195, 207-208 (CA2 1983). In light of the explicit congressional endorsement in § 107, the purpose for which Ford's literary form was borrowed strongly favors a finding of fair use.

The Court concedes the validity of the news reporting purpose n15 but then quickly offsets it against three purportedly countervailing considerations. First, the Court asserts that because The Nation publishes for profit, its publication of [592] the Ford quotes is a presumptively unfair commercial use. Second, the Court claims that The Nation's stated desire to create a "news event" signaled an illegitimate purpose of supplanting the copyright owner's right of first publication. Ante , at 562-563. Third, The Nation acted in bad faith, the Court claims, because its editor "knowingly exploited a purloined manuscript." Ante, at 563.[15]

The Court's reliance on the commercial nature of The Nation's use as "a separate factor that tends to weigh against a finding of fair use," ante, at 562, is inappropriate in the present context. Many uses § 107 lists as paradigmatic examples of fair use, including criticism, comment, and news reporting , are generally conducted for profit in this country, a fact of which Congress was obviously aware when it enacted § 107. To negate any argument favoring fair use based on news reporting or criticism because that reporting or criticism was published for profit is to render meaningless the congressional imprimatur placed on such uses.[16]

Nor should The Nation's intent to create a "news event" weigh against a finding of fair use. Such a rule, like the [593] Court's automatic presumption against news reporting for profit, would undermine the congressional validation of the news reporting purpose. A news business earns its reputation, and therefore its readership, through consistent prompt publication of news – and often through "scooping" rivals. More importantly, the Court's failure to maintain the distinction between information and literary form colors the analysis of this point. Because Harper & Row had no legitimate copyright interest in the information and ideas in the Ford manuscript, The Nation had every right to seek to be the first to disclose these facts and ideas to the public. The record suggests only that The Nation sought to be the first to reveal the information in the Ford manuscript. The Nation's stated purpose of scooping the competition should under those circumstances have no negative bearing on the claim of fair use. Indeed the Court's reliance on this factor would seem to amount to little more than distaste for the standard journalistic practice of seeking to be the first to publish news.

---

[14] E.g., N.Y. Times, Aug. 2, 1984, p. C20, col. 5 (article about revelations in forthcoming biography of Cardinal Spellman); N.Y. Times, Dec. 10, 1981, p. A18, col. 1 (article about revelations in forthcoming book by John Erlichman); N.Y. Times, Sept. 29, 1976, p. 1, col. 2 (article about revelations in forthcoming autobiography of President Nixon); N.Y. Times, Mar. 27, 1976, p. 9, col. 1 (article about revelations concerning President Nixon's resignation in forthcoming book The Final Days); N.Y. Times, Sept. 23, 1976, p. 36, col. 1 (article about revelations concerning President Ford in forthcoming book Blind Ambition by John Dean).

[15] The Court properly rejects the argument that this is not legitimate news. Courts have no business making such evaluations of journalistic quality. See ante, at 561. The Court also properly rejects the argument that this use is nonproductive. See ibid. News reporting, which encompasses journalistic judgment with respect to selection, organization, and presentation of facts and ideas, is certainly a productive use. See Sony Corp. of America v. Universal City Studios, Inc., 464 U.S., at 478-479 (BLACKMUN, J., dissenting).

[16] To support this claim the Court refers to some language in Sony Corp. of America v. Universal City Studios, Inc., supra, to the effect that "every commercial use of copyrighted material is presumptively an unfair exploitation." Id., at 451. See ante, at 562. Properly understood, this language does not support the Court's position in this case. The Court in Sony Corp. dealt with a use – video recording of copyrighted television programs for personal use – about which Congress had expressed no policy judgment. When a court evaluates uses that Congress has not specifically addressed, the presumption articulated in Sony Corp. is appropriate to effectuate the congressional instruction to consider "whether such use is of a commercial nature." 17 U. S. C. § 107(1). Also, the Court made that statement in the course of evaluating a use that appropriated the entirety of the copyrighted work in a form identical to that of the original; the presumption articulated may well have been intended to apply to takings under these circumstances. But, in light of the specific language of § 107, this presumption is not appropriately employed to negate the weight Congress explicitly gave to news reporting as a justification for limited use of another's expression.

The Court's reliance on The Nation's putative bad faith is equally unwarranted. No court has found that The Nation possessed the Ford manuscript illegally or in violation of any common-law interest of Harper & Row; all common-law causes of action have been abandoned or dismissed in this case. 723 F.2d, at 199-201. Even if the manuscript had been "purloined" by someone, nothing in this record imputes culpability to The Nation.[17] On the basis of the record in this case, the most that can be said is that The Nation made use of the contents of the manuscript knowing the copyright owner would not sanction the use.

[594]At several points the Court brands this conduct thievery. See, e.g., ante, at 556, 563. This judgment is unsupportable, and is perhaps influenced by the Court's unspoken tendency in this case to find infringement based on the taking of information and ideas. With respect to the appropriation of information and ideas other than the quoted words, The Nation's use was perfectly legitimate despite the copyright owner's objection because no copyright can be claimed in ideas or information. Whether the quotation of 300 words was an infringement or a fair use within the meaning of § 107 is a close question that has produced sharp division in both this Court and the Court of Appeals. If the Copyright Act were held not to prohibit the use, then the copyright owner would have had no basis in law for objecting. The Nation's awareness of an objection that has a significant chance of being adjudged unfounded cannot amount to bad faith. Imputing bad faith on the basis of no more than knowledge of such an objection, the Court impermissibly prejudices the inquiry and impedes arrival at the proper conclusion that the "purpose" factor of the statutorily prescribed analysis strongly favors a finding of fair use in this case.

The Nature of the Copyrighted Work. In Sony Corp. of America v. Universal City Studios, Inc., we stated that "not ... all copyrights are fungible" and that "[copying] a news broadcast may have a stronger claim to fair use than copying a motion picture." 464 U.S., at 455, n. 40. These statements reflect the principle, suggested in § 107(2) of the Act, that the scope of fair use is generally broader when the source of borrowed

expression is a factual or historical work. See 3 Nimmer §13.05[A][2], at 13-73 – 13-74. "[Informational] works," like the Ford manuscript, "that readily lend themselves to productive use by others, are less protected." Sony Corp. of America v. Universal City Studios, Inc., 464 U.S., at 496-497 (BLACKMUN, J., dissenting). Thus the second statutory factor also favors a finding of fair use in this case.

[595] The Court acknowledges that "[the] law generally recognizes a greater need to disseminate factual works than works of fiction or fantasy," ante, at 563, and that "[some] of the briefer quotations from the memoir are arguably necessary to convey the facts," ibid. But the Court discounts the force of this consideration, primarily on the ground that "[the] fact that a work is unpublished is a crucial element of its 'nature.'" Ante, at 564.[18] At this point the Court introduces into analysis of this case a categorical presumption against prepublication fair use. See ante, at 555 ("Under ordinary circumstances, the author's right to control the first public appearance of his undisseminated expression will outweigh a claim of fair use").

This categorical presumption is unwarranted on its own terms and unfaithful to congressional intent.[19] Whether a [596] particular prepublication

---

[17] This case is a far cry from Time Inc. v. Bernard Geis Associates, 293 F.Supp. 130, 146 (SDNY 1968), the only case the Court cites to support consideration of The Nation's purported bad faith. In that case the publisher claiming fair use had personally stolen film negatives from the offices of Time and then published graphic representations of the stolen photographic images. And the court found fair use despite these circumstances. Ibid.

[18] The Court also discounts this factor in part because the appropriation of The Nation, "focusing on the most expressive elements of the work, exceeds that necessary to disseminate the facts." Ante, at 564. Whatever the propriety of this view of The Nation's use, it is properly analyzed under the third statutory fair use factor – the amount and substantiality of the expression taken in relation to the copyrighted work as a whole, 17 U. S. C. § 107(3) – and will be analyzed as such in this opinion.

[19] The Court lays claim to specific congressional intent supporting the presumption against prepublication fair use. See ante, at 553, quoting S. Rep. No. 94-473, p. 64 (1975); ante, at 551, n. 4, 553-554. The argument based on congressional intent is unpersuasive for three reasons. First, the face of the statute clearly allows for prepublication fair use. The right of first publication, like all other rights § 106 of the Act specifically grants copyright owners, is explicitly made "subject to section 107," the statutory fair use provision. See 17 U. S. C. § 106.
Second, the language from the Senate Report on which the Court relies so heavily, see ante, at 553, simply will not bear the weight the Court places on it. The Senate Report merely suggests that prepublication photocopying for classroom purposes will not generally constitute fair use when the author has an interest in the confidentiality of the unpublished work, evidenced by the author's "deliberate choice" not to publish. Given that the face of § 106 specifically allows for prepublication fair use, it would be unfaithful to the intent of Congress to draw from this circumscribed suggestion in the Senate Report a blanket presumption against any amount of prepublication fair use for any purpose and irrespective of the effect of that use on the copyright owner's privacy, editorial, or

use will impair any interest the Court identifies as encompassed with in the right of first publication, see ante, at 552-555,[20] will depend on the nature of the copyrighted work, the timing of prepublication use, the amount of expression used, and the medium in which the second author communicates. Also, certain uses might be tolerable for some purposes but not for others. See Sony Corp. of America v. Universal City Studios, Inc., supra, at 490, n. 40. The Court is ambiguous as to whether it relies on the force of the presumption against prepublication fair use or an analysis of the purpose and effect of this particular use. Compare ante, at 552-555, with ante, at 564. To the extent the Court relies on the presumption, it presumes intolerable [597] injury – in particular the usurpation of the economic interest[21] – based on no more than a quick litmus

test for prepublication timing. Because "Congress has plainly instructed us that fair use analysis calls for a sensitive balancing of interests," we held last Term that the fair use inquiry could never be resolved on the basis of such a "two dimensional" categorical approach. See Sony Corp. of America v. Universal City Studios, Inc., 464 U.S., at 455, n. 40 (rejecting categorical requirement of "productive use").

To the extent the Court purports to evaluate the facts of this case, its analysis relies on sheer speculation. The quotation of 300 words from the manuscript infringed no privacy interest of Mr. Ford. This author intended the words in the manuscript to be a public statement about his Presidency. Lacking, therefore, is the "deliberate choice on the part of the copyright owner" to keep expression confidential, a consideration that the Senate Report – in the passage on which the Court places great reliance, see ante, at 553 – recognized as the impetus behind narrowing fair use for unpublished works. See S. Rep. No. 94-473, at 64. See also 3 Nimmer § 13.05[A], at 13-73 ("[The] scope of the fair use doctrine is considerably narrower with respect to unpublished works which are held confidential by their copyright owners") (emphasis added). What the Court depicts as the copyright owner's "confidentiality" interest, see ante, at 564, is not a privacy interest at all. Rather, it is no more than an economic interest in capturing the full value of initial release of information to [598] the public, and is properly analyzed as such. See infra, at 602-603. Lacking too is any suggestion that The Nation's use interfered with the copyright owner's interest in editorial control of the manuscript. The Nation made use of the Ford quotes on the eve of official publication.

Thus, the only interest The Nation's prepublication use might have infringed is the copyright owner's interest in capturing the full economic value of initial release. By considering this interest as a component of the "nature" of the copyrighted work, the Court's analysis deflates The Nation's claim that the informational nature of the work supports fair use without any inquiry into the actual or potential economic harm of The Nation's particular prepublication use. For this reason, the question of economic harm is properly considered under the fourth statutory factor – the effect on the value of or market for the copyrighted work, 17 U. S. C. § 107(4) – and not as a presumed element of the "nature" of the copyright.

---

economic interests. Third, the Court's reliance on congressional adoption of the common law is also unpersuasive. The common law did not set up the monolithic barrier to prepublication fair use that the Court wishes it did. See, e.g., Estate of Hemingway v. Random House, Inc., 53 Misc. 2d 462, 279 N.Y. S. 2d 51 (S. Ct. N.Y. Cty.), aff'd, 29 App. Div. 2d 633, 285 N.Y. S. 2d 568 (1st Jud. Dept. 1967), aff'd on other grounds, 23 N.Y. 2d 341, 244 N. E. 2d 250 (1968). The statements of general principle the Court cites to support its contrary representation of the common law, see ante, at 551, n. 4, are themselves unsupported by reference to substantial judicial authority. Congressional endorsement of the common law of fair use should not be read as adoption of any rigid presumption against prepublication use. If read that way, the broad statement that the Copyright Act was intended to incorporate the common law would in effect be given the force of nullifying Congress' repeated methodological prescription that definite rules are inappropriate and fact-specific analysis is required. The broad language adopting the common-law approach to fair use is best understood as an endorsement of the essential fact-specificity and case-by-case methodology of the common law of fair use.

[20] The Court finds the right of first publication particularly weighty because it encompasses three important interests: (i) a privacy interest in whether to make expression public at all; (ii) an editorial interest in ensuring control over the work while it is being groomed for public dissemination; and (iii) an economic interest in capturing the full remunerative potential of initial release to the public. Ante, at 552-555.

[21] Perhaps most inappropriate is the Court's apocalyptic prophesy that permitting any prepublication use for news reporting will "effectively destroy any expectation of copyright protection in the work of a public figure." Ante, at 557. The impact of a prepublication use for purposes of news reporting will obviously vary with the circumstances. A claim of news reporting should not be a fig leaf for substantial plagiarism, see Wainwright Securities Inc. v. Wall Street Transcript Corp., 558 F.2d 91 (CA2 1977), but there is no warrant for concluding that prepublication quotation of a few sentences will usually

drain all value from a copyright owner's right of first publication.

The Amount and Substantiality of the Portion Used. More difficult questions arise with respect to judgments about the importance to this case of the amount and substantiality of the quotations used. The Nation quoted only approximately 300 words from a manuscript of more than 200,000 words, and the quotes are drawn from isolated passages in disparate sections of the work. The judgment that this taking was quantitatively "infinitesimal," 723 F.2d, at 209, does not dispose of the inquiry, however. An evaluation of substantiality in qualitative terms is also required. Much of the quoted material was Mr. Ford's matter-of-fact representation of the words of others in conversations with him; such quotations are "arguably necessary adequately to convey the facts," ante, at 563, and are not rich in expressive content. Beyond these quotations a portion of the quoted material was drawn from the most poignant expression in the Ford manuscript; in particular The Nation made use of six examples of Mr. Ford's expression of his reflections on [599] events or perceptions about President Nixon.[22] The fair use inquiry turns on the propriety of the use of these quotations with admittedly strong expressive content.

The Court holds that "in view of the expressive value of the excerpts and their key role in the infringing work," this third statutory factor

---

[22] These six quotes are:
(1) "'[Compassion] for Nixon as an individual hadn't prompted my decision at all.' Rather, he did it because he had 'to get the monkey off my back one way or the other.'" Ante, at 572-573.
(2) "Nixon 'would not spend the time quietly in San Clemente,' and 'it would be virtually impossible for me to direct public attention on anything else.'" Ante, at 573.
(3) "'I learned that public policy often took precedence over a rule of law. Although I respected the tenet that no man should be above the law, public policy demanded that I put Nixon – and Watergate – behind us as quickly as possible.'" Ante, at 575.
(4) "'If I made the trip it would remind everybody of Watergate and the pardon. If I didn't people would say I lacked compassion.'" Ibid.
(5) "'He was stretched out flat on his back. There were tubes in his nose and mouth, and wires led from his arms, chest and legs to machines with orange lights that blinked on and off. His face was ashen, and I thought I had never seen anyone closer to death.'" Ibid.
(6) "'A terribly proud man,' writes Ford, 'he detested weakness in other people. I'd often heard him speak disparagingly of those whom he felt to be soft and expedient. (Curiously, he didn't feel that the press was weak. Reporters, he sensed, were his adversaries. He knew they didn't like him, and he responded with reciprocal disdain.)' . . . 'His pride and personal contempt for weakness had overcome his ability to tell the difference between right and wrong.' . . . 'Nixon was out of touch with reality.'" Ante, at 578.

---

disfavors a finding of fair use.[23] To support [600] this conclusion, the Court purports to rely on the District Court factual findings that The Nation had taken "the heart of the book." 557 F.Supp. 1062, 1072 (SDNY 1983). This reliance is misplaced, and would appear to be another result of the Court's failure to distinguish between information and literary form. When the District Court made this finding, it was evaluating not the quoted words at issue here but the "totality" of the information and reflective commentary in the Ford work. Ibid. The vast majority of what the District Court considered the heart of the Ford work, therefore, consisted of ideas and information The Nation was free to use. It may well be that, as a qualitative matter, most of the value of the manuscript did lie in the information and ideas The Nation used. But appropriation of the "heart" of the manuscript in this sense is irrelevant to copyright analysis because copyright does not preclude a second author's use of information and ideas.

Perhaps tacitly recognizing that reliance on the District Court finding is unjustifiable, the Court goes on to evaluate independently the quality of the expression appearing in The Nation's article. The Court states that "[the] portions actually quoted were selected by Mr. Navasky as among the most powerful passages." Ante, at 565. On the basis of no more than this observation, and perhaps also inference from the fact that the quotes were important to The Nation's article,[24] the Court adheres to its conclusion that The Nation appropriated the heart of the Ford manuscript.

[601] At least with respect to the six particular quotes of Mr. Ford's observations and reflections about President Nixon, I agree with the Court's

---

[23] The Court places some emphasis on the fact that the quotations from the Ford work constituted a substantial portion of The Nation's article. Superficially, the Court would thus appear to be evaluating The Nation's quotation of 300 words in relation to the amount and substantiality of expression used in relation to the second author's work as a whole. The statute directs the inquiry into "the amount and substantiality of the portion used in relation to the copyrighted work as a whole," 17 U. S. C. § 107(3) (emphasis added). As the statutory directive implies, it matters little whether the second author's use is 1- or 100-percent appropriated expression if the taking of that expression had no adverse effect on the copyrighted work. See Sony Corp. of America v. Universal City Studios, Inc., 464 U.S. 417 (1984) (100% of expression taken). I presume, therefore, that the Court considered the role of the expression "in the infringing work" only as indirect evidence of the qualitative value of the expression taken in this case. If read this way, the point dovetails with the Court's major argument that The Nation appropriated the most valuable sentences of the work.
[24] See n. 23, supra.

conclusion that The Nation appropriated some literary form of substantial quality. I do not agree, however, that the substantiality of the expression taken was clearly excessive or inappropriate to The Nation's news reporting purpose.

Had these quotations been used in the context of a critical book review of the Ford work, there is little question that such a use would be fair use within the meaning of § 107 of the Act. The amount and substantiality of the use – in both quantitative and qualitative terms – would have certainly been appropriate to the purpose of such a use. It is difficult to see how the use of these quoted words in a news report is less appropriate. The Court acknowledges as much: "[Even] substantial quotations might qualify as a fair use in a review of a published work or a news account of a speech that had been delivered to the public." See ante, at 564. With respect to the motivation for the pardon and the insights into the psyche of the fallen President, for example, Mr. Ford's reflections and perceptions are so laden with emotion and deeply personal value judgments that full understanding is immeasurably enhanced by reproducing a limited portion of Mr. Ford's own words. The importance of the work, after all, lies not only in revelation of previously unknown fact but also in revelation of the thoughts, ideas, motivations, and fears of two Presidents at a critical moment in our national history. Thus, while the question is not easily resolved, it is difficult to say that the use of the six quotations was gratuitous in relation to the news reporting purpose.

Conceding that even substantial quotation is appropriate in a news report of a published work, the Court would seem to agree that this quotation was not clearly inappropriate in relation to The Nation's news reporting purpose. For the Court, the determinative factor is again that the substantiality of the use was inappropriate in relation to the prepublication [602] timing of that use. That is really an objection to the effect of this use on the market for the copyrighted work, and is properly evaluated as such.

The Effect on the Market. The Court correctly notes that the effect on the market "is undoubtedly the single most important element of fair use." Ante, at 566, citing 3 Nimmer § 13.05[A], at 13-76, and the Court properly focuses on whether The Nation's use adversely affected Harper & Row's serialization potential and not merely the market for sales of the Ford work itself. Ante, at 566-567. Unfortunately, the Court's failure to distinguish between the use of information and the appropriation of literary form badly skews its analysis of this factor.

For purposes of fair use analysis, the Court holds, it is sufficient that the entire article containing the quotes eroded the serialization market potential of Mr. Ford's work. Ante, at 567. On the basis of Time's cancellation of its serialization agreement, the Court finds that "[rarely] will a case of copyright infringement present such clear-cut evidence of actual damage." Ibid. In essence, the Court finds that by using some quotes in a story about the Nixon pardon, The Nation "competed for a share of the market of prepublication excerpts" ante, at 568, because Time planned to excerpt from the chapters about the pardon.

The Nation's publication indisputably precipitated Time's eventual cancellation. But that does not mean that The Nation's use of the 300 quoted words caused this injury to Harper & Row. Wholly apart from these quoted words, The Nation published significant information and ideas from the Ford manuscript. If it was this publication of information, and not the publication of the few quotations, that caused Time to abrogate its serialization agreement, then whatever the negative effect on the serialization market, that effect was the product of wholly legitimate activity.

The Court of Appeals specifically held that "the evidence does not support a finding that it was the very limited use of expression per se which led to Time's decision not to print excerpts." [603] 723 F.2d, at 208. I fully agree with this holding. If The Nation competed with Time, the competition was not for a share of the market in excerpts of literary form but for a share of the market in the new information in the Ford work. That the information, and not the literary form, represents most of the real value of the work in this case is perhaps best revealed by the following provision in the contract between Harper & Row and Mr. Ford:

"Author acknowledges that the value of the rights granted to publisher hereunder would be substantially diminished by Author's public discussion of the unique information not previously disclosed about Author's career and personal life which will be included in the Work, and Author agrees that Author will endeavor not to disseminate any such information in any media, including television, radio and newspaper and magazine interviews prior to the first publication of the work hereunder." App. 484.

The contract thus makes clear that Harper & Row sought to benefit substantially from monopolizing the initial revelation of information known only to Ford.

Because The Nation was the first to convey the information in this case, it did perhaps take from

Harper & Row some of the value that publisher sought to garner for itself through the contractual arrangement with Ford and the license to Time. Harper & Row had every right to seek to monopolize revenue from that potential market through contractual arrangements but it has no right to set up copyright as a shield from competition in that market because copyright does not protect information. The Nation had every right to seek to be the first to publish that information.[25]

[604] Balancing the Interests. Once the distinction between information and literary form is made clear, the statutorily prescribed process of weighing the four statutory fair use factors discussed above leads naturally to a conclusion that The Nation's limited use of literary form was not an infringement. Both the purpose of the use and the nature of the copyrighted work strongly favor the fair use defense here. The Nation appropriated Mr. Ford's expression for a purpose Congress expressly authorized in § 107 and borrowed from a work whose nature justifies some appropriation to facilitate the spread of information. The factor that is perhaps least favorable to the claim of fair use is the amount and substantiality of the expression used. Without question, a portion of the expression appropriated was among the most poignant in the Ford manuscript. But it is difficult to conclude that this taking was excessive in relation to the news reporting purpose. In any event, because the appropriation of literary form – as opposed to the use of information – was not shown to injure Harper & Row's economic interest, any uncertainty with respect to the propriety of the amount of expression borrowed should be resolved in favor of a finding of fair use.[26] In light of the circumscribed scope of the quotation in The Nation's article and the undoubted validity of the purpose [605] motivating that quotation, I must conclude that the Court has simply adopted an exceedingly narrow view of fair use in order to impose liability for what was in essence a taking of unprotected information.

III. The Court's exceedingly narrow approach to fair use permits Harper & Row to monopolize information. This holding "[effects] an important extension of property rights and a corresponding curtailment in the free use of knowledge and of ideas." International News Service v. Associated Press, 248 U.S., at 263 (Brandeis, J., dissenting). The Court has perhaps advanced the ability of the historian – or at least the public official who has recently left office – to capture the full economic value of information in his or her possession. But the Court does so only by risking the robust debate of public issues that is the "essence of self-government." Garrison v. Louisiana, 379 U.S., at 74-75. The Nation was providing the grist for that robust debate. The Court imposes liability upon The Nation for no other reason than that The Nation succeeded in being the first to provide certain information to the public. I dissent.

---

[25] The Court's reliance on the principle that "an infringer who mingles infringing and noninfringing elements 'must abide the consequences,'" ante, at 567 (citation omitted), is misconceived. Once infringement of a § 106 exclusive right has been shown, it is entirely appropriate to shift to the infringer the burden of showing that the infringement did not cause all the damages shown. But the question in this case is whether this particular use infringed any § 106 rights. Harper & Row may have shown actual damage flowing from The Nation's use of information, but they have not shown actual damage flowing from an infringement of a § 106 exclusive right.

[26] Had The Nation sought to justify a more substantial appropriation of expression on a news reporting rationale, a different case might be presented. The substantiality of the taking would certainly dilute the claim of need to use the first author's exact words to convey a particular thought or sentiment. Even if the claim of need were plausible, the equities would have to favor the copyright owner in order to prevent erosion of virtually all copyright protection for works of former public officials. In this case, however, the need is manifest and the integrity of copyright protection for the works of public officials is not threatened.

Universal City Studios v. Corley
273 F.3d 429
(2nd Cir. 2001)
(Excerpts only. Footnotes omitted.)

SUBSEQUENT HISTORY: As Amended January 29, 2002.

PRIOR HISTORY: Appeal from the amended final judgment of the United States District Court for the Southern District of New York (Lewis A. Kaplan, District Judge), entered August 23, 2000, enjoining Appellants from posting on their web site a computer program that decrypts the encryption code limiting access to DVD movies, and from linking to other web sites containing the decryption program. Universal City Studios, Inc. v. Reimerdes, 111 F. Supp. 2d 346, 2000 U.S. Dist. LEXIS 11949 (S.D.N.Y. 2000)

JUDGES: Before: NEWMAN and CABRANES, Circuit Judges, and THOMPSON, * District Judge.
* United States District Court for the District of Connecticut, sitting by designation.

OPINION: [434] JON O. NEWMAN, Circuit Judge.
…This appeal raises significant First Amendment issues concerning one aspect of computer technology – encryption to protect materials in digital form from unauthorized access. The appeal challenges the constitutionality of the Digital Millennium Copyright Act ("DMCA"), 17 U.S.C. § 1201 et seq. (Supp. V 1999) and the validity of an injunction entered to enforce the DMCA. … [435] We affirm.
… This appeal concerns the anti-trafficking provisions of the DMCA, which Congress enacted in 1998 to strengthen copyright protection in the digital age. Fearful that the ease with which pirates could copy and distribute a copyrightable work in digital form was overwhelming the capacity of conventional copyright enforcement to find and enjoin unlawfully copied material, Congress sought to combat copyright piracy in its earlier stages, before the work was even copied. The DMCA therefore backed with legal sanctions the efforts of copyright owners to protect their works from piracy behind digital walls such as encryption codes or password protections. In so doing, Congress targeted not only those pirates who would circumvent these digital walls (the "anti-circumvention provisions," contained in 17 U.S.C. § 1201 (a)(1)), but also anyone who would traffic in a technology primarily designed to circumvent a digital wall (the "anti-trafficking provisions," contained in 17 U.S.C. § 1201 (a)(2), (b)(1)).

Corley publishes a print magazine and maintains an affiliated web site geared towards "hackers…" In November 1999, Corley posted a copy of the decryption computer program "DeCSS" on his web site, http://www.2600.com ("2600.com"). DeCSS is designed to circumvent "CSS," the encryption technology [436] that motion picture studios place on DVDs to prevent the unauthorized viewing and copying of motion pictures. Corley also posted on his web site links to other web sites where DeCSS could be found.

Plaintiffs-Appellees are eight motion picture studios…. Following a full non-jury trial, the District Court entered a permanent injunction barring Corley from posting DeCSS on his web site or from knowingly linking via a hyperlink to any other web site containing DeCSS. …Corley renews his constitutional challenges on appeal. Specifically, he argues primarily that: (1) the DMCA oversteps limits in the Copyright Clause on the duration of copyright protection; (2) the DMCA as applied to his dissemination of DeCSS violates the First Amendment because computer code is "speech" entitled to full First Amendment protection and the DMCA fails to survive the exacting scrutiny accorded statutes that regulate "speech"; and (3) the DMCA violates the First Amendment and the Copyright Clause by unduly obstructing the "fair use" of copyrighted materials…. [437]

If a user runs the DeCSS program … with a DVD in the computer's disk drive, DeCSS will decrypt the DVD's CSS protection, allowing the user to copy the DVD's files and place the copy on the user's hard drive. The result is a very large computer file that can be played on a non-CSS-compliant player and copied, manipulated, and transferred just like any [438] other computer file. …The quality of the resulting decrypted movie is "virtually identical" to that of the encrypted movie on the DVD. And the file produced by DeCSS, while large, can be compressed to a manageable size by a compression software called "DivX," available at no cost on the Internet. This compressed file can be copied onto a DVD, or transferred over the Internet (with some patience).

Johansen posted the executable object code, but not the source code, for DeCSS on his web site. ... [439] Since computer languages range in complexity, object code can be placed on one end of a spectrum, and different kinds of source code can be arrayed across the spectrum according to the ease with which they are read and understood by humans. Within months of its appearance in executable form on Johansen's web site, DeCSS was widely available on the Internet, in both object code and various forms of source code. [Later,] the Defendants posted copies of the object and source code of DeCSS. ... Corley also added ... links that he explained would take the reader to other web sites where DeCSS could be found.

2600.com was only one of hundreds of web sites that began posting DeCSS near the end of 1999. The movie industry tried to stem the tide by sending cease-and-desist letters to many of these sites. These efforts met with only partial success; a number of sites refused to remove [440] DeCSS. In January 2000, the studios filed this lawsuit. ...

The DMCA was enacted in 1998 to implement the World Intellectual Property Organization Copyright Treaty ("WIPO Treaty"), which requires contracting parties to "provide adequate legal protection and effective legal remedies against the circumvention of effective technological measures that are used by authors in connection with the exercise of their rights under this Treaty or the Berne Convention and that restrict acts, in respect of their works, which are not authorized by the authors concerned or permitted by law." Even before the treaty, Congress had been devoting attention to the problems faced by copyright enforcement in the digital age. Hearings on the topic have spanned several years....

The Act contains three provisions targeted at the circumvention of technological protections. The first is subsection 1201(a)(1)(A), the anti-circumvention provision. This provision prohibits a person from "circumventing a technological measure that effectively controls access to a work protected under [Title 17, governing copyright]." The Librarian of Congress is required to promulgate regulations every three years exempting from this subsection individuals who would otherwise be "adversely affected" in "their ability to make noninfringing uses." ... The second and third provisions are subsections 1201(a)(2) and 1201(b)(1), the "anti-trafficking provisions." Subsection 1201(a)(2), the provision at issue in this case, provides:

No person shall manufacture, import, offer to the public, provide, or otherwise traffic in any technology, product, service, device, component, or part thereof, that–

(A) is primarily designed or produced for the purpose of circumventing a technological measure that effectively controls access to a work protected under this title;

(B) has only limited commercially significant purpose or use other than to circumvent a technological measure that effectively controls access to a work protected under this title; or

(C) is marketed by that person or another acting in concert with that person with that person's knowledge for use in circumventing a technological measure [441] that effectively controls access to a work protected under this title. Id. § 1201(a)(2).

To "circumvent a technological measure" is defined, in pertinent part, as "to descramble a scrambled work . . . or otherwise to . . . bypass . . . a technological measure, without the authority of the copyright owner." Id. § 1201(a)(3)(A).

Subsection 1201(b)(1) is similar to subsection 1201(a)(2), except that subsection 1201(a)(2) covers those who traffic in technology that can circumvent "a technological measure that effectively controls access to a work protected under" Title 17, whereas subsection 1201(b)(1) covers those who traffic in technology that can circumvent "protection afforded by a technological measure that effectively protects a right of a copyright owner under" Title 17. Id. § 1201(a)(2), (b)(1). In other words, although both subsections prohibit trafficking in a circumvention technology, the focus of subsection 1201(a)(2) is circumvention of technologies designed to prevent access to a work, and the focus of subsection 1201(b)(1) is circumvention of technologies designed to permit access to a work but prevent copying of the work or some other act that infringes a copyright. Subsection 1201(a)(1) differs from both of these anti-trafficking subsections in that it targets the use of a circumvention technology, not the trafficking in such a technology.

The DMCA contains exceptions for schools and libraries that want to use circumvention technologies to determine whether to purchase a copyrighted product, 17 U.S.C. § 1201 (d); individuals using circumvention technology "for the sole purpose" of trying to achieve "interoperability" of computer programs through reverse-engineering, id. § 1201(f); encryption research aimed at identifying flaws in encryption technology, if the research is conducted to advance the state of knowledge in the field, id. § 1201(g); and several other exceptions not relevant here.

The DMCA creates civil remedies, id. § 1203, and criminal sanctions, id. § 1204. It specifically authorizes a court to "grant temporary and permanent injunctions on such terms as it deems reasonable to prevent or restrain a violation." Id. §1203(b)(1).

...On January 20, 2000, after a hearing, the District Court issued a preliminary injunction barring the Defendants from posting DeCSS. The Defendants complied with the preliminary injunction, but continued to post links to other web sites carrying DeCSS, an action they termed "electronic civil disobedience." Under the heading "Stop the MPAA [(Motion Picture Association of America)]," Corley urged other web sites to post DeCSS lest "we . . . be forced into submission."

The Plaintiffs then sought a permanent injunction barring the Defendants from both posting DeCSS and linking to sites containing DeCSS. After a trial on the merits, the Court issued a comprehensive opinion and granted a permanent injunction.

The Court explained that the Defendants' posting of DeCSS on their web site clearly falls within section 1201(a)(2)(A) of the DMCA, ... [442] and that the alleged importance of DeCSS to certain fair uses of encrypted copyrighted material was immaterial to their statutory liability. The Court went on to hold that when the Defendants "proclaimed on their own site that DeCSS could be had by clicking on the hyperlinks" on their site, they were trafficking in DeCSS, and therefore liable for their linking as well as their posting.

Turning to the Defendants' numerous constitutional arguments, the Court first held that computer code like DeCSS is "speech" that is "protected" (in the sense of "covered") by the First Amendment, but that because the DMCA is targeting the "functional" aspect of that speech, it is "content neutral," and the intermediate scrutiny of United States v. O'Brien applies. The Court concluded that the DMCA survives this scrutiny and also rejected prior restraint, overbreadth, and vagueness challenges.

The Court upheld the constitutionality of the DMCA's application to linking on similar grounds: linking, the Court concluded, is "speech," but the DMCA is content-neutral, targeting only the functional components of that speech. Therefore, its application to linking is also evaluated under O'Brien, and, thus evaluated, survives intermediate scrutiny. However, the Court concluded that a blanket proscription on linking would create a risk of chilling legitimate linking on the web. The Court therefore crafted a restrictive test for linking liability (discussed below) that it believed sufficiently mitigated that risk. The Court then found its test satisfied in this case.

Finally, the Court concluded that an injunction was highly appropriate in this case. The Court observed that DeCSS was harming the Plaintiffs, not only because they were now exposed to the possibility of piracy and therefore were obliged to develop costly new safeguards for DVDs, but also because, even if there was only indirect evidence that DeCSS availability actually facilitated DVD piracy, the threat of piracy was very real, particularly as Internet transmission speeds continue to increase. Acknowledging that DeCSS was (and still is) widely available on the Internet, the Court expressed confidence in "the likelihood . . . that this decision will serve notice on others that 'the strong right arm of equity' may be brought to bear against them absent a change in their conduct and thus contribute to a climate of appropriate respect for intellectual property rights in an age in which the excitement of ready access to [443] untold quantities of information has blurred in some minds the fact that taking what is not yours and not freely offered to you is stealing."

The Court's injunction barred the Defendants from: "posting on any Internet web site" DeCSS; "in any other way . . . offering to the public, providing, or otherwise trafficking in DeCSS"; violating the anti-trafficking provisions of the DMCA in any other manner, and finally "knowingly linking any Internet web site operated by them to any other web site containing DeCSS, or knowingly maintaining any such link, for the purpose of disseminating DeCSS."

The Appellants have appealed from the permanent injunction. The United States has intervened in support of the constitutionality of the DMCA. We have also had the benefit of a number of amicus curiae briefs, supporting and opposing the District Court's judgment. ... [444]

In a footnote to their brief, the Appellants appear to contend that the DMCA, as construed by the District Court, exceeds the constitutional authority [445] of Congress to grant authors copyrights for a "limited time," U.S. Const. art. I, § 8, cl. 8, because it "empowers copyright owners to effectively secure perpetual protection by mixing public domain works with copyrighted materials, then locking both up with technological protection measures."...[T]he possibility that encryption would preclude access to public domain works "does not yet appear to be a problem, although it may emerge as one in the future." ...

Last year, in one of our Court's first forays into First Amendment law in the digital age, we took an "evolutionary" approach to the task of tailoring familiar constitutional rules to novel technological circumstances, favoring "narrow" holdings that would permit the law to mature on a "case-by-case" basis. ... [The] issues, which we consider only to the extent necessary to resolve the pending appeal, are whether computer code is speech, whether computer programs are speech, the scope of First Amendment protection for computer code, and the scope of First Amendment protection for decryption code. ...

Communication does not lose constitutional protection as "speech" simply because it is expressed in the language of computer code. Mathematical formulae and musical scores are written in "code," i.e., symbolic notations not comprehensible to the uninitiated, and yet both are covered by the First Amendment. If someone [446] chose to write a novel entirely in computer object code by using strings of 1's and 0's for each letter of each word, the resulting work would be no different for constitutional purposes than if it had been written in English. The "object code" version would be incomprehensible to readers outside the programming community (and tedious to read even for most within the community), but it would be no more incomprehensible than a work written in Sanskrit for those unversed in that language. The undisputed evidence reveals that even pure object code can be, and often is, read and understood by experienced programmers. And source code (in any of its various levels of complexity) can be read by many more. Ultimately, however, the ease with which a work is comprehended is irrelevant to the constitutional inquiry. If computer code is distinguishable from conventional speech for First Amendment purposes, it is not because it is written in an obscure language.

Of course, computer code is not likely to be the language in which a work of literature is written. Instead, it is primarily the language for programs executable by a computer. These programs are essentially instructions to a computer. In general, programs may give instructions either to perform a task or series of tasks when initiated by a single (or double) click of a mouse or, once a program is operational ("launched"), to manipulate data that the user enters into the computer. Whether computer code that gives a computer instructions is "speech" within the meaning of the First Amendment requires consideration of the scope of the Constitution's protection of speech.

..."Speech" is an elusive term, and judges and scholars have debated its bounds for two centuries. Some would confine First Amendment protection to political speech. Others would extend it further to artistic expression. Whatever might be the merits of these and other approaches, the law has not been so limited. Even dry information, devoid of advocacy, political relevance, or artistic expression, has been accorded First Amendment protection. [447] Thus, for example, courts have subjected to First Amendment scrutiny restrictions on the dissemination of technical scientific information, and scientific research, and attempts to regulate the publication of instructions.

Computer programs are not exempted from the category of First Amendment speech simply because their instructions require use of a computer. A recipe is no less "speech" because it calls for the use of an oven, and a musical score is no less "speech" because it specifies performance on an electric guitar. Arguably distinguishing computer programs from conventional language instructions is the fact that programs are executable on a computer. But the fact that a program has the capacity to direct the functioning of a computer does not mean that it lacks the additional capacity to convey information, and it is the conveying of information that renders instructions "speech" for purposes of the First Amendment. ... [448]

[P]rogrammers communicating ideas to one another almost inevitably communicate in code, much as musicians use notes. Limiting First Amendment protection of programmers to descriptions of computer code (but not the code itself) would impede discourse among computer scholars, just as limiting protection for musicians to descriptions of musical scores (but not sequences of notes) would impede their exchange of ideas and expression. Instructions that communicate information comprehensible to a human qualify as speech whether the instructions are designed for execution by a computer or a human (or both).

...[449] For all of these reasons, we join the other courts that have concluded that computer code, and computer programs constructed from code, can merit First Amendment protection, although the scope of such protection remains to be determined. ...[450]

As the District Court recognized, the scope of protection for speech generally depends on whether the restriction is imposed because of the content of the speech. Content-based restrictions are permissible only if they serve compelling state interests and do so by the least restrictive means available. A content-neutral restriction is permissible if it serves a substantial governmental interest, the interest is unrelated to the suppression of free expression, and the regulation is narrowly tailored, which "in this context requires . . . that the means chosen do not 'burden substantially more speech than is necessary to further the government's legitimate interests.'"

"Government regulation of expressive activity is 'content neutral' if it is justified without reference to the content of regulated speech." The government's purpose is the controlling consideration. A regulation that serves purposes unrelated to the content of expression is deemed neutral, even if it has an incidental effect on some speakers or messages but not others."

To determine whether regulation of computer code is content-neutral, the initial inquiry must be whether the regulated activity is "sufficiently imbued with elements of communication to fall within the scope of the First . . . Amendment." Computer code, as we have noted, often conveys information comprehensible to human beings, even as it also directs a computer to perform various functions. Once a speech component [451] is identified, the inquiry then proceeds to whether the regulation is "justified without reference to the content of regulated speech."

The Appellants vigorously reject the idea that computer code can be regulated according to any different standard than that applicable to pure speech, i.e., speech that lacks a nonspeech component. ... We disagree. Unlike a blueprint or a recipe, which cannot yield any functional result without human comprehension of its content, human decision-making, and human action, computer code can instantly cause a computer to accomplish tasks and instantly render the results of those tasks available throughout the world via the Internet. The only human action required to achieve these results can be as limited and instantaneous as a single click of a mouse. These realities of what code is and what its normal functions are require a First Amendment analysis that treats code as combining nonspeech and speech elements, i.e., functional and expressive elements.

... "[Functionality is really 'a proxy for effects or harm....' Society increasingly depends upon technological means of controlling access to digital files and systems, whether they are military computers, bank records, academic records, copyrighted works or something else entirely. There are far too many who, given any opportunity, will bypass security measures, [452] some for the sheer joy of doing it, some for innocuous reasons, and others for more malevolent purposes. Given the virtually instantaneous and worldwide dissemination widely available via the Internet, the only rational assumption is that once a computer program capable of bypassing such an access control system is disseminated, it will be used. And that is not all.

"There was a time when copyright infringement could be dealt with quite adequately by focusing on the infringing act. If someone wished to make and sell high quality but unauthorized copies of a copyrighted book, for example, the infringer needed a printing press. The copyright holder, once aware of the appearance of infringing copies, usually was able to trace the copies up the chain of distribution, find and prosecute the infringer, and shut off the infringement at the source.

In principle, the digital world is very different. Once a decryption program like DeCSS is written, it quickly can be sent all over the world. Every recipient is capable not only of decrypting and perfectly copying plaintiffs' copyrighted DVDs, but also of retransmitting perfect copies of DeCSS and thus enabling every recipient to do the same. They likewise are capable of transmitting perfect copies of the decrypted DVD. The process potentially is exponential rather than linear....

"These considerations drastically alter consideration of the causal link between dissemination of computer programs such as this and their illicit use. Causation in the law ultimately involves practical policy judgments. Here, dissemination itself carries very substantial risk of imminent harm because the mechanism is so unusual by which dissemination of means of circumventing access controls to copyrighted works threatens to produce virtually unstoppable infringement of copyright. In consequence, the causal link between the dissemination of circumvention computer programs and their improper use is more than sufficiently close to warrant selection of a level of constitutional scrutiny based on the programs' functionality."

In considering the scope of First Amendment protection for a decryption program like DeCSS, we must recognize that the essential purpose of encryption code is to prevent unauthorized access. Owners of all property rights are entitled to prohibit access to their property by unauthorized persons. Homeowners can install locks on the doors of their houses. Custodians of valuables can place them in safes. Stores can attach to products security devices that will activate alarms if the products are taken away without purchase. These and similar security devices can be circumvented. Burglars can use skeleton keys to open door locks. Thieves can obtain the combinations to safes. Product security devices can be neutralized.

Our case concerns a security device, CSS computer code, that prevents access by unauthorized persons to DVD movies. ... In its basic function, [453] CSS is like a lock on a homeowner's door, a combination of a safe, or a security device attached to a store's products.

DeCSS is computer code that can decrypt CSS. In its basic function, it is like a skeleton key that can open a locked door, a combination that can open a safe, or a device that can neutralize the security device attached to a store's products.

The initial use of DeCSS to gain access to a DVD movie creates no loss to movie producers because the initial user must purchase the DVD. However, once the DVD is purchased, DeCSS enables the initial user to copy the movie in digital form and transmit it instantly in virtually limitless quantity, thereby depriving the movie producer of sales. The advent of the Internet creates the potential for instantaneous worldwide distribution of the copied material.

At first glance, one might think that Congress has as much authority to regulate the distribution of computer code to decrypt DVD movies as it has to regulate distribution of skeleton keys, combinations to safes, or devices to neutralize store product security devices. However, despite the evident legitimacy of protection against unauthorized access to DVD movies, just like any other property, regulation of decryption code like DeCSS is challenged in this case because DeCSS differs from a skeleton key in one important respect: it not only is capable of performing the function of unlocking the encrypted DVD movie, it also is a form of communication, albeit written in a language not understood by the general public. As a communication, the DeCSS code has a claim to being "speech," and as "speech," it has a claim to being protected by the First Amendment. But just as the realities of what any computer code can accomplish must inform the scope of its constitutional protection, so the capacity of a decryption program like DeCSS to accomplish unauthorized – indeed, unlawful – access to materials in which the Plaintiffs have intellectual property rights must inform and limit the scope of its First Amendment protection. ...

The initial issue is whether the [lower court's] posting prohibition is content-neutral. ... [454] [T]he target of the posting provisions of the injunction – DeCSS – has both a nonspeech and a speech component, and that the DMCA, as applied to the Appellants, and the posting prohibition of the injunction target only the nonspeech component. Neither the DMCA nor the posting prohibition is concerned with whatever capacity DeCSS might have for conveying information to a human being, and that capacity, as previously explained, is what arguably creates a speech component of the decryption code. The DMCA and the posting prohibition are applied to DeCSS solely because of its capacity to instruct a computer to decrypt CSS. That functional capability is not speech within the meaning of the First Amendment. The Government seeks to "justify" both the application of the DMCA and the posting prohibition to the Appellants solely on the basis of the functional capability of DeCSS to instruct a computer to decrypt CSS "without reference to the content of the regulated speech." This type of regulation is therefore content-neutral, just as would be a

restriction on trafficking in skeleton keys identified because of their capacity to unlock jail cells, even though some of the keys happened to bear a slogan ... that qualified as a speech component.

As a content-neutral regulation with an incidental effect on a speech component, the regulation must serve a substantial governmental interest, the interest must be unrelated to the suppression of free expression, and the incidental restriction on speech must not burden substantially more speech than is necessary to further that interest. The Government's interest in preventing unauthorized access to encrypted copyrighted material is unquestionably substantial, and the regulation of DeCSS by the posting prohibition plainly serves that interest. Moreover, that interest is unrelated to the suppression of free expression. The injunction regulates the posting of DeCSS, regardless of whether DeCSS code contains any information comprehensible by human beings that would qualify as speech.

Whether the incidental regulation on speech burdens substantially more speech than is necessary to further the interest in preventing unauthorized access to copyrighted materials requires some elaboration.... Although the prohibition on posting prevents the Appellants from conveying to others the speech component of DeCSS, the Appellants have not suggested, much less shown, any technique for barring them from making this instantaneous worldwide distribution of a decryption code that makes a lesser restriction on the code's speech component. It is true that the [455] Government has alternative means of prohibiting unauthorized access to copyrighted materials. For example, it can create criminal and civil liability for those who gain unauthorized access, and thus it can be argued that the restriction on posting DeCSS is not absolutely necessary to preventing unauthorized access to copyrighted materials. But a content-neutral regulation need not employ the least restrictive means of accomplishing the governmental objective. It need only avoid burdening "substantially more speech than is necessary to further the government's legitimate interests." The prohibition on the Defendants' posting of DeCSS satisfies that standard.... [456]

...[A] hyperlink has both a speech and a nonspeech component. It conveys information, the Internet address of the linked web page, and has the functional capacity to bring the content of the linked web page to the user's computer screen.... [A]pplication of the DMCA to the Defendants' linking to web sites containing DeCSS is content-neutral because it is justified without regard to the speech component of the hyperlink. The linking prohibition applies whether or not the hyperlink contains any information, comprehensible to a human being, as to the Internet address of the web page being accessed. The linking prohibition is justified solely by the functional capability of the hyperlink.

... [T]he DMCA, as applied to the Defendants' linking, served substantial governmental interests and was unrelated to the suppression of free expression.... [S]trict liability for linking to web sites containing DeCSS would risk two impairments of free expression. Web site operators would be inhibited from displaying links to various web pages for fear that a linked page might contain DeCSS, and a prohibition on linking to a web site containing DeCSS would curtail access to whatever other information was contained at the accessed site.... [457] Mindful of the cautious approach to First Amendment claims involving computer technology..., we... reject the Appellants' contention that an intent to cause harm is required and that linking can be enjoined only under circumstances applicable to a print medium. ... [T]he injunction's linking prohibition validly regulates the Appellants' opportunity instantly to enable anyone anywhere to gain unauthorized access to copyrighted movies on DVDs.

At oral argument, we asked the Government whether its undoubted power to punish the distribution of obscene materials would permit an injunction prohibiting a newspaper from printing addresses of bookstore locations carrying such materials.... Like many analogies posited to illuminate legal issues, the bookstore analogy is helpful primarily in identifying characteristics that distinguish it from the context of the pending dispute. If a bookstore proprietor is knowingly selling obscene materials, the evil of distributing such materials can be prevented by injunctive relief against the unlawful distribution (and similar distribution by others can be deterred by punishment of the distributor). And if others publish the location of the bookstore, preventive relief against a distributor can be effective before any significant distribution of the prohibited materials has occurred. The digital world, however, creates a very different problem. If obscene materials are posted on one web site and other sites post hyperlinks to the first site, the materials are available for instantaneous worldwide distribution before any preventive measures can be effectively taken.

This reality obliges courts considering First Amendment claims in the context of the pending case to choose between two unattractive alternatives: either tolerate some impairment of communication in order [458] to permit Congress to prohibit decryption that may lawfully be prevented, or tolerate some decryption in order to avoid some impairment of communication. Although the parties dispute the extent of impairment of communication if the injunction is upheld and the extent of decryption if it is vacated, and differ on the availability and effectiveness of techniques for minimizing both consequences, the fundamental choice between impairing some communication and tolerating decryption cannot be entirely avoided.

In facing this choice, we are mindful that it is not for us to resolve the issues of public policy implicated by the choice we have identified. Those issues are for Congress. Our task is to determine whether the legislative solution adopted by Congress, as applied to the Appellants by the District Court's injunction, is consistent with the limitations of the First Amendment, and we are satisfied that it is.

...Asserting that fair use "is rooted in and required by both the Copyright Clause and the First Amendment," the Appellants contend that the DMCA, as applied by the District Court, unconstitutionally "eliminates fair use" of copyrighted materials. We reject this extravagant claim....

[W]e note that the Supreme Court has never held that fair use is constitutionally required, although some isolated statements in its opinions might arguably be enlisted for such a requirement.

...We need not explore the extent to which fair use might have constitutional protection, grounded on either the First Amendment or the Copyright Clause, because whatever validity a constitutional claim might have as to an application of the DMCA that impairs fair use of copyrighted materials, such matters are far beyond the [459] scope of this lawsuit.... [T]he Appellants have provided no support for their premise that fair use of DVD movies is constitutionally required to be made by copying the original work in its original format.... We know of no authority for the proposition that fair use, as protected by the Copyright Act, much less the Constitution, guarantees copying by the optimum method or in the identical format of the original. ... A film critic making fair use of a movie by quoting selected lines of dialogue has no constitutionally valid claim that the review (in print or on television) would be technologically superior if the reviewer had not been prevented from using a movie camera in the theater, nor has an art student a valid constitutional claim to fair use of a painting by photographing it in a museum. Fair use has never been held to be a guarantee of access to copyrighted material in order to copy it by the fair user's preferred technique or in the format of the original.... [460]

[T]he judgment is affirmed.

Access to Government

Advancing the people's right to know

Focal case:
Dept. of Justice v. Reporters Committee for Freedom of Press, 489 U.S. 749 (1989)

F undamental democratic theory holds that an informed polity is the key to self-governance. An informed polity, in turn, rests on broad public access to government information and unfettered citizen ability to oversee government processes and to hold government accountable for its actions. Government information also is a vital component of the political discussion revered under the First Amendment. Moreover, the transparency of government actions is therapeutic; the sunlight of openness cleanses government of malfeasance and abuse.[1]

Government transparency, however, is not without cost. Broad citizen access to government demands timely agency responsiveness to requests, requires certain types of record keeping, and dictates procedures that may delay decision-making and involve real financial and opportunity costs. Most individuals would accept that completely open government would threaten legitimate interests in personal privacy, effective law enforcement and national security. These are the crux of most access debates. Legal battles surround the proper balance between personal privacy or anti-terrorist initiatives, for example, and legitimate public concern with what information government has collected and what actions officials are taking in the name of the people.

The Constitution does not balance these countervailing interests. Indeed, neither the First Amendment[2] nor the common law provides a right of access to government records or meetings beyond a limited common law right of access to records about oneself and a right of access to criminal trials that have been open historically and in which openness serves a multiplicity of

---

[1] *See generally* Harold Cross, The People's Right to Know (1953).

[2] *See, e.g.,* Zemel v. Rusk, 381 U.S. 1 (1964); Kleindienst v. Mandel, 408 U.S. 753 (1972); Branzburg v. Hayes, 408 U.S. 665, 681(acknowledging some First Amendment interest in news gathering) (1972); Saxbe v. Washington Post, 417 U.S. 843 (1974); Houchins v. KQED, 438 U.S. 1, 8 (1978) (dismissing notion that press is critical fourth estate or "adjunct" of government); Pell v. Procunier, 417 U.S. 817 (1984). *See also* First National Bank of Boston v. Bellotti, 435 U.S. 765, 798-88, 901 (1978) (Burger, C.J., concurring) (finding no special status, privileges or rights of access for the institutional press).

laudatory purposes.[3] (See Chap. 18 for more information on open courts.) As Supreme Court Justice Potter Stewart once wrote, "The Constitution itself is neither a Freedom of Information Act nor an Official Secrets Act. The Constitution, in other words, establishes the contest, not its resolution."[4]

While the media may function as the eyes and ears of the citizenry, their function as the "fourth estate" watchdog of government is informal. Courts have refused to allow government to exclude journalists arbitrarily or discriminatorily from news locales and public records,[5] but journalists enjoy no special access privileges beyond those available to the public at large.[6] The Constitution not only fails to provide an affirmative right for journalists to gather news information from government agencies, it also fails to provide a defense or exemption for members of the press from prosecution under general laws that may hamper information gathering. Thus, as mentioned earlier, journalists are subject to prosecution for trespass, failure to obey an officer of the law, fraud, wiretapping, contempt, harassment or stalking if their news-gathering techniques become excessively zealous.[7]

Yet, citizens and journalists alike benefit from statutes that dictate broad public access to government records and meetings. In the 1950s, '60s and '70s, the federal government, the District of Columbia, and all 50 states enacted laws embodying a philosophical commitment to the broadest possible openness in government. These state laws vary greatly in detail and depth, as do the court applications and interpretations of those statutes. As a result, the law of access in the United States is one of the more complex areas of communication law. The Federal Freedom of Information Act and the Government in Sunshine Act, however, provided models for many state statutes, and understanding their provisions provides helpful insight into access issues generally.

THE FEDERAL FREEDOM OF INFORMATION ACT

Congress enacted the federal Freedom of Information Act in 1966[8] to prevent abuse of power by the executive branch of federal government by requiring it to disclose its deliberative processes and its decisions to the people. Similar laws were later adopted to extend these provisions of openness to the proliferating committees, boards, commissions and councils within the executive branch that proffer expert advice or administer specific areas.[9] These laws generally require information held by federal agencies to be available to the public unless the information falls within one of nine specific categories of exemptions.[10] Explicit congressional language and

---

[3] Richmond Newspapers v. Virginia, 448 U.S. 1 (1978).

[4] Potter Stewart, *Or of the Press*, 26 Hastings L. J. 631 (1975) (affirming special constitutional role of the press as an additional check on abuse of government power).

[5] *See* Borreca v. Fasi, 369 F. Supp. 906 (D. Haw. 1974); Ludtke v. Kuhn, 461 F. Supp. 86 (S.D. N.Y. 1978); CNN v. ABC, 518 F. Supp. 1238 (N.D. Ga. 1981) (enjoining White House from excluding broadcast journalist from pool coverage). But see Los Angeles Free Press v. Los Angeles, 88 Cal. Rptr. 605 (Cal. Ct. App. 1970).

[6] Branzburg at 684-85. *But see* Saxbe at 841 (Douglas, J., dissenting).

[7] *See, e.g.,* Food Lion v. Capital Cities/ABC, 194 F.3d 505 (4th Cir. 1999); Wolfson v. Lewis, 924 F. Supp. 1413 (E.D. Penn. 1996). *See also* Howard Troxler, Congress can't diminish freedom of press; neither can local judge, St. Petersburg Times (Dec. 16, 2002) (describing anti-stalking injunction imposed by local judge on reporter for filming and attempting to question a repeat DUI offender).

[8] 5 U.S.C. §§ 552 *et seq.*

[9] *See* Federal Advisory Committee Act, 5 U.S.C. App. 2 requiring advisory committees to make public all reports, records, or other documents used by the committee, provided they do not fall within any Freedom of Information Act exemptions but exempting from its purview advisory committees "composed wholly of full-time officers or employees of the Federal Government" 5 U.S.C. App. 2, § 3(2)(iii)); Administrative Procedure Act, 5 U.S.C. § 701 *et seq.*

[10] 5 U.S.C.A. § 552.

public policy establish openness as the "dominant objective"[11] of these laws, dictating a narrow reading of exemptions.

Individual federal agencies or Congress, however, may take steps that erode the broad presumption of openness in government. In January 2003, for example, a rule issued by the director of the newly created cabinet-level Department of Homeland Security eliminated public scrutiny of the department's classification process.[12] According to the interim final rule on Classified National Security Information, "[T]he department ... determined that notice and public procedure are impracticable, unnecessary and contrary to the public interest" in efficient and effective protection of national security. In addition, bills proposed in Congress in the spring of 2003 would remove virtually all reporting requirements from the Pentagon[13] and exempt from disclosure nearly all operational files of the National Security Agency.[14]

The access mandate of FOIA also is subject to interpretation by each administration. Shortly after the attacks on the Pentagon and the World Trade Center in September 2001, the Bush administration announced its policy to favor the safekeeping of information over disclosure. Attorney General John Ashcroft encouraged federal agencies to withhold records whenever a "sound legal basis" might justify secrecy. The new FOIA interpretation required record keepers to review all applicable FOIA exemptions and conduct a "full and deliberate consideration of the institutional, commercial and personal privacy interests that could be implicated" prior to any records disclosure.[15] In addition, the Justice Department said it would support any agency sued for withholding information except in the rare case when a lawsuit might jeopardize the government's ability to withhold additional information in the future.

A closer examination of FOIA will demonstrate how the inherent flexibility of statutory language permitted this shift away from the Clinton Administration's practice of disclosing information under FOIA absent a clear, "foreseeable harm."

DEFINITION OF FOIA PROVISIONS

Records

Public records generally are defined under FOIA as those records – regardless of their physical form – prepared, owned, used or kept by government agencies that document transactions of public business or that are necessary to conduct the agency's business. A record is any document, paper, letter, map, book, photograph, film, tape, data-processing record, artifact or other material.[16] All such records are subject to disclosure under FOIA, but agencies do not need to compile or create new records to respond to FOIA requests.

The Electronic Freedom of Information Act of 1996[17] expressly provides access to records held in digital form. Under this amendment to FOIA, any agency-held information, "in any format, including an electronic format,"[18] that is not otherwise exempt is a record subject to

---

[11] Dept. of Air Force v. Rose, 425 U.S. 352 (1976).

[12] Office of the Secretary, Homeland Security, Interim final rule on Classified National Security Information, 68:17 Fed. Reg., 6 C.F.R. Part 7, (Jan. 27, 2003) available at http://www.fas.org/sgp/news/2003/01/dhsnsi.html.

[13] *See* http://daniel.cornwall.home.att.net/DOD Reports Concern.html.

[14] *See* S. 747 § 933.

[15] New Attorney General FOIA Memorandum Issued available at www.usdoj.gov/oip/foiapost/2001foiapost19.htm.

[16] *See* Long v. IRS, 596 F.2d 362 (D.C. Cir. 1979).

[17] Pub. L. No. 104-231, 110 Stat. 3048, *amend'g* 5. U.S.C.§552.

[18] Electronic Freedom of Information Act Amendments of 1996, Pub. L. No. 104-231, § 3, 110 Stat. 3048 (1996).

disclosure under FOIA provisions.[19] In addition, E-FOIA assists requesters by mandating indexing of major records and information systems and by encouraging agencies to provide records in the format preferred by the requester when that format is readily available.[20] Indeed, E-FOIA encourages the creation and storage of government records in electronic formats because of the greater ease of searching records electronically.

Agency

FOIA does not apply to Congress or to the federal courts. The Constitution establishes that Congress can make its own rules about what sessions and records should be public, except that Congress is required to publish a "journal of its proceedings."[21] Both houses of Congress generally conduct business in the open – and under the watchful eye of C-SPAN – and conference meetings between the two houses, committee and subcommittee meetings of the Senate, and committee meetings of the House of Representatives are open unless the members expressly vote for closure.

Agencies covered by FOIA include all federal executive branch agencies (e.g., the FBI, the CIA, the National Security Council,[22] the Office of the President, the Office of Management and Budget, etc.) and all independent regulatory agencies (the Federal Communication Commission, the Federal Trade Commission, the Securities and Exchange Commission, etc.) with the exception of advisory agencies comprised entirely of government employees.[23] In 1996, The U.S. Court of Appeals for the District of Columbia Circuit established three factors to determine whether a group serving the president constituted an agency under FOIA. If the group 1) operates closely with or under the supervision of the president, 2) fails to exercise independent authority, and 3) has no autonomous structure, it is does not qualify as an agency. [24]

A case involving the determination of what constitutes an agency under federal access laws has been pending since the early days of the Bush Administration. In January 2001, President Bush established the National Energy Policy Development Group, headed by Vice President Dick Cheney, which issued a report recommending a set of energy policies "designed to help the private sector, and government at all levels, promote dependable, affordable and environmentally sound production and distribution of energy for the future."[25] A non-profit watchdog group sued to gain access to records of the group's meetings, arguing that the records were subject to disclosure because non-governmental employees participated in the deliberations.[26]

---

[19] *See* Armstrong v. Executive Office of the President, 1 F.3d 1274 (D.C. Cir. 1993).

[20] *See* TPS v. U.S. Dept. of Defense, 330 F.3d 1191 (9th Cir. 2003) (remanding for determination of whether a "zipped" files are "readily reproducible" by the agency and, therefore, must be provided to requester).

[21] U.S. Const. art I, § 5.

[22] *See* Armstrong v. Executive Office of the President, 877 F.Supp. 690 (1995); 897 F.Supp 10 (1995); 1 F. 3d 1274 (1993); 90 F.3d 553 (D.C. Cir. 1996); 97 F.3d 575 (1997). *See also* Energy Research Foundation v. Defense Nuclear Facilities Safety Board, 917 F.2d 581 (D.C. Cir. 1990) (finding nuclear safety board an agency covered by FOIA).

[23] *See* Rushforth v. Council of Economic Advisors, 762 F.2d 1038 (D.C. Cir. 1985) (excluding the Council of Economic Advisors from FOIA). *See also* National Security Archives v. U.S. Archivist, 909 F.2d 541 (D.C. Cir. 1990) (Office of Counsel to President purely advisory and not agency under FOIA).

[24] *See* Armstrong v. Executive Office of the President, 90 F.3d 553 (D.C. Cir. 1996).

[25] *See* Memorandum Establishing National Energy Policy Development Group (Jan. 29, 2001); NATIONAL ENERGY POLICY DEVELOPMENT GROUP, NATIONAL ENERGY POLICY: REPORT OF THE NATIONAL ENERGY POLICY DEVELOPMENT GROUP (2001), available at http://www.whitehouse.gov/energy/National- Energy-Policy.pdf.

[26] Judicial Watch v. National Energy Policy Development Group, 219 F. Supp. 2d 20 (D. D.C. 2002); 230 F. Supp. 2d 12 (D.D.C. 2002).

For two years, the administration argued that release of any information about the group was unwarranted because the group was purely advisory and membership was limited to government employees. The government also asserted that release of information, even to the court for review, would jeopardize executive privilege and cause irreparable harm to the president's ability to gather expert advice.[27] After several procedural battles, the U.S. Court of Appeals for the D.C. Circuit said that courts deciding which groups are exempt as purely advisory must "look beyond formal membership" and determine whether the "involvement and role" of consultants to the group "are functionally indistinguishable from those of the other members."[28] The court in July 2003 ordered Vice President Dick Cheney to provide the lower court with records on the membership and functioning of the energy task force to enable a decision on whether non-government officials were *de facto* members of the group.

Agency record

Records created, possessed and controlled by a federal executive branch agency are subject to FOIA.[29] Records in the physical possession of an agency tend to qualify as agency records if they relate to official business of the agency but not if the agency holds them inadvertently or without any relation to the agency's responsibilities and duties.[30] Records created but not held by covered agencies generally are not agency records under the law. Thus, data gathered and held by a federally funded private consultant is not "possessed" by the agency and is not subject to FOIA even if the agency develops federal policies from the consultant's report based on this data.[31] In addition, records created by an office subject to FOIA but transferred to and held by a FOIA-exempt organization are not agency records subject to disclosure.[32] In contrast, a government agency subject to FOIA must disclose records originated by the courts but possessed and controlled by the agency even if the records are also publicly available from the courts.[33]

Agency response

FOIA mandates prompt reply to requests that provide a "reasonable" description of the information sought. Prompt means an agency has 20 days to determine whether the material is exempt, except in "unusual circumstances." In addition, agencies must expedite requests from individuals who demonstrate an "urgen[t need] to inform the public concerning actual or alleged federal government activity"[34] or to protect against imminent harm to personal safety. Courts,

---

[27] In re Cheney, 2003 U.S. App. LEXIS 13702 (D.C. Cir. July 8, 2003) (dismissing Cheney request for writ of mandamus vacating lower court discovery order). *See* Henri. E. Cauvin, Court rejects bid to stop Cheney lawsuit, Washington Post (July 8, 2003) available at www.washingtonpost.com/wp-dyn/articles/A26381-2003Jul8.html?nav:hptop_tb

[28] In re Cheney, 2003 U.S. App. LEXIS 13702, *17-18 (D.C. Cir. July 8, 2003)

[29] *See* Missouri v. U.S. Dept. of Interior, 297 F.3d 745 (8th Cir. 2002) (records maintained by U.S. Fish and Wildlife Service employee acting as full-time coordinator of non-profit agency are not agency records).

[30] BNA v. Baxter, 742 F.2d 1848 (D.C. Cir. 1984) (phone memos and calendar notes are not agency records); Wolfe v. Dept. of Health and Human Services, 711 F.2d 1077 (D.C. Cir. 1983) (records physically held but not used by agency are not agency records).

[31] Forsham v. Harris, 445 U.S. 169 (1980) (finding data gathered by and held by an independent group to develop a government-funded report are not agency records).

[32] Kissinger v. Reporters Committee for Freedom of Press, 445 U.S. 136 (1980) (finding letters of former Sec. of State Henry Kissinger not agency records after their transferal to the Library of Congress).

[33] Dept. of Justice v. Tax Analysts, 492 U.S. 136 (1989) (records obtained and controlled by agency are agency record subject to disclosure), *contra* Dept. of Justice v. Reporters Committee for Freedom of Press, 489 U.S. 749 (1989) (rap sheet data available through local and state agencies not subject to FOIA disclosure from federal database). *See also* Forsham v. Harris, 445 U.S. 169 (1980). *But see* United States (In re Boston Herald) v. Connolly, 321 F.3d 174 (1st Cir. 2003) (denying access to personal financial records filed with the court).

[34] U.S.C.S. § 522 (a) (6) (E).

however, generally have tolerated lengthy delays in response to FOIA queries so long as the agency can demonstrate that it is acting with "due diligence" and that delays are neither intentional circumvention of the law nor motivated by ill will.

FOIA EXEMPTIONS

The nine exemptions to FOIA establish types of records that agencies are permitted, but not mandated, to withhold from the public. As discretionary guidelines, the nine exemptions are subject to different spin from different administrations, agencies and courts. The nine FOIA exemptions, often referred to by number, shield:

1. Protected national security and foreign intelligence information.
2. Internal agency rules and practices.
3. Statutorily exempted material.
4. Mandatory business disclosures of proprietary information.
5. Working papers, drafts, and inter- or intra-agency memos.
6. Private personal information in personnel, medical and similar files.
7. Sensitive law enforcement records.
8. Records of financial institutions.
9. Drilling information.

As outlined below, a variety of executive, legislative and judicial branch actions modify and clarify the application of FOIA's nine exemptions.

1. Protected national security and foreign intelligence information.[35]

Records in this area are expressly protected by executive orders of the president, who determines the standards for secrecy classification of federal records subject only to limited review by the courts.

In March 2002, Bush Chief of Staff Andrew Card issued a memo establishing the administration policy of placing priority on assuring the security, rather than the public availability, of government information.[36] The memo re-established a practice adopted by the Reagan Administration of excluding from public view information the government deems to be "sensitive but unclassified." The undefined term "sensitive" affords federal officials broad discretion to determine when information that does not meet national security classification standards but "that could be misused to harm the security of our nation and the safety of our people"[37] may be withheld from the public. Provisions of the Homeland Security Act of 2002 also establish express provisions protecting "sensitive" information about critical infrastructure in the United States.

In March 2003, President Bush issued Executive Order 13292[38] expanding the breadth and duration of national security classification but maintaining some sunset provisions that now

---

[35] *See, e.g.,* Homeland Security Act of 2002, Public Law 107-296, Freedom of Information Act, 5 U.S.C. § 552(b)(3) (2000) (establishing new exemption for critical infrastructure information held by the Dept. of Homeland Security).

[36] ANDREW H. CARD, JR., Assistant to the President and Chief of Staff, Memo: Action to Safeguard Information Regarding Weapons of Mass Destruction and Other Sensitive Documents Related to Homeland Security (March 19, 2002) available at http://www.fas.org/sgp/bush/wh031902.html. *See also* Homeland Security Act, Pub. L. No. 107-296, 116 Stat. 2135 §§ 891-93, 6 U.S.C. §§ 481-83 (requiring establishment of procedures to protect "sensitive but unclassified" information and to share it among government agencies for homeland security purposes).

[37] *Ibid.*

[38] 68 Fed. Reg. 15,315 (March 25, 2003).

trigger declassification after 25 years.[39] The new classification standard eliminates a presumption toward openness adopted by the Clinton administration[40] in order to "optimize the safeguarding" of information.[41]

2. Internal agency rules and practices.[42]

This exemption, sometimes called the "housekeeping" exclusion, shields from disclosure the voluminous material of little or no public concern generated by agencies to facilitate daily operations. Records related to routine matters of "merely internal significance," such as schedules for purchasing coffee for the communal coffee pot, are not subject to disclosure because the records are not of genuine public interest and requiring their disclosure would unduly burden agencies.[43] However, the exemption also permits law enforcement agencies to withhold certain portions of training manuals related to investigative procedures,[44] and Attorney General John Ashcroft encouraged use of this exemption to protect a diversity of information with "heightened sensitivity."[45]

3. Statutorily exempted material.

This exemption provides for the withholding of materials Congress expressly excludes from disclosure. For example, critical infrastructure information,[46] tax returns, census bureau records,[47] patent applications, some records of the U.S. Post Office, most information related to the CIA[48] and records of the National Security Agency all fall under statutory exemptions to disclosure.

Statutory exemptions proliferate, especially during a period of heightened concern for national security. As mentioned above, provisions of the Homeland Security Act exempt all critical infrastructure information voluntarily submitted to the Department of Homeland Security[49] from FOIA disclosure. The statute also preempts state and local access laws by requiring continued confidentiality of the information even when state or local laws would mandate that non-federal agencies disclose the records.[50] The law also imposes criminal sanctions

---

[39] *Ibid* at §§ 1.5 (b), 3.1 (e).

[40] Executive Order 12958 on Classified National Security Information (1995).

[41] *Ibid*. at § 5.4 (c). *See also* §§ 1.3 (d), 5.1 (a) (2).

[42] *See, e.g.,* Proposed rule, Freedom of Information Act and Privacy Act Requests: Removal of Rules, Bureau of Prisons, Department of Justice, 28 C.F.R. § 513 (D) (May 13, 2003) (proposing to eliminate prison rules and regulations regarding Privacy Act and Freedom of Information Act requests for information as repetitive and solely related to internal practice and procedure).

[43] *See* Dept. of Air Force v. Rose, 425 U.S. 352, 369-70 (1976).

[44] *See* Hardy v. Bureau of Alcohol, Tobacco and Firearms, 631 F. 2d 653 (D.C. Cir. 1980).

[45] New Attorney General FOIA Memorandum Issued available at www.usdoj.gov/oip/foiapost/2001foiapost19.htm. *See* Coastal Delivery, Corp. v. U.S. Customs Service, No. 02-3838 (C.D. Cal. 2003) (protecting the frequency of customs inspections of ports to prevent disclosure of more vulnerable locations).

[46] Homeland Security Act, Pub. L. No. 107-296, 116 Stat. 2135, §214, 6 U.S.C. §133 (prohibits disclosure of critical infrastructure information voluntarily submitted to the Office of Homeland Security). *See also* Procedures for Handling Critical Infrastructure Information; Proposed Rule, 68 Fed. Reb. 18,524 (April 15, 2003).

[47] *But see* Carter v. U.S. Dept. of Commerce, 2002 U.S. App. Lexis (9th Cir. Oct. 8, 2002) (finding adjusted 2000 census data must be released because they are not pre-decisional or deliberative and release would not reveal any protected process).

[48] 50 U.S.C.S. §§ 403g, 403-3 (c) (5). *See also* CIA v. Sims, 471 U.S. 159 (1985) (affirming confidentiality of participants in CIA drug tests under intelligence exemption)

[49] Pub. L. No. 107-296, 116 Stat. 2135, § 214(a)(1)(A) (to be codified at 6 U.S.C. § 133(a)(1)(A)).

[50] Pub. L. No. 107-296, 116 Stat. 2135, § 214(a)(1)(E)(i); *see also id.* at § 214(a)(1)(F) (guarding against "waiver of any applicable privilege or protection provided under law").

on federal employees who "knowingly . . . disclose" any protected critical infrastructure information.[51]

In addition, an executive order issued by President Bush late in 2001 effectively revised the Presidential Records Act to permit non-disclosure of records of legal advice and legal work for the president and communications between the president and his advisers.[52]

4. Mandatory business disclosures of proprietary information.

Trade secrets – which are defined as unpatented, proprietary formulas that result from significant investment or initiative and that contribute to producing a commercial product[53] – or commercial and financial information the government requires individuals or firms to submit for licensing, government contracts and statistical and other purposes may be withheld if the disclosure would cause competitive harm or undermine the government's ability to continue to gather such information.[54] Some businesses have protested government's mandatory disclosures of proprietary information because agencies have discretion to release the information under FOIA.[55] In response, Congress enacted the Trade Secrets Act to prohibit and punish government disclosure of trade secrets.[56] Under a 1988 executive order, agencies also must alert businesses when they receive requests for disclosure of proprietary or confidential information.[57]

5. Working papers, drafts, and inter- or intra-agency memos.

This exemption protects records related to the internal deliberative processes of agencies that do not shed light on or become part of final decisions, opinions or dispositions. The goal of this exemption is to encourage wide-open brainstorming by government without fear of publicity and criticism of offbeat ideas.[58] This provision does not exempt records of final decisions or pre-decision documents that explain, embody or elaborate the agency's policy basis after a decision is reached because such disclosures would not undermine creative thinking by the agency.[59] This provision allows agencies to withhold documents that are protected by executive privilege or by attorney-client privilege.[60] The exemption incorporates attorney-client privilege so litigants cannot use FOIA to gather information they could not obtain through the discovery process in a civil lawsuit.[61]

6. Private personal information in personnel, medical and similar files.

This protects from disclosure highly personal material in medical files or information in employment files – such as performance evaluations or disciplinary procedures – the release of

---

[51] Pub. L. No. 107-296, 116 Stat. 2135, § 214(f).

[52] *See* Executive Order 13233, Further Implementation of the Presidential Records Act of 1978, 66 Fed. Reg. 56,025 (2001) (Nov. 1, 2001).

[53] *See* Public Citizen Health Research Group v. Food and Drug Administration, 704 F.2d 180 (D.C. Cir. 1983).

[54] *See, e.g.,* Miami Herald v. Small Business Administration, 670 F.2d 65 (D.C. Cir. 1987).

[55] Chrysler Corp. v. Brown, 441 U.S. 281 (1979).

[56] 18 U.S.C.S. § 1905.

[57] Exec. Order No. 12, 600 (1988).

[58] *See* Russell v. Air Force, 682 F.2d 1045 (D.C. Cir. 1982).

[59] NLRB v. Sears, Roebuck & Co., 421 U.S. 132, 152-3 (1975) (distinguishing memos that do and do not fall under exemption 5 of FOIA).

[60] *See* Tax Analysts v. IRS, 294 F.3d 71 (D.C. Cir. 2002) (affirming non-disclosure of legal memoranda and certain technical assistance documents under attorney work-product privilege).

[61] *But see* Dept. of the Interior v. Klamath Water Users, 532 U.S. 1 (2001) (rejecting both attorney-client and consultant-client analogies to justify non-disclosure of records of communications between the Bureau of Indian Affairs and certain tribes).

which "would constitute a clearly unwarranted invasion of personal privacy."[62] It also keeps confidential social security numbers, personal finances and a wide array of personal information – including address and marital status – when that information is linked to specific individuals.[63] This exemption does not create a categorical shield for all information in these files.[64] Courts must determine the need to maintain the confidentiality of information based on *ad hoc* balancing between the public interest served by disclosure of information about the functioning of government and the privacy interest.[65]

7. Sensitive law enforcement records.

This is not a blanket exemption for all records related to law enforcement or even to ongoing investigations.[66] Rather, this exemption allows government to withhold records compiled for law enforcement purposes[67] when release would "reasonably" a) interfere with ongoing investigations or anticipated legal proceedings,[68] b) deprive an individual of a fair trial,[69] c) invade personal privacy,[70] d) reveal the identity of a source expressly promised confidentiality,[71] e) reveal sensitive law enforcement procedures,[72] or f) endanger someone's safety.[73] Government

---

[62] Dept. of Air Force v. Rose, 425 U.S. 352, 370-71 (1976).

[63] *See* Dept. of State v. Washington Post, 456 U.S. 595 (1982); U.S. Dept. of State v. Ray, 502 U.S. 164 (1991); Dept. of Defense v. Federal Labor Relations Authority, 510 U.S.487 (1994). *See also* Driver's Privacy Protection Act of 1994 , 18 U.S.C. §§ 2721-25 (prohibiting most disclosure of personal information in driver's licensing records without express permission of the individual).

[64] *See* 5 U.S.C.S. § 522 a (t) (establishing that disclosure provisions of FOIA take precedent over the non-disclosure presumptions in the federal Privacy Act of 1974 when the two conflict).

[65] *See* Dept. of Air Force v. Rose, 425 U.S. 352, 372 (1976); Dept. of Justice v. Reporters Committee for Freedom of Press, 489 U.S. 749 (1989); Dept. of Defense v. Federal Labor Relations Authority, 510 U.S. 487 (1994). *See also* Accuracy in Media v. Office of the Independent Counsel, 2003 U.S. App. LEXIS 7682 (D.C. Cir. Apr. 22, 2003) (maintaining secrecy of autopsy photo of former Deputy White House Counsel Vince Foster and rejecting claim that privacy interest is *de minimis*).

[66] *See* 20 U.S.C. § 1232 g (a) (4) (B) (ii) (establishing campus law enforcement records as public records *not* kept confidential by the Family Educational Rights and Privacy Act, 5. U.S.C.S. § 522 a (t)); 20 U.S.C. § 1092 (f) (requiring campuses to maintain a timely public log and to publish an annual statistical report of campus crime, subject only to non-disclosure of information that would violate provisions of FOIA exemption 7).

[67] *See* Tax Analysts v. IRS, 294 F.3d 71 (D.C. Cir. 2002) (finding IRS compiles information for law enforcement purposes).

[68] § 7(a). *See* Center for National Security Studies v. U.S. Dept. of Justice, 2003 U.S. App. LEXIS 11910 (D.C. Cir. 2003) (declaring broad deference to executive branch interpretation of FOIA exemptions 1 and 3 and upholding nondisclosure of identities of immigrants detained post 9/11 on grounds that disclosure would allow terrorists to create composite of and impede terrorist investigations).

[69] § 7(b).

[70] § 7(c). *See* Dept. of Justice v. Reporters Committee for Freedom of Press, 489 U.S. 749 (1989) (finding heightened privacy interest in federal computerized compilation of records and effectively limiting disclosures under FOIA to those that inform citizens about the functioning of government); Chicago v. U.S. Dept. of Treasury, 287 F.3d 628 (7th Cir. 2002) (affirming summary judgment that neither privacy nor law enforcement exemptions of FOIA permit non-disclosure of names and addresses in ATF gun-trafficking database), *cert. revoked, vacated and remanded*, 123 S. Ct. 1352 (2003). *See also* Center for National Security Studies v. U.S. Dept. of Justice, 2003 U.S. App. LEXIS 11910 (D.C. Cir. 2003); Accuracy in Media v. Office of the Independent Counsel, 2003 U.S. App. LEXIS 7682 (D.C. Cir. Apr. 22, 2003); Office of Independent Counsel v. Favish, 217 F.3d 1168 (9th Cir. 2000), *cert. grant'd* 123 S. Ct. 1928 (May 5, 2003) (whether personal privacy protection for graphic law enforcement photographs extends to the family of the deceased). *But see* Electronic Freedom of Information Act (re-establishing FOIA's purpose as providing access to government information for any purpose).

[71] § 7(d). *See* U.S. Dept. of Justice v. Landano, 508 U.S. 165 (1993).

[72] § 7(e).

concern for the highly sensitive nature of investigative procedures enables agencies to refuse to either confirm or deny the existence of records related to certain criminal investigations, informants, foreign intelligence, counterintelligence or terrorism. Information exempted under this provision may remain confidential even after it is shared with other units of government that use the information for non-law enforcement reasons.[74] Often, however, the key question in determining the application of this exemption is whether the information is *used* for law enforcement purposes.[75]

The Supreme Court granted *certiorari* and several media organizations filed friend of the court briefs in a challenge to the use of Exemption 7(c) to withhold photographs related to the death of White House staffer Vincent W. Foster, Jr.[76]

8. Records of financial institutions.

This exemption is designed to protect the stability of the banking system by avoiding dissemination of information that would undermine public faith in the system. It broadly exempts from disclosure financial reports, audits, and mandatory filing information provided to government by banks, credit unions, trust companies and other regulated financial institutions.

9. Drilling information.

Maps, descriptions and geological data related to the locations of natural resources such as oil, natural gas and water may be kept confidential.

THE APPLICATION OF FOIA

To avoid chilling public interest in obtaining government interest, the law does not require requesters to provide information about themselves or the reason for their requests.[77] Instead, "any person"[78] may make a request through FOIA to obtain government information "for any public or private use." In 2003, however, Congress amended FOIA to impose a restriction on certain requesters. As amended, the law prevents representatives of foreign governments from using FOIA to obtain records from federal agencies that have any relation to "an element of ... the intelligence community."[79]

Costs

When Congress enacted FOIA nearly 40 years ago to assist broad public access to government information, it provided no special appropriation to cover agency expenses associated with maintaining records or retrieving and delivering them to requesters. Instead, FOIA expenses are covered by the general operating funds of each agency and are subject to the pressures of shrinking budgets.[80] In 2003, Congress used its "power of the purse" to curtail some

---

[73] § 7(f). *See* Living Rivers v. U.S. Bureau of Reclamation, No. 2:02CV644 (D. Utah 2003) (finding flood maps below Hoover and Glen Canyon dams qualify as law enforcement records and permitting non-disclosure to prevent aiding terrorist attacks on these dams that would endanger lives).

[74] *See* FBI v. Abramson, 456 U.S. 615 (1982) (affirming White House nondisclosure of FBI enemies list).

[75] *See* John Doe Agency v. John Doe Corp., 493 U.S. 146 (1989).

[76] Office of Independent Counsel v. Favish, 123 S.Ct. 1928 (2003).

[77] *See* Dept. of Justice v. Reporters Committee for Freedom of Press, 489 U.S. 749 (1989).

[78] 5 U.S.C.S. § 552 (a) (3).

[79] *See* Intelligence Authorization Act for Fiscal Year 2003, Pub. L. No. 107-306, 116 Stat. 2383, § 312, 5. U.S.C.§ 552 (a) (3) (A), (E) (Supp. 1 2003).

[80] Note: The same is true at the state level, and absence of funding is sometimes used to justify non-responsiveness to requests. *See, e.g.,* comments of Jeff Stier, Public Records CLE, Lacey, Wash. (May 28, 2003).

FOIA disclosures by expressly prohibiting the Bureau of Alcohol, Tobacco and Firearms from using federal appropriations to fund FOIA activities.[81]

Congress has said public policy favoring and encouraging citizen access to government requires that government limit the costs passed on to FOIA users. Accordingly, agencies require only commercial users of FOIA to pay the full, actual costs of search, redaction and copying. Non-commercial users, media, schools and research institutions receive up to two hours of search time, redaction and 100 pages of records free. In addition, agencies may reduce or waive fees when they determine that disclosure is intended primarily to serve a public interest in government. While some agencies apply this fee waiver broadly to all media requests, others define fee categories very rigidly[82] and may refuse to fulfill FOIA queries while they engage in lengthy haggling over fee classifications.[83]

Remedies for denial or high fees

Individuals who wish to challenge denial of records, fee classifications or excessive fees may appeal the ruling through agency channels or file suit in federal district court. The courts generally conduct *in camera de novo* review even of classified documents to determine whether the records were properly withheld. However, especially in the case of classified records, courts tend to defer to the expertise of agency judgments. Individuals who win FOIA lawsuits may recoup attorney's fees and costs. In some cases of egregious conduct by a federal agency, a court may issue contempt citations against agency officials.

THE FEDERAL GOVERNMENT IN SUNSHINE ACT

The Government in Sunshine Act[84] adopted in 1976 and the Federal Advisory Committee Act of 1972 govern access to meetings of boards of federal government agencies and officials. Like FOIA, the Sunshine Act embodies a broad commitment to open meetings and a narrow interpretation of the act's ten areas of exemption. Under the law, the public "is entitled to the fullest practicable information" about the decision-making processes of covered agencies and those "authorized to act on behalf of the agency." However, the Sunshine Act covers only about fifty boards of administrative agencies or executive branch operations that have independent authority and are presided over by two or more people, where most members are appointed by the president and confirmed by the Senate. Notably, this includes the Federal Communications Commission and the Securities and Exchange Commission. The Federal Advisory Committee Act applies to citizen groups established by Congress, the president or an executive branch agency to advise the president or executive agencies.[85]

The law requires that groups provide public notice of meetings one week in advance (fifteen days in the case of advisory committees) and conduct business before the public unless any of the exceptions applies. Many laws prohibit informal communications about group business among members or with interested parties unless the communications are recorded and included in the

---

[81] H.J. Res. 2, § 644, Appropriation for Fiscal Year 2003. *See also* H.R. 2658, § 8124, Dept. of Defense Appropriation Act of 2004 (limiting access to information on the Terrorism Information Awareness program).

[82] *See* Judicial Watch v. U.S. Dept. of Justice, 2000 U.S. Dist. Lexis 19789, *11 (limiting the "news media" requester category to those with a firm plan and intent to publish information that "pertain[s] to a particular topic of current interest").

[83] Michael Ravnitzky, New Justice Department Definition of News Media for FOIA Fee Categorization, available from mikerav@mindspring.com.

[84] 90 Stat. 1241, 5 U.S.C.S. § 522b.

[85] *See* Assoc. of American physicians and Surveons v. Clinton, 997 F.2d 898 (D.C. Cir. 1993) (finding meetings of Clinton's task force on health care reform not subject to FACA because its head, Hillary Clinton, was considered a government employee).

public record. Groups covered by these laws must provide a specific reason and vote to close a meeting before excluding the public from sessions. Seven of the act's ten exemptions parallel those of FOIA: classified information, housekeeping discussions, areas exempted by statute, sensitive business records, private personal information, law enforcement investigations and banking reports. The remaining three exceptions permit closed meetings when boards discuss: formal reprimands or criminal accusations; litigation in which the agency is involved; and regulatory matters when disclosure might disrupt financial markets, undermine agency action or prompt financial speculation.

Individuals may challenge the closure of meetings or seek transcripts of closed sessions by filing suit in federal district court. Courts may enjoin boards from conducting business in private sessions and may award attorney's fees and court costs but do not levy fines against violators of open meetings statutes. On the other hand, those bringing "frivolous" suits under the law may be assessed the costs associated with the suit.

STATE AND LOCAL OPEN RECORDS AND OPEN MEETINGS STATUTES

Hundreds of statutes control access to records and meetings at the state and local levels. These laws share some general characteristics and often incorporate many of the provisions of federal access laws. However, state access laws are subject to nearly continuous amendment, and court interpretations reshape their meaning so that facially similar statutes may differ greatly in their application in different states. As they say, the devil is in the details, and the details of access and exclusion vary enormously from one state to another and even among localities within a given state.[86] Readers are encouraged to examine their local and state laws carefully and to use the following discussion mostly as an indicator of where those laws exceed or fail to meet norms across the country.

Strong access laws generally adopt a policy that meetings and records are presumptively open unless they fall into a specific category of exemption. Such laws also include strong statements of public policy in favor of openness to guide the application and interpretation of the law. Many state statutes include preambles or statements of intent and purpose that state explicitly that the access provisions of the law should be construed liberally and exemptions interpreted narrowly to provide the greatest possible public access to the functioning of government.

State laws on open records

Individuals with a legal interest in particular government actions generally have a common law right of access to the related records agencies are legally required to keep. In addition, all fifty states and the District of Columbia have enacted state laws mandating that local, county and state records be open to the public. State open records laws generally pertain to the records of executive and administrative agencies and of groups created by these agencies that expend public moneys or perform governmental functions. They do not apply to state legislatures or to the courts.

Some states enumerate the specific records that are public. More laws, however, require that all records related to public business that are made, received or possessed by a government agency must be public. Not all state laws cover records in every format. The vast majority of open records laws cover physical records, including audio and video tapes and computer disks, but many state laws do not expressly require disclosure of "records" created or transmitted electronically and stored only in computer memory. Increasingly, however, state laws consider

---

[86] *See generally* The Reporters Committee on Freedom of Press, Tapping Officials Secrets (offering a comparative survey of state open meetings and open records laws).

email exchanges among government employees to constitute public records, and a few states mandate public disclosure of government electronic databases. A few states also require agencies to compile an index of public records to facilitate access.

Access to records generally is open to anyone and does not require requestors to provide their name or the reason for the request. Some states, however, limit access to citizens and either require commercial users to identify themselves and pay heightened fees or reduce commercial access to certain types of records. Most states allow both informal and written requests and provide for copying of public records at cost.

Every state law includes some exemptions to public disclosure, and many laws follow the guidance of FOIA. In most states, scores of other laws create exceptions to augment the exemptions enumerated in the open records statute.[87] In some states, confidentiality is mandatory for exempt records; other state laws merely permit non-disclosure. Some state laws do not require agencies to give reasons for non-disclosure.

Penalties for violations of state open records laws rarely are stiff. A few states provide for payment of attorney's fees and costs to successful litigants, and a handful impose criminal sanctions on officials who knowingly or repeatedly violate the law.

State laws on open meetings

Careful statutory definitions of agencies covered by the law, meetings, and exceptions to openness reduce the possibility for government officials to knowingly or unintentionally exclude the public from important government processes. For example, some state access laws cover all meetings of any agency or board supported by public funds or performing a government function. Others define covered agencies much more narrowly or do not apply to advisory groups, quasi-governmental agencies or private organizations performing the functions of government, such as private prisons.

Open meetings laws ensure the greatest public access to the deliberative process – but may squelch networking by government employees – when they define meetings as gatherings of two or more members of a covered board discussing business related to the board regardless of the manner in which the discussion is conducted. In contrast, when meetings are defined as physical gatherings of a quorum of a board, consensus may be achieved outside public scrutiny through serial meetings of fewer members or through electronic meetings via the Internet. In addition, laws that cover all deliberations related to public business rather than merely the decision-making vote broadly protect the right of citizens to oversee, and possibly influence, government actions. Some laws expressly exempt social meetings from the law's purview, while others intentionally include social gatherings to prevent evasion of the law.

In addition to requiring boards and governmental bodies to conduct business in public, open meetings laws generally require public notification of meetings in advance to permit public attendance and participation.

Most state open meeting statutes allow cameras and broadcast equipment as well as the public, and most require the legislative to operate in the open. Laws in many states close parole hearings, jury deliberations and many juvenile sessions, and most states permit covered bodies to meet in closed executive sessions.

As with other exceptions to openness, well-drafted provisions for executive sessions narrowly define and carefully detail the conditions under which closed sessions may be held and clarify who may participate in such sessions. In general, a strong open meetings law will require

---

[87] *See, e.g.,* Attorney Training Committee, Office of the Attorney General of the State of Washington, Statutes Relating to Confidential or Privileged Documents, Information or Communications (April 2003) (offering a 39-page list of relevant state and federal statutory exceptions).

boards to state publicly the topics to be discussed and the exemption that permits closure. Discussion during closed sessions is limited to the stated topics. Strong laws also require boards to vote publicly to go into executive session before closure and to keep records of the business conducted during the closed session. Some laws require disclosure of these records after the reason for closure is no longer relevant or if closure is improper. Most open meetings laws also mandate that no official action be taken during the closed session, and they require boards to reconvene in public to reach a final decision on issues deliberated in private.

To be effective, state access laws should impose sanctions on violators. Laws that levy heavy fines or even jail terms on repeat violators,[88] that enjoin boards from future improper meetings, and that nullify actions taken during illegally closed sessions encourage greater compliance than do laws without such penalties, although these sanctions are rarely imposed.

ADDITIONAL CASE READINGS

This chapter provides but a summary of the expansive law of access. Reading the cases in the list below and the case that follows will provide additional detail about this complex and evolving area of the law. However, thorough understanding of the scope of access in your locality also requires a careful reading of the rulings of the state and federal courts in your region.

- *Center for National Security Studies v. U.S. Dept. of Justice*, 2003 U.S. App. LEXIS 11910 (D.C. Cir. 2003) (rejecting First Amendment, common law and FOIA challenge to nondisclosure of information about immigrants detained post 9/11).
- *TPS, Inc. v. U.S. Dept. of Defense*, 330 F.3d 1191 (9th Cir. 2003) (remanding to determine whether "zipped" files are part of business "as usual," requiring disclosure in that format upon FOIA request).
- *Chicago v. U.S. Dept. of Treasury*, 287 F.3d 628 (7th Cir. 2002), *cert. revoked, vacated and remanded*, 123 S. Ct. 1352 (2003) (affirming summary judgment that FOIA exemptions do not shield names and addresses in ATF gun-trafficking database).
- *Food Lion v. Capital Cities/ABC*, 194 F.3d 505 (4th Cir. 1999) (affirming finding of breach of loyalty and trespass but not fraud or unfair labor practices against media).
- *Dept. of Defense v. Federal Labor Relations Authority*, 510 U.S.487 (1994) (privacy act protects federal employee addresses from disclosure to labor unions).
- *U.S. Dept. of Justice v. Landano*, 508 U.S. 165 (1993) (rejecting assumption that all FBI information sources are confidential).
- *U.S. Dept. of State v. Ray*, 502 U.S. 164 (1991) (affirming that identities of returned Haitian nationals are exempt under FOIA).
- *John Doe Agency v. John Doe Corp.*, 493 U.S. 146 (1989) (finding FOIA exemption for law-enforcement records inapplicable to documents originally collected for non-law enforcement reasons).
- *Dept. of Justice v. Tax Analysts*, 492 U.S. 136 (1989) (copies of court decisions are agency records subject to disclosure under FOIA).
- *FBI v. Abramson*, 456 U.S. 615 (1982) (finding FOIA law enforcement exemption properly applies when FBI enemies list shared with White House for non-law enforcement purpose).
- *Dept. of State v. Washington Post*, 456 U.S. 595 (1982) (finding privacy exemption protects citizenship information of non-nationals).

---

[88] *See* Florida Stat. § 112.52 (providing for criminal penalties).

- *Forsham v. Harris*, 445 U.S. 169 (1980) (affirming that data gathered by and held by an independent group to develop a government-funded report do not constitute agency record).
- *Kissinger v. Reporters Committee for Freedom of Press*, 445 U.S. 136 (1980) (finding letters of former Sec. of State Henry Kissinger not agency records of Dept. of State and not withheld by agency after their transfer to the Library of Congress).
- *Chrysler Corp. v. Brown*, 441 U.S. 281 (1979) (finding no individual right of action to prevent agency disclosures under FOIA).
- *Dept. of Air Force v. Rose*, 425 U.S. 352 (1976) (affirming that summaries of disciplinary records of Air Force Academy not exempt under either personal privacy or internal records exclusions).
- *NLRB v. Sears, Roebuck & Co.*, 421 U.S. 132 (1975) (clarifying the application of the internal records exemption to FOIA).

The following questions will help focus your reading of the case below.

- How does this decision define a "record" for purposes of FOIA?
- What work, if any, is required of agency officials to produce a record in response to a FOIA request?
- What is the Court's concern with "compiled" records, and do you believe it is legitimate?
- Who enjoys "privacy" rights under FOIA, according to this decision?
- How does the Court define the privacy interests and the public interest in the information at issue in this case?
- Does the Court, as Justice Blackmun suggests, adopt a "bright line rule" and engage in "categorical balancing"? If so, what are the benefits and disadvantages of this approach?

U.S. Dept. of Justice v. Reporters Committee for Freedom of Press
489 U.S. 749
(1989)

PRIOR HISTORY: Certiorari to the United States Court of Appeals for the District of Columbia Circuit.

JUDGES: Stevens, J., delivered the opinion of the Court, in which Rehnquist, C.J., and White, Marshall, O'Connor, Scalia, and Kennedy, JJ., joined. Black-mun, J., filed an opinion concurring in the judgment, in which Brennan, J., joined.

OPINION: [751] JUSTICE STEVENS delivered the opinion of the Court.

[1A] The Federal Bureau of Investigation (FBI) has accumulated and maintains criminal identification records, sometimes referred to as "rap sheets," on over 24 million persons. The question presented by this case is whether the disclosure of the contents of such a file to a third party "could reasonably be expected to constitute an unwarranted invasion of personal privacy" within the meaning of the Freedom of Information Act (FOIA), 5 U. S. C. § 552(b)(7)(C) (1982 ed., Supp. V).

I. In 1924 Congress appropriated funds to enable the Department of Justice (Department) to establish a program to collect and preserve fingerprints and other criminal identification records. 43 Stat. 217. That statute authorized the Department to exchange such information with "officials of States, cities and other institutions." Ibid. Six years later Congress created the FBI's identification division, and gave it responsibility for "acquiring, collecting, classifying, and preserving criminal identification and other crime records and the exchanging of said criminal identification records with the duly authorized officials of governmental agencies, [752] of States, cities, and penal institutions." Ch. 455, 46 Stat. 554 (codified at 5 U. S. C. § 340 (1934 ed.)); see 28 U. S. C. § 534(a)(4) (providing for exchange of rap-sheet information among "authorized officials of the Federal Government, the States, cities, and penal and other institutions"). Rap sheets compiled pursuant to such authority contain certain descriptive information, such as date of birth and physical characteristics, as well as a history of arrests, charges, convictions, and incarcerations of the subject. Normally a rap sheet is preserved until its subject attains age 80. Because of the volume of rap sheets, they are sometimes incorrect or incomplete and sometimes contain information about other persons with similar names.

The local, state, and federal law enforcement agencies throughout the Nation that exchange rap-sheet data with the FBI do so on a voluntary basis. The principal use of the information is to assist in the detection and prosecution of offenders; it is also used by courts and corrections officials in connection with sentencing and parole decisions. As a matter of executive policy, the Department has generally treated rap sheets as confidential and, with certain exceptions, has restricted their use to governmental purposes. Consistent with the Department's basic policy of treating these records as confidential, Congress in 1957 amended the basic statute to provide that the FBI's exchange of rap-sheet information with any other agency is subject to cancellation "if dissemination is made outside the receiving departments or related agencies." 71 Stat. 61; see 28 U. S. C. § 534(b).

As a matter of Department policy, the FBI has made two exceptions to its general practice of prohibiting unofficial access to rap sheets. First, it allows the subject of a rap sheet to obtain a copy, see 28 CFR §§ 16.30-16.34 (1988); and second, it occasionally allows rap sheets to be used in the preparation of press releases and publicity designed to assist in the apprehension of wanted persons or fugitives. See § 20.33(a)(4).

[753] In addition, on three separate occasions Congress has expressly authorized the release of rap sheets for other limited purposes. In 1972 it provided for such release to officials of federally chartered or insured banking institutions and "if authorized by State statute and approved by the Attorney General, to officials of State and local governments for purposes of employment and licensing...." 86 Stat. 1115. In 1975, in an amendment to the Securities Exchange Act of 1934, Congress permitted the Attorney General to release rap sheets to self-regulatory organizations in the securities industry. See 15 U. S. C. § 78q(f)(2) (1982 ed., Supp V). And finally, in 1986 Congress authorized release of criminal-history information to licensees or applicants before the Nuclear Regulatory Commission. See 42 U. S. C. § 2169(a). These three targeted enactments – all adopted after the FOIA was passed in 1966 – are consistent with the view that Congress understood and did not disapprove the FBI's general policy of treating rap sheets as nonpublic documents.

Although much rap-sheet information is a matter of public record, the availability and dissemination of the actual rap sheet to the public is limited. Arrests, indictments, convictions, and sentences are public events that are usually documented in court records. In addition, if a person's entire criminal history transpired in a single jurisdiction, all of the contents of his or her rap sheet may be available upon request in that jurisdiction. That possibility, however, is present in only three States.[1] All of the other 47 States place substantial restrictions on the availability of criminal-history summaries even though individual events in those summaries are matters of public record. Moreover, even in Florida, Wisconsin, and Oklahoma, the publicly available [754] summaries may not include information about out-of-state arrests or convictions.[2]

II. The statute known as the FOIA is actually a part of the Administrative Procedure Act (APA). Section 3 of the APA as enacted in 1946 gave agencies broad discretion concerning the publication of governmental records.[3] In 1966 Congress amended that section to implement "'a general philosophy of full agency disclosure.'"[4] The amendment required agencies to publish their rules of procedure in the Federal Register, 5 U. S. C. § 552(a)(1)(C), and to make available for public inspection and copying their opinions, statements of policy, interpretations, and staff manuals and instructions that are not published in the Federal Register, § 552(a)(2). In addition, § 552(a)(3) requires every agency "upon any request for [755] records which . . . reasonably describes such records" to make such records "promptly available to any person."[5] If an agency improperly withholds any documents, the district court has jurisdiction to order their production. Unlike the review of other agency action that must be upheld if supported by substantial evidence and not arbitrary or capricious, the FOIA expressly places the burden "on the agency to sustain its action" and directs the district courts to "determine the matter de novo."[6]

Congress exempted nine categories of documents from the FOIA's broad disclosure requirements. Three of those exemptions are arguably relevant to this case. Exemption 3 applies to documents that are specifically exempted from disclosure by another statute. §552(b)(3). Exemption 6 protects "personnel and medical files and similar files the disclosure of which would constitute a clearly unwarranted invasion of personal privacy." §552(b)(6).[7] Exemption [756] 7(C) excludes records or information compiled for law enforcement purposes, "but only to the extent that the production of such [materials] . . . could reasonably be expected to constitute an unwarranted invasion of personal privacy." § 552(b)(7)(C).

[2A] Exemption 7(C)'s privacy language is broader than the comparable language in Exemption 6 in two respects. First, whereas

---

[1] See Fla. Stat. § 943.053(3) (1987); Wis. Stat. § 19.35 (1987-1988); and Okla. Stat., Tit. 51, § 24A.8 (Supp. 1988).

[2] The brief filed on behalf of Search Group, Inc., and other amici curiae contains the following summary description of the dissemination policies in 47 States:

"Conviction data, although generally unavailable to the public, is often available to governmental non-criminal justice agencies and even private employers. In general, conviction data is far more available outside the criminal justice system than is non-conviction data. By contrast, in all 47 states non-conviction data cannot be disclosed at all for non-criminal justice purposes, or may be disclosed only in narrowly defined circumstances, for specified purposes." Brief for Search Group, Inc., et al. as amici curiae 40 (footnotes omitted); see also Brief for Petitioner 27, n. 13. A number of States, while requiring disclosure of police blotters and event-based information, deny the public access to personal arrest data such as rap sheets. See Houston Chronicle Publishing Co. v. Houston, 531 S. W. 2d 177 (Tex. Civ. App. 1975), aff'd, 536 S. W. 2d 559 (Tex. 1976); Stephens v. Van Arsdale, 227 Kan. 676, 608 P. 2d 972 (1980).

[3] "The section was plagued with vague phrases, such as that exempting from disclosure 'any function of the United States requiring secrecy in the public interest.' Moreover, even 'matters of official record' were only to be made available to 'persons properly and directly concerned' with the information. And the section provided no remedy for wrongful withholding of information." EPA v. Mink, 410 U.S. 73, 79 (1973).

[4] Department of Air Force v. Rose, 425 U.S. 352, 360 (1976) (quoting S. Rep. No. 813, 89th Cong., 1st Sess., 3 (1965)).

[5] Title 5 U. S. C. § 552(a)(3) provides:
"Except with respect to the records made available under paragraphs (1) and (2) of this subsection, each agency, upon any request for records which (A) reasonably describes such records and (B) is made in accordance with published rules stating the time, place, fees (if any), and procedures to be followed, shall make the records promptly available to any person."

[6] Section 552(a)(4)(B) provides:
"(B) On complaint, the district court . . . has jurisdiction to enjoin the agency from withholding agency records and to order the production of any agency records improperly withheld from the complainant. In such a case the court shall determine the matter de novo, and may examine the contents of such agency records in camera to determine whether such records or any part thereof shall be withheld under any of the exemptions set forth in subsection (b) of this section, and the burden is on the agency to sustain its action."

[7] Congress employed similar language earlier in the statute to authorize an agency to delete identifying details that might otherwise offend an individual's privacy:
"To the extent required to prevent a clearly unwarranted invasion of personal privacy, an agency may delete identifying details when it makes available or publishes an opinion, statement of policy, interpretation, or staff manual or instruction." § 552(a)(2).

Exemption 6 requires that the invasion of privacy be "clearly unwarranted," the adverb "clearly" is omitted from Exemption 7(C). This omission is the product of a 1974 amendment adopted in response to concerns expressed by the President.[8] Second, whereas Exemption 6 refers to disclosures that "would constitute" an invasion of privacy, Exemption 7(C) encompasses any disclosure that "could reasonably be expected to constitute" such an invasion. This difference is also the product of a specific amendment.[9] Thus, the standard for evaluating a threatened invasion of privacy interests resulting from the disclosure of records compiled for law enforcement purposes is somewhat broader than the standard applicable to personnel, medical, and similar files. [757]

III. [2B] This case arises out of requests made by a CBS news correspondent and the Reporters Committee for Freedom of the Press (respondents) for information concerning the criminal records of four members of the Medico family. The Pennsylvania Crime Commission had identified the family's company, Medico Industries, as a legitimate business dominated by organized crime figures. Moreover, the company allegedly had obtained a number of defense contracts as a result of an improper arrangement with a corrupt Congressman.

The FOIA requests sought disclosure of any arrests, indictments, acquittals, convictions, and sentences of any of the four Medicos. Although the FBI originally denied the requests, it provided the requested data concerning three of the Medicos after their deaths. In their complaint in the District Court, respondents sought the rap sheet for the fourth, Charles Medico (Medico), insofar as it contained "matters of public record." App. 33.

The parties filed cross-motions for summary judgment. Respondents urged that any information regarding "a record of bribery, embezzlement or

other financial crime" would potentially be a matter of special public interest. Id., at 97. In answer to that argument, the Department advised respondents and the District Court that it had no record of any financial crimes concerning Medico, but the Department continued to refuse to confirm or deny whether it had any information concerning nonfinancial crimes. Thus, the issue was narrowed to Medico's nonfinancial-crime history insofar as it is a matter of public record.

The District Court granted the Department's motion for summary judgment, relying on three separate grounds. First, it concluded that 28 U. S. C. § 534, the statute that authorizes the exchange of rap-sheet information with other official agencies, also prohibits the release of such information to members of the public, and therefore that Exemption 3 [758] was applicable.[10] Second, it decided that files containing rap sheets were included within the category of "personnel and medical files and similar files the disclosure of which would constitute an unwarranted invasion of privacy," and therefore that Exemption 6 was applicable. The term "similar files" applied because rap-sheet information "is personal to the individual named therein." App. to Pet. for Cert. 56a. After balancing Medico's privacy interest against the public interest in disclosure, the District Court concluded that the invasion of privacy was "clearly unwarranted."[11] Finally, the court held that

---

[8] See 120 Cong. Rec. 33158-33159 and 34162-34163 (1974).
[9] See 132 Cong. Rec. 27189 and 31414-31415 (1986). Although the move from the "would constitute" standard to the "could reasonably be expected to constitute" standard represents a considered congressional effort "to ease considerably a Federal law enforcement agency's burden in invoking [Exemption 7]," id., at 31424, there is no indication that the shift was intended to eliminate de novo review in favor of agency deference in Exemption 7(C) cases. Rather, although district courts still operate under the general de novo review standard of 5 U. S. C. § 552(a)(4)(B), in determining the impact on personal privacy from disclosure of law enforcement records or information, the stricter standard of whether such disclosure "would" constitute an unwarranted invasion of such privacy gives way to the more flexible standard of whether such disclosure "could reasonably be expected to" constitute such an invasion.

[10] "The duty to compile such records is set forth in 28 U. S. C. § 534. That section provides that the Attorney General is to 'acquire, collect, classify, and preserve identification, criminal identification, crime and other records' and that he is to 'exchange these records with, and for the official use of, authorized officials of the Federal Government, the States, cities, and penal and other institutions.' Significantly, however, the section goes on to provide that '[t]he exchange of records authorized by [the section] is subject to cancellation if dissemination is made outside the receiving departments or related agencies.' Section 534(b). "This Court is satisfied that pursuant to the above section, the information acquired and collected by the Attorney General may be released only to the agencies, organizations or states set forth in that section, and may not be released to the general public. Thus, the information is '[s]pecifically exempted from disclosure by statute [28 U. S. C. § 534]' which 'requires that the matters be withheld from the public in such a manner as to leave no discretion on the issue.' The Court therefore concludes that if the defendants have collected and maintained a rap sheet related to Charles Medico, that rap sheet is exempt from disclosure pursuant to Exemption 3." App. to Pet. for Cert. 55a.

[11] "It seems highly unlikely that information about offenses which may have occurred 30 or 40 years ago, as in the case of William Medico, would have any relevance or public interest. The same can be said for information relating to the arrest or conviction of persons for minor criminal offenses or offenses which are completely unrelated to anything now under consideration by the plaintiffs. That

the rap sheet was also protected by Exemption [759] 7(C), but it ordered the Department to file a statement containing the requested data in camera to give it an opportunity to reconsider the issue if, after reviewing that statement, such action seemed appropriate. After the Department made that filing, the District Court advised the parties that it would not reconsider the matter, but it did seal the in camera submission and make it part of the record on appeal.

The Court of Appeals reversed. 259 U. S. App. D. C. 426, 816 F. 2d 730 (1987). It held that an individual's privacy interest in criminal-history information that is a matter of public record was minimal at best. Noting the absence of any statutory standards by which to judge the public interest in disclosure, the Court of Appeals concluded that it should be bound by the state and local determinations that such information should be made available to the general public. Accordingly, it held that Exemptions 6 and 7(C) were inapplicable. It also agreed with respondents that Exemption 3 did not apply because 28 U. S. C. § 534 did not qualify as a statute "specifically" exempting rap sheets from disclosure.

In response to rehearing petitions advising the court that, contrary to its original understanding, most States had adopted policies of refusing to provide members of the public with criminal-history summaries, the Court of Appeals modified its holding. 265 U. S. App. D. C. 365, 831 F. 2d 1124 (1987). With regard to the public interest side of the balance, the court now recognized that it could not rely upon state policies of disclosure. However, it adhered to its view that federal judges are not in a position to make "idiosyncratic" evaluations of the public interest in particular disclosures, see 259 U. S. App. D. C., at 437, 816 F. 2d, at 741; instead, it directed district courts to consider "the general disclosure policies of the statute." 265 U. S. App. D. C., at 367, 831 F. 2d, at 1126. With regard to the privacy interest in nondisclosure of rap sheets, the court told the District Court "only to make a factual determination in these kinds of [760] cases: Has a legitimate privacy interest of the subject in his rap sheets faded because they appear on the public record?" Id., at 368, 831 F. 2d, at 1127. In accordance with its initial opinion, it remanded the case to the District Court to determine whether the

withheld information is publicly available at its source, and if so, whether the Department might satisfy its statutory obligation by referring respondents to the enforcement agency or agencies that had provided the original information.

Although he had concurred in the Court of Appeals' original disposition, Judge Starr dissented, expressing disagreement with the majority on three points. First, he rejected the argument that there is no privacy interest in "cumulative, indexed, computerized" data simply because the underlying information is on record at local courthouses or police stations:

"As I see it, computerized data banks of the sort involved here present issues considerably more difficult than, and certainly very different from, a case involving the source records themselves. This conclusion is buttressed by what I now know to be the host of state laws requiring that cumulative, indexed criminal history information be kept confidential, as well as by general Congressional indications of concern about the privacy implications of computerized data banks. See H. R. Rep. No. 1416, 93d Cong., 2d Sess. 3, 6-9 (1974), reprinted in Legislative History of the Privacy Act of 1974, Source Book on Privacy, 296, 299-302 (1974)." Id., at 369, 831 F. 2d, at 1128.

Second, Judge Starr concluded that the statute required the District Court to make a separate evaluation of the public interest in disclosure depending upon the kind of use that would be made of the information and the identity of the subject:

[761] "Although there may be no public interest in disclosure of the FBI rap sheet of one's otherwise inconspicuously anonymous next-door neighbor, there may be a significant public interest – one that overcomes the substantial privacy interest at stake – in the rap sheet of a public figure or an official holding high governmental office. For guidance in fleshing out that analysis, it seems sensible to me to draw upon the substantial body of defamation law dealing with 'public personages.'" Id., at 370, 831 F. 2d, at 1129.

[3A] Finally, he questioned the feasibility of requiring the Department to determine the availability of the requested material at its source, and expressed concern that the majority's approach departed from the original purpose of the FOIA and threatened to convert the Federal Government into a clearinghouse for personal information that had been collected about millions of persons under a variety of different situations:

"We are now informed that many federal agencies collect items of information on individuals that are ostensibly matters of public record. For example, Veterans Administration and Social Security records include birth certificates, marriage licenses, and divorce decrees (which may

---

information is personal to the third party (Charles Medico), and it if [sic] exists, its release would constitute 'a clearly unwarranted invasion of personal privacy.' The Court concludes therefore that those documents and that information are exempt from disclosure pursuant to 5 U. S. C. § 552(b)(6) and (7)(C)." Id., at 57a.

recite findings of fault); the Department of Housing and Urban Development maintains data on millions of home mortgages that are presumably 'public records' at county clerks' offices. . . . Under the majority's approach, in the absence of state confidentiality laws, there would appear to be a virtual per se rule requiring all such information to be released. The federal government is thereby transformed in one fell swoop into the clearinghouse for highly personal information, releasing records on any person, to any requester, for any purpose. This Congress did not intend." Id., at 371, 831 F. 2d, at 1130 (emphasis in original).

[762] The Court of Appeals denied rehearing en banc, with four judges dissenting. App. to Pet. for Cert. 64a-66a. Because of the potential effect of the Court of Appeals' opinion on values of personal privacy, we granted certiorari. 485 U.S. 1005 (1988). We now reverse.[12]

IV. [3B][4A] Exemption 7(C) requires us to balance the privacy interest in maintaining, as the Government puts it, the "practical obscurity" of the rap sheets against the public interest in their release.

[5A] [6A] The preliminary question is whether Medico's interest in the nondisclosure of any rap sheet the FBI might have on him is the sort of "personal privacy" interest that Congress intended Exemption 7(C) to protect.[13] As we have pointed out before, "[t]he cases sometimes characterized as protecting 'privacy' have in fact involved at least two different kinds of interests. One is the individual interest in avoiding disclosure of personal matters, and another is the interest in independence in making certain kinds of important decisions." Whalen v. Roe, 429 U.S. 589, 598-600 (1977) (footnotes omitted). Here, the former interest, "in avoiding disclosure of personal matters," is implicated. Because events summarized in a rap sheet have been previously disclosed to the public, respondents contend that Medico's privacy interest in avoiding disclosure of a federal compilation of these events [763] approaches zero. We reject respondents' cramped notion of personal privacy.

---

[12] Because Exemption 7(C) covers this case, there is no occasion to address the application of Exemption 6.

[13] The question of the statutory meaning of privacy under the FOIA is, of course, not the same as the question whether a tort action might lie for invasion of privacy or the question whether an individual's interest in privacy is protected by the Constitution. See, e.g., Cox Broadcasting Corp. v. Cohn, 420 U.S. 469 (1975) (Constitution prohibits State from penalizing publication of name of deceased rape victim obtained from public records); Paul v. Davis, 424 U.S. 693, 712-714 (1976) (no constitutional privacy right affected by publication of name of arrested but untried shoplifter).

[6B] [5B] [7] To begin with, both the common law and the literal understandings of privacy encompass the individual's control of information concerning his or her person. In an organized society, there are few facts that are not at one time or another divulged to another.[14] Thus the extent of the protection accorded a privacy right at common law rested in part on the degree of dissemination of the allegedly private fact and the extent to which the passage of time rendered it private.[15] According to Webster's initial definition, information may be classified as "private" if it is "intended for or restricted to [764] the use of a particular person or group or class of persons: not freely available to the public."[16]

---

[14] See Karst, "The Files": Legal Controls Over the Accuracy and Accessibility of Stored Personal Data, 31 Law & Contemp. Prob. 342, 343-344 (1966) ("Hardly anyone in our society can keep altogether secret very many facts about himself. Almost every such fact, however personal or sensitive, is known to someone else. Meaningful discussion of privacy, therefore, requires the recognition that ordinarily we deal not with an interest in total nondisclosure but with an interest in selective disclosure").

[15] See Warren & Brandeis, The Right to Privacy, 4 Harv. L. Rev. 193, 198 (1890-1891) ("The common law secures to each individual the right of determining, ordinarily, to what extent his thoughts, sentiments, and emotions shall be communicated to others. . . . [E]ven if he has chosen to give them expression, he generally retains the power to fix the limits of the publicity which shall be given them"). The common law recognized that one did not necessarily forfeit a privacy interest in matters made part of the public record, albeit the privacy interest was diminished and another who obtained the facts from the public record might be privileged to publish it. See Cox Broadcasting Corp. v. Cohn, 420 U.S., at 494-495 ("[T]he interests in privacy fade when the information involved already appears on the public record") (emphasis supplied). See also Restatement (Second) of Torts § 652D, pp. 385-386 (1977) ("[T]here is no liability for giving publicity to facts about the plaintiff's life that are matters of public record, such as the date of his birth . . . . On the other hand, if the record is not open to public inspection, as in the case of income tax returns, it is not public and there is an invasion of privacy when it is made so"); W. Keeton, D. Dobbs, R. Keeton, & D. Owens, Prosser & Keeton on Law of Torts § 117, p. 859 (5th ed. 1984) ("[M]erely because [a fact] can be found in a public recor[d] does not mean that it should receive widespread publicity if it does not involve a matter of public concern").

[16] See Webster's Third New International Dictionary 1804 (1976). See also A. Breckenridge, The Right to Privacy 1 (1970) ("Privacy, in my view, is the rightful claim of the individual to determine the extent to which he wishes to share of himself with others. . . . It is also the individual's right to control dissemination of information about himself"); A. Westin, Privacy and Freedom 7 (1967) ("Privacy is the claim of individuals . . . to determine for themselves when, how, and to what extent information about them is communicated to others"); Project, Government Information and the Rights of Citizens, 73 Mich. L. Rev. 971, 1225 (1974-1975) ("[T]he right of privacy

Recognition of this attribute of a privacy interest supports the distinction, in terms of personal privacy, between scattered disclosure of the bits of information contained in a rap sheet and revelation of the rap sheet as a whole. The very fact that federal funds have been spent to prepare, index, and maintain these criminal-history files demonstrates that the individual items of information in the summaries would not otherwise be "freely available" either to the officials who have access to the underlying files or to the general public. Indeed, if the summaries were "freely available," there would be no reason to invoke the FOIA to obtain access to the information they contain. Granted, in many contexts the fact that information is not freely available is no reason to exempt that information from a statute generally requiring its dissemination. But the issue here is whether the compilation of otherwise hard-to-obtain information alters the privacy interest implicated by disclosure of that information. Plainly there is a vast difference between the public records that might be found after a diligent search of courthouse files, county archives, and local police stations throughout the country and a computerized summary located in a single clearinghouse of information.

[5C] This conclusion is supported by the web of federal statutory and regulatory provisions that limits the disclosure of [765] rap-sheet information. That is, Congress has authorized rap-sheet dissemination to banks, local licensing officials, the securities industry, the nuclear-power industry, and other law enforcement agencies. See supra, at 752-753. Further, the FBI has permitted such disclosure to the subject of the rap sheet and, more generally, to assist in the apprehension of wanted persons or fugitives. See supra, at 752. Finally, the FBI's exchange of rap-sheet information "is subject to cancellation if dissemination is made outside the receiving departments or related agencies." 28 U. S. C. §534(b). This careful and limited pattern of authorized rap-sheet disclosure fits the dictionary definition of privacy as involving a restriction of information "to the use of a particular person or group or class of persons." Moreover, although perhaps not specific enough to constitute a statutory exemption under FOIA Exemption 3, 5 U. S. C. § 552(b)(3),[17] these statutes and regulations, taken as a whole, evidence a congressional intent to

protect the privacy of rap-sheet subjects, and a concomitant recognition of the power of compilations to affect personal privacy that outstrips the combined power of the bits of information contained within.

Other portions of the FOIA itself bolster the conclusion that disclosure of records regarding private citizens, identifiable by name, is not what the framers of the FOIA had in mind. Specifically, the FOIA provides that "[t]o the extent required to prevent a clearly unwarranted invasion of personal privacy, an agency may delete identifying details when it makes available or publishes an opinion, statement of policy, interpretation, or staff manual or instruction." 5 U. S. C. §552(a)(2). Additionally, the FOIA assures that "[a]ny reasonably segregable portion of a record shall be provided to any person requesting such record after deletion of the portions which are exempt under [§ (b)]." 5 U. S. C. [766] § 552(b) (1982 ed., Supp. V). These provisions, for deletion of identifying references and disclosure of segregable portions of records with exempt information deleted, reflect a congressional understanding that disclosure of records containing personal details about private citizens can infringe significant privacy interests.[18]

Also supporting our conclusion that a strong privacy interest inheres in the nondisclosure of compiled computerized information is the Privacy Act of 1974, codified at 5 U. S. C. § 552a (1982 ed. and Supp. V). The Privacy Act was passed largely out of concern over "the impact of computer data banks on individual privacy." H. R. Rep. No.

---

is the right to control the flow of information concerning the details of one's individuality").

[17] The Court of Appeals reversed the District Court's holding in favor of petitioners on the Exemption 3 issue, and petitioners do not renew their Exemption 3 argument before this Court. See Pet. for Cert. 6, n. 1.

[18] See S. Rep. No. 813, 89th Cong., 1st Sess., 7 (1965) ("The authority to delete identifying details after written justification is necessary in order to be able to balance the public's right to know with the private citizen's right to be secure in his personal affairs which have no bearing or effect on the general public. For example, it may be pertinent to know that unseasonably harsh weather has caused an increase in public relief costs; but it is not necessary that the identity of any person so affected be made public"); H. R. Rep. No. 1497, 89th Cong., 2d Sess., 8 (1966) ("The public has a need to know, for example, the details of an agency opinion or statement of policy on an income tax matter, but there is no need to identify the individuals involved in a tax matter if the identification has no bearing or effect on the general public"). Both public relief and income tax assessments – like law enforcement – are proper subjects of public concern. But just as the identity of the individuals given public relief or involved in tax matters is irrelevant to the public's understanding of the Government's operation, so too is the identity of individuals who are the subjects of rap sheets irrelevant to the public's understanding of the system of law enforcement. For rap sheets reveal only the dry, chronological, personal history of individuals who have had brushes with the law, and tell us nothing about matters of substantive law enforcement policy that are properly the subject of public concern.

93-1416, p. 7 (1974). The Privacy Act provides generally that "[n]o agency shall disclose any record which is contained in a system of records . . . except pursuant to a written request by, or with the prior written consent of, the individual to whom the record pertains." 5 U. S. C. § 552a(b) (1982 ed., Supp. V). Although the Privacy Act contains a variety of exceptions [767] to this rule, including an exemption for information required to be disclosed under the FOIA, see 5 U. S. C. §552a(b)(2), Congress' basic policy concern regarding the implications of computerized data banks for personal privacy is certainly relevant in our consideration of the privacy interest affected by dissemination of rap sheets from the FBI computer.

[8] Given this level of federal concern over centralized data bases, the fact that most States deny the general public access to their criminal-history summaries should not be surprising. As we have pointed out, see supra, at 753, and n. 2, in 47 States nonconviction data from criminal-history summaries are not available at all, and even conviction data are "generally unavailable to the public." See n. 2, supra. State policies, of course, do not determine the meaning of a federal statute, but they provide evidence that the law enforcement profession generally assumes – as has the Department of Justice – that individual subjects have a significant privacy interest in their criminal histories. It is reasonable to presume that Congress legislated with an understanding of this professional point of view.

In addition to the common-law and dictionary understandings, the basic difference between scattered bits of criminal history and a federal compilation, federal statutory provisions, and state policies, our cases have also recognized the privacy interest inherent in the nondisclosure of certain information even where the information may have been at one time public. Most apposite for present purposes is our decision in Department of Air Force v. Rose, 425 U.S. 352 (1976). New York University law students sought Air Force Academy Honor and Ethics Code case summaries for a law review project on military discipline. The Academy had already publicly posted these summaries on 40 squadron bulletin boards, usually with identifying names redacted (names were posted for cadets who were found guilty and who left the Academy), and with instructions that cadets should read [768] the summaries only if necessary.

Although the opinion dealt with Exemption 6's exception for "personnel and medical files and similar files the disclosure of which would constitute a clearly unwarranted invasion of personal privacy," and our opinion today deals with Exemption 7(C), much of our discussion in Rose is applicable here. We explained that the

FOIA permits release of a segregable portion of a record with other portions deleted, and that in camera inspection was proper to determine whether parts of a record could be released while keeping other parts secret. See id., at 373-377; 5 U. S. C. §§ 552(b) and (a)(4)(B) (1982 ed. and Supp. V). We emphasized the FOIA's segregability and in camera provisions in order to explain that the case summaries, with identifying names redacted, were generally disclosable. We then offered guidance to lower courts in determining whether disclosure of all or part of such case summaries would constitute a "clearly unwarranted invasion of personal privacy" under Exemption 6:

"Respondents sought only such disclosure as was consistent with[the Academy tradition of keeping identities confidential within the Academy]. Their request for access to summaries 'with personal references or other identifying information deleted,' respected the confidentiality interests embodied in Exemption 6. As the Court of Appeals recognized, however, what constitutes identifying information regarding a subject cadet must be weighed not only from the viewpoint of the public, but also from the vantage of those who would have been familiar, as fellow cadets or Academy staff, with other aspects of his career at the Academy. Despite the summaries' distribution within the Academy, many of this group with earlier access to summaries may never have identified a particular cadet, or may have wholly forgotten his encounter with Academy discipline. And the risk to the privacy interests of a former cadet, particularly one who has remained in the military, posed by his [769] identification by otherwise unknowing former colleagues or instructors cannot be rejected as trivial.

We nevertheless conclude that consideration of the policies underlying the Freedom of Information Act, to open public business to public view when no 'clearly unwarranted' invasion of privacy will result, requires affirmance of the holding of the Court of Appeals . . . that although 'no one can guarantee that all those who are "in the know" will hold their tongues, particularly years later when time may have eroded the fabric of cadet loyalty,' it sufficed to protect privacy at this stage in these proceedings by enjoining the District Court . . . that if in its opinion deletion of personal references and other identifying information 'is not sufficient to safeguard privacy, then the summaries should not be disclosed to [respondents].'" 425 U.S., at 380-381. See also id., at 387-388 (Blackmun, J., dissenting); id., at 389-390 (Rehnquist, J., dissenting).

In this passage we doubly stressed the importance of the privacy interest implicated by disclosure of the case summaries. First: We praised the Academy's tradition of protecting personal privacy through redaction of names from the case summaries. But even with names redacted, subjects of such summaries can often be identified through other, disclosed information. So, second: Even though the summaries, with only names redacted, had once been public, we recognized the potential invasion of privacy through later recognition of identifying details, and approved the Court of Appeals' rule permitting the District Court to delete "other identifying information" in order to safeguard this privacy interest. If a cadet has a privacy interest in past discipline that was once public but may have been "wholly forgotten," the ordinary citizen surely has a similar interest in the aspects of his or her criminal history that may have been wholly forgotten.

We have also recognized the privacy interest in keeping personal facts away from the public eye. In Whalen v. Roe, [770] 429 U.S. 589 (1977), we held that "the State of New York may record, in a centralized computer file, the names and addresses of all persons who have obtained, pursuant to a doctor's prescription, certain drugs for which there is both a lawful and an unlawful market." Id., at 591. In holding only that the Federal Constitution does not prohibit such a compilation, we recognized that such a centralized computer file posed a "threat to privacy":

"We are not unaware of the threat to privacy implicit in the accumulation of vast amounts of personal information in computerized data banks or other massive government files. The collection of taxes, the distribution of welfare and social security benefits, the supervision of public health, the direction of our Armed Forces, and the enforcement of the criminal laws all require the orderly preservation of great quantities of information, much of which is personal in character and potentially embarrassing or harmful if disclosed. The right to collect and use such data for public purposes is typically accompanied by a concomitant statutory or regulatory duty to avoid unwarranted disclosures. Recognizing that in some circumstances that duty arguably has its roots in the Constitution, nevertheless New York's statutory scheme, and its implementing administrative procedures, evidence a proper concern with, and protection of, the individual's interest in privacy." Id., at 605 (footnote omitted); see also id., at 607 (Brennan, J., concurring) ("The central storage and easy accessibility of computerized data vastly increase the potential for abuse of that information...").

[5D] [9] In sum, the fact that "an event is not wholly 'private' does not mean that an individual has no interest in limiting disclosure or dissemination of the information." Rehnquist, Is an

Expanded Right of Privacy Consistent with Fair and Effective Law Enforcement?, Nelson Timothy Stephens Lectures, University of Kansas Law School, pt. 1, p. 13 (Sept. 26-27, [771] 1974). The privacy interest in a rap sheet is substantial. The substantial character of that interest is affected by the fact that in today's society the computer can accumulate and store information that would otherwise have surely been forgotten long before a person attains age 80, when the FBI's rap sheets are discarded.

V. Exemption 7(C), by its terms, permits an agency to withhold a document only when revelation "could reasonably be expected to constitute an unwarranted invasion of personal privacy." We must next address what factors might warrant an invasion of the interest described in Part IV, supra.

[10A] [11] [12] Our previous decisions establish that whether an invasion of privacy is warranted cannot turn on the purposes for which the request for information is made. Except for cases in which the objection to disclosure is based on a claim of privilege and the person requesting disclosure is the party protected by the privilege, the identity of the requesting party has no bearing on the merits of his or her FOIA request. Thus, although the subject of a presentence report can waive a privilege that might defeat a third party's access to that report, United States Department of Justice v. Julian, 486 U.S. 1, 13-14 (1988), and although the FBI's policy of granting the subject of a rap sheet access to his own criminal history is consistent with its policy of denying access to all other members of the general public, see supra, at 752, the rights of the two press respondents in this case are no different from those that might be asserted by any other third party, such as a neighbor or prospective employer. As we have repeatedly stated, Congress "clearly intended" the FOIA "to give any member of the public as much right to disclosure as one with a special interest [in a particular document]." NLRB v. Sears, Roebuck & Co., 421 U.S. 132, 149 (1975); see NLRB v. Robbins Tire & Rubber Co., 437 U.S. 214, 221 (1978); FBI v. Abramson, 456 U.S. 615 (1982). As Professor [772] Davis explained: "The Act's sole concern is with what must be made public or not made public."[19]

[10B] [13] Thus whether disclosure of a private document under Exemption 7(C) is warranted must turn on the nature of the requested document and its relationship to "the basic purpose of the Freedom of Information Act 'to open agency action

---

[19] Davis, The Information Act: A Preliminary Analysis, 34 U. Chi. L. Rev. 761, 765 (1966-1967), quoted in Justice Scalia's dissenting opinion in United States Department of Justice v. Julian, 486 U.S. 1, 17 (1988).

to the light of public scrutiny.'" Department of Air Force v. Rose, 425 U.S., at 372, rather than on the particular purpose for which the document is being requested. In our leading case on the FOIA, we declared that the Act was designed to create a broad right of access to "official information." EPA v. Mink, 410 U.S. 73, 80 (1973).[20] In his dissent in that case, Justice Douglas characterized the philosophy of the statute by quoting this comment by Henry Steele Commager:

"'The generation that made the nation thought secrecy in government one of the instruments of Old World tyranny and committed itself to the principle that a democracy cannot function unless the people are permitted [773] to know what their government is up to.'" Id., at 105 (quoting from The New York Review of Books, Oct. 5, 1972, p. 7) (emphasis added).

This basic policy of "'full agency disclosure unless information is exempted under clearly delineated statutory language,'" Department of Air Force v. Rose, 425 U.S., at 360-361 (quoting S. Rep. No. 813, 89th Cong., 1st Sess., 3 (1965)), indeed focuses on the citizens' right to be informed about "what their government is up to." Official information that sheds light on an agency's performance of its statutory duties falls squarely within that statutory purpose. That purpose, however, is not fostered by disclosure of information about private citizens that is accumulated in various governmental files but that reveals little or nothing about an agency's own conduct. In this case – and presumably in the typical case in which one private citizen is seeking information about another – the requester does not intend to discover anything about the conduct of the agency that has possession of the requested

---

[20] Cf. Easterbrook, Privacy and the Optimal Extent of Disclosure Under the Freedom of Information Act, 9 J. Legal Studies 775, 777 (1980) ("The act's indexing and reading-room rules indicate that the primary objective is the elimination of 'secret law.' Under the FOIA an agency must disclose its rules governing relationships with private parties and its demands on private conduct"); Kronman, The Privacy Exemption to the Freedom of Information Act, 9 J. Legal Studies 727, 733 (1980) ("The act's first and most obvious goal (reflected in its basic disclosure requirements) is to promote honesty and reduce waste in government by exposing official conduct to public scrutiny"); Comment, The Freedom of Information Act's Privacy Exemption and the Privacy Act of 1974, 11 Harv. Civ. Rights-Civ. Lib. L. Rev. 596, 608 (1976) ("No statement was made in Congress that the Act was designed for a broader purpose such as making the government's collection of data available to anyone who has any socially useful purpose for it. For example, it was never suggested that the FOIA would be a boon to academic researchers, by eliminating their need to assemble on their own data which the government has already collected").

records. Indeed, response to this request would not shed any light on the conduct of any Government agency or official.

The point is illustrated by our decision in Rose, supra. As discussed earlier, we held that the FOIA required the United States Air Force to honor a request for in camera submission of disciplinary-hearing summaries maintained in the Academy's Honors and Ethics Code reading files. The summaries obviously contained information that would explain how the disciplinary procedures actually functioned and therefore were an appropriate subject of a FOIA request. All parties, however, agreed that the files should be redacted by deleting information that would identify the particular cadets to whom the summaries related. The deletions were unquestionably appropriate because the names of the particular cadets were irrelevant to the inquiry into the way the Air Force Academy administered its Honor Code; leaving the identifying material in the summaries would therefore have been a "clearly unwarranted" [774] invasion of individual privacy. If, instead of seeking information about the Academy's own conduct, the requests had asked for specific files to obtain information about the persons to whom those files related, the public interest that supported the decision in Rose would have been inapplicable. In fact, we explicitly recognized that "the basic purpose of the [FOIA is] to open agency action to the light of public scrutiny." Id., at 372.

[14] Respondents argue that there is a twofold public interest in learning about Medico's past arrests or convictions: He allegedly had improper dealings with a corrupt Congressman, and he is an officer of a corporation with defense contracts. But if Medico has, in fact, been arrested or convicted of certain crimes, that information would neither aggravate nor mitigate his allegedly improper relationship with the Congressman; more specifically, it would tell us nothing directly about the character of the Congressman's behavior. Nor would it tell us anything about the conduct of the Department of Defense (DOD) in awarding one or more contracts to the Medico Company. Arguably a FOIA request to the DOD for records relating to those contracts, or for documents describing the agency's procedures, if any, for determining whether officers of a prospective contractor have criminal records, would constitute an appropriate request for "official information." Conceivably Medico's rap sheet would provide details to include in a news story, but, in itself, this is not the kind of public interest for which Congress enacted the FOIA.

In other words, although there is undoubtedly some public interest in anyone's criminal history, especially if the history is in some way related to the subject's dealing with a public official or agency, the FOIA's central purpose is to ensure that the Government's activities be opened to the sharp eye of public scrutiny, not that information about private citizens that happens to be in the warehouse of the Government be so disclosed. Thus, it should come as no surprise that in none of our cases construing the FOIA have we found it appropriate [775] to order a Government agency to honor a FOIA request for information about a particular private citizen.[21]

What we have said should make clear that the public interest in the release of any rap sheet on Medico that may exist is not the type of interest protected by the FOIA. Medico may or may not be one of the 24 million persons for whom the FBI has a rap sheet. If respondents are entitled to have the FBI tell them what it knows about Medico's criminal history, any other member of the public is entitled to the same disclosure — whether for writing a news story, for deciding whether to employ Medico, to rent a house to him, to extend credit to him, or simply to confirm or deny a suspicion. There is, unquestionably, some public interest in providing interested citizens with answers to their questions about Medico. But that interest falls outside the ambit of the public interest that the FOIA was enacted to serve.

Finally, we note that Congress has provided that the standard fees for production of documents under the FOIA shall be waived or reduced "if disclosure of the information is in the public interest because it is likely to contribute significantly to public understanding of the operations or activities of the government and is not primarily in the commercial interest of the requester." 5 U. S. C. § 552(a)(4)(A)(iii) (1982 ed., Supp. V). Although such a provision obviously implies that there will be requests that do not meet such a "public interest" standard, we think it relevant to today's inquiry regarding the public interest in release of rap sheets on private citizens that Congress once again expressed the core purpose of the FOIA as "contribut[ing] significantly to public understanding of the operations or activities of the government." [776]

VI. [4B] [15A]   Both the general requirement that a court "shall determine the matter de novo" and the specific reference to an "unwarranted" invasion of privacy in Exemption 7(C) indicate that a court must balance the public interest in disclosure against the interest Congress intended

the Exemption to protect. Although both sides agree that such a balance must be undertaken, how such a balance should be done is in dispute. The Court of Appeals majority expressed concern about assigning federal judges the task of striking a proper case-by-case, or ad hoc, balance between individual privacy interests and the public interest in the disclosure of criminal-history information without providing those judges standards to assist in performing that task. Our cases provide support for the proposition that categorical decisions may be appropriate and individual circumstances disregarded when a case fits into a genus in which the balance characteristically tips in one direction. The point is well illustrated by both the majority and dissenting opinions in NLRB v. Robbins Tire & Rubber Co., 437 U.S. 214 (1978).

[15B] In Robbins, the majority held that Exemption 7(A), which protects from disclosure law enforcement records or information that "could reasonably be expected to interfere with enforcement proceedings," applied to statements of witnesses whom the National Labor Relations Board (NLRB or Board) intended to call at an unfair-labor-practice hearing. Although we noted that the language of Exemptions 7(B), (C), and (D) seems to contemplate a case-by-case showing "that the factors made relevant by the statute are present in each distinct situation," id., at 223; see id., at 234, we concluded that Exemption 7(A) "appears to contemplate that certain generic determinations might be made." Id., at 224. Thus, our ruling encompassed the entire category of NLRB witness statements, and a concurring opinion pointed out that the category embraced enforcement proceedings by other agencies [777] as well. See id., at 243 (Stevens, J., concurring). In his partial dissent, Justice Powell endorsed the Court's "generic" approach to the issue, id., at 244; he agreed that "the congressional requirement of a specific showing of harm does not prevent determinations of likely harm with respect to prehearing release of particular categories of documents." Id., at 249. In his view, however, the exempt category should have been limited to statements of witnesses who were currently employed by the respondent. To be sure, the majority opinion in Robbins noted that the phrases "'a person,'" "'an unwarranted invasion,'" and "'a confidential source,'" in Exemptions 7(B), (C), and (D), respectively, seem to imply a need for an individualized showing in every case (whereas the plural "'enforcement proceedings'" in Exemption 7(A) implies a categorical determination). See id., at 223-224. But since only an Exemption 7(A) question was presented in Robbins, we conclude today, upon closer inspection of Exemption 7(C), that for an appropriate class of law enforcement

---

[21] In fact, in at least three cases we have specifically rejected requests for information about private citizens. See CIA v. Sims, 471 U.S. 159 (1985); FBI v. Abramson, 456 U.S. 615 (1982); United States Department of State v. Washington Post Co., 456 U.S. 595 (1982).

records or information a categorical balance may be undertaken there as well.[22]

[15C] [778] First: A separate discussion in Robbins applies properly to Exemption 7(C) as well as to Exemption 7(A). Respondent had argued that "because FOIA expressly provides for disclosure of segregable portions of records and for in camera review of documents, and because the statute places the burden of justifying non-disclosure on the Government, 5 U. S. C. §§ 552(a)(4)(B), (b) (1976 ed.), the Act necessarily contemplates that the Board must specifically demonstrate in each case that disclosure of the particular witness' statement would interfere with a pending enforcement proceeding." 437 U.S., at 224. We rejected this argument, holding instead that these provisions could equally well apply to categorical balancing. This holding – that the provisions regarding segregability, in camera inspections, and burden of proof do not by themselves mandate case-by-case balancing – is a general one that applies to all exemptions.

---

[22] Our willingness to permit categorical balancing in Robbins itself was a departure from earlier dicta. In NLRB v. Sears, Roebuck & Co., 421 U.S. 132, 162-165 (1975), we decided not to decide an Exemption 7 issue. In so doing, we responded to the NLRB General Counsel's argument that "once a certain type of document is determined to fall into the category of 'investigatory files' the courts are not to inquire whether the disclosure of the particular document in question would contravene any of the purposes of Exemption 7." Id., at 163 (emphases in original). In other words, the General Counsel argued for categorical balancing throughout Exemption 7. We rejected this argument: "The legislative history clearly indicates that Congress disapproves of those cases, relied on by the General Counsel, . . . which relieve the Government of the obligation to show that disclosure of a particular investigatory file would contravene the purposes of Exemption 7." Id., at 164. The legislative history cited, S. Conf. Rep. No. 93-1200 (1974), is in fact not clear on the question whether categorical balancing may be appropriate in Exemption 7 or elsewhere. In 1986, moreover, Congress amended Exemption 7(C) to give the Government greater flexibility in responding to FOIA requests for law enforcement records or information. Whereas previously the Government was required to show that disclosure of a law enforcement record "would" constitute an unwarranted invasion of personal privacy, under amended Exemption 7(C) the Government need only establish that production "could reasonably be expected" to cause such an invasion. The amendment was originally proposed by the Senate which intended to replace a focus on the effect of a particular disclosure "with a standard of reasonableness... based on an objective test." S. Rep. No. 98-221, p. 24 (1983). This reasonableness standard, focusing on whether disclosure of a particular type of document would tend to cause an unwarranted invasion of privacy, amply supports a categorical approach to the balance of private and public interests in Exemption 7(C).

Second: Although Robbins noted that Exemption 7(C) speaks of "an unwarranted invasion of personal privacy" (emphasis added), we do not think that the Exemption's use of the singular mandates ad hoc balancing. The Exemption in full provides: "This section does not apply to matters that are – records or information compiled for law enforcement purposes, but only to the extent that the production of such law enforcement records or information . . . could reasonably be expected to constitute an unwarranted invasion of personal [779] privacy." Just as one can ask whether a particular rap sheet is a "law enforcement record" that meets the requirements of this Exemption, so too can one ask whether rap sheets in general (or at least on private citizens) are "law enforcement records" that meet the stated criteria. If it is always true that the damage to a private citizen's privacy interest from a rap sheet's production outweighs the FOIA-based public value of such disclosure, then it is perfectly appropriate to conclude as a categorical matter that "production of such [rap sheets] could reasonably be expected to constitute an unwarranted invasion of personal privacy." In sum, Robbins' focus on the singular "an" in the phrase "an unwarranted invasion of personal privacy" is not a sufficient reason to hold that Exemption 7(C) requires ad hoc balancing.

Third: In FTC v. Grolier Inc., 462 U.S. 19 (1983), we also supported categorical balancing. Respondent sought FTC documents concerning an investigation of a subsidiary. At issue were seven documents that would normally be exempt from disclosure under Exemption 5, which protects "inter-agency or intra-agency memo-randums or letters which would not be available by law to a party other than an agency in litigation with the agency." 5 U. S. C. § 552(b)(5). The Court of Appeals held that four of the documents "could not be withheld on the basis of the work-product rule unless the Commission could show that 'litigation related to the terminated action exists or potentially exists.'" 462 U.S., at 22. We reversed, concluding that even if in some instances civil-discovery rules would permit such disclosure, "[s]uch materials are . . . not 'routinely' or 'normally' available to parties in litigation and hence are exempt under Exemption 5." Id., at 27. We added that "[t]his result, by establishing a discrete category of exempt information, implements the congressional intent to provide 'workable' rules. . . . Only by construing the Exemption to provide a categorical rule can the Act's purpose of expediting disclosure by means of workable rules be furthered." Id., at 27-28 (emphasis added).

[780] [1B] Finally: The privacy interest in maintaining the practical obscurity of rap-sheet information will always be high. When the subject of such a rap sheet is a private citizen and when the information is in the Government's control as a compilation, rather than as a record of "what the Government is up to," the privacy interest protected by Exemption 7(C) is in fact at its apex while the FOIA-based public interest in disclosure is at its nadir. See Parts IV and V, supra. Such a disparity on the scales of justice holds for a class of cases without regard to individual circumstances; the standard virtues of bright-line rules are thus present, and the difficulties attendant to ad hoc adjudication may be avoided. Accordingly, we hold as a categorical matter that a third party's request for law enforcement records or information about a private citizen can reasonably be expected to invade that citizen's privacy, and that when the request seeks no "official information" about a Government agency, but merely records that the Government happens to be storing, the invasion of privacy is "unwarranted." The judgment of the Court of Appeals is reversed.

It is so ordered.

CONCUR: JUSTICE BLACKMUN, with whom JUSTICE BRENNAN joins, concurring in the judgment.

I concur in the result the Court reaches in this case, but I cannot follow the route the Court takes to reach that result. In other words, the Court's use of "categorical balancing" under Exemption 7(C), I think, is not basically sound. Such a bright-line rule obviously has its appeal, but I wonder whether it would not run aground on occasion, such as in a situation where a rap sheet discloses a congressional candidate's conviction of tax fraud five years before. Surely, the FBI's disclosure of that information could not "reasonably be expected" to constitute an invasion of personal privacy, much less an unwarranted invasion, inasmuch as the candidate relinquished any interest in preventing the dissemination of this information when he chose to run for Congress. [781] In short, I do not believe that Exemption 7(C)'s language and its legislative history, or the case law, support interpreting that provision as exempting all rap-sheet information from the FOIA's disclosure requirements. See H. R. Rep. No. 1497, 89th Cong., 2d Sess., 11 (1966); S. Rep. No. 813, 89th Cong., 1st Sess., 3, 9 (1965); Department of Air Force v. Rose, 425 U.S. 352, 372 (1976); Lesar v. United States Dept. of Justice, 204 U. S. App. D. C. 200, 214, n. 80, 636 F. 2d 472, 486, n. 80 (1980).

It might be possible to mount a substantial argument in favor of interpreting Exemption 3 and 28 U. S. C. § 534 as exempting all rap-sheet information from the FOIA, especially in the light of the presence of the three post-FOIA enactments the Court mentions, ante, at 753. But the federal parties before this Court have abandoned the Exemption 3 issue they presented to the Court of Appeals and lost, and it perhaps would be inappropriate for us to pursue an inquiry along this line in the present case.

For these reasons, I would not adopt the Court's bright-line approach but would leave the door open for the disclosure of rap-sheet information in some circumstances. Nonetheless, even a more flexible balancing approach would still require reversing the Court of Appeals in this case. I, therefore, concur in the judgment, but do not join the Court's opinion.

Chapter

18

Open Courts

Balancing free press and fair trials

Focal cases:
Richmond Newspapers v. Virginia, 448 U.S. 555 (1980)
Detroit Free Press v. Ashcroft, 303 F.3d 681 (6th Cir. 2002)
North Jersey Media Group v. Ashcroft, 308 F.3d 198 (3rd Cir. 2002)

The Sixth Amendment to the Constitution protects the right to a speedy public trial by an impartial jury in the district where the crime was committed. Under this constitutional mandate, judges are obligated to protect a fair trial by protecting juror impartiality, maintaining order in the courtroom and preserving the decorum of the judicial process. In 1966, the Supreme Court established this responsibility when it criticized a judge for allowing a murder trial to become a media circus and a "Roman holiday."[1] The Court said the judge in *Sheppard v. Maxwell* had permitted massive publicity before and during the trial to bias the jury and frequent media disruptions of the trial to violate the defendant's constitutional right to a fair process.

In overturning the guilty verdict, the Supreme Court said the judge should reasonably have protected the defendant's Sixth Amendment rights by controlling the courtroom atmosphere, the information released to the press and the jury pool's and jury's access to potentially prejudicial publicity. The Supreme Court said judges should limit the number, movement and location of media representatives in a courtroom during a trial. In cases of extreme publicity, the Court said judges also should use any of 10 steps to assure fair trials:
1. Change the *venue* of the trial;[2]
2. Change the *venire* of the jury;
3. Issue a continuance (delay) in the trial;
4. Sever proceedings of multiple defendants to try each defendant separately;
5. Conduct exacting *voir dire* of the jury pool;[3]

---

[1] Sheppard v. Maxwell, 384 U.S. 333, 356 (1966).
[2] *See* Rideau v. Louisiana, 373 U.S. 723 (1963) (finding refusal to relocate trial after repeated publicity of defendant's confession violates right to fair trial).
[3] *See* Mu'Min v. Virginia, 500 U.S. 415 (1991); Irvin v. Dowd, 366 U.S. 717 (1961).

6. Give detailed instructions and admonishments to the jury;
7. Sequester the jury;
8. Order trial participants not to talk to the media about the trial;
9. Cite participants or the media with contempt for jeopardizing the trial process; or
10. Schedule a new trial.

PREJUDICIAL PUBLICITY

Although research is inconclusive about the influence of media coverage on juror attitudes or trial outcomes, the Supreme Court in *Sheppard* accepted the prejudicial impact of publicity and told judges they must assure that media coverage does not prevent fair trials.[4] Under the law, an unbiased juror does not need to be completely unfamiliar with the case before the trial. Rather, an impartial juror is someone who is free of fixed opinions about the defendant's guilt or innocence and who believes he can reach a verdict based solely on the evidence presented in court.[5] The American Bar Association, for example, is most concerned about the effect on jurors of extensive publicity about a defendant's confessions, prior criminal record, and lifestyle or personality traits. In addition, the ABA has encouraged its members not to discuss and the media not to publish information about evidence, testimony, law enforcement officers' speculations and the results of various tests and investigative procedures (e.g., blood tests, lie detector tests, forensics, etc.) until this information is disclosed in court.

While media behavior in the *Sheppard* case was extreme, some observers argue that little has changed in the nearly four decades since. Certainly, Judge Lance Ito believed media coverage threatened his ability to oversee a fair trial in the O. J. Simpson case. However, the Supreme Court has said courts may not presume the detrimental effects of publicity. Rather, for reversible error in the form of jury prejudice to exist, courts must show that individual jurors have identifiable bias or that extreme publicity saturates an entire community and creates an overwhelming presumption of prejudice at the time of the trial.[6]

Protection of fair trials, therefore, does not require – or even permit – judges to stop all potentially prejudicial publicity. In fact, the Supreme Court has said public scrutiny of the judicial system is vital to its proper functioning,[7] and the Court consistently has refused to categorically privilege either Sixth Amendment fair trial rights or First Amendment interests in information about trials. Achieving the proper balance between these sometimes complementary, sometimes conflicting rights requires a delicate hand.

PUBLIC AND PRESS ACCESS TO TRIALS

Both the First and the Sixth Amendments to the Constitution provide some right of public access to court proceedings, but the right is far from absolute. Penumbral rights under the First Amendment protect some right to gather newsworthy information essential to public oversight of the courts, while the Sixth Amendment protects the public's right to an open proceeding. The media share these rights with all members of the public.

The Supreme Court first asserted the public's right to attend criminal trials in 1980.[8] In *Richmond Newspapers v. Virginia*, the Court applied something close to strict scrutiny to find that

---

[4] *See also* Estes v. Texas, 381 U.S. 532 (1965); Rideau v. Louisiana, 373 U.S. 723 (1963); Irvin v. Dowd, 366 U.S. 717 (1961); Marshall v. United States, 360 U.S. 310 (1959).

[5] *See, e.g.,* United States v. Burr, 24 F. Cas. 49 (1807); Patterson v. Colorado, 205 U.S. 454 (1907); Murphy v. Florida, 421 U.S. 794 (1975).

[6] *See, e.g.,* Irvin v. Dowd, 366 U.S. 717 (1961); Estes v. Texas, 381 U.S. 532 (1965); Patton v. Yount, 467 U.S. 1025 (1984).

[7] *See, e.g.,* Sheppard v. Maxwell, 384 U.S. 333 (1966); Cox Broadcasting Corp. v. Cohn, 420 U.S. 469 (1975).

[8] 448 U.S. 555 (1980).

the state trial judge had improperly agreed to a defense request to close a murder trial to the public and the press. The Court said criminal trials are presumptively open to the public under both the First and Sixth Amendments because 1) of experience, e.g., these proceedings have been open historically, and 2) logic, e.g., openness contributes to the proper functioning of justice and to public faith in the process.

The decisions in *Richmond Newspapers* and in *Globe Newspaper v. Superior Court*[9] two years later established that the strong public interest in and uninterrupted history of open criminal proceedings required individuals seeking to close criminal trials to show 1) with specific findings of fact that 2) closure was vital to serve a compelling government interest and 3) was narrowly tailored to achieve that interest. The Supreme Court said judges must support orders closing criminal trials with empirical findings that closure would advance the asserted government interest and that no alternatives that would protect the public right of access would serve that interest. Although many states presumptively close juvenile proceedings,[10] the Supreme Court in *Globe Newspaper* struck down a state law *mandating* closure of courts during testimony by juveniles.[11] The Supreme Court has not ruled directly on whether juvenile proceedings and civil trials are presumptively open.

The Court also has never asserted a broad constitutional right of access to all judicial proceedings. To the contrary, the Court has found it constitutionally acceptable to *permit* closed proceedings when circumstances demonstrate that a compelling government interest justifies closure.

ACCESS TO PRETRIAL PROCEEDINGS

In ruling that many pretrial proceedings are presumptively open, the Court relied on the similarity of pretrial hearings to trials, the determinative effect of many pretrial proceedings, their unbroken history of openness, and the contribution of openness to their proper functioning.[12] Moreover, the Court said, courts cannot presume that publicity generated by open pretrial hearings will automatically prejudice a jury and undermine the right to a fair trial. To protect First Amendment interests in overseeing court processes, the Court said, those seeking to close pretrial proceedings must show that "there is a substantial probability" that publicity is likely to cause prejudice and that closure is the only reasonable means to effectively avoid this harm.[13] Employing similar reasoning, the U.S. Court of Appeals for the Ninth Circuit in 2002 ruled that executions must be public because they are a vital part of the justice system and have been historically open.[14]

However, two appeals courts reviewing the mandatory closure of all deportation hearings of "special interest" to federal anti-terrorist initiatives disagreed on whether blanket closure violated

---

[9] Globe Newspaper v. Superior Court, 457 U.S. 596 (1982) (overturning a state statute that required court closure in certain types of trials).

[10] *See, e.g.,* Stephan E. Oestreicher, Jr., Toward Fundamental Fairness In The Kangaroo Courtroom: The Case Against Statutes Presumptively Closing Juvenile Proceedings, 54 Vand. L. Rev. 1751, 1755 (2001) (noting 19 states that retain presumptive closure of juvenile proceedings).

[11] *Ibid.*

[12] *See, e.g.,* Press-Enterprise v. Riverside County Superior Court, 464 U.S. 501 (1984) (finding presumption of openness in *voir dire* proceedings) [Press-Enterprise I]; Press-Enterprise v. Riverside County Superior Court, 478 U.S. 1 (1986) [Press-Enterprise I] (finding general right of access to transcripts of preliminary hearing in criminal case).

[13] Press-Enterprise II at 14.

[14] California First Amendment Coalition v. Woodford, 299 F.3d 868 (9th Cir. 2002).

the First Amendment.[15] The Supreme Court denied *certiorari* in the appeal to the decision of the U.S. Court of Appeals for the Third Circuit that the First Amendment permitted the U.S. Immigration and Naturalization Service to close all special interest deportation hearings. However, one justice of the Supreme Court recently said there is "no basis in the Constitution for a 'right of access to courts' that effectively imposes an affirmative duty on Government officials ... to disclose matters concerning national security."[16]

The disagreement between the circuits relates to their differing interpretations of whether deportation proceedings enjoy a history of openness and whether openness advances the effectiveness of the judicial process or other compelling government interests. Historically closed proceedings, such as suppression hearings and grand jury sessions, generally may be kept secret and their records sealed.[17]

CAMERAS IN COURTROOMS

Although many court proceedings are presumptively open, the Supreme Court ruled in 1981 that the public right of access does not include a requirement that cameras be permitted in courtrooms.[18] Broadcasting clearly has changed greatly since the days of the highly intrusive and intimidating technology epitomized by massive, floor-mounted cameras, cords snaking across courtroom floors, and floodlights blinding jurors and witnesses at issue in *Sheppard*.[19] In fact, the Court in *Chandler v. Florida* acknowledged the changes in technology and said cameras are not *per se* prejudicial to trials. Yet, some judges maintain that cameras do not belong in courts because they inherently undermine the solemnity of the process, affect the content of testimony, encourage attorney grandstanding and fundamentally alter the order of the court.[20]

To this day, the U.S. Supreme Court and federal trial courts prohibit camera coverage of their proceedings. Indeed, in 1996 testimony before a congressional committee, Supreme Court Justice David Souter said, "The day you see a camera coming into our courtroom, it's going to roll over my dead body."[21] In federal courts of appeal and in most state courts, judges use their own discretion to determine whether, when, and how they will permit cameras in their courtrooms.

GAG ORDERS

Although the Supreme Court in *Sheppard* affirmed the authority of judges to use restrictive, or gag, orders to protect trials from prejudicial extra-judicial comments and disclosures, the Court since has said virtually all gags that directly restrict media coverage of trials violate the First Amendment's ban on prior restraints.[22] In 1976, the Court in *Nebraska Press Association v. Stuart* said the heavy presumption against prior restraints precludes gag orders that limit press coverage

---

[15] *See* Detroit Free Press v. Ashcroft, 303 F.3d 681 (6th Cir. 2002) (finding blanket closure unconstitutional); North Jersey Media Group v. Ashcroft, 308 F.3d 198 (3rd Cir. 2002), *cert. den'd*, 2003 U.S. LEXIS 4082 (May 27, 2003) (finding no constitutional infirmity in blanket closures).

[16] Christopher v. Harbury, 536 U.S. 403, 422 (2002) (Thomas, J., concurring) (finding no cause of action against government for failure to disclose information about foreign torture of dissident).

[17] *See* Gannett v. DePasquale, 443 U.S. 368 (1979) (finding closure of pretrial suppression hearing does not violate the Constitution); Newark Morning Ledger, 260 F.3d 217 (3rd Cir. 2001) (affirming order sealing filings associated with contempt motion related to grand jury materials).

[18] Chandler v. Florida, 449 U.S. 560 (1981).

[19] *See* Estes v. Texas, 381 U.S. 532 (1965); Chandler v. Florida, 449 U.S. 560 (1981).

[20] *See* Sheppard v. Maxwell, 384 U.S. 333 (1966).

[21] Tim O'Brien, *High Court TV*, N.Y. TIMES, Jan. 6, 1997, at A17; Editorial, *Open Up the Courts to Cameras, the Public*, SEATTLE TIMES, March 16, 1998, at B6; *High Court Rules Out Cameras For Debate*, U.S.A. TODAY, Nov. 27, 2000.

[22] *See, e.g.*, Nebraska Press Association v. Stuart, 427 U.S. 539 (1976).

of the courts unless judges first conduct a hearing that shows convincingly that pervasive media coverage 1) is likely to occur and 2) will pose a clear and present danger to a fair trial.[23] In addition, the Court said judges seeking to impose gags on media dissemination of information must show the gag will be effective and alternatives will not protect the fairness of the court proceeding.

Gags imposed on the media without such findings are presumptively unconstitutional. However, the collateral bar rule, sometimes called the Dickinson rule, requires individuals to obey even these facially unconstitutional orders until they are overturned.[24]

In fact, however, not all gags on media discussion of judicial procedures are unconstitutional, and the Supreme Court in 1984 upheld a gag on media to protect a vital component of the judicial process. The Court let stand a ban on newspaper dissemination of information received through discovery as a party to a lawsuit.[25] In allowing the restraining order to stand against the media, the Supreme Court said the ban was not a classic prior restraint because it did not prevent the publication of specific content. Instead, the ban punished only the improper use of judicial discovery and left the media free to publish the same information if obtained from another source. In another ruling suggesting that some media gags may be constitutional, one justice of the Court in 1995 refused to stay a temporary restraining order preventing Business Week from publishing sealed documents inadvertently disclosed by an attorney.[26] The U.S. Court of Appeals for the Sixth Circuit subsequently found the restraining order unconstitutional.[27]

Judicial restraining orders that forbid attorneys, jurors and other trial participants from discussing ongoing trials are less constitutionally problematic.[28] To some extent, the Court has viewed the speech of parties to trials in much the same way it views the speech of government employees; because insiders have access to sensitive information and their speech implicates the functioning of government, this speech is subject to limits that would otherwise be unconstitutional. However, direct restrictions on the speech of trial participants generally must end as soon as the threat to a fair trial passes. Thus, the Supreme Court found it unconstitutional for a state to prohibit grand jury witnesses to discuss their testimony after the grand jury's term expired.[29]

CONTEMPT CITATIONS AND OTHER SANCTIONS

Judges enjoy broad discretion to cite individuals for contempt of court. Criminal contempt punishes disruptive behavior, while civil contempt citations pressure people to comply with court orders, such as gag orders, orders to disclose information or orders not to publish information sealed by the court. The Supreme Court has said judges may impose contempt citations only on

---

[23] *See* Nebraska Press Association v. Stuart, 427 U.S. 539 (1976).

[24] *See* United States v. Dickinson, 465 U.S. F.2d 496 (5th Cir. 1972); United States v. CNN, 865 F. Supp. 1549 (S.D. Fla. 1994); United States v. Noriega, 917 F.2d 1543 (11th Cir. 1990) (upholding contempt citation against CNN). *But see* In re Providence Journal, 820 F.2d 1354 (1st Cir. 1987) (finding a facially unconstitutional court order cannot be the basis for contempt citation).

[25] Seattle Times v. Rhinehart, 467 U.S. 20 (1984) (unanimously finding Constitution does not prohibit ban on dissemination of information mandatorily disclosed during discovery). *See also* New Jersey v. Neulander, 801 A.2d 255 (N.J. 2002) (affirming court order preventing media disclosure of juror IDs not in public record and prohibiting contact with jurors after hung jury) cert. den'd sub nom Philadelphia Newspapers v. Neulander, 123 S.Ct. 1281 (2003).

[26] McGraw-Hill v. Procter & Gamble, 515 U.S. 1309 (1995).

[27] Procter & Gamble v. Bankers Trust, 78 F.3d 219 (6th Cir. 1996).

[28] *See* Gentile v. State Bar of Nevada, 501 U.S. 1030 (1991). *But see* United States v. Scarfo, 263 F.3d 80 (3rd Cir. 2001) (finding a gag on former attorney of defendant in ongoing trial imposed without finding of jeopardy to trial or impairment of judicial process violates the First Amendment).

[29] Butterworth v. Smith, 494 U.S. 624 (1990).

behavior in or physically adjacent to the courtroom.[30] The Court also has said judges may not impose jail terms of greater than six months for contempt without conducting a jury trial.[31]

In addition, the First Amendment limits use of contempt orders against the media to instances in which the press coverage poses a serious threat to the judicial process.[32] More than fifty years ago the Court established that the Constitution does not permit judges to use contempt orders to punish media criticism of judicial conduct unless the publicity presents a "clear and present danger to the fair administration of justice."[33] In 1991, the Supreme Court ruled that this standard permitted the court to sanction a defense attorney for extra-judicial comments that had a "substantial likelihood of materially prejudicing" the ongoing trial.[34]

The Supreme Court generally has held that First Amendment protection of open discussion about judicial proceedings also mandates a showing of imminent harm to a compelling government interest before courts may impose sanctions on media for publication of legally obtained confidential information.[35]

ACCESS TO COURT RECORDS

Official court records are presumptively open to the public unless the court finds an inescapable necessity to seal them to preserve fair process.[36] The right to view and copy court records extends to transcripts of open court proceedings, including pretrial hearings.[37] This constitutional and common law right of access requires that orders sealing records be as narrow as possible[38] and that records of sealed portions of open proceedings be made public if the government's justification for closure abates.[39]

The right of access to court records does not necessarily cover public inspection of evidence. For example, in a case involving the White House tapes of former president Richard Nixon, the Supreme Court ruled that the presentation of evidence in open courtrooms adequately protects the public's constitutional right of access to evidence.[40] Broadcasters had no right to copy and disseminate the tapes themselves.

Lower courts tend to balance personal interests in privacy against the public benefit of access to determine whether evidence and other judicial materials should be available for copying.[41] However, federal appeals courts disagree on the proper judicial standard to determine when

---

[30] Nye v. U.S. 313 U.S. 33 (1941).

[31] Cheff v. Schnackenberg, 384 U.S. 373 (1966); Bloom v. Illinois, 392 U.S. 194 (1968).

[32] *See* Bridges v. California, 314 U.S. 252 (1941); Craig v. Harney, 331 U.S. 367 (1947).

[33] Pennekamp v. Florida, 328 U.S. 331, 348, 353 (1946). *See also* Bridges v. California & Times Mirror Co. v. Superior Court, 314 U.S. 252 (1941).

[34] *See* Gentile v. State Bar of Nevada 501 U.S. 1030, 1033 (1991) (finding, however, that the rules at issue in this case were void for vagueness).

[35] *See* Landmark Communications v. Virginia, 435 U.S. 829 (1978); Smith v. Daily Mail Publishing, 443 U.S. 97 (1979).

[36] *See* Associated Press v. U.S. Dist. Court, 705 F.2d 1143 (9th Cir. 1983).

[37] *See* Press-Enterprise I, 464 U.S. at 510-511.

[38] *See* In re ABC (United States v. Moussaoui), 31 Med. L. Rep. 1705 (May 13, 2003); 2003 U.S. Dist. LEXIS 9457 (E.D. Va. June 2, 2003) (granting access to non-classified portions of 28 records and oral argument in appeal in trial of alleged participant in Sept. 11, 2001, terrorist attacks)

[39] *See* Gannett v. DePasquale, 443 U.S. at 445 (Blackmun, J., dissenting).

[40] Nixon v. Warner Communications, 435 U.S. 589 (1978). *See also* In re Providence Journal, 293 F.3d 1 (1st Cir. 2002) (finding blanket denial of access to mandatory legal memos violates the First Amendment but affirming court's refusal to grant access to audio and video taped evidence in political corruption trial).

[41] *See, e.g.,* In re Boston Herald (United States v. Connolly), 321 F.3d 174 (1st Cir. 2003) (finding no constitutional right of access and limited common law right of access to criminal defendant's mandatory financial filings not violated by sealing these records); United States v. Loeper, 132 F. Supp. 2d 337 (E.D. Penn. 2001); In re Knoxville News-Sentinel, 723 F.2d 470 (6th Cir. 1983).

courts may seal evidence presented in court.[42] For example, courts historically have viewed settlements in civil suits as private, but a few appeals courts have ruled that once settlements that implicate important public interests are filed with the court, they are open to the public.[43] Records in court files that have not been presented in open court may not be open to the public.

READING THE CASES

The cases listed below and those that follow afford insight into the differing application of legal tests to determine when judicial proceedings and records may constitutionally be closed. As with other areas of constitutional law, courts differ in the degree of deference they give to the executive branch when case facts relate to international terrorism or national security. Decisions on access sometimes reflect the political climate of the nation.

- *In re ABC* (United States v. Moussaoui), 31 Med. L. Rep. 1705 (May 13, 2003) (granting access to redacted classified documents filed with court).
- *Gentile v. State Bar of Nevada*, 501 U.S. 1030 (1991) (finding state bar rule limiting attorney extra-judicial comment constitutional).
- *Mu'Min v. Virginia*, 500 U.S. 415 (1991) (rejecting claim that refusal to ask specific questions during voir dire is unconstitutional).
- *Butterworth v. Smith*, 494 U.S. 624 (1990) (finding Constitution prevents state ban on grand jury witness discussion of testimony after grand jury session ends).
- *United States v. Noriega*, 917 F.2d 1543 (11th Cir. 1990) (upholding contempt citation against CNN for violating gag order).
- *In re Providence Journal*, 820 F.2d 1354 (1st Cir. 1987) (finding a facially unconstitutional court order cannot be the basis for contempt citation).
- *Press-Enterprise v. Riverside County Superior Court*, 478 U.S. 1 (1986) [Press-Enterprise I] (finding limited Constitutional right of access to preliminary hearing in criminal case).
- *Press-Enterprise v. Riverside County Superior Court*, 464 U.S. 501 (1984) [Press-Enterprise I] (finding presumption of openness in *voir dire* proceedings).
- *Seattle Times v. Rhinehart*, 467 U.S. 20 (1984) (unanimously finding Constitution does not prohibit ban on dissemination of information mandatorily disclosed during discovery).
- *Patton v. Yount*, 467 U.S. 1025 (1984) (rejecting presumption of prejudice absent findings).
- *Globe Newspaper v. Superior Court*, 457 U.S. 596 (1982) (overturning a state statute mandating court closure in certain types of trials).
- *Chandler v. Florida*, 449 U.S. 560 (1981) (finding broadcast coverage of courts is not inherently prejudicial).
- *Gannett v. DePasquale*, 443 U.S. 368 (1979) (finding closure of pretrial suppression hearing does not violate the Constitution).
- *Smith v. Daily Mail Publishing*, 443 U.S. 97 (1979) (holding state ban on newspaper dissemination of legally obtained information about juvenile proceedings unconstitutional).

---

[42] *See* United States v. Jenrette, 653 F.2d 609 (D.C. Cir. 1981); In re NBC, 648 F.2d 814 (3rd Cir. 1981); Belo Broadcasting v. Clark, 654 F.2d 423 (5th Cir. 1981); United States v. Beckham, 789 F.2d 401 (6th Cir. 1986); Public Citizen v. Liggett Group, 858 F.2d 775 (1st Cir. 1988); United States v. McVeigh, 119 F.3d 806 (10th Cir. 1997).

[43] *See, e.g.,* Bank of America v. Hotel Rittenhouse, 800 F.2d 339, 344-45 (3rd Cir. 1986); United States v. Smith, 787 F.2d 111 (3d Cir. 1986); EEOC v. The Erection Co., 900 F.2d 168, 170 (9th Cir. 1990); Pansy v. Stroudsburg, 22 F.3d 772 (3rd Cir.1994).

- *Landmark Communications v. Virginia*, 435 U.S. 829 (1978) (finding unconstitutional post-publication sanctions for publication of legally obtained information about confidential proceedings).
- *Nixon v. Warner Communications*, 435 U.S. 589 (1978) (finding right of access to trials does not require release of taped evidence presented in open court).
- *Nebraska Press Association v. Stuart*, 427 U.S. 539 (1976) (finding gags imposed on media presumptively invalid prior restraints).
- *Cox Broadcasting Corp. v. Cohn*, 420 U.S. 469 (1975) (finding punishment for publication of confidential information gathered from court records violates the First Amendment).
- *Sheppard v. Maxwell*, 384 U.S. 333 (1966) (finding court's failure to prevent prejudicial publicity violates Sixth Amendment right to fair trial).
- *Estes v. Texas*, 381 U.S. 532 (1965) (finding intensive broadcast coverage of trial violates defendant's Sixth Amendment rights).
- *Rideau v. Louisiana*, 373 U.S. 723 (1963) (finding refusal to relocate trial after repeated publicity of defendant's confession violates right to fair trial).
- *Irvin v. Dowd*, 366 U.S. 717 (1961) (finding failure to change venue in highly publicized trial violates defendant's Sixth Amendment rights).
- *Pennekamp v. Florida*, 328 U.S. 331 (1946) (finding use of contempt to punish media criticism of court violates First Amendment).

In reading the following three cases, focus on how the different courts define and apply the two-prong experience and logic test established in *Richmond Newspapers*.

- What is the test established in *Richmond Newspapers* and to what kinds of judicial proceedings does it apply?
- How many of the justices in *Richmond Newspapers* endorse the test, and in what ways, if any, do they disagree about its use?
- Do the three courts ruling in the following cases differ in their definitions of the test or in its specific application to the facts in the cases?
- Do differences in the use of the *Richmond Newspapers* test pertain to the meanings of the two prongs, their relative weight in determining access rights or both?
- In what ways do the two appeals courts disagree about the history of deportation hearings and the benefits of their openness?
- In the final analysis, what determines the outcome of the two appeals courts' rulings?
- What do the three cases, taken as a group, suggest about the predictability of the application of the "experience and logic" test?
- What, if anything, might these cases indicate more broadly about the constitutional protection for public access to judicial processes?

Richmond Newspapers v. Virginia
448 U.S. 555
(1980)

PRIOR HISTORY: Appeal from the Supreme Court of Virginia.

DECISION: State trial judge's order, at request of accused, closing murder trial to public and press, held violative of First and Fourteenth Amendments.

JUDGES: BURGER, C. J., announced the Court's judgment and delivered an opinion, in which WHITE and STEVENS, JJ., joined. WHITE, J., and STEVENS, J., , filed concurring opinions. BRENNAN, J., filed an opinion concurring in the judgment, in which MARSHALL, J., joined. STEWART, J., and BLACKMUN, J., filed opinions concurring in the judgment. REHNQUIST, J., filed a dissenting opinion. POWELL, J., took no part in the consideration or decision of the case.

OPINION: [558] MR. CHIEF JUSTICE BURGER announced the judgment of the Court and delivered an opinion, in which MR. JUSTICE WHITE and MR. JUSTICE STEVENS joined.

The narrow question presented in this case is whether the right of the public and press to attend criminal trials is guaranteed under the United States Constitution. [559]

I. In March 1976, one Stevenson was indicted for the murder of a hotel manager who had been found stabbed to death on December 2, 1975. Tried promptly in July 1976, Stevenson was convicted of second-degree murder in the Circuit Court of Hanover County, Va. The Virginia Supreme Court reversed the conviction in October 1977, holding that a bloodstained shirt purportedly belonging to Stevenson had been improperly admitted into evidence. *Stevenson* v. *Commonwealth*, 218 Va. 462, 237 S. E. 2d 779.

Stevenson was retried in the same court. This second trial ended in a mistrial on May 30, 1978, when a juror asked to be excused after trial had begun and no alternate was available.[1]

A third trial, which began in the same court on June 6, 1978, also ended in a mistrial. It appears that the mistrial may have been declared because a prospective juror had read about Stevenson's previous trials in a newspaper and had told other prospective jurors about the case before the retrial began. See App. 35a-36a.

Stevenson was tried in the same court for a fourth time beginning on September 11, 1978. Present in the courtroom when the case was called were appellants Wheeler and McCarthy, reporters for appellant Richmond Newspapers, Inc. Before the trial began, counsel for the defendant moved that it be closed to the public:

"[There] was this woman that was with the family of the deceased when we were here before. She had sat in the Courtroom. I would like to ask that everybody be excluded from the Courtroom because I don't want any information being shuffled back and forth when we have [560] a recess as to what – who testified to what." Tr. of Sept. 11, 1978 Hearing on Defendant's Motion to Close Trial to the Public 2-3.

The trial judge, who had presided over two of the three previous trials, asked if the prosecution had any objection to clearing the courtroom. The prosecutor stated he had no objection and would leave it to the discretion of the court. *Id.*, at 4. Presumably referring to Va. Code § 19.2-266 (Supp. 1980), the trial judge then announced: "[The] statute gives me that power specifically and the defendant has made the motion." He then ordered "that the Courtroom be kept clear of all parties except the witnesses when they testify." Tr., *supra*, at 4-5.[2] The record does not show that any objections to the closure order were made by anyone present at the time, including appellants Wheeler and McCarthy.

Later that same day, however, appellants sought a hearing on a motion to vacate the closure order. The trial judge granted the request and scheduled a hearing to follow the close of the day's proceedings. When the hearing began, the court ruled that the hearing was to be treated as part of the trial; accordingly, he again ordered the reporters to leave the courtroom, and they complied.

---

[1] A newspaper account published the next day reported the mistrial and went on to note that "[a] key piece of evidence in Stevenson's original conviction was a bloodstained shirt obtained from Stevenson's wife soon after the killing. The Virginia Supreme Court, however, ruled that the shirt was entered into evidence improperly." App. 34a.

[2] Virginia Code § 19.2-266 (Supp. 1980) provides in part: "In the trial of all criminal cases, whether the same be felony or misdemeanor cases, the court may, in its discretion, exclude from the trial any persons whose presence would impair the conduct of a fair trial, provided that the right of the accused to a public trial shall not be violated."

At the closed hearing, counsel for appellants observed that no evidentiary findings had been made by the court prior to the entry of its closure order and pointed out that the court had failed to consider any other, less drastic measures within its power to ensure a fair trial. Tr. of Sept. 11, 1978 Hearing on Motion to Vacate 11-12. Counsel for appellants argued that constitutional considerations mandated that before ordering closure, the court should first decide that the rights of the defendant could be protected in no other way.

[561] Counsel for defendant Stevenson pointed out that this was the fourth time he was standing trial. He also referred to "difficulty with information between the jurors," and stated that he "didn't want information to leak out," be published by the media, perhaps inaccurately, and then be seen by the jurors. Defense counsel argued that these things, plus the fact that "this is a small community," made this a proper case for closure. *Id.*, at 16-18.

The trial judge noted that counsel for the defendant had made similar statements at the morning hearing. The court also stated:

"[One] of the other points that we take into consideration in this particular Courtroom is layout of the Courtroom. I think that having people in the Courtroom is distracting to the jury. Now, we have to have certain people in here and maybe that's not a very good reason. When we get into our new Court Building, people can sit in the audience so the jury can't see them. The rule of the Court may be different under those circumstances." *Id.*, at 19.

The prosecutor again declined comment, and the court summed up by saying: "I'm inclined to agree with [defense counsel] that, if I feel that the rights of the defendant are infringed in any way, [when] he makes the motion to do something and it doesn't completely override all rights of everyone else, then I'm inclined to go along with the defendant's motion." *Id.*, at 20.

The court denied the motion to vacate and ordered the trial to continue the following morning "with the press and public excluded." *Id.*, at 27; App. 21a.

What transpired when the closed trial resumed the next day was disclosed in the following manner by an order of the court entered September 12, 1978: "[In] the absence of the jury, the defendant by counsel [562] made a Motion that a mistrial be declared, which motion was taken under advisement.

"At the conclusion of the Commonwealth's evidence, the attorney for the defendant moved the Court to strike the Commonwealth's evidence on grounds stated to the record, which Motion was sustained by the Court.

"And the jury having been excused, the Court doth find the accused NOT GUILTY of Murder, as charged in the Indictment, and he was allowed to depart." *Id.*, at 22a.[3]

On September 27, 1978, the trial court granted appellants' motion to intervene *nunc pro tunc* in the Stevenson case. Appellants then petitioned the Virginia Supreme Court for writs of mandamus and prohibition and filed an appeal from the trial court's closure order. On July 9, 1979, the Virginia Supreme Court dismissed the mandamus and prohibition petitions and, finding no reversible error, denied the petition for appeal. *Id.*, at 23a-28a.

Appellants then sought review in this Court, invoking both our appellate, 28 U. S. C. § 1257 (2), and certiorari jurisdiction. §1257 (3). We postponed further consideration of the question of our jurisdiction to the hearing of the case on the merits. 444 U.S. 896 (1979). We conclude that jurisdiction by appeal does not lie;[4] however, treating the filed [563] papers as a petition for a writ of certiorari pursuant to 28 U. S. C. § 2103, we grant the petition.

The criminal trial which appellants sought to attend has long since ended, and there is thus some suggestion that the case is moot. This Court has frequently recognized, however, that its jurisdiction is not necessarily defeated by the practical termination of a contest which is short-lived by

---

[3] At oral argument, it was represented to the Court that tapes of the trial were available to the public as soon as the trial terminated. Tr. of Oral Arg. 36.

[4] In our view, the validity of Va. Code § 19.2-266 (Supp. 1980) was not sufficiently drawn in question by appellants before the Virginia courts to invoke our appellate jurisdiction. "It is essential to our jurisdiction on appeal . . . that there be an explicit and timely insistence in the state courts that a state statute, as applied, is repugnant to the federal Constitution, treaties or laws." *Charleston Federal Savings & Loan Assn.* v. *Alderson*, 324 U.S. 182, 185 (1945). Appellants never explicitly challenged the statute's validity. In both the trial court and the State Supreme Court, appellants argued that constitutional rights of the public and the press prevented the court from closing a trial without first giving notice and an opportunity for a hearing to the public and the press and exhausting every alternative means of protecting the defendant's right to a fair trial. Given appellants' failure explicitly to challenge the statute, we view these arguments as constituting claims of rights under the Constitution, which rights are said to limit the exercise of the discretion conferred by the statute on the trial court. Cf. *Phillips* v. *United States*, 312 U.S. 246, 252 (1941) ("[An] attack on lawless exercise of authority in a particular case is not an attack upon the constitutionality of a statute conferring the authority . . ."). Such claims are properly brought before this Court by way of our certiorari, rather than appellate, jurisdiction. See, *e.g.*, *Kulko* v. *California Superior Court*, 436 U.S. 84, 90, n. 4 (1978); *Hanson* v. *Denckla*, 357 U.S. 235, 244, and n. 4 (1958). We shall, however, continue to refer to the parties as appellants and appellee. See *Kulko, supra.*

nature. See, *e.g., Gannett Co.* v. *DePasquale,* 443 U.S. 368, 377-378 (1979); *Nebraska Press Assn.* v. *Stuart,* 427 U.S. 539, 546-547 (1976). If the underlying dispute is "capable of repetition, yet evading review," *Southern Pacific Terminal Co.* v. *ICC,* 219 U.S. 498, 515 (1911), it is not moot.

Since the Virginia Supreme Court declined plenary review, it is reasonably foreseeable that other trials may be closed by other judges without any more showing of need than is presented on this record. More often than not, criminal trials will be of sufficiently short duration that a closure order "will evade review, or at least considered plenary review in this Court." *Nebraska Press, supra,* at 547. Accordingly, we turn to the merits.

II. We begin consideration of this case by noting that the precise issue presented here has not previously been before this [564] Court for decision. In *Gannett Co.* v. *DePasquale, supra,* the Court was not required to decide whether a right of access to *trials,* as distinguished from hearings on pretrial motions, was constitutionally guaranteed. The Court held that the Sixth Amendment's guarantee to the accused of a public trial gave neither the public nor the press an enforceable right of access to a pretrial suppression hearing. One concurring opinion specifically emphasized that "a hearing on a motion before trial to suppress evidence is not a *trial. . . .*" 443 U.S., at 394 (BURGER, C. J., concurring). Moreover, the Court did not decide whether the First and Fourteenth Amendments guarantee a right of the public to attend trials, *id.,* at 392, and n. 24; nor did the dissenting opinion reach this issue. *Id.,* at 447 (opinion of BLACKMUN, J.).

In prior cases the Court has treated questions involving conflicts between publicity and a defendant's right to a fair trial; as we observed in *Nebraska Press Assn.* v. *Stuart, supra,* at 547, "[the] problems presented by this [conflict] are almost as old as the Republic." See also, *e.g., Gannett, supra; Murphy* v. *Florida,* 421 U.S. 794 (1975); *Sheppard* v. *Maxwell,* 384 U.S. 333 (1966); *Estes* v. *Texas,* 381 U.S. 532 (1965). But here for the first time the Court is asked to decide whether a criminal trial itself may be closed to the public upon the unopposed request of a defendant, without any demonstration that closure is required to protect the defendant's superior right to a fair trial, or that some other overriding consideration requires closure.

A The origins of the proceeding which has become the modern criminal trial in Anglo-American justice can be traced back beyond reliable historical records. We need not here review all details of its development, but a summary of that history is instructive. What is significant for present purposes is that throughout its evolution, the trial has been open to all who cared to observe.

[565] In the days before the Norman Conquest, cases in England were generally brought before moots, such as the local court of the hundred or the county court, which were attended by the freemen of the community. Pollock, English Law Before the Norman Conquest, in 1 Select Essays in Anglo-American Legal History 88, 89 (1907). Somewhat like modern jury duty, attendance at these early meetings was compulsory on the part of the freemen, who were called upon to render judgment. *Id.,* at 89-90; see also 1 W. Holdsworth, A History of English Law 10, 12 (1927).[5]

With the gradual evolution of the jury system in the years after the Norman Conquest, see, *e.g., id.,* at 316, the duty of all freemen to attend trials to render judgment was relaxed, but there is no indication that criminal trials did not remain public. When certain groups were excused from compelled attendance, see the Statute of Marlborough, 52 Hen. 3, ch. 10 (1267); 1 Holdsworth, *supra,* at 79, and n. 4, the statutory exemption did not prevent them from attending; Lord Coke observed that those excused "are not compellable to come, but left to their own liberty." 2 E. Coke, Institutes of the Laws of England 121 (6th ed. 1681).[6]

Although there appear to be few contemporary statements [566] on the subject, reports of the Eyre of Kent, a general court held in 1313-1314, evince a recognition of the importance of public attendance apart from the "jury duty" aspect. It was explained that "the King's will was that all evil doers should be punished after their deserts, and that justice should be ministered indifferently to rich as to poor; *and for the better accomplishing of this,* he prayed the community of the county *by their attendance* there to lend him their aid in the establishing of a happy and certain peace that should be both for the honour of the realm and for their own welfare." 1 Holdsworth, *supra,* at 268,

---

[5] That there is little in the way of a contemporary record from this period is not surprising. It has been noted by historians, see E. Jenks, A Short History of English Law 3-4 (2d ed. 1922), that the early Anglo-Saxon laws "deal rather with the novel and uncertain, than with the normal and undoubted rules of law. . . . Why trouble to record that which every village elder knows? Only when a disputed point has long caused bloodshed and disturbance, or when a successful invader . . . insists on a change, is it necessary to draw up a code." *Ibid.*

[6] Coke interpreted certain language of an earlier chapter of the same statute as specifically indicating that court proceedings were to be public in nature: "These words [*In curia Domini Regis*] are of great importance, for all Causes ought to be heard, ordered, and determined before the Judges of the King's Courts *openly* in the King's Courts, *whither all persons may resort.* . . . "2 E. Coke, Institutes of the Laws of England 103 (6th ed. 1681) (emphasis added).

quoting from the S.S. edition of the Eyre of Kent, vol. i., p. 2 (emphasis added).

From these early times, although great changes in courts and procedure took place, one thing remained constant: the public character of the trial at which guilt or innocence was decided. Sir Thomas Smith, writing in 1565 about "the definitive proceedings in causes criminal," explained that, while the indictment was put in writing as in civil law countries:

"All the rest is done openly in the presence of the Judges, the Justices, the enquest, the prisoner, *and so manie as will or can come so neare as to heare it,* and all depositions and witnesses given aloud, *that all men may heare from the mouth of the depositors and witnesses what is saide.*" T. Smith, De Republica Anglorum 101 (Alston ed. 1972) (emphasis added).

Three centuries later, Sir Frederick Pollock was able to state of the "rule of publicity" that, "[here] we have one tradition, at any rate, which has persisted through all changes." F. Pollock, The Expansion of the Common Law 31-32 (1904). See also E. Jenks, The Book of English Law 73-74 (6th ed. 1967): "[One] of the most conspicuous features of English justice, that all judicial trials are held in open court, to which the [567] public have free access, . . . appears to have been the rule in England from time immemorial."

We have found nothing to suggest that the presumptive openness of the trial, which English courts were later to call "one of the essential qualities of a court of justice," *Daubney* v. *Cooper,* 10 B. & C. 237, 240, 109 Eng. Rep. 438, 440 (K.B. 1829), was not also an attribute of the judicial systems of colonial America. In Virginia, for example, such records as there are of early criminal trials indicate that they were open, and nothing to the contrary has been cited. See A. Scott, Criminal Law in Colonial Virginia 128-129 (1930); Reinsch, The English Common Law in the Early American Colonies, in 1 Select Essays in Anglo-American Legal History 367, 405 (1907). Indeed, when in the mid-1600's the Virginia Assembly felt that the respect due the courts was "by the clamorous unmannerlynes of the people lost, and order, gravity and decoram which should manifest the authority of a court in the court it selfe neglected," the response was not to restrict the openness of the trials to the public, but instead to prescribe rules for the conduct of those attending them. See Scott, *supra,* at 132.

In some instances, the openness of trials was explicitly recognized as part of the fundamental law of the Colony. The 1677 Concessions and Agreements of West New Jersey, for example, provided:

"That in all publick courts of justice for tryals of causes, civil or criminal, any person or persons, inhabitants of the said Province may freely come into, and attend the said courts, and hear and be present, at all or any such tryals as shall be there had or passed, that justice may not be done in a corner nor in any covert manner." Reprinted in Sources of Our Liberties 188 (R. Perry ed. 1959). See also 1 B. Schwartz, The Bill of Rights: A Documentary History 129 (1971). [568] The Pennsylvania Frame of Government of 1682 also provided "[that] all courts shall be open . . . ," Sources of Our Liberties, *supra,* at 217; 1 Schwartz, *supra,* at 140, and this declaration was reaffirmed in § 26 of the Constitution adopted by Pennsylvania in 1776. See 1 Schwartz, *supra,* at 271. See also §§ 12 and 76 of the Massachusetts Body of Liberties, 1641, reprinted in 1 Schwartz, *supra,* at 73, 80.

Other contemporary writings confirm the recognition that part of the very nature of a criminal trial was its openness to those who wished to attend. Perhaps the best indication of this is found in an address to the inhabitants of Quebec which was drafted by a committee consisting of Thomas Cushing, Richard Henry Lee, and John Dickinson and approved by the First Continental Congress on October 26, 1774. 1 Journals of the Continental Congress, 1774-1789, pp. 101, 105 (1904) (Journals). This address, written to explain the position of the Colonies and to gain the support of the people of Quebec, is an "exposition of the fundamental rights of the colonists, as they were understood by a representative assembly chosen from all the colonies." 1 Schwartz, *supra,* at 221. Because it was intended for the inhabitants of Quebec, who had been "educated under another form of government" and had only recently become English subjects, it was thought desirable for the Continental Congress to explain "the inestimable advantages of a free English constitution of government, which it is the privilege of all English subjects to enjoy." 1 Journals 106.

"[One] great right is that of trial by jury. This provides, that neither life, liberty nor property, can be taken from the possessor, until twelve of his unexceptionable countrymen and peers of his vicinage, who from that neighbourhood may reasonably be supposed to be acquainted with his character, and the characters of the witnesses, upon a fair trial, and full enquiry, face to face, *in open Court, before as many of the people as chuse to* [569] *attend,* shall pass their sentence upon oath against him. . . ." *Id.,* at 107 (emphasis added).

B   As we have shown, and as was shown in both the Court's opinion and the dissent in *Gannett,* 443 U.S., at 384, 386, n. 15, 418-425, the historical evidence demonstrates conclusively that at the time when our organic laws were adopted, criminal trials both here and in England had long been presumptively open. This is no quirk of history; rather, it has long been recognized as an indispensable attribute of an Anglo-American trial. Both Hale in the 17th century and Blackstone in the 18th saw the importance of openness to the proper functioning of a trial; it gave assurance that the proceedings were conducted fairly to all concerned, and it discouraged perjury, the misconduct of participants, and decisions based on secret bias or partiality. See, e.g., M. Hale, The History of the Common Law of England 343-345 (6th ed. 1820); 3 W. Blackstone, Commentaries *372-*373. Jeremy Bentham not only recognized the therapeutic value of open justice but regarded it as the keystone: "Without publicity, all other checks are insufficient: in comparison of publicity, all other checks are of small account. Recordation, appeal, whatever other institutions might present themselves in the character of checks, would be found to operate rather as cloaks than checks; as cloaks in reality, as checks only in appearance." 1 J. Bentham, Rationale of Judicial Evidence 524 (1827).[7]

Panegyrics on the values of openness were by no means confined to self-praise by the English. Foreign observers of English criminal procedure in the 18th and early 19th centuries [570] came away impressed by the very fact that they had been freely admitted to the courts, as many were not in their own homelands. See L. Radzinowicz, A History of English Criminal Law 715, and n. 96 (1948). They marveled that "the whole juridical procedure passes in public," 2 P. Grosley, A Tour to London; or New Observations on England 142 (Nugent trans. 1772), quoted in Radzinowicz, supra, at 717, and one commentator declared:

"The main excellence of the English judicature consists in publicity, in the free trial by jury, and in the extraordinary despatch with which business is transacted. The publicity of their proceedings is indeed astonishing. Free access to the courts is universally granted." C. Goede, A Foreigner's Opinion of England 214 (Horne trans. 1822). (Emphasis added.)

The nexus between openness, fairness, and the perception of fairness was not lost on them:

"[The] judge, the counsel, and the jury, are constantly exposed to public animadversion; and this greatly tends to augment the extraordinary confidence, which the English repose in the administration of justice." Id., at 215.

This observation raises the important point that "[the] publicity of a judicial proceeding is a requirement of much broader bearing than its mere effect upon the quality of testimony." 6 J. Wigmore, Evidence § 1834, p. 435 (J. Chadbourn rev. 1976).[8] The early history of open trials in part reflects the widespread acknowledgment, long before there were behavioral scientists, that public trials had significant community therapeutic value. Even without such experts to frame [571] the concept in words, people sensed from experience and observation that, especially in the administration of criminal justice, the means used to achieve justice must have the support derived from public acceptance of both the process and its results.

When a shocking crime occurs, a community reaction of outrage and public protest often follows. See H. Weihofen, The Urge to Punish 130-131 (1956). Thereafter the open processes of justice serve an important prophylactic purpose, providing an outlet for community concern, hostility, and emotion. Without an awareness that society's responses to criminal conduct are underway, natural human reactions of outrage and protest are frustrated and may manifest themselves in some form of vengeful "self-help," as indeed they did regularly in the activities of vigilante "committees" on our frontiers. "The accusation and conviction or acquittal, as much perhaps as the execution of punishment, [operate] to restore the imbalance which was created by the offense or public charge, to reaffirm the temporarily lost feeling of security and, perhaps, to satisfy that latent 'urge to punish.'" Mueller, Problems Posed by Publicity to Crime and Criminal Proceedings, 110 U. Pa. L. Rev. 1, 6 (1961).

Civilized societies withdraw both from the victim and the vigilante the enforcement of criminal laws, but they cannot erase from people's consciousness the fundamental, natural yearning to see justice done – or even the urge for retribution. The crucial prophylactic aspects of the administration of justice cannot function in the dark; no community catharsis can occur if justice is "done in a corner [or] in any covert manner." Supra, at 567. It is not enough to say that results alone will satiate the natural community desire for "satisfaction." A result considered untoward may undermine public confidence, and where the trial has been concealed from public view an unexpected outcome can cause a reaction that the

---

[7] Bentham also emphasized that open proceedings enhanced the performance of all involved, protected the judge from imputations of dishonesty, and served to educate the public. Rationale of Judicial Evidence, at 522-525.

[8] A collateral aspect seen by Wigmore was the possibility that someone in attendance at the trial or who learns of the proceedings through publicity may be able to furnish evidence in chief or contradict "falsifiers." 6 Wigmore, at 436. Wigmore gives examples of such occurrences. Id., at 436, and n. 2.

system at best has failed and at worst has been corrupted. To work effectively, it is important that society's criminal [572] process "satisfy the appearance of justice," *Offutt* v. *United States*, 348 U.S. 11, 14 (1954), and the appearance of justice can best be provided by allowing people to observe it.

Looking back, we see that when the ancient "town meeting" form of trial became too cumbersome, 12 members of the community were delegated to act as its surrogates, but the community did not surrender its right to observe the conduct of trials. The people retained a "right of visitation" which enabled them to satisfy themselves that justice was in fact being done.

People in an open society do not demand infallibility from their institutions, but it is difficult for them to accept what they are prohibited from observing. When a criminal trial is conducted in the open, there is at least an opportunity both for understanding the system in general and its workings in a particular case:

"The educative effect of public attendance is a material advantage. Not only is respect for the law increased and intelligent acquaintance acquired with the methods of government, but a strong confidence in judicial remedies is secured which could never be inspired by a system of secrecy." 6 Wigmore, *supra*, at 438. See also 1 J. Bentham, Rationale of Judicial Evidence, at 525.

In earlier times, both in England and America, attendance at court was a common mode of "passing the time." See, *e.g.*, 6 Wigmore, *supra*, at 436; Mueller, *supra*, at 6. With the press, cinema, and electronic media now supplying the representations or reality of the real life drama once available only in the courtroom, attendance at court is no longer a widespread pastime. Yet "[it] is not unrealistic even in this day to believe that public inclusion affords citizens a form of legal education and hopefully promotes confidence in the fair administration of justice." *State* v. *Schmit*, 273 Minn. 78, 87-88, 139 N. W. 2d 800, 807 (1966). Instead of acquiring information about trials by firsthand observation or by word [573] of mouth from those who attended, people now acquire it chiefly through the print and electronic media. In a sense, this validates the media claim of functioning as surrogates for the public. While media representatives enjoy the same right of access as the public, they often are provided special seating and priority of entry so that they may report what people in attendance have seen and heard. This "[contributes] to public understanding of the rule of law and to comprehension of the functioning of the entire criminal justice system. . . ." *Nebraska Press Assn.* v. *Stuart*, 427 U.S., at 587 (BRENNAN, J., concurring in judgment).

C From this unbroken, uncontradicted history, supported by reasons as valid today as in centuries past, we are bound to conclude that a presumption of openness inheres in the very nature of a criminal trial under our system of justice. This conclusion is hardly novel; without a direct holding on the issue, the Court has voiced its recognition of it in a variety of contexts over the years.[9] Even while holding, in *Levine* v. [574] *United States*, 362 U.S. 610 (1960), that a criminal contempt proceeding was not a "criminal prosecution" within the meaning of the Sixth Amendment, the Court was careful to note that more than the Sixth Amendment was involved:

"[While] the right to a 'public trial' is explicitly guaranteed by the Sixth Amendment only for 'criminal prosecutions,' that provision is a reflection of the notion, deeply rooted in the common law, that 'justice must satisfy the appearance of justice.' . . . [Due] process demands appropriate regard for the requirements of a public proceeding in cases of criminal contempt . . . as it does for all

---

[9] "Of course trials must be public and the public have a deep interest in trials." *Pennekamp* v. *Florida*, 328 U.S. 331, 361 (1946) (Frankfurter, J., concurring).

"A trial is a public event. What transpires in the court room is public property." *Craig* v. *Harney*, 331 U.S. 367, 374 (1947) (Douglas, J.).

"[We] have been unable to find a single instance of a criminal trial conducted in camera in any federal, state, or municipal court during the history of this country. Nor have we found any record of even one such secret criminal trial in England since abolition of the Court of Star Chamber in 1641, and whether that court ever convicted people secretly is in dispute. . . .

"This nation's accepted practice of guaranteeing a public trial to an accused has its roots in our English common law heritage. The exact date of its origin is obscure, but it likely evolved long before the settlement of our land as an accompaniment of the ancient institution of jury trial." *In re Oliver*, 333 U.S. 257, 266 (1948) (Black, J.) (footnotes omitted).

"One of the demands of a democratic society is that the public should know what goes on in courts by being told by the press what happens there, to the end that the public may judge whether our system of criminal justice is fair and right." *Maryland* v. *Baltimore Radio Show, Inc.*, 338 U.S. 912, 920 (1950) (Frankfurter, J., dissenting from denial of certiorari).

"It is true that the public has the right to be informed as to what occurs in its courts, . . . reporters of all media, including television, are always present if they wish to be and are plainly free to report whatever occurs in open court. . . ." *Estes* v. *Texas*, 381 U.S. 532, 541-542 (1965) (Clark, J.); see also *id.*, at 583-584 (Warren, C. J., concurring). (The Court ruled, however, that the televising of the criminal trial over the defendant's objections violated his due process right to a fair trial.)

"The principle that justice cannot survive behind walls of silence has long been reflected in the 'Anglo-American distrust for secret trials.'" *Sheppard* v. *Maxwell*, 384 U.S. 333, 349 (1966) (Clark, J.).

adjudications through the exercise of the judicial power, barring narrowly limited categories of exceptions. . . ." *Id.*, at 616.[10]

And recently in *Gannett Co.* v. *DePasquale*, 443 U.S. 368 (1979), both the majority and dissenting opinion, *id.*, at 423, agreed that open trials were part of the common-law tradition.

[575] Despite the history of criminal trials being presumptively open since long before the Constitution, the State presses its contention that neither the Constitution nor the Bill of Rights contains any provision which by its terms guarantees to the public the right to attend criminal trials. Standing alone, this is correct, but there remains the question whether, absent an explicit provision, the Constitution affords protection against exclusion of the public from criminal trials. III. A   The First Amendment, in conjunction with the Fourteenth, prohibits governments from "abridging the freedom of speech, or of the press; or the right of the people peaceably to assemble, and to petition the Government for a redress of grievances." These expressly guaranteed freedoms share a common core purpose of assuring freedom of communication on matters relating to the functioning of government. Plainly it would be difficult to single out any aspect of government of higher concern and importance to the people than the manner in which criminal trials are conducted; as we have shown, recognition of this pervades the centuries-old history of open trials and the opinions of this Court. *Supra*, at 564-575, and n. 9.

The Bill of Rights was enacted against the backdrop of the long history of trials being presumptively open. Public access to trials was then regarded as an important aspect of the process itself; the conduct of trials "before as many of the people as chuse to attend" was regarded as one of "the inestimable advantages of a free English constitution of government." 1 Journals 106, 107. In guaranteeing freedoms such as those of speech and press, the First Amendment can be read as protecting the right of everyone to attend trials so as to give meaning to those explicit guarantees. "[The] First Amendment goes beyond protection of the press and the self-expression [576] of individuals to prohibit government from limiting the stock of information from which members of the public may draw." *First National Bank of Boston* v. *Bellotti*, 435 U.S. 765, 783 (1978). Free speech carries with it some freedom to listen. "In a

variety of contexts this Court has referred to a First Amendment right to 'receive information and ideas.'" *Kleindienst* v. *Mandel*, 408 U.S. 753, 762 (1972). What this means in the context of trials is that the First Amendment guarantees of speech and press, standing alone, prohibit government from summarily closing courtroom doors which had long been open to the public at the time that Amendment was adopted. "For the First Amendment does not speak equivocally. . . . It must be taken as a command of the broadest scope that explicit language, read in the context of a liberty-loving society, will allow." *Bridges* v. *California*, 314 U.S. 252, 263 (1941) (footnote omitted).

It is not crucial whether we describe this right to attend criminal trials to hear, see, and communicate observations concerning them as a "right of access," cf. *Gannett, supra*, at 397 (POWELL, J., concurring); *Saxbe* v. *Washington Post Co.*, 417 U.S. 843 (1974); *Pell* v. *Procunier*, 417 U.S. 817 (1974),[11] or a "right to gather information," for we have recognized that "without some protection for seeking out the news, freedom of the press could be eviscerated." *Branzburg* v. *Hayes*, 408 U.S. 665, 681 (1972). The explicit, guaranteed rights to speak and to publish concerning what takes place at a [577] trial would lose much meaning if access to observe the trial could, as it was here, be foreclosed arbitrarily.[12]

B   The right of access to places traditionally open to the public, as criminal trials have long been, may be seen as assured by the amalgam of the First Amendment guarantees of speech and press; and their affinity to the right of assembly is not without relevance. From the outset, the right of assembly was regarded not only as an independent right but also as a catalyst to augment the free exercise of

---

[10] The Court went on to hold that, "on the particular circumstances of the case," 362 U.S., at 616, the accused could not complain on appeal of the "so-called 'secrecy' of the proceedings," *id.*, at 617, because, with counsel present, he had failed to object or to request the judge to open the courtroom at the time.

---

[11] *Procunier* and *Saxbe* are distinguishable in the sense that they were concerned with penal institutions which, by definition, are not "open" or public places. Penal institutions do not share the long tradition of openness, although traditionally there have been visiting committees of citizens, and there is no doubt that legislative committees could exercise plenary oversight and "visitation rights." *Saxbe*, 417 U.S., at 849, noted that "limitation on visitations is justified by what the Court of Appeals acknowledged as 'the truism that prisons are institutions where public access is generally limited.' 161 U. S. App. D. C., at 80, 494 F.2d, at 999. See *Adderley* v. *Florida*, 385 U.S. 39, 41 (1966) [jails]." See also *Greer* v. *Spock*, 424 U.S. 828 (1976) (military bases).
[12] That the right to attend may be exercised by people less frequently today when information as to trials generally reaches them by way of print and electronic media in no way alters the basic right. Instead of relying on personal observation or reports from neighbors as in the past, most people receive information concerning trials through the media whose representatives "are entitled to the same rights [to attend trials] as the general public." *Estes* v. *Texas*, 381 U.S., at 540.

the other First Amendment rights with which it was deliberately linked by the draftsmen.[13] [578] "The right of peaceable assembly is a right cognate to those of free speech and free press and is equally fundamental." *De Jonge* v. *Oregon*, 299 U.S. 353, 364 (1937). People assemble in public places not only to speak or to take action, but also to listen, observe, and learn; indeed, they may "[assemble] for any lawful purpose," *Hague* v. *CIO*, 307 U.S. 496, 519 (1939) (opinion of Stone, J.). Subject to the traditional time, place, and manner restrictions, see, *e.g.*, *Cox* v. *New Hampshire*, 312 U.S. 569 (1941); see also *Cox* v. *Louisiana*, 379 U.S. 559, 560-564 (1965), streets, sidewalks, and parks are places traditionally open, where First Amendment rights may be exercised, see *Hague* v. *CIO, supra*, at 515 (opinion of Roberts, J.); a trial courtroom also is a public place where the people generally – and representatives of the media – have a right to be present, and where their presence historically has been thought to enhance the integrity and quality of what takes place.[14] [579]

C The State argues that the Constitution nowhere spells out a guarantee for the right of the public to attend trials, and that accordingly no such right is protected. The possibility that such a contention could be made did not escape the notice of the Constitution's draftsmen; they were concerned that some important rights might be thought disparaged because not specifically guaranteed. It was even argued that because of this danger no Bill of Rights should be adopted. See, *e.g.*, The Federalist No. 84 (A. Hamilton). In a letter to Thomas Jefferson in October 1788, James Madison explained why he, although "in favor of a bill of rights," had "not viewed it in an important light" up to that time: "I conceive that in a certain degree . . . the rights in question are reserved by the manner in which the federal powers are granted." He went on to state that "there is great reason to fear that a positive declaration of some of the most essential rights could not be obtained in the requisite latitude." 5 Writings of James Madison 271 (G. Hunt ed. 1904).[15]

But arguments such as the State makes have not precluded recognition of important rights not enumerated. Notwithstanding the appropriate caution against reading into the Constitution rights not explicitly defined, the Court has acknowledged that certain unarticulated rights are implicit in enumerated guarantees. For example, the rights of association and of privacy, the right to be presumed innocent, and the right to be judged by a standard of proof beyond a reasonable [580] doubt in a criminal trial, as well as the right to travel, appear nowhere in the Constitution or Bill of Rights. Yet these important but unarticulated rights have nonetheless been found to share constitutional

---

[13] When the First Congress was debating the Bill of Rights, it was contended that there was no need separately to assert the right of assembly because it was subsumed in freedom of speech. Mr. Sedgwick of Massachusetts argued that inclusion of "assembly" among the enumerated rights would tend to make the Congress "appear trifling in the eyes of their constituents. . . . If people freely converse together, they must assemble for that purpose; it is a self-evident, unalienable right which the people possess; it is certainly a thing that never would be called in question. . . ." 1 Annals of Cong. 731 (1789).

Since the right existed independent of any written guarantee, Sedgwick went on to argue that if it were the drafting committee's purpose to protect all inherent rights of the people by listing them, "they might have gone into a very lengthy enumeration of rights," but this was unnecessary, he said, "in a Government where none of them were intended to be infringed." *Id.*, at 732.

Mr. Page of Virginia responded, however, that at times "such rights have been opposed," and that "people have . . . been prevented from assembling together on their lawful occasions":

"[Therefore] it is well to guard against such stretches of authority, by inserting the privilege in the declaration of rights. If the people could be deprived of the power of assembling under any pretext whatsoever, they might be deprived of every other privilege contained in the clause." *Ibid.*

The motion to strike "assembly" was defeated. *Id.*, at 733.

[14] It is of course true that the right of assembly in our Bill of Rights was in large part drafted in reaction to restrictions on such rights in England. See, *e.g.*, 1 Geo. 1, stat. 2, ch. 5 (1714); cf. 36 Geo. 3, ch. 8 (1795). As we have shown, the right of Englishmen to attend trials was not similarly limited; but it would be ironic indeed if the very historic openness of the trial could militate against protection of the right to attend it. The Constitution guarantees more than simply freedom from those abuses which led the Framers to single out particular rights. The very purpose of the First Amendment is to guarantee all facets of each right

described; its draftsmen sought both to protect the "rights of Englishmen" and to enlarge their scope. See *Bridges* v. *California*, 314 U.S. 252, 263-265 (1941). "There are no contrary implications in any part of the history of the period in which the First Amendment was framed and adopted. No purpose in ratifying the Bill of Rights was clearer than that of securing for the people of the United States much greater freedom of religion, expression, assembly, and petition than the people of Great Britain had ever enjoyed." *Id.*, at 265.

[15] Madison's comments in Congress also reveal the perceived need for some sort of constitutional "saving clause," which, among other things, would serve to foreclose application to the Bill of Rights of the maxim that the affirmation of particular rights implies a negation of those not expressly defined. See 1 Annals of Cong. 438-440 (1789). See also, *e.g.*, 2 J. Story, Commentaries on the Constitution of the United States 651 (5th ed. 1891). Madison's efforts, culminating in the Ninth Amendment, served to allay the fears of those who were concerned that expressing certain guarantees could be read as excluding others.

protection in common with explicit guarantees.[16] The concerns expressed by Madison and others have thus been resolved; fundamental rights, even though not expressly guaranteed, have been recognized by the Court as indispensable to the enjoyment of rights explicitly defined.

We hold that the right to attend criminal trials[17] is implicit in the guarantees of the First Amendment; without the freedom to attend such trials, which people have exercised for centuries, important aspects of freedom of speech and "of the press could be eviscerated." *Branzburg*, 408 U.S., at 681.

D Having concluded there was a guaranteed right of the public under the First and Fourteenth Amendments to attend the trial of Stevenson's case, we return to the closure order challenged by appellants. The Court in *Gannett* made clear that although the Sixth Amendment guarantees the accused a right to a public trial, it does not give a right to a private trial. 443 U.S., at 382. Despite the fact that this was the fourth trial of the accused, the trial judge made no findings to support closure; no inquiry was made as to whether alternative [581] solutions would have met the need to ensure fairness; there was no recognition of any right under the Constitution for the public or press to attend the trial. In contrast to the pretrial proceeding dealt with in *Gannett*, there exist in the context of the trial itself various tested alternatives to satisfy the constitutional demands of fairness. See, *e.g., Nebraska Press Assn.* v. *Stuart*, 427 U.S., at 563-565; *Sheppard* v. *Maxwell*, 384 U.S., at 357-362. There was no suggestion that any problems with witnesses could not have been dealt with by their exclusion from the courtroom or their sequestration during the trial. See *id.*, at 359. Nor is there anything to indicate that sequestration of the jurors would not have guarded against their being subjected to any improper information. All of the alternatives admittedly present difficulties for trial courts, but none of the factors relied on here was beyond the realm of the manageable. Absent an overriding interest articulated in findings, the trial

of a criminal case must be open to the public.[18] Accordingly, the judgment under review is *Reversed.*

MR. JUSTICE POWELL took no part in the consideration or decision of this case.

CONCUR BY: WHITE; STEVENS; BRENNAN; STEWART; BLACKMUN

CONCUR: MR. JUSTICE WHITE, concurring.

This case would have been unnecessary had *Gannett Co.* v. *DePasquale*, 443 U.S. 368 (1979), construed the Sixth [582] Amendment to forbid excluding the public from criminal proceedings except in narrowly defined circumstances. But the Court there rejected the submission of four of us to this effect, thus requiring that the First Amendment issue involved here be addressed. On this issue, I concur in the opinion of THE CHIEF JUSTICE.

MR. JUSTICE STEVENS, concurring.

This is a watershed case. Until today the Court has accorded virtually absolute protection to the dissemination of information or ideas, but never before has it squarely held that the acquisition of newsworthy matter is entitled to any constitutional protection whatsoever. An additional word of emphasis is therefore appropriate.

---

[16] See, *e.g., NAACP* v. *Alabama*, 357 U.S. 449 (1958) (right of association); *Griswold* v. *Connecticut*, 381 U.S. 479 (1965), and *Stanley* v. *Georgia*, 394 U.S. 557 (1969) (right to privacy); *Estelle* v. *Williams*, 425 U.S. 501, 503 (1976), and *Taylor* v. *Kentucky*, 436 U.S. 478, 483-486 (1978) (presumption of innocence); *In re Winship*, 397 U.S. 358 (1970) (standard of proof beyond a reasonable doubt); *United States* v. *Guest*, 383 U.S. 745, 757-759 (1966), and *Shapiro* v. *Thompson*, 394 U.S. 618, 630 (1969) (right to interstate travel).

[17] Whether the public has a right to attend trials of civil cases is a question not raised by this case, but we note that historically both civil and criminal trials have been presumptively open.

[18] We have no occasion here to define the circumstances in which all or parts of a criminal trial may be closed to the public, cf., *e.g.,* 6 J. Wigmore, Evidence § 1835 (J. Chadbourn rev. 1976), but our holding today does not mean that the First Amendment rights of the public and representatives of the press are absolute. Just as a government may impose reasonable time, place, and manner restrictions upon the use of its streets in the interest of such objectives as the free flow of traffic, see, *e.g., Cox* v. *New Hampshire*, 312 U.S. 569 (1941), so may a trial judge, in the interest of the fair administration of justice, impose reasonable limitations on access to a trial. "[The] question in a particular case is whether that control is exerted so as not to deny or unwarrantedly abridge . . . the opportunities for the communication of thought and the discussion of public questions immemorially associated with resort to public places." *Id.*, at 574. It is far more important that trials be conducted in a quiet and orderly setting than it is to preserve that atmosphere on city streets. Compare, *e.g., Kovacs* v. *Cooper*, 336 U.S. 77 (1949), with *Illinois* v. *Allen*, 397 U.S. 337 (1970), and *Estes* v. *Texas*, 381 U.S. 532 (1965). Moreover, since courtrooms have limited capacity, there may be occasions when not every person who wishes to attend can be accommodated. In such situations, reasonable restrictions on general access are traditionally imposed, including preferential seating for media representatives. Cf. *Gannett*, 443 U.S., at 397-398 (POWELL, J., concurring); *Houchins* v. *KQED, Inc.*, 438 U.S. 1, 17 (1978) (STEWART, J., concurring in judgment); *id.*, at 32 (STEVENS, J., dissenting).

Twice before, the Court has implied that any governmental restriction on access to information, no matter how severe and no matter how unjustified, would be constitutionally acceptable so long as it did not single out the press for special disabilities not applicable to the public at large. In a dissent joined by MR. JUSTICE BRENNAN and MR. JUSTICE MARSHALL in *Saxbe* v. *Washington Post Co.*, 417 U.S. 843, 850, MR. JUSTICE POWELL unequivocally rejected the conclusion that *"any governmental restriction on press access to information, [583] so long as it is nondiscriminatory, falls outside the purview of First Amendment concern."* *Id.*, at 857 (emphasis in original). And in *Houchins* v. *KQED, Inc.*, 438 U.S. 1, 19-40, I explained at length why MR. JUSTICE BRENNAN, MR. JUSTICE POWELL, and I were convinced that "[an] official prison policy of concealing . . . knowledge from the public by arbitrarily cutting off the flow of information at its source abridges the freedom of speech and of the press protected by the First and Fourteenth Amendments to the Constitution." *Id.*, at 38.

Since MR. JUSTICE MARSHALL and MR. JUSTICE BLACKMUN were unable to participate in that case, a majority of the Court neither accepted nor rejected that conclusion or the contrary conclusion expressed in the prevailing opinions.[1] Today, however, for the first time, the Court unequivocally holds that an arbitrary interference with access to important information is an abridgment of the freedoms of speech and of the press protected by the First Amendment.

It is somewhat ironic that the Court should find more reason to recognize a right of access today than it did in *Houchins*. For *Houchins* involved the plight of a segment of society least able to protect itself, an attack on a longstanding policy of concealment, and an absence of any legitimate justification for abridging public access to information about how government operates.

In this case we are protecting the interests of the most powerful voices in the community, we are concerned with an almost unique exception to an established tradition of openness in the conduct of criminal [584] trials, and it is likely that the closure order was motivated by the judge's desire to protect

the individual defendant from the burden of a fourth criminal trial.[2]

In any event, for the reasons stated in Part II of my *Houchins* opinion, 438 U.S., at 30-38, as well as those stated by THE CHIEF JUSTICE today, I agree that the First Amendment protects the public and the press from abridgment of their rights of access to information about the operation of their government, including the Judicial Branch; given the total absence of any record justification for the closure order entered in this case, that order violated the First Amendment.

MR. JUSTICE BRENNAN, with whom MR. JUSTICE MARSHALL joins, concurring in the judgment.

Gannett Co. v. *DePasquale*, 443 U.S. 368 (1979), held that the Sixth Amendment right to a public trial was personal to the accused, conferring no right of access to pretrial proceedings that is separately enforceable by the public or the press. The instant case raises the question whether the First Amendment, of its own force and as applied to the States through [585] the Fourteenth Amendment, secures the public an independent right of access to trial proceedings. Because I believe that the First Amendment – of itself and as applied to the States through the Fourteenth Amendment – secures such a public right of access, I agree with those of my Brethren who hold that, without more, agreement of the trial judge and the

---

[1] "Neither the First Amendment nor the Fourteenth Amendment mandates a right of access to government information or sources of information within the government's control." 438 U.S., at 15 (opinion of BURGER, C. J.).
"The First and Fourteenth Amendments do not guarantee the public a right of access to information generated or controlled by government. . . . The Constitution does no more than assure the public and the press equal access once government has opened its doors." *Id.*, at 16 (STEWART, J., concurring in judgment).

[2] Neither that likely motivation nor facts showing the risk that a fifth trial would have been necessary without closure of the fourth are disclosed in this record, however. The absence of any articulated reason for the closure order is a sufficient basis for distinguishing this case from *Gannett Co.* v. *DePasquale*, 443 U.S. 368. The decision today is in no way inconsistent with the perfectly unambiguous holding in *Gannett* that the rights guaranteed by the Sixth Amendment are rights that may be asserted by the accused rather than members of the general public. In my opinion the Framers quite properly identified the party who has the greatest interest in the right to a public trial. The language of the Sixth Amendment is worth emphasizing:
"In all criminal prosecutions, *the accused* shall enjoy the right to a speedy and public trial, by an impartial jury of the State and district wherein the crime shall have been committed, which district shall have been previously ascertained by law, and to be informed of the nature and cause of the accusation; to be confronted with the witnesses against him; to have compulsory process for obtaining witnesses in his favor, and to have the Assistance of Counsel for his defence." (Emphasis added.)

parties cannot constitutionally close a trial to the public.[1]

While freedom of expression is made inviolate by the First Amendment, and, with only rare and stringent exceptions, may not be suppressed, see, *e.g.*, *Brown* v. *Glines*, 444 U.S. 348, 364 (1980) (BRENNAN, J., dissenting); *Nebraska Press Assn.* v. *Stuart*, 427 U.S. 539, 558-559 (1976); *id.*, at 590 (BRENNAN, J., concurring in judgment); *New York Times Co.* v. *United States*, 403 U.S. 713, 714 (1971) (*per curiam* opinion); *Near* v. *Minnesota ex rel. Olson*, 283 U.S. 697, 715-716 (1931), the First Amendment has not been viewed by the Court in all settings as providing an equally categorical assurance of the correlative freedom of access to information, see, *e.g.*, *Saxbe* v. *Washington Post Co.*, 417 U.S. 843, 849 [586] (1974); *Zemel* v. *Rusk*, 381 U.S. 1, 16-17 (1965); see also *Houchins* v. *KQED, Inc.*, 438 U.S. 1, 8-9 (1978) (opinion of BURGER, C. J.); *id.*, at 16 (STEWART, J., concurring in judgment); *Gannett Co.* v. *DePasquale*, 433 U.S., at 404-405 (REHNQUIST, J. , concurring). But cf. *id.*, at 397-398 (POWELL, J., concurring); *Houchins, supra*, at 27-38 (STEVENS, J., dissenting); *Saxbe, supra*, at 856-864 (POWELL, J., dissenting); *Pell* v. *Procunier*, 417 U.S. 817, 839-842 (1974) (Douglas, J., dissenting).[2] Yet the Court has not ruled out a public access component to the First Amendment

---

[1] Of course, the Sixth Amendment remains the source of the *accused*'s own right to insist upon public judicial proceedings. *Gannett Co.* v. *DePasquale*, 443 U.S. 368 (1979). That the Sixth Amendment explicitly establishes a public trial right does not impliedly foreclose the derivation of such a right from other provisions of the Constitution. The Constitution was not framed as a work of carpentry, in which all joints must fit snugly without overlapping. Of necessity, a document that designs a form of government will address central political concerns from a variety of perspectives. Significantly, this Court has recognized the open trial right both as a matter of the Sixth Amendment and as an ingredient in Fifth Amendment due process. See *Levine* v. *United States*, 362 U.S. 610, 614, 616 (1960); cf. *In re Oliver*, 333 U.S. 257 (1948) (Fourteenth Amendment due process). Analogously, racial segregation has been found independently offensive to the Equal Protection and Fifth Amendment Due Process Clauses. Compare *Brown* v. *Board of Education*, 347 U.S. 483, 495 (1954), with *Bolling* v. *Sharpe*, 347 U.S. 497, 499-500 (1954).

[2] A conceptually separate, yet related, question is whether the media should enjoy greater access rights than the general public. See, *e.g.*, *Saxbe* v. *Washington Post Co.*, 417 U.S., at 850; *Pell* v. *Procunier*, 417 U.S., at 834-835. But no such contention is at stake here. Since the media's right of access is at least equal to that of the general public, see *ibid.*, this case is resolved by a decision that the state statute unconstitutionally restricts public access to trials. As a practical matter, however, the institutional press is the likely, and fitting, chief beneficiary of a right of access because it serves as the "agent" of interested citizens, and funnels information about trials to a large number of individuals.

in every circumstance. Read with care and in context, our decisions must therefore be understood as holding only that any privilege of access to governmental information is subject to a degree of restraint dictated by the nature of the information and countervailing interests in security or confidentiality. See *Houchins, supra*, at 8-9 (opinion of BURGER, C. J.) (access to prisons); *Saxbe, supra*, at 849 (same); *Pell, supra*, at 831-832 (same); *Estes* v. *Texas*, 381 U.S. 532, 541-542 (1965) (television in courtroom); *Zemel* v. *Rusk, supra*, at 16-17 (validation of passport to unfriendly country). These cases neither comprehensively nor absolutely deny that public access to information may at times be implied by the First Amendment and the principles which animate it.

The Court's approach in right-of-access cases simply reflects the special nature of a claim of First Amendment right to gather information. Customarily, First Amendment guarantees are interposed to protect communication between speaker [587] and listener. When so employed against prior restraints, free speech protections are almost insurmountable. See *Nebraska Press Assn.* v. *Stuart, supra*, at 558-559; *New York Times Co.* v. *United States, supra*, at 714 (*per curiam* opinion). See generally Brennan, Address, 32 Rutgers L. Rev. 173, 176 (1979). But the First Amendment embodies more than a commitment to free expression and communicative interchange for their own sakes; it has a *structural* role to play in securing and fostering our republican system of self-government. See *United States* v. *Carolene Products Co.*, 304 U.S. 144, 152-153, n. 4 (1938); *Grosjean* v. *American Press Co.*, 297 U.S. 233, 249-250 (1936); *Stromberg* v. *California*, 283 U.S. 359, 369 (1931); Brennan, *supra*, at 176-177; J. Ely, Democracy and Distrust 93-94 (1980); T. Emerson, The System of Freedom of Expression 7 (1970); A. Meiklejohn, Free Speech and Its Relation to Self-Government (1948); Bork, Neutral Principles and Some First Amendment Problems, 47 Ind. L.J. 1, 23 (1971). Implicit in this structural role is not only "the principle that debate on public issues should be uninhibited, robust, and wide-open," *New York Times Co.* v. *Sullivan*, 376 U.S. 254, 270 (1964), but also the antecedent assumption that valuable public debate – as well as other civic behavior – must be informed.[3] The

---

[3] This idea has been foreshadowed in MR. JUSTICE POWELL's dissent in *Saxbe* v. *Washington Post Co., supra*, at 862-863:

"What is at stake here is the societal function of the First Amendment in preserving free public discussion of governmental affairs. No aspect of that constitutional guarantee is more rightly treasured than its protection of the ability of our people through free and open debate to

structural [588] model links the First Amendment to that process of communication necessary for a democracy to survive, and thus entails solicitude not only for communication itself, but also for the indispensable conditions of meaningful communication.[4]

However, because "the stretch of this protection is theoretically endless," Brennan, supra, at 177, it must be invoked with discrimination and temperance. For so far as the participating citizen's need for information is concerned, "[there] are few restrictions on action which could not be clothed by ingenious argument in the garb of decreased data flow." Zemel v. Rusk, supra, at 16-17. An assertion of the prerogative to gather information must accordingly be assayed by considering the information sought and the opposing interests invaded.[5]

This judicial task is as much a matter of sensitivity to practical necessities as it is of abstract reasoning. But at least [589] two helpful principles may be sketched. First, the case for a right of access has special force when drawn from an

---

consider and resolve their own destiny. . . . '[The] First Amendment is one of the vital bulwarks of our national commitment to intelligent self-government.' . . . It embodies our Nation's commitment to popular self-determination and our abiding faith that the surest course for developing sound national policy lies in a free exchange of views on public issues. And public debate must not only be unfettered; it must also be informed. For that reason this Court has repeatedly stated that First Amendment concerns encompass the receipt of information and ideas as well as the right of free expression." (Footnote omitted.)

[4] The technique of deriving specific rights from the structure of our constitutional government, or from other explicit rights, is not novel. The right of suffrage has been inferred from the nature of "a free and democratic society" and from its importance as a "preservative of other basic civil and political rights. . . ." Reynolds v. Sims, 377 U.S. 533, 561-562 (1964); San Antonio Independent School Dist. v. Rodriguez, 411 U.S. 1, 34, n. 74 (1973). So, too, the explicit freedoms of speech, petition, and assembly have yielded a correlative guarantee of certain associational activities. NAACP v. Button, 371 U.S. 415, 430 (1963). See also Rodriguez, supra, at 33-34 (indicating that rights may be implicitly embedded in the Constitution); 411 U.S., at 62-63 (BRENNAN, J., dissenting); id., at 112-115 (MARSHALL, J., dissenting); Lamont v. Postmaster General, 381 U.S. 301, 308 (1965) (BRENNAN, J., concurring).

[5] Analogously, we have been somewhat cautious in applying First Amendment protections to communication by way of nonverbal and nonpictorial conduct. Some behavior is so intimately connected with expression that for practical purposes it partakes of the same transcendental constitutional value as pure speech. See, e.g., Tinker v. Des Moines School District, 393 U.S. 503, 505-506 (1969). Yet where the connection between expression and action is perceived as more tenuous, communicative interests may be overridden by competing social values. See, e.g., Hughes v. Superior Court, 339 U.S. 460, 464-465 (1950).

---

enduring and vital tradition of public entree to particular proceedings or information. Cf. In re Winship, 397 U.S. 358, 361-362 (1970). Such a tradition commands respect in part because the Constitution carries the gloss of history. More importantly, a tradition of accessibility implies the favorable judgment of experience. Second, the value of access must be measured in specifics. Analysis is not advanced by rhetorical statements that all information bears upon public issues; what is crucial in individual cases is whether access to a particular government process is important in terms of that very process.

To resolve the case before us, therefore, we must consult historical and current practice with respect to open trials, and weigh the importance of public access to the trial process itself.

II. "This nation's accepted practice of guaranteeing a public trial to an accused has its roots in our English common law heritage." In re Oliver, 333 U.S. 257, 266 (1948); see Gannett Co. v. DePasquale, 443 U.S., at 419-420 (BLACK-MUN, J., concurring and dissenting). Indeed, historically and functionally, open trials have been closely associated with the development of the fundamental procedure of trial by jury. In re Oliver, supra, at 266; Radin, The Right to a Public Trial, 6 Temp. L.Q. 381, 388 (1932).[6] Pre-eminent English legal observers and commentators have unreservedly acknowledged and applauded the public character of the common-law [590] trial process. See T. Smith, De Republica Anglorum 77, 81-82 (1970);[7] 2 E. Coke, Institutes of the Laws of England 103 (6th ed. 1681); 3 W. Blackstone, Commentaries *372-*373;[8] M. Hale, The History of the Common Law of England 342-344 (6th ed. 1820);[9] 1 J. Bentham, Rationale of Judicial Evidence 584-585 (1827). And it appears that "there is little record, if any, of secret proceedings, criminal or civil, having occurred at any time in known English history." Gannett, supra, at 420 (BLACKMUN, J., concurring and dissenting); see also In re Oliver, supra, at 269, n. 22; Radin, supra, at 386-387.

This legacy of open justice was inherited by the English settlers in America. The earliest charters of

---

[6] "[The public trial] seems almost a necessary incident of jury trials, since the presence of a jury . . . already insured the presence of a large part of the public. We need scarcely be reminded that the jury was the patria, the 'country' and that it was in that capacity and not as judges, that it was summoned." Radin, The Right to a Public Trial, 6 Temp. L.Q. 381, 388 (1932); see 3 W. Blackstone, Commentaries * 349 ("trial by jury; called also the trial per pais, or by the country"); T. Smith, De Republica Anglorum 79 (1970).

[7] First published in 1583.

[8] First published in 1765.

[9] First edition published in 1713.

colonial government expressly perpetuated the accepted practice of public trials. See Concessions and Agreements of West New Jersey, 1677, ch. XXIII;[10] Pennsylvania Frame of Government, 1682, Laws Agreed Upon in England, V.[11] "There is no evidence that any colonial court conducted criminal trials behind closed doors. . . ." *Gannett Co.* v. *DePasquale, supra,* at 425 (BLACKMUN, J., concurring and dissenting). Subsequently framed state constitutions also prescribed open trial proceedings. See, *e.g.,* Pennsylvania Declaration of Rights, 1776, IX;[12] North Carolina Declaration of Rights, 1776, IX;[13] Vermont Declaration of Rights, X (1777);[14] see also *In re Oliver,* 333 U.S., at 267. "Following the ratification in 1791 of the Federal Constitution's Sixth Amendment, ...most of the original states and those subsequently admitted to [591] the Union adopted similar constitutional provisions." *Ibid.*[15] Today, the overwhelming majority of States secure the right to public trials. *Gannett, supra,* at 414-415, n. 3 (BLACKMUN, J., concurring and dissenting); see also *In re Oliver, supra,* at 267-268, 271, and nn. 17-20.

This Court too has persistently defended the public character of the trial process. *In re Oliver* established that the Due Process Clause of the Fourteenth Amendment forbids closed criminal trials. Noting the "universal rule against secret trials," 333 U.S., at 266, the Court held that

"[in] view of this nation's historic distrust of secret proceedings, their inherent dangers to freedom, and the universal requirement of our federal and state governments that criminal trials be public, the Fourteenth Amendment's guarantee that no one shall be deprived of his liberty without due

process of law means at least that an accused cannot be thus sentenced to prison." *Id.,* at 273.[16]

[592] Even more significantly for our present purpose, *Oliver* recognized that open trials are bulwarks of our free and democratic government: public access to court proceedings is one of the numerous "checks and balances" of our system, because "contemporaneous review in the forum of public opinion is an effective restraint on possible abuse of judicial power," *id.,* at 270. See *Sheppard* v. *Maxwell,* 384 U.S. 333, 350 (1966). Indeed, the Court focused with particularity upon the public trial guarantee "as a safeguard against any attempt to employ our courts as instruments of persecution," or "for the suppression of political and religious heresies." *Oliver, supra,* at 270. Thus, *Oliver* acknowledged that open trials are indispensable to First Amendment political and religious freedoms.

By the same token, a special solicitude for the public character of judicial proceedings is evident in the Court's rulings upholding the right to report about the administration of justice. While these decisions are impelled by the classic protections afforded by the First Amendment to pure communication, they are also bottomed upon a keen appreciation of the structural interest served in opening the judicial system to public inspection.[17] So, in upholding a privilege for reporting truthful information about judicial misconduct proceedings, *Landmark Communications, Inc.* v. *Virginia,* 435 U.S. 829 (1978), emphasized that public scrutiny of the operation of a judicial disciplinary body implicates a major purpose of the First Amendment – "discussion of governmental affairs," *id.,* at 839. Again, *Nebraska Press Assn.* v. *Stuart,* 427 U.S., at 559, noted that the traditional guarantee against prior restraint "should have particular force as applied to reporting of criminal proceedings. . . ." And *Cox Broadcasting Corp.* v. *Cohn,* 420 U.S. 469, 492 (1975), instructed that [593] "[with] respect to judicial proceedings in particular, the function of the press serves to guarantee the fairness of trials and to bring to bear the beneficial effects of public scrutiny upon the administration

---

[10] Quoted in 1 B. Schwartz, The Bill of Rights: A Documentary History 129 (1971).

[11] *Id.,* at 140.

[12] *Id.,* at 265.

[13] *Id.,* at 287.

[14] *Id.,* at 323.

[15] To be sure, some of these constitutions, such as the Pennsylvania Declaration of Rights, couched their public trial guarantees in the language of the accused's rights. But although the Court has read the Federal Constitution's explicit public trial provision, U.S. Const., Amdt. 6, as benefiting the defendant alone, it does not follow that comparably worded state guarantees must be so construed. See *Gannett Co.* v. *DePasquale,* 443 U.S., at 425, and n. 9 (BLACKMUN, J., concurring and dissenting); cf. also *Mallott* v. *State,* 608 P. 2d 737, 745, n. 12 (Alaska 1980). And even if the specific state public trial protections must be invoked by defendants, those state constitutional clauses still provide evidence of the importance attached to open trials by the founders of our state governments. Indeed, it may have been thought that linking public trials to the accused's privileges was the most effective way of assuring a vigorous representative for the popular interest.

[16] Notably, *Oliver* did not rest upon the simple incorportaion of the Sixth Amendment into the Fourteenth, but upon notions intrinsic to due process, because the criminal contempt proceedings at issue in the case were "not within 'all criminal prosecutions' to which [the Sixth] . . . Amendment applies." *Levine* v. *United States,* 362 U.S. 610, 616 (1960); see also n. 1, *supra.*

[17] As Mr. Justice Holmes pointed out in his opinion for the Massachusetts Supreme Judicial Court in *Cowley* v. *Pulsifer,* 137 Mass. 392, 394 (1884), "the privilege [to publish reports of judicial proceedings] and the access of the public to the courts stand in reason upon common ground." See *Lewis* v. *Levy,* El., Bl., & El. 537, 120 Eng. Rep. 610 (K.B. 1858).

of justice." See *Time, Inc.* v. *Firestone*, 424 U.S. 448, 473-474, 476-478 (1976) (BRENNAN, J., dissenting) (open judicial process is essential to fulfill "the First Amendment guarantees to the people of this Nation that they shall retain the necessary means of control over their institutions...").

Tradition, contemporaneous state practice, and this Court's own decisions manifest a common understanding that "[a] trial is a public event. What transpires in the court room is public property." *Craig* v. *Harney*, 331 U.S. 367, 374 (1947). As a matter of law and virtually immemorial custom, public trials have been the essentially unwavering rule in ancestral England and in our own Nation. See *In re Oliver*, 333 U.S., at 266-268; *Gannett Co.* v. *DePasquale*, 443 U.S., at 386, n. 15; *id.*, at 418-432, and n. 11 (BLACKMUN, J., concurring and dissenting).[18] Such abiding adherence to the principle of open trials "[reflects] a profound judgment about the way in which law should be enforced and justice administered." *Duncan* v. *Louisiana*, 391 U.S. 145, 155 (1968).

III. Publicity serves to advance several of the particular purposes of the trial (and, indeed, the judicial) process. Open trials play a fundamental role in furthering the efforts of our judicial system to assure the criminal defendant a fair and accurate adjudication of guilt or innocence. See, *e.g., Estes* v. *Texas*, 381 U.S., at 538-539. But, as a feature of our [594] governing system of justice, the trial process serves other, broadly political, interests, and public access advances these objectives as well. To that extent, trial access possesses specific structural significance.[19]

---

[18] The dictum in *Branzburg* v. *Hayes*, 408 U.S. 665, 684-685 (1972), that "[newsmen] . . . may be prohibited from attending or publishing information about trials if such restrictions are necessary to assure a defendant a fair trial . . . ," is not to the contrary; it simply notes that rights of access may be curtailed where there are sufficiently powerful countervailing considerations. See *supra*, at 588.
[19] By way of analogy, we have fashioned rules of criminal procedure to serve interests implicated in the trial process beside those of the defendant. For example, the exclusionary rule is prompted not only by the accused's interest in vindicating his own rights, but also in part by the independent "'imperative of judicial integrity.'" See, *e.g., Terry* v. *Ohio*, 392 U.S. 1, 12-13 (1968), quoting *Elkins* v. *United States*, 364 U.S. 206, 222 (1960); *United States* v. *Calandra*, 414 U.S. 338, 357-359 (1974) (BRENNAN, J., dissenting); *Olmstead* v. *United States*, 277 U.S. 438, 484-485 (1928) (Brandeis, J., dissenting); *id.*, at 470 (Holmes, J., dissenting). And several Members of this Court have insisted that criminal entrapment cannot be "countenanced" because the "obligation" to avoid "enforcement of the law by lawless means . . . goes beyond the conviction of the particular defendant before the court. Public confidence in the fair and honorable administration of justice . . . is the transcending value at stake." *Sherman* v. *United States*, 356 U.S. 369, 380 (1958) (Frankfurter, J., concurring in result);

The trial is a means of meeting "the notion, deeply rooted in the common law, that 'justice must satisfy the appearance of justice.'" *Levine* v. *United States*, 362 U.S. 610, 616 (1960), quoting *Offutt* v. *United States*, 348 U.S. 11, 14 (1954); accord, *Gannett Co.* v. *DePasquale, supra*, at 429 (BLACKMUN, J., concurring and dissenting); see *Cowley* v. *Pulsifer*, 137 Mass. 392, 394 (1884) (Holmes, J.). For a civilization founded upon principles of ordered liberty to survive and flourish, its members must share the conviction that they are governed equitably. That necessity underlies constitutional provisions as diverse as the rule against takings without just compensation, see *Prune Yard Shopping Center* v. *Robins*, 447 U.S. 74, 82-83, and n. 7 (1980), and the Equal Protection Clause. It also mandates a system of justice that demonstrates the fairness of the law to our citizens. One [595] major function of the trial, hedged with procedural protections and conducted with conspicuous respect for the rule of law, is to make that demonstration. See *In re Oliver, supra*, at 270, n. 24.

Secrecy is profoundly inimical to this demonstrative purpose of the trial process. Open trials assure the public that procedural rights are respected, and that justice is afforded equally. Closed trials breed suspicion of prejudice and arbitrariness, which in turn spawns disrespect for law. Public access is essential, therefore, if trial adjudication is to achieve the objective of maintaining public confidence in the administration of justice. See *Gannett, supra*, at 428-429 (BLACKMUN, J., concurring and dissenting).

But the trial is more than a demonstrably just method of adjudicating disputes and protecting rights. It plays a pivotal role in the entire judicial process, and, by extension, in our form of government. Under our system, judges are not mere umpires, but, in their own sphere, lawmakers – a coordinate branch of *government*.[20] While

---

see *United States* v. *Russell*, 411 U.S. 423, 436-439 (1973) (Douglas, J., dissenting); *id.*, at 442-443 (STEWART, J., dissenting); *Sorrells* v. *United States*, 287 U.S. 435, 455 (1932) (opinion of Roberts, J.); *Casey* v. *United States*, 276 U.S. 413, 423, 425 (1928) (Brandeis, J., dissenting).
[20] The interpretation and application of constitutional and statutory law, while not legislation, is lawmaking, albeit of a kind that is subject to special constraints and informed by unique considerations. Guided and confined by the Constitution and pertinent statutes, judges are obliged to be discerning, to exercise judgment, and to prescribe rules. Indeed, at times judges wield considerable authority to formulate legal policy in designated areas. See, *e.g., Moragne* v. *States Marine Lines*, 398 U.S. 375 (1970); *Banco Nacional de Cuba* v. *Sabbatino*, 376 U.S. 398 (1964); *Textile Workers* v. *Lincoln Mills*, 353 U.S. 448, 456-457 (1957); P. Areeda, Antitrust Analysis 45-46 (2d ed. 1974) ("Sherman Act [is] . . . a general authority to do what common law courts usually

individual cases turn upon the controversies between parties, or involve particular prosecutions, court rulings impose official and practical consequences upon members of society at large. Moreover, judges bear responsibility for the vitally important task of construing and securing constitutional rights. Thus, so far as the [596] trial is the mechanism for judicial factfinding, as well as the initial forum for legal decision making, it is a genuine governmental proceeding.

It follows that the conduct of the trial is pre-eminently a matter of public interest. See *Cox Broadcasting Corp.* v. *Cohn,* 420 U.S., at 491-492; *Maryland* v. *Baltimore Radio Show, Inc.,* 338 U.S. 912, 920 (1950) (opinion of Frankfurter, J., respecting denial of certiorari). More importantly, public access to trials acts as an important check, akin in purpose to the other checks and balances that infuse our system of government. "The knowledge that every criminal trial is subject to contemporaneous review in the forum of public opinion is an effective restraint on possible abuse of judicial power," *In re Oliver,* 333 U.S., at 270 – an abuse that, in many cases, would have ramifications beyond the impact upon the parties before the court. Indeed, "'[without] publicity, all other checks are insufficient: in comparison of publicity, all other checks are of small account.'" *Id.,* at 271, quoting 1 J. Bentham, Rationale of Judicial Evidence 524 (1827); see 3 W. Blackstone, Commentaries *372; M. Hale, History of the Common Law of England 344 (6th ed. 1820); 1 J. Bryce, The American Commonwealth 514 (rev. 1931).

Finally, with some limitations, a trial aims at true and accurate factfinding. Of course, proper factfinding is to the benefit of criminal defendants and of the parties in civil proceedings. But other, comparably urgent, interests are also often at stake. A miscarriage of justice that imprisons an innocent accused also leaves a guilty party at large, a continuing threat to society. Also, mistakes of fact in civil litigation may inflict costs upon others than the plaintiff and defendant. Facilitation of the trial factfinding process, therefore, is of concern to the public as well as to the parties.[21]

Publicizing trial proceedings aids accurate factfinding. "Public trials come to the attention of key witnesses unknown [597] to the parties." *In re Oliver, supra,* at 270, n. 24; see *Tanksley* v. *United States,* 145 F.2d 58, 59 (CA9 1944); 6 J. Wigmore,

Evidence § 1834 (J. Chadbourn rev. 1976). Shrewd legal observers have averred that "open examination of witnesses *viva voce,* in the presence of all mankind, is much more conducive to the clearing up of truth, than the private and secret examination . . . where a witness may frequently depose that in private, which he will be ashamed to testify in a public and solemn tribunal." 3 Blackstone, *supra,* at *373.

See *Tanksley* v. *United States, supra,* at 59-60; Hale, *supra,* at 345; 1 Bentham, *supra,* at 522-523. And experience has borne out these assertions about the truthfinding role of publicity. See Hearings on S. 290 before the Subcommittee on Constitutional Rights and the Subcommittee on Improvements in Judicial Machinery of the Senate Judiciary Committee, 89th Cong., 1st Sess., pt. 2, pp. 433-434, 437-438 (1966).

Popular attendance at trials, in sum, substantially furthers the particular public purposes of that critical judicial proceeding.[22] In that sense, public access is an indispensable element of the trial process itself. Trial access, therefore, assumes structural importance in our "government of laws," *Marbury* v. *Madison,* 1 Cranch 137, 163 (1803).

IV. As previously noted, resolution of First Amendment public access claims in individual cases must be strongly influenced [598] by the weight of historical practice and by an assessment of the specific structural value of public access in the circumstances. With regard to the case at hand, our ingrained tradition of public trials and the importance of public access to the broader purposes of the trial process, tip the balance strongly toward the rule that trials be open.[23] What countervailing interests might be sufficiently compelling to reverse this presumption of openness need not concern us now,[24] for the statute at stake here

---

[22] In advancing these purposes, the availability of a trial transcript is no substitute for a public presence at the trial itself. As any experienced appellate judge can attest, the "cold" record is a very imperfect reproduction of events that transpire in the courtroom. Indeed, to the extent that publicity serves as a check upon trial officials, "[recordation] . . . would be found to operate rather as [cloak] than [check]; as [cloak] in reality, as [check] only in appearance." *In re Oliver,* 333 U.S., at 271, quoting 1 J. Bentham, Rationale of Judicial Evidence 524 (1827); see *id.,* at 577-578.

[23] The presumption of public trials is, of course, not at all incompatible with reasonable restrictions imposed upon courtroom behavior in the interests of decorum. Cf. *Illinois* v. *Allen,* 397 U.S. 337 (1970). Thus, when engaging in interchanges at the bench, the trial judge is not required to allow public or press intrusion upon the huddle. Nor does this opinion intimate that judges are restricted in their ability to conduct conferences in chambers, inasmuch as such conferences are distinct from trial proceedings.

[24] For example, national security concerns about confidentiality may sometimes warrant closures during

---

do: to use certain customary techniques of judicial reasoning . . . and to develop, refine, and innovate in the dynamic common law tradition").

[21] Further, the interest in insuring that the innocent are not punished may be shared by the general public, in addition to the accused himself.

authorizes trial closures at the unfettered discretion of the judge and parties.[25] Accordingly, Va. Code § 19.2-266 (Supp. 1980) violates the First and Fourteenth Amendments, and the decision of the Virginia Supreme Court to the contrary should be reversed.

MR. JUSTICE STEWART, concurring in the judgment.

In *Gannett Co.* v. *DePasquale*, 443 U.S. 368, the Court held that the Sixth Amendment, which guarantees "the accused" the right to a public trial, does not confer upon representatives of the press or members of the general public any right of access to a trial.[1] But the Court explicitly left [599] open the question whether such a right of access may be guaranteed by other provisions of the Constitution, *id.*, at 391-393. MR. JUSTICE POWELL expressed the view that the First and Fourteenth Amendments do extend at least a limited right of access even to pretrial suppression hearings in criminal cases, *id.*, at 397-403 (concurring opinion). MR. JUSTICE REHNQUIST expressed a contrary view, *id.*, at 403-406 (concurring opinion). The remaining Members of the Court were silent on the question.

Whatever the ultimate answer to that question may be with respect to pretrial suppression hearings in criminal cases, the First and Fourteenth Amendments clearly give the press and the public a right of access to trials themselves, civil as well as criminal.[2] As has been abundantly demonstrated in Part II of the opinion of THE CHIEF JUSTICE, in MR. JUSTICE BRENNAN's opinion concurring in the judgment, and in MR. JUSTICE BLACK-MUN's opinion dissenting in part last Term in the

Gannett case, *supra*, at 406, it has for centuries been a basic presupposition of the Anglo-American legal system that trials shall be public trials. The opinions referred to also convincingly explain the many good reasons why this is so. With us, a trial is by very definition a proceeding open to the press and to the public.

In conspicuous contrast to a military base, *Greer* v. *Spock*, 424 U.S. 828; a jail, *Adderley* v. *Florida*, 385 U.S. 39; or a prison, *Pell* v. *Procunier*, 417 U.S. 817, a trial courtroom is a public place. Even more than city streets, sidewalks, and [600] parks as areas of traditional First Amendment activity, *e.g.*, *Shuttlesworth* v. *Birmingham*, 394 U.S. 147, a trial courtroom is a place where representatives of the press and of the public are not only free to be, but where their presence serves to assure the integrity of what goes on.

But this does not mean that the First Amendment right of members of the public and representatives of the press to attend civil and criminal trials is absolute. Just as a legislature may impose reasonable time, place, and manner restrictions upon the exercise of First Amendment freedoms, so may a trial judge impose reasonable limitations upon the unrestricted occupation of a courtroom by representatives of the press and members of the public. Cf. *Sheppard* v. *Maxwell*, 384 U.S. 333. Much more than a city street, a trial courtroom must be a quiet and orderly place. Compare *Kovacs* v. *Cooper*, 336 U.S. 77, with *Illinois* v. *Allen*, 397 U.S. 337, and *Estes* v. *Texas*, 381 U.S. 532. Moreover, every courtroom has a finite physical capacity, and there may be occasions when not all who wish to attend a trial may do so.[3] And while there exist many alternative ways to satisfy the constitutional demands of a fair trial,[4] those demands may also sometimes justify limitations upon the unrestricted presence of spectators in the courtroom.[5]

Since in the present case the trial judge appears to have [601] given no recognition to the right of representatives of the press and members of the public to be present at the Virginia murder trial

---

sensitive portions of trial proceedings, such as testimony about state secrets. Cf. *United States* v. *Nixon*, 418 U.S. 683, 714-716 (1974).

[25] Significantly, closing a trial lacks even the justification for barring the door to pretrial hearings: the necessity of preventing dissemination of suppressible prejudicial evidence to the public before the jury pool has become, in a practical sense, finite and subject to sequestration.

[1] The Court also made clear that the Sixth Amendment does not give the accused the right to a *private* trial. 443 U.S., at 382. Cf. *Singer* v. *United States*, 380 U.S. 24 (Sixth Amendment right of trial by jury does not include right to be tried without a jury).

[2] It has long been established that the protections of the First Amendment are guaranteed by the Fourteenth Amendment against invasion by the States. *E.g.*, *Gitlow* v. *New York*, 268 U.S. 652. The First Amendment provisions relevant to this case are those protecting free speech and a free press. The right to speak implies a freedom to listen, *Kleindienst* v. *Mandel*, 408 U.S. 753. The right to publish implies a freedom to gather information, *Branzburg* v. *Hayes*, 408 U.S. 665, 681. See opinion of MR. JUSTICE BRENNAN concurring in the judgment, *ante*, p. 584, *passim*.

---

[3] In such situations, representatives of the press must be assured access. *Houchins* v. *KQED, Inc.*, 438 U.S. 1, 16 (opinion concurring in judgment).
[4] Such alternatives include sequestration of juries, continuances, and changes of venue.
[5] This is not to say that only constitutional considerations can justify such restrictions. The preservation of trade secrets, for example, might justify the exclusion of the public from at least some segments of a civil trial. And the sensibilities of a youthful prosecution witness, for example, might justify similar exclusion in a criminal trial for rape, so long as the defendant's Sixth Amendment right to a public trial were not impaired. See, *e.g.*, *Stamicarbon, N. V.* v. *American Cyanamid Co.*, 506 F.2d 532, 539-542 (CA2 1974).

over which he was presiding, the judgment under review must be reversed.

It is upon the basis of these principles that I concur in the judgment.

MR. JUSTICE BLACKMUN, concurring in the judgment.

My opinion and vote in partial dissent last Term in *Gannett Co.* v. *DePasquale*, 443 U.S. 368, 406 (1979), compels my vote to reverse the judgment of the Supreme Court of Virginia.

I. The decision in this case is gratifying for me for two reasons:

It is gratifying, first, to see the Court now looking to and relying upon legal history in determining the fundamental public character of the criminal trial. *Ante*, at 564-569, 572-574, and n. 9. The partial dissent in *Gannett*, 443 U.S., at 419-433, took great pains in assembling − I believe adequately − the historical material and in stressing its importance to this area of the law. See also MR. JUSTICE BRENNAN's helpful review set forth as Part II of his opinion in the present case. *Ante*, at 589-593. Although the Court in *Gannett* gave a modicum of lip service to legal history, 443 U.S., at 386, n. 15, it denied its obvious application when the defense and the prosecution, with no resistance by the trial judge, agreed that the proceeding should be closed.

The Court's return to history is a welcome change in direction. It is gratifying, second, to see the Court wash away at least some of the graffiti that marred the prevailing opinions in *Gannett*.[1] No fewer than 12 times in the primary opinion in that case, the Court (albeit in what seems now to have become [602] clear dicta) observed that its Sixth Amendment closure ruling applied to the *trial* itself. The author of the first concurring opinion was fully aware of this and would have restricted the Court's observations and ruling to the

suppression hearing. *Id.*, at 394. Nonetheless, he *joined* the Court's opinion, *ibid.*, with its multiple references to the trial itself; the opinion was not a mere concurrence in the Court's judgment. And MR. JUSTICE REHNQUIST, in his separate concurring opinion, quite understandably observed, as a consequence, that the Court was holding "without qualification," that "'members of the public have no constitutional right under the Sixth and Fourteenth Amendments to attend criminal trials,'" *id.*, at 403, quoting from the primary opinion, *id.*, at 391. The resulting confusion among commentators n1 and journalists[2] was not surprising. [603]

II. The Court's ultimate ruling in *Gannett*, with such clarification as is provided by the opinions in this case today, apparently is now to the effect that there is no *Sixth* Amendment right on the part of the public − or the press − to an open hearing on a motion to suppress. I, of course, continue to believe that *Gannett* was in error, both in its interpretation of the Sixth Amendment generally, and in its application to the suppression hearing, for I remain convinced that the right to a public trial is to be found where the Constitution explicitly placed it − in the Sixth Amendment.[3]

The Court, however, has eschewed the Sixth Amendment route. The plurality turns to other possible constitutional sources and invokes a veritable potpourri of them − the Speech Clause of the First Amendment, the Press Clause, the Assembly Clause, the Ninth Amendment, and a cluster of penumbral guarantees recognized in past decisions. This course is troublesome, but it is the route that has been selected and, at least for now, we must live with it. No purpose would be served by my spelling out at length here the reasons for my saying that the course is troublesome. I need do no more than observe that uncertainty marks the nature − and strictness − of the standard of closure the Court adopts. The plurality opinion speaks of "an overriding interest articulated in findings," *ante*, at 581; MR. JUSTICE STEWART reserves,

---

[1] See, *e.g.*, Stephenson, Fair Trial-Free Press: Rights in Continuing Conflict, 46 Brooklyn L. Rev. 39, 63 (1979) ("intended reach of the majority opinion is unclear" (footnote omitted)); The Supreme Court, 1978 Term, 93 Harv. L. Rev. 60, 65 (1979) ("widespread uncertainty over what the Court held"); Note, 51 U. Colo. L. Rev. 425, 432-433 (1980) (*"Gannett* can be interpreted to sanction the closing of trials"; citing "the uncertainty of the language in *Gannett*," and its "ambiguous sixth amendment holding"); Note, 11 Tex. Tech. L. Rev. 159, 170-171 (1979) ("perhaps much of the present and imminent confusion lies in the Court's own statement of its holding"); Borow & Kruth, Closed Preliminary Hearings, 55 Calif. State Bar J. 18, 23 (1980) ("Despite the public disclaimers . . . , the majority holding appears to embrace the right of access to trials as well as pretrial hearings"); Goodale, Gannett Means What it Says; But Who Knows What it Says?, Nat. L.J., Oct. 15, 1979, p. 20; see also Keeffe, The Boner Called Gannett, 66 A.B.A.J. 227 (1980).

[2] The press − perhaps the segment of society most profoundly affected by *Gannett* − has called the Court's decision "cloudy," Birmingham Post-Herald, Aug. 21, 1979, p. A4; "confused," Chicago Sun-Times, Sept. 20, 1979, p. 56 (cartoon); "incoherent," Baltimore Sun, Sept. 22, 1979, p. A14; "mushy," Washington Post, Aug. 10, 1979, p. A15; and a "muddle," Time, Sept. 17, 1979, p. 82, and Newsweek, Aug. 27, 1979, p. 69.

[3] I shall not again seek to demonstrate the errors of analysis in the Court's opinion in *Gannett*. I note, however, that the very existence of the present case illustrates the utter fallacy of thinking, in this context, that "the public interest is fully protected by the participants in the litigation." *Gannett Co.* v. *DePasquale*, 443 U.S., at 384. Cf. *id.*, at 438-439 (opinion in partial dissent).

perhaps not inappropriately, "reasonable limitations," *ante*, at 600; MR. JUSTICE BRENNAN presents his separate analytical framework; MR. JUSTICE POWELL in *Gannett* was critical of those Justices who, relying on the Sixth Amendment, concluded [604] that closure is authorized only when "strictly and inescapably necessary," 443 U.S., at 339-400; and MR. JUSTICE REHNQUIST continues his flat rejection of, among others, the First Amendment avenue.

Having said all this, and with the Sixth Amendment set to one side in this case, I am driven to conclude, as a secondary position, that the First Amendment must provide some measure of protection for public access to the trial. The opinion in partial dissent in *Gannett* explained that the public has an intense need and a deserved right to know about the administration of justice in general; about the prosecution of local crimes in particular; about the conduct of the judge, the prosecutor, defense counsel, police officers, other public servants, and all the actors in the judicial arena; and about the trial itself. See 443 U.S., at 413, and n. 2, 414, 428-429, 448. See also *Cox Broadcasting Corp.* v. *Cohn*, 420 U.S. 469, 492 (1975). It is clear and obvious to me, on the approach the Court has chosen to take, that, by closing this criminal trial, the trial judge abridged these First Amendment interests of the public.

I also would reverse, and I join the judgment of the Court.

DISSENT: MR. JUSTICE REHNQUIST, dissenting.

In the Gilbert and Sullivan operetta "Iolanthe," the Lord Chancellor recites:

"The Law is the true embodiment of everything that's excellent,

It has no kind of fault or flaw,

And I, my Lords, embody the Law."

It is difficult not to derive more than a little of this flavor from the various opinions supporting the judgment in this case. The opinion of THE CHIEF JUSTICE states: "[Here] for the first time the Court is asked to decide whether a criminal trial itself may be closed to the public upon the unopposed request of a defendant, without any [605] demonstration that closure is required to protect the defendant's superior right to a fair trial, or that some other overriding consideration requires closure." *Ante*, at 564.

The opinion of MR. JUSTICE BRENNAN states: "Read with care and in context, our decisions must therefore be understood as holding only that any privilege of access to governmental information is subject to a degree of restraint dictated by the nature of the information and countervailing interests in security or confidentiality." *Ante*, at 586.

For the reasons stated in my separate concurrence in *Gannett Co.* v. *DePasquale*, 443 U.S. 368, 403 (1979), I do not believe that either the First or Sixth Amendment, as made applicable to the States by the Fourteenth, requires that a State's reasons for denying public access to a trial, where both the prosecuting attorney and the defendant have consented to an order of closure approved by the judge, are subject to any additional constitutional review at our hands. And I most certainly do not believe that the Ninth Amendment confers upon us any such power to review orders of state trial judges closing trials in such situations. See *ante*, at 579, n. 15.

We have at present 50 state judicial systems and one federal judicial system in the United States, and our authority to reverse a decision by the highest court of the State is limited to only those occasions when the state decision violates some provision of the United States Constitution. And that authority should be exercised with a full sense that the judges whose decisions we review are making the same effort as we to uphold the Constitution. As said by Mr. Justice Jackson, concurring in the result in *Brown* v. *Allen*, 344 U.S. 443, 540 (1953), "we are not final because we are infallible, but we are infallible only because we are final."

The proper administration of justice in any nation is bound to be a matter of the highest concern to all thinking citizens. [606]But to gradually rein in, as this Court has done over the past generation, all of the ultimate decisionmaking power over how justice shall be administered, not merely in the federal system but in each of the 50 States, is a task that no Court consisting of nine persons, however gifted, is equal to. Nor is it desirable that such authority be exercised by such a tiny numerical fragment of the 220 million people who compose the population of this country. In the same concurrence just quoted, Mr. Justice Jackson accurately observed that "[the] generalities of the Fourteenth Amendment are so indeterminate as to what state actions are forbidden that this Court has found it a ready instrument, in one field or another, to magnify federal, and incidentally its own, authority over the states." *id.*, at 534.

However high-minded the impulses which originally spawned this trend may have been, and which impulses have been accentuated since the time Mr. Justice Jackson wrote, it is basically unhealthy to have so much authority concentrated in a small group of lawyers who have been appointed to the Supreme Court and enjoy virtual life tenure. Nothing in the reasoning of Mr. Chief Justice Marshall in *Marbury* v. *Madison*, 1 Cranch

137 (1803), requires that this Court through ever-broadening use of the Supremacy Clause smother a healthy pluralism which would ordinarily exist in a national government embracing 50 States.

The issue here is not whether the "right" to freedom of the press conferred by the First Amendment to the Constitution overrides the defendant's "right" to a fair trial conferred by other Amendments to the Constitution; it is instead whether any provision in the Constitution may fairly be read to prohibit what the trial judge in the Virginia state-court system did in this case. Being unable to find any such prohibition in the First, Sixth, Ninth, or any other Amendment to the United States Constitution, or in the Constitution itself, I dissent.

Detroit Free Press v. Ashcroft
303 F.3d 681
(6th Cir. 2002)
(Excerpts only. Footnotes omitted.)

PRIOR HISTORY: Appeal from the United States District Court for the Eastern District of Michigan at Detroit. Detroit Free Press v. Ashcroft, 195 F. Supp. 2d 937 (E.D. Mich. 2002).

JUDGES: Before: KEITH and DAUGHTREY, Circuit Judges; CARR, District Judge.

OPINION: [682] DAMON J. KEITH, Circuit Judge.

The primary issue on appeal in this case is whether the First Amendment to the United States Constitution confers a public right of access to deportation hearings. If it does, then the Government must make a showing to overcome that right.

No one will ever forget the egregious, deplorable, and despicable terrorist attacks of September 11, 2001. These were cowardly acts. In response, our government launched an extensive investigation into the attacks, future threats, conspiracies, and attempts to come. As part of this effort, immigration laws are prosecuted with increased vigor. The issue before us today involves these efforts.

The political branches of our government enjoy near-unrestrained ability to control our borders. "These are policy questions entrusted exclusively to the political branches of our government." Fiallo v. Bell, 430 U.S. 787, 798 (1977). Since the end of the 19th Century, our government has enacted immigration laws banishing, or deporting, [683] non-citizens because of their race and their beliefs. ...While the Bill of Rights zealously protects citizens from such laws, it has never protected non-citizens facing deportation in the same way. In our democracy, based on checks and balances, neither the Bill of Rights nor the judiciary can second-guess government's choices. The only safeguard on this extraordinary governmental power is the public, deputizing the press as the guardians of their liberty. "An informed public is the most potent of all restraints upon misgovernment[.]" Grosjean v. Am. Press Co., 297 U.S. 233, 250 (1936). "[They] alone can here protect the values of democratic government." New York Times v. United States, 403 U.S. 713, 728 (1971) (per curiam) (Stewart, J., concurring).

Today, the Executive Branch seeks to take this safeguard away from the public by placing its actions beyond public scrutiny. Against non-citizens, it seeks the power to secretly deport a class if it unilaterally calls them "special interest" cases. The Executive Branch seeks to uproot people's lives, outside the public eye, and behind a closed door. Democracies die behind closed doors. The First Amendment, through a free press, protects the people's right to know that their government acts fairly, lawfully, and accurately in deportation proceedings. When government begins closing doors, it selectively controls information rightfully belonging to the people. Selective information is misinformation. The Framers of the First Amendment "did not trust any government to separate the true from the false for us." Kleindienst v. Mandel, 408 U.S. 753, 773 (1972). They protected the people against secret government.

The Office of the Chief Immigration Judge, under the authorization of Attorney General John Ashcroft, designates certain cases to be special interest cases, conducted in secret, closed off from the public. Arguing that closure of these hearings was unconstitutional, plaintiffs in three separate cases sought an injunction against such action. The Government filed a motion to dismiss, arguing that closing special interest cases was not unconstitutional.

The district court granted the injunction, finding blanket closure of deportation hearings in "special interest" cases unconstitutional. For the reasons that follow, we AFFIRM the district court's order granting Plaintiffs a preliminary injunction. ...

On September 21, 2001, Chief Immigration Judge Michael Creppy issued a directive (the

"Creppy directive") to all United States Immigration Judges requiring closure of special interest cases. [684] ... On December 19, 2002, Immigration Judge Elizabeth Hacker conducted a bond hearing for Rabih Haddad ("Haddad"), one such special interest case.... Without prior notice to the public, Haddad, or his attorney, courtroom security officers announced that the hearing was closed to the public and the press. Haddad was denied bail, detained, and has since been in the government's custody....

Among the claims asserted, the Newspaper Plaintiffs ... sought a declaratory judgment that the Creppy directive, facially and as applied, violated their First Amendment right of access to Haddad's deportation proceedings. They further sought to enjoin subsequent closures of proceedings in Haddad's case and a release of all transcripts and documents from previous proceedings.

The district court granted the Newspaper Plaintiffs' motion. Finding that the Newspaper Plaintiffs had a First Amendment right of access to the proceedings under *Richmond Newspapers Inc., v. Virginia,* 448 U.S. 555 (1980), and its progeny. ... [685]

We review the grant of a preliminary injunction for an abuse of discretion, but questions of law are reviewed de novo. *Gonzales v. National Board of Medical Examiners,* 225 F.3d 620, 625 (6th Cir. 2000).... [686]

[W]hether or not there is a First Amendment right of access to deportation proceedings, the Government argues, it can implement any non-substantive policy infringing upon that right if it is "facially legitimate and bona fide."

...Were we to adopt the Government's position, one would wonder whether and how the Constitution could limit the political branches' power over immigration matters. Similarly, that position would undercut the force of the First Amendment. "The dominant purpose of the First Amendment was to prohibit the widespread practice of governmental suppression of embarrassing information." *New York Times,* 403 U.S. at 723-24 (Douglas, J., concurring). It would be ironic, indeed, to allow the Government's assertion of plenary power to transform the First Amendment from the great instrument of open democracy to a safe harbor from public scrutiny. In the words of Justice Murphy, "[such a] conclusion would make our constitutional safeguards transitory and discriminatory in nature.... [We] cannot agree that the framers of the Constitution meant to make such an empty mockery of human freedom." *Bridges v. Wixon,* 326 U.S. 135, 162 (1945) (Murphy, J., concurring). As a result, the Government's stated position finds no authority in the Constitution and is untenable.... [688]

The Supreme Court has always interpreted the Constitution meaningfully to limit non-substantive immigration laws, without granting the Government special deference. ...First, the Supreme Court has explicitly stated that non-citizens are afforded "the same constitutional protections of due process that we accord citizens." *Hellenic Lines Ltd. v. Rhoditis,* 398 U.S. 306, 309 (1970). As old as the first immigration laws of this country is the recognition that non-citizens, even if illegally present in the United States, are "persons" entitled to the Fifth Amendment right of due process in deportation proceedings.... Therefore, the Fifth Amendment limits non-substantive immigration laws.... [690]

Non-deferential review does not begin and end with the Fifth Amendment. As long ago as 1896, the Supreme Court recognized that the Fifth and Sixth Amendments limited Congress from enforcing its powers over immigration.... While noting the broad powers enjoyed by the political branches to expel and exclude aliens, the Court held that such powers were limited by the Fifth and Sixth Amendments: "But to declare unlawful residence within the country to be an infamous crime, punishable by deprivation of liberty and property, would be to pass out of the sphere of constitutional legislation, unless provision were made that the fact of guilt should first be established by a judicial trial." 163 U.S. at 237.

Although the question had never been addressed specifically, there is ample foundation to conclude that the Supreme Court would also recognize that non-citizens enjoy unrestrained First Amendment rights in deportation proceedings. For example, in *Bridges v. Wixon,* 326 U.S. 135 [691] ...[a] concurrence by Justice Murphy, however, noted that deportees had unqualified First Amendment rights in deportation hearings:

Once an alien lawfully enters and resides in this country he becomes invested with the rights guaranteed by the Constitution to all people within our borders. Such rights include those protected by the First and Fifth Amendments and by the due process clause of the Fourteenth Amendment. None of these provisions acknowledges any distinction between citizens and resident aliens. They extend their inalienable privileges to all "persons" and guard against any encroachment on those rights by federal or state authority. *Id.* at 161 (Murphy, J., concurring).

This statement has since been adopted by the full court. *See Hellenic Lines Ltd.,* 398 U.S. at 310 n.5 (1970); *see also Reno v. American-Arab Anti-Discrimination Committee,* 525 U.S. 471, 142 L. Ed. 2d 940, 119 S. Ct. 936 (1999) (Ginsburg, J., concurring) (recognizing First Amendment restrictions on the political branches' authority over deportation)....[692]

The Government correctly notes that the Court in *Zadvydas* twice indicated that it might be deferential in situations involving terrorism. *See* 533 U.S. at 691, 696.... However, nothing in *Zadvydas* indicates that given such a situation, the Court would defer to the political branches' determination of who belongs in that "small segment of particularly dangerous individuals" without judicial review of the individual circumstances of each case, something that the Creppy directive strikingly lacks. The Court repeated the importance of strong procedural protections when constitutional rights were involved: "The Constitution may well preclude granting 'an administrative body the unreviewable authority to make determinations implicating fundamental rights.'" *See* 533 U.S. at 692.

Importantly, the Creppy directive does not apply to "a small segment of particularly dangerous" information, but a broad, indiscriminate range of information, including information likely to be entirely innocuous. Similarly, no definable standards used to determine whether a case is of "special interest" have been articulated.... In fact, the Government so much as argues that certain non-citizens known to have no links to terrorism will be designated "special interest" cases. Supposedly, closing a more targeted class would allow terrorists to draw inferences from which hearings are open and which are closed.

While we sympathize and share the Government's fear that dangerous information might be disclosed in some of these hearings, we feel that the ordinary process of determining whether closure is warranted on a case-by-case basis sufficiently addresses [693] their concerns. Using this stricter standard does not mean that information helpful to terrorists will be disclosed, only that the Government must be more targeted and precise in its approach. Given the importance of the constitutional rights involved, such safeguards must be vigorously guarded, lest the First Amendment turn into another balancing test. In the words of Justice Black: "The word 'security' is a broad, vague generality whose contours should not be invoked to abrogate the fundamental law embodied in the First Amendment. The guarding of military and diplomatic secrets at the expense of informed representative government provides no real security for our Republic." *New York Times*, 403 U.S. at 719 (Black, J., concurring)....

Finally, ...were the political branches' decisions not subject to certain basic procedural requirements, the government could act arbitrarily and behind closed doors, leaving unsettled the lives of thousands of immigrants. Even though the political branches may have unfettered discretion to deport and exclude certain people, requiring the Government to account for their choices assures an informed public – a foundational principle of democracy....

[I]f a First Amendment right of access exists, the Government must show that it is a narrowly tailored means of advancing a compelling interest. *See Globe Newspaper*, 457 U.S. at 606. [694] ...

We next consider whether the First Amendment affords the press and public a right of access to deportation hearings. The Newspaper Plaintiffs argue that the right of access should be governed by the standards set forth in *Richmond Newspapers, Inc. v. Virginia*, 448 U.S. 555 (1980), and its progeny. The Government, on the other hand, contends that *Richmond Newspapers* and its progeny are limited to judicial proceedings, and therefore, the standards articulated in these cases do not apply to deportation hearings, which are administrative proceedings. According to the Government, review of claims of access to administrative proceedings are governed by the more deferential standard articulated in *Houchins v. KQED*, Inc., 438 U.S. 1 (1978). The Government also argues that even if the standard articulated in *Richmond Newspapers* and its progeny is the appropriate test, the Newspaper Plaintiffs cannot demonstrate a right of access to deportation hearings by the standards articulated therein.

We do not agree that the standard articulated in *Houchins* is the applicable standard for reviewing First Amendment claims of access to administrative proceedings. First, we find both the issues and facts in *Houchins* distinguishable from those present in this case. Second, assuming without deciding that *Houchins* may be applicable to administrative proceedings, we do not find it applicable to administrative proceedings that exhibit substantial quasi-judicial characteristics....

The issue before the Court in *Houchins*, decided two years before *Richmond Newspapers*, was "whether the news media have a constitutional right of access to a county jail, *over and above that of other persons*, to interview inmates and make sound recordings, films and photographs for publication and broadcasting by newspapers, radio and television." 438 U.S. at 3. (emphasis added). Here, the Newspaper Plaintiffs do not claim a "special privilege of access" to the deportations hearings. Rather, the Newspaper Plaintiffs simply request that they be able to attend the hearings on equal footing with the public.

Next, ... *Houchins* represented a plurality opinion of the Court, and as such, the conclusion that the First and Fourteenth Amendments do not guarantee the public a right of access to information generated or controlled by the government was neither accepted nor rejected by a majority of the Court.... Additionally, ... we question the vitality of the standard articulated in *Houchins*, at least with respect to cases such as the one presently [695] before us. The *Richmond Newspapers's* two-part "experience and logic" test sufficiently addresses all of the *Houchins* Court's concerns for the implications of a constitutionally mandated general right of access to government information. And in repeatedly applying *Richmond Newspapers's* two-part "experience and logic" test to assess the merits of cases claiming First Amendment access rights to different government proceedings, it is clear that the Court has since moved away from its position in *Houchins* and recognizes that there is a limited constitutional right to some government information....

[W]e reject the Government's assertion that a line has been drawn between judicial and administrative proceedings, with the First Amendment guaranteeing access to the former but not the latter. "The First Amendment question cannot be resolved solely on the label we give the event, i.e., 'trial' or otherwise." *Press-Enterprise II*, 478 U.S. at 7. Moreover, the Government cites no cases explicitly stating such a categorical distinction – that the political branches of government are completely immune from the First Amendment guarantee of access recognized in *Richmond Newspapers*. On the contrary, we believe that there is a limited First Amendment right of access to certain aspects of the executive and legislative branches. *See Richmond Newspapers*, 448 U.S. at 584 [696] ....

Finally, to the extent that the standard in *Houchins* remains good law, we do not find *Houchins* applicable to the facts of the present case. Here, the Newspaper Plaintiffs seek access to a demonstrably quasi-judicial government administrative proceeding normally open to the public, as opposed to *Houchins*, where the plaintiffs sought access to a government facility normally restricted to the public.

Deportation hearings, as quasi-judicial proceedings, are fundamentally different than a prison facility. "The distinction between trials and other official proceedings is not necessarily dispositive, or even important, in evaluating First Amendment issues." *Press-Enterprise I*, 464 U.S. at 516 (Stevens, J., concurring). Drawing sharp lines between administrative and judicial proceedings would allow the legislature to artfully craft information out of the public eye.

A deportation proceeding, although administrative, is an adversarial, adjudicative process, designed to expel non-citizens from this country. "The ultimate individual stake in these proceedings is the same as or greater than in

criminal or civil actions." *See N. Media Jersey Media Group, Inc. v. Ashcroft*, 205 F. Supp. 2d 288, 301 (D.N.J. 2002)....

Two recent Supreme Court cases and one of our recent decisions that turned on the precise substance of particular administrative proceedings are instructive. The holdings in these cases did not rest on the simple determination that the proceedings were administrative. Rather, in each of these cases, the courts looked to the adjudicative characteristics of the proceedings in reaching their final decisions....

[699] [T]here are many similarities between judicial proceedings and deportation proceedings. ... We are not convinced that the *Houchins* test should be applied to deportation hearings, being exceedingly formal and adversarial. The Government rests its argument regarding the inapplicability of the *Richmond Newspapers* two-part test to deportation proceedings on cases that we find readily distinguishable. All the cases cited by the Government concern purported rights of access to, or disclosure of, government-held *investigatory* information and *not* access to information relating to a governmental *adjudicative* process, which is at issue here.... [700]

[T]he line of cases from *Richmond Newspapers* to *Press-Enterprise II* recognize that there is in fact a *limited* constitutional right to *some* government information and also provide a test of general applicability for making that determination. Accordingly, we must assess whether the Newspaper Plaintiffs enjoy a First Amendment right of access to deportation hearings under the two-part test of *Richmond Newspapers* and its progeny.

Under the two-part "experience and logic" test from *Richmond Newspapers*, we conclude that there is a First Amendment right of access to deportation proceedings. Deportation hearings, and similar proceedings, have traditionally been open to the public, and openness undoubtedly plays a significant positive role in this process....

[701] First, the case for a right of access has special force when drawn from an enduring and vital tradition of public entree to particular proceedings or information.... Such a tradition commands respect in part because the Constitution carries the gloss of history. *More importantly, a tradition of accessibility implies the favorable judgment of experience.* Second, the value of access must be measured in specifics. Analysis is not advanced by rhetorical statements that all information bears upon public issues; *what is crucial in individual cases is whether access to particular government process is important in terms of that very process. Richmond Newspapers,*

448 U.S. at 589 (Brennan, J., concurring) (emphasis added).

Therefore, although historical context is important, a brief historical tradition might be sufficient to establish a First Amendment right of access where the beneficial effects of access to that process are overwhelming and uncontradicted....

Nonetheless, deportation proceedings historically have been open. Although exceptions may have been allowed, the general policy has been one of openness.... Since 1965, INS regulations have explicitly required deportation proceedings to be presumptively open. Since that time, Congress has revised the Immigration and Nationality Act at least 53 times without indicating that the INS had judged their intent incorrectly.... [702] To the extent that their actions were ambiguous, the Supreme Court has repeated "the long standing principle of construing any lingering ambiguities in deportation statutes in favor of the alien." *See INS v. Cardoza-Fonseca*, 480 U.S. 421, 459 (1987) ....

Moreover, the history of immigration law informs Congress's legislation. Open hearings, apart from their value to the community, have long been considered to advance fairness to the parties.... Additionally, Congress has long been aware that deportees are constitutionally guaranteed greater procedural rights than those excluded upon initial entry....

As stated earlier, to paraphrase the Supreme Court, deportation hearings "walk, talk, and squawk" very much like a judicial proceeding.... [703] It bears note that the history of administrative proceedings is briskly evolving to embrace open hearings....

Next, we turn to the "logic" prong, which asks "whether public access plays a significant positive role in the functioning of the particular process in question." *Press-Enter. II*, 478 U.S. at 8-9. Public access undoubtedly enhances the quality of deportation proceedings. Much of the reasoning from *Richmond Newspapers* is also applicable to this context.

First, public access acts as a check on the actions of the Executive by assuring us that proceedings are conducted fairly and [704] properly.... In an area such as immigration, where the government has nearly unlimited authority, the press and the public serve as perhaps the only check on abusive government practices.

Second, openness ensures that government does its job properly; that it does not make mistakes.... These first two concerns are magnified by the fact that deportees have no right to an attorney at the government's expense. Effectively, the press and the public may be their only guardian.

Third, after the devastation of September 11 and the massive investigation that followed, the cathartic effect of open deportations cannot be overstated. They serve a "therapeutic" purpose as outlets for "community concern, hostility, and emotions." *Richmond Newspapers*, 448 U.S. at 571. As the district court stated:

It is important for the public, particularly individuals who feel that they are being targeted by the Government as a result of the terrorist attacks of September 11, to know that even during these sensitive times the Government is adhering to immigration procedures and respecting individuals' rights.... *Detroit Free Press*, 195 F. Supp. 2d at 944.

Fourth, openness enhances the perception of integrity and fairness. "The value of openness lies in the fact that people not actually attending trials can have confidence that standards of fairness are being observed; the sure knowledge that *anyone* is free to attend gives assurance that established procedures are being followed and that deviations will become known." *Press-Enter.*, 464 U.S. at 508. The most stringent safeguards for a deportee "would be of limited worth if the public is not persuaded that the standards are being fairly enforced. Legitimacy rests in large part on public understanding." *See First Amendment Coalition*, 784 F.2d at 486 (Adams, J., concurring in part, dissenting in part).

Fifth, public access helps ensure that "the individual citizen can effectively participate in and contribute to our republican system of self-government." *Globe Newspaper*, 457 U.S. at 604. "[A] major purpose of [the First Amendment] was to protect the free discussion of governmental affairs." *Id.* Public access [705] to deportation proceedings helps inform the public of the affairs of the government. Direct knowledge of how their government is operating enhances the public's ability to affirm or protest government's efforts. When government selectively chooses what information it allows the public to see, it can become a powerful tool for deception.

Additionally, the Government has not identified one persuasive reason why openness would play a negative role in the process....

Having found a First Amendment right of access to deportation hearings, we now determine whether the Government has made a sufficient showing to overcome that right.

Under the standard articulated in *Globe Newspaper*, government action that curtails a First Amendment right of access "in order to inhibit the disclosure of sensitive information" must be supported by a showing "that denial is necessitated by a compelling governmental interest, and is narrowly tailored to serve that interest." *Globe Newspaper Co.*, 457 U.S. at 606-07. Moreover, "the interest is to be articulated along with findings specific enough that a reviewing court can determine whether the closure order was properly entered." *Press-Enter. II,* 478 U.S. at 10. The Government's ongoing anti-terrorism investigation certainly implicates a compelling interest. However, the Creppy directive is neither narrowly tailored, nor does it require particularized findings. Therefore, it impermissibly infringes on the Newspaper Plaintiffs' First Amendment right of access.... [706]

The Government certainly has a compelling interest in preventing terrorism. ...According to... affidavits, public access to removal proceedings would disclose the following information that would impede the Government's investigation:

"Bits and pieces of information that may appear innocuous in isolation," but used by terrorist groups to help form a "bigger picture" of the Government's terrorism investigation, would be disclosed. The Government describes this type of intelligence gathering as "akin to the construction of a mosaic," where an individual piece of information is not of obvious importance until pieced together with other pieces of information....

The identifications of the detainees, witnesses, and investigative sources would be disclosed. Terrorist groups could subject these individuals or their families to intimidation or harm and discourage them from cooperating with the Government.

Methods of entry to the country, communicating, or funding could be revealed. This information could allow terrorist organizations to alter their patterns of activity to find the most effective means of evading detection. "Information that is *not* presented at the hearings also might provide important clues to terrorist, because it could reveal what the investigation has not yet discovered." The Government provides this example: "If the government discloses the evidence it has about a particular [707] member of a terrorist organization, but fails to mention that the detainee is involved in an impending attack, the other members of the organization may be able to infer that the government is not yet aware of the attack." *See* Gov't Brief at 47-49.

Inasmuch as these agents' declarations establish that certain information revealed during removal proceedings could impede the ongoing anti-terrorism investigation, we defer to their judgment. These agents are certainly in a better position to understand the contours of the investigation and the intelligence capabilities of terrorist organizations....

Although the Government is able to demonstrate a compelling interest for closure, the immigration judge, Defendant Hacker, failed to make specific findings before closing Haddad's deportation proceedings. *Press-Enterprise II* instructs that in cases where partial or complete closure is warranted, there must be specific findings on the record so that a reviewing court can determine whether closure was proper and whether less restrictive alternatives exist. *Press- Enter. II,* 478 U.S. at 13. Similarly, the Creppy directive fails this requirement.

Finally, the blanket closure rule mandated by the Creppy directive is not narrowly tailored. The Government offers no persuasive argument as to why the Government's concerns cannot be addressed on a case-by-case basis. The Newspaper Plaintiffs argue, and the district court agreed, that the Creppy directive is ineffective in achieving its purported goals because the detainees and their lawyers are allowed to publicize the proceedings. According to the Newspaper Plaintiffs, to the extent that Haddad had discussed his proceedings (and disclosed documents) with family, friends and the media, the information that the Government seeks to protect is disclosed to the public anyway. We are not persuaded by the Government's argument in response that few detainees will disclose any information and that their disclosure will be less than complete public access. This contention is, at best, speculative and belies the Government's assertion that *any* information disclosed, even bits and pieces that seem innocuous, will be detrimental to the anti-terrorism investigation.

The recent interim rule promulgated by the Department of Justice ("DOJ") regarding protective orders and sealing of documents in these special interest cases does not fully address our concern that the Creppy directive is under-inclusive. The parties do not dispute that the rule is meant to work in tandem with the Creppy directive. The interim DOJ rule authorizes immigration judges to issue protective orders and seal documents relating to law enforcement or national security information in the course of immigration proceedings. *See* 67 Fed. Reg. 36799. Pursuant to the interim rules, the immigration judge is authorized to order that detainees [708] and their attorneys refrain from disclosing certain confidential information....

These prohibitions are impermissible to the extent that they indefinitely restrain a deportee's ability to divulge all information, including information obtained independently from the deportation proceedings.... The Government argues that its interests include concerns about dangers associated with disclosing the deportees' names, as well as the dates and places of arrest. Such information is known independently from the proceedings. Therefore, such information cannot properly be protected. To avoid this constitutional problem, we construe the orders to terminate when the deportation proceedings end. At this juncture, nothing precludes the deportee from disclosing this information. Thus, the interim rule does not remedy the under-inclusiveness of the Creppy directive.

The interim rule notwithstanding, the Creppy directive is also over-inclusive, being too broad and indiscriminate.... It is clear that certain types of information that the Government seeks to keep confidential could be kept from the public on a case-by-case basis through protective orders or in camera review – for example, the identification of investigative sources and witnesses. The Government, however, argues that it is impossible to keep some sensitive information confidential if any portion of a hearing is open or if the immigration court conducts a hearing to determine if closure is proper. Stated differently, the Government argues that there is sensitive information that would be disclosed if closure occurred on a case-by-case basis. First, the Government contends that the identities of the detainees would be revealed if closure occurred on a case-by-case basis, and such information would impede the anti-terrorism investigation. This information, however, is already being disclosed to the public through the detainees themselves or their counsel. Even if, as a result of the interim rule, a detainee remains silent, a terrorist group capable of sophisticated intelligence-gathering would certainly be made aware that one of its operatives, or someone connected to a particular terrorist plot, has disappeared into the Government's custody. Moreover, if a deportee does have links to terrorist organizations, there is nothing to stop that deportee from divulging the information learned from these proceedings once deported.

[709] ... Finally, the Government seeks to protect from disclosure the bits and pieces of information that seem innocuous in isolation, but when pieced together with other bits and pieces aid in creating a bigger picture of the Government's anti-terrorism investigation, i.e., the "mosaic intelligence." Mindful of the Government's concerns, we must nevertheless conclude that the Creppy directive is over-inclusive. While the risk of "mosaic intelligence" may exist, we do not believe speculation should form the basis for such a drastic restriction of the public's First Amendment rights.... Fittingly, in this case, the Government subsequently admitted that there was no information disclosed in any of Haddad's first three hearings that threatened "national security or the safety of the American people." U.S. Dept. of Justice, *Statement of Associate Attorney General Jay Stephens Regarding the Sixth Circuit Decision in the Haddad Case*, (last modified 8/20/02) <http://www.usdoj.gov/opa/*pr/2002/April/02_ag_2 38.htm*>. Yet, all these hearings were closed. The only reason offered for closing the hearings has been that the presiding immigration judge was told do it by the chief immigration judge, who in turn was told to do it by the Attorney General.

Furthermore, there seems to be no limit to the Government's argument. The Government could use its "mosaic intelligence" argument as a justification to close any public hearing completely and categorically, including criminal proceedings. The Government could operate in virtual secrecy in all matters dealing, even remotely, with "national security," resulting in a [710] wholesale suspension of First Amendment rights. By the simple assertion of "national security," the Government seeks a process where it may, without review, designate certain classes of cases as "special interest cases" and, behind closed doors, adjudicate the merits of these cases to deprive non-citizens of their fundamental liberty interests.

This, we simply may not countenance. A government operating in the shadow of secrecy stands in complete opposition to the society envisioned by the Framers of our Constitution. "Fully aware of both the need to defend a new nation and the abuses of the English and Colonial governments, [the Framers of the First Amendment] sought to give this new society strength and security by providing that freedom of speech, press, religion, and assembly should not be abridged." *See New York Times*, 403 U.S. at 719 (Black, J., concurring).

Moreover, we find unpersuasive the Government's argument that the closure of special interest hearings has been accomplished on a case-by-case basis. ... Assuming such an evaluation has occurred, we find that problems still remain. The task of designating a case special interest is performed in secret, without any established standards or procedures, and the process is, thus, not subject to any sort of review, either by another administrative entity or the courts. Therefore, no real safeguard on this exercise of authority exists. ... The Government states that special interest cases represent "a small, carefully chosen subset of the universe of aliens facing removal proceedings." Yet, to date, the Government has failed to disclose the actual number of special interest cases it has designated.

In sum, we find that the Government's attempt to establish a narrowly tailored restriction has failed. The Creppy directive is under-inclusive by permitting the disclosure of sensitive information while at the same time drastically restricting First Amendment rights. The directive is over-inclusive by categorically and completely closing all special interest hearings without demonstrating, beyond speculation, that such a closure is absolutely necessary....

The Newspaper Plaintiffs will undoubtedly suffer irreparable injury if they are denied access to Haddad's upcoming hearings. The Supreme Court has held that even a minimal infringement upon First Amendment rights constitutes irreparable injury sufficient to justify injunctive relief.... As the district court noted, no [711] subsequent measures can cure this loss, because the information contained in the appeal or transcripts will be stale, and there is no assurance that they will completely detail the proceedings.

Lastly, the public's interests are best served by open proceedings. A true democracy is one that operates on faith - faith that government officials are forthcoming and honest, and faith that informed citizens will arrive at logical conclusions. This is a vital reciprocity that America should not discard in these troubling times. Without question, the events of September 11, 2001, left an indelible mark on our nation, but we as a people are united in the wake of the destruction to demonstrate to the world that we are a country deeply committed to preserving the rights and freedoms guaranteed by our democracy. Today, we reflect our commitment to those democratic values by ensuring that our government is held accountable to the people and that First Amendment rights are not impermissibly compromised. Open proceedings, with a vigorous and scrutinizing press, serve to ensure the durability of our democracy.

For the foregoing reasons, we AFFIRM.

North Jersey Media Group v. Ashcroft
308 F.3d 198
(3rd Cir. 2002)
(Excerpts only. Footnotes omitted.)

SUBSEQUENT HISTORY: US Supreme Court certiorari denied by N. Jersey Media Group v. Ashcroft, 2003 U.S. LEXIS 4082 (U.S., May 27, 2003)

PRIOR HISTORY: On Appeal From the United States District Court For the District of New Jersey.

JUDGES: Before: BECKER, Chief Judge, SCIRICA and GREENBERG, Circuit Judges. SCIRICA, Circuit Judge, dissenting.

[199] OPINION OF THE COURT: BECKER, Chief Judge.

This civil action was brought in the District Court for the District of New Jersey by a consortium of media groups seeking access to "special interest" deportation hearings involving persons whom the Attorney General has determined might have connections to or knowledge of the September 11, 2001 terrorist attacks.... The District Court found for the media plaintiffs and issued an order enjoining the Attorney General from denying access, from which he now appeals.

The District Court ... held that the case was governed by the test developed in Richmond Newspapers, Inc. v. Virginia.... [T]he District Court rejected the Government's argument that administrative hearings in general, and deportation hearings in particular, are not subject to the Richmond Newspapers two-part "experience and logic" test because they are of a fundamentally different nature.... [and] applying Richmond Newspapers, found that there was a sufficient history of open deportation proceedings to satisfy the Richmond Newspapers experience test.

Turning to the logic prong, the District Court held that policy considerations strongly favored media access. Significantly, however, in evaluating the logic prong, the Court did not consider the policies militating against media access, including ... the danger of security breaches entailed in opening the hearings. In brief, ... insight gleaned from open proceedings might alert vigilant terrorists to the United States' investigative tactics and could easily betray what knowledge the government does – or does not – possess.... [E]ven details that seem innocuous in isolation, such as the names of those detained, might be pieced together by knowledgeable persons within the terrorist network, who could in turn shift activities to a yet-undiscovered terrorist cell. Because immigration judges cannot be expected accurately to assess the harm that might result from disclosing seemingly trivial facts, ... seeking closure on a case-by-case basis would ineffectively protect the nation's interests.

Although existing caselaw on the logic prong has discussed only the policies favoring openness, we are satisfied that the logic prong must consider the flip side of the coin. Indeed, the Supreme Court seems to have contemplated this, for in formulating the Richmond Newspapers test it asked "whether public access plays a significant positive role in the functioning of the particular process in question." Press-Enterprise Co. v. Superior Court, 478 U.S. 1, 8 (1986). Any inquiry into whether a role is positive must perforce [201] consider whether it is potentially harmful....

While we believe that the notion that Richmond Newspapers applies is open to debate as a theoretical matter, we must yield to the prior precedent of this Court, and hence will apply it to the facts.... In our view the tradition of openness of deportation proceedings does not meet the standard required.... Deportation procedures have been codified for approximately 100 years but, despite their constant reenactment during that time, Congress has never explicitly guaranteed public access. Indeed, deportation cases involving abused alien children are mandatorily closed by statute, and hearings are often conducted in places generally inaccessible to the public. While INS regulations promulgated in 1964 create a rebuttable presumption of openness for most deportation cases, we conclude that a recently-created regulatory presumption of openness with significant statutory exceptions does not present the type of "unbroken, uncontradicted history" that Richmond Newspapers and its progeny require to establish a First Amendment right of access....

We recognize that, at least since the 1960s, formalized deportation proceedings have borne an undeniable procedural resemblance to civil trials.... [T]here has never been a fundamental right of access to all government proceedings. Even today, many are closed by statute, including such frequent and important matters as Social Security hearings.... [202]

We note preliminarily that, in the jurisprudence developed thus far, the logic prong does not appear to do much work in the Richmond Newspapers approach, for we have not found a case in which a proceeding passed the experience test through its history of openness yet failed the logic test by not serving community values. Under the reported cases, the second prong of the Richmond Newspapers test has been applied to inquire whether openness plays a positive policy role in a given proceeding. But, as we have explained, that calculus perforce must take account of the flip side – the extent to which openness impairs the public good.

This case arises in the wake of September 11, 2001, a day on which American life changed drastically and dramatically. The era that dawned on September 11th, and the war against terrorism that has pervaded the sinews of our national life since that day, are reflected in thousands of ways in legislative and national policy, the habits of daily living, and our collective psyches. Since the primary national policy must be self-preservation, it seems elementary that, to the extent open deportation hearings might impair national security, that security is implicated in the logic test.

When it is factored in, given due consideration to the attorney general's statements of the threat, we do not believe that the Richmond Newspapers logic prong test favors the media either.

As we will now explain in detail, we find that the application of the Richmond Newspapers experience and logic tests does not compel us to declare the Creppy Directive unconstitutional. We will therefore reverse the Order of the District Court.... [203]

The [Creppy] Directive requires immigration judges "to close the hearings to the public, and to avoid discussing the cases or otherwise disclosing any information about the cases to anyone outside the Immigration Court." It further instructs that "the courtroom must be closed for these cases – no visitors, no family, and no press," and explains that the restriction even "includes confirming or denying whether such a case is on the docket or scheduled for a hearing." In short, the Directive contemplates a complete information blackout along both substantive and procedural dimensions.

In closing special interest deportation hearings, the Government's stated purpose is to avoid disclosing potentially sensitive information to those who may pose an ongoing security threat to the United States and its interests.... The Government offers a litany of harms that might flow from open hearings. Most obviously, terrorist organizations could alter future attack plans, or devise new, easier ways to enter the country through channels they learn are relatively unguarded by the Department of Justice. They might also obstruct or disrupt pending proceedings by destroying evidence, threatening potential witnesses, or targeting the hearings themselves. Finally, if the government cannot guarantee a closed hearing, aliens might be deterred from cooperating with the ongoing investigation.... [204]

[T]he District Court ... clarified that its injunction [on application of the Creppy Directive] has nationwide scope, applies to all proceedings regardless of whether plaintiffs seek to attend, and requires proceedings to be open to all members of the press and public.... [T]he Supreme Court granted a stay of the District Court's injunction pending the final disposition of this appeal.... [209]

Richmond Newspapers requires that when a court assesses a claimed First Amendment right of access, it must "consider[ ] whether the place and process have historically been open to the press and general public . . . [and] whether public access plays a significant positive role in the functioning of the particular process in question." Press-Enterprise II, 478 U.S. at 8. This language seems to place the burden of proof on the party alleging a First Amendment right. While we acknowledge a current presumption of openness in most deportation proceedings, we find that this presumption has neither the pedigree nor uniformity necessary to satisfy Richmond Newspapers's first prong. We also conclude that under a logic inquiry properly acknowledging both community benefits and potential harms, public access does not serve a "significant positive role" in deportation hearings....

In Richmond Newspapers, 448 U.S. at 575, the Supreme Court acknowledged the State's argument that the Constitution nowhere explicitly guarantees the public's right to attend criminal trials, but it found that right implicit because the Framers drafted the Constitution against a backdrop of longstanding popular access to criminal trials.... The history of access to political branch proceedings is quite different. The Government correctly notes that the Framers themselves rejected any unqualified right of access to the political branches....

Congressional practice confirms that there is no general right of public access to governmental proceedings or information. The members of the First Congress did not open their own proceedings to the [210] public – the Senate met behind closed doors until 1794, and the House did likewise until after the War of 1812.... [C]ommittee sessions remained closed and were not routinely opened to the public until the mid-1970s.... Even today, the Senate operates under a resolution limiting public access to "routine Senate records" for 20 years after their creation and to "sensitive records, such as investigative files" for 50 years after their creation, and each Senate committee retains the right to extend that access period for its own records....

This tradition of closing sensitive proceedings extends to many hearings before administrative agencies.... Faced with this litany of administrative hearings that are closed to the public, the Newspapers cannot claim a general First Amendment right of access to government proceedings without urging a judicially-imposed revolution in the administrative state.... Instead they submit that, [211] despite frequent closures throughout the administrative realm, deportation proceedings in particular boast a history of openness sufficient to meet the Richmond Newspapers requirement. We now assess that claim, and find that we disagree....

For a First Amendment right of access to vest under Richmond Newspapers, we must consider whether "the place and process have historically been open to the press and general public," because such a "tradition of accessibility implies the favorable judgment of experience." Press-Enterprise II, 478 U.S. at 8. ... [T]he tradition of open deportation hearings is too recent and inconsistent to support a First Amendment right of access.

The strongest historical evidence of open deportation proceedings is that since the 1890s, when Congress first codified deportation procedures, "the governing statutes have always expressly closed exclusion hearings, but have never closed deportation hearings." ... The current Justice Department regulations provide explicitly that "all hearings, other than exclusion hearings, shall be open to the public except that . . . for the purpose of protecting . . . the public interest, the Immigration Judge may limit attendance or hold a closed hearing." 8 C.F.R. 3.27. From this they conclude that the regulations state explicitly what the statutes had long said implicitly, namely that deportation hearings are to be open unless an individualized case is made for closure.

But there is also evidence that, in practice, deportation hearings have frequently been closed to the general public. From the early 1900s, the government has often conducted deportation hearings in prisons, hospitals, or private homes, places where there is no general right of public access. Even in recent times, the government has continued to hold thousands of deportation hearings each year in federal and state prisons.... Moreover, hearings involving abused alien children are closed by regulation no matter where they are held, and those involving abused alien spouses are closed presumptively. See 8 C.F.R. 3.27(c).

We ultimately do not believe that deportation hearings boast a tradition of openness sufficient to satisfy Richmond Newspapers.... [213] [W]e are unwilling effectively to craft a constitutional right from mere Congressional silence, especially when faced with evidence that some deportation proceedings were, and are, explicitly closed to the public or conducted in places unlikely to allow general public access. Although the 1964 Department of Justice regulations did create a presumption of openness, a recent – and rebuttable – regulatory presumption is hardly the stuff of which Constitutional rights are forged....

[A] 1000-year history is unnecessary, and ... in some cases, largely limited to the criminal context, relatively little history is required. These cases do not, however, allow us to dispense with the Richmond Newspapers "experience" requirement where history is ambiguous or lacking, and to recognize a First Amendment right based solely on the "logic" inquiry.... [215]

Although we are confident that our precedents do not allow us to find a First Amendment right of access to deportation hearings absent strong historical evidence, the Supreme Court's recent ruling in FMC v. South Carolina Ports Authority, 122 S. Ct. at 1864, gives us pause.... Ports

Authority had not been decided when the District Court heard this case, and the Newspapers now assert that it forces us to distinguish the procedures in deportation hearings from those in civil trials before finding that different rights exist in each context. Were this suggestion correct, we would indeed be hard pressed to find meaningful differences between the two types of proceedings.... [215]

Despite these undeniable similarities, however, we do not believe that the Supreme Court intended in Ports Authority to import the full panoply of constitutional rights to any administrative proceeding that resembles a civil trial... [T]here is no fundamental right to attend government proceedings underpinning the Newspapers' alleged right to attend deportation proceedings.... This is not a situation where the Framers contemplated a perfectly transparent government, only to have deportation proceedings, which they did not foresee, jeopardize that intended scheme. This is also not a situation involving allegations that the government assigned to an administrative agency a function that courts historically performed in order to deprive the public of an access right it once possessed. And most importantly, this is not a situation that risks affront to states' "residual and inviolable sovereignty." ... We therefore decline to loose the Ports Authority analysis from its Eleventh Amendment moorings. Instead of analogizing procedures, the proper approach is that developed in Richmond Newspapers, and as we have explained, under that test we find an insufficient tradition of openness to support the right....

The Government [216] contends that by relaxing the need for a "1000-year tradition of public access" ... we would permanently constitutionalize a right of access whenever an executive agency does not consistently bar all public access to a particular proceeding. We do not adopt this reasoning in its entirety.... Nevertheless, we agree with the Government that a rigorous experience test is necessary to preserve the "basic tenet of administrative law that agencies should be free to fashion their own rules of procedure." ... Were we to adopt the Newspapers' view that we can recognize a First Amendment right based solely on the logic prong if there is no history of closure, we would effectively compel the Executive to close its proceedings to the public ab initio or risk creating a constitutional right of access that would preclude it from closing them in the future. Under such a system, reserved powers of closure would be meaningless. It seems possible that, ironically, such a system would result in less public access than one in which a constitutional right of access is more difficult to create....

Even if we could find a right of access under the Richmond Newspapers logic prong, absent a strong showing of openness under the experience prong, a proposition we do not embrace, we would find no such right here. The logic test compels us to consider "whether public access plays a significant positive role in the functioning of the particular process in question." Press-Enterprise II, 478 U.S. at 8....

In Press-Enterprise II, the case that formalized the Richmond Newspapers test, the Court identified several reasons that openness plays a significant positive role in preliminary hearings. It recognized that "because of its extensive scope, the preliminary hearing is often the final and most important step in the criminal proceeding," and in many cases it "provides the sole occasion for public observation [217] of the criminal justice system." 478 U.S. at 12 (citation omitted). Similarly, it found that "the absence of a jury, long recognized as an inestimable safeguard against the corrupt or overzealous prosecutor and against the compliant, biased, or eccentric judge, makes the importance of public access to a preliminary hearing even more significant." 478 U.S. at 12-13 (citations omitted). Summarizing that "denying the transcript of a preliminary hearing would frustrate what we have characterized as the 'community therapeutic value' of openness," it concluded that a qualified First Amendment right of access attaches to preliminary hearings. 478 U.S. at 13.

In subsequent cases, this Court has noted six values typically served by openness: "[1] promotion of informed discussion of governmental affairs by providing the public with the more complete understanding of the judicial system; [2] promotion of the public perception of fairness which can be achieved only by permitting full public view of the proceedings; [3] providing a significant community therapeutic value as an outlet for community concern, hostility and emotion; [4] serving as a check on corrupt practices by exposing the judicial process to public scrutiny; [5] enhancement of the performance of all involved; and [6] discouragement of perjury." Simone, 14 F.3d at 839.

We agree with the District Court and the Sixth Circuit that openness in deportation hearings performs each of these salutary functions, but we are troubled by our sense that the logic inquiry, as currently conducted, does not do much work in the Richmond Newspapers test. We have not found a case in which a proceeding passed the experience test through its history of openness yet failed the logic test by not serving community values. Under the reported cases, whenever a court has found that openness serves community values, it has concluded that openness plays a "significant positive role" in that proceeding. But that cannot be the story's end, for to gauge accurately whether a role is positive, the calculus must perforce take account of the flip side – the extent to which openness impairs the public good. We note in this respect that, were the logic prong only to determine whether openness serves some good, it is difficult to conceive of a government proceeding to which the public would not have a First Amendment right of access. For example, public access to any government affair, even internal CIA deliberations, would "promote informed discussion" among the citizenry. It is unlikely the Supreme Court intended this result.

In this case the Government presented substantial evidence that open deportation hearings would threaten national security. Although the District Court discussed these concerns as part of its strict scrutiny analysis, they are equally applicable to the question whether openness, on balance, serves a positive role in removal hearings. We find that upon factoring them into the logic equation, it is doubtful that openness promotes the public good in this context. [218]

The Government's security evidence is contained in the declaration of Dale Watson, the FBI's Executive Assistant Director for Counterterrorism and Counterintelligence. Watson presents a range of potential dangers, the most pressing of which we rescribe here.

First, public hearings would necessarily reveal sources and methods of investigation.... Second, ... putting entry information into the public realm regarding all 'special interest cases' would allow the terrorist organization to see patterns of entry, what works and what doesn't." That information would allow it to tailor future entries to exploit weaknesses in the United States immigration system. Third, "information about what evidence the United States has against members of a particular cell collectively will inform the terrorist organization as to what cells to use and which not to use for further plots and attacks." A related concern is that open hearings would reveal what evidence the government lacks.... Fourth, if a terrorist organization discovers that a particular member is detained, or that information about a plot is known, it may accelerate the timing of a planned attack, thus reducing the amount of time the government has to detect and prevent it. If acceleration is impossible, it may still be able to shift the planned activity to a yet-undiscovered cell. 478 U.S. at 7. Fifth, a public hearing involving evidence about terrorist links could allow terrorist organizations to interfere with the pending proceedings by creating false or misleading evidence. Even more likely, a terrorist might destroy existing evidence or make it more difficult

to obtain, such as by threatening or tampering with potential witnesses. Should potential informants not feel secure in coming forward, that would greatly impair the ongoing investigation. Sixth, INS detainees have a substantial privacy interest in having their possible connection to the ongoing investigation kept undisclosed.... [219] Finally, ... "the government cannot proceed to close hearings on a case-by-case basis, as the identification of certain cases for closure, and the introduction of evidence to support that closure, could itself expose critical information about which activities and patterns of behavior merit such closure." Moreover, he explains, given judges' relative lack of expertise regarding national security and their inability to see the mosaic, we should not entrust to them the decision whether an isolated fact is sensitive enough to warrant closure.

The Newspapers are undoubtedly correct that the representations of the Watson Declaration are to some degree speculative, at least insofar as there is no concrete evidence that closed deportation hearings have prevented, or will prevent, terrorist attacks. But the Richmond Newspapers logic prong is unavoidably speculative, for it is impossible to weigh objectively, for example, the community benefit of emotional catharsis against the security risk of disclosing the United States' methods of investigation and the extent of its knowledge. We are quite hesitant to conduct a judicial inquiry into the credibility of these security concerns, as national security is an area where courts have traditionally extended great deference to Executive expertise.... The assessments before us have been made by senior government officials responsible for investigating the events of September 11th and for preventing future attacks. These officials believe that closure of special interest hearings is necessary to advance these goals, and their concerns ... have gone unrebutted. To the extent that the Attorney General's national security concerns seem credible, we will not lightly second-guess them. [220]

We are keenly aware of the dangers presented by deference to the executive branch when constitutional liberties are at stake, especially in times of national crisis, when those liberties are likely in greatest jeopardy. On balance, however, we are unable to conclude that openness plays a positive role in special interest deportation hearings at a time when our nation is faced with threats of such profound and unknown dimension.

Whatever the outer bounds of Richmond Newspapers might be, they do not envelop us here. Deportation proceedings' history of openness is quite limited, and their presumption of openness quite weak. They plainly do not present the type of "unbroken, uncontradicted history" that Richmond

Newspapers and its progeny require to establish a First Amendment right of access. We do not decide that there is no right to attend administrative proceedings, or even that there is no right to attend any immigration proceeding. Our judgment is confined to the extremely narrow class of deportation cases that are determined by the Attorney General to present significant national security concerns. In recognition of his experience (and our lack of experience) in this field, we will defer to his judgment. We note that although there may be no judicial remedy for these closures, there is, as always, the powerful check of political accountability on Executive discretion.

The importance of this case has not escaped us.... Democracy in America does at this moment face a serious threat.... It is true that last September's [221] unprecedented mass-slaughter of American citizens on American soil inevitably forced the government to take security measures that infringed on some rights and privileges. But these do not in themselves represent any real threat to democracy. A real threat could arise, however, should the government fail in its mission to prevent another September 11. If that happens, the public will demand, and will get, immense restrictions on liberties....

Because we find that open deportation hearings do not pass the two-part Richmond Newspapers test, we hold that the press and public possess no First Amendment right of access. In the absence of such a right, we need not reach the subsequent questions whether the Creppy Directive's closures would pass a strict scrutiny analysis and whether the District Court's "national in scope" injunction was too broad.

The judgment of the District Court will be reversed.

DISSENT: SCIRICA, Circuit Judge, dissenting:

At issue is not whether some or all deportation hearings of special interest aliens should be closed, but who makes that determination. The answer depends on how we interpret the First Amendment of the Constitution.

The Constitution is silent on the right to public access. But the Supreme Court has framed a qualified right of access that may be overcome by sound reasons. Because no reason is more compelling than national security, closure of special interest alien deportation hearings may well be warranted.

The Supreme Court's test in Richmond Newspapers – when a right of access attaches to a particular type of proceeding and whether it may be overcome – applies here. Therefore, I agree with the majority that this test applies to deportation hearings. But I believe the requirements of that test

are met. Consequently, I would find a qualified right of access to deportation hearings. Because I believe that Immigration Judges can make these determinations with substantial deference to national security, I would affirm the District Court's judgment. [222]

... Deportation hearings have a consistent history of openness. Congress first adopted immigration statutes at the end of the nineteenth century. In so doing, Congress expressly closed exclusion proceedings while leaving deportation hearings presumptively open. For at least one hundred years, deportation hearings have remained presumptively open to the public.... The Supreme Court has noted that we must assess history "because a tradition of accessibility implies the favorable judgment of experience." Press-Enterprise II, 478 U.S. at 8.... But this historical assessment does not cabin our review only to proceedings with a pre-constitutional history of openness. Other factors may reveal a favorable judgment of experience for presumptive access to deportation hearings.

Notably, Press-Enterprise II relies upon nineteenth and twentieth century history to find a tradition of openness for criminal preliminary hearings.... Furthermore, the Supreme Court has recognized that the Founders "could not [223] have anticipated the vast growth of the administrative state." For administrative proceedings, therefore, it would appear that the experience inquiry should consider the tradition of access to a particular proceeding within the history of the modern administrative state.... [224]

Congress has provided for presumptively open deportation proceedings from the moment that it first enacted an immigration statutory framework. This century of unbroken openness, especially within the nascent tradition of the administrative state, "implies the favorable judgment of experience" under the Richmond Newspapers test.

Public access to deportation hearings serves the same positive functions as does openness in criminal and civil trials. But the logic inquiry cannot consist merely of a recitation of the factors supporting open proceedings. "An assertion of the prerogative to gather information must . . . be assayed by considering the information sought and the opposing interests invaded." Richmond Newspapers, 448 U.S. at 588 (Brennan, J., concurring).... [225]

At this stage, we must consider the value of openness in deportation hearings generally, not its benefits and detriments in "special interest" deportation hearings in particular. If a qualified right of access is found to attach to deportation hearings generally, the analysis then turns to whether particular issues raised in individual cases override the general limited right of access.

Were the logic analysis focused only on special interest cases, I would agree that national security would likely trump the arguments in favor of access. Although paramount in certain deportation cases–like terrorism–national security is not generally implicated in the panoply of deportation hearings that occur throughout the United States.... Accordingly, the demands of national security under the logic prong of Richmond Newspapers do not provide sufficient justification for rejecting a qualified right of access to deportation hearings in general. To conclude otherwise would permit concerns relevant only to a discrete class of cases to determine there is no qualified right of access to any of the broad range of deportation proceedings, a departure from Richmond Newspapers. Whether national security interests justify closure of individual deportation hearings is a question properly addressed in the next step's more particularized inquiry.

Having found a qualified right of access to deportation hearings, the question remains whether the government has a sufficient justification to "override the qualified First Amendment right of access" by application of the Creppy Directive. Press-Enterprise II, 478 U.S. at 509.

Where a qualified right of access has been found, courts ordinarily have required a substantial showing to deny access. "The presumption of openness may be overcome only by an overriding interest based on findings that closure is essential to preserve higher values and is narrowly tailored to serve that interest." Press-Enterprise I, 464 U.S. at 510. There must be "a substantial probability" that openness will interfere with these interests. Press-Enterprise II, 478 U.S. at 14. Closure is appropriate only if "reasonable alternatives [226] to closure" are not available to protect the government's interests. Id. It bears noting, however, that these cases have not considered the deference due the government in matters involving national security.... [227]

In this case, the government's asserted interest–national security–is exceedingly compelling. Closure in some–or perhaps all–special interest cases may be necessary and appropriate. In fact, the Department of Justice regulations, enacted in 1964, expressly authorize an Immigration Judge to hold closed hearings to protect the public interest. But the question remains whether the Creppy Directive's blanket closure rule–which removes the decision to close the hearing from the Immigration Judge on a case-by-case basis–is reasonably necessary for the protection of national security.

The government contends that a case-by-case closure of removal proceedings would permit the release of sensitive information, potentially revealing sources, patterns and methods of investigation. But there is no reason that all of the information related to a particular detainee cannot be kept from public view. Even the initial determination to close a proceeding – and to seal the entire record – can be accomplished in camera and under seal. The government need only make the required showing of special interest, under seal to the Immigration Judge, subject to appellate review. In making their determinations, Immigration Judges should grant substantial deference to national security interests. A similar procedural framework has proven workable with criminal prosecutions.

The government maintains that these protections would be ineffective given the complexities in combating terrorism. It contends that individual, seemingly innocuous pieces of information, including a special interest alien's name, could be harmful to national security when compiled by terrorists into a mosaic. This seems correct. Nevertheless, the government could make the same argument to an Immigration Judge, who could determine, with substantial deference, that the apparently innocuous [228] information provides appropriate grounds for closure....

The Creppy Directive and the pre-existing Department of Justice regulations both accommodate the government's national security responsibilities. But a case-by-case approach would permit an Immigration Judge to independently assess the balance of these fundamental values. Because this is a reasonable alternative, the Creppy Directive's blanket closure rule is constitutionally infirm. As the Supreme Court reasoned in Globe Newspaper: "We emphasize that our holding is a narrow one: that a rule of mandatory closure . . . is constitutionally infirm. In individual cases, and under appropriate circumstances, the First Amendment does not necessarily stand as a bar to the exclusion from the courtroom of the press and general public . . . . But a mandatory rule, requiring no particularized determinations in individual cases, is unconstitutional." 457 U.S. at 611 n.27.

The stakes are high. Cherished traditions of openness have come up against the vital and compelling imperatives of national security. Because I believe national security interests can be fully accommodated on a case-by-case basis, I would affirm that part of the District Court's judgment.

Chapter

19

Press Privileges and Limits

Journalists as citizens

Focal case:
Branzburg v. Hayes, 408 U.S. 665 (1972)

Many journalists and observers of the press believe the First Amendment's explicit mention of the freedom of the press confers a special role for the press as the "fourth estate" watchdog of government. The Supreme Court at times has advocated this reading of the Constitution. In 1966, for example, the Court said: "The Constitution specifically selected the press . . . to play an important role in the discussion of public affairs. Thus the press serves and was designed to serve as a powerful antidote to any abuses of power by governmental officials and as a constitutionally chosen means for keeping officials elected by the people responsible to all the people whom they were selected to serve."[1]

Media disclosure of government misrepresentation of Vietnam War casualties and the political break-in at the Watergate Hotel during the re-election campaign of President Nixon are two prominent examples of the vital government information investigative journalism provided to the American public. In the late 1960s and '70s, however, aggressive journalism prompted overt hostility from the Nixon Administration and generated landmark Supreme Court rulings on the rights and responsibilities of the press in America.[2]

The tension between media watchdogs and government officials reached its contemporary apex when Vice President Spiro T. Agnew railed repeatedly against the "little group of men" he said dictated the nation's news. In one speech, Agnew called the "liberal press" an "effete corps of impudent snobs who characterize themselves as intellectuals."[3] Agnew accused these "nattering nabobs of negativism"[4] of disgorging a "cacophony of seditious drivel" that fomented

---

[1] Mills v. Alabama, 384 U.S. 214, 219 (1966).

[2] *See* United State v. New York Times, 403 U.S. 713 (1971) (protecting media dissemination of information about the Viet Nam conflict from government prior restraint); Nixon v. Admin. of General Services, 433 U.S. 425 (1977) (affirming public access to Nixon's official documents); Nixon v. Warner Communications, 435 U.S. 589 (1978) (denying access to Nixon tapes presented as evidence in Watergate conspiracy trial).

[3] Address in Des Moines, Iowa (Nov. 13, 1969).

[4] Address in San Diego, Cal. (Sept. 11, 1970) (phrase originally attributed to William Safire).

national discontent and perpetuated "national masochism."[5] He called repeatedly for more media responsibility, a term he often equated with reduced media criticism of the White House.

During these years, the executive branch and the courts[6] increasingly suggested the rights of a free press carried concomitant responsibilities.[7] The High Court did not consistently require all media to behave responsibly, but it considered the degree to which "the First Amendment was intended to guarantee free expression, not to create a privileged industry."[8] Its decision in *Red Lion Broadcasting v. FCC* is a clear example of the Supreme Court's willingness to subordinate the interests of some media owners to the public's interest.[9]

In contrast, journalists emphasized the First Amendment's edict that "Congress shall make no law ... abridging the freedom ... of the press." Media asserted common law privilege from government intrusions into their content and constitutional protection for their newsgathering processes.[10] Media argued, for example, that their ultimate responsibility as government watchdog afforded them a privilege to withhold confidential sources and information from grand juries because compelled disclosure and the appearance of government cooperation would undermine their relationships with sources and destroy important streams of news critical to citizens.[11] In their role as the eyes and ears of the public, journalists also said they deserved a special right of access to closed pretrial proceedings[12] and to parts of government facilities and prisons not afforded to the general public.[13] With very few exceptions, the Court disagreed.

CONSTITUTIONAL PRIVILEGE

In 1972, the Supreme Court in *Branzburg v. Hayes* held that no special First Amendment privilege released reporters from a citizen's duty to appear before a grand jury and provide evidence.[14] The Court said: "We do not question the significance of free speech, press or assembly to the country's welfare. Nor is it suggested that newsgathering does not qualify for First Amendment protection; without some protection for seeking out the news, freedom of the press could be eviscerated."[15] However, the Court was unconvinced that requiring reporters to provide confidential testimony – including the names of confidential sources – to assist criminal investigations would impede the flow of information to the public or cause significant harm to journalists' ability to gather news. Moreover, the Court refused to establish a constitutional shield for the confidentiality of news sources when Congress had considered and rejected legislation that would have provided that protection.[16] Finally, the Court said it would not enter the morass

---

[5] *But see, e.g.,* Eric Alterman, What Liberal Media? The Truth about Bias and the News (2003) (arguing that media liberalism is a myth perpetuated by the conservative right to cow the media into increased coverage of conservatives).

[6] *See, e.g.,* Miami Herald v. Tornilla, 418 U.S. 241 (1974); Gertz v. Welch, 418 U.S. 323 (1974).

[7] *See, e.g.,* Robert M. Hutchins, The Report of the Commission on Freedom of the Press: A Free and Responsible Press (1947); J. Coons, ed., Freedom and Responsibility in Broadcasting (1961); W. Emery, Broadcasting and Government: Responsibilities and Regulations (1961).

[8] Miami Herald, 418 U.S. at 399 (White, J., dissenting) (citing Commission on Freedom of the Press, A Free and Responsible Press 130, 81 (1947)).

[9] 395 U.S. 367 (1969). *But see* Miami Herald v. Tornillo, 418 U.S. 241 (1974).

[10] *See* United States v. Matthews, 209 F.3d 338 (2000) (finding First Amendment does not shield reporter from prosecution for trading in pornography even as part of the newsgathering process).

[11] *See* Branzburg v. Hayes, 408 U.S. 665 (1972).

[12] *See* Gannett v. DePasquale, 443 U.S. 368 (1979).

[13] *See* Houchins v. KQED, 438 U.S. 1 (1978); Saxbe v. Washington Post, 417 U.S. 843 (1974); Pell v. Procunier, 417 U.S. 817 (1974).

[14] 408 U.S. 665 (1972).

[15] 408 U.S. at 681.

[16] 408 U.S. at 690 (noting that 17 states had enacted shield laws and referencing seven bills presented in Congress between 1959 and 1971).

of determining which individuals in which contexts would constitute members of "the press" who warranted privilege. Reluctance to define journalists and distinguish them from the general public is a factor in the Court's continuing refusal to recognize even a qualified First Amendment privilege for journalists.[17]

In contrast, virtually all federal courts of appeal[18] and state courts recognize some limited constitutionally based media privilege.[19] This privilege, in fact, grows from part of Justice Stewart's dissent in *Branzburg* in which he argues that the First Amendment imposes a serious obstacle to government subpoenas likely to impede newsgathering. Justice Stewart set out three criteria government should demonstrate before requiring journalists to disclose confidential information. He argued, and most courts have accepted, that journalists may be compelled to testify only after government clearly shows:

1. Probable cause to believe the reporter has material information "clearly relevant to a specific probable violation of law;"
2. The absence of alternative sources of the information that would raise fewer First Amendment concerns; and
3. A compelling and overriding government interest in the information.[20]

In applying the test, courts generally have not allowed journalists to withhold information from grand juries, particularly when the journalist has first-hand knowledge of alleged criminal activity.[21] Many courts also require journalists to disclose non-confidential information[22] or information critical to determining the media's own liability for defamation or other harm.[23] The qualified constitutional journalists privilege articulated in *Branzburg* seems to apply most strongly in civil proceedings (where important interests of criminal defendants are not jeopardized) in which the journalist is not a party.[24] However, courts also are highly critical when government appears to use its power of subpoena to harass journalists.

STATE STATUTORY PRIVILEGE

Twenty-nine states and the District of Columbia have enacted shield laws to give qualified protection to journalists from judicially compelled disclosure of news sources. Typical shield statutes provide protection from testifying only for individuals explicitly categorized as journalists in the law. Most of these state statutes cover full-time journalists employed by news organizations, not freelancers or reporters for entertainment publications, for example. Others

---

[17] *See,* Herbert v. Lando, 441 U.S. 153 (1979) (refusing to find constitutional privilege shields editorial process from intrusive discovery in defamation case); University of Pennsylvania v. EEOC, 493 U.S. 182, 189 (1990) (reiterating its Branzburg refusal to establish a constitutional privilege); Bartnicki v. Vopper, 532 U.S. 514 (2001) (citing Branzburg to establish lack of constitutional protection regardless of impact on news flow). *But see* In re Roche, 448 U.S. 1312 (1980) (in which single justice grants stay against contempt citation for reporter refusal to divulge sources regarding judicial disciplinary action and noting "the First Amendment interposes a threshold barrier to the subpoenaing of confidential information and work product from a newsgatherer" at 1315); 381 Mass. 624 (1980) (affirming contempt citation for non-disclosure of facts unrelated to confidential sources).

[18] *See* In re Grand Jury Proceedings, 810 F.2d 580 (6th Cir. 1987) (finding no First Amendment journalists' privilege).

[19] *See, e.g.,* Zelenka v. State, 266 N.W.2d 279 (Wis. 1978) (finding state constitutional reporters' privilege); Sinear v. Daily Journal-American, 641 P.2d 1180 (Wash. 1982) (finding state common law privilege).

[20] 408 U.S. at 713.

[21] *See, e.g.,* Miami Herald Publishing v. Morejon, 561 So. 2d 577 (Fla. 1990).

[22] *See, e.g.,* Gonzales v. NBC, 194 F.3d 29 (2nd Cir. 1999); Reporters Committee for Freedom of Press v. AT&T, 593 F.2d 1030 (D.C. Cir. 1978).

[23] *See, e.g.,* Herbert v. Lando, 441 U.S. 153 (1979); Star Editorial v. U.S. District Court, 7 F.3d 856 (9th Cir. 1993).

[24] *See* In re Roche, 448 U.S. 1312 (1980); Baker v. F & F Investment, 470 F.2d 778 (2nd Cir. 1972).

protect anyone involved in the news process or anyone employed by the news media. Some shield only the names of confidential sources that provided information publicized by the news organization. Others cover all confidential, or even non-confidential, information possessed by the reporter.

PROMISES TO SOURCES

Although the First Amendment generally does not bar courts from requiring journalists to disclose confidential sources and information, journalists may be legally liable for damages to sources whose names they publicize after giving a clear promise of anonymity. The Supreme Court ruled in 1991 that media are liable for damages to sources that suffer harm because of broken promises of confidentiality.[25] When people rely on verbal promises to guide their behavior, courts may enforce the promises under the common law doctrine of promissory estoppel. Thus, when a journalist's promise of confidentiality is a condition for obtaining information, the promise is enforceable under common law in much the same way as a written contract. Here again the Court reasoned that while this doctrine may implicate First Amendment interests, the Constitution does not establish reporters as a special, privileged class immune from laws of general applicability that curtail the behavior of all citizens.

Since 1991, at least one federal appeals court reviewing a claim of promissory estoppel brought against the media sent the case forward to jury trial.[26]

SEARCH WARRANTS

Investigative officers who wish to examine a specific location without providing warning to the occupants rely on search warrants. The Fourth Amendment of the Constitution says courts may issue search warrants only upon a showing of probable cause that a crime has occurred and that the warrant will uncover specific items related to criminal acts. However, Section 213 of the USA PATRIOT Act[27] of 2001 (see Chap. 15) for the first time expressly permits a secret court to issue "sneak and peek" search warrants, which allow law officers to covertly search a person's home or office and conduct phone and Internet wiretaps when it is "reasonable" such a search may provide evidence related to any federal crime. These searches occur without the occupant's permission or knowledge, and officers may delay notifying the occupant that a search has occurred if "the court finds reasonable cause to believe that providing immediate notification of the execution of the warrant may have an adverse result."[28]

Historically, newsroom searches have been exceptional. In 1978, the Supreme Court issued its sole decision in the area, establishing the authority of law officers to search for evidence of criminal activity on the premises of law-abiding third parties, including journalists.[29]

Given the secrecy surrounding the issuance of search warrants under the PATRIOT Act, the Reporters Committee for Freedom of Press is concerned. According to the RCFP, "It is still unclear how or when the FBI's expanded wiretapping powers will affect journalists, but the Justice Department has shown that it intends to use its powers aggressively."[30] In response to

---

[25] Cohen v. Cowles Media, 501 U.S. 663 (1991).

[26] Ruzicka v. Conde Nast Publications, 999 F.2d 1319 (8th Cir. 1993) (no subsequent court decisions appear to have been published).

[27] The Uniting and Strengthening America by Providing Appropriate Tools Required to Intercept and Obstruct Terrorism Act, Pub. L. No. 107-56.

[28] § 213 (1), amending 18 U. S. C. § 3103a.

[29] Zurcher v. Stanford Daily, 436 U.S. 547 (1978).

[30] See http://www.rcfp.org/homefrontconfidential/usapatriot.html, accessed July 18, 2003. See also American Civil Liberties Union v. Department of Justice, (D.D.C. Oct. 4, 2002), available at http://www.eff.org/pub/Legal/Cases/EFF_ACLU_v_DoJ/ or

litigation and requests under the federal Freedom of Information Act, the U.S. Department of Justice and the Office of the Attorney General indicated in 2003 that the attorney general's office had initiated searches and surveillance unilaterally without court approval.[31] The Department of Justice refused to indicate how extensively it had used this authority, but it acknowledged that an 18-page document detailed only the authorizations issued to obtain reporters' telephone records during the previous two years.[32]

The Privacy Protection Act of 1980[33] provides some compensation to news media harmed by unreasonable searches or seizures. In 1994, a federal appeals court found this law obligated the Secret Service to pay damages to the distributor of an electronic bulletin board and publisher of a magazine on computer gaming for the seizure of work products, including computer disks and drafts of magazine articles.[34] The Secret Service had obtained a search warrant prior to the seizures, but the court said materials that include the original ideas of journalists may be seized only when there is evidence the journalists themselves committed a crime. In contrast, even when journalists are innocent of any criminal activity, government may seize the documentary materials used in the news process if the materials provide evidence of the crimes of others.[35] In addition, journalists cannot invoke the protections of The Privacy Protection Act if they are the targets of "sneak and peek" searches.

READING THE CASES

The cases in this list and the case below provide a good overview of the federal case law related to reporters privilege and search and seizure of journalists' materials. However, state courts also have produced a wealth of case law on these topics. Thorough understanding of the rights and privileges of journalists warrants a reading of state law as well as the numerous federal district court decisions not listed here.

- *Gonzales v. NBC*, 194 F.3d 29 (2nd Cir. 1999) (finding qualified privilege for non-confidential information overcome).
- *Steve Jackson Games v. U. S. Secret Service*, 36 F.3d 457 (5th Cir. 1994) (affirming finding that seizure of unread emails is not an illegal wiretap but seizure of work product violates Privacy Protection Act).
- *Star Editorial v. U.S. District Court*, 7 F.3d 856 (9th Cir. 1993) (finding no privilege shields confidential sources in story at issue in defamation suit by Rodney Dangerfield).
- *Cohen v. Cowles Media*, 501 U.S. 663 (1991) (finding promissory estoppel enforceable against media).
- *In re Grand Jury Proceedings (Storer Communications v. Giovan)*, 810 F.2d 580 (6th Cir. 1987) (finding no First Amendment journalists' privilege not to provide evidence to grand jury and finding rational the Mich. statutory privilege limitation to print journalists).

---

www.epic.org/privacy/terrorism/usapatriot/foia/ (attempting to force the release of statistics related to the use of the new search powers under the PATRIOT Act).

[31] *See, e.g.,* http://www.aclu.org/SafeandFree/SafeandFree.cfm?ID=12166&c=206.

[32] *See* case numbers AG/03-R0313, DAG/03-R0314, PAO/03-R0317. *See also* Reporters Committee for Freedom of Press v. AT&T, 593 F. 2d 1030 (D.C. Cir. 1978) (finding no constitutional infirmity in telephone company delivery of private telephone records in response to subpoena without notifying subscriber).

[33] 42 U.S.C. §2000aa (1988).

[34] *See* Steve Jackson Games v. United States Secret Service, 816 F. Supp. 432 (W.D. Texas 1993), *aff'd* 36 F.3d 457 (5th Cir. 1994).

[35] Citicasters v. McCaskill, 883 F. Supp. 1282 (W.D. Mo. 1995) (defining work product as materials intended for dissemination to the public and awarding damages for seizure of documentary materials when search responded neither to imminent threat to human safety nor likely destruction of the materials).

- *In re Roche*, 448 U.S. 1312 (1980) (entering a stay to contempt citation for non-disclosure of confidential sources pending adjudication).
- *Herbert v. Lando*, 441 U.S. 153 (1979) (refusing to find constitutional privilege shields editorial process from intrusive discovery in defamation case).
- *Houchins v. KQED*, 438 U.S. 1 (1978) (finding Constitution does not provide press right of access to the jail superior to that of the public generally).
- *Zurcher v. Stanford Daily*, 436 U.S. 547 (1978) (finding First Amendment does not prohibit newsroom searches).
- *Reporters Committee for Freedom of Press v. AT&T*, 593 F.2d 1030 (D.C. Cir. 1978) (finding no constitutional infirmity in telephone company delivery of private telephone records in response to subpoena without notifying subscriber).
- *Saxbe v. Washington Post*, 417 U.S. 843 (1974) (finding prison policy limiting public access does not abridge freedom of the press).
- *Pell v. Procunier*, 417 U.S. 817 (1974) (finding ban on face-to-face interviews with named inmates does not violate inmates' or media's First Amendment rights).
- *Baker v. F & F Investment*, 470 F.2d 778 (2nd Cir. 1972) (refusing to require journalist to disclose sources in civil deposition).

In reading *Branzburg v. Hayes*, consider the following questions.

- Does the Court in *Branzburg* find a First Amendment interest in confidentiality as a part of newsgathering?
- How does the Court characterize subpoenas that require journalists to testify? Are they prior restraints? Are they direct infringement on First Amendment rights? Are they content-based restrictions? Are they a form of punishment? Why?
- What is the significance of the government interest involved in grand juries?
- Does the Court balance the First Amendment interests in this case against the grand jury interests? Why?
- What affect might it have had on the Court's ruling if the confidential informants at issue in *Branzburg* were not engaged in criminal conduct? Why?
- What test does the Court establish in *Branzburg* to determine when a reporter should testify?
- What are the primary points of contention between the dissenters and the majority of the Court?
- In what ways is the Court's view of the First Amendment "crabbed," and what are the potential deleterious effects of this view?

Branzburg v. Hayes
408 U.S. 665
(1972)

PRIOR HISTORY: Certiorari to the Court of Appeals of Kentucky.

JUDGES: White, J., wrote the opinion of the Court, in which Burger, C. J., and Blackmun, Powell, and Rehnquist, JJ., joined. Powell, J., filed a concurring opinion, post. Douglas, J., filed a dissenting opinion, post. Stewart, J., filed a dissenting opinion, in which Brennan and Marshall, JJ., joined.

OPINION: [667] Opinion of the Court by MR. JUSTICE WHITE, announced by THE CHIEF JUSTICE.

[1A] The issue in these cases is whether requiring newsmen to appear and testify before state or federal grand juries abridges the freedom of speech and press guaranteed by the First Amendment. We hold that it does not.

I. The writ of certiorari in No. 70-85, Branzburg v. Hayes and Meigs, brings before us two judgments of the Kentucky Court of Appeals, both involving petitioner Branzburg, a staff reporter for the Courier-Journal, a daily newspaper published in Louisville, Kentucky.

On November 15, 1969, the Courier-Journal carried a story under petitioner's by-line describing in detail his observations of two young residents of Jefferson County synthesizing hashish from marihuana, an activity which, they asserted, earned them about $5,000 in three weeks. The article included a photograph of a pair of hands working above a laboratory table on which was a substance identified by the caption as hashish. The article stated that petitioner had promised not to [668] reveal the identity of the two hashish makers.[1] Petitioner was shortly subpoenaed by the Jefferson County grand jury; he appeared, but refused to identify the individuals he had seen possessing marihuana or the persons he had seen making hashish from marihuana.[2] A state trial court

judge[3] ordered petitioner to answer these questions and rejected his contention that the Kentucky reporters' privilege statute, Ky. Rev. Stat. §421.100 (1962),[4] the First Amendment of the United States Constitution, or §§ 1, 2, and 8 of the Kentucky Constitution authorized his refusal to answer. Petitioner then sought prohibition and mandamus in the Kentucky Court of Appeals on the same grounds, but the Court of Appeals denied the petition. Branzburg v. [669] Pound, 461 S. W. 2d 345 (1970), as modified on denial of rehearing, Jan. 22, 1971. It held that petitioner had abandoned his First Amendment argument in a supplemental memorandum he had filed and tacitly rejected his argument based on the Kentucky Constitution. It also construed Ky. Rev. Stat. §421.100 as affording a newsman the privilege of refusing to divulge the identity of an informant who supplied him with information, but held that the statute did not permit a reporter to refuse to testify about events he had observed personally, including the identities of those persons he had observed.

The second case involving petitioner Branzburg arose out of his later story published on January 10, 1971, which described in detail the use of drugs in Frankfort, Kentucky. The article reported that in order to provide a comprehensive survey of the "drug scene" in Frankfort, petitioner had "spent two weeks interviewing several dozen drug users in the capital city" and had seen some of them smoking marihuana. A number of conversations with and observations of several unnamed drug users were recounted. Subpoenaed to appear before a Franklin County grand jury "to testify in the matter of violation of statutes concerning use and sale of drugs," petitioner Branzburg moved to quash the

---

[1] The article contained the following paragraph: "'I don't know why I'm letting you do this story,' [one informant] said quietly. 'To make the narcs (narcotics detectives) mad, I guess. That's the main reason.' However, Larry and his partner asked for and received a promise that their names would be changed." App. 3-4.

[2] The Foreman of the grand jury reported that petitioner Branzburg had refused to answer the following two questions: "#1. On November 12, or 13, 1969, who was the person or persons you observed in possession of Marijuana, about which you wrote an article in the Courier-Journal on November 15, 1969? #2. On November 12, or 13, 1969,

who was the person or persons you observed compounding Marijuana, producing same to a compound known as Hashish?" App. 6.

[3] Judge J. Miles Pound. The respondent in this case, Hon. John P. Hayes, is the successor of Judge Pound.

[4] Ky. Rev. Stat. § 421.100 provides:
"No person shall be compelled to disclose in any legal proceeding or trial before any court, or before any grand or petit jury, or before the presiding officer of any tribunal, or his agent or agents, or before the General Assembly, or any committee thereof, or before any city or county legislative body, or any committee thereof, or elsewhere, the source of any information procured or obtained by him, and published in a newspaper or by a radio or television broadcasting station by which he is engaged or employed, or with which he is connected."

summons;[5] the motion was denied, although [670] an order was issued protecting Branzburg from revealing "confidential associations, sources or information" but requiring that he "answer any questions which concern or pertain to any criminal act, the commission of which was actually observed by [him]." Prior to the time he was slated to appear before the grand jury, petitioner sought mandamus and prohibition from the Kentucky Court of Appeals, arguing that if he were forced to go before the grand jury or to answer questions regarding the identity of informants or disclose information given to him in confidence, his effectiveness as a reporter would be greatly damaged.

The Court of Appeals once again denied the requested writs, reaffirming its construction of Ky. Rev. Stat. § 421.100, and rejecting petitioner's claim of a First Amendment privilege. It distinguished Caldwell v. United States, 434 F.2d 1081 (CA9 1970), and it also announced its "misgivings" about that decision, asserting that it represented "a drastic departure from the generally recognized rule that the sources of information of a newspaper reporter are not privileged under the First Amendment." It characterized petitioner's fear that his ability to obtain [671] news would be destroyed as "so tenuous that it does not, in the opinion of this court, present an issue of abridgement of the freedom of the press within the

meaning of that term as used in the Constitution of the United States."[6]

[2A] Petitioner sought a writ of certiorari to review both judgments of the Kentucky Court of Appeals, and we granted the writ. n6 402 U.S. 942 (1971).

[2B] [672] In re Pappas, No. 70-94, originated when petitioner Pappas, a television newsman-photographer working out of the Providence, Rhode Island, office of a New Bedford, Massachusetts, television station, was called to

---

[5] Petitioner's Motion to Quash argued:

"If Mr. Branzburg were required to disclose these confidences to the Grand Jury, or any other person, he would thereby destroy the relationship of trust which he presently enjoys with those in the drug culture. They would refuse to speak to him; they would become even more reluctant than they are now to speak to any newsman; and the news media would thereby be vitally hampered in their ability to cover the views and activities of those involved in the drug culture.

"The inevitable effect of the subpoena issued to Mr. Branzburg, if it not be quashed by this Court, will be to suppress vital First Amendment freedoms of Mr. Branzburg, of the Courier-Journal, of the news media, and of those involved in the drug culture by driving a wedge of distrust and silence between the news media and the drug culture. This Court should not sanction a use of its process entailing so drastic an incursion upon First Amendment freedoms in the absence of compelling Commonwealth interest in requiring Mr. Branzburg's appearance before the Grand Jury. It is insufficient merely to protect Mr. Branzburg's right to silence after he appears before the Grand Jury. This Court should totally excuse Mr. Branzburg from responding to the subpoena and even entering the Grand Jury room. Once Mr. Branzburg is required to go behind the closed doors of the Grand Jury room, his effectiveness as a reporter in these areas is totally destroyed. The secrecy that surrounds Grand Jury testimony necessarily introduces uncertainties in the minds of those who fear a betrayal of their confidences." App. 43-44.

---

[6] After the Kentucky Court of Appeals' decision in Branzburg v. Meigs was announced, petitioner filed a rehearing motion in Branzburg v. Pound suggesting that the court had not passed upon his First Amendment argument and calling to the court's attention the recent Ninth Circuit decision in Caldwell v. United States, 434 F.2d 1081 (1970). On Jan. 22, 1971, the court denied petitioner's motion and filed an amended opinion in the case, adding a footnote, 461 S. W. 2d 345, 346 n. 1, to indicate that petitioner had abandoned his First Amendment argument and elected to rely wholly on Ky. Rev. Stat. § 421.100 when he filed a Supplemental Memorandum before oral argument. In his Petition for Prohibition and Mandamus, petitioner had clearly relied on the First Amendment, and he had filed his Supplemental Memorandum in response to the State's Memorandum in Opposition to the granting of the writs. As its title indicates, this Memorandum was complementary to petitioner's earlier Petition, and it dealt primarily with the State's construction of the phrase "source of any information" in Ky. Rev. Stat. § 421.100. The passage that the Kentucky Court of Appeals cited to indicate abandonment of petitioner's First Amendment claim is as follows:

"Thus, the controversy continues as to whether a newsman's source of information should be privileged. However, that question is not before the Court in this case. The Legislature of Kentucky has settled the issue, having decided that a newsman's source of information is to be privileged. Because of this there is no point in citing Professor Wigmore and other authorities who speak against the grant of such a privilege. The question has been many times debated, and the Legislature has spoken. The only question before the Court is the construction of the term 'source of information' as it was intended by the Legislature." Though the passage itself is somewhat unclear, the surrounding discussion indicates that petitioner was asserting here that the question of whether a common-law privilege should be recognized was irrelevant since the legislature had already enacted a statute. In his earlier discussion, petitioner had analyzed certain cases in which the First Amendment argument was made but indicated that it was not necessary to reach this question if the statutory phrase "source of any information" were interpreted expansively. We do not interpret this discussion as indicating that petitioner was abandoning his First Amendment claim if the Kentucky Court of Appeals did not agree with his statutory interpretation argument, and we hold that the constitutional question in Branzburg v. Pound was properly preserved for review.

New Bedford on July 30, 1970, to report on civil disorders there which involved fires and other turmoil. He intended to cover a Black Panther news conference at that group's headquarters in a boarded-up store. Petitioner found the streets around the store barricaded, but he ultimately gained entrance to the area and recorded and photographed a prepared statement read by one of the Black Panther leaders at about 3 p. m.[7] He then asked for and received permission to reenter the area. Returning at about 9 o'clock, he was allowed to enter and remain inside Panther headquarters. As a condition of entry, Pappas agreed not to disclose anything he saw or heard inside the store except an anticipated police raid, which Pappas, "on his own," was free to photograph and report as he wished. Pappas stayed inside the headquarters for about three hours, but there was no police raid, and petitioner wrote no story and did not otherwise reveal what had occurred in the store while he was there. Two months later, petitioner was summoned before the Bristol [673] County Grand Jury and appeared, answered questions as to his name, address, employment, and what he had seen and heard outside Panther headquarters, but refused to answer any questions about what had taken place inside headquarters while he was there, claiming that the First Amendment afforded him a privilege to protect confidential informants and their information.

A second summons was then served upon him, again directing him to appear before the grand jury and "to give such evidence as he knows relating to any matters which may be inquired of on behalf of the Commonwealth before . . . the Grand Jury." His motion to quash on First Amendment and other grounds was denied by the trial judge who, noting the absence of a statutory newsman's privilege in Massachusetts, ruled that petitioner had no constitutional privilege to refuse to divulge to the grand jury what he had seen and heard, including the identity of persons he had observed. The case was reported for decision to the Supreme Judicial Court of Massachusetts.[8] The record there did not include a transcript of the hearing on the motion to quash, nor did it reveal the specific questions petitioner had refused to answer, the expected nature of his testimony, the nature of the grand jury investigation, or the likelihood of the

grand jury's securing the information it sought from petitioner by other means.[9]

The [674] Supreme Judicial Court, however, took "judicial notice that in July, 1970, there were serious civil disorders in New Bedford, which involved street barricades, exclusion of the public from certain streets, fires, and similar turmoil. We were told at the arguments that there was gunfire in certain streets. We assume that the grand jury investigation was an appropriate effort to discover and indict those responsible for criminal acts." 358 Mass. 604, 607, 266 N. E. 2d 297, 299 (1971). The court then reaffirmed prior Massachusetts holdings that testimonial privileges were "exceptional" and "limited," stating that "the principle that the public 'has a right to every man's evidence'" had usually been preferred, in the Commonwealth, to countervailing interests. Ibid.

The court rejected the holding of the Ninth Circuit in Caldwell v. United States, supra, and "adhere[d] to the view that there exists no constitutional newsman's privilege, either qualified or absolute, to refuse to appear and testify before a court or grand jury."[10] 358 Mass., at 612, 266 N. E. 2d, at 302-303. Any adverse effect upon the free dissemination of news by virtue of petitioner's being called to testify was deemed to be only "indirect, theoretical, and uncertain." Id., at 612, 266 N. E. 2d, at 302. The court concluded that "the obligation of newsmen . . . is that of every citizen . . . to appear when summoned, with relevant written or other material when required, and to answer relevant and reasonable inquiries." Id., at 612, 266 N. E. 2d, at 303. The court nevertheless noted that grand juries were subject to supervision by the presiding [675] judge, who had the duty "to prevent oppressive, unnecessary, irrelevant, and other improper inquiry and investigation," ibid., to insure that a witness' Fifth Amendment rights were not infringed, and to assess the propriety, necessity, and pertinence of the probable testimony to the investigation in progress.[11] The burden was deemed

---

[7] Petitioner's news films of this event were made available to the Bristol County District Attorney. App. 4.

[8] The case was reported by the superior court directly to the Supreme Judicial Court for an interlocutory ruling under Mass. Gen. Laws, c. 278, § 30A and Mass. Gen. Laws, c. 231, § 111 (1959). The Supreme Judicial Court's decision appears at 358 Mass. 604, 266 N. E. 2d 297 (1971).

[9] "We do not have before us the text of any specific questions which Pappas has refused to answer before the grand jury, or any petition to hold him for contempt for his refusal. We have only general statements concerning (a) the inquiries of the grand jury, and (b) the materiality of the testimony sought from Pappas. The record does not show the expected nature of his testimony or what likelihood there is of being able to obtain that testimony from persons other than news gatherers." 358 Mass., at 606-607, 266 N. E. 2d, at 299 (footnote omitted).

[10] The court expressly declined to consider, however, appearances of newsmen before legislative or administrative bodies. Id., at 612 n. 10, 266 N. E. 2d, at 303 n. 10.

[11] The court noted that "a presiding judge may consider in his discretion" the argument that the use of newsmen as witnesses is likely to result in unnecessary or burdensome

to be on the witness to establish the impropriety of the summons or the questions asked. The denial of the motion to quash was affirmed and we granted a writ of certiorari to petitioner Pappas. 402 U.S. 942 (1971).

United States v. Caldwell, No. 70-57, arose from subpoenas issued by a federal grand jury in the Northern District of California to respondent Earl Caldwell, a reporter for the New York Times assigned to cover the Black Panther Party and other black militant groups. A subpoena duces tecum was served on respondent on February 2, 1970, ordering him to appear before the grand jury to testify and to bring with him notes and tape recordings of interviews given him for publication by officers and spokesmen of the Black Panther Party concerning the aims, purposes, and activities of that organization.[12] Respondent objected to the scope [676] of this subpoena, and an agreement between his counsel and the Government attorneys resulted in a continuance. A second subpoena, served on March 16, omitted the documentary requirement and simply ordered Caldwell "to appear . . . to testify before the Grand Jury." Respondent and his employer, the New York Times,[13] moved to quash on the ground that the unlimited breadth of the subpoenas and the fact that Caldwell would have to appear in secret before the grand jury would destroy his working relationship with the Black Panther Party and "suppress vital First Amendment freedoms ... by driving a wedge of distrust and silence between the news media and the militants." App. 7.

Respondent argued that "so drastic an incursion upon First Amendment freedoms" should not be permitted "in the absence of a compelling

use of their work product, id., at 614 n. 13, 266 N. E. 2d, at 304 n. 13, and cautioned that: "We do not suggest that a general investigation of mere political or group association of persons, without substantial relation to criminal events, may not be viewed by a judge in a somewhat different manner from an investigation of particular criminal events concerning which a newsman may have knowledge." Id., at 614 n. 14, 266 N. E. 2d, at 304 n. 14.

[12] The subpoena ordered production of "notes and tape recordings of interviews covering the period from January 1, 1969, to date, reflecting statements made for publication by officers and spokesmen for the Black Panther Party concerning the aims and purposes of said organization and the activities of said organization, its officers, staff, personnel, and members, including specifically but not limited to interviews given by David Hilliard and Raymond 'Masai' Hewitt." App. 20.

[13] The New York Times was granted standing to intervene as a party on the motion to quash the subpoenas. Application of Caldwell, 311 F.Supp. 358, 359 (ND Cal. 1970). It did not file an appeal from the District Court's contempt citation, and it did not seek certiorari here. It has filed an amicus curiae brief, however.

governmental interest – not shown here – in requiring Mr. Caldwell's appearance before the grand jury." Ibid. The motion was supported by amicus curiae memoranda from other publishing concerns and by affidavits from newsmen asserting the unfavorable impact on news sources of requiring reporters to appear before grand juries. The Government filed three memoranda in opposition to the motion to quash, each supported by affidavits. These documents stated that the grand jury was investigating, among other things, possible violations of a number of criminal statutes, including 18 U. S. C. §871 (threats against the President), 18 U.S.C. [677] §1751 (assassination, attempts to assassinate, conspiracy to assassinate the President), 18 U. S. C. §231 (civil disorders), 18 U. S. C. § 2101 (interstate travel to incite a riot), and 18 U. S. C. §1341 (mail frauds and swindles).

It was recited that on November 15, 1969, an officer of the Black Panther Party made a publicly televised speech in which he had declared that "we will kill Richard Nixon" and that this threat had been repeated in three subsequent issues of the Party newspaper. App. 66, 77. Also referred to were various writings by Caldwell about the Black Panther Party, including an article published in the New York Times on December 14, 1969, stating that "in their role as the vanguard in a revolutionary struggle the Panthers have picked up guns," and quoting the Chief of Staff of the Party as declaring: "We advocate the very direct overthrow of the Government by way of force and violence. By picking up guns and moving against it because we recognize it as being oppressive and in recognizing that we know that the only solution to it is armed struggle [sic]." App. 62. The Government also stated that the Chief of Staff of the Party had been indicted by the grand jury on December 3, 1969, for uttering threats against the life of the President in violation of 18 U. S. C. § 871 and that various efforts had been made to secure evidence of crimes under investigation through the immunization of persons allegedly associated with the Black Panther Party.

On April 6, the District Court denied the motion to quash, Application of Caldwell, 311 F.Supp. 358 (ND Cal. 1970), on the ground that "every person within the jurisdiction of the government" is bound to testify upon being properly summoned. Id., at 360 (emphasis in original). Nevertheless, the court accepted respondent's First Amendment arguments to the extent of issuing a protective order providing that although respondent had to divulge [678] whatever information had been given to him for publication, he "shall not be required to reveal confidential associations, sources or information received, developed or maintained by him as a professional journalist in the course of his efforts to gather news for dissemination to the public through the press or other news media." The court held that the First Amendment afforded respondent a privilege to refuse disclosure of such confidential information until there had been "a showing by the Government of a compelling and overriding national interest in requiring Mr. Caldwell's testimony which cannot be served by any alternative means." Id., at 362.

Subsequently,[14] the term of the grand jury expired, a new grand jury was convened, and a new subpoena ad testificandum was issued and served on May 22, 1970. A new motion to quash by respondent and memorandum in opposition by the Government were filed, and, by stipulation of the parties, the motion was submitted on the prior record. The court denied the motion to quash, repeating the protective provisions in its prior order but this time directing Caldwell to appear before the grand jury pursuant to the May 22 subpoena. Respondent refused to appear before the grand jury, and the court issued an order to show cause why he should not be held in contempt. Upon his further refusal to go before the grand jury, respondent was ordered committed for contempt until such time as he complied with the court's order or until the expiration of the term of the grand jury.

[679] Respondent Caldwell appealed the contempt order,[15] and the Court of Appeals reversed. Caldwell v. United States, 434 F.2d 1081 (CA9 1970). Viewing the issue before it as whether Caldwell was required to appear before the grand jury at all, rather than the scope of permissible interrogation, the court first determined that the First Amendment provided a qualified testimonial privilege to newsmen; in its view, requiring a reporter like Caldwell to testify would deter his informants from communicating with him in the future and would cause him to censor his writings in an effort to avoid being subpoenaed.

Absent compelling reasons for requiring his testimony, he was held privileged to withhold it. The court also held, for similar First Amendment reasons, that, absent some special showing of necessity by the Government, attendance by Caldwell at a secret meeting of the grand jury was something he was privileged to refuse because of the potential impact of such an appearance on the

flow of news to the public. We granted the United States' petition for certiorari.[16] 402 U.S. 942 (1971).

II. Petitioners Branzburg and Pappas and respondent Caldwell press First Amendment claims that may be simply put: that to gather news it is often necessary to agree either not to identify the source of information published or to publish only part of the facts revealed, or both; that if the reporter is nevertheless [680] forced to reveal these confidences to a grand jury, the source so identified and other confidential sources of other reporters will be measurably deterred from furnishing publishable information, all to the detriment of the free flow of information protected by the First Amendment. Although the newsmen in these cases do not claim an absolute privilege against official interrogation in all circumstances, they assert that the reporter should not be forced either to appear or to testify before a grand jury or at trial until and unless sufficient grounds are shown for believing that the reporter possesses information relevant to a crime the grand jury is investigating, that the information the reporter has is unavailable from other sources, and that the need for the information is sufficiently compelling to override the claimed invasion of First Amendment interests occasioned by the disclosure.

Principally relied upon are prior cases emphasizing the importance of the First Amendment guarantees to individual development and to our system of representative government,[17] decisions requiring that official action with adverse impact on First Amendment rights be justified by a public interest that is "compelling" or "paramount,"[18] and those precedents establishing the principle that justifiable governmental goals may not be achieved by unduly broad means having an unnecessary impact [681] on protected rights of speech, press, or association.[19]

---

[14] Respondent appealed from the District Court's April 6 denial of his motion to quash on April 17, 1970, and the Government moved to dismiss that appeal on the ground that the order was interlocutory. On May 12, 1970, the Ninth Circuit dismissed the appeal without opinion.
[15] The Government did not file a cross-appeal and did not challenge the validity of the District Court protective order in the Court of Appeals.

[16] The petition presented a single question: "Whether a newspaper reporter who has published articles about an organization can, under the First Amendment, properly refuse to appear before a grand jury investigating possible crimes by members of that organization who have been quoted in the published articles."
[17] urtis Publishing Co. v. Butts, 388 U.S. 130, 145 (1967) (opinion of Harlan, J.); New York Times Co. v. Sullivan, 376 U.S. 254, 270 (1964); Talley v. California, 362 U.S. 60, 64-65 (1960); Bridges v. California, 314 U.S. 252, 263 (1941); Grosjean v. American Press Co., 297 U.S. 233, 250 (1936); Near v. Minnesota, 283 U.S. 697, 722 (1931).
[18] NAACP v. Button, 371 U.S. 415, 439 (1963); Thomas v. Collins, 323 U.S. 516, 530 (1945); DeGregory v. Attorney General of New Hampshire, 383 U.S. 825, 829 (1966); Bates v. Little Rock, 361 U.S. 516, 524 (1960); Schneider v. State, 308 U.S. 147, 161 (1939); NAACP v. Alabama, 357 U.S. 449, 464 (1958).
[19] Freedman v. Maryland, 380 U.S. 51, 56 (1965); NAACP v. Alabama, 377 U.S. 288, 307 (1964); Martin v. City of

The heart of the claim is that the burden on news gathering resulting from compelling reporters to disclose confidential information outweighs any public interest in obtaining the information.[20]

We do not question the significance of free speech, press, or assembly to the country's welfare. Nor is it suggested that news gathering does not qualify for First Amendment protection; without some protection for seeking out the news, freedom of the press could be eviscerated. But these cases involve no intrusions upon speech or assembly, no prior restraint or restriction on what the press may publish, and no express or implied command that the press publish what it prefers to withhold. No exaction or tax for the privilege of publishing, and no penalty, civil or criminal, related to the content of published material is at issue here. The use of confidential sources by the press is not forbidden or restricted; reporters remain free to seek news from [682] any source by means within the law. No attempt is made to require the press to publish its sources of information or indiscriminately to disclose them on request.

[3] The sole issue before us is the obligation of reporters to respond to grand jury subpoenas as other citizens do and to answer questions relevant to an investigation into the commission of crime. Citizens generally are not constitutionally immune from grand jury subpoenas; and neither the First Amendment nor any other constitutional provision protects the average citizen from disclosing to a grand jury information that he has received in confidence.[21] The claim is, however, that

reporters are exempt from these obligations because if forced to respond to subpoenas and identify their sources or disclose other confidences, their informants will refuse or be reluctant to furnish newsworthy information in the future. This asserted burden on news gathering is said to make compelled testimony from newsmen constitutionally suspect and to require a privileged position for them.

[4] [5] [6] It is clear that the First Amendment does not invalidate every incidental burdening of the press that may result from the enforcement of civil or criminal statutes of general applicability. Under prior cases, otherwise valid laws serving substantial public interests may be enforced against the press as against others, despite [683] the possible burden that may be imposed. The Court has emphasized that "the publisher of a newspaper has no special immunity from the application of general laws. He has no special privilege to invade the rights and liberties of others." Associated Press v. NLRB, 301 U.S. 103, 132-133 (1937). It was there held that the Associated Press, a news-gathering and disseminating organization, was not exempt from the requirements of the National Labor Relations Act. The holding was reaffirmed in Oklahoma Press Publishing Co. v. Walling, 327 U.S. 186, 192-193 (1946), where the Court rejected the claim that applying the Fair Labor Standards Act to a newspaper publishing business would abridge the freedom of press guaranteed by the First Amendment. See also Mabee v. White Plains Publishing Co., 327 U.S. 178 (1946). Associated Press v. United States, 326 U.S. 1 (1945), similarly overruled assertions that the First Amendment precluded application of the Sherman Act to a newsgathering and disseminating organization. Cf. Indiana Farmer's Guide Publishing Co. v. Prairie Farmer Publishing Co., 293 U.S. 268, 276 (1934); Citizen Publishing Co. v. United States, 394 U.S. 131, 139 (1969); Lorain Journal Co. v. United States, 342 U.S. 143, 155-156 (1951). Likewise, a newspaper may be subjected to nondiscriminatory forms of general taxation. Grosjean v. American Press Co., 297 U.S. 233, 250 (1936); Murdock v. Pennsylvania, 319 U.S. 105, 112 (1943).

[7] [8] [9] The prevailing view is that the press is not free to publish with impunity everything and anything it desires to publish. Although it may deter or regulate what is said or published, the

---

Struthers, 319 U.S. 141, 147 (1943); Elfbrandt v. Russell, 384 U.S. 11, 18 (1966).

[20] There has been a great deal of writing in recent years on the existence of a newsman's constitutional right of nondisclosure of confidential information. See, e.g., Beaver, The Newsman's Code, The Claim of Privilege and Everyman's Right to Evidence, 47 Ore. L. Rev. 243 (1968); Guest & Stanzler, The Constitutional Argument for Newsmen Concealing Their Sources, 64 Nw. U. L. Rev. 18 (1969); Note, Reporters and Their Sources: The Constitutional Right to a Confidential Relationship, 80 Yale L. J. 317 (1970); Comment, The Newsman's Privilege: Government Investigations, Criminal Prosecutions and Private Litigation, 58 Calif. L. Rev. 1198 (1970); Note, The Right of the Press to Gather Information, 71 Col. L. Rev. 838 (1971); Nelson, The Newsmen's Privilege Against Disclosure of Confidential Sources and Information, 24 Vand. L. Rev. 667 (1971).

[21] "In general, then, the mere fact that a communication was made in express confidence, or in the implied confidence of a confidential relation, does not create a privilege.

". . . No pledge of privacy nor oath of secrecy can avail against demand for the truth in a court of justice." 8 J. Wigmore, Evidence § 2286 (McNaughton rev. 1961). This was not always the rule at common law, however. In 17th century England, the obligations of honor among

gentlemen were occasionally recognized as privileging from compulsory disclosure information obtained in exchange for a promise of confidence. See Bulstrod v. Letchmere, 2 Freem. 6, 22 Eng. Rep. 1019 (1676); Lord Grey's Trial, 9 How. St. Tr. 127 (1682).

press may not circulate knowing or reckless falsehoods damaging to private reputation without subjecting itself to liability for damages, including punitive damages, or even criminal prosecution. See New York Times Co. v. Sullivan, 376 U.S. 254, [684] 279-280 (1964); Garrison v. Louisiana, 379 U.S. 64, 74 (1964); Curtis Publishing Co. v. Butts, 388 U.S. 130, 147 (1967) (opinion of Harlan, J.,); Monitor Patriot Co. v. Roy, 401 U.S. 265, 277 (1971). A newspaper or a journalist may also be punished for contempt of court, in appropriate circumstances. Craig v. Harney, 331 U.S. 367, 377-378 (1947).

[10] [11] It has generally been held that the First Amendment does not guarantee the press a constitutional right of special access to information not available to the public generally. Zemel v. Rusk, 381 U.S. 1, 16-17 (1965); New York Times Co. v. United States, 403 U.S. 713, 728-730 (1971), (STEWART, J., concurring); Tribune Review Publishing Co. v. Thomas, 254 F.2d 883, 885 (CA3 1958); In the Matter of United Press Assns. v. Valente, 308 N.Y. 71, 77, 123 N. E. 2d 777, 778 (1954). In Zemel v. Rusk, supra, for example, the Court sustained the Government's refusal to validate passports to Cuba even though that restriction "render[ed] less than wholly free the flow of information concerning that country." Id., at 16. The ban on travel was held constitutional, for "the right to speak and publish does not carry with it the unrestrained right to gather information." Id., at 17.[22]

[12] [13] [14] Despite the fact that news gathering may be hampered, the press is regularly excluded from grand jury proceedings, our own conferences, the meetings of other official bodies gathered in executive session, and the meetings of private organizations. Newsmen have no constitutional right of access to the scenes of crime or [685] disaster when the general public is excluded, and they may be prohibited from attending or publishing information about trials if such restrictions are necessary to assure a defendant a fair trial before an impartial tribunal. In Sheppard v. Maxwell, 384 U.S. 333 (1966), for example, the Court reversed a state court conviction where the trial court failed to adopt "stricter rules governing the use of the courtroom by newsmen, as Sheppard's counsel requested,"

---

22 "There are few restrictions on action which could not be clothed by ingenious argument in the garb of decreased data flow. For example, the prohibition of unauthorized entry into the White House diminishes the citizen's opportunities to gather information he might find relevant to his opinion of the way the country is being run, but that does not make entry into the White House a First Amendment right." 381 U.S., at 16-17.

neglected to insulate witnesses from the press, and made no "effort to control the release of leads, information, and gossip to the press by police officers, witnesses, and the counsel for both sides." Id., at 358, 359. "The trial court might well have proscribed extrajudicial statements by any lawyer, party, witness, or court official which divulged prejudicial matters." Id., at 361. See also Estes v. Texas, 381 U.S. 532, 539-540 (1965); Rideau v. Louisiana, 373 U.S. 723, 726 (1963).

[15] [16] It is thus not surprising that the great weight of authority is that newsmen are not exempt from the normal duty of appearing before a grand jury and answering questions relevant to a criminal investigation. At common law, courts consistently refused to recognize the existence of any privilege authorizing a newsman to refuse to reveal confidential information to a grand jury. See, e.g., Ex parte Lawrence, 116 Cal. 298, 48 P. 124 (1897); Plunkett v. Hamilton, 136 Ga. 72, 70 S. E. 781 (1911); Clein v. State, 52 So. 2d 117 (Fla. 1950); In re Grunow, 84 N. J. L. 235, 85 A. 1011 (1913); People ex rel. Mooney v. Sheriff, 269 N.Y. 291, 199 N. E. 415 (1936); Joslyn v. People, 67 Colo. 297, 184 P. 375 (1919); Adams v. Associated Press, 46 F.R.D. 439 (SD Tex. 1969); Brewster v. Boston Herald-Traveler Corp., 20 F.R.D. 416 (Mass. 1957). See generally Annot., 7 A. L. R. 3d 591 (1966). In 1958, a news gatherer asserted for the first time that the First Amendment [686] exempted confidential information from public disclosure pursuant to a subpoena issued in a civil suit, Garland v. Torre, 259 F.2d 545 (CA2), cert. denied, 358 U.S. 910 (1958), but the claim was denied, and this argument has been almost uniformly rejected since then, although there are occasional dicta that, in circumstances not presented here, a newsman might be excused. In re Goodfader, 45 Haw. 317, 367 P. 2d 472 (1961); In re Taylor, 412 Pa. 32, 193 A. 2d 181 (1963); State v. Buchanan, 250 Ore. 244, 436 P. 2d 729, cert. denied, 392 U.S. 905 (1968); Murphy v. Colorado (No. 19604, Sup. Ct. Colo.), cert. denied, 365 U.S. 843 (1961) (unreported, discussed in In re Goodfader, supra, at 366, 367 P. 2d, at 498 (Mizuha, J., dissenting)).

These courts have applied the presumption against the existence of an asserted testimonial privilege, United States v. Bryan, 339 U.S. 323, 331 (1950), and have concluded that the First Amendment interest asserted by the newsman was outweighed by the general obligation of a citizen to appear before a grand jury or at trial, pursuant to a subpoena, and give what information he possesses. The opinions of the state courts in Branzburg and Pappas are typical of the prevailing view, although a few recent cases, such as Caldwell, have recognized and given effect to some form of constitutional newsman's privilege. See State v. Knops, 49 Wis. 2d 647, 183 N. W. 2d 93 (1971) (dictum); Alioto v. Cowles Communications, Inc., C. A. No. 52150 (ND Cal. 1969); In re Grand Jury Witnesses, 322 F.Supp. 573 (ND Cal. 1970); People v. Dohrn, Crim. No. 69-3808 (Cook County, Ill., Cir. Ct. 1970).

[17] [18] [19A] [20] [21A] [22A] [23] [24] The prevailing constitutional view of the newsman's privilege is very much rooted in the ancient role of the grand jury that has the dual function of determining if there is probable cause to believe that a crime has been committed and of protecting citizens against unfounded [687] criminal prosecutions.[23] Grand jury proceedings are constitutionally mandated for the institution of federal criminal prosecutions for capital or other serious crimes, and "its constitutional prerogatives are rooted in long centuries of Anglo-American history." Hannah v. Larche, 363 U.S. 420, 489-490 (1960) (Frankfurter, J., concurring in result). The Fifth Amendment provides that "no person shall be held to answer for a capital, or otherwise infamous crime, unless on a presentment or indictment of a Grand Jury."[24] The adoption of the grand jury "in our Constitution as the sole method for preferring charges in serious criminal cases shows the high place it held as an instrument of justice." Costello v. United States, 350 U.S. 359, 362 (1956).

Although state systems of criminal procedure differ greatly among themselves, the grand jury is similarly guaranteed by many state constitutions and plays an important role in fair and effective law enforcement in the overwhelming [688]majority of the States.[25] Because its task is to inquire into the existence of possible criminal conduct and to return only well-founded indictments, its investigative powers are necessarily broad. "It is a grand inquest, a body with powers of investigation and inquisition, the scope of whose inquiries is not to be limited narrowly by questions of propriety or forecasts of the probable result of the investigation, or by doubts whether any particular individual will be found properly subject to an accusation of crime." Blair v. United States, 250 U.S. 273, 282 (1919). Hence, the grand jury's authority to subpoena witnesses is not only historic, id., at 279-281, but essential to its task. Although the powers of the grand jury are not unlimited and are subject to the supervision of a judge, the longstanding principle that "the public . . . has a right to every man's evidence," except for those persons protected by a constitutional, common-law, or statutory privilege, United States v. Bryan, 339 U.S., at 331; Blackmer v. United States, 284 U.S. 421, 438 (1932); 8 J. Wigmore, Evidence §2192 (McNaughton rev. 1961), is particularly applicable to grand jury proceedings.[26]

[19B] [21B] [689][1B] [25] A number of States have provided newsmen a statutory privilege of varying breadth,[27] but the majority have not done

---

[23] "Historically, [the grand jury] has been regarded as a primary security to the innocent against hasty, malicious and oppressive persecution; it serves the invaluable function in our society of standing between the accuser and the accused . . . to determine whether a charge is founded upon reason or was dictated by an intimidating power or by malice and personal ill will." Wood v. Georgia, 370 U.S. 375, 390 (1962) (footnote omitted).

[24] It has been held that "infamous" punishments include confinement at hard labor, United States v. Moreland, 258 U.S. 433 (1922); incarceration in a penitentiary, Mackin v. United States, 117 U.S. 348 (1886); and imprisonment for more than a year, Barkman v. Sanford, 162 F.2d 592 (CA5), cert. denied, 332 U.S. 816 (1947). Fed. Rule Crim. Proc. 7 (a) has codified these holdings: "An offense which may be punished by death shall be prosecuted by indictment. An offense which may be punished by imprisonment for a term exceeding one year or at hard labor shall be prosecuted by indictment or, if indictment is waived, it may be prosecuted by information. Any other offense may be prosecuted by indictment or by information."

[25] Although indictment by grand jury is not part of the due process of law guaranteed to state criminal defendants by the Fourteenth Amendment, Hurtado v. California, 110 U.S. 516 (1884), a recent study reveals that 32 States require that certain kinds of criminal prosecutions be initiated by indictment. Spain, The Grand Jury, Past and Present: A Survey, 2 Am. Crim. L. Q. 119, 126-142 (1964). In the 18 States in which the prosecutor may proceed by information, the grand jury is retained as an alternative means of invoking the criminal process and as an investigative tool. Ibid.

[26] Jeremy Bentham vividly illustrated this maxim: "Are men of the first rank and consideration – are men high in office – men whose time is not less valuable to the public than to themselves – are such men to be forced to quit their business, their functions, and what is more than all, their pleasure, at the beck of every idle or malicious adversary, to dance attendance upon every petty cause? Yes, as far as it is necessary, they and everybody. . . . Were the Prince of Wales, the Archbishop of Canterbury, and the Lord High Chancellor, to be passing by in the same coach, while a chimney-sweeper and a barrow-woman were in dispute about a halfpennyworth of apples, and the chimney-sweeper or the barrow-woman were to think proper to call upon them for their evidence, could they refuse it? No, most certainly." 4 The Works of Jeremy Bentham 320-321 (J. Bowring ed. 1843).

In United States v. Burr, 25 F. Cas. 30, 34 (No. 14,692d) (CC Va. 1807), Chief Justice Marshall, sitting on Circuit, opined that in proper circumstances a subpoena could be issued to the President of the United States.

[27] Thus far, 17 States have provided some type of statutory protection to a newsman's confidential sources:

so, and none has been provided by federal statute.[28] Until now the only testimonial privilege for unofficial witnesses that is rooted in the Federal Constitution [690] is the Fifth Amendment privilege against compelled self-incrimination. We are asked to create another by interpreting the First Amendment to grant newsmen a testimonial privilege that other citizens do not enjoy. This we decline to do.[29] Fair and effective law enforcement aimed at providing security for the person and property of the individual is a fundamental function of government, and the grand jury plays an important, constitutionally mandated role in this

---

Ala. Code, Tit. 7, § 370 (1960); Alaska Stat. § 09.25.150 (Supp. 1971); Ariz. Rev. Stat. Ann. § 12-2237 (Supp. 1971-1972); Ark. Stat. Ann. § 43-917 (1964); Cal. Evid. Code § 1070 (Supp. 1972); Ind. Ann. Stat. § 2-1733 (1968); Ky. Rev. Stat. § 421.100 (1962); La. Rev. Stat. Ann. §§ 45:1451-45:1454 (Supp. 1972); Md. Ann. Code, Art. 35, § 2 (1971); Mich. Comp. Laws § 767.5a (Supp. 1956), Mich. Stat. Ann. § 28.945 (1) (1954); Mont. Rev. Codes Ann. § 93-601-2 (1964); Nev. Rev. Stat. § 49.275 (1971); N. J. Rev. Stat. §§ 2A:84A-21, 2A:84A-29 (Supp. 1972-1973); N. M. Stat. Ann. § 20-1-12.1 (1970); N.Y. Civ. Rights Law § 79-h (Supp. 1971-1972); Ohio Rev. Code Ann. § 2739.12 (1954); Pa. Stat. Ann., Tit. 28, § 330 (Supp. 1972-1973).

[28] Such legislation has been introduced, however. See, e.g., S. 1311, 92d Cong., 1st Sess. (1971); S. 3552, 91st Cong., 2d Sess. (1970); H. R. 16328, H. R. 16704, 91st Cong., 2d Sess. (1970); S. 1851, 88th Cong., 1st Sess. (1963); H. R. 8519, H. R. 7787, 88th Cong., 1st Sess. (1963); S. 965, 86th Cong., 1st Sess. (1959); H. R. 355, 86th Cong., 1st Sess. (1959). For a general analysis of proposed congressional legislation, see Staff of Senate Committee on the Judiciary, 89th Cong., 2d Sess., The Newsman's Privilege (Comm. Print 1966).

[29] The creation of new testimonial privileges has been met with disfavor by commentators since such privileges obstruct the search for truth. Wigmore condemns such privileges as "so many derogations from a positive general rule [that everyone is obligated to testify when properly summoned]" and as "obstacle[s] to the administration of justice." 8 J. Wigmore, Evidence § 2192 (McNaughton rev. 1961). His criticism that "all privileges of exemption from this duty are exceptional, and are therefore to be discountenanced," id., at § 2192, p. 73 (emphasis in original) has been frequently echoed. Morgan, Foreword, Model Code of Evidence 22-30 (1942); 2 Z. Chafee, Government and Mass Communications 496-497 (1947); Report of ABA Committee on Improvements in the Law of Evidence, 63 A. B. A. Reports 595 (1938); C. McCormick, Evidence 159 (2d ed. 1972); Chafee, Privileged Communications: Is Justice Served or Obstructed by Closing the Doctor's Mouth on the Witness Stand?, 52 Yale L. J. 607 (1943); Ladd, Privileges, 1969 Law & the Social Order 555, 556; 58 Am. Jur., Witnesses § 546 (1948); 97 C. J. S., Witnesses § 259 (1957); McMann v. Securities and Exchange Commission, 87 F.2d 377, 378 (CA2 1937) (L. Hand, J.). Neither the ALI's Model Code of Evidence (1942), the Uniform Rules of Evidence of the National Conference of Commissioners on Uniform State Laws (1953), nor the Proposed Rules of Evidence for the United States Courts and Magistrates (rev. ed. 1971) has included a newsman's privilege.

---

process. On the records now before us, we perceive no basis for holding that the public interest in law enforcement and in ensuring effective grand jury proceedings is insufficient to override the consequential, but uncertain, burden on news gathering that is said to result from insisting that reporters, like other citizens, respond to relevant [691] questions put to them in the course of a valid grand jury investigation or criminal trial.

This conclusion itself involves no restraint on what newspapers may publish or on the type or quality of information reporters may seek to acquire, nor does it threaten the vast bulk of confidential relationships between reporters and their sources. Grand juries address themselves to the issues of whether crimes have been committed and who committed them. Only where news sources themselves are implicated in crime or possess information relevant to the grand jury's task need they or the reporter be concerned about grand jury subpoenas. Nothing before us indicates that a large number or percentage of all confidential news sources falls into either category and would in any way be deterred by our holding that the Constitution does not, as it never has, exempt the newsman from performing the citizen's normal duty of appearing and furnishing information relevant to the grand jury's task.

[26][27][28] The preference for anonymity of those confidential informants involved in actual criminal conduct is presumably a product of their desire to escape criminal prosecution, and this preference, while understandable, is hardly deserving of constitutional protection. It would be frivolous to assert – and no one does in these cases – that the First Amendment, in the interest of securing news or otherwise, confers a license on either the reporter or his news sources to violate valid criminal laws. Although stealing documents or private wiretapping could provide newsworthy information, neither reporter nor source is immune from conviction for such conduct, whatever the impact on the flow of news. Neither is immune, on First Amendment grounds, from testifying against the other, before the grand jury or at a criminal trial. The Amendment does not reach so far as to override the interest of the public in ensuring [692] that neither reporter nor source is invading the rights of other citizens through reprehensible conduct forbidden to all other persons. To assert the contrary proposition "is to answer it, since it involves in its very statement the contention that the freedom of the press is the freedom to do wrong with impunity and implies the right to frustrate and defeat the discharge of those governmental duties upon the performance of which the freedom of all, including that of the press, depends. . . . It suffices to say that, however

complete is the right of the press to state public things and discuss them, that right, as every other right enjoyed in human society, is subject to the restraints which separate right from wrong-doing." Toledo Newspaper Co. v. United States, 247 U.S. 402, 419-420 (1918).[30]

[29] Thus, we cannot seriously entertain the notion that the First Amendment protects a newsman's agreement to conceal the criminal conduct of his source, or evidence thereof, on the theory that it is better to write about crime than to do something about it. Insofar as any reporter in these cases undertook not to reveal or testify about the crime he witnessed, his claim of privilege under the First Amendment presents no substantial question. The crimes of news sources are no less reprehensible and threatening to the public interest when witnessed by a reporter than when they are not.

[693] There remain those situations where a source is not engaged in criminal conduct but has information suggesting illegal conduct by others. Newsmen frequently receive information from such sources pursuant to a tacit or express agreement to withhold the source's name and suppress any information that the source wishes not published. Such informants presumably desire anonymity in order to avoid being entangled as a witness in a criminal trial or grand jury investigation. They may fear that disclosure will threaten their job security or personal safety or that it will simply result in dishonor or embarrassment.

The argument that the flow of news will be diminished by compelling reporters to aid the grand jury in a criminal investigation is not irrational, nor are the records before us silent on the matter. But we remain unclear how often and to what extent informers are actually deterred from furnishing information when newsmen are forced to testify before a grand jury. The available data indicate that some newsmen rely a great deal on confidential sources and that some informants are particularly sensitive to the threat of exposure and may be silenced if it is held by this Court that, ordinarily, newsmen must testify pursuant to subpoenas,[31] but

the evidence fails to demonstrate that there would be a significant constriction of the flow of news to the public if this Court reaffirms the prior common-law and constitutional rule regarding the testimonial obligations of newsmen. Estimates of the inhibiting effect of such subpoenas on the willingness of informants to make disclosures to newsmen are widely divergent and [694] to a great extent speculative.[32]

It would be difficult to canvass the views of the informants themselves; surveys of reporters on this topic are chiefly opinions of predicted informant behavior and must be viewed in the light of the professional self-interest of the interviewees.[33] Reliance by the press on confidential informants does not mean that all such sources will in fact dry up because of the later possible appearance of the newsman before a grand jury. The reporter may never be called and if he objects to testifying, the prosecution may not insist. Also, the relationship of many informants to the press is a symbiotic one which is unlikely to be greatly inhibited by the threat of subpoena: quite often, such informants are members of a minority political or cultural group that [695] relies heavily on the media to propagate its views, publicize its aims, and magnify its exposure to the public. Moreover, grand juries characteristically conduct secret proceedings, and law enforcement officers are themselves experienced in dealing with informers, and have their own methods for protecting them without interference with the effective administration of justice. There is little before us indicating that

---

[30] The holding in this case involved a construction of the Contempt of Court Act of 1831, 4 Stat. 487, which permitted summary trial of contempts "so near [to the court] as to obstruct the administration of justice." The Court held that the Act required only that the conduct have a "direct tendency to prevent and obstruct the discharge of judicial duty." 247 U.S., at 419. This view was overruled and the Act given a much narrower reading in Nye v. United States, 313 U.S. 33, 47-52 (1941). See Bloom v. Illinois, 391 U.S. 194, 205-206 (1968).

[31] Respondent Caldwell attached a number of affidavits from prominent newsmen to his initial motion to quash, which detail the experiences of such journalists after they have been subpoenaed. Appendix to No. 70-57, pp. 22-61.

[32] Cf., e.g., the results of a study conducted by Guest & Stanzler, which appears as an appendix to their article, supra, n. 20. A number of editors of daily newspapers of varying circulation were asked the question, "Excluding one- or two-sentence gossip items, on the average how many stories based on information received in confidence are published in your paper each year? Very rough estimate." Answers varied significantly, e.g., "Virtually innumerable," Tucson Daily Citizen (41,969 daily circ.), "Too many to remember," Los Angeles Herald-Examiner (718,221 daily circ.), "Occasionally," Denver Post (252,084 daily circ.), "Rarely," Cleveland Plain Dealer (370,499 daily circ.), "Very rare, some politics," Oregon Journal (146,403 daily circ.). This study did not purport to measure the extent of deterrence of informants caused by subpoenas to the press.

[33] In his Press Subpoenas: An Empirical and Legal Analysis, Study Report of the Reporters' Committee on Freedom of the Press 6-12, Prof. Vince Blasi discusses these methodological problems. Prof. Blasi's survey found that slightly more than half of the 975 reporters questioned said that they relied on regular confidential sources for at least 10% of their stories. Id., at 21. Of this group of reporters, only 8% were able to say with some certainty that their professional functioning had been adversely affected by the threat of subpoena; another 11% were not certain whether or not they had been adversely affected. Id., at 53.

informants whose interest in avoiding exposure is that it may threaten job security, personal safety, or peace of mind, would in fact be in a worse position, or would think they would be, if they risked placing their trust in public officials as well as reporters. We doubt if the informer who prefers anonymity but is sincerely interested in furnishing evidence of crime will always or very often be deterred by the prospect of dealing with those public authorities characteristically charged with the duty to protect the public interest as well as his.

[30] Accepting the fact, however, that an undetermined number of informants not themselves implicated in crime will nevertheless, for whatever reason, refuse to talk to newsmen if they fear identification by a reporter in an official investigation, we cannot accept the argument that the public interest in possible future news about crime from undisclosed, unverified sources must take precedence over the public interest in pursuing and prosecuting those crimes reported to the press by informants and in thus deterring the commission of such crimes in the future.

We note first that the privilege claimed is that of the reporter, not the informant, and that if the authorities independently identify the informant, neither his own reluctance to testify nor the objection of the newsman would shield him from grand jury inquiry, whatever the impact on the flow of news or on his future usefulness as a secret source of information. More important, [696] it is obvious that agreements to conceal information relevant to commission of crime have very little to recommend them from the standpoint of public policy. Historically, the common law recognized a duty to raise the "hue and cry" and report felonies to the authorities.[34] Misprision of a felony – that is, the concealment of a felony "which a man knows, but never assented to . . . [so as to become] either principal or accessory," 4 W. Blackstone, Commentaries *121, was often said to be a common-law crime.[35] The first Congress passed a statute, 1 Stat. 113, §6, as amended, 35 Stat. 1114,

§146, 62 Stat. 684, which is still in effect, defining a federal crime of misprision:

"Whoever, having knowledge of the actual commission of a felony cognizable by a court of the United States, conceals and does not as soon as possible make known the same to some judge or other person in civil or military authority under the United States, shall be [guilty of misprision]." 18 U. S. C. §4.[36]

[697] It is apparent from this statute, as well as from our history and that of England, that concealment of crime and agreements to do so are not looked upon with favor. Such conduct deserves no encomium, and we decline now to afford it First Amendment protection by denigrating the duty of a citizen, whether reporter or informer, to respond to grand jury subpoena and answer relevant questions put to him.

Of course, the press has the right to abide by its agreement not to publish all the information it has, but the right to withhold news is not equivalent to a First Amendment exemption from the ordinary duty of all other citizens to furnish relevant information to a grand jury performing an important public function. Private restraints on the flow of information are not so favored by the First Amendment that they override all other public interests. As Mr. Justice Black declared in another context, "freedom of the press from governmental interference under the First Amendment does not sanction repression of that freedom by private interests." Associated Press v. United States, 326 U.S., at 20.

[31] [32] Neither are we now convinced that a virtually impenetrable constitutional shield, beyond legislative or judicial control, should be forged to protect a private system of informers operated by the press to report on criminal conduct, a system that would be unaccountable to the public, would pose a threat to the citizen's justifiable expectations of privacy, and would equally protect well-intentioned informants and those who for pay or otherwise betray their trust to their employer or associates. The public through its elected and appointed [698] law enforcement officers regularly utilizes informers, and in proper circumstances may assert a privilege against disclosing the identity of these informers. But "the purpose of the privilege is the furtherance and protection of the public interest

---

[34] See Statute of Westminster First, 3 Edw. 1, c. 9, p. 43 (1275); Statute of Westminster Second, 13 Edw. 1, c. 6, pp. 114-115 (1285); Sheriffs Act of 1887, 50 & 51 Vict., c. 55, § 8 (1); 4 W. Blackstone, Commentaries * 293-295; 2 W. Holdsworth, History of English Law 80-81, 101-102 (3d ed. 1927); 4 id., at 521-522.

[35] See, e.g., Scrope's Case, referred to in 3 Coke's Institute 36; Rex v. Cowper, 5 Mod. 206, 87 Eng. Rep. 611 (1696); Proceedings under a Special Commission for the County of York, 31 How. St. Tr. 965, 969 (1813); Sykes v. Director of Public Prosecutions, [1961] 3 W. L. R. 371. But see Glazebrook, Misprision of Felony – Shadow or Phantom?, 8 Am. J. Legal Hist. 189 (1964). See also Act 5 & 6 Edw. 6, c. 11 (1552).

[36] This statute has been construed, however, to require both knowledge of a crime and some affirmative act of concealment or participation. Bratton v. United States, 73 F.2d 795 (CA10 1934); United States v. Farrar, 38 F.2d 515, 516 (Mass.), aff'd on other grounds, 281 U.S. 624 (1930); United States v. Norman, 391 F.2d 212 (CA6), cert. denied, 390 U.S. 1014 (1968); Lancey v. United States, 356 F.2d 407 (CA9), cert. denied, 385 U.S. 922 (1966). Cf. Marbury v. Brooks, 7 Wheat. 556, 575 (1822) (Marshall, C. J.).

in effective law enforcement. The privilege recognizes the obligation of citizens to communicate their knowledge of the commission of crimes to law-enforcement officials and, by preserving their anonymity, encourages them to perform that obligation." Roviaro v. United States, 353 U.S. 53, 59 (1957).

Such informers enjoy no constitutional protection. Their testimony is available to the public when desired by grand juries or at criminal trials; their identity cannot be concealed from the defendant when it is critical to his case. Id., at 60-61, 62; McCray v. Illinois, 386 U.S. 300, 310 (1967); Smith v. Illinois, 390 U.S. 129, 131 (1968); Alford v. United States, 282 U.S. 687, 693 (1931). Clearly, this system is not impervious to control by the judiciary and the decision whether to unmask an informer or to continue to profit by his anonymity is in public, not private, hands. We think that it should remain there and that public authorities should retain the options of either insisting on the informer's testimony relevant to the prosecution of crime or of seeking the benefit of further information that his exposure might prevent.

We are admonished that refusal to provide a First Amendment reporter's privilege will undermine the freedom of the press to collect and disseminate news. But this is not the lesson history teaches us. As noted previously, the common law recognized no such privilege, and the constitutional argument was not even asserted until 1958. From the beginning of our country the press has operated without constitutional protection [699] for press informants, and the press has flourished. The existing constitutional rules have not been a serious obstacle to either the development or retention of confidential news sources by the press.[37]

It is said that currently press subpoenas have multiplied,[38] that mutual distrust and tension between press and officialdom have increased, that reporting styles have changed, and that there is now more need for confidential sources, particularly where the press seeks news about minority cultural and political groups or dissident organizations

suspicious of the law and public officials. These developments, even if true, are treacherous grounds for a far-reaching interpretation of the First Amendment fastening a nationwide rule on courts, grand juries, and prosecuting officials everywhere. The obligation to testify in response to grand jury subpoenas will not threaten these sources not involved with criminal conduct and without information relevant to grand jury investigations, and we cannot hold that the Constitution places the sources in these two categories either above the law or beyond its reach.

[22B] The argument for such a constitutional privilege rests heavily on those cases holding that the infringement of protected First Amendment rights must be no broader than necessary to achieve a permissible governmental purpose, see cases cited at n. 19, supra. We do not deal, however, with a governmental institution that has abused [700] its proper function, as a legislative committee does when it "expose[s] for the sake of exposure." Watkins v. United States, 354 U.S. 178, 200 (1957). Nothing in the record indicates that these grand juries were "prob[ing] at will and without relation to existing need." DeGregory v. Attorney General of New Hampshire, 383 U.S. 825, 829 (1966). Nor did the grand juries attempt to invade protected First Amendment rights by forcing wholesale disclosure of names and organizational affiliations for a purpose that was not germane to the determination of whether crime has been committed, cf. NAACP v. Alabama, 357 U.S. 449 (1958); NAACP v. Button, 371 U.S. 415 (1963); Bates v. Little Rock, 361 U.S. 516 (1960), and the characteristic secrecy of grand jury proceedings is a further protection against the undue invasion of such rights. See Fed. Rule Crim. Proc. 6 (e). The investigative power of the grand jury is necessarily broad if its public responsibility is to be adequately discharged. Costello v. United States, 350 U.S., at 364.

The requirements of those cases, see n. 18, supra, which hold that a State's interest must be "compelling" or "paramount" to justify even an indirect burden on First Amendment rights, are also met here. As we have indicated, the investigation of crime by the grand jury implements a fundamental governmental role of securing the safety of the person and property of the citizen, and it appears to us that calling reporters to give testimony in the manner and for the reasons that other citizens are called "bears a reasonable relationship to the achievement of the governmental purpose asserted as its justification." Bates v. Little Rock, supra, at 525. If the test is that the government "convincingly show a substantial relation between the information sought and a subject of overriding and compelling state interest,"

---

[37] Though the constitutional argument for a newsman's privilege has been put forward very recently, newsmen have contended for a number of years that such a privilege was desirable. See, e.g., Siebert & Ryniker, Press Winning Fight to Guard Sources, Editor & Publisher, Sept. 1, 1934, pp. 9, 36-37; G. Bird & F. Merwin, The Press and Society 592 (1971). The first newsman's privilege statute was enacted by Maryland in 1896, and currently is codified as Md. Ann. Code, Art. 35, § 2 (1971).

[38] A list of recent subpoenas to the news media is contained in the appendix to the brief of amicus New York Times in No. 70-57.

Gibson v. Florida Legislative Investigation Committee, [701] 372 U.S. 539, 546 (1963), it is quite apparent (1) that the State has the necessary interest in extirpating the traffic in illegal drugs, in forestalling assassination attempts on the President, and in preventing the community from being disrupted by violent disorders endangering both persons and property; and (2) that, based on the stories Branzburg and Caldwell wrote and Pappas' admitted conduct, the grand jury called these reporters as they would others − because it was likely that they could supply information to help the government determine whether illegal conduct had occurred and, if it had, whether there was sufficient evidence to return an indictment.

[33] [34] [35] [36] [37] Similar considerations dispose of the reporters' claims that preliminary to requiring their grand jury appearance, the State must show that a crime has been committed and that they possess relevant information not available from other sources, for only the grand jury itself can make this determination. The role of the grand jury as an important instrument of effective law enforcement necessarily includes an investigatory function with respect to determining whether a crime has been committed and who committed it. To this end it must call witnesses, in the manner best suited to perform its task. "When the grand jury is performing its investigatory function into a general problem area . . . society's interest is best served by a thorough and extensive investigation." Wood v. Georgia, 370 U.S. 375, 392 (1962). A grand jury investigation "is not fully carried out until every available clue has been run down and all witnesses examined in every proper way to find if a crime has been committed." United States v. Stone, 429 F.2d 138, 140 (CA2 1970). Such an investigation may be triggered by tips, rumors, evidence proffered by the prosecutor, or the personal knowledge of the grand jurors. Costello v. United States, 350 U.S., at 362. It is [702] only after the grand jury has examined the evidence that a determination of whether the proceeding will result in an indictment can be made.

"It is impossible to conceive that in such cases the examination of witnesses must be stopped until a basis is laid by an indictment formally preferred, when the very object of the examination is to ascertain who shall be indicted." Hale v. Henkel, 201 U.S. 43, 65 (1906). See also Hendricks v. United States, 223 U.S. 178 (1912); Blair v. United States, 250 U.S., at 282-283. We see no reason to hold that these reporters, any more than other citizens, should be excused from furnishing information that may help the grand jury in arriving at its initial determinations.

The privilege claimed here is conditional, not absolute; given the suggested preliminary showings

and compelling need, the reporter would be required to testify. Presumably, such a rule would reduce the instances in which reporters could be required to appear, but predicting in advance when and in what circumstances they could be compelled to do so would be difficult. Such a rule would also have implications for the issuance of compulsory process to reporters at civil and criminal trials and at legislative hearings. If newsmen's confidential sources are as sensitive as they are claimed to be, the prospect of being unmasked whenever a judge determines the situation justifies it is hardly a satisfactory solution to the problem.[39] For them, it would appear that only an absolute privilege would suffice.

---

[39] "Under the case-by-case method of developing rules," it will be difficult for potential informants and reporters to predict whether testimony will be compelled since the decision will turn on the judge's ad hoc assessment in different fact settings of 'importance' or 'relevance' in relation to the free press interest. A 'general' deterrent effect is likely to result. This type of effect stems from the vagueness of the tests and from the uncertainty attending their application. For example, if a reporter's information goes to the 'heart of the matter' in Situation X, another reporter and informant who subsequently are in Situation Y will not know if 'heart of the matter rule X' will be extended to them, and deterrence will thereby result. Leaving substantial discretion with judges to delineate those 'situations' in which rules of 'relevance' or 'importance' apply would therefore seem to undermine significantly the effectiveness of a reporter-informer privilege." Note, Reporters and Their Sources: The Constitutional Right to a Confidential Relationship, 80 Yale L. J. 317, 341 (1970).

In re Grand Jury Witnesses, 322 F.Supp. 573 (ND Cal. 1970), illustrates the impact of this ad hoc approach. Here, the grand jury was, as in Caldwell, investigating the Black Panther Party, and was "inquiring into matters which involve possible violations of Congressional acts passed to protect the person of the President (18 U. S. C. § 1751), to free him from threats (18 U. S. C. § 871), to protect our armed forces from unlawful interference (18 U. S. C. § 2387), conspiracy to commit the foregoing offenses (18 U. S. C. § 371), and related statutes prohibiting acts directed against the security of the government." Id., at 577. The two witnesses, reporters for a Black Panther Party newspaper, were subpoenaed and given Fifth Amendment immunity against criminal prosecution, and they claimed a First Amendment journalist's privilege. The District Court entered a protective order, allowing them to refuse to divulge confidential information until the Government demonstrated "a compelling and overriding national interest in requiring the testimony of [the witnesses] which cannot be served by any alternative means." Id., at 574. The Government claimed that it had information that the witnesses had associated with persons who had conspired to perform some of the criminal acts that the grand jury was investigating. The court held the Government had met its burden and ordered the witnesses to testify:

[703] [38] [39A] We are unwilling to embark the judiciary on a long and difficult journey to such an uncertain destination. The administration of a constitutional newsman's privilege [704] would present practical and conceptual difficulties of a high order. Sooner or later, it would be necessary to define those categories of newsmen who qualified for the privilege, a questionable procedure in light of the traditional doctrine that liberty of the press is the right of the lonely pamphleteer who uses carbon paper or a mimeograph just as much as of the large metropolitan publisher who utilizes the latest photocomposition methods. Cf. In re Grand Jury Witnesses, 322 F.Supp. 573, 574 (ND Cal. 1970). Freedom of the press is a "fundamental personal right" which "is not confined to newspapers and periodicals. It necessarily embraces pamphlets and leaflets. . . . The press in its historic connotation comprehends every sort of publication which affords a vehicle of information and opinion." Lovell v. Griffin, 303 U.S. 444, 450, 452 (1938). See also Mills [705] v. Alabama, 384 U.S. 214, 219 (1966); Murdock v. Pennsylvania, 319 U.S. 105, 111 (1943). The informative function asserted by representatives of the organized press in the present cases is also performed by lecturers, political pollsters, novelists, academic researchers, and dramatists. Almost any author may quite accurately assert that he is contributing to the flow of information to the public, that he relies on confidential sources of information, and that these sources will be silenced if he is forced to make disclosures before a grand jury.[40]

[39B] In each instance where a reporter is subpoenaed to testify, the courts would also be embroiled in preliminary factual and legal determinations with respect to whether the proper predicate had been laid for the reporter's appearance: Is there probable cause to believe a crime has been committed? Is it likely that the reporter has useful information gained in confidence? Could the grand jury obtain the information elsewhere? Is the official interest sufficient to outweigh the claimed privilege?

Thus, in the end, by considering whether enforcement of a particular law served a "compelling" governmental interest, the courts would be inextricably involved in [706] distinguishing between the value of enforcing different criminal laws. By requiring testimony from a reporter in investigations involving some crimes but not in others, they would be making a value judgment that a legislature had declined to make, since in each case the criminal law involved would represent a considered legislative judgment, not constitutionally suspect, of what conduct is liable to criminal prosecution. The task of judges, like other officials outside the legislative branch, is not to make the law but to uphold it in accordance with their oaths.

[40] [41] At the federal level, Congress has freedom to determine whether a statutory newsman's privilege is necessary and desirable and to fashion standards and rules as narrow or broad as deemed necessary to deal with the evil discerned and, equally important, to refashion those rules as experience from time to time may dictate. There is also merit in leaving state legislatures free, within First Amendment limits, to fashion their own standards in light of the conditions and problems with respect to the relations between law enforcement officials and press in their own areas. It goes without saying, of course, that we are

---

"The whole point of the investigation is to identify persons known to the [witnesses] who may have engaged in activities violative of the above indicated statutes, and also to ascertain the details of their alleged unlawful activities. All questions directed to such objectives of the investigation are unquestionably relevant, and any other evaluation thereof by the Court without knowledge of the facts before the Grand Jury would clearly constitute 'undue interference of the Court.'" Id., at 577.

Another illustration is provided by State v. Knops, 49 Wis. 2d 647, 183 N. W. 2d 93 (1971), in which a grand jury was investigating the August 24, 1970, bombing of Sterling Hall on the University of Wisconsin Madison campus. On August 26, 1970, an "underground" newspaper, the Madison Kaleidoscope, printed a front-page story entitled "The Bombers Tell Why and What Next – Exclusive to Kaleidoscope." An editor of the Kaleidoscope was subpoenaed, appeared, asserted his Fifth Amendment right against self-incrimination, was given immunity, and then pleaded that he had a First Amendment privilege against disclosing his confidential informants. The Wisconsin Supreme Court rejected his claim and upheld his contempt sentence: "[Appellant] faces five very narrow and specific questions, all of which are founded on information which he himself has already volunteered. The purpose of these questions is very clear. The need for answers to them is 'overriding,' to say the least. The need for these answers is nothing short of the public's need (and right) to protect itself from physical attack by apprehending the perpetrators of such attacks." 49 Wis. 2d, at 658, 183 N. W. 2d., at 98-99.

---

[40] Such a privilege might be claimed by groups that set up newspapers in order to engage in criminal activity and to therefore be insulated from grand jury inquiry, regardless of Fifth Amendment grants of immunity. It might appear that such "sham" newspapers would be easily distinguishable, yet the First Amendment ordinarily prohibits courts from inquiring into the content of expression, except in cases of obscenity or libel, and protects speech and publications regardless of their motivation, orthodoxy, truthfulness, timeliness, or taste. New York Times Co. v. Sullivan, 376 U.S., at 269-270; Kingsley Pictures Corp. v. Regents, 360 U.S. 684, 689 (1959); Winters v. New York, 333 U.S. 507, 510 (1948); Thomas v. Collins, 323 U.S., at 537. By affording a privilege to some organs of communication but not to others, courts would inevitably be discriminating on the basis of content.

powerless to bar state courts from responding in their own way and construing their own constitutions so as to recognize a newsman's privilege, either qualified or absolute.

In addition, there is much force in the pragmatic view that the press has at its disposal powerful mechanisms of communication and is far from helpless to protect itself from harassment or substantial harm. Furthermore, if what the newsmen urged in these cases is true – that law enforcement cannot hope to gain and may suffer from subpoenaing newsmen before grand juries – prosecutors will be loath to risk so much for so little. Thus, at the federal level the Attorney General has already fashioned a set of rules for federal officials in connection [707] with subpoenaing members of the press to testify before grand juries or at criminal trials.[41] These rules are a major step in the direction the reporters herein desire to move. They may prove wholly sufficient to resolve the bulk of disagreements and controversies between press and federal officials.

[42] Finally, as we have earlier indicated, news gathering is not without its First Amendment protections, and grand jury investigations if instituted or conducted other than in good faith, would pose wholly different issues for resolution under the First Amendment.[42] Official harassment of the press undertaken not for purposes of law enforcement but to disrupt a reporter's relationship

---

[41] The Guidelines for Subpoenas to the News Media were first announced in a speech by the Attorney General on August 10, 1970, and then were expressed in Department of Justice Memo. No. 692 (Sept. 2, 1970), which was sent to all United States Attorneys by the Assistant Attorney General in charge of the Criminal Division. The Guidelines state that: "The Department of Justice recognizes that compulsory process in some circumstances may have a limiting effect on the exercise of First Amendment rights. In determining whether to request issuance of a subpoena to the press, the approach in every case must be to weigh that limiting effect against the public interest to be served in the fair administration of justice" and that: "The Department of Justice does not consider the press 'an investigative arm of the government.' Therefore, all reasonable attempts should be made to obtain information from non-press sources before there is any consideration of subpoenaing the press." The Guidelines provide for negotiations with the press and require the express authorization of the Attorney General for such subpoenas. The principles to be applied in authorizing such subpoenas are stated to be whether there is "sufficient reason to believe that the information sought [from the journalist] is essential to a successful investigation," and whether the Government has unsuccessfully attempted to obtain the information from alternative non-press sources. The Guidelines provide, however, that in "emergencies and other unusual situations," subpoenas may be issued which do not exactly conform to the Guidelines.

[42] Cf. Younger v. Harris, 401 U.S. 37, 49, 53-54 (1971).

[708] with his news sources would have no justification. Grand juries are subject to judicial control and subpoenas to motions to quash. We do not expect courts will forget that grand juries must operate within the limits of the First Amendment as well as the Fifth.

III. [43] We turn, therefore, to the disposition of the cases before us. From what we have said, it necessarily follows that the decision in United States v. Caldwell, No. 70-57, must be reversed. If there is no First Amendment privilege to refuse to answer the relevant and material questions asked during a good-faith grand jury investigation, then it is a fortiori true that there is no privilege to refuse to appear before such a grand jury until the Government demonstrates some "compelling need" for a newsman's testimony. Other issues were urged upon us, but since they were not passed upon by the Court of Appeals, we decline to address them in the first instance.

The decisions in No. 70-85, Branzburg v. Hayes and Branzburg v. Meigs, must be affirmed. Here, petitioner refused to answer questions that directly related to criminal conduct that he had observed and written about. The Kentucky Court of Appeals noted that marihuana is defined as a narcotic drug by statute, Ky. Rev. Stat. §218.010 (14) (1962), and that unlicensed possession or compounding of it is a felony punishable by both fine and imprisonment. Ky. Rev. Stat. §218.210 (1962). It held that petitioner "saw the commission of the statutory felonies of unlawful possession of marijuana and the unlawful conversion of it into hashish," in Branzburg v. Pound, 461 S. W. 2d, at 346. Petitioner may be presumed to have observed similar violations of the state narcotics laws during the research he did for the story that forms the basis of the subpoena in Branzburg v. Meigs. In both cases, if what petitioner wrote was true, [709] he had direct information to provide the grand jury concerning the commission of serious crimes.

The only question presented at the present time in In re Pappas, No. 70-94, is whether petitioner Pappas must appear before the grand jury to testify pursuant to subpoena. The Massachusetts Supreme Judicial Court characterized the record in this case as "meager," and it is not clear what petitioner will be asked by the grand jury. It is not even clear that he will be asked to divulge information received in confidence. We affirm the decision of the Massachusetts Supreme Judicial Court and hold that petitioner must appear before the grand jury to answer the questions put to him, subject, of course, to the supervision of the presiding judge as to "the propriety, purposes, and scope of the grand jury inquiry and the pertinence of the probable testimony." 358 Mass., at 614, 266 N. E. 2d, at 303-304.   So ordered.

CONCUR: MR. JUSTICE POWELL, concurring.

I add this brief statement to emphasize what seems to me to be the limited nature of the Court's holding. The Court does not hold that newsmen, subpoenaed to testify before a grand jury, are without constitutional rights with respect to the gathering of news or in safeguarding their sources. Certainly, we do not hold, as suggested in MR. JUSTICE STEWART's dissenting opinion, that state and federal authorities are free to "annex" the news media as "an investigative arm of government." The solicitude repeatedly shown by this Court for First Amendment freedoms should be sufficient assurance against any such effort, even if one seriously believed that the media – properly free and untrammeled in the fullest sense of these terms – were not able to protect themselves.

As indicated in the concluding portion of the opinion, the Court states that no harassment of newsmen will [710] be tolerated. If a newsman believes that the grand jury investigation is not being conducted in good faith he is not without remedy. Indeed, if the newsman is called upon to give information bearing only a remote and tenuous relationship to the subject of the investigation, or if he has some other reason to believe that his testimony implicates confidential source relationships without a legitimate need of law enforcement, he will have access to the court on a motion to quash and an appropriate protective order may be entered. The asserted claim to privilege should be judged on its facts by the striking of a proper balance between freedom of the press and the obligation of all citizens to give relevant testimony with respect to criminal conduct. The balance of these vital constitutional and societal interests on a case-by-case basis accords with the tried and traditional way of adjudicating such questions.[*]

---

[*] It is to be remembered that Caldwell asserts a constitutional privilege not even to appear before the grand jury unless a court decides that the Government has made a showing that meets the three preconditions specified in the dissenting opinion of MR. JUSTICE STEWART. To be sure, this would require a "balancing" of interests by the court, but under circumstances and constraints significantly different from the balancing that will be appropriate under the court's decision. The newsman witness, like all other witnesses, will have to appear; he will not be in a position to litigate at the threshold the State's very authority to subpoena him. Moreover, absent the constitutional preconditions that Caldwell and that dissenting opinion would impose as heavy burdens of proof to be carried by the State, the court – when called upon to protect a newsman from improper or prejudicial questioning – would be free to balance the competing interests on their merits in the particular case. The new constitutional rule endorsed by that dissenting opinion would, as a practical matter, defeat

In short, the courts will be available to newsmen under circumstances where legitimate First Amendment interests require protection.

DISSENT BY: DOUGLAS; STEWART
DISSENT: [711] MR. JUSTICE DOUGLAS, dissenting in No. 70-57, United States v. Caldwell.

Caldwell, a black, is a reporter for the New York Times and was assigned to San Francisco with the hope that he could report on the activities and attitudes of the Black Panther Party. Caldwell in time gained the complete confidence of its members and wrote in-depth articles about them.

He was subpoenaed to appear and testify before a federal grand jury and to bring with him notes and tapes covering interviews with its members. A hearing on a motion to quash was held. The District Court ruled that while Caldwell had to appear before the grand jury, he did not have to reveal confidential communications unless the court was satisfied that there was a "compelling and overriding national interest." See 311 F.Supp. 358, 362. Caldwell filed a notice of appeal and the Court of Appeals dismissed the appeal without opinion.

Shortly thereafter a new grand jury was impaneled and it issued a new subpoena for Caldwell to testify. On a motion to quash, the District Court issued an order substantially identical to its earlier one.

Caldwell refused to appear and was held in contempt. On appeal, the Court of Appeals vacated the judgment of contempt. It said that the revealing of confidential sources of information jeopardized a First Amendment freedom and that Caldwell did not have to appear before the grand jury absent a showing that there was a "compelling and overriding national interest" in pursuing such an interrogation.

The District Court had found that Caldwell's knowledge of the activities of the Black Panthers "derived in substantial part" from information obtained "within the scope of a relationship of trust and confidence." Id., at 361. It also found that confidential relationships of this sort are commonly developed and maintained by [712] professional journalists, and are indispensable to their work of gathering, analyzing, and publishing the news.

The District Court further had found that compelled disclosure of information received by a journalist within the scope of such confidential

---

such a fair balancing and the essential societal interest in the detection and prosecution of crime would be heavily subordinated.

relationships jeopardized those relationships and thereby impaired the journalist's ability to gather, analyze, and publish the news.

The District Court, finally, had found that, without a protective order delimiting the scope of interrogation of Earl Caldwell by the grand jury, his appearance and examination before the jury would severely impair and damage his confidential relationships with members of the Black Panther Party and other militants, and thereby severely impair and damage his ability to gather, analyze, and publish news concerning them; and that it would also damage and impair the abilities of all reporters to gather, analyze, and publish news concerning them.

The Court of Appeals agreed with the findings of the District Court but held that Caldwell did not have to appear at all before the grand jury absent a "compelling need" shown by the Government. 434 F.2d 1081.

It is my view that there is no "compelling need" that can be shown which qualifies the reporter's immunity from appearing or testifying before a grand jury, unless the reporter himself is implicated in a crime. His immunity in my view is therefore quite complete, for, absent his involvement in a crime, the First Amendment protects him against an appearance before a grand jury and if he is involved in a crime, the Fifth Amendment stands as a barrier. Since in my view there is no area of inquiry not protected by a privilege, the reporter need not appear for the futile purpose of invoking one to each question. And, since in my view a newsman has an absolute right not to appear before a grand jury, it follows for me that a journalist who voluntarily appears before that body may invoke his First Amendment privilege to specific questions. [713] The basic issue is the extent to which the First Amendment (which is applicable to investigating committees, Watkins v. United States, 354 U.S. 178; NAACP v. Alabama, 357 U.S. 449, 463; Gibson v. Florida Legislative Investigation Committee, 372 U.S. 539; Baird v. State Bar of Arizona, 401 U.S. 1, 6-7; In re Stolar, 401 U.S. 23) must yield to the Government's asserted need to know a reporter's unprinted information.

The starting point for decision pretty well marks the range within which the end result lies. The New York Times, whose reporting functions are at issue here, takes the amazing position that First Amendment rights are to be balanced against other needs or conveniences of government.[1] My belief

is that all of the "balancing" was done by those who wrote the Bill of Rights. By casting the First Amendment in absolute terms, they repudiated the timid, watered-down, emasculated versions of the First Amendment which both the Government and the New York Times advance in the case.

My view is close to that of the late Alexander Meiklejohn:[2] "For the understanding of these principles it is essential to keep clear the crucial difference between 'the rights' of the governed and 'the powers' of the governors. And at this point, the title 'Bill of Rights' is lamentably inaccurate as a designation [714] of the first ten amendments. They are not a 'Bill of Rights' but a 'Bill of Powers and Rights.' The Second through the Ninth Amendments limit the powers of the subordinate agencies in order that due regard shall be paid to the private 'rights of the governed.' The First and Tenth Amendments protect the governing 'powers' of the people from abridgment by the agencies which are established as their servants. In the field of our 'rights,' each one of us can claim 'due process of law.' In the field of our governing 'powers,' the notion of 'due process' is irrelevant."

He also believed that "self-government can exist only insofar as the voters acquire the intelligence, integrity, sensitivity, and generous devotion to the general welfare that, in theory, casting a ballot is assumed to express,"[3] and that "public discussions of public issues, together with the spreading of information and opinion bearing on those issues, must have a freedom unabridged by our agents. Though they govern us, we, in a deeper sense, govern them. Over our governing, they have no power. Over their governing we have sovereign power."[4]

Two principles which follow from this understanding of the First Amendment are at stake here. One is that the people, the ultimate governors, must have absolute freedom of, and therefore privacy of, their individual opinions and beliefs regardless of how suspect or strange they may appear to others. Ancillary to that principle is the conclusion that an individual must also have absolute privacy over whatever information he

---

[1] "The three minimal tests we contend must be met before testimony divulging confidences may be compelled from a reporter are these: 1. The government must clearly show that there is probable cause to believe that the reporter

possesses information which is specifically relevant to a specific probable violation of law. 2. The government must clearly show that the information it seeks cannot be obtained by alternative means, which is to say, from sources other than the reporter. 3. The government must clearly demonstrate a compelling and overriding interest in the information." Brief for New York Times as Amicus Curiae 29.

[2] The First Amendment Is An Absolute, 1961 Sup. Ct. Rev. 245, 254.

[3] Id., at 255.

[4] Id., at 257.

may generate in the course of testing his opinions and beliefs. In this regard, Caldwell's status as a reporter is less relevant than is his status as a student who affirmatively pursued empirical research to enlarge his own intellectual viewpoint. [715] The second principle is that effective self-government cannot succeed unless the people are immersed in a steady, robust, unimpeded, and uncensored flow of opinion and reporting which are continuously subjected to critique, rebuttal, and re-examination. In this respect, Caldwell's status as a news gatherer and an integral part of that process becomes critical.

I. Government has many interests that compete with the First Amendment. Congressional investigations determine how existing laws actually operate or whether new laws are needed. While congressional committees have broad powers, they are subject to the restraints of the First Amendment. As we said in Watkins v. United States, 354 U.S., at 197: "Clearly, an investigation is subject to the command that the Congress shall make no law abridging freedom of speech or press or assembly. While it is true that there is no statute to be reviewed, and that an investigation is not a law, nevertheless an investigation is part of lawmaking. It is justified solely as an adjunct to the legislative process. The First Amendment may be invoked against infringement of the protected freedoms by law or by lawmaking."

Hence, matters of belief, ideology, religious practices, social philosophy, and the like are beyond the pale and of no rightful concern of government, unless the belief or the speech, or other expression has been translated into action. West Virginia State Board of Education v. Barnette, 319 U.S. 624, 642; Baird v. State Bar of Arizona, 401 U.S., at 6-7; In re Stolar, 401 U.S. 23.

Also at stake here is Caldwell's privacy of association. We have held that "inviolability of privacy in group association may in many circumstances be indispensable to preservation of freedom of association, particularly where a group espouses dissident beliefs." NAACP v. [716] Alabama, 357 U.S., at 462; NAACP v. Button, 371 U.S. 415.

As I said in Gibson v. Florida Legislative Investigation Committee, 372 U.S., at 565: "the associational rights protected by the First Amendment . . . cover the entire spectrum in political ideology as well as in art, in journalism, in teaching, and in religion. . . . Government is . . . precluded from probing the intimacies of spiritual and intellectual relationships in the myriad of such societies and groups that exist in this country, regardless of the legislative purpose sought to be served. . . . If that is not true, I see no barrier to investigation of newspapers, churches, political parties, clubs, societies, unions, and any other association for their political, economic, social, philosophical, or religious views." (Concurring opinion.) (Emphasis added.)

The Court has not always been consistent in its protection of these First Amendment rights and has sometimes allowed a government interest to override the absolutes of the First Amendment. For example, under the banner of the "clear and present danger" test,[5] and later under the influence of the "balancing" formula,[6] the [717] Court has permitted men to be penalized not for any harmful conduct but solely for holding unpopular beliefs.

In recent years we have said over and over again that where First Amendment rights are concerned any regulation "narrowly drawn,"[7] must be

---

[5] E.g., Schenck v. United States, 249 U.S. 47 (wartime antidraft "leafleting"); Debs v. United States, 249 U.S. 211 (wartime anti-draft speech); Abrams v. United States, 250 U.S. 616 (wartime leafleting calling for general strike); Feiner v. New York, 340 U.S. 315 (arrest of radical speaker without attempt to protect him from hostile audience); Dennis v. United States, 341 U.S. 494 (reformulation of test as "not improbable" rule to sustain conviction of knowing advocacy of overthrow); Scales v. United States, 367 U.S. 203 (knowing membership in group which espouses forbidden advocacy is punishable). For a more detailed account of the infamy of the "clear and present danger" test see my concurring opinion in Brandenburg v. Ohio, 395 U.S. 444, 450.

[6] E.g., Adler v. Board of Education, 342 U.S. 485 (protection of schools from "pollution" outweighs public teachers' freedom to advocate violent overthrow); Uphaus v. Wyman, 360 U.S. 72, 79, 81 (preserving security of New Hampshire from subversives outweighs privacy of list of participants in suspect summer camp); Barenblatt v. United States, 360 U.S. 109 (legislative inquiry more important than protecting HUAC witness' refusal to answer whether a third person had been a Communist); Wilkinson v. United States, 365 U.S. 399 (legislative inquiry more important than protecting HUAC witness' refusal to state whether he was currently a member of the Communist Party); Braden v. United States, 365 U.S. 431, 435 (legislative inquiry more important than protecting HUAC witness' refusal to state whether he had once been a member of the Communist Party); Konigsberg v. State Bar, 366 U.S. 36 (regulating membership of bar outweighs interest of applicants in refusing to answer question concerning Communist affiliations); In re Anastaplo, 366 U.S. 82 (regulating membership of bar outweighs protection of applicant's belief in Declaration of Independence that citizens should revolt against an oppressive government); Communist Party v. Subversive Activities Control Board, 367 U.S. 1 (national security outweighs privacy of association of leaders of suspect groups); Law Students Research Council v. Wadmond, 401 U.S. 154 (regulating membership of bar outweighs privacy of applicants' views on the soundness of the Constitution).

[7] Thus, we have held "overbroad" measures which unduly restricted the time, place, and manner of expression. Schneider v. State, 308 U.S. 147, 161 (anti-leafleting law); Thornhill v. Alabama, 310 U.S. 88, 102 (anti-boycott statute); Cantwell v. Connecticut, 310 U.S. 296 (breach-of-

"compelling" and not [718] merely "rational" as is the case where other activities are concerned.[8] But

---

peace measure); Cox v. Louisiana, 379 U.S. 536 (breach-of-peace measure); Edwards v. South Carolina, 372 U.S. 229 (breach-of-peace statute); Cohen v. California, 403 U.S. 15, 22 (breach-of-peace statute); Gooding v. Wilson, 405 U.S. 518 (breach-of-peace statute). But insofar as penalizing the content of thought and opinion is concerned, the Court has not in recent Terms permitted any interest to override the absolute privacy of one's philosophy. To be sure, opinions have often adverted to the absence of a compelling justification for attempted intrusions into philosophical or associational privacy. E.g., Bates v. Little Rock, 361 U.S. 516, 523 (disclosure of NAACP membership lists to city officials); Gibson v. Florida Legislative Investigation Committee, 372 U.S. 539, 546 (disclosure of NAACP membership list to state legislature); DeGregory v. Attorney General of New Hampshire, 383 U.S. 825, 829 (witness' refusal to state whether he had been a member of the Communist Party three years earlier); Baird v. State Bar of Arizona, 401 U.S. 1, 6-7 (refusal of bar applicant to state whether she had been a member of the Communist Party); In re Stolar, 401 U.S. 23 (refusal of bar applicant to state whether he was "loyal" to the Government); see also Street v. New York, 394 U.S. 576 (expression of disgust for flag). Yet, while the rhetoric of these opinions did not expressly embrace an absolute privilege for the privacy of opinions and philosophy, the trend of those results was not inconsistent with and in their totality appeared to be approaching such a doctrine. Moreover, in another group of opinions invalidating for overbreadth intrusions into the realm of belief and association, there was no specification of whether a danger test, a balancing process, an absolute doctrine, or a compelling justification inquiry had been used to detect invalid applications comprehended by the challenged measures. E.g., Wieman v. Updegraff, 344 U.S. 183 (loyalty test which condemned mere unknowing membership in a suspect group); Shelton v. Tucker, 364 U.S. 479 (requirement that public teachers disclose all affiliations); Louisiana ex rel. Gremillion v. NAACP, 366 U.S. 293, 296 (disclosure of NAACP membership lists); Whitehill v. Elkins, 389 U.S. 54, 59 (nonactive membership in a suspect group a predicate for refusing employment as a public teacher); United States v. Robel, 389 U.S. 258 (mere membership in Communist Party a sole ground for exclusion from employment in defense facility). Regrettably, the vitality of the overdue trend toward a complete privilege in this area has been drawn into question by quite recent decisions of the Court, Law Students Research Council v. Wadmond, 401 U.S. 154, holding that bar applicants may be turned away for refusing to disclose their opinions on the soundness of the Constitution; Cole v. Richardson, 405 U.S. 676, sustaining an oath required of public employees that they will "oppose" a violent overthrow; and, of course, by today's decision.

[8] Where no more than economic interests were affected this Court has upheld legislation only upon a showing that it was "rationally connected" to some permissible state objective. E.g., United States v. Carolene Products Co., 304 U.S. 144, 152; Goesaert v. Cleary, 335 U.S. 464; Williamson v. Lee Optical Co., 348 U.S. 483; McGowan v. Maryland, 366 U.S. 420; McDonald v. Board of Election Comm'rs, 394 U.S. 802; United States v. Maryland Savings-Share Ins.

---

the "compelling" interest in regulation neither includes paring down or diluting the right, nor [719] embraces penalizing one solely for his intellectual viewpoint; it concerns the State's interest, for example, in regulating the time and place or perhaps manner of exercising First Amendment rights. Thus, one has an undoubted right to read and proclaim the First Amendment in the classroom or in a park. But he would not have the right to blare it forth from a sound truck rolling through the village or city at 2 a. m. The distinction drawn in Cantwell v. Connecticut, 310 U.S. 296, 303-304, should still stand: "The Amendment embraces two concepts, – freedom to believe and freedom to act. The first is absolute but, in the nature of things, the second cannot be."[9]

Under these precedents there is no doubt that Caldwell could not be brought before the grand jury for the sole purpose of exposing his political beliefs. Yet today the Court effectively permits that result under the guise of allowing an attempt to elicit from him "factual information." To be sure, the inquiry will be couched only in terms of extracting Caldwell's recollection of what was said to him during the interviews, but the fact remains that his questions to the Panthers and therefore the respective answers were guided by Caldwell's own preconceptions and views about the Black Panthers. His [720] entire experience was shaped by his intellectual viewpoint. Unlike the random bystander, those who affirmatively set out to test a hypothesis, as here, have no tidy means of segregating subjective opinion from objective facts.

Sooner or later, any test which provides less than blanket protection to beliefs and associations will be twisted and relaxed so as to provide virtually no protection at all. As Justice Holmes noted in Abrams v. United States, 250 U.S. 616, 624, such was the fate of the "clear and present danger" test which he had coined in Schenck v. United States, 249 U.S. 47. Eventually, that formula was so watered down that the danger had to be neither clear nor present but merely "not improbable." Dennis v. United States, 341 U.S. 494, 510. See my concurring opinion in Brandenburg v. Ohio, 395 U.S. 444, 450. A compelling-interest test may prove as pliable as did the clear-and-present-danger test. Perceptions of

---

Corp., 400 U.S. 4; Richardson v. Belcher, 404 U.S. 78; Schilb v. Kuebel, 404 U.S. 357.

[9] The majority cites several cases which held that certain burdens on the press were permissible despite incidental burdens on its news-gathering ability. For example, see Sheppard v. Maxwell, 384 U.S. 333, 358. Even assuming that those cases were rightly decided, the fact remains that in none of them was the Government attempting to extract personal belief from a witness and the privacy of a citizen's personal intellectual viewpoint was not implicated.

the worth of state objectives will change with the composition of the Court and with the intensity of the politics of the times. For example, in Uphaus v. Wyman, 360 U.S. 72, sustaining an attempt to compel a witness to divulge the names of participants in a summer political camp, JUSTICE BRENNAN dissented on the ground that "it is patent that there is really no subordinating interest . . . demonstrated on the part of the State." Id., at 106.

The majority, however, found that "the governmental interest in self-preservation is sufficiently compelling to subordinate the interest in associational privacy . . . ." Id., at 81. That is to enter the world of "make believe," for New Hampshire, the State involved in Uphaus, was never in fear of being overthrown.

II. Today's decision will impede the wide-open and robust dissemination of ideas and counter-thought which [721] a free press both fosters and protects and which is essential to the success of intelligent self-government. Forcing a reporter before a grand jury will have two retarding effects upon the ear and the pen of the press. Fear of exposure will cause dissidents to communicate less openly to trusted reporters. And, fear of accountability will cause editors and critics to write with more restrained pens.

I see no way of making mandatory the disclosure of a reporter's confidential source of the information on which he bases his news story. The press has a preferred position in our constitutional scheme, not to enable it to make money, not to set newsmen apart as a favored class, but to bring fulfillment to the public's right to know. The right to know is crucial to the governing powers of the people, to paraphrase Alexander Meiklejohn. Knowledge is essential to informed decisions.

As Mr. Justice Black said in New York Times Co. v. United States, 403 U.S. 713, 717 (concurring opinion), "The press was to serve the governed, not the governors. . . . The press was protected so that it could bare the secrets of government and inform the people."

Government has an interest in law and order; and history shows that the trend of rulers — the bureaucracy and the police — is to suppress the radical and his ideas and to arrest him rather than the hostile audience. See Feiner v. New York, 340 U.S. 315. Yet, as held in Terminiello v. Chicago, 337 U.S. 1, 4, one "function of free speech under our system of government is to invite dispute." We went on to say, "It may indeed best serve its high purpose when it induces a condition of unrest, creates dissatisfaction with conditions as they are, or even stirs people to anger. Speech is often provocative and challenging. It may strike at prejudices and preconceptions [722] and have

profound unsettling effects as it presses for acceptance of an idea."

The people who govern are often far removed from the cabals that threaten the regime; the people are often remote from the sources of truth even though they live in the city where the forces that would undermine society operate. The function of the press is to explore and investigate events, inform the people what is going on, and to expose the harmful as well as the good influences at work. There is no higher function performed under our constitutional regime. Its performance means that the press is often engaged in projects that bring anxiety or even fear to the bureaucracies, departments, or officials of government. The whole weight of government is therefore often brought to bear against a paper or a reporter.

A reporter is no better than his source of information. Unless he has a privilege to withhold the identity of his source, he will be the victim of governmental intrigue or aggression. If he can be summoned to testify in secret before a grand jury, his sources will dry up and the attempted exposure, the effort to enlighten the public, will be ended. If what the Court sanctions today becomes settled law, then the reporter's main function in American society will be to pass on to the public the press releases which the various departments of government issue.

It is no answer to reply that the risk that a newsman will divulge one's secrets to the grand jury is no greater than the threat that he will in any event inform to the police. Even the most trustworthy reporter may not be able to withstand relentless badgering before a grand jury.[10]

[723] The record in this case is replete with weighty affidavits from responsible newsmen, telling how important is the sanctity of their

---

[10] "The secrecy of the [grand jury's] proceedings and the possibility of a jail sentence for contempt so intimidate the witness that he may be led into answering questions which pry into his personal life and associations and which, in the bargain, are frequently immaterial and vague. Alone and faced by either hostile or apathetic grand juries, the witness is frequently undone by his experience. Life in a relatively open society makes him especially vulnerable to a secret appearance before a body that is considering criminal charges. And the very body toward which he could once look for protection has become a weapon of the prosecution. When he seeks protective guidance from his lawyer he learns that the judicial broadening of due process which has occurred in the past two decades has largely ignored grand jury matters, precisely because it was assumed that the grand jury still functioned as a guardian of the rights of potential defendants." Donner & Cerruti, The Grand Jury Network: How the Nixon Administration Has Secretly Perverted A Traditional Safeguard of Individual Rights, 214 The Nation 5, 6 (1972).

sources of information.[11] When we deny newsmen that protection, we deprive the people of the information needed to run the affairs of the Nation in an intelligent way.

Madison said: "A popular Government, without popular information, or the means of acquiring it, is but a Prologue to a Farce or a Tragedy; or, perhaps both. Knowledge will forever govern ignorance: And a people who mean to be their own Governors, must arm themselves with the power which knowledge gives." (To W. T. Barry, Aug. 4, 1822). 9 Writings of James Madison 103 (G. Hunt ed. 1910).

[724] Today's decision is more than a clog upon news gathering. It is a signal to publishers and editors that they should exercise caution in how they use whatever information they can obtain. Without immunity they may be summoned to account for their criticism. Entrenched officers have been quick to crash their powers down upon unfriendly commentators.[12] E.g., New York Times Co. v. Sullivan, 376 U.S. 254; Garrison v.

---

[11] It is said that "we remain unclear how often and to what extent informers are actually deterred from furnishing information when newsmen are forced to testify before a grand jury." Ante, at 693. But the majority need look no further than its holdings that prosecutors need not disclose informers' names because disclosure would (a) terminate the usefulness of an exposed informant inasmuch as others would no longer confide in him, and (b) it would generally inhibit persons from becoming confidential informers. McCray v. Illinois, 386 U.S. 300; Scher v. United States, 305 U.S. 251; cf. Roviaro v. United States, 353 U.S. 53.

[12] For a summary of early reprisals against the press, such as the John Peter Zenger trial, the Alien and Sedition Acts prosecutions, and Civil War suppression of newspapers, see Press Freedoms Under Pressure, Report of the Twentieth Century Fund Task Force on the Government and the Press 3-5 (1972). We have not outlived the tendency of officials to retaliate against critics. For recent examples see J. Wiggins, Freedom or Secrecy 87 (1956) ("New Mexico, in 1954, furnished a striking example of government reprisal against . . . a teacher in the state reform school [who] wrote a letter to the New Mexican, confirming stories it had printed about mistreatment of inmates by guards. . . . [Two days later he] was notified of his dismissal."); Note, The Right of Government Employees to Furnish Information to Congress: Statutory and Constitutional Aspects, 57 Va. L. Rev. 885-886 (1971) (dismissal of an Air Force employee who testified before a Senate committee with respect to C-5A cargo plane cost overruns and firing of an FBI agent who wrote Senators complaining of the Bureau's personnel practices); N.Y. Times, Nov. 8, 1967, p. 1, col. 2; id., Nov. 9, 1967, p. 2, col. 4 (Selective Service directive to local draft boards requiring conscription of those who protested war); N.Y. Times, Nov. 11, 1971, p. 95, col. 4; id., Nov. 12, 1971, p. 13, col. 1; id., Nov. 14, 1971, pt. 4, p. 13, col. 1 (FBI investigation of a television commentator who criticized administration policies); id., Nov. 14, 1971, p. 75, col. 3 (denial of White House press pass to underground journalist).

Louisiana, 379 U.S. 64; Pickering v. Board of Education, 391 U.S. 563; Gravel v. United States, ante, p. 606.

The intrusion of government into this domain is symptomatic of the disease of this society. As the years pass the power of government becomes more and more pervasive. It is a power to suffocate both people and causes. Those in power, whatever their politics, want only to perpetuate [725] it. Now that the fences of the law and the tradition that has protected the press are broken down, the people are the victims. The First Amendment, as I read it, was designed precisely to prevent that tragedy.

I would also reverse the judgments in No. 70-85, Branzburg v. Hayes, and No. 70-94, In re Pappas, for the reasons stated in the above dissent in No. 70-57, United States v. Caldwell.

MR. JUSTICE STEWART, with whom MR. JUSTICE BRENNAN and MR. JUSTICE MARSHALL join, dissenting.

The Court's crabbed view of the First Amendment reflects a disturbing insensitivity to the critical role of an independent press in our society. The question whether a reporter has a constitutional right to a confidential relationship with his source is of first impression here, but the principles that should guide our decision are as basic as any to be found in the Constitution.

While MR. JUSTICE POWELL's enigmatic concurring opinion gives some hope of a more flexible view in the future, the Court in these cases holds that a newsman has no First Amendment right to protect his sources when called before a grand jury. The Court thus invites state and federal authorities to undermine the historic independence of the press by attempting to annex the journalistic profession as an investigative arm of government. Not only will this decision impair performance of the press' constitutionally protected functions, but it will, I am convinced, in the long run harm rather than help the administration of justice.

I respectfully dissent.

I. The reporter's constitutional right to a confidential relationship with his source stems from the broad societal interest in a full and free flow of information to the public. It is this basic concern that underlies the Constitution's [726] protection of a free press, Grosjean v. American Press Co., 297 U.S. 233, 250; New York

Times Co. v. Sullivan, 376 U.S. 254, 269,[1] because the guarantee is "not for the benefit of the press so much as for the benefit of all of us." Time, Inc. v. Hill, 385 U.S. 374, 389.[2]

Enlightened choice by an informed citizenry is the basic ideal upon which an open society is premised,[3] and a free press is thus indispensable to a free society. Not only does the press enhance personal self-fulfillment [727] by providing the people with the widest possible range of fact and opinion, but it also is an incontestable precondition of self-government. The press "has been a mighty catalyst in awakening public interest in governmental affairs, exposing corruption among public officers and employees and generally informing the citizenry of public events and occurrences . . . ." Estes v. Texas, 381 U.S. 532, 539; Mills v. Alabama, 384 U.S. 214, 219; Grosjean, supra, at 250. As private and public aggregations of power burgeon in size and the pressures for conformity necessarily mount, there is obviously a continuing need for an independent press to disseminate a robust variety of information and opinion through reportage, investigation, and criticism, if we are to preserve our constitutional tradition of maximizing freedom of choice by encouraging diversity of expression.

A In keeping with this tradition, we have held that the right to publish is central to the First Amendment and basic to the existence of constitutional democracy. Grosjean, supra, at 250; New York Times, supra, at 270.

A corollary of the right to publish must be the right to gather news. The full flow of information to the public protected by the free-press guarantee would be severely curtailed if no protection whatever were afforded to the process by which news is assembled and disseminated. We have, therefore, recognized that there is a right to publish without prior governmental approval, Near v. Minnesota, 283 U.S. 697; New York Times Co. v. United States, 403 U.S. 713, a right to distribute information, see, e.g., Lovell v. Griffin, 303 U.S. 444, 452; Marsh v. Alabama, 326 U.S. 501; Martin v. City of Struthers, 319 U.S. 141; Grosjean, supra, and a right to receive printed matter, Lamont v. Postmaster General, 381 U.S. 301.

[728] No less important to the news dissemination process is the gathering of information. News must not be unnecessarily cut off at its source, for without freedom to acquire information the right to publish would be impermissibly compromised. Accordingly, a right to gather news, of some dimensions, must exist. Zemel v. Rusk, 381 U.S. 1.[4] Note, The Right of the Press to Gather Information, 71 Col. L. Rev. 838 (1971). As Madison wrote: "A popular Government, without popular information, or the means of acquiring it, is but a Prologue to a Farce or a Tragedy; or, perhaps both." 9 Writings of James Madison 103 (G. Hunt ed. 1910).

B The right to gather news implies, in turn, a right to a confidential relationship between a reporter and his source. This proposition follows as a matter of simple logic once three factual predicates are recognized: (1) newsmen require informants to gather news; (2) confidentiality – the promise or understanding that names or certain aspects of communications will be kept off the record – is essential to the creation and maintenance of a news-gathering relationship with informants; and (3) an unbridled subpoena power – the absence of a constitutional right protecting, in any way, a confidential relationship from

---

[1] We have often described the process of informing the public as the core purpose of the constitutional guarantee of free speech and a free press. See, e.g., Stromberg v. California, 283 U.S. 359, 369; De Jonge v. Oregon, 299 U.S. 353, 365; Smith v. California, 361 U.S. 147, 153.

[2] As I see it, a reporter's right to protect his source is bottomed on the constitutional guarantee of a full flow of information to the public. A newsman's personal First Amendment rights or the associational rights of the newsman and the source are subsumed under that broad societal interest protected by the First Amendment. Obviously, we are not here concerned with the parochial personal concerns of particular newsmen or informants. "The newsman-informer relationship is different from . . . other relationships whose confidentiality is protected by statute, such as the attorney-client and physician-patient relationships. In the case of other statutory privileges, the right of nondisclosure is granted to the person making the communication in order that he will be encouraged by strong assurances of confidentiality to seek such relationships which contribute to his personal well-being. The judgment is made that the interests of society will be served when individuals consult physicians and lawyers; the public interest is thus advanced by creating a zone of privacy that the individual can control. However, in the case of the reporter-informer relationship, society's interest is not in the welfare of the informant per se, but rather in creating conditions in which information possessed by news sources can reach public attention." Note, 80 Yale L.J. 317, 343 (1970) (footnotes omitted) (hereinafter Yale Note).

[3] See generally Z. Chafee, Free Speech in the United States (1941); A. Meikeljohn, Free Speech and Its Relation to Self-Government (1948); T. Emerson, Toward a General Theory of the First Amendment (1963).

---

[4] In Zemel v. Rusk, 381 U.S. 1, we held that the Secretary of State's denial of a passport for travel to Cuba did not violate a citizen's First Amendment rights. The rule was justified by the "weightiest considerations of national security" and we concluded that the "right to speak and publish does not carry with it the unrestrained right to gather information." Id., at 16-17 (emphasis supplied). The necessary implication is that some right to gather information does exist.

compulsory process – will either deter sources from divulging information or deter reporters from gathering and publishing information.

[729] It is obvious that informants are necessary to the news-gathering process as we know it today. If it is to perform its constitutional mission, the press must do far more than merely print public statements or publish prepared handouts. Familiarity with the people and circumstances involved in the myriad background activities that result in the final product called "news" is vital to complete and responsible journalism, unless the press is to be a captive mouthpiece of "newsmakers."[5]

It is equally obvious that the promise of confidentiality may be a necessary prerequisite to a productive relationship between a newsman and his informants. An officeholder may fear his superior; a member of the bureaucracy, his associates; a dissident, the scorn of majority opinion. All may have information valuable to the public discourse, yet each may be willing to relate that information only in confidence to a reporter whom he trusts, either because of excessive caution or because of a reasonable fear of reprisals or censure for unorthodox [730] views. The First Amendment concern must not be with the motives of any particular news source, but rather with the conditions in which informants of all shades of the spectrum may make information available through the press to the public. Cf. Talley v. California, 362 U.S. 60, 65; Bates v. Little Rock, 361 U.S. 516; NAACP v. Alabama, 357 U.S. 449.[6]

In Caldwell, the District Court found that "confidential relationships . . . are commonly developed and maintained by professional journalists, and are indispensable to their work of gathering, analyzing and publishing the news."[7] Commentators and individual reporters have repeatedly noted the importance of confidentiality.[8] [731]And surveys among reporters and editors indicate that the promise of nondisclosure is necessary for many types of news gathering.[9]

Finally, and most important, when governmental officials possess an unchecked power to compel newsmen to disclose information received in confidence, sources will clearly be deterred from giving information, and reporters will clearly be deterred from publishing it, because uncertainty about exercise of the power will lead to "self-censorship." Smith v. California, 361 U.S. 147, 149-154; New York Times Co. v. Sullivan, 376 U.S., at 279. The uncertainty arises, of course, because the judiciary has traditionally imposed virtually no limitations on the grand jury's broad investigatory powers. See Antell, The Modern Grand Jury: Benighted Super-government, 51 A. B. A. J. 153 (1965). See also Part II, infra.

After today's decision, the potential informant can never be sure that his identity or off-the-record communications will not subsequently be revealed

---

[5] In Caldwell v. United States, 434 F.2d 1081, the Government claimed that Caldwell did not have to maintain a confidential relationship with members of the Black Panther Party and provide independent reporting of their activities, since the Party and its leaders could issue statements on their own. But, as the Court of Appeals for the Ninth Circuit correctly observed:

"It is not enough that Black Panther press releases and public addresses by Panther leaders may continue unabated in the wake of subpoenas such as the one here in question. It is not enough that the public's knowledge of groups such as the Black Panthers should be confined to their deliberate public pronouncements or distant news accounts of their occasional dramatic forays into the public view.

"The need for an untrammeled press takes on special urgency in times of widespread protest and dissent. In such times the First Amendment protections exist to maintain communication with dissenting groups and to provide the public with a wide range of information about the nature of protest and heterodoxy." Citing Associated Press v. United States, 326 U.S. 1, 20; Thornhill v. Alabama, 310 U.S. 88, 102. Id., at 1084-1085.

[6] As we observed in Talley v. California, 362 U.S. 60, "Anonymous pamphlets, leaflets, brochures and even books have played an important role in the progress of mankind. . . Before the Revolutionary War colonial patriots frequently

had to conceal their authorship or distribution of literature that easily could have brought down on them prosecutions by English-controlled courts. . . . Even the Federalist Papers, written in favor of the adoption of our Constitution, were published under fictitious names. It is plain that anonymity has sometimes been assumed for the most constructive purposes." Id., at 64-65. And in Lamont v. Postmaster General, 381 U.S. 301, we recognized the importance to First Amendment values of the right to receive information anonymously.

[7] Application of Caldwell, 311 F.Supp. 358, 361.

[8] See, e.g., F. Chalmers, A Gentleman of the Press: The Biography of Colonel John Bayne MacLean 74-75 (1969); H. Klurfeld, Behind the Lines: The World of Drew Pearson 50, 52-55 (1968); A. Krock, Memoirs: Sixty Years on the Firing Line 181, 184-185 (1968); E. Larsen, First with the Truth 22-23 (1968); R. Ottley, The Lonely Warrior – The Life and Times of Robert S. Abbott 143-145 (1955); C. Sulzberger, A Long Row of Candles; Memoirs and Diaries 241 (1969).

As Walter Cronkite, a network television reporter, said in an affidavit in Caldwell: "In doing my work, I (and those who assist me) depend constantly on information, ideas, leads and opinions received in confidence. Such material is essential in digging out newsworthy facts and, equally important, in assessing the importance and analyzing the significance of public events." App. 52.

[9] See Guest & Stanzler, The Constitutional Argument for Newsmen Concealing Their Sources, 64 Nw. U. L. Rev. 18 (1969); V. Blasi, Press Subpoenas: An Empirical and Legal Analysis, Study Report of the Reporters' Committee on Freedom of the Press 20-29 (hereinafter Blasi).

through the compelled testimony of a newsman. A public-spirited person inside government, who is not implicated in any crime, will now be fearful of revealing corruption or other governmental wrongdoing, because he will now know he can subsequently be identified by use of compulsory process. The potential source must, therefore, choose between risking exposure by giving information or avoiding the risk by remaining silent.

The reporter must speculate about whether contact with a controversial source or publication of controversial material will lead to a subpoena. In the event of a [732] subpoena, under today's decision, the newsman will know that he must choose between being punished for contempt if he refuses to testify, or violating his profession's ethics[10] and impairing his resourcefulness as a reporter if he discloses confidential information.[11]

Again, the commonsense understanding that such deterrence will occur is buttressed by concrete evidence. The existence of deterrent effects through fear and self-censorship was impressively developed in the District Court in Caldwell.[12] Individual reporters[13] and commentators[14] have

---

[10] The American Newspaper Guild has adopted the following rule as part of the newsman's code of ethics: "Newspapermen shall refuse to reveal confidences or disclose sources of confidential information in court or before other judicial or investigating bodies." G. Bird & F. Merwin, The Press and Society 592 (1971).

[11] Obviously, if a newsman does not honor a confidence he will have difficulty establishing other confidential relationships necessary for obtaining information in the future. See Siebert & Ryniker, Press Winning Fight to Guard Sources, Editor & Publisher, Sept. 1, 1934, pp. 9, 36-37.

[12] The court found that "compelled disclosure of information received by a journalist within the scope of ... confidential relationships jeopardizes those relationships and thereby impairs the journalist's ability to gather, analyze and publish the news." Application of Caldwell, 311 F.Supp., at 361.

[13] See n. 8, supra.

[14] Recent commentary is nearly unanimous in urging either an absolute or qualified newsman's privilege. See, e.g., Goldstein, Newsmen and Their Confidential Sources, New Republic, Mar. 21, 1970, pp. 13-14; Yale Note, supra, n. 2; Comment, 46 N.Y. U. L. Rev. 617 (1971); Nelson, The Newsmen's Privilege Against Disclosure of Confidential Sources and Information, 24 Vand. L. Rev. 667 (1971); Note, The Right of the Press to Gather Information, 71 Col. L. Rev. 838 (1971); Comment, 4 U. Mich. J. L. Ref. 85 (1970); Comment, 6 Harv. Civ. Rights-Civ. Lib. L. Rev. 119 (1970); Comment, The Newsman's Privilege: Government Investigations, Criminal Prosecutions and Private Litigation, 58 Calif. L. Rev. 1198 (1970). But see the Court's opinion, ante, at 690 n. 29. And see generally articles collected in Yale Note, supra, n. 2.
Recent decisions are in conflict both as to the importance of the deterrent effects and, a fortiori, as to the existence of a constitutional right to a confidential reporter-source

noted such effects. Surveys have verified that an unbridled subpoena power will substantially [733] impair the flow of news to the public, especially in sensitive areas involving governmental officials, financial affairs, political figures, dissidents, or minority groups that require in-depth, investigative reporting.[15] And the Justice Department has recognized that "compulsory process in some circumstances may have a limiting effect on the exercise of First Amendment rights."[16] No evidence contradicting the existence of such deterrent effects was offered at the trials or in the briefs here by the petitioner in Caldwell or by the respondents in Branzburg and Pappas.

The impairment of the flow of news cannot, of course, be proved with scientific precision, as the Court seems to demand. Obviously, not every news-gathering relationship requires confidentiality. And it is difficult to pinpoint precisely how many relationships do require a promise or understanding of nondisclosure. But we have never before demanded that First Amendment rights rest on elaborate empirical studies demonstrating beyond any conceivable doubt that deterrent effects exist; we have never before required proof of the exact number of people potentially affected by governmental action, who would actually be dissuaded from engaging in First Amendment activity.

Rather, on the basis of common sense and available information, we have asked, often implicitly, (1) whether there was a rational connection between the cause (the governmental action) and the effect (the deterrence or [734] impairment of First Amendment activity), and (2) whether the effect would occur with some regularity, i.e., would not be de minimis. See, e.g., Grosjean v. American Press Co., 297 U.S., at 244-245; Burstyn, Inc. v. Wilson, 343 U.S. 495, 503; Sweezy v. New Hampshire, 354 U.S. 234, 248 (plurality opinion); NAACP v. Alabama, 357 U.S., at 461-466; Smith v. California, 361 U.S., at 150-154; Bates v. Little Rock, 361 U.S., at 523-524; Talley v. California, 362 U.S., at 64-65; Shelton v. Tucker, 364 U.S. 479, 485-486; Cramp v. Board of Public Instruction, 368 U.S. 278, 286; NAACP v. Button, 371 U.S. 415, 431-438; Gibson v. Florida Legislative Investigation Committee, 372 U.S. 539, 555-557; New York Times Co. v. Sullivan, 376 U.S., at 277-278; Freedman v. Maryland, 380 U.S. 51, 59; DeGregory v. New Hampshire Attorney General, 383 U.S. 825; Elfbrandt v. Russell, 384 U.S. 11, 16-19. And, in making this determination,

---

relationship. See the Court's opinion, ante, at 686, and cases collected in Yale Note, at 318 nn. 6-7.

[15] See Blasi 6-71; Guest & Stanzler, supra, n. 9, at 43-50.

[16] Department of Justice Memo. No. 692 (Sept. 2, 1970).

we have shown a special solicitude towards the "indispensable liberties" protected by the First Amendment, NAACP v. Alabama, supra, at 461; Bantam Books, Inc. v. Sullivan, 372 U.S. 58, 66, for "freedoms such as these are protected not only against heavy-handed frontal attack, but also from being stifled by more subtle governmental interference." Bates, supra, at 523.[17] Once this threshold inquiry has been satisfied, we have then examined the competing interests in determining whether [735] there is an unconstitutional infringement of First Amendment freedoms.

For example, in NAACP v. Alabama, supra, we found that compelled disclosure of the names of those in Alabama who belonged to the NAACP "is likely to affect adversely the ability [of the NAACP] and its members to pursue their . . . beliefs which they admittedly have the right to advocate, in that it may induce members to withdraw from the Association and dissuade others from joining it because of fear of exposure of their beliefs shown through their associations and of the consequences of this exposure." Id., at 462-463. In Talley, supra, we held invalid a city ordinance that forbade circulation of any handbill that did not have the distributor's name on it, for there was "no doubt that such an identification requirement would tend to restrict freedom to distribute information and thereby freedom of expression." Id., at 64. And in Burstyn, Inc., supra, we found deterrence of First Amendment activity inherent in a censor's power to exercise unbridled discretion under an overbroad statute. Id., at 503.

Surely the analogous claim of deterrence here is as securely grounded in evidence and common sense as the claims in the cases cited above, although the Court calls the claim "speculative." See ante, at 694. The deterrence may not occur in every confidential relationship between a reporter and his source.[18] But it will certainly [736] occur

in certain types of relationships involving sensitive and controversial matters. And such relationships are vital to the free flow of information.

To require any greater burden of proof is to shirk our duty to protect values securely embedded in the Constitution. We cannot await an unequivocal – and therefore unattainable – imprimatur from empirical studies.[19] We can and must accept the evidence developed in the record, and elsewhere, that overwhelmingly supports the premise that deterrence will occur with regularity in important types of news-gathering relationships.[20]

Thus, we cannot escape the conclusion that when neither the reporter nor his source can rely on the shield of confidentiality against unrestrained use of the grand jury's subpoena power, valuable information will not be published and the public dialogue will inevitably be impoverished.

II. Posed against the First Amendment's protection of the newsman's confidential relationships in these cases is society's interest in the use of the grand jury to administer [737] justice fairly and effectively. The grand jury serves two important functions: "to examine into the commission of crimes" and "to stand between the prosecutor and the accused, and to determine whether the charge was founded upon credible testimony or was dictated by malice or personal ill will." Hale v. Henkel, 201 U.S. 43, 59. And to perform these functions the grand jury must have available to it every man's relevant evidence. See Blair v. United States, 250 U.S. 273, 281; Blackmer v. United States, 284 U.S. 421, 438.

Yet the longstanding rule making every person's evidence available to the grand jury is not absolute.

---

[17] Although, as the Court points out, we have held that the press is not free from the requirements of the National Labor Relations Act, the Fair Labor Standards Act, the antitrust laws, or nondiscriminatory taxation, ante, at 683, these decisions were concerned "only with restraints on certain business or commercial practices" of the press. Citizen Publishing Co. v. United States, 394 U.S. 131, 139. And due weight was given to First Amendment interests. For example, "The First Amendment, far from providing an argument against application of the Sherman Act . . . provides powerful reasons to the contrary." Associated Press v. United States, 326 U.S., at 20.

[18] The fact that some informants will not be deterred from giving information by the prospect of the unbridled exercise of the subpoena power only means that there will not always be a conflict between the grand jury's inquiry and the protection of First Amendment activities. But even if the percentage of such informants is relatively large compared to the total "universe" of potential informants, there will

remain a large number of people in "absolute" terms who will be deterred, and the flow of news through mass circulation newspapers and electronic media will inevitably be impaired.

[19] Empirical studies, after all, can only provide facts. It is the duty of courts to give legal significance to facts; and it is the special duty of this Court to understand the constitutional significance of facts. We must often proceed in a state of less than perfect knowledge, either because the facts are murky or the methodology used in obtaining the facts is open to question. It is then that we must look to the Constitution for the values that inform our presumptions. And the importance to our society of the full flow of information to the public has buttressed this Court's historic presumption in favor of First Amendment values.

[20] See, e.g., the uncontradicted evidence presented in affidavits from newsmen in Caldwell, Appendix to No. 70-57, pp. 22-61 (statements from Gerald Fraser, Thomas Johnson, John Kifner, Timothy Knight, Nicholas Proffitt, Anthony Ripley, Wallace Turner, Gilbert Noble, Anthony Lukas, Martin Arnold, David Burnham, Jon Lowell, Frank Morgan, Min Yee, Walter Cronkite, Eric Sevareid, Mike Wallace, Dan Rather, Marvin Kalb).

The rule has been limited by the Fifth Amendment,[21] the Fourth Amendment,[22] and the evidentiary privileges of the common law.[23] So it was that in Blair, supra, after recognizing that the right against compulsory self-incrimination prohibited certain inquiries, the Court noted that "some confidential matters are shielded from considerations of policy, and perhaps in other cases for special reasons a witness may be excused from telling all that he knows." Id., at 281 (emphasis supplied). And in United States v. Bryan, 339 U.S. 323, the Court observed that any exemption from the duty to testify before the grand jury "presupposes a very real interest to be protected." Id., at 332.

Such an interest must surely be the First Amendment protection of a confidential relationship that I have discussed above in Part I. As noted there, this protection does not exist for the purely private interests of the [738] newsman or his informant, nor even, at bottom, for the First Amendment interests of either partner in the news-gathering relationship.[24] Rather, it functions to insure nothing less than democratic decisionmaking through the free flow of information to the public, and it serves, thereby, to honor the "profound national commitment to the principle that debate on public issues should be uninhibited, robust, and wide-open." New York Times Co. v. Sullivan, 376 U.S., at 270.

In striking the proper balance between the public interest in the efficient administration of justice and the First Amendment guarantee of the fullest flow of information, we must begin with the basic proposition that because of their "delicate and vulnerable" nature, NAACP v. Button, 371 U.S., at 433, and their transcendent importance for the just functioning of our society, First Amendment rights require special safeguards.

A This Court has erected such safeguards when government, by legislative investigation or other investigative means, has attempted to pierce the shield of privacy inherent in freedom of association.[25] In no previous case have we considered the extent to which the First Amendment limits the grand jury subpoena power. But the [739] Court has said that "the Bill of Rights is applicable to investigations as to all forms of governmental action. Witnesses cannot be compelled to give evidence against themselves. They cannot be subjected to unreasonable search and seizure. Nor can the First Amendment freedoms of speech, press ... or political belief and association be abridged." Watkins v. United States, 354 U.S. 178, 188.And in Sweezy v. New Hampshire it was stated: "It is particularly important that the exercise of the power of compulsory process be carefully circumscribed when the investigative process tends to impinge upon such highly sensitive areas as freedom of speech or press, freedom of political association, and freedom of communication of ideas." 354 U.S., at 245 (plurality opinion).

The established method of "carefully" circumscribing investigative powers is to place a heavy burden of justification on government officials when First Amendment rights are impaired. The decisions of this Court have "consistently held that only a compelling state interest in the regulation of a subject within the State's constitutional power to regulate can justify limiting First Amendment freedoms." NAACP v. Button, 371 U.S., at 438. And "it is an essential prerequisite to the validity of an investigation which intrudes into the area of constitutionally protected rights of speech, press, association and petition that the State convincingly show a substantial relation between the information sought and a subject of overriding and compelling state interest." Gibson v. Florida Legislative Investigation Committee, 372 U.S., at 546 (emphasis supplied). See also DeGregory v. Attorney General of New Hampshire, 383 U.S. 825; NAACP v. Alabama, 357 U.S. 449; Sweezy, supra; Watkins, supra.

Thus, when an investigation impinges on First Amendment rights, the government must not only show that [740] the inquiry is of "compelling and overriding importance" but it must also "convincingly" demonstrate that the investigation is "substantially related" to the information sought.

---

[21] See Blau v. United States, 340 U.S. 159; Quinn v. United States, 349 U.S. 155; Curcio v. United States, 354 U.S. 118; Malloy v. Hogan, 378 U.S. 1.

[22] See Silverthorne Lumber Co. v. United States, 251 U.S. 385.

[23] See Committee on Rules of Practice and Procedure of Judicial Conference of the United States, Revised Draft of Proposed Rules of Evidence for the United States Courts and Magistrates (1971); 8 J. Wigmore, Evidence §§ 2290-2391 (McNaughton rev. 1961).

[24] Although there is a longstanding presumption against creation of common-law testimonial privileges, United States v. Bryan, 339 U.S. 323, these privileges are grounded in an "individual interest which has been found ... to outweigh the public interest in the search for truth" rather than in the broad public concerns that inform the First Amendment. Id., at 331.

[25] The protection of information from compelled disclosure for broad purposes of public policy has been recognized in decisions involving police informers, see Roviaro v. United States, 353 U.S. 53, United States v. Ventresca, 380 U.S. 102, 108, Aguilar v. Texas, 378 U.S. 108, 114, McCray v. Illinois, 386 U.S. 300, and military and state secrets, United States v. Reynolds, 345 U.S. 1.

Governmental officials must, therefore, demonstrate that the information sought is clearly relevant to a precisely defined subject of governmental inquiry. Watkins, supra; Sweezy, supra.[26] They must demonstrate that it is reasonable to think the witness in question has that information. Sweezy, supra; Gibson, supra.[27] And they must show that there is not any means of obtaining the information less destructive of First Amendment liberties. Shelton v. Tucker, 364 U.S., at 488; Louisiana ex rel. Gremillion v. NAACP, 366 U.S. 293, 296-297.[28]

These requirements, which we have recognized in decisions involving legislative and executive investigations, serve established policies reflected in numerous First [741] Amendment decisions arising in other contexts. The requirements militate against vague investigations that, like vague laws, create uncertainty and needlessly discourage First Amendment activity.[29] They also insure that a legitimate governmental purpose will not be pursued by means that "broadly stifle fundamental personal liberties when the end can be more narrowly achieved." Shelton, supra, at 488.[30]

As we said in Gibson, supra, "Of course, a legislative investigation – as any investigation – must proceed 'step by step,' . . . but step by step or in totality, an adequate foundation for inquiry must be laid before proceeding in such a manner as will substantially intrude upon and severely curtail or inhibit constitutionally protected activities or seriously interfere with similarly protected associational rights." 372 U.S., at 557.

I believe the safeguards developed in our decisions involving governmental investigations must apply to the grand jury inquiries in these cases. Surely the function of the grand jury to aid in the enforcement of the law is no more important than the function of the legislature, and its committees, to make the law. We have long recognized the value of the role played by legislative investigations, see, e.g., United States v. Rumely, [742] 345 U.S. 41, 43; Barenblatt v. United States, 360 U.S. 109, 111-112, for the "power of the Congress to conduct investigations is inherent . . . [encompassing] surveys of defects in our social, economic or political system for the purpose of enabling the Congress to remedy them." Watkins, supra, at 187. Similarly, the associational rights of private individuals, which have been the prime focus of our First Amendment decisions in the investigative sphere, are hardly more important than the First Amendment rights of mass circulation newspapers and electronic media to disseminate ideas and information, and of the general public to receive them. Moreover, the vices of vagueness and overbreadth that legislative investigations may manifest are also exhibited by grand jury inquiries, since grand jury investigations are not limited in scope to specific criminal acts, see, e.g., Wilson v. United States, 221 U.S. 361, Hendricks v. United States, 223 U.S. 178, 184, United States v. Johnson, 319 U.S. 503, and since standards of materiality and relevance are greatly relaxed. Holt v. United States, 218 U.S. 245; Costello v. United States, 350 U.S. 359. See generally Note, The Grand Jury as an Investigatory Body, 74 Harv. L. Rev. 590, 591-592 (1961).[31] For,

---

[26] As we said in Watkins v. United States, 354 U.S. 178, "When First Amendment rights are threatened, the delegation of power to the [legislative] committee must be clearly revealed in its charter." "It is the responsibility of the Congress . . . to insure that compulsory process is used only in furtherance of a legislative purpose. That requires that the instructions to an investigating committee spell out the group's jurisdiction and purpose with sufficient particularity. . . . The more vague the committee's charter is, the greater becomes the possibility that the committee's specific actions are not in conformity with the will of the parent House of Congress." Id., at 198, 201.

[27] We noted in Sweezy v. New Hampshire, 354 U.S. 234: "The State Supreme Court itself recognized that there was a weakness in its conclusion that the menace of forcible overthrow of the government justified sacrificing constitutional rights. There was a missing link in the chain of reasoning. The syllogism was not complete. There was nothing to connect the questioning of petitioner with this fundamental interest of the State." Id., at 251 (emphasis supplied).

[28] See generally Note, Less Drastic Means and the First Amendment, 78 Yale L. J. 464 (1969).

[29] See Watkins, supra, at 208-209. See generally Baggett v. Bullitt, 377 U.S. 360, 372; Speiser v. Randall, 357 U.S. 513, 526; Ashton v. Kentucky, 384 U.S. 195, 200-201; Dombrowski v. Pfister, 380 U.S. 479, 486; Smith v. California, 361 U.S., at 150-152; Winters v. New York, 333 U.S. 507; Stromberg v. California, 283 U.S., at 369. See also Note, The Chilling Effect in Constitutional Law, 69 Col. L. Rev. 808 (1969).

[30] See generally Zwickler v. Koota, 389 U.S. 241, 249-250, and cases cited therein; Coates v. Cincinnati, 402 U.S. 611, 616; Cantwell v. Connecticut, 310 U.S. 296, 307; De Jonge v. Oregon, 299 U.S., at 364-365; Schneider v. State, 308 U.S. 147, 164; Cox v. Louisiana, 379 U.S. 559, 562-564. Cf. NAACP v. Button, 371 U.S. 415, 438. See also Note,

The First Amendment Overbreadth Doctrine, 83 Harv. L. Rev. 844 (1970).

[31] In addition, witnesses customarily are not allowed to object to questions on the grounds of materiality or relevance, since the scope of the grand jury inquiry is deemed to be of no concern to the witness. Carter v. United States, 417 F.2d 384, cert. denied, 399 U.S. 935. Nor is counsel permitted to be present to aid a witness. See In re Groban, 352 U.S. 330.

See generally Younger, The Grand Jury Under Attack, pt. 3, 46 J. Crim. L. C. & P. S. 214 (1955); Recent Cases, 104 U. Pa. L. Rev. 429 (1955); Watts, Grand Jury: Sleeping Watchdog or Expensive Antique, 37 N. C. L. Rev. 290 (1959); Whyte, Is the Grand Jury Necessary?, 45 Va. L.

as the United States notes in its brief in Caldwell, the [743]grand jury "need establish no factual basis for commencing an investigation, and can pursue rumors which further investigation may prove groundless."

Accordingly, when a reporter is asked to appear before a grand jury and reveal confidences, I would hold that the government must (1) show that there is probable cause to believe that the newsman has information that is clearly relevant to a specific probable violation of law;[32] (2) demonstrate that the information sought cannot be obtained by alternative means less destructive of First Amendment rights; and (3) demonstrate a compelling and overriding interest in the information.[33]

This is not to say that a grand jury could not issue a subpoena until such a showing were made, and it is not to say that a newsman would be in any way privileged to ignore any subpoena that was issued. Obviously, before the government's burden to make such a showing were triggered, the reporter would have to move to quash the subpoena, asserting the basis on which he considered the particular relationship a confidential one. [744]

B   The crux of the Court's rejection of any newsman's privilege is its observation that only "where news sources themselves are implicated in crime or possess information relevant to the grand jury's task need they or the reporter be concerned about grand jury subpoenas." See ante, at 691 (emphasis supplied). But this is a most misleading construct. For it is obviously not true that the only persons about whom reporters will be

forced to testify will be those "confidential informants involved in actual criminal conduct" and those having "information suggesting illegal conduct by others." See ante, at 691, 693. As noted above, given the grand jury's extraordinarily broad investigative powers and the weak standards of relevance and materiality that apply during such inquiries, reporters, if they have no testimonial privilege, will be called to give information about informants who have neither committed crimes nor have information about crime. It is to avoid deterrence of such sources and thus to prevent needless injury to First Amendment values that I think the government must be required to show probable cause that the newsman has information that is clearly relevant to a specific probable violation of criminal law.[34]

[745] Similarly, a reporter may have information from a confidential source that is "related" to the commission of crime, but the government may be able to obtain an indictment or otherwise achieve its purposes by subpoenaing persons other than the reporter. It is an obvious but important truism that when government aims have been fully served, there can be no legitimate reason to disrupt a confidential relationship between a reporter and his source. To do so would not aid the administration of justice and would only impair the flow of information to the public. Thus, it is to avoid deterrence of such sources that I think the government must show that there are no alternative means for the grand jury to obtain the information sought.

Rev. 461 (1959); Note, 2 Col. J. Law & Soc. Prob. 47, 58 (1966); Antell, The Modern Grand Jury: Benighted Supergovernment, 51 A. B. A. J. 153 (1965); Orfield, The Federal Grand Jury, 22 F.R.D. 343.

[32] The standard of proof employed by most grand juries, federal and State, is simply "probable cause" to believe that the accused has committed a crime. See Note, 1963 Wash. U. L. Q. 102; L. Hall et al., Modern Criminal Procedure 793-794 (1969). Generally speaking, it is extremely difficult to challenge indictments on the ground that they are not supported by adequate or competent evidence. Cf. Costello v. United States, 350 U.S. 359; Beck v. Washington, 369 U.S. 541.

[33] Cf. Garland v. Torre, 259 F.2d 545. The Court of Appeals for the Second Circuit declined to provide a testimonial privilege to a newsman called to testify at a civil trial. But the court recognized a newsman's First Amendment right to a confidential relationship with his source and concluded: "It is to be noted that we are not dealing here with the use of the judicial process to force a wholesale disclosure of a newspaper's confidential sources of news, nor with a case where the identity of the news source is of doubtful relevance or materiality. . . . The question asked . . . went to the heart of the plaintiff's claim." Id., at 549-550 (citations omitted).

[34] If this requirement is not met, then the government will basically be allowed to undertake a "fishing expedition" at the expense of the press. Such general, exploratory investigations will be most damaging to confidential news-gathering relationships, since they will create great uncertainty in both reporters and their sources. The Court sanctions such explorations, by refusing to apply a meaningful "probable cause" requirement. See ante, at 701-702. As the Court states, a grand jury investigation "may be triggered by tips, rumors, evidence proffered by the prosecutor, or the personal knowledge of the grand jurors." Ante, at 701. It thereby invites government to try to annex the press as an investigative arm, since any time government wants to probe the relationships between the newsman and his source, it can, on virtually any pretext, convene a grand jury and compel the journalist to testify.

The Court fails to recognize that under the guise of "investigating crime" vindictive prosecutors can, using the broad powers of the grand jury which are, in effect, immune from judicial supervision, explore the newsman's sources at will, with no serious law enforcement purpose. The secrecy of grand jury proceedings affords little consolation to a news source; the prosecutor obviously will, in most cases, have knowledge of testimony given by grand jury witnesses.

Both the "probable cause" and "alternative means" requirements would thus serve the vital function of mediating between the public interest in the administration of justice and the constitutional protection of the full flow of information. These requirements would avoid a direct conflict between these competing concerns, and they would generally provide adequate protection for newsmen. See Part III, infra.[35] No doubt the courts would be required to make some delicate judgments in working out this accommodation. But that, after all, [746] is the function of courts of law. Better such judgments, however difficult, than the simplistic and stultifying absolutism adopted by the Court in denying any force to the First Amendment in these cases.[36]

The error in the Court's absolute rejection of First Amendment interests in these cases seems to me to be most profound. For in the name of advancing the administration of justice, the Court's decision, I think, will only impair the achievement of that goal. People entrusted with law enforcement responsibility, no less than private citizens, need general information relating to controversial social problems. Obviously, press reports have great value to government, even when the newsman cannot be compelled to testify before a grand jury. The sad paradox of the Court's position is that when a grand jury may exercise an unbridled subpoena power, and sources involved in sensitive matters become fearful of disclosing information, the newsman will not only cease to be a useful grand jury witness; he will cease to investigate and publish information about issues of public import. I cannot subscribe to such an anomalous result, for, in my view, the interests protected by the First Amendment are not antagonistic to the administration of justice. Rather, they can, in the long run, only be complementary, and for that reason must be given great "breathing space." NAACP v. Button, 371 U.S., at 433.

III. In deciding what protection should be given to information a reporter receives in confidence from a news source, the Court of Appeals for the Ninth Circuit affirmed the holding of the District Court that the grand [747] jury power of testimonial compulsion must not be exercised in a manner likely to impair First Amendment interests "until there has been a clear showing of a compelling and overriding national interest that cannot be served by any alternative means." Caldwell v. United States, 434 F.2d 1081, 1086. It approved the request of respondent Caldwell for specification by the government of the "subject, direction or scope of the Grand Jury inquiry." Id., at 1085. And it held that in the circumstances of this case Caldwell need not divulge confidential information.

I think this decision was correct. On the record before us the United States has not met the burden that I think the appropriate newsman's privilege should require.

In affidavits before the District Court, the United States said it was investigating possible violations of 18 U. S. C. §871 (threats against the President), 18 U. S. C. §1751 (assassination, attempts to assassinate, conspiracy to assassinate the President), 18 U. S. C. §231 (civil disorders), 18 U. S. C. § 2101 (interstate travel to incite a riot), 18 U. S. C. §1341 (mail fraud and swindles) and other crimes that were not specified. But, with one exception, there has been no factual showing in this case of the probable commission of, or of attempts to commit, any crimes.[37] The single exception relates to the allegation that a Black Panther Party leader, David Hilliard, violated 18 U. S. C. §871 during the course of a speech in November 1969. But Caldwell was subpoenaed two months after an indictment was returned against Hilliard, and that charge could not, subsequent to the indictment, be investigated by a grand jury. See In re National Window Glass Workers, 287 F. 219; United [748]States v. Dardi, 330 F.2d 316, 336.[38] Furthermore, the record before us does not show that Caldwell probably had any information about the violation of any other federal criminal

---

[35] We need not, therefore, reach the question of whether government's interest in these cases is "overriding and compelling." I do not, however, believe, as the Court does, that all grand jury investigations automatically would override the newsman's testimonial privilege.

[36] The disclaimers in MR. JUSTICE POWELL's concurring opinion leave room for the hope that in some future case the Court may take a less absolute position in this area.

---

[37] See Blasi 61 et seq.

[38] After Caldwell was first subpoenaed to appear before the grand jury, the Government did undertake, by affidavits, to "set forth facts indicating the general nature of the grand jury's investigation [and] witness Earl Caldwell's possession of information relevant to this general inquiry." In detailing the basis for the belief that a crime had probably been committed, the Government simply asserted that certain actions had previously been taken by other grand juries, and by Government counsel, with respect to certain members of the Black Panther Party (i.e., immunity grants for certain Black Panthers were sought; the Government moved to compel party members to testify before grand juries; and contempt citations were sought when party members refused to testify). No facts were asserted suggesting the actual commission of crime. The exception, as noted, involved David Hilliard's speech and its republication in the party newspaper, the Black Panther, for which Hilliard had been indicted before Caldwell was subpoenaed.

laws,[39] or that alternative [749] means of obtaining the desired information were pursued.[40]

In the Caldwell case, the Court of Appeals further found that Caldwell's confidential relationship with the leaders of the Black Panther Party would be impaired if he appeared before the grand jury at all to answer questions, even though not privileged. Caldwell v. United States, 434 F.2d, at 1088. On the particular facts before it,[41] the court concluded that the very [750] appearance by Caldwell before the grand jury would jeopardize his relationship with his sources, leading to a severance of the news-gathering relationship and impairment of the flow of news to the public:[42]

"Appellant asserted in affidavit that there is nothing to which he could testify (beyond that which he has already made public and for which, therefore, his appearance is unnecessary) that is not protected by the District Court's order. If this is true – and the Government apparently has not believed it necessary to dispute it – appellant's response to the subpoena would be a barren performance – [751] one of no benefit to the Grand Jury. To destroy appellant's capacity as news gatherer for such a return hardly makes sense. Since the cost to the public of excusing his attendance is so slight, it may be said that there is here no public interest of real substance in

---

[39] In its affidavits, the Government placed primary reliance on certain articles published by Caldwell in the New York Times during 1969 (on June 15, July 20, July 22, July 27, and Dec. 14). On Dec. 14, 1969, Caldwell wrote:

"'We are special,' Mr. Hilliard said recently 'We advocate the very direct overthrow of the Government by way of force and violence. By picking up guns and moving against it because we recognize it as being oppressive and in recognizing that we know that the only solution to it is armed struggle.'

"In their role as the vanguard in a revolutionary struggle, the Panthers have picked up guns.

"Last week two of their leaders were killed during the police raid on one of their offices in Chicago. And in Los Angeles a few days earlier, three officers and three Panthers were wounded in a similar shooting incident. In these and in some other raids, the police have found caches of weapons, including high-powered rifles." App. in No. 70-57, p. 13.

In my view, this should be read as indicating that Caldwell had interviewed Panther leaders. It does not indicate that he probably had knowledge of the crimes being investigated by the Government. And, to repeat, to the extent it does relate to Hilliard's threat, an indictment had already been brought in that matter. The other articles merely demonstrate that Black Panther Party leaders had told Caldwell their ideological beliefs – beliefs that were readily available to the Government through other sources, like the party newspaper.

[40] The Government did not attempt to show that means less impinging upon First Amendment interests had been pursued.

[41] In an affidavit filed with the District Court, Caldwell stated:

"I began covering and writing articles about the Black Panthers almost from the time of their inception, and I myself found that in those first months . . . they were very brief and reluctant to discuss any substantive matter with me. However, as they realized I could be trusted and that my sole purpose was to collect my information and present it objectively in the newspaper and that I had no other motive, I found that not only were the party leaders available for in-depth interviews but also the rank and file members were cooperative in aiding me in the newspaper stories that I wanted to do. During the time that I have been covering the party, I have noticed other newspapermen representing legitimate organizations in the news media being turned away because they were not known and trusted by the party leadership.

"As a result of the relationship that I have developed, I have been able to write lengthy stories about the Panthers that have appeared in The New York Times and have been of such a nature that other reporters who have not known the Panthers have not been able to write. Many of these stories have appeared in up to 50 or 60 other newspapers around the country.

"The Black Panther Party's method of operation with regard to members of the press is significantly different from that of other organizations. For instance, press credentials are not recognized as being of any significance. In addition, interviews are not normally designated as being 'backgrounders' or 'off the record' or 'for publication' or 'on the record.' Because no substantive interviews are given until a relationship of trust and confidence is developed between the Black Panther Party members and a reporter, statements are rarely made to such reporters on an expressed 'on' or 'off' the record basis. Instead, an understanding is developed over a period of time between the Black Panther Party members and the reporter as to matters which the Black Panther Party wishes to disclose for publications and those matters which are given in confidence. . . . Indeed, if I am forced to appear in secret grand jury proceedings, my appearance alone would be interpreted by the Black Panthers and other dissident groups as a possible disclosure of confidences and trusts and would similarly destroy my effectiveness as a newspaperman."

The Government did not contradict this affidavit.

[42] "Militant groups might very understandably fear that, under the pressure of examination before a Grand Jury, the witness may fail to protect their confidences . . . . The Government characterizes this anticipated loss of communication as Black Panther reprisal . . . . But it is not an extortionate threat we face. It is human reaction as reasonable to expect as that a client will leave his lawyer when his confidence is shaken. . . . As the Government points out, loss of such a sensitive news source can also result from its reaction to indiscreet or unfavorable reporting or from a reporter's association with Government agents or persons disapproved of by the news source. Loss in such a case, however, results from an exercise of the choice and prerogative of a free press. It is not the result of Government compulsion." Caldwell v. United States, 434 F.2d, at 1088.

competition with the First Amendment freedoms that are jeopardized.

"If any competing public interest is ever to arise in a case such as this (where First Amendment liberties are threatened by mere appearance at a Grand Jury investigation) it will be on an occasion in which the witness, armed with his privilege, can still serve a useful purpose before the Grand Jury. Considering the scope of the privilege embodied in the protective order, these occasions would seem to be unusual. It is not asking too much of the Government to show that such an occasion is presented here." Id., at 1089.

I think this ruling was also correct in light of the particularized circumstances of the Caldwell case. Obviously, only in very rare circumstances would a confidential relationship between a reporter and his source be so sensitive that mere appearance before the grand jury by the newsman would substantially impair his news-gathering function. But in this case, the reporter made out a prima facie case that the flow of news to the public would be curtailed. And he stated, without contradiction, that the only nonconfidential material about which he could testify was already printed in his newspaper articles.[43] Since the United States has not attempted to [752] refute this assertion, the appearance of Caldwell would, on these facts, indeed be a "barren performance." But this aspect of the Caldwell judgment I would confine to its own facts. As the Court of Appeals appropriately observed: "The rule of this case is a narrow one. . . ." Caldwell, supra, at 1090.

Accordingly, I would affirm the judgment of the Court of Appeals in No. 70-57, United States v. Caldwell.[44] In the other two cases before us, No. 70-85, Branzburg v. Hayes and Meigs, and No. 70-94, In re Pappas, I would vacate the judgments and remand the cases for further proceedings not inconsistent with the views I have expressed in this opinion.

---

[43] Caldwell stated in his affidavit filed with the District Court, see n. 40, supra:
"It would be virtually impossible for me to recall whether any particular matter disclosed to me by members of the Black Panther Party since January 1, 1969, was based on an understanding that it would or would not be confidential. Generally, those matters which were made on a non-confidential or 'for publication' basis have been published in articles I have written in The New York Times; conversely, any matters which I have not thus far disclosed in published articles would have been given to me based on the understanding that they were confidential and would not be published."

[44] The District Court reserved jurisdiction to modify its order on a showing of a governmental interest which cannot be served by means other than Caldwell's grand jury testimony. The Government would thus have further opportunity in that court to meet the burden that, I think, protection of First Amendment rights requires.

Glossary

A

Absolutism. Relying on a literal reading of the First Amendment, this stance insists that proper application of its command dictates that government action may never infringe the amendment's enumerated rights.

Actual damages. Also compensatory damages because they compensate for actual injuries or loss, as opposed to punitive damages.

Actual malice. A libel standard requiring proof that publication occurred with knowledge of the falsity of its contents or with reckless disregard of whether the contents were true or false.

Ad hoc. Literally, "for this particular purpose." Hence, case decisions based on the particulars of the case rather than more general principles.

Ad libitum. Literally, "at pleasure."

Administrative adjudication. The process through which an administrative agency issues an order.

Administrative agency. An executive branch agency established by law to provide specialized knowledge over specified subjects and vested with discretionary power to exercise authority in this field.

Administrative hearing. Hearing in which administrative agencies grant relief, resolve disputes and levy fines or penalties to apply and enforce administrative law.

Administrative law. The orders, rules and regulations promulgated by executive branch administrative agencies to carry out their delegated duties.

Amicus curiae. Literally, "friends of the court." Referring to those who file briefs on issues pending before a court.

Annotation. Comments designed to summarize and/or explain and clarify an article, book, case decision, statute or the like.

Arguendo. Literally, "as a matter of argument" or "hypothetically."

Arraignment. A court proceeding in which formal charges are read against the defendant, and the defendant enters a plea of guilty or not guilty.

B

Balancing. This approach acknowledges that other important rights may conflict with the rights enumerated in the First Amendment. In determining the proper application of the First Amendment, judges must weigh the enumerated individual rights against societal rights to arrive at a logical compromise.

Beyond a reasonable doubt. The standard of proof required to establish guilt in a criminal trial.

Black letter law. Law that is formally enacted, written down and available in legal reporters or other documents.

Breach of the peace. Disturbing public tranquility by force, riot or illegal act.

Bright line. A term of art used to describe a clearly delineated distinction between legal concepts.

Burden of proof. The obligation of one party to establish, by convincing evidence, a key point of law. The necessity to explain or refute the legal presumption.

C

Categorical balancing. A hierarchical classification of types of speech to assist in First Amendment decision making.

Chilling effect. Refers to any practice that seriously discourages the exercise of a constitutional right.

Circuit courts. The intermediate-level federal courts of appeal.

Common carrier. Under First Amendment jurisprudence, an entity that transports the speech of others on an equitable basis without interference or oversight of the content.

Common law. Unwritten law comprised of judicial decisions and the reasoning for them. Law created by judges from case precedent.

Concurrence or **concurring opinion.** A separate opinion of a minority of the court or a single justice agreeing with the court's judgment but applying different reasoning or legal principles.

Consent decree. A judgment reached through agreement of the parties in which the litigation ends and the defendant stops the alleged illegal activity without admitting guilt.

Conspiracy. The concerted and collaborative effort of two or more people to plan, assist or commit a criminal act.

Constitution. Legal pact that outlines the form and functions of government and guarantees the rights of the people.

Contempt, power of. Each house of Congress and every court has inherent power to punish individuals for conduct in or near its halls that willfully disregards, disobeys or interferes with its authority.

Core purpose. In determining the proper application of the First Amendment, judges grant stronger protection to speech that is more proximate to the amendment's perceived central intent.

D

Damages. Financial payments ordered by the court to compensate for injury or loss.

Decision. A popular term for a judicial judgment, decree or order.

De facto. Literally, "in fact." A corporation, person or state of affairs that exists in reality though perhaps not officially; a matter of conduct or practice not founded upon law.

Defamation. A false communication that harms another's reputation and subjects him/her to ridicule and scorn. Incorporates both libel and slander.

Defendant. The party against whom either a civil or criminal action is brought. In criminal cases, also called the accused.

Deference. The inclination of courts to give weight to the judgment of expert administrative agencies or legislative policies and strategies.

De jure. Literally, "by right." A corporation, person or state of affairs functioning in accordance with the law.

De minimis. Related to small or trifling matters with which the law need not contend.

Demurrer. A motion to dismiss a case on the grounds that although the claims are true they are insufficient to warrant a judgment against the defendant.

De novo review. Literally, a fresh or "new" review. Thus, on appeal, the court reviews the facts rather than simply the legal posture and process of the case.

Dicta. Comments in a court opinion that go beyond the issue before the court and represent the individual opinion of the author rather than the binding precedent of the court.

Discovery. In trial preparation, the process through which one party obtains information about the case from the other party. In criminal proceedings, the defense has the right to obtain evidence necessary to prepare its case.

Dispositive. Facts or issues that create, modify or otherwise determine legal decisions.

Dissent or **dissenting opinion.** A separate opinion of a minority of the court or a single justice disagreeing with the result reached by the majority and challenging the majority's reasoning or legal basis.

District courts. The federal trial-level courts.

Doctrine. A principle or theory of law, e.g. doctrine of content neutrality.

Due process. The constitutional requirement, under the 5th and 14th amendments, that individuals be guaranteed a fair legal process.

E

***En banc* review.** A hearing by all the judges of a circuit court of appeals to decide important or controversial cases.

Equity law. Law that empowers judges to issue decrees and remedies to assure fair outcomes that would not otherwise be addressed by law.

Ex parte. Literally, by or for or "on the behalf of" someone. In a case heading, the name following this phrase is the party who applied for the legal hearing.

F

Facial meaning. The surface, apparent or obvious meaning of a legal text.

Federal depository library. Any of 1,300 libraries around the country designated to maintain federal government documents available to the public.

First impression. Identifying a question of law that has been presented for the court for the first time. A case that presents an entirely novel question of law not governed by precedent.

G

Gravamen. The essence or gist of a complaint.

H

Heresy. In English law, the offense of publishing or expressing opinions contrary to church doctrine.

I

Illicit motive. Impermissible, improper or prohibited motivation. Generally relates to government legislative goals.

Impartial juror. An individual having no fixed opinion of the guilt or innocence of the defendant and able to render a verdict solely on the basis of evidence presented in court.

Indecent. Offensive to common decency, modesty or delicacy.

In camera. Literally, "in chambers."

Injunction. A court order prohibiting someone from doing something. Generally intended to stop a present or future harmful action.

Intermediate scrutiny. Also called heightened review, this standard is applied by the courts to the review of laws that implicate core constitutional values.

Intrusion. The wrongful entry onto or possession of another's property.

J

Judgment. The final and official decision or conclusion of a court on the issue submitted for its determination.

Judicial review. The power of the U.S. Supreme Court to determine the meaning of the language of the Constitution and to assure that no laws violate constitutional dictates.

Jurisdiction. The geographic or topical area of responsibility and authority of a court.

Jurisprudence. The philosophy or science of law.

Jury nullification. The power of a jury in criminal cases to acquit the defendant regardless of the strength of the evidence against him. The setting aside of the law.

K

L

Law of general application. A law that applies equally to the community in its entirety or to all individuals or actions within a natural class as distinguished from a law that relates to a specialized group.

Liability. Responsibility for any of a vast range of debts and obligations.

M

Mandamus. Literally, "we order" or "we command." Generally used with various types of orders that compel parties to perform certain acts.

Marketplace of ideas. A theory that compares the functioning of free speech to a free market economy and suggests that the speech market generates optimal results for society when government intervention is kept to a minimum.

Mootness. When a legal controversy is no longer "live" and a court decision would have no real effect on its resolution.

N

Narrow tailoring. A requirement of intermediate judicial scrutiny that laws be carefully crafted to achieve their objectives.

Natural rights. Rights that exist in nature that are inherent to humanity as opposed to rights created by positive laws enacted by government authority.

Negligence. Acting or failing to act in the way a reasonable or prudent person would be expected to. Failure to use reasonable care.

Nunc pro tunc. Literally, "now for then." Referring to acts or entries of decrees or judgments made retroactive to an earlier date.

O

Obscenity. A legal category defined by *Miller v. California*, 413 U.S. 15 (1973), to include material that, taken as a whole, (1) lacks serious value (2) appeals to prurient interests, and (3) describes or depicts sexual or excretory organs or functions in a manner patently offensive to the average person applying contemporary community standards.

Opinion. The statement of the decision of the court, or some members of the court, and an explanation of why the decision was reached.

Original intent. A concept that relies on the perceived meaning and intent given the First Amendment by its Framers to guide contemporary First Amendment application and interpretation.

Original jurisdiction. The jurisdiction to hear a case at its inception, as distinct from appellate jurisdiction.

Overbreadth or **Overinclusiveness.** A First Amendment doctrine concerned with the facial validity of laws that target legitimate government interests but pose an unacceptable danger of significantly compromising protected speech. The doctrine dictates precision and specificity in legislation.

P

Pari material. Literally, "on the same subject" or "related."

Per curiam **opinion.** An unsigned opinion of the whole court.

Petitioner. The party filing an appeal. Also known as the appellant.

Plaintiff. The party who sues in a civil action. Sometimes called the complainant.

Plurality opinion. An opinion in which a majority of the court agree on the outcome but only a minority agree on the reasoning. Plurality opinions do not establish binding precedent.

Post hoc. Literally, "after the fact" or "after this."

Precedent. A case judgment that establishes binding authority and guiding principles for cases to follow on closely analogous questions of law within the court's jurisdiction.

Preponderance of evidence. The standard of proof required to sustain a claim in civil cases.

Presumed damages. Alternately called presumptive or punitive damages.

Presumption. An assumption in the absence of contrary proof to favor a certain reading of the law or evidence.

Primary legal resources. The law itself; the actual documents that constitute the law.

Prior restraint. A system in which government officials exercise power to restrain or censor expression before it occurs.

Private figure. Used in libel and privacy law to describe those individuals who are neither public officials nor public figures.

Probable cause. The standard of evidence needed for an arrest or to issue a search warrant. A showing through reasonably trustworthy information that a crime has been or is being committed. More than mere suspicion.

Pro forma. Literally, "as a matter of form." Referring to processes designed to facilitate further proceedings rather than as an end in themselves.

Public figure. Under libel law, someone who has chosen a role of special prominence or has thrust himself into a public controversy to influence its outcome. Under privacy law, famous individuals whose position focuses public attention on them.

Public official. Under libel and privacy law, someone who occupies a public office and exercises some power and responsibility.

Publici juris. In the public interest, the public's right, a public (as differentiated from a private) good, e.g., the air.

Punitive damages. Damages awarded over and above the amount of actual harm to give increased solace to the plaintiff or to punish the defendant and make an example of him. Also called exemplary damages.

Q

Qualified privilege. Also know as journalist's privilege. A conditional privilege or immunity from liability for defamation based on fair and accurate reporting of communications originally protected by absolute privilege, e.g., comments during an open public meeting.

R

Rational review. A standard of judicial review that assumes the wisdom of legislative or administrative enactments.

Remand. The act of an appellate court to send a case back to the trial court for further action.

Respondent. The party fighting the appeal and seeking to have the lower court opinion upheld. Also known as the appellee.

Ripeness. When a case is ready for appellate review because it presents a real and present controversy.

Rule of law. A legal principle of general application that establishes a norm or guides future legal decisions. Also the framework of a society in which pre-established norms and procedures provide for consistent, neutral decision making.

S

Scienter. With guilty knowledge. A term used to describe defendants' prior knowledge of the harmful effects of their actions.

Secondary legal resources. Documents about the law; legal treatises, horn books, scholarly articles, legal encyclopedias, summaries, commentaries and the like.

Seditious libel. Communication that defames or criticizes government or that advocates or incites others to overthrow government.

Special damages. Compensation for the actual, though unusual, damages that resulted from the injury in a specific case.

Stare decisis. The doctrine of abiding by precedent fundamental to common law.

Statutory construction. The review of statutes in which courts determine the meaning and application of statutes. Courts tend to engage in strict construction, which narrowly defines laws to their clear letter and intent.

Statutory law. Written law formally adopted by representative legislatures.

Strict scrutiny. A standard of judicial review that places the burden on government to establish the need for government actions that adversely affect fundamental constitutional interests.

Strict liability. Liability without fault; liability for any and all harms, foreseeable or unforeseen, that result from a product or action.

Subpoena. An order to appear and testify or produce materials in court on a certain matter.

Summary judgment. A judicial decree ending a lawsuit when the judge determines there is no dispute over the facts in the case and those facts legally support one party.

Symbolic speech. Action that warrants First Amendment protection because its primary purpose is to express ideas.

T

TPM or time/place/manner restrictions. A doctrine that permits regulation of the form of a message to address harmful, incidental effects of speech so long as the law does not overburden the constitutionally protected content of the message.

Tailoring. Crafting of laws to regulate only those people or activities necessary to achieve the government's identified goals.

Terrorism. Generally, a violent act that endangers the lives of civilians, that is intended to intimidate the population and coerce government policy, and that violates state or federal criminal laws. Threats of terrorism are criminal under federal law.

Textualism. An interpretative approach that relies exclusively on a careful reading of legal texts to determine the meaning of the law.

True threat. A serious statement of intent to injure that, when taken in context, conveys menace to a reasonable person and harms the tranquility, security or freedom of action of the person to whom it is addressed.

U

Underinclusive. A First Amendment doctrine that disfavors laws that target a subset of a natural group for discriminatory treatment.

V

Vagueness. The First Amendment principle that laws are facially invalid if they are insufficiently clear to inform citizens of the line between proper and improper expression.

Venire. Literally, "to come" or "to appear." The term used for the location from which a court draws its pool of potential jurors, who must then appear in court for voir dire. Thus a change of venire means a change of the location from which potential jurors are drawn.

Venue. Location. The locality of a lawsuit and of the court hearing the suit. Thus, a change of venue means a relocation of a trial.

Voir dire. Literally, "to speak the truth." Refers to the preliminary examination of potential jurors to assess their suitability.

W

Writ of certiorari. Certiorari, literally, means "to be informed of." Used to refer to a petition for review by the Supreme Court of the United States.

Table of Cases

T

Index

O